EXPLORING HUMAN SEXUALITY

EXPLORING HUMAN SEXUALITY

Kathryn Kelley . Donn Byrne

THE UNIVERSITY AT ALBANY
STATE UNIVERSITY OF NEW YORK

 Prentice Hall, Englewood Cliffs, New Jersey 07632

Library of Congress Cataloging-in-Publication Data

Kelley, Kathryn.
  Exploring human sexuality / Kathryn Kelley, Donn Byrne.
    p.   cm.
  Includes bibliographical references and indexes.
  ISBN 0-13-445438-3
  1. Sex instruction for youth--United States.   2. Sex.   3. Sex
(Biology)   4. Sex (Psychology)   5. Hygiene, Sexual.   6. Birth
control.   I. Byrne, Donn Erwin.   II. Title.
  HQ35.2.K45   1992
  613.9'5--dc20   91-20398
                                                         CIP

TO OUR PARENTS

Johnnie and Lawrence Kelley
Rebecca and Bernard Byrne

Production Editor: Mary Kathryn L. Bsales
Acquisitions Editor: Susan Finnemore
Editor-in-Chief: Charlyce Jones Owen
Development Editor: Marilyn Miller
Senior Development Editor: Leslie Carr
Marketing Manager: Tracey McPeake
Copy Editor: Nancy Savio-Marcello
Designers: Lee Cohen and Lisa A. Domínguez
Cover Designer: Bruce Kenselaar
Photo Editor: Rona Tuccillo
Photo Researcher: Teri Stratford
Prepress Buyers: Debra Kesar and Kelly Behr
Manufacturing Buyer: Mary Ann Gloriande
Supplements Editor: Sharon Chambliss
Editorial Assistant: Jennie Katsaros

Cover photo: *Two Figures* by Diana Ong, 1940.
  Private Collection. Photo from *SuperStock*.

© 1992 by Prentice-Hall, Inc.
A Simon & Schuster Company
Englewood Cliffs, New Jersey 07632

Printed in the United States of America
10 9 8 7 6 5 4 3 2 1

ISBN   0-13-445438-3

Prentice-Hall International (UK) Limited, *London*
Prentice-Hall of Australia Pty. Limited, *Sydney*
Prentice-Hall Canada Inc., *Toronto*
Prentice-Hall Hispanoamericana, S.A., *Mexico*
Prentice-Hall of India Private Limited, *New Delhi*
Prentice-Hall of Japan, Inc., *Tokyo*
Simon & Schuster Asia Pte. Ltd., *Singapore*
Editora Prentice-Hall do Brasil, Ltda., *Rio de Janeiro*

BRIEF CONTENTS

CONTENTS

CHAPTER SEVEN
SEXUALITY IN CHILDHOOD AND ADOLESCENCE
169

CHAPTER EIGHT
SEXUAL ATTITUDES AND BEHAVIOR
196

CHAPTER NINE
SEXUAL RELATIONSHIPS AMONG ADULTS
220

ABOUT THE AUTHORS

Kathryn Kelley is currently Associate Professor of Psychology at the University at Albany, State University of New York, and she served as Director of the doctoral program in Industrial/Organizational Psychology. She received the Ph.D. degree from Purdue University and has held academic positions in the graduate and undergraduate programs at Marquette University and the University of Wisconsin–Milwaukee. The author of over fifty articles, invited chapters, and books, she is on the Editorial Board of the *Journal of Sex Research*. She has also presented research findings to Attorney General Meese's Commission on Pornography for the U.S. Justice Department and was an invited participant in Surgeon General Koop's Workshop on Pornography and Health. Her current research interests include sex roles and gender, sexual attitudes and behavior, and chronic self-destructiveness.

Donn Byrne is currently Professor of Psychology at the University at Albany, State University of New York, and Director of the doctoral program in Social-Personality Psychology. He received the Ph.D. degree from Stanford University and has held academic positions in the graduate and undergraduate programs at the California State University at San Francisco, the University of Texas, Stanford University, the University of Hawaii, and Purdue University. He is a past president of the Midwestern Psychological Association and is currently the president of the Society for the Scientific Study of Sex. The author of numerous articles, invited chapters, and books, he is on the Editorial Boards of several psychological journals (including the *Journal of Sex Research*), and has conducted research for President Johnson's Commission on Obscenity and Pornography, participated in the summer sex research program of the Institute for Sex Research at Indiana University, presented research findings to Attorney General Meese's Commission on Pornography for the U.S. Justice Department, was an invited participant in Surgeon General Koop's Workshop on Pornography and Health, and recieved the Distinguished Scientific Achievement Award from the Society for the Scientific Study of Sex. His current research interests include interpersonal attraction, close relationships, and sexual coercion.

Among the other books written by Kelley and Byrne are

Byrne, D. (1971). *The attraction paradigm*. New York: Academic Press.

Byrne, D., & Kelley, K. (1981). *An introduction to personality* (3rd ed.). Englewood Cliffs, NJ: Prentice Hall.

Byrne, D., & Fisher, W. A. (Eds.). (1983). *Adolescents, sex, and contraception*. Hillsdale, NJ: Lawrence Erlbaum Associates.

Byrne, D., & Kelley, K. (Eds.). (1986). *Alternative approaches to the study of sexual behavior*. Hillsdale, NJ: Lawrence Erlbaum Associates.

Kelley, K. (Ed.). (1987). *Females, males, and sexuality*. Albany, NY: SUNY Press.

Baron, R. A., & Byrne, D. (1991). *Social psychology: Understanding human interaction* (6th ed.). Boston: Allyn and Bacon.

Kelley, K. (Ed.). (1991). *Issues, theory, and research in industrial/organizational psychology*. Amsterdam: North Holland.

PREFACE

Studying Human Sexuality

When we began conducting empirical studies of human sexuality in the 1970s and also teaching undergraduate courses on this topic, we underestimated some of the difficulties and some of the rewards. This book represents a portion of what we learned over the past two decades. Here in the preface, we'll share some of the "backstage secrets" about this enterprise.

■ Studying Sex Is Not Like Studying Mathematics or Geography

First, we quickly discovered that anything having to do with sex causes a great many people to feel embarrassed—even today. Among the other negative reactions are guilt, anxiety, anger, and disgust. For those students and colleagues who intellectualize their aversive feelings, their discomfort tends to be expressed in the judgment that the study of sexual behavior is somehow not quite scientific or at least not quite respectable. At the opposite attitudinal extreme are people who react with considerable interest and curiosity, including the countless students who enroll in sex courses plus those who cannot (because each semester a great many prospective students find that all of the sections are filled to capacity). Sometimes, the positive feelings and expectations are excessive, and some students are disappointed to learn that sex research involves the same basic elements as all other scientific investigations. Neither sex research

nor sex education bears any resemblance to Roman orgies.

Second, the study of sexuality cuts across many fields and traditional disciplines, so it is necessary to become aware of some aspects of the work of psychologists, sociologists, anthropologists, biologists, historians, and medical scientists—among others—just to master the basic elements of the subject. Consider just a few of the topics covered in this book, and you will see that the study of sexuality covers a broad array of human behavior: the physical underpinnings of sexual functioning, the behavioral effects of erotic books and movies, sexually transmissible diseases, reproduction, sex guilt, the similarities and differences of males and females, homosexuality, attraction and love, rape and other sexual crimes, fetishism, marriage and parenthood, contraception, sexual dysfunctions, prostitution, and on and on. Though it is not at all unusual to hear someone assert that "I know all there is to know about sex," the fact is that each of us has a great deal to learn about this aspect of human behavior.

Third, a sex course differs from most other courses in the extent to which it can affect your life. Many of us have studied algebra or learned the location of the Hanging Gardens of Babylon without behaving much differently afterward. In contrast, sex plays a central role in our lives, and its positive and negative implications are neither abstract nor distant from one's everyday world. Though it makes us slightly uncomfortable to realize this—as you learn bits and pieces of what is currently known about human sexuality, you may find yourself changing with respect to a few aspects of what you think, feel, and do. Frankly, the possibility of causing such effects is one of the most challenging but also most sobering aspects of teaching a course or writing a book about sexuality.

■ The Goals of This Book

Besides gathering much of what is known about sexuality and attempting to communicate such material in ways that are both informative and interesting, we have a more basic goal. We hope that you learn to pay attention to *how* knowledge is obtained and become sophisticated in *evaluating* its reliability and validity. There is no reason for everyone to become a behavioral scientist, but it is extremely important for everyone to be able to distinguish assertions based on unsubstantiated opinions from assertions based on careful investigations. In the future, if someone tells you or you read that pornography causes sex crimes, conception cannot occur if you have intercourse standing up, homosexuals are maladjusted, heterosexuals cannot contract AIDS, all sexual interest and desire ceases at age 45, masturbation causes pimples, or anything else about sex, we hope you don't just say, "my, my, isn't that interesting!" Instead, we hope you inquire about the basis on which any such assertion is made. Is the statement based on someone's beliefs, biases, and fantasies or on empirical data? If there are data, how were they gathered? Was there an experiment, a correlational investigation, a descriptive survey, or behavioral observations? How were the subjects selected? How were the responses measured? Are there any alternative explanations for the findings?

Even after you learn to question and seek the objective basis of any sweeping conclusion, it is important to consider two additional factors. (1) No single experiment or survey answers all of the relevant questions; for this reason, a series of different investigations by a variety of investigators is more convincing than any single, isolated finding. (2) Scientific inquiry is an ongoing activity in which new findings and new interpretations are the rule. Don't for a moment assume that everything is known about sex as of 1992. New information is constantly being generated, and the content of a human sexuality text written in 1950 is as out of date four decades later as the electronics of 1950. The same will soon be true of this text. Don't think of education as a set of facts to be learned and retained for all time but rather as a way of finding out about anything and everything of interest—a process that, under the best of circumstances, will continue throughout your life.

■ Easing the Pain of Learning

No matter how fascinating and important the topic, professors are able to transform any subject matter into a dull learning experience, even when the topic is sex. In fact, we can be guilty of that ourselves, but we have tried very hard to make this material as interesting and as personally relevant to the student as possible. Let us point out some of the specific features that were designed to help you learn with a minimum of discomfort.

1. Each chapter begins with a *brief vignette* in which an individual describes an incident in his or her life that deals with some aspect of sexuality. These stories are true, but they have of course been modified to disguise the identity of each person. That is, names, locations, and irrelevant details have changed, but not the basic content. We hope that these accounts help remind you that sex involves real people and not simply technical terms and statistics.

2. Speaking of *technical terms,* there are a lot of them. We have attempted to emphasize the most important and least familiar ones throughout the text by printing them in **boldface**. This should help alert you to their importance and also to the fact they are defined in the Glossary appearing at the end of the book. In that Glossary, when appropriate, we indicate how the less familiar words are pronounced.

3. Each chapter is organized in *sections,* and you will see this organization in the *contents* preceding each chapter, the *headings* throughout each chapter, and the *summaries* that follow each chapter. By the way, some students find it helpful to read the summary before reading the chapter. Being aware of this organization is important because you will get an idea of where the authors are going with each discussion—it enables you to keep track of the forest rather

than become lost in examining individual trees. We'll also let you in on a secret: when instructors make up exams, the *technical terms* and the *headings* often guide them in focusing on specific content and in devising questions.

4. The *graphs, tables, flow charts, drawings, photographs,* and *cartoons* in each chapter (most often, in full color) are designed to make the material more understandable or interesting or both. We have also taken special care to clarify the content of each graph and table so that you will know exactly what was found.

5. All chapters contain one or more *special sections* that draw attention and expand on particular aspects of a given subject. There are three varieties of such sections:

HIGHLIGHTING RESEARCH Specific research findings or a series of findings are described in enough details to let you understand how and why particular conclusions have been drawn.

TAKING RESPONSIBILITY AND PROTECTING YOURSELF Sexual interactions can have negative consequences, and a theme throughout the book is the necessity for you to know enough about potential pitfalls to be able to take responsibility and protect yourself and your partner with respect to conception, health, victimization, and so forth.

INCREASING ENJOYMENT Despite unwanted pregnancies, fatal diseases, and sex crimes, sex can be and *should be* fun. You heard it here first. Accurate knowledge can help make any sexual expression (petting, oral sex, intercourse, fantasizing, orgasm, etc.) even more enjoyable, and we provide a few guidelines.

6. At the end of every chapter, you will find suggestions for *additional readings.* We know that students usually ignore such material because "it isn't going to be on the test." Believe us when we say that this book doesn't cover everything about sex, and you are likely to want to know more about certain topics. The sources we list can be very helpful in providing more information. Beyond these references, each student will receive a group of informative pamphlets produced by various agencies and organizations dealing with specific sex-related issues.

7. Finally, for the instructors who adopt this text, a full teaching and learning package is available to enhance your classroom experience. In answer to multiple requests for good instructional videos, our publisher is providing the ABC News/Prentice Hall Video Library for Human Sexuality, a series of videos which include recent ABC news programs about topics addressed in this book. For more information, see the end of this preface or contact your local P-H representative.

To further enchance your audio visual program, a full set of color transparencies is available, many of which come from sources outside this text. For qualifying adopters, 50 color slides of issues relating to AIDS and STDs will be provided. Informative pamphlets from government and health agencies can act as a reference for students, and the Study Guide should help them master the content material. Our Instructor's Resource and Testing Manual and computerized testing for IBM or Macintosh computers offer support by providing lecture topics, test questions, and listings of audio-visual material, as well as a user-friendly and flexible means for administering exams. We hope that all of this support will make using our text as easy and effective as possible.

Acknowledgments

Many people have contributed to this book in many different ways, and we would like to express our special thanks to:

Our daughters, Lindsey Kelley Byrne and Rebecka Byrne Kelley, who had to put up with two parents working at two word processors.

Some exceptionally nice and able people who helped care for and entertain Lindsey, Becka, or both during the writing process: Barbara Levin, Donna Levin, Rebecca Levin, Ginger Nestlen, Linda Pearson, and Ruth Van Wagenen.

Several very conscientious colleagues who read the manuscript and made numerous suggestions and comments: Joseph R. Heller, California State University-Sacramento; Thomas E. Billimek, San Antonio College; Beverly B. Palmer, California State University-Dominguez Hills; Irvin W. Brandel, University of Akron; David A. Edwards, Emory University; M. Andrew Berisford, University of Houston; Michael Walraven, Jackson Community College; Michael Campbell, Highline Community College; M. O'Neal Weeks, University of Kentucky; Alan G. Glaros, University of Missouri-Kansas City; Luis Garcia, Rutgers University-Camden; Karen G. Duffy, SUNY at Geneseo; and John DeLamater, University of Wisconsin.

The professionals at Prentice Hall who were involved at every step of the project: John Isley whose original interest and unending patience made the book possible, along with a succession of individuals who each made essential contributions—Susan Finnemore, Psychology Editor; Leslie Carr, College Editor; Marilyn Miller, Developmental Editor; and Katy Bsales, Production Editor.

Tell Us What You Think

We know all too well that despite more hours of hard work than we care to remember, this book is far from perfect. We can improve it in future editions with your help. We hope that students and instructors alike will take the time to write us with any reactions that occur while reading this text. Constructive criticisms are most welcome, and we hope to hear from you.

Kathryn Kelley and Donn Byrne
Department of Psychology
The University at Albany
State University of New York
Albany, NY 12222

ABC NEWS / PRENTICE HALL VIDEO LIBRARY FOR HUMAN SEXUALITY

Video is the most dynamic of all the supplements you can use to enhance your class. But the quality of the video material and how well it relates to your course can make all the difference. For these reasons, Prentice Hall and ABC News have decided to work together to bring you the best and most comprehensive video ancillaries available in the college market.

Through its wide variety of award-winning programs—*Nightline, 20/20, World News Tonight,* and *The Health Show*—ABC offers a resource for feature and documentary-style videos related to text concepts and applications. The programs have extremely high production quality, present substantial content, and are hosted by well-versed, well-known anchors. Prentice Hall, its authors, and its editors provide the benefit of having selected videos on topics that will work well with this course and this text.

CHAPTER ONE

INTRODUCING SEX RESEARCH
History, Procedures, and Problems

Even today, sex is an emotionally loaded topic; as a result, it is sometimes difficult to find the answer to what appears to be a seemingly simple and straightforward question. A male college student describes his attempt to obtain some basic, objective information about average penis length. When you read Neil's account, see if you notice anything about the procedures he used that might affect his results.

Not long after I began my first semester at the university, a bunch of us were sitting around the dorm one night talking and joking. Somehow the conversation drifted to the topic of sex and specifically to penis size. The big question was how long most penises are—what's the average length and things like that.

For some reason, I had never thought about it before. It suddenly occurred to me that maybe I didn't "measure up" to other guys in this respect. I wondered how it was possible to find out such information. You can look up the facts about most things fairly easily—the average height of guys your age or the average score of college students on an I.Q. test. Some things you can find out roughly just by looking—how big most noses are compared to yours or whether most men wear shoes that are a larger or smaller size than yours.

I wondered, how in the world could you find out about penis length? Guys wouldn't think of staring at each other in the john or when they're taking a shower. Besides, the crucial question was length of an erection, and I've never seen anyone's erection besides my own. It's not something you could seriously ask very many people about. The idea of going around with a ruler to measure erections is out of the question. So, how could I ever get the answer?

My curiosity led me to my first college research project. At the time, I was pretty proud of my idea. It occurred to me that the letters people write to Penthouse magazine (the "Forum" and "Call Me Madam" columns) often mentioned penis length. I decided to look at every letter written over the past year and write down the length in inches whenever that information appeared in a letter. I began with the November 1987 issue that I bought and worked backward to December 1986 with copies in the library. I discovered that the letters reported penis length forty-one times during those twelve months. In two letters, the writer gave an uncertain range ("six or eight inches" and "nine or eleven inches"), so I didn't count either one of those.

After getting the information from all twelve issues, I made a little chart and computed the average length. It was very upsetting to me because the average was 8.6 inches, and I had already measured myself one night as being six-and-a-half inches. For a while I was totally convinced that I was a freak who would be ridiculed by any girl who saw me with my clothes off. You can imagine my relief when I took a human sexuality course in the spring semester and found out that "the average length of the erect penis of white college males is 6.2 inches" (see Table 1-1). I was actually above-average. The only thing I can't understand is—what did I do wrong and how could my numbers have been so far off?

Neil, age 18

Like Neil, many people have questions about sex but discover that it is difficult to obtain accurate answers. The basic problem is the emotional nature of this topic. Sex has become an acceptable target of scientific inquiry only in the past

TABLE 1-1 **Average Penis Length: Penthouse Letters versus Kinsey**

There is a remarkable difference between average penis length as reported in letters to *Penthouse* magazine (December 1986 through November 1987) and average penis length as reported by Kinsey's subjects (Gebhard and Johnson, 1979), who measured their own erections according to directions from the investigators. Why do you think there is more than a 2-inch difference in the mean penis lengths reported in these two samples?

LENGTH OF ERECT PENIS IN INCHES	PERCENTAGE OF WHITE COLLEGE MALES REPORTING EACH LENGTH	PERCENTAGE OF PENTHOUSE LETTERS REPORTING EACH LENGTH
12.00–12.75	0.0	.2
11.00–11.75	0.0	4.9
10.00–10.75	0.0	12.2
9.00–9.75	.1	31.7
8.00–8.75	1.7	29.3
7.00–7.75	15.2	14.6
6.00–6.75	52.7	4.9
5.00–5.75	27.3	0.0
4.00–4.75	3.0	0.0
3.00–3.75	.2	0.0
Mean Length	6.2 in	8.6 in

several decades, so even the most knowledgeable experts in this field still have a lot to learn. As Figure 1-1 suggests, nonexperts are even more likely to lack knowledge about sex.

This chapter describes how scientists establish the basic facts about sex—just as they establish the basic facts about everything else, including other aspects of human functioning. We begin by discussing the *evolution of sex research* over the past several decades—a period during which this topic slowly became an acceptable one for scientific investigation. We then describe some of the procedures and issues involved in *conducting sex research*, providing a basis that will help you evaluate such work now and in the future. Because sexuality is a sensitive and intimate aspect of our private lives, some unique *problems arise in conducting sex research*, and we will outline some of

them. In special sections we emphasize the value of the *sexual advice and information* provided by popular newspaper columnists. We also point out the difficulties encountered in *breaking research taboos* by pioneers who began to study human sexuality before either the scientific community or society in general was prepared to accept such investigations.

In Neil's *Penthouse* study, he tried to use a scientific procedure, but his findings were not at all like those of Kinsey. What went wrong? His plan was reasonable, but there were problems with the data—specifically, sampling and validity problems. By **sampling**, we mean that any study of human beings must

FIGURE 1-1 *WHO KNOWS EVERYTHING ABOUT SEX?* Scientific information about sex has gradually become available during the last several decades, and our knowledge is constantly expanding. Hagar the Horrible isn't the only one who doesn't know "everything" about the birds and the bees.

select some small portion of the 5 billion people now living on this planet. Ideally, scientists would obtain a random sample of this enormous group, but of course that is essentially impossible. Later in this chapter, we will describe how samples are actually obtained, the special sampling problems that arise in sex research, and the possible reasons that Neil's study ran into difficulties. By **validity**, we mean that the measures used in research must be accurate. A valid measure of intercourse frequency among married couples, for example, is one that corresponds to the actual frequency with which they engage in intercourse. Unless there is direct observation in bedrooms by bystanders, cameras, or whatever, we must depend on verbal reports. When studying sexual behavior, investigators usually must rely on what subjects say. Later in the chapter we will describe the issues involved in obtaining valid measures of sexual variables and some possible reasons for the discrepancies between the Kinsey data and what Neil found.

The Evolution of Sex Research: From Case Histories to Laboratory Experiments

Many of you would probably agree that scientific methods and procedures are the best way humans have devised to obtain information about our world. Ideally, science allows investigators to describe phenomena precisely, to determine relationships between and among events, to predict consequences, and sometimes to exert control over physical and biological occurrences. The attempts to build and test theoretical formulations, the constantly developing technology, the sophisticated statistical and mathematical tools, and the procedural rules and safeguards all constitute part of a wide-ranging activity whose goal is to gain and expand knowledge.

Among most scientists, the term **research** refers to **empirical** investigations. Although there are many types of empirical research, the process always involves the gathering of **data** (information or facts) about observable phenomena. Examples of empirical research include observing the planets, discovering new insect species, ascertaining the association between climate and aggressive behavior, and determin-

ing the effect of violent pornography on attitudes about rape. This type of research is distinguished from "library research" in which one examines what others have written about a given topic.

■ Finding Out about Sex

It is generally true that human anatomy and human behavior were among the last phenomena to receive scientific attention. It was acceptable to study the stars, chemical compounds, and the behavior of other animals, for example, long before human beings could be similarly scrutinized. Among the reasons for the avoidance of research on humans were restrictive religious beliefs and the possible threat that arises if each human being is viewed as simply one more predictable object in the universe. In the late 15th century, for example, Leonardo da Vinci had to ignore the objections of the Church to study human anatomy by dissecting human corpses, but he felt that the genitals were too repulsive to examine in detail (Hughes, 1984). Despite the problems, the breakthrough in the scientific study of humans began with early attempts to map human anatomy, describe human physiology, and find cures for various physical illnesses. The study of human *behavior* did not, however, really begin until the end of the last century. The most taboo aspect of human functioning is sex (McDonald, 1988; Mosher, 1988). A body of knowledge has, nevertheless, gradually accumulated.

For a scientist engaged in sex research, the realization that the field is young and much remains to be learned constitutes an exciting challenge. In contrast, people in general simply want specific answers to specific questions about some aspect of their sexuality. As a consequence, most individuals may not be interested in reviewing the entire area of human sexuality in a course or in a text such as the one you are now reading. Instead of wanting to become experts, people sometimes simply need an understandable answer as quickly as possible. We feel strongly, however, that it is to your benefit to know as much as possible about the topic and about how such information was originally obtained.

Even though you are enrolled in a sex course, a question may come up about a topic that is not covered in adequate detail. Or, after the course is over, you may want the answer to a question that seemed uninteresting or irrelevant when you encountered it during the course and then rapidly forgot it. For example, we feel confident that some of the material on conception, pregnancy, and childbirth (in Chapter 4) may seem irrelevant to you today, but it may be of vital interest in a few years.

The authors of this book are frequently approached by students and former students who want to know something very specific about sex. For example, a former student in our undergraduate sex course telephoned on the eve of his wedding to ask for precise directions on how to locate his bride's clitoris; he remembered something about it from the material on female anatomy but hadn't paid much attention at the time. (See Chapter 2 for information about the external sexual organs of females.) Another student

phoned late at night from his girlfriend's apartment; he was unable to attain an erection and wanted to know why and what to do about it. (See Chapter 17 for information about dysfunctions.) A female student came to see one of us, obviously embarrassed, to ask why during cunnilingus she suddenly seemed to lose control and "urinate." (Information about female ejaculation is provided in a later section of this chapter.)

For those who have not taken a sex course, one responsible way to obtain information about sex is to write to one of the popular newspaper columnists or to read the questions raised by others. The responses to such questions help educate the public and to provide reassurance when it is needed. In the special section, ***Taking Responsibility and Protecting Yourself,*** on pages 5–7, we present examples of how useful and informative such columns can be.

Taking Responsibility and Protecting Yourself

DEAR ABBY, ANN, AND DR. RUTH

Where do most people turn for answers to questions about sex? Often, they find that parents, clergy, and physicians are unable to tell them what they need to know. Even worse is the situation in which bad advice and incorrect information are given. Consider the worried parents at the turn of the century who consulted a physician, W. H. Walling, M.D., to find out about their offspring's masturbation. The doctor's beliefs about this practice were published in 1904 in a widely read book, *Sexology*:

(about their sons, parents were told:)

"Viewing the world over, this shameful and criminal act is the most frequent, as well as the most fatal, of all vices" (p. 34).

(about their daughters, parents were told:)

"The moral symptoms are similar to those of the opposite sex. They are sadness or melancholy, solitude or indifference, an aversion to legitimate pleasures, and a host of other characteristics common to the two sexes. The condition called 'nymphomania' sometimes ensues. . ." (p. 46).

Today, it is possible to obtain much better information from an advice-giver on the radio, television, or in newspaper columns. The following are examples of the kinds of questions and comments received and answered by three of the better-known columnists (pictured in Figure 1-2).

DEAR ABBY: Maybe I can share my experience.

While in graduate school, a fellow student (a good friend I'll call Dora) and I were enrolled in a course together.

During the semester, Dora became involved with the professor—a 40-year-old man. When the course ended, the professor ended their relationship. Dora was crushed.

I still remember going to Dora's apartment at midnight to talk her out of committing suicide. She's fine now, but it taught me a big lesson.

Students run the risk of getting hurt if they become involved with instructors. Likewise, professors' feelings can be hurt,

too, not to mention the possibility of an unscrupulous student threatening blackmail for a better grade—or even money.

Even though they both may be consenting adults, it's best to stay away from the other side of the desk.—JOE IN NEBRASKA

DEAR JOE: You're right. If a student and professor become mutually attracted, they should put their relationship on "hold" until she (or he) is no longer a student. If they're right for each other, it will last.

* * *

In this reply, Abigail Van Buren reinforces the opinions expressed by a reader and goes on to suggest how to deal with such situations should genuine attraction arise. We will return to the topic of faculty-student relationships in Chapter 14, discussing the issue of sexual harassment.

* * *

DEAR ANN LANDERS: I have never seen this problem in your column and

FIGURE 1-2 *COLUMNISTS AS SEX EDUCATORS* For many people, accurate information about sex is most available in the writings of nationally known newspaper columnists. The three women pictured here provide facts, expert knowledge, and reassurance each day not only to those who write to them but also to millions of readers who may have similar questions.

hope you will be able to help us. My husband and I are terribly distressed.

Nearly three years ago we had our first child. My husband was in the delivery room with me and when the doctor said, "It's a girl!" we were both thrilled.

The next morning the pediatrician came in to give the baby a physical. When he told my husband and me that our child might be a boy, we were shocked. He said he wasn't sure and was calling in a specialist.

I had noticed that the genitalia didn't look right and I mentioned it to my obstetrician. He said it was probably swollen as a result of birth trauma and not to worry about it.

When the specialist came in the next day he examined the baby and said, "I'm not sure. We will have to do some further investigating." The ultrasound test at Children's Hospital in San Diego revealed that our baby had no internal female organs. They still would not say for sure if we had a boy or a girl.

A chromosome study was done and the results showed all male chromosomes but still a sex determination was not made. Testosterone shots were given at three-week intervals, and it was then decided

that our baby was a boy. Since that time the child has had two operations and one more is scheduled for 1988.

We were told that this condition is called ambiguous genitalia. We had never heard of it before. We were also told that it was due to a recessive gene that my husband and I share. When we asked about future pregnancies, they said, "You run a 25 percent chance of having it happen again."

We are still shaken up by all this and would like to know if there are any support groups for parents like us. Please, Ann, can you help?—BARSTOW, CALIF.

DEAR FRIENDS: I spoke with Dr. George M. Ryan, Jr., professor of obstetrics and gynecology at the University of Tennessee at Memphis. Dr. Ryan explained that all fetuses, both male and female, go through the same early developmental process, but the male develops differently in later stages of pregnancy. In some cases, this differentiation is not apparent at birth. For this reason all newborns should be examined at birth. If there is any question regarding gender, a pediatric gynecologist or an endocrinologist should be called in.

Dr. Joe Leigh Simpson, a geneticist and chairman of ob-gyn at the University of

Tennessee at Memphis, said that he knows of no support groups and that it is just as well.

Dr. Simpson believes that parents should get counseling, stick to the sex determination designated by the doctor and not view this occurrence as a continuing problem.

* * *

This is an example of a very serious concern that involves a relatively rare medical condition. It is not likely to be covered in any detail in a human sexuality course, but for some new parents it can suddenly become a matter of central concern. Ann Landers was able to provide useful factual information by contacting medical experts. In Chapter 4, we describe some of the possible complications that occur during pregnancy and childbirth.

* * *

Question for Dr. Ruth: Up until what age does a male have wet dreams? I am 23 and a little confused because I thought wet dreams were confined to the teen years, but for me this is not the case.

A: Wet dreams will not be confined to any age bracket just because some expert says they will. Whoever told you they were a teenage phenomenon was speaking generally. They seem to be a teen thing because when they first happen in a male's life it is a dramatic event. This usually occurs around 12 or 13, or sometimes earlier.

When they occur later in life it is only a sign of sexual vigor. I can't say a sign of sexual inactivity because this does happen sometimes to men who have just fallen asleep after having sex. Don't worry about

this innocent and harmless happening. The recommended thing to do is to go back to sleep smiling.

* * *

To this question, Dr. Ruth Westheimer responds with her usual mix of information and humor. Presumably, the writer was reassured to find that he was not unusual or abnormal simply because he'd had an orgasm while he was asleep. The very common and natural experience of

nocturnal orgasm is discussed in Chapter 7.

* * *

Though there may well be uninformed, potentially harmful individuals who give sexual advice, responsible writers such as the three just quoted serve a helpful and important function in our society. Sex information can now be obtained from such sources just as easily as information about gardening, repairing your car, or making investment decisions.

■ Early Sex Research

Because the topic of sex can be emotionally upsetting, each step in the growth of this field of study has been marked by extremely cautious scientific steps, often followed by condemnation from fellow scientists and the public at large. Tolerance for sex research has gradually increased, however, and work that would have been unthinkable and even illegal forty or fifty years ago is now conducted routinely. Increased sexual tolerance has occurred throughout our society and is summed up by Krassner's (1987, p. 46) observation, "Lenny Bruce got arrested for saying *cocksucker* in the Sixties, but Meryl Streep got an Academy Award for saying it in the Eighties." Given past intolerance and other difficulties involved in conducting sex research, how did we ever begin to acquire scientific knowledge about it? We will briefly trace the history of this struggle.

Medical Case Histories: Sex Lives of the Weird and Infamous. At the end of the nineteenth century, a number of medical practitioners interested in sexuality followed the established procedure of describing patients in detailed case histories—in this instance, focusing on the individual's sexual abnormalities. Descriptions that would have been considered legally obscene as fiction were tolerated because they constituted a scholarly medical description of deviation. These medical scholars began to document the detailed sex lives of patients whose behavior they defined as abnormal.

One physician, a German neurologist-psychiatrist, Richard von Krafft-Ebing (1886), compiled a detailed classification of sexual disorders. This book, *Psychopathia Sexualis,* greatly influenced public atti-

tudes, as well as medical and legal attitudes about sex. Krafft-Ebing proposed that all sexual deviations and "perversions" were caused by genetic weakness or by the "loathsome" practice of masturbation. He described cunnilingus and fellatio as "horrible sexual acts." He also used extreme examples such as sexual murders and intercourse with dead bodies to illustrate his points.

In contrast, one of his contemporaries in England, Henry Havelock Ellis (1899), was convinced that variations in sexual behavior were simply different expressions of a basic human need; his approach to sexual behavior emphasized tolerance and sexual freedom (Brecher, 1969). Ellis discussed topics like childhood sexuality in his writings in ways that resemble the views that would soon appear in Freud's case studies. According to Ellis, masturbation commonly occurred among males and females across the life span. He sought psychological explanations for personal problems while his contemporaries preferred physiological ones. His work had a surprisingly modern flavor, and many of his views are still accepted almost 100 years later.

The Role of Case Histories in Sexual Science. The scholars who compiled these case histories wrote about their patients in a somber and nontitillating manner, but libraries nevertheless attempted to protect their general patrons from possible exposure to such "unsuitable" material by placing it in locked cabinets to which only professionals had access. Despite the extremely limited nature of the subject matter covered and the extremely limited readership to whom these books were addressed, a bridgehead had been created. It became *possible* for the first time to examine certain types of human sexual behavior.

Freud used the study of individual cases extensively to promote his theoretical view that sexuality existed in infants and small children. In his publications between 1880 and 1905, he eloquently added to the growing evidence that sexuality was a primary motivator of human behavior. He proposed that anxiety about sexuality can lead to neurotic behavior in which generalized anxiety distorts the individual's ability to cope.

The case history approach played a crucial historical role in the study of sexuality, but this does not imply that it has no current value. A fairly recent example is provided by Abramson (1984) who has published a book-length "sexual biography" of Sarah, a college student. Her experiences as an abused child and her subsequent life offer valuable insights into some aspects of sexuality. By the age of 21, for example, Sarah had been a victim of childhood molestation, engaged in prostitution, had two pregnancies and two abortions, and undergone a wide variety of other traumatic sexual interactions. Sarah's description of her stepfather's behavior is simply one of the many abusive events in her early childhood years:

> *Much worse things happened with my stepfather. In fact, this is one of my most vivid memories . . . I had no idea of what was going on. I remember him (his name was Al) waking me up and telling me to come into the living room. It was very late and my mother was asleep in the bedroom. Actually, she would sleep in the bedroom, and he would sleep in the living room. (This part really makes me sick. It's funny, it's not the physical act that makes me sick, it's the things he said that turn my stomach.) When Al woke me up he said, "Do you want some Italian sausage?" I didn't know what he was talking about so I said, "Sure." He then took his pants off and he made me touch his penis. Next, he made me put my mouth around his penis . . . and I was getting very sick. He then came. I thought it was urine, but it doesn't make any difference. I didn't particularly care. I was being tortured . . . I just felt sick. He then told me not tell my mother [Abramson, 1984, pp. 21–22].*

Such descriptions of one individual's life story not only are the source of hypotheses about sexual behavior but also often suggest that the most de-plorable events can be overcome. As Abramson (1984, p. 140) concludes, ". . . against all odds Sarah made it. Consequently, it offers hope to others." That is, other victims of abuse may be strengthened by her story.

Sexual Behavior in Other Species. In addition to abnormal sexuality, scientists in several fields found another "respectable" way to study sex—by examining it in nonhumans.

Much of the earliest work on animal sexuality consisted of descriptive observational studies of mating patterns. From this large body of data, scientists accumulated an amazing array of facts about what different animals do and do not do sexually, and animal research continues today. A simple listing of some of this information reads somewhat like Ripley's *Believe It or Not* or perhaps as source material for a Trivial Pursuit game. Table 1-2 presents a sampling of facts about the sexual behavior of animals.

There are two major applications of this information to human behavior. First, the higher a species is on the phylogenetic scale, the more the animals in question are similar to human beings. As a consequence, their sexual patterns may tell us something basic about our own behavior. For example, some species at the lower end of the scale (e.g., salmon) mate only once in their entire lifetime; others (e.g., the sea worm) mate once a year. At higher stages of evolution (e.g., deer), some animals mate several times during an annual mating season, and still others (e.g., dogs) have intercourse periodically throughout the year whenever a female is fertile. Among many species of primates sexual activity occurs throughout the cycle, but the frequency increases at ovulation when the female genitals redden and swell (Gallup, 1982). It should not be surprising, then, that the frequency with which humans engage in sexual intercourse resembles primates more closely than salmon or sea worms. Humans are similar to their primate relatives in showing an increase in intercourse frequency at midcycle (during ovulation), presumably for biological reasons. Unlike primates or people living in very primitive societies, however, those whose culture forbids intercourse during the menstrual period also show an increased frequency just before menstruation, presumably to compensate for the nonsexual days ahead (Manson, 1986).

TABLE 1.2 **A Sampling of Sexual Characteristics of Other Species**

In the study of the sexual behavior of other animal species, many of the countless findings can be treated at the simplest level much like Fun Facts to be inserted in bubble gum packs. Much more importantly, knowledge of animal sexuality can provide basic information about human sexuality.

FINDING	SOURCE
The male desert tortoise nips the female's legs and head until she withdraws into her shell. He then mounts her from the rear, grunting, stamping his feet, and knocking on her back with his front feet.	Scott (1961)
A long-term homosexual relationship has been observed in pairs of ducks.	Lorenz (1966)
The male sea otter bites the female on the nose until she bleeds, causing her to ovulate.	Witters and Jones-Witters (1980)
The male moose makes a depression in the ground (a "wallow"), urinates in it, and rolls around in the mud he has created. He then pushes the female near the wallow, mounts her, and completes the sexual act in about three minutes.	Scott (1961)
Minks copulate for up to eight hours before the male withdraws.	Ford and Beach (1951)
Ferenuk antelopes copulate while in motion, and the act lasts only a fraction of a second.	Geer, Heiman, and Leitenberg (1984)
Two male monkeys in captivity may engage in anal intercourse.	Erwin and Maple (1976)

The second application of animal research leads us to question the meaning of "natural" versus "unnatural" as labels for sexual behavior. That other species commonly engage in specific practices we term unnatural suggests that such practices are in fact natural, that is, a familiar part of nature. For example, because young monkeys (and other primates) frequently masturbate (Harlow, 1975), it is difficult to conclude that human masturbation is a horrifying crime against nature (see Figure 1-3).

Among the more recent applications of animal research is Gallup's (1986) examination of human sexuality in the context of evolution. The general perspective is that any genetic aspects of sexual anatomy or sexual behavior associated with reproductive success will be passed on to subsequent generations. The following example illustrates this process.

There is a tendency among most vertebrates for sexual intercourse to occur when a female invites or selects a partner. Males, on the other hand, tend to be much less selective. Underlying this difference is the fact that males produce billions of sperm cells throughout their life span while females produce a much smaller number of egg cells during a limited number of reproductive years. Thus, whereas a male can potentially father hundreds or thousands of offspring, a female can mother only a relatively minute proportion of this number. Because of this difference,

FIGURE 1-3 *NATURAL SEXUALITY OR "LOATHSOME PRACTICE"?*
One benefit of studying the behavior of animals is in establishing definitions of "natural behavior." When, for example, masturbation is observed in various species, it becomes difficult to define this activity in humans as a "perversion" or a "crime against nature." Source: Harlow, 1975.

we would expect males and females to have developed different reproductive strategies. For males, the best strategy to ensure that their genes are well represented in subsequent generations is to engage in sex frequently with as many partners as possible. For females, the best reproductive strategy to pass on *their* genes is to choose only the best partners so that their offspring will have the greatest chance to survive.

For many species, this means that the female should select males who are dominant, healthy, and strong. Thus, among Wyoming sage grouse, males fight for status, and the most successful 3 percent are most likely to be selected as mates—they father 87 percent of the next generation of sage grouse (Allee, 1938). Among chimpanzees, the same principle applies, but with an additional focus on the intellect. Chimps who are smart have greater success in attracting partners, and intelligence, rather than simply strength or size, often leads to a dominant position in the group (Goodall, 1971).

Are any of these tendencies reflected in human behavior? Men certainly appear to be less selective than women with respect to sex partners and are more likely than women to have multiple partners prior to marriage and, subsequently, to engage in extramarital affairs. When Gallup and Suarez (1983) asked college students to name the characteristics of the opposite sex they find most attractive, females usually listed intelligence and a sense of humor, while males emphasized breasts. Perhaps these answers indicate that college females respond to an important aspect of dominance and success in our species (intelligence), while college males respond to the only overt indicator of fertility in human females (Gallup, 1982). We are obviously not *aware* of the reasons we respond as we do to the opposite sex. Instead, our evolutionary history is such that males have been "programmed" by hundreds of thousands of years of reproductive history to seek partners most likely to be fertile, while females have been programmed to seek the partners most likely to succeed and thus to be able to provide for their offspring.

Early Anthropological Studies of Sexuality. A third approach to the study of sex is to study it cross-culturally to determine which behaviors may be termed universal. This type of research has been conducted primarily by anthropologists traveling to the Pacific Islands, Africa, Latin America, and elsewhere to describe (among other things) the sexual habits of quite different cultural groups. The subjects and their behavior were distant from the everyday lives of the investigators and their readers—primarily Europeans and North Americans—and therefore the subject matter was not especially threatening. It was socially acceptable to read about sex in Samoa (Mead, 1928) or about sexual variations in the underdeveloped world (Ford and Beach, 1951) long before similar descriptions of the sexual habits of one's family, friends, and neighbors were permissible. In an analogous way, (see Figure 1-4) *National Geographic* published photographs of bare-breasted African and Polynesian women for decades before a magazine like *Playboy* (which first appeared in 1953) could legally present similar pictures of the bare-breasted girl next door.

FIGURE 1-4 *NUDITY: ACCEPTABLE IF IT'S THEM, OBSCENE IF IT'S US* Anthropological studies of the sexual behavior of groups geographically and socially distant from us were acceptable long before similar studies of European and North American populations could be conducted. Perhaps, for the same reasons, magazines such as *National Geographic* could publish revealing photographs of "natives" long before any magazine could publish similar photographs of "us."

Like the study of abnormal sex and animal sex, cross-cultural studies could also be viewed as a collection of the strange and marvelous details of individuals geographically and socially far removed from our lives. Table 1-3 presents a sampling of such findings.

This research also served a more general purpose than providing interesting descriptive information. The major implications of animal research may be said to involve the similarities among various species based on genetic predispositions. Much of human sexual behavior can thus be viewed as being impelled by biological forces. Anthropological studies of different cultures provide a contrasting message. That people differ widely in what they do sexually suggests that a great many of our practices are learned. Instead of discovering universal characteristics of human nature, scientists such as Margaret Mead found evidence that different cultures can create different and even opposite behavioral patterns:

TABLE 1-3 **Cultural Variations in Sexual Expression**

Anthropological research provides numerous details about sexual practices in other cultures. Of significance is the resulting evidence pointing to the very different ways humans learn to express their sexual needs.

FINDING	GROUP	SOURCE
Children and young adolescents spend their evenings together in the *ghotul* in sexual play and lovemaking	Muria, a nonHindu tribal group in India	Elwin (1968)
The young are kept ignorant about sex, sex play and premarital sex are prohibited, and sexual pleasure in adulthood is devalued—sex occurs only to have offspring.	Cheyenne Indians in North America	Hoebel (1960)
During foreplay, female bites off pieces of male's eyebrow and spits them aside.	Apinaye in Brazil	Goldstein (1976)
The sight of a navel is sexually arousing, so this portion of the body must be covered in public.	Samoa	Gebhard (1985)
Only weak males get engaged in order to have sex; masculine males "sleep crawl" to girl's house at night, quietly sweet-talk her out of resisting, and have sex silently so as not to wake her parents.	Mangaias in Polynesia	Ortner and Whitehead (1981)
As part of the marriage ceremony, groom is insulted by bride's family and vice versa. After ceremony, groom tries to hurt bride by thrusting roughly while she cries and resists, often being held down by groom's friends.	Gusii in Kenya	Levine (1959)

If those temperamental attitudues which we have traditionally regarded as feminine—such as passivity, responsiveness, and a willingness to cherish children—can so easily be set up as the masculine pattern in one tribe, and in another be outlawed for the majority of women as well as the majority of men, we no longer have any basis for regarding such aspects of behavior as sex-linked [Mead, 1935, pp. 279–280].

As Gregersen (1986, p. 88) points out, "Just on an ideological level, we find tremendous variation: societies that encourage premarital promiscuity and those that require nonvirgin brides to be killed, societies that permit polygamy and those that insist on monogamy, societies that make homosexual acts compulsory for all its members and others that condemn all such acts for any member." He concludes that these dramatic differences from group to group make it very difficult to create a theory based on universal patterns of human behavior.

To take just one example—you might assume that oral contact is a basic part of human sexual interaction, for example, kissing your partner on the mouth. There are, nevertheless, some societies in which people do not kiss at all—the Somali of Africa, the Lepcha of Asia, and the Siriono of South America (Gregersen, 1982). Similarly, other oral activity, such as fellatio and cunnilingus, may be practiced by most individuals in one culture (in the present-day United States, for example) and be totally unknown in another. It is also of interest to find that although fellatio may be common in a culture in which cunnilingus is unknown, the opposite pattern has never been reported (Gregersen, 1986).

Altogether, it is clear that standards of what is acceptable and unacceptable sexually vary across time and place. We will return to this point in discussing topics such as homosexual behavior, sexual techniques, and laws about sex in later chapters.

■ Moving Toward Modern Sex Research: Pioneering on a Rocky Road

Sex research that focuses on the normal human behavior of people in one's own culture has threatening implications (Gagnon, 1975). The findings are potentially about *your* most private thoughts and activities—not to mention those of your parents, your children, and everyone else you know. It is scarcely surprising, then, that those who first bridged this scientific gap met with resistance, criticism, and sometimes violent condemnation. We will mention three examples of these pioneering efforts, though these individuals are obviously not the only ones who blazed trails.

Freud: Psychoanalytic Patients in Austria. One of the first was Sigmund Freud (1856–1939), whose work with emotionally disturbed patients could have fit comfortably within the accepted medical tradition of his era in detailing their sexual peculiarities. Instead, his work developed in a quite different way. As a young physician, he worked as a neurologist; among his patients, he discovered many instances in which there were no *physical* causes of paralysis, blindness, and other dysfunctions. As a result, he turned to psychological explanations of the physical symptoms. He was interested in a "talking cure" used by others, and he developed the technique that became **psychoanalysis**, as shown in Figure 1-5. One of Freud's early proposals was that sexual frustration led to psychological disorders.

In addition to treating and trying to understand neurological illness, Freud also had other goals, and he soon became involved in constructing the first comprehensive theory of personality. He wanted to describe and explain the psychological functioning of *all* human beings, not just those who were functioning abnormally. When he began writing and lecturing about such topics as the sexual attraction of small children toward their parents, the resentment felt by females from early childhood about not possessing a penis, or males' anxiety about the threat of castration, his audiences were shocked, offended, and often unwilling to consider him as a serious, respected professional. Today, concepts such as the Oedipal and Electra complexes, penis envy, and castration anxiety are no longer shocking. They were innovative in their time and led to a considerable amount of sexual research and theorizing.

Kinsey: Surveys in Indiana. The next quantum leap in sex research took place far from Freud's Vienna in Bloomington, Indiana (see Figure 1–6). Alfred Kinsey (1894–1956), an entomologist at Indiana University, was asked in 1938 to create a noncredit course on the subject of marriage. In attempting to prepare lectures,

FIGURE 1-5 *FREUDIAN THEORY: SEX AS A BASIC FORCE IN OUR LIVES* In developing the therapeutic procedures of psychoanalysis and the (psychoanalytic) personality theory that grew out of his practice, Sigmund Freud emphasized conscious and unconscious sexual motivation, early sexual experiences, and sexual frustrations. These themes were not initially well received by his medical colleagues or by the general public.

Kinsey discovered that almost nothing was known about the sexual behavior of the nondeviant American population. Although some survey work had been done in the study of marital compatibility (e.g., Davis, 1929; Hamilton, 1929; Terman et al., 1938), the content was much less detailed and less generally applicable than Kinsey desired.

To remedy the situation, Kinsey began to collect data himself, first administering questionnaires to some of the students in his class and then expanding his investigations to subjects beyond the campus. He also began to use personal interviews to obtain the desired information. He felt that this technique was more flexible and provided greater detail. These initial efforts grew into an interview procedure lasting several hours and covering hundreds of questions that were administered to 12,000 men and women from various social classes and races in the United States (Gebhard, 1976). The aim was to obtain objec-

tive descriptive data dealing with a multitude of intimate sexual activities such as masturbation, premarital sex, intercourse frequency among married couples, oral sex, extramarital sex, homosexual acts, and much more. Kinsey's first major publication of his findings was the book, *Sexual Behavior in the Human Male* (Kinsey et al., 1948), followed five years later by the companion volume, *Sexual Behavior in the Human Female* (Kinsey et al., 1953). For the first time, there was an enormous amount of very specific information covering numerous aspects of the sexual experiences and practices of the general population.

As did Freud at the beginning of the century, Kinsey found himself at the center of criticism and controversy. One problem, pointed out by Gregersen (1986), was that the American ideals of appropriate and legal sexual activity did not match the actual behavior reported by these subjects. Many officially condemned behaviors such as adultery, homosexual-

FIGURE 1-6 *KINSEY'S SURVEYS: DETERMINING SEXUAL PRAC-TICES ON MAIN STREET* Faced with the request to teach a course on marriage, Alfred Kinsey found that very little was known about human sexual behavior. He began conducting survey research, and this effort grew into his milestone nationwide studies in the 1940s and 1950s. The Institute for Sex Research at Indiana University remains as a major research center.

ity, and oral sex were found to be common activities in our culture. Americans were startled to learn that six out of ten women had masturbated, three out of ten post-pubescent men had experienced orgasm with a partner of their own sex, and four out of ten husbands had engaged in sex with women other than their wives. Kinsey's research was not well received by his colleagues on the Indiana faculty, and funding was always difficult. Then, in the 1950s, several right-wing politicians decided that the findings of such research would weaken the moral fiber of American citizens and make the nation an easy target for a Communist takeover (Gebhard, 1976). The F.B.I. actually monitored Kinsey's work because they feared

that it would corrupt and endanger the nation's children (Sonenschein, 1987). The work continued despite these problems primarily because of the support of the university's president and the money generated by the surprising popularity of the "Kinsey reports." Presumably these books sold well because such information was novel at the time, and a great many people wanted to learn as much as possible about sexuality.

Kinsey improved the survey method by repeating sensitive questions in order to obtain more reliable data. He also placed the most threatening questions (for example, about homosexual experiences) near the end of the survey. Nonetheless, his methodology was criticized because he was unable to sample all of the groups in his original plan and because the total sample was smaller than he would have liked. Today, though Kinsey died over thirty years ago, the Institute for Sex Research remains an active scientific center, and its research is no longer viewed as scandalous.

Masters and Johnson: Laboratory Sex in Missouri. Though Freud's emphasis on childhood sexuality and the Kinsey approach to sexual surveys gradually became part of the mainstream, a third scientific breakthrough caused another shockwave of disapproval and criticism. As noted earlier, the study of sexual behavior usually relies on verbal reports of what individuals *say* they have done, want to do, fantasize about, and so forth. In the 1960s in a St. Louis laboratory, the now famous physician-psychologist team of William Masters and Virginia Johnson carried sex research to the "last frontier" by directly observing and measuring the physical bodily changes that occur during sexual acts, as Figure 1-7 shows.

In their first series of studies, the investigators asked men and women volunteers to engage in masturbation and intercourse in the laboratory while various bodily changes were assessed physiologically and through visual observation. After studying over 10,000 episodes of sexual activity involving 382 women and 312 men, Masters and Johnson (1966) published their best-selling book, *Human Sexual Response.* Among the many findings (see Chapter 3 for additional details) were the unexpected similarities of male and female arousal, the four stages of the sexual response cycle, and the capacity of females to experi-

FIGURE 1-7 *MASTERS AND JOHNSON: SEX-UAL BEHAVIOR IN THE LABORATORY* The re-search of Masters and Johnson crossed the "final frontier" of sexual investigations with the direct observation of volunteers engaged in masturbation and sexual interactions with partners.

ence repeated orgasms in contrast to males, whose re-sponsiveness is limited by the refractory period following orgasm (Masters and Johnson, 1966).

Even in the "swinging sixties," direct observation of sexual activity elicited the kind of negative response previously experienced by Freud and by Kinsey. Once again, the furor eventually died down, and this work has continued and been expanded to include homosexual behavior, the treatment of sexual

dysfunctions, and the importance of long-term sexual relationships (Masters and Johnson, 1970, 1976, 1979).

Timing is obviously crucial in determining the fate of controversial research endeavors. The special section, *Highlighting Research,* on pages 15–17, offers some historical insight into what happens when scientists are too far in advance of what their cultures will accept at the time.

Highlighting Research

BREAKING RESEARCH TABOOS

As you've seen, many now famous and respected research pioneeers met with extremely negative responses that included editorial attacks, dislike masked as scientific criticism, political controversy, and withdrawal of grant funds. Other pioneers in sex research ran into even worse difficulties. A crucial factor in the response to scientific breakthroughs is timing. Though it is difficult or impossible to predict in advance how negative the reaction may be to a new line of controversial research, experience tells us that dramatic societal changes pave the way for later scientific innovation.

Sex is not the only topic that has been studied before the culture was prepared to accept it. In the seventeenth century, Galileo (see Figure 1–8), the first individual to use a telescope to study the heavens, became convinced on the basis of his observations that Copernicus was correct that the earth orbited the sun and was not the center of the universe. The Church officially condemned this view in 1616, and Galileo was told to desist from expressing these views. Because he failed to obey, Galileo was summoned to Rome in 1633, tried, and placed under house arrest for the remainder of his life. The ban on

Copernican views, partially lifted by the Church over a century later in 1757, was finally removed entirely in 1820. Strangely enough, recent historical research suggests that this familiar version of Galileo's difficulties with the Church constitutes a cover story—a sort of plea bargaining for Galileo (Redondi, 1987). Galileo's real threat to the religious beliefs of his day was in advocating that matter is made of atoms; for the Church, such an idea was incompatible with the doctrine that bread and wine are changed (transsubstantiated) into the body and blood of Christ at communion. Galileo's views constituted heresy and

FIGURE 1-8 *GALILEO: ASTRONOMY AND ATOMIC THEORY BEFORE HIS CULTURE WAS READY*   Scientific research and scientific theories can be premature in the sense of being too far in advance of what the scientist's culture is willing to tolerate. This interaction between science and culture is not confined to sex. One example of nonsexual prematurity was Galileo's attempt to spread the concepts of Copernican astronomy and of the atomic theory of matter.

would have led to his execution. To prevent this outcome, a secret compromise was reached about what to tell the public, and a milder punishment (to the milder crime) was agreed upon. Though sex research has not led to threats of house arrest or the death penalty, such investigations have been the focus of heated controversy.

Even when sex research has not led to negative consequences, it has remained unpublished and unknown because the time was not "right." For example, in 1892, Clelia Mosher, a Stanford undergraduate, conducted a sex survey using forty-seven married women. The subjects (most of whom were born before 1870) reported that they usually had orgasm during intercourse, desired sexual rela-

tions, and used birth control (Jacob, 1979). Although many of Mosher's findings were remarkably similar to Kinsey's fifty years later, one interesting difference involved frequency of intercourse. As Table 1-4 shows, Mosher found a decrease in frequency related to age (as did more recent studies), but the rise in frequency from 1892 to 1953 to 1970 suggests increases in sexual interactions within marriage from generation to generation. In any event, Mosher later became one of the first women to obtain an M.D. degree at Johns Hopkins University.

The famous American psychologist, John B. Watson, undertook more controversial research than Mosher did and suffered negative consequences. Watson became interested in various questions

involving sex during World War I, long before Americans were prepared to permit such inquiry (Magoun, 1981). Watson investigated the way military audiences responded to films graphically depicting the dangers of venereal disease (Cohen, 1979).

One of the first problems Watson encountered with this research was the response of physicians who generally reacted quite negatively to material about genital diseases and other sexual matters in professional publications (Watson and Lashley, 1919). Watson (1929), as a consequence, decided that human sexual behavior should be studied by psychologists instead of by the medical profession.

While at Johns Hopkins University, Watson extended his faith in the behaviorist approach to the study of sex. That is,

TABLE 1-4   **Sex Surveys: Unpublished in 1892, Commonplace Today**

The earliest known survey of sexual behavior is an unpublished study conducted by Clelia Mosher in 1892. It is interesting to compare intercourse frequencies reported in the nineteenth century with those of Kinsey in 1953 and a national survey in 1970. The studies are consistent in showing a slight drop in frequency with age (roughly dividing the groups as above and below age thirty-five). There is also a steady increase in intercourse frequency over the decades.

	MARRIED FEMALES' SELF-REPORT OF INTERCOURSE FREQUENCY PER MONTH	
	Younger Women	Older Women
Mosher (1892)	4–5	3–4
Kinsey (1953)	7	5.5
National Fertility Survey (1970)	8.5	6.4

rather than rely on subjective verbal reports, he decided to deal directly with sexual behavior. Interestingly enough, this same idea appealed to Kinsey in the 1950s; he even designed space in the Institute for Sex Research to be used as a physiological laboratory to measure sexual responses directly (Pomeroy, 1966, 1972). The project was abandoned as too controversial, however.

If direct observation of sex was perceived as infeasible in the 1950s, Watson's decision to proceed with it in 1919 does not in retrospect seem wise. He went further astray in his choice of research subjects whose sexual interactions were to be monitored—he and a female graduate student were the only participants.

When university officials became aware of this research, he was dismissed, and his wife filed for divorce. All of Watson's data, including physiological recordings of sexual arousal, were seized by his wife and destroyed. Whatever his data may have revealed, information about bodily responses during sexual intercourse would be unavailable to science until almost a half century later when Masters and Johnson undertook similar research in a much more ethical fashion.

Conducting Sex Research: Observing, Correlating, and Experimenting

The basic process of research in behavioral science (as in other scientific research) involves systematic observation under specified conditions that can be repeated (or **replicated**) by other investigators (Mosher, 1989). Such research takes many forms, and we will describe how it is applied to sex research.

Scientific knowledge includes numerous components; at the simplest level there is careful observation of the basic phenomena being investigated. In sex research, much of the historical work we have described is of this variety. Observational research includes the examination and description of sexual anatomy and physiological functioning, the examination of sexual practices within a given culture, and the surveying of the sexual practices of a given popu-

lation. Research almost always involves speculation as well as data gathering. Scientists continually seek explanations and attempt to establish relationships between and among variables. We will examine a few brief examples of the way in which observational research is conducted and the way that such activity can lead to more general questions.

▪ Mapping Sexual Anatomy and Functioning

As previously suggested, sexual taboos prevented any detailed study of the sexual aspects of anatomy and physiology. In medical practice, cultural values interfered with diagnosis and treatment. For example, until the stethoscope was introduced in 1816, physicians placed an ear directly on the chest of each male patient to listen to the sounds made by his heart and lungs (Rosenberg, 1987). To examine a female patient, however, a physician was expected to place his ear on a handkerchief draped across her fully clothed chest.

Because of such restrictions in the past, much of the information described in Chapters 2 and 3 of this book is relatively recent. Additional anatomical knowledge is still being generated. For example, one basic question is still disputed (Alzate, 1985). Some women appear to expel a fluid (not urine) from the genital region during some orgasms (Belzer et al., 1984; Bohlen, 1982; Goldberg et al., 1983; Perry and Whipple, 1981; Sevely and Bennett, 1978). The mechanism for this may involve an area within the vagina. Grafenberg (1950) identified an erotically sensitive spot on the anterior (toward the front) wall of the vagina, near the external opening. The tissue here differs from that of the remainder of the vaginal lining. This portion of the vagina became known as the **Grafenberg spot**, or the **G spot** (see Figure 1-9), and some investigators believe that it represents the female prostate gland. It lies close to the underside of the urethra (the tube through which urine passes) and is 2 cm long and 1.5 cm wide. Stimulation of this area is reported to be sexually arousing, and such stimulation results in its temporary increase in size by about 50 percent (Hoch, 1980).

In response to G–spot stimulation, some women apparently ejaculate fluid at orgasm through the urethral opening. (Perry and Whipple, 1981). Though this expulsion of liquid was once believed to constitute a medical problem requiring surgery (Novicki, 1983), we now know that this response is a normal (though not universal) aspect of female sexual functioning (Zaviacic et al., 1988).

With the controversial discovery of a previously unknown anatomical feature and an explanation of why females may expel a liquid during sexual activity, the question is raised as to whether stimulation of the *male* prostate gland also leads to excitement and orgasm. Unlike the female's G spot, the male prostate is not ordinarily stimulated during intercourse. Contact with the male prostate usually occurs only (1) during a medical examination in which the physician inserts a gloved finger through the patient's anus to examine this organ, (2) during anal intercourse between gay males, (3) with digital stimulation of the anus by self or partner, or (4) when mechanical devices such as a dildo or string of beads are inserted

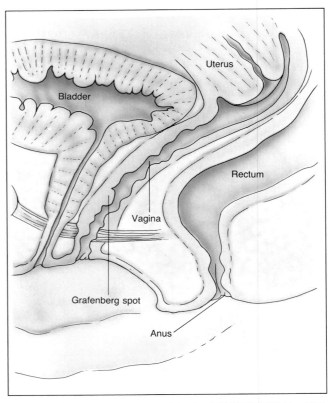

FIGURE 1-9 *GRAFENBERG SPOT: A CONTROVERSIAL ANATOMICAL FINDING* Though many of the findings are still a matter of dispute, the Grafenberg spot, a small body of cells on the anterior wall of the vagina, has been proposed as (1) especially sensitive to erotic stimulation, (2) a triggering area for female ejaculation, and (3) the female counterpart of the male prostate gland.

anally. In such instances, stimulation of the prostate can lead to sexual arousal, and this kind of manipulation can elicit orgasm and ejaculation. One possible conclusion is that males and females are quite similar in possessing a prostate gland and in how they respond when it is stimulated; the primary way the gland differs between the sexes is simply with respect to its location.

Sex in Other Cultures

Anthropological descriptions of cultures quite different from our own may seem like the content of a novel or a travelogue—exotic natives behaving in interesting ways. As we noted earlier, such investigations aim at something considerably beyond providing entertaining reading. Very often, these studies demonstrate that the same broad principles apply to very different cultures. They also demonstrate that human beings can learn to express their sexual needs in quite different ways.

We will describe one example of this type of research. Money et al. (1970) spent a considerable amount of time studying the Yolngu on Elcho Island, near the coast of the Northern Territory of Australia. These aborigines were found to be quite different from ourselves in their attitudes about childhood sexuality.

The scientists reported a classroom experience in which an eight-year-old described how two six-year-olds demonstrated "nigi nigi" (sexual intercourse) at the previous night's campfire. The adults who saw their demonstration and the children who heard the story thought it hilarious. Adults believe it is quite acceptable, though amusing, for children to pretend to have intercourse. In our culture, children can pretend to cook mud pies or pretend to shoot one another (as in Figure 1-10), but most adults would be quite uncomfortable watching children embracing on the floor, making pelvic thrusts, and otherwise imitating adult sexual interactions.

There are many ways in which the Yolngu are extremely permissive about childhood sex. Crying infants are soothed by an adult stroking their genitals. Nudity—at least until the European settlers fought against the custom—was accepted from infancy through old age. Children of both sexes shower together, experience no confusion about the anatomical differences between males and females, and do not respond negatively to public urination and defecation. Sex play is common throughout childhood with both same-sex and opposite-sex partners, as is masturbation, and the details of menstruation are taught to females long before puberty. If many of *our* sexual problems are caused by repressive attitudes, lack of information, and the resultant anxiety, then, by contrast, the Yolngu should have no sexual problems.

Yet they do, and this is by no means a "sexual paradise." In a culture where males are dominant, each can have several wives, usually women who are sisters. The Yolngu's *polygamous promise system* gives the female no choice as to her mate, and she is expected to marry as soon as she reaches puberty. A very young girl frequently must accept a relatively old man as her husband, and she is then supposed to have as many children as possible.

One outcome of this situation is that the sexually free female child becomes a woman who is apathetic about sex, no longer able to have an orgasm, and generally unhappy. In this male-oriented society, men—as you may expect—are well adjusted sexually and generally have a happy life. They don't have to take care of the children or supply the family's food (unless they decide to go hunting or fishing for fun). Males have sex whenever they wish with whichever wife they choose, and report no sexual dysfunctions or loss of sexual interest. Except in childhood and

FIGURE 1-10   *PLAYING AT ADULTHOOD: COOKING AND KILLING—YES, MAKING LOVE—NO*   In our society, children are encouraged to rehearse many aspects of adult behavior in their play activities. We do not, however, allow children to rehearse adult sexual activity even though such childhood play is common in many other cultures.

adolescent play, homosexuality is unknown. Sex crimes such as rape or child abuse do not seem to occur.

Altogether, an investigation such as this provides information that leads to the proposal that sexual problems in adulthood are the result not simply of sexual restrictiveness but also stem from other factors such as the respective power the culture grants men and women. Despite similar childhood experiences, very different adult experiences for males and females seem to result in good sexual adjustment for Yolngu men though not for Yolngu women.

■ Surveying Sexual Behavior

One of the most efficient ways to find out about the sexual activities of large numbers of individuals in our own society is to ask them to respond to a series of questions. These investigations use **surveys** that contain questions about past and present behavior, preferences, attitudes, beliefs, thoughts and fantasies, or whatever. Among the many technical aspects of survey research is the necessity of asking questions in

such a way (under appropriate conditions) that respondents will be likely to give truthful answers to each item (*not* as in Figure 1-11). We will look at an example of such research.

In human sexual functioning, it is becoming increasingly clear that fantasy and imagination are of considerable importance. Though detailed data are still relatively rare, there is now reason to believe that there is some connection between the content of our sexual fantasies and the type of behavior we engage in. For example, Greendlinger and Byrne (1987) investigated the relationship between the self-reported coercive fantasies of males and their self-reported experience with initiating coercive sexual behavior. The hypothesis was that the more males engage in fantasies involving coercion, the more they would act in a sexually coercive fashion.

Subjects were male undergraduates enrolled in junior- and senior-level psychology courses. They were given several surveys and tests under conditions of anonymity, but we will focus here on only two measures. With respect to fantasies, subjects were asked to indicate the extent to which they think

"Would you say Attila is doing an excellent job, a good job, a fair job, or a poor job?"

FIGURE 1-11 *SURVEYS: WHO ASKS WHICH QUESTIONS UNDER WHAT CONDITIONS?* Survey research must be conducted in such a way that the respondents can give honest and truthful answers that are not distorted by the way the questions are worded, the position of the person who asks the questions, or anticipation of future consequences for expressing a particular opinion. That Attila's survey represents a valid assessment of opinion is doubtful.
Source: *New Yorker*, November 29, 1982, p. 37.

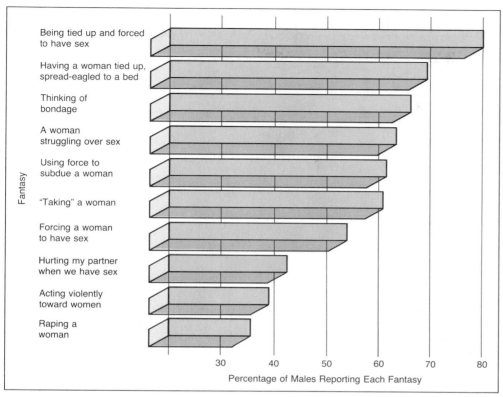

FIGURE 1-12 *MALE SEXUAL FANTASIES: FORCE, VIOLENCE, COERCION* A survey of 114 anonymous male undergraduates revealed that sexual fantasies with themes of force and violence are relatively common.
Source: Data from Greendlinger & Byrne, 1987.

about several types of sexual scenarios. Ten of these fantasy themes were found to be associated with one another, and they have in common some aspect of force, domination, and coercion. The fantasy plots are listed in Figure 1-12, along with an indication of how commonly each particular fantasy was reported among these subjects.

These same male subjects were also asked about the extent to which they had engaged in various coercive techniques in an effort to obtain sex from a female against her will. Figure 1-13 shows their responses to these questions.

The two figures indicate the relative frequency with which the fantasies are experienced and the relative frequency with which coercive behaviors occur, but more information is needed. It is important to determine whether these two events are related to one another. Throughout this book, we will indicate whether or not two variables are associated. Statisti-

cally, this is most often expressed as a **correlation**. In the study just described, the fantasies and the coercive acts *were* significantly correlated. That is, males who generate coercive sexual fantasies most often are also most likely to engage in coercive sexual behavior; those who have such fantasies least often are least likely to coerce females. A finding is labeled **significant** if analysis indicates it is sufficiently strong that it probably represents a real, nonchance occurrence.

■ Experimental Research: Manipulating an Independent Variable to Determine Its Effect

Many of the studies discussed so far are simply descriptive (e.g., comparing the tissue of the Grafenberg spot with surrounding vaginal tissue) or **correlational** (e.g., the relationship between fantasies and behavior). Correlational research informs us that cer-

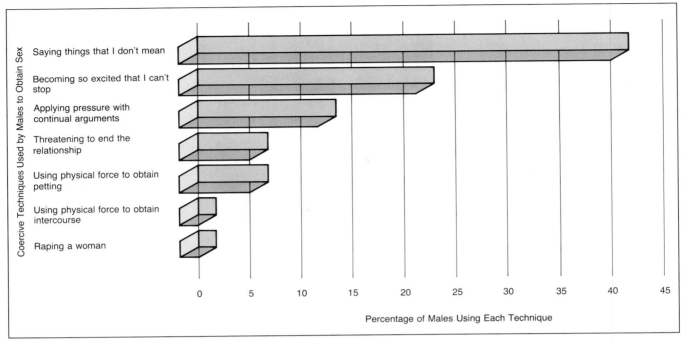

FIGURE 1-13 *MALE COERCIVE TECHNIQUES: LIES, THREATS, FORCE* A survey of 114 anonymous male undergraduates revealed that a variety of verbal and physical means are used in attempts to persuade or force females to engage in sexual activity.
Source: Data from Greendlinger & Byrne, 1987.

tain events tend to occur together. In correlational research, we cannot determine whether event A (such as coercive fantasies) leads to or "causes" event B (such as coercive behavior), or vice versa, or whether some third factor is responsible for both A and B (such as exposure to particular themes in movies and on television).

Stimulus or response dimensions that can vary are called *variables*. The only way to determine that changes in one variable are responsible for changes in another variable is to manipulate one event (the **independent variable**) in a controlled **experimental** setting to determine its effect on a second event (the **dependent variable**). In this type of research, if B is consistently affected whenever we make changes in A, it can be concluded that A and B have an **antecedent-consequent relationship**. In everyday language, we usually say that A causes B.

In discussing work on the Grafenberg spot, we indicated that manual stimulation of this tissue is followed by an increase in the size of the spot and by self-reported increases in sexual excitement. This procedure is, roughly speaking, an experiment. When the independent variable (manual stimulation) is in-

troduced, there is an effect on two dependent variables (physical changes in the tissue and changes in reported arousal level). When the stimulation is stopped, these responses stop.

Most experimental investigations are somewhat more elaborate in design, but the basic principles are the same. Commonly, there are at least two conditions, involving an **experimental group** and **control group**. Subjects are placed in one of these groups by **random assignment**. This assignment is one of the ways that the experimenter exerts control over other variables that could possibly affect the dependent variable. For example, you would not want the experimental group to consist of only Catholics and the control group of only Unitarians. You would not want the experimental group to be recruited from a human sexuality class and the control group from an accounting course. Beyond the subjects, it is also necessary to control the external conditions so that they are the same for the experimental and control groups. You would not want the experimental group to be run on New Year's Eve and the control group on July 4. The general idea is simply to make the two groups as similar as possible with respect to everything that might be relevant *except* the introduction of the independent variable in the experimental group.

We will turn to a brief example of an idea that led to correlational research and also to experimental research. It has been known for some time that when people think about sexual matters, they become sexually excited, both as indicated by self-reported arousal and by physiological measures (Kelley and Byrne, 1983). This general finding has led some to propose that individual differences in sex drive (defined as the frequency with which people engage in sexual activity) may be based on individual differences in thinking about sex (daydreams, memories of past sexual experiences, creation of imagined sexual scenes, and so on). Supporting this hypothesis are several correlational findings. For example, men typically exhibit a higher sex drive than women; in addition, male college students are found to have about twice as many sexual fantasies each day as women (Jones and Barlow 1987). In another correlational study using only females, it was found that women who read soft-core erotic romances have sexual intercourse twice as often as women who do not (Coles and Shamp, 1984). The results of both studies are consistent with the proposal that sex fantasies lead to sexual behavior, but many other explanations are also possible.

More convincing data would be provided by an experiment in which fantasies are induced in an experimental group versus no fantasies in a control group, followed by a determination of whether the two groups differ in their subsequent sexual behavior. Eisenman (1982) did just that by having some college students write sexual fantasies during a twenty-minute experimental session; other college students (the control group) wrote about nonsexual topics. During the week following the writing experience, the experimental group engaged in more sexual acts than the control group. These results strongly suggest that sexual fantasies serve as an antecedent causing sexual behavior to occur.

Problems that Arise in Conducting Sex Research

The issues discussed in this section are common to all research on human behavior but cause special problems in sex research. The reason for indicating these problems is to emphasize the difficulties that are encountered in conducting research in this area of inquiry and to encourage you to ask meaningful questions whenever you read about research findings.

■ Sampling Problems

As previously noted, all research projects choose a group of subjects (a sample) who constitute only a very limited portion of the total population. In the best of all possible worlds, the sample would be randomly chosen and be a **representative sample** of the total group (see Figure 1-14). Thus, a representative sample of American citizens would match the total array of Americans in terms of age, sex, race, education, marital status, income, political affiliation, religious beliefs, geographic location, and any other obvious characteristics that we may expect to affect the behavior under investigation. The absolute number of respondents is not as critical as is their representativeness (though an extremely small sample is usually inadequate). If you wanted to know the average

FIGURE 1-14 *OBTAINING A REPRESENTATIVE SAMPLE OF STUDENTS* If you wanted to learn about the sexual attitudes and practices of students on a college campus, which of these samples would you use for a survey? Why?

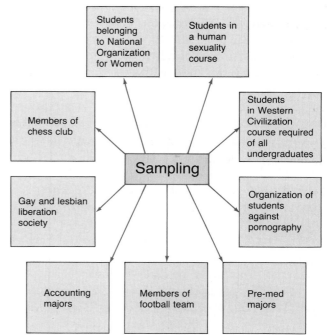

height of males, a sample of 1,000 basketball players would not provide any better data than a sample of 10 basketball players, because neither sample is representative of males in general.

Sampling in Sexual Research.   With sexual behavior, the goal of **random**, representative sampling is essentially impossible to obtain because many people do not want to be asked questions about sex, to read or view erotic material, to reveal intimate details of their private lives, and/or to have an experimenter attach a measuring device to their genitals. Further, evidence suggests that people who avoid participating in sex research are different in several respects from those who do participate. Subjects taking part in sex research are more sexually tolerant, experienced, and liberal than those who refuse (Saunders et al., 1985; Wolchik et al., 1985). When we extrapolate from these participants to characterize people in general, Americans in general, or whomever, mistakes are very likely to be made. No sexual investigation is able to obtain a random sample in which each person in the total population has an equal chance of being selected.

To cite one example of the sampling problem, Hite (1987) published a popular book that reports survey data involving female experiences with love, relationships, and marriage. Her findings include some startling and discouraging figures—88 percent of single women believe they are picking the wrong men to date, 70 percent of women who have been married at least five years are having extramarital affairs, and 92 percent of all divorces are initiated by women. A basic weakness with these percentages and others that the author reports rests in the sampling. Subjects were drawn from feminist organizations. Even if every woman contacted actually responded to the questionnaires, they would not be representative. As sociologist Arlie Russell Hochschild (1987, p. 3) says, "Ms. Hite could only talk about women in these organizations, unless these members 'represent' all women. How many women join feminist organizations? Or, *any* organization, for that matter?" Altogether, Hite's method represents volunteer bias, in which the respondents have characteristics that set them apart from other possible volunteers.

Beyond that problem, Hite did not obtain the responses of all or even very many of these potential subjects. Though 100,000 questionnaires were dis-

tributed, only 4.5 percent were returned. In most survey research, the return rate usually ranges between 40 and 70 percent. Is it possible that those who were motivated enough to respond to Hite's 127 essay questions were the women most likely to have problems with love, relationships, and marriage? If so, that could well explain why her figures on adultery, divorce, and so forth differ greatly from those reported by other investigators.

Surveys versus Experiments.   Though sampling issues apply to all types of research, they are more crucial in some instances than others. In a survey study, we usually want to report what people do, when they do it, how often, their attitudes about it, and so forth. Thus, if Kinsey indicates that one third of American males have had a homosexual experience or if Hite indicates that 81 percent of women are in unequal emotional relationships, it is essential to know how representative the sample is. In contrast, if an experimenter finds that a given stimulus (e.g., sexually explicit films) affects a specific response (e.g., penile erection), it is possible—though doubtful—that this antecedent-consequent relationship is limited to a specific sample of the population. More likely, this relationship would be found among a wide range of male subjects, even if the subjects in the original experiment were not a representative sample.

Perhaps a helpful analogy is a *survey* that asks whether an individual has received an electric shock in the past year. If the sample consisted of electricians, the percentage reporting that experience might well differ greatly from a sample of bartenders. On the other hand, if an *experiment* were conducted, and it was found that electrical shock led to pain, withdrawal from the electric stimulus, and a blister on the skin, the findings would probably be very similar for electricians and bartenders.

Neil's Sampling Difficulties.   In the *Penthouse* project described at the beginning of this chapter, the sample used was not at all representative. First, the initial self-selected pool consisted of individuals who decided to write about sexual matters in a letter to the magazine. Second, only some of these writers elected to mention penis length in specific terms. Third, only some of their letters were then selected by the editors to be printed. Among other considerations, perhaps only men with longer-than-average penises have exciting sexual adventures to write about, perhaps only those with longer-than-average penises elect to mention length, and/or perhaps the editors are more inclined to select letters in which long rather than short penises are described.

For all of these reasons, the sample used by Neil was unsatisfactory.

■ Validity and Reliability

The term *validity* refers to the extent to which a measure actually assesses what it purports to assess. Thus, a test that is supposed to predict success in college should, in fact, predict success in college. **Reliability** refers to the consistency of a measuring device. For example, an instrument that measures air pressure in your tires should give the same reading at one o'clock and at two o'clock—unless something has occurred in between. For example, your car may have run over a nail. Consistency also means that two such devices should indicate the same air pressure reading if they are used at the same time, and two individuals looking at the same gauge should report the same air pressure.

Sex Research: Validity and Reliability. As mentioned, we often must deal with data that are based on verbal self-reports about sex. If a subject is asked how frequently he or she engaged in sexual intercourse last month, the answer may or may not correspond with reality for a number of reasons. For example, the subject may not remember accurately, or the subject might lie. The same is true in experiments when subjects are asked about their sexual preferences, emotions, or beliefs. What is said to the experimenter may or may not correspond to what the subject actually prefers, feels, or believes. Among other possibilities, the subject may be trying to please or impress the experimenter, or trying to report what seems most socially desirable, and/or trying unsuccessfully to be honest. Given the way people respond to sexual matters, we would probably have less difficulty believing that a subject is giving a valid answer about his or her feelings about a given political candidate than about anal intercourse.

Reliability can also be a problem. As an example, when Kinsey asked male subjects to go home, measure their erect penises along the top side, and write down the length in inches, it is quite possible that reliability was less than perfect. Inconsistency of measurement could easily occur, depending on whether the ruler was pressed into the abdomen or allowed to rest gently on the skin surface, how carefully the measure was taken as to the location of the tip of the penis, whether each subject rounded up or down to the nearest half-inch, and so forth.

Neil's Validity and Reliability Difficulties. Even if you could set aside the sampling problems with the magazine study, you would still have good reason to question the validity of the letters that stated penis length. Men would seem likely to give an exaggerated version of their genital size, especially when there is no way to check the validity of their statements. We would also have reason to question the study's reliability. Why? We have no idea whether a person describing a "9-inch penis" actually measured penis length or simply estimated it. If a measurement was taken, we do not know whether it was made along the top side, bottom side, or where.

In summary, the data leave much to be desired, and the discrepancies between the magazine data and the Kinsey data suggest that deficiencies in sampling, validity, and reliability may have played a role in producing Neil's unusual findings.

■ Ethical Issues in Sex Research

Ethics must be considered in all research, and we will briefly outline some of the most important such issues in sex research, as Table 1-5 summarizes. Organizations such as the Society for the Scientific Study of Sex, the American Psychological Association, the American Psychological Society, and the American Psychiatric Association have developed guidelines for conducting sexual research.

1. Subjects must be *fully informed* about the nature of the research beforehand. No participant in sex research should be in the position of being surprised and potentially offended by the nature of the questions asked, the content of any stimulus material such as pictures or stories, or by the way his or her responses are measured. Deception as to research procedures and methods is unacceptable.

2. Subjects must participate *voluntarily* and be permitted to *refuse to answer* any and all questions

TABLE 1-5 **Ethical Considerations in Sex Research**

All research must be conducted according to explicit ethical standards, and these considerations are of special importance when the subject matter is sex.

ETHICAL SEX RESEARCH	UNETHICAL SEX RESEARCH
Subjects are told beforehand that they will be viewing a sexually explicit film depicting oral sex and intercourse.	Subjects are told beforehand that they will be viewing a *National Geographic* film but are actually shown a sexually explicit film.
Subjects volunteer to participate in research and are told that they can omit answering questions if they wish and may terminate their participation in the study at any time.	Subjects are required to participate in research and are told that they must answer every question and cannot terminate their participation in the study until it is completed.
Subjects who have experienced sexual trauma are asked questions about the event only if they wish to deal with it and if the inquiry is conducted for very important research reasons.	Victims of sexual trauma are asked to describe all of the details of their experience simply because the investigator is curious about male-female differences in dealing with emotional events.
Subjects participate anonymously and all responses are strictly confidential.	Subjects' names are attached to all data, and this information is available to school authorities, police, and parents.
Subjects are fully debriefed when the investigation ends so they will know what the research was all about and why each procedure was used.	Subjects are told that the research is too complicated for them to understand and that the experimenter needs to run the next batch of subjects as quickly as possible.

and even to *terminate participation* in the study freely without interference. Even those who have been fully informed about the research may become upset or disturbed by certain questions, certain movie scenes, or by the reality of using a genital measuring device. They must be assured that they will not be forced to remain in an unpleasant situation.

3. Any survey or experiment that deals with subject matter that might cause distress must be conducted with *very special care*. Victims of child abuse, incest, or rape, for example, should be asked about or otherwise reminded of their experiences only if they have expressed willingness to deal with such matters and only if it is extremely important to a given investigation to obtain those data. Supportive assistance should be readily available if a subject appears to become emotionally upset, and access to such support should be available even after the research is concluded.

4. All data provided by subjects must be totally *confidential* so that no one can ever link a particular response to a specific individual. Ideally, the subjects participate *anonymously*, and their names are never recorded in association with any of the data they provide. In addition to pro-

tecting the subjects, these procedures help reduce any tendency to lie or otherwise distort answers (Tice, 1987).

5. Subjects should be fully *debriefed* at the conclusion of the research so that they learn something as a function of serving as a subject. There are good reasons for the investigator to withhold some types of information beforehand; responses can be badly distorted if the subjects know what the experimenter expects to find or if they know the details of the research design. Afterward, however, they should be told every detail—or at least as much as they want to know. Those who take part as research subjects are providing an extremely important service to the scientific enterprise, and it is appropriate to let them know the vital part they have played in expanding knowledge.

Our emphasis on cautions and ethical concerns may suggest that those who serve as subjects in sex research are often devastated by the experience. In fact, follow-up studies of such subjects indicate neither discomfort during the experiment nor negative aftereffects. Instead, participants perceive their research experience as personally rewarding (Alzate and Londono, 1987).

Summarizing the Information about Sex Research . . .

Science provides a way to obtain and advance information about our world, but sexuality was not scientifically investigated until relatively recently. The study of sex began by focusing on subject populations that were different from and so not threatening to those conducting the research. The earliest acceptable approaches involved medical case histories of patients engaged in abnormal sexual practices, the sexual behavior of nonhuman species, and the sexual customs practiced in primitive cultures. In time, investigations began to include the normal sexual activities of Europeans and North Americans. Both the general public and the scientific community responded negatively, at least initially, to such pioneers as Freud, Kinsey, and Masters and Johnson.

Modern sex research continues all of the early lines of investigation (work with abnormal populations, other species, other cultures, and so on) as well as new approaches that would have been condemned as unethical and even illegal until relatively recently. Examples of current investigations include the study of sexual anatomy and physiology that resulted in the identification of the **Grafenberg spot** in the vagina and laboratory studies of subjective and physiological responses to explicit sexual slides and movies. Anthropological observations provide evidence of the diverse possibilities of human sexual development and functioning. Detailed **survey** research inquiries into the past and present acts, relationships, thoughts, and desires of all segments of the population, and we can determine the **correlations** among the variables studied. In **experimental** research, scientists manipulate an **independent variable** to determine its effect on a **dependent variable** and thus establish **antecedent-consequent relationships**.

Sex research is not different in principle from any other research, but the taboo nature of the topic clearly adds to the problems raised in obtaining a **representative sample** of subjects and developing response measures that are acceptable with respect to **validity** and **reliability**. Ethical issues are also acute in this area, so it is important to use only fully informed volunteer subjects who may withdraw from participation in the research whenever they wish. Special care must be taken not to cause distress to the subjects, to treat all information as confidential, and to debrief the participants afterward about all aspects of the study.

To Find Out More about Sex Research . . . .

Bullough, V. L. (1989). *The Society for the Scientific Study of Sex: A brief history*. Mt. Vernon, IA: Foundation for the Scientific Study of Sexuality.

   The history of modern sex research is summarized, beginning with work in 19th century Germany. The role of professional organizations is emphasized, focusing on the Society for the Scientific Study of Sex in the United States.

Byrne, D., & Kelley, K. (Eds.)(1986). *Alternative approaches to the study of sexual behavior*. Hillsdale, N. J.: Lawrence Erlbaum.

   This collection of chapters by psychologists, an anthropologist, and a sociologist provides a good view of the various ways that sexual behavior is investigated in three different fields of behavioral science.

Davis, C. M., Yarber, W. L. & Davis, S. L. (Eds.). (1988). *Sexuality related measures*. Mt. Vernon, IA: Foundation for the Scientific Study of Sexuality.

   This publication contains a valuable collection of over 100 paper and pencil measures of sexual attitudes, beliefs, emotional responses, and reported behaviors. All scales are reproduced along with information about their development, use, and scoring plus reliability and validity data.

Geer, J. H., & O'Donohue, W. (Eds.)(1987). *Theories of human sexuality*. New York: Plenum.

   This volume contains chapters by experts from a variety of fields. The focus is on the kinds of questions that are asked, the differing research methods, and what has been learned. Among the fourteen approaches covered are theological, feminist/political, evolutionary, anthropological, sociocultural, learning and physiological.

SEXUAL ANATOMY

The details of sexual anatomy can seem both daunting and unrelated to the process of sexual enjoyment. Nevertheless, as we point out in this chapter, learning something about your sexual anatomy and that of your partner can help increase your pleasure and also protect you from unnecessary problems and worries. In the following account, a female student believed that anatomical facts were uninteresting and far removed from her everyday concerns. She discovered that such information was necessary in order to help her overcome a specific fear based on lack of knowledge. You may discover similar gaps in what you know about bodily structures.

I'm embarrassed to tell this story, but it's true. In my high school you could get by without taking a lot of boring courses in biology; I dodged them because they seemed like nothing more than dull memory work that had nothing to do with my life.

During my first year in college I finally met someone really special. I knew that we were likely to end up having a sexual relationship. Steve would be my first—we were in love, and sex seemed to be the obvious way to express our feelings.

I knew I didn't want to get pregnant, but I was pretty ignorant about birth control. I had heard that the pill could be bad for you. I had also heard stories about women who used diaphragms that somehow broke loose and became lost inside them, causing a lot of problems.

That scared me, and I mentioned it to the physician at the Student Health Service. She must have heard all kinds of stories because, thank goodness, she didn't laugh at me. Instead, she showed me a plastic model of a woman's anatomy, pointed out how and where a diaphragm is inserted. She explained that there was no way it could float into your abdomen.

I decided to use a diaphragm, in part because it is an effective method of birth control and also because it provides some protection against disease, especially if your partner uses a condom at the same time. Back then, I was as ignorant about the inside of my body as most of us are about the geography of Central America. Looking back, I don't know how I ever thought that there was no need for me to know about my own body.

Now I know a lot more about biology; as a result, I'm much more confident about protecting myself and much less nervous about sex. Who knows, some day I may discover that knowing about Central America is relevant, too.

Barbara, age 19

Like Barbara, many people decide that anatomy and physiology are of little interest or relevance to them. Also like Barbara, many discover through experience that they were wrong. We strongly believe that information about sexual anatomy and functioning is of major importance to your health and enjoyment. By analogy, you can drive a car without any knowledge of what lies under the hood, but the consequences of lacking information about automobiles can be as negative as the consequences of lacking information about your body.

The basic structures that make it possible for human beings to experience sexual pleasure and to become parents are described in this chapter as we outline the details of *female sexual anatomy* and *male sexual anatomy*. For men, sexual arousal generally occurs in response to stimulation of the penis, especially the glans and the underside of the penile shaft, but there has been controversy concerning the precise location of comparable areas in women. In the special section on *female orgasm*, we provide information about the erotic sensitivity of women's anatomical structures.

Female Sexual Anatomy

Female sexual organs are usually divided into internal and external structures.

■ External Sexual Organs

In females the external structures include the mons pubis, labia majora and minora, vaginal introitus, hymen, and clitoris. Figure 2-1 depicts these genital structures—known collectively as the **vulva**.

Mons Pubis. The **mons pubis**, also called the **mons veneris**, a Latin term for the mountain of Venus, the Roman goddess of love. This cushion of fat lies over the pubic bone and, after puberty, is covered by pubic hair that varies from person to person in amount, color, texture, and curliness. A few shave it off because they or their partners believe that a hairless mons is sexually attractive (Winick, 1983). Twenty-five percent of women have a pubic hairline which extends to the navel.

Because the skin covering the mons has considerable sensitivity to sensations of touch, it can be sexually arousing to caress it. Though the mons itself is not erotically sensitive to pressure, such stimulation can transfer to the nearby clitoral area, thus providing an indirect sexual stimulus (Sorg, 1982).

Labia Majora. **Labia majora** is the Latin term for large lips. This structure is also called the outer lips. It consists of a fold of tissue surrounding the vaginal and urethral openings on each side. The labia majora vary among women in shape, color, and hairiness. Size does not vary greatly from individual to individ-

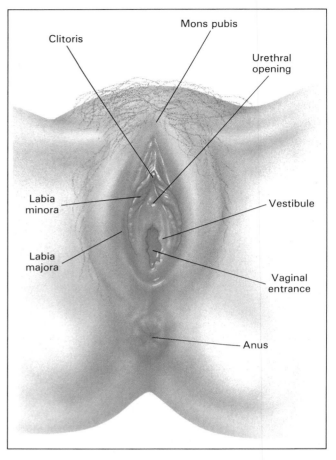

FIGURE 2-1 *EXTERNAL FEMALE SEXUAL ANATOMY* The external female sexual organs include the mons pubis, labia majora and minora, clitoris, clitoral hood, and vaginal introitus.

ual. The variations are not related to sexual pleasure in any significant way, in part because the labia majora are not as sensitive to touch as the skin covering the mons.

Labia Minora. The labia majora surround the smaller, inner lips called **labia minora**. During sexual excitement, both sets of labia swell slightly and unfold, exposing the vaginal and urethral openings. Oil glands are located underneath the skin surface of the labia minora, but this oil does not appear to affect the ease of vaginal intercourse directly. Rather, lubrication of the labia minora keeps them flexible by making the tissue more pliable. After menopause (the biological end of fertility), some of this flexibility is lost because of reduced oil production. One result is painful intercourse in postmenopausal women.

Clitoral Hood. The labia minora meet above the clitoris and form the skin fold known as the *clitoral hood*. It covers most of the clitoris during peak levels of sexual excitement; if it did not, direct stimulation of the clitoris at this time would tend to be painfully intense.

Clitoris. The **clitoris** lies in the area where the left and right portions of the labia majora join above the vestibule, as Figure 2-2 shows. Although the clitoris varies in size among different women, it is typically about 1 inch long and 0.5 inch wide. The clitoral shaft contains spongy cylinders, or **corpora cavernosa**, that fill with blood during sexual excitement, causing clitoral erection. When the shaft becomes erect, the **glans clitoris** (the head or tip of the clitoris) also enlarges and becomes increasingly sensitive to touch.

The clitoral glans, which is visible beneath the clitoral head, has the same density of nerve endings on its surface as the glans penis in males, though the male glans is about twenty times larger. Altogether, the clitoris has more dense nerve endings than any other surface of the female body, making it a crucially sensitive component of sexual arousal (D'Encarnacao and D'Encarnacao, 1979; Trainer, 1981). The clitoris has no reproductive function.

FIGURE 2-2 *THE ANATOMY OF THE CLITORIS* The clitoris is the most erotically sensitive portion of the female's genitals.

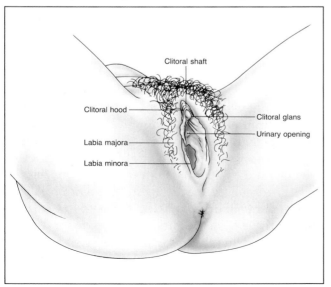

Secretions in the genital area sometimes collect under the clitoral hood, binding it to the shaft and glans, thereby producing pain during sexual stimulation. Surgery can remove this sticky, hardened substance, called smegma (Graber and Kline-Graber, 1979), but, preferably, this condition can be prevented by gently washing the area regularly.

The strong connection between the sensitivity of the clitoris and female sexual pleasure combined with cultural beliefs about the dangers of female sexuality have periodically led to the practice of surgical removal of this organ. Known as clitoridectomy, this procedure has been performed on an estimated 30 million women in 26 countries (Leo, 1980), though international efforts are now underway to stop this practice.

In Egypt, for example, clitoridectomy is expected to help preserve a young girl's virginity until marriage because it limits her ability to become sexually aroused. An even more radical procedure is to remove the clitoris and both labia among girls aged six to ten in order to prevent any sexual arousal prior to marriage (Assaad, 1980). An Egyptian woman, forced to undergo this surgery as a nine-year-old, described the experience:

> *I realized they were planning to [remove my clitoris] . . . I screamed and tried to run away . . . Both my aunt and the doctor explained that this was necessary for my future, to guarantee my marriage . . . The male assistant took me on his lap and stretched my legs apart. The doctor cut off the tip of my clitoris with his scissors . . . I could never submit my daughters to such brutality [Assaad, 1980, pp. 10–11].*

It should be noted that removal of the clitoris, labia, or both, limits but does not destroy a female's response to sexual stimulation. The remainder of the vulva, the outer portion of the vagina, and other parts of the body also can be sources of sexual arousal and enjoyment.

Vaginal Introitus. The term **vaginal introitus** means the entrance to the vagina. Between the inner lips is a recessed area known as the vestibule that contains the clitoris and the urethral opening. Along the sides of the introitus are openings to a pair of glands, **Bartholin's glands**, which ordinarily secrete a small amount of mucus. These openings can become plugged and infected if this area is insufficiently clean. Two more glands are situated on either side of the urethral orifice—the opening through which urine is expelled. These organs, *Skene's glands,* secrete a small amount of fluid. Together, the Bartholin's and Skene's glands are known as the *vestibular glands*; their contribution to a female's lubrication during sexual excitement is relatively minor.

Especially in young, sexually inexperienced females, tissue known as the **hymen** may partly cover the vaginal introitus. When the hymen completely covers the introitus, it is called *imperforate*. Because this condition can block menstrual flow, minor surgery is advised for an imperforate hymen. More common is an incomplete hymen (see Figure 2-3). Such tissue can be torn open by one's initial experiences with intercourse, during a fall, through the insertion of a tampon or fingers into the introitus, or by participation in active sports. Despite centuries of folklore, the absence of a hymen does not necessarily indicate that sexual intercourse has occured, nor do female virgins typically bleed at first intercourse when the hymen is torn. The appearance of blood is more

FIGURE 2-3 *THE HYMEN: MYTHS AND MISUNDERSTANDINGS*
The hymen is a thin tissue covering the introitus. Not all females have hymens; thus, its absence does not reliably indicate that vaginal intercourse has occured.

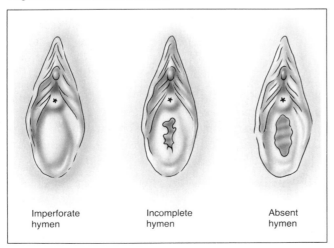

Imperforate hymen   Incomplete hymen   Absent hymen

likely to be the result of broken blood vessels within the vagina or the onset of menstruation.

The introitus is more important for sexual pleasure than was believed for many years. It is supplied with many nerve endings that increase responsiveness to touch. The **pubococcygeus muscle** (PC muscle), surrounding the introitus is also sensitive to the stretching that occurs during sexual arousal (Kroop, 1981). When the penis initially penetrates the introitus, the female is aroused and feels pleasure as the PC muscle is pressed so long as there is enough excitement to bring about lubrication and widening of the introitus (Graber, 1982). (Both males and females have PC muscles; in males these surround the base of the penis.) Experts disagree about whether exercising these muscles improves sexual functioning.

Between the vaginal introitus and the anus is the **perineum**, another sexually sensitive area. A portion of the PC muscle lies beneath it. As is discussed in Chapter 4, the woman's perineum is typically cut surgically during childbirth to provide a larger passage for the newborn infant. (In males, the perineum is the area between the scrotum and the anus.)

Internal Sexual Organs

The female's internal sexual organs include the vagina, uterus, oviducts, and ovaries.

Vagina. The **vagina** is a 4- to 6-inch tube located between the urinary bladder and the rectum. It is described as a potential rather than an actual space (see Figure 2-4); that is, the tube is ordinarily collapsed, but opens when penetrated—for example, by intercourse, the insertion of a tampon, medical examinations, and childbirth. When a woman is sexually aroused, a small amount of fluid originating in the engorged blood vessels percolates through the vaginal wall and produces lubrication.

The muscular walls of the vagina unfold and stretch during arousal. The depth, or length, of the vagina varies slightly from woman to woman, and may change over the life span. For example, pregnancy and childbirth increase its length. Weight gain creates the illusion of a longer vagina because of the extra fat padding the mons and labia. Conversely, the vagina may shorten because of reduced hormonal lev-

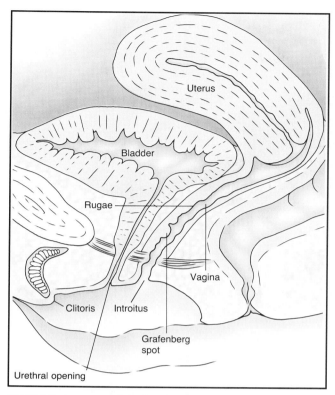

FIGURE 2-4 *STRUCTURE OF THE VAGINA* The vagina's structure reflects both its reproductive and pleasure functions.

Labels in figure: Uterus, Bladder, Rugae, Vagina, Clitoris, Introitus, Grafenberg spot, Urethral opening

els or a decrease in intercourse frequency, particularly in older women (Linton, 1981).

The vagina is a highly sensitive organ, though you may have read otherwise. Evidence about the role of the vagina and other areas in producing orgasm is described in the special section, *Increasing Enjoyment,* on pages 33–34.

Uterus. The **uterus** is a pear-shaped organ that houses the fetus during pregnancy. About 3 inches long and 2 inches wide, it is also called the womb. The uterus is located in the middle part of the lower abdomen, where it is supported by ligaments.

Its lower opening, the **cervix**, connects the uterus to the vagina. On the uterine side, this opening is called the internal **cervical os.** On the vaginal side, it is called the external cervical os and its diameter is about one eighth of an inch.

The upper, widest portion of the uterus is the fundus, as Figure 2-6 (see page 35) shows. The middle layer of the uterine wall, called the myometrium, consists of smooth muscle tissue that contracts during orgasm, stretches during pregnancy, and strongly contracts during labor. In the inner layer of the uterine wall, called the endometrium, are blood vessels that contribute to the menstrual flow. During each

Increasing Enjoyment

FEMALE ORGASM: LOCATING AREAS OF SENSITIVITY TO EROTIC STIMULATION

Emphasis on the relative importance of the clitoris versus the vagina in female sexual arousal has shifted periodically over the past decades. Freud proposed that orgasms produced by clitoral stimulation were "less mature" than those produced by vaginal stimulation. His distinction strongly implied that women should value intercourse in preference to masturbation or oral-genital stimulation (Robertiello, 1970). The sexual politics of this characterization seem clear—mature women can best function sexually if they have intercourse with a male partner while immature women masturbate or engage in manual or oral sex with other females.

A generation ago, there was a complete reversal of expert opinion. Sex pioneers Masters and Johnson (1966) ruled out the vagina as a site for sexual pleasure. Such pronouncements happened to fit in well with the woman's movement and with attitudes that devalued the role of males as essential in providing sexual excitement. The concept of females having to depend on males for their pleasure had become an unpopular one.

The most recent research reveals that the vagina does, in fact, contain several areas of special sensitivity. If the Masters and Johnson deemphasis of the vagina was based on solid laboratory research, how could they have been mistaken? Their conclusion turned out to be faulty because they studied vaginal sensitivity by holding the vagina open with a speculum (a metal or plastic device used in medical examinations) and stroking various sites with a cotton swab (Jayne, 1981). This is a relatively uncomfortable procedure, and the most sensitive areas were blocked off by the speculum. For these reasons, producing an erotic response would have been very difficult using this technique. So, how can vaginal sensitivity be determined?

One way is to interview women and ask them about the relative pleasures of clitoral and vaginal stimulation. Women who have experienced orgasm from both types of stimulation usually report that one is more pleasurable than the other. They do not agree, however, about which is better. Some like clitoral stimulation better, and others favor the vagina. Actually, most prefer to have both the clitoris and the vagina stimulated, reporting that this produces a more intense, *blended orgasm* (Sholty et al., 1984). Many women say that a blended orgasm is "more complete."

The other way to answer the question is by direct stimulation of the vagina by the subject's sexual partner or by a medical researcher wearing rubber gloves—but not using a speculum. In one study, sexually experienced women had their vaginas manually stimulated by a physician; twenty-four out of twenty-seven experienced at least one orgasm during this procedure (Alzate, 1985). The two most sensitive areas were found to be located on the lower posterior and the upper anterior of the vagina. (The posterior side is toward the woman's back; the anterior side toward the front, or abdomen.)

Using this direct method, the vagina has been "mapped" with respect to areas of sensitivity. Zones of the vaginal barrel are identified as though they were positions on a clock. Imagine that you are looking directly into the vagina with the clitoris labeled as 12 o'clock. The 12 o'clock location has been pinpointed as the primary region of sensitivity (Schultz et al., 1989). This area underlies the *urethral sponge* (see Figure 2-5) and has been given the name *Grafenberg spot* (or *G-spot*) as discussed in Chapter 1.

Figure 2-5 also identifies another vaginal site whose stimulation leads to high

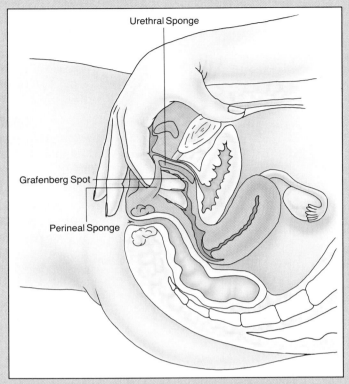

FIGURE 2-5 *PLEASURE CENTERS IN THE VAGINA* In the vagina are erotically sensitive areas, such as the Grafenberg spot, that feel slightly rough when touched.

levels of excitement—the 6 o'clock position just inside the vaginal opening. The **perineal sponge** is located here. Some obstetricians check whether the birth canal is wide enough for the passage of the fetus during childbirth by rubbing the perineal sponge and noting the extent to which the vagina expands. A woman can locate this area herself by inserting her thumb and pressing down toward her spine.

Though research on vaginal sensitivity has revealed some useful information, it has also had an unfortunate and unintended side effect. Some women and their partners who are aware of these findings create new expectations and standards for their sexual performance (Segraves, 1985).

Clearly, no one should have to feel anxious about being unable to reach (or help a partner reach) orgasm through stimulation of particular vaginal areas. In this, as in other human sexual responses, women vary widely in what they find most exciting. There is no "right" or "wrong," "mature" or "immature" way to become aroused and to reach orgasm.

An additional finding of interest is that stimulation of the vaginal walls or of the clitoris raises a woman's pain threshold (Whipple & Komisaruk, 1988). In other words, pleasurable stimulation of the genitals has an analgesic effect—a decreased sensitivity to pain.

menstrual cycle, the wall's old lining is replaced with a new one.

Oviducts. Directly below the fundus, the **oviducts** extend to each ovary. Also known as Fallopian tubes

in honor of a sixteenth-century anatomist, these ducts resemble 4-inch straws. Near the ovaries, each oviduct expands to form small projections, or fimbriae, which look like fingers. Fimbriae help move

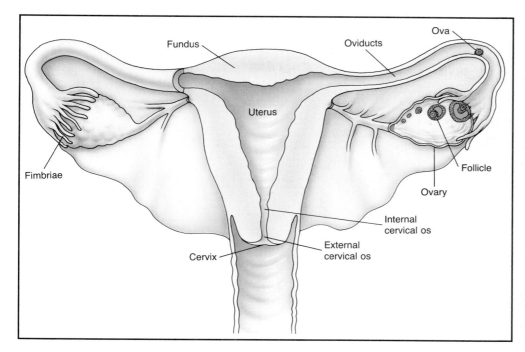

FIGURE 2-6 *INTERNAL FEMALE SEXUAL ANATOMY* The uterus, oviducts, and ovaries play a central role in sexual and reproductive functioning.

each egg from ovary to oviduct. From there, the smooth muscles of the oviducts contract to transport eggs to the uterus along with any sperm that have entered the tubes. On the innermost surface of each oviduct, cilia with hairlike tails also aid the transportation process. The cilia swirl the mucus containing sperm and egg to their destination.

Ovaries. The **ovaries** lie on each side of the uterus and are about the size and shape of almonds, 1 inch in length. Ligaments connect them to the pelvic wall and uterus. When a female is born, each ovary contains about half a million **follicles**, small sacs containing immature eggs, or **ova**. During the individual's lifetime, no new follicles are created, and many die. By age thirty-five, the average female has only about 30,000 follicles remaining in each ovary. During the menstrual cycle, the ovaries release mature ova and secrete the female sex hormones, estrogen and progesterone. This process will be described more fully in Chapter 4.

■ The Mammary Glands

The mammary glands, located within the breasts, are not sexual organs, but play a role in both reproduction and sexual arousal. Their major func-

tion is the secretion of milk for infants. Males' mammary glands ordinarily do not secrete milk, but certain hormones can stimulate them to do so, and male infants frequently produce breast milk. Chapter 4 discusses the production of breast milk in detail. **Nipples** project from each breast and contain the ducts from the mammary glands.

Humans most often have only a single pair of breasts, but a few have an extra nipple or an extra pair of breasts. This condition is known as **polythelia,** and about 1 to 2 percent of each sex have at least one extra nipple, or **supernumerary breast** (Marchant, 1983). This structure may be so small that it can be detected only by a trained specialist.

Figure 2-7 depicts some of the major parts of the mammary glands. The glands contain fat that varies in amount from woman to woman. The amount of fat accumulation is determined by hereditary factors as well as by the woman's weight. Within each breast, mammary ducts extend from the nipple to the *mammary alveoli* where milk is produced. Regardless of size, mammary glands produce roughly equal amounts of milk. Some cultures attribute erotic significance to large breasts, but they can be a source of headaches and muscular pain for some (Zohn, 1979). Wearing a properly fitted bra can help prevent

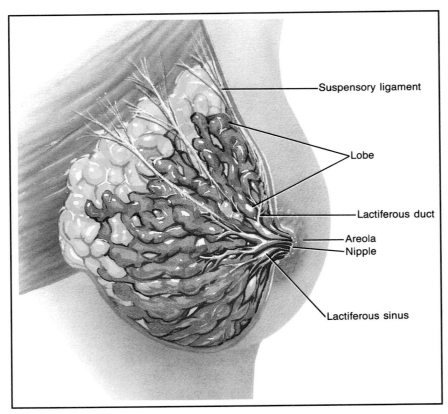

Suspensory ligament

Lobe

Lactiferous duct

Areola
Nipple

Lactiferous sinus

FIGURE 2-7 *THE BREAST: MILK FROM THE MAMMARY GLANDS* The mammary glands function primarily to produce and deliver milk for infants.

or delay sagging breasts which occur when the ligaments and muscles underlying them fail to provide enough support (Ellenbogen, 1979).

For half of the female population, the breasts are approximately matched in size. The other 50 percent have two visibly different breasts. In about one out of four women, this disparity is great enough to cause worries about attractiveness (Ellenbogen, 1982). For many, breast asymmetry begins at puberty and disappears by the end of adolescence. If the condition hasn't changed by age twenty to thirty, it is not likely to do so without cosmetic surgery.

Some women have inverted nipples which become erect during sexual excitement and breast-feeding and then recede afterward. Though female breasts tend to be hairless, 15 to 20 percent of women have hair around the **areola**, the pigmented area surrounding the nipple, and also between the breasts. Oil glands just below the surface of the areola give it a bumpy texture. For a breast-feeding infant, breast size, asymmetry, nipple inversion, and the presence of hair are irrelevant. Adults, however, may

learn to respond to such cues with sexual excitement or with self-doubts and fears that advertisers regularly exploit (Stone, 1982).

Male Sexual Anatomy

In males the external sexual organs include the penis and scrotum. The scrotum contains a pair of testicles.

■ External Sexual Organs

The Penis. The **penis**, as Figure 2-8 depicts, consists of a **penile shaft** extending from the male's body to the enlarged tip, the **glans penis**. Despite numerous jokes and slang expressions, the human penis contains no bones. Males commonly report that the glans is the most sensitive part of their penis, and it does contain nerve endings that are extremely responsive to touch. Also especially sensitive to stimulation by touch are the **corona**, a raised ridge separating the glans from the shaft, and the underside of the shaft.

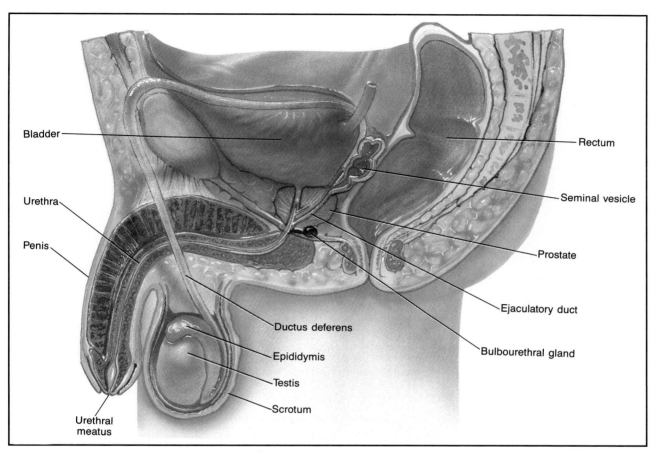

FIGURE 2-8 *EXTERNAL MALE SEXUAL ANATOMY* The scrotum contains the testes in two separate pouches, and the glans penis is the area of male genitalia most sensitive to tactile stimulation.

At birth, the glans penis is covered by an easily retractable layer of skin, called the **foreskin**. For both religious and medical reasons, the foreskin may be removed by circumcision. (See Chapter 5 for a detailed discussion of this practice.) A small triangle of skin, called the **frenulum**, connects the glans with the foreskin on the underside of the penis.

Like females, males have a triangle of pubic hair, though the penis itself is hairless. At the tip of the glans, the **meatus** forms the urethral opening through which both urine and semen are expelled from the body. This constitutes one basic anatomical difference between the sexes—males have one external opening for urinary and reproductive fluids, whereas females have two separate structures—the urethral and vaginal openings. Males and females are similar in secreting oil, perspiring, and urinating; as a result, cleanliness is crucial for both sexes (see Chapter 15 for additional information).

As Figure 2-9 illustrates, inside the shaft are three cylinders containing spongy tissue, richly supplied with blood vessels; the cylinders fill with blood to stiffen and enlarge the penis to produce an erection. Two of these cylinders, the **corpora cavernosa**, lie on each side of the penis. The third, the **corpus spongiosum**, runs along the underside of the shaft. These spongy tissues attach to the pelvic bone. The corpus spongiosum contains the **urethra**, the passageway for both urine and semen.

Just as females often become concerned and overconcerned about breast size, male fears and myths may center on penis size. Despite what you may encounter in erotic stories and photographs (see Chapter 1), the erect penis averages about 6 to 6.5

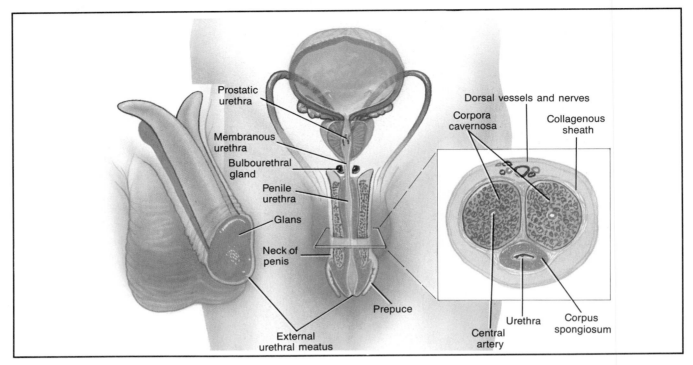

FIGURE 2-9 *THE STRUCTURE OF THE PENIS* Within the penis, the spongy chambers fill with blood during sexual excitement and produce an erection. Both urine and semen are expelled through the urethra.

inches in length, approximately twice the length of a flaccid, or nonerect, penis. Figure 2-10 provides data on erect penis length among college males. Penis size actually varies most when the organ is flaccid; erection tends to neutralize differences in length among individuals (Jamison and Gebhard, 1988). Males who primarily see their genitals when looking down tend to underestimate length as the result of an optical illusion—looking at one's penis in a mirror provides a more realistic view. Interestingly, infant penis size predicts the size of the adult penis (Allen, 1979), but it is a myth that a male's penis length can be predicted from his height or the size of his hands or his feet (Cantrell, 1979).

The various devices and techniques advertised to lengthen a male's genitals are much more likely to cause physical harm than penis enlargement (Kupperman, 1983). Obesity reduces the effective length of the shaft because part of the penis becomes hidden in the fatty layers of the abdomen and therefore remains unavilable for vaginal penetration. Obviously, weight loss corrects the problem. Men sometimes trim or

shave their pubic hair in part to make the penis appear larger.

Most women report that the size of a partner's penis makes little or no difference in their sexual satisfaction. (Henker, 1982). In general, the length of the penis is irrelevant to sexual pleasure for either sex; it is only important if people have learned to believe it is.

In describing their own bodies, most people tend to use the same agreed-upon terminology—head, nose, hand, knee, and so forth. For the penis, in contrast, private names such as "John Thomas" or "joystick" are common. Females apply pet names to their vaginas much less often (Cornog, 1981). Males, however, refer to the female genitalia with numerous slang terms such as "snatch" and "pussy." They employ even more such terms in describing breasts—such as "bazooms" and "jugs" (Bennett & Mannis, 1986).

The Scrotum. The **scrotum** is a sacklike fold of loose skin underneath the penis, containing the two **testes,** or **testicles,** in pouches on either side. The

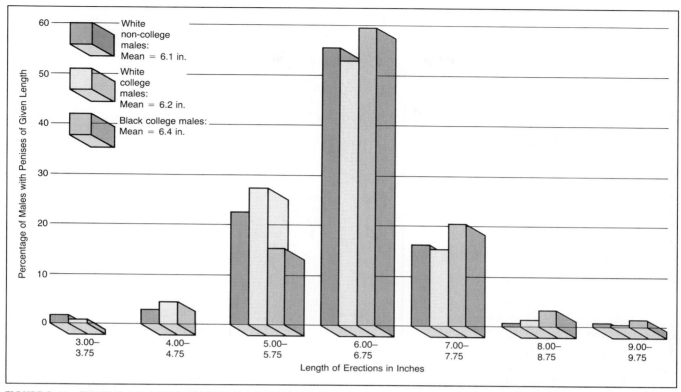

FIGURE 2-10 *WHAT IS THE AVERAGE LENGTH OF AN ERECT PENIS?* The length of an erect penis does not vary greatly from male to male. In a study of over 2,000 subjects, over 90 percent reported lengths ranging from 5 to 7.75 inches—regardless of race and of college versus noncollege status.
Source: Data from Gebhard & Johnson, 1979.

left testis usually hangs slightly lower than the right. In the middle of the scrotum, a ridge called the **raphe,** separates the pouches. The skin of the scrotum is pigmented. Beneath the skin, a layer of muscle, the *dartos muscle,* contracts the scrotum during sexual stimulation, as Figure 2-11 illustrates. When the male is frightened, sexually aroused, or cold, this muscle raises the testes. For example, the scrotum and testes draw closer to the body when their temperature is lowered by a plunge into a cold swimming pool. Such reflexes serve to keep testicular temperature relatively constant and thus help to maintain sperm production. Heat, as well as cold, reduces the number of sperm. Thus, decreased fertility can result from a hot shower or from wearing tight briefs.

■ Internal Sexual Organs

The Testicles. Testicles have two major functions. First, the male hormone testosterone—affecting both sexual development and interest—is produced in the Leydig cells. Testicles are oval shaped, about 1.5 by 1.0 inches. Second, **sperm** cells are produced within the testicles. Each testicle contains approximately 250 separate compartments with several coiled **seminiferous tubules.** These tubules are each about 1 to 3 feet long, and all of them stretched end-to-end would exceed the length of a soccer field.

Sperm production begins at puberty and, under normal conditions, continues throughout the male's entire life. After sperm are produced, the **epididymis** stores them briefly before they are transported into the body. The epididymis is a network of tubes coiled against the back of each testicle. The entire production process for each sperm takes about two months and occurs constantly. Approximately 200 million sperm reach the final stage of production each day. Sperm are then transported from each epididymis to the seminal vesicles and prostate gland through one of the vas deferens, each about 16 inches long. Chapter 4 describes the process in greater detail.

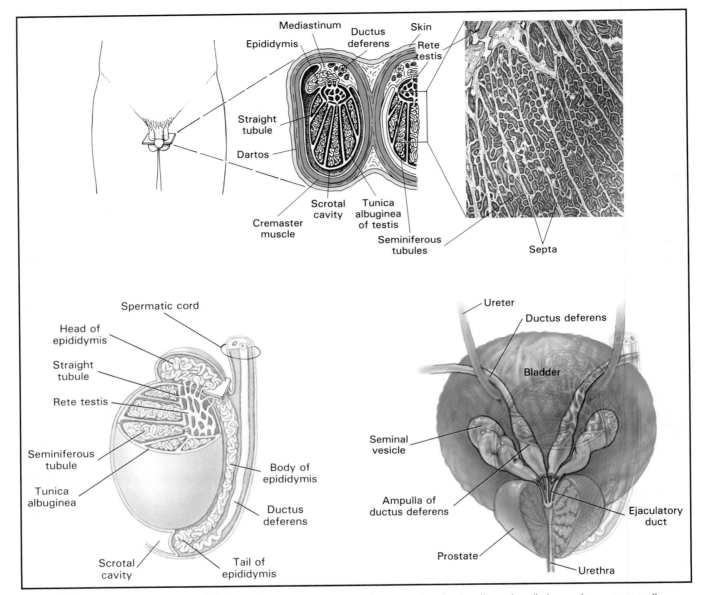

FIGURE 2-11 *INTERNAL MALE SEXUAL ANATOMY* The internal sexual organs of males function primarily to produce sperm cells and the other substances contained in semen.

The testicles are extremely sensitive to pressure, as many males know from having been hit there while engaging in sports or other strenuous activity. Painful sensitivity is primarily caused by deep pressure; in contrast, gentle touch or stroking is pleasurably stimulating (F. B. Scott, 1979). The phrase "I've got him by the balls" rings true for males, as squeezing the testicles may produce a severe reaction, including an aching abdomen, nausea, vomiting, fainting, or physiological shock. To stabilize the testicles and prevent pain and accidental injury, males are advised to wear an athletic supporter (Bunge, 1984).

Men differ a great deal in the size of their testes, and some racial differences are found. For example, the testes of adult Danes are more than twice the size of the Chinese testes and produce about twice as many sperm each day (Harvey & May, 1989).

■ Producing Seminal Fluid

Each testicle is suspended from a spermatic cord, which surrounds blood vessels and nerves. The **vas deferens** also runs through the spermatic cord and is the transportation route for sperm to reach a reservoir where they remain until they enter the urethra. About 30 percent of the **semen**, or **seminal fluid**, originates from the nearby **prostate gland**, which contributes mainly water plus a bicarbonate substance that neutralizes the acid environments of the male's urethra and the female's vagina. Because the prostate is located in front of the rectum, a physician can examine it during a rectal examination. The prostate also secretes small amounts of an unidentified substance that acts as an antibiotic, helping to prevent urinary tract infections in males (Martini, 1989).

Most of the remaining fluid forming the ejaculate comes from the **seminal vesicles**. They secrete a liquid containing fructose to nourish the sperm, thus helping them to become highly mobile. The seminal vesicles and the prostate also contribute hormones (prostaglandins). These stimulate contractions of the pelvis that help to expel semen during ejaculation. Each seminal vesicle is about 6 inches long but folds itself into a smaller overall size.

The **bulbourethral (Cowper's) glands** add lubrication to the urethra, and some of this mucus substance is also ejaculated. These two glands, resembling round half-inch beads, lie at each side of the base of the penis. Their ducts empty a thick sticky mucus into the urethra, providing lubrication just before ejaculation.

To summarize, the ejaculated fluid comes primarily from the seminal vesicles and the prostate gland. The smallest contribution to the volume of the semen consists of a few drops of mucus from the bulbourethral glands and the millions of microscopic sperm that originated in the testicles and passed through the vas deferens.

Semen does not contain urine; valves known as prostatic sphincters are located in the prostate at the base of the urinary bladder. These sphincters normally prevent urine from entering the urethra during ejaculation; they also keep semen out of the bladder. At ejaculation, one set of sphincters blocks off the bladder, while another set opens the entrance that permits semen to enter the urethra. Each ejaculation consists of approximately one teaspoonful of fluid that contains about twenty calories. Seminal fluid, usually a white or yellowish color, has the consistency of egg whites.

Summarizing the Information about Sexual Anatomy . . .

In females the external genital organs (the **vulva**) include the **mons pubis, labia majora, labia minora,** and **clitoris**. The last of these is the most sensitive portion of the vulva, although each area plays a role in sexual excitement. The erotically sensitive **vagina**, together with the **uterus, oviducts,** and **ovaries** make up the female's internal sexual anatomy. The mammary glands, within the breasts, are also considered sexual in many cultures, although their primary function is to produce milk for infants.

In males the external sexual anatomy includes the **penis** as well as the **scrotum**, with two **testicles** inside it. The penis is composed of spongy tissue which becomes engorged with blood during excitement to produce an erection. Sperm are produced and stored temporarily in the testicles. The tubes known as the **vas deferens** transport the newly produced sperm out of the testes to be combined with the nutritive and lubricatory secretions of the **bulbourethral glands, seminal vesicles,** and **prostate gland** before the ejaculation of **semen**, as this mixture of substances is called.

To Find Out More About Sexual Anatomy . . .

Haeberle, E. J. (1982). *The sex atlas*. New York: Continuum.
    This is a basic sourcebook of information about human sexuality. Included are text and illustrations covering the details of male and female sexual anatomy.
Martini, F. (1989). *Fundamentals of anatomy and physiology*. Englewood Cliffs, N.J.: Prentice Hall.
    An up-to-date and comprehensive text that provides detailed information about human anatomy and physiology, including sexual and reproductive structures and processes.

SEXUAL FUNCTIONING

Despite the many similarities between males and females in sexual functioning, there are also some differences. When partners are unaware of these differences, it is easy enough to misperceive the other person's responses and to make incorrect attributions about what is happening and why. A young married woman describes how her lack of knowledge led to incorrect assumptions and unnecessary fears about her husband's apparent unresponsiveness following orgasm.

I think something is wrong with my marriage, and I don't know what to do about it. When my husband is ready to have sex with me, he is just perfect. He is affectionate, and he kisses me and hugs me and wants to touch every inch of my body. He's never in a hurry (not like a guy I used to date), so he can drive me wild when he builds me up. After I get to a certain point, it's even exciting when he kisses the back of my neck or sucks on my earlobes. I usually have to tell him to do it NOW!

None of that is the problem. And I almost always climax, so that's not the problem either.

What bothers me is that after he comes, that's the end of the story for Jim. I am usually still turned on and want to keep kissing and touching. A lot of times I want to make love again, but Jim doesn't.

When he's through, he's through. He seems to lose all interest in sex and in me. In fact, he usually does one of two things. Most nights, he just rolls over and quickly goes to sleep. I lay there wondering what's wrong. I think that maybe he doesn't really love me—maybe he just uses me. On the weekends, when he doesn't have to get up the next morning and go to work, it's even worse. He gets out of bed, fixes himself something to eat, and sits in front of the TV. He has a wife who wants more sex, and he's in there watching the Lakers or somebody.

One Saturday, when he was busy with his after-sex pizza and basketball, I was so upset about it that I decided to take care of myself. I left the bedroom door open so he would hear me moaning and sighing. I thought surely that would bring him in and get him excited. He didn't move. The next morning he just said he hoped I had had a good time.

How could he be so excited about making love one minute—then a little later, have no desire? What's wrong?

Dina, age 25

What Dina describes is a basic male–female difference in how the body responds following orgasm. Masters and Johnson reported that males experience a *refractory period* during which further stimulation fails to create excitement. As we point out in this chapter, for the average woman, orgasm is *not* usually followed by the kind of rapid decrease in sexual responsivity that is typical for men; instead, further stimulation for her can lead to continued arousal and sometimes to additional orgasms. In this respect, neither Jim nor Dina is doing anything wrong—their bodies are responding naturally, though in different ways, to erotic stimulation.

As we will discuss shortly, however, some aspects of Jim's behavior are not based on physiology, and he would benefit by realizing that Dina is interested in *afterplay*—cuddling and hugging and talking to her partner following orgasm. When a sexual act is completed, it is pleasant and comforting to continue loving and affectionate interactions without necessarily resuming intercourse, oral sex, or whatever.

Continuing the automobile analogy suggested in Chapter 2, once you know something about the parts of a car, you are ready to learn about how it functions. This chapter describes how the sexual system functions. We discuss what causes *sexual desire*. When desire leads to sexual acts, they involve a specific pattern of physical and psychological arousal—the *sexual response cycle*—that has been descibed in somewhat different ways by various sexual scientists. We next focus on male–female similarities and differences in *orgasm, resolution, and the refractory period.* The modern scientific devices used in *assessing sexual excitement and orgasm* also are described. Special sections discuss alternative ways to *obtain sexual excitement* and examine the importance of communication in *detecting your partner's sexual excitement and orgasm*.

Sexual Desire

The need for sexual gratification is a natural phenomenon, but the sexual motives of others can be observed only indirectly; that is, we can ask them to describe their feelings or we can infer such feelings on the basis of what they do and say, but we cannot really know what they feel. What, then, do we mean by "sexual desire"?

■ Can Libido Be Measured?

Sigmund Freud proposed the existence of a special energy, **libido,** that motivates each of us to seek gratification. Freud conceptualized this energy as an instinct, but around the world people differ greatly in the degree of sexual interest they profess and in the frequency of their sexual acts. To take two extreme examples reported by anthropologists, men and women in one Irish village, Inis Beag, receive strong warnings to restrict sexual activity to intercourse within marriage solely for the purpose of creating offspring. Thus, these villagers rarely reported engaging

in masturbation, oral sex, premarital intercourse, or extramarital affairs (Messenger, 1971). By contrast, on the South Pacific island of Mangaia, premarital sexual activity begins immediately after the onset of puberty, and those not engaging in frequent sex are subjected to ridicule (Marshall, 1971). Thus, a person born and raised in the Irish village engages in sexual acts infrequently and with minimal pleasure while a person born and raised on the Pacific island has sex often and with great enjoyment. Chapter 8 discusses crosscultural variations in learned sexual patterns.

As suggested by these examples, even though our sexual desire has a biological base, it is greatly influenced by what we have been taught. Therefore, sexual needs and the frequency of sexual activity differ widely from culture to culture and person to person.

One approach to the study of sexual desire is to ask people, "If you had your wishes, how many times per month would you like to have sex?" (Frauman, 1982, p. 43). In a group of 78 college students, 65 percent said that they desired sex two to thirteen times per month; males and females did not differ in how often they desired it. These students also reported that they actually engaged in sexual activity less often (one to about eight times per month) than they desired.

More detailed questions about the activities that people find sexually arousing may provide a better idea of what determines sexual desire. Is it exciting to kiss and be kissed? Is it enticing to touch and be touched by your partner? In responding to such questions, middle-aged people differed in their responses, depending on whether they had problems in satisfying their sexual needs. Those with no major sexual problems indicated the greatest interest and enjoyment in response to these questions, as Figure 3-1 shows. In contrast, for males and females with a relatively low frequency of orgasms (those who were dysfunctional—see Chapter 17), kissing and other acts were much less appealing (Harbison et al., 1974).

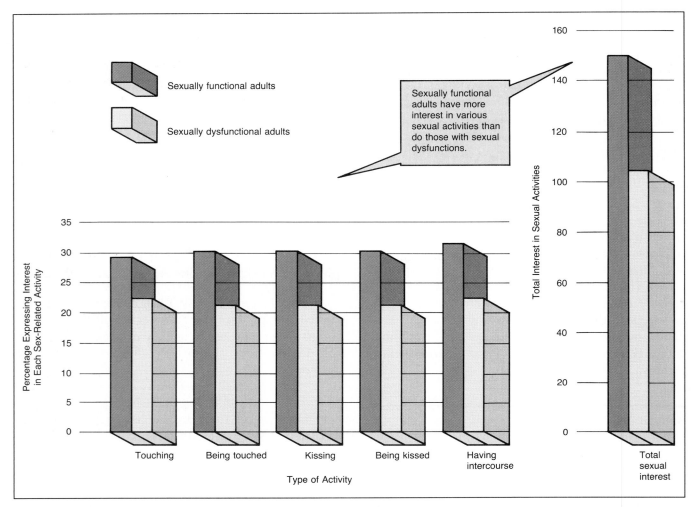

FIGURE 3-1 *WHAT DO YOU LIKE—KISSING, TOUCHING, HAVING INTERCOURSE?*   A group of 40 sexually functional adults and a group of 35 who were sexually dysfunctional were asked about their interest in a variety of sex-related activities. Those without dysfunctions had greater interest in each activity and expressed greater sexual interest overall than the dysfunctional group.
Source: Data from Harbison et al., 1974.

■ **Desire: Physical, Emotional, and Cognitive Aspects**

Kaplan (1979) proposes that dysfunctional people have decided, perhaps unknowingly, that sex is unenjoyable. Their sexual problems stem from their decision "not to feel sexual" (p. 110). Kaplan recommends that therapists convince them that they should enjoy sex because they miss a lot of pleasure by not doing so. Also, avoidance of sex can contribute to difficulties in their marital relationships, as discussed in Chapter 9.

These ideas suggest that what people think about sex can strongly affect their desire for it. Mosher's (1980) theory about sexual involvement states that two sets of emotions—excitement and enjoyment—affect how we respond to erotic situations. The interest and excitement factor provides the motivation to seek out sexual experience. After sexual activity has begun, enjoyment occurs and peaks at orgasm. Sexual desire increases when excitement and enjoyment combine with love for a partner, as described in Chapter 10.

Levine (1987) separates desire into two components. The drive component consists of the physiological experience of desire—the need for the physical release of sexual tension. The wish component refers to the cognitive aspects of drive, including feelings, thoughts, and fantasies connected with a partner.

Sexual excitement is the natural outcome of desire, depending on the circumstances and the availability of a willing sexual partner. Feeling "horny" is no justification for forcing anyone to engage in sex or for indiscriminate sexual acts at odd places or times. Even the most sexually permissive people do not advocate coercive sex or "doing it in the road."

Under ordinary circumstances with a cooperative partner, what *does* happen when desire leads to excitement?

The Sexual Response Cycle

Sexual stimulation is conceptualized as the beginning of a sequence that includes increasing levels of excitement, ordinarily culminating in orgasm and the release of built-up sexual tension. Several attempts have been made to describe this process, called the *sexual response cycle,* and Figure 3-2 outlines three of these descriptions. We will discuss the basic elements of each.

■   Theories of Sexual Functioning: Ellis, Kaplan, and Masters and Johnson

Ellis: Two Stages.   An early sexologist, Ellis (1942), proposed only two stages. He indicated that sexual

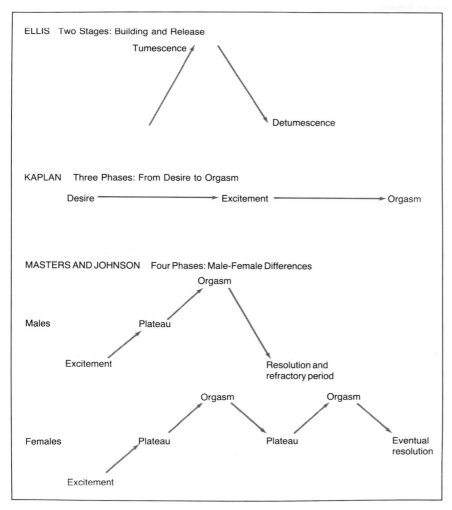

FIGURE 3-2 *THREE DESCRIPTIONS OF THE SEXUAL RESPONSE CYCLE*   At the turn of the century, a pioneer sexologist named Havelock Ellis proposed a male-oriented model of tumescence and detumescence. Sex therapist Helen Singer Kaplan emphasized desire as a prelude to excitement and orgasm. Physician William Masters and psychologist Virginia Johnson omitted desire, but observed differences in males and females in the resolution phase, observing that the male response cycle includes a refractory period.

ELLIS   Two Stages: Building and Release

Tumescence

Detumescence

KAPLAN   Three Phases: From Desire to Orgasm

Desire ⟶ Excitement ⟶ Orgasm

MASTERS AND JOHNSON   Four Phases: Male-Female Differences

Males

Orgasm

Plateau

Excitement

Resolution and refractory period

Females

Orgasm

Plateau

Orgasm

Plateau

Excitement

Eventual resolution

tension builds and then is released through the processes of *tumescence* and *detumescence*. Tumescence, or swelling, occurs when blood flows into the pelvic area during arousal. Detumescence, or diminution of the swelling, represents the discharge of energy following orgasm. In describing sexual responses, Ellis focused more on male than on female sexuality even though the general process applies to both sexes.

Kaplan: Three Phases. According to Kaplan (1979), the sequence involves three independent phases. As a sex therapist, she worked with dysfunctional clients for whom sexual problems tended to involve lack of desire, difficulties in becoming excited, and/or inability to obtain orgasm. In her theoretical model, she applied these three components of sexual response to normal as well as to dysfunctional behavior. According to Kaplan, then, the three stages of sexual response are desire, excitement, and orgasm. Kaplan describes sexual response as including more than genital changes, because desire also involves the individual's feelings about a specific partner or act.

Masters and Johnson: Four Phases. Probably the best-known and most widely quoted model of the sexual behavior sequence is that of Masters and Johnson (1966), who observed the sexual acts of individual men and women as well as couples in their laboratory. Masters and Johnson describe four phases of sexual response as excitement, plateau, orgasm, and resolution. In the first phase, excitement, blood flows into the genitals and elsewhere, resulting in swelling for such organs as the clitoris and penis. In the second phase, plateau, stimulation generally continues until orgasm, the third phase, is reached. Following orgasm is the resolution, or fourth phase, characterized by a gradual loss of excitement and sexual tension.

The Masters and Johnson model has been criticized because it leaves out a beginning phase, desire. Another criticism is that the **plateau phase** applies primarily to women—the walls of the vagina balloon out at the peak of excitement—but males exhibit no analogous physical response. In fact, this difference in sexual response between men and women can lead to problems when partners do not understand what is happening. In the plateau phase, the vaginal walls can expand sufficiently to lose contact with the penis, leaving the male puzzled as to why he experiences less friction (Wolkoff, 1977).

We have combined the most useful elements of the Kaplan and the Masters and Johnson models in Figure 3-3. One sequence typically occurs for

FIGURE 3-3 *THE SEXUAL RESPONSE CYCLE: MALE AND FEMALE PHASES* A composite model of the sexual response cycle depicts a series of phases for males and a slightly different series of *phases* for females. Females who receive additional stimulation after an initial orgasm may experience repeated additional orgasms before entering the resolution phase.

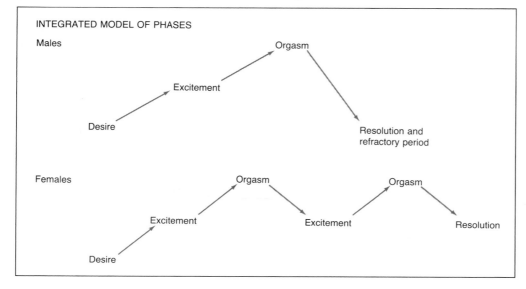

males—desire, excitement, orgasm, and resolution with a refractory period. The term **refractory period** refers to the period immediately after orgasm during which males are generally unresponsive to further stimulation.

Females have a more variable response pattern than males in that they do not have a refractory period. Instead, they *are* responsive to continued stimulation and may experience additional periods of excitement and additional orgasms before reaching a final resolution phase. Having discussed desire previously, we will now turn to the remaining elements of the cycle—excitement, orgasm, and resolution.

■ **Excitement: Getting There Is Half the Fun**

Sexual excitement is the way we respond to erotic cues, either psychological or physical. The two primary physiological responses occurring during sexual excitement are **vasocongestion** and **myotonia**. Vasocongestion of the genital organs results when, engorged with blood, they become erect, lubricate, and swell. It is the parasympathetic nervous system's response to erotic stimulation. Myotonia is the tension in voluntary muscles, occurring throughout the body, especially in the large muscles of the legs, buttocks, and arms. Besides these general responses, there are other responses, which we describe separately for males and females.

The special section, *Taking Responsibility and Protecting Yourself,* on pages 49–50, describes other sources of sexual excitement besides touch, including one that can be fatal.

Excitement in Males. Erection of the penis is the most obvious physical sign of sexual excitement in men (Batra & Lue, 1990). At the lower end of the

Taking Responsibility and Protecting Yourself

SEXUAL EXCITEMENT: FANTASY, NOCTURNAL AROUSAL, AND SELF-STRANGULATION

Because touch initiates many of our sexual experiences, you might assume that touching yourself or someone else is the only way to produce sexual excitement. In fact, several other means exist. For example, exposure to fantasies presented in erotica or created in their own imagination is sexually exciting for both males (Harrell and Stolp, 1985) and females (Heiman and Hatch, 1980). For some, fantasizing about erotic interactions can even produce orgasm, without any physical stimulation of the genitals. People usually report that they have erotic thoughts during genital stimulation, thus experiencing two simultaneous sources of arousal. In humans, then, the brain plays a major role in sexual responsivity. (Chapter 11 discusses the use of fantasy as a sexual technique in greater detail.)

Another indication of the role of mental processes in sexuality is the occurrence of orgasm during sleep. In young males, **nocturnal emissions,** or "wet dreams," begin shortly after puberty. This perfectly normal process was once thought to be a sign of "impure thoughts" and a danger to one's health. By the age of sixteen, more than one out of two males (55 percent) have experienced them (Truxal, 1983). Sometimes the individual is awakened by the orgasm; at other times he discovers dried semen on his sheets or pajamas in the morning. Erections also occur throughout much of the dreaming phase of sleep—usually three to five episodes during about one fourth of a normal night's sleep (McCarley, 1978). Somewhat surprisingly, there is no relationship between the amount of sexual activity during a man's waking hours and either the duration or the strength of his nocturnal erections (Rosen et al., 1986). Abstaining from sexual acts does not necessarily increase the frequency of nocturnal emissions, because built-up sperm and semen can be absorbed by the body or expelled during urination (Diamond, 1979).

Females also report having orgasms during sleep (Jeffress, 1981). They may notice lubrication seeping from their vaginas afterward or be awakened by their own pelvic thrusting. Women, in fact, become sexually excited during sleep as often as men (C. Fisher et al., 1983). A study of university women found that 37 percent had experienced nocturnal orgasms, and those with positive sexual attitudes were most likely to report such experiences (Wells, 1986).

Sexual asphyxia (also called *asphyxiophilia* and *autoerotic asphyxia*) is an extremely dangerous form of stimulation. The victims are usually young males who hang themselves, or bind their necks and bodies, to produce erection and orgasm. In doing so they deprive their brains of adequate amounts of oxygen. When victims struggle to free themselves from the noose or bindings, they may accidentally tighten them, causing not only ejaculation but also death (Innala and Ernulf, 1989).

A few female cases have also been reported, and some investigators believe that the actual number of female victims is higher than the records indicate (Byard & Bramwell, 1988).

It is hypothesized that those who use such means of arousal want to avoid any guilt associated with masturbating to orgasm and also to experience the added thrill of risking death (Faber and Rosenblum, 1978). When the victim is discovered by family members, they may attempt to hide the bizarre sexual elements of the death. It is estimated that such asphyxia claims the lives of about 500 to 1,000 males a year in the United States (Hazelwood and Burgess, 1984). The death rate from sexual asphyxia in Scandinavia is about half that in the United States, suggesting the role of cultural influences on such behavior (Innala & Ernulf, 1989).

Electrocution also produces sexual asphyxia. Witnesses have frequently noted that male criminals executed by hanging or the electric chair respond with erections and ejaculation.

spinal cord, an *erection center* activates the reflex that results in erection. As more blood flows into the corpora cavernosa and corpus spongiosum than flows out, an erection results (see Figure 3-4). One chamber may fill faster than another so that the erection leans to one side before full vasocongestion has occurred. Until higher levels of excitement are reached, an erection may sometimes soften temporarily. Though such a response is not at all unusual, an unknowing male may interpret it as an erectile problem, or an unknowing partner may believe that she is not exciting him.

One question often asked about erections has to do with "staying power." How long can or should a male be able to maintain an erection before experiencing orgasm? Concern about this issue reflects the realization that females may require stimulation over a longer period than males to reach orgasm, and also that females may not be fully satisfied with only one orgasm. In Kinsey's (1948) survey of males, young adults sometimes reported erections lasting up to one hour, but this figure was reduced by 50 percent for men in their late forties. In contrast, Masters and Johnson (1966) found in their laboratory observations that younger men had orgasms more quickly than older men. Perhaps the inconsistent evidence is a function of survey data versus direct observation—nevertheless, there is no definitive answer to the aver-

FIGURE 3-4 *MALE SEXUAL EXCITEMENT: ERECTION, TESTICULAR CONTRACTION, AND LUBRICATION* With sexual arousal, the penis becomes erect, the testicles and scrotum contract toward the body, and lubricatory fluid appears at the meatus.

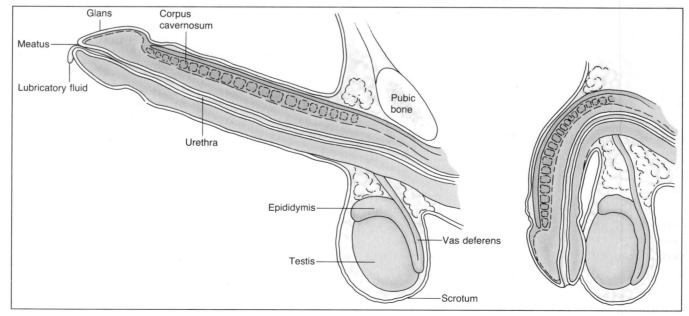

age duration of erections or the effect of age on maintaining them. Some men use mechanical devices to maintain their erections, but these can be dangerous (see Chapter 11).

Other signs of male sexual excitement are nipple erection and **sex flush**, which occurs in about three out of five men as the result of vasocongestion. The blood vessels near the surface of the skin dilate or widen, and a red rash appears on the male's face, neck, back, and chest. The sex flush may spread over the entire body surface. It is most likely to occur when the man is in a relatively warm place and when his anticipation of sexual pleasure is intense.

A few drops of lubrication secreted from the bulbourethral glands may appear at the meatus. The fact that some sperm are contained in this fluid is one reason that withdrawal of the penis from the vagina prior to ejaculation is ineffective in preventing conception. As excitement continues to mount, the male's arms and legs extend more stiffly because of increased myotonia. The dartos and cremaster muscles retract the scrotum and testes toward the body, and the testes rise to a position that makes their swollen size prominent, as Figure 3-4 shows.

Excitement in Females. The first response of a woman to effective erotic stimulation is vaginal lubrication, which appears after approximately thirty seconds. In consistency, quantity, and odor, the lubricating fluid varies from one woman to another. The vaginal walls moisten after fluid seeps through them as a result of vasocongestion (see Figure 3-5). Though lubrication is a sign of excitement, its quantity is not necessarily indicative of a woman's level of arousal. Other bodily reactions to excitement are a sex flush, myotonia, nipple erection (caused by contractions of small muscle fibers), and an approximately 25 percent increase in breast size. The clitoris and labia also darken and swell because of vasocongestion, and the clitoral hood, after initially retracting, begins to draw over the glans.

Sexual excitement also affects women internally. The vagina widens past the introitus, which itself relaxes as the PC muscles respond to stimulation. The vagina's length increases as the uterus elevates into the abdomen, a reaction known as the *tenting effect*. The uterus also enlarges and contracts painlessly and irregularly, as Figure 3-6 shows. Because the vagina

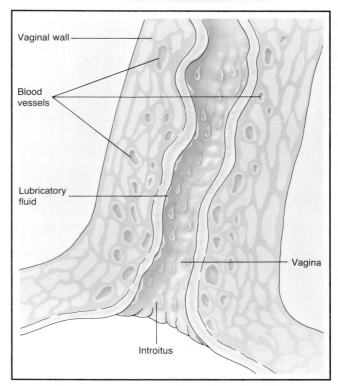

FIGURE 3-5 *THE SOURCE OF VAGINAL LUBRICATION* Vaginal lubrication occurs when blood collects in the vaginal walls. Mucus percolates through these walls, coating them with a thin layer of lubricatory fluid.

continues to engorge with blood, its internal space becomes narrower. For the same reason, the labia minora swell even more than during early excitement. The **orgasmic platform** is created by the swelling and thickening of the labia minora and the outer third of the vagina, causing the opening of the vagina to decrease by 30 percent or more. Her vagina now grips the penis more tightly. When the woman's excitement level reaches that of the orgasmic platform, it signals that orgasm will occur soon—if there is continued stimulation.

Because much of a woman's body is involved in sexual excitement, you can see why the idea of special "erogenous zones" is probably mistaken (de Moya, 1984). Erogenous zones were thought to be a few sensitive areas of the body, such as the inner thigh, which are extremely responsive to erotic stimulation. In reality, as long as a woman derives pleasure from the activity, touching any part of the body will

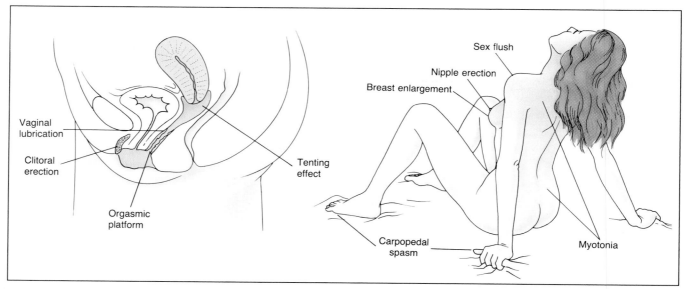

FIGURE 3-6 *FEMALE SEXUAL EXCITEMENT: MULTIPLE PHYSICAL SIGNS* The effects of sexual excitement in females involve both internal and external physical responses.

increase excitement. The areas that produce pleasure when stimulated vary from one woman to another and in the same woman from time to time, as Figure 3-7 suggests. For example, breasts may swell premenstrually and touching at that time can cause pain as Chapter 4 discusses. Besides genitals and breasts, sensitive areas include ear lobes, neck, buttocks and anus, elbow, the creases behind each knee, thighs, and—in fact—the entire surface of the body.

Orgasm, Resolution, and the Refractory Period

Most often, the stimulation that causes sexual excitement results in orgasm, and, then, decreased excitement. Males and females differ physiologically in their post-orgasmic responses.

■ Orgasm: Physiology and Experience

The term **orgasm** derives from the Greek word *orgasmos,* meaning "to be lustful" or "to swell." It occurs at the peak of sexual excitement when the body suddenly releases the built-up vasocongestive and muscular tension that accompanied desire and excitement. Biologically the briefest phase of the sexual response cycle, orgasm usually continues for only a few seconds. It is characterized by rhythmic muscular contractions, followed by relaxation.

Most orgasms are experienced as intensely pleasurable, although some men and women have learned to dread having them because they perceive orgasm as something negative (Kroop, 1980a; O'Connor and

FIGURE 3-7 *EROGENOUS ZONES: WHERE ARE THEY?* Though it has often been suggested that there are a limited number of special bodily areas that are sensitive to sexual stimulation—erogenous zones—the entire body can respond in this way.

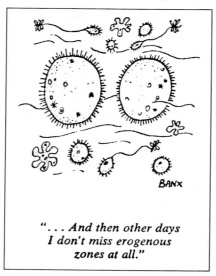

"... And then other days I don't miss erogenous zones at all."

TABLE 3-1 **Males and Females: How Does an Orgasm Feel?**

Descriptions of orgasms written by males and females are surprisingly similar, and experts were unable to distinguish them by sex. How well did you do?

For each description of orgasm, indicate whether you believe it was written by a male or a female. After you have responded, check your answers below.

1. An orgasm feels extremely pleasurable, yet it can be so violent that the feeling of uncontrol is frightening. It also is hard to describe because it is as if I am in limbo—only conscious of release.

2. I really think it defies description by words. Combinations of waves of very pleasurable sensations and mounting of tensions culminating in a fantastic sensation and release of tension.

3. Often loss of contact with reality. All senses acute. Sight becomes patterns of color, but often very difficult to explain because words were made to fit in the real world.

4. A feeling of intense physical and mental satisfaction. The height of a sexual encounter. Words can hardly describe feeling so great.

5. A building up of tensions—like getting ready for takeoff from a launching pad, then a sudden blossoming relief that extends all over the body.

6. An orgasm is a very quick release of sexual tension which results in a kind of flash of pleasure.

1 = F, 2 = M, 3 = M, 4 = F, 5 = F, 6 = M

O'Connor, 1980). For such people, losing control—and orgasm does involve a brief loss of control—causes panic. Research indicates that women willing to give up self-control are more easily hypnotized, use alcohol more frequently for relaxation, and have orgasms more often during intercourse than women who strive to maintain self-control (Bridges et al., 1985).

The pelvic contractions that force the blood out of the swollen tissues are **clonic**—that is, contractions are stimulated until an appropriate reduction in vasocongestion has occurred. The pelvic muscles have stretched to accommodate the increased pool of blood, and the orgasmic response to prolonged stimulation—relayed through the lower spinal cord—signals the brain to begin these contractions.

How does an orgasm feel, and is it different for the two sexes? No one can possibly answer these questions directly, but men and women have been asked to describe the feeling of orgasm (Vance and Wagner, 1976). Table 3-1 contains some of their descriptions. Surprisingly, male and female medical students, obstetricians, and psychologists were unable to distinguish the male from the female descriptions. Among those presented in the table, can you identify which were written by which sex?

Among heterosexual college couples, orgasm tends to occur more consistently among men than women (Waterman et al., 1979). For couples having sexual interactions about four times weekly, just over half of the men indicated that their orgasms always occurred with intercourse, oral-genital sex, or manual stimulation of their genitals, as Figure 3-8 indicates. Women say that their orgasms occur less consistently than is true for men, and those reporting the most frequent orgasms express greater satisfaction with their sexual activities than do those with relatively infrequent orgasms (Waterman and Chiauzzi, 1982). Also, those women who have had a relatively large number of sexual partners (six or more) express more sexual satisfaction and are more likely to reach orgasms before their partners do (Davidson & Darling, 1988). Chapter 17 discusses some factors that interfere with having orgasms.

■ **Similarities and Differences in Male and Female Physical Responses to Orgasm**

In both sexes, these physical responses accompany orgasm:

1. Heart rate and blood pressure increase to about 50 or 60 percent above normal levels and then return to near normal within about two minutes following orgasm (Nemec et al., 1976). The sex flush is greatest at orgasm.

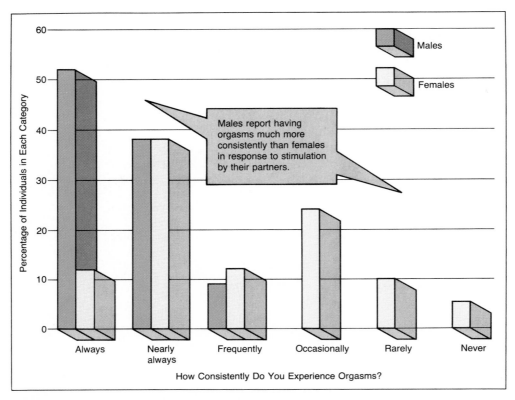

Males report having orgasms much more consistently than females in response to stimulation by their partners.

FIGURE 3-8 *ORGASM CONSISTENCY: MALES AND FEMALES DIFFER* In a study of 42 couples, males reported having orgasms much more consistently than was true for females, in sexual interactions.
Source: Data from Waterman et al., 1979.

2. *Carpopedal spasm* produces an arching of the foot, with the toes curling under to assume a clawlike appearance. The hands tend to clutch the other person or adjacent surfaces such as sheets or pillows.

3. Facial muscles contract involuntarily, making it appear that the person is frowning or grimacing. It is difficult to distinguish the expression of an individual experiencing orgasm from that of someone in pain. The director of the movie *Ecstasy* took advantage of this similarity. So that actress Hedy Lamarr would appear to be experiencing orgasm, he stuck her with a pin out of the sight of the camera.

4. *Anoxia* may occur, in that some people momentarily stop breathing. Following orgasm, they tend to open their mouths, gasping for breath.

5. *Hyperventilation* is caused by the greatly increased breathing rate, which reaches forty

breaths per minute compared to the normal respiratory rate of ten to twelve per minute.

6. Muscles contract involuntarily in the anus, limbs, and back, a response known as *myotonia*. A partner might view this orgasmic effect as indicating discomfort or dislike, but it simply reveals a high level of sexual excitement.

If sexual excitement continues over an extended period of time without an orgasm, pelvic congestion can result—in both sexes. Genital vasocongestion is not released, and blood lodges in the genital organs. Less formal names for this condition in males—blue balls and stone ache—refer to the pooling of blood in the testicles, which can enlarge by 50 percent because of unresolved excitement. If instances of prolonged excitement without orgasm occur repeatedly, medical complications such as infection, pain, or infertility can result. More often, vasocongestion slowly de-

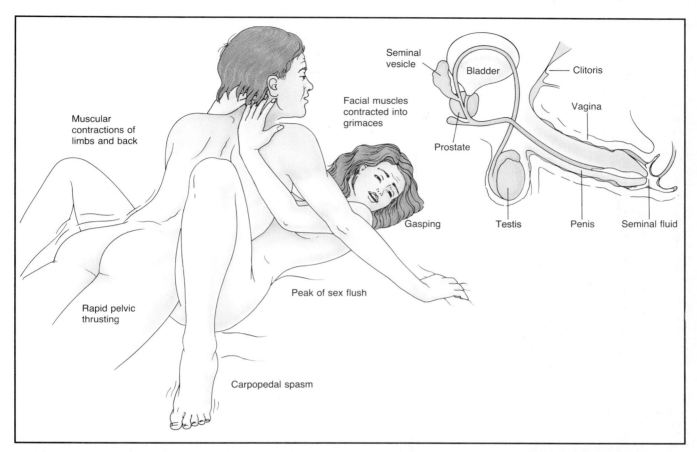

FIGURE 3-9 *THE MANY FACETS OF ORGASM* The physical signs of orgasm include the various responses depicted here. You can understand why orgasm is often described as producing a "total body response."
Source: Based on *Medical Aspects of Human Sexuality*, 1979, *13*(9), 136–137.

creases even without orgasm, causing no negative effects.

These various physical reactions to orgasm and nonorgasm occur in both sexes. Even among other mammals, such as rats, the mechanics of sexual climax are remarkably similar for males and females (Schmeck, 1989). Nevertheless, some effects differ, as indicated in the following discussion.

Males: Pelvic Thrusting and Ejaculation.
Immediately before orgasm, males rhythmically and rapidly thrust the pelvis several times, as Figure 3-9 illustrates. They also experience a period of **ejaculatory inevitability** for about two to four seconds (Masters and Johnson, 1966); at this point, they know that orgasm is imminent and unstoppable. This period corresponds to the first, or *emission*, stage of ejaculation (see Figure 3-10). In this stage, the mus-

cles surrounding the pathways taken by sperm and semen contract (partially in response to hormones). One such hormone is oxytocin, which also stimulates labor; others are prostaglandins, which produce uterine and tubal contractions in females. Once the emission stage begins, orgasm will occur. Even if someone were to shout "Fire!" during a man's emission stage, he would ejaculate and have an orgasm—though less pleasurably (Jensen, 1981).

During the emission stage, genital contractions push the semen toward the urethra. In the second, or *expulsion*, stage semen is discharged from the urethra. The **bulbocavernosus muscle** at the base of the penis contracts strongly three or four times at intervals of about .8 seconds, expelling most of the semen. At that point, a few additional contractions occur at longer intervals, producing only a small amount of

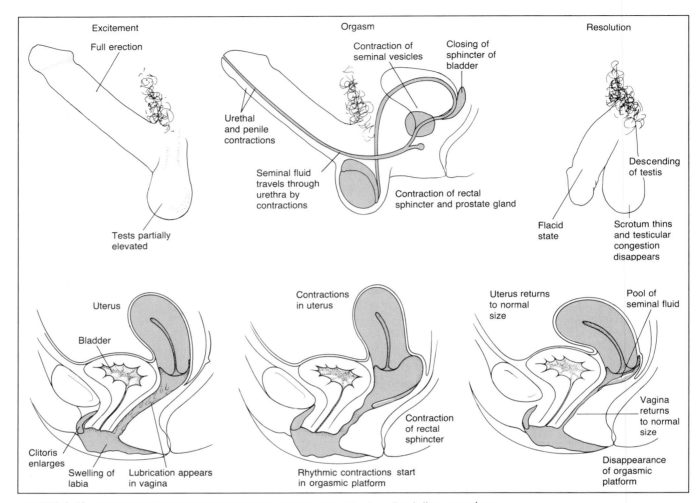

FIGURE 3-10 *REVIEWING THE SEXUAL RESPONSE CYCLE* With effective stimulation, sexual excitement culminates in orgasm.

fluid. Repeated ejaculations within a twenty-four-hour period will reduce the total volume of semen expelled during each orgasm and the number of sperm contained in the ejaculate. Men generally report intense feelings of pleasure from the muscle contractions in the pelvis and the tension release within the urethra (Bensimon, 1984).

Variations in Male Orgasmic Behavior. Ejaculation does not always accompany orgasm. A man may have the sensations of orgasm without semen expulsion. Among the possible reasons for this is **retrograde ejaculation;** emission occurs, but semen is expelled inward to the urinary bladder rather than outward through the urethra. The explanation for this type of ejaculation is that the bladder neck closes improperly

during orgasm, causing the semen to flow backward. A "dry" orgasm can also occur if the male has recently ejaculated.

Some males have learned to have **multiple orgasms** without losing an erection and without ejaculating until a final intensely pleasurable orgasm occurs (Hartman and Fithian, 1984). Others report that nonejaculatory orgasms occur after one involving ejaculation (Dunn & Trost, 1989). Only a small percentage of males have been able to master this technique (Robbins and Jensen, 1978). Thus, neither males nor their partners should feel that multiple orgasm represents a new standard for evaluating male sexual performance. Somewhat related is the practice of *coitus reservatus* in which intercourse is prolonged by slow movements and frequent pauses, thus delaying orgasm for long periods.

A widespread myth is that the experience of orgasm somehow saps males of their strength. As a result, many people believe that men should refrain from sexual contact before an important athletic contest or other major physical activity. For example, the Minnesota Vikings football players were required to sleep apart from their wives and girlfriends the night before each of their four Super Bowl games (Mirkin, 1980). They lost all four, and the separation may actually have impaired performance for a number of reasons unrelated to sex—for example, disruption of their usual routines or getting less sleep than normal. Because during ten minutes of sexual intercourse each partner expends only about fifty calories (Wise, 1979), this would not appear to be enough to interfere with a player's overall energy level. A survey of college coaches indicates that the traditional negative assumptions about pregame sex are rapidly disappearing (Gordon, 1988). One football coach suggested a more realistic connection between sexual and athletic activities: "It's not the sex before a game that ruins a player's performance; it's the time that he wastes looking for it" (Colt, 1981, p. 25).

Females: Pelvic Contractions. Orgasm in women resembles that of males, except that women don't ejaculate semen. First, the outer one third of the vagina contracts strongly, and this first contraction lasts two to four seconds. Next, the vagina rhythmically contracts up to ten to fifteen times at .8-second intervals. As orgasm continues, the intensity and duration of these contractions gradually declines, and they occur less regularly (Bohlen et al., 1982).

At orgasm, the woman's brain releases a small amount of oxytocin in response to cervical stimulation during intercourse. Oxytocin is a hormone which strengthens uterine contractions. The thrusting of the penis against the cervix produces this effect, and it is absent when the male partner has a shorter than average penis while the female partner has a longer than average vagina. Oxytocin quickly travels through the bloodstream where it stimulates stronger contractions of the uterus than would have otherwise occurred (Fox and Knaggs, 1969). The vagina and the uterus both have contractions during orgasm, aiding

sperm in their movement toward the oviducts where fertilization occurs. Thus, the female's orgasm is **proceptive** in that it promotes conception. Male orgasms are obviously proceptive because they ordinarily include the ejaculation of semen containing sperm.

A longer than average continuation of pelvic contractions—one minute or more—is called **status orgasmus.** Many females have the capacity for several orgasms in a short time period without notable loss of excitement. The ability to have multiple orgasms is much more common among females than males. Still another pattern for females is **sequential orgasms,** which occur when there are brief pauses between periods of stimulation (Amberson and Hoon, 1985). Thus, multiple orgasms occur during continuous stimulation, whereas sequential orgasms involve periodic drops to lower levels of excitement within a single sequence of sexual activity (Hite, 1976; Masters and Johnson, 1966).

The special section, *Increasing Enjoyment,* on page 58, describes how to recognize a partner's level of sexual excitement and his or her orgasm.

■ Resolution and the Refractory Period: A Renewable Cycle

Orgasm is followed by the **resolution phase.** This is the time during which arousal returns to the previous resting or nonaroused state. Muscles relax, vasocongestion is reversed, and the sex flush disappears within about five minutes. In women, the internal cervical os widens, and the cervix moves down into the pool of semen deposited at the back of the vagina. As a result, conception becomes more likely, and this response occurs only when a woman experiences orgasm. Once again, evidence suggests that the female orgasm has proceptive qualities despite the widespread belief that such a response is irrelevant to conception (Van Buren, 1986).

For men, erections diminish during the resolution phase, but a complete return to normal size can sometimes take an hour or two. By then, all genital organs have returned to their unaroused state. About a third of both sexes perspire heavily during resolution, and some individuals become very sleepy. Why people sweat or desire sleep after orgasm is unclear,

Increasing Enjoyment

DETECTING YOUR PARTNER'S SEXUAL EXCITEMENT AND ORGASM: A WORD IS WORTH A THOUSAND PICTURES

During a sexual interaction, how can you accurately gauge the excitement of your partner? For example, how do you know when he or she has reached a stage of excitement that indicates readiness for intercourse? Premature attempts at penetration can be embarrassing for the male whose erection begins to soften and painful for the female whose vagina is insufficiently lubricated.

Male and female nipple erection is sometimes used as an index of sexual excitement. This is not, however, a perfect indicator, because not everyone's nipples become erect when excited and also because other factors such as low skin temperature can produce that same physical response (Steinberger, 1981). The latter effect is used by photographers of nude females—ice cubes are rubbed on their nipples to make the models appear to be sexually excited. Nipple erection is sometimes masked by the swelling of the areola during the intense excitement of an approaching orgasm (Barbach, 1982). Some people, moreover, have flat areolas while others have more rounded and prominent ones, again making nipple erection an unreliable indicator of excitement (de Moya and de Moya, 1981). In addition, it should be noted that attempts to monitor a partner's nipples throughout a sexual interaction can be a serious distraction.

For males, the appearance of preejaculatory fluid from the bulbourethral glands can indicate an advanced level of excitement and an approaching orgasm.

TABLE 3-2 **Reading Your Partner's Sexual Signals**

Detecting physical signs of sexual excitement and of orgasm is easier with respect to males than females. For both sexes, verbal indications are more reliable than physical ones.

	PHYSICAL SIGNS OF SEXUAL EXCITEMENT	PHYSICAL SIGNS OF ORGASM
Males	Penis uniformly erect, no periods of softening, appearance of preejaculatory fluid	Ejaculation, but orgasm can occur without ejaculation
Females	Vaginal lubrication and the tenting effect	None

How can a man determine whether a woman is sufficiently excited that intercourse can begin? One sign is vaginal lubrication, which can be determined by the gentle insertion of a finger (Nadelson, 1978). Once intercourse is underway, lubrication tends to decrease despite the fact that the female may remain highly aroused (Keye, 1983). The most reliable sign of readiness for penetration, however, is the ballooning of the vaginal walls (James, 1982a). If the male's finger encounters an empty space beyond the introitus, the tenting effect has begun, and the female has reached a highly excited state.

As Table 3-2 suggests, unless monitoring devices were attached to each individual to measure heart rate and vaginal contractions, there is no infallible way to discern whether or not one's partner has had an orgasm (Keller, 1985).

The surest, and for many the most embarrassing, way to determine a partner's excitement and readiness and also to determine whether he or she has had an orgasm is through direct communication. The same approach applies in determining each partner's preferences—positions, pace, areas of touch, whether to verbalize, or whatever. Such communication is more efficient and accurate than searching for physical signs and signals. If two people know each other well enough to engage in sex, they should know each other well enough to converse about its details from time to time and to verbalize their feelings during sexual interactions.

but the reasons may be related to neurological stimulation.

A **refractory period** is very common among males. This is the period immediately after orgasm during which men are physically unresponsive to ad-

ditional sexual stimulation. Young men may not notice a refractory period because, up to age twenty, it may last less than ten minutes. With hormonal changes during aging, it gradually lengthens to several hours. When a man urinates half an hour or so after ejaculation, this helps the urinary sphincters (muscular valves) relax and thus speeds up resolution (Kaufman, 1981).

Why do males have a refractory period? A possible explanation is based on evolutionary theorizing. Human males share with other primates, such as the chimpanzee, the tendency to copulate and then to remain sexually inactive for a half hour or more (Jensen, 1981). Among the earliest humans, after orgasm females could potentially engage in intercourse with additional partners while the original partner became sexually uninterested. Such a pattern increased the possibilities for insemination by more than one male, thus increasing the odds that the female would conceive and the species would survive (Gallup, 1986).

A second explanation is based on experimental studies of other mammals such as rats. Research shows that a specific brain structure, the ventral medial lemniscus, controls whether males are interested in sex following orgasm—its destruction reduces the refractory period (Barfield et al., 1975). The refractory period, then, may be beneficial for males, providing a rest period during which their physiological resources are restored and thus permitting subsequent sexual encounters.

A third explanation, compatible with the first two, is based on the fact that after ejaculation few sperm are present in the remaining semen. The refractory period would thus be reproductively adaptive because males would not engage in further intercourse until their sperm count rose to a useful level for fertilization.

Assessing Sexual Excitement and Orgasm

In studying human motivation and emotion, behavioral scientists must rely on one of several indirect approaches. In investigations of anger, for example, an experimenter can (1) ask people how angry they are, (2) identify certain aggressive behaviors that usually accompany anger, or (3) use specific experimental manipulations that reliably elicit anger—such as insulting remarks. Physiological measures such as blood pressure or heart rate can be utilized, but they are not *specific* to anger; other events also affect their occur-

rence. With sexual responding, as we shall describe, it is not necessary to use such indirect and nonspecific measuring devices.

■ Psychophysiology of the Response Cycle

Sexual arousal is unique in that very specific bodily changes occur when an individual is stimulated. The development of measuring instruments to record these changes objectively has meant that those conducting sex research are able to determine an individual's level of physiological arousal precisely.

Instruments for Sexologists. Measuring the male sexual response has been relatively easy. In 1963, Freund indicated that male arousal could be assessed by determining increases in the volume or circumference of the penis as it changes from a flaccid to an erect state. Some of the earliest devices used for this purpose, each known as a **penile plethysmograph,** were relatively cumbersome and awkward (Freund et al., 1965; Fisher et al., 1965).

An improved mechanical strain gauge to measure changes in circumference (see Figure 3-11) was reported by Barlow et al., (1970). The gauge is encompassed in a ring made of pliant material that encircles the penis. When any degree of erection occurs, the ring expands. This expansion is recorded automatically on a polygraph, producing a line drawing that parallels the sexual response cycle (Earls et al., 1987).

Throughout this book, we will refer to research in which this and similar instruments are used to measure male arousal (McConaghy, 1989). It is obvious that a physical measure, unlike verbal reports, is not influenced by a subject's willingness to report arousal, by his desire to impress the experimenter, or by a faulty perception of his own bodily response.

Female arousal is also accompanied by physiological changes, as has just been described. For anatomical reasons, these changes in a female's body are more difficult to observe than is true for males; thus, they are more difficult to measure. Some of the earliest attempts included sampling vaginal secretions (Shapiro et al., 1968), using a balloon-like **kolpograph** to assess vaginal contractions (Jovanovic, 1971), and inserting a mechanical diaphragm to de-

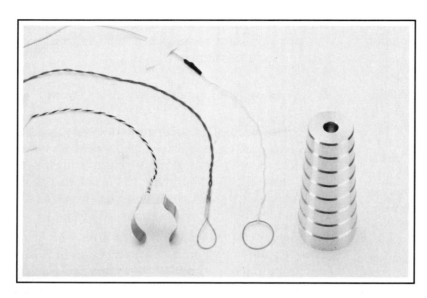

FIGURE 3-11 *PENILE PLETHYSMOGRAPH: MEASURING ERECTIONS* Physical measurement of male sexual arousal is relatively easy. Most versions of the penile plethysmograph record changes in the circumference or volume of the penis in various stages of excitement.

termine vaginal blood flow (Cohen and Shapiro, 1970).

Such devices were far from satisfactory, and a much better measuring instrument was developed by Geer (1975). The **vaginal photoplethysmograph** (see Figure 3-12) measures the degree of vasocongestion in the vaginal walls (Sintchak and Geer, 1975). A female volunteer in a laboratory study of sexuality inserts an acrylic probe the size of a tampon into her vagina. The probe contains a photoelectric transducer and emits a light, which is reflected back into the probe. A sensor then measures how much light has been reflected toward it. As vasocongestion increases, more light is reflected back into the sensor, and its amount is entered on a polygraph. Figure 3-13 shows graphs of the sexual response cycles of a male and a female who masturbated while attached to these devices.

Despite the successful use of Geer's technique in many investigations, this approach has several drawbacks (Beck et al., 1983). For example, even without being attached to anyone, when placed in a cylinder

in a dark, temperature-controlled room, the instrument indicates changes over time just as if a female subject were becoming slowly aroused. Also, when room temperature varies, the instrument also responds as if arousal were varying. Because such effects can be misinterpreted as changes in sexual arousal, additional technical improvements are needed before female responsiveness can be measured as accurately as male responsiveness.

■ The Accuracy of Subjective Estimates of Sexual Arousal

Females tend to be less accurate in assessing their level of physical excitement than are males (Rosen and Beck, 1986), and they are also less factually accurate about their orgasms. For example, when women have been asked to estimate how long their orgasms lasted, the average estimated duration (twelve seconds) was only about half of the actual duration of twenty seconds (Levin and Wagner, 1985). The less sexual experience a male has had, the less

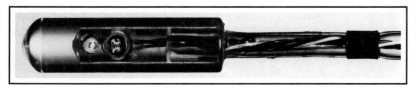

FIGURE 3-12 *MEASURING FEMALE AROUSAL: THE VAGINAL PHOTOPLETHYSMOGRAPH* The vaginal probe for a photoplethysmograph contains a light source and a light-sensitive spot in an acrylic tube. The probe is inserted into the vagina to measure the vasocongestion occurring during the sexual response cycle.

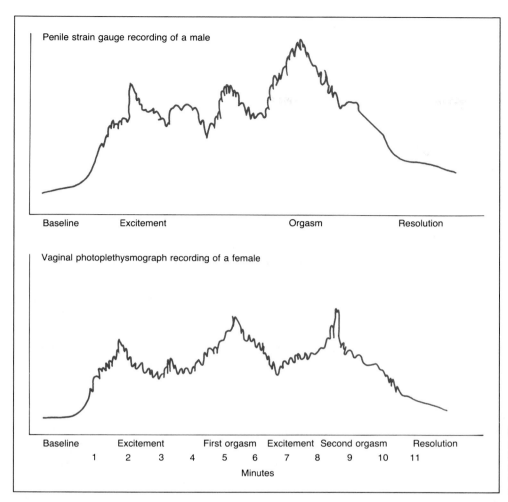

Penile strain gauge recording of a male

Baseline   Excitement   Orgasm   Resolution

Vaginal photoplethysmograph recording of a female

Baseline   Excitement   First orgasm   Excitement   Second orgasm   Resolution
         1   2   3   4   5   6   7   8   9   10   11
                                          Minutes

FIGURE 3-13 *EXCITEMENT, OR-GASM, AND RESOLUTION: A PLAY-BY-PLAY ACCOUNT* Patterns of sexual excitement as indicated by a penile strain gauge and a vaginal photoplethysmograph.

correspondence between his self-reported and physiological arousal levels (Sakheim et al., 1985).

With respect to both excitement and orgasm, females have less obvious external physical evidence than is true for males. That is, an erection and ejaculation are clearly much easier to perceive than vaginal lubrication and a female's climax. What would happen if males had less information about their erections than they normally do? Would they be less accurate in recognizing their physical excitement? This is precisely what happened to males whose genitals were hidden by a sheet while they watched a sexy movie. Their arousal as indicated by the strain gauge was actually reduced when they had no visual evidence of their erections, and they were less accurate in estimating their physical excitement (Sakheim et al., 1984). These findings suggest that sex differences in awareness of sexual arousal occur because of anatomically different cues. Perhaps the same would

be true of orgasm if males did not have the informational cues provided by ejaculation.

Because sexual excitement is associated with vasocongestion, temperature rises in those areas of the body, such as the genitals, with the greatest increase in the amount of blood. One approach to measuring excitement, **thermography**, takes advantage of this phenomenon (Abramson et al., 1981). It has been used for decades to detect breast lumps, because these growths are warmer than the surrounding region. In one sexual investigation using this technique, each subject was asked to masturbate while standing behind a screen through which the temperature changes could be monitored. As Figure 3-14 indicates, vasocongestion appears as a darkened (warmer) area in the genital region. Thermography, unlike the strain gauge and the photoplethysmograph, permits the use of the same measuring device for both males and females.

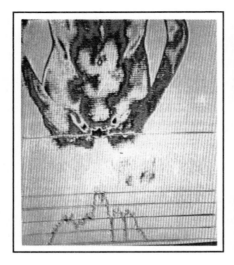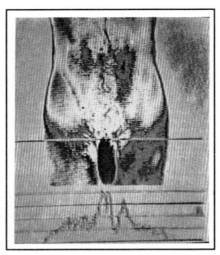

FIGURE 3-14 *SMILE—YOU'RE ON CANDID THERMOGRAPHY* Thermography provides a clear picture of the temperature changes in the genital organs and elsewhere during the sexual response cycle for both males and females.

Summarizing the Information about Sexual Functioning...

To describe the *sexual response cycle,* we combine the model of Kaplan with that of Masters and Johnson. *Sexual desire* varies from person to person and across situations, and it involves the motivation to seek sexual gratification. *Sexual excitement* results from physical or mental stimulation producing **vasocongestion** and **myotonia.** Among the signs of sexual excitement are sex flush, nipple erection, penile erection, and vaginal lubrication.

When **orgasm** occurs, pelvic congestion is relieved through muscle contractions, and *ejaculation* usually accompanies orgasm in males. Besides the pleasure caused by orgasm, it has various bodily effects such as increased respiration and heart rates. Females have the capacity for **multiple orgasms** if stimulation continues, but males usually have a **refractory period** during which they are not responsive to further stimulation. For either sex, long periods of stimulation that do not result in orgasm may cause *pelvic congestion.*

Psychophysiologists assess sexual excitement and orgasm directly using such devices as the **penile plethysmograph, vaginal photoplethysmograph,** and **thermography.**

To Find Out More about Sexual Functioning...

Hite, S. (1976). *The Hite report: A nationwide study of female sexuality.* New York: Dell.

   This report deals with the sexual feelings and experiences of 3,000 women who were interviewed. What females say about excitement and orgasm is described in detail.

Kothari, P. (1989). *Orgasm—New dimensions.* Bombay: VRP.

   This book presents detailed information about male orgasms including multiple orgasms and the relationship between desire and arousal.

Masters, W. H., & Johnson, V. E. (1966). *Human sexual response.* Boston: Little, Brown.

   This pioneering technical description of human sexual functioning became a surprise best-seller. It documents years of laboratory observations of men and women engaging in sexual acts.

Scruton, R. (1986). *Sexual desire: A moral philosophy of the erotic.* New York: Free Press.

   A philosopher examines arousal, desire, and love as expressed in quite different ways including chastity, paraphilias, masturbation, homosexuality, and incest. He presents a perspective on sexual ethics based on a moral philosophy.

Zilbergeld, B. (1978). *Male sexuality: A guide to sexual fulfillment.* Boston: Little, Brown.

   The sexuality of males is examined with numerous case studies and detailed factual information. The author also examines how masculine roles may create unnecessary problems.

CHAPTER FOUR

REPRODUCTION:
Conception, Pregnancy, Parenthood, and Infertility

For any sexually active person, pleasure in heterosexual interactions is (or should be) combined with considerations involving conception. For those who don't wish to conceive, there is the fear of an accidental pregnancy. For those who *do* want to become parents, there can be concern about the possibility of being unable to create an offspring. In the following narrative, a married man describes his own experiences with both situations.

Before I was married the news I feared most was when a woman said her period was late, raising the awful question, "What will we do if I really am pregnant?" Eventually I got married, but avoiding pregnancy was still a big deal, because Sue and I didn't have much money. We had a nice apartment and were buying a car, plus there were a million other things we wanted to do before we settled down to parenthood. A late period was still bad news.

After we had been married about five years, I was promoted, and Sue was ready to quit her job and have a baby, so we decided to go for it—no more pill, no more worries. Now we could make love freely and look forward to her getting pregnant. The only problem was, nothing happened. Every month, her period arrived "like clockwork."

When a few months had passed, we both were feeling a little spooked about the whole thing. We didn't know what was wrong or what to do. It began to strain our relationship; I think we both felt like failures. Once I said something about her not being able to have kids, and we had a hell of a fight. Then, she began seeing a doctor who sent her for a lot of tests, but there didn't seem to be anything wrong.

Next, her doctor said that I should make an appointment with an andrologist (whatever that was) to get a sperm count. This was maybe the most embarrassing experience in my life. To find out if I was man enough to father a kid, I had to make myself come in a little glass jar. It was like a nightmare when the doctor told me that I had a low sperm count. I just shut down. I didn't even hear the rest of his spiel.

Luckily, Sue was more sensible than I was. She paid attention and found out what to do. We "abstained" several days at a time, kept records of Sue's temperature to try to hit the magic moment when she was ready, and I even switched from wearing briefs to boxer shorts. It worked, and Timmy is running around the house as living proof. The effort we put into solving the problem now seems worth it, and I feel a lot better about the whole process than I did at the time.

Steve, age 32

As Steve found out, conception can be a problem whether it is something a couple wants or wants to avoid. Today's medical technology makes pregnancy possible among couples who in past decades would have remained childless. The desire to become a parent is likely to be strong at some point in your life, so it is worth your while to know as much as possible about the factors affecting fertility and infertility as an investment in that future prospect.

For our species the basic purpose of sexual anatomy, functioning, and behavior is to reproduce. In this chapter, we provide detailed information about the reproductive process: *the biological foundations*, the way in which *human life begins,* the process of *pregnancy*, and several aspects of *childbirth and parenthood.* Because reproduction may be difficult or impossible for a variety of reasons, we also discuss the problem of *infertility* and various remedies for it. Though conception is a biological process, parenthood represents a complex, emotionally involving, and long-lasting undertaking for human beings; we discuss some of the relevant issues in a special section on *the decision to become a parent.* Another such section outlines the scientific technology that makes it possible to conceive *test-tube babies.*

Biological Foundations: Sperm Production, Egg Ripening, and the Menstrual Cycle

To begin the story of reproduction, we will look at how the basic elements of conception are created and how they then join together. First, sperm must be produced, and an ovum must reach maturity.

■ Developing Sperm Cells

At the base of the human brain lies the **pituitary gland**, just below the **hypothalamus**. The pituitary is sufficiently important that it has been nicknamed the "master gland." Without the pituitary (e.g., if it has been removed), the person loses the potential to reproduce.

The biology of sexual reproduction is fairly complex; to explain it, we will start with a few basic concepts and build from there.

Based on instructions from the hypothalamus, the acorn-size pituitary secretes hormones which control the functions of the ovaries and the testes, as Figure 4-1 outlines. It also controls such things as growth rate, reactions to stress, and so forth, but in our discussion we will concentrate on reproduction. Thus, the neuroendocrine system lays the foundation for the reproductive organs to grow and for sperm and ova to be produced.

A Sperm Factory at Work. Hormones stimulate the functioning of the testes. The hypothalamus produces

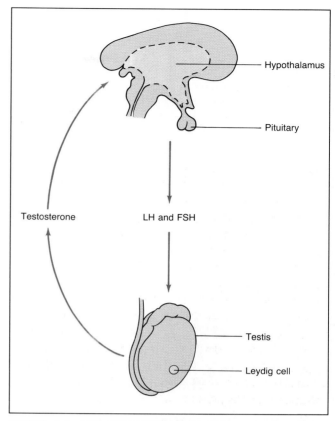

FIGURE 4-1 *SEX HORMONES AND SPERM PRODUCTION: A WELL-REGULATED PROCESS* The hormonal control of male reproduction depends on this feedback loop. Luteinizing hormone-releasing hormone (LHRH) signals the pituitary to begin a cycle which reduces testosterone level whenever necessary to maintain a constant production of sperm.
Source: Adapted from Svare and Kinsley, 1987.

luteinizing hormone-releasing hormone (LHRH) which signals the anterior part of the pituitary to secrete two hormones called **gonadotropins**, so called because they influence the gonads (Svare and Kinsley, 1987). These two hormones are the **follicle stimulating hormone (FSH)** and the **luteinizing hormone (LH)**, and in the male they cause the testes to produce **testosterone** and **sperm**. Testosterone circulates in the bloodstream, and it can relay a message to the hypothalamus to reduce its secretion of LHRH if such a reduction is needed. A message to reduce a hormone level is called a **negative feedback loop**. In contrast, a message to increase a hormone level is called a **positive feedback loop**. Because of feedback loops, a fairly stable level of testosterone and LH circulates in human males (Ramey, 1972). The levels of these two male sex hormones increase

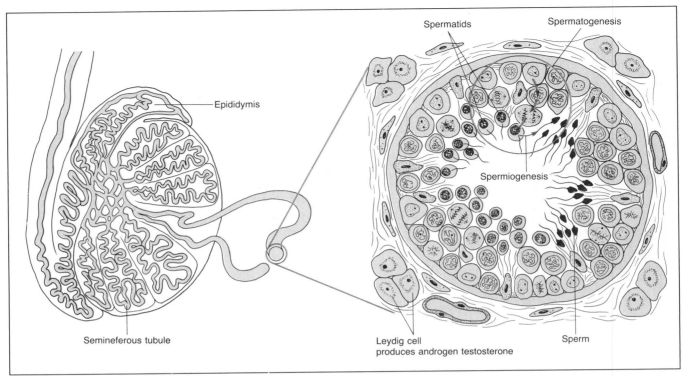

FIGURE 4-2   *SPERM PRODUCTION: A CONTINUOUS BIOLOGICAL ASSEMBLY LINE*   Sperm production involves a series of steps in growth and maturation over a two-month period.

slightly during the night, and testosterone peaks in autumn. However, such daily and seasonal changes do not seem to be directly related to sexual behavior.

Production of Sperm.   The initial steps in sperm production occur in the seminiferous tubules, where **spermatogenesis** and **spermiogenesis** occur. In spermatogenesis, a germ cell is transformed into four new cells called **spermatids** (see Figure 4-2). The spermatids mature and become sperm cells through spermiogenesis. Together, spermatogenesis and spermiogenesis take about two weeks.

The next steps of sperm production occur in the *interstitial spaces*, or the spaces between the seminiferous tubules. The interstitial spaces contain **Leydig cells,** which manufacture and secrete male sex hormones called **androgens**. These hormones, including testosterone, stimulate male tissues to grow. Leydig cells produce most (95 percent) of the testosterone in the blood of males, with the remainder coming from the adrenal glands, located just above the kidneys. Testosterone contributes to the growth of male physi-

cal characteristics such as facial hair, the penis, and the scrotum, so the Leydig cells are a crucial element in male sexuality. See Chapter 6 for a further discussion of the role of testosterone in male sexuality.

Sperm continue their development another six weeks before they are ready to be ejaculated. As was noted in Chapter 2, they are produced almost continuously from puberty to death. Sperm grow and mature in the Leydig cells and then in the epididymis. At first, they simply go in circles, but they soon begin to swim in a forward direction by moving in a spiral fashion, lashing their tails. The head contains genetic material called **chromosomes**. As Figure 4-3 shows, a sperm is only about 1/500 of an inch long—a mature ovum, or egg, is about 2.5 times larger than this.

After about eight weeks of this production process, sperm are ready for their reproductive function. Following ejaculation, each sperm is potentially ready to join with a partner (an ovum) in conception. Before discussing this union, we will describe the preparation of an egg—in the ovary.

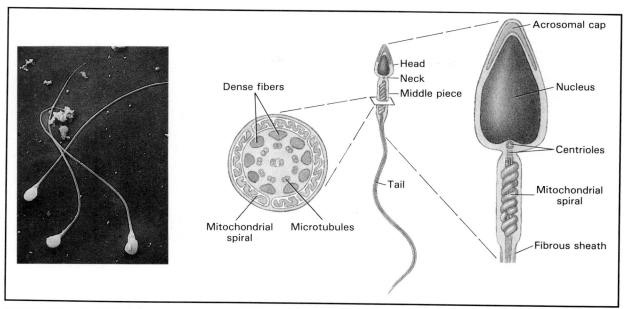

FIGURE 4-3 *HUMAN SPERM: TRANSPORTING GENETIC MATERIAL FROM THE MALE* The sperm's genetic message is contained in its head, while the middle section provides the energy for the whip-like tail that propels it in a spiral movement. The sperm here are magnified tens of thousands of times by an electron microscope.

The Menstrual Cycle

Several events occur during the menstrual cycle that culminate in the production of a mature egg, a process called **oogenesis**. Oogenesis requires the stimulation of hormones that are released in a series of steps as Figure 4-4 shows. Women ovulate about once every four weeks, alternating between the left and right ovaries. In other species, ovulation is often more frequent—female rats, for example, ovulate every four to five days.

The menstrual cycle consists of three phases: the *menstrual phase* during which menstrual flow appears; the *follicular phase* in the second week of the cycle when the ovum matures and **ovulation** occurs; and the *luteal phase* in the last two weeks when the uterus prepares to receive a fertilized egg.

Hormonal Control of the Menstrual Cycle. At the beginning of a menstrual cycle, the release of LHRH from the hypothalamus stimulates the pituitary to secrete a follicle stimulating hormone into the woman's bloodstream. Each of the two ovaries contains one **follicle** for each germ cell. At puberty there are about 80 to 90 thousand potential eggs in the ovaries, and

these small sacs serve as incubation chambers. During a menstrual cycle usually only one follicle becomes activated to ripen its ovum. When activated by FSH, a follicle swells to the size of a half-inch pellet. This stimulates the ovary to secrete estrogen into the bloodstream. Estrogen signals the hypothalamus to stop producing FSH and, instead, to begin producing luteinizing hormone.

With the resulting surge of LH, the follicle releases its mature ovum from the ovary, and the ovary secretes progesterone. When progesterone reaches the hypothalamus, this causes it to stop producing LH. The ovum then uses the walls of the old follicle to form the protective, nourishing **corpus luteum** (Latin for "yellow body") around itself. If the egg is not fertilized, the corpus luteum changes from yellow to white and degenerates.

The Phases of the Menstrual Cycle. During the **menstrual phase**, the unfertilized products of the previous cycle (blood and blood clots) are expelled from the uterus by way of the vagina. **Menstruation** usually takes about four or five days. The fluid consists of about four to six tablespoons of blood from the uterine lining (Grimes, 1980). This lining, called

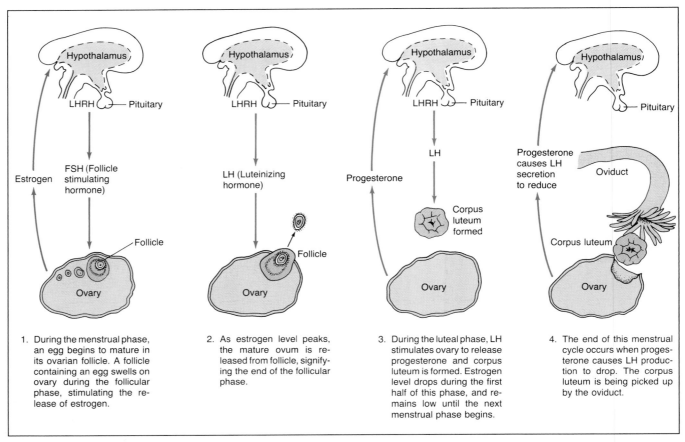

1. During the menstrual phase, an egg begins to mature in its ovarian follicle. A follicle containing an egg swells on ovary during the follicular phase, stimulating the release of estrogen.

2. As estrogen level peaks, the mature ovum is released from follicle, signifying the end of the follicular phase.

3. During the luteal phase, LH stimulates ovary to release progesterone and corpus luteum is formed. Estrogen level drops during the first half of this phase, and remains low until the next menstrual phase begins.

4. The end of this menstrual cycle occurs when progesterone causes LH production to drop. The corpus luteum is being picked up by the oviduct.

FIGURE 4-4 *THE MENSTRUAL CYCLE UNDER HORMONAL CONTROL*   The events outlined here indicate the hormonal basis for the menstrual cycle.
Source: Adapted from Svare and Kinsley, 1987.

the **endometrium**, builds up from the nutrients provided during the previous luteal phase, and is designed to receive the newly fertilized egg. Without fertilization, it simply sloughs off slowly to produce the menstrual flow. The ovarian follicle that will rupture during the next ovulation begins to mature during menstruation, and continues the process during the follicular phase.

During most of the menstrual cycle, the female ordinarily has few obvious clues about its progression (see Figure 4-5). In the middle of the cycle, ovulation occurs and can cause some abdominal pain on the side where the ovulating ovary is located. Known as *mittelschmerz* (the German term for "middle pain"), it is caused by the rupture of the follicle. When the pain is unusually intense and centered in the right ovary, it can be mistaken for symptoms of an

inflamed appendix. Ovulation occurs during the **follicular phase**, which ocupies the second week of the cycle.

The **luteal phase**, which occurs during the last two weeks of a twenty-eight-day cycle, gets its name from the corpus luteum, which consists of the cells that remain in the ovary after ovulation when the follicle ruptures. During the luteal phase, the level of progesterone circulating in the woman's blood increases, because the hormone is produced by the cells of the corpus luteum. The circulation of progesterone results in a reduction of LH level. Near the end of the luteal phase, progesterone secretion drops and the next menstrual phase occurs.

Ninety percent of menstruating women have cycles that last 24 to 32 days (Worley, 1980), indicating that the 28–day cycle depicted in Figure 4–5 is the

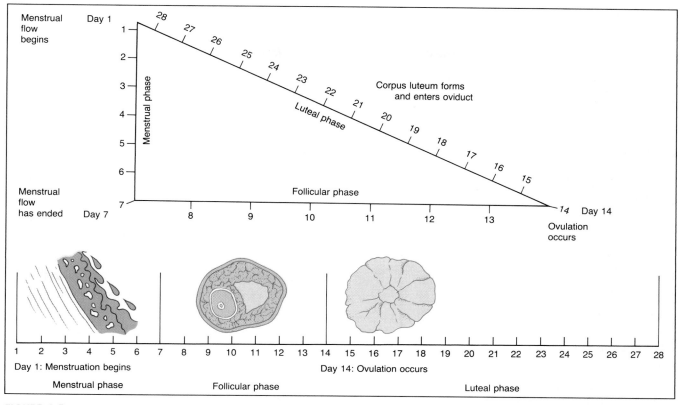

FIGURE 4-5 *THE THREE PHASES OF THE MENSTRUAL CYCLE* The menstrual cycle is divided into these three phases. Ovulation typically occurs about fourteen days before the next menstruation.

norm but not the universal rule. Cycles shorter than 21 days indicate the need for a gynecological examination, because a menstrual disorder may have developed.

■ The Physical and Psychological Effects of Menstruation

The blood and lining from the uterus have a characteristic, musty odor caused by bacteria that occur naturally in this bodily product. In order to catch the discharge, women use external products such as pads (some of which contain a deodorant to mask the odor) or internal products such as tampons inserted in the vagina. Others employ contraceptive devices such as cervical caps or diaphragms to catch the menstrual flow. Among these products, only pads are free from potential health problems. There can be an overgrowth of harmful bacteria with the prolonged use of a highly absorbent, thick tampon, and either of the contraceptive devices can promote bacteria overgrowth. Chapter 15 discusses this health problem. It should also be noted that those women with a heavier than average blood flow are at risk for developing anemia.

Menstrual Taboos. Taboos about menstruation have been common since ancient times, and they still exist today. Phrases like "the curse" and "being on the rag" continue to be applied to menstruation. The cultural taboos often indicate that a menstruating woman must be avoided; such fears seem likely to create generally negative attitudes about the female sex. For example, a student in one of our human sexuality classes asked, "Doesn't the fact that women menstruate make them inferior to men?" The obvious answer is "No," but there are data that indicate widespread support for such evaluations of this normal function. In a survey of women in fourteen different cultures, most indicated that even though menstruation was not a sickness, it *was* physically dirty (World Health Organization, 1981b). Although menstruation was considered a necessary outcome of being a female and being able to bear children, it also was perceived as inconvenient and the cause of hygiene problems. Among 260 college women in the United States, 75 percent expressed at least some negative feelings about the process while only 25 percent viewed it positively (Larsen, 1965).

In some cultures, the negative attitudes are more extreme. Among Orthodox Jews, for example, menstruating women are considered sufficiently unclean that a husband may not touch his wife at all, not even her little finger (Whelan, 1975). For the same reasons, Orthodox Jewish women tend to reject using IUDs as contraceptive devices because they cause an increased blood flow. Among Muslims, women are believed to be polluted, not only during their periods, but for an additional seven days after the menstrual flow stops. At this point, they must undergo a ritual washing before having sex.

Because of the combination of taboos and the reality of messiness during intercourse, sexual activity is least likely to occur during this phase of the cycle (Bachmann, 1983). There is, however, no actual health concern that dictates the avoidance of intercourse despite beliefs among both sexes that intercourse will cause cramping or prolonged menstruation (Snow and Johnson, 1978). Orgasm in a menstruating woman can, in fact, help to reduce some of the feeling of heaviness that is produced by vasocongestion (Ansbacher, 1982), and some women masturbate to relieve menstrual cramps.

The Premenstrual Syndrome (PMS). Most women indicate that they experience some physical discomfort in the last few days before, and often during, menstruation. In the fourteen-culture survey mentioned earlier, 51 to 70 percent of the women said they had *menstrual cramps*, with pain in the back or abdomen (World Health Organization, 1981b). The medical term for painful menstruation is **dysmenorrhea**.

The **premenstrual syndrome** consists of those symptoms of pain plus headaches, breast tenderness, irritability, tension, or depression that occur two to five days before menstruation, decreasing during or just after it (Brody, 1989). The premenstrual syndrome (or PMS) was first described in 1931 (Rolker-Dolinsky, 1987a), but only recently has it attracted much scientific interest. It can be severe, interfering with normal daily activities; a few women spend the worst days in bed. Even the criminal justice system recognizes its importance; a court in Great Britain agreed that PMS could have caused diminished capacity and thus it was used as part of the defense for a woman accused of murder (Laws, 1983; Lewis, 1990). Estimates of the incidence of PMS range from 20 to 75 percent of women, occurring equally often among blacks and whites.

More than 150 symptoms have been attributed to PMS, but, of course, not every sufferer experiences all of them. Beyond the physical complaints, PMS is believed to have a negative effect on concentration, mood, and feelings of control (Moos, 1969).

It may seem surprising, but there have been very few scientifically valid studies of PMS. Valid studies involve the daily recording of symptoms by women who are unaware of the intent of the study. One such investigation (Rossi and Rossi, 1980) has documented differences in mood state during the menstrual cycle. For eighty-two college women, positive moods were common around the time of ovulation, but negative moods such as sadness prevailed on several days before and during menstruation. These mood changes did not occur among women taking birth control pills, presumably because the pill creates a steady level of sex hormones—without the natural fluctuations of estrogen and progesterone, PMS does not occur. For whatever reason, adolescent women report fewer mood changes than are experienced by those of college age and beyond (Golub and Harrington, 1981).

Research on PMS is difficult because women's responses related to menstruation are affected by their negative beliefs about it. If women mistakenly believe they are about to menstruate, they report PMS symptoms even though they are actually at a totally different point in the cycle (Ruble, 1977). Memory is also faulty, and symptoms recorded daily are not the same as symptoms recalled from a previous cycle (Parlee, 1974). Expectations about PMS apparently have more to do with stereotypes about it than with objective physiological events.

Psychological characteristics such as mood and symptom reporting vary with the menstrual cycle. Does performance on the job or in school also depend on where a woman is in her cycle? Studies show that the menstrual cycle does not affect learning ability, memory, or decision making (Asso, 1983). Exam scores in a psychology class also are found to be unaffected by the cycle (Bernstein, 1977).

The causes of PMS are not clear, and the findings are quite inconsistent (Rolker-Dolinsky, 1987a). Whenever an investigator shows that PMS is caused by certain hormonal combinations or psychological factors, another study shows the opposite pattern of results. Evidence exists that PMS may consist of one or more entities that differ for different women.

Because a large number of symptoms are associated with PMS, it is possible that more than one syndrome exists. Premenstrual sufferers tend to fit at least one of the following subtypes:

FIGURE 4-6 *FIVE SUBTYPES OF PMS* The five subtypes of premenstrual responses lead to the conclusion that there are several premenstrual syndromes. Can you name each subtype shown in the photographs? (The answers appear below.)

(a)

(b)

(c)

(d)

(e)

1. general discomfort   2. impaired social functioning   3. impulsive   4. depressive   5. water retention

1. A depressive syndrome involving a negative mood state and changes in appetite;
2. A water retention syndrome resulting in breast pain and weight gain;
3. A general discomfort syndrome including pains primarily in the head, back, and abdomen;
4. An impulsive syndrome associated with irritability, lack of control, and violence;
5. An impaired social-functioning syndrome adversely affecting interpersonal behavior, decision making, performance, and the woman's usual social activities.

There is evidence supporting the existence of each subtype: Figure 4-6 shows some of the effects of each. The importance of the depressive subtype is suggested by the fact that women attempt and are successful in committing suicide more often around menstruation than at other points in the cycle (Mandell and Mandell, 1967). The water retention subtype seems to explain the painful response to breast stimulation by some females just prior to menstruation. Women with the impulsive subtype may be more likely to commit violent crimes than other women (Dalton, 1982) or if imprisoned more likely to behave violently than other female prisoners near the time of their periods (Hands et al., 1974). The impaired social-functioning subtype may be the reason that women most often are admitted to psychiatric hospitals during menstruation.

The concept of multiple types also suggests that different causes may be involved for each subtype, and therefore, that different treatments need to be sought for each. Progesterone therapy may lessen the symptoms of one PMS sufferer, but not for another individual whose problem involves a different subtype. Research on the water retention syndrome is centered on aldosterone, a hormone which causes retention of salt and water; some women with PMS are found to have an excess of this hormone (Janowsky et al., 1973). Such excess can be treated with Vitamin B6, yielding positive effects (Abraham, 1983).

PMS is obviously real and a source of discomfort and difficulty for some women. Recent research is promising and suggests that a combination of everyday stresses and hormonal irregularities are the basis of the problem.

Human Life Begins

The creation and nurturance of a new human being constitute extremely basic activities in the lives of most of us.

■ Conception

Though both sperm and ova are each obviously alive, the potential for the development of a human begins with the union of these two germ cells—conception. The egg is drawn into the oviduct after ovulation; there tiny cilia (hairlike growths) propel it toward the uterus. If fertilization occurs, this process takes place in the upper part of the oviduct, before it reaches the uterus.

Fertilization: A Microscopic Battle for Survival and Union. Within five minutes after semen is ejaculated into the vagina or even onto a moist portion of the vulva, sperm can reach the uterus (Worley, 1979). On the way, sperm face a potentially hostile environment—the acidic content of vaginal secretions is sufficiently high to kill or immobilize half of the sperm deposited there (Marmar, 1980). Bacteria within the vagina can also impede their progress. The survivors among the original 100 to 250 million sperm need sufficient *motility*, or ability to move, to travel from the vagina through the cervix. If they are able to navigate this entrance, they then must move through the uterus to reach the openings to the oviducts, where (if ovulation has occurred recently and if they are on the side of the woman's body in which ovulation occurred that month) the sperm might meet a mature egg that has been journeying in the opposite direction. Female orgasm and the associated uterine contractions help propel sperm toward the oviducts but are not essential for conception to occur.

The survival rate for sperm is enhanced just after ovulation because cervical mucus increases in volume and changes from acid to base at that time. Cervical mucus is also thicker and more "stretchy" at this point, a characteristic that is called *spinnbarkeit*. Such alterations in the mucus offer a more hospitable environment to sperm than they do at other parts of the menstrual cycle.

When sperm enter the uterus, the rest of the seminal fluid is left behind. After ejaculation, semen initially turns into a gel that helps protect sperm in the highly acid environment. Within thirty minutes, the gel liquifies and will seep or drip from the vagina, especially if the woman stands up or moves around following intercourse (Wild, 1983).

During this time, a complex change occurs in the metabolism of the sperm. For example, they develop the capacity to fertilize as the semen changes from a gel to a liquid. This process, called **capacitation**, enables sperm to penetrate the egg (Roland, 1984). Substances secreted by the ovum appear to aid capacitation.

The ovum is able to be fertilized for only about forty-eight hours after ovulation while sperm retain the ability to fertilize for 72 hours. During these overlapping time spans, these two elements must meet, like strangers in the night, or at least strangers in the oviduct. It is believed that the swirling fluids in the oviduct create a "backwater" area and that the ovum and sperm collide in an enlarged area of the tube, called the *ampulla* (see Figure 4-7).

Ordinarily, a number of sperm reach the egg and swarm around it. One sperm then succeeds in burrowing its head into the **zona pellucida**, a thin, jellylike coating around the egg. The sperm is propelled by the corkscrew-like motion of its tail. Penetration takes about ten minutes, although the entire fertilization process continues for twenty-four hours. Almost immediately after penetration, the zona pellucida forms a chemical crust that prevents other sperm from gaining entry. The unsuccessful thousands that have reached the threshold of conception are left outside the egg to die.

The period of gestation, from conception to

FIGURE 4-7 *SPERM PENETRATES OVUM: FIRST COME, FIRST SERVED* Conception is the outcome of a series of steps in the reproductive process.

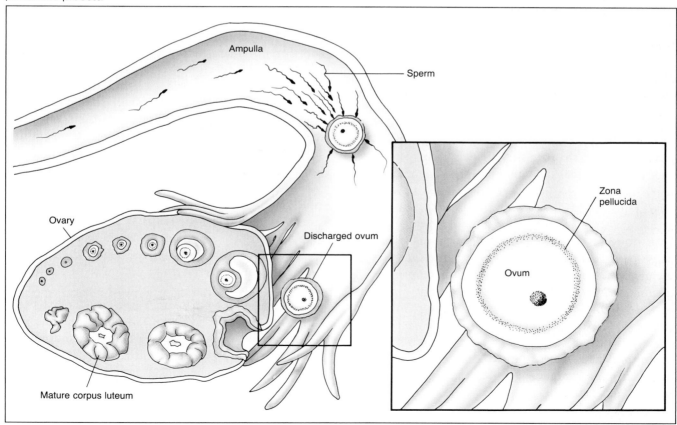

birth, typically takes 266 days. A woman's expected due date can be calculated by counting forward nine months plus one week from the first day of her last menstrual period. For example, if conception occurred during a menstrual cycle that started on January 1, the due date would be approximately October 8.

The Story Continues: The Drama of Conception.
Sperm and ova are specialized cells that each contain twenty-three chromosomes; all of our other cells contain forty-six chromosomes arranged in pairs. Chromosomes are strands of genetic material. When sperm and egg join at conception, the result is a **zygote**, a forty-six-chromosome cell that is able to develop into a human being. Twenty-three of these chromosomes are contributed by the egg, twenty-three by the sperm; they provide the programming for all inherited characteristics.

When both the egg and sperm contain X sex chromosomes, a zygote with two X sex chromosomes results, creating a female. Half of the sperm cells ejaculated into the vagina contain a Y sex chromosome; if one of these fertilizes the egg (which always contains an X sex chromosome), the result is an XY zygote, creating a male. Therefore, the sex of the offspring is determined by the sperm cell contributed by the father to fertilization. Chapter 6 discusses the biological origins of maleness and femaleness in more detail.

Many of our characteristics, especially physical ones, are clearly inherited—these make up the *genotype*, or genetic constitution, for each individual. The genotype has a major effect on many characteristics such as eye color, height, the color and texture of hair, and even whether a person is likely to become bald (Murphy, 1978). Despite the genetic "blueprint," actual development may vary to some degree on the basis of events that occur after fertilization. The *phenotype*, or observable characteristics, can differ from the genotype for various reasons. For example, an individual may not grow as tall as the genotype permits because he or she is malnourished during childhood and adolescence. The extent to which behavioral characteristics are genetic in origin has long been a matter of debate, speculation, and even political argument. Existing evidence suggests that individual differences in behavior are often based on learning rather than on information stored in our chromosomes (Lewin, 1981a). Human characteristics most often result from multiple determinants, both hereditary and environmental (Plomin, 1990).

Only one egg is usually released from an ovary at a time, but occasionally two are expelled. If this happens, both can be fertilized and thus produce twins with different genotypes. These are *fraternal (dyzygotic) twins*. They are no more similar genetically than any other siblings, and they may be of the same or opposite sex. In some cases, a second fertilized egg only survives during part of the pregnancy and then disintegrates without disturbing the healthier twin (Harris, 1983). Sometimes a single fertilized ovum separates into two; the result is *identical (monozygotic) twins* with exactly the same genotype. Twins occur in about one out of every eighty to ninety pregnancies, but the incidence increases as the mother's age increases (Mincer, 1988).

Multiple births of triplets, quadruplets, and so forth occur much less frequently than single or twin births. For women who take drugs to treat infertility, ovulation can produce more than one egg, and the probability of multiple births increases. Even birth control pills affect the rate of multiple births; women who become pregnant within a month or two after stopping the pill have an increased likelihood of conceiving twins (Rothman, 1978). It should be noted that when a pregnancy involves multiple offspring, there is a greater than normal risk of problems during pregnancy and delivery, including an early labor, because of the extra strain placed on the mother.

The genetic resemblance between parent and child is obvious, but it becomes a legal question when the identity of the father is in question. For example, a mother may charge that a specific man fathered her child and should be required to provide financial support. A paternity test involves a comparison of the blood types of the child and the possible father. The only totally conclusive result of this test, called an "exclusion," is the indication that the man *could not* have been the child's father. In the remaining instances (72 percent of the tests), all that can be determined is that the alleged father *could be* the biological parent (Walker, 1982).

■ Pregnancy: Detection and Trimesters

How can you determine whether conception has occurred, and, if it has, what exactly happens during the ensuing pregnancy?

Detecting Pregnancy. Among the early indications of pregnancy, called *presumptive signs*, the most obvious is the absence of menstruation. In addition, placental hormones stimulate growth of the mammary glands in preparation for milk production, and the breasts have a tingling sensation. Some of the early signs are likely to be noticed only by a physician—the darkening of the vagina and cervix to a bluish tinge because of increased blood flow (*Chadwick's sign*) and the softening of the area between the cervix and uterus (*Hegar's sign*) (Panter, 1981a).

Other early symptoms are more apparent to the individual herself, such as the nausea and vomiting experienced by half of those who become pregnant. The causes of this reaction are not well understood (Panter, 1982), though it may be the result of high hormone levels. Some women are helped by eating small carbohydrate snacks throughout the day. Additional presumptive signs are more frequent urination, fatigue, and an increased need for sleep. Some women also begin to leak small amounts of urine because of the pressure exerted by the developing embryo on the bladder and because hormones lead to a relaxation of the PC muscles surrounding the introitus (Freese and Levitt, 1984). The increase in fatigue seems to be the result of physical strain and muscle relaxation during pregnancy.

Some women need to have a definite answer very early in pregnancy—are they pregnant or not? A pregnancy only two weeks old can be detected by evidence that *human chorionic gonadotropin* (HCG) has entered the woman's bloodstream. HCG is secreted by the placenta, and determining its presence requires a sensitive laboratory test. After the first month of pregnancy, home pregnancy test kits can detect HCG in the woman's urine, but these kits tend to be less accurate than laboratory blood tests. The test kits give accurate results 80 percent of the time, while blood tests are 98 percent accurate.

Not until the third month of pregnancy, when the embryo is designated as a **fetus**, do *positive signs of pregnancy* appear. These include a fetal heartbeat and bodily movement. An X-ray or sonogram can produce a recognizable picture of the fetus. A sonogram uses high-frequency (ultrasonic) sound waves to produce these images, which can even show the fetus sucking its thumb (Hillard, 1983). Ultrasound creates shock waves in liquid, including the **amniotic fluid** in which the fetus floats. Because this procedure delivers ultrasonic waves to the fetus and there are no long-term data about its safety, *sonography* should be used only when problems with the pregnancy are suspected.

In a woman's first pregnancy, she usually becomes aware of fetal movement sometimes during the fifth month (Hillard, 1984). It feels like a gentle knocking at first, but progresses to bigger bumps as the fetus gains weight and strength. After their first experience with motherhood, women tend to recognize these movements at an earlier point in subsequent pregnancies.

Sometimes a woman senses the presumptive signs of pregnancy, but she is not in fact pregnant. A false pregnancy, or *pseudocyesis*, can be accompanied by weight gain, an enlarged abdomen, sore breasts, and so on. In extreme cases, women have even reported to a hospital in apparent labor following nine months of false pregnancy. This psychosomatic condition is usually interpreted as a maladaptive response to the failure to conceive (Murray, 1979). Freud designated this condition as "hysterical pregnancy" when one of his patients, Anna O., developed it (Sloan, 1982a).

Development in the First Trimester. On the third or fourth day after fertilization, the small mass of cells that has grown from the original sperm–egg union enters the uterus where growth and division continue. One week after fertilization, the developing embryo burrows itself into the endometrium. This implantation causes a small amount of bleeding, which the woman may assume is a light menstrual period. Unlike menstruation, however, there is a rise rather than a fall in progesterone level, and other hormones are secreted to aid the development of the implanted cells. Two weeks after fertilization, the **pla-**

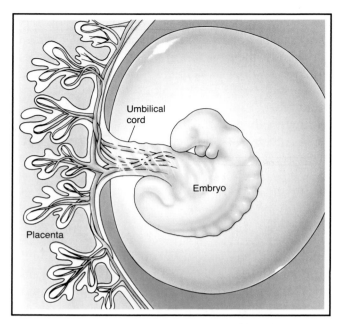

FIGURE 4-8 *EARLY IN PREGNANCY: THE EMBRYO DEVELOPS*
Formed during the first trimester of pregnancy, the embryo's life-support system consists of the placenta and umbilical cord.

centa (the organ formed during pregnancy to nourish the fetus) begins to develop, as Figure 4-8 illustrates. The placenta attaches to the inner surface of the uterus and is connected to the fetus by means of a tube called the **umbilical cord**. The placenta makes possible fetal respiration, excretion, and nutrition, and it also secretes hormones needed during pregnancy. Despite the transport of materials to and from the fetus through the mother's blood, using the placenta as a bridge, the blood of mother and fetus are separate and do not mix. At delivery, the normal placenta resembles a four-inch disk, weighing about one pound and having a grayish, veined appearance.

Pregnancy is usually divided into **trimesters**—three 3-month segments. During the first two months of the first trimester, the embryo develops to the point at which organ systems start forming. The fetus' central nervous system and heart form during the third month. When the *blastocyst* implants in the uterus, it has a .04-inch (<1 mm) diameter. By the end of the first trimester, the fetus has grown to 3.5 inches (9 cm) in length, .04 ounces (1 gm) in weight, and has a distinct human appearance.

Development in the Second Trimester.   In the second trimester, limbs, ears, and eyes near completion.

The fetus sucks its thumbs and moves actively within its amniotic sac. During these three months the fetus grows to a foot-long (30 cm), 1.4 pound (650 gm) organism which ordinarily cannot survive outside the uterus. Its organ systems are still too immature, and breathing would be impaired.

This trimester may be the most enjoyable of the three for the healthy mother—fatigue and nausea usually have been replaced by increased energy, better resistance to common, contagious illnesses, and more optimism about the upcoming birth. Shopping and other preparations for the new baby are more easily accomplished now than they will be in the following trimester. The woman should avoid contact with noxious substances such as paint throughout pregnancy (Shinkle, 1990). Strenuous exercise does not seem to harm the pregnant woman, but overdoing it can reduce the amount of blood available to the fetus (Stockton, 1989). Figure 4-9 shows embryonic and fetal development through the second trimester.

Development in the Third Trimester.   The average newborn has grown to 20 inches (50 cm) and 7 pounds (3,300 gm) at forty weeks of gestation. Its chances of survival, if delivered, increase from 10 percent in the seventh month to 70 percent in the eighth month, when the fetus' head usually begins to point downward in the uterus. Because of its increased size, freedom of movement within the uterus is restricted. Increased attention to sounds may compensate for the relative lack of movement, because the fetus can hear loud sounds outside the mother's body. The fetus often knocks with its hands, feet, and head on the uterine wall, and the mother looks forward to delivery more and more. In any high-risk pregnancy, airplane flights should be avoided at this time (Tomer, 1989).

The Father's Role During the Trimesters.   The father's initial reaction to pregnancy may range from surprise, joy, and elation to more negative responses such as worry or fear of the financial consequences of increasing family size (Shapiro, 1987).

Men become involved in pregnancy, too. Among husbands, for example, 25 percent experience some of the same symptoms as their pregnant wives—nausea, indigestion, and pain (Hillard and Hillard, 1983). In the ritual known as **couvade**, his symptoms may mimic not only pregnancy but also childbirth.

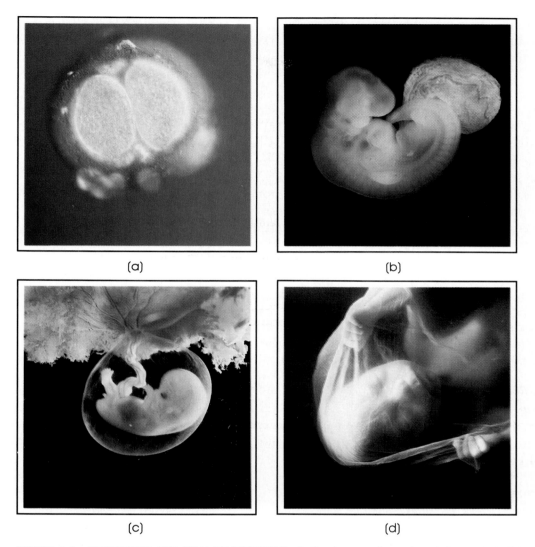

FIGURE 4-9 *EMBRYONIC AND FETAL DEVELOPMENT*   A. On day one, the embryo is two cells. B. By the fourth week, the spinal cord is recognizable. C. By the eighth week, the head, limbs, and genitalia can be identified. D. By the sixteenth week, the fetus appears human.

There is no apparent physiological basis for this sympathetic behavior among men, but the "power of suggestion" can clearly cause such symptoms when the man is constantly around a pregnant woman who is undergoing various bodily and mood changes.

Changes in his partner's body become more obvious during the second trimester, and he can come to appreciate the increase in her breast size, rounded abdomen, and the opportunity to feel fetal movement. His earlier anxiety usually is replaced by optimistic feelings about fatherhood.

The third trimester may be associated with decreases in his desire for her expanded body or in her interest in sexual activity. The pregnant woman feels more dependent on her mate, whom she needs even more at this physically and psychologically stressful time in her life. The prospect of the totally helpless baby about to arrive also increases her dependency needs, even among career-minded, independent women. The father may feel isolated from the relationship she has with her physician, although childbirth classes and joining his wife in visiting the doctor may help reduce this feeling. Numerous situation comedies have portrayed the loyalty, unease, and closeness the expectant father feels about his mate and the pregnancy.

Adapting to Pregnancy and Parenthood. The reactions of most women to their first few pregnancies are usually positive, as shown in Figure 4-10. As the number of children increase, reactions become more negative. Social class also affects attitudes toward pregnancy. The higher the social class, the more accepting and positive the attitudes. Pregnant women whose incomes place them in the upper middle class are more pleased with their pregnancy, feel sexier, and enjoy being treated as someone special more than is true of lower-class women. Such differences in self-perception partially reflect the attitudes of those around them. One intriguing index of socioeconomic effects is that in higher status stores, maternity clothes are usually located near lingerie or loungewear; budget stores tend to place them near uniforms or larger size clothes (Horgan, 1983).

The special section, ***Taking Responsibility and Protecting Yourself*** on pages 79 to 80, explores the process by which a couple decides to have a child and factors that enter into family planning.

Nutrition during Pregnancy. The pregnant woman requires more nutrients than the nonpregnant one in order to satisfy the needs of her developing baby and to maintain her own health. If good nutrition is lacking, the fetus may grow more slowly, be delivered prematurely, and have low birth weight with its attendant problems (including mental retardation in some cases).

Pregnant women need 300 extra calories daily and should increase their intake of minerals such as iron and calcium in food and in vitamin supplements. Calcium contributes to growth of fetal bones; if the mother eats too little of calcium-rich foods such as almonds and sesame seeds, she will experience cramping of her lower legs as the fetus absorbs the calcium stored in the mother's body. A balanced diet will usually provide the necessary nutrients including protein

FIGURE 4-10 *REACTIONS TO PREGNANCY: FAMILY SIZE MAKES A DIFFERENCE* Women express feelings about their pregnancies that range from highly positive to highly negative. In this survey, 2,846 white, married women were asked about their pregnancies. The numbers above each bar indicate the number of children each woman had (including her current pregnancy). Positive feelings decreased as the number of children increased, with negative feelings becoming more frequent.
Source: Based on data in Westoff, 1980.

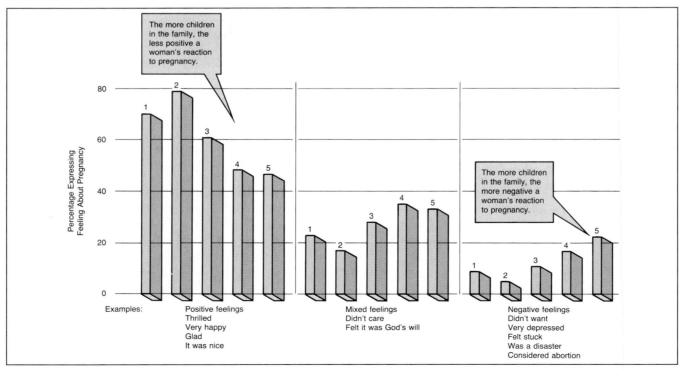

Taking Responsibility and Protecting Yourself

THE DECISION TO BECOME A PARENT: WHO, WHEN, WHY?

Our society's attitudes toward pregnancy are shown by the way we treat pregnant women. In contrast to most industrialized nations, the United States has not developed a national policy providing parental job leave in late pregnancy or after childbirth (Scott, 1979a). Such a bill was passed by Congress in 1990 but was then vetoed by President Bush. Even at the personal level, adults tend to avoid being near pregnant women. In a field study, passengers in an elevator were found to stand farther away from a female experimenter wearing a device that made her look pregnant than fellow passengers did when she did not appear to be pregnant (Taylor and Langer, 1977).

Parenthood remains a desirable role for adults, at least for females. College women, for example, plan to have children, though at a later age than their mothers did (Knaub et al., 1983). For these women, motherhood is not the only life choice that promises happiness and fulfillment, however; career interests and successful marriages are equally important. For men, parenthood is perceived as leading to less satisfaction with their lives than childlessness (Ross and Kahan, 1983), as Figure 4-11 indicates. Once a married couple has a child, their motivation to have additional children drops dramatically (Beckman, 1987).

One option for any couple is to remain childless, and couples without children are as happy and as successful as those who become parents (Peterson, 1983). Only 1 or 2 percent of married couples currently have no children by choice, but childlessness may become increasingly common (Bloom, 1981).

One reason is that young professional women under the age of forty express doubts about their ability to combine motherhood and career successfully. At Northwestern University, two thirds of young female professors had no children whereas only 22 percent of older faculty

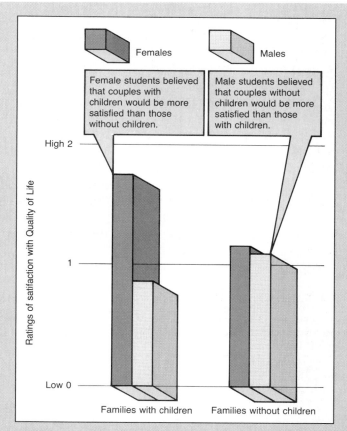

FIGURE 4-11 *SEX DIFFERENCES IN PERCEPTIONS ABOUT THE EFFECTS OF CHILDREN* A sample of forty-four college females expressed the belief that a couple with children would be more satisfied with their lives than if they had none. A group of sixty-eight college males, in contrast, indicated that having children would *decrease* the couple's satisfaction.
Source: Data from Ross and Kahan, 1983.

women were childless (Yogev and Vierra, 1983). Women who choose not to become mothers usually believe that family life would interfere with their careers and with independence (Gaylin, 1977). Women who have had several children, however, express confidence that it is possible to juggle marriage, job, and offspring (Booth and Duvall, 1981).

One factor important to couples in de-

ciding about parenthood is cost. Today in the United States, about a quarter of a million dollars is spent raising a college-educated son to age twenty-two—about a fourth of a middle-class family's total lifetime income (Olson, 1983). Daughters cost an additional $20,000, reflecting the greater expenditures on clothing, dance lessons, and other female-associated possessions and activities.

There are also nonfinancial costs of parenting such as the fears that one's children will turn out badly, the responsibilities of parenthood, and the greater difficulty in ending a bad marriage (Gerson, 1984). Nevertheless, various pressures encourage parenthood; for example, people consider those without children as maladjusted or misguided. College students describe people without offspring who accidentally conceive as "living happily ever after." As most parents could tell them, this is an unrealistic view of the effects of having children.

By the time a female begins to menstruate and is able to conceive, she has a good idea of the number of children she would like to have (Philliber, 1980). A young girl's own family background has an effect on these projections—those with at least one sibling tend to want the average, two-child family (Clay and Zuiches, 1980). The perceived financial and emotional costs of children also affect expectations about ideal family size. Those who have less education and who are religious, older, and from rural backgrounds want a larger number of offspring than others. If they were given more accurate information about costs, their views could conceivably change (Scott and Morgan, 1983).

Desires about family size are not very good predictors of the actual number of children a couple has (Trent, 1980). Factors such as divorce or infertility can interfere with the firmest of plans (Bongaarts, 1984). Ideal goals about family size are also not as predictive of number of children as are specific intentions to have specific numbers (Jaccard, 1981). Before having children, a couple might usefully expore their intentions together and come to, if possible, a "meeting of the minds" (see Figure 4-12).

Techniques have been developed to help couples make such decisions. There is an exercise in which couples rate the *subjective expected utility* of having children versus remaining without (Beach et al., 1982). Subjective expected utility is defined as the value placed on the payoff for making a certain choice. The idea is that the best decision for a couple is one in which the rewards exceed the costs. Some people agonize for years about whether to become parents; for example, a teacher in his early thirties said, "We made lists, we talked to friends with children . . . but the more we knew the harder it became" (Rosenblum, 1979, p. 58). Such a rational, logical approach to parenthood is probably rare. Most of us make such highly personal decisions based on emotional reactions, not necessarily sensible ones. We become parents because we want to, our friends or siblings have already done so, or it seems like something we *ought* to do. Considering the high stakes involved for parents and their children, it is probably wise to consider as many aspects of childbearing as possible before plunging into the new, demanding, and long-term role of parenthood.

FIGURE 4-12 *PARENTHOOD: WHY DO YOU WANT TO HAVE CHILDREN?* The decision to have children is extremely important, and couples need to discuss the issue thoroughly before marriage and, especially, before parenthood. There are many possible motives for having offspring, including the desire to reproduce young ones just like yourselves—as suggested here. Such a desire is perfectly reasonable, but the serious and long-lasting responsibilities of being a parent are likely to require a more thoughtful analysis of what is involved.

"Ooh! How cute!"

for growth of the placenta and uterus. Pregnant women who prefer a mainly vegetarian diet should consult with their physician to be sure they are getting sufficient nourishment.

Some of the Effects of Pregnancy: Appearance, Behavior, and Sexuality. Women quite naturally have special concerns about their bodies during pregnancy. A central question often involves fears of a change for the worse in appearance. Varicose veins, hemorrhoids (Panter, 1981b), and stretch marks (Millen, 1982) appear during the last half of pregnancy, but such problems usually disappear or subside in the months following delivery. While they are pregnant, women's hair grows more rapidly, and its general condition improves because of higher hormone levels (Hillard, 1982). Two to seven months after delivery, however, hormone reductions lead to hair loss. This condition, called *postpartum alopecia,* clears up a few months later.

Women tolerate pain better during pregnancy than before, because levels of pain-killing *endorphin* increase. Endorphins help make tolerable the increased crowding within her body as well as the pain of childbirth (Gintzler, 1980). *Braxton-Hicks contractions* of the uterus occur spontaneously from time to time. These contractions tend to be mildly painful, and consist of short periods of tightening of the uterus. They are not a sign of labor and are thought to help strengthen the uterus for labor.

A common concern during pregnancy centers on the couple's sexual activity, as Figure 4-13 suggests. Should sexual practices change during pregnancy because of concerns about the health of the mother and of the unborn child? The answer is "yes"; some changes should occur. For example, from the fourth month until about six weeks after delivery, the

FIGURE 4-13 *SEX DURING PREGNANCY: TO HAVE OR NOT TO HAVE ISN'T USUALLY THE QUESTION* For many couples, sexual activity during pregnancy involves changes in frequency, positions of intercourse, and enjoyment. Nevertheless, vaginal intercourse usually does not have any negative side effects on a normal pregnancy.

missionary position of intercourse is to be avoided (Fertel, 1983a). The side-by-side or rear-entry positions are preferable to avoid pressure on the enlarging uterus so as not to reduce the blood supply to the mother and the fetus (Solberg et al., 1973). During the first trimester, persistent nausea and fatigue may interfere with the woman's sexual interest, and the frequency of sexual interactions most often declines. As the delivery date approaches, pregnancy has an increasingly negative effect on sexual desire, activity, and enjoyment (Reamy & White, 1987). This effect tends to be more dramatic in the first pregnancy than in later ones (Masters and Johnson, 1966). Most women (82 percent) feel that sexual activity should *not* continue through all nine months of pregnancy (Kenny, 1973).

During the second trimester, there is usually a sexual bonus for couples in that sexual frequency tends to return to the pre-pregnancy level (Calhoun et al., 1981). Women say that they especially like their partners to hold and stroke them (White and Reamy, 1982). Women continue to have erotic dreams during pregnancy, but when orgasm occurs, painful uterine contractions may result (Duenhoelter, 1978). Neither female orgasm nor male ejaculation tend to initiate miscarriages or labor in women unless their pregnancies are abnormal in some way or if they have a history of miscarriage.

A special caution is that cunnilingus must be performed carefully in order to avoid blowing air into the vagina. The danger is that air bubbles can be absorbed through the uterine lining and enter the blood vessels of the lungs, brain, or heart—a condition known as air embolism. Aronson and Nelson (1967) reported several cases of maternal deaths caused in this way.

A major danger from intercourse during pregnancy is the transmission of infections from the male to his partner and the unborn child, causing a *septic pregnancy* (infection of the uterus). Such infections can be treated, but the treatment may damage the fetus. For this reason, couples should be sure that they are free of infection before they attempt to conceive. Masters and Johnson (1966) found that 18 out of 71 husbands engaged in extramarital sexual interactions before or just after delivery, while their wives were unable to engage in intercourse. At the very least men who have sex with outside partners (as well as those using intravenous drugs) should wear condoms to lessen the probability of transmitting an infection to their spouses.

By the last six weeks of the third trimester, sexual activity of all kinds decreases for most pregnant women. Intercourse, especially, becomes less frequent because of the discomfort involved. Both males and females differ widely in their perceptions of the woman's appearance at this point. Some regard late pregnancy as an unattractive stage, responding negatively to the swollen belly, enlarged arms and legs, and puffy face. Some women, however, feel glorious and as beautiful as ever, and some men see them as glowing in a very special way. If you have not had the experience and a pregnancy is in your future, how do you think you will respond?

■ Problems during Pregnancy

Ectopic Pregnancy.   A not uncommon, and very serious, physical problem is an **ectopic** (misplaced) **pregnancy** in which the embryo is implanted outside the uterus and begins to develop and grow. This can take place, for example, in the oviducts or elsewhere in the abdomen. Ectopic pregnancy can create a medical emergency and may cause the mother's death. If the oviduct ruptures, for example, the blood loss can be very dangerous. An embryo growing in the abdomen can calcify into a "stone baby." In the last twenty-five years, the incidence of ectopic implantations has doubled and now occurs in about one of every 100 pregnancies (Ziff, 1984). Among the causes are pelvic disease and repeated abortions. A woman with presumptive signs of pregnancy who also has pain in her lower abdomen should consult a physician immediately about the possibility of an ectopic pregnancy and its surgical removal.

Defective Sperm.   Though the topic has been neglected until recent years, research indicates that sperm can be damaged by alcohol, opiates, various gases, lead, pesticides, and industrial chemicals (Blakeslee, 1991). When such sperm fertilize an egg, the results can range from spontaneous abortions to birth defects.

Alcohol as a Teratogen.   An important aspect of fetal development should not be missed by potential

FIGURE 4-14   *TERATOGENS DURING PREGNANCY: PHYSICAL DAMAGE TO THE DEVELOPING CHILD*   The effects of teratogens on the embryo and fetus depend on which organ system is developing most rapidly at the time of contact with the substance. Except during the first two weeks of pregnancy, the organs and structures in the solid boxes are vulnerable to major deformities. (CNS means central nervous system, and the palate is the roof of the mouth.) The organ systems in the darkened boxes may suffer minor structural and physiological defects.
Source: Based on Moore, 1982.

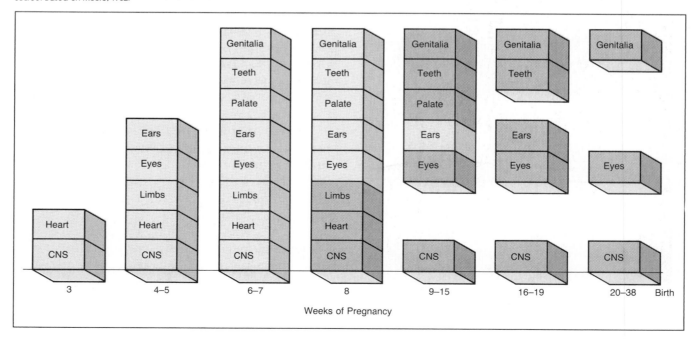

parents. Rapidly developing organ systems are most susceptible to damage from a number of toxic substances, known as **teratogens** (see Figure 4-14). Some teratogens, such as environmental pollutants, cannot be avoided by the average individual, but the consumption of drugs *is* under the control of each individual mother. A good rule is that no drugs should be used during pregnancy unless the risk of not using them exceeds the risk of using them. An example of a worthwhile drug is medication needed to control a physical condition that could harm the fetus.

An unnecessary and dangerous drug is alcohol, and it can create severe damage in newborns. The **fetal alcohol syndrome (FAS)** (see Figure 4-15) can occur after significant alcohol use during pregnancy. The effects of FAS occur when the mother has consumed one or more drinks daily, although milder forms of FAS have been associated with lighter and binge drinking. The best advice is to avoid alcohol

use during pregnancy. FAS results in a smaller than average infant, permanent mental retardation, facial abnormalities including those affecting the eyes, and childhood behavior problems such as irritability in infancy and hyperactivity in later childhood (Streissguth et al., 1984). The leaflet, *Alcohol and Your Unborn Baby,* is available from the U.S. Public Health Service.

In addition to alcohol, the consumption of marijuana (Fried, 1982) or fish from water contaminated by metals or other toxins (Jacobson et al., 1984) is associated with defects in newborns. In addition, various psychotropic drugs and even some legal medications (such as Accutane, used in treating acne) can pose dangers (Raeburn, 1988). Certain infections, including Lyme disease and hepatitis B can cause equally serious birth defects (Altman, 1988; Sweet, 1988).

Smoking. Smoking also affects the unborn child by shortening the pregnancy, which may result in health problems or even death. Babies born to mothers who smoked during pregnancy have lower *Apgar scores* than those with nonsmoking mothers (Garn, 1981). This rating, made within the first few minutes after birth, indicates the physical condition of a newborn infant and includes an assessment of respiration, muscle tone, and reflex irritability, heart rate, and skin color.

Drug Addiction. Addiction to drugs during pregnancy can result in serious problems for the baby, who may be born addicted to the drug and suffering from birth defects. Drugs having such effects include amphetamines, barbiturates, heroin, cocaine, codeine, and morphine. Birth defects connected with drug use are low birth weight and abnormalities of the nervous system such as learning disabilities. The infant's addiction leads to withdrawal characterized by tremors and disturbances of normal sleep and feeding patterns.

Miscarriage. By the fifth month, the risk of *miscarriage* decreases. Miscarriage, or spontaneous abortion, occurs when a pregnancy is terminated because of natural causes though the reason for its occurrence is not clear. Sometimes the fetus is defective, and abortion is a natural process that eliminates the problem.

About 31 percent of all conceptions end in miscarriage, frequently before the woman even knows she is pregnant (Kolata, 1988). If heavy or prolonged

FIGURE 4-15 *DRINKING AND SMOKING: NO WAY TO TREAT A BABY* Use of alcohol or tobacco during pregnancy can have severe negative effects on the child's development before and after birth.

bleeding and severe cramping occur during pregnancy, a spontaneous abortion may follow. In some instances, bed rest and avoidance of sexual intercourse may prevent the miscarriage. More often, the mother's activities have no bearing on the threatened miscarriage. When a spontaneous abortion occurs, the uterine contents (including the placenta) may have to be removed using a minor surgical procedure (discussed in Chapter 5) known as D & C (**dilation and curettage** or *dilatation and curettage*). Most miscarriages occur during the first trimester. Miscarriages can cause both the woman and her partner a deep sense of loss, especially when they have experienced difficulty in conceiving. In many instances, parents mourn as they would when a child dies, and counseling is sometime helpful.

Birth Defects.   If there is any reason to suspect that the fetus may have genetic defects, there are two procedures to detect them (Lehman, 1989). Tissue surrounding the eight- to ten-week-old embryo can be removed in a **chorionic villus biopsy.** In order to provide accurate results, the test must be done at this stage of gestation, before the chorionic villi transform into part of the placenta (Kolata, 1983b). When serious defects are discovered, parents face the dilemma of whether to abort the fetus. Because this test yields information early, those who decide to have an abortion can do it during the first trimester when the risk is lowest. A more familiar test, **amniocentesis,** is performed fifteen to sixteen weeks into the pregnancy, though an abortion during the second trimester is more dangerous for the mother. A sample of amniotic fluid is obtained through a long needle, and several weeks are required for a complete analysis (Elias, 1980). Both tests involve some risk in that complications such as miscarriage or stillbirth occur following 7.2 percent of chorionic villus biopsies and 5.7 percent of amniocentesis tests (Brown, 1989).

Such procedures can provide evidence for problems like chromosomal abnormalities that result in mental retardation associated with Down syndrome, also called mongolism. This condition becomes increasingly more common with older parents (Kaye, 1983). The incidence of Down syndrome, due to trisomy of the 21st chromosome, is about 1 in 1,500 births to mothers under age thirty, 1 in 300 births by age thirty-five, and 1 in about 50 births at age forty-five. About 3 percent of newborns have some genetic disorder (Kaye, 1981), ranging from cleft palate and club feet to cystic fibrosis. Professionals trained in *genetic counseling* can aid parents in making decisions about whether to have offspring if their family history reveals genetic problems (Lewis, 1986).

Toxemia and Eclampsia.   Ideally, any pregnancy should be watched closely by an obstetrician, especially if there is any indication of a high risk. For example, 5 to 7 percent of pregnancies are complicated by **toxemia,** a condition in which blood pressure and weight rise rapidly, severe swelling in the limbs occurs, and the kidneys spill protein into the mother's urine. This is most likely to occur during the last trimester, and it can lead to life-threatening **eclampsia** (Hillard, 1983).

Eclampsia is often preceded by preeclampsia, consisting of weight gain of more than four pounds weekly and swelling of the joints and face. The disease disappears when the fetus is delivered, though premature delivery and resultant low birth weight under five pounds are obviously also possibilities. The *breast stimulation stress test* can assess whether eclampsia is likely to harm the fetus. The woman stimulates her breasts in the doctor's office until the uterus starts contracting (Hill, 1985). If the pregnancy is still progressing well, the fetal heart rate will increase in response to the uterine contractions.

Prematurity.   The onset of labor before thirty-seven to thirty-eight weeks of gestation can cause several problems. Among the signs that this process is beginning are a vaginal discharge of small amounts of amniotic fluid that feels slippery like glycerin or is pinkish in color, and rhythmic pains that begin to increase in intensity. When these symptoms occur, medical help should be sought immediately so that an effort can be made to forestall prematurity. Labor which occurs prematurely can result in the birth of a *low-birth-weight* baby (one weighing 5 pounds or less). These infants can develop a number of immediate physical problems and face the prospect of long-term difficulties.

Today, compared to even the recent past, the baby's chances of survival are greatly improved, even for infants weighing as little as two pounds (Burns et al., 1983). For example, placing these tiny babies on waterbeds and providing rhythmic sounds mimics the uterine environment and is helpfully stimulating. Because low-birth-weight and high infant-mortality rates are most common among low-income groups in the United States (Spitz et al., 1983), better prenatal care for such mothers should be a national priority.

Pregnancy Ends, Parenthood Begins

As startling as pregnancy may be as a new experience for both men and women, even more dramatic events are in store with the birth process and the reality of becoming parents.

Labor and Delivery

Delivery usually occurs thirty-eight weeks (nine months) after conception. Though babies can be born anytime, the birth is most likely to occur at night, between 1:00 A.M. and 7:00 A.M., and the odds are better than chance that it will happen during late December or early January or in mid-summer, at least for those living in the Northern Hemisphere (Angier, 1990). This means that conception is most likely in March or in mid-Fall—times when the sun shines about 12 hours daily and the temperature is between 50 and 70 degrees. Conception is twice as likely on such days, compared to the rest of the year.

The seasonal pattern may reflect the sun's influence on sperm production, and giving birth at night may have been a useful protection against daytime predators for our prehistoric ancestors.

The Onset of Labor. **Labor** occurs when regular contractions of the uterus cause the cervix to dilate (widen) and thin, permitting the fetus to pass through. The fetus moves down the birth canal when it is expelled from the uterus. Surprisingly, the way in which this process is initiated is not yet understood. The level of the hormone **oxytocin,** secreted by the pituitary gland, rises at the onset of labor and stimulates uterine contractions, but what causes oxytocin secretion (Panter, 1980)?

One possibility is that the aging of the placenta reaches a point where it is unable to prevent the start of labor. Another hypothesis centers on the role of the fetus itself; it may become ready for delivery and therefore begins to secrete oxytocin (Fuchs et al., 1982). Still a third potential initiator of labor is the layer of the uterus called the *decidua,* which forms during pregnancy as the site where the placenta becomes implanted. The decidua may collect a contraction-stimulating hormone called *prostaglandin,* which starts labor when it is released. Some evidence for the third hypothesis is that the onset of labor is delayed for pregnant women who take large amounts of aspirin to relieve arthritis pain—aspirin stops the production of prostaglandin.

Whatever the trigger mechanism, physicians do know how to stimulate labor artificially: They inject prostaglandin or synthetic oxytocin (Rindfuss et al., 1978, 1979). Several medical complications make it advisable to induce labor. For example, if delivery is overdue by two or three weeks, the placenta may no longer be able to support fetal life adequately; the fetus then begins to swallow fluid containing its own waste, *meconium.* Another complication involves bursting of the amniotic sac and the release of its fluid; if labor fails to begin within twenty-four hours, infections threaten the fetus. Artificial onset of labor should not be undertaken simply for reasons of convenience such as avoiding birth on a holiday or accommodating the physician's vacation schedule; the danger is a lowering of the newborn's Apgar score, a risk that is justified only on medical grounds.

About two weeks before normal labor, the fetus drops from its position high in the uterus to rest down in the pelvic cavity. This change, called *lightening,* has the effect of making it easier for the woman to breathe deeply because the fetus puts less pressure on her diaphragm. Another effect of lightening is increased pressure on the urinary bladder, resulting in the need to urinate more frequently. When labor begins, three stages occur, and these will be described next.

Stage One: The Cervix Changes in Preparation for Delivery. The Bible states that "In sorrow thou shalt bring forth children," and the first stage of labor usually involves the greatest amount of prolonged pain. Painful menstrual cramps that build to a severe level during a period of several hours might be a useful way to characterize the pain of labor. For first-time mothers, this involves about eight to fourteen hours of hard work; in subsequent deliveries only about four to nine hours are required. The earliest contractions of the uterus last twenty to forty seconds and are fairly mild, and they produce the thinning of the cervix, known as **effacement**, and its widening, known as **dilation**.

During the five to twenty minutes between contractions, the mother is able to walk around, to talk, and even to respond with laughter when something amusing is said. At this stage the plug in the cervix loosens, and a pink discharge (colorfully labeled a *bloody show*) is expelled through the vagina. The amniotic sac, or bag of waters, breaks and releases its fluid. One sleeping father-to-be reported being awakened by his wife's announcement that "the water broke." He was on his way to call the plumber before realizing that she was going into labor.

During the first part of stage one, uterine contractions serve to dilate the cervix from its normal 1/25 of an inch (.3 cm) to about 2 inches (7 cm) in diameter. These dilation contractions typically cause considerably more pain than effacement does (see Figure 4-16). By the end of the dilation, pain occurs only one or two minutes apart. Mothers-to-be who have planned hospital births should have checked in by this point. The physician periodically determines the degree of cervical dilation by placing his or her fingers on the cervix. In some hospitals the patient is prepared for delivery by having her pubic hair shaved in order to reduce the risk of infection, but other facilities have stopped this practice because it is considered medically unnecessary—the vulva is thoroughly cleaned instead. Fluids are usually provided intravenously, but natural endorphins make the needle insertion practically painless. Because defecation commonly occurs during first deliveries, an enema may be given. The mother receives an identification band with her last name on it, a birth certificate with the same name is prepared, and the newborn baby will be given his or her own ID band soon after birth; it is obviously very difficult to "go home with the wrong baby" in today's maternity wards.

The last part of stage one, *transition,* completes cervical dilation to 3.9 inches (10 cm), with the help of very strong contractions. These contractions occur almost continuously for the duration of the transition phase, which averages forty minutes for first pregnancies and twenty minutes for later ones. If the fetus is facing toward the mother's spine, she feels these contractions in her abdomen. When its head is turned toward the mother's abdomen, the contractions center in the woman's lower back (*back labor*) and are even more severe than abdominal ones.

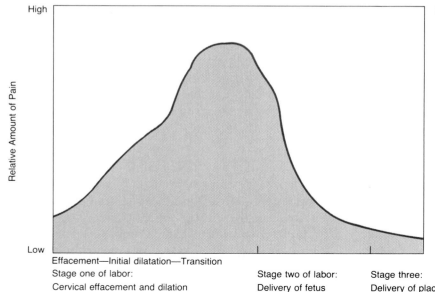

FIGURE 4-16 *THE PAIN OF LABOR* The stages of labor and the relative amount of pain experienced by an unanesthetized woman are shown in this diagram.

High

Relative Amount of Pain

Low

Effacement—Initial dilatation—Transition

Stage one of labor:
Cervical effacement and dilation

Stage two of labor:
Delivery of fetus

Stage three:
Delivery of placenta

Near the end of transition, the persistent nausea that accompanies labor usually ends in a reflexive vomiting response. The cervix is fully dilated at this point. As Figure 4-17 shows, the fetus' head drops to rest on the pelvis, causing the woman to have an urge to push during each contraction. This pushing feels like the need to defecate. Any attempts to push before full dilation will not move the fetus, and the resulting fatigue can prevent the mother from exerting her remaining strength during delivery. Cervical swelling can also result from premature pushing, impeding the passage of the fetus out of the uterus.

Some women are given a pain-killing (anesthetic) drug before transition. These drugs have adverse effects on the newborn, and they interfere with the woman's active participation, through pushing for example. Anesthetized women also give birth to babies with lower Apgar scores than women who do not receive anesthesia. One of three basic types of *conduction anesthetics* is usually given by injection. In the outside membranes of the spinal cord, an *epidural* or *caudal* anesthetic numbs the pain and other sensations below the point of injection, but muscle movement is still possible. Injected under the membranes around the spinal cord are the *spinal anesthetic* (center of the back) or *saddle block* (lower in the back). These injections numb not only sensory but also motor nerves, so the woman is unable to use her muscles to participate in the delivery. Other approaches to reducing the pain of childbirth are the *paracervical block* (anesthetic in both sides of the cervix) and the *pudendal block* (anesthetic on each side of the vagina). The paracervical type blocks pain in the uterus and cervix, but is ineffective in the late part of stage one labor. A pudendal block counteracts pain in the perineum and vulva for about half of those women who receive it.

Births in hospitals usually include **fetal monitoring** during the latter parts of stage one. Electrodes are attached to a band around the mother's abdomen

FIGURE 4-17 *THE BIRTH PROCESS* The three stages of labor function to ensure a slow, safe birth.

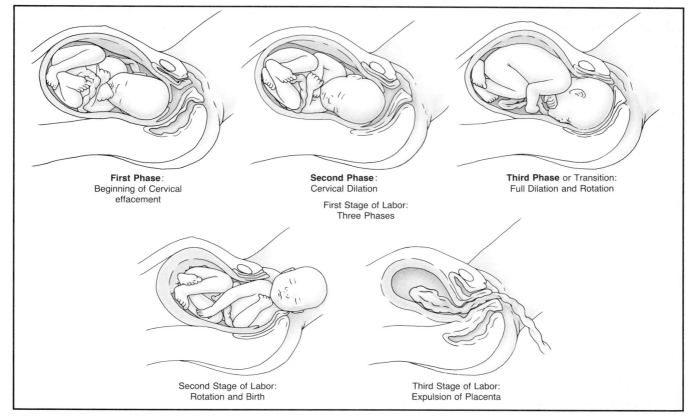

First Phase:
Beginning of Cervical
effacement

Second Phase:
Cervical Dilation

Third Phase or Transition:
Full Dilation and Rotation

First Stage of Labor:
Three Phases

Second Stage of Labor:
Rotation and Birth

Third Stage of Labor:
Expulsion of Placenta

or screwed into the fetus's scalp in order to assess its heart rate for signs of trouble. Routine use of fetal monitoring is controversial. At the very least, the band is uncomfortable. The physician must be able to differentiate signs of a minor problem from those of major emergency requiring a surgical delivery. Such a delivery is known as a *Cesarean* section; instead of a vaginal birth, the infant is removed through a surgical incision in the woman's abdomen. In the United States, a sharp rise in Cesarean deliveries has occurred since 1970—from 5.5 percent of all deliveries to over 24 percent in 1987 (Grisanti, 1989). This procedure is believed to have gotten its name from a Roman law, supported by Julius Caesar, that required surgical delivery of all babies whose mothers died in advanced pregnancy.

The phrase "once a Cesarean, always a Cesarean" is incorrect. Following this type of birth, most women can safely have vaginal deliveries of subsequent pregnancies without tearing the site of the old incision (Kolata, 1980b). Cesareans should be used only when absolutely necessary because several problems are associated with the procedure. First, this surgery requires several more weeks of recovery for the mother than with ordinary births and exposes her to an increased risk of complications. Second, maternal deaths occur two to four times more often with Cesarean than with vaginal delivery.

One valid reason for deciding on a Cesarean section is that the fetus is in the **breech position** (Hillard, 1985b); this means that the feet or buttocks will emerge from the vagina before the head. This creates a serious problem, because it interferes with the baby's passage through the 10 cm. cervical opening. The breech position occurs in about 3 to 5 percent of all full-term deliveries. Sometimes the fetus can be turned manually into a normal position within the uterus. Turning is usually performed several weeks before delivery if the breech position is detected.

Stage Two: Delivery. Once the cervix has fully dilated and the physician has felt the fetus' head, and not its buttocks at the cervix, the team heads for the delivery room. In stage two of labor, delivery occurs. The period between full cervical dilation and birth of the baby lasts for an average of eighty minutes for first pregnancies and thirty minutes for later ones.

Most births in the United States involve an **episiotomy**, the surgical cutting of the perineum to avoid its being torn during birth and to allow more room for passage of the baby (see Figure 4-18). The incision, usually about 1 or 2 inches (2 to 5 cm) long, is made at the time the head shows through the cervix, called **crowning.** Usually, the area is naturally numb at this stage of labor, just before delivery, but sometimes a local anesthetic is used. The practice of episiotomy is not performed very commonly in Western Europe; there, small vaginal tears are believed preferable to a relatively large surgical incision. Following delivery, the cut area is numbed with a local anesthetic and then sutured with a material that is gradually absorbed in the tissues—thus, no stitches have to

FIGURE 4-18 *EPISIOTOMY: FOR SOME, A SURGICAL STITCH IN TIME* An episiotomy is performed just before delivery to avoid tearing the vagina and perineum.

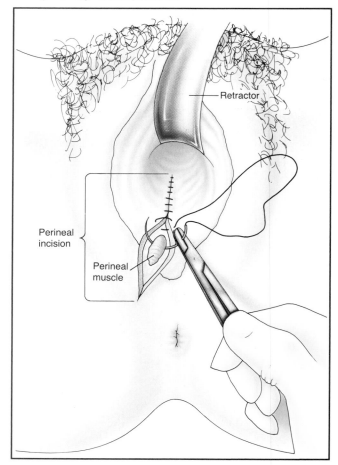

be removed later. Mothers experience significant pain for the next week as the episiotomy slowly heals. Some continue to experience pain and numbness when sexual activity resumes because of scar tissue or severed nerves (Lehfeldt, 1982).

When labor is quite difficult (termed *dystocia*), it is sometimes necessary to use *forceps,* an instrument resembling large ice tongs. They are placed around the baby's head after it has crowned to help with pulling and rotation. Babies delivered in this way have pressure marks on their heads, and their heads may be molded into an elongated shape because of the longer than average time spent in the restricted space of the mother's pelvis (Hillard, 1984). Because the use of forceps can result in brain damage, a Cesarean is usually the preferred solution to prolonged dystocia.

During delivery, the fetus rotates so that one shoulder appears after the head. As soon as the body is out, blood and mucus are wiped from the baby's mouth. Silver nitrate or antibiotic drops are placed in the eyes to prevent blindness resulting from a bacterial infection such as gonorrhea. All states in the United States require this last procedure. Most *neonates* (the term for babies during their first three months of life) cry and breathe automatically, so it is not usually necessary to slap them to start respiration, despite the frequency of such scenes in movies and on television. The baby's skin becomes pink in response to oxygen unless there is a medical problem. The umbilical cord is cut and clamped a couple of inches (5 cm) from the baby's abdomen. The other end of the umbilical cord is attached to the placenta, still in the uterus. The baby receives a shot of Vitamin K to prevent bleeding and a medical examination to check for possible problems.

Stage Three: The Placenta Is Expelled. The placenta is expelled from the body with a few uterine contractions over about a twelve-minute period. The whole placenta must be expelled; bleeding can result if pieces of it remain in the uterus. The episiotomy and any tears in the vagina are repaired at this time. Because mothers normally lose about one pint of blood during delivery, a nurse usually rubs the abdomen in order to stimulate more contractions, in order to stop the blood flow. This massaging, by the way, can be painful to the exhausted, drug-free mother.

Despite the discomfort and pain, most mothers describe childbirth as one of life's highlights—birth is perceived as exhilarating.

■ Methods of Childbirth

Several styles of childbirth have been developed to help the laboring mother. Parents have a variety of options in planning for this event, including the setting in which it occurs. Historically, childbirth changed from a female-controlled home procedure to a male-controlled medical procedure in the 20th century for those living in the United States (Leavitt, 1987).

Birthing Centers. For pregnancies free of complicating factors, when the delivery is expected to progress normally, the couple may choose to have the birth outside of a hospital. It may be difficult to believe, but Jimmy Carter was the first United States president to have been born in a hospital rather than at home. Birthing centers are special clinics designed with an atmosphere that is more homelike than the typical hospital. The major problem with giving birth at home or in a birthing center is that advanced medical equipment is not available should an emergency arise (Brown, 1985).

Midwifery. Another variation on the traditional hospital delivery is midwifery. *Midwives,* usually women trained by observing other midwives, handled deliveries for centuries before physicians took over the role (Courter, 1982). Some midwives lack formal medical education, and they have difficulty obtaining adequate malpractice insurance. Certified training programs for midwifery have graduated several thousand in the last twenty years, and these trained professionals work in hospitals and physicians' offices. Many midwives have bachelors' degrees in nursing or are registered nurses. At one New York City hospital, they assist in nine out of ten births (Norwood, 1982).

Midwives encourage prenatal education, as do obstetricians, but use less intervention than the traditional hospital delivery. They typically remain with the laboring mother as a monitor and cheerleader, preferring to keep her mobile throughout labor as long as possible to facilitate the birth process. The medical establishment in some states has welcomed the practice of midwifery by providing insurance coverage for their services, which are still controversial and resisted in other states.

The Birthing Chair. A *birthing chair* gives the mother the opportunity to sit up during delivery, a position that facilitates the fetus' descent through the help of gravity (Lowe, 1982). Actually, women sat up to deliver babies in Western societies until 1738, when the obstetrician to the Queen of France decided they should lie down in order to make his job easier (Wertz and Wertz, 1977). Another feature that makes the chair technique less appealing to physicians is that it makes the episiotomy more difficult to stitch.

The Birthing Room. Because delivery in a hospital can seem far from relaxing and homey, some hospitals have introduced the *birthing room.* It is offered as an option to prospective parents who can reserve the room and its more comfortable furnishings for their due date. The birthing room can be visited by children and other close relatives during labor and delivery, but it has safeguards for the one in five cases that need them—oxygen, anesthesia, provisions for surgical delivery, and other medical necessities are nearby. The cost of using this room usually is the same as the more hospital-like facilities for labor and delivery.

The Leboyer Method. Several procedures have been developed to make birth less stressful. The *Leboyer method* was first described by the French physician Frederick Leboyer (1975) in his book, *Birth without Violence.* Leboyer's approach is based on his belief that birth is a traumatic event for the baby. His method dictates dim lights, warm temperatures, and immersion in warm water immediately after birth to help the neonate adjust to life outside of the womb. After delivery, a lot of physical contact between the mother and neonate is recommended to bond close emotional ties between the two. Leboyer claims that his method produces children free of health problems and conflict, but studies have not supported this assumption.

Close attachment between the newborn infant and his or her parents help the child develop normally and to remain alert. Two other methods advise that the mother have a companion present during labor and delivery. The companion, whether a husband, other relative, or friend, offers reassurance and praise, helping the woman relax so contractions can do the work of labor. It is found that women who have no companion suffer complications of delivery or problems with the neonate twice as often as those who do have a companion (Kennel, 1981). There are two major variations in instructing the woman and her companion how to behave during childbirth.

The Lamaze Method. The *Lamaze method* uses the companion as a coach, usually the husband or partner or another person if she is unmarried or her husband is unavailable. The companion times the woman's contractions, monitors her breathing patterns, and helps her relax (see Figure 4-19).

FIGURE 4-19 *THE CHILDBIRTH COACH HELPS WITH RELAXATION* Most methods of childbirth (such as Lamaze) involve the cooperation of a supportive coach who helps the woman relax as a way to minimize pain. In this cartoon, Adam is depicted as a not very satisfactory coach for his wife.

Fernand Lamaze developed this method in the 1950s and 1960s in France, similar to that which a British obstetrician, Grantly Dick-Read, introduced in the 1930s. Dick-Read proposed that the use of natural childbirth techniques would help reduce fear through both prenatal education and relaxation during childbirth. The coach and woman learn this procedure in prenatal training sessions that are required by most hospitals if the companion is to be present during delivery. Pregnant women are taught to pant and distract themselves from awareness of pain during labor. They use **effleurage**, rubbing their abdomens with their hands as an additional distraction from the pain. Coaches also learn about the details of childbirth as well as how to record the duration of contractions and the intervals between them. Although there have been few studies of the effectiveness of the Lamaze method, the general approach helps increase tolerance to pain, although it is not eliminated (Worthington et al., 1983). The Lamaze method promotes education and exercises to increase the self-control that the woman can have during labor.

The Bradley Method.   For some women, Lamaze is ineffective (Gaylin, 1985). An alternative is the *Bradley method* of husband-coached childbirth. Obstetrician Robert Bradley (1981) observed that farm animals became very still and quiet during labor, and he developed a technique for humans that promotes relaxation and helps the cervix dilate more efficiently. The method has three major components: the running, fetal-like position resembling the posture of a runner, as shown in Figure 4-20; slow, deep breathing during contractions; and the single-minded devotion and admiration of a companion. Bradley recommends that parents learn both Lamaze and his own method so that they can experiment with them during the early phases of stage one labor. At that point, the decision can be made as to which method is working best for them. Bradley discusses informal comparisons of his method to others, but no large-scale research has been reported on its use.

Circumcision.   One of the common differences in the treatment of newborn males and females is **circumcision**, shown in Figure 4-21. This surgery is performed (usually about twenty-four hours after birth) on 1.3 million male infants in the United States

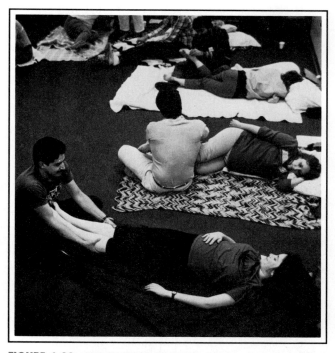

FIGURE 4-20   *THE BRADLEY METHOD: USING THE WISDOM OF ANIMALS*   The Bradley method of childbirth prescribes the fetal (or running) position and deep, slow breathing for relaxation to help uterine contractions become more efficient in dilating the cervix.

every year, making it the most common of all surgical procedures.

Approximately one third of an inch (1 cm) is cut from the newborn's foreskin, sometimes without any anesthesia although some obstetricians inject a painkiller. When circumcision is part of a religious rite, wine often serves as the anesthetic. The baby is restrained by being tied to a board during circumcision. After removing the foreskin, the obstetrician places a clamp on the severed blood vessels. The cutting and clamping apparently is painful to the newborn, because he cries and thrashes his limbs. One in every 500 circumcisions causes complications such as heavy bleeding or infection.

Figure 4-22 shows the appearance of a circumcized and an uncircumsized penis. Without circumcision, the male may have more difficulty in cleaning the area under the foreskin. When oily secretions called *smegma* collect and bind the foreskin and penis, the condition is known as *phimosis*. It can be prevented if the foreskin is routinely pulled back for

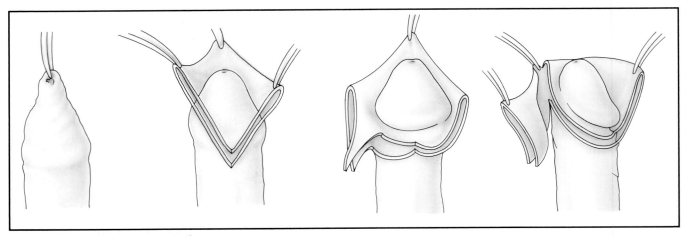

FIGURE 4-21 *PERFORMING CIRCUMCISION* Most circumcisions in the United States today are performed by obstetricians, because pediatricians usually prefer not to do them. The questionable medical value of circumcision is reflected in the refusal of some health insurance companies to pay for circumcision unless it is done while the newborn is still in the hospital, not eight days after birth in accordance with the Jewish ceremonial rite.

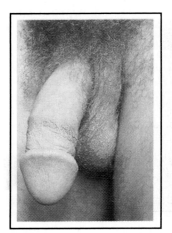
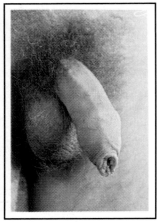

FIGURE 4-22 *CIRCUMCISION—REMOVING THE FORESKIN* During circumcision the male's foreskin is removed, leaving the glans exposed. Some circumcisions are performed for religious reasons, but there is controversy about whether it should be done simply for health reasons.

cleaning. King Louis XVI of France had painful erections and avoided intercourse as a result of phimosis. After surgery corrected the condition, this eighteenth century monarch reportedly "partook of the diversion" repeatedly with his wife, Marie Antoinette (Shearn and Shearn, 1983).

■   The Postpartum Period

After the baby has been delivered, there are a number of new challenges for the woman and her partner.

How Does It Feel to Be a New Mother? Physical Changes. During the *postpartum period* which follows birth, the woman experiences a variety of physical and emotional changes. Delivery of the placenta is accompanied by a rapid drop in levels of hormones such as estrogen and progesterone circulating in the bloodstream, and one reaction is several minutes of shivering. For the next several days there are *afterpains*, uterine contractions of the same intensity as in early labor, but these taper off as the uterus begins to shrink. Few women who have had vaginal deliveries develop serious medical complications after birth. Only 2 to 3 percent have postpartum infections of the uterine lining. This condition, called puerperal or childbed fever, was common before the days of sterile medical techniques and antibiotics and the leading cause of maternal deaths (Panter, 1981c).

Psychological Changes after Childbirth. On the second day after childbirth, the hormone levels that maintained pregnancy continue to decline slowly to near normal, prepregnancy levels. This change often produces feelings of depression that contrast sharply with the elation of childbirth. Mothers of ill or low-birth-weight neonates have a higher risk of developing depression or anxiety and of feeling more negatively about their infants (Blumberg, 1980), as Figure 4-23 indicates.

Other possible causes of temporary depression are physical exhaustion resulting from the new schedule oriented around the baby's needs and the pres-

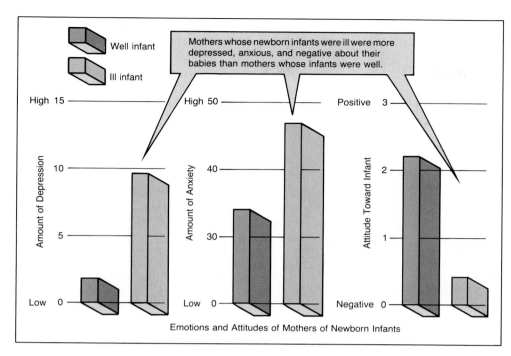

FIGURE 4-23 *THE HEALTHIER THE BABY, THE MORE POSITIVE THE MOTHER* During the first five days following birth, new mothers with a baby who is ill or low-birth-weight experience more depression and anxiety than those whose babies are well. For 100 mothers surveyed, women with well babies also expressed more positive attitudes toward them. Having a newborn whose health is at risk can add significantly to the stresses of the postpartum period.
Source: Data from Blumberg, 1980.

sure of making numerous decisions such as breast versus bottle feeding. Some new mothers have a bout with **postpartum depression** that is so intense that counseling is needed. This is a feeling of sadness, and at times emotional withdrawal, which a new mother may experience soon after childbirth and which usually lasts a few days. Some women experience more severe depression during the postpartum period of the first six weeks following childbirth. The frequency of admission to psychiatric hospitals increases by at least 50 percent during the three months following childbirth (David et al., 1981), as shown in Figure 4-24.

For new mothers who do not have a husband, the rate of postpartum depression is more than double that of new mothers who are married (Blumberg, 1980). The percentage of women who experience depression lasting at least one month also depends on their psychological characteristics and work plans. Pfost et al. (1989) surveyed sixty-nine women twice, one month before and one month after delivery. New mothers who had described themselves in feminine terms and who intended to return to work after delivery experienced less depression than those who neither included femininity in their self-descriptions nor

FIGURE 4-24 *THE STRESSES OF THE POSTPARTUM PERIOD* During the three months following birth, rates of admission to psychiatric hospitals increase by at least 50 percent among thousands of both married and unmarried women living in Denmark. The highest rate was found for those who were separated, divorced, or widowed. The postpartum period can be a difficult one for the new mother, and it is even more difficult without the support of a partner.
Source: Data from David et al., 1981.

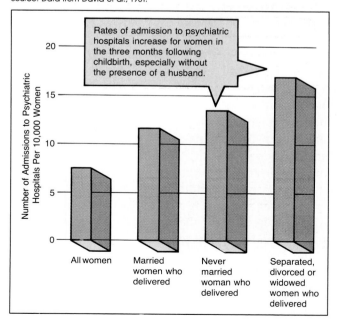

intended to work outside the home. Both of these variables, femininity and work plans, may provide some protection against postpartum depression, by helping women to adapt successfully to the caretaking role and to continue their career roles simultaneously.

What can be done to prevent the development of long-term depression after childbirth? For most new mothers, depressed feelings are temporary, and a few simple preventive techniques can be surprisingly valuable. Socializing with other parents and their children also helps, while a move to a new neighborhood just before or after birth increases stress. It helps to make advance arrangements for babysitters and other household help, if possible. Caring for a newborn infant is a full-time job, and the mother needs extra rest and sleep; she might be well advised to lower her standards for household neatness (Eheart and Martel, 1983). It is also useful to try to maintain some interests outside of the home. It is important to continue the intensely satisfying and close relationship between mother and child. Close contact alternated with a few short breaks in the daily routine can help both mother and child through this demanding period. The infant is adjusting to new life, and the mother is adapting to the all encompassing needs of her new baby.

Sex after Childbirth.   Within three weeks or so, the episiotomy stitches have healed, and the pinkish vaginal discharge, *lochia,* has diminished. It is then usually safe to resume sexual intercourse. The average interval between delivery and first postpartum intercourse is five weeks (Grudzinskas and Atkinson, 1984). Because ovulation can occur then, effective contraception is necessary. Neither the diaphragm nor intrauterine device (see Chapter 5) can be used until the pelvic organs return to normal size—about six weeks postpartum. Mothers who have more than one child tend to resume intercourse slightly sooner than inexperienced mothers (Kenny, 1973).

In general, this is a period when the new father may feel left out of the intimate mother-child relationship and not in great demand as a sexual partner. Some men begin to perceive themselves in competition with their newborn infants. Several factors, including fatigue and physical discomfort, can interfere with the new mother's sexual desire during the post-partum period (Nelson, 1983). She sometimes fails to have orgasms as easily or as frequently as before (Flowers and Flowers, 1978). In addition, the man will probably notice that the vagina does not encircle his penis as tightly as in the past because of the natural relaxation of the PC muscles after birth (Levitt et al., 1979), but there are contraction exercises that improve the tone and gripping power of these muscles (Linton, 1982).

The relationship between new parents sometimes takes a turn for the worse during the first three months after the child is born. Moderate changes occur in their interactions, which become less satisfying and more conflicted. The wife, especially, may express less love for the spouse than before childbirth. The division of labor in the family becomes more traditional because the husband typically contributes less to housework in this period than in the past (Belsky et al., 1990). Relationships which were difficult before the birth—for example, having a low income or lacking sensitivity to each other's needs—are most likely to undergo the postpartum decline in satisfaction and love (Belsky and Rovine, in press 1990). Having a baby whose temperament is difficult and tense instead of easy and flexible also contributes to negative changes in the couple's relationship.

Lactation

Mothers who choose to breastfeed their infants give them a better physical start in life than those who do not (Burros, 1990). Human milk cannot be made artificially, and the milk of other animals does not contain all of the same nutrients and other beneficial ingredients. This is the reason that mothers who cannot produce milk (lactate) for their newborn often seek surplus milk from other lactating mothers. Breast milk, but not the formula used in bottle feeding, protects the neonate from infections because mothers develop antibodies during the first three postpartum months which then transfer to their breast milk, thus protecting the newborn. Breast feeding even results in straighter teeth for the child than bottle feeding (Breast-feeding linked . . . , 1987). One half to three fourths of mothers in the United States are reluctant to breastfeed; as a result, many infants are exposed to inferior diets (Wholey, 1983). In less developed countries, breast-feeding protects infants from severe intestinal disease (Gillin et al., 1983) and reduces their death rate (Knodel, 1977).

Certain advantages do exist for bottle feeding using formula compared to breast-feeding. These include convenience, less fatigue in the nursing mother, and the possibility of both parents' participating equally in close contact with the baby during feeding.

Milk Production. Lactation begins during pregnancy, when small amounts of milk are produced. The hormone *prolactin* causes larger amounts of milk to be secreted after birth, unless a hormone or drug is used to prevent it. Following delivery, **colostrum** is secreted for two or three days. It is rich in nutrients such as protein and contains a sweet mixture that is highly beneficial to the newborn infant. During the next few days, the milk becomes thinner, but its sugary taste (lactose) is clearly enjoyable for the infant. As the breasts become engorged with milk, they increase in size and become tender. If the first few weeks of breastfeeding are too painful, a rubber nipple shield can be used to lessen the pain. The discomfort of sore nipples can be relieved by rubbing them with breast milk (Eiger, 1987). With continued feeding this pain decreases and the breasts soften. Pregnant women find it helpful to start preparing their nipples for sucking—toughening them by rolling and gently pinching them.

Milk production adjusts to the infant's needs, thus avoiding overfilling or underfilling the breasts. Prolactin travels through the bloodstream to the mammary glands in a matter of seconds once sucking begins. This causes the let-down response, a reflex in which milk is ejected through the nipple, as shown in Figure 4-25. Psychological factors such as anxiety or embarrassment can delay or prevent this reflex. A lactating mother with full breasts may be surprised to find that the sound of her baby's crying can cause milk ejection.

Factors which decrease the amount of milk produced include an interference with frequent, relaxed feedings (Huffman, 1984). When the infant is given other food supplements such as canned milk or even a pacifier to suck on, milk production is reduced. Women who have negative or mixed feelings about nursing produce less milk (Newton and Newton, 1978). Mothers who work may have difficulty arrang-

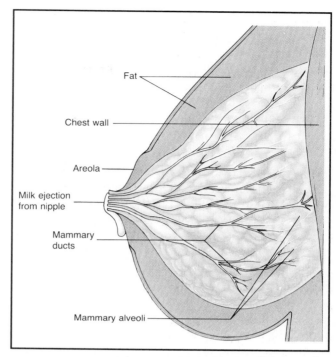

FIGURE 4-25 *MILK EJECTION: IT CAN BE A SURPRISE* The let-down response causes ejection of milk from the mammary glands. This reflex also occurs during sleep, when the breasts fill with milk.

ing their schedules to fit the baby's nursing schedule. One solution is for them to "express" milk, using a manual or electric pump; the milk is then refrigerated or frozen for a later bottle feeding. Brochures about many aspects of breast-feeding are available from La Leche League International in Franklin Park, Illinois.

Sexuality and Lactation. Though mothers in the United States who breastfeed tend to stop by the end of the second month, those in developing countries typically continue for much longer. In Bangladesh, for example, two years is common (Jain and Bongaarts, 1981). Lactation usually suspends the menstrual cycle, producing *amenorrhea*. In undernourished women, at least, this provides a contraceptive effect and lengthens the interval between births (Laukaran and Winikoff, 1985). By the time six months have passed following birth, half of those women who are lactating resume ovulation (Tyrer, 1984a). Because this return to fertility is unpredictable, lactating women who don't wish to conceive need to use contraception. Some contraceptives should be avoided because they include substances that can enter the milk through the mother's bloodstream and harm the infant—hormonal pills, intrauterine devices, and spermicides used with either the diaphragm or a condom are examples.

Because sucking causes oxytocin to be released by the pituitary, the uterus contracts, and women may experience orgasm during the feeding session. Very little estrogen is secreted during lactation; as a result, vaginal lubrication diminishes and the vagina thins. The result is pain during intercourse for many lactating women (Youngs, 1979). The solution is to engage in other forms of sexual interaction at this time or to use vaginal lubricants. When the male sucks his partner's milk as part of their sexual play, a practice called *milk cannabalism,* the outcome can be an insufficient amount of milk for their baby.

Concerns about appearance lead to questions as to the eventual effect of breast-feeding on the shape and size of the breasts. It is true that breasts may droop and flatten for a few weeks after lactation ceases (Gall, 1983), but they usually return to their prepregnancy shape soon afterward. Lying down during feedings rather than sitting up can help prevent some sagging (Figure 4-26). Breast-feeding also has some positive effects on appearance. The abdomen reduces in size more quickly than otherwise because of the uterine contractions during feeding. Because lactation uses calories (the equivalent of three hours of daily cycling), it helps the mother's return to normal weight without severe dieting. Keep in mind that this energy expenditure also leads to fatigue and the need for extra rest.

Altogether, if it can be managed, breast-feeding has lasting benefits for both mother and child.

The Heartbreak of Infertility

For those who have tried to conceive but have not succeeded, **infertility** is a serious disappointment (Fleming, 1989). Those who have never had a child are described as having *primary infertility,* while those who have conceived previously are designated as having *secondary infertility.* Technically, a couple is medically described as infertile only if they are childless after engaging in sexual intercourse at least three times weekly for a year without using contraception. Based on data obtained over the past twenty years, one in

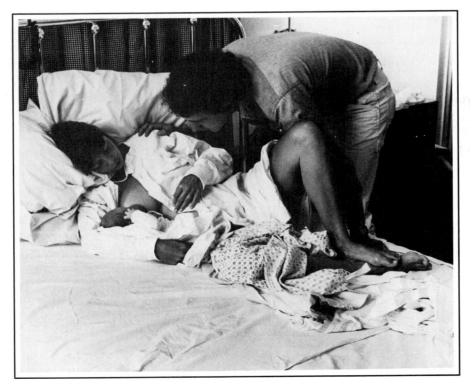

FIGURE 4-26 *THE BEST POSITION FOR BREAST-FEEDING* Using the proper position during breast-feeding can help reduce the tendency of breasts to sag (a common problem when feeding occurs in an upright position).

ten married couples in the United States is infertile (Mosher, 1985). The greatest rise in infertility rate has occurred among the youngest couples—from 4 percent in 1965 to 10 percent in 1982. An even more dramatic increase in infertility is reported for young black couples, with a change from 3 percent in 1965 to 15 percent in 1976 (Mosher, 1982). We will examine the effects of infertility on males and females as well as its causes and treatments.

■ Effects on the Couple

In 90 percent of all infertile couples, the problem can be traced to one or more physical factors, while no specific cause can be identified in the remaining couples (Mazor, 1980). The physical basis of this condition is consistent with the fact that infertile couples are *not* found to differ from fertile couples in how happy they are in their marriages or in whether psychological problems exist (Adler and Boxley, 1985).

While psychological difficulties do not seem to cause infertility, this condition frequently creates interpersonal problems, especially with respect to sex. Infertile couples tend to label their efforts to have a child as a failure, and anxieties about sexual performance often develop. A physician is likely to question them closely about the most private aspects of their sexual interactions such as how often they have intercourse and in what positions. Such inquiries are so threatening that some men later experience difficulty in having erections or they ejaculate too quickly; some women experience increased difficulty in reaching orgasm.

■ Causes of Infertility

It is commonly assumed that failure to conceive results from a physical problem in the woman, such as failure to ovulate or blockage of the oviducts. In fact, the causes of infertility are found to be equally traced to men and women, and sometimes to both spouses.

Biological Limits.   Men do not have a biological limitation on fertility; testes continue to produce viable sperm well into old age. In contrast, the reproductive years of women end at about age forty-eight to fifty, when menstrual cycles cease. Also, women become

pregnant less easily after they reach the age of thirty (Konner, 1987). For childless women, conceiving after age thirty is even less likely than for women who have already had at least one child—a *parous* woman (Hendershot et al., 1982). In general, a female's fertility decreases with age, as Figure 4-27 indicates. College-educated women in the thirty- to forty-five-year-old age range are quite likely to postpone childbearing until their careers are established; as a result, they may find they have become infertile (O'Connell and Rogers, 1982). It is the cumulative damage to their reproductive systems that leads to infertility because of the long-term effects of genital infections or hormonal imbalance, for example. In the 1980s women bore their first child in their early thirties twice as often as was true in 1970 (Ventura, 1982); thus, it can be expected that infertility rates will be even higher if they attempt to have a second child when they are a few years older.

FIGURE 4-27 *INFERTILITY: AGE MAKES A DIFFERENCE* Women over age twenty-four who have not conceived after one year of attempting to do so tend not to have conceived three years later. The women in this investigation did not receive treatment for infertility, and they would be described as reproductively sterile.
Source: Data from Hendershot, 1982.

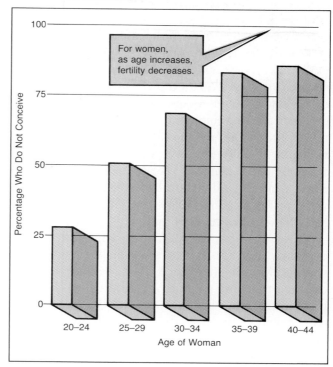

For women, as age increases, fertility decreases.

Percentage Who Do Not Conceive

Age of Woman

Characteristics of the Couple.   Physical or behavioral characteristics in a given couple can cause infertility; for example, a woman may be allergic to her partner's semen. Her blood then creates antibodies that kill sperm before they can reach the ovum. Desensitization treatment can alleviate this problem as it does with other allergies (Bernstein, 1984). The sexual habits of the couple can also cause infertility. Some couples have intercourse too infrequently to conceive easily, but such behavior can easily be changed once they are given appropriate information. The opposite sexual extreme, having intercourse several times each day, can reduce the number of sperm below the minimum number of 60 million per ejaculation that is usually necessary for fertilization to occurr (Bensimon, 1981). Treatment consists of counseling the male member of such a couple to ejaculate no more than once every other day during the week of ovulation in order to increase his sperm count.

Intercourse position also affects conception. Use of the male superior position makes it more likely that sperm will remain deep in the vagina and make their way through the cervix, especially if the woman remains lying down for thirty minutes following the man's ejaculation (Langmyhr, 1981).

Infections.   A common cause of female infertility is blockage of the oviducts. Usually, this results from scarring caused by a previous infection in the pelvic area (see Chapter 15). One of the most devastating examples of such an infection is *pelvic inflammatory disease* (PID), in which the woman's genital tract becomes infected with a disease such as gonorrhea. The eventual scarring and resultant blocking of the interior wall of the oviducts can occur without the woman's knowledge, until perhaps years later when she attempts to conceive. Treatment of this condition consists of surgical removal of scar tissue, but even with treatment about 20 percent of those who have had PID remain permanently infertile (Curran, 1980).

The bacterial infection caused by T-strain mycoplasma also reduces fertility, perhaps by interfering with fertilization and implantation. Because very specialized laboratory facilities are required to detect its presence in either males or females, this infection often remains undetected despite routine testing (Chlamydial, Mycoplasmal, 1984). Infection from T-strain mycoplasma has been blamed for turning marginally fertile people into infertile ones and for the occurrence of repeated miscarriages (Cohn, 1983). Antibiotic therapy for *both* the male and female is required to cure the problem (Knudsin et al., 1981).

The Reproductive System.   Another cause of infertility is a condition known as *endometriosis,* which involves the implanting of uterine tissue outside the uterus—for example, in the oviducts and ovaries. This tissue then blocks the movement of egg and sperm. During menstruation the extra tissue also contributes to the menstrual flow, increasing the number of days in the woman's period. Endometriosis occurs in 10 to 20 percent of women in their thirties and forties, probably as the result of an imbalance of sex hormones. The disease can be slowed or temporarily corrected by hormonal treatments, surgical removal of the extra tissue, and also by pregnancy. The U.S.–Canadian Endometriosis Association, located in Milwaukee, Wisconsin, can provide information for sufferers regarding treatment and counseling.

Toxic substances such as drugs and other chemicals not only affect sexual functioning (see Chapter 16), they also interfere with fertility. The role of toxins in the reduced fertility rate of young women and in the decreased sperm production of young men is suspected (Smith, 1978), in part caused by the increased use of potent chemicals in agriculture and industry. In addition, such substances as tobacco (Sterling and Kobayashi, 1975), marijuana (Hembree, 1980; Smith et al., 1983), caffeine (Weathersbee and Lodge, 1980), and alcohol (Maugh, 1981a) can lower fertility rates. These products have a negative effect on both sperm production and ovulation; in addition, they increase the number of defective sperm and eggs, impairing both the quantity and the quality of germ cells. Much of the research on such effects is based on work with animals, but prospective parents seem well advised to stop the use of drugs several months before any attempt to conceive.

■ Treating Infertility

A couple's decision to seek the help of a physician specializing in assessing and treating infertility is not usually based on factual knowledge. They simply want to have a child, preferably their own, and even if treatment is unsuccessful, they may persist for years before giving up.

Figure 4-28 outlines the steps involved in the medical evaluation of infertility before treatment begins. At each step, if a problem is identified, corrective action is taken. Treatment does not guarantee success, of course. An example of diagnosis would be a test after ovulation which would show insufficient levels of progesterone, making it impossible for a pregnancy to survive. Treatment would consist of hormonal therapy to boost progesterone to the required level.

In a medical workup for infertility, three major questions must be answered (Pfeffer, 1980). Most often, the process begins when the female visits a *gynecologist,* who carries out the initial examination. The first question is whether the woman is ovulating regularly, and whether sufficient numbers of viable sperm are being produced. Evidence of ovulation comes from charting for at least three menstrual cycles the woman's body temperature each morning before she gets out of bed. A drop followed by a rise in morning temperature at midcycle indicates that ovulation will probably occur within twenty-four hours.

The absence of such a pattern strongly suggests that the woman is not ovulating. If ovulation *does* seem to be occurring, women are still advised to continue recording their temperatures daily in order to time intercourse to coincide with the presence of a mature egg in the oviducts.

The man at this point is usually asked to see an **andrologist,** a physician specializing in urology and male reproductive disorders. A *semen analysis* is performed to determine the approximate number of sperm in a sample of freshly ejaculated seminal fluid. The man is asked to masturbate to orgasm into a sterile jar which must be transported within the next two hours to a laboratory for microscopic examination. Viable sperm are motile (they move around), numerous, and normal in shape. Even for men with a low sperm count, conception is possible through new techniques such as *zona puncturing* in which holes are made in the zona pellucida and *sperm microinjection* in which a needle is used to inject a sperm in the egg membrane (Goben, 1990).

A second question focuses on whether sperm and egg are able to reach one another for fertilization to occur. This is determined by a *postcoital test.* The couple is instructed to have intercourse near the time

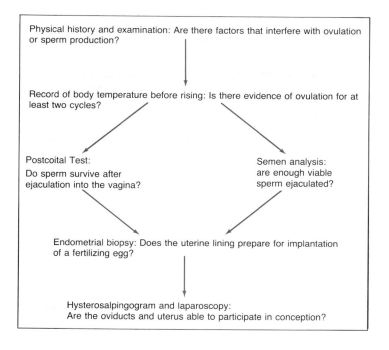

FIGURE 4-28 *THE INFERTILITY WORKUP: PROBLEM SOLVING, NOT ROMANCE* The steps involved in a medical evaluation of infertility require several months of assessment. In looking over this outline of the steps, you can imagine how some couples might become discouraged about the process.

Physical history and examination: Are there factors that interfere with ovulation or sperm production?

Record of body temperature before rising: Is there evidence of ovulation for at least two cycles?

Postcoital Test:
Do sperm survive after ejaculation into the vagina?

Semen analysis:
are enough viable sperm ejaculated?

Endometrial biopsy: Does the uterine lining prepare for implantation of a fertilizing egg?

Hysterosalpingogram and laparoscopy:
Are the oviducts and uterus able to participate in conception?

of ovulation, during the follicular phase of the menstrual cycle (see Figure 4-29). After intercourse, the woman must reach the physician's office as quickly as possible. There, a sample of vaginal fluid is taken to determine how well the sperm have survived. As you may guess, many couples find it difficult or embarrassing to have sexual relations at a specified time and then to rush off immediately to be tested in a laboratory; as a result, appointments for these tests tend to be repeatedly cancelled and rescheduled.

The condition of the uterus and oviducts is then assessed by two procedures which involve slightly more risk than the previously mentioned tests. The **hysterosalpingogram** uses a dye to fill the uterus and oviducts by means of a tube inserted through the vagina and cervix. The insertion process can be quite painful. The flow of dye through the oviducts is shown on an X-ray screen. **Laparoscopy** involves surgery under general anesthesia; a small telescope is inserted into the abdominal wall for direct inspection of the female's reproductive organs. Both procedures can reveal sources of blockage in the uterus or oviducts.

If answers to the first two questions indicate that fertilization *can* occur, a third question is asked: Is the uterus able to receive the fertilized egg? Normally a sufficient amount of the hormone progesterone, secreted by the corpus luteum, aids in preparing the uterus. Infertility can result from the level of progesterone being too low. To determine whether infertility is based on this source of hormonal and uterine problems, an *endometrial biopsy* removes a fiber from the endometrium—a painful procedure. This sample is obtained during the height of the luteal phase about one week after ovulation—this is the time when progesterone level peaks. Combined with a blood test, the biopsy can indicate whether the uterine lining would be able to nourish a fertilized egg should it be implanted there.

The results of these various infertility tests indicate what sort of treatment should be used. Failure to ovulate can sometimes be corrected by taking fertility drugs such as Clomid (Radwanska, 1980). This drug stimulates the pituitary gland in the brain to secrete LH and FSH (luteinizing and follicle stimulating hormones). About half the women who take Clomid become pregnant, with multiple births in about 10 percent, compared to the average 1.2 percent giving birth to more than one child at a time. Clomid does not increase the incidence of birth defects or spontaneous abortion (miscarriage).

The two major causes of infertility in women—absence of ovulation and blocked oviducts—can often be corrected. Blocked oviducts were formerly treated by surgery, but a tiny balloon can now be inserted and the tubes unclogged in a procedure similar to that used with blocked arteries (Elmer-Dewitt, 1990). In one study, approximately one-third of those who were treated became pregnant within a year. An ovulating woman with blocked oviducts can turn to *in vitro fertilization* as a solution, and this procedure is discussed in the special section **Highlighting Research,** on page 101 to 102.

Technology for Treating Male Infertility: Artificial Insemination. Problems with sperm production have not been treated very successfully (Bouton, 1982). One solution is to use *artificial insemination* in

FIGURE 4-29 *INFERTILITY TESTING: INTERCOURSE ON SCHEDULE* Couples undergoing an evaluation of their infertility problem schedule intercourse to occur at ovulation followed by a postcoital test of sperm survival in the vagina. The endometrial biopsy takes a sample of the uterine lining for examination midway through the luteal phase, when the nutritive progesterone level peaks.

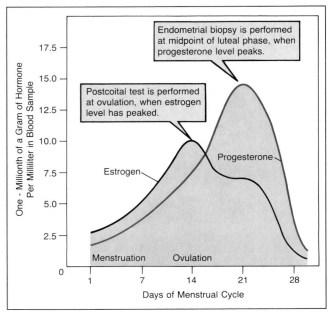

Highlighting Research

TEST-TUBE BABIES: A NEW FRONTIER IN CONCEPTION

The problem of blocked oviducts can be overcome by women who wish to conceive their own offspring by turning to a new technique that involves fertilization in the laboratory rather than in the oviducts: **in vitro fertilization** (Yulsman, 1990). This procedure can be used if microsurgery cannot correct the problem. Despite the success of this technique, for many individuals it raises questions about how much, or even whether, medical science should experiment with the human reproductive process.

With in vitro fertilization, a mature egg is surgically removed from the ovary, as shown in Figure 4-30. Actually, eggs are removed from several follicles that appear close to rupturing. These eggs, along with live sperm, are placed in a laboratory dish containing a nutrient solution designed to resemble the environment of the oviducts. These germ cells are left to mingle for two to three days, and if all goes well, fertilization occurs. The fertilized egg is allowed to subdivide a few times. At the next stage, it is called a *blastocyst* consisting of about fifty cells. It is placed in the woman's uterus, and from then on the process continues like any other pregnancy.

The entire procedure usually has to be repeated three or four times before it succeeds. For a given attempt, the average success rate is 13 percent, though at specific institutions, the range is from 0 to 17 percent (Leary, 1989). By the end of the 1980's, more than 10,000 babies had been conceived using this procedure (Bazell, 1988). Private, commercial laboratories and clinics commonly charge a fee of $3,000 to $5,000 for each attempt at fertilization (Kolata, 1983a). The obstetrical course of pregnancies started through in vitro fertilization progresses like those conceived naturally. Because in vitro pregnancies involve mothers older than the average and a pregnancy that the parents value perhaps even more than usual, sur-

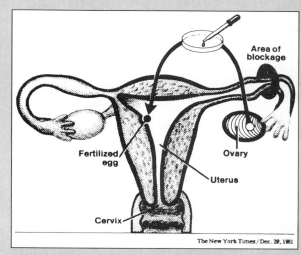

Area of blockage

Fertilized egg

Ovary

Uterus

Cervix

The New York Times / Dec. 29, 1981

FIGURE 4-30 REPRODUCTIVE TECHNOLOGY: CONCEIVING BABIES IN A DISH The procedure for in vitro fertilization consists of removing a mature egg from an ovary. The ovum and sperm are then placed in a laboratory dish for fertilization to occur. The fertilized egg is afterward placed in the uterus.

gical deliveries occur more frequently (56 percent) than is typical of ordinary pregnancies.

A new variation of this approach permits post–menopausal women to bear children. Eggs are obtained from a younger woman and mixed with the husband's sperm. After an egg is fertilized, the process is like that of an ordinary in vitro fertilization except that the older woman is given hormones to prepare her body for conception and pregnancy (Elmer-Dewitt, 1990).

Two recent advances have made it possible to place gametes (sperm and eggs) or zygotes directly into the healthy oviducts of women who are experiencing fertility problems. The sperm or eggs (or both) may come from potential parents or from donors. When ripe ova and sperm are injected through a very thin catheter tube into the oviduct to await fertilization, the

procedure is known as Gamete Intrafallopian Transfer (or GIFT). In Zygote Intrafallopian Transfer (ZIFT), fertilization occurs in a laboratory dish, and then one–celled zygotes are placed in the oviduct. Success rates for these two techniques are expected to be higher than for regular in vitro fertilization (Elmer–Dewitt, 1990).

Reservations about in vitro fertilization and its newer variations center around moral and practical issues. The cost of this procedure is not typically covered by most insurance companies or by the government, making it available mainly to a select group who can afford it.

Simply because we possess the technology for the procedure, under what conditions should it be used? One Roman Catholic priest, a Jesuit, has pointed out the moral difficulties that arise when unneeded or defective embryos are discarded (Marchell, 1981). The success rate after placing the embryo in the uterus averages about 15 to 20 percent (Grobstein et al., 1983), so most embryos do not survive the process. The counterargument to this objection is that at least 15 percent of ordinary pregnancies end in a natural, spontaneous abortion (Hillard, 1984). Is one type of embryo loss less acceptable than another?

Where should experimentation on fertility stop? Consider a few possibilities. If cloning becomes possible with humans as it has with mice, do we want to be able to produce offspring genetically identical to ourselves? Experimenters have suggested that a human female could be created by combining two ova rather than an ovum and a sperm. Genetic engineering theoretically can allow us to produce a new version of our species able to manufacture food directly by photosynthesis from sunlight as plants do (Andrews, 1981). The image of a human supermarket with a frozen embryo section may be more than the basis of a science-fiction story. These and other dramatically new aspects of conception must be evaluated by our society, and the answers require more than the knowledge of what *can* be done. Difficult ethical questions such as these have created the need for sympathetic, sensible guidelines to deal with these and future questions about reproductive technology.

which a quantity of semen is injected into the vagina by a syringe at the time of ovulation. In addition to artificial insemination from a donor (AID) or from the husband (AIH), other methods for correcting low sperm count or quality, depending on the cause, include testosterone therapy and surgery on varicose veins in the testes.

If the husband's sperm quality is zero or too low, if he has had a vasectomy, if he has a known genetic defect, or if a single female desires motherhood but not marriage, a donor's sperm can be used. For artifical insemination, the woman must of course be fertile. Usually the identity of a donor is unknown to the recipient, and he must meet certain health requirements, including tests to rule out AIDS. The donor would be expected to have at least average intelligence, be in excellent health, and resemble the husband physically. In return for a fee, a donor may contribute sperm to a sperm bank, where sperm is frozen and stored or the donor may provide sperm directly to the doctor's office. The rate of resultant pregnancy using fresh, unfrozen sperm exceeds that for sperm from a bank. One sperm bank, located in California, tries to acquire semen only from Nobel Prize winners (Andrews, 1980). The goal is to produce highly intelligent offspring for those who use this bank, but the link between the genetic characteristics of any given sperm and subsequent intellectual behavior is not direct enough to guarantee the desired outcome.

Of practical concern are the success rate and emotional effects of artifical insemination. The woman typically has to be inseminated for three successive cycles before pregnancy occurs; after three inseminations 60 to 70 percent of fertile women conceive. Most couples do not reveal that they have undergone this procedure because they do not want it known that the husband did not father the child (Rosenfeld, 1980).

If the husband's sperm count is low but more than 10 million per cubic centimeter, or if sperm motility is low, artificial insemination using semen from the husband can be tried (Shapiro, 1980). Semen is collected and then placed on the cervix at the time of ovulation. The semen is not placed into the uterus directly because of the side effects of cramping and infection that could result.

Surrogate Motherhood. When the man is fertile and the women is not, some couples have elected to use a *surrogate mother* to bear their child. By means of artificial insemination, sperm are placed in the surrogate mother's vagina near the time of her ovulation. The biological mother continues as a surrogate with the pregnancy, delivers the baby, and then allows the couple to adopt him or her. A new variation is known as gestational surrogacy (Lawson, 1990). The husband and wife conceive by means of in vitro fertilization, and the blastocyst is placed in the uterus of another woman, one who is genetically unrelated to the fetus she is carrying.

Adoption. Adoption is obviously one answer for sterile couples, though adopting a healthy child is likely to cost $5,000 to $12,000 (Cole, 1987). It should be noted that, despite a popular belief, couples with fertility problems do not conceive more often after they adopt than before (Ansbacher, 1984).

When one of the various forms of technology is

used instead of adoption as a solution to infertility, the couple can be brought closer together. The joint effort and shared anxiety may affect their relationship for the better. The decision to proceed with IVF, AI, surrogacy, or future reproductive technologies, should be made jointly; it may not be the right thing to do for either one or both persons for a variety of reasons. The initially infertile couple can later become fertile through treatment, and the decision to use reproductive technology may be premature in some cases.

■ Legal Aspects of Reproductive Technology

In Vitro Fertilization.   Legal and ethical issues have been raised about IVF (Chartrand, 1989). When ova are removed and combined with sperm, several may be fertilized. Unneeded zygotes are frozen for later use. If the couple divorces, controversy exists about which spouse should be awarded the fertilized egg by the court. In 1988 one hotly contested case on Long Island in New York resulted in the ex-wife receiving the frozen, fertilized egg.

Artificial Insemination.   After conceiving through AID, the woman frequently worries about whether her partner will reject a child conceived in this way. In the United States, some localities require a husband who consents to AID to agree beforehand to support the offspring financially even if the child has a birth defect such as mental retardation (Andrews, 1981).

Surrogate Motherhood.   Some couples arrange for surrogate motherhood privately, while others use an attorney for this purpose. The surrogate usually receives a fee of $10,000 plus expenses connected with the pregnancy. The issues connected with surrogacy are complex and unsettled, as states consider laws concerning whether to ban or regulate the practice. The use of a legal contract to regulate parenthood, as has occurred in hundreds of cases so far, creates enormous complications in the lives of those involved (Andrews, 1989). For example, the child may someday try to find his or her surrogate mother, but the legal contract may not allow her identity to be revealed. In one case ("Baby M"), the surrogate mother refused to give up the newborn infant, and the court had to decide who was the rightful parent (Kolbert, 1987).

Summarizing the Information about Reproduction . . .

The hormonal systems that control sperm production and the menstrual cycle are produced by the central nervous system. The testes produce sperm and secrete male sex hormones called **androgens**. The beginning of a menstrual cycle occurs with the stimulation of a **follicle** to mature its ovum. As the ovum is released, **luteinizing hormone** stimulates the **corpus luteum** to form and the secretion of progesterone by the ovary. The **luteal phase** of the menstrual cycle follows, and an unfertilized egg disintegrates to be shed along with menstrual blood and tissue from the **endometrium**. A number of symptoms have been identified as part of the **premenstrual syndrome**. Despite popular beliefs, women's performance on many types of tasks is not negatively affected. The causes of the syndrome are not well understood, and different patterns of this syndrome occur in different women.

Conception is aided by a number of factors, including physical changes in the vagina at ovulation. The genetic combination of sperm and ovum constitutes the *genotype* of the developing infant. The offspring's *phenotype* is affected by genes and by experiences occurring after conception. Detection of pregnancy is based on both *presumptive* and *positive signs*. The **trimesters** of pregnancy are the setting for different aspects of *embryonic* and *fetal* development. The effects of toxins on the organism depend on the timing of contact with them. Defects can be assessed by **chorionic villus biopsy** in the first trimester and by **amniocentesis** in the second.

The precise mechanism by which labor is initiated is not well understood, but its progress can be accurately described. Stage one of labor is characterized by contractions associateed with cervical **effacement** and **dilation**. In stages two and three, respectively, the *neonate* and **placenta** are expelled from the uterus through the vagina. The Lamaze and Bradley methods of childbirth aim for increased tolerance to pain without drugs. In the *postpartum period,* adjustments occur to the new feelings about parenthood and sexuality. *Lactation* has benefits for the neonate's health and the mother's appearance, but several factors interfere with successful breastfeeding, including the mother's emotional state and work schedule.

A rise in infertility rates among younger couples has been attributed to the effects of disease, environmental and dietary toxins, and drugs. Treatment of infertility depends on its causes, including inadequate sperm production, problems with the transportation of sperm and egg, and poor maintenance of a fertilized egg within the uterus. In addition to the more traditional treatments, the controversial procedure known as **in vitro fertilization** has solved the infertility problems of some couples.

To Find Out More about Reproduction . . .

Andrews, L. (1989). *Between strangers: Surrogate mothers, expectant fathers, and brave new babies.* New York: Harper and Row.

Using the experiences of six women as examples, the author describes the phenomenon of surrogacy, covering such topics as surrogate agencies, court cases, and organized objections to the practice.

Bradley, R. A. (1981). *Husband-coached childbirth* (3rd ed.). New York: Harper & Row.

Bradley discusses a method of husband-coached childbirth which promotes relaxation and avoidance of drug use. The book also informs the reader about many health issues concerning pregnancy and the postpartum period.

La Leche League International. (1981). *The womanly art of breastfeeding.* Frankling Park, Ill.: La Leche League International.

La Leche League documents the benefits and techniques of successful breastfeeding in this volume. It gives a woman encouragement and supportive tips in making the decision to nurse her infant.

Stangel, J. J. (1979). *Fertility and conception.* New York: New American Library.

For couples who face infertility, this book has a detailed description of the evaluation and treatment of the problem.

Stern, P. N. (Ed.). (1989). *Pregnancy and parenting.* New York: Hemisphere.

This useful collection of chapters covers many aspects of pregnancy and beyond, including sexual intercourse, breastfeeding, and the stresses of parenthood.

BIRTH CONTROL

The decision to become heterosexually active necessarily raises the issue of birth control. To avoid unwanted pregnancies, the couple must think about the possibility of conception and make appropriate plans., One young woman told us about her initial experiences with contraceptive use.

When Alex and I made love the first time, it wasn't planned at all—at least not by me. We had been dating off and on for some time. I was in my junior year in high school, and he was a senior. One Saturday night, after a party where we had been drinking beer, Alex grew more insistent than ever. I loved him a lot and started feeling really excited about sex.

To be honest, we didn't talk about birth control or even think about it. I just wanted to show him how much I loved him, and I was only worried about doing it right and not making a fool of myself.

The next day, though, I began to worry about being pregnant. I wasn't, but I was scared enough to make Alex hold off on more sex until we could do something. His only contribution was that he wouldn't use a condom because "it was like taking a shower with a raincoat on." I was naive enough to think he had said something original and even sensible. Anyway, I was the one who had to take the big step.

I didn't want to go to our family doctor because I had known him since I was a kid. Besides, he might think he had to tell my Mom. Instead, I went across town to a clinic that one of my friends told me about. Alex wouldn't go with me because he said it would make him nervous.

I was really worried about what it would be like. I kept imagining terrible scenes like having to tell the receptionist what I wanted while everyone in the waiting room stared at me. Even worse—maybe the doctor would give a lecture about morals. In fact, there were no problems, and a very understanding doctor examined me and prescribed a diaphragm. Afterward, I went to a pharmacy to buy it along with the jelly, a plastic thing to insert it, and so forth.

The first time I was with Alex after that, I was almost too nervous to use the thing. It seemed so mechanical to stop what we were doing and go through this unromantic procedure. I had practiced inserting it at home after my parents were asleep, but it was still hard to get it just right. It didn't take long before Alex and I were comfortable with the whole idea and were even able to joke about it.

Now, four years later, I'm going with a different guy and hardly ever think about Alex anymore. I know now that getting pregnant back then would have been the worst thing that ever happened to me. Thank goodness I was smart enough to do the sensible thing about birth control.

Carla, age 20

Carla is fortunate to live at a time when several effective ways to prevent conception are available, but she still has had to deal with the embarrassing emotional aspects of obtaining and using the available technology. As she makes clear, such concerns were much less serious than the possibility of an unwanted pregnancy.

When a man and a woman decide to engage in vaginal intercourse, they must face the possibility of conception. The desire to separate sexual enjoyment from reproduction is an ancient human goal, and though today's technology makes such a goal increasingly possible, no current method of contraception is perfect. In addition, emotional barriers can make it difficult to obtain and use birth control devices. We discuss the technical and the psychological aspects of contraception in this chapter. Specifically, we summarize the primary methods of *preventing conception* and the emotional issues surrounding *abortion;* we also describe individual differences in *contraceptive attitudes and behavior.* In special sections we focus on the imbalance between the relative number of *contraceptives for males and for females,* the most *recent contraceptive developments,* and the issues involved in making a *contraceptive choice.*

Before discussing the details of contraception, it is important to get beyond the widespread myth that contraceptives are risky whereas pregnancy and childbirth are safe (Hofmann, 1982). Exactly the opposite is true: It has been known for a long time that the possibility of death from pregnancy and childbirth is several times greater than the possibility of death from the use of any modern contraceptive (Hatcher et al., 1990). A generation ago, Peel and Potts (1970, p. 254) wrote:

> *The woman who begins taking oral contraceptives has a greater likelihood of being alive one year later than has her sister who chooses to have a baby or to use some less effective method of contraception.*

Preventing Conception

The effectiveness of modern contraceptives is impressive, but throughout most of human history this was not the case.

■ Contraceptive Methods: A Brief History

Some of the earliest attempts at contraception were ineffective and dangerous, and their use suggests how desperate people were to enjoy sex without conceiving offspring. Many of the ancient methods had only a partial contraceptive effect. For example, 3,000 years ago in ancient Egypt, a common contraceptive was a paste consisting of honey or oil mixed with animal feces (Schneider, 1978). This crude *spermicide* raised the acidic level of the vagina, making it slightly more difficult for sperm to survive.

Superstitions and myths often raised false hopes in women wishing to avoid conception. In Rome in A.D. 50, Pliny the Elder advised tying a piece of deerskin to the woman's body after intercourse and before the next sunrise (Schneider, 1978). Other Romans recommended that the man spit into the mouth of a female toad three times before and three times after coitus. An equally useless alternative was for the woman to hold a pebble in her hand while having sex. Still other futile contraceptive attempts in various cultures included eating a hen's oviduct, consuming gun powder, and inserting crocodile dung in the vagina (Newman, 1990)

Albert the Great, a thirteenth-century physician and the tutor of Thomas Aquinas, prescribed the eating of bees by both partners as a way of preventing conception. The compulsive Italian lover of the eighteenth century, Casanova (see Figure 5-1), used a primitive diaphragm (Greenblatt, 1980); it consisted of half a lemon which he placed over the woman's cervix, thereby attempting to block the passage of sperm and to create a more acidic environment. He claimed never to have impregnated a woman, but infertility, rather than the lemons, was probably the explanation.

The only truly effective approaches used by the ancient Greeks and Romans to prevent unwanted offspring were infanticide and abortion. It was not until the late 1800s that effective contraceptives were developed. Except for the pill, every major type of contraception used today was available in some form at that time. Unfortunately, information about contraceptives was banned in the United States and some parts of Europe. For example, the Comstock Act of 1873 made it illegal to use the U.S. postal system to distribute contraceptive knowledge. In Britain at the same time, the first users of effective birth control devices were physicians and ministers, but both groups strongly opposed allowing others to use or even to learn about them (Peel and Potts, 1970).

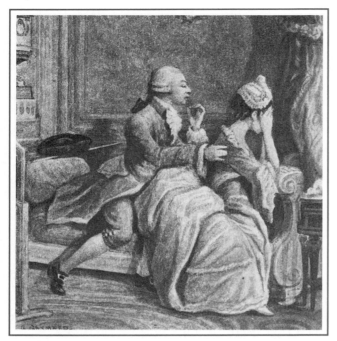

FIGURE 5-1 *SEX WITHOUT PREGNANCY: A QUEST OVER THE CENTURIES* The desire to have sex while avoiding conception has been a challenge to men and women for at least 3,000 years. In the eighteenth century, Casanova, attempting to avoid impregnating his many sexual partners, placed half a lemon over each woman's cervix prior to intercourse as a kind of primitive diaphragm. Only in the late nineteenth century were effective contraceptive techniques developed.

Social attitudes changed gradually, and the family planning movement slowly became accepted in Western countries (Dawson et al., 1980). An American birth control advocate, Margaret Sanger, campaigned worldwide for the removal of sanctions against the ban on contraceptive information and products. Despite being repeatedly jailed, punished, and attacked by opponents, her crusade gained widespread support. In 1948, Sanger formed the organization that later became the International Planned Parenthood Foundation. Even today, there is controversy surrounding the work of this group.

We will now describe the primary methods of birth control that are currently available.

■ Scheduling Sex to Avoid Ovulation

Because conception can occur only when a mature egg is present to be fertilized, the female's menstrual cycle can be used as a rough indication as to "safe" (infertile) versus "unsafe" (fertile) days for intercourse—the **rhythm method**. There is one major side effect to contraception based on scheduling—each year about 20 to 40 percent of those women who use this technique become pregnant (Reinisch, 1984). Though this approach to birth control is frustrating, inexact, unreliable, and is the one least liked by Americans, it is the only method officially approved by the Roman Catholic Church for its members. Local priests in the United States often accept women's choice of other methods, however. There are three variations of this approach. Though we will describe them in terms of birth control, couples who wish to conceive use these same guidelines to determine when intercourse *should* occur to maximize the chance of pregnancy.

Calendar Method. In the **calendar method of family planning** the woman charts the menstrual cycle to identify those days that are safe for intercourse, that is, the days when she is not ovulating. Conception generally occurs in midcycle for women with completely regular, twenty-eight-day cycles. The fertile period occurs approximately thirteen to fifteen days before menstruation begins.

How many days should a couple abstain from intercourse to avoid pregnancy? Besides the three days when ovulation usually occurs, sperm can survive in the woman's body for up to six days (Johnston et al., 1980), and some eggs live as long as two days. Thus, a couple is advised to abstain from intercourse for fourteen days of each cycle, or days eight to twenty-one of a twenty-eight-day cycle. Any irregularity or variation in the cycle can of course create havoc with this careful planning.

Temperature Method. Instead of relying on the calendar, some couples use the **temperature method of family planning** to identify the appropriate days for abstinence. The idea is to use temperature changes as an indication of when ovulation occurs. During the two weeks prior to ovulation, the woman's morning body temperature, called *basal body temperature* (BBT), is usually at a fairly constant level. On the day of ovulation, it usually drops a degree or so on the Fahrenheit scale, followed by an increase of at least .3 degrees Fahrenheit above the level during the follicular phase.

Because the temperature changes occur in tenths

of a degree, a thermometer with gradations that are easy to read should be used. Until that temperature rise occurs, conception is possible. Intercourse should be avoided for six days before the expected ovulation. If the temperature remains constant, intercourse should not be resumed for at least three days. The temperature method can determine safe days after but not before ovulation, and about one in five ovulatory cycles do not show a pattern indicating ovulation. Thus the temperature method is generally considered inaccurate and unreliable.

Checking Cervical Mucus. The **natural (Billings) method of family planning** was developed by Drs. John and Evelyn Billings in Australia. It requires women to check the consistency and appearance of cervical mucus. Between menstruation and ovulation, the vagina is relatively free of mucus. A day or two before ovulation, increased estrogen levels in the bloodstream cause the vagina to become more moist and the mucus to increase and resemble stringy, raw egg whites (Klaus, 1984). Ovulation is expected to occur within one day after the peak day for heavier

mucus at midcycle. Intercourse is avoided during the increased discharge of cloudy mucus and for four additional days (Betts, 1984).

Less than 10 percent of couples use any of these methods, but some use two or even all three (Betts, 1984; Klaus, 1984). In Figure 5-2 the days of abstinence and the methods of scheduling intercourse are compared. Under the best of circumstances, however, the predictability of the menstrual cycle and ovulation is poor. It may be difficult to note the changes in cervical mucus. Stress, fatigue, illness, vaginal infection, or fever can affect the various signs of ovulation. Thus, the "safe" days for intercourse may become unsafe, and using a rhythm method can restrict the couple's spontaneity. There are no medical side effects other than pregnancy.

■ **Withdrawal and Douching**

When couples find scheduling methods too complicated and too demanding and contraceptive devices too embarrassing or too expensive, they of-

FIGURE 5-2 *TRYING TO AVOID FERTILE OVA* Three methods of natural family planning prescribe the avoidance of intercourse during ovulation, which occurs at midcycle. These charts assume completely regular twenty-eight-day menstrual cycles, but one of the most consistent features of the menstrual cycle is its irregularity from month to month. The methods of scheduling intercourse require cooperation and planning of sexual activity by the couple, something which the young and uncommitted may find difficult to do.

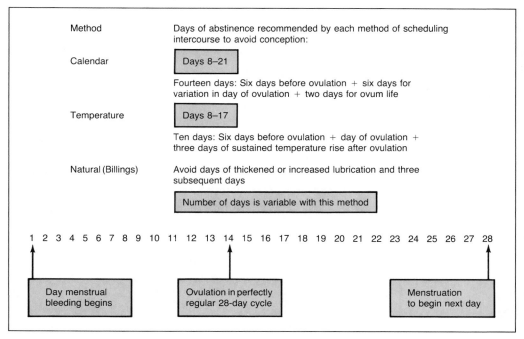

ten turn to one of two simple but quite ineffective methods of birth control.

Withdrawal. The formal name for withdrawal is **coitus interruptus** (interrupted intercourse), and this practice consists of the man removing his penis from the vagina just before he ejaculates. Each year about one fourth of the couples using it are faced with pregnancy. With this 25 percent failure rate, withdrawal is scarcely a method to recommend.

The ineffectiveness of withdrawal has three causes. First, the preejaculatory fluid that appears at the tip of the penis prior to orgasm often contains enough sperm to produce conception. Second, the male may not withdraw quickly enough to avoid at least partial ejaculation in the vagina; in about 90 percent of men, the first two spurts of ejaculate contain most of the sperm (Gordon, 1981). Third, even if the man does withdraw, his penis may be close to the woman's moist vulva, thus permitting sperm to enter the vagina from outside. In the same way, interfemoral stimulation (rubbing the penis between the female's thighs without vaginal penetration) also can lead to pregnancy (Crist, 1984).

In addition to these contraceptive problems, the psychological effect of the male's efforts to monitor his excitement to predict the point at which ejaculation will occur can easily contribute to erectile or orgasmic dysfunctions. This method also creates tension for the woman; concern about whether her partner will withdraw at the right time hardly contributes to the full enjoyment of the sexual experience (Roen, 1983). In addition, the shortened time period of the interrupted act is likely to leave the female without an orgasm. The only advantage of withdrawal is that it is better to use it than no contraceptive at all.

Taking Responsibility and Protecting Yourself

WHY DO WOMEN USUALLY HAVE THE RESPONSIBILITY FOR CONTRACEPTION?

One answer to the question of male-female differences in contraceptive availability is that more money is spent on research and development of female contraceptives than is spent on male contraceptives, as Figure 5-3 indicates. There has, however, been some shift toward the male side since 1978. The ratio of female to male expenditures before that date was about twelve to one (Atkinson et al., 1980), compared to nearly seven to one in 1980–1983 (Atkinson et al., 1985). This change is not as great as it appears, though, because more money is currently being spent in the "general" category that applies to both sexes. The monetary difference leads to the next question—why are there more funds available for research on female than on male methods of contraception?

One reason is the difficulty in finding an effective method for males. It has proved to be difficult to inhibit sperm production because of the way that the male

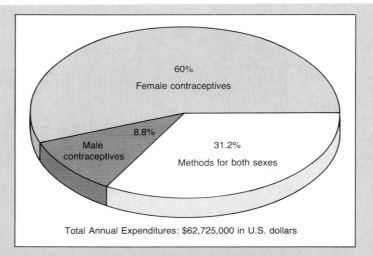

FIGURE 5-3 *MONEY FOR CONTRACEPTIVE RESEARCH: SEX DIFFERENCES* Most expenditures for contraceptive research and development are aimed at methods for female use. The annual average amount spent during 1980–1983 worldwide (figures for the Soviet bloc countries are unavailable) indicate 60 percent of the funds committed to female contraceptives and 8.8 percent for exclusively male contraceptives. Methods involving both sexes accounted for the other 31.2 percent. Source: Atkinson et al., 1985.

reproductive system functions. For example, consider the use of luteinizing hormone-releasing hormone (LHRH—see Chapter 4) in synthetic form. LHRH stimulates the release of two hormones, luteinizing (LH) and follicle stimulating (FSH) hormones in both sexes. In males, LH and FSH are involved in sperm production; thus, lowering their levels would have a contraceptive effect. Yet reducing LH (and subsequently, testosterone) also can result in undesirable side effects: erectile difficulties and the development of female secondary sexual characteristics such as enlarged breasts (Benditt, 1980). If a way can be found to lower FSH while not affecting LH levels, the contraceptive goal might be accomplished. One result of the relative neglect of research on male contraception is that we now know much more about female reproductive physiology than we do about the male system.

Assuming that an appropriate chemical contraceptive for men could be developed, would they be willing to use it? Among married couples in the United States, both men and women express favorable attitudes about using a male pill (Marsiglio and Menaghen, 1987). Studies of middle-aged men in five countries (Fiji, India, Iran, Mexico, and Korea) indicate that between 41 and 74 percent would be willing to use a pill or have an injection to provide contraception (World Health Organization, 1978). It seems that men are increasingly ready to try new methods (Prendergast, 1990). The majority of men surveyed in six countries indicated that controlling fertility is the responsibility of the male alone or of both partners. As Figure 5-4 shows, these men say they intend to use new chemical methods in the future in preference to a condom or a vasectomy. It only can be hoped that such options are actually available in the near future.

FIGURE 5-4 MALES ARE WILLING TO TRY SOMETHING NEW A group of 119 men in several countries stated that they viewed using pills or having hormones injected more favorably than undergoing a vasectomy or wearing a condom.
Source: Based on data from World Health Organization, 1982.

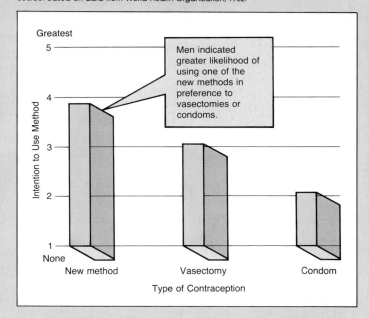

Withdrawal is one of the three methods of birth control available to men, the others being the condom and sterilization. The other methods all depend on women. In the special section, **Taking Responsibility and Protecting Yourself**, on pages 110 to 111, we explore some of the reasons for this sex difference.

Douching to Kill or Remove Sperm. Many people believe that douching (flushing the vagina with a liquid after intercourse) provides contraceptive protection. The force of the liquid, however, can help push sperm toward their destination rather than remove them. Acid solutions such as vinegar and water do provide an inhospitable environment for sperm, but these organisms move with remarkable speed. Even if a woman rushes to douche immediately after her partner has ejaculated, she is likely to be too late to prevent a large number of the fastest sperm from entering the uterus. Douching has a 50 percent failure rate; half of women who use it would become pregnant within a year (Hatcher et al., 1988).

Not only are homemade and commercial douche products unreliable as contraceptives, they can also increase the probability of infection because they irritate the vaginal lining and change its normal bacterial composition. Even plain water may have this negative effect. Appropriate genital hygiene for females should be limited to washing the vulva with soap and then rinsing.

■ Barrier Methods

Three methods of contraception are designed to prevent sperm from reaching an ovum—the condom, the diaphragm, and the sponge. Spermicides can also be used either alone or in combination with these devices. The advantages of the three methods are the absence of any negative effects on a fetus accidentally conceived during their use and some protection against sexually transmitted disease. Among the disadvantages are interference with spontaneity in sexual activity through the interruption of foreplay to install the device; possible allergies to spermicide; and the possibility of their breaking or slipping during use.

Condoms. A condom ("rubber," "safe," or "prophylactic") is a sheath that fits snugly over the penis. The Italian physician for whom the oviducts were named, Fallopius, provided the first written description of a condom-like device in 1564. He suggested that males place moist linen sheaths over the head of the penis to prevent the spread of venereal disease. The name "condom" may be based on the Latin word *condus* (collector), or it could have originated in England in the seventeenth century with Dr. Condom (or Conton).

Whatever their origin, most condoms today are made from one of two materials, either latex rubber or skin from lamb intestines. The former is produced by dipping glass molds into liquid latex. This is done at an angle so that the substance collects at the mold tip, creating a reservoir for semen. The resulting thin sheath is dried, rolled, and sometimes lubricated and perfumed before being stored in individual packets.

Only about 5 percent of condom users select the lambskin variety, which costs about three times more than a latex condom. Men who prefer the skins say that they allow greater sensitivity during intercourse, presumably because they conduct body heat more readily. Lambskin condoms also tend to be less reliable than latex, because the natural variations in the consistency of skin results in slightly more breakage ("Can you rely?", 1989). This problem is relevant both to birth control and the prevention of diseases such as AIDS.

Condoms are available on drug store shelves without prescription, from family planning clinics, in dispensing machines, at the college health service facilities, some supermarkets, and through mail-order firms. The user can choose from a wide variety of shapes and textures, either lubricated or not, and with or without spermicide applied on the outside, as Figure 5-5 shows. Despite erotic myths and glowing advertising claims, there is no evidence that finger-

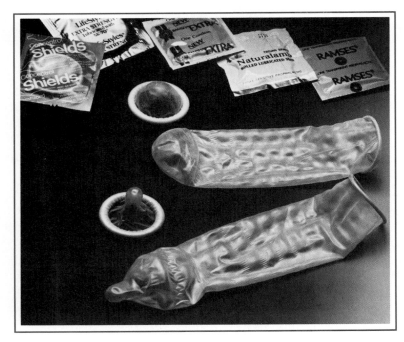

FIGURE 5-5 *THE WONDERFUL WORLD OF CONDOMS* Condoms are manufactured in a variety of shapes, colors, and textures, but such characteristics have no effect on sexual pleasure or contraceptive value. Only spermicides enhance contraceptive effectiveness.

like projections ("French ticklers") or ribbing on condoms adds to either partner's physical pleasure. Some couples might be intrigued by the novelty of sampling one or more of the many available colors.

How to Use a Condom. Though men may feel that instructions are unnecessary for such a simple device, there are several important cautions (Brody, 1987). In opening the package, care should be taken to tear only the wrapper, not the condom; it should then be unrolled over an erect penis. As indicated in discussing the withdrawal method, sperm are present in preejaculatory fluid and need only reach the vulva in order to be able to race toward the egg. It follows that the condom must be in place before the man's penis approaches his partner's genitals in order to prevent this from occurring. If there is no built-in reservoir at the tip, enough room should be left in the condom at the end of the glans penis to catch the ejaculate. It is also important to make sure that the unrolled rim clings tightly to the base of the penis during intercourse and to withdraw the penis after ejaculation and before detumescence begins, preferably while holding the condom in place on the penis. Some condoms now have an adhesive strip to prevent slippage. Water soluble lubrication on the condom helps prevent breakage, but keep in mind that oil based lubricants such as petroleum jelly can destroy a condom. These precautions are obviously aimed at keeping the sperm within the condom and away from the female's vagina. Nonoxynol-9, a spermicide, is applied during manufacture to the surface and helps improve effectiveness. Finally, condoms should never be reused. Some men try to save money by stretching and drying them after intercourse, but used condoms are likely to have a "blowout."

Men complain about the loss of sensitivity caused by condoms, as Carla's boyfriend indicated in the opening chapter vignette. The reduced sensation, however, also allows a man using a condom to maintain an erection for a longer time prior to ejaculation than a man not using one (Roen, 1981). The most frequent complaint, though, is that condom use interrupts lovemaking because it must be rolled onto the erect penis prior to penetration (Condoms, 1979). The only negative physical side effect is that either the man or woman may have an allergic reaction to the material itself or to the spermicide, but this problem can often be solved simply by switching brands (Fisher, 1984).

How Effective Is the Condom? Theoretically, the condom has a 97 percent effectiveness rate; in other words, it fails to prevent conception for only three out of 100 users over a one-year period (Condoms, 1979). Because of inconvenience or carelessness, however, men often do not use them during every act of intercourse or use them incorrectly. Actual effectiveness depends on proper use. As a result, condoms have an actual effectiveness rate of about 85 to 90 percent. Condoms with spermicide applied to their surfaces or that are used along with contraceptive jelly have a slightly higher actual effectiveness rate: 90 to 95 percent (Friedman, 1983; Tyrer, 1982). An additional benefit of this form of contraception is that condoms also block the passage of viruses and therefore are helpful in preventing sexually transmissible diseases (Gamson, 1990).

The manufacture of condoms is quality controlled. Samples are tested for "bursting strength" by filling each with water; they are also examined for electrical conductance in salt water. Other tests determine the rate of deterioration when exposed to heat or light. Men who carry condoms in their wallets for months may end up with a defective product. It is possible to test an old, unused condom for water leakage, but it is safer and less trouble simply to replace it (Tietze, 1981).

A "female condom" has recently become available for use (Detjen, 1990). It looks like an extra large male condom, is inserted in the vagina, and, following intercourse, is discarded. Tests in 11 countries indicate that it is more effective than the ordinary male condom.

The Diaphragm. Another barrier to contact between sperm and ovum is the diaphragm used in combination with spermidical cream or jelly. The diaphragm is a round, rubber dome of thin rubber with a flexible rim. After it is filled with a spermicidal cream or jelly, it is inserted inside the vagina so that the rim snugly covers the cervix. Spermicide is required because some sperm are able to slip behind the diaphragm to reach the cervix. The cream and jelly forms of spermicide are equally effective; your personal preference for a white cream or a colored jelly is the only basis for deciding which to use.

Because of fears about the side effects of the pill, this method of contraception has shown a slight increase in popularity (Bachrach, 1984). A prescription is required because a trained health care professional has to fit it to the anatomy of the individual woman so that the device covers the cervix and fits against the vaginal walls. The heavier the woman, the smaller the appropriate diaphragm, so weight gains or losses of 10 pounds or more—as well as childbirth—result in the need for refitting. An improperly fitted diaphragm can result not only in contraceptive failure but also in repeated urinary bladder infections (Tyrer, 1981).

How to Use the Diaphragm. The diaphragm should be inserted no more than one hour prior to intercourse. The cup is filled with spermicide, and some is applied to the inner rim. Then the diaphragm is folded once to insert with the fingers or with a plastic device. Figure 5-6 illustrates the proper position after insertion. If the diaphragm is properly inserted, the woman or her partner should be able to feel the rim directly behind the pubic bone with the fingers. After ejaculation, the diaphragm should be left in place for another six to eight hours. To remove it, the woman uses a finger to break the suction and then gently withdraws the diaphragm. If intercourse is repeated before the six-hour period ends, the diaphragm should be left in place and another application of spermicide should be inserted in the vagina with the applicator tube supplied with it.

Because rubber deteriorates over time or can be punctured, a woman should inspect her diaphragm periodically by holding it up to light or filling it with water to see if there is a leak (Lane, 1980). Even if no holes appear, it is best to replace a diaphragm annually.

Some women wear their diaphragms during menstruation to catch the discharge. This is not recommended because such use may contribute to endometriosis—see Chapter 4 (Keith, 1979).

The **cervical cap** is a smaller and more rigid version of the diaphragm that provides greater suction around the cervix. Though it is very popular among European women, the cervical cap was not approved for use in the United States until recently (Lohr, 1988). It has to be replaced less frequently than the diaphragm, so it is less expensive to use (Toufexis, 1988). Like the diaphragm, it needs to be fitted so that the appropriate size is used.

Effectiveness, Advantages, and Disadvantages of the Diaphragm and Cervical Cap. The theoretical effectiveness rate for the diaphragm is 97 percent. If the woman fails to use the diaphragm or spermicide during every act of intercourse, the actual effectiveness (85 percent) is lower than the theoretical rate. The

FIGURE 5-6 *PREPARING AND INSERTING A DIAPHRAGM* Inserting a diaphragm containing spermicide involves folding it and then pushing it into proper position in the vagina. If the diaphragm is the appropriate size for the woman's vagina and is placed correctly, her partner should not be able to detect its presence during intercourse.
Source: Fertel, 1983.

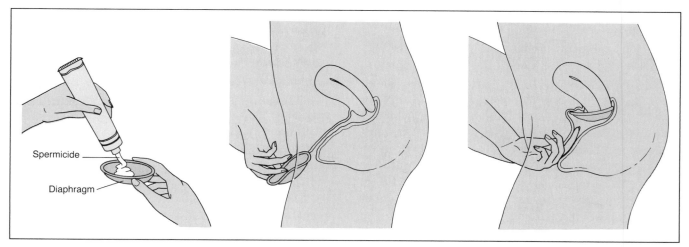

cervical cap's actual effectiveness rate is 80 percent (Koch, 1982).

Both the spermicide-bearing diaphragm and the cervical cap have advantages in that they do not have major side effects. But their inconvenience, cost, and messiness through leakage of spermicide after intercourse could be considered drawbacks.

The Sponge. In some respects, the contraceptive sponge is the female analogue of the condom in that it is available without prescription. Inserted into the vagina, the soft, disposable sponge partially blocks the cervix, releasing the spermicide it contains, and absorbing a portion of the semen. Made of the synthetic polyurethane, it must be moistened with water prior to insertion to activate the spermicide; the sponge remains effective in the vagina for up to twenty-four hours, permitting repeated acts of intercourse. After use, the woman should discard it. This device should not be left in place more than six hours during menstruation because bacteria grow rapidly in blood. It is removed by pulling on a short ribbon attached to one side.

The sponge is as effective as the diaphragm with an 85 percent actual effectiveness rate among *nulliparous* women (those who have never given birth). Women who have had offspring (*parous*) have an enlarged vaginal barrel; as a result, the effectiveness rate drops to 70 to 75 percent (Failure rate, 1985).

Spermicides: How to Use. Each of the barrier methods just discussed is often or always used in conjunction with spermicides in the form of foams, jellies, suppositories, tablets, or creams. Sperm-killing foams (a nonprescription drug) can also be used alone. Foam coats the cervix and is deposited into the vagina before penetration with a special applicator that accompanies the product. Repeated intercourse should be preceded by a new application of foam each time. Spermicide should not be used during pregnancy or if pregnancy is suspected because of the danger that it may produce birth defects.

A newer version of spermicide is the contraceptive vaginal tablet that dissolves after insertion. This is simpler than foam, but less effective because the substance may not remain in place over the cervix. It is also important to delay intercourse for ten to fifteen minutes after the tablet is inserted so that it has time to melt, as the result of a heat reaction called efferves-

cence. A man who ignores this instruction may discover that his penis is slightly burned.

Effectiveness of Spermicides. The actual effectiveness rate of such spermicides is about 80 percent (Christakos, 1983). As you might guess from the discussion of douching, the side effects of spermicides used either alone or with barrier devices can include vaginal irritation and infections. They also discourage males from engaging in cunnilingus, because of the lingering unpleasant taste. When the man uses a condom in conjunction with his female partner's spermicidal foam, the effectiveness rates of both methods get a boost, to 99 percent in theory. When failure to use and inappropriate use are taken into account, the combination of condom with foam still has an impressive 95 to 97 percent actual effectiveness rate.

■ IUD—Barrier to Conception or Built-in Abortion?

Intrauterine devices (IUDs), small plastic objects inserted into the uterus by a doctor, have progressed considerably since Arabs and Turks first placed pebbles into the uteruses of camels to prevent pregnancy, which would have interfered with the work of the caravans. No one then understood precisely how such a contraceptive device worked, and there is still controversy about the functioning of IUDs. Some regard them as an additional barrier to conception in that they may simply destroy sperm, but that does not appear to be accurate. Instead, it is more probable that the presence of an intrauterine device somehow destroys eggs that have been fertilized or prevents the usual development of the uterine lining so that a newly fertilized egg cannot become implanted into the uterus (Shepard, 1980). Because the effect does occur after fertilization, some opponents of abortion classify the IUD as unacceptable.

How the IUD Works. IUDs are a popular form of birth control. The most recent IUDs release tiny amounts of copper or hormone into the uterus, creating a slight inflammation there. It is this inflammation that prevents pregnancy. The small devices, which vary in size and composition, are usually shaped like the number seven (for the Copper-7) or the letter T (for the hormone-containing Progestasert). Figure 5-7 shows the T-shaped Progestasert IUD.

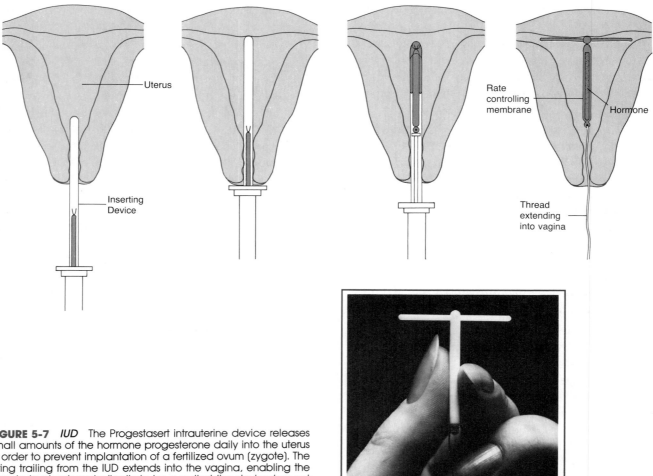

Uterus

Inserting Device

Rate controlling membrane

Hormone

Thread extending into vagina

FIGURE 5-7 *IUD* The Progestasert intrauterine device releases small amounts of the hormone progesterone daily into the uterus in order to prevent implantation of a fertilized ovum (zygote). The string trailing from the IUD extends into the vagina, enabling the female to check periodically to be sure that the device has not been expelled.

How the IUD Is Used. The IUD is commonly inserted during menstruation when the cervix is slightly dilated, which makes the process easier and less painful. Insertion by an experienced physician costs about $60. The Progestasert device should be replaced annually because the active ingredient, a synthetic form of progesterone, dissipates over time.

In the unlikely event of a pregnancy occurring while the IUD is in place, it should be removed to prevent a possible infection or puncturing of the uterus. For reasons that are unclear, women with IUDs who have more than one sexual partner (PID risk, 1981) or who use an IUD that does not contain copper (Washington et al., 1985) are at risk for developing pelvic infections that can cause infertility.

Advantages and Disadvantages of the IUD. A main advantage of the IUD is that its use does not interfere with lovemaking; it is already in place when intercourse occurs. Also, the IUD does not interfere with ovulatory menstrual cycling, but various side effects, such as heavy bleeding and cramping, may create the impression that the cycles are irregular.

Expulsion of the device from the uterus occurs in 5 to 20 percent of users during the first year after insertion. Expulsion is more likely among nulliparous (who have not given birth) than parous women, probably because of their smaller uteruses. Expulsion can be detected by noting the absence of the safety string that may be felt protruding from the cervix. A woman using this device should be shown by her doctor (after insertion) how to detect whether the string is still in place; she should return for a checkup if it is missing or feels longer than before. If no string can be felt, it may simply have contracted into the uterus, but a physician needs to determine this (Tyrer, 1980). Rarely, the device is partially expelled, and the sharp, rigid object protruding through the cervix may be noted by the woman when she checks the safety string or by the man when his penis makes painful contact with the IUD. Immediate removal of the device by a professional is then necessary.

Altogether, then, the best prospect for IUD use are women who are parous and monogamous. About one woman out of five is not a good candidate for the IUD because of preexisting conditions such as a pelvic infection. The possibility of such an infection being *caused* by the IUD has been of even wider concern, because pelvic inflammatory disease can lead to scarring of the oviducts and infertility. One IUD, the Dalkon shield, was removed from the market because of its association with pelvic infections. Similarly, Searle Pharmaceuticals removed its copper device from the U.S. market in 1986 because of the high cost of defense against lawsuits by women (Searle removes, 1986). It is, nevertheless, still available by prescription in other countries, including Canada.

A new IUD, the T Cu 380A, contains copper; its use in the United States was approved by the Food and Drug Administration in 1984 (Hutchings et al., 1985). The device remains in place for up to four years.

Effectiveness of the IUD. The 95 percent actual effectiveness rate of the IUD in preventing pregnancy is close to its 99 percent theoretical rate of effectiveness, perhaps because women with IUDs do not have to insert it themselves before engaging in intercourse, which is required for barrier contraceptives for women. The 95 percent rate of actual effectiveness is second only to birth control pills in preventing pregnancy. This figure means that in one year of IUD use, one in twenty women would conceive.

■ Oral Contraceptives

How the Oral Contraceptive Works. The *combination birth control pill* prevents pregnancy by inhibiting the release of mature eggs from the ovaries. The com-

bination pill contains synthetic versions of two hormones, estrogen and progesterone, that are normally present in varying levels across the menstrual cycle. Instead of normal fluctuations during the cycle, estrogen and progestrogen are present in constant amounts when the pill is taken daily during the first three weeks of the menstrual cycle. During the fourth week, the woman stops taking the pill, and the resultant lower hormone level leads to a flow resembling a usual menstrual period. She then starts a new set of pills after day 28—the first day of her next cycle. Some brands or oral contraception include pills for the fourth week that contain only an inert substance or an iron supplement rather than hormones. When first introduced, combination pills contained relatively high doses of estrogen (2 mg) and progestogen (10 mg). Today's oral contraceptives contain smaller amounts of each hormone, 1/2 mg of estrogen and 1 mg of progestogen, which are high enough to be effective but low enough to reduce side effects (Mischell, 1989).

The artificially high level of estrogen following menstruation prevents a follicle from preparing an egg for release. The normal cycling of follicle stimulating hormone (FSH) and lutenizing hormone (LH) are blocked, preventing ovulation. In addition, the pill has backup mechanisms in case ovulation does occur. Cervical mucus also thickens in response to progestogen and provides a barrier to sperm entry into the uterus. Progestogen creates a reproductive environment that discourages conception—in addition to the heavy cervical mucus that prevents sperm entry, it sets up hormonal barriers to fertilization and implantation. If an egg is released during pill use and fertilized, the pill could be viewed as a drug that aborts the conceptus; if abortion is made illegal, some people contend that the combination pill would be unlawful.

The contraceptive *minipill* contains a small amount of the hormone progestogen. It is less effective than the combination pill and must be taken daily. A backup contraceptive (such as one of the barrier methods) is recommended during its first cycle of use. Most of our discussion will focus on the more widely used combination pill.

Triphasic combination pills contain estrogen and levels of progestogen that vary across different parts of the cycle. The variation in progestogen level allows the risk of related side effects to be lower than for regular combination pills. Triphasic pills have been used in Europe since the 1970s, and U.S. women first used them in the 1980s. Neither regular combination pills nor triphasic combination pills are taken during the fourth week of the cycle.

How to Use the Pill.   In summary, starting on the fifth day of the menstrual cycle, contraceptive combination pills are taken for twenty-one consecutive days and then discontinued for the next seven days so that the uterine lining can be discharged through menstrual bleeding. If a user misses one pill, she should take two pills the next day. If a user for some reason misses taking more than two pills during a cycle, she or her partner should use a barrier contraceptive to be safe. Birth control pills, particularly the minipill, should be taken at the same time daily to maintain a constant level in the woman's bloodstream and to help her remember to take it (Hatcher et al., 1990).

Advantages and Disadvantages of the Oral Contraceptive.   Because of its potency, the pill is available by prescription only. If a user has minor, negative side effects such as irregular bleeding while taking one brand of pill, the physician may recommend she switch to another of the more than twenty brands. Some side effects, such as a slight increase in blood pressure, normally occur during pill use.

The major side effects of oral contraceptives are described in leaflets distributed with each packet of pills. Serious problems caused by birth control pills include blood clotting in lungs or legs, which may be associated with pain in the chest or leg, respectively; disease of the gallbladder or liver, with severe abdominal pain as a symptom; and stroke or high blood pressure, which may be signaled by headaches or blurrred vision. For some groups of users, especially smokers (see Figure 5-8) or women over the age of forty, taking the pill increases the risk of heart disease, internal blood clots, and death. Women not in

FIGURE 5-8   *SMOKING AND THE PILL DON'T MIX*   "Half of all deaths associated with pill use would be avoided if women on the pill would not smoke."

these categories have no significant risk from using oral contraceptives. The pill contributes to circulatory disorders, which cause death at a rate four times more often in users than nonusers; one in 27,000 women dies annually from this cause.

Using a contraceptive pill creates a hormonal condition similar to that of early pregnancy. The woman's body undergoes adjustments in adapting to the pill, which can result in weight gain, nausea, and water retention. There is a slight, long-term effect on fertility related to the pill. After stopping the pill, women find that pregnancy is delayed by six to eight months compared to those who have not been using the pill (Nelson, 1982), although their pregnancies are normal in development and duration.

Users of hormonal contraception may be surprised to find that other drugs interfere with the contraceptive usefulness of the combination pills. For example, some antihistamines, antibiotics, and mood-altering drugs have this effect. Appendix A at the end of this book lists some of these drugs plus a list of medications whose effectiveness is reduced by the contraceptive pill. Before using a prescription drug, a woman taking the pill should ask her doctor to check a reference manual such as the *Physician's Desk Reference* to determine whether there is any interference with the contraceptive effect. If so, the supplementary use of a barrier method is advised.

Perhaps increased awareness of possible side effects accounts for the 20 percent reduction in the pill's use between 1975 and 1981 in the United States (Scrimshaw, 1981). The list of the pill's advantages and disadvantages is long. For every noncontraceptive benefit such as increased menstrual regularity and lighter bleeding for many (but not all) users, there is a disadvantage such as reduced resistance to break-through bleeding for some users or vaginal infections caused by chemical changes in vaginal lining. Compared to nonusers, those using the birth control pill develop more precancerous cervical conditions but less ovarian and endometrial cancer (Schlesselman et al., 1988). Whether or not the pill increases the odds of developing breast cancer remains unclear because existing data are not conclusive (Toufexis, 1989).

Other advantages of pill use are a reduction in abdominal pain during ovulation and menstruation, when the amount and duration of flow can be less-

ened; fewer symptoms of premenstrual tension; a reduction in benign breast disease; a lowered incidence of rheumatoid arthritis; and a reduction in endometriosis, ovarian cysts, and iron-deficiency anemia (Duchin et al., 1989). Also on the positive side of pill use are its convenience and lack of messiness, compared to most barrier methods. The cost of the prescription could be a problem for some users.

Effectiveness of the Pill. The combination pill's 97 to 98 percent actual effectiveness rate is almost perfect, and its theoretical effectiveness rate of 99.5 percent is even better. The minipill's effectiveness rate is 98 to 99 percent in theory, and 90 to 95 percent when actual use and failure to use are taken into account.

■ Sterilization: The Ultimate Birth Control

Sterilization, a surgical procedure that prevents impregnation, is viewed as the most effective method of contraception. Though in males it sometimes can be reversed (Willscher, 1980), it is more often permanent, so it tends to be chosen only by those who wish never to have children or by those who do not want additional ones. The popularity of sterilization has grown in the United States since 1970—previously only 11 to 14 percent of married persons chose sterilization; by 1982, 41 percent relied on it (Bachrach, 1984). Worldwide, sterilization is the most popular method of birth control, with twice as many couples choosing sterilization rather than the pill (Johnson, 1983).

Obviously, every prospective patient should be fully informed as to the implications of this surgery. About one in ten sterilized men and women later regrets having had the procedure (Philliber and Philliber, 1985).

Male Sterilization: How Vasectomy Is Done. For male sterilization, the operation, a **vasectomy**, is performed in about thirty minutes—64 percent of them in a physician's office (Orr et al., 1985). There is considerable pain involved, beginning with the insertion of the hypodermic needle in the scrotum to inject Novocain and ending with post-operative discomfort when the injection wears off (Hoose, 1990). Small incisions in the upper part of the scrotum are made. Each vas deferens (see Figure 5–9) is located, tied,

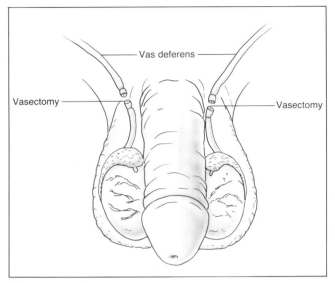

FIGURE 5-9 *VASECTOMY: A MINOR SURGICAL PROCEDURE*
The vasectomy of males involves the severing and tying of the vas deferens.
Source: *Medical Aspects of Human Sexuality,* Volume 13, No. 6, p. 91.

and cut through. The cut ends are then clipped, tied, or burned off (cauterized) to prevent rejoining. The patient is advised to avoid strenuous activity for a couple of days to protect the stitches and to abstain from intercourse for a week to allow for complete healing. Semen analysis should confirm the absence of all sperm in about six weeks, and the man is instructed to use other contraceptive methods for two or three months after surgery to be completely safe (Blaivas, 1981). It is rare, though possible, for the vas deferens spontaneously to rejoin, requiring an additional vasectomy.

Reversal of vasectomy can be attempted by reconnecting the ends of the vas deferens in a microsurgical procedure called *vasovasotomy.* It results in the production of viable sperm in 29 to 85 percent of attempts (Hatcher et al., 1990), although its success rate increases the sooner it is attempted after the original vasectomy. Some experimentation is being done with the insertion of blocking agents into the vas deferens that prevent the passage of sperm. These blocking agents dissolve slowly, and would be reapplied at intervals, providing temporary sterilization.

Advantages and Disadvantages of Vasectomy. Although sterilized male monkeys have been found to be more likely than nonsterilized male monkeys to

develop blocked arteries on a fatty diet (Alexander and Clarkson, 1978), this effect does not seem to occur among humans (Linnet et al., 1982; Pettiti, 1982). Male sterilization, in fact, most often has no physical side effects, although in rare cases the epididymis or testicle becomes inflamed or the area around the surgical stitches becomes infected. Other possible complications of surgery include blood clots at the site which can enter the man's bloodstream and threaten his life. Altogether, however, vasectomy is considered a low-risk procedure.

Following a vasectomy, the man continues to produce sperm normally, but they are absorbed by the body instead of becoming part of the ejaculate (Ansong and Smith, 1982). Despite the absence of sperm, the volume of semen ejaculated is not noticeably reduced (Brosman, 1982). Vasectomy has no physical effect on erection, ejaculation, or sex drive (Glenn, 1980). There *can be* psychological effects, however. Masculine identity often is associated with the ability to reproduce, and after the operation a man can experience anxiety and self-doubt. Unrealistic fears of impotence can become self-fulfilling prophecies, especially if men confuse sterilization with castration (the removal of the testicles).

Because of such effects, men tend to require more social support for undergoing sterilization than is true for women (Clark et al., 1979). When men are uninformed about the effects of vasectomy, they frequently rely on other males to tell them such things as whether intercourse and ejaculation are still possible (Mumford, 1983).

The failure rate of vasectomy is less than 1 percent, and it has not been shown to have long-term side effects. The temporary swelling or bruising in the lower abdomen subsides a few days after surgery.

Female Sterilization. Female sterilization involves the severing of the oviducts to prevent the mature egg and sperm from making contact. This type of **tubal ligation,** called **laparotomy,** is a more complex and risky procedure than vasectomy is for men—it requires abdominal incisions under general anesthesia; 93 percent are performed in a hospital (Orr et al., 1985). Few women experience post-operative complications (Johnson, 1982), but there is a longer recovery time after this operation than after a vasectomy. Nevertheless, more women than men undergo sterilization, possibly because women are relatively less threatened by "loss of femininity" and more concerned about having additional offspring whereas men fear "loss of masculinity" but not their mate's pregnancy (Philliber and Philliber, 1985).

How Female Sterilization Is Done. In laparotomy, illustrated in Figure 5-10, small sections of each of the oviducts are removed and the ends tied; colloquially the procedure is known as "tying the tubes." During surgery a small amount of gaseous carbon dioxide is pumped through a long, thin needle into the women's abdomen through a small incision just below her navel. The gas inflates the abdomen to make the surgery easier. The ends of the oviducts are cut and cauterized rather than tied. Afterward, the carbon dioxide gas is released and a small bandage is applied to the incision, giving tubal ligation another name, "the Band-Aid operation."

Some surgeons use an endoscope, a cigar-size tube with a light on the tip in order to illuminate the abdomen; it is inserted through a small abdominal incision. This procedure, called **laparoscopy**, results in more complications and more contraceptive failures than the ordinary laparotomy (McCann and Cole, 1980; Mumford et al., 1980). When the surgeon enters the abdomen through an incision in the vagina, the procedure is called a *culpotomy* or (if a lighted endoscope is used) a *culdoscopy*.

Advantages and Disadvantages of Female Sterilization. None of these methods of sterilization cause a change in the menstrual cycle (Cole et al., 1984) or in sexual activity level. Only removal of the ovaries (see Chapter 16 for a discussion of oophorectomy) affects the menstrual cycle, in that it ceases. One apparent side effect for women who are sterilized before the age of 30 is an increased risk of needing a hysterectomy later in their lives (Cohen, 1987).

Surgical sterilization of women is effective nearly 100 percent of the time. In the future, reversible sterilization may be accomplished through the injection of chemicals into the oviducts (Klitsch, 1982). Surgical reversal of female sterilization is sometimes successful depending, for example, on precisely how the previous procedure severed and sealed the ends of the oviducts. Reversal of tubal ligation has made it possible for conception to occur in one-fourth of women seeking to become fertile after sterilization.

Women who choose sterilization usually express certainty about wanting to end their potential for childbearing (Nickerson and McClelland, 1987). Those who have no offspring are likely to express

FIGURE 5-10 *FEMALE STERILIZATION* The procedure of laparotomy consists of severing the oviducts on each side of the abdomen, and then cauterizing the ends to close them. As a result, ova and sperm are unable to unite.

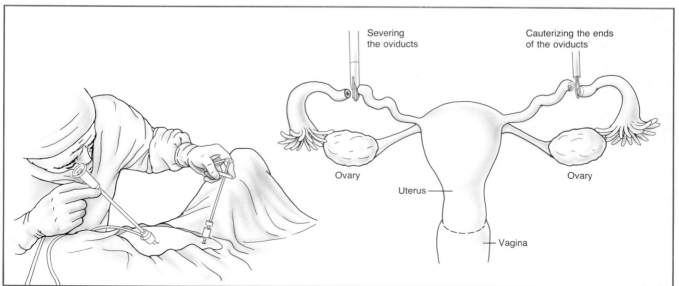

negative, nontraditional attitudes about the prospect of having a husband and family. Women interviewed six months after the surgery report no regrets about the decision. Instead, they say that they experience greater sexual pleasure and increased confidence about being able to control their own lives (Philliber and Philliber, 1985). For women who are sure that they do not want children in the future, sterilization appears to have primarily positive effects on their lives.

Nevertheless, one-fourth of women who have had sterilization express a desire for a child a few years later (Mosher, 1985). Women who had been sterilized before age twenty-five were especially likely to be dissatisfied with their premature decision to end their ability to conceive.

The special section, *Hightlighting Research*, on pages 122 to 123, discusses recent technological developments that are yielding new contraceptives.

Highlighting Research

NEW AND FUTURE CONTRACEPTIVES

Any new contraceptive is costly and time-consuming to develop and test. Annual expenditures on the development of better contraceptives worldwide only equals what is spent on military supplies every twenty minutes (Potts and Wheeler, 1981), so innovative methods are slow to appear. The goal is a perfect contraceptive—highly effective, reversible, completely safe, easy to use, and free from all side effects. Although current methods are reasonably suitable for those residing in developed countries, they are frequently inadequate in societies with high rates of illiteracy and poor medical services. Despite scarce resources, a very real need exists for a simple method such as a long-acting, injectable hormone or skin implant (Crabbe et al., 1980).

There is also an increasing demand for more variety in male contraceptives, which are now limited to condoms, withdrawal, and vasectomies,—from women who are reluctant or unable to use current female contraceptives, from men who are sympathetic to the plight of women, and from men who wish to take contraceptive responsibility themselves. At present, research is underway to improve the contraceptive effects of chemicals on male sexuality and health before they are released for general use.

Four chemicals may provide solutions to the long-awaited male contraceptive:

1. One substance, gossypol, is a compound derived from cottonseed oil. In the People's Republic of China, tests on its effect in reducing sperm production began in 1972 (Benditt, 1980), and a great many Chinese men use it (Maugh, 1981b). A serious difficulty, discovered in research with animals, is that this product can cause cancer and birth defects (Ames, 1983). There is also evidence that it causes a drastic reduction in potassium levels and can cause irreversible sterility (Prendergast, 1990).

2. The male hormone testosterone also can reduce sperm production when taken in higher amounts than the body normally produces. A synthetic version, *testosterone enanthate*, is injected in the buttocks each week (Prendergast, 1990). A variation of this procedure involves a testosterone enanthate shot every four weeks plus a daily pill containing the hormone *danazol*; this combination is found to be effective and has no negative effects on sexual functioning (Wiest and Webster, 1988).

3. A third possibility is a combination pill composed of synthetic testosterone and progesterone. It temporarily reduces sperm production, but it also tends to cause acne (Paulsen, 1981), weight gain, and breast enlargement (Benditt,

1980). The latter two side effects are similar to those experienced by women taking the pill.

4. An artificial form of luteinizing hormone-releasing hormone (see Chapter 4) stops sperm production just as it stops ovulation (Atkinson et al., 1980). Still in the testing stage, this chemical may be administered as a pill or a nasal spray, or implanted under the skin.

The search is also underway for a female chemical contraceptive that inhibits fertility for long periods with only one dose. Among the recent developments:

1. Antiprogestin, a synthetic inhibitor of progesterone, is taken once a month in pill form. First produced in the early 1980s, it is still undergoing extensive testing (Spitz and Bardin, 1985).

2. Depo-Provera, a synthetic progesterone, is injected once every three months. It suppresses ovulation by blocking maturation of the follicle. Among the suspected side effects of this drug is cancer (Sun, 1984). It is currently used in several countries, but not in the United States (National Research Council Committee on Contraceptive Developments, 1990).

3. NORPLANT consists of six rubber capsules containing progestin implanted under the skin of a woman's arm. The

contraceptive effect begins within twenty-four hours, lasts for five years, and, when the capsules are removed, there is an immediate return to fertility. Tests indicate that NORPLANT's effectiveness in preventing pregnancy is the highest of any contraceptive ever marketed (Hilts, 1990). Though there are some minor side effects, such as abnormal menstrual flow during the first year of use, women report more satisfaction with it than with other chemical methods or with barrier methods (Sivin et al., 1983). The United States Food and Drug Administration approved its use in December, 1990. It is generally believed that this approach may soon be used widely.

4. Noristerat is an injectable steroid that lasts two months. With a 98 percent effectiveness rate, it has been used by 800,000 women in countries other than the United States (National Research Council Committee on Contraceptive Developments, 1990).

5. China and France have approved the use of a chemical contraceptive with the trade name Mifegyne. It is an antiprogesterone called RU 486 and is taken in pill form up to three weeks after a missed menstrual period. It starts the menstrual flow and prevents a fertilized egg from implanting or remaining implanted in the uterine wall. The woman takes three of these pills, usually followed by an injection of the hormone prostaglandin to stimulate uterine contractions. Ninety percent of women treated with RU 486 have a spontaneous abortion, with bleeding comparable to heavy menstrual flow. The availability of this contraceptive in the United States is controversial, because groups opposing abortion also oppose using this substance. The National Right to Life Committee, for example, wants to prevent its sale because it can induce an early abortion (Murphy, 1986). As of 1990 the French government reimburses clinics and compensates for their loss of income for using the drug instead of a surgical abortion, at a rate which amounts to 80 percent of the usual cost ($247) (Riding, 1990). RU 486 faces years of testing by the Food and Drug Administration before it could be approved in the United States. Anti-abortion activists threaten to boycott any pharmaceutical company that even applies for government approval (Abortion, ..., 1988).

Work is also in progress on new mechanical devices (Benditt, 1980). For example, progestin can be released from a vaginal ring or a cylinder protruding from the cervix into the uterus, serving to thicken cervical mucus and thus preventing sperm entry. Another possibility is to vaccinate a woman against her partner's sperm.

As you may have concluded, no perfect contraceptive now exists or is even on the horizon. Women and men will continue to choose among a variety of methods, weighing their relative advantages and disadvantages.

Aborting the Fetus

Abortion is not a means of contraception, but is a completely effective way to terminate an existing pregnancy. Abortions may be spontaneous or induced. In a **spontaneous abortion**, the pregnancy is ended by a miscarriage. In an **induced abortion**, the pregnancy is terminated by medical or surgical means, and the procedure is relatively risk-free for the woman (Thompson, 1989).

The typical woman who seeks an induced abortion is white, fifteen to twenty-four years old, single, childless, lives in an urban area, and qualifies for welfare services (Henshaw et al., 1985). Women who seek abortions have a record of using contraception ineffectively in the past (Westoff et al., 1981).

■ Abortion Activism: "Pro-Choice" versus "Pro-Life"

Strong emotions are characteristic of any discussion of a woman's right to have an abortion. On the anti-abortion (or right-to-life) side there is concern about protecting the rights of the unborn fetus (Donovan, 1983). As a political force, the anti-abortion movement has attempted to convince others that abortion should be illegal. The argument is that the right of the pregnant woman to make decisions about her own body should be given less weight than the right of the unborn child to exist (Tyre, 1989; Williams, 1979).

Advocates of the pro-choice movement, in contrast, want women to be able to exercise their freedom of choice to control their own bodies and futures. Public opinion polls indicate that about 88 percent of Americans favor abortion rights in some form while about 10 percent oppose abortion under all circumstances (Greenhouse, 1988). Surveys indicate that the majority of Americans believe that abortion should be an available option when the mother's health is endangered, a birth defect exists, or if the pregnancy is the result of rape or incest (Majority of Americans, 1989). Figure 5-11 suggests the strength

FIGURE 5-11 *ABORTION ACTIVISTS: RIGHT TO LIFE OR RIGHT TO CHOOSE?*   Opposing views on the right of women to control their bodies versus the right of the unborn to live clearly elicit strong emotions on each side. These issues are of great importance, and they cannot be resolved scientifically. Each individual and each society must decide on the basis of subjective values rather than objective evidence.

of the feelings generated by disagreements about abortion.

These opposing arguments clearly cannot be settled on the basis of scientific evidence. Less obviously, there is also no way that science can determine "when life begins" or "when the developing fetus becomes a human being"—such questions are a matter of how you define "life" and "human being." What each individual (and eventually our society) decides is necessarily based on values rather than on empirical evidence (Steinfels, 1990).

Illegal abortions were common in the United States and investigations as early as 1878 indicated that one-third of all pregnancies were terminated in this way; Kinsey reported a comparable figure (28 percent) in 1958 (The history of. . . , 1989). Abortion was legalized by the United States government in 1973 when the U.S. Supreme Court ruled in *Roe vs. Wade* that state anti-abortion laws may interfere with an individual's freedom of self-expression as outlined in the First Amendment of the Constitution. Abortion was already legal in many states before this decision, but the effect of nationwide legalized abortion on the birth rate among unmarried women has been dramatic. One result is that the large number of induced abortions has created a severe shortage of healthy, white infants available for adoption (McGee, 1982). On the other hand, fewer women are dying from illegal abortions. Studies of both high school and college women indicate that about 25 percent report having had an abortion (Costa et al., 1987).

Despite its legality, poor women and adolescents still find it difficult to obtain an abortion because services are limited. In 1977, for example, half a million such women who wanted abortions could not get them (Seims, 1980). One reason is that state laws often restrict the timing or setting for the operation, making it less likely that poor women could be accommodated in an approved clinic or that adolescents would recognize the signs of pregnancy and then act on the information quickly enough to terminate pregnancy in the first trimester. For those under 18 years of age, almost half of the states in the United States require either that parents give their consent for an abortion or be notified of their daughter's plan (Bishop, 1987). In states with restrictions, the rate of abortions is relatively low (Richards, 1978).

Medical personnel who perform abortions also influence the availability of the procedure indirectly because of their attitudes about it. Although half of all private physicians deliver babies, only one in ten performs abortions (Orr and Forrest, 1985). In hospitals where physicians disapprove of the procedure, the frequency of abortions is low (Nathanson and Becker, 1980). Nurses who express moral disapproval of abortion evaluate abortion patients more negatively compared to their evaluations of other patients, and even more negatively for those who are married than for single patients (Fischer, 1979). Such findings suggest that negative responses from physicians and nurses may operate against terminating a pregnancy, even when abortion is legal.

In 1989 the controversy about abortion returned to the political arena in full force, when the U.S. Supreme Court narrowed the previous decision in *Roe v. Wade*. It ruled that state governments could restrict women's right to abortion and could forbid the use of public funds to pay for abortions. Advocates on both sides of the issue predict heated political battles before a final outcome is reached. If medical abortions should become illegal again, some feminists propose that women learn how to perform safe abortions on one another (Toufexis, 1989)

■ **Methods Of Abortion**

When and where abortions are illegal, women tend to abort themselves in extremely dangerous ways, sometimes resulting in excessive bleeding or fatal infections. For example, they may force a coat hanger into the uterus, deliberately and repeatedly fall down, or seek unlicensed, untrained abortionists. With legalization and the development of improved medical procedures, abortion is a relatively safe procedure for the patient and unlikely to lead to future problems in subsequent pregnancies (Tietze, 1984).

Vacuum Aspiration. While the embryo is still quite small during the first trimester of pregnancy, the most common method of abortion is **vacuum aspiration**, or suction. The cervix is widened, or dilated, and suction is applied to remove the contents of the uterus (Hogue et al., 1983). This method usually takes about ten to fifteen minutes and can be performed in a hospital's outpatient surgical unit, using local anesthesia. Figure 5-12 illustrates the vacuum aspiration method.

Drug-Induced Abortion.   The sooner after conception that an unwanted pregnancy is terminated, the fewer the possible complications. *Abortifacients* are drugs used to induce abortion, typically during the first trimester. For example, diethylstilbestrol (DES) is commonly used in cases of rape and incest. In such emergency situations large doses of the drug are given within three days following intercourse; uterine contractions are stimulated, thus preventing implantation. As a "morning-after" method of abortion, a major drawback of DES is the risk of birth defects and maternal breast cancer if the fetus fails to abort (Johnson, 1984).

Other abortifacients such as the hormone prostaglandin induce uterine contractions and bleeding, with the embryo or fetus usually expelled within twenty-four hours. Prostaglandin works with few side effects during the first two months of pregnancy, although it also can be used in the second trimester with close medical supervision. Artificial versions of this hormone, given in the form of vaginal suppositories or by injection, have a 90 percent effectiveness rate in evacuating the embryo from the uterus (Atkinson et al, 1980).

Dilation and Curettage.   One method of induced abortion used in the first trimester, **dilation and curettage** (or *D and C*), involves dilating the cervix and scraping out the uterine contents with a spoon-shaped surgical instrument. Repeated dilation of the cervix during two or more abortions can contribute to difficulties in future pregnancies if the woman decides to have a child (Levin et al., 1980). This procedure is more commonly used to diagnose or correct medical problems such as endometriosis than for abortion.

Dilation and Evacuation.   During the second trimester, the fetus grows rapidly and develops bones, so extraction becomes more difficult. *Dilation and evacuation* (or *D and E*) usually is done during the fourth and fifth months of pregnancy. After the cervix is dilated, a curette is used to remove the fetus. At this point the bodily parts of the fetus have become too large to pass through the small cervical opening, so segments—including the skull—must be separated and crushed. Such chilling terms as *utero decapitation* and *fetal pulverization* are used to describe these procedures. The fetal parts are then removed carefully to avoid tearing the cervix. If the uterus is not completely emptied or if the uterus or cervix is torn, an infection can result (Benditt, 1979).

Instillation.   Abortion during the fifth and sixth months of pregnancy is usually by *instillation* of a substance such as a saline solution into the uterus to kill the fetus and to cause contractions to start. The woman's body then expels the fetus in the next couple of days just as if the woman were having a spontaneous abortion. Another method is to inject a hormone such as prostaglandin into the woman's bloodstream, which produces contractions similar to labor. In a few instances the fetus survives these procedures, presenting a moral and legal problem (Donovan, 1984). Fewer than 1 percent of abortions in the United States occur after twenty weeks of pregnancy (Rhoden, 1985).

Compared to the techniques used early in pregnancy, D and E as well as instillation are physically and emotionally more difficult for the woman, who by this time has probably felt fetal movements. Psy-

FIGURE 5-12 *VACUUM ASPIRATION ABORTION DURING THE FIRST TRIMESTER*   Induced abortions, such as the vacuum aspiration method shown here, result in fewer complications if conducted during the first trimester of pregnancy than abortions conducted later in the pregnancy.

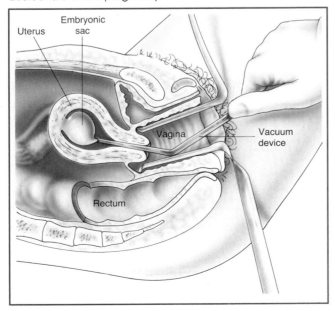

chologically, such abortions are more likely to be perceived as losing one's child. The medical risks of instillation (such as heavy bleeding) are as high as those of childbirth (Grimes, 1984).

■ Psychological Effects of Having an Abortion

Despite much speculation to the contrary, studies indicate that few women who have chosen to have abortions express regrets, and their attitudes about the experience are relatively positive (Rosen and von Knorring, 1989). Counseling can help relieve the temporary feelings of loss or guilt that may result (Lemkau, 1988). Compared to women who have completed unwanted pregnancies, those who chose to terminate them are better adjusted and happier about their decision (Nadelson, 1978). It should be noted that women who are most conflicted about undergoing an abortion tend to avoid being interviewed after surgery (Adler, 1976), so their postabortion reactions are not included in the studies. Such women are likely to be younger and more religious and to have had abortions in the second trimester. Because of these sampling problems, the average emotional effects of abortion are possibly more negative than suggested by current investigations.

Although very little is known about the reactions of men to their partner's abortion, they also may experience psychological aftereffects such as anger and guilt (Shotak et al., 1984). In a survey of several hundred college students about their opinions of the man's role in abortion decisions, the intimacy of the couple's relationship was perceived as a crucial variable. In more intimate relationships lasting six months or longer, they indicated that the woman should take into account his opinion about the issue but the final decision about whether to obtain the abortion should be hers (Rosenwasser et al., 1987). In brief, relatively casual relationships, the woman was not necessarily expected to consider her partner's wishes.

Both pro-life and pro-choice advocates agree that the best solution to the problems of unwanted pregnancy is to prevent the need for abortion by changing either sexual or contraceptive habits. Sexual behavior is clearly difficult to change, but there *are* ways to increase the use of contraception. For example, when women who had undergone abortions were educated about effective contraceptive techniques and the health dangers of abortion, 86 pecent switched to a better method of contraception than they had used previously (Bulut, 1984).

Contraceptive Attitudes and Behavior

Contraception involves more than technology; its use also depends on what people know, how they respond emotionally, and how they actually behave. The statistics on unwanted and unplanned pregnancies are alarming.

Of the babies born each year in the United States, over 13 percent are born to young women in their teens, including .3 percent under age 15 (National Center for Health Statistics, 1987). An average of 3,231 women have abortions each day. Every twenty-four hours, 2,740 adolescent pregnancies begin. Our country spends over $16 billion yearly on teenage mothers and their offspring in the form of welfare payments and other benefits (Teen childbearing. . . , 1986). Such reproductive and contraceptive statistics suggest that a great many maladaptive decisions are being made, creating serious problems for the individuals involved and for society. The emotions, thoughts, and experiences of individuals and couples are clearly as important as the statistical data (Kelley, 1983).

■ Unwanted Adolescent Pregnancy

Much of the public concern and much of the behavioral research has centered on the "adolescent pregnancy epidemic." Though the teenage pregnancy rate has dropped in the United States since the 1970s, it is still higher than in any other industrialized nation (Teen-age pregnancy. . . , 1987).

The Problem of Premature Pregnancy. Before effective contraception became widely available in the 1960s, most births were unintended, unplanned, and seemingly unwanted (Westoff, 1976). Couples had few options beyond that of abstinence. In the present post-contraception era, only about one in ten children born to married couples are reported to be unwanted when conceived (Forrest, 1987).

Despite this positive description of marital parenthood, unwanted pregnancies among adolescents represent a serious social problem. The average age for first intercourse has decreased, and younger and younger individuals are facing this problem. For example, one in five 15-year-olds is now sexually experienced (Moore et al., 1989).

Most sexually active adolescents do not use effective contraception, and they continue to avoid birth control for the first year or more of sexual activity. As a result, it is not surprising that about 10 percent of all teenage females conceive every year. The number of adolescent pregnancies in the United States is about 1,100,000 each year. The vast majority of these pregnancies are unplanned and unwanted. Two-thirds of first babies born to teenagers are conceived outside of marriage (O'Connell and Rogers, 1984), and these births represent problems for the parents, the infants, and all of us.

The Effects of Unwanted Adolescent Pregnancy. Many teenage parents are married when their child is born. For example, in 1975, four out of ten live births were to teenage mothers with teenage husbands. Why should adolescent married couples be considered a problem? As Figure 5-13 suggests, even when they marry, adolescents have more problems than older parents. Early parenthood means greater health risks for both mothers and their babies. Babies born to these mothers also have a greater frequency of low birth weight, resulting in a higher incidence of infant death or mental retardation (Scales and Gordon, 1979). The incidence of spontaneous abortion and of complications of pregnancy such as **toxemia** is higher in adolescence than among women in their twenties (see Chapter 4). Because of poverty or unsupportive families, many adolescent mothers-to-be fail to seek medical advice or examinations until the sixth month of pregnancy. By then, it is often too late to correct the damage caused by malnutrition, drug abuse, or other health hazards. Infants born to adolescent mothers have a death rate almost twice that of infants born to women in their twenties.

The typical teenage marriage is vulnerable on other fronts besides the health of mother and child. Compared to mothers over age twenty, married adolescent mothers are more likely to separate from their husbands. The divorce rate (60 percent within five years) for teenage couples is much higher than for older couples (20 percent) (Scales and Gordon, 1979). Young wives with children also have difficulty

FIGURE 5-13 *UNWANTED ADOLESCENT PREGNANCY: A SERIOUS PROBLEM FOR THE INDIVIDUAL AND FOR SOCIETY* Adolescent pregnancy almost always has negative consequences on the social, educational, and economic aspects of young women's lives—even when the couple decides to marry and have the baby.

continuing their education (McCarthy and Radish, 1982). They drop out of school twice as often as young, unmarried women, thus adding the problem of inadequate education to the other problems of parenthood and marriage. Arranging a quick wedding is clearly not a perfect solution to the problem of an unwanted teenage pregnancy (Marsiglio, 1987).

Married or unmarried, young mothers and their children face more problems than either older mothers or young, childless women. Child abuse rates among young mothers are high, whereas their educational level remains low. The welfare system becomes the main salvation for many. Young mothers are also likely to have additional unwanted children, and these offspring frequently model their parents' behavior and become teenage parents themselves. In addition to these personal costs, the financial cost of unwanted, premature pregnancies is high—teen mothers often become dependent on government support. In the United States, taxpayers spend over $8,000 yearly for each young mother and her child (Ellwood and Bane, 1985).

It is not easy for an adolescent to obtain and pay for an abortion. In some states, parental consent is required (Roemer, 1985). Those who do have an abortion are likely to go through at least one additional unwanted pregnancy and abortion.

Possible Solutions to the Problem. This dismal overall picture leads to the question, "Why do teenagers take such chances, playing roulette with conception?" One reason is inadequate information about the consequences of intercourse (Gerrard, 1987; Reis and Herz, 1989). For example, many teenagers may believe a myth such as "You can't get pregnant if you do it standing up" and rely on that position as the only "contraceptive protection." Teenagers are also generally uninformed about the relationship between intercourse frequency and the chances of conception (Kelley, 1982b). Each act of intercourse involves the risk of pregnancy, of course, but risk rises as frequency rises. Weekly intercourse without effective contraception means that about one couple out of six will conceive within a year (Nakashima, 1980). If unprotected intercourse occurs twice weekly, 51 percent will experience pregnancy, while four times weekly raises the risk to 83 percent. Young people also have the false belief that they are uniquely invulnerable to accidents, diseases, and other misfortunes. With respect to pregnancy, a sexually active college woman believes that she is less likely to become pregnant than other students, other women her age, or women in general (Burger and Burns, 1988).

Another reason for the problem of teenage pregnancy may be our society's mixed messages about sex (Haddad, 1986):

> *U.S. teenagers . . . have inherited the worst of all possible worlds . . . Movies, music, radio, and TV tell them that sex is romantic, exciting, titillating . . . Yet, at the same time, young people get the message that good girls should say no [Jones et al., 1985].*

Further studies show that the typical TV viewer receives 14,000 sexual messages each year. Only 165 of these refer to such unromantic concepts as birth control, abortion, disease, or sex education (Nolan, 1988).

Advertisements for birth control have portrayed its use in a variety of different themes, showing how the media use mixed messages to sell a product. Condoms have been shown as making sex more fun, romantic, or adventuresome. Ads for female contraceptives such as spermicidal foam or the sponge often appeal to the sensible, responsible side of thoughts about sex, discussing their lack of side effects and convenience.

How can adolescents be encouraged to avoid unwanted pregnancy? Several solutions have been proposed over the past few years: abstinence, nonprocreative sexual acts such as fellatio and cunnilingus or heterosexual anal intercourse, and contraception. Any such message can be effective only if there is improved communication about sexuality and conception. Parents would seem to be the obvious first choice for information, but female adolescents who discuss sex and contraception with their mothers are no more apt to use contraceptives than those who do not (Furstenberg et al., 1984). In Western European countries, acceptable sex education and easily available contraception *have* resulted in a decline in adolescent pregnancy rates. In contrast, American television networks seem to push the message that sex is fun while contraception is taboo. They have been extremely reluctant to air contraceptive commercials (Donovan, 1982), although the threat of AIDS (Chapter 15) may be breaking down this barrier (Toufexis, 1987). Such advertising has long been accepted in other countries (Boone et al., 1985).

One innovative, although controversial, strategy has been employed in the attempt to reduce unwanted adolescent pregnancy. Several cities whose high schools have educational programs and contraceptive clinics show a 50 percent decrease in teenage pregnancy rates (Dryfoos, 1985). It seems clear that school-based clinic and educational programs result in decreased sexual activity among the youngest teenagers and a drop in unwanted pregnancies (Eisen et al., 1990; Miller, 1990). Figure 5-14 summarizes some of those findings. In a study of older adolescents attending college, Fisher (1989) found that a massive educational effort decreased the rate of unwanted pregnancies on campus. The technique used rehearsal of the appropriate behaviors, practice in communication with the partner, and training in how to have thoughts, feelings, and fantasies that would promote contraceptive use. Clearly this type of behavior change is a major undertaking (Beck & Davies, 1987).

FIGURE 5-14 *THE POSITIVE EFFECT OF CONTRACEPTIVE HEALTH CLINICS IN HIGH SCHOOLS* The availability of a high school health clinic providing contraceptive information and services was found to lead to lower pregnancy rates. In St. Paul, Minnesota, pregnancies fell from 59 to 26 per 1,000 females after the clinic opened. In West Dallas, Texas, those who did not use the clinic in 1977 had significantly more pregnancies (112 per 1,000) than those who did use it (58 per 1,000).
Source: Based on data from Dryfoos, 1985.

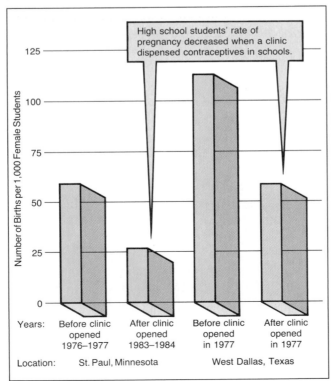

High school students' rate of pregnancy decreased when a clinic dispensed contraceptives in schools.

Number of Births per 1,000 Female Students

| Years: | Before clinic opened 1976–1977 | After clinic opened 1983–1984 | Before clinic opened in 1977 | After clinic opened in 1977 |
| Location: | St. Paul, Minnesota | | West Dallas, Texas | |

A quite different (and so far less successful) emphasis involves redirecting the lives of lower-class mothers in an attempt to increase happiness and productivity. An intensive program to help unwed adolescent mothers obtain job training, education, and group support had only temporary effects (Polit and Kahn, 1985). In the year following one such program, participants were likely to hold a job or remain in school, and to use contraceptives when having intercourse—two years later, however, they were no different from nonparticipants.

■ **Attitudes about Contraception**

An individual's attitude about contraception is based partially on the importance he or she places on the various benefits and disadvantages of using a particular contraceptive. For example, how important is avoiding an unwanted pregnancy compared to avoiding the embarrassment of buying a condom in a drug store? Also, how likely do you think it is that pregnancy will occur and how likely is it that you will be embarrassed by buying a condom? The combination of such positive and negative attitudes and beliefs is called the *expectancy-value* theory of evaluation. The expected outcome of an action and the value placed on that outcome determine the individual's behavior (Cohen et al., 1978).

This theory identifies expectancies as a major factor influencing decisions. Expectancies are most influenced by what one knows, and incorrect information leads to unrealistic expectancies. Education and other informational sources are able to change in expectancies. Decisions are also affected by values, based on a person's emotional responses, which are much more resistant to change (Kalmuss et al., 1987).

The decisions one person makes about sexuality and contraception may be quite different from those of another because each of them differs in her or his expectancies and the values placed on given outcomes. For some adolescent females, premature parenthood is perceived as a major disaster; for others, it is an avenue to marriage, an act of rebellion against parents, an escape from school, evidence of femininity, and the source of added excitement in their life (Reis and Herz, 1989). For some, the risk of pregnancy is frightening enough that intercourse is avoided; for others, the risk adds to their sexual pleasure.

Detailed research from the expectancy-value approach tries to identify precisely how individuals respond to specific contraceptive choices. A study of attitudes about using a male pill illustrates how this is done. College students rated health and safety concerns as the most important consideration in deciding whether to use such a product. A moderate probability of minor side effects was acceptable, but even a small probability of major side effects was considered unacceptable (Jaccard et al., 1981) The second most important consideration was effectiveness. Least important considerations were cost and convenience. Also, the partner not using the product (in this instance, the woman) is less concerned about side effects and more concerned about effectiveness.

■ The Five Steps of Contraceptive Behavior

Success or failure in using contraception is a fairly complex process, involving knowledge, emotions, the situation, and previous experiences. The assumption is generally made that ignorance is a primary reason for the high rate of unwanted pregnancies—insufficient knowledge about the effects of unprotected intercourse and about the use of contraceptives. In fact, most sexually active individuals know these basic facts. Other obstacles to birth control do exist, however, especially for young people.

For example, only 20 percent of colleges and universities include contraception as a regular part of their health-care programs.

Nevertheless, better education and more available contraception are not the only answers to preventing unwanted pregnancies. At Indiana University, where birth control services and educational programs have long been available, sexually active coeds would logically be expected to use effective contraception. In a survey of 150 single females, the majority (61 percent) reported engaging in sexual intercourse, but less than one-third of these young women used contraceptives regularly (Byrne and Fisher, 1983). The remaining two-thirds reported using contraceptives only occasionally or not at all. Later surveys sampling students at several state and private universities revealed a similar pattern of contraceptive use (Kelley et al., 1987; McCormick and Gaeddert, 1989). Intelligence, education, and availability of contraception obviously do not guarantee that sexual intercourse will be accompanied by adequate protection against conception. How might we explain this behavior? The *five steps of contraceptive behavior* describe the essential conditions necessary for successful contraceptive behavior (Byrne, 1983); sexual inhibitions and negative sexual attitudes interfere with each step (Harvey and Scrimshaw, 1988; Strassberg and Mahoney, 1988). Figure 5-15 summarizes these steps.

FIGURE 5-15 *BEHAVIORAL STEPS TOWARD EFFECTIVE CONTRACEPTION* The behaviors necessary to engage in effective contraception can be grouped into the five-step process outlined here.

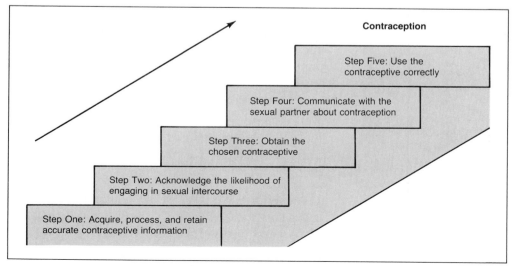

Step One: Acquire, Process, and Retain Accurate Contraceptive Information. Learning about the need for and the specific methods of contraception rarely occurs at the appropriate time for young people. Most of them must seek such information informally at home, in church, and among friends, but parents feel uncomfortable discussing sexual topics with their offspring, schools are criticized for providing explicit sexual information, television avoids contraceptive themes, and peers are frequently misinformed. Consequently, it is not surprising that many adolescents possess inadequate and inaccurate knowledge.

Further, negative emotions interfere with the desire to seek and the ability to learn sexual and contraceptive information, as is discussed in Chapter 8. For this reason, individual differences in sexual attitudes are related to remembering and using the appropriate knowledge (Goldfarb et al., 1988).

Step Two: Acknowledge the Likelihood of Engaging in Sexual Intercourse. Those who engage in premarital intercourse stress spontaneity as a highly desirable quality. Among young people there is a widespread tendency not to plan ahead with respect to sex, especially at the beginning of a relationship. Planning makes it clear that you deliberately intend to participate in a sexual relationship. Many do not want their sex lives determined by a cold, calculating plan; they want to be carried away by love and passion instead of having to consider clinical details. They also do not want to surprise a partner by suddenly producing a contraceptive device, perhaps leading to rejection. A 17-year-old Midwestern young man said:

> *It is easier to read if it is a girl you've been going out with—so then you are likely to bring a condom along, and she probably is not going to be so shocked [Kisker, 1985].*

Some of the facts and figures on contraceptive behavior are consistent with our common experiences about how people behave. For example, sexually inexperienced adolescents are least likely to use contraception when they have intercourse. One investiga-

tion indicated that Canadian college students who engage in intercourse regularly are likely to use contraception more effectively than those having it for the first time or infrequently (Barrett, 1980). Usually, the younger a person is when he or she becomes sexually active, the less likely is contraception to be used. Even those who first become sexually active at ages eighteen to twenty used more effective contraception later in their sexual interactions compared with those who first have intercourse at ages fourteen to sixteen.

Casual sexual involvement is associated with less contraceptive use than is true for a committed relationship (DeLamater and MacCorquodale, 1978; Harvey and Scrimshaw, 1988; Sack et al., 1985). Among single undergraduates involved in an ongoing relationship, 77 percent used condoms or pills while, in contrast, only 58 percent in casual, uncommitted relationships used contraception (Fisher et al., 1979).

Sexual attitudes also play an important role in determining contraceptive use. Male undergraduates with positive attitudes toward sexuality are more accurate in predicting their upcoming sexual activity than those with negative attitudes (Fisher, 1984). None of the positive males had sexual intercourse over a month's period when they didn't expect to, but 17 percent of the males with negative attitudes unexpectedly did so. It is obviously easier to arrange for contraception beforehand if you know what you will do sexually.

Many adolescents fail to plan ahead and consider the long-term consequences of their actions, and unwanted conception is one such consequence. Compared to effective contraceptors using a Planned Parenthood clinic, pregnant teenagers believed that "the good life" would be theirs much sooner. For example, they expected to have a great apartment and a wardrobe of clothes by age thirty-three; those who used contraception expected such things by age thirty-seven and a-half (Mindick et al., 1977). Pregnant females also dismiss the idea of negative future events; they are less likely to expect to be refused credit or to have a divorce than do those using contraception. If you expect only good things to happen in the future, it makes sense not to be concerned about the consequences of unprotected intercourse (Burger and Burns, 1988).

Step Three: Obtain the Chosen Contraceptive. After an individual acknowledges the need for birth control, he or she must do something to obtain the relevant materials. Inertia has a powerful effect on behavior—it is usually easier to do nothing than to act in time to prevent a problem from occurring. According to family planning clinics across the nation, female adolescents usually seek contraception about one year *after* they first become sexually active (Zelnik, 1980). Of those adolescents visiting a birth control clinic for the first time, only 14 percent had previously used *any* contraceptive (Zabin and Clark, 1983). Many adolescents say they avoid using birth control because they fear that their parents will become aware of their sexual activity. Usually, the shock of a late menstrual period convinces young females to seek help. Unfortunately, a great many find themselves having to decide between abortion and childbirth.

A major obstacle to contraceptive use, especially among the young and unmarried, is the sheer embarrassment of revealing one's intentions to be sexually active. Few of us would respond like the sitter in Figure 5-16, who phones her employers to ask about condoms. More commonly, in order to use birth control, a person has to consult a physician, go to a drugstore, or whatever. A study by Fisher et al. (1977) asked college males to purchase condoms in a drugstore near the campus. The money for this purchase was supplied by the experimenters. Sexually negative males disliked the experience a great deal, and they also expressed negative evaluations of the drugstore and of condoms; in addition, they thought that the pharmacist would consider them immoral and immature. Although no research has been reported, the possibility of purchasing condoms by mail or from a vending machine should reduce the anxiety associated with obtaining contraception.

Once the device is purchased, the pills, diaphragm, condoms, and so forth must be kept somewhere for future use. For adolescents, storing such items in a wallet, handbag, or dresser drawer means that a family member or friend can come across them and become aware of their activities or their intentions. Parents may react with dismay and disapproval, and peers may make negative attributions about moral character (Beck and Davies, 1987).

Step Four: Communicate with the Sexual Partner about Contraception. If an individual assumes total responsibility for contraception, he or she would not

"It's the sitter. She wants to know where we keep the condoms!"

FIGURE 5-16 *POTENTIAL EMBARRASSMENT IN COMMUNICATING ABOUT SEX TO ADULTS* A major difficulty in obtaining contraceptives is the negative influence of emotional factors. A young person must face the problem of communicating his or her sexual secrets to an adult, often in a relatively public setting. Clearly, the baby sitter in this cartoon is *not* embarrassed about such a communication.

Source: Reproduced by Special Permission of PLAYBOY Magazine: Copyright © 1977 by PLAYBOY.

FIGURE 5-17 *CAN ROMANCE AND CONTRACEPTION GO TOGETHER* Especially in a new sexual relationship, discussions of contraception are not considered romantic or sexy. There is a fear of "spoiling the mood." As suggested in this cartoon, any introduction of the topic seems intrusive and a little strange. It would probably be helpful if movie and television presentations of sexual relationships provided a model for such interactions. If they did, we could learn to associate romance with contraception, thus making it easier to use contraception effectively.
Source: Reproduced by Special Permission of PLAYBOY Magazine: Copyright © 1989 by PLAYBOY.

need to communicate with a partner about the topic. If, however, one person incorrectly assumes that his or her partner is taking responsibility, communication becomes vital.

Conversations about contraception in the context of sexual excitement and burning romance are usually considered inappropriate and counterproductive. There seem to be few socially acceptable ways to introduce the topic (see Figure 5-17). Not only do sexually active individuals tend to avoid talking about birth control, they don't even talk about sex itself. Only later in a relationship are partners inclined to talk about sexual matters, including contraception (Burger and Inderbitzen, 1985).

Step Five: Use the Contraceptive Correctly. If an individual successfully completes the preceding four steps, he or she must now actually use the contraceptive and use it correctly. This is the obvious, but nevertheless *crucial*, final step in avoiding unwanted pregnancy. As discussed in this chapter, such use involves a considerable amount of knowledge plus the self-discipline to use it consistently. Also, to use contraception correctly, the person needs to overcome

his or her possible anxiety and awkwardness about dealing with a barrier method in the presence of a partner.

Also, males and females react somewhat differently to the use of contraception. In one experiment, college students viewed an explicit film depicting intercourse. Some subjects were told that the male and female were married, and some that they were single; some were told the female was taking the pill, and others that no contraception was used (Jazwinski and Byrne, 1978). Males enjoyed the film most when the actors were described as single and using contraception; they believed, however, that the couple cared more for one another if they were not using contraception. Females, in contrast, interpreted contraception as an indication of greater caring. It appeared that males interpreted the risk-taking as a sign of true love, while females, who are vulnerable to pregnancy, interpret protection as a sign of true love.

The special section, *Increasing Enjoyment*, on pages 135 to 136, explains more about the process of selecting and successfully using a particular method of contraception.

Increasing Enjoyment

Contraceptive Choice

The many details of contraceptive information can be lost in the barrage of facts about the different methods. They vary in advantages, disadvantages, side effects, and effectiveness. We have already explored these aspects of each method, and Table 5-1 summarizes comparisons among them.

In addition, those using one contraceptive rather than another differ in their attitudes and concerns. Some males, for example, may be reluctant to use condoms because of beliefs such as these expressed on Brown's (1984) Attitudes toward Condoms Scale:

"In my opinion, condoms are too much trouble."

"Condoms ruin the sex act."

"Most women don't like their partners to use condoms."

Considering the value of contraception to those who do not wish to become parents during a certain period in their lives, it might be helpful to provide accurate contraceptive information as a regular part of the school curriculum along with driver education, home economics, and typing. One objection to such education is that it is assumed to produce sexually wild, promiscuous young people. As we have pointed out, however, most adolescents are already sexually active when they first seek contraception. In other words, contraceptives do not lead to sex, though sex eventually leads to contraceptive use. Also, having birth control devices does not in-

TABLE 5-1   Comparing Different Approaches to Birth Control

Making decisions about which method of birth control to use is made difficult by the fact that no contraceptive is perfect. The different types vary in their effectiveness and in possible side effects. Each individual (and couple) must weigh the many positive and negative factors of each and make a decision based on what they feel is most important. Sexual enjoyment is not enhanced by ignorance or by the use of a form of contraception that is perceived as unpleasant, uncomfortable, unethical, or unreliable. In the United States, the most used methods of birth control are sterilization (34 percent), the pill (30 percent) the condom (13 percent), the diaphragm (9 percent), IUD (8 percent), and rhythm (4 percent), as reported by women aged 15 to 44 (National Center for Health Statistics, 1987).

METHOD	OVERALL EFFECTIVENESS	SOME SIDE EFFECTS	MAIN STRENGTHS (+) & WEAKNESSES (−)
Douching	Poor (50% failure)	Can encourage infection	+ low cost − unreliable
Withdrawal	Fair (25% failure)	None	+ no cost − unreliable
Rhythm	Poor to Fair (20% to 40% failure)	No major side effects	+ independent of intercourse, low cost, accepted by Catholic Church − unreliable, interferes with sexual pleasure, periods of abstinence required
Spermicide	Poor to Fair (20% to 40% failure)	No major side effects	+ low cost − unpleasant to some
Diaphragm and Spermicide	Good (15% failure)	No major side effects	+ moderate cost − unpleasant to some
Sponge	Good (15% failure)	No major side effects	+ simple to use, 24 hours of contraception − can be messy, unpleasant to some

TABLE 5-1   (cont'd)

Condom	Good (10–15% failure)	No major side effects	+ no prescription required, man's responsibility, simple to use, helps prevent STDs – unpleasant to some, reduces man's pleasure
Condom plus Foam Spermicide	Excellent (3–5% failure)	No major side effects	+ no prescription required, shared responsibility, helps prevent STDs – see condom, spermicide above
Condom and Diaphragm plus Spermicide	Excellent (3–5% failure)	No major side effects	+ see condom, diaphragm above – see condom, diaphragm above
Minipill	Very Good (5–10% failure)	Few side effects	+ independent of intercourse – continued cost, daily dose, breakthrough bleeding
IUD	Excellent (5% failure)	Bleeding, cramping, expulsion	+ independent of intercourse, reliable, minimal trouble after insertion – risk of pelvic infection
Oral Combination Pill	Excellent (2–3% failure)	Risk of blood clotting, gallbladder or liver disease, stroke or high blood pressure	+ independent of intercourse – continued cost, daily dose
Vasectomy	Excellent (<1% failure)	Possible complications of surgery	+ reliable, independent of intercourse – relatively expensive, usually not reversible
Tubal Ligation	Excellent (<1% fialure)	Possible complications of surgery	+ reliable, independent of intercourse – relatively expensive, usually not reversible

crease the number of sexual partners one has. New contraceptors, for example, have an average of 1.1 partners both before and after starting the pill (Reichelt, 1978). The major behavioral effect of the pill was simply to increase the frequency of intercourse from 4.3 times per month to 6.8 times. The negative effects of nonuse of contraception are clear: unwanted pregnancy.

Each method has special requirements which may or may not fit the needs, beliefs, values, and capabilities of a given user (Murray et al., 1989; Nickerson and McClelland, 1987). One goal is to seek the best fit between the individual and the method of contraception. Birth control pills can be taken in a totally nonsexual and nonembarrassing context, but keeping a regular schedule is essential whether or not sexual activity is contemplated. If such regularity is impossible and if sexual encounters are infrequent, the use of an IUD provides continuing protection without special effort by the user, though she must remember to check for the safety string each month.

When medical reasons suggest prob-lems with the pill or the IUD, then diaphragms, condoms, and spermicides can be considered. These methods require advance planning and involve interrupting foreplay prior to intercourse. These methods also require the user to touch his or her genitalia. Some people consider that aspect of contraceptive use distasteful. Negative attitudes about masturbation and about touching yourself "down there" make these methods quite unappealing to some (Kelley, 1979; Mosher and Vonderheide, 1985).

Summarizing the Information about Birth Control . . .

Concern about access to effective, safe forms of contraception is common; in the pre-pill era, all the other major forms of today's contraceptives were used. These techniques vary in effectiveness with the least effective being withdrawal, douching, and scheduling intercourse. Barrier methods are much more reliable and have no major side effects, but using the condom, diaphragm, and/or *spermicides* interrupts ongoing sexual activity. The **intrauterine device** and the contraceptive pill are effective and nonintrusive, but they *do* involve a number of side effects. For those who intend never to conceive (or never to conceive again), **sterilization** is a possibility; it involves greater expense and greater risk for women than for men. New contraceptive methods are being developed and tested for both sexes, but the greatest emphasis continues to be on female contraception.

The methods of **induced abortion** vary with the stage of pregnancy. **Vacuum aspiration** and **dilation and curettage** are performed in the first trimester. In the second trimester, *dilation and evacuation* or *instillation* can be performed. The use of abortion remains a controversial issue with strong emotional reactions emphasizing either the right of the pregnant woman to make choices about her own body or the right of the unborn fetus to live.

The reasons for the epidemic of unwanted adolescent pregnancy include both emotional and informational factors. Attitudes toward sex and toward contraception vary greatly, and these attitudes affect the use or nonuse of birth control. The behaviors necessary for contraception are described in five basic steps: (1) acquire, process, and retain accurate contraceptive information; (2) acknowledge the likelihood of engaging in sexual intercourse; (3) obtain the chosen contraceptive; (4) communicate with the sexual partner about contraception; and (5) use the contraceptive correctly. Emotional factors such as sexual attitudes have an impact on each of these steps.

To Find Out More about Birth Control . . .

Aguilar, N. (1986). *The new no-pill no-risk birth control.* New York: Rawson.

Natural family planning methods of scheduling intercourse are described in detail. Cervical mucus changes and temperature variations during the menstrual cycle are used to detect fertility.

Byrne, D., & Fisher, W. A. (Eds.). (1983). *Adolescents, sex, and contraception.* Hillsdale, N. J.: Lawrence Erlbaum.

Organized around the problem of unwanted adolescent pregnancy, this book contains chapters by a number of authors. They explain how adolescents fail to use effective contraception, drawing from social, psychological, and historical sources.

Cleland, J., & Hobcraft, J. (Eds.). (1985). *Reproductive change in developing countries: Insights from the World Fertility Survey.* New York: Oxford University Press.

This volume examines the roles that economic and political factors play in the high fertility rates in Third World developing countries.

Shapiro, H. I. (1988). *The new birth-control book: A complete guide for women and men.* Englewood Cliffs, N. J.: Prentice Hall.

This book gives useful, practical information about brands and types of contraceptives on the market today.

Tribe, L. H. (1990). *Abortion: The clash of absolutes.* New York: W.W. Norton.

The author makes a comprehensive and impartial attempt to present both sides of the abortion issue, though he personally favors the pro-choice position.

CHAPTER SIX

FEMALES AND MALES

One of the first questions about a newborn infant is whether it's a boy or girl. That single classification affects the child's name, clothing, playthings, and a host of assumptions and expectations about behavior and personality. Despite cultural differences and changes within our own culture, a great many parents view their children much like the following father who provided us with his observations.

I have two kids, a boy and a girl, and they are as different as night and day. From the time Rick was only a toddler, he was a real boy—always in motion and ready to fight back if he didn't like what was happening to him. He climbed on the furniture as soon as he was strong enough to pull himself up, and he loved to roughhouse with me. His favorite toys were guns and trucks and his G.I. Joe collection.

Now he's in junior high, on the football team, and I pity the girls when he turns his attention to the opposite sex. He's going to make his old dad look like a pansy, and I was pretty hot stuff myself a few years back.

My daughter, Jennifer, is a totally different story. She was always gentle and quiet; she spent hours and hours playing with her dolls and dressing them up. When she was just barely able to walk, she began to imitate her mother around the house—cleaning and cooking and such. She was so proud when she was big enough to help set the table and clear the dishes after dinner. She's in the fifth grade now, and all of her teachers have commented on how polite and well-behaved she is.

I know that I'm old fashioned, but I'm against either of my kids getting carried away by some extreme like women's liberation. There's no reason in the world for my son to learn sewing or to become so "sensitive" he can cry whenever someone hurts his feelings. And, there's no reason for my little girl to sign up for the Marines. They're regular kids, the way God made them, and I thank my lucky stars for that.

Sam, age 36

The basic ideas about males and females that are expressed by Sam are common ones. Many believe that the two sexes are not at all alike and that their differences are biologically determined. From childhood on, males and females are perceived as having different interests, as behaving differently, and as being different in their sexuality. In contrast to these views, some people hold quite different attitudes about the two sexes, assuming that boys and girls differ primarily because we treat them differently and have different expectations for males and females. The traditional way of thinking about the roles of men and women contrasts with many current ideas about what is appropriate. No one yet has all the answers, but we will describe what is known about the relationship between a person's sex and his or her behavior.

What are the implications of being a man versus being a woman? That question may not seem meaningful until you consider that maleness and femaleness include not only anatomical features but also personality characteristics, behavior, thought processes, and perceptions that may or may not be related to physical differences between the sexes. In this chapter, we first describe the biological underpinnings involved in *creating males and females,* including sexual anatomy and the possibility of "built-in" behavioral differences between the sexes. Because male and female behavior is not the same in all cultures, we also examine how girls and boys are taught to behave in specific ways that provide each of us with a *gender identity.* We also describe *transsexualism* in which a person's biological sex is inconsistent with his or her gender identity. We then compare men and women with respect to *sex, gender, and sexuality.* Special sections discuss the kind of prejudice and discrimination involved in *sexism* and inequalities in *the division of labor* between the sexes.

Creating Males and Females

Parents sometimes want to know their baby's sex even before he or she is born, and the first thing they announce to others is their child's sex. What determines whether an infant begins life as a boy or a girl?

■ **Sexual Differentiation**

At conception, the genetic information contained in a single sperm determines the sex of the person-to-be.

Genes as the Basic Determinant.   In each cell of the body except for sperm and eggs, there are twenty-three pairs of *chromosomes* containing genetic information. One member of each matched pair was con-

tributed by the person's mother and the other by the father. One pair constitutes the **sex chromosomes**, and these determine an individual's sex and sex-linked characteristics (such as color-blindness). In females, the two sex chromosomes are alike, and each is designated as an X cell. Her chromosomal type is 46;XX. The 46 refers to the twenty-three pairs of chromosomes, and the XX to the dual sex chromosomes. In males, the two sex chromosomes are different; one is an X and the other is a Y, giving him a chromosomal type of 46;XY. When the sex chromosomes are both X, the person is female; when they are X and Y, the person is male.

As described in Chapter 4, humans have two kinds of *reproductive cells* (ova and sperm) which unite to produce offspring. These reproductive cells do not have twenty-three chromosome pairs. Each sperm and each egg has only half as many chromosomes as the other cells of the body, because the twenty-three pairs split when each sperm and egg form. After the split every egg has an X chromosome: each is 23;X. Because a male has one X and one Y chromosome, half of the sperm carry twenty-two plus a Y chromosome, making half the sperm 23;X and the other half 23;Y. So, when a sperm fertilizes an egg, half of the time the fertilized egg consists of an XX combination, creating a new female. Half of the time the fertilized egg is made up of an XY combination, creating a new male. Figure 6-1 shows this process.

Before their child is born, prospective parents

FIGURE 6-1 *GIRL OR BOY? XX OR XY GENE PAIRS* At conception, two germ cells (a sperm and an ovum) unite, producing a zygote that first develops into an embryo, then a fetus, and eventually a newborn infant. Each germ cell contains twenty-three chromosomes, so the zygote contains forty-six chromosomes. The determination of the offspring's sex is based on whether the sperm contains a Y gene or an X gene (all ova contain an X gene). At conception, an XY pair of genes constitutes a male, while an XX pair constitutes a female.

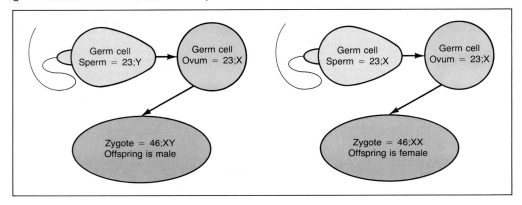

often want to know what its sex will be. A genetic analysis providing a *karyotype,* based on cells in the amniotic fluid surrounding the fetus in the uterus, is obtained by means of an *amniocentesis* (see Chapter 4). A controversial use of this information occurs when parents decide to abort the fetus if it is not found to be the sex they desire (Kolata, 1988).

Some parents wishing to avoid such tests may turn to questionable techniques such as suspending the mother's wedding ring on a string above her abdomen, allowing it to move freely. According to myth, a back and forth motion supposedly means that the baby will be a boy, and a circular motion means it will be a girl. There is no evidence that such predictions are any better than chance, but presumably no harm is done. A second inaccurate and generally harmless myth is that the fetus' sex is shown by how high in the abdomen the pregnant women carries the fetus. One current myth *is* dangerous, however. Some pregnant women mix their saliva with a small amount of drain cleaner; supposedly, no change in color indicates a girl. This mixture creates heat and fumes that can be toxic when they are inhaled (Edmondson, 1984).

Concern about the sex of a child leads some couples to attempt to conceive one sex or the other deliberately. Parents usually want their first child to be a boy, and their second child to be the opposite sex of whatever the first turned out to be (Callen and Kee, 1981).

There are techniques designed to preselect sex, based on differences between X and Y sperm. In the widely used method developed by Dr. Ronald J. Ericsson, the likelihood of conceiving a male offspring is increased by spreading semen on a special protein solution, allowing the sperm to swim into the liquid. They are then extracted by spinning the mixture in a centrifuge. The survivors are placed on a thicker protein solution; most of the sperm who penetrate it during the next hour carry a Y chromosome and therefore will create males if they fertilize an egg. A variation on this procedure, developed by Dr. Rihachi Iizuka in Japan, separates two layers of sperm, one that is 85 percent Y-carriers and another that is 95 percent X-carriers (Sullivan, 1987). The next step, using either method, is artificial insemination.

For couples not wanting to undergo this laboratory procedure, less formal methods are possible. If the woman takes an alkaline, or chemically "basic," douche just prior to coitus, she increases the chances, if she becomes pregnant, of the offspring being male. The reason is that Y sperm survive better in an alkaline environment than X sperm. The douche consists of five teaspoons of baking soda in a quart of warm water. To increase the odds of a female offspring, the opposite is recommended—an acidic douche consisting of five teaspoons of distilled white vinegar in a quart of warm water. Such douches, developed by Landrum B. Shettles (Shettles and Rorvik, 1970), appear to be less effective than centrifuge separation in increasing a couple's chance to produce an offspring of the desired sex. Further, as indicated elsewhere in this book, repeated douching is not recommended because it can cause vaginal irritation.

Other factors that may help Y sperm reach the ovum before X sperm include deep penetration of the vagina and the occurrence of an orgasm in the female. Couples are also often advised to have intercourse as close as possible to the time of ovulation, but this recommendation conflicts with a study of several thousand births in which more males were born when intercourse had occurred two or more days after ovulation rather than close to it (Harlap, 1979).

Success with any of these methods may create a new problem. Because of a general preference worldwide for boys (Burton, 1990; Freed and Freed, 1989), some express fears that deliberate sex-selection at conception or through abortion will result in the overproduction of men and underproduction of women (Brody, 1990).

In females, who have the XX pattern of sex chromosomes, one of the X chromosomes is not needed, so it is inactivated by *Barr bodies,* or *sex chromatin,* which appear only in the cells of females. Barr bodies are inactive X-chromosome material, found in all biologically normal females. A *buccal smear test,* in which a few cells are scraped from the lining of the mouth, can test for the presence of Barr bodies. The test is used to determine the sex of athletes when the question arises. Male athletes, for example, sometimes claim they are females in order to take advantage of sex differences in running speed and upper body muscle strength.

Development of Genitalia and Internal Structures. Until eight weeks after conception, female and male embryos are identical except for the presence of Barr bodies in female cells. Then, the genitalia and other sex-related structures develop in one of two directions. **Mullerian ducts** are embryonic structures that degenerate in males, but in females they develop into the oviducts, uterus, cervix, and upper portion of the vagina. When a Y chromosome is present, however, the embryonic structures known as **Wolffian ducts** (which degenerate in females) develop into the epididymis, vas deferens, and seminal vesicles. It appears that a single gene (called the *testes determining factor*), located on the Y chromosome, is responsible for the development of a male rather than a female fetus (Schmeck, 1987).

The sex hormone *testosterone* is needed to create male genitals. It causes the penis, scrotum, testes, and other male organs to grow. Without testosterone, the embryo's undeveloped genital organ, known as the **genital tubercle**, becomes a clitoris instead of a penis. Figure 6-2 compares some *homologous structures* of female and male genitalia. These organs develop from the same embryonic structures, but become male or female as directed by genetic coding that operates in part through differential hormone production.

During the last seven months of prenatal development, the testes descend from the abdomen into the scrotum. If one or both fail to descend, **cryptorchidism**, or undescended testes, results. This condition, occurring in about 2 percent of all males, can cause infertility or cancer unless it is corrected by the age of five. Surgery is used in more severe cases, and hormonal therapy can correct milder instances (Lee, 1985).

■ Errors in Sexual Differentiation

Errors sometimes occur during fetal development, resulting in incomplete sexual differentiation. The newborn's genitals may resemble those of both sexes, and the unsure physician may have to announce, "It's a boy *or* maybe a girl."

Hormonal Errors.   The rare condition of **hermaphroditism**, in which a person has ambiguous sex organs, is also known as **intersexuality**. Hermaphrodites have both male and female genitalia; they may have a vaginal opening and also menstruate, in addition to having a penis, testicles, and scrotum. If both an ovary and a testis develop in the abdomen, the

FIGURE 6-2   *WHAT ARE LITTLE BOYS AND GIRLS MADE OF? IN PART, HOMOLOGOUS GENITAL STRUCTURES*   Male and female genitals develop from the same embryonic tissue, and many specific structures are homologous. Those structures indicated on the left for males correspond to the ones on the right for females.

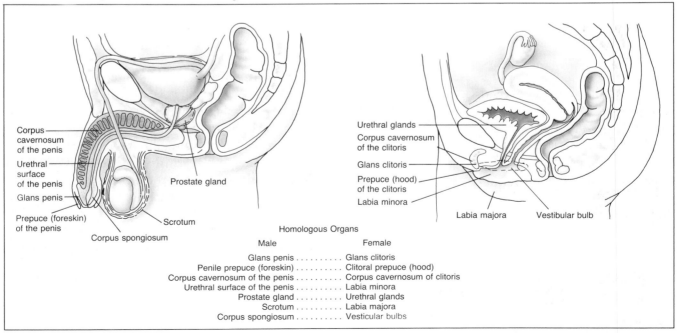

Homologous Organs	
Male	Female
Glans penis	Glans clitoris
Penile prepuce (foreskin)	Clitoral prepuce (hood)
Corpus cavernosum of the penis	Corpus cavernosum of clitoris
Urethral surface of the penis	Labia minora
Prostate gland	Urethral glands
Scrotum	Labia majora
Corpus spongiosum	Vesticular bulbs

person is a **true hermaphrodite.** The cause of hermaphroditism can be a lack of *androgen,* a masculinizing hormone, during fetal development.

A **pseudohermaphrodite** has the internal sexual organs of one sex and the external genitals of the other sex. The male pseudohermaphrodite has a Y chromosome and testes and no ovaries or uterus, but develops breasts and labia. Some pseudohermaphrodites have incomplete male or female structures.

The female pseudohermaphrodite has ovaries but also can develop a "penis." This combination may be produced by the **androgenital syndrome** when the female fetus is exposed to excess androgen before or shortly after birth. For example, the fetus' own adrenal glands could malfunction because of an inherited defect, producing abnormally high amounts of androgen. A malformation of the fetal clitoris similar to this syndrome also can occur if the mother takes birth control pills during pregnancy; the progestogen in the pill stimulates the release of excess androgen in the fetus (Young, 1983). These females have an enlarged clitoris that resembles a penis, and surgery can correct this problem. Other masculine characteristics such as thick body hair, called *hirsutism,* can be controlled by hormonal treatment (Galle et al., 1984). The female pseudohermaphrodite's labia may fuse and resemble a scrotum, which can be changed by surgery. Such an individual can reproduce and is likely to have a heterosexual orientation (Money and Mathews, 1982). Figure 6-3 shows the external genitals of a female pseudohermaphrodite.

In cases of ambiguous genitalia such as these, *sex reassignment* was used until the 1970s. The individual was raised as a boy or as a girl on the basis of the appearance of the genitals despite the fact that this did not correspond with the person's genetic sex. For example, a male child with the usual 46;XY pattern, but with a very small penis, called **microphallus,** could be classified as a female. If such sex reassignment begins before age three and is followed by appropriate surgery and hormone treatments, the outcome tends to be successful (Rosenbaum, 1982). Today doctors study the individual's chromosomal makeup and gonadal structure, in order to identify the child's sex correctly and to recommend that he or she be reared accordingly. The boy with microphal-

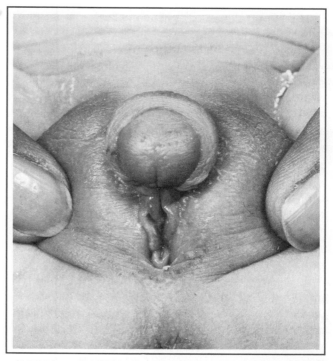

FIGURE 6-3 *AMBIGUOUS GENITALS—GIRL OR BOY?* Female pseudohermaphrodites, like the one depicted here, may have an enlarged clitoris which resembles a penis.

lus, for example, today would be raised as a boy and given hormonal treatment to increase the size of his penis, if necessary.

Genetic Errors. Several kinds of genetic errors interfere with genital development and the ability to reproduce. For example, hermaphroditism can be caused by an error at the time of conception, resulting in a zygote containing both XX and XY chromosomes. We will discuss two other such errors, each involving an abnormal number of sex chromosomes.

In **Turner's syndrome,** which occurs rarely, the genetic composition is 45;XO. The O refers to a missing sex chromosome. A person suffering from it has only 22 pairs of chromosomes per cell, is missing a Y chromosome or a second X, and has no Barr bodies (Mosley, 1984). The person has the genitals of a female, no functioning ovaries, is unusually short, has a deformed face and neck, and develops a series of organic problems including malfunctioning heart and kidneys (Reindollar and McDonough, 1981). The person with Turner's syndrome may develop breasts in response to hormonal therapy.

About one out of 700 males have **Klinefelter's syndrome.** Such men have 47;XXY cells. The extra X is associated with small penis size, undescended testicles, infertility, lack of sexual desire, and mental retardation. Penis growth can be stimulated by the application of testosterone cream to the young boy's penis (Weldon, 1980). Half of these males also develop **gynecomastia,** in which their breasts increase in size; a number even have their breasts removed to reduce the risk of cancer (Cherlin, 1984). Some males with Klinefelter's syndrome also have excessively long arms and legs relative to the individual's height (Karpas, 1981a). Testosterone therapy is started after puberty to stimulate sexual interest and development of secondary sexual characteristics such as beard growth.

In some males having this syndrome, the penis curves when erect. In addition, the meatus is often located in the wrong place on the glans or may even appear along the shaft, causing the individual to feel embarrassed when urinating in a public rest room. This problem, called *hypospadia,* occurs once in every 350 male births (Horton and Devine, 1981). It usually can be corrected with plastic surgery during childhood. Without surgery, the curved penis can cause pain to both partners during intercourse, but ejaculation is unimpaired. (Curvature of the erect penis can also be caused by **Peyronie's disease,** in which foreign tissue growing inside the penis makes it bend during erection. Surgery can correct the problem [Miller, 1984].)

■ Hormonal Effects on the Sexual Activity of Males and Females

In lower mammals, hormones play a very important role in sexual behavior. In male mice and rhesus monkeys, for example, a rise in testosterone clearly activates sexual activity. These males respond to the hormone increase by attempting to mount and penetrate any females who are nearby. In the females of these species, estrogens and progesterone levels determine the sexual cycles of reproduction. During *estrus,* when hormone levels increase, females become receptive to being mounted by a male, and they are simultaneously able to conceive (Dixon, 1990; Svare and Kinsley, 1987). Female rodents, like many other mammalian females, advertise their receptivity during estrus by bending over and displaying their genitals, a response known as *lordosis.*

In contrast, no clear correlation exists between testosterone level and male sexual activity in humans nor do human females have estrus or respond with lordosis. How much, then, if at all, does human sexuality depend on sex hormones? Numerous studies have tried to answer that question, with conflicting results. We will summarize several of these investigations that have attempted to determine the role of hormones in human sexual behavior.

Hormones and Sexuality. There are some cautions to keep in mind in examining the effects of sex hormones on human behavior. First, few people have sufficiently low or high levels of sex hormones to affect their sexual behavior adversely. Most people fall in the broad, normal range, and the over- or under-production of hormones seldom is found to be the cause of any sexual problems. Second, hormones affect not only sexuality but also our general health and well-being. Recipients of hormone therapy may become more healthy, and any benefits to their sexuality simply may be side effects of this overall improvement in functioning (Hammond, 1981). Third, sex hormones have multiple and sometimes complex effects on our bodies (Whalen, 1984), and our knowledge about them is rapidly expanding. As recently as 1961, Stedman's *Medical Dictionary* defined androgen as that which "makes a man," and estrogen as that which "begets mad desire." We no longer assume that hormones are this simple. For example, the androgen testosterone masculinizes sex organs during gestation but also increases lordosis in female rodents without ovaries. Sex hormones may transform from one type to another before they act on a specific organ in a specific way. For example, testosterone can metabolize into estrogen and affect estrogen-sensitive sites.

Intercourse rates decline during menstruation and peak during midcycle (Spitz et al., 1975). This pattern does not seem to be based on physiological determinants; rather, couples are often reluctant to have sexual intercourse during the female's period for esthetic reasons, and "make up for lost time" afterward. If humans were primarily driven to sexual activity for reproductive reasons rather than pleasure, intercourse frequency would peak at ovulation when an egg is released and a woman's estrogen level is highest; but it does not.

It may surprise you, but in neither males nor females does castration necessarily block sexual desire or excitement, as discussed in Chapter 16. Adults without functioning ovaries or testes, both of which secrete sex hormones, can continue to perform sexually. Once again, we see that in human beings, sexual behavior is not a direct function of hormone level.

In Chapter 4, the role of the hormone, *oxytocin*, was described in terms of precipitating childbirth. This same hormone is also found to facilitate sexual arousal, orgasm, and the feeling of relaxation that follows a sexual act (Angier, 1991). Those who study physiological functioning suggest that estrogen and testosterone prepare the body for reproduction whereas oxytocin motivates the individual to seek a partner, behave affectionately, and care for offspring.

Other Evidence for Hormone Effects. Pseudohermaphrodites usually learn to function as a member of the sex indicated by their external genitals, although they cannot reproduce. An unusual group of twenty-four girls living in the Dominican Republic did not fit this pattern. These girls had a rare genetic defect which interfered with their bodies' ability to use testosterone. At puberty, a sudden increase in testosterone level caused their clitoral-like penises to grow into a relatively normal masculine appearance. Even though they had been reared as females until puberty, they reacted to their physical changes by adopting the male identity. So, twenty-four pseudohermaphroditic females suddenly became twenty-four males (Imperato-McGinley et al., 1974, 1976). The investigators claimed that the altered identity of these individuals was based on hormonal changes. Equally possible, however, is that they developed serious doubts about their femaleness after discovering that they possessed penises (Money, 1976; Feder, 1984).

There are instances in which hormones have been misused as a way to increase athletic prowess. Androgens and other hormones can temporarily increase the strength and endurance of trained athletes (Karpas, 1981b). Serious long-term side effects can result, however, including cancer, infertility, and birth defects in the user's offspring (Holub, 1982) plus cardiovascular disease, aggressive behavior, and a reduction in the size of the testes (O'Shea, 1989).

Sociobiology versus Socialization: A Continuing Debate. A general question is: To what extent is human sexuality based on biological determinants instead of on learning experiences? Do you believe that differences between males and females in behavior, attitudes, interests, or emotional responses are the result of biological factors or of learning experiences? This question restates an old, never-ending debate about the origin of human characteristics. One fallacy involved in such questions is the assumption that either heredity *or* socialization accounts for most of our behavior—in fact, both are major contributors. Perhaps the most accurate statement is that genetic encodings lay the basis for certain traits, whereas social experiences route behaviors in different directions within the limits set by biological factors (Wyers et al., 1980).

Some behavioral scientists are attracted to the proposition that complex social behavior is determined by genetically based patterns that were adaptive in previous generations of our own and other species. This general approach describes that field of **sociobiology** (Lumsden and Wilson, 1981). An example of such work was described in Chapter 1 dealing with sex differences in that males are found to be much less selective than females about sexual partners. According to sociobiologists, any behavior that enhances both conception and the survival of offspring to maturity tends to persist across generations, while behavior that interferes with reproduction and survival gradually disappears from the species.

Although our anatomy and physiology derive largely from genetic determinants, the idea that complex behavior is equally dependent on inherited factors is more problematic. Let us examine some of the criticisms of sociobiology.

1. Hereditary explanations have a common-sense appeal. We easily can believe, for example, that males are aggressive because aggressive male forebears were best able to survive and to mate. In this way, we can "explain" male predominance in contact sports, crime, and war. However, we are unable to test such an explanation scientifically. Social explanations of sex differences are much more complex and tend to rest on a large body of psychological and sociological findings. Considerable evidence suggests that

males and females have quite different socialization histories with respect to aggressive behavior—different rewards and punishments, different models, and so forth—and that both aggressive and nonaggressive behaviors are subject to the laws of learning.

2. The untested assertions of sociobiology can be used to support social policies based on political values rather than scientific fact (Lewin, 1981b; Rogers, 1983). If sex, racial, or cultural differences exist in a given place at a given time, we may conceivably assume that they represent unalterable biological differences. This may lead to the conclusion that there is no reason even to attempt to alter the status quo concerning male and female job opportunities, black and white educational attainment, or the economic progress of nations. Other more extreme possible consequences are possible—for example, forbidding females to practice law or medicine, making it illegal for blacks to learn how to read, and colonizing underdeveloped nations to dispossess and exploit their citizens. These actions are not fictional; all have occurred and were declared to be justified on the basis of inborn sexual, racial, and cultural superiority. Explanations based on biological imperatives are obviously most appealing to the group in power. For example, men find the theoretical argument that they are biologically driven to have sex with multiple partners and that their wives are biologically motivated to remain at home and raise offspring more compelling than women do.

   Assigning differences in behavior to genetic causes often requires that the actions of previous generations be ignored whenever they do not support the thesis (Jahoda, 1979). For example, during the hunter-gatherer stage of human history, both sexes wielded considerable power. Females had economic independence and chose their own spouses (Lee, 1974). Patriarchal societies (those based on male dominance and lines of inheritance) were instituted much later. However, sociobiologists still use an inaccurate description of hunter-gatherers as biological justification for male dominance in our society.

3. When the behavior of lower animals is used to support sociobiological propositions, the examples tend to be selected because they appear to fit a particular theory. For example, male seals tend to have harems containing multiple females while pairs of geese mate for life. Which model do you choose as the most relevant to human behavior?

Also, sociobiology tends to confirm the all-too-human tendency to assume that when groups differ, they can be ordered along a dimension of good–bad or superior–inferior (Gould, 1981). In our culture, maleness tends to be valued over femaleness, so male characteristics are preferable to those of females (Fausto-Sterling, 1985). For example, it is "better" to be *assertive* than to be *sensitive*. Even such acts as promiscuity and sexual coercion can be characterized as positive; males who are sexually active and aggressive are often described as being virile, supermasculine studs—make-out artists. Females who have multiple sex partners are sluts, bitches, tramps, or nymphos; if they are sexually aggressive, they are ball-busters.

Evidence suggests that sex differences in sexuality instilled through socialization outnumber those determined genetically (Kelley, 1987a). For example, females learn not to seek out or respond positively to pictures of couples interacting sexually. Males learn the opposite. Neither sex is born with such preferences or expectancies, nor do their hormones direct them to respond positively or negatively to sexual images.

You may find it enlightening, in this context, to examine the children's book by Stan and Jan Berenstain, *He Bear, She Bear*. The authors make the point that the main difference between the sexes is that boy bears can become fathers and girl bears can become mothers. For all other activities, the individual's sex is irrelevant: "There's *nothing* that we cannot try. We can do all these things you see, whether we are he OR she" (Berenstain and Berenstain, 1974).

Gender Identity: The Origins of Masculinity and Femininity

How and when do we figure out to which sex we belong? The labeling of ourselves as female or male, called **gender identity**, generally occurs at the age of two-and-one-half to three years. After age 3, a child initially focuses on **gender** differences and only later

TABLE 6-1 **Men and Women in the Eyes of Children**

Three-year-olds perceive few differences or similarities in what men and women do. By age five, more boys than girls believe that men are different from women, although some similarities are perceived. Seven-year-olds think that adults are more alike than different. The characteristics are listed in order of how often 140 children cited each—the first in each list was mentioned most frequently, and so forth.

	Boys, Age Three	Girls, Age Three	Boys, Age Five	Girls, Age Five	Boys, Age Seven	Girls, Age Seven
Differences between men and women	1. Men fix things		1. Men fix things 2. Men are brave 3. Men are strong 4. Women are gentle	1. Men are strong	1. Men fix things 2. Men are brave 3. Men are strong	1. Men are strong 2. Men are brave 3. Men fix things
Similarities between men and women			1. Adults take care of children	1. Adults are polite 2. Adults are brave 3. Adults take care of children	1. Adults are polite 2. Adults are gentle 3. Adults fix things 4. Adults can do anything 5. Adults make money	1. Adults are polite 2. Adults are gentle 3. Adults need others 4. Adults can do anything 5. Adults make money

Source: Based on data in Urberg, 1982.

on their similarities. In a study of three-, five-, and seven-year-olds, men and women are perceived as most different by five-year-old boys, while seven-year-olds of both sexes perceived the greatest number of male-female similarities (Urberg, 1982). Table 6-1 gives examples of the effects of age on perceiving sex differences.

Children also learn to identify activities as appropriate or inappropriate, according to their sex. Over four grade levels, boys choose increasingly masculine tasks as they grow older. Shown pictures of objects (as in Figure 6-4), they express a preference for using tools while avoiding kitchen implements. Similarly, girls select objects appropriate to traditionally feminine tasks like sewing in preference to traditionally masculine objects like house paint and brushes. Figure 6-5 depicts these findings. By the eleventh grade, boys prefer masculine activities almost exclusively and avoid feminine ones (Brinn et al., 1984). Adolescent boys express interests that are more stereotypically sex-typed than younger age groups. Although girls follow a similar pattern in having traditionally feminine interests, they do not avoid opposite-sex activities as strongly as boys do.

■ Physical Factors as the Basis for Divergence

As you might surmise from the discussion of sociobiology, there are two opposing explanations for sex differences in behavior. One view holds that biological factors, such as hormones, are the key. The other argues that environmental factors can encourage or discourage children's specific behavior, sometimes consistent with possible hormonal influences and sometimes not (Ehrhardt et al., 1981).

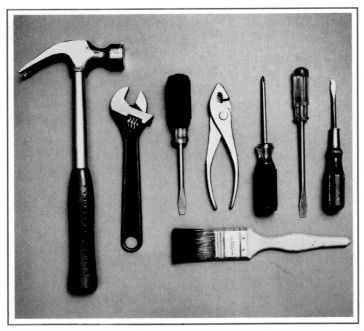
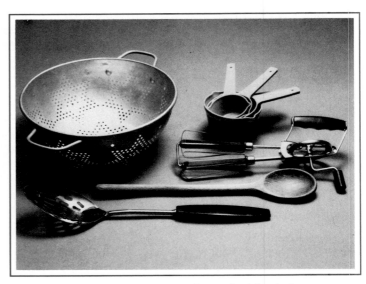

FIGURE 6-4 *WOULD YOU RATHER HAMMER A NAIL OR BEAT AN EGG?* Children's preference for masculine or feminine tasks can be tested by showing pictures such as these. The child is asked whether or not using each item shown in the picture is appealing. A series of such pictures is used in a test known as the It Scale for Children.
Source: Brown, 1956a, b.

FIGURE 6-5 *THE DIVERGING INTERESTS OF MALE AND FEMALE YOUNGSTERS* At each grade level, children preferred tasks that matched their own sex with respect to what is considered appropriate in our culture for males and females.
Source: Based on data in Brinn et al., 1984.

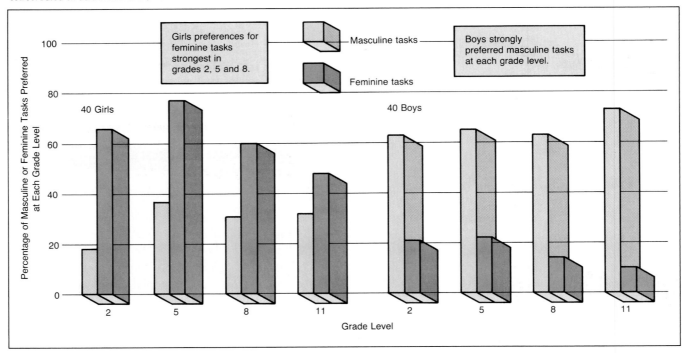

Does biology explain sex differences in behavior? To take one example, aggressiveness is usually more characteristic of boys than girls, and testosterone seems to be related to this difference. Testosterone may simply *cause* aggression, but it should be noted that its presence also causes boys to be more physically active than girls. If boys engage in more active play because of testosterone, such play is likely to include more aggression as well as more running and other nonaggressive acts. Thus, a basic, early physical difference between the sexes in activity level can set the stage for later divergence in aggressiveness because highly active boys have more experience with such behavior than do less active girls. As studies of young baboons show, however, hormonal and activity level differences need *not* develop into differences in aggressiveness (Young and Bramblett, 1977); such findings are not consistent with the theory that hormones are all-important as determinants (Lynn, 1973).

Twin studies also indicate the limits of biological explanations of gender identity. Identical twins have the same genetic makeup and experienced the same uterine environment. Nevertheless, sometimes identical twins express different gender preferences from one another. Even if both twins are biologically male, one can consider himself a female and have feminine interests while his identical twin can express strongly masculine preferences (Diamond, 1982; Green and Stoller, 1971). Such findings raise doubts about biological factors as the only determinant of maleness and femaleness.

■ The Socialization of Sex Differences

If biological factors do not totally explain how sex differences develop, what is the evidence for the importance of socialization experiences?

Sex-Typing. Research has shown that we form concepts of what it means to be male or female as early as age three; subsequently, we conform to these expectations. Kohlberg (1966) used the term **sex-typing** to indicate the categories used for maleness and femaleness. Sex-typing becomes the primary guide for acquiring attitudes associated with our own sex (Cahill, 1983). In the sex-typing process, a person

learns to value the qualities considered appropriate for his or her sex in a given culture.

Being a boy or a girl becomes most obvious to a child living in a household that consists primarily of the opposite sex. If all of a boy's siblings are female, the fact that he and his father are the only males emphasizes their sex. When such a boy is asked to "Tell us about yourself," he mentions that he is a boy more often than do boys who have brothers (McGuire et al., 1979).

Training for gender characteristics is more strict and less flexible for males than for females. For example, boys who step out of the culturally approved role for males by engaging in traditionally feminine behavior can expect a much more negative reaction, such as punishment, ridicule, or rejection, than girls who engage in traditionally masculine behavior (Feinman, 1981). By adolescence, many girls conform more strongly to traditional feminine roles than at early ages when many adopt the role of tomboys.

Lessons in sex-typing begin as early as infancy. The label *boy* or *girl* applied to an infant affects how the baby is dressed and treated. The custom of blue clothing—the color of the sky and good spirits—for boys began in ancient times as a protection against evil spirits. Baby girls were considered less valuable and therefore not worth protecting. Several centuries later, pink clothing for girls became popular in Europe, based on a folk tale in which female babies were born inside pink roses (Blue for boys . . . , 1989).

A study in a suburban shopping mall revealed that 90 percent of infants wore or carried items that were sex-appropriate (Shakin et al., 1985). Girls were dressed in pink and yellow with ruffles, puffed sleeves, and dresses. Boys wore mostly blue or red. Such differences provide cues to adults that a girl is more fragile than a boy and should be treated differently. Despite these overwhelming differences in clothing and so forth, parents claim that they do *not* buy clothing to correspond to the baby's sex and that they would not be bothered if a stranger identified the child's sex incorrectly.

Memory for gender-related information in young children influences the strength of beliefs about it. Among eighty-three children three to seven years of age, memory was tested to determine how well they recognized males and females performing activities consistent with their sex. Recognition memory improved when the child had strong preferences for playing with toys that had gender-related labels, such as a doll for girls and a rifle for boys (Levy, 1989). Such early learning about what is desired and appropriate for each sex may well set the stage for later sex differences in specific abilities.

Throughout childhood, sex-related cues are emphasized, including the kinds of toys that are "appropriate" for each sex (Lawson, 1989). For a group of five-year-old preschoolers, identifying an object as appropriate for a specific sex affected their responses to it (Bradbard and Endsley, 1983). Items such as a pizza cutter and hole puncher were placed in separate boxes. The children were told that each box contained things that boys or girls would like. They could touch the objects and ask questions about them; their task was to remember what was in the boxes. As Figure 6-6 shows, both boys and girls spent more time touching and asking about things that

FIGURE 6-6 *RESPONDING TO SAME-SEX AND OPPOSITE-SEX ITEMS* Five-year-olds are found to explore and ask questions about objects identified as appropriate for their own sex more than is true for objects appropriate for the opposite sex. Recall of the objects also is affected by the child's sex. When objects were described as appropriate for both sexes, these thirty-six children tended to respond as they did for own-sex objects.
Source: Based on data in Bradbard and Endsley, 1983.

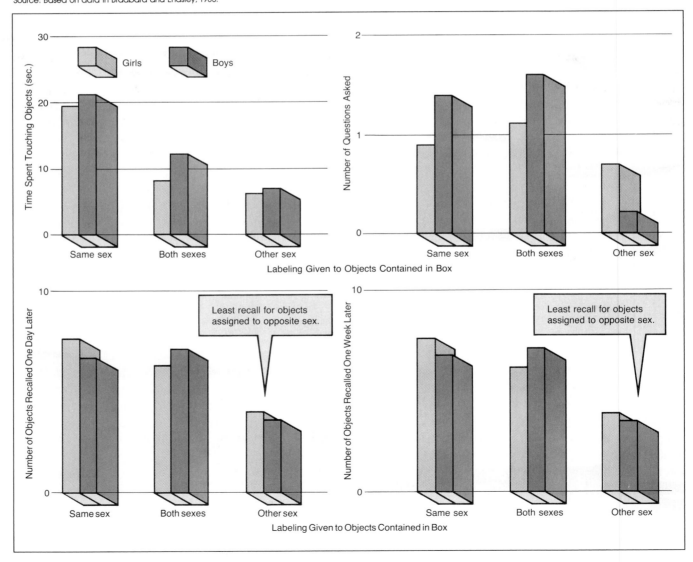

were supposedly liked by their own sex rather than by the opposite sex. The children also recalled the names of these objects better. All it took to improve the children's memory for these objects was a sex-typed label, suggesting the impact that such labeling can have on learning.

Beyond simple sex-typing, children also try to explain why males and females differ (Smith and Russell, 1984). Responses depend on the child's sex, as Figure 6-7 shows. Four different categories of reasons are given. Boys favor biological, physical, or personality differences. Girls favor explanations based on differences in experience.

Learning Experiences. By late adolescence, countless learning experiences have strengthened the initial sex-typing received by most children. For example, daughters start to resemble their mothers in attitudes about marriage, children, and careers (Rollins and White, 1982). Mothers from lower socioeconomic backgrounds tend to believe strongly that preschool boys and girls differ dramatically as a function of their sex. They expect girls to cry and to enjoy being held more than boys who are described as rougher

and noisier (Brooks-Gunn, 1986). By the time children enter elementary school, however, mothers from higher socioeconomic backgrounds are increasingly likely to agree with mothers from lower socioeconomic backgrounds that boys and girls have little in common and should be treated quite differently.

Fathers also contribute to sex-typing. They tend to play with their offspring in ways "appropriate" to the child's sex—they play dolls with their daughters and cowboys with their sons (Jacklin et al., 1984). Fathers also treat their sons more roughly than their daughters. Presumably because of how they are treated, parents regard girls as more trustworthy, responsible, and dependable than boys (Block, 1973).

Having an active, adventuresome son attunes parents to the risk that a child faces in certain situations; thus, they intervene more quickly when a child faces danger than parents without a son (Kronsberg et al., 1985), as Figure 6-8 shows. When the child in danger is identified as a boy instead of a girl, parents generally help twice as rapidly—seventy-eight seconds pass before they help a girl, while boys are helped in thirty-eight seconds. It would be interesting

FIGURE 6-7 *WHY ARE BOYS AND GIRLS DIFFERENT?* Male fifteen-year-olds explain sex differences on biological, physical, or personality bases. Females tend to cite learning experiences as the cause of boy–girl differences.
Source: Based on data in Smith and Russell, 1984.

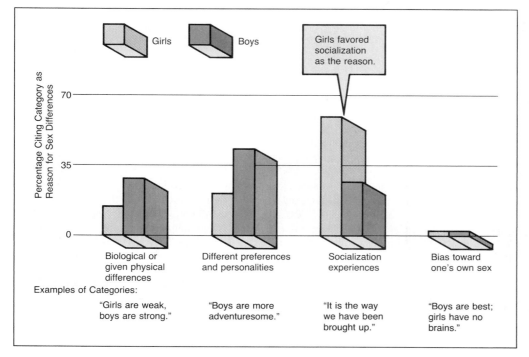

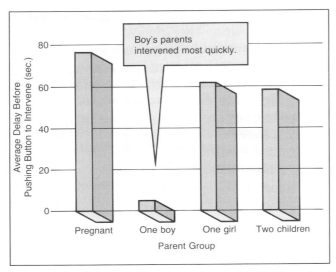

FIGURE 6-8   *STOP! THE CHILD'S IN DANGER*   Thirty parents of young children or parents-to-be viewed a videotape of a child riding a tricycle into a street. By pressing a button, subjects signaled when they wanted to intervene to stop the child. Parents of boys intervened most quickly, suggesting that they had been sensitized to risk by their son's previous behavior.
Source: Based on data in Kronsberg et al., 1985.

to know whether these reactions would be reversed for adolescents. At older ages, females might seem more vulnerable than males.

Besides parents, many other sources bombard youngsters with preconceived notions about how males and females should behave, including rock music videos (Hansen and Hansen, 1988). The more young people are exposed to television in general, the more stereotyped their views of males and females by college age (Ross et al., 1982). Can you guess why television might contribute to sex-typing? Think of the probable effect of repeated commercials portraying women in one of three roles—mother, housekeeper, or sex object. Research suggests the strong effect of such portrayals on stereotyped attitudes about men and women (Jennings et al., 1980). Annual studies of prime time TV indicate that the presentation of traditional sex role images has remained relatively unchanged over the past 10 to 15 years (Signorielli, 1989). Teachers also are influential in directing their students' interests toward sex-typed career choices, such as nursing for girls and construction for boys. When the sex of the student matches

Highlighting Research

SHADES OF SEXISM: TOWARD EQUALITY

The prejudiced attitude that results in the derogation of one sex, usually but not always women, is known as **sexism**. This type of prejudice is found worldwide and has been documented in places as different as Greece (Balswick, 1978), various African nations (Mendonsa, 1981), and Thailand (Springer and Gable, 1981). Evidence of the existence of sexism is easy to find, but women perceive incidents of sexism much more readily than men (Smith and Byrne, 1988). Also, men are more amused by sexist humor than are women (Neuliep, 1987). Male college students in the United States and in the People's Republic of China agree that being male is far preferable to being female, but female students were not equally favorable about their own sex (Lii and Wong, 1982). College students of both sexes also still describe typical men and typical women according to the stereotyped traits shown in Table 6-2 (Ruble, 1983). Because the masculine characteristics are more highly valued than the feminine ones, such stereotypes result in the devaluation of women and their activities, despite the superiority of women in several respects. As Strickland (1983) puts it, "Females appear to have a biological or environmental advantage over males, which leads them to be less vulnerable to accident, disease and disorder." Two to three males are conceived for every female, but only 106 males are born for every 100 females. Men commit suicide twice as often as women, and they die in preventable accidents three or four times as often as women do. Women outlive men, and by age 100, there are five times as many females as males. Physically, the "weaker sex" does very well. In the social environment, however, women are clearly disadvantaged as a result of sexist attitudes, beliefs, and behaviors.

Many studies have shown how sexism affects hiring decisions and career advancement. In the typical experiment, a resume is prepared that summarizes the qualifications of an applicant for a job or promotion. The resume is the same for both sexes. The applicant's sex is indicated by using a name or picture that is clearly either male or female. After seeing the resume, subjects offer jobs to males more often than to females and offer males higher starting salaries than females (Firth, 1982;

TABLE 6-2   **Gender Roles—The Good and the Bad**

The attributes used to define masculinity and femininity are either positively or negatively valued, and this table identifies the traits commonly used to define gender roles. Among several thousand students in high school and college, most individuals describe themselves as having both good and bad characteristics, although they may not easily admit negative traits.

POSITIVELY VALUED FEMININE CHARACTERISTICS	POSITIVELY VALUED MASCULINE CHARACTERISTICS
Emotional	Stands up under pressure
Warm	Independent
Able to devote self to others	Dominant
Gentle	Active
Helpful to others	Competitive
Kind	Feels superior
Understanding	Self-confident
Aware of feelings of others	Never gives up
	Decisive

NEGATIVELY VALUED FEMININE CHARACTERISTICS	NEGATIVELY VALUED MASCULINE CHARACTERISTICS
Whiny	Arrogant
Complaining	Boastful
Nagging	Egotistical
Fussy	Greedy
Spineless	Dictatorial
Subordinates self	Cynical
Servile	Unprincipled
Guillible	Hostile

Source: Based on Helmreich et al., 1981.

Gerdes and Garber, 1983). Actual managers make the same kind of sexist decisions as college students. Discrimination against women is most likely to occur where it does the most damage—in the job setting; there, power-holders make crucial decisions affecting the careers of women (Lott, 1985). In academia, male professors are rated as doing a better job than female professors by students of both sexes (Sidanius and Crane, 1989).

The more favorable evaluation of masculine traits results in a *halo effect* benefitting men (Kelley, 1987b). The negative side of this effect is that women's efforts are devalued, whether as homemaker or engineer. As with all stereotypes, one doesn't have to think—an individual can be viewed simply as an example of what most men or women are like. **Social categorization** of people to fit our stereotypes obviously involves erroneous assumptions about a world much more simplistic than

is actually the case. This unrealistic world consists of masculine men and feminine women, and ne'er the twain shall meet, except in bed.

One possible way to break through sexism is constantly to remind decision makers that only objective data are valid. Personal biases should not contaminate their decisions, and criteria for evaluating individuals must be consistently and universally applied. In one experiment, when researchers instructed college students about how to rank applicants fairly and about the specific requirements needed for job success, the students' tendency to prefer males to equally qualified females disappeared (Siegfried, 1982).

Men are also victimized by sexism at times. Men are usually expected not to show their emotions, not to be good or trusted as caretakers for children, and to have the primary responsibility for providing for their families (Farrell, 1986). Such

assumptions are unfair, and it is clear that the problem of sexism affects both men and women.

Given the widespread existence of sexism, how optimistic are you about its future? Will most people learn to correct their way of thinking once they are made aware of their tendency to stereotype? Will they stop placing obstacles in the paths of females, or will sexism persist for generations to come? One key to the future involves our fantasies. If we regularly fantasize equally positive attitudes about males and females, we may move away from sexism. An example of how this process may work can be seen in how males and females are presented in comic strips. Here, female characters are portrayed in less demeaning, sexist ways than in the past. In a 1976 study by Brabant, college students of both sexes rated female comic strip characters more negatively than male characters. A few years later (Potkay et al.,

1982), no difference was found in students' ratings of primary male and female characters, as Figure 6-9 illustrates. Surprisingly, ratings of secondary characters like Peppermint Patty in *Peanuts* actually reversed the previous trend, with females perceived more favorably than males. For whatever reasons—the women's movement, new legal standards, or other societal changes—the devaluation of females has decreased in comic strips.

The content of prime-time dramas on network television has not generally undergone a shift away from sexism, however. Further, frequent viewers of such shows (compared to those who watch less TV) express more sexist opinions of women (Signorielli, 1989). This kind of relationship does not, of course, establish cause and effect. That is, the viewers' sexism may make such programs seem appealing, or the TV content may increase the sexism of viewers.

If the change in the treatment of the two sexes spreads from comic strips to television, advertising, movies, and so on, perhaps we will gradually be moving toward a society that does not denigrate or exploit either sex.

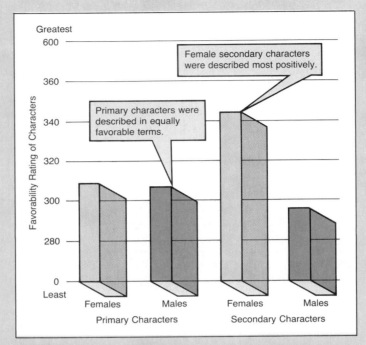

FIGURE 6-9 *SEXUAL EQUALITY IN THE COMICS* Major comic strip characters were described by thirty college students of each sex in equally positive terms, regardless of the character's or the rater's sex. For example, students of both sexes typically described both Superman (75 percent) and Wonder Woman (52 percent) as strong. Minor (secondary) characters were rated more positively if they were female rather than male. Perhaps nonsexist fantasies in current comics may be a sign of a future trend toward less sexism in behavior.
Source: Based on data in Potkay et al., 1982.

that of the teacher, this effect is greater than when they are different sexes (Stake and Noonan, 1985).

The special section, *Highlighting Research,* on pages 152 to 154, describes other ways in which distinctions are made between the sexes.

Transsexualism

People who are overwhelmingly motivated to be members of the opposite sex are known as **transsexuals.** In other words, their gender identity does not match their genes, their genitals, nor their secondary sex characteristics. We will examine the effects of transsexualism in childhood and in adulthood. Transsexuals want to change their sexual anatomy to match

gender identity and to live as a member of the opposite sex, and we will discuss how such changes are accomplished.

■ Gender Identity Disorder of Childhood

The first indication of transsexualism often occurs early in life—before puberty—and the official label is *gender identity disorder of childhood* (Blanchard, 1989; Tsoi, 1990).

Beliefs Associated with the Disorder. Among the first indications of such problems is the expression of various beliefs related to gender issues, as Table 6-3 summarizes. The child insists that he or she is actually a member of the opposite sex or states repeatedly the desire to be one. This is more than a casual thought or simple belief that the other sex has certain

TABLE 6-3   **Beliefs as Warning Signs
of Gender Identity Disorder of Childhood**

Children with gender identity disorder have a strong, persistent desire to be
a member of the opposite sex, and this desire begins before puberty. The
beliefs listed below tend to be associated with this disorder.

GIRLS STRONGLY BELIEVE ONE OR MORE OF THESE

I will grow up to be a man.
I can't become pregnant.
I won't have breasts.
I have no vagina.
I have or will grow a penis.

*BOYS STRONGLY BELIEVE ONE OR MORE OF THESE,
OR STRONGLY PREFER TO DRESS, PLAY,
OR OTHERWISE BEHAVE AS GIRLS DO*

I will grow up to be a woman.
My testes or penis is disgusting or will disappear.
I wish I didn't have a penis or testes.

Source: American Psychiatric Association, 1987.

advantages in our society. The transsexual girl truly believes that she should have the physical characteristics of boys, and the transsexual boy similarly desires to have the physical characteristics of girls.

Possible Causes of the Disorder. Speculations about the causes of gender identity disorder of childhood have focused primarily on experiences during that period, as we will discuss. There is no consistent evidence that transsexualism is related to physical factors such as hormonal imbalance (Aiman and Boyar, 1982; Boyar and Aiman, 1982).

Children with gender identity disorder play with toys ordinarily associated with the opposite sex more than or as frequently as with toys "appropriate" to their biological sex. The siblings of transsexuals, in contrast, play with sex-typed toys in the usual way (Zucker at al., 1982). Figure 6-10 illustrates the differences in amount of time children with gender identity disorder, their siblings, and a control group of emotionally disturbed seven-year-olds played with female toys such as dolls and with male toys such as plastic cowboys and army helmets.

Transsexual children frequently *cross-dress,* or wear clothes of the other sex; thus, boys wear skirts and girls wear boys' outfits (Blanchard et al., 1987). Adult transsexuals say that they remember dressing in this way as well as putting on the underwear and

shoes of the other sex (Ehrhardt et al., 1979). While some parents are upset by such behavior, others strongly encourage it because they would prefer having a child of the other sex.

It is easy to confuse transsexuals with transvestites, who cross-dress primarily to increase their sexual arousal. Transvestites usually do not want to have their anatomy or appearance changed permanently, however. Chapter 13 discusses transvestism in greater detail.

It has been suggested that the absence of one parent leads to gender identity problems, but the origins of transsexualism do not appear to be that simple. Boys whose fathers are absent because of death, divorce, or other causes tend to develop a less strong masculine gender identity than boys whose fathers are present, but this does not constitute a gender identity disorder (Kagel and Schilling, 1985). As college students, these young men often have more feminine interests than the average male, but they do not usually wish to be females. Females reared without a father miss various interactions with an adult male, but are no more likely to develop gender identity disorder than girls in two-parent families (Green et al., 1982). Similarly, girls raised without a mother at home do not become transsexuals any more frequently than those whose mothers are present.

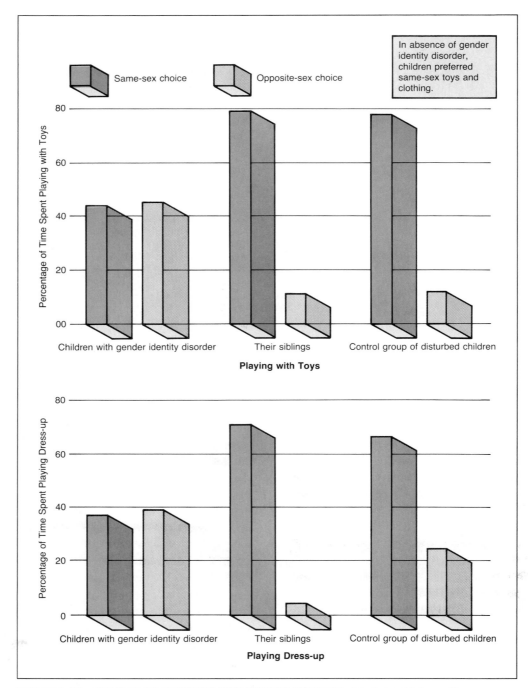

FIGURE 6-10 *THE PLAY OF CHILDREN WITH GENDER DISORDER*   Fourteen children with gender identity disorder played equally often with same- and opposite-sex toys and dressed up equally often in same- and opposite-sex clothing. Their sixteen siblings and a control group of thirteen emotionally disturbed children avoided opposite-sex toys and clothing. This pattern of not differentiating sex-appropriate items is characteristic of children who have difficulty in establishing the expected gender identity.
Source: Based on data in Zucker et al., 1982.

So—why do some individuals develop gender identity disorder in early childhood? The simple answer is that no one as yet knows.

■ Adult Transsexuals

Transsexualism is not a new phenomenon; cases have been recorded for at least the past 200 years. For example, a young woman joined the Russian cavalry in 1806 and fought against Napoleon's army during the following decade—her comrades never knew their fellow officer was a woman (Durova, 1988). Similarly, James Barry, a surgeon in the English army, was revealed to be a woman only after she died in 1865 (Bullough, 1975). Apparently, Barry's parents reared her as a boy and then sent her to medical school as a young man, because, at that time, women were not allowed to attend medical school or to practice medicine. Much more recently, a jazz musician named Billy Tipton had a successful career, a wife, and three adopted sons, but was discovered to be a woman when "he" died at age 74 (Musician's death . . . , 1989).

Incidence and Attitudes. How common, or how rare, is transsexualism? No one can be certain, because mental health and medical professionals tend to become aware of transsexuals only when they are experiencing extreme stress involving gender identity. Some data indicate that transsexualism is present in one in 100,000 males and in one in 130,000 females (Pauly, 1974).

Most transsexuals do not feel the need for help. In the early 1970s, clinics reported that male transsexuals outnumbered females by three to one—at least among people seeking psychological or medical assistance. More recent data indicate an equal number of male and female transsexuals (Roberto, 1983). It is not clear, of course, whether the population of transsexuals is changing, the relative discomfort of male and female transsexuals is shifting, or diagnostic criteria have changed.

Although people usually tend to be disconcerted by the idea of someone being a transsexual, attitudes are slightly less negative than toward homosexuals. For example, 20 percent of college students believe that transsexualism is always wrong whereas 30 per-

cent believe that homosexuality is (Leitenberg and Slavin, 1983). Though most students do not favor barring either group from most occupations (including judges, doctors, and government officials), men do not approve of transsexuals and homosexuals becoming teachers or ministers. Most students of both sexes also feel that neither group should be allowed to adopt a child. Clearly, our society has ambivalent attitudes toward transsexuality. Such conflict may originate from our perceiving an implied threat in someone very different from ourselves. The existence of transsexuals also can be threatening to some people's gender identity. If our genes and our anatomy do not guarantee which sex we are, then *anybody* could potentially be a male or a female.

The Lives of Transsexuals. When transsexualism persists into adulthood, it is categorized by the American Psychiatric Association (1987) as a *gender identity disorder*. This does not imply that most transsexuals are mentally disturbed or suffering from neurosis or psychosis (Hoenig and Kenna, 1974). Most transsexuals are employed at regular jobs and have developed relatively stable lifestyles; they have fewer emotional conflicts than many other groups in our society (Levine et al., 1976). When a transsexual does not begin cross-dressing until adulthood, he or she tends to have more negative self-attitudes than transsexuals who have cross-dressed since childhood (Lutz et al., 1984).

Adult transsexuals usually want to establish themselves in society as members of the opposite sex and to live and function as that sex does. Some are bisexual, engaging in sexual acts with partners of both sexes (Bullough et al., 1983). As Figure 6-11 shows, most male transsexuals report sexual attraction to other males, making them homosexual transsexuals; out of 163 transsexual men, 100 were found to be sexually attracted to other men. A surprisingly large proportion (44 percent) of these individuals abstain from sexual activity altogether (Leavitt and Berger, 1990). The vast majority say they do not become sexually aroused when they dress in women's clothing, suggesting that cross-dressing serves to confirm their identity as females rather than as a source of sexual excitement (Blanchard, 1985).

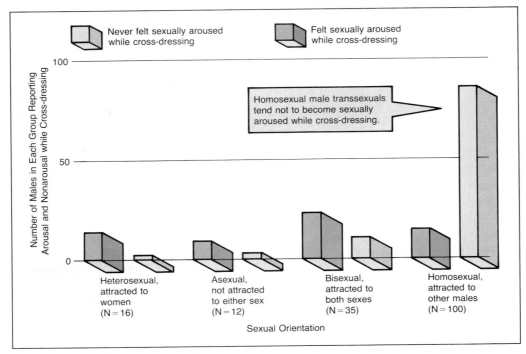

FIGURE 6-11 *CROSS-DRESSING: A SOURCE OF SEXUAL EXCITEMENT FOR MANY TRANSSEXUALS*
Males who have a female gender identity typically cross-dress. Among 163 male-to-female transsexuals, wearing female clothing tended to be sexually arousing to those who were heterosexual,
asexual, or bisexual, but not to those who were homosexual.
Source: Based on data in Blanchard, 1985.

■ Treating Transsexuals

For many transsexuals, *sex change* has become
the ultimate goal now that medical technology provides such a possibility. Changing one's sex physically
involves several components, and we will outline the
procedures and their effects.

Centers for the treatment of transsexuals began
to spring up in many parts of the world following the
highly publicized male-to-female sex change of the
late Christine Jorgensen in Denmark in 1951
(Sorensen and Heroft, 1982). In the United States,
university medical centers did not perform sex-reas-
signment surgery until 1966 (Green and Fleming,
1990), and the first such operation in China occurred
in 1988 (Ruan and Bullough, 1988). Such clinics vary
greatly in quality, effectiveness, and cost. The entire
sex-change procedure, with counseling, hormonal
treatment, surgery, and gender reorientation is likely
to cost $100,000 or more. Information about these
clinics can be obtained from two organizations: The
Harry Benjamin International Gender Dysphoria As-

sociation, Inc., in Stanford, California, and the Janus
Information Facility in San Francisco, California.

Hormonal Treatment. Sex hormones initiate changes
in secondary sexual characteristics for those who wish
to change their sex. For male-to-female change, estrogen and *spironolactone* are given daily to produce
breast growth and to slow the growth of facial and
body hair (Prior et al., 1989). Electrolysis is used to
complete the removal of hair from the face and body.
One effect of estrogen is a decline in the frequency of
erections, and transsexuals perceive this as a positive
feature (Kwan et al., 1985). Many of them had previously avoided sexual contacts because their natural
erections disgusted them (Sorensen and Hertoft,
1982). Estrogen also causes the prostate gland and
seminal vesicles to shrink.

Female-to-male transsexuals are given testosterone to stimulate growth of body muscles and hair;
this hormone also increases the length of the clitoris
to 1.5 inches (4 cm) (Meyer et al., 1981) and also
causes menstrual periods to cease and the voice to
deepen. Such transsexuals tend to have had frequent

sexual contacts with other women, and these hormone-induced changes enhance their sexuality (Meyer et al., 1986).

Gender Reorientation. *Gender reorientation* is an important psychological step in the process of sex change for transsexuals—the person learns to live in society as a member of the opposite sex.

When a person seeks sex change surgery, a common rule is that a transsexual must spend at least one year living successfully as a member of the opposite sex before the operation is performed. Thus, if problems arise, hormone treatments can be stopped and their effects reversed. It is obviously better to discover problems prior to irreversible surgery.

During the year of *gender reorientation*, the person receives help in learning the mannerisms and behaviors appropriate to his or her new sex. Ruth, a male-to-female transsexual, described the beginning of the process as follows:

> *My determination to complete my program gathered momentum. . . . I settled an array of personal matters, including the sale of my rural estate, relocation, family, divorce, name change, and cosmetic adjustments such as electrolysis. . . . I left work Friday as a man, and returned Monday in a dress [Levine and Shumaker, 1983, pp. 255–256].*

Males take voice lessons, learning how to raise the pitch of their voices so that they sound more feminine. Because of the anatomy of the voice box, men have greater difficulty in sounding female than women do in sounding male (Coleman, 1983).

People can undergo gender reorientation at almost any age, but this does not necessarily involve changing one's biological sex. For example, Steve, a ten-year-old, wavered between being a boy and a girl. He thought that life as a girl would be fun, but he also wanted to remain a boy. Beginning at the age of three, his interests and mannerisms differed from those of his siblings who were all appropriately sex-typed. In contrast, Steve began to cross-dress in his mother's panty hose and high heels, and used her makeup. His parents placed him in therapy where he was asked to imagine and then practice boyish behaviors that were shown on videotape. He was taught to talk, stand, sit, gesture, and carry books in the ways

typical of boys rather than girls (Hay et al., 1981). Steve completed therapy, and his parents were pleased to find that their son continued to behave as a boy.

Sex Change Surgery. Female-to-male transsexuals have their breasts amputated, and their ovaries, oviducts, uterus, and vagina removed. A penis is constructed from a tube made from their abdominal skin or from tissue from the vaginal labia and perineum. Because the female's urethra cannot extend as far as the outer end of the new penis, the urethral opening is placed at the base. There are no nerve endings in this penis, so it is not a source of sexual stimulation. A special danger is that the transsexual can catch the penis in a zipper or cut off the blood supply by wearing tight pants and be unaware of the problem. Constructed penises can be made erect by using a removable prosthesis that can be inserted when desired (DeCecco and Ricketts, 1982). Because of the difficulty in creating such a penis surgically, the results are far from ideal. Moreover, ejaculation is not possible. Perhaps in response to these problems, many female-to-male transsexuals decide not to have an artificial penis.

Male-to-female transsexual surgery is simpler to perform than female-to-male surgery. The male-to-female version includes removal of the testes, scrotum, and penis. Breasts are constructed by means of plastic surgery. One problem for males is the surgical difficulty in reducing the size of the Adam's apple that remains visible in their necks. Also, continued injections of high doses of estrogens can cause various medical problems for these castrated men (Goh and Ratnam, 1990). An artificial vagina is created within the abdomen, along with female-appearing genitals. Ruth described the effects of her surgery in the following way:

> *Having a vagina is an existential necessity; I now feel whole, in a way that eluded me before. . . . I now have orgasms that are more intense and of longer duration than those I experienced before. Simply stated, my vagina allows me to feel good about myself [Levine and Shumaker, 1983, p. 257].*

Evaluation of Sex Change Procedures. Not all applicants for sex change have their request fulfilled. At one Danish clinic, the screening process excludes one half to two thirds of those seeking surgery because they are diagnosed as emotionally disturbed (Sorensen and Hertoft, 1982). Surgery cannot be expected to help in such cases. Across nine gender clinics, the approval rate varied from 15 to 27 percent for 1,356 biological males and for 281 biological females (Roback et al., 1984). More males than females request sex change, but the reasons for this sex difference are not clear. Transsexuals may be aware that surgery on biological females is more complex and less successful than surgery on biological males. Males also may be more motivated than females to achieve a physical sex change.

Sex change surgery has both critics and advocates in the medical community. The absence of standardized criteria for selecting applicants for surgery and for evaluating their post-operative adjustment makes agreement difficult or impossible (Green and Fleming, 1990). On the negative side is a report from the clinic at Johns Hopkins Hospital. Out of fifty transsexuals (forty males, ten females), fifteen had sex change surgery while thirty-five had only psychotherapy. Those receiving psychotherapy without surgery actually benefitted more, as indicated by follow-up information. Compared to the surgery group, they had fewer psychiatric hospitalizations and arrests, better employment records, as well as more successful intimate relationships (Holden, 1979).

Other studies, however, support the advocates of surgery. Following a sex change operation, female-to-male transsexuals who marry women are found to have marriages as satisfying as ordinary marriages (Fleming et al., 1985). As for male-to-female success, it seems to depend on the person's emotional adjustment, because depression often occurs and interferes with establishing a satisfying indentity as a woman (Blanchard et al., 1983). The better the surgical transformation and the more social acceptance the man receives, the better his adjustment as a female following the operation (Ross and Need, 1989).

Sex, Gender, and Sexuality

When we compare the sexes, both differences and similarities emerge. In other chapters, we describe how males and females are similar or different in re-

sponding to explicit sexual material (Chapter 13), the opposite sex (Chapter 10), and sexual information of various kinds (Chapters 2, 3, 4, and 8). The following section explores some of the reasons that men and women may differ.

■ Comparing Males and Females

What are some of the major male-female differences that can affect their sexuality?

Emotional Expression. Emotional responses differ between the sexes. You are undoubtedly familiar with the stereotypes of women as emotional and men as being in control of their feelings. Figure 6-12 illustrates the dissimilar responses of males and females to pain. Why should they differ? Perhaps the process begins in early childhood when we are exposed to nursery rhymes with models such as Georgie Porgie who kissed the girls and made them cry (Pollitt, 1990).

Sex differences in emotional expression seem to be based on learning experiences. In infancy, males express their feelings more obviously and more frequently than females. Later, boys are taught strict control of their emotions—boys are not supposed to be crybabies, for example. In contrast, girls are permitted to weep, giggle, shriek, and otherwise express themselves. Such training of emotional expression is apparently successful; by puberty, observers rate boys as considerably less emotional than girls (Brody, 1985). Societal customs often reflect extremes of those stereotypes. Consider a football game in which the masculine players behave aggressively and endure pain without complaint while feminine cheerleaders scream and cry while jumping up and down in scanty clothing (McLaughlin, 1990). Emotional learning is also colored by society's preconceptions about what males and females supposedly do best in terms of daily tasks and future careers. In the special section, ***Taking Responsibility and Protecting Yourself*** on pages 162 to 163, we discuss the division of labor between the sexes.

Physical and Intellectual Abilities. Sex differences in physical ability begin to appear in puberty. At that point, the upper body strength of boys, and later men, surpasses that of the opposite sex because of male hormones and engaging in more physical activity that promotes muscular strength.

FIGURE 6-12 *BIG, STRONG, TRADITIONAL MALES* Stereotypes influence how boys and girls are taught to respond emotionally. Emotional expression is much more acceptable for females than for males. Denial of feelings by males can lead to extremes, as illustrated by Duffy's denial of pain.

Few differences in intellectual abilities exist between the sexes. Two that do consistently appear in many studies concern early, stable female superiority in verbal skills and later male superiority in math-related skills (Fennema, 1980; Maccoby and Jacklin, 1974; Sherman, 1980). The differences in math ability are related to age. On achievement tests, girls perform better than boys in fourth and sixth grades in both math and English tests, but fall behind in math by the end of high school. Despite these average differences, some boys have higher verbal achievement scores than most girls; and some girls score higher on math achievement tests than most boys (Deaux, 1984).

What can be concluded from these sex differences in math and verbal abilities? One consideration is the difference between taking an achievement test and taking a course. Sex differences on achievement tests do not generalize to classroom performance in high school, girls make better grades in all subjects including math throughout elementary and secondary education (Stockard and Wood, 1984). In a longitu-

Taking Responsibility and Protecting Yourself

THE DIVISION OF LABOR: AN APPROPRIATE ARENA FOR SEX DIFFERENCES?

It is often assumed that in the typical family, women do housework and care for the children while men work outside the home to provide financial support for the family (Janman, 1989). In the United States today, this division of labor characterizes only 20 percent of all families, because almost 60 percent of working age women have entered the labor force (Uchitelle, 1990). Figure 6-13 suggests that, nevertheless, most women still do housework in addition to their outside employment, and they often feel dissatisfied about the situation (Levine, 1990).

Sex differences in work around the home is not just a cartoon fantasy. Despite holding jobs outside the home, the typical working wife cooks, cleans, and does other household chores. In one survey, only two out of 164 couples reported that husbands performed most or even half of the daily housework (Nyquist et al., 1985). In studies conducted over two decades, there is evidence of a steady trend toward men doing an increased share of the work around the house. The

female to male ratio of hours spent was 6 to 1 in 1965, 3 to 1 in 1975, and 2 to 1 in 1985 (Survey says men . . . , 1988). Husbands are found to contribute more than half of the time and effort only with respect to yard work and traditionally masculine tasks such as home repairs. Even when loving couples plan to be liberated and share household work evenly, they tend to revert to the traditional division of labor after they marry (Kelley and Rolker-Dolinsky, 1986). An equal division of labor is found only for dealing with bills, gardening, and pet care. There is an apparent effort to share the child care, but women actually have more responsibility for this task. As the number of children increases, husbands help less with both housework and child care (Perrucci et al., 1978).

The work patterns of unmarried couples who are cohabitants do not differ much from those of married partners. Unmarried females spend twice as many hours doing housework every week (24.5) as their boyfriends (Denmark et al., 1985).

Working outside the home can provide

significant rewards for both sexes. Besides expanding their interests, they raise their standard of living. Because both spouses contribute to the family income, they are able to live less well if either spouse gives up the outside job. Employment can, however, also create stresses for the couple.

In the workplace, men sometimes face more problems than women. A study of almost 500 Canadian teachers found that men reported more work stress than women, felt less stimulated and fulfilled on the job, and were less able to cope with such difficulties (Ogus et al., 1990). These men expressed stronger feelings of depersonalization and were more likely to respond with absenteeism and a higher consumption of caffeine, tobacco, and alcohol. Women, however, are likely to feel overextended with too much to accomplish in too short a time (House, 1986). The problem is alleviated to some extent if the woman has a professional career or at least an interesting rather than a lackluster job; the quality of life is higher, and the negative effects on the marriage are fewer

FIGURE 6-13 *HOUSEWORK = WOMEN'S WORK FOR MOST COUPLES* "Husbands generate, by their presence, more hours of housework than they contribute" (Spitze and South, 1985, p. 311). When females work outside the home, their housework activities continue; what is reduced is the amount of time for such things as sleep and leisure.

HI AND LOIS   BY MORT WALKER AND DIK BROWNE

(Sekaran, 1986; Yogev, 1982). Women with menial jobs, where the only reward is money, report less satisfaction at home and work (Meeker, 1983).

Why are women expected to do most of the housework? Hiller (1984) proposes that two factors combine to determine the sex differential. First, having money or the skills to make money is a source of power that reduces dependence in a relationship. Men have more often been the principal or sole wage earner in the family, and the power derived from this has led them to avoid distasteful, low prestige tasks such as housework. Young women desire to have this kind of economic power (Merriam and Hyer, 1984), whereas older women place a greater value on marriage, family, and home. If a woman sees parenting as a major source of reward, she feels that a career is less important (Jensen et al., 1985). Some husbands, especially those holding progressive attitudes about women, want their wives to be employed (Smith, 1985). Nevertheless, women are finding it increasingly difficult to "have it all," particularly when their children are very young (Hock et al., 1980).

The second factor that Hiller proposes to explain sex differences in household work relates to affective commitment. Women strongly committed to their romantic relationship perform more housework than less committed women (Stafford et al., 1977). Unfair treatment, or women's perception of it, reduces their short-term commitment and makes divorce more likely (Hatfield et al., 1982). The probability of divorce rises when middle-class wives work longer hours or when husbands disapprove of their wives' employment (Spitze and South, 1985). Such couples often cannot afford to hire others to do the housework, and the husbands refuse to share the labor. Under these conditions, the marriage deteriorates.

Other than traditional ideas about sex differences, how may a couple divide tasks fairly? One solution involves taking the interests and talents of each partner into account. If one partner enjoys cooking, or at least does not consider it onerous, he or she can take on this job and learn to do it well. If the other partner dislikes cooking, he or she can agree to do the cleaning and to wash the clothes. By giving each person the task he or she finds less objectionable, both gain some compensation for doing specific kinds of household work.

These matters may appear trivial to couples contemplating a life of love and happiness, but questions of who does the grocery shopping and who cleans the bathroom, and how fairly these tasks are divided, seem to be essential to a successful marriage.

dinal study of thirty boys and thirty girls in high school, girls made better grades but their achievment test scores declined slightly in both subjects. Boys' grades and test scores remained stable (Wentzel, 1988). For middle-class boys at this age, achievement becomes very important in traditionally male areas such as math, but not necessarily in the classroom, especially with female teachers. For girls, impressing peers and cooperating with adult authority may become more important than mastery of subjects they perceive to be masculine.

Sex Differences in Communication. As they approach adulthood, females surpass males in their ability to communicate with others. It seems likely that female experience in expressing feelings explains their later skills in sending and receiving interpersonal messages (Dalton, 1983). Females are better than males at detecting when others are lying, and they talk about their personal concerns more than males do (Derlega et al., 1981).

Women also talk more; for example, they gossip at greater length than men. The two sexes gossip about similar topics, however; both tell secrets about close friends and family members, and don't hesitate to make negative remarks about others (Levin and Arluke, 1985). Both males and females say more unpleasant things about others when talking to a man than to a woman (Hall and Braunwald, 1981), presumably because women are expected to get upset (and perhaps cry) while men are expected to maintain self-control.

Sexual Interests. Young males receive much more encouragement than young females to attend to sexual cues. For males, sexuality is pervasive, and male behavior mirrors this. For example, women college students use less profanity and use it in fewer situations than their male peers (Selnow, 1985). Despite having better verbal abilities, women also make sexual references in their conversations less frequently than men (Singer et al., 1977). In ranking twenty possible goals of a college education, men rank "developing social relations with the opposite sex" as the sixth most important goal while women rank this as twelfth in importance (Goldberg and Shiflett, 1981).

Although some women are more concerned about sex than some men, the general tendency is for men to have the most intense sexual preoccupations.

For example, men view the interactions of others in more sexual terms than women do. Men rate female strangers as sexy and seductive, especially if they wear revealing clothes; women do not respond to male strangers in this way (Abbey et al., 1987). Women are skilled, however, in communicating, expressing emotions, and managing the behavior of others, thus helping them to control men's sexual initiatives (Saranson et al., 1985).

Among young adults, men usually initiate and escalate sexual activity (Kelley et al., 1981). This does not necessarily mean that they routinely either take advantage of women or coerce them sexually: Women, for example, typically limit the sexual advances of men (DeLamater, 1987). Men intentionally plan to initiate sexual activity with a partner more frequently than women do, and they do so more often in new than in older, established relationships (Byers and Heinlein, 1989). Once men decide to initiate sex, they estimate whether their intended partner would be receptive and act accordingly (Perper and Weis, 1987). By middle age, however, women initiate sexual activity more often than in their youth; thus, both sexes become initiators (Kelley and Rolker-Dolinsky, 1986). It is interesting that it takes half a lifetime to change these socially imposed roles specifying who initiates sex.

Once sex has been initiated, women and men express similar amounts of desire for caring and closeness (Hatfield et al., 1988). In recent decades sexual encounters have moved toward more equality and interchangeable roles for women and men in their sexual relationships (Macklin, 1983).

■ The Power of Gender Roles through Socialization

The term **gender role** refers to the personality attributes that are correlated with maleness or femaleness.

Masculinity and Femininity. When we respond to someone of either sex, we react to more than their biological sex. We also perceive traits, behavioral tendencies, and attitudes as characteristic of their sex. You may recall that Table 6-2 presented traits regarded as typical of most males and most females. Persons who describe themselves primarily in mascu-

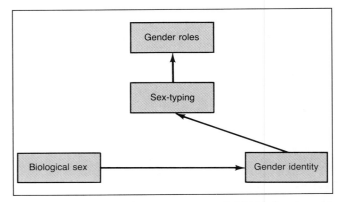

FIGURE 6-14 *CONSTRUCTING A GENDER ROLE* *Gender roles* originate from learning which behaviors and attitudes society considers appropriate for males and females. Parents and others identify our *biological sex,* from which we establish *gender identity.* In childhood, gender identity determines *sex-typing.* Gender roles arise from this foundation, allowing maleness or femaleness to affect our everyday lives.

line terms are said to have a *masculine gender role,* and feminine self-descriptions indicate a *feminine gender role.* The masculine role involves instrumental traits—getting things done and overcoming obstacles (Managan and Walvin, 1987; Seidler, 1989). The feminine role is primarily concerned with feelings and relationships. Figure 6-14 suggests how biological sex and gender identity contribute to sex-typing which, in turn, forms the basis for gender roles.

Nonverbal Behavior and Traditional Roles. Others observe us and make decisions as to our gender roles. Once made, that classification influences how they respond to us. Table 6-4 lists nonverbal behaviors that we perceive as signs of masculine and feminine gender roles.

If an individual is dissatisfied with his or her gender role, it is possible to learn behaviors that conform more closely with the desired role. In one study, college students of both sexes were able to relearn their styles of standing, walking, and sitting to fit the feminine or masculine gender role they wanted to adopt (Hayes et al., 1984). They selected which gender role to emphasize because of their dissatisfaction with their own behavior and with feedback from others; feminine behavior by a male and masculine behavior by a female frequently elicit negative reactions from others.

TABLE 6-4 **Nonverbal Clues to Gender Roles**

Nonverbal behaviors provide observers with clues as to a person's masculine or feminine gender role. The assumptions made on the basis of such behaviors may or may not be accurate. These data are based on forty-three observers of both sexes.

BEHAVIOR	RATED FEMININE	RATED MASCULINE
While standing	Feet together Arm movements from elbow Limp wrist action Frequent arm movement	Feet apart Arm movements from shoulder Firm wrist action Hand(s) in pocket
While walking	Short stride Pronounced hip movement Arms held closely to body	Long stride Minimum hip movement Arms hang loosely
While sitting	Buttocks close to back of chair Legs uncrossed and together, or leg crossed, knee on knee Graceful hand motions, with fingers bent	Buttocks away from back of chair Legs uncrossed and apart, or leg cross, ankle on knee Precise hand motions, fingers straight

Source: Based on data in Barlow et al., 1979.

In one experiment, college students serving as confederates agreed to learn extremely masculine or feminine behavioral styles such as those indicated in Table 6-4 (Hayes and Leonard, 1983). After they had learned these styles, subjects watched videotapes of confederates exhibiting the different styles and made judgments about them. As Figure 6-15 illustrates, feminine females and masculine males tended to be perceived as heterosexual, while feminine males and masculine females were viewed as probably homosexual (Hayes and Leonard, 1983). When these confederates approached strangers on the campus and asked for help in filling out a 200-item questionnaire, subjects gave most help to confederates of both sexes who behaved in a masculine way. The least help was given to male confederates who behaved in a feminine way; subjects also disliked these "feminine" men and perceived them to be unnatural and unconfident. It appears that femininity in men elicits negative interpersonal reactions (Beck and Barlow, 1983). For these reasons, many men have learned to hide any trace of femininity (O'Neil et al., 1986).

■ Androgyny: A Gender-role Alternative

It may have occurred to you that many people do not seem to be either strongly masculine or strongly feminine. They belong to a third gender category, **androgyny**, which refers to those who possess *both* masculine and feminine traits (Cook, 1985). The word *androgyn* originates from two Greek roots, *andro* translated as male, and *gyn* translated as female. Among college students, the three gender roles (masculine, feminine, and androgynous) occur in almost equal proportions. The androgynous individual blends the masculine and feminine gender roles together. Thus, androgyns have a gender role consisting of both masculine and feminine traits. Androgyny does not mean that the person is bisexual, hermaphroditic, or an activist for economic equality. This person, like those with traditional gender roles, has a strong gender identity of femaleness or maleness based on her or his biological sex. Androgynous persons develop some of the qualities characteristic of the opposite sex, while simultaneously behaving in ways consistent with their own sex.

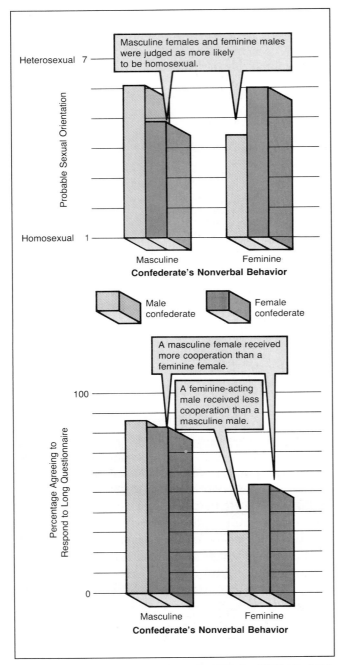

FIGURE 6-15 *THE EFFECTS OF NONVERBAL CUES TO MASCULINITY AND FEMININITY* Confederates were trained to stand and to walk in traditional masculine or feminine ways. Such behavioral differences influenced how they were judged and how much cooperation they received from observers.
Source: Based on data in Hayes and Leonard, 1983.

On the basis of research initiated by Bem (1975), psychologists have tended to define androgyny as the ideal gender role for both sexes. A number of empirical studies support that view. For example, people like androgynous individuals better than masculine or feminine ones (Major et al., 1981). Psychotherapists also generally view them as standard models for mental health (Thomas, 1985). Androgyns adapt to the demands of many kinds of situations better than primarily masculine or primarily feminine persons (Prager and Bailey, 1985). Also, across many situations, violence is more often a response of highly masculine men than of androgynous men (Finn, 1986). Despite these studies, it may well be inaccurate to conclude that androgyny is the best gender role for everyone to adopt. Some individuals are much more comfortable with the more traditional masculine or feminine roles.

The Socialization of Androgyny. Why do some people develop androgynous roles while others do not? For men, ego development seems to be an important factor. The term *ego* does not mean conceited or being overly sensitive, but something quite different. Men with highly masculine gender roles tend to have a low level of ego development—meaning that they have little self-control and are dependent on others. In contrast, men with highly developed egos are flexible in considering options and in respecting the rights of others; they are generally androgynous (Costos, 1986). For women, ego development is a less important determinant of their behavior than the gender role adopted by their mothers. Women with androgynous mothers tend to become androgynous; traditionally feminine mothers also produce daughters like themselves.

The Sexuality of Androgyns. Androgyns have relatively positive attitudes about sex, ranging from homosexuality to heterosexual relationships. They tend to be more comfortable with their sexuality than highly masculine or feminine persons (Garcia, 1982; Walfish and Myerson, 1980). Androgyns also say they would prefer having an androgynous spouse (Pursell et al., 1981).

Falling in love, interacting with a loved partner, and continuing a close relationship depend on gender role more strongly than on the sex of the person involved (Coleman and Ganong, 1985). For example, both men and women who express androgynous gender roles are more satisfied interpersonally and sexually than highly masculine or feminine persons (Rosenzweig and Daley, 1989). Couples in which one or both partners are androgynous are more sexually satisfied than those with nonandrogynous partners (Safir et al., 1982). When both partners are androgynous, marital satisfaction is higher than for either sex-typed pairs or mixed pairs (Zammichieli et al., 1988).

A clue to the interpersonal success of androgyns comes from a study of married couples, in which androgynous pairs were found to divide decision-making power evenly. In traditional couples, the man usually has this power. As you may expect, androgyns express more satisfaction with their marriages than do traditional individuals. They are also more

sexually satisfied than persons who are *neither* especially masculine or feminine—having an *undifferentiated gender role* (Cooper et al., 1985). When it comes to happiness in marriage, it appears that androgynous couples generally have an advantage.

This body of research sheds light on the function of masculinity and femininity within androgyny. Persons who are either masculine or androgynous have higher self-esteem than feminine or undifferentiated individuals (Lau, 1989). The positive effect of androgyny on behavior could depend on possessing masculine traits tempered by feminine qualities like sensitivity. In effect, traditional masculine and feminine gender roles can combine in interesting and productive ways to help the individual realize his or her own goals.

Summarizing the Information about Females and Males . . .

Sexual differentiation of the fetus depends on distinct genetic differences that can be assessed by examining fetal cells obtained through *amniocentesis*. *Homologous* organs arise from the same fetal tissue for the two sexes. Errors in sexual differentiation produce **hermaphroditism**, **Klinefelter's syndrome**, and **Turner's syndrome**. Although lower animals' sexual responses vary with hormonal changes, human sexuality is influenced more strongly by social factors and dispositional differences than by normal variations in levels of sex hormones.

Gender identity originates from the labels given to our biological sex, and the meaning attached to those labels. Physical differences between very young males and females, including activity level, may contribute to later sex differences in behavior. In **sex-typing**, values are attached to the labels of maleness and femaleness, and the child is socialized in ways considered appropriate for each sex in a given culture. Multiple learning experiences reinforce the initial sex-typing. **Sociobiology** and socialization are the two competing explanations of sex differences.

Transsexualism, a gender identity disorder, probably originates in the individual's early training that leads to his or her consequent preferences for acting as a member of the opposite sex. *Gender identity disorder of childhood* begins before puberty and is associated with early cross-dressing, either encouraged by parents or chosen by the child for unknown reasons. Adult transsexualism is somewhat threatening to others. **Transsexuals** strongly desire to establish themselves in society as members of the opposite sex. Treatment of transsexuals consists of therapeutic counseling, use of sex hormones, surgery for sex change, and reorientation for living as a member of the opposite sex. The total sex change procedure varies in effectiveness, cost, and suitability for specific individuals.

For females and males with typical gender identity, sex differences influence several aspects of sexuality and interpersonal behavior, but similarities between the sexes are also common. The division of labor for men and women reflects our expectancies about what each sex should do, and this can affect satisfaction in marriage. **Sexism** appears in our daily lives, but some encouraging signs suggest that sexual exploitation may gradually be decreasing.

Gender roles refer to the pattern of masculine and/or feminine traits. Behaviors associated with gen-der roles include nonverbal acts and interactions with intimate partners, and such roles affect marital happiness. Growing evidence supports the idea that **androgynous** individuals adjust better than those who are more traditionally masculine or feminine.

To Find Out More about Females and Males . . .

Bleier, R. (1984). *Science and gender: A critique of biology and its theories on women.* New York: Pergamon.

This book reviews cross-cultural, historical, and biological data about women and their roles. The history of sexism throughout science is traced.

Cook, E. P. (1985). *Psychological androgyny.* New York: Pergamon.

The gender role of androgyny is examined extensively. The author compares and contrasts androgyns to masculine and feminine persons with respect to social behaviors, thoughts, and attitudes.

Kelley, K. (Ed.). (1987). *Females, males, and sexuality.* Albany, N. Y.: State University of New York Press.

A series of experts write about gender influences on sexuality. Reviews of the biological, social, and psychological data indicate how strongly being male or female affects sexual responding.

McGill, M. E. (1990). *The McGill report on male intimacy.* New York: Harper-Collins.

Based on surveys of over 5000 men and women, this book describes sex differences in caring behavior, emotional expression, and feelings of intimacy.

Williams, J. E. & Best, D. L. (1990). *Measuring sex stereotypes: A multination study.* Newbury Park, CA: Sage.

With data from 30 nations, the authors report stereotypes about males and females that are held by children and adults. Though some stereotypes are unique to a particular culture, others are held cross-culturally.

Zilbergeld, B. (1978). *Male sexuality: A guide to sexual fulfillment.* New York: Little, Brown.

The experience of being male is closely scrutinized, especially the subject of how expectations about one's sexual performance affect masculinity.

CHAPTER SEVEN

SEXUALITY IN CHILDHOOD AND ADOLESCENCE

For most people, "sex education" begins neither in school nor in carefully planned discussions with parents. Instead, as the following reminiscence by a young college professor illustrates, we are likely to learn bits and pieces of sexual information by accident in interacting with our peers and through exposure to a portion of the secret world of adults.

I'm always surprised when people talk about the innocence of children with respect to sex. For me, sex was a topic of interest at least as far back as my preschool days— long before I had even heard the word sex. My first real memory of such things was when I was about three, spending the afternoon with the daughter of my mother's best friend. Our mothers and two other women were playing bridge in the living room, and Nancy and I went upstairs to find something to do. Somehow, we decided to play doctor, and that mainly involved taking off our clothes and examining one another. I had no sisters, and Nancy had no brothers, so we each discovered the amazing world of physical sex differences that afternoon. I remember feeling that being a boy was better than being a girl because I had more to show than she did.

The experience was interesting, it satisfied some of my curiosity, and I don't think there was any feeling of doing something wrong or expecting to be punished. No one saw us, so there were no adult reactions to deal with. If our mothers actually had interrupted our game and responded with anger or shock, I can imagine that could have had a negative effect on my feelings about sex. Instead, we just examined and explored for a while, and I decided that naked girls were fun to look at. In fact, I still think so. I sometimes wonder what Nancy remembers about that afternoon and how she feels about sex.

One other childhood experience stands out in my memory. I was about ten and had only the vaguest idea of the details of intercourse despite having heard many dirty jokes and stories. I was familiar with erections even though I was not really aware of masturbation yet and was not old enough to ejaculate. I also knew that sex more or less involved an erect penis being inserted somehow, somewhere in the folds of female anatomy. Enough stories were passed around at school that I knew the term for this even though I long believed the word for it was fluck.

No one had ever explained the process to me in any detail. My parents answered most of my questions by saying that they would tell me all about it when I was twenty one; actually, I don't think they told me then either. I would never ask my friends because they all pretended to know everything, and I didn't want to be the only one dumb enough to need further information. Walking to school one morning I stopped at a service station on the way to use the restroom. Above the urinal was a very large and anatomically detailed drawing of a couple having intercourse. This unknown artist provided at least one grateful child with some vivid information about adult male–female genitalia, the precise way in which people copulate (I later learned there are other ways), and the fact that both participants seemed to be having a good time.

For quite a while after discovering this masterpiece, I found it necessary to stop at that restroom on my way to and from school. I guess sex education is very often a matter of chance events.

Bill, age 30

What are your earliest sexual memories? How did you feel? Perhaps your parents saw you rubbing your genitals or interacting with a playmate. How did they react? Often, sex play may be fun but the reactions, or anticipated reactions, of others tend to cause anxiety, guilt, and shame. Some of these early experiences and the associated feelings are sufficiently intense that they have lasting effects on our sexual attitudes and emotions.

Despite the widespread assumption that children are not concerned with sexual matters until they reach puberty, we now know that sexuality plays an important role throughout the lifespan. In this chapter, we first describe *sexual behavior from infancy to puberty*. Because sexual interest, reproductive capability, and interpersonal expectations reach new highs after puberty, *adolescent sexuality* often presents an especially difficult problem for teenagers and their parents, and we discuss several aspects of this developmental stage. We also describe the various ways that young people obtain *sexual knowledge,* including *sex education.* In special sections, we discuss the effects of a youngster witnessing his or her parents engaging in sex (*the primal scene*) and what is known about *the effects of sex education.*

Sexual Behavior from Infancy to Puberty

Although a great deal has been written about sexuality in childhood, such material contains more speculation than fact (Kilpatrick, 1987). Why are only limited facts about childhood sexuality available? Consider for a minute the scientific procedures discussed in Chapter 1 and try to imagine how anyone would investigate the sexual lives of children. Would a survey be appropriate, and, if so, would parents want their offspring surveyed? The answer is probably "no" to both questions. Sometimes it is possible to observe what children do and say, but observations of sexual acts are rarely possible, and the ethical problems of doing so are obvious. Equally questionable would be to use children as subjects in experimental studies of sexuality.

The most common way to gather facts about childhood sexuality is to ask adults to recollect their childhood experiences, though faulty memory and embarrassment undoubtedly affect what is recalled. You can see that empirical data about childhood sexuality are scarce because solid information is very difficult to obtain. Despite the problems, we will outline what is known.

■ Sexual Beginnings

Infancy. Male fetuses have been observed to have erections in the uterus, and some males are born with an erect penis (Halverson, 1940). During the months following birth, infantile erections commonly occur. Female babies probably do not have vaginal lubrication, because this response is dependent on hormonal secretions. It is believed, however, that they have clitoral erections.

Infants of both sexes can become sexually excited and reach orgasm, though males do not ejaculate semen until puberty. It is estimated that at least half of all boys have experienced orgasm by the age of three or four (Kinsey et al., 1948). For girls, the rate is much lower, with only 14 percent recalling having a childhood orgasm (Kinsey et al., 1953). These early sexual climaxes are almost always the result of masturbation, which typically begins around eight months of age. Babies massage their genitals with their hands and also rub against objects such as toys or the sides of a crib. Kinsey directly observed infant masturbation of this sort along with the accompanying buildup and sudden release of tension. Some babies use masturbation to soothe and comfort themselves in the same way that other babies suck their thumbs or a pacifier (Kestenberg, 1979).

Genital play is most likely to occur among babies who live at home as opposed to those in institutions such as an orphanage (Spitz, 1949). It seems that close contact with parent figures stimulates infants; in contrast, institutionalized babies tend to become depressed and inactive. Babies thrive on attention and affection, and physical contact with a caressing, cuddling father or mother is extremely beneficial (Grossman et al., 1981). One, probably unintended, effect of such closeness is an increase in self-stimulation.

Early Childhood.   Toddlers aged one to three continue to masturbate, and they add some new sexual behaviors as well. Because they can move about and do more than is possible for infants, their sexual activity becomes more obvious to adults. Among a sample of sixty preschool teachers in Norway, 85 percent reported that the children in their classes masturbated at least occasionally (Gundersen et al., 1981). The reactions of the teachers probably have a more lasting effect on the children than does the masturbation itself. Almost half (40 percent) responded negatively and used words like "nasty" to describe the preschoolers' behavior.

Many parents prefer to discourage such behavior, but there are vast differences among adults in their attitudes about a child who plays with his or her genitals. Though some react to their offspring's sexual

activity with shock or surprise, it may be helpful for adults to realize that this is a normal aspect of human development. Guilt about masturbation is discussed in more detail in Chapter 8.

Beyond masturbation, young children also engage in sex play with other children of both sexes—either their siblings or friends. Such sexual interactions may start as early as two or three, but more commonly occur between ages four and seven. This activity satisfies curiosity about genitals and provides pleasurable genital stimulation. One female college student reported that she discovered the existence of the vagina while engaging in sexual exploration with her friends. When another girl pulled her pants down and bent over, "We were amazed to see she had an extra opening down there we didn't know about" (Morrison et al., 1980, p. 19).

In the Norwegian study of preschool teachers, 65 percent said they observed the children playing sexual games like doctor-nurse (see Figure 7-1) and father-mother (Gunderson et al., 1981). Teachers were most likely to stop the game if a child was being

FIGURE 7-1 *I'LL BE THE DOCTOR*   In sexual play, children satisfy their curiosity and obtain sexual stimulation. The only negative effects for non-forced, same-aged sex play seem to be those elicited by the negative reactions of adults, especially parents.

ROTHCO
ORIGINAL

*"Sure, I'll play doctor with you,
but only if I'm the doctor."*

© Zahn

forced to play or if fingers or objects were being inserted into bodily orifices. Four-year-olds have many questions about sexuality and reproduction. At age five, children begin to joke about sexual topics, including the function of genitalia and breasts. Five-to seven-year-olds play house and sometimes include sexual themes in their fantasies.

Sexual play among young children of the same age occurs spontaneously and naturally. It typically has little impact, either positive or negative, on later sexual functioning during young adulthood unless force or domination is involved (Leitenberg et al., 1989). When there is an age difference between the participants of four years or more, however, negative effects are more likely. Examples include incest or the sexual abuse of children by adults (see Chapter 14). Negative outcomes also occur when an adult punishes a child for sexual play or otherwise communicates the idea that a wrong has been committed. Sexual guilt and other negative feelings about sex may be taught in this way.

Later Childhood.   By the age of ten, most children have passed a series of sexual milestones. They have seen, done, and fantasized about many sexual activities. Eight- and nine-year-olds tend to play with peers of their own sex rather than those of the opposite sex. Adults do not tend to think of young children as "sexually experienced," but they often have explored several aspects of sexuality by this point in their lives. Table 7-1 outlines the sexual acts and thoughts common to most ten-year-olds, as reported retrospectively by college students in Oklahoma and New York (Green, 1985). Strongly religious backgrounds were more common in the Oklahoma sample than in the New York one, but this difference did not affect early sexual activity.

For most children, their initial sexual explorations are not labeled as sexual either by themselves or by adults who observe them. Children do recognize the pleasure they feel but are frequently aware that others react negatively to the activity. In the survey of childhood memories of college students, the recollections of their first act of masturbating was more likely to be perceived as sexual by the New Yorkers than by the Oklahomans, as Figure 7-2 shows. There was also a sex difference, in that females were less likely to apply a sexual label to the behavior than males. Parents tend to avoid educating their children about such matters. When parents also avoid using the appropriate words to describe sex and masturbation, children usually do not categorize their behavior in sexual terms either. As adults, many of us are able to recall the early experiences and the accompanying sensations, and perhaps realize only later that it was a sexual experience after all. Whether young children do or do not have sexual experiences

TABLE 7-1   **Sexual Experiences in Childhood**

By the age of ten, some sexual activities commonly occur while others are unusual, according to self-reports of over 1,200 college students.

MOST STUDENTS REPORTED THAT THEY HAD ENGAGED IN THE FOLLOWING SEXUAL ACTIVITIES BY THE AGE OF TEN:

Became aware that the opposite sex had genitals different from their own
Looked at a nude picture of someone of the opposite sex
Observed a nude opposite-sex individual
Examined his or her own genitalia closely
Masturbated without reaching orgasm

MOST STUDENTS REPORTED THAT THEY HAD NOT ENGAGED IN THE FOLLOWING SEXUAL ACTIVITIES BY THE AGE OF TEN:

Had intercourse
Engaged in petting
Masturbated to orgasm

Source: Data from Green, 1985.

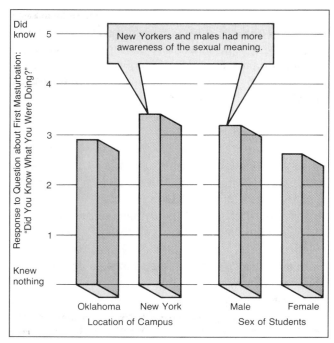

FIGURE 7-2 *PERCEIVING MASTURBATION AS A SEXUAL EXPER-IENCE* College students were asked whether they understood the sexual meaning of their first masturbation experience. Among almost 200 New York students, masturbation was more likely to be perceived as sexual than was true for over 1,000 Oklahoma students. Across locations, males were more likely to report it as sexual than were females.
Source: Data from Green, 1985.

is found to have little effect—positive or negative—on their later sexual adjustment (Leitenberg et al., 1989).

At ages ten and eleven, children eagerly antici-pate the bodily changes that will prepare them for adolescence. Modesty may increase at this age; they become self-conscious about their bodies and don't want to expose them. Boys and girls tend to avoid one another and to interact primarily with those of their own sex.

Today, children are much less likely to be shel-tered from sexual references in movies, songs, and television programs than in the past, and images of children such as those in Figure 7-3 are not uncom-mon. As an example of the changes in acceptability, the youth-oriented *Mad* magazine satirized the film, *Little Darlings,* which told the story of two young fe-male campers competing over who would lose her virginity first. The magazine has also advertised "training diaphragms" and has depicted a little girl

spying on an adolescent couple engaged in inter-course. In the late 1950s, fifteen- and sixteen-year-olds bought *Mad,* but by the 1980s eleven- to thir-teen-year-olds accounted for most of its readers (Winn, 1981). In effect, childhood seems to have been shortened, and such problems as premarital pregnancy (Chapter 5) and sexually transmissible diseases (Chapter 15) are increasingly familiar to youngsters.

■ Puberty

Because we now know that infancy and child-hood are far from nonsexual periods of life, it no longer makes sense to describe **puberty** as the time of sexual awakening. Instead, puberty is defined simply as the developmental stage during which physical maturation results in the ability to reproduce. Accom-panying reproductive capacity are such physical

FIGURE 7-3 *SEXUAL IMAGES OF SCHOOL CHILDREN* Pre-adolescents today often appear to be worldly and sexual. No one knows yet how this type of accelerated social development may affect them in adolescence and adulthood.

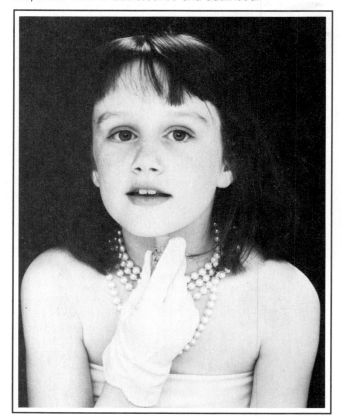

changes as breast development, an increase in genital size, and the growth of body hair, especially in the genital and axillary (armpit) areas. Table 7-2 outlines some of the observable bodily changes among males and females. Stage 1 includes childhood, in which there is no physical maturation of sexual organs. Adolescence occupies the teenage years, from ages 12 to 19. Puberty and adolescence occupy the middle three stages during which sexual maturation occurs, and the development is completed in Stage 5 (Tanner, 1962). Physicians use this classification system to describe their patients' level of physical maturity, which is not necessarily related to social or emotional maturity.

It is interesting to note that the inceased production of sex hormones at puberty is associated with anatomical changes and with an increase in sexual drive. Nevertheless, such hormones do not seem to have a direct effect on personality characteristics (Udry and Talbert, 1988).

Male Puberty. The physical changes of puberty occur among males when the levels of masculinizing hormones rise. Between ages six and ten, the adrenal glands begin to secrete androgens. Other hormones (FSH and LH—see Chapter 3) are produced by the pituitary. By the age of eleven for most boys, the pubertal time clock is ticking. One result is genital growth, and the **primary sexual characteristics**

(genitals and internal sexual anatomy) show rapid development. The boy becomes able to produce semen containing sperm. Other physical changes for males, the **secondary sexual characteristics**, also develop at this time—enlarged body muscles, increased height, facial hair, and a deeper voice.

Though puberty is sometimes described as if it happens suddenly one spring afternoon, it is actually a gradual process that takes place over an extended span of time. For example, boys' voices may waver between soprano and tenor for a lengthy period before reaching a stable plateau. A very light growth of hair ("peach fuzz") appears on their upper lips before darker, coarser facial hair begins to grow. Many boys are anxious to mature quickly and often begin to shave before they have enough beard to justify the effort.

Before puberty, males do not produce sperm. Their first ejaculation typically occurs at about the same time that pubic hair appears, between ages eleven and fifteen for 90 percent of males (Harlan, 1980). The first ejaculation of semen, called **thorarche**, is usually a memorable event for most males. In one study, four out of five college students were able to recall the circumstances of their own thorarche, which most often occurred during masturbation. For 25 percent of the sample, thorarche occurred during sleep; nocturnal emissions are common

TABLE 7-2 **Stages of Physical Sexual Maturity**

Tanner (1962) described the normal progression of genital maturation and identified five developmental stages. Stage 1 includes infancy and childhood, before sexual development has begun. At Stage 2, physical maturation gets underway. In Stage 3 girls begin to ovulate and menstruate, while boys for the first time produce semen containing sperm. Genital and breast growth continue during Stage 4, the adolescent years. Stage 5 is defined as the time when full physical maturity has been reached.

| | STAGES OF SEXUAL DEVELOPMENT | | | | |
	1	2	3	4	5
Both Sexes: Pubic Hair	None	Little growth, light color, straight	Heavier growth, some curl	Course, curly, not as thick as adults	Thick, coarse, curly
Males: Penis and testes	No enlargement	Slight enlargement	Longer penis, larger testes	Growth continues, scrotum darkens	Adult appearance
Females: Breasts	No enlargement	Small mound forms	Enlarged breast and areola	Areola forms its own mound on breast	Nipple projects, areola and breast form one contour

during this developmental period. As inevitable and important as this milestone is, few males (28 percent) report being given any advance information about it (Levin, 1976). Such deliberate avoidance of the topic by parents, teachers, and others probably explains why only one in eight boys tells anyone about the event, and half try to hide any sign that it happened.

In decades past, negative beliefs about "self-abuse" and nocturnal emissions were prevalent. For example, a marine, Philip C. Van Buskirk, during the 1850s, kept a detailed record of his voluntary and involuntary orgasms because he was struggling to avoid the presumed health hazards of losing semen. He wrote that, "The loss of one ounce of this fluid . . . weakens the system more completely than the abstraction of forty ounces of blood" (Burg, 1988, p. 217).

Puberty is a gradual process and the exact timing of the changes varies widely, leading to anxiety among late developers. Though such worry is usually unnecessary, sometimes a hormonal problem or other physical disorder *does* cause the delay (Reiter, 1981). Male genital growth usually begins between ages ten to fourteen-and-a-half, pubic hair appears between ten to fifteen years of age (Goldstein, 1976), and puberty is typically completed by age seventeen (Rosenfeld, 1983). A boy is able to reproduce when he begins to produce sperm (called the *spermarche*); this occurs about age fourteen as evidenced by the presence of sperm in the urine (Brown, 1989).

One worrisome side effect of the hormonal changes is that male breasts may become enlarged for a time, and this can be sufficiently embarrassing that a boy doesn't want to take his clothes off in gym class. The percentage of males whose breasts become enlarged has been reported as between 8 and 39 percent in different studies (Harlan, 1980; Karpas, 1982). Such breast growth peaks at age fourteen to fourteen-and-a-half, and usually declines by age sixteen without requiring medical treatment (Silber, 1985).

Some cultures and some religions recognize puberty with rituals that mark the passage from childhood to young manhood. In many groups, young males are temporarily separated from females to undergo what is essentially an initiation ceremony. They may be tattooed, circumsized, hazed, or educated about sex and manhood. Among Australian bushmen,

subincision rites initiate young men into adulthood. The subincision ceremony consists of slitting the underside of the penis with a sharp instrument, using no anesthesia. The urethra becomes an open channel instead of a closed tube for the passage of urine and semen to the meatus (Lobdell, 1975). Other rites involve no pain; for example, when a Jewish boy is bar mitzvahed at age thirteen, friends and family gather to celebrate his new status as an adult male.

Female Puberty.   The beginning of puberty in females is identified with the **menarche,** the first menstruation. Approximately two years before menarche, height increases rapidly. Breasts begin to enlarge between ages eight and thirteen for most girls, and their pubic hair begins growing beteween ages eight and fourteen (Goldstein, 1976). Because of improvements in diet, the age of menarche has dropped over the last century (Wyshak and Frisch, 1982). In the United States, the average girl began menstruating at age 14 in the late 1800s, but it begins years earlier today, the average occurring at the average age of 12.8 (Tanner, 1981).

During the first year of menstruation, half or more of the cycles do not include ovulation (Brennock, 1982). Despite this, sexually active girls who have recently begun to menstruate should not assume that contraception is unnecessary. Ovulation does occur about half the time, and conception is obviously possible during the first year after menarche (Reyniak, 1984). Five years after puberty begins, hormonal control starts to stabilize, cycles become more regular, and most cycles consistently result in fertility with regular ovulation at midcycle.

Though boys may be uninformed that ejaculation will occur, most (over 90 percent) females report having received at least some information about menstruation beforehand. There is also less secrecy about it afterward than about the first male ejaculation. It appears that half of the girls tell their girlfriends about the onset of menstruation. Rituals celebrating the physical changes of puberty are less common for females than males, though some groups do have female ceremonies analogous to those for males. Among Jews, for example, the female equivalent of the bar mitzvah is the bat mitzvah.

If a girl's breasts haven't enlarged by age thirteen or if she has not begun to menstruate by age fifteen-and-a-half, a medical examination should be conducted (Mitchell, 1982). If a girl is very thin (with less than 18 percent of her total weight consisting of body fat), menarche may be delayed. Secondary sexual characteristics such as breast growth and a padding of fat on the hips should nevertheless appear on schedule (Coryllos, 1980).

The opposite problem is early puberty. When sexual maturation begins before age nine in females (age ten in males), this condition is called **precocious puberty**. Such early physical maturation occurs in less than 1 percent of girls and even more rarely among boys (Sanfilippo, 1984), and hormonal treatment can usually reduce any problems that arise. When precocious puberty occurs, sexual behavior does not usually accompany the physical changes. Hormonal changes do not seem to be sufficient to bring about behavior for which the child is not psychologically and socially ready.

Girls commonly worry about their appearance and have physical and psychological doubts about themselves in early adolescence. At twelve and thirteen, they describe themselves in more negative terms than boys describe themselves (Simmons and Rosenberg, 1975). Females perceive their body proportions as inappropriate, feel they are too fat or too thin, and worry about their popularity. A girl who begins the growth spurt earlier than most of her peers can suffer special discomfort. For example, girls prefer to be shorter than boys of their own age, not taller. Because girls reach puberty about two years earlier than boys, they will temporarily tower over their male classmates by a couple of inches. Girls who reach puberty early have to endure this situation for a longer period of time than their peers. Fortunately, this seemingly endless misery eventually ends (Brooks-Gunn and Ruble, 1982).

The sexual signs of puberty for females tend to center around breast development, beginning with the appearance of "breast buds" typically around the age of ten or eleven. A training bra often makes a young girl more comfortable because scratchy clothes can irritate the sensitive areola and nipples as they grow. Girls who develop large breasts may suddenly discover that older males are interested in them; some young females welcome the attention, but others dislike it. Whatever the reaction, girls learn for the first time what it means to be a "sex object" whose primary value lies in specific physical attributes. Family

members also react; fathers, for example, may feel threatened that their little girls have been replaced by attractive young women (Berger, 1978). The possibility of sexual attraction to a daughter is especially confusing, and some fathers avoid their daughters as a way to control such incestuous thoughts. Recognizing these impulses as natural and controllable can reduce these paternal conflicts and help spare their daughters the experience of apparent rejection (Benedek, 1983).

■ Theories of Psychosexual Development

Theoretical descriptions of sexual development attempt to explain the psychological changes that accompany the events we have just described. Two such accounts will be examined here—Freud's **psychoanalytic theory** and the **sexual scripts** theory of Simon and Gagnon.

Psychoanalytic Theory of Development. One of the main points made by Freud is clearly consistent with our description of sexual behavior in infancy and young childhood. Freud shocked much of his contemporary world by emphasizing infantile sexuality, suggesting that even babies and toddlers have strong, biologically based, erotic interests and inclinations.

Freud conceptualized five stages of psychosexual development beginning in earliest infancy and centering around the control of strong sexual urges. According to Freud, in the **oral stage**, infants during their first year focused attention primarily on oral stimulation. Although babies nurse and try to put most objects into their mouths, this is clearly not *all* that they do. For a generation now, scientists have known that infants are also busy with many nonoral exploratory activities, such as intense looking and listening (Piaget, 1951). In the second period of development, the **anal stage**, from ages one to three, the primary source of sexual gratification is the anus. While being toilet trained, the child for the first time may assert his or her independence by withholding or releasing feces. Freud's insistence that events at this stage affect later sexuality, however, seems to be largely inaccurate (Caldwell, 1964, Juni and Cohen, 1985). In the **phallic stage**, from ages four to six, sensual pleasure focuses on the genitals, thus evoking the Oedipal and Elektra complexes (see Figure 7-4). During this stage, children identify with the same-sex

FIGURE 7-4   OEDIPAL FEELINGS: FATHER AS A SEXUAL RIVAL   Freud postulated the Oedipal complex to explain such behavior as the objection expressed by male children to affectionate displays between their parents. Sexual attraction toward the mother was hypothesized to be the basis of attempts to interfere with, or at least be included in, their hugging and kissing. Boys were also said to fear retaliation by the powerful father who might castrate them. The conflict is solved when the boy identifies with his father. For girls, the Elektra complex is somewhat similar, and is resolved by identification with the mother.

parent in order to ward off that parent's anger caused by the offspring's unacceptable sexual attraction to the opposite-sex parent. Boys supposedly respond to anticipations of their fathers' jealous hostility with **castration anxiety.** These observations of typical concerns among therapy patients in Vienna at the turn of the century may have been accurate, but they have since been found not to apply to all cultures. Such behavior is clearly not a universal part of human development.

The **latency period,** usually after age six, supposedly follows the phallic stage and lasts throughout the remainder of childhood. Sexual interests are repressed in order to avoid the threats raised in the phallic stage. Despite Freud's description of this nonsexual phase, children are found to engage in sexual play, masturbation, and sexual fantasies during this period (Broderick, 1966; Janus and Bess, 1981). Some support for the concept has been provided by Harlow (1975). He observed that preadolescent monkeys usually separate into all-male and all-female play groups. The reason, however, does not involve sexual repression; rather, it occurs because males are rougher and more aggressive than females, so the recreational interests of the two sexes differ.

Freud indicated that puberty and adolescence revive the submerged sexual interests of the young person as he or she moves into the **genital stage.** Intimate partnerships with the opposite sex become important if the complexes of the previous stages have been successfully resolved.

Another part of psychoanalytic theory concerns the perceptions of and reactions to anatomical differences between the sexes. When children discover that boys and girls are genitally different, girls are said to respond with **penis envy,** consisting of the strong desire to have this "missing" organ as part of their own bodies. Evidence supporting Freud's concept of penis envy comes from observations of girls' curiosity about penises and their unsuccessful attempts to urinate while standing up at the toilet as boys do. Such behavior need not indicate penis envy, however. It may simply mean that a girl is curious about the male's sex organ and that she imitates the behavior of playmates. The concept of "envy" was much more believable when male superiority was generally accepted;

the idea that females should want to be as much like males as possible seemed obvious. Freud suggested that girls compensated for their lack of a male phallus by producing creative things like arts and crafts (as adults, a similar compensation was provided by creating a child). Girls were also said to develop nervous habits such as nail-biting to occupy themselves in their unhappy hours of longing for a penis. As you may already have guessed, the proposed associations among penis envy, creativity, motherhood, and nail-biting have not been supported by scientific data.

Despite criticisms directed at many specific details of Freud's ideas about sexuality in childhood and adolescence, his theories have exerted a profound influence on the modern study of sexuality. Freud realized that his concepts were incomplete, and he welcomed new information that required their revision.

Sexual Scripts. Do we learn how to behave sexually because of the expectations of those around us? If we do, socialization experiences must play a major role in our patterns of sexual behavior throughout life. Two theorists, William Simon and John Gagnon (1986), have proposed that sexual scripts guide our feelings and our behavior. These scripts have three components, as Figure 7-5 shows—cultural scenarios, interpersonal scripts, and intrapsychic scripting. Gagnon (1990, p. 34) points out that this theoretical perspective" . . . allows one to organize and link together what people think, what they do, and how

FIGURE 7-5 *SEXUAL SCRIPTS: LEARNING TO PLAY ONE'S SEXUAL ROLE* According to Simon and Gagnon (1986), sexual scripts have three components. Cultural scenarios reflect general themes provided by one's society. Interpersonal scripts originate from the attempts of each individual to adapt his or her sexual needs to the expectations of others. Intrapsychic scripts represent one's private sexual thoughts, feelings, and fantasies.

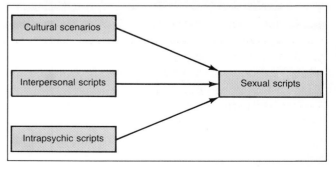

they are affected by the socio-cultural context in which they live."

Cultural scenarios guide us by providing instruction as to appropriate behavior in our particular society. Some societies provide more explicit, detailed information than others, and are best able to coerce their members into behaving as expected. Highly religious or politically totalitarian societies operate in this fashion. Fundamentalist Muslim societies, such as Iran, provide examples. Many Western societies have fewer restrictions about sexual behavior and fewer punishments for violating the restrictions. As a result, many individuals receive conflicting messages from parents, the media, school, and their own religion. Sexuality is both extremely positive (a wonderland of pleasure and romance) and extremely negative (combining sin, unwanted pregnancy, and disease). In this context, any confusion felt by children and adolescents in such an environment is entirely understandable.

The social rules that we learn are adapted to the situations we encounter via **interpersonal scripts.** In effect, we write some portion of the scripts that we follow in our everyday sexual lives. When details are not provided by religious doctrine, parents, or the educational system, we turn elsewhere—for example, to movies and television—for guidance. What we learn must then be applied to a specific situation as we decide what we are supposed to do and how we are supposed to react. Young people often discuss options with their friends or siblings: Is it all right to deep kiss on the first date? If you are in love, are you expected to have sexual intercourse? Is oral sex okay because then you are still a virgin? How do people decide what to do when such questions arise?

Intrapsychic scripting provides a clue as to how an individual reacts to such situations, thereby answering the questions for himself or herself. Fantasies, thoughts, and feelings about sexual matters depend on cultural and interpersonal scenarios, and, moreover, are revised by individuals. A young person might listen to his or her friends' speculations about kissing, intercourse, and oral sex, think about them privately, and then develop an internal script that may be a blend of what they say and what seems reasonable according to his or her own background. As scripting occurs, intrapsychic scripting also takes place in that the individual begins to rehearse inter-

nally the appropriate behavior in the situation. We all have fantasies about what we will say and do in future situations, and to some degree we act on our projections of the future.

Adolescence

Adolescents emerge from childhood to face many challenges. In highly developed societies, where adulthood is postponed, **adolescence** can be relatively complex and stressful. Teenagers no longer have the protected status of childhood, but at the same time there is general agreement that adolescents are not yet ready to function as adults in a fast-paced, technological society. Nevertheless, the "storm and stress" of this period probably has been exaggerated over the years. Many adolescents simply do not conform to the myth of rebelliousness and aggressiveness (Kutner, 1989).

■ Concerns of the Teen Years

Whatever any particular culture may add to the problems of this period, all adolescents must face the reality of continued physical growth. Full height is not reached until the late teens or early twenties. In fact, bones continue to thicken as late as the mid-thirties. The effects of continued social and physical growth and change may create identity questions: Who am I? What should I do? What do I really want? Who is the real me? These concerns often occupy the attention of adolescents for an extended period of time.

Today, in the United States, it is common for 12- and 13-year-olds to begin going to parties and school dances where both sexes are present. By the time girls are 14 to 15 and boys 15 to 16, dating is likely to start (Kutner, 1989). During these years, concerns involving popularity, love, and sex become all-important. Whether or not an adolescent becomes sexually active depends on several factors, including self-acceptance, competence in interacting with the opposite sex, and the belief that dating is important (Newcomb et al., 1986).

Even more than in childhood or later in adulthood, the teen's peer group is the primary source of information, of misinformation, and of most crucial rewards and punishments. Friends also serve as models, and an adolescent's sexual behavior is strongly affected by what his or her friends do (Wilcox and Udry, 1986). Personal appearance receives a great deal of attention, and wearing the right (or wrong) clothing can be a major determinant of a happy (or unhappy) day at school. For the adolescent, not looking "right" can place formidable barriers in the way of gaining acceptance. This is a major reason why acne, a common affliction among teenagers, can be extremely upsetting to its sufferers. Only one in seven adolescents has no acne at all, whereas 3 to 5 percent have very serious cases. Acne results from the androgen hormones which increase in both sexes during adolescence, though males tend to develop more problems than females (Kligman, 1977). Cases of acne peak in frequency between ages sixteen and nineteen in boys, with girls having the greatest problems between fourteen and seventeen (Wessel, 1980). Several effective medical treatments exist, so it is possible for teenagers with acne to avoid the negative effects on self-esteem and self-perceptions of attractiveness.

■ **First Intercourse and Other Sexual Activities**

Because sexual preoccupation and acne occur simultaneously for many adolescents, the myth developed that sexual thoughts and desires *cause* acne. Because acne begins to clear up in late adolescence when many young men and women are likely to become sexually active, a related myth was that engaging in sexual intercourse *cures* acne. Neither fable is true, of course.

Masturbation in Adolescence. Most adolescents masturbate, though they may not experience intercourse until after age nineteen. A survey of teenage males found that they masturbated five times weekly as an average (Lopresto et al., 1985). Females tend to masturbate less frequently than males in all age groups, including adolescence. By the end of adolescence, two thirds of females and almost all males have stimulated themselves to orgasm (Hunt, 1974). This kind of sexual experience can be a positive way to learn about sexuality, and in Chapter 11 we discuss various techniques of masturbation. As discussed more fully in Chapter 8, guilt and anxiety are aroused in some individuals because of negative beliefs about such behavior.

Petting and Necking. Petting is defined as sexual contact below the waist; necking involves kissing on the lips and above-the-waist sexual touching. According to the survey conducted by Hunt in 1974, two thirds of boys and half of girls had orgasm in response to some form of petting by age twenty.

The incidence of oral sex has risen dramatically since the Kinsey data were reported in 1948 and 1953. Adolescents today engage in oral-genital sex about two to three times more frequently than was true of Kinsey's adults (Gagnon and Simon, 1987; Newcomer and Udry, 1985). Females are more likely to receive oral stimulation of their genitals (cunnilingus) than males are to receive fellatio. Those who smoke marijuana tend to have more sexual experience than those who do not (Kolodny, 1981c).

Homosexual Interactions. During adolescence, 6 percent of girls and 11 percent of boys have one or more same-sex sexual partners (Sorenson, 1973), a lower rate than was true when the Kinsey studies were conducted. Other surveys indicate that 11 percent of adolescent girls and 14 percent of adolescent boys have one or more sexual encounters with someone of their own sex (Hass, 1979). Perhaps the most accurate statement is that about one in ten adolescents has at least one homosexual experience, with boys being slightly more likely than girls to do so (DeLameter and MacCorquodale, 1979).

Homosexual experience in adolescence may simply represent experimentation, or it may be an expression of a more permanent sexual orientation. Many adolescents who engage in homosexual interactions do not continue this activity in adulthood. Finding someone with whom to discuss such matters can be difficult. Talking about homosexual experiences to peers, parents, teachers, or ministers may elicit a very negative reaction. Even homosexual organizations are reluctant to provide assistance and support to young people because of legal restrictions centered on "contributing to the delinquency of a minor." Chapter 12 discusses homosexual behavior in greater detail.

First Intercourse. In many societies premarital intercourse has become an increasingly likely experience for young people. The first act of intercourse represents a major event in one's life. Because the transition from virgin to nonvirgin status is treated as a matter of great significance in our society, research has often centered on that topic. Table 7-3 summarizes some common experiences associated with first intercourse.

When teenagers are asked *why* they engage in sex (Stark, 1989), what reasons do you think they give? Girls and boys differ somewhat, but the major reason is peer pressure (34 percent of girls, 26 percent of boys) and—for girls—pressure from boys (17 percent). Both sexes also say that it's because "everyone is doing it" (14 percent of girls, 10 percent of boys), curiosity (14 percent of girls, 16 percent of boys), the need for sexual gratification (5 percent of girls, 10 percent of boys), and love (11 percent of girls, 6 percent of boys). When behavioral scientists seek to identify objective variables associated with becoming sexually active, the best predictors are permissive attitudes about sex and a low level of church attendance (Miller and Olson, 1988).

Because most Americans of both sexes engage in intercourse before marriage and before the age of 20, adult advice to abstain from sex seems to be useless (Barringer, 1990). Many sex educators, such as Carol Cassell, suggest instead that parents encourage their daughters to say "not now" and their sons to consider how girls feel rather than simply to focus on their own physiological needs and the desire to bolster a masculine image (Cook, 1989). Because of problems such as level of emotional maturity, acquiring a bad reputation, and the difficulties involved in obtaining adequate contraceptives, teenagers are well advised to postpone sexual intercourse at least until they leave high school.

A woman's first partner averages nineteen years of age while a man's first partner averages sixteen years (Zelnik and Shah, 1983). At the time Kinsey et al. (1948) gathered their data, about 75 percent of unmarried men had intercourse by the time they were age twenty-five; for women the figure was about 33 percent. By the 1970s, these figures had risen to 97 percent for men and 67 percent for women (Hunt, 1974). Today, 66 percent of both sexes have had intercourse before their *twentieth* birthday (Shearer, 1989). In Germany the number of sexually active unmarried students is found to be above 75 percent for both sexes (Clement et al., 1984). In Sweden, almost 95 percent of the young women report having sexual relations before age twenty (Shearer, 1989).

Men tend to become sexually active at a slightly younger age than do women (Green, 1985), and there has been a tendency for intercourse to begin at increasingly younger ages, especially for women (Wielandt et al., 1989). Now, that trend may be reversing. In the late 1970s, 26.2 percent of American males had at least one sexual experience by the time they reached age fifteen; by the late 1980s, only 19.3 percent reported having sex by that age (Maugh, 1990).

In various Western cultures, then, virginity is quite likely to end during adolescence and prior to marriage. This is not, however, a universal pattern. Only 17 percent of unmarried Japanese females are sexually experienced by age 20, for example (Shearer, 1989). In the Peoples Republic of China, most females have intercourse for the first time when they marry, usually at about age twenty-four. At the opposite extreme, in parts of Black Africa, menarche and first intercourse coincide (Fiedler, 1978).

Effects of First Intercourse. Males and females tend to perceive their first intercourse differently (DeLamater, 1987). As Table 7-3 indicated, females most often describe their first intercourse partner as someone they love, but most males do not. Immediate sexual gratification is the primary goal of males, not romance. The sexes also differ in whether first intercourse culminates in orgasm; 80 percent of college males report an orgasm as part of this experience, while only 7 to 22 percent of females do so (Simon and Gagnon, 1968). Probably, this is one reason that males report more enjoyment. First intercourse is associated with different thoughts and feelings among adolescent males and females (Sorenson, 1973). Boys attach more significance to it than girls, and they usually react positively with joyful emotions and a sense of maturity. Girls often react with negative feelings that include guilt or sorrow, reactions that their partners may not realize.

Neither males nor females tend to plan their first sexual interaction ahead of time. For 75 percent it is a spur-of-the-moment event (Zelnik and Shah, 1983). Sullivan (1984, p. 200) describes the typical

TABLE 7-3 **The First Time: Differences between Males and Females**

An individual's first experience with intercourse commonly occurs during adolescence. This event differs for males and females with respect to the age when it occurs, the role of affection toward the partner, enjoyment, and whether the facts are shared with others.

	FIRST INTERCOURSE	
	Boys	Girls
Average age	15	16
In love with, engaged to, or married to first partner	30–41%	66–82%
Experience was enjoyable and satisfying	75–90%	50–75%
Told others about it	60% told someone; most told five or more friends; 66% of parents found out	40% told someone; 22% told five or more friends; 40% of parents found out

Source: Data from Athanasiou et al., 1970; Bell et al., 1981; Carns, 1973; DeLamater and MacCorquodale, 1979; Green, 1985; Simon and Gagnon, 1968; Sorensen, 1973

initial sexual encounter as "those first awkward, guilt-ridden probings in the suboptimum setting of a makeshift surrounding." Chapter 5 discusses one consequence of the lack of preparation: the high rates of unwanted teenage pregnancy.

Failure to plan and prepare also means that many females feel pain, guilt, and anxiety about what has happened (Weis, 1983a, 1985). Most males are quite uninformed about how best to stimulate a female in order to create sexual excitement, and, consequently, must learn by doing. The result is often pain rather than pleasure for the female, and the younger the girl the worse the pain. Pain is also more likely among those who have negative attitudes about sexuality, as Chapter 8 explores.

For males, sexual intercourse is more of an end in itself than is true for females among both black and white adolescents (Zelnik and Shah, 1983). Sexual success is a positive aspect of a male's public image; therefore, males are much more likely to "advertise" their activity to their friends than are females. Also, male friends tend to express approval and admiration when learning of such sexual feats. In other words, males brag about having intercourse, and their friends congratulate them. It is "good" to make out like a bandit, to score, to be a stud. In deciding whether to have intercourse with an adolescent boy, a teenage girl might consider how she might feel about the subsequent public descriptions of her behavior.

Whatever the effects, sexual intercourse is now a common occurrence early in one's life. According to one survey of over 5,000 Israeli teenagers, the answer to the question, "How far have you gone?" means something different to them than to earlier generations (Antonovsky, 1982). When their parents were teenagers, how far one had gotten with the opposite sex referred to articles of clothing removed or parts of the body that had been touched; for the younger generation, the answer is intercourse, which is increasingly accepted as part of adolescence.

Obtaining Sexual Knowledge

Though it reminds us of a congressional hearing, we must ask the questions—what do children know about sex, when do they know it, and what is the source of their information? Answers are explored in the following section.

■ Sexual Information in Childhood

A child's ability to think and to make sense of any information increases and matures as he or she ages. An explanation that is useful to an eight-year-old may be totally inappropriate for a four-year-old, for example. With increasing maturity, a child can understand and remember more detailed facts and can deal with more complex material about sex or any other subject. A very young girl may find it difficult to understand how the same woman can be her mother as well as someone's wife and someone else's daughter; this information sinks in quite easily a few years later.

Understanding Sexual Matters. Because of the gradual development of thinking capacity, children's understanding of sex gradually changes. Even though sexual learning tends to occur earlier now than in the past (Gebhard, 1977), parents and sex educators need to fit what they teach about sex to the child's age level. An old joke illustrates the general point that it is not always easy to guess what children want to know and what information they are able to process. A preschooler asks his mother, "Where did I come from?" Having prepared carefully for this moment,

she tells him a beautiful story about Daddy planting a seed, the tiny child growing slowly inside of Mommy, and the infant finally emerging from between his mother's legs to enter the world. Afterward, the boy responds, "Oh. I just wondered because Johnnie said that he came from Cleveland."

Once a child—usually about age four—begins asking questions about conception, her or she is ready to hear that babies are made, not delivered by storks or purchased at the hospital. The same child, nevertheless, probably cannot yet understand just how love, sexual intercourse, and biological processes combine to produce a new human being (Bernstein and Cowan, 1975). At times, education occurs accidentally through exposure to the sexual interactions of others. As is pointed out in the special section, ***Taking Responsibility and Protecting Yourself,*** on pages 184 to 185, special concerns are raised when a child chances to witness his or her parents engaged in sex.

Taking Responsibility and Protecting Yourself

EXPOSURE TO THE PRIMAL SCENE: CONTROLLING ITS IMPACT

Many children have experienced what Freud (1918/1955) labeled the **primal scene**—they enter a room and find their parents engaged in sexual acts, including intercourse. Such exposure usually occurs accidentally in the United States because parents and children tend not to share the same bedroom. In other parts of the world, including Japan, sharing a bedroom is quite common, and this arrangement does not seem to have a negative effect on children (Laury, 1978). Research indicates that neither sleeping in the parents' bed nor occasionally seeing them nude leads to sexual dysfunction or maladjustment (Lewis and Janda, 1988). In our culture, the child's reactions to witnessing parental sex is more extreme than in cultures where the incident is considered natural. What is the impact of this experience, and what can be done to prevent a negative outcome?

Despite Freud's insistence on the lasting importance of this event on children, there is little evidence to support that proposition. Figure 7-6 provides an example of a child's reaction to discovering this strange thing that his or her parents are doing. The response is more likely to be great curiosity and wonder instead of fear or anxiety.

Only a minority of college students report any memory of perceiving any sexual interaction between their parents. In a group of 345 U.S. students, 18.5 percent remembered such an event. Most of these (70 percent) heard the sound their parents made, while less than half (44 percent) actually saw the sexual activity in progress. The average age for witnessing parental sex was 11.6 years, but some had observed their parents as early as age 3 (Hoyt, 1978). In a group of upper-middle-

class youngsters, the figures were similar in that 20 percent had perceived their parents engaged in sex (Rosenfeld, 1984). Thus, the experience is not rare, but most people either do not have the experience or fail to remember it.

Exposure to the primal scene does not usually produce a lasting emotional disturbance. Nevertheless, many children who are exposed to the primal scene *do* have a negative emotional reaction, having some feelings of distress. They are shocked by such a scene, even when questioned years later (Hoyt, 1979a). One reason that parental sex seems to be of special importance is they have not previously observed their parents together in the nude (Hoyt, 1979b).

College students who had observed parental sex during childhood rated sexuality as a more important part of their par-

Gaining a Realistic Understanding of Sexuality. Children's thought processes progress from relatively less realistic to more realistic. In early childhood, they emphasize minor characteristics of things in an attempt to understand them. For example, a daughter thinks she is like her mother because they both have blue dresses, not necessarily because they are females or from the same family. When investigators asked questions of over 800 children and adolescents from four different countries (Australia, Great Britain, the United States, and Sweden) to test their sexual knowledge, their answers differed across age groups. The subjects were asked, "Do the bodies of boys and girls grow differently as they grow older?" Five-year-olds answered by pointing out differences that were nonsexual, or vaguely physical, saying that boys and girls wear different clothes or that boys are bigger than girls. Between age five and adolescence, children focused more on primary or secondary sexual characteristics of just one sex—men have a deep voice or women have breasts. In contrast, adolescents focused on sexual functioning to describe both sexes, saying for example that "Girls menstruate, and boys have wet dreams" (Goldman and Goldman, 1983).

In the absence of information, young children sometimes gave nonsensical answers. When asked, "How long does it take a baby to grow before it is born?" Some five-year-olds said "a few minutes" whereas others said "a hundred years." Some seven-year-olds occasionally gave answers similar to these, but generally the responses of older children reflected much more realism and accuracy.

Learning Sexual Terminology. Can you remember when you first learned the correct names for male and female genitalia? It may seem surprising, but most adults indicate that they didn't learn these until late childhood or adolescence. They first were taught euphemisms for sexual anatomy, such as the terms listed in Table 7-4. It seems that while parents are eager to teach their offspring the correct names for the rest of the body—from forehead to toes—they fail to include the area between the navel and the knees.

FIGURE 7-6 *EXPOSURE TO "THE PRIMAL SCENE": PUZZLING BUT NOT TRAUMATIC* When a child accidentally witnesses his or her parents engaged in sexual activity, only rarely are there any long-term effects on the child.

ents' lives than did those who had not had this experience. The two groups did not differ, however, in how important they considered sex in their own lives or in how happy they felt. The primal scene appears to cause only temporary upset, but has no apparent long-term effects on the observer's sexual or emotional development.

What can parents do to minimize the effects of such an experience on a child? An angry response is obviously inappropriate. The child can calmly be asked to return to his or her room where a quiet explanation of what is happening helps to soothe the child's fears. The parents may want to ask later what the child observed, and what he or she thought was happening. The child frequently misinterprets the interaction as aggressive rather than sexual (Rosenfeld, 1984). Two writhing, groaning bodies can appear to be experiencing pain rather than pleasure. An explanation that the adults enjoy this vigorous activity, similar to the way the child enjoys playful wrestling or being thrown up in the air, is helpful (Brooks, 1984). The child needs to associate what was observed with pleasure, love, and caring between the parents rather than with anger, shame, and unhappiness.

Some children may ask to be included in something that sounds this nice. They can be told that when they grow up and find someone they love, they can also enjoy such experiences. A child who is simply told to go away without a chance to ask questions or receive explanations may have a hard time in understanding the event and his or her feelings about it.

Though a locked door is an obvious way to prevent the potential problem from arising, that can also be a mysterious signal that something special and secret is going on behind it. Children can be taught that they cannot share in every part of their parents' relationship and, therefore, should knock before entering a closed room (Cantrell, 1982). If this procedure is followed, parents should also be careful to knock on their offspring's closed doors—they too deserve privacy.

TABLE 7-4 What's That? For Genitals, Children Learn Special Words

In a survey of over 200 adults, they reported using these terms for their genitals during childhood. It seems clear that parents are willing to teach their offspring the correct words to identify all parts of the body except those related to sexuality.

FEMALES		MALES	
Bunny	Pocketbook	Bimpus	Peter
Christmas	Toy-toy	Dick	Go-go
Doty	Wee-wee-er	Ding-ding	Pipi
Down there	Shame	Peepee button	Puppy
Nasty	Tush	Piddler	Thing

Source: Adapted from Gartell and Mosbacher, 1984.

Similarly, most male and female dolls are blank in this region of the body.

Adult males report that they knew the meaning of the words *penis, testes,* and *anus* at an average age of 11.5. In contrast, adult females report not having known the meaning of *clitoris, vagina,* or *vulva* until 15.6 years on the average (Gartrell and Mosbacher, 1984). Childhood sex differences are even more striking. Among girls, 44 percent learned no names at all to designate their genitals; whereas among boys only 19 percent did not know the terms for their genitals. Inaccurate information or total silence on the subject could easily give girls the impression that their sexuality is shameful or unimportant.

Most young people, adolescents included, also lack general information about sexuality. For example, they often are misinformed about homosexuality, masturbation, and conception (Grace, 1981). Try to imagine the suffering of a youngster who believes that having only same-sex friends indicates homosexuality, that masturbation causes insanity or weak eyesight, or that a soda pop douche prevents conception. The consequences of such misinformation about pregnancy and sexually transmissible disease can have lifetime consequences (Millard, 1980; Rollin, 1980). The teenage father or mother who has to quit school or the adolescent girl who becomes permanently infertile because of pelvic infection represent just two possible examples of damaging results. Adolescents lacking sexual information may also suffer from the effects of sexual exploitation or unenjoyable sexual interactions.

■ Sources of Sexual Information

Where do we obtain our sexual facts and false-hoods? Most are learned from other people, typically from childhood peers. As Figure 7-7 illustrates, a study of over 1,000 college students found that young friends were the major source of information about intercourse. Boys learned from fellow children slightly more often than girls did. Girls were likely to receive information from their parents—usually their mothers—more than twice as frequently as was true for boys. Less common sources for finding out about intercourse were books or magazines, self-discovery through intercourse itself, formal sex education, and so on. Peers were the major source, however, by a two-to-one margin. They are also the major source of information about other sexual matters, such as puberty and contraception (Weis, 1975).

In the past, attempts at providing accurate information about sex were strongly discouraged. When Margaret Sanger wrote *What Every Girl Should Know* in weekly installments in 1912 and 1913, such "obscene, lewd, and lascivious" material as the section on venereal disease was banned by the United States Post Office (Robertson, 1980). A quarter of a century later, the situation had not changed markedly. Campion (1989) described her college "hygiene" course in

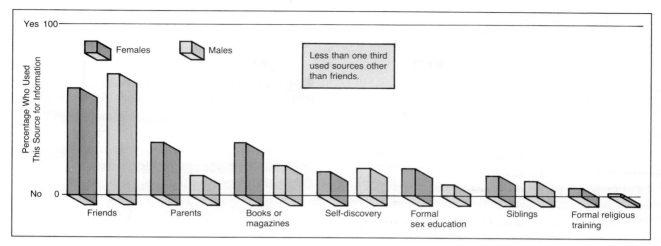

FIGURE 7-7 *LEARNING ABOUT SEX: FRIENDS AS SEX EDUCATORS* The primary source of information about sexual intercourse, according to a study of over 1,200 college students, was their friends. All other sources were much less relevant for learning about this topic.
Source: Data from Green, 1985.

the late 1930s. Her professor at Wellesley College warned the freshmen women never to wear red satin because it arouses men and to avoid dancing because it "leads to babies." You may well question the usefulness of this kind of sex education.

A complete absence of information is rare but potentially dangerous. One student's case history illustrates this, though it is clearly not a typical experience. Tony was a twenty-two-year-old graduate student who sought counseling because he suspected

that he was gay. Not only had Tony been totally uninformed about sex by his parents, he had also been isolated from the influence of peers and even written material dealing with sex. Consequently, he did not know that males and females had different genitals, and he believed that birth occurred through the woman's anus. The counselor gave him a great deal of information and as much reassurance as possible. Despite this help, Tony continued to feel anxious around women, interpreting his response as an indi-

TABLE 7-5 **Sexual Knowledge: How Accurate Is Your Information?**

These items from a survey of sexual knowledge for college students represent statements answered incorrectly by a substantial proportion of students in a preliminary study. The correct answers are "true" for the first item and "false" for the other three.

SAMPLE ITEMS FROM A SURVEY OF SEXUAL KNOWLEDGE

1. Women can become sexually aroused when breast-feeding an infant.
   T   F
2. There are physiological differences in orgasms attained through sexual intercourse, masturbation, or any other technique.   T   F
3. Nocturnal emissions or "wet dreams" are indicative of sexual problems.
   T   F
4. Frequent masturbation is one of the most common causes of premature ejaculation in the male.   T   F

Source: Allgeier, 1978.

cation of homosexual tendencies even though he had no intimate contacts with any male (Chisholm, 1981). Tony was not homosexual, and his experience illustrates an extreme instance of how unnecessary suffering and insecurity can result from not being informed about sex.

At the opposite extreme, you may wonder about the effect of exposing a young person to a great deal of accurate information. Many opponents of sex education express the fear that the more that young people are taught about sex, the more likely they are to respond by trying it. Research indicates that college students who perform well on a test of sexual knowledge do in fact have different sexual histories than their less knowledgeable peers (Allgeier, 1978), though not in the way that might be expected. Students with high scores on the test (see Table 7-5, p. 187 for examples of test items) began masturbating one year *later* than students with low scores (13.03 versus 11.86 years of age, respectively), and they also had intercourse for the first time 1.5 years *later* than was true of students who knew less about sex (17.51 versus 16 years of age, respectively). In summary, then, young people who possess accurate information typically engage in sexual acts later than do those who lack dependable information.

Sex Education

When asked, "Would you be for or against sex education in public schools?", 1,200 out of 1,500 adults said they were in favor (Mahoney, 1979). Other research shows that between 60 and 70 percent of adult Americans approve sex education and even birth control services for adolescents (Reichelt, 1986). Active opposition to formal sex education is confined to a minority who expressed extremely traditional, conservative opinions about many moral issues. For example, they also oppose women working outside the home, premarital sexual activity, and permissive divorce laws. Even among those who favor sex education in the school system, the details of the process provoke heated controversies. Few parents agree about how, when, or what the schools should teach *their* children about sex.

■   **Attitudes toward Formal Sex Education**

Parents worry about what their children might learn, or fail to learn, in sex education classes. Because sexuality goes beyond biology and anatomy to include moral, religious, and social values, fears about whose values are to be taught are legitimate (Szasz, 1981). Parents clearly want only their own opinions and attitudes represented. In contrast, sex educators want to point out the errors in sexual myths, enlighten students about sexual decision making and its effects, and inform them about the emotional and interpersonal aspects of sexuality (Passmore, 1980). Some sex educators would add a fourth goal to this list: to provide information about contraception and contraceptive services (Roemer and Paxman, 1985).

Even among those who share such goals, there is much disagreement about how to accomplish them. Public school administrators in the United States indicate that opposition from their communities is the greatest obstacle to effective sex education (Scales and Kirby, 1983). Principals and their staffs fear the public's reactions to programs that are needed to deal with problems such as unwanted teenage pregnancy. Reflecting the conflict between the pressing need and the fear of criticism, most (75 percent) big city school districts do have sex education classes, but only one in ten includes detailed information about contraception prior to the high school level. Though this topic may be avoided, the number of pregnancies in the earlier grade levels is steadily increasing (Sonenstein and Pittman, 1984). AIDS adds a new dimension to the problem, and indications of the presence of the AIDS-causing virus (HIV) are expected to become more common among sexually active adolescents in the 1990s.

■   **The Mechanics of Formal Sex Education**

How can sex educators accomplish their educational goals? A common research finding is that the information in sex courses must be tailored to the students' needs and competencies.

Course Content.   Elementary school children in the early grades have many questions and they need honest answers ("How does a baby get out?"). By the middle grades (fourth through sixth), students want to know about their own and others' feelings and responsibilities ("At what age is a girl too young to have sex?") In a number of communities, parents have been asked to meet with teachers to help in designing the sexuality curriculum for grades one through twelve (Brick, 1985). The courses are designed to include information about practical matters such as how children may protect themselves from unwanted sexual advances and from the persuasive influences of peers and the media about sex.

When parents and other adults object to sex education or to particular aspects of it, their concern often focuses on its possible effects on their children. What do we know about the effects of sex education? The special section, *Highlighting Research,* on pages 189 to 190, explores the effects of sex education on knowledge, attitudes, and behavior.

Highlighting Research

THE EFFECTS OF SEX EDUCATION: KNOWLEDGE, ATTITUDES, AND BEHAVIOR

Perhaps the biggest fear about sex education is that students will become sexually active at earlier ages than if sex education were not part of the school curriculum. "What they don't know can't hurt them." The president of the Eagle Forum, Phyllis Schafly, has fought all sex education in the public schools because "sex education is a principal cause of teenage pregnancy" (Allgeier, 1982, p.7). Beyond behavioral effects, many adults believe that sex education will instill a permissive attitude in children and adolescents about activities of which they as parents do not approve—masturbation, prostitution, oral sex, homosexuality, and so forth (Gordon, 1986; Kerrison, 1988). In one heated controversy, educators in New Hampshire discovered that if homosexuality is not described as abnormal and unhealthy, a storm of public protest is likely to follow (Paul, 1988). What are the facts about the results of sex education?

First, sexuality courses produce gains in knowledge about the topic (Kilmann et al., 1981). Before and after measures of the sex information possessed by students show significant improvement. Students are more accurate in their knowledge afterward, believing fewer sexual myths. Such educational benefits tend to last at least as long as a year after the course is over. (It might be noted that these evaluation studies are confined to college sex-education courses, because at lower grade levels there is resistance to evaluating the effects of such courses.)

Second, sexual attitudes are found to change in the direction of greater approval of and comfort with various sexual topics. Specifically, students become more tolerant of others' engaging in many types of sexual acts, and this more permissive outlook persists for at least two years after the course is completed. Such tolerance does not, interestingly enough, extend to the individual's own behavior (Story, 1979). Thus, students express more permissive attitudes about others (not themselves) with respect to:

1. mutual masturbation with someone of the same or opposite sex

2. engaging in sex with one's partner in the presence of others

3. maintaining more than one sexual relationship simultaneously

This greater tolerance by students does not mean that sex education encourages acceptance of these or any other sexual activities. The tolerant attitudes seem to result from the general freedom to talk about and think about sexual matters. The increased permissiveness is most likely to occur in classes including discussion of the course material as well as lectures (Wanlass et al., 1983). Neither lecture by itself nor discussion by itself has this effect. The combination of hard facts and the opportunity to discuss them causes the attitudinal shift.

These changes have been documented in research on the effects of college sexuality courses. Other research has dealt with medical students who usually spend only about eighteen hours in a minicourse on sex (Cross, 1983). The majority (80 to 90 percent) of U.S. medical schools offer at least this minimal training in the sexual area to future physicians (Lief, 1979). Even with this limited exposure to sexuality, medical students gain some knowledge of the subject, and their sexual attitudes become slightly more tolerant and liberal (Alzate, 1982; Schnarch and Jones, 1981). It is worth noting that medical students generally hold more restrictive and conservative views about sex than the general population; nevertheless, they believe their patients to be even more restrictive and conservative than themselves (Schnarch, 1981).

Despite becoming more permissive, students in sex education courses do not dramatically change their preexisting patterns of sexual behavior (Eisen and Zellman, 1987). Only one investigation found an increase in students' sexual activity after they had completed a college sex course, and this change occurred only among males (Zuckerman et al., 1976). These men reported an increase in total number of orgasms, frequency of masturbation, and heterosexual contacts after the course compared to the pre-course period. In a control group of students taking a personality course, males also increased their frequency of heterosexual contacts during the semester. Thus, some of the observed changes were a function of factors (for example, the length of time in college) other than sex education itself. Comparisons of students in sex courses with those in other courses also must take into account that those taking sex education are generally more permissive and tolerant about sexual matters *before* the course than students in general. Any effects therefore may partly reflect the personality characteristics of students who are interested in courses concerned with sexual behavior.

Two crucial questions are asked about sex education: (1) Does it make premarital intercourse more likely to occur? (2) Does it increase the risk of unwanted pregnancy? Young people in one study were asked to indicate whether they had taken any formal sex courses and also to provide information about their experiences with intercourse and pregnancy. Figure 7-8 illustrates the association between sex education and behavior. The incidence of premarital intercourse was the same for students who had taken such a course as for those who had not. A more surprising finding was that fewer females taking a course in sexuality became pregnant than females not taking sex education (Zelnik and Kim, 1982). A possible reason for this difference is that women taking a formal sex course are provided with information about contraception.

We can conclude that formal sex education increases knowledge and leads to more permissive attitudes about the behavior of others. The only behavioral effects are a mild increase in the sexual activity of males and a slight decrease in pregnancy rates for females.

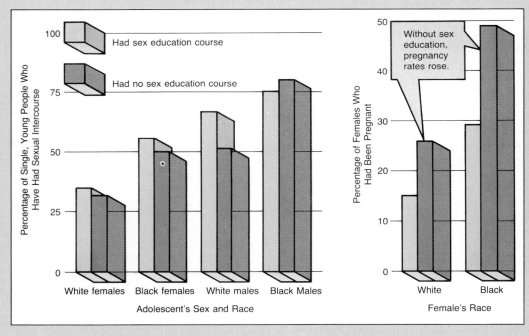

FIGURE 7-8 *SEX EDUCATION: NO EFFECT ON INTERCOURSE, BUT FEWER PREGNANCIES* Several hundred black and white adolescents, females aged fifteen to seventeen and males aged seventeen to eighteen, reported whether they had taken formal sex education courses and whether they had engaged in sexual intercourse. Females also were asked if they had ever been pregnant. Although sex education had no effect on the likelihood of intercourse, it was associated with lower pregnancy rates, regardless of race. Racial differences in pregnancy rates are believed to be based on differences in social class.
Source: Data from Zelnik and Kim, 1982.

Controversies. Information generally is most effective when it is available to those who most need it. For example, sexually active adolescents find birth control information to be extremely valuable, but adolescents who are virgins do not find it particularly meaningful (Kallen et al., 1983).

Teachers and the general public agree that adolescents should receive instruction about birth control and several other topics as Figure 7-9 shows. For elementary school children, however, only instruction about reproductive biology receives high approval ratings from both groups (Gallup, 1984; 1985a,b). Teachers expressed more conservative views than parents as to whether elementary schools should teach sex education. Possibly in stating these views teachers hoped to avoid criticism, or they may simply have felt

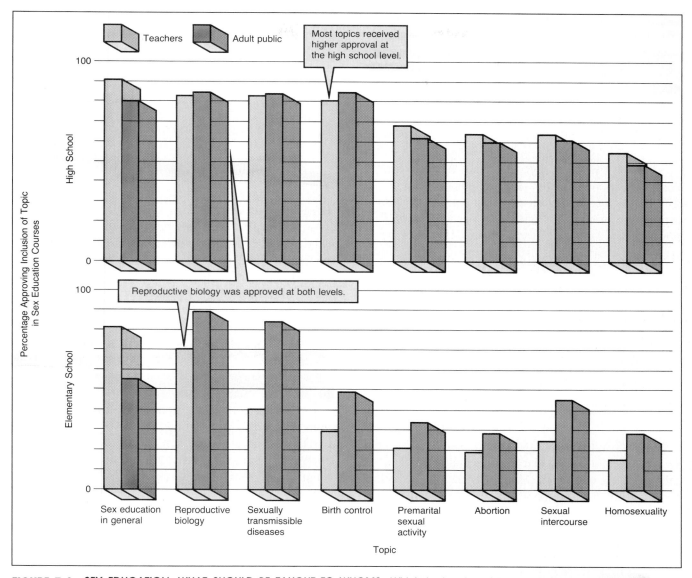

FIGURE 7-9 *SEX EDUCATION: WHAT SHOULD BE TAUGHT TO WHOM?* Which topics should be covered in sex education courses in elementary and high schools? When over 800 public school teachers and over 1,500 other adults were surveyed, both groups approved all but one (homosexuality) of the topics shown here for high school courses. Although a bare majority of teachers wanted information about gays and lesbians included in the curriculum, most of the general public were opposed. For elementary school courses, only general sex education and reproductive biology were approved by both groups; only nonteachers strongly favored including the topic of sexually transmissible diseases.
Source: Data from Gallup, 1984, 1985a, 1985b.

embarrassed about discussing such topics with young children (Yarber and McCabe, 1981). The lowest approval rating by both teachers and other adults is for teaching about homosexuality. Most elementary and high school sex education classes omit this subject (Newton, 1982). As we suggest throughout this text, controversial sexual topics can provoke negative feel-

ings and the expression of hostility by people who are offended by such material.

The books available for sexuality classes at the elementary school level leave much to be desired. A review of twenty-three such texts for children revealed two major problems (Rindskopf, 1981). First, they generally depict men and women in quite traditional roles—women have babies and care for families, while men dominate the couples' sexual activity. Second, the books frequently define sexual acts with euphemistic words and avoid relevant illustrations. When children read that heterosexual intercourse means "making love for baby's future" and see an accompanying picture of two faces (one male, one female) in close proximity, one wonders just what they might be learning.

There are many diverse resources that describe the publications available for sex education. For example, religious books on sexuality contain the teachings of many different faiths. A *Bibliography of Religious Publications on Sexuality and Sex Education* is available from SIECUS (Sex Information and Education Council of the United States) Resource Center and Library at New York University in New York City. The same organization publishes a list of nonreligious, general handbooks on sex education: *Sexuality and Family Life Education: An Annotated Bibliography of Curricula Available for Purchase.*

■ Professional Training for Sex Educators

How does a person become a sex educator? An initial question to consider is "What are the desirable qualities of sex educators?" Although no research has yet focused on the personal characteristics of those in this field, sex educators clearly should have sufficient background in the biological and behavioral sciences to enable them to provide accurate information. This background is necessary because sex educators help shape a very important aspect of the lives of their students.

For elementary and high school sex educators, college courses are often available that help prepare them to teach about human sexuality. Students wanting to be trained in sex education at the college level have two options. One is to seek graduate training in university departments where individuals are engaged in teaching and research dealing with sexuality. (No one field has a monopoly on the topic of sex; thus, relevant experts may be found in departments of psychology, sociology, biology, and physical education, among others.) Those writing books, chapters, and journal articles about sexuality often are based in colleges and universities, and many examples of such work are contained in the bibliography of this text-

book. A second option for the interested student is to compare doctoral programs in human sexuality education at the handful of universities offering such training. The Society for the Scientific Study of Sex maintains a list of these programs, and its address is P. O. Box 208, Mount Vernon, Iowa 52314.

■ Parents as Sex Educators

In addition to peers, parents also may teach their youngsters about sex. What are the effects of such learning? One problem is that parents are usually in conflict about taking on this task themselves.

Four out of five parents agree that they—rather than schools, peers, or other sources—should educate their children sexually (McConnell, 1974). Despite this general belief, many parents do not talk to their children about sexual matters. If the topic *does* arise, the information given is often relatively vague and negative: don't have sex, don't become pregnant, don't acquire a disease, or don't get a bad reputation. Parents over the past several years have agreed that they should discuss sex with their offspring more often than is actually the case (Fox and Inazu, 1980). Today, such communications are much more common, according to Planned Parenthood surveys of parents (Talking about sex . . . , 1989). The most common topics are love, responsibility, and commitment (88 percent), followed closely by pregnancy and sexually transmissible diseases. Abortion, birth control, and dating behavior is discussed by 60 percent of the parents, and only 14 percent say that they never discuss sex with their children.

If parents and their offspring are asked separately about sex education in the home and parent-child discussions of sexuality, they disagree a great deal about what occurred. As Figure 7-10 shows, a survey of over 700 pairs of mothers and their teens in the United States revealed that 33 to 50 percent of mothers and their adolescent sons and daughters did not agree about whether they had ever discussed sexuality or birth control (Newcomer and Udry, 1985). Usually mothers thought they had discussed it, but their adolescents denied that such communications were given. Adolescents also think that their mothers have opinions about sexual topics that they do not actually have, as summarized in Figure 7-11.

Considering the misinformation that many teen-

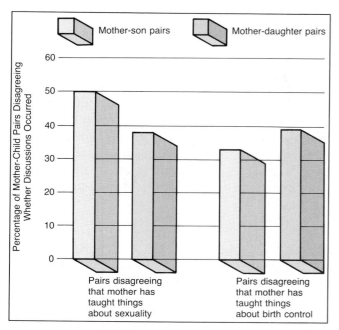

FIGURE 7-10 *WHEN MOM TALKS TO TEENAGERS ABOUT SEX: DID THEY OR DIDN'T THEY?* Mothers and their adolescent sons and daughters don't agree about whether they have discussed sexual topics such as birth control. Among over 700 pairs of mothers and their offspring, from one third to one half disagreed about having discussed specific sexual topics.
Source: Data from Newcomer and Udry, 1985.

agers have about what their parents think about sexuality, would you expect sex education by one's mother and father to change behavior? What results can parents expect if they become sex educators? Mothers and fathers believe that sex education in the home reduces the likelihood of sexual activity (Dickman, 1982) and increases responsible behavior. Thus, they expect their family-educated teenagers to refrain from potentially harmful sexual relations and to use effective contraceptives if they should have sex (Inazu and Fox, 1980).

Studies have evaluated the practical value of such heart-to-heart talks about the birds and bees. Boys showed no change in sexual behavior during the two years following discussions with their parents, even when there was parent-son agreement about what had been discussed. For girls, there *were* some effects, depending on who reported the discussions. When mothers said that they had discussed intercourse, their daughters tended to refrain from engaging in it. When daughters said that contraception was

discussed, they tended to use effective methods of birth control.

Other research indicates that both male and female adolescents who are sexually active use contraceptives more effectively if they have had open discussion with their parents about sex and contraception (Baker et al., 1988; Milan and Kilmann, 1987). Such discussions do not, however, seem to alter the likelihood of adolescents having intercourse (Fisher, 1987, 1988).

Even if parental education does not greatly affect adolescent sexual behavior, it may have another sort of positive effect. Such discussions help teenagers view their parents as approachable adults to confide in if sexual problems arise. If basic sexual information is withheld by parents, they should not be surprised when their offspring fail to share with them their sexual concerns. Parents might find it helpful to prepare beforehand just how they want to communicate with their sons and daughters about sex, and there are books that provide useful guidelines—one example is a publication by Planned Parenthood (1986).

FIGURE 7-11 *WHAT ARE YOUR MOTHER'S REAL ATTITUDES ABOUT SEX?* A study of over 700 adolescents found that a large minority (26 to 40 percent) were inaccurate in describing their mothers' views about sexuality.
Source: Data from Newcomer and Udry, 1985.

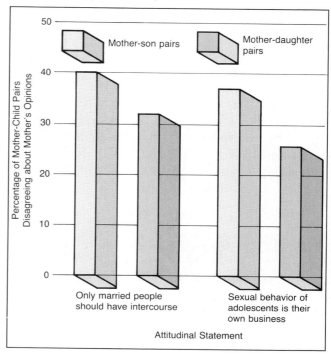

Obviously, there are differences among families in how parents approach sex education. These differences are not, however, related to such factors as ethnic background (Abramson et al., 1983). Other characteristics determine responses to sexual questions asked by their children. For fathers, education was a major factor; men who had more than the average amount (fourteen to fifteen years) expressed greater comfort in talking about subjects such as nudity and masturbation with their children than was true for fathers with less education. For mothers, religion was a major factor determining the ease with which they could discuss sex with their sons and daughters.

Mothers with a strongly religious background were less comfortable with these topics and less likely to be available to talk about sexuality than were mothers with a less religious background.

A study of 22 12- to 14-year-olds and their parents found that parent-child communication about sex did not have a measurable effect on the adolescents' sexual knowledge or attitudes (Fisher, 1986). For those families who do communicate, however, there is much more similarity in parent-offspring sexual values than is true for the non-communicating families.

Summarizing the Information about Sexuality in Childhood and Adolescence. . .

Sexuality is in evidence throughout infancy and childhood, and masturbation demonstrates the motivation of youngsters to obtain sexual stimulation. Later, sexual play with other children also provides stimulation as well as information about physical differences and similarities in genitalia.

In **puberty** physical maturation of the reproductive organs occurs, but social and emotional development usually lags behind. **Thorarche** and **menarche** are sexual milestones for males and females, respectively, but most children do not receive adequate information to prepare them for adjusting emotionally to such changes. Theories of psychosexual development include Freud's **psychoanalytic** formulation and **sexual scripting** by Simon and Gagnon. The latter involves three major components—**cultural scenarios, interpersonal scripts**, and **intrapsychic scripting**. Among the psychosexual hurdles of adolescence are continued physical development and the conflicts surrounding first intercourse.

Sexual knowledge advances in childhood, becoming increasingly complex and conventional. Misconceptions about sexuality arise and persist well into **adolescence** and beyond. Because of reluctance to discuss sexuality with their children, most parents do not fulfill the responsibility they assert to be important—to educate their offspring about sex. Much of the information and misinformation about sex that most of us receive is from our peers.

Formal sex education provokes a number of controversies, including the value of including it in the school curriculum, which topics should be covered, and fears about its effects. Research indicates that formal sex education in college enhances knowledge and increases tolerance of the sexual practices of others, but it does not lead to dramatic changes in sexual behavior. Professional training programs for sex educators have been developed in various institutions to fill the need for sex education.

To Find Out More about Sexuality in Childhood and Adolescence. . .

Brooks-Gunn, J., & Peterson, A. C. (Eds.). (1983). *Girls at puberty: Biological and psychosocial perspectives*. New York: Plenum Press.
    Various experts on female sexual development comment on the experience of puberty. Topics such as early and late puberty and attitudes toward sexual maturation are covered.

Gay, P. (Ed.) (1989). *The Freud reader*. New York: W. W. Norton.
    This selection of original contributions by Freud permits the reader to have direct contact with some of his proposals about psychosexual development as well as many other aspects of psychoanalytic theory.
Kirby, D. (1984). *Sexuality education: An evaluation of programs and their*

effects. Santa Cruz, Calif.: Network Publications.

This volume summarizes a large-scale study of formal sex education at the elementary and high school levels. Ways to improve such education and to enlist parental support are discussed.

Morrison, E. S., Starks, K., Hyndman, C., & Ronzio, N. (1980). *Growing up sexual.* New York: D. Van Nostrand.

College students reminisce about their sexual development from childhood onward. They express the fears, joys, and challenges of growing up in a highly sexualized society.

CHAPTER EIGHT

SEXUAL ATTITUDES AND BEHAVIOR

There is a general human tendency (known as the "false consensus effect") for each person to believe that most other people share his or her views about various topics, including sex. As one college freshman discovered, however, such attitudes can vary widely from person to person and from community to community.

Before coming to this university, my whole life was spent in a very small New England town that looks like something painted by Norman Rockwell or Grandma Moses. Where I come from, people all know one another, they go to church every Sunday, and they talk to one another without having to use profanity or "bathroom language" as we call it. The best description that comes to mind are words like clean *and* wholesome. *I've learned not to say such things here at school because people only make fun of me.*

In my high school, there wasn't much real dating. The girls would go to dances in groups and so would the guys. Sex was just not part of our lives, and the most I had ever done with a boy was hold hands, except when a good friend—Phil—kissed me after our senior picnic. It was sweet and not at all steamy.

With that background, you can imagine what a shock this university was to me. Everyone goes around talking like a sailor, and my roommate's adventures make her sound like a prostitute to me—excuse the language. Even some of the TV soaps that they watch in the dorm lounge are enough to make you blush. So, I have been pretty unhappy at school and plan to leave at the end of the semester and transfer to the college where my sister graduated.

The final straw here was something that happened a couple of weeks ago. I still can't quite believe it, and wouldn't dare tell my parents any of the worst details.

Two weeks ago on a Friday night my roommate and some of her friends asked if I wanted to go with them to see a movie that the Student Association was showing in the Campus Center. That sounded fun, so I agreed without even finding out that it was one of those for adults only. That turned out to be the worst night of my life—one I'll never forget. The story was supposed to be something about stewardesses. I didn't stay more than about ten minutes but that was enough time for two cheap-looking "stewardesses" and a "pilot" to go to a hotel room and take off their clothes. I'm sure I was blushing already, because no one in my family ever went around the house naked. In the movie—you may not be surprised, but I was—one girl actually put the man's private parts in her mouth while the other girl was on the bed digging at herself with her fingers. I got up and left, and the other girls just looked at me as though I was from Mars. I felt so dirty that I went back to the dorm and took a hot shower. There must be something seriously wrong with these people around here.

Carol, age 17

Perhaps you may feel the way Carol does about sex or you react to such matters more like her roommate does. There is no "standard" or "natural" reaction to sexual words, kissing, nudity, explicit films, oral sex, and so forth. We each react in the way we have learned from parents, schools, our peers, religion, the media, and all the other elements in our specific experiences. It's easy to decide that people who are very different from you sexually are odd or maladjusted, but don't be surprised if they think the same about you.

People differ greatly in their attitudes about sex and about specific aspects of sexuality. As a result, emotional reactions, beliefs, and behaviors range from positive to negative extremes on almost any sexual topic you can name. In this chapter we examine some of these *variations in attitudes and behavior* across several social groups. In the 1960s dramatic shifts in attitudes about sex in much of Western Europe and North America were characterized as the *sexual revolution*. Today, attitudes seem to be moving in the opposite direction. We next describe what is known about how *positive and negative sexual attitudes* are learned, and we also examine the effects of different attitudes about the sometimes embarrassing topic of *masturbation*. A special section deals with *the relationship between sexual attitudes and physical health*.

Variations in Attitudes and Behavior: Comparisons across Social Groups

In Chapter 1, we discussed some of the variations in sexual behavior from culture to culture, and now we will describe how other categories of people—such as racial or religious groups—also vary in their sexual attitudes and behavior. Despite the underlying biological need for sexual expression, the way we respond to this need emotionally and behaviorally is determined much more by psychological and social factors than by physiological ones.

■ Cultural Variations in Sexuality

Most people hold an **ethnocentric bias**; that is, each person believes that his or her own cultural views and practices are preferable to those of other groups (Gregerson, 1986). While the puberty rites of some nonindustrialized cultures may seem strange to many of us, our premarital sexual rituals may appear equally curious to them. Our own behavioral norms, or typical patterns of behavior, become the standard that we use to judge others.

The fact that cultural differences are based on learning is fairly obvious. Cross-cultural differences in intercourse frequency, oral-genital stimulation, and other aspects of sexual behavior demonstrate the way that cultural standards affect our private, intimate lives.

Differences in Oral Sexuality. According to the Communist party's rule of "oral chastity," even the most innocent kiss on the lips is not permitted in public in the People's Republic of China. This same restriction also is followed in traditional Indian society. In some societies, kissing is unknown or considered disgusting, as among the Thonga of South Africa. In contrast, all Western societies include kissing on the mouth as an acceptable and expected part of romantic and sexual interactions. Further, a sex manual written in ancient Persia (now Iran) prescribes the deep (soul, tongue, or French) kiss as the only type that should be performed during intercourse. The smell or olfactory kiss (smelling the partner's face) was common in Egypt. In a similar fashion, Eskimos and a few other cultural groups rub noses.

Though oral-genital acts have clearly had a place in human sexuality for thousands of years, as recorded in erotic drawings, the frequency of this behavior has been increasing in Western societies over the past few decades. Oral stimulation of the female genitals (**cunnilingus**) and of the male genitals (**fellatio**) occurs on all continents. Both types of oral stimulation are popular not only in most Western societies, but also in northern Africa, in the South Pacific, and in the industrialized countries of Asia. The practice of fellatio in a given society does not necessarily mean that cunnilingus also occurs there, but fellatio invariably occurs wherever cunnilingus is common (Gebhard, 1971).

Differences in Other Sexual Behaviors. Males throughout the world use their hands to stimulate female breasts, but contact between mouth and breast is less common—perhaps because sucking the breasts is associated with infancy. Most societies also report that males manually stimulate the female's genitals and that females—at least experienced ones—manually stimulate the penis.

Several cultures historically associated sexuality with agriculture. In some American Indian tribes, sexual acts took place just before seeds were planted; in other tribes, however, it was important to abstain from sex at planting time. The ancient Sumerians required that religious dignitaries perform sexual intercourse with each other as a way of ensuring a bountiful crop.

Virginity. In some parts of the world, female virginity has been considered especially important, and virgins were thought to hold special powers. In feudal Europe, the *droit du seigneur* was the custom that gave the lord of the manor the right to be the first to violate the virginity of any bride in his domain on her wedding night. In Victorian England virgins were especially valued (and priced accordingly) in brothels. Even today, some men seek out virgin females to "deflower."

Cultural standards attempt to regulate premarital sexuality in many societies. Generally, as the complexity of a culture increases, so does its restrictiveness about virginity. It seems that if young people have to learn a great deal in order to survive in an economically difficult environment, the society considers it important to teach discipline, in part by controlling sexual impulses. In a simpler environment, discipline and sexual control are less vital.

Homosexuality. Homosexuality is a special issue in most societies, although many forbid or severely restrict such behavior. More is known, however, about gay males than about lesbians. **Anal intercourse** is the most common male homosexual act in nonindustrialized, tribal societies (Gregersen, 1983). Another fairly common practice is **interfemoral foration**, in which the male rubs his penis between the thighs of his partner. In the United States, fellatio is the most popular sexual act among gays. European gays, as a result, have labeled such oral sex "the American vice."

Because the Ila of Africa believe that men can become pregnant, they forbid homosexual intercourse between males. In New Guinea, the Keraki hold similar beliefs, and they have developed a homosexual ritual in which boys drink a contraceptive potion.

Anthropologists have not found any society in which homosexual behavior is the dominant form of sexual activity among adults. There is, however, considerable variation in the percentage of males who engage in homosexual acts at some point in their lives. For example, none do so in Mangaia while virtually all males have such experiences in the East Bay society of Melanesia (Davenport, 1965). Still another pattern is common among the Sambians living in the mountains of New Guinea; homosexual activity is required among males from the age of seven until they marry, at which time they shift to exclusively heterosexual behavior (Stoller and Herdt, 1985). Overall, the lowest proportion of active homosexuals are found in underdeveloped societies in the South Pacific and in Africa.

Sex Drive. Something as seemingly biological as the strength of one's sex drive also varies considerably across cultures, once again demonstrating the powerful effect of environmental factors such as cultural practices on sexuality. As strong as sexual needs are for many people throughout the world, the Dani of West Irian (near New Guinea) appear relatively uninterested in sexual expression. During the first two years of marriage, for example, the Dani couple has no sexual interaction; after a child is born, the husband and wife abstain from sex during the following four to six years ("Abstemious Dani," 1976). In contrast, for many Polynesian groups, the norm is having intercourse at least once a day.

Sex in Industrialized Nations. Beginning in the 1940s, the sexual behavior of those living in modern, developed societies has been investigated in great detail. It has been well documented that sexual permissiveness and experimentation have increased dramatically over the past several decades. The first clear indication of change was in Western Europe, and then the Scandinavian countries, the United States, and later Japan followed the same trend (Christensen, 1969; Leo, 1983; Perlman et al., 1978; Sigusch and Schmidt, 1973).

In contrast, many Communist societies such as the U.S.S.R. (Orinova, 1981) and the People's Republic of China (Butterfield, 1980) remained sexually unpermissive over those same decades. For example, the norm in those societies remained negative with respect to nudity, sexual explicitness, and premarital sexual interactions. In the wake of political changes occurring in many parts of the Communist world, it is interesting to observe parallel sexual changes. For example, recent large-scale Chinese surveys indicate the kind of permissive shifts observed earlier in Western nations (Burton, 1988). Among over 1,200 respondents in 41 Chinese cities, there are now favorable attitudes toward premarital sex (86 percent approve) and extramarital sex (69 percent see nothing wrong with it); behavioral changes include confidential abortions for unmarried pregnant women, the use of varied intercourse positions by 60 percent of married couples, and the practice of heterosexual anal intercourse by 70 percent of the subjects (Burton, 1990).

Among the developing nations such as Colombia, sexual patterns have resembled those of the United States in the 1950s. Alzate (1984) reported that, among Colombians, more unmarried males (94 percent) engage in heterosexual acts than do unmarried females (38 percent). Because of such a sexual double standard, a minority of females—some of them prostitutes—have multiple sexual partners, while most females remain virginal until marriage. Rapid changes are occurring, however, in that five

years later almost 65 percent of unmarried women reported engaging in premarital sex (Alzate, 1989).

In sum, cross-cultural studies show that we can learn many quite different ways to interact sexually. As you may expect, sexual beliefs vary across cultures as much as do sexual practices. Table 8-1 presents a sampling of such variations.

■ Sexuality and Social Class

Beyond cultural variations, **demographic variables** also affect sexuality. In effect, subgroups within the broader culture develop their own standards for what to do or avoid doing. In the United States, the demographic variables of social class, race or ethnicity, and religion have a major impact on sexuality, presumably through shared attitudes and beliefs. If, however, the attitudes or beliefs of an individual are known, they predict behavior more accurately than do such broad categories as social class (Miller et al., 1987). For example, intercourse frequency is more closely associated with a person's attitudes than with his or her demographic characteristics (Hornick, 1978).

Socioeconomic class is defined by such indicators as income, occupational status, and education.

TABLE 8.1 **Cultural Variations in Sexual Beliefs and Practices**

Sexual beliefs and practices vary greatly across societies. Norms establish the standards for what individuals believe and do sexually in a given culture.

BELIEF OR PRACTICE	AREA(S) IN WHICH IT OCCURRED
1. Belief that sexual intercourse with a virgin is dangerous	In parts of Siberia and among Kagaba of South America
2. Belief that intercourse causes menstruation to begin	At least twelve societies, including the Tepoztecans of Mexico and the Murngin of Australia
3. Belief that men can become pregnant	Ila of Africa, Keraki of New Guinea, and some black male homosexuals in the United States (Money and Hosta, 1968)
4. Practice of ritual sexual acts associated with agriculture	Some Native American Indian groups and the ancient Sumerians of the Middle East
5. Practice of prostitution	In many areas of the world, including some American Indian groups (Aztecs, Maya, Inca, and others) prior to contacts with Europeans

Source: Adapted from Gregersen, 1986.

The higher an individual's socioeconomic level, the more he or she tends to hold permissive attitudes about sex. Among lower socioeconomic couples, sex usually focuses on the gratification of the male's physical needs, often ignoring the female's wishes and desires. Sexual interactions are more likely to include closeness and intimacy among middle- and upper-class partners than among lower-class pairs (Burgoyne, 1982). It has been suggested that education level is the crucial determinant of class differences in sexual attitudes and practices (Blumstein and Schwartz, 1983).

Some sexual patterns, such as premarital intercourse, occur in all social classes. At present, singles usually engage in intercourse regardless of their economic status. Upper-class males have the highest rate of extramarital relationships, with middle-class males "catching up" by the time they reach middle age (Hunt, 1974; Kinsey et al., 1948). Such differences may partially reflect differences in opportunities, money, and leisure time across classes. Middle-aged women have one or more extramarital sexual relationships at almost the same rate as their husbands, although exact figures on the percentages are lacking (Seagraves, 1989). In Chapter 9, additional information on adult sexual patterns is provided.

■ Racial and Ethnic Sexual Patterns

Whites in the United States hold a few common stereotypes about the sexual practices of blacks, Hispanics, and other subgroups, but survey data often contradict prevailing beliefs.

Although blacks hold slightly more liberal attitudes about some sexual matters such as premarital intercourse than whites, the two races share quite similar attitudes about homosexuality (Glenn and Weaver, 1979), as Figure 8-1 indicates. In their general sexual behavior, blacks and whites in the United States are also quite similar (Belcastro, 1985; Robinson and Calhoun, 1983). Blacks have been reported to engage in premarital sex at a younger age and to have premarital intercourse more frequently than whites. Blacks also discuss sex more openly and report fewer sexual problems (Weinberg and Williams, 1988).

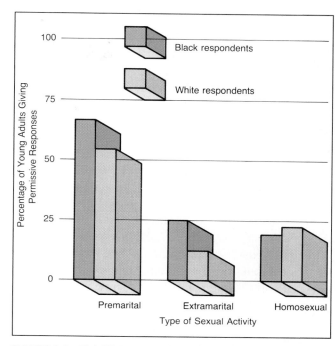

FIGURE 8-1 *BLACK AND WHITE SEXUAL ATTITUDES* A survey of several thousand young adults in the United States revealed that blacks expressed only slightly more positive opinions about premarital and extramarital sexual activity than whites. Both groups generally approve of premarital sex and disapprove of extramarital and homosexual sex.
Source: Adapted from Glenn and Weaver, 1979.

Whites uphold the double standard for men and women more strongly than is true for blacks; as a result, black women more easily and openly than white women express their sexual needs to their partners.

Societal changes since mid-century have affected both races in similar ways. For example, compared to the black females in Kinsey's 1953 survey, Wyatt et al. (1988) found that black women today have more sexual experience with more partners at younger ages. Other factors also affect blacks and whites similarly. Males of both races are more positive about premarital sex than females of both races. In addition, the sexual behavior of middle-class blacks resembles that of middle-class whites in age of first intercourse, for example, and both groups differ from lower-class whites and blacks (Wyatt, 1989).

Some investigators propose that genetic factors account for racial differences in sexual behavior patterns (for example, Rushton, 1988b, 1989a, b; Rushton and Bogaert, 1987, 1988). Specifically, Rushton

(1988a) concludes that blacks, orientals, and whites differ in such inherited characteristics as age of puberty, sperm and egg production, intercourse frequency, size of genitalia, and marital stability. In each instance, blacks are the most sexually expressive (early puberty, larger genitals, etc.) and orientals the least so; whites fall in the middle on each characteristic. Other investigators dispute the methods and conclusions leading to a biological explanation of behavioral differences (for example, Lynn, 1989a, b; Zuckerman and Brody, 1988).

Whites often stereotype blacks and Hispanic-Americans as sexually immoral and promiscuous. Hispanic college students in reality express more conservative sexual opinions and engage in sexual activity less frequently than their Anglo-American peers (Padilla and O'Grady, 1987), as Figure 8-2 illustrates. Hispanics also differ from their Anglo peers in having less factual knowledge about sex and in accepting more sexual myths (such as the harmfulness of masturbation).

■ The Effect of Religious Affiliation on Sexuality

Organized Religions. Sexual customs have historically been influenced by religious doctrine. We will describe how three religions—Judaism, Christianity, and Mohammedanism—affect the sexual attitudes and behavior of their adherents.

Judaism takes its rituals and moral guidelines about sex from two sources: the Old Testament of the Bible and more recent Jewish law (Glasner, 1961). The teachings include encouraging sexual activity for married couples and advising women to adopt traditional roles of modesty and motherhood. Adultery is forbidden by Judaism. Some of the older sexual rules were quite negative and restrictive. For example, warnings about masturbation were especially harsh; some sects of Judaism even forbade touching the penis during urination. Traditionally, those committing male homosexual acts were put to death while lesbians were punished by a lashing (Artson, 1988). The three major divisions of U.S. Judaism (Orthodox,

FIGURE 8-2 *HISPANIC-AMERICANS: STEREOTYPES VERSUS REALITY* The responses of 165 college students who were Hispanic-Americans were compared to those of 99 white (Anglo) students. It was found that the Hispanic students held more conservative sexual attitudes than white students.
Source: Adapted from Padilla and O'Grady, 1983.

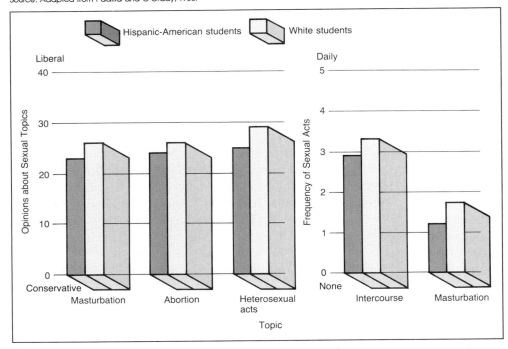

Conservative, and Reformed) no longer condemn all homosexuality; among Reformed Jews, homosexuals can even be ordained as Rabbis. In general, there is a somewhat mixed message about sex. One rabbi has characterized the Jewish outlook on sexuality as involving frank, nonpuritanical acceptance, accompanied by a rather rigid, self-imposed discipline of sexual restraint (Glasner, 1961).

Early Christianity capitalized on the concept of sin, laying the basis for self-imposed guilt. If external punishment in the form of penance or other negative controls could not be applied immediately in every situation, the religious person was expected to punish his or her own impure thoughts, words, or deeds (Bullough, 1977). The Christian New Testament placed a high value on celibacy and distinguished spiritual from physical love. An influential Christian source, St. Augustine, condemned all sex as evil, though he classified marital sex as slightly less sinful than other varieties. An underlying Christian theme has been the conceptualization of the human body and its functions as nasty and disgusting (Delumeau, 1990). A widely read religious treatise from the 13th century proposed that "Man is naught but fetid sperm, a bag of excrement, and food for worms . . . In life, he produces dung and vomit. In death, he will produce stench and decay" (Doniger, 1990, p. 27).

Between the 3rd and 10th centuries, church authorities issued many edicts forbidding sex on certain days for religious reasons—Saturdays, Sundays, Wednesdays, and Fridays; during 40-day fasts before Easter, Christmas, and Witsuntide; during menstruation, pregnancy, a month post-partum, and while a mother was breastfeeding. The couple who obeyed all these injunctions would have been able to engage in acceptable marital sex only 21 to 44 days each year (Stone, 1989).

During the Protestant Reformation in the sixteenth century, schisms in Christianity led to some variations in views about sexuality. Protestants continued to emphasize guilt as a means of controlling behavior, along with the promise of a rewarding afterlife for the truly repentant sinner. The leading reformer, Martin Luther, softened the teachings about the inherently evil nature of sex and did not consider celibacy as necessarily virtuous. Catholic-Protestant differences also were reflected in attitudes about mas-

turbation and premarital sex, with Catholics holding less permissive attitudes.

One of the results of the Christian focus on sin has been the generally more negative sexual views among Catholics and Protestants than among Jews (Glenn and Weaver, 1979). Recently, a Catholic theologian wrote a book denouncing the church's official stance on sexuality (Ranke-Heinemann, 1990). She suggests that the basic problem is priestly celibacy that results in a generalized hostility toward sex. Such hostility leads to "pleasure-hating" and specific bans on divorce, birth control, and premarital sex. The church's response to these charges is reflected in Cardinal O'Connor's accusation that the book's publisher is purveying "hatred and scandal and malice and libel and calumny" (Ostling, 1990, p. 92). The most liberal sexual outlook is held by individuals who report no religious affiliation.

Almost one quarter of the world's 5 billion people identify themselves as Moslem. The Moslem religion dominates North Africa, the Middle and Near East, Pakistan, and the islands making up Indonesia and Malaysia. Mohammed, the Moslem prophet, taught that sexual intercourse was one of life's highest pleasures. In much of the Moslem world, relationships between men and women are dictated by the custom of **purdah**. Purdah involves the separation of the sexes, isolating or hiding women from the sight of males beyond their own relatives. Women wear a veil or a loose-fitting garment, called a *chador,* over their body and most of the face as a protection against the prying eyes of the outside world, as Figure 8-3 illustrates. Such customs are designed to control the sexuality of Moslem women, who are regarded as more powerful, less intelligent, and potentially more dangerous than men. For both men and women, sexual pleasure is considered to be more important than love or caring in a relationship.

Religiosity and Sexuality. For both Jews and Christians, more conservative sexual attitudes are held by believers who regularly attend religious services than by those who attend periodically (Robinson and Calhoun, 1983). Such attitudes affect behavior. Adolescents in Australia, for example, engage in fewer heterosexual acts if they regularly attend religious services (McCabe and Collins, 1983).

Besides attendance, those individuals who rate

FIGURE 8-3 *SECLUDING MOSLEM WOMEN FROM THE PRYING EYES OF MALES* Moslem women wear a garment known as a chador to cover their bodies and faces in public. Men who are not relatives—including male physicians—may not look at them.

religion as most important and meaningful in their lives also are less sexually permissive (Paxton and Turner, 1978). One compromise is for those who are religious to maintain *technical virginity*. For example, couples can engage in petting or oral-genital contact rather than intercourse and remain virgins (Clement, 1990; Mahoney, 1980). Highly religious male undergraduates seem to place the highest value on technical virginity.

The Sexual Revolution in the United States: Has It Ended?

Throughout history, societies have undergone change in their general attitudes about sex and their sexual practices. Sometimes the changes are abrupt; a restrictive society suddenly becomes permissive or vice versa. Thus, in the twentieth century, a **sexual revolution** occurred in most of Western civilization, al-

though the reasons for this change are not at all clear. What *is* clear is that an increase in sexual freedom and tolerance followed World War I. This steadily more permissive trend continued for several decades and reached a peak in the late 1960s and early 1970s. By the 1980s, a reverse movement, toward increased conservatism, apparently began. Evidence about both types of change will be examined in this section.

■ Decades of Attitudinal and Cultural Change

No one is able to say whether broad cultural shifts lead to changes in the behavior of individuals or whether individuals begin to behave differently and subsequently bring about changes in the culture. Perhaps many quite different kinds of change occur simultaneously—the widespread use of automobiles for dating, the gradually increasing sexual explicitness of movies and printed material, and the development of easily available contraceptives—and each of them facilitates tolerant and permissive sexual attitudes and sexual practices.

There are well-documented changes in American attitudes about sex between Kinsey's surveys (in the late 1940s and early 1950s) and Hunt's (1974) work a quarter of a century later. The most consistent change was in the new willingness to tolerate the sexual practices of others (Bauman and Wilson, 1976). Whatever consenting adults did behind closed doors was in effect no longer of concern to most other adults.

Other attitudinal changes were signs of the new sexual openness. A poll of over 1,500 American adults showed that acceptance of premarital sex increased from 24 to 58 percent between 1969 and 1985. Generational differences in these views are apparent—81 percent of those aged eighteen to thirty found nothing wrong with premarital sex, but only 37 percent of those over age fifty agreed with them (Gallup, 1985c). Besides age, geography also affected permissiveness, as Figure 8-4 shows. Adults living in the western part of the United States have the most permissive attitudes, and southerners the least permissive.

Despite the sexual changes of the 1960s and 1970s, differences associated with religion, social class, and sex remained consistent.

Sexual liberalization was also studied by Krause

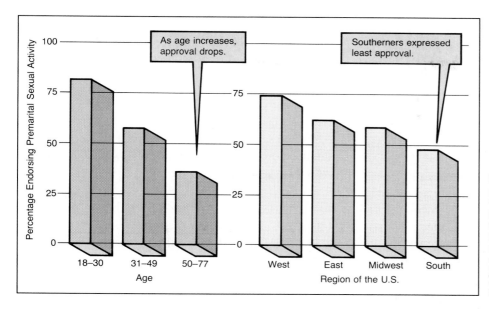

FIGURE 8-4 *A SEXUAL REVOLUTION IN PERMISSIVE ATTITUDES* More young adults in the United States believe that premarital sexual activity is acceptable than do adults over age fifty. Westerners have the most permissive attitudes, and only in the South is approval expressed by less than a majority (48 percent) among over 1,500 adults surveyed.
Source: Adapted from Gallup, 1985c.

(1978), who investigated three generations of American women from a variety of ethnic backgrounds. Women whose average age was twenty-five, their mothers (average age of fifty-two), and their maternal grandmothers (average age of seventy-seven) were interviewed. As Figure 8-5 illustrates, the young adult daughters expressed the least conservative opinions about premarital sexual activity, though they valued fidelity within marriage. Other studies of attitudinal change within Japanese-American families (Abram-

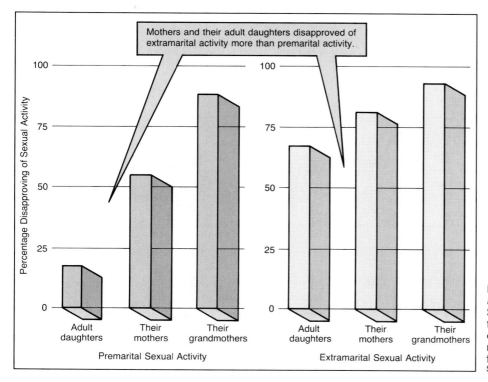

FIGURE 8-5 *SEXUAL TOLERANCE DIFFERS ACROSS GENERATIONS* Spanning three generations within families, 225 women provided evidence that younger women have more tolerant sexual attitudes than their mothers and grandmothers.
Source: Adapted from Krause, 1978.

son, 1982; Abramson and Imai-Marquex, 1982) similarly reveal a steady increase in permissive attitudes from the generation that emigrated from Japan through their children and grandchildren.

One component of the changes in attitudes across generations is a pervasive difficulty in communicating about sex between parents and offspring as well as the existence of misperceptions on both sides. For example, most parents do not believe that their college-age sons and daughters are sexually active (McConnell, 1974). Conversely, students are equally uncomfortable in thinking about their own parents having sex (see Figure 8-6). College students consistently underestimate how often their parents engage in intimate acts, by at least 50 percent (Murnen and Allgeier, 1986; Pocs and Godow 1977; Zeiss, 1982).

Beginning about 1980, attitude surveys began to show a shift toward less liberal views. For example, more individuals began to express the belief that premarital sexual relations are immoral than was true in

the late 1970s (Robinson and Jedlicka, 1983). Despite this recent decline in permissiveness, at the moment there is still more acceptance of premarital intercourse now than there was several decades ago.

■ Shifts in Behavior

The sexual revolution involved more than attitudinal changes. Profound changes in sexual behavior were also reported.

Premarital Sex. Only one third of college males had experienced sexual intercourse before marriage in the 1940s. By the time they graduated from college, about one half had had some premarital sexual experience, averaging about once every three weeks (Kinsey, 1948). Their usual sexual interactions consisted of petting to orgasm, with intercourse saved until shortly before marriage. Three decades later, most college men (72 percent) had experienced intercourse, and they reported having sex at least once a

FIGURE 8-6 *NOT MY PARENTS!* Perhaps it has always been difficult for parents and their children to communicate about sex, but the generational changes reflected in the sexual revolution make such communication especially difficult. Not only do parents resist perceiving their sons and daughters to be sexual, but, as shown here, their children are equally upset about parental sexuality.

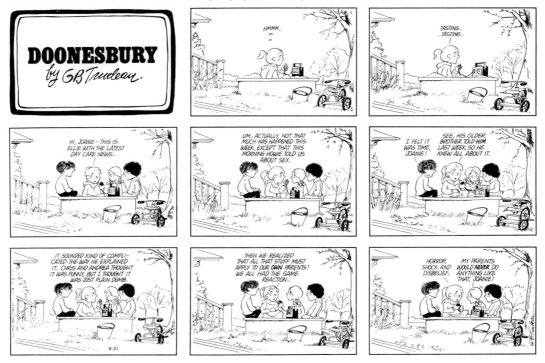

week. About half (51 percent) of them had only one partner. Thus, the increased freedom seems to have led to selectivity rather than promiscuity (Leslie, 1978).

The frequency of other sexual acts such as masturbation and oral-genital sex is not much higher than in earlier generations (Downey, 1980). It is interesting to note that the incidence of homosexual acts has not shown any increase or decrease.

Male-Female Similarity. The traditional double standard means greater permissiveness for men than for women; for example, men were expected to become sexually active earlier and to have more partners. Such sex differences in expectations have narrowed as a result of the sexual revolution. In one study, over 650 college students indicated how much permissiveness was acceptable for male or female siblings, friends, and people in general. Women expressed less permissiveness about *themselves* than men did about *themselves;* in evaluating *other people,* however, the sex of the individual was unrelated to how much permissiveness was acceptable (Sprecher, 1989).

Clement (1989), on the basis of complex quantitative analyses of changes in sexual behavior over the past forty years, concluded that the liberation of females from the behavioral double standard was the key factor in producing the sexual revolution.

In any event, to a greater extent than previously, males and females now are similar in their sexual habits, ranging from masturbation to premarital intercourse (Phillis and Gromko, 1985). By the late 1970s, the majority of both sexes reported engaging in intercourse prior to marriage (King et al., 1977). In West Germany between 1966 and 1981, the percentage of college males who had premarital intercourse rose by 22 percent. For West German college females, the figure rose 35 percent during the same period (Clement et al., 1984). In a similar fashion, the age of first coitus has been dropping steadily for both sexes in societies as diverse as Japan (Asayama, 1976), Czechoslovakia (Raboch and Bartok, 1980), and the United States (Reed and Weinberg, 1984), with the greatest changes occurring for females.

Women not only engage in sexual activity at an earlier age and more frequently, but their reactions to the experience are increasingly similar to those of males. The readers of *Cosmopolitan* magazine may not represent all American females, but only 3 percent of them say that they do not enjoy intercourse and only 23 percent believe that love is necessary for sexual pleasure to occur (Wolfe, 1980).

The sexual revolution has affected our daily lives in many ways. Examples are the rise in the number of single couples who cohabit (see Chapter 9) and new technology for contraception and reproduction (see Chapter 5). There is now greater awareness of sexual victimization such as date rape and sexual harassment (see Chapter 14). Also note the liberalization of laws about abortion and the fact that the American Psychiatric Association stopped classifying homosexuality as a mental disorder. Whatever one's personal views on such topics, the changes are obviously major ones.

The Negative Side of Liberated Sexuality. Despite these changes, the sexual revolution has not led to entirely carefree sexuality. Negative reactions to sex are common. Two thirds of sexually active, unmarried couples report some problems; these often focus on the differences between males and females in sexual interest (Schreiner-Engle and Schiavi, 1986). Females also frequently develop feelings of guilt, anxiety, and fear about being exploited in their intimate relationships (Weis, 1983). Other negative components of sexual interactions include concerns about contraceptives having side effects, unwanted pregnancies, sexually transmissible diseases, and whether to have an abortion.

Young people who have intercourse in their early teens feel independent and distant from their parents. They place a relatively low value on religion and academic achievement, and they are more likely to use alcohol, marijuana, and other illegal drugs than do adolescents who do not become sexually active until they are older (Jessor et al., 1983). The problems are compounded because more of them fail to use contraceptives than is true of those who begin sexual activity at a later age (Cvetkovich and Grote, 1983).

Recent Decreases in Sexual Activity. A number of indicators suggest that the pendulum is swinging away from the sexual revolution at its peak. For example, the five-year span between 1978 and 1983 revealed a slight decline in premarital sexual activity of young women in the United States (O'Connell and Rogers, 1984; Pratt et al., 1984). Speculation about the reasons for broad social changes is risky, but conservative movements such as the Moral Majority and the anti-abortion right-to-life organizations may have played a role. Further, the threat of contracting AIDS undoubtedly has facilitated the development of more cautious attitudes and behaviors.

Less sexual involvement is also indicated in a study of coeds at the University of Texas (Gerrard, 1987). Figure 8-7 compares the heterosexual activity of single females taking sophomore-level courses during each of three different time periods. The percentage of college females who had engaged in intercourse rose rapidly during the five years from the early 1970s to the late 1970s and then dropped just as rapidly over the following five years. This shift may represent temporary changes, or it may constitute the beginning of a long-term reversal in behavioral trends.

FIGURE 8-7 *PREMARITAL INTERCOURSE INCREASED AND THEN DECREASED AMONG COLLEGE FEMALES* Three groups of female college students (approximately 100 in each group) were surveyed during the year they were enrolled as sophomores at the University of Texas. Results over the decade indicated a rise in sexual activity in the late 1970s and a drop in the early 1980s, suggesting that the sexual revolution has peaked and begun to reverse itself.
Source: Adapted from Gerrard, 1987.

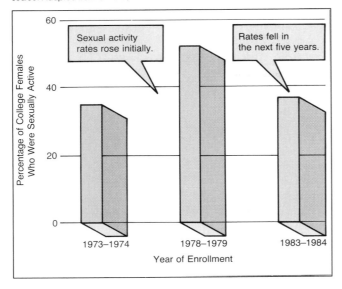

Positive and Negative Attitudes about Sex

Most aspects of sexuality elicit strong emotional reactions, some positive and some quite negative (Hudson et al., 1983). When we think about sexual topics, our feelings are seldom neutral; they consist instead of a mixture of anxiety, fear, guilt, disgust, curiosity, joy, excitement, and interest. Presumably on the basis of our childhood experiences and our family backgrounds, each of us develops attitudes about sexual matters that fall at some point along a continuum from extremely negative to extremely positive. In this section we will examine how individual differences along this dimension influence our sexuality in a great many ways.

■   Measuring Sexual Attitudes

Two widely used psychological tests have been developed to assess positive versus negative sexual attitudes: the **Sex Guilt Scale** (Mosher, 1968) and the **Sexual Opinion Survey** (Fisher et al., 1988). Each contains a series of statements about diverse aspects of sexuality such as pornography, masturbation, oral sex, homosexuality, and prostitution. Table 8-2 provides examples of items found in each test. Responses indicate a relatively positive or negative reaction to each topic. In describing some of the research conducted with each scale, we will use the term **erotophilic** to indicate positive attitudes (those low in sex guilt) and **erotophobic** to indicate negative attitudes (those high in sex guilt). People who are erotophilic tend to respond to sexual cues with positive emotions and to approach or seek out sexual experiences. In contrast, those who are erotophobic avoid sexual cues; if they can't avoid them in thoughts, words, or deeds, these individuals experience negative feelings (Griffitt and Kaiser, 1978; O'Grady, 1982a).

■   How Do Sexual Attitudes Develop?

Religion and Social Conservatism. Erotophobic attitudes are most likely to be acquired when a person's family background is oriented toward traditional, conservative values. For example, a family with a reli-

TABLE 8-2 **Measuring Sexual Attitudes: Sample Items**

These items appear in two widely used scales to assess sexual attitudes. The Sex Guilt Scale is scored by giving a point for each choice that indicates feelings of guilt. Here, a subject choosing B for each item would indicate negative, guilty responses. The Sexual Opinion Survey is scored according to the degree of positiveness in responding to each item. Answering "I strongly agree" to each of these three items indicates positive attitudes, while "I strongly disagree" indicates negative attitudes.

The Sex Guilt Scale

1. If in the future I committed adultery, . . .
   a. I won't feel bad about it.
   b. it would be sinful.
2. Unusual sex practices . . .
   a. might be interesting.
   b. don't interest me.
3. Sex relations before marriage . . .
   a. are practiced too much to be wrong.
   b. should not be permitted, in my opinion.

Sexual Opinion Survey

1. I think it would be very entertaining to look at hard-core pornography.
   I strongly agree :__:__:__:__:__:__: I strongly disagree
2. Masturbation can be an exciting experience.
   I strongly agree :__:__:__:__:__:__: I strongly disagree
3. Thoughts that I may have homosexual tendencies would not worry me at all.
   I strongly agree :__:__:__:__:__:__: I strongly disagree

Source: Adapted from Mosher, 1968, and Byrne and Fisher, 1983.

gious orientation and a pattern of regular church attendance is more likely to produce erotophobic than erotophilic offspring. College students having this general background say that they were told of the perils of various sexual activities and of the importance of keeping sexual feelings in check with self-imposed guilt. Religiously devout college students express more negative sexual attitudes and engage in fewer sexual acts than the nondevout (Troiden and Jendrek, 1987).

Socialization. As expected, erotophobic parents provide their children with relatively little sexual information. Compared to erotophilic mothers and fathers, parents with negative attitudes about sex usually give evasive rather than frank answers when their children ask the inevitable questions about sexuality (Yarber and Whitehill, 1981; Lemery, 1983). When a child wonders, "Where do babies come from?" an

erotophobic parent is likely to say something like, "We'll talk about that when you're older." Such responses suggest to the child that certain concerns are somehow shameful and are not to be discussed.

Husbands and wives most often have similar rather than dissimilar sexual attitudes (Byrne et al., 1986; Fisher and Gray, 1988; Smith et al., 1990). For this reason, a child's mother and father are likely to respond consistently to sexual issues. Thus, two erotophobic parents can "teach" their child that the appropriate response to sex is avoidance, guilt, and negative emotions (Daugherty and Burger, 1984).

Societal factors also influence sexual attitudes. Besides the messages of parents and others, each of us receives information about sex from television, movies, and other media sources. A study of college females (Gerrard, 1987) found that erotophobia had increased between 1978 and 1983. One possible explanation is that changes in the political climate in

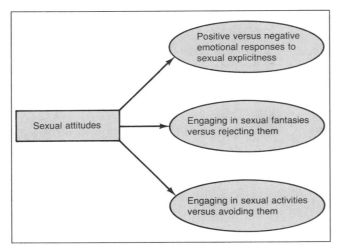

FIGURE 8-8 *SEXUAL ATTITUDES: A CENTRAL CONCEPT* Sexual attitudes influence many feelings, thoughts, and overt behaviors involving sexuality. Among these are emotional responses to sexual cues, generating sexual fantasies, and engaging in sexual acts.

the United States affected the attitudes of young people growing up during that period. The threat of AIDS that became widely publicized by the second half of the 1980s probably has helped to legitimize relatively conservative sexual attitudes and activities for those who are basically ambivalent about expressing their sexuality.

Behavioral Effects of Sexual Attitudes

Once an individual has developed an erotophobic or erotophilic orientation to sex, these attitudes have an impact on a wide range of sexual behaviors (Fisher et al., 1988), as Figure 8-8 suggests. Erotophobic attitudes lead to negative responses to sexual cues and to the avoidance of sexual thoughts, fantasies, and behaviors. Erotophilic attitudes, in contrast, lead to positive emotions and approach behavior (Fisher et al., 1988).

Attitudes and Sexual Expression. Erotophobes, as may be expected, experience difficulty in talking about sex. In one study, when erotophobic students were given the task of reading a prepared description that was either sexually explicit or neutral, the sexual message evoked much more negative feelings (Fisher et al., 1980). As they read about heterosexual foreplay and other acts, many of these subjects mispronounced words; for example, *scrotum* became

"scotrum," and *vagina* was read as "virginia." Those erotophobes who read the sexual speech aloud felt embarrassed and frightened, but not those who had to read the neutral speech (about the mechanisms of voice production). The discomfort about the sexual theme also led erotophobes to believe that the audience would respond to them negatively. It seems reasonable to expect that erotophobic parents would have similar difficulties in attempting to discuss sexual matters with their children.

Drawing a human figure represents a quite different behavior influenced by sexual attitudes. A small number of male and female undergraduates were asked to draw nude figures of each sex. Erotophiles produced pictures with larger and more detailed genitalia as well as detailed secondary sexual characteristics such as pubic and chest hair in contrast to erotophobes who produced figures with smaller penises, testicles, breasts, and mons (Przybyla et al., 1988). Presumably, other forms of creative expression involving sex are also affected by one's attitudes.

The effect of positive and negative sexual attitudes extends beyond verbal behavior and figure drawing. Erotophobics masturbate less often (Fisher et al., 1983) and are less likely to have premarital intercourse than erotophiles (Gerrard, 1987; Gerrard and Gibbons, 1982). Among female college students who become sexually active, those who are erotophobic engage in sexual intercourse less frequently than those who are erotophilic (Gerrard, 1982). As the cultural norm shifted toward increased permissiveness, abstaining from sex became more difficult, and a higher level of erotophobia was required to resist the temptation to engage in sex.

Not only are erotophilic individuals more likely to engage in sex and to do so more frequently than those who are erotophobic, their sexual experiences are also more varied. Positive sexual attitudes are associated with having more sexual partners (Fisher et al., 1983) and engaging in more varied sexual acts, including oral sex and intercourse in varied positions (Troiden and Jendrek, 1987). Finally, erotophile–erotophobe differences in frequency of sexual activity is not limited to college students; the difference also persists among older adults, even those in their early seventies (DiVasto et al., 1981).

Responding to Explicit Sexual Material. Females generally report feeling more guilty about sexual matters than males do (Evans, 1984). Such sex differences exist in various parts of the world; for example, Brazilian college men are substantially more erotophilic than their female classmates (Hutz, 1990). In fact, the negative response of females is even greater than most people assume. When college students are asked to estimate the level of erotophobia of the typical male and female student, both sexes underestimate the degree of negativism that females actually report, as Figure 8-9 shows (Evans, 1984). Women, in contrast, *over*estimate the negative attitudes of males, thinking that they are less positive about sex than they really are.

On many different measures, men are consistently found to be more permissive and liberal in their sexual attitudes than women (Hendrick and Hendrick, 1987; Sprecher, 1989). Among medical students in the 1980s, women still differ from men in their attitudes about entering a sexual relationship—women are more cautious and selective and are more likely to assume that sex is a prelude to a marriage (Townsend, 1987). Men also indicate that they are

more preoccupied about sex than is true for women (Snell and Papini, 1989).

Are these sex differences in attitudes a function of biological differences or of what is taught to males versus females about what is sexually appropriate? Although there are very cogent arguments supporting the role of our evolutionary history in producing these differences (Gallup, 1986), considerable evidence suggests that males and females do not receive the same cultural "lessons" about sex. For example, the widespread belief that female sexual expression needs to be restricted and protected may cause parents to give more negative sexual messages to daughters than to sons. Such differences may, in turn, underlie the male-female differences in attitudes.

Another way to answer the question is to examine the traditional sex roles of masculinity and femininity. Females who feel more feminine than average are relatively erotophobic, regardless of their biological sex. It seems that femininity and erotophobia accompany one another, based on cultural expectations of what it means to be female. Females are taught to be more passive, sensitive, and less interested than males in sex. Masculinity, in contrast, is associated

FIGURE 8-9 *JUDGING THE EROTOPHOBIA OF OTHERS: MISCONCEPTIONS BY BOTH SEXES*
Females tend to be more erotophobic than males. Both sexes also have misconceptions about each other's sexual attitudes. Would males and females communicate better if they knew the actual responses of the opposite sex?
Source: Adapted from Evans, 1984.

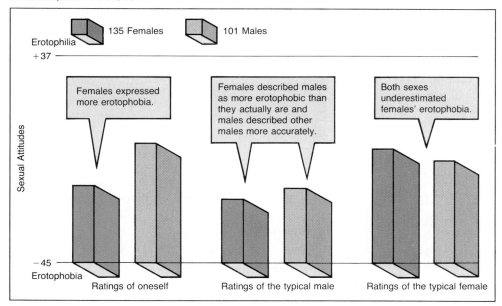

with erotophilia in both sexes. (See Chapter 6 for a further discussion of these topics.)

Whatever the reason, females are more erotophobic than males, and such negative attitudes promote dislike of sexually explicit films. Explicit erotica elicits feelings of disgust and fear in both males and females who have a negative sexual orientation (Mosher and O'Grady, 1979a,b). As Figure 8-10 indicates, erotophobic females report less sexual arousal when viewing a film showing nude petting and oral-genital acts than erotophilic females. Erotophobic females not only felt less aroused during the film but also experienced only mild genital sensations. Erotophilic females in contrast reported moderate to prolonged genital sensations, including warmth, itching, and vaginal lubrication.

Erotophobic individuals, besides being less responsive to erotic material, actually feel relieved when they are able to avoid sexually explicit content. If given a free choice as to how much time they can spend looking at explicit sexual slides, erotophobes choose a briefer viewing time than erotophiles

(Becker and Byrne, 1985). Such avoidance behavior probably explains why erotophobes are found to recall the content of the erotic pictures less accurately than erotophiles do (Becker and Byrne, 1985). That same difference shows up in response to sexually explicit stories. Erotophobes make more mistakes in recalling the story's details, although their memory of nonsexual stories does not differ from that of erotophiles (Bakaitis and Abramson, 1986).

Fantasies about Sex.   Sexual attitudes also affect the fantasies that people create for themselves. The greater an individual's guilt, the less frequently he or she has sexual fantasies, the more limited the variety of fantasies, and the less erotic the content (Pelletier and Herold, 1988). Erotophiles write more explicit sexual stories than erotophobes (Walker, 1983). They also include more details involving positive emotions such as enjoyment and caring (Kelley, 1985a). Erotophiles are also more likely than erotophobes to respond to their own fantasies by becoming sexually aroused (Green and Mosher, 1985)—they write material that interests and arouses them. If a story, picture, or fantasy involves explicit sexuality, it generally evokes interest in erotophiles and avoidance in erotophobes. Among conservative Christians, sexual fantasies occur, but these individuals react with strong negative affect and guilt (Gil, 1990).

The way sexual attitudes influence sexual behavior, response to erotic materials, and fantasizing does not imply that either erotophobic or erotophilic attitudes represent a "better" or more well-adjusted response to sex. Depending on a person's values, one or the other reaction may be preferable. There is one area of behavior, however, in which individuals with erotophobic attitudes seem at a disadvantage. As discussed in the special section, **Taking Responsibility and Protecting Yourself,** on pages 213 to 214, negative sexual attitudes have an adverse effect on sex-related health practices, apparently because of the same kind of emotional and cognitive processes that have just been discussed.

■   The Effects of Sexual Attitudes on Marriage

When couples in a close relationship pause to consider how well or how poorly they are getting along, some may be disappointed with what they

FIGURE 8-10 *EROTOPHOBIA AND FEMALES' RESPONSES TO A SEXUAL FILM* In a study of eighty college women, erotophilic females indicated feelings of greater sexual arousal and more intense genital sensations than did erotophobic females, after viewing a sexually explicit film. They also felt less guilty and disgusted by the film than was true for erotophobes.
Source: Adapted from Mosher and O'Grady, 1979b.

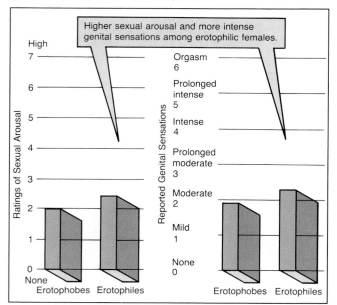

Taking Responsibility and Protecting Yourself

HOW DO SEXUAL ATTITUDES AFFECT OUR PHYSICAL HEALTH?

The link between sexual attitudes and health may not be immediately obvious. They are, however, connected, and the explanation is that erotophiles respond to sexual cues as a source of reward, while erotophobes respond to the same cues as a source of punishment (Griffitt & Kaiser, 1978). That basic difference has many implications, as we have seen. Consider what it means, then, when a person is exposed to material covering a topic combining sex and health. Because negative attitudes result in the avoidance of sex-related content and difficulty in learning such details when avoidance is not possible, erotophobic individuals tend to know less and hold more incorrect beliefs about sex than erotophilic individuals (Mosher, 1979). As Table 8-3 indicates, some of these incorrect beliefs have health implications.

In addition, erotophobic avoidance tendencies interfere with many health-related behaviors. Most of us feel some re-

luctance about visiting a doctor's office; as a result, we sometimes delay seeking appropriate health care (Kelley, 1987c). When the problem involves sexual anatomy or functioning, erotophobia sharply increases this avoidance tendency, thus postponing medical diagnosis and treatment. For example, surveys of college women indicate that erotophobes obtain gynecological examinations less frequently than erotophiles (Fisher et al., 1983). Erotophilic females do not enjoy such examinations, either, viewing them as painful and embarrassing, but they nevertheless visit a gynecologist regularly (Kelley, 1987d). Even private, nonpainful medical procedures are avoided by those with negative attitudes; the frequency of breast self-examination is greater for erotophilic than for erotophobic women.

Like their female counterparts, erotophobic men are more upset by having their breasts examined by a physician than

are erotophilics. They also are more embarrassed about ejaculating into a sterile jar when a medical analysis of their semen is required.

Erotophobe–erotophile differences similarly affect responses to sexually transmitted diseases. Erotophobes are less likely than erotophiles to take preventive measures against them (Kelley and Streeter, 1990; Yarber and Fisher, 1983).

Sexual attitudes also are found to affect behavior during pregnancy and following childbirth. During pregnancy, erotophobic couples tend to restrict their sexual activity more than is true for erotophilic couples (Fisher and Gray, 1988). Erotophilic fathers also are more likely to choose to be present in the delivery room during childbirth; erotophobic fathers prefer to stay away.

We have previously discussed the positive benefits of breast-feeding on the health of the infant. In this context, ero-

TABLE 8-3 **Sex and Health: What You Don't Know Can Hurt You**

Sexual attitudes influence what we know and believe about sex, and the more negative the attitudes the less accurate our beliefs. Of the statements below, #4 and #7 are true while the rest are false. Because of the number of sexual beliefs that have health implications, sexual attitudes clearly affect our physical well-being.

EXAMPLES OF SEX BELIEFS

Directly Related to Health	*Not Directly Related to Health*
1. Boys who masturbate excessively harm themselves by losing protein and blood through the semen which is ejaculated.	**7.** It is the man who determines the sex of the child.
2. If heart patients remain physically inactive and quiet during sexual intercourse, they need not worry that sexual activity will be detrimental to their health.	**8.** Virginity of the woman is one of the more important factors in the success of a marriage.
3. The best health is enjoyed by people who abstain from sex.	**9.** Oral-genital sex between a man and a woman indicates homosexual tendencies.
4. If a man urinates after sexual intercouse, it will reduce his chances of contracting some venereal disease.	
5. Masturbation causes pimples and acne.	
6. It is dangerous to have sexual intercourse during menstruation because of harmful wastes in the menstrual fluid.	

Source: Adapted from Mosher, 1979.

tophilic mothers are more likely to breast-feed their babies than are erotophobic mothers (Fisher and Gray, 1988). This difference is accurately anticipated by women prior to experiencing pregnancy and childbirth. Female undergraduates with erotophilic attitudes expect to breastfeed longer than do female undergraduates with erotophobic attitudes (Kelley, 1987d).

The same attitudinal factors that interfere with sex-related behaviors in the general population also operate among health practitioners. Studies of medical students find that those who are most erotophobic know less about sexual matters, are less likely to take an elective human sexuality course in med school, and indicate less willingness to treat patients with sexual concerns (Fisher et al., 1988).

find. Among the common problems with relationships are those involving sex. Though there is obviously more to a relationship than sex, it is an extremely important component of marriage. A happy marriage is most likely to include a successful sexual relationship, and that requires, among other things, **sexual compatibility**—the correspondence between partners in sexual attitudes and preferences.

Marital Success and Failure. How each partner expresses his or her sexual attitudes and preferences is central in determining how their relationship functions. When partners begin commanding or criticizing each other sexually, their problems are probably sufficiently severe that professional counseling is advised (Haynes et al., 1981). Fewer problems arise if they communicate their desires positively, if they agree about sexual matters, and if the humorous aspects of sexual interactions can be emphasized.

Married couples do not tend to tally their daily successes and disappointments. Instead, each partner responds globally to the overall positive and negative elements of the relationship (Martin, 1985). The perception of the degree to which the marriage provides rewards such as love, status, money, sexuality, and so on matters a great deal—this seems to affect a couple's general satisfaction with the marriage.

Husband-wife Sexual Similarity. Spouses resemble one another in many ways sexually (Murstein, 1974). For example, they are similar in how much they are aroused by sexually explicit pictures and in their emotional judgments of such stimuli (Byrne et al., 1973). Couples who are dissimilar in responding to erotic stimuli are in fact likely to be dissatisfied with their marriages (Miller and Byrne, 1985). Husbands and wives who perceive that sexual activity occurs too infrequently also dislike their marriages more than do couples who say that sex occurs acceptably often (Myers, 1981). The association between frequency of sexual activity and marital satisfaction persists whether there are children at home or not (Schenck et al., 1983). The evidence is clear that sexual satisfaction is more characteristic of happy than of unhappy relationships. It should be noted, however, that research consistently finds that wives perceive the sexual component of marriage as less important than their husbands do (Schenck et al., 1983).

Most people seem to be successful in seeking and finding intimate partners whose sexual attitudes are similar to their own (Grush and Yehl, 1979). College students with erotophilic attitudes strongly desire to date, love, and interact sexually with an opposite-sex person who is described as having attitudes like their own. Married couples in their thirties reveal considerable husband-wife agreement about pornography, sexual techniques, and other aspects of sexuality (Smith et al., 1990). Spouses with positive sexual attitudes have a more accurate perception of each other's sexual preferences, suggesting that they would be able to fulfill their partner's sexual needs more adequately than spouses with a negative sexual orientation. An erotophilic partner is found to think about sex more often than an erotophobic one, both during sexual interactions and at other times. Such individuals also initiate marital sex more often.

What is the effect on marriage of agreements and disagreements about erotic matters? Spouses with dissimilar sexual attitudes express increased dissatisfaction with their sex lives, with their marriages, and with life in general (Smith et al., 1990). In the most successful marriages, partners also make sure they set aside time to enjoy their sexuality (Becker and Byrne, 1984).

Masturbation: An Anxiety-Arousing Topic

The topic of masturbation (also called *autoeroticism* or *autosexuality*) arouses strongly negative feelings in many people, perhaps more than any other normal sexual activity. In this section, we will discuss such reactions and also point out the way in which a person's experience with masturbation contributes to his or her own sexual adjustment. Chapter 11 includes information about masturbation techniques.

■ **Pervasive Negative Attitudes toward Masturbation**

Several sources have contributed to the view that masturbation is bad and bad for you.

Masturbation as a Sin and a Health Hazard. Negative responses to masturbation have a long history. For centuries, it was commonly termed "Onanism" among Jews and Christians, on the basis of the Old Testament account of Onan, who "spilled his seed upon the ground" and aroused God's anger. Onan's sin was not actually masturbation but an act of disobeying the Lord by practicing coitus interruptus with his brother's widow rather than impregnating her as God had instructed. The idea that Onan masturbated and that what he did was a sin was, nevertheless, firmly established by tradition. Roman Catholic doctrine still identifies masturbation as an "intrinsically and seriously disordered act" that has no reproductive function (Thou shalt not, 1976).

The medical field also played a strong role in creating a negative view of masturbation. Well-meaning physicians at the end of the nineteenth and beginning of the twentieth centuries began warning parents that children who masturbated were likely to experience loss of memory, lowered intelligence, depression, nymphomania, retarded growth, headaches, poor eyesight, stooped shoulders, sleeplessness, pain, weakness in the back and genitalia, cowardice, dry hair with split ends, heart pains, constipation, coughing, epilepsy, paralysis, premature old age, and death (Stout, 1885; Walling, 1904).

That masturbation was both sinful and physically harmful caused many parents to "protect" their children by attempting to stop such dangerous behav-ior. Various strategies were developed to prevent masturbation or to punish it when it occurred. Children in Victorian England had their wrists and ankles tied to the bedposts, received severe beatings, or were subjected to food deprivation (Hartman, 1976). Ingenious devices—one had spokes that caused pain whenever the penis became erect—were attached to young males to prevent sexual arousal, even during sleep.

In more recent times, novelist James Jones recalled that his mother warned him that masturbation would cause his hand to turn black; to convince him this was true, she painted his hand black when he was asleep (MacShane, 1985). Though most people today realize that the supposed negative effects of masturbation constitute a myth, it is still unacceptable to discuss self-stimulation in social settings and especially to say positive things about it. In a 1988 article, writer N. W. Aldrich described journalist Jane Grant (one of the founders of the White Flower Farm nursery) as "bizarre," "peculiar," and "eccentric" based on the fact that she played poker, drank, met her deadlines at the *New York Times,* and kept her maiden name after marriage. Yet, the most upsetting part of her behavior seemed to be something else—her attitude about autosexuality:

> *Even odder, perhaps, was Grant's enthusiastic advocacy of masturbation. "Jane believed that everyone should masturbate," a neighbor remembers. "At dinner parties she would argue strenuously that masturbation was good for the figure and for the complexion, and wonderful exercise for the mind. 'I do it all the time in the shower,' she would say, 'Don't you?'"* [Aldrich, 1988, p. 43].

Masturbation Today. Despite the sexual revolution, the masturbation taboo still remains surprisingly strong. For example, in 1982 it was reported that a male babysitter beat a three-year-old who masturbated, striking him so hard in the groin that the boy's genitals swelled and became discolored (DeMare, 1982). The sitter felt justified in punishing him as a way to prevent such behavior in the future; the fact that the babysitter was arrested for assault suggests that society's views on masturbation have progressed to some degree. Compared to the 1940s, for example, many more people today say that they approve of masturbation and practice it themselves. This is true of both college students seeking "safe sex" and those over 60 who want to relieve sexual tension when a partner is unavailable, ill, or disinterested (Brody, 1987).

Even without having experienced physical punishment for touching our genitals, many of us still learn that masturbation is shameful. Sometimes young people are warned only to avoid "excessive" masturbation, but the question of how much is *too much* generally remains unanswered. Among college students, exposure to pictures of others masturbating often produces feelings of guilt and discomfort. In one experiment, slides showing autosexual acts produced more negative feelings than did pictures of heterosexual intercouse or oral sex (Kelley, 1985b). Seeing a picture of someone of one's own sex masturbating is particularly upsetting, especially among males.

Most parents today deny that they would tell their children that masturbation will harm them, but only 5 percent or less communicate to the child that they approve of it (Gagnon, 1985). (For the record, there is no scientific evidence of any physical problem caused by masturbation.) Sometimes the "enlightened" modern message seems to be almost as bad as that shown in Figure 8-11.

In a survey of over 1,400 parents of three- to eleven-year-olds, most reported that they ignore their child's masturbation or try to distract him or her to another activity. A relatively small number of parents

FIGURE 8-11 *NEGATIVE MESSAGES ABOUT MASTURBATION* Would you expect that this young boy may get the message that masturbation is wrong or dangerous because of what his father says?

Source: Reproduced by Special Permission of PLAY-BOY Magazine: Copyright © 1984 by PLAYBOY.

*"It's perfectly normal and healthy,
son—providing you don't do it to excess,
or have perverted or neurotic thoughts
while doing it, or do it with other kids, or use foreign
objects, or make a mess on the bed, or
neglect to wash yourself afterward, or let
Mommy or sister catch you doing it, or. . . ."*

(20 to 25 percent) tell the child that it is acceptable to masturbate privately. Even more rare is a positive message that self-stimulation is a powerful source of pleasure. What many parents do not realize is that failure to communicate a positive message about masturbation forces children to reach their own conclusions—usually negative—about such behavior. Actor Donald Sutherland has described his own reactions at age thirteen:

> . . . *someone told me about masturbation. I had no idea what he was talking about. Nevertheless, I went home and masturbated. And, God, I have to tell you, it was the hugest shock! I never expected anything to come out from where I peed! When I suddenly had this overwhelming explosion, I nearly died of a heart attack. Needless to say, I felt this was original sin— this had to be, if anything was . . .* [*Playboy* interview, 1981, pp. 78–79].

There is a useful pamphlet for parents who want to discuss masturbation with their children. It is called "Talking with Your Young Child about Sex" prepared by the Family Life Education Cooperative and available from Network Publications in Santa Cruz, California.

The issue of masturbating in public is one that even the most permissive and tolerant parents may have difficulty facing. What is the best response if a child persistently plays with himself or herself without regard to time or place? In a classroom or other public setting, children may ride on furniture or stimulate their genitals using a hand, toy, or pillow (McCray, 1981). In our culture, these activities cause discomfort to others in the same way as would urinating or defecating in public. Techniques have been developed by behavioral therapists that discourage public masturbation without resorting to fear and punishment. For example, a four-year-old girl upset her preschool teachers by almost constant masturbation that she called "itchy-itching." She was expelled from school, and her mother sought professional help. Tina's mother was instructed to give her two M & M candies whenever the child refrained from masturbating in public for at least fifteen minutes. After three months of this procedure, the child openly masturbated only about once a week, and she was able to return to school.

There is obviously a fine line between discouraging public acts that upset others and communicating that the act itself is acceptable. Most parents are not, however, really interested in encouraging their children to have positive attitudes about masturbation. Studies of young adults indicate the rarity of positive views about stimulating one's own genitals. Table 8-4 presents several statements used to assess negative attitudes about masturbation. Guilt and disgust often accompany this kind of sexual pleasure, even though most college men (92 percent) and women (72 percent) report that they masturbate (Abramson and Mosher, 1975). Ironically, masturbation is perceived as negative and intercourse as positive, but self-stimulation is a much more common activity among students than coitus.

TABLE 8-4 **Masturbation: Good or Bad?**

These statements assess positive and negative attitudes about masturbation. Strong agreement with the first two items, and strong disagreement with the second two, indicate very negative attitudes about genital self-stimulation.

SAMPLE STATEMENTS FROM THE SCALE OF NEGATIVE ATTITUDES TOWARD MASTURBATION

1. Any masturbation is too much.
2. Masturbation is a sin against yourself.
3. Masturbation is a normal sexual outlet.
4. Masturbation can teach you to enjoy the sensuousness of your own body.

Source: Abramson and Mosher, 1975.

How Masturbation Contributes to Sexual Adjustment

What benefits, other than pleasure, do people derive from masturbation? Despite the general discouragement provided by parents and other adults and the disgust people commonly express about doing such a thing, masturbation is frequently practiced because it feels good and releases sexual tension (Clifford, 1978). For males, even extremely negative attitudes about this activity do not inhibit the behavior; females with negative attitudes, in contrast, tend to find masturbation less arousing and to engage in this behavior less often than those with positive attitudes (Abramson et al., 1981).

Many sexologists encourage masturbation as a part of sexual therapy for clients who are having sexual difficulties (Chapter 17 discusses this further). Masturbation is also regarded as an important foundation for later sexuality (Kelley, 1983b). Most people find out about sexual pleasure and what it means to have an orgasm through masturbation rather than in interacting with a partner. It seems likely that our emotional responses to sex and sexuality are based on how we feel about masturbation. As you may guess, erotophiles express more positive attitudes about masturbation than erotophobes (Byrne et al., 1990).

What can be done to encourage more positive and less threatening attitudes toward masturbation?

In one innovative experiment, 115 male high school students participated in a forty-minute session with their parents' consent. Two adult males explored the following ideas with these adolescent boys:

1. Masturbation occurs quite commonly among adolescents.
2. Beliefs that masturbation is associated with consequences such as sexual dysfunctions or homosexuality are simply myths.
3. Masturbation is an acceptable alternative to intercourse, and it has the advantage of avoiding the risk of pregnancy and disease.
4. Someone who masturbates can learn a great deal about his or her own sexual responses and thus be better prepared for later sexuality.
5. Guilt feelings about masturbation are unreasonable; they are based on out-of-date societal beliefs.

The boys who participated in this experiment developed more positive attitudes and believed fewer myths about masturbation three weeks later than comparable boys in a control group (Lo Presto et al., 1985). Neither group of subjects showed any change in the frequency of masturbation during this period; the change was in their feelings and beliefs about it. Most sex therapists would view this emotional and intellectual change as beneficial.

Summarizing the Information about Sexual Attitudes and Behavior . . .

Wide variations in sexual attitudes and behavior occur across cultures and throughout different periods of history. People tend to have an **ethnocentric bias that leads them to believe that their own cultural norms are simply natural expressions of basic human behavior. Cross-cultural and historical comparisons make it clear, however, that such self-centered beliefs are incorrect.**

Demographic variables influence sexuality, too, with social class, race or ethnicity, and religious orientation each playing a role. More positive attitudes about sex are associated with higher socioeconomic levels, and education seems to be the primary reason

for this relationship. Blacks and whites hold fairly similar attitudes about sex, with blacks being somewhat more permissive about certain sexual matters. Hispanic-Americans, despite stereotypes to the contrary, tend to be more conservative than Anglo-Americans. Traditional Catholic and Protestant beliefs contain much that is sexually negative, while Moslems stress differences between males and females, requiring the separation of the sexes.

Society-wide changes in sexual permissiveness were reflected in attitudes and in behavior that characterized the **sexual revolution. After decades of a steady increase in tolerance for the sexual proclivites** of others, the incidence of premarital sex, and the frequency and variety of sexual interactions, recent data suggest that a reverse shift in the conservative direction is underway.

Positive (**erotophilic**) and negative (**erotophobic**) sexual attitudes influence many aspects of sexuality. Erotophobes generally avoid sexual cues; when avoidance is not possible, they experience negative emotional reactions to such cues. Erotophiles experience positive emotions to sexual cues and engage in approach behavior. Conservative sexual training apparently underlies erotophobic attitudes. These nega-tive attitudes reduce the frequency of sexual activity, encourage less exposure to internal or external erotic fantasies, and interfere with various health-related behaviors involving sexual anatomy or functioning.

Although most individuals masturbate, negative attitudes about the act are widespread. There are ways to teach children that masturbation in a public setting is not socially acceptable without inducing fear, guilt, and conflict about it. As a learning experience, masturbation provides a basic introduction to sexual sensation and erotic pleasure for most people.

To Find Out More about Sexual Attitudes and Behavior . . .

Brown, P. (1988). *The body and society: Men, women and sexual renunciation*. New York: Columbia University Press.

This historian describes the early Christian church and the development of religious beliefs involving celibacy and the renunciation of sex.

Freedman, E., & D'Emilio, J. (1989). *Intimate matters: A history of sexuality in America*. New York: Harper and Row.

This book covers American sexual history, beginning with Native Americans and the English colonists. The authors describe the way in which race, social class, and gender have affected sexuality in this country.

Kitzinger, S. (1983) *Women's experience of sex*. New York: G. P. Putnam.

The author provides a source book on women's sexuality. Included are many informative illustrations.

Money, J. (1985). *The destroying anger: Sex, fitness, and food in the legacy of degeneracy theory, graham crackers, Kellogg's corn flakes, and American health history*. Buffalo, N.Y.: Prometheus.

Medical psychologist John Money traces the history of the effects of negative sexual attitudes on health care in the United States. One amusing example is the way in which Kellogg's corn flakes were touted in 1898 as an "anti-masturbation food and extinguisher of sexual desire."

Pogrebin, L. C. (1980). *Growing up free: Raising your child in the '80s*. New York: Bantam.

This book discusses how parents may educate their children without sexism or negativism. It encompasses the spectrum of sexual development from conception to maturity.

Reiss, I. L. (1990). *An end to shame: Shaping our next sexual revolution*. Buffalo, N.Y.: Prometheus.

Sociologist Ira Reiss, in a very readable style, predicts that a new sexual revolution will occur out of necessity—one based on tolerance and the principles of honesty, equality, and responsibility. Rather than imposing anyone's sexual values on others, people would be better off if each person were free to choose his or her own lifestyle.

CHAPTER NINE

SEXUAL RELATIONSHIPS AMONG ADULTS

Relationships begin in many different ways, and two people often are brought together by accident. A young executive describes how he and his future wife first became aware of each other as potential spouses rather than simply as two people who were employed by the same firm.

Last summer, we had a big power blackout after a thunderstorm, and I found myself stuck at the office downtown. I knew that transportation in and out of the city was a total mess, so I couldn't get to my apartment in the suburbs. The safest thing to do was to get a hotel room for the night.

The trouble with my plan turned out to be that I wasn't the only one who decided to go to a hotel. My secretary, Janet, must have called over a dozen nearby places, and every one was full—even a couple of fairly junky ones. I was beginning to consider camping out in my office when Janet said, "My apartment is only a few blocks from here. You're welcome to spend the night on my couch." I only hesitated a minute. It sounded a lot better than curling up on the rug next to my desk.

I took her to dinner at a small Japanese restaurant where we sat at low tables with our shoes off. I don't know whether it was the saki or our feet touching under the table or what, but we talked and laughed more during that meal than we had in the eight months she'd worked for me. She's about ten years younger than I am, a real knock-out, and at dinner I discovered how much fun she could be. It was one of the nicest evenings I had spent in a long time.

Things were kind of awkward when we first got to her place. She sat next to me on the sofa, and I could smell her perfume as we talked. We both had recently gone through relationships that ended badly, and I told her things about my feelings and disappointments that I had never shared with anyone. About midnight, I noticed the time and said, "I should be shot for boring you with all of this. Maybe it's time for me to shut up and let you get some sleep."

I was trying not to be obvious about being attracted to her. After all, there was no reason to think that this beautiful young woman was interested in me just because she offered me a couch to sleep on. Frankly, I don't know exactly what happened next. I was helping her put sheets on the foldout couch, we kissed, and I began caressing her firm breasts and her rounded bottom. Then, we were out of our clothes and in bed. For the next two or three hours, we did everything a man and woman can do without getting arrested. She wasn't inhibited in the least. I was overjoyed with her and wanted the evening never to end.

In a way, it hasn't. Two weeks later, she moved into my apartment, and we have been living together for five or six months. I feel that being with Janet is the only sensible thing I've done for years. She's fun, she's sexy, she's smart, and most important, she is loving and affectionate—and, I'm unhappy whenever we are not together.

What will happen next? I don't know, but we both would like to have kids, and marriage seems more and more where we are headed.

Warner, age 32

Increasingly, couples follow the pattern of Warner and Janet—sexual intimacy followed by cohabitation and then marriage. Most people want to be part of a marriage in which two loving individuals remain together, sexually faithful, for a lifetime. We also know, of course, that no relationship is guaranteed to last. Relationships may deteriorate and sometimes come to an end—it is also possible for love and intimacy to last a lifetime, as we will discuss shortly.

Perhaps the most important, and undoubtedly most difficult, interpersonal decisions that we make involve establishing or not establishing intimate relationships. In this chapter, we examine the lifestyles of those who remain *single*, including couples who live together (cohabit) but avoid formal commitments. We also discuss *marriage*, including the decision of two individuals to marry, variations in the sexual interactions of spouses, and a summary of the causes of marital dissatisfaction. Among the common responses to an unhappy marriage are divorce and sexual relationships *outside of marriage*. In addition, we deal with *sexual life beyond young adulthood*, including sexuality among middle-aged and elderly adults. Special sections discuss the unpleasant realities of *spouse abuse*, speculations about future sexual *lifestyles*, and research documenting the *effects of divorce on children and adolescents*.

Singlehood

Though most people in our society view marriage as a primary goal, a great many individuals remain single. What is it like to be part of the unmarried minority?

▪ Single Lifestyles

It is not common today to speak of singles as spinsters or bachelors, though these terms *were* common a generation ago. During this last decade of the twentieth century, more Americans remain single, or live alone, than ever before. Of every ninety-eight households in the United States, twenty-two are composed of one individual. Among adults, 10 to 15 percent live alone or with a nonrelative. Even among those who will eventually marry or who have been married, the single lifestyle spans a greater portion of their lives than was true in the past.

The married majority often react negatively to those who are single. Married couples tend to avoid single women, even widows; they are perceived by wives as potentially threatening (Stolk and Brother-

ton, 1981). A survey in Australia found that men evaluated single women even more negatively than women did.

Because of divorce, premarital pregnancy, or personal choice, more single parents are raising their children alone than ever before. Single-parent households increased dramatically between 1960 and 1986 in the United States, with about 15 million youngsters under age 18 living with only one parent (Schmid, 1988). Though most children (63 percent) live with both parents in the home, 20 percent of those under eighteen live with only their mothers and two percent with only their fathers, as Figure 9-1 illustrates.

Singlehood is a viable option for many adults, either as an alternative to marriage or as a way of life following divorce. Some women and men prefer to focus on careers and deliberately choose the single life, finding it preferable to marriage and parenthood.

Today, singles are likely to be as sexually active as those who marry (More single women..., 1988; Petersen 1983), although finding suitable partners is often a continuing concern. The typical "singles scene" in bars may be unappealing, and singles increasingly turn to dating services and personal ads. It is also possible to meet others through current friends, on the job, and through group activities (Austrom and Hanel, 1985). Most singles eventually enter into long-term relationships, and many decide to live together, as is discussed in the following section.

A growing, but unknown, number of unmarried adults seek parenthood without the ties of either marriage or cohabitation. A single woman is most likely to obtain artificial insemination at a fertility clinic, while a single man is likely to advertise in order to find a woman willing to bear his child and then give it to him. Singles of either sex also may elect to seek an adoptive child. Altogether, these "elective parents" or "parents by choice," as some call themselves, are entering parenthood relatively easily. It helps, of course, to live in an era when the concept of illegitimacy carries little, if any, stigma.

FIGURE 9-1 *SINGLE-PARENT HOUSEHOLDS: A STEADILY GROWING PATTERN*   Single-parent households have become increasingly common in the United States and most such families consist of children living with their mothers.

■   Cohabitation

It may seem strange in the 1990s, but only a relatively few years ago, an unmarried couple who shared the same house or apartment were described as "living in sin" or "shacking up." **Cohabitation** was a daring act—and it was a violation of the law in many parts of the United States. Today, about 80 percent of the college couples who live together are married while 20 percent are not. The percentage of unmarried couples who engage in cohabitation (unmarried, heterosexual couples living together and engaging in sex) has risen dramatically—a figure about ten times greater now than in the 1950s.

One of the less serious problems is what to call the person with whom you are living—significant other, lover, roommate, housemate, cohabitor? The U.S. Census Bureau uses POSSLQ (Persons of the Opposite Sex Sharing Living Quarters), but no one else seems to. Another possible term that is growing in popularity is *spousal equivalent* (Keeney, 1990).

What are the implications of this increasingly familiar lifestyle for the institution of marriage?

Effects of Cohabitation.   Those who cohabit are very likely to marry eventually, either the partner with whom they live or someone else. Does the experience of cohabitation affect a subsequent marriage? If marriages are enhanced by previous cohabitation, the effect is extremely small. Several studies comparing couples who did and did not live together prior to marriage showed no differences between them in emotional closeness, satisfaction, number of conflicts, or equality of sharing (Watson, 1983). There was slightly less marital satisfaction among those who had lived together before marrying, but this may simply reflect the typical decrease in satisfaction found during the first decade of intimate relationships. Perhaps for the same reasons, those who do cohabit and then marry later on are found to have a divorce rate 80 percent higher than those who did not live together, premaritally, according to a Swedish study of over

4000 adults between the ages of 20 and 44 (Ex-unwed couples..., 1987).

Among the differences that have been identified, cohabitors are found to "give in" less often to their partners' desires (Macklin, 1978), but this behavior may indicate only that those individuals who choose to cohabit are more independent than those who decide not to live together until after marriage. As is also true of married couples, the men in a cohabiting relationship tend to initiate sex more often than the women do; one difference is that sex is initiated more frequently in cohabitation than in marriage (Byers and Heinlein, 1989). Cohabitors begin engaging in sex at an earlier age and have greater sexual experience than a comparable group of married couples, but the two groups do not differ in how much love they express for their partners (Newcomb, 1986).

Social and Legal Aspects of Cohabitation.   Among the reasons for the increased popularity of cohabitation are the appeal of a seemingly uncomplicated alternative to marriage and the current acceptance of such living arrangements.

For example, college housing regulations have become less restrictive about cohabitation on most campuses. This change may represent a delayed effect of the politically active climate of the 1960s, including an emphasis by the women's movement supporting greater responsibility for women. Also, the availability of effective birth control methods makes it easier for those who are not married to engage in intercourse with relative safety.

A couple planning to cohabit could benefit, however, by considering some of the legal and practical issues involved. Couples who live together and then break up do not have the same legal rights as do married couples seeking a divorce. When there is joint property to be divided or the question of a monetary settlement, for example, the law is much less clear about cohabitors than about spouses. Other issues include such matters as insurance and health benefits, discriminatory tax laws, and inheritance in the absence of a will. For the loving couple embarking on a new life of romance and sexuality, these issues are seldom discussed or even thought about, but they can eventually arise as matters of extreme importance.

Within Marriage

As will be discussed shortly, most people want to marry, and most do find an acceptable and accepting partner. Marriage may be the norm, but there are no generally accepted rules or customs governing this crucial aspect of one's life—deciding to marry, developing appropriate patterns of marital sexuality, maximizing marital satisfaction while minimizing dissatisfaction, and communicating with one's spouse.

■ The Decision to Marry

In some respects, we probably select our cars more carefully and rationally than we do our spouses. How *are* marital decisions made?

Social Trends and Contrasts.   In some cultures, the decision to marry is based on negotiations and agreements between the parents of the potential bride and groom (see Figure 9-2). In some places—such as Turkey—a price is paid for the bride. Howe (1980) describes a young Turkish couple who attempted suicide when their families could not agree as to how much the prospective groom's relatives should pay the girl's family for the privilege of marrying a virgin.

Parental negotiations and payments may seem odd to us, but such customs provide stability to those who accept them. For example, where such practices prevail, premarital sex occurs much less frequently, divorce and remarriage are strongly discouraged, and a paternal family structure ensures clear guidelines involving male control of the family's assets.

A paternalistic marriage may appear to apply only to other, quite different cultures, but marriage manuals in the nineteenth-century United States recommended that a wife show obedience, submission, and reverence toward her husband. He, in turn, should behave as a kindly ruler:

> *Husbands should remember that in order to have the submission of their wives they must temper their authority with love, prudence, and wisdom [Brandt, 1892, p. 121, cf. Gordon and Bernstein, 1970].*

> *The wife . . . loves to be guided by the clearer intellect of her husband, and to receive the protection of his firmer and more aggressive nature [Reed, 1870, p. 42, cf. Gordon and Bernstein, 1970].*

FIGURE 9-2 *ARRANGING A MARRIAGE: PARENTS KNOW BEST* In many cultures other than our own, marriages are arranged in the traditional way by parents and do not depend on a couple "falling in love" or even necessarily knowing each other.

In England, writing in the period just before World War I, author H. H. Munro frequently poked fun at the prevailing view among the privileged classes that a man's only pressing courtship problem was to select a suitable wife who would presumably be an asset to him socially and economically. In his play, *The Watched Pot,* a young man named Trevor is discussing the difficulties involved in selecting the right woman to marry. Trevor says:

> *Oh, I suppose I shall marry somebody some day, but it's the choosing business that is so beastly compli-cated. Think of the millions and millions of nice women there are in the world, and then of the fact that one can only marry one of them—it makes mar-rying an awfully ticklish matter. It's like choosing which puppies you're going to keep out of a large lit-ter; you can never be sure that you haven't drowned the wrong ones [Munro, reprinted 1988, p. 892].*

The view that a wife resembles a household pet has been replaced for some men by the view that she should be a motherly servant who also provides extra

money for the family. In a survey of middle-class males aged eighteen to fifty in twenty U.S. cities, more than three fourths expressed admiration and desire for an ideal wife who would be a good mother more than anything else, cook dinner, do all the laun-dry, clean the bathroom, and also work outside the home (Scott, 1979b). Unlike men, women want to share household duties with a spouse. This is a fairly recent development, as discussed in more detail in Chapter 6.

Marriage is, nevertheless, still highly valued by most young Americans. More than 90 percent of a group of eighteen-year-olds expected to marry even-tually, and only 3 percent thought they would remain single (Thornton and Freedman, 1982). The major at-titude change that has in fact occurred does not con-cern whether to marry but at what age to do so. Be-tween 1960 and 1980, the expected age rose a year or more, to 24.7 for men and age 23.1 for women. Ac-cording to the U.S. Bureau of the Census (1981a), as recently as 1970, young adults married at a younger age than they did in the early 1980s.

The entry of more women into careers, the increased acceptability of premarital sex, and a delay in the age when individuals want to have children all seem to contribute to the rising age of first marriages—but there is an additional reason. Single men in the twenty to twenty-nine age bracket outnumber single women of that age. In 1988 in the United States, there were 122 single men in their twenties for every 100 single women (Bradsher, 1990). As a result, marriages may be delayed as women become more selective in their choices, and males wait for a younger group of females to "come of age."

The chances are high that most of us will marry at least once by the time we reach middle age. As Figure 9-3 shows, most twenty- to twenty-four-year-olds have not yet married. By the ages of forty-five to fifty-four, however, fewer than 10 percent have remained single. Couples who marry in their teens have a much higher risk of divorce. Their youth, financial difficulties, and early parenthood contribute to less successful marriages.

The typical groom is about two years older than

FIGURE 9-3 *POSTPONING THE AGE OF MARRIAGE* Though most individuals in the United States have married by the time they are in their late fortys and early fiftys, most people in their early twentys are postponing when they first marry.
Source: Based on data in Thornton and Freedman, 1982.

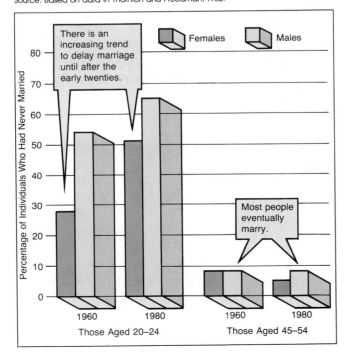

his bride; age-discrepant marriages are much less common. In 1977, the husband was younger than his wife in only 14.4 percent of first marriages (U.S. Bureau of the Census, 1981b). When partners' ages differ by ten or more years (most often an older man and a younger woman), the woman faces certain problems. Surveys in Detroit and in Tokyo indicate that young wives with older husbands feel less companionship with their husbands than do wives whose husbands are closer to them in age (Blood, 1982).

Older husbands in age-discrepant marriages (see Figure 9-4) benefit in that they live longer than other married men their age; men with younger wives have a 13 percent reduction in death rate (Foster et al., 1984). That finding does not have to be interpreted to mean that a young wife prolongs a man's life. Men who select such a mate may differ from other men in other important ways. For example, they may be healthier than other men even *before* they marry.

The opposite pattern, a woman marrying a younger man (also depicted in Figure 9-4), is far less common. Nevertheless, the trend is growing. In 1970, 16 percent of all U.S. marriages involved older women and younger men; by the late 1980s, 22 percent of all marriages involved such couples (Toufexis, 1987). Men who marry older women are 20 percent more likely to die at any given age than are men in same-age couples. College students expect pairs in which the wife is older than the husband to be more likely to divorce than any other age combination (Cowan, 1984). Because women live longer than men and because men often seek younger women as mates, older women encounter special problems if they are seeking a mate. In the competition between older and younger women for the same men, younger women usually have the advantage.

Although most people marry someone of their own race, when there are racial differences, you might expect there to be a negative effect on marriages. There is, however, little research support for that expectation. Sociologist Ernest Porterfield interviewed mixed (black–white) couples and found these marriages to be as happy and strong as those of same-race couples (cf. Snider, 1973). It is interesting to note that black–white couples tend to live in a white neighborhood if the husband is white and in a black neighborhood if he is black (Porterfield, 1973). The

FIGURE 9-4 *TOO OLD FOR HIM OR FOR HER—OR JUST RIGHT?* When an age discrepancy exists between husband and wife, the couple experiences a few specific problems and benefits that are different from those of couples who are about the same age. Generally, when the woman is older than her husband, others respond somewhat negatively to the relationship. In contrast, others find a union between an older man and a younger woman relatively acceptable, and there is evidence that men in such marriages actually live longer than men with same-age spouses.

most negative effect on mixed marriages is disapproval from family members on both sides who feel that a same-race partner would have been preferable. Another potential problem is prejudice encountered by the children of mixed-race marriages.

Changing the Woman's Last Name. One decision that is increasingly faced by couples is whether the woman should keep her last name after marriage or adopt her husband's name. Only 8 percent of college men express interest in changing their own surnames, but 61 percent of college women expect to change their names when they marry. Despite these figures, women attach more significance to their maiden names than is generally realized (Intons-Peterson and Crawford, 1985). A related problem is the identity shift that accompanies a change of names. Your name affects your sense of who you are, and women have unfairly been expected to undergo such change while men have not (Quindlen, 1987).

A married woman who retains her own family name helps clarify her status as a financially independent individual, and she need not make name changes on her drivers' license, credit cards, and other documents after marriage. Information about the right of women to keep their surnames is provided by organizations such as the Lucy Stone League in New York City and The Center for Women's Own Name in Marrington, Illinois (James, 1982b).

The authors of this text can provide a word of warning from their own experience. Many obstetrics wards assign the mother's name to the newborn baby. If the couple wants their child to have the father's name, the wife may have to be admitted to the hospital under that name no matter what she ordinarily calls herself. If she does this, however, other complications arise. For example, the physician may not recognize the patient's "new," temporary name. We now know the importance of notifying the physician about such matters long before entering the labor room; those in a similar situation might benefit from our mistakes.

Spousal Similarity. As we will point out in Chapter 10, similarity between partners improves the chances that a relationship will grow and prosper, and the same is true for a marital relationship. There is substantial overlap in the personalities of married couples (Buss, 1984; Smith et al., 1990). Dominant men tend to marry dominant women, extraverts marry extraverts, quarrelsome people marry quarrelsome people, and so on. Spouses even resemble one another in the amount of time they want to spend conversing (Thelen et al., 1985).

Wives generally perceive the feelings of their husbands more accurately than husbands know their wives' feelings (White, 1985). Women also have a better idea than men about where their partners stand on important issues. Table 9-1 presents the four most important and four least important issues that a sample of married couples reported having discussed. The success of the relationship is determined in part by agreement on the important issues.

Spouses who reciprocate their positive feelings about each other tend to have better marriages than those who don't (Rosenthal, 1984). In other words, "If you love and value me, say it and show it." As with any other close relationship, unpleasant inter-personal interactions lead to the relationship's deterioration. In general, dissimilarity lays the groundwork for additional problems.

A few specific characteristics of potential spouses are more highly valued than others. When college students were asked about their preferences for the qualities of their future spouses, they responded as shown in Table 9-2 (Buss and Barnes, 1986). Three of the characteristics were emphasized by one sex more than the other. Men expressed more interest in physically attractive mates than women did. Women were more likely to mention a mate's good earning capacity and a college degree than were men. Such responses suggest some well-established stereotypes in which males are viewed as well-educated bread winners who come home to their sexually appealing partners. In the total list of preferred characteristics, however, most were expressed by both sexes, suggesting that men and women agree about who would make a good or bad partner.

Cultural Arrangements for Marriage. In Western societies, the legally recognized form of marriage is **monogamy,** in which one man and one woman are legally joined. Of the 862 cultures across the world described in Murdock (1981), only 16 percent require monogamy. **Polygamy,** in which a person is married to more than one spouse at a time, is the norm in 44 percent of the cultures. A choice of either

---

TABLE 9-1 **Crucial Issues for Husbands and Wives**

Married couples rated various issues as to their importance in their relationship. There was fairly good agreement among men and women as to which were most and least important. Husbands and wives differed with respect to women's rights (wives rated this topic more important than their husbands did), and men rated work as more important than women did.

	ISSUES IN A MARITAL RELATIONSHIP
The four most important issues	Family size
	Physical discipline of children
	Leisure time activities
	Economic contribution of each partner
The four least important issues	Chores
	Who gives more to the relationship
	Women's rights
	Work

Source: Based on data in White, 1985a.

TABLE 9-2 **What Do You Want in a Future Spouse?**

According to almost 300 college students, certain qualities are perceived as important in their future spouses. Several personality characteristics top the list.

DESIRABILITY OF CHARACTERISTICS OF A FUTURE SPOUSE

Rank	Characteristic
1 (most desirable)	Kind and understanding
2	Exciting personality (warm, extraverted)
3	Intelligent
4	Physically attractive
5	Healthy
6	Easygoing
7	Creative
8	Wants children
9	College graduate
10	Good earning capacity
11	Good heredity (no skeletons in family closet)
12	Good housekeeper
13	Religious

Source: Based on data in Buss and Barnes, 1986.

monogamy or polygamy is permitted in 39 percent of all cultures. Undeveloped agricultural societies are most likely to adopt **polygyny**, in which a man has multiple wives. The presence of several wives and many offspring to cultivate the crops is economically useful. For the man it is also a sign of status to have a large family (Emlen and Oring, 1977). In some cultures—parts of China for example—men of extremely high status may have a harem with as many as 800 partners (Gregersen, 1983).

Polygyny is relatively common around the world, and about 400 cultures permit it. Much less common—only four societies allow it—is **polyandry**, the form of polygamy in which a woman has two or more husbands. One society in northern India also permits **polygynandry**, a group marriage in which several men and several women form the family unit.

The relatively high rate of divorce and remarriage in Western societies has resulted in the concept of **serial monogamy**, which means that an individual may legally be a partner in multiple marriages (one at a time) during his or her lifetime. Serial monogamy also is practiced among the Hopi Indians of North America and the Siwans of Egypt.

■ Marital Sexuality

Whatever you may believe constitutes the "typical" marriage in our own culture, married couples in fact vary a great deal in their sexual patterns. Intercourse rates differ widely—some couples even avoid it altogether, and most married partners masturbate. We will explore these and other aspects of marital sexuality.

Marital Intercourse and Oral-Genital Sex. People are often interested in the average figures for various kinds of marital sex. How many people engage in various sexual acts, and how frequently? One reason for such interest seems to be our desire to evaluate ourselves or our partners as "normal" or "abnormal." Terms such as *oversexed* and *undersexed* appear frequently in letters to advice columnists when the writer is describing and complaining about a spouse. In reality, there is no rule book to guide any of us, and survey data merely indicate what a given sample of people in a given culture at a given time report about their behavior. The averages detailed in such research do not necessarily represent what everyone *should* do, but rather what other people say they are doing. Using such information to evaluate the sexual preferences of yourself or of someone else is risky.

Even the basic data of these studies are not entirely accurate. For example, spouses give different estimates as to how often they have sexual intercourse. In one study, wives reported having intercourse with their husbands 7.78 times per month while their husbands reported the frequency as 6.98 times per month (Levinger, 1970). Spouses' estimates of intercourse frequency agree exactly only about half the time (Udry, 1980).

Many studies suggest that intercourse frequency decreases over the course of a marriage. In a sample of approximately 500 married women in sixteen U.S. cities, frequency declined from 10.01 times per four weeks to 7.75 times per four weeks over a four-year span (Udry, 1980). Women who, at the beginning of the study, had been married the shortest time, reported the greatest decrease in frequency over the four years, as Figure 9-5 shows.

Intercourse frequency is highest among newly married couples. Within the first month of marriage,

eleven out of twenty-one couples said that they had intercourse more than seventeen times. One year later, the rate dropped to half that; pregnancy or the birth of a baby caused the rate to decline even more (James, 1981). Factors such as boredom and fatigue also contribute to decreases in sexual frequency.

Oral-genital sex is common in about half of the marriages according to the Hunt (1974) survey of American adults, with the unmarried engaging in oral sex as frequently as those who are married. College-educated partners are more likely to practice fellatio and cunnilingus than less educated partners.

Masturbation within Marriage.   As Figure 9-6 illustrates, most married men and women sometimes masturbate. The changes in sexual attitudes in the 1960s and 1970s made masturbation more acceptable; for that reason, the rates increased among those who are married *and* those who are not.

Married partners, then, can and do masturbate, and not necessarily because they are sexually dissatisfied. Masturbation is a simple alternative when a partner is temporarily absent or unmotivated to en-

FIGURE 9-5   *DECLINING FREQUENCY OF MARITAL INTERCOURSE OVER TIME*   The frequency of marital intercourse decreases over time, with the greatest decrease occurring during the first four years of marriage. These data are based on the reports of several hundred wives under the age of thirty in 1974.
Source: Based on data in Udry, 1980.

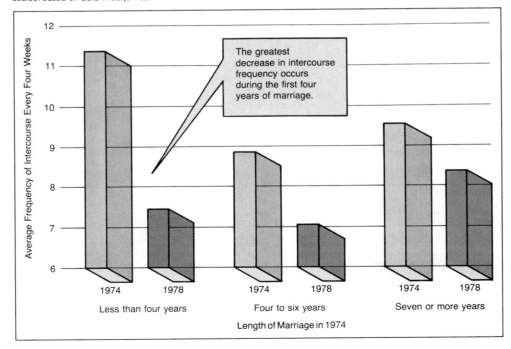

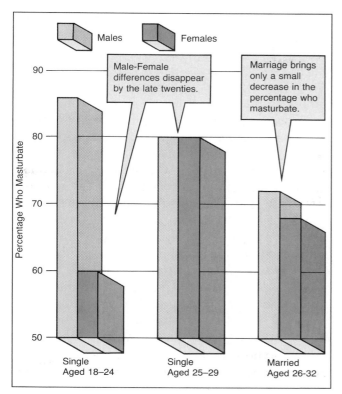

FIGURE 9-6 *MASTURBATION IN YOUNG ADULTHOOD* Young adult men and women, whether single or married, masturbate, and the incidence shows only a slight decrease with marriage. Source: Based on data in Hunt, 1974.

gage in sex (Jensen, 1978). Or, it may be enjoyed at times for its own sake as an element of variety in addition to other forms of marital sex. *Sometimes,* masturbation is a response to an unsatisfactory marriage. The frequency of masturbation is, however, unrelated to whether the marriage is happy or unhappy.

Celibate Marriage. The exact frequency of **celibate marriage** is unknown. When such couples seek therapy, the professionals they contact usually interpret the absence of sex as a sign of problems within the marriage. This arrangement, it turns out, is usually not really acceptable to both partners (Goldsmith, 1982), and one of them tends to express dissatisfaction. Couples sometimes live in this way (besides having a mutual disinterest in sex) because of a sexual dysfunction (see Chapter 17) or a psychological disturbance such as depression (Martin, 1981). A less common reason for celibacy is the expression of a **madonna-whore syndrome** by the husband (Stay-

ton, 1984). Some men think that women are either sexless saints like the Virgin Mary or passionate whores with whom sex is appropriate; if a man perceives his wife as a saint, he seeks sex elsewhere with "bad" women.

■ Satisfaction . . . and Dissatisfaction

Satisfaction with one's marriage tends to be a pivotal factor in each individual's overall happiness. What do we know about marital satisfaction? Sadly enough, research shows that during the first year of marriage about half of all couples say they have serious problems, over a third of the newlyweds are more critical of their spouses than prior to marriage, and more than one of every four couples report an increase in arguments (Burden, 1989).

Satisfaction within Marriage. **Marital satisfaction** is defined as having positive feelings about the relationship, as expressed in the behaviors, the emotions, and the thoughts of the two partners (Snyder et al., 1981). Specifically, these include how adaptively the partners say they communicate, solve problems, spend their leisure time, deal with their children, and interact sexually. If negative emotions characterize these interactions, **marital dissatisfaction** is indicated. A dissatisfied spouse is likely to agree with statements such as "My spouse frequently misinterprets the way I really feel when we are arguing," "My marriage is an unhappy one" (Snyder and Regts, 1982). In unhappy marriages, it is more common to blame the spouse for all of the problems than in happy marriages (Fincham et al., 1987).

Sexual Satisfaction. Sexual interactions within marriage can satisfy both individuals, one of them, or neither. Once two people are married, sex sometimes becomes less interesting or exciting; for others, sex becomes better and better over time. Conflicts about sex may be a sign of more general problems in the relationship, or they may simply reflect unhappiness about sex itself (Sloan, 1982b).

A recurring problem is figuring out what the partner really wants sexually. For example, husbands typically underestimate how frequently their wives want intercourse while wives overestimate their husbands' sexual desires (Levinger, 1970). Measures of sexual satisfaction (Hudson et al., 1981) ask spouses to indicate agreement or disagreement in responding to such statements as "My partner is very sensitive to my sexual needs and desires," and "I feel that my sex life is boring." A satisfied partner is likely to agree with the first statement and disagree with the second. Partners who report the greatest sexual satisfaction also have more orgasms than partners who are dissatisfied (Perlman and Abramson, 1981).

The general quality of a relationship influences sexual satisfaction. When everyday interactions create problems, the couple is said to experience *role strain*. If either partner, for example, believes that it is the husband's role to determine how money is spent when the wife actually makes the money decisions, role strain results. The greater the role strain in whatever areas of their lives, the greater the dissatisfaction with sexual interactions (Frank et al., 1979; Heath, 1978).

Among the many specific areas of interaction that can provoke disharmony and a lessening of affection are those involving children.

The Impact of Parenthood. While the addition of a child to the family can create happiness and satisfaction, it also can cause a husband and wife to feel less satisfied with one another (Goldberg, 1981).

Most new parents report enjoying their infant and the experience of parenthood (Feldman and Nash, 1984). New mothers say that they feel fulfilled, and new fathers say they are more at ease with themselves. However, becoming parents also has its drawbacks. New mothers feel fatigued and desire to be alone after spending many hours meeting the constant needs of a young infant. New fathers feel tense, and they too want to be alone. For most couples, the positive feelings that accompany parenthood outweigh the negative ones.

There are other sacrifices that parents must make, and sometimes these come as a surprise to them. Their social activities change drastically; financially, too, there may be strains, especially if a working wife opts to stay at home. A less common but increasingly observed phenomenon is for the man to give up his job to become a "househusband." When men take on this role, they seem to be able to adapt readily to the child's needs.

Some couples obviously have an easier time adjusting to parenthood than others. The support, encouragement, and advice of friends and family also can help the couple get through the transition from being childless to being parents (Power and Parke, 1984). If a marriage was functioning poorly before and during pregnancy, a newborn infant only adds to the problem (Heinicke, 1984). Frequent bickering and arguing can make the period of early parenthood and infancy extremely unhappy, as Figure 9-7 suggests.

When a child is old enough to enter school, parents may encounter another kind of stress, especially if they are already dissatisfied with the relationship (Anderson, 1985). The adjustments they made in accepting the role of full-time parents, with a child always present, must be altered to meet the requirement of being part-time parents, because their child is now away from home most of the day. Adults with traditional sex roles (see Chapter 6) experience more marital dissatisfaction at this point than do those with androgynous sex roles. In a similar way, women who reached adulthood at a time when the maternal role was considered all important find it difficult to adjust to the final departure of their offspring from home (the *empty nest* phenomenon) when they enter college, marry, establish their own households, and so forth (Adelmann et al., 1989).

■ Marital Communication

Marital dissatisfaction goes beyond the expression of negative feelings or attitudes. A couple's problems are expressed in the way they communicate, and negative communications serve to make the problems worse.

Characteristics of Unhappy Relationships. Evidence of a couple's unhappiness permeates most of their interactions. Such partners communicate poorly (Noller, 1980, 1981) and avoid disclosing personal information to one another (Hendrick, 1981). They avoid topics such as their feelings, love, or the state of their marriage. Anger may arise during arguments characterized by exchanges of insults (Siegel, 1986). During such arguments, both are physically upset, and their feelings are strongly negative (Levenson and Gottman, 1983). Instead of reciprocating positive

FIGURE 9-7 *PARENTHOOD CAN ADD TO MARITAL PROBLEMS* This scene is all too typical when early parenthood results in poor marital functioning. Hostility, suspicion, and worry in mothers, especially when unwarranted, contribute not only to marital dissatisfaction but also to negative thoughts about the infant. For example, worried mothers report that their infants are fussier than those of unworried mothers (Dorman and Olds, 1983). The infant may in fact be responding to the parents' unhappiness or the mother's perception may be based on the couple's own unhappy feelings.

feelings and loving evaluations, such couples repeatedly exchange barbs and criticisms (Gottman, 1980; Kirchler, 1988).

Happy partners make helpful, relationship-positive attributions about behavior—good events are attributed to the other person's traits, and bad events are attributed to accident, a temporary emotional state, or outside events (Fletcher et al., 1990). In contrast, unhappy partners make behavioral attributions that maintain relationship-negative assumptions—good events are attributed to accident, outside events, etc., and bad events are attributed to traits and intentional acts. These different kinds of attributions have effects on each partner that depend, in part, on personality characteristics (Fincham and Bradbury, 1989).

Such verbal messages are extremely important, but nonverbal behavior also can damage the relationship. Dissatisfied couples maintain less eye contact with one another and place more distance between themselves (Lochman and Allen, 1981). Even when talking about neutral or positive topics, their tone of voice creates the impression of hostility (Noller, 1985). A question about what to have for dinner can sound more like a hostile attack than a search for information. Figure 9-8 compares satisfied and dissatisfied spouses in their communication styles. In instances where only one partner expresses negative feelings or uses a hostile tone of voice, the other partner is likely to reciprocate (Pike and Sillars, 1985). Each tries to pay the other back for the last hurtful thing he or she said.

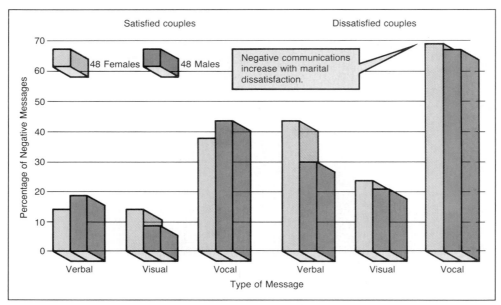

FIGURE 9-8 *COMMUNICATION PATTERNS OF DISSATISFIED VERSUS SATISFIED SPOUSES*
Dissatisfaction within a marriage can surface in the ways a husband and wife communicate with each other. Dissatisfied partners of both sexes talk to their partner more negatively, avoid eye contact, and use a more negative tone of voice than satisfied couples do. Although it may be important to disclose your feelings to a spouse, how this is done can exert a crucial impact on the relationship.
Source: Based on data in Noller, 1985.

The extreme of such negative interactions involves physical acts that hurt the partner. In the special section, *Highlighting Research*, on pages 235 to 236, we discuss some of the recent research findings dealing with spouse abuse.

Improving Marital Communication. In **marital therapy** distressed couples can learn how to communicate and interact more effectively. They learn to behave intimately with a partner in ways that are not self-centered. Each partner learns to take the blame for some problems; the therapist also stresses the importance of bringing partners together by encouraging them to think in terms of "we" rather than of "me" (Fichten, 1984; McAdams and Powers, 1981). Couples also learn how to avoid overreacting to the inevitable negative events that occur in any marriage and to find ways to communicate positive feelings toward one another (Hahlweg and Markman, 1988; Jacobson et al., 1982; Robinson and Price, 1980). Married partners also learn to communicate in ways that clarify and solve problems rather than simply assigning blame and expressing criticism (Gottman et al., 1976; Markman et al., 1988). Table 9-3 gives examples of a range of positive and negative communications.

It is extremely helpful to improve the way the couple solves problems. They must learn to discuss issues instead of avoiding them (Miller et al., 1986). For example, when partners discuss where to take a vacation or what to do about troublesome in-laws, each benefits from becoming aware of the tactics he or she employs to influence the other. A study of heterosexual and homosexual (male and female) couples indicates consistent differences in how partners try to "get their way." Regardless of sexual orientation, a partner who depends on or is less powerful than the other uses one of two tactics: **supplication** (pleading, crying, acting ill or helpless) or **manipulation** (hinting, flattering, behaving seductively, reminding the other of past favors). The more dominant partners use **bullying** (making threats, insulting, committing violence, ridiculing) and **autocratic tactics** (insisting, asserting authority, and claiming greater knowledge) (Howard et al., 1986). The worse the relationship, the more frequently the latter two tactics are employed. As two individuals learn to reason and compromise,

TABLE 9-3   **Speak Your Mind, but Do It in a Positive Way**

Very positive communications were found to occur most frequently among forty satisfied married couples, while twenty dissatisfied couples consistently communicated more negatively.

CATEGORIES OF COMMUNICATION	EXAMPLES
Very positive	Summarizing each other's opinion Asking how the partner feels about an issue Proposing a specific plan or giving specific feedback to the partner
Moderately positive	Stating one's own feelings Accepting responsibility Using humor, showing empathy, or asking for clarification Agreeing or disagreeing and providing reasons for one's position
Neutral	Asking a question Agreeing without providing reasons for doing so Giving information
Moderately negative	Stating opinions without explaining them Disagreeing without providing reasons for doing so Negative nonverbal behavior such as frown, a cold tone of voice, or rude gestures
Very negative	Insulting Blaming Attempting to read the other person's mind in a negative way Yes, but . . .

Source: Floyd and Markman, 1984; Gottman et al., 1976.

Highlighting Research

SPOUSE ABUSE

The physical abuse of one's spouse is disturbingly common—it occurs in about one marriage out of three (Arias and Beach, 1986), and the same figure holds for unmarried couples whether the partners are dating, engaged, or cohabiting (Sachs, 1988). As high as that figure is, it represents a reduction of 27 percent between 1975 and 1985 in cases of severe abuse of wives by husbands (Straus and Gelles, 1986, 1989). Severe abuse is defined as violence that has a high probabil-

ity of causing an injury; kicking the other person is an example. Minor violence, such as light slapping, is also painful, unpleasant, and degrading, but medical treatment is not likely to be required.

As many husbands as wives report being the victim of their partner's physical aggression at least once. In one third of the cases of marital abuse, both spouses commit acts of aggression against each other. Repeated acts of violence (with homicide as the extreme example) are,

however, more often committed by men than by women, with the attacks reaching a peak when the temperatures are highest (Spencer, 1987). Figure 9-9 illustrates the devastating effects of physical abuse.

Are there any characteristics differentiating abusive couples from nonabusive ones? Such behavior occurs in every social class, and at least one in ten professional men beat their wives (Fedders, 1987). Abusers commonly drink excessive amounts of alcohol (Okum, 1986), have a

FIGURE 9-9 *SPOUSE ABUSE: VIOLENCE AS A RESPONSE TO DISSATISFACTION* Spouse abuse is an all too common part of many marriages. Both aggressors and victims in abusive marriages report low satisfaction with their marital relationship and strong feelings of hostility, compared to spouses in nonabusive marriages (Arias and Beach, 1986).

history of abuse as children, or have witnessed spouse abuse during their childhood.

Sexism, power differences between the spouses, and poor communication have each been identified as contributing to abuse. A familiar question is, "Why does the victim remain in an abusive relationship?" Victims often feel trapped by death threats, actual violence in response to attempts to leave, or fear of losing financial support. Battered wives suffer emotional trauma similar to that of prisoners of war (Romero, 1985). Both groups feel isolated from supportive friends and both experience lowered self-esteem and a loss of identity. Information can be helpful to victims; one source is a pamphlet, "Plain Talk about Wife Abuse," available from the Public Health Service in Rockville, Maryland.

More male than female undergraduates feel that it is acceptable for a husband to use physical force against his wife. Men are more likely than women to endorse statements such as "Sometimes a husband must hit his wife so that she will respect him." For both sexes, acceptance of spouse abuse is greatest among those holding traditional sex-role stereotypes in which the husband is viewed as superior and the one with decision-making power (Finn, 1986).

they may discover **bargaining** to be an effective substitute.

Even with training and improved communication and problem-solving skills, difficulties are likely to arise in the relationship. No marriage is perfect, but techniques *can* be learned to improve marital interactions.

Outside of Marriage: Extramarital Sexuality and Divorce

One of the potential side effects of an unhappy marriage is for one or sometimes both partners to seek a sexual relationship with someone else. We will discuss several aspects of extramarital sex and its possible effects. We also will examine divorce and its consequences.

■ Extramarital Sexuality

An *extramarital relationship* exists when someone who is married interacts sexually with an individual other than his or her spouse. Sexual involvement with a new partner raises numerous problems involving both moral and emotional issues. Adultery also may end the marriage, and in about half of the states in the United States, it is a crime to engage in extramarital sex (Sachs, 1990). Extramarital sex is, nevertheless, common in our society.

A local television news show in New York City provided clues to help viewers determine whether or not a spouse was unfaithful (Duffy, 1990), including such questions as—Does he or she: come home smelling of perfume or alcohol? want too much or too little sex? spend more time than usual at work? race to answer the telephone?

Secret Extramarital Sex. Most adults (60 to 80 percent) in this country say that they disapprove of sexual interactions outside of marriage for either men or women (Glenn, 1979; Weis and Slosnerick, 1981). Yet, in various surveys, 50 to 70 percent of American husbands and 45 to 65 percent of their wives report having one or more extramarital sexual relationships (Stayton, 1984). The frequency of extramarital sex has changed since Kinsey's data in 1948 and 1953 indicated that 50 percent of married men and 26 percent of married women interacted sexually with another partner. In the 1980s, the figures rose to two thirds of married men (Hite, 1981) and 43 percent of married women (Grosskopf, 1983). Note that some extramarital affairs involve same-sex rather than opposite-sex partners.

Because a spouse who has been "cheated on" is expected to react negatively to a partner's adultery, most of these relationships involve secrecy and deception. Although an unhappy marriage may be one of the underlying reasons for adultery, the marriage is likely to suffer even greater damage because of the time spent by the straying spouse with his or her new lover; additional stress is caused by the effort to hide the fact that a new relationship is underway.

When a spouse feels underrewarded by his or her partner, an extramarital affair becomes more likely (Walster et al., 1978). In addition, McDonald and McDonald (1978) identify fifty-three factors that contribute to infidelity, including sexual boredom, hostility, and husband–wife dissimilarities. The more dissatisfied one partner is with the marriage, the greater the likelihood that he or she will seek emotional as well as sexual intimacy with an extramarital partner (Glass and Wright, 1985). Women tend to stress their emotional closeness with a lover, while men stress the amount of sexual activity in the love affair.

The husband or wife who seeks an outside relationship tends to view the cause as marital dissatisfaction and to deny the negative effect of the affair on the marriage; the partner whose spouse has an outside relationship, however, perceives that as the basic cause of marital problems (Spanier and Margolis, 1983). Extramarital sex tends to create guilt feelings, especially for women. The guilt is usually insufficient to prevent the behavior from occurring, and most (86 percent of both sexes) describe their extramarital sexual activity as extremely satisfying.

Some personal characteristics are associated with the increased likelihood of an individual engaging in extramarital sex. The most consistent predictor is premarital sexual permissiveness (Thompson, 1983). Also, people who are nonreligious tend to seek an outside relationship relatively early in their marriage (during the first four years), while very religious individuals avoid adultery until later in the marriage (Spanier and Margolis, 1983). Although it

might help prevent an outside affair, most couples find it difficult to discuss beforehand the possibility of either partner's sexual attraction to another person or how they would respond to infidelity.

Sexually Open Marriages. In contrast to secret affairs, some married couples agree to have an **open marriage**. Each partner is free to establish sexually and even emotionally intimate relationships with others, though the spouses continue to live together (Knapp, 1976). A study of over 3,500 heterosexual couples revealed that 15 percent of them found such an arrangement acceptable under certain circumstances.

In 1972, Nena and George O'Neill published the book, *Open Marriage*. They describe how each partner is allowed the freedom of developing close extramarital relationships without damaging the marital relationship. The O'Neills suggested that such outside arrangements can help fill the gaps created in the marriage and that over time one person may be unable to fulfill all of the partner's intimacy needs.

Some feel that an open marriage will solve their marital problems, but this arrangement usually does not save a poorly functioning relationship (Stayton, 1983). Despite mutual agreement about sexual openness, many individuals become very upset when their partners actually follow through and engage in extramarital sex (McGinnis, 1981).

At the peak of the sexual revolution, open marriages appeared to some as the wave of the future. Now, in the post-revolutionary days of fatal diseases transmitted sexually, this lifestyle seems to have represented only a passing fad. In the special section, **Increasing Enjoyment**, on page 238, we discuss possible future patterns of alternative sexual behavior.

Comarital Sexual Activity. *Swingers* are couples who engage in sexual acts with someone other than their own spouse, most often as couples interacting with other couples. According to some estimates, 2 to 5 percent of all husband-wife pairs exchange sexual partners with other couples, using **comarital sexual behavior** as a recreational outlet for their sexual desires (Stayton, 1984). Typically, these exchanges occur on an occasional basis rather than regularly. When they meet with other couples and pair off in various combinations with new partners for the night, the process is known as **mate-swapping**.

Increasing Enjoyment

LIFESTYLES: A LOOK AT THE FUTURE OF SEXUAL RELATIONSHIPS

Realistic concerns about health hazards as well as a cultural shift toward more conservative values are often given as reasons for what is sometimes termed the counterrevolution in sexuality. Indeed, considerable evidence suggests at the very least that the revolution has ended, as described in Chapter 8. Americans increasingly favor monogomy and sexual restrictiveness (Brody, 1983; Frank, 1983). Many experts predict that marriage will become even more popular, replacing both cohabitation and the single life (Leo, 1985). Some even proclaim that celibacy will become widely popular (Brown, 1980; Hanaver, 1985; Lee, 1980), but total abstinence from sex seems unlikely to become an overwhelmingly desirable option.

In addition to the attitudinal and behavioral changes described in Chapter 8, there is evidence that on college campuses, sexual conservatism is on the rise. Psychologist Bernard Murstein reported several sexual differences between students in 1979 versus 1986. The number of sexually experienced undergraduates dropped about 13 percent over that time period. Also, sex is first experienced when students are older than was true previously. At the end of the

1970s, 66 percent of the females began having intercourse when they were sixteen or younger. That figure dropped to 20 percent in 1986. For males, the figures for intercourse before age seventeen decreased from 70 percent in 1979 to 43 percent in 1986. The 1986 pattern, Murstein noted, closely resembles that of 1974. Perhaps the shift toward sexual restraint is simply a return to the values and behaviors common before the peak of the sexual revolution. Only continued research over a longer period of time will reveal whether these behavioral changes are temporary or a more lasting shift.

Some propose that sexual activity in the future will become more spontaneous and *less* exclusive. *Improvisational sex* occurs when circumstances call for a change in usual patterns (Ruefli, 1985). Examples include masturbation while talking erotically to a partner on the telephone or caressing a partner's genitals through his or her clothing. Another example is *couch dancing* (McWalter, 1987); men sit on couches in a cocktail bar while scantily clad female dancers perform very close to them for a fee. There is no physical contact and no possibility of a disease or a relationship.

Other predictions suggest a quite different sexual future involving nonexclusive sexual behavior in which people have several partners both serially and simultaneously at different times in their lives. According to Weis (1983b, p. 208): "The increased isolation of the nuclear family, the growing egalitarianism of male/female relationships, the greater acceptability of premarital sex, the increasing mobility of American society, the advent of contraceptive technology, and the increased alienation of contemporary society have all been offered as possible factors leading to increases in nonexclusive behavior."

While divergent views of the future are interesting and while some may even be accurate, few in the conservative 1950s would have foreseen free love and flower children in the following decades. Similarly, at the height of the sexual revolution, who would have guessed that a disease such as AIDS would soon cast a pall over sexual interactions with anyone but a monogomous mate? It seems safest, then, to predict that sexual attitudes and sexual behavior patterns will continue to change over time, but your guess is as good as ours as to the nature of those changes.

Outsiders usually assume that swingers are political liberals, drug users, and/or suffering from emotional disturbances. None of these attributes is characteristic of swingers. Most fall in the twenty-eight- to forty-five-year old age range, and are otherwise average, upper- or middle-class white Americans (Gilmartin, 1977). Swingers are more politically conservative, less religious, less interested in alcohol and drugs, and better educated than nonswingers (Jenks, 1985a, 1985b).

Swingers locate one another through friends or through organizations devoted to this activity. Explicit sex magazines and newspapers often carry ads with information such as:

He, a 6' hunk with blue eyes and flaming red hair. She, a fun, busty blond with voracious appetite. Call for coffee date.

It is usually the male partner who initiates swinging in the attempt to experience new sexual sensations. When wives overcome their initial misgivings and inhibitions, they often report an increase in sexual satisfaction as the result of repeated sexual encounters with partners of both sexes. Some women adopt a bisexual orientation as a result of their swinging experiences (Dixon, 1984). In contrast, men are likely to become jealous, feel envious of the sexual capacity of their partners, and to initiate withdrawal from swinging (Bartell, 1970).

Swingers appear to be more interested in sex, but they also communicate less well with their spouses than is true for other couples. In a comparison of thirty-five married swingers with thirty-five married nonswingers, the swinging group indicated that sex was more satisfying to them, and they expressed more positive attitudes about a variety of heterosexual acts (Wheeler and Kilmann, 1983). In a test of how to solve marital problems, however, the swinger did less well in finding effective solutions. Their interactions included more disagreements, negative statements, and interruptions than occurred among the nonswingers.

■ Divorce

About 2.4 million marriages are performed in the United States each year, while about 1.2 million divorces are granted during the same time period. It may seem surprising, but almost twice as many divorces in the United States are filed by women as by men (Women began..., 1989). After rising for many years, the divorce rate seemed to stabilize in the late 1970s (Levitan and Belous, 1981). Then, however, it began to rise again, and as Figure 9-10 indicates, the greatest increase between 1970 and 1980 occurred among black Americans rather than among whites or Hispanics (U.S. Bureau of the Census, 1981b). These data indicate the number of divorces that are granted in a given year per 1,000 married persons. In 1980, for example, 110 out of every 1,000 married white women (11 percent) and 74 out of every 1,000 married white men (7.4 percent) were divorced. The highest divorce rate occurred among black women in 1980, reaching 257 (25.7 percent).

The "divorce rate" does *not* refer to the ratio of marriages to divorces per year or to the annual number of divorces among married couples. Instead, demographers use a *life table* approach (Bennett, 1990). That is, a sample of couples who marry at a given

FIGURE 9-10 *DIVORCE IN AMERICA* The surging rate of divorce in the 1970s hit the black population hardest in the United States, rising by over 140 percent.
Source: Based on data from U.S. Bureau of the Census, 1981.

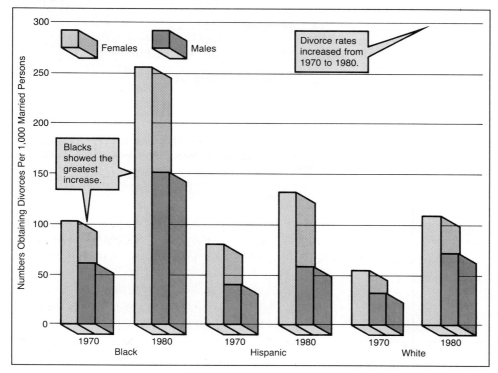

time are followed for a specific number of years (for example, 20) to determine how many of the marriages end in divorce. On the basis of such studies, the United States divorce rate is found to be approximately 50 percent. Thus, out of every two marriages, one remains intact and the other terminates in divorce. Americans currently have a higher divorce rate than the citizens of all other major industrialized nations (O'Leary and Smith, 1991).

Couples between the ages of thirty to forty-four are most likely to obtain a divorce, and the breakup occurs most frequently during the second to sixth years of a marriage (Glick, 1983). Only 4 percent of divorces occur during the first year of marriage. The familiar idea of a "seven-year itch" is incorrect; in fact, the probability of divorce actually begins to decrease in the seventh year. Divorce is found to be less common in big cities than in rural settings (Kelley, 1985d). One possible reason is that rural residents have fewer distractions, so they focus on their relationship and its shortcomings.

When 600 divorced men and women were asked to explain why their marriages failed, the most common responses included communication difficulties, unhappiness, and incompatibilities (Cleek and Pearson, 1985). Other, less personal explanations for the increased number of divorces are higher incomes that make it possible to support more than one family and the greater economic independence of women. Also, in the 1970s U.S. divorce laws were liberalized, along with a decrease in negative attitudes about ending a marriage. Still another possible contribution to divorce is an increase in the expectation that a relationship will permit both partners to fulfill all of their emotional, sexual, and personal needs. When reality does not live up to this expectation, a new relationship is sought.

The Legal and Social Aspects of Divorce. Some divorces are very traumatic (Horn, 1979), but the relief at ending an unhappy marriage becomes more clear as time passes.

A few individuals going through the divorce process do rash things they might not otherwise do. One spouse may remove items of property that belong to the other. This kind of theft is common, and a judicial process called **replevin** orders the return of the property until the court decides ownership

(Slovenko, 1982b). At the opposite extreme is the partner who tells the departing spouse to "take everything you want," only to regret it later. An inventory of all property and a written agreement about who owns what is advised for couples getting a divorce (Keeney, 1986). Even under the best of circumstances, the resolution of many issues involving credit, property, debts, and other legal considerations may take a great deal of time. A growing trend is the attempt to foresee the various problems *prior to* marriage and spell out the solution in *prenuptial agreements*. These contracts, however, may well be challenged and contested in bitter divorce battles (Smolowe, 1990).

Before a divorce is granted, a period of separation is usually required by state law. In some instances, the couple is directed to obtain counseling during this period. If they cannot afford separate living quarters, an *in-house separation* is possible, with specific rooms assigned to the husband or wife or scheduled for use at different times. Despite good intentions, most of these arrangements seem to lead to additional stress for both parties.

Divorce laws vary from state to state, but strict legal rules designed to discourage divorce do not stop the breakup of marriages (Stetson, 1979). The trend in the United States has been toward increasingly easy divorce procedures. **No-fault divorce laws** are now characteristic of most states. Those filing for divorce no longer have to prove infidelity or mental cruelty. Instead, divorce is granted on the basis of any kind of incompatibility or simply a mutual agreement to end the marriage.

The dependent spouse—nearly always the wife—may receive **alimony**, but it has become much more common for short-term payments to be specified until she is able to develop financial independence. One study in California revealed that women experienced a 73 percent decline in their standard of living during the first year following a no-fault divorce (Weitzman, 1985). When a husband agrees to pay child support, etc., his disposable income may also drop, but not as much as that of his ex-wife. Most states attempt to guide an equitable division of marital property, recognizing the earning power of each spouse (Tippins, 1986) and even the financial value of "fame" if one spouse becomes a celebrity during the marriage (Margolick, 1990). In such agreements, for example, a former wife who is working for the minimum wage would receive more of the property than her highly paid husband.

In *divorce mediation,* an attorney or counselor functions as a mediator between the divorcing spouses to help them arrive at a mutually agreeable settlement, avoiding the need for a court trial (Emery and Wyer, 1987). This procedure for resolving conflicts differs from the two traditional methods for reaching a settlement. In both *litigation* and *out-of-court negotiation* between the spouses' attorneys, an adversarial, competitive stance is assumed. In contrast, divorce mediation operates on the assumption of cooperation as the best way to serve the interests of the couple and of their children.

Even the smoothest of arrangements for divorce cannot avoid the possibility of an emotional toll on innocent victims. Children of divorced parents often suffer unduly, as is pointed out in the special section, **Taking Responsibility and Protecting Yourself**, on pages 241 to 242.

Adjusting to Divorce. The consequences of divorce for the ex-spouses can include loneliness for those who do not remarry (Renshaw, 1982) and long-lasting anger for both individuals, as long as ten years for 30 to 40 percent of those who divorce (Fischman, 1986). Some divorced people become depressed, and they smoke more and consume more alcohol than before (Furstenberg and Spanier, 1984). Medical research suggests the possibility of even worse effects. An internist, James Goodwin, examined 25,000 patients with cancer and compared the survival rates of various groups. Married individuals have the greatest chance of surviving cancer, while those who were divorced are most likely to die (Benderly, 1988). The investigators proposed that the difference may be based on such factors as economic status or health habits, but the stress of divorce may well play a major role.

How do most people explain the failure of their marriages? The most usual response (60 percent) is to blame the ex-spouse (Newman and Langer, 1981). Among a sample of divorced women ranging in age from twenty-five to fifty-seven, the spouse was perceived as being emotionally immature, having psychological problems, being selfish, drinking excessively, and so on. The husband-blaming women were more unhappy and less optimistic than divorced

Taking Responsibility and Protecting Yourself

THE EFFECTS OF DIVORCE ON OFFSPRING

When their parents break up, children tend to evaluate divorce negatively, and such attitudes are maintained for years afterward (Kurdek et al., 1981). Although they come to understand why their parents are no longer together and do not blame themselves for what happened, divorce is still perceived in negative terms. As Figure 9-11 suggests, the post-divorce period can also be confusing for a child, especially if the parents remarry. Further, labels such as "stepmother" or "stepfather" have negative connotations in our society (Ganong et al., 1990).

It may not be obvious, but children also suffer for economic reasons. A single parent is likely to have a lower income than two working parents, and this difference can be noticeable. For the reasons noted above, the economic drop tends to be greatest for women, so offspring staying with their mother face this problem most often (Arendell, 1986). In one study (Guidubaldi et al., 1987), boys were found to suffer more than girls following a divorce in both academic achievement and in social rejection by their peers.

Economic issues are not, of course, the only factors determining a child's response. Children who live with the parent of their own sex tend to fare better than children living with the opposite-sex parent (Buie, 1988). For example, boys living with their mothers have more discipline problems than boys residing with their fathers. According to a 1985 report of the U.S. Bureau of the Census, 87 percent of divorced or separated mothers are awarded custody of their children, making it unlikely that a boy will be living with his divorced father. Counseling may be helpful—the books *Helping Children of Divorce* (Diamond, 1985) and *Interventions for Children of Divorce* (Hodges, 1986) explain the techniques that can be used.

Even adolescent offspring react badly to their parents' divorce. If the amount of conflict between ex-spouses is great, their teenagers are found to be more anxious and negative about themselves, as well as feeling less in control of their lives (Slater

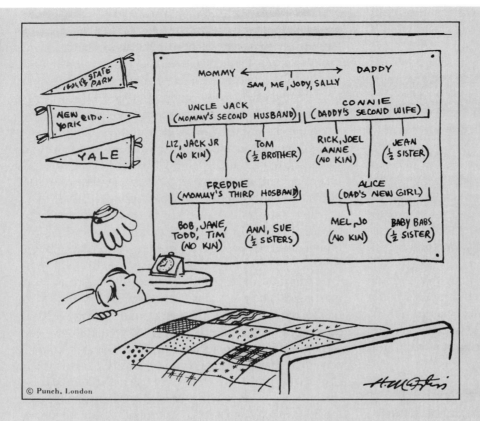

© Punch, London

FIGURE 9-11 *ADJUSTING TO THE NEW FAMILY* The child whose divorced parents remarry can often expect a blending of a new family with his or her own. After divorce, children frequently develop behavioral problems (Fergusson et al., 1986).

and Haber, 1984). When the mother's experience with divorce is especially bad, her adolescent offspring express the belief that few marriages are happy, and they express the belief that they will never want to get married (Thornton and Freedman, 1982). Female college students whose parents divorce express more anger toward their fathers than toward their mothers. Their anger toward their fathers is greater than that of males toward either parent (Bales, 1984). Clearly, regardless of age, having one's parents get divorced leads to an emotional upheaval.

women who blamed their divorce on the relationship (citing mutual incompatibility, money problems, a lack of love, and problems with communication).

One crucial factor affecting reactions to the process is who initiates the divorce. When the husband seeks to end the marriage, the wife is inclined to place all of the blame on him and to feel inferior, as Figure 9-12 indicates.

Sexual Involvements Following Divorce. Immediately after a divorce, men and women are likely to have a larger number of sexual partners than those of the same age who never were married (Feldman-Summers, 1985). One possible reason for the high level of sexual activity following divorce is the use of sex as a substitute for emotional closeness; the loss of such closeness is threatening to the newly divorced person (Suarez and Weston, 1978). Success in finding sexual partners also can help the divorced person prove to himself or herself that he or she is still attractive and desirable despite the former mate's lack of interest.

A few divorced couples continue having sex with one another, attempting to maintain some last threads of the former relationship (Hawkins, 1982). Even without sexual interactions, some former spouses find it possible to maintain cordial personal or business relationships (Masheter and Harris, 1986). Altogether, though, post-marital harmony is characteristic of only a small minority of couples (Ambert, 1988).

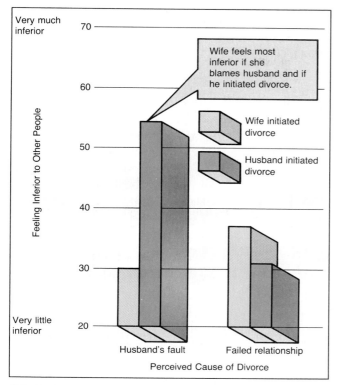

FIGURE 9-12 *DIVORCE: YOUR FAULT OR OUR FAULT?* In this survey of seventy-seven divorced women, they expressed more positive attitudes about themselves if they had initiated the divorce or, even if their husbands had, the blame was placed on the relationship. The greatest feelings of inferiority were expressed by women whose spouse had initiated the divorce and was perceived as the cause of the failed marriage.
Source: Based on data in Newman and Langer, 1981.

When there are children, divorced parents often worry about possible problems created by new romantic relationships (Deutsch, 1981). Until everyone concerned feels comfortable with the new partner, the question of allowing him or her to remain overnight can create considerable conflict between parent and child. A study of single-parent families in which the mother had custody of the children was conducted by Isaacs and Leon (King, 1989). They compared the adjustment of the children over the first five years of separation from their fathers. Over this time span, 13 percent of the mothers were cohabiting with a new partner, 20 percent had remarried, 22 percent were seriously involved with a dating partner, and almost half had no serious relationships with men. It was found that children in the last group, those whose mothers had no romantic involvements, were the best adjusted. Children were least well adjusted if their mothers had a live-in boyfriend, and that arrangement was especially hard on teenagers.

Remarriage. Despite the failure of the previous marriage and various reservations about trying it again, the usual pattern is for divorced men and women to enter a new marriage. The length of time passing before remarriage depends in part on age. Among those in their thirties, most men (57 percent) and women (51 percent) remarry within four years of their divorce (Goode, 1981). The comparable figures for divorced people in their late fifties are 43 percent for men and 36 percent for women. You may have noticed that the figures for men are higher than those for women in each age group; divorced husbands tend to remarry sooner than divorced wives, selecting new mates who are slightly younger than their original ones (Davidson, 1983).

In various ways, women tend to be more disadvantaged by divorce than men. Currently, 14 million American women are divorced or separated, and it is projected that 28 percent of them will remain single. The remarriage rate for divorced women dropped 33 percent between 1965 and 1984. One explanation for these changes is a positive one. Sociologist Larry Bumpass, who reported these data, suggests that marriage is not as necessary for women today because they are more economically independent. An alternative, and less positive, explanation is a shortage of men. Once women pass age 35, they begin to outnumber men of the same age by a ratio of 5 to 4; at 45, the ratio is 2 to 1; and at 65, it is 4 to 1 (Lovenheim, 1987).

If the first marriage does not work out, do people who remarry have similar experiences the second time in selecting a new mate who resembles the first, getting divorced again, and so on? The answer is yes and no. Most (60 percent) second husbands and wives are dissimilar to the first spouse in appearance, personality, and temperament (Pietropinto and Simenauer, 1981). Second marriages are, nevertheless, more likely to end in divorce than first marriages (McKenry, 1979). For those who then go on to a third marriage, however, divorce becomes much more unlikely.

Some of the problems of the first marriage also can affect the second, including alcohol abuse, sexual difficulties, poor communication, and selfishness. Some of the new challenges (including the financial costs of alimony, demands made by the ex-spouse, and problems with the children of the earlier marriage) may not be resolved successfully, thus contributing to the failure of the second marriage.

Sexual Life beyond Young Adulthood

As people age, bodily changes gradually cause some problems such as a loss of physical strength and a decreased ability to deal with stress. There may actually be an increased feeling of happiness, however, as Figure 9-13 shows (Sheehy, 1981). Adults in the United States over age sixty-three express a greater sense of well-being than all other age groups. We will look at some of the possible reasons for this somewhat surprising finding.

■ Physical Changes Related to Sexuality

Most people believe that age and the resulting changes in the reproductive system destroy both sexual functioning and sexual interest. In fact, the physical changes experienced by men and women represent special aspects of the developmental process but not the end of sexuality. **Climacteric**, from the Greek word for "rungs of a ladder," refers to life changes involving sexuality and aging in both men and women.

Females: The Effects of Menopause. **Menopause**, the female climacteric, refers to the end of a woman's ability to reproduce. Menstruation ceases, the ovaries

FIGURE 9-13 *INCREASING HAPPINESS WITH INCREASING AGE* A survey of several thousand U.S. citizens of different ages revealed that older persons express the greatest degree of happiness. This seems surprising, but the various challenges faced by those at younger age levels may interfere with feelings of contentment.
Source: Based on data in Sheehy, 1981.

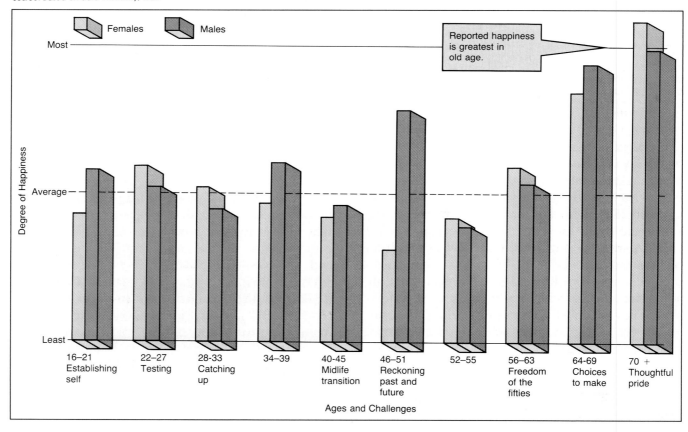

stop releasing mature eggs, and the level of sex hormones drops. These changes generally occur between the ages of forty-eight and fifty-five (Ansbacher, 1983). Just as the age of first menstruation has fallen during the last century, the age of menopause has gradually increased in the United States. These changes, for women in industrialized countries—versus women in developing countries—probably are based on nutritional and other health-related factors.

The most obvious indication of menopause is the absence of menstrual periods. When menstruation is absent for ninety days among women at age forty-five, menopause is the accurate explanation for only 13 percent (Wallace, 1980). After 180 consecutive days without menstruation, menopause is the reason in about half of the cases; after 300 days, over 90 percent are experiencing menopause. Other reasons for the absence of menstruation (not based on menopause) include pregnancy and several kinds of medical problems (such as severe anemia or endocrine abnormalities) for which expert help is needed.

During the seven years preceding menopause, the woman's sexual desire, activity level, and satisfaction do not fluctuate, even though hormonal levels have begun to drop (Cutler et al., 1987). Once again, it is clear that human sexuality is not strongly related to hormone levels. After menopause, the ovaries no longer function. The ovaries of postmenopausal women do not respond to the hormones FSH and LH (see Chapter 3), and the ovarian blood supply decreases. A high level of FSH in the blood indicates that menopause has actually taken place. Note that the sex lives of most women are not adversely affected by these changes unless *estradiol* (an estrogen) level is especially low (Cutler et al., 1987).

Other physical symptoms of menopause include *hot flashes;* about three fourths of all menopausal women report profuse sweating, sensations of warmth in the skin, and a one degree Fahrenheit rise in body temperature (McCoy et al., 1985). The exact cause of hot flashes is unclear, but fluctuations in sex hormone levels probably cause an expansion of blood vessels in the skin, resulting in an increase in temperature. Hot flashes occur more frequently when alcohol is consumed, because this also acts to dilate blood vessels. Menopause is not the direct cause of either

depression or other forms of psychological distress (Lennon, 1987; Siegal, 1990). When such reactions occur, they may be traced to other changes going on in the woman's life, such as her children growing up and leaving home.

The absence of estrogens allows androgenic hormones to exert a greater effect, and the result among some women is the growth of facial hair, a deepening of the voice, and an enlargement of the clitoris. Menopausal women also may gain weight, experience a reduction in the size of their breasts and vaginal lips, and have an *atrophic vagina.*

This last condition refers to a thinning and drying of the vaginal walls; one result is pain during intercourse because of reduced elasticity and inadequate vaginal lubrication. Women with atrophic vaginas have been successfully treated with estrogen, but one side effect of this treatment is uterine cancer and a slightly increased risk for breast cancer (Kolata, 1990). A safer treatment is the internal application of commercial lubricants (Mozley, 1983). Atrophy is also less of a problem if the female frequently engages in vaginal intercourse (McCoy et al., 1985). The vagina is lubricated and stretched during sexual arousal, and the increased blood flow seems to slow the process of atrophy. For this reason, the phrase "use it or lose it" is often applied to menopausal women (Notelovitz, 1978). Though some women believe that menopause ends their sexual interest and activity, many others feel liberated by the ending of their childbearing years and actually increase their level of sexual activity.

The Male Climacteric. Menopause lasts for a few months, but an analogous phenomenon in males occurs gradually over a period of years. In the man's forties or later, the **male climacteric** is characterized by a decline in sexual responsiveness (Mulligan and Moss, 1991; Schiavi, 1990). A longer time is required to develop an erection, and more active stimulation of the penis during foreplay is required (Jacobs, 1980). In one experimental investigation of this change, two groups of men watched a sexually explicit movie. Those aged nineteen to thirty had erections almost six times more rapidly than those aged forty-eight to sixty-five (Solnick and Birren, 1977). The younger men also had fuller erections and a greater increase in penile temperature than the older men.

Other effects of aging in males include a shrinking of the scrotum, testicles, and penis. When the male stands upright with an erection, its angle is lower. Figure 9-14 illustrates the changes in the angle of an erect penis at varying ages; sexual performance is not in any way affected by these changes, however (Roen, 1978). After the climacteric, a smaller amount of semen is ejaculated than previously, and orgasm may produce slightly less pleasure (Wise, 1978).

Older men often can maintain erections for prolonged time periods without the urge to ejaculate (Laury, 1982). If ejaculation fails to occur or is delayed, the refractory period also is absent or delayed. One result is a more extended period of active lovemaking, a bonus for both the man and his partner (Laury, 1981). Ejaculations occur less forcefully than at younger ages. The refractory period lengthens, and an elderly man may have fewer erections in a twenty-four-hour period than when he was young.

One explanation for the changes associated with the male climacteric is the lower levels of the male sex hormone, testosterone, along with the general physical effects of aging. With less testosterone, estrogen has an increased effect, causing a rise in the man's voice pitch and a decrease in facial hair. The severity of the male climacteric is reduced by maintaining good health, avoiding obesity, and drinking only moderate amounts of alcohol. The better one's overall health, the less the decrease in testosterone level (Futterweit, 1984; Marx, 1979).

Another way for men, as well as women, to decrease the negative effects of aging is to engage in regular, frequent sexual activity (Martin, 1981; Trainer, 1980). Dr. Mary Calderone suggests that, "Sex adds years to our lives, and life to our years." For many people, there is a generally negative view of sexual activity for either men or women once they reach age 65. Sex for older individuals is perceived as immoral, inappropriate, and a foolish attempt to regain lost youth (Covey, 1989; Whitbourne, 1990).

Although administering testosterone can be helpful (Harman, 1981), most men do not require such treatment unless there are severe physical problems (Campden-Main and Sara, 1983). The testicles continue to produce sperm, though there is a gradual decrease in quantity (Harman, 1981). These sperm can still fertilize ova well into the man's oldest years.

■   Relationships in Later Life

As signs of aging begin to appear, people must make the transition from youth and wrinkle-free attractiveness to an emphasis on self-worth that is independent of personal appearance. The value of such characteristics as competence and wisdom and a good

FIGURE 9-14   *CHANGES IN THE ANGLE OF ERECTION WITH AGE*   As a man ages, the erect penile angle changes from almost vertical to a position below the horizontal. This change has no effect on sexual performance.

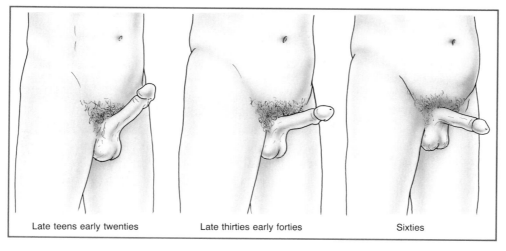

Late teens early twenties   Late thirties early forties   Sixties

disposition becomes more obvious to the individual and to others (Appleton, 1983). Reactions to the physical changes can cause problems such as seeking reassurance in extramarital affairs, a loss of interest in sex, and depression—but aging need not be disruptive.

Reactions to Aging.   The most familiar physical sign of aging is caused by the deterioration of underlying layers of skin, resulting in wrinkles. The process is gradual, as Figure 9-15 illustrates; thus, a person has time to adapt to a new image (Castelnuovo-Tedesco, 1979). Whether an individual responds to aging positively or negatively depends in large part on how old age is viewed in the society in which he or she lives.

The transition to later life is marked in very specific ways in different cultures. Among native Mexicans in Tepoztlan, for example, old men and women are granted increased freedom and allowed to get drunk, use obscene language, and urinate in public. In one South American tribe, postmenopausal women are honored by being granted the legal status of men (Griffen, 1977). In contrast, some societies treat aging negatively. The Tiu send postmenopausal females to live with their brothers, and in rural Ire-

land older women are expected to spend their final years in bed. A study of over 100 tribal societies reported that most encouraged sexual activity among their oldest members (Winn and Newton, 1982). In many Western societies, aging tends to be accompanied by negative stereotypes that are shared by both the old and the young (Griffitt, 1981).

In the United States, the perception of older people by the young seems to be affected by the presence of others. The most harsh judgments occur in public rather than in private settings. In an experiment, several hundred college students were shown facial pictures of middle-aged men and women and asked to rate their attractiveness. When the ratings were made, the students were either alone, in a group of other students of their own sex, or in a mixed-sex group of students (Berman et al., 1981). Figure 9-16 shows the outcome. When alone, students rated the older women as more attractive than the older men, but the reverse occurred when the ratings were made in groups. Older women were rated most negatively by male students in all-male groups. Regardless of how attractive an older woman may be perceived by an individual privately, the presence of other young

FIGURE 9-15 *FACIAL CHANGES AS AN INDIVIDUAL GROWS OLDER*   Aging changes the appearance of a person's face. The chin recedes, wrinkles appear, and the facial muscles sag.

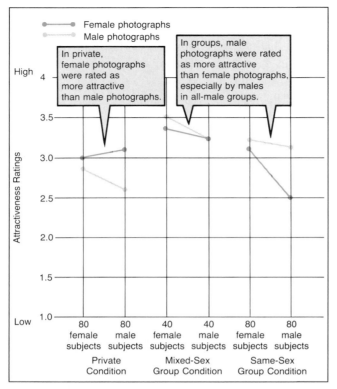

FIGURE 9-16 *NEGATIVE STEREOTYPES ABOUT OLDER FEMALES*
Negative stereotypes about the attractiveness of middle-aged women are expressed most strongly by young men when they rate photographs in a group of other young males. In private, college students rated pictures of middle-aged women as more attractive than those of middle-aged men.
Source: Based on data in Berman et al., 1981.

people seems to generate reliance on negative stereotypes.

In 1745, Benjamin Franklin counseled a young man to seek an older woman as a sexual partner. He explained that "even though the face, neck, breasts, and arms grow lank and wrinkled, the lower parts would continue to last as plump as ever. And, as in the Dark all Cats are Gray, the pleasure of Corporal Enjoyment with an old Woman is at least equal, and frequently superior, every knack of practice being by Practice capable of improvement" (Ben Franklin's advice, 1983, p. 162). While an experimental test of these observations cannot be reasonably carried out with human subjects, old male monkeys are found to be equally attracted sexually to old and young females (Chambers and Phoenix, 1982).

Adjusting to the Death of a Spouse. Because men have an average life span that is several years shorter

than that of women, wives are six times more likely to become widows than husbands are to become widowers (U.S. Bureau of the Census, 1988b). Widowhood can, of course, happen at any age, but it most often occurs late in a woman's life. Older women who become widows report feeling more lonely than older men who are widowers. Among widows, 32 percent express loneliness, while only 10 percent of widowers do, perhaps because of differing perceptions of male–female attractiveness in old age and because women are more likely than men to be at an economic disadvantage (Baum, 1983). Social support from siblings, children and their families, and religious groups can help the widow experience psychological well-being (McGloshen and O'Bryant, 1988). Despite sex differences in feelings, older men report fewer close friends and less social activity than do older women. Possibly because women have historically defined their lives in terms of family and friends while men emphasized their careers, they perceive the loss of close relationships as more of a problem than men would. The effects of divorce and widowhood are somewhat similar in that both require adjustments to a new way of life.

Widowers may not report feeling lonely, but they are clearly affected by the loss of a spouse. Men whose wives die have a much higher chance of dying in the next few years than is true for males of the same age whose spouses remain alive (Helsing et al., 1981). Widowers die at a rate 28 to 60 percent higher than married men; the older the male, the more likely he is to die after losing a spouse (Greenberg, 1981). In contrast, becoming a widow does not increase the death rate for women (Greenberg, 1981). It is possible that men simply do not admit their loneliness as easily as women do, but they may suffer as much or more when they lose companionship (Burgess, 1983). Or, perhaps men are more dependent on the special relationship with a spouse than women are. In any event, health and happiness are clearly damaged by the loss of one's spouse (Laudenslager and Reite, 1984).

Remarriage for those over sixty-five has a positive effect on widowers and improves their chances of staying alive (Vinick, 1983). Males typically remarry sooner after a spouse's death than females. Those women who do remarry express great satisfaction and say that they would remarry again if the second husband died. In the United States, prior to 1979, widows who remarried lost their former husband's social security benefits, but then the government changed the rules. Considering the fact that half of the females over age 65 are widowed, this change was extremely important in removing an economic barrier to remarriage.

■ Sexuality among the Elderly

The concept of older people having an active sex life is usually unpleasant for those who are young. College students, for example, seem to feel that sex is appropriate only for young people; thus, they respond very negatively to explicit depictions of sex among senior citizens (Przybyla and Byrne, 1989) and to the idea that people as old as their parents would engage in erotic acts (Allgeier and Murnen, 1985; Pocs and Godow, 1977).

Despite these negative reactions and the widespread belief that older people lose their sexual drive, sex can be a source of continuing excitement and pleasure throughout life. Figure 9-17 summarizes the results of a survey of sexual activity in middle-aged and older individuals over a six-year period. Up to age sixty-five, most reported stable levels of sexual interactions (George and Weiler, 1981). Past age sixty-five, a great many individuals (33 percent of women and 42 percent of men) indicate little change. Only in

FIGURE 9-17 *SEXUAL ACTIVITY ACROSS THE ADULT YEARS* Changes in level of sexual activity are relatively uncommon before the age of sixty-six. Only in their late sixties do some individuals begin to "slow down."
Source: Based on data in George and Weiler, 1981.

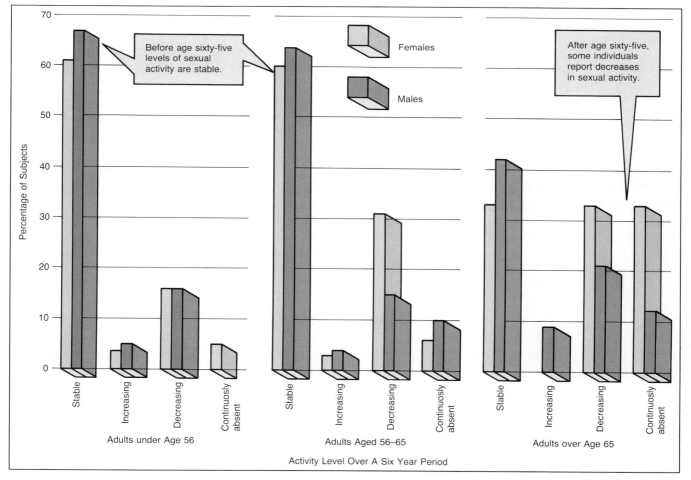

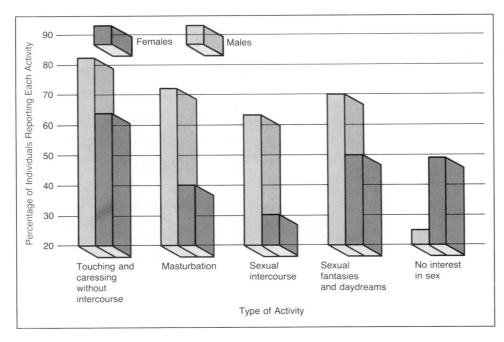

FIGURE 9-18 *ACTIVE SEX AMONG THE ELDERLY* In a permissive setting, elderly retirement home residents (aged 80 to 102) reported strong sexual interests and an active sex life. Over half (63 percent) of them felt that the retirement home did not interfere with their sexual activity, and 42 percent said that the institutional living arrangements increased their opportunities to have sex.
Source: Based on data in Bretschneidert and McCoy, 1988.

the oldest group was there any reported decline in sexual activity.

If senility develops in advanced old age, some individuals begin to perform inappropriate sexual acts for the first time in their lives (Grauer, 1978). The percentage of elderly people who suddenly begin to expose themselves, approach children sexually, and so forth is undoubtedly small, but the precise figures are unknown.

In institutions for the elderly such as nursing homes, sexual interactions are common. In a study of twenty-two nursing homes in Texas, 10 percent of the population indicated they were sexually active, primarily engaging in masturbation (White, 1980). People confined to nursing homes not only find masturbation to be sexually gratifying, but it is also one of the few aspects of their lives totally under their control (Adams and Turner, 1985; Catania and White, 1982).

It seems likely that the actual rates of masturbation and intercourse in such settings may be higher than the data indicate because of the elderly's embarrassment about revealing their private acts and fear of getting into trouble for breaking the anti-sex institutional rules. A more recent study in California asked retirement home residents aged 80 to 102 about their sex lives. Most of the residents were upper middle

class, half had college degrees, and about one third were retired professionals. Altogether, this group would be expected to be more secure about their living arrangements and more willing to discuss their sexuality. As Figure 9-18 shows, these elderly men and women reported a considerable amount of sexual

FIGURE 9-19 *MULTIPLE DETERMINANTS OF SEXUAL ACTIVITY IN OLD AGE* Whether an active sex life is continued in old age depends on the degree of physical deterioration, one's attitudes and expectations about sex in old age, and the availability of a willing sexual partner.

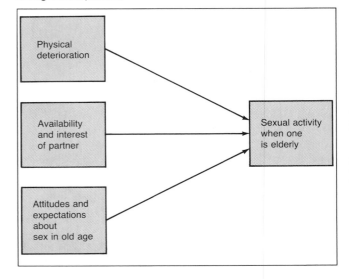

interest and activity (Bretschneider and McCoy, 1988; McCoy, 1989).

Sexual activity in old age is facilitated by good health and the availability of a willing partner, as outlined in Figure 9-19 (see p. 250).

In addition, the elderly individual's own personal attitudes about sexuality help determine how much sexual activity occurs in old age. One instrument measuring these attitudes contains items such as, "Aged people have little interest in sexuality." "An aged person who shows sexual interest brings disgrace to himself/herself" (White, 1982a, p. 496). People who answer such items negatively are expressing negative attitudes about sexuality and the elderly. In old age, life satisfaction is greatest among those who

are sexually active, especially if coitus is the preferred sexual act (Turner and Adams, 1988).

A survey of male and female nursing home residents whose average age was over eighty found that attitudes combined with other factors in predicting who was sexually active (White, 1982b). Having positive attitudes, expressing interest in sexuality, and having an active sexual history were characteristic of those who continued to engage in sex but not of those who had abandoned their sex lives. Young people who expect a decline in sexual interest and sexual ability as they age (Zeiss, 1982) indeed may find themselves having a sexless old age. Such a fate is unnecessary and can be prevented if more people develop positive expectations about sex and aging.

Summarizing the Information about Sexual Relationships among Adults . . .

Cohabitation seems to have little effect, either positive or negative, on later marital relationships. Living life as a single person is increasingly common, and some singles elect to become parents without the entanglements of a spouse or cohabitant.

The decision to marry a particular person is influenced by societal standards regarding the appropriateness of that individual's socioeconomic status, age, race, and religion. Age discrepancies between marital partners is usually viewed more positively if the man is older than the woman rather than vice versa, reflecting cultural stereotypes. Only a minority of societies require **monogamy** in marriage. A larger percentage permit **polygamy**, usually **polygyny** but rarely **polyandry** or **polygynandry**. **Serial monogamy** is common in industrialized Western societies. Marital sex involves not only interactions between spouses but also masturbation. Intercourse frequency tends to decline over the course of a marriage. The amount of oral-genital activity is higher among couples with the greatest amount of education. **Marital satisfaction** or **dissatisfaction** is based on multiple factors, including those that affect any type of relationship. Additionally, the presence of children affects marital happiness. Attempts to influence one's spouse with a tactic such as **bargaining** has a more positive

effect on the relationship than the use of **supplication**, **manipulation**, **bullying**, or **autocratic tactics**. **Marital therapy** attempts to improve the marital relationship, by, for example, enhancing communication skills.

Secret extramarital activity and marital dissatisfaction often are associated with each other. Nonreligious individuals and those who have positive attitudes toward premarital sex are more likely to engage in extramarital sex than others. For a small percentage of couples, extramarital involvement includes **open marriages**, and **comarital sexual activity** such as **mate-swapping**. The rate of divorce in the United States is high, and one of the most serious negative consequences is the effect on children. Divorce is most likely to occur during the second through the sixth year of marriage. For ex-wives, financial problems are common. The emotional suffering caused by divorce is associated with the pattern of blame each person uses to explain a failed marriage. Men tend to remarry more often and more quickly than women do.

Sexuality in middle and old age revolves partly around the physical and psychological effects of **menopause** and the **male climacteric**. Regular sexual activity can prevent the loss of sexual responsiveness and interest in both sexes. Stereotypes about the physical signs of aging tend to be negative in our culture, especially among young 'males surrounded by their peers. Older widows experience loneliness more than widowers do, while men who lose a spouse are more likely to die soon afterward. Aged persons usually retain their sexual interests and continue to engage in sex. Active sex in later life is highly probable if the individual is in good health, has an available partner, and has a positive attitude about sex.

To Find Out More about Sexual Relationships among Adults . . .

Duck, S. (Ed.). (1982). *Personal relationships 4: Dissolving personal relationships.* New York: Academic Press.

How, when, and why relationships deteriorate are explained in a series of chapters written by behavioral scientists who actively conduct research on this topic. Commitment, blaming, and breaking up are included in the coverage.

Folberg, J., & Milne, A. L. (Eds.). (1988). *Divorce mediation: Theory and practice.* New York: Guilford.

The many aspects of divorce mediation are discussed in this edited book. Topics include the theory and practice of mediation, ethical issues, and research on the success of mediation.

Gurman, A. S. (1985). *Casebook of marital therapy.* New York: Guilford.

Descriptions of troubled marriages are provided, and marital therapists comment on their techniques for building trust and mutual understanding. The role of physical illness is also discussed.

Nadelson, C. C., & Polonsky, D. C. (Eds.). (1984). *Marriage and divorce: A contemporary perspective.* New York: Guilford.

This books examines marriage in the context of health, personal change, and adultery. Other topics include the effects of divorce on children and on the divorced woman.

Sarrel, L., & Sarrel, P. (1984). *Sexual turning points: The seven stages of adult sexuality.* New York: Macmillan.

The different stages of adulthood and sexuality are described. Important topics include first love, the decision to marry, divorce, and widowhood.

Schiavi, R. C. (1990). Sexuality and aging in men. In J. Bancroft, C. M. Davis, & D. Weinstein (Eds.), *Annual review of sex research,* Vol. 1 (pp. 227–249). Mt. Vernon, IA: Foundation for the Scientific Study of Sexuality.

An up-to-date review of what is known about male sexuality in the later stages of the life span. Included are discussions of reproductive hormones, the nervous system, the vascular system, and psychobiological research.

ATTRACTION AND LOVE

Men and women sometimes respond to members of the opposite sex in different ways, and their divergent expectations about the meaning of attraction can be confusing and frustrating. A male graduate student describes one such experience with a fellow student and his feelings of resentment and puzzlement.

There are hundreds of young, healthy members of both sexes here in graduate school, and we all have sexual needs. What's the big deal about getting together, having sex, and making everyone feel good? Instead, the typical woman wants to make everything complicated with love and respect and commitment and all the rest. I don't want a relationship; I want sex.

Betty and I are both in the Anthro department, working on our Ph.Ds. We take a lot of the same classes, work on the same field project upstate, and usually go to the same student get-togethers. One night we were at a party at Professor Hanson's, and we spent a lot of time with each other—talking, drinking, and playing table tennis. We got along very well, and I was more and more turned on. I kept picturing her out of those clothes, romping around my apartment.

It was about midnight when I told her that my ride had disappeared and asked if she could drop me off on her way home. She said, "Sure," and we were soon cruising along in her Honda. As she drove, I stroked her arm lightly and began talking about how much I liked her. She laughed and said, "You barely know me. You probably just like my body." I agreed that I liked her body, but I reminded her of the things we had in common and of the fun we'd had together.

As we reached my apartment complex, I asked her to come on up to share a joint or open a bottle of wine or whatever. "It's the 'whatever' that's the problem," she told me. "I've had a good time tonight, Ted, but I don't want to go to your place and jump in the sack."

"Why not? That's part of getting to know one another."

"Not in my rule book. Let's get to know each other first, and then see what develops. If all goes well, we might find ourselves in a closer relationship one of these days."

"Do you want me to lie a little and tell you I'm head over heels in love and will probably die on the spot if we don't make it tonight?"

"No, thanks. Just be yourself, and take it easy. We'll see what happens. Let's have a cup of coffee after our nine o'clock Monday. Goodnight."

I got out of the car, tried to sound pleasant, and walked toward my building. Actually, I felt horny and more than a little angry. Why couldn't she just come in and give us both a little pleasure? Like the professor asks in My Fair Lady, "Why can't a woman be more like a man?"

Ted, age 22

In our complex society, conflicting norms guide beliefs about what constitutes appropriate sexual behavior for singles. These norms range from total chastity before marriage to casual sex of the kind Ted wants. For most people in the United States during the last decades of this century, the pattern has been more or less the one suggested by Betty. Typically, people meet, become acquainted, form friendships, fall in love, and then may become sexually intimate. More men than women share Ted's viewpoint about sex, but members of both sexes express a variety of beliefs about what is appropriate, what is right, and what they feel comfortable doing.

In order to enter a sexual relationship, a person must first identify a suitable partner. In this chapter, we describe the determinants of *interpersonal attraction*—the way that people become acquainted, develop friendships, and experience sexual attraction. *Love* plays a crucial role in our culture; we discuss its different forms, how it develops, and how it can evaporate. Today, there are no generally accepted guidelines about premarital sex activity, and each person's *sexual decision making* is affected by social factors, personal values, and his or her moral standards. Special sections focus on the meaning of *physical attractiveness* and the efforts people make to change how they look, what is known about *keeping relationships together,* and a consideration of current standards of *premarital permissiveness.*

Interpersonal Attraction: Taking the First Steps toward Friendship

During your lifetime, how many of the 5 billion people on this planet will you meet? Obviously, you will have contact with a very small percentage of them; any one of us is likely to interact with only a few thousand other people. Of these, we will come to know personally an extremely limited sample. This very small subgroup will provide our friends, lovers, and enemies. Why do we select them and tend to ignore all the rest? A century of research indicates that both the external situation and specific personal characteristics influence the selection process. In this section, we identify and describe the factors that encourage and discourage acquaintanceship, friendship, and intimacy.

■ Setting the Stage by Becoming Acquainted

Before any two people can become acquainted, form a friendship, become lovers, spouses, or whatever, they must somehow come into contact with each other. In the late 1800s, psychologists, sociologists, and others began studying the details of this process. The three basic factors are propinquity, affect, and the need for affiliation.

Propinquity: Environmental Determinants of Interpersonal Contact. Think of a large apartment building, several stories high, located in a busy city (see Figure 10-1). Imagine its residents going about their daily lives within each individual apartment. What

FIGURE 10-1 *ACQUAINTANCESHIP: PROPINQUITY IS THE KEY* In an apartment building housing many strangers, the initial determinants of who becomes acquainted with whom are based largely on physical factors. The greater the propinquity of any two people, the more likely they are to form some kind of relationship. These same factors operate in classrooms, college dormitories, work settings, and neighborhoods.

are the chances that any two of these individuals will become acquainted? Within the building, casual interactions are primarily determined by the physical arrangement of the apartments, doorways, passageways, stairs, elevators, and so on. Though most of us don't think much about such seemingly trivial elements in our surroundings, **propinquity,** or proximity, tends to dictate whether two people begin to interact or simply remain total strangers. Anything that brings them into close contact increases the probability that they will notice one another, accept each other as "a familiar face," and possibly begin to communicate. Residents who live on the same floor, ride the elevator at the same time, or use the laundry room simultaneously are much more likely to get to know one another than residents who live on different floors or have different schedules for using the elevator or laundry room.

The distance between two apartments can be crucial. People whose apartment entrances are within 22 feet of one another are likely to become friends. If, however, their entrances are separated by 88 feet or more, they are unlikely ever to meet (Festinger et al., 1950). Such physical determinants operate in all settings—dormitories, neighborhoods, and the work place. In classrooms, for example, students assigned side-by-side seats are much more likely to become acquainted than students whose seats are separated by as little as one seat (Byrne, 1961; Byrne and Buehler, 1955; Segal, 1974). Friendships, romance, and even future marital partners very often are determined by just such environmental factors.

You may wonder *why* propinquity should affect our friendships. Besides the obvious necessity for contact to precede becoming acquainted, the casual interactions dictated by physical surroundings also play an active role in increasing attraction. Propinquity results in **repeated exposure** to specific people. Repeated exposure causes increasingly favorable evaluations of a person and of other stimuli as well. We even respond positively to a person who simply *resembles* someone we like; that is, a stranger seems to be familiar (White and Shapiro, 1987). As Figure 10-2 illustrates, multiple exposures to pictures, advertisements, political candidates, words, and so forth lead us to evaluate them positively (Moreland and Zajonc, 1979, 1982; Zajonc, 1968).

Why should exposure be positive? Strangers—or any other unknown elements in the environment—evoke at least a little anxiety, perhaps because anything new is a potential source of danger. Our response is to reject anyone who makes us feel uneasy. With repeated contact, provided the stranger does nothing to frighten or anger us, our anxiety gradually disappears. The negative feelings are replaced by positive ones in response to someone who is now familiar (Bornstein et al., 1987).

Affect: Feelings Determine Liking and Disliking. Not only does the change from negative to positive feelings explain the repeated exposure effect, our **af-**

FIGURE 10-2 *THE MORE I SEE IT, THE MORE I LIKE IT* Repeated exposure to any stimulus, including another person, can increase positive feelings, including interpersonal attraction.

fective state (emotions, feelings, mood) generally influences whom we like or dislike. Sometimes we know why we are in a good or bad mood and sometimes we don't. Either way, research indicates that we make much more positive interpersonal evaluations when our affective state is positive than when it is negative (Shapiro, 1988; Swallow and Kuiper, 1987).

For example, merchants use background music to lull shoppers into a pleasant mood so they will buy more. Also, in bars sad music results in a higher level of alcohol consumption than fast, loud music; those feeling sad tend to drink while those feeling happy would rather dance (Littlel, 1981). Clearly, bar owners prefer drinkers to dancers. Mood has an equally strong effect on attraction. May and Hamilton (1980) showed how mood-inducing music influences interpersonal judgments. They asked female undergraduates to rate photographs of male strangers under one of three different conditions: no music, music they liked (rock), or music they disliked (avant-garde classical). Subjects rated the males in the photographs as most likable and physically attractive when rock music was playing, and rated them most negatively when classical music was playing. If the subjects had hated rock and loved the classical selections, the ratings would presumably have been reversed. What is crucial is that music arouses feelings, and these feelings in turn determine how people respond to strangers.

Music is, of course, only one determinant of emotions. It seems that anything that influences affect also influences attraction and other interpersonal judgments. Experiments indicate that hot and humid rooms, sad movies, bad news on the radio, and exposure to depressed people cause us to dislike others, whereas comfortable rooms, funny movies, good news, and exposure to happy people cause us to like others (Gouaux, 1971; Griffitt, 1970; Winer et al., 1981; Veitch and Griffitt, 1976). In addition to liking others when our emotional state is positive, we communicate more easily, disclose more about ourselves, and are more likely to interact socially (Clark and Watson, 1988; Cunningham, 1988).

The theory underlying such findings is the **reinforcement-affect model of interpersonal attraction**. According to this formulation, all evaluative judgments, including attraction, are based on our positive or negative emotions. If someone or some-

thing makes us feel good, we like it; if it makes us feel bad, we dislike it. Even if another person does nothing to arouse our positive or negative feelings, we associate him or her with any affect aroused by other events (a toothache, a good grade on a test, music, temperature, and so forth) when that person happens to be present. As a result, we like those associated with positive feelings and dislike those associated with negative feelings. Attraction toward others can range from love to hate, based on affect ranging from extremely positive to extremely negative.

Need for Affiliation: How Badly Do You Want Friends? For most of us, having friends is a central part of our lives (Wright, 1984). We want to interact with others, share our feelings with them, and know that they like us (Research and Forecasts, 1981). Though most people want to have friends, the **need for affiliation** (the motivation to seek friendships and other close relationships) varies in strength from person to person. Although some of us are satisfied with one or two friends, others want many. For some, affiliation is a driving force in their lives while others assign it a much lower priority. Table 10-1 presents test items that differentiate people with high versus low affiliative needs.

In the acquaintance process, propinquity and positive emotions encourage two people to form a relationship, but unless they have strong affiliation needs, they may never interact. In one study, students high in need for affiliation made more friends within a psychology class during the semester than did those low in need for affiliation (Greendlinger and Byrne, 1989). Hill (1987) suggests that people are affiliative to the extent that they want other people to provide information, stimulation, emotional support, and attention.

The need to affiliate is also influenced by external factors. Whenever people encounter uncertain, anxiety-arousing conditions, they are likely to seek interpersonal contact (Schachter, 1959). An external threat makes us want to engage in **social comparison**; we discuss the situation with others to help discover what exactly is happening, how they feel about it, and what to do about it. By this process, we reduce anxiety (Kulik and Mahler, 1989). This explains why people frequently initiate new relationships during

TABLE 10-1 **How Strong Is Your Need to Affiliate?**

These statements are part of a personality scale used to measure need for affiliation. Agreement with the first and third statements, and disagreement with the other three indicates a tendency to prefer affiliation to being alone.

TEST ITEMS USED TO MEASURE NEED FOR AFFILIATION

1. I think that any experience is more significant when shared with a friend.

2. At parties, I prefer to talk to one person for the entire evening instead of participating in different conversations.

3. I like to make as many friends as I can.

4. I prefer the independence which comes from lack of attachments to the good and warm feelings associated with close ties.

5. If I had to choose between the two, I would rather be considered intelligent than sociable.

Source: Mehrabian, 1970.

any kind of unexpected, frightening experience such as a power blackout or a snowstorm.

Loneliness: When Affiliation Fails. If someone has difficulty making friends, the result is **loneliness**. It is possible, of course, to be alone and not feel lonely. Sometimes, for example, we prefer to be by ourselves to read, walk, think, or listen to music. Loneliness occurs when we *want* to be with others but cannot. A person feels lonely when existing social relationships fail to meet his or her expectations (Marangoni and Ickes, 1989; Rook, 1984).

Lonely people are unable to make friends easily or to interact smoothly with others (Berg and Mc-Quinn, 1989; Suedfeld, 1982), and they tend not to make disclosures about themselves (Davis and Franzoi, 1986). Loneliness reaches a peak in adolescence, a period when peers become more important than parents (Brennan, 1982; Brennan and Auslander, 1979). For young men and women whose social skills are poor, high school and college can be a time of lonely alienation (Riggio, 1986).

The study of loneliness and what to do about it began with the development of a way to measure this state. The **UCLA Loneliness Scale** (Russell, 1982) assesses loneliness by asking respondents to agree or disagree with twenty statements such as "I feel left out" and "I have a lot in common with the people around me." A lonely person's answers indicate that he or she feels left out and different from others. People of all ages who are lonely feel socially anxious, dissatisfied, negative about themselves, and depressed (Hojat and Crandall, 1987; Jones et al., 1981; Russell, 1982; Weeks et al., 1980), as Figure 10-3 suggests.

Both men and women experience loneliness in dealing with the opposite sex. Because men are expected to face the risks involved in initiating heterosexual relationships, they can become lonely either because they are afraid to seize the initiative or because they make the attempt and then are rejected. Men, as a consequence, are especially likely to feel unhappy and lonely (Schultz and Moore, 1986).

Adolescent and adult loneliness seem to originate in the person's failure to learn appropriate social skills in childhood (Bruch et al., 1989; Check et al., 1985; Hansson et al., 1984; Hill, 1989; Rubin, 1982). How do we learn effective ways to deal with others? No one is systematically instructed in such skills, but some are lucky enough to have good role models of positive social behavior in their families or among their acquaintances (Burns and Farina, 1984). When children enter nursery school or kindergarten and are away from their family for the first time, they often must learn how to "sink or swim" in the social world. Some never quite get the knack of dealing successfully with peers, and the result is loneliness (Spitzberg and Canary, 1985; Wittenberg and Reis, 1986).

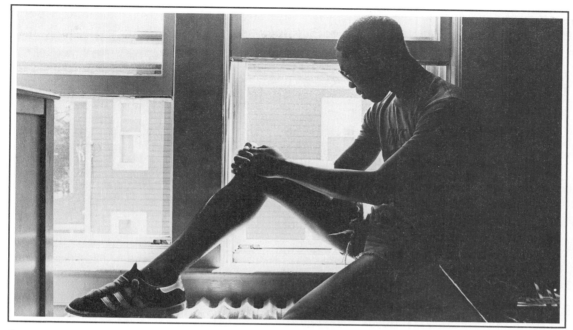

FIGURE 10-3 *THE MISERY OF FEELING LONELY* Loneliness is a source of considerable unhappiness, and its emotional toll can be devastating. Past failures with making and keeping friends compound the difficulty.

What happens to lonely adults? They usually doubt that their state will ever change, and they become increasingly pessimistic as they grow older. Many assume that others feel as shy and lonely as themselves (Harris and Wilshire, 1988). Some respond with wish-fulfilling fantasies about having friends (Revenson, 1981), others try to lose themselves in work or in alcohol or other drugs (Paloutzian and Ellison, 1979), and still others turn to sad music, but this makes them feel even more lonely (Davis and Kraus, 1989). There *are,* however, two effective solutions to the problem: **cognitive therapy,** in which false beliefs about interpersonal interactions are replaced with effective views (Asendorpf, 1989; Jones et al., 1981; Young, 1982), and **social skills training,** in which clients are taught how to deal with social situations (Heimberg and Hope 1989; Rook and Peplau, 1982; Thoits, 1984).

■ Forming a Friendship

Once two people meet and begin to interact because of propinquity, positive feelings, and the need to affiliate, several additional factors come into play, influencing how the relationship develops. First, our initial impressions of others depend in large part on *appearance* (Perdue and Gurtmann, 1990). If our reactions are negative, the process stops. If we respond positively, the second factor comes into play: the extent to which we discover that we share *similar* beliefs and attitudes with the other person. Third, the final step in forming a close friendship occurs when we and the other person each feel and express a *positive evaluation* of the other. We will now examine these three factors in greater detail.

Physical Attractiveness: Life as a Beauty Contest. On first coming in contact with someone, we have a strong tendency to respond to **physical attractiveness**—that combination of facial features, body configuration, and general appearance that our culture defines as pleasing (Albright et al., 1988). We all have learned that "Beauty is only skin deep" and "You can't judge a book by its cover"; nevertheless, most people respond most positively to those they perceive as attractive (Calvert, 1988). Even in childhood, attractive pre-school girls are treated better than their less attractive peers by other children; the physically attractive children are helped more and hurt less (Smith, 1985). Also, attractiveness and unattractiveness remain as fairly stable characteristics throughout childhood and adolescence (Pittenger et al., 1989).

Other species also respond to overt physical characteristics—a peacock's tail, a deer's antlers, a swordtail fish's tail fin—suggesting an inherited tendency to select mates on the basis of such cues (Gould, 1991).

Our culture also emphasizes the value of beauty, as Figure 10-4 illustrates. For example, advertisements instruct women to cover their embarrassing

FIGURE 10-4 *SELLING PRODUCTS THAT INCREASE SEX APPEAL* Advertising repeatedly informs both men and women that it is possible to increase their sex appeal by using the appropriate products. [Copyright: Quintessance, 1989.]

age spots, lose weight, change their hair style and color, wear the right makeup, and so on (Downs and Harrison, 1985). The mass media are found to stress slimness for women much more strongly than for men (Silverstein et al., 1986). Men, too, are told to take steps to avoid gray hair, dandruff, insufficiently white teeth, underdeveloped muscles, and a host of other "defects." One result is that both men and women focus on the attractiveness of the opposite sex in most of their interactions (Hatfield and Sprecher, 1986b; Smith, 1985). Not surprisingly, then, attractive men and women receive more invitations for dates in a video-dating service than unattractive ones (Green et al., 1984). Women, are, however, able to overlook male unattractiveness if the men possess compensatory attributes such as status, money, power, or prestige. People differ in the emphasis they place on attractiveness; men and women who are most traditional in their masculinity and femininity are more concerned with attractiveness than their less traditional, androgynous counterparts (Andersen and Bem, 1981).

Physical attractiveness creates a halo around those who possess it. Both men and women assume that good-looking people also have a great many positive personal qualities (Dion and Dion, 1987), as Table 10-2 shows. Our inflated view of attractive peo-

ple can best be overcome if we learn to pay more attention to their behavior than to their appearance.

Altogether, beauty has a number of benefits, however unfair this may be. Attractive men and women have more success with the opposite sex, including more dates (Reis et al., 1980), and they succeed in many other social situations as well (Abbott and Sebastian, 1981). One explanation is that those who are attractive behave differently than those who are unattractive. For example, attractive males are relatively assertive and unafraid of rejection, and attractive women are relatively unassertive (Reis et al., 1982; Riggio and Friedman, 1986; Sadalla et al., 1987), and these are precisely the qualities each sex most prefers in the other in a dating situation. Beyond the dating age, the greater a person's physical attractiveness, the better off he or she is in educational level, income, status, and mental health (Umberson and Hughes, 1984).

The strong effects of physical attractiveness might seem to imply that each of us would seek only an incredibly attractive individual as a partner. One barrier to doing so is the fear of being rejected by someone who is extremely good-looking (Bernstein et al., 1983). People tend, in fact, to prefer partners similar to themselves in attractiveness. Because of this tendency, pairs of friends, dating partners, and

TABLE 10-2   **Does Attractiveness Indicate Your Character?**

These stereotypes about physically attractive or unattractive people are based on beliefs about the value of physical beauty.

ATTRACTIVE INDIVIDUALS OF BOTH SEXES ARE DESCRIBED AS:

> Poised
> Interesting
> Sociable
> Independent
> Exciting
> Sexually warm

LESS ATTRACTIVE INDIVIDUALS OF BOTH SEXES ARE DESCRIBED AS:

> Psychologically unhealthy
> Politically radical
> Homosexual

Source: Based on data from Brigham, 1980; Jones et al., 1978; Unger et al., 1982.

spouses are found to be relatively similar to each other in physical attractiveness (Berscheid et al., 1971; Feingold, 1988; Kalick and Hamilton, 1988; Zajonc et al., 1987). Couples who are most similar in attractiveness, moreover, have a greater chance of maintaining their relationship than mismatched couples (White, 1980a).

Because of the value we place on attractiveness, it follows that self-perceptions of deficiencies in appearance lower self-esteem and lead to efforts to improve how we look. This topic is discussed in the special section, *Highlighting Research,* on pages 262 to 263.

Similarity: Seeking Those Most Like Ourselves. Attraction toward a similar partner goes beyond physical appearance. Once we begin interacting with someone new, we try to discover as much as possible about his or her likes and dislikes. Throughout history it has been observed that people respond most positively to other individuals who are most similar to themselves, especially those who hold similar attitudes, beliefs, and values (Smeaton et al., 1989).

Research consistently finds that **attitude similarity** leads to attraction (Byrne, 1971; Newcomb, 1961). You may hear that "opposites attract," but such mismatching works better in fiction than in real

Highlighting Research

IDENTIFYING ATTRACTIVENESS . . . AND IMPROVING IT

What specific elements of a person's appearance lead us to conclude that he or she is attractive? Neither sex finds obesity appealing (Franzoi and Herzog, 1987; Harris et al., 1982), and women respond most positively to men with a V-shaped torso—broad shoulders and a thin waist (Beck et al., 1976). Also, neither a straight, non-V physique nor the bulging, muscular appearance of the body builder interests most women; they prefer small buttocks and thin legs (Horvath, 1979; Lavrakas, 1975). Similarly, women like men of medium height, preferably about 2 inches taller than themselves (Gillis and Avis,

1980; Graziano et al., 1978; Sheppard and Strathman, 1989).

Although you might not guess it on the basis of centerfolds in magazines such as *Playboy,* men are most attracted to women with medium-sized breasts, legs, and buttocks (Kleinke and Staneski, 1980; Wiggins et al., 1968). A study of ads in the personals section found that men were more likely to make contact with women whose ads indicated that they had red hair than to those who stated they were either blond or brunette (Lynn and Shurgot, 1984).

Men find two kinds of female faces es-

pecially attractive. On the one hand, they like childlike features such as large, widely spaced eyes and a small nose and chin. They also like women with mature features such as prominent cheekbones, narrow cheeks, high eyebrows, and large pupils (Cunningham, 1986).

We also respond to our own appearance, either by being relatively satisfied or dissatisfied with our body image. Having a poor body image means that you dislike various parts of your body. Table 10-3 lists some of the elements people view as important in evaluating themselves physically. For example, college students of

TABLE 10-3 **Mirror, Mirror . . . Tell Me I'm OK**

A person's body image depends on these components. Attitudes toward our physical selves are important to self-concept.

BODY IMAGE: FIVE CONCERNS OR CAPABILITIES	SPECIFICS:
1. Physical skills and fitness	Stamina, coordination, and energy level
2. Face and overall appearance	Hair, complexion, profile, height
3. Weight and lower body (mostly of concern to women)	Hips, legs, waist
4. Physique and muscular strength (mostly of concern to men)	Body build, chest, arms, shoulders
5. Miscellaneous	Chin, ears, genitals

Source: Based on Tucker, 1983, 1985.

both sexes are most satisfied with their faces and overall appearance. In contrast, college men are least satisfied by their physique and muscular strength; college women express unhappiness about their weight and lower body proportions (Tucker, 1983, 1985). One solution to the perceived problems is for males to exercise and for females to diet. Such attempts at self-improvement can be carried to unrealistic and excessive lengths as when men take dangerous steroids to build muscles and women diet to the point of **anorexia**, sometimes becoming fatally undernourished.

Many women focus on their breast size, either considering them too large or too small. Weight loss can reduce breast size, and isometric exercises (depicted in Figure 10-5) can increase apparent breast size through expansion of the pectoral muscles under the breasts. Such exercise also reduces the tendency of breasts to sag with age.

In addition to dieting, exercise, and cosmetics (Cox and Glick, 1986), some people go to even greater lengths to change their appearance. Plastic surgery can alter a person's face, breasts, and almost any other part of the body. Because of the risks, it is recommended that cosmetic surgery be performed only by surgeons who are board-certified in that specialty. Some of the most common forms of plastic surgery (Zarem, 1982) reshape the nose (*rhinoplasty*), increase or decrease breast size (*mammoplasty*), and alter various other physical features (*body contouring*) usually by removing pockets of fat. Interestingly, in China, women seek cosmetic surgery to make them look more Western—rounder eyes and larger noses (Kristof, 1987).

With mammoplasty, scarring is more common when a woman's breasts are made smaller than when they are enlarged. To make breasts larger, the plastic surgeon usually implants silicone. After the operation the patient experiences about two days of pain, but can resume her usual physical and sexual activity in two weeks. One fourth of women who have mammoplasties form a thick covering around the implant because their bodies attempt to reject the foreign object; massage or additional surgery can solve this problem (Imber, 1980). Unless the plastic surgeon has made the incision in or near the areola, the woman can usually breast-feed normally. Implants also carry such risks as inflammation, blood clots, and even cancer (Blakeslee, 1989).

Besides the pain and possible after-effects, cost is an additional factor in considering whether to obtain plastic surgery. As of 1990, a forehead lift to raise eyebrows costs about $2,000, and the fee for body contouring ranges from $5,000 to $6,000—and medical insurance generally does not cover such elective surgery. For United States tax payers, this kind of surgery can no longer be used as a medical deduction, thus increasing a patient's total expenditure (Cowan, 1990). For most people, the potential importance of improved looks is outweighed by the medical risks and the expense of plastic surgery.

FIGURE 10-5 *EXERCISES TO CREATE THE BODY BEAUTIFUL: EASIER THAN SURGERY* Isometric exercises such as these can reshape body contours. Flexing the pectoral (chest) muscles as in (1) and exercising those same muscles as in (2) can help increase chest circumference by thickening the muscles underneath fatty breast tissue. The third exercise (3) creates a more pleasing leg contour if done slowly a few times each day.

life. As Figure 10-6 suggests, attraction is a direct consequence of similar attitudes. Thus, friends, lovers, and spouses have similar views on most issues (Feingold, 1989).

In addition to similarity of attitudes, beliefs, and values, other kinds of similarity also facilitate attraction. For example, the needs of spouses tend to match. Thus, *need compatibility* outweighs *need complementarity*. Husbands and wives whose needs are similar have fewer marital problems than couples whose needs differ (Meyer and Pepper, 1977). Also, female undergraduates prefer roommates with social backgrounds similar to their own (Hill and Stull, 1981). People with similar personalities are mutually attracted (Smith, 1989), and such similarity actually increases when two people interact over a long period of time (Blankenship et al., 1984). We not only prefer to have friends who are similar, we believe that similarity exists when it does not (Dawes, 1989).

Matching also occurs between friends whose daily habits are similar (Jamieson et al., 1987). We like friends who behave as we do and who make decisions similar to our own. High school friends resemble each other in drug use, for example (Kandel et al., 1976). At least among women, patterns of smoking, drinking, and premarital sexual activity are more similar among groups of friends than among classmates in general (Rodgers et al., 1984). People who live together are more satisfied with the relationship if they have similar preferences about when to sleep and when to be active (Watts, 1982). For most characteristics that have been studied, similarity leads to attraction (Griffin and Sparks, 1990).

Why is similarity so crucial in relationships? It appears that similarity has a positive effect because it helps confirm our judgments about the world. When another person agrees with us, he or she affirms or "validates" our views about politics, religion, and so on and also provides evidence that our judgments, tastes, and style of behavior are reasonable, normal, and wise (Byrne, 1971; Goethals, 1986). We find it rewarding when others provide this positive information (Davis, 1981). As a result, similarity creates a state of **positive affect**, and comfortable, good feelings form the basis of a successful relationship (Clore and Byrne, 1974; Cramer, 1985). Conversely, friendships deteriorate if they are characterized by **negative affect**—unpleasant emotions created in part by dissimilarities (Byrne et al., 1986; Rosenbaum, 1986).

A quite different explanation is provided by sociobiologists. Rushton (1989) suggests that people prefer mates who are genetically similar to themselves, and the consequence is enhancement and survival of their own segment of the gene pool.

Reciprocity of Positive Evaluations: If You Like Me, Let Me Know. If someone is really your friend and if your interactions are positive, would you expect that person to evaluate you positively, help you whenever possible, and let you know you are liked? Many studies indicate that the communication of such positive evaluations between partners is the most crucial characteristic of a successful relationship (Coleman et al., 1987; Condon et al., 1988)

Even when two people are dissimilar in their attitudes, a man will be attracted to a woman if she shows interest in him by maintaining eye contact, talking to him, and leaning toward him (Gold et al., 1984). When **reciprocity** of positive reactions occurs, either verbally or nonverbally, the relationship is strengthened for both individuals. Flattery, a desire to be together and to communicate, and any sign of affection indicate clearly that positive affect is operating in the friendship (Drachman et al., 1978; Hays, 1984). In contrast, hostility, negative evaluations, or refusal to be helpful to one another, creates negative

FIGURE 10-6 *ATTRACTION INCREASES AS SIMILARITY INCREASES* The higher the proportion of attitude similarity between two individuals, the greater their attraction toward one another (Byrne, 1971). For example, you will like a stranger who is 60 percent similar to you much better than a stranger who is 20 percent similar to you—with all other factors held constant.

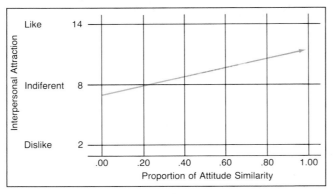

affect, which clearly endangers the relationship (Amabile, 1983; Byrne and Murnen, 1988; Riordan et al., 1982).

■ Sexual Attraction

Sexual attraction goes beyond simply liking another person and becoming friends; it includes a desire for physical intimacy. At present, we know more about why two people like each other than why they find each other sexy. One explanation is provided by Singer (1984), who proposes that three steps are necessary for sexual attraction to occur. First, there is the *aesthetic response* based on physical attractiveness, including the other person's face, physique, voice, and so forth. We usually equate attractiveness with sexiness. Second, after this initial positive impression, there is likely to be an *approach response*—we try to get physically close to the attractive individual. Third, if two people are mutually attracted, the next step is a *genital response,* as described in Chapter 3.

The aesthetic component of sexual attraction helps us decide about the sex appeal of another person. Sexiness lies in the eye of the beholder ("What in

the world does she see in him?"), but there is some consistency about what people in a given culture at a given time regard as sexy. For example, undergraduates of both sexes agree about the kind of female clothing that "turns men on." Women who perceive themselves as sexy tend to wear such clothes (Edmonds and Cahoon, 1984). Also, men assume that a woman who wears revealing clothing is sending the message that she desires sexual activity, but women do not make the same assumption about the meaning of what females wear (Goodchilds and Zellman, 1984; Griffitt, 1986). In a similar way, a man will regard a woman's friendliness as a sign of sexual interest; he is often surprised and disbelieving if she subsequently refuses to have intercourse with him (Abbey, 1982). Excitement also affects sexual attraction. When men have been exposed to erotic material and become sexually aroused, attraction toward physically attractive females increases while attraction toward unattractive females decreases (Istvan et al., 1983).

As Figure 10-7 suggests, certain postures provide cues to sexual interest between a male and a female. Men and women in a superior, dominant pose are perceived as sexually experienced (Garcia

FIGURE 10-7 *NONVERBAL MESSAGES PROVIDE CUES* A superior, dominant pose is perceived as an indication of sexual experience and interest. Individuals in an inferior, more submissive pose are presumed to be less experienced and less interested in a sexual relationship.

and Derfel, 1983). In contrast, those in an inferior, submissive stance are perceived as unappealing and inexperienced.

Sexual attraction is also affected by assumptions about the sexual history of the other person. Women perceive men as very experienced sexually, and they overestimate what men have done and how many partners they have had (Griffitt, 1973). Both sexes show much greater interest in the meaning of a woman's sexual history. For example, undergraduates of both sexes express the need for more information about a female's sexual past in order to be able to describe her, but such information is not required in order to be able to describe a male (Garcia et al., 1983). The information that a woman has had little sexual experience results in the perception that she is pure, even when she is known to become excited in response to explicit erotic material (Garcia, 1983).

In Chapter 9 we referred to the belief held by some men that that women are either virginal madonnas or sexually experienced whores driven by their animal instincts. On the basis of such stereotypical views, some men place a woman in the experienced category on the basis of how she behaves and dresses, as well as on the basis of the attitudes she expresses (Garcia, 1984). For example, men holding these stereotypes believe that feminist women have more sexual experience than nonfeminists. One result is that a woman wearing a T-shirt with a positive message about women's liberation can be perceived by some (however incorrectly) as sexually loose (Janda, 1982).

Approach behavior that brings two people physically close is characteristic of couples who are sexually attracted to one another (McAdams and Powers, 1981). In one experiment, male–female pairs were introduced for the first time and sent on a thirty-minute "Coke date." When they returned to report to the experimenter, those who felt the most mutual attraction stood closer to one another than those who were not attracted (Byrne et al., 1970). Even attitude similarity induces people of the opposite sex to sit close to one another (Allgeier and Byrne, 1973). Generally, the factors that enhance friendships—such as similarity, positive affect, and physical attractiveness—also contribute to sexual attraction.

Some theorists propose a **sociobiological perspective on sexual attraction**—the theory that inherited traits associated with historically successful reproductive strategies for our species influence today's human behavior. Thus, we unconsciously select mates primarily to improve our chances of reproducing ourselves with the best possible mate we can attract (Kenrick and Trost, 1986). According to this perspective, the best reproductive strategy for men is to have intercourse with as many fertile young females as possible, while the best strategy for women is be very selective in mating and to make sure that the male has the resources (strength, intelligence, status, and so forth) to protect her and their offspring (Buss, 1988; Kenrick and Keefe, 1990).

Evidence supporting genetically driven sexual interactions is most clear among animals lower than ourselves on the phylogenetic scale. The behavior of relatively simple species is controlled by the overwhelming power of hormones and built-in behavioral patterns. For example, insects respond automatically to chemical attractants that are effective only within a species—**sexual pheromones**. Pests such as the boll weevil can be controlled better by baiting traps with sexual pheromones than by spraying crops with insecticides (Abelson, 1985). Even mammals such as rodents, pigs, dogs, and cats are strongly responsive to sexual odors, as anyone knows who has witnessed the response of a male pet to a female in heat. The evidence that humans emit or are affected by such pheromones is, however, limited and inconsistent. Nevertheless, humans spend a great deal of money on perfume, after-shave lotion, and other products because they are convinced that smelling like flowers, pine trees, lemons, or musk increases sexual attractiveness.

Falling In—and Out—of Love

Love combines liking, sexual attraction, and the intense emotional interaction of two partners (see Figure 10-8). Love is more affected by appearance and less affected by similarity than is friendship (Aron et al., 1989). Behavioral scientists began investigating love extensively only in the last couple of decades.

FIGURE 10-8 *LOVE AS THE BASIS FOR SEX AND MARRIAGE* Over the past several hundred years, the concept of love has developed and become an accepted part of many cultures. The ideal involves two people who like each other, feel mutual sexual attraction, and are emotionally aroused in response to each other. Love is commonly viewed as the prerequisite for a sexual relationship and/or marriage.

The following section describes how love develops and affects those experiencing it. We also discuss how love may evaporate and what partners can do to help maintain a loving relationship.

■ Passionate Love versus Companionate Love

In attempting to understand human behavior, observers over the centuries have speculated about several different kinds of love.

Varieties of Love. The ancient Greeks described four types of love (Lewis, 1960). **Storge** indicates affection and caring, the way a parent might feel about an offspring. In a similar way, we can "love" a pet or even an inanimate object, expecting nothing in return. **Philia** refers to the feeling between friends and seems to be what we have described as interpersonal attraction. **Eros** is romantic love, characterized by a person's total preoccupation with the loved one. Recent research has focused on this kind of love, and we will describe it in more detail shortly. **Agape** is a charitable, concerned feeling toward others. Goodness and decency result from agape, and it sometimes seems to be in short supply in modern societies.

Hendrick and Hendrick (1986) present a similar system that outlines six types of love: passionate, game-playing, friendship, logical, possessive, and selfless. On tests that measure these kinds of loving, men score higher than women in passionate and game-playing love, while women outscore men in friendship, logical, and possessive love (Hendrick et al., 1984). Romantic partners tend to be similar in the kind of love they feel (Hendrick et al., 1988). Relationships are most likely to last when the partners are high in passionate love and low in game-playing love.

Abraham Maslow, in contrast, suggested that there are only two kinds of love. **B-love (being-love)** was his term for love that is unselfish, healthy, and concerned with the needs and the successes of the other person rather than oneself. In contrast is **D-love (deficiency-love)**, a selfish kind of love whose primary goal is to satisfy one's own interests and needs. Relationships suffer when one or both partners are narcissistically centered on themselves rather than being truly concerned about the best interests of the other person (Wright, 1984).

Without minimizing the importance of these varieties of love, a great deal of current interest centers on the emotional state of **passionate love.**

Passionate Love. People in love may not think logically or practically about the object of that love, but obsessive thoughts about that person occupy much of their attention (Milardo et al., 1983). Other activities and relationships are abandoned in favor of interacting with the lover. Some people experience passionate love more intensely than others; for example, those who think about love a lot are the most likely to fall in love (Tesser and Paulhus, 1976). Being "head over heels in love" has been termed *limerance* by Tennov (1979). Those who have experienced limerance tend to agree with such statements as "I love everything about someone to whom I am strongly attracted" and "I have felt an intense attraction for someone I hardly knew." Such feelings have been compared to accidents such as slipping on a banana peel—and some people slip more often than others (Solomon, 1981).

Passionate love is clearly different from simply liking. Liking refers to a positive evaluation of the other person and a desire to spend time with him or her (Byrne, 1971) while passionate love involves much more intense feelings as well as sexual desire (Hatfield and Rapson, 1987). One measure of this love includes items such as "Since I've been with _____, my emotions have been on a roller coaster," and "Sometimes I can't control my thoughts; they are obsessively on _____" (Hatfield and Sprecher, 1986a). Figure 10-9 illustrates the kind of response most common when passionate love is aroused.

One theory of passionate love has received considerable attention from behavioral scientists. The **three-factor theory of passionate love** states three conditions that must precede its development (Hatfield, 1988). First, for an individual to fall in love, he or she must live in a culture that provides the information that romantic love occurs as an expected and desirable part of male–female relationships (Dion and Dion, 1988). Love may seem natural to us, but the concept is a relatively new one in human history, becoming generally accepted in France in the eleventh century (Gregersen, 1983) as the idealized, nonsexual passion of knights for untouchable married ladies. In societies where economic necessity was the basis for marriage, passionate love was unknown. Not until the seventeenth century was love considered to be the basis for an ideal marriage in Western Europe. In North America, European settlers accepted arranged marriages for at least a century before love became the accepted reason to marry.

Today, in most Western societies, young people are well prepared to experience love by a lifetime of exposure to fairy tales, songs, television shows, and movies that present it as the norm—the necessary prerequisite for sex and marriage (Dion and Dion, 1975). India, a country in which arranged marriages were the rule, only in fairly recent years has begun making the transition to marriages based on love. As a result, movies depicting passionate love and defiance of parents' wishes have become popular among young people in the Indian middle class (Kaufman, 1980).

Second, an appropriate love object must be present for passionate love to occur. In one study of adults of various ages and backgrounds, about half

FIGURE 10-9 *PASSIONATE LOVE AND IRRATIONAL RESPONSES* Does passionate love lead us to respond irrationally? Love is not only blind, but it also may be a bit like temporary insanity.

reported experiencing "love at first sight" at least once in their lives (Averill and Boothroyd, 1977). Even in a laboratory setting, when two opposite-sex strangers are instructed to look into each other's eyes for two minutes, feelings of passionate love are aroused (Kellerman et al., 1989). It is as though we have been programmed to expect a specific kind of love object—usually a member of the opposite sex who is sexually attractive and not already involved in a close relationship. When that person comes along, bingo—we fall in love! But what makes someone an appropriate love object? Men tend to emphasize the physical characteristics of an ideal romantic partner as shown in a study of undergraduates (Nevid, 1984). They were most concerned about the partner's face, weight, attractiveness, and other bodily characteristics. Females stress attractiveness as well, but they also want a partner who is warm, gentle, and kind. For both sexes, honesty, fidelity, and personality were described as important in meaningful, long-term relationships. Buss' (1988, 1989b) sociobiological approach suggests that our choices are based on men looking for a mate who is young and healthy enough

FIGURE 10-10 *THE CONDITIONS NECESSARY FOR PASSION-ATE LOVE* The three preconditions for passionate love are outlined in a theory first proposed by Elaine Hatfield and Ellen Berscheid (1971).

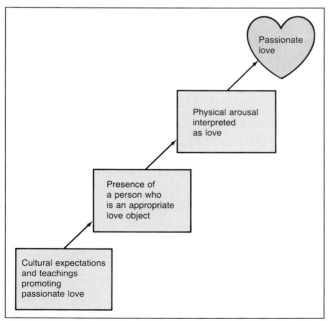

to reproduce and on women looking for a mate who is able and willing to protect her and their offspring.

The third factor in promoting the intense feelings of passionate love is any kind of intense emotional arousal that is interpreted as love (see Figure 10-10). Earlier, we described how anxiety and fear increase the desire to affiliate with others (Riordan and Tedeschi, 1983). In a similar way, when the first two factors are present, and a strong emotion is aroused, affiliative needs are activated—at that point the situation is defined as falling in love.

Thus, emotional arousal can provide the final ingredient for instant infatuation. In such circumstances, we easily can interpret our arousal not as anxiety, fear, or whatever but as *love*. Research has shown that when people are aroused in various ways—by erotic material, by being in an embarrassing situation, by a frightening circumstance—they respond with increased romantic interest in a member of the opposite sex (Dutton and Aron, 1974; Istvan et al., 1983; Przybyla et al., 1985). Even the anger generated by parental interference in a love affair can be reinterpreted by the lovers as a sign that their intense feelings indicate love—a phenomenon known as the **Romeo and Juliet effect** (Driscoll et al., 1972). Other investigators also have found that arousal leads to passionate love, but they explain it simply as a matter of facilitating whatever responses the individuals are already making (Allen et al., 1989).

Because passionate love is intense and based partially on unrealistic expectations and misinterpreted emotions, couples are unable to continue indefinitely in this emotional state. They either lose interest as the love affair dies ("It was too hot not to cool down"), or they move on to a more realistic kind of love that *can* endure: **companionate love.**

Companionate Love. Even though a relationship may begin passionately, it can evolve into companionate love—a relationship that resembles a close, affectionate, caring friendship with positive emotions, similarity on many dimensions, and reciprocal liking and respect. These deep, lasting feelings are suggested when someone says that "my lover—or my spouse—is my best friend." Caring between two people makes durable relationships possible (Steck et al., 1982). Also, because companionate love is less consuming and possessive than passionate romance, it makes it possible for partners to concentrate on work, friends, and children as well as on each other. Companionate love can include an exciting and satisfying sex life along with continuous evidence that your partner cares for you. It also follows that the best message you can give is that you care for your partner as well (Hatfield, 1988).

Sternberg (1986, 1988) describes the ideal loving relationship as consisting of three balanced components. The first two correspond to passionate and companionate love, which he labels as passion and intimacy. He adds a third component, *decision/commitment*—partners rationally make a commitment to maintain a loving relationship and to make every effort to solve and overcome problems when they arise. When all three components are present and equally strong, the result is *consummate love,* a perfect relationship that partners can strive to attain.

Communication between Companionate Lovers. Lovers discuss extremely intimate personal matters with one another (Sollie and Fischer, 1985). Ideally, lovers know that their partner will not use such disclosures to criticize, ridicule, or put them down. Lovers are expected to accept us, even our faults. Early in a relationship, one partner's self-disclosure can actually arouse the other partner's interest in him or her. The lover to whom intimacies are revealed assumes that the partner is disclosing such information because he or she is attracted; men typically reveal

more personal details about themselves than women do early in a relationship (Derlega et al., 1985).

Even lovers have "taboo topics," as Table 10-4 shows; most of them concern aspects of their own relationship (Baxter and Wilmot, 1985). The most common reason subjects gave for avoiding such discussions—41 percent of those surveyed—was that discussing the relationship would destroy it. For example, one subject said, "It's hard to talk about what is going to happen in the future in the relationship," and another indicated that "It would ruin a carefree relationship" (Baxter and Wilmot, 1985, p. 260). Subjects also said that they avoided talking about prior relationships because this might threaten their current involvement. Among these respondents, 63 percent expressed fear about a partner's possible anger or jealousy, especially concerning extra-relationship activity. Among the statements made by these undergraduates were:

I wouldn't tell this to my boyfriend because I don't want to hurt him.

His aggressive behavior . . . If it came up he'd get mad and become very defensive [Baxter and Wilmot, 1985, pp. 262–263].

Although some topics may be unpleasant to discuss, couples who do not open up or who cease communicating are most likely to break up (Tolstedt and Stokes, 1984). As you might expect, a decrease in

TABLE 10-4 **Don't Even Ask!**

Certain topics are avoided in love relationships. The percentages do not add up to 100 because 4 percent of the avoided topics did not fit any category.

TABOO TOPICS FOR LOVERS	EXAMPLES	PERCENTAGE
1. State of the relationship	Do we love each other? Will we marry?	34
2. Extra-relationship activities	Are you having an affair? Do you want to be with someone else?	16
3. Relationship norms	How should we treat each other?	13
4. Prior relationships	Tell me about your previous boyfriend (girlfriend).	13
5. Conflictful topics	How dissimilar are we?	11
6. Negative self-disclosure	I have a police record. Are you on the pill?	9

Source: Based on data from Baxter and Wilmot, 1985.

feelings of love is associated with a decrease in self-disclosure.

■ Changes in Love Relationships

Five stages characterize relationships over time: initial attraction, building the relationship, and continuation; then, if too many problems arise, deterioration and ending (Levinger, 1980). Having described the first two stages, we will now briefly explore the last three (Duck et al., 1984). Although most of our knowledge is based on investigations of male-female pairs, the findings seem to apply to homosexual couples equally well (Schullo and Alperson, 1984).

Continuing a Relationship: The Role of Equity. Although you might expect passionate love to fade easily, companionate love also may fail. Many elements of a relationship are crucial to its success. Each partner desires both love and sexual rewards. People want intimacy and the power to determine what happens within the interaction (Kelley and Rolker-Dolinsky, 1986). Partners who feel satisfied with the rewards they receive relative to their contribution to the relationship experience *equity* (Hatfield, 1983). Those who feel that their contributions outweigh their rewards feel *inequity,* and they are likely to become increasingly dissatisfied with the relationship (Clark and Waddell, 1985). Love is best maintained when partners treat each other sensitively and fairly (Tesch, 1985).

Two people need to feel they are contributing equally to the relationship in attractiveness, abilities, daily efforts, income, and so forth. Over time, one partner may begin to feel inequitably treated, undervalued, unwanted, or overcommitted compared to the other partner. If, for example, one individual earns considerably more money than the other or does all of the housework, he or she begins to feel inequity (McAdams, 1982). Both dating and married couples need to experience equity (Utne et al., 1984).

Men and women want to have a sense of control or power in the relationship, but the sexes differ about their perceptions of the most important sources of power. In a survey of fifty dating couples, women who said they contributed more to the relationship than the male partner felt that they had relatively less power. Those who undercontributed to the relation-ship felt more powerful. Women identified love and affection as their source of power and control. Men felt most powerful and in control when they had "other irons in the fire," such as a romantic interest in other women (Sprecher, 1985). Consistently, when women believe they are treated inequitably, they tend to withhold love; when men perceive inequity, they threaten their current partner with interest in an alternative lover.

Jealousy as a Threat. **Jealousy** is common in close relationships, as Figure 10-11 suggests (White and Mullen, 1990). If the partners feel committed to their relationship, they are less likely to become involved with alternative partners (Johnson and Rusbult, 1989). When you believe that a rival exists—whether or not this perception is accurate—emotional pain results. A person suffering from extreme jealousy may even exhibit physical symptoms such as a rapid heartbeat or a feeling of emptiness in the stomach (Pines and Aronson, 1983). The thought that a loved one might potentially seek a new partner can cause feelings of anxiety, fear, anger, and lowered self-esteem (Buunk and Bringle, 1987; Smith et al.,. 1988; Mathes et al., 1985).

Research indicates that about one third of female undergraduates and one fifth of the males deliberately try to induce jealousy in their partners (White, 1980b). They flirt, discuss their present and past attraction toward others, date others, or invent happenings of this sort. Why? The goal is to gain self-esteem, attention, or revenge and to test how their partner "really" feels about them. Such games may be the first step in the deterioration of a relationship. A similar risk is run by partners who repeatedly bring up the other person's past loves.

Some people are more likely to experience jealousy than others. Slightly more than half of the adults in one survey described themselves as jealous (Pines and Aronson, 1983). People planning an extramarital affair show the least jealousy (Buunk, 1982). At the other extreme, people who demand sexual exclusivity rather than simply expecting or requesting it show the greatest jealousy (White, 1980b). Excessively jealous people often feel inadequate and dependent, and jealousy is more common among traditionally masculine males and feminine females (Hansen, 1985). When parents express feelings of jealousy toward one

FIGURE 10-11 *TRYING TO ASSERT POWER IN A RELATIONSHIP* Women in dating relationships sometimes manipulate their expressions of love by withholding affection and sex, whereas men threaten to seek other partners. Both techniques represent ways to assert power in the relationship, and both pose dangers for the continuation of the relationship (Sprecher, 1985).

another, they unwittingly teach their offspring to respond to their future partners in the same way (Bringle and Williams, 1979).

Deterioration and Ending. When love relationships deteriorate, the process is painful. The romance may slowly lose its appeal over a period of time, or it may fall apart quickly. About one fourth of all relationships suddenly disintegrate after a critical incident, including the revelation of an outside affair (Baxter, 1984). The following examples illustrate the two types of ending:

> *The first thing that upset me was that she didn't like my dog. . . . Then I discovered that she had been married before. . . . We argued a lot and things were tense between us then. I finally decided that I'd had it and wanted out.*
>
> *From a mutual friend, she found out that I had been seeing other people while she was away at school. She confronted me and it was all over [Baxter, 1984, p. 35].*

In troubled premarital relationships, partners spend a lot of time arguing (Lloyd and Cate, 1985a), and the amount of conflict in a relationship before marriage predicts dissatisfaction after marriage (Kelly et al., 1985). When doubts about the relationship continue, love decreases and conflict escalates. The two partners may respond actively or passively to this conflict (Rusbult et al., 1986: Rusbult and Zembrodt, 1983). Active responses consist of "exit," or ending the relationship, and "voice," or working to improve it. Passive responses are "loyalty," or waiting for improvement, and "neglect," or allowing deterioration to run its course. The most constructive alternatives are loyalty and voice; these represent possible ways to save the relationship. The lower a person's self-esteem, the more likely he or she is to respond with neglect or exit (Rusbult et al., 1990).

Breakups are most likely to occur when partners do not feel mutually committed to the relationship (Lund, 1985). Love may not keep couples together, but commitment may do so. Love does, however, make breakups more painful for the two individuals (Lee, 1984).

Even with strong commitment, the relationship still may fail. Initial attraction and desire may not be sufficient to provide long-term rewards, and alternative partners may appear more desirable to one or both of the partners (Rusbult, 1983). In addition, men commonly complain that their partners reject them sexually and are moody and self-absorbed, while women complain that their partners demand sex, ignore their opinions, and are neglectful and thoughtless (Buss, 1989a). Specific events—the first big fight, an affair, or whatever—may act as turning points, leading the couple to greater closeness or to increasing the distance between them (Lloyd and Cate, 1985b). Maintaining a relationship requires hard work by two committed persons, and conflicts are almost certain to arise in intimate relationships (Baxter, 1990). Table 10-5 summarizes the elements involved in the development, maintenance, and downfall of close relationships.

What can lovers do to avoid a breakup? Several investigations have identified some of crucial elements that help hold relationships together. The special section, *Increasing Enjoyment,* on pages 274 to 275, describes techniques for improving the chances of "keeping love alive."

TABLE 10-5   **Stages of a Relationship: Helpful and Harmful Behaviors**

Relationships often progress through a series of five stages, from initial attraction to the possibility of ending altogether. At each stage, some factors benefit the relationship, while others increase the likelihood of its failure.

RELATIONSHIP STAGE				
Initial Attraction	*Building the Relationship*	*Continuation*	*Deterioration*	*Ending*
These benefit the relationship:				
1. Propinquity, repeated exposure	1. Similarity in physical attitudes, and personality	1. Interest, variety, and mutual satisfaction	1. Continuous work toward improving relationship	1. Rewards continue in existing relationship
2. Positive affect	2. Reciprocity	2. Lack of jealousy		2. Commitment toward continuing relationship; expecting it to succeed
3. Strong need for affiliation		3. Equity and positive evaluation		3. Alternative partners unavailable
These detract from the relationship:				
1. Absence of propinquity and repeated exposure	1. Dissimilarity	1. Little interest, variety, or mutual satisfaction	1. Little or no work toward improving relationship	1. Seeking rewards in a new life
2. Negative affect	2. Lack of reciprocity	2. Jealousy		2. Decision to end relationship or expecting it to fail
3. Weak need for affiliation		3. Inequity and negative evaluation		3. Alternative partners available

Source: Adapted from Baron and Byrne, 1987.

Increasing Enjoyment

KEEPING A RELATIONSHIP TOGETHER

It seems totally impossible at the beginning of a love affair, but the warm feelings frequently turn to indifference, dislike, and even hatred. A love affair between unmarried college students has approximately a 50 percent chance of dissolving within two years (Hill et al., 1976). Over time, people change, and relationships do, too. Why do relationships fail, and what, if anything, can be done about it? Three general danger zones have been identified (Byrne and Murnen, 1988).

First, the lovers may discover too many dissimilarities as they get to know each other better over time. Considering the importance of similarity in influencing liking, you can see how the realization of major dissimilarities would interfere with an ongoing relationship (Hill et al., 1976). Not only is it impossible to know *everything* about another person at the beginning of a relationship, the strong emotions associated with passionate love interfere with logic and rational thought. This may make it difficult for either the man or the woman honestly to appraise how similar the two of them are. When the initial infatuation fades and the couple begins to perceive that the basic elements of a friendship are absent, love can die. Clearly, it is extremely important for two people to know as much as possible about each other before becoming too involved, and this is especially crucial with respect to beliefs, attitudes, and values that are directly relevant to the relationship (Jones and Stanton, 1988).

A related difficulty in long-term relationships is that two similar people can become dissimilar if one partner changes while the other does not. Even the best-matched pair at the beginning of an affair may find that they are mismatched at a later time (Levinger, 1988). The way for couples to avoid this kind of dissimilarity problem is to be attuned to the pitfalls of change. For example, if one individual pursues further education, embarks on a new avocation, or develops a new area of interest, the partner should at least consider joining in rather than risk being left behind.

The second general area of concern has seldom been investigated—*boredom* (Skinner, 1986). One study of failed college love affairs found that this was the most frequently cited cause of breakup (Hill et al., 1976). Continual contact with the same partner and repeatedly doing the same things in the same way can contribute to declining interest in each other. When people feel that they are in a rut, negative affect is aroused. The unhappiness is then unfairly attributed to the partner who has "failed to measure up."

Not much is known about solving the boredom problem, but an awareness of its dangers can motivate couples to seek ways to avoid or overcome it. For example, couples may develop new hobbies, recreational activities, and educational pursuits. In daily life—having sex, talking, planning weekend activities, preparing meals, taking vacations, or whatever—couples might do well to remember the importance of variety. Novelty is usually preferable to monotony. Feelings of boredom may otherwise intensify, and suddenly a new partner appears to be the only solution.

The third, and perhaps most crucial, problem for maintaining a smooth relationship is a decrease in the exchange of positive evaluations. Remember that friendships are initiated and endure because of continuing indications of mutual liking and respect. People in long-term romantic relationships often forget this. When people say, "The honeymoon is over," they mean that a positive, loving interaction has shifted to a negative one. Amazingly, partners often feel that it is acceptable to criticize, nag, complain, and

---

TABLE 10-6 **Promoting a Positive Relationship**

These guidelines suggest behaviors that help promote friendly feelings rather than interfering with them. Friendships deteriorate to the extent that they involve the opposite behaviors.

HELPFUL BEHAVIOR IN RELATIONSHIPS	
Behavior	*Examples*
Exchange of positive affect	Share good news
	Show emotional support and caring
	Offer help when it is needed
	Try to make partner happy when together
	Avoid nagging
	Repay favors
Intimacy	Trust each other
	Confide in each other
	Respect privacy
Interactions with others	Defend the partner in his or her absence
	Show tolerance of partner's friends
	Don't criticize partner to others
	Keep each other's secrets
	Avoid jealousy and criticism of other relationships

Source: Based on data from Argyle and Henderson, 1985.

find fault with each other. Two people who begin to treat each other in such a way may not only feel less loving but also may cease even being friends (Baucom et al., 1989; Margolin et al., 1989).

If lovers and spouses continued to be as nice, as polite, as complimentary, and as friendly as they were on their first date, they would much more easily maintain a positive relationship.

In summary, dissimilarity, boredom, and the substitution of negative for positive evaluations each contribute to the fail-ure of a relationship. To avoid the pain of a breakup, partners must be aware of these three problem areas and make a continual effort to avoid them.

Can couples do anything else to promote their relationship? Because most of us do not receive any formal instruction about the rules of friendship, learning how successful pairs interact may be helpful. Studies of hundreds of friends in Japan showed that certain behaviors characterized successful friendships, as Table 10-6 summarizes (Argyle and Henderson, 1985).

Pairs who had ceased interacting did not engage in these behaviors, and they admitted their failure to abide by these informal guidelines. A group of 351 American couples who had been married at least 15 years agreed that the secret of marital success was based on friendship, commitment, similarity, and the frequent arousal of positive affect (Lauer and Lauer, 1985). Both of these studies provide descriptions of positive ways in which two people can most harmoniously interact.

Sexual Decision Making

What factors influence us to engage in some specific sexual activity or to avoid it? In this section, we will outline the external and internal factors that affect such decision making.

Perspectives on Sexual Relationships

Many social factors influence our sexuality (De-Lamater, 1981). Through religion, family, and peers we learn how we are supposed to respond to sexual needs. Most religions emphasize the **procreational orientation** toward sex. This means that sexual intercourse should occur solely within the context of marriage for the purpose of producing children (Comfort, 1973). Masturbation, oral-genital stimulation, anal intercourse, or sex outside of marriage are disapproved within these religious traditions. As discussed in Chapter 8, those with a religious affiliation are likely to be more sexually conservative in their attitudes and behaviors than those without such affiliations. Even so, the meaning of religion to the person is the crucial element in determining its effect (Falbo and Shepperd, 1986).

Instead of a procreational approach to sex, many have a **relational orientation.** Such a perspective emphasizes the quality of the relationship between partners in making decisions about whether, when, and with whom to engage in sexual acts (Reiss, 1960). A majority of college students prefer having intercourse with a loved person rather than with someone toward whom they are indifferent (Sherwin and Corbett, 1985). One reason is that most of us have been exposed to many messages from parents, magazines (Lantz et al., 1977), and soap operas (Sexy soaps, 1981) favoring romantic love rather than casual sex.

If a romantic partner is unavailable, men are more willing than women to settle for sex without love. This preference suggests that men are more likely than women to have a **recreational orientation** to sex. According to this view, physical pleasure with a partner is adequate justification for sex. That men—more than women—are likely to have peers as the major source of sexual information increases the possibility of their developing a recreational style (Reiss, 1967). In future years we expect that recreational sex between uncommitted partners will decrease in frequency in response to increasing fears about AIDS.

The three orientations—procreational, relational, and recreational—affect the sexual behavior of young couples. Procreational couples refrain from intercourse until after marriage. Relational couples tend to engage in intercourse after professing love for one another, usually after about six months of dating (Peplau et al., 1977). Recreational couples have intercourse within the first week of the relationship.

Premarital sexuality creates conflicts about the "right thing to do," and this issue is examined in the special section, *Taking Responsibility and Protecting Yourself,* on pages 276 to 277. Among other concerns are the long-term and short-term effects of premarital sexual decisions.

Taking Responsibility and Protecting Yourself

PREMARITAL PERMISSIVENESS: SEX AMONG THE YOUNG AND SINGLE

How do you decide whether or not to engage in premarital sex? The decision to become sexually active is based partially on physical desire, the wishes of one's partner, peer pressure, and the perceived values of one's society (DeLamater, 1981; Randolph and Winstead, 1988). Whatever the influences, however, the implications of this decision extend far beyond an immediate sexual interaction with a given partner. Among the immediate possible effects are feelings of guilt or shame if the decision conflicts with religious or parental teachings, a new vulnerability to the fear of a breakup, and loss of independence (McCormack, 1980). The dangers of an unwanted conception and of contracting a sexually transmissible disease also must be considered.

There are long-term effects as well—such as consequences for health and reproductive fertility. For example, the "marriageability" of young women who have become sexually active may change. Even though college men rank the chastity of their potential spouses as much less important today than was true four decades ago (Hudson, 1980), virginity still influences perceptions about a female's suitability as a marriage partner. Both sexes also express doubts about the sexual past of a possible mate. Sexually inexperienced undergraduates consider those with a great deal of sexual experience to be undesirable as either dates or spouses (Istvan and Griffitt, 1980).

One approach to decision-making involves learning how to reason using a cost-benefit analysis (Larrick et al., 1990). The assumption is that if individuals are taught to consider the probabilities of various short-term and long-term outcomes along with the value of each (how costly or how beneficial?), they will act so as to maximize their overall welfare. Research indicates that the abstract rules of such decision-making can be learned and then applied to a variety of situations, including

totally new ones such as the person's first sexual interactions.

Young people who become sexually involved tend to emphasize the quality of the current relationship. Women, more than men, report greater concern about their attraction and love for the partner (Christopher and Cate, 1984). Feelings of closeness tend to be a prerequisite for sex among women and sexually inexperienced men. Figure 10-12 indicates at what point in the relationship a sample of sexually active couples began having intercourse (Christopher and Cate, 1985). Once sexual intimacy began, both sexes reported an increase in conflicts, arguments, and the

expression of negative feelings along with an increase in love. The fireworks of a mutually desired romantic sexual relationship seem to result from a complicated mixture of love, erotic activity, and conflict.

Does premarital sexual activity affect later sexual behavior? Some evidence suggests it may. People who have several sexual partners before marriage are most likely to express dissatisfaction with their marriages and to engage in extramarital sex (Athanasiou and Sarkin, 1974). Expectations about the role of sex in marriage and about the value of variety may also be altered by extensive premarital sex, though premarital petting does not seem to have

FIGURE 10-12 *COUPLE STATUS FIRST, THEN INTERCOURSE* Sexual involvement begins for most college couples only after they have "become a couple" or are considering becoming one.
Source: Based on data from Christopher and Cate, 1985.

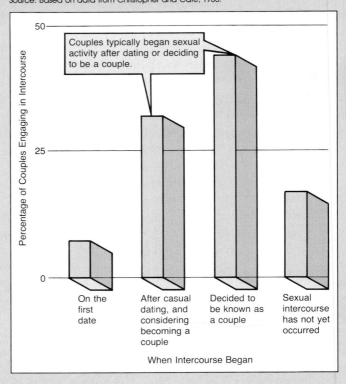

this same effect (Reevy, 1972). Cohabitation before marriage (discussed in Chapter 9) does not appear to influence later marriage either positively or negatively, but premarital pregnancy adds to the likelihood of divorce by interfering with the relationship and adding financial burdens (Furstenberg, 1976).

If the evidence to date were summarized simply, it might be said that the ability to get along with a partner and to communicate (Markman, 1981) are more important for later satisfaction than whether or not the couple decides to "do it."

■ Egocentrism versus Situation Ethics

Although the influences on our sexual values begin operating early in childhood, they affect our actual behavior some years later (Reiss and Miller, 1979; Singh and Forsyth, 1989). Meanwhile, other factors influence our sexual decision making.

Certain principles cut across cultural boundaries as influences on sexuality. Piaget described how, with increasing maturity, a child moves away from **egocentrism**. An egocentric view of the world is selfish, uncaring, and self-centered. Immaturity prevents an egocentric child from sharing, taking the perspective of another person, and behaving altruistically. Further development leads to **conventional moral reasoning**, in which feelings of empathy become more common. How do the differences between egocentrism and conventional moral reasoning apply to sexual decision making?

One possible answer is provided by philosophical formulations about moral behavior. In 1966, a Protestant minister named Joseph Fletcher formulated the moral philosophy known as **situation ethics**, reflecting the need to act out of concern for the welfare of others—something like the concept of agape discussed earlier. We can evaluate whether we are engaging in the most caring, ethical possible behavior by examining the immediate and long-term effects of our actions. An example of how situation ethics might operate would be to delay sexual intercourse until both partners are sure they want to add this dimension to their relationship, have discussed contraception and taken steps to prevent unwanted pregnancy, and have had medical examinations to ensure the absence of sexually transmissible diseases. Figure 10-13 illustrates an unhappy outcome that could have been prevented by adherence to situation ethics.

FIGURE 10-13 *LOVE ENDING IN SADNESS: WHAT CAN PREVENT IT?* Could this couple's distress have been prevented by thinking ahead and avoiding some of the known causes of a failed relationship? Current knowledge about sexual decision making and relationship-maintenance suggest that it may have been.

Fletcher's position has frequently been misinterpreted as "if it feels good, do it," but that message is actually consistent with egocentrism and a recreational orientation, *not* situation ethics. Fletcher emphasizes behaving in ways that are the most loving and best in the short- and long-term for each consenting participant. Situation ethics does, however, pose a valid problem. It is impossible for anyone to know with certainty all the potentially harmful effects of a given sexual interaction or how sexual desire and strong emotions may have affected his or her judgment (Nelson, 1978). In many instances—not only involving sex—we easily can persuade ourselves that we are acting for "good" reasons and not simply because we want to do a particular thing.

Jean Piaget, a Swiss developmental psychologist, introduced decision-making concepts that were consistent with Fletcher's position. Piaget distinguished two types of justice that define morality. **Retributive justice** consists of decisions based on the outcome of our actions, and we are motivated to avoid being punished. **Distributive justice** leads to moral judgments that depend on our intentions not to cause harm rather than to avoid punishment. People differ in the kind of justice that guides their actions. One person avoids premarital sex because his or her parents would strongly disapprove—behavior based on retributive justice. Another person avoids premarital sex because he or she wants sex only in the context of a close, loving relationship—behavior based on distributive justice. Notice that the behavior is the same in these examples, and both individuals refrain from having intercourse. Their reasons differ greatly, however, and this is the key to understanding the motivations underlying such sexual decision making.

■ **Responsibility and the Individual**

Kohlberg (1981, 1984) conceptualized moral reasoning as developing over a series of six stages, in-

TABLE 10-7 **Moral Reasoning at Each Stage of Development**

Six stages of moral reasoning about sexuality differ in the reasons people give for their behavior. Here, abortion is used as an example of the justifications typical of each stage.

	ORIENTATION OF THIS STAGE	*EXAMPLE OF REASONING*
Preconventional level		
Stage 1	Punishment and obdience: Avoid punishment, respect power	An unmarried, pregnant teenager should have an abortion because: . . . it would be a sin for her to have a baby.
Stage 2	Instrumental relativist: Satisfy one's own needs first	. . . having a baby now would ruin her life.
Conventional level		
Stage 3	Good boy–nice girl: Conformity and intention; do as others do, and mean no harm	An unmarried, pregnant teenager should have an abortion because: . . . she thought she loved her partner.
Stage 4	Law and order: Do your duty; keep social order	An unmarried, pregnant teenager should *not* have an abortion because: . . . it's taking life, even if it's right for her to have an abortion
Postconventional level		
Stage 5	Social-contract legalistic: Personal values should reflect prevailing laws	. . . getting married and giving birth wouldn't work. The next step would be a divorce.
Stage 6	Universal ethical principle: Self-chosen ethical principles use justice, reciprocity, and equality as ideals	. . . it's her and her boyfriend's responsibility to take the consequences and have the baby, maybe put it up for adoption.

Source: Based on data from Gilligan et al., 1970.

volving three levels. Table 10-7 suggests how these stages may apply to sexual problems (Gilligan et al., 1970). In the first, or **preconventional level of moral reasoning,** morality is egocentric, centering on pursuing pleasure and avoiding pain. In the second, or **conventional level of moral reasoning,** morality is characterized by conformity to law and order and adherence to rules set by authority figures. Although most adults remain at the second level, a few advance to the third, or **postconventional level of moral reasoning,** in which they seek solutions to moral problems based on universal ethical principles that are higher and more abstract than simple rules of right and wrong.

Changes in Moral Reasoning.   The ability to reason effectively about sexual issues changes dramatically in early adolescence. Between ages eleven and seventeen, conventional reasoning develops. Most eleven-year-olds believe that sexuality is procreational, thus ruling out sexual intercourse for teenagers; by age fifteen or sixteen most apply relational concepts that justify sexual pleasure as an expression of love (Schoof-Tams et al., 1976).

Whatever the sexual standards of teenagers, they may have difficulty planning ahead and effectively avoiding the problems that are frequently created by sexuality (Zabin et al., 1984).

Effects of Moral Reasoning on Sexual Decision Making.   Some evidence suggests that the sexual decision making of college students is related to their stage of moral reasoning, especially for men. Figure 10-14 shows that young men at stage 4, law and order, have significantly less sexual experience than young men at earlier or later stages. Both sexes at stage 4 also feel guilty about their sexual acts and expect to be punished for them (D'Augelli and Cross, 1975).

A moralistic stand on sexual issues, typical in stage 4, leads to condemning those who engage in socially disapproved behaviors (Reeder and Coovert, 1986). People in this stage also attempt to direct the behavior of others. Some evidence shows that sex

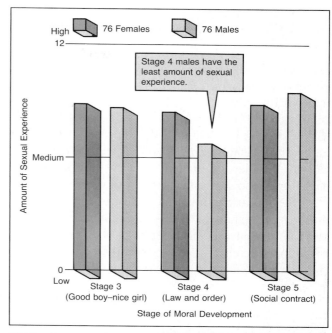

FIGURE 10-14 *MORAL DEVELOPMENT AND MALE SEXUAL EXPERIENCE* A man's sexual experience varies according to his stage of moral development. College men at Kohlberg's stage 4 are the least sexually experienced and those at stage 5, the most sexually experienced.
Source: Based on data from D'Augelli and Cross, 1975.

guilt contributes to this tendency. In an experiment, college women were asked to make a tape giving sexual advice to a thirteen-year-old girl who had just begun menstruating. Subjects high in sex guilt argued that premarital intercourse should be avoided whether or not two people were in love (Mendelsohn and Mosher, 1979). In a similar way, those with guilty and negative sexual attitudes tend to favor censorship and to advocate punishment for those who violate strict sexual standards (Fisher et al., 1988).

In sum, young people often feel confused and anxious in making sexual decisions because of the conflicting societal messages concerning sex. These decisions are also affected by the individual's egocentrism and level of moral reasoning (Forsyth and Nye, 1990). The best society can offer is to help increase awareness of the issues involved.

Summarizing the Information about Attraction and Love . . .

Interpersonal attraction is facilitated by **propinquity, positive affect,** and **need for affiliation.** Propinquity and positive affect set the stage for meeting and liking other people. Affiliation need varies across people and different types of situations. We are most likely to develop a friendship with someone who is physically attractive, similar to ourselves along various dimensions, and who expresses positive evaluations of us.

Sexual attraction leads to aesthetic, approach, and genital responses. The **sociobiological perspective on sexual attraction** stresses the possibility of evolutionary contributions to the process based on reproductive strategies. **Sexual pheromones** act as strong sources of attraction in various species.

Passionate love is an overpowering emotional response to another person. According to the **three-factor theory of passionate love,** the necessary conditions for this reaction are cultural expectations, the presence of an appropriate love object, and various types of emotional arousal interpreted as love. **Com-** **panionate love** refers to the closeness and emotional rewards characteristic of long-term, committed relationships. **Jealousy** often interferes with feelings of love. The deterioration of a love relationship is caused by disagreements, conflict, lack of commitment, dissimilarity, and boredom.

Society attempts to control sexuality through family and religious influences, but the effects of peers and the media may be even more important. Individuals develop **procreational, relational,** or **recreational orientations** to sexuality. **Egocentrism** contrasts with **conventional moral reasoning** in response to sexual issues. **Situation ethics** requires people to have a great deal of knowledge about the impact of their sexual behavior and to apply this knowledge appropriately. Kohlberg's theory of sexual moral reasoning includes three levels, the **preconventional, conventional,** and **postconventional,** and the level of each person's development affects what he or she does sexually.

To Find Out More about Attraction and Love . . .

Brehm, S. S. (1985). *Intimate relationships.* New York: Random House.

    This book describes how close relationships begin, thrive, and often falter. It contains a great deal of information about the factors that produce successful and unsuccessful relationships.

Fishkin, J. S. (1985). *Beyond subjective morality: Ethical reasoning and political philosophy.* New Haven, Conn.: Yale University Press.

    This book explores the philosophical issues behind moral reasoning and decision making. The author distinguishes between facts and feelings as the basis for morality.

Hatfield, E., & Sprecher, S. (1986). *Mirror, mirror. . . The importance of looks in everyday life.* Albany, NY: SUNY Press.

    An interesting review of research on the role of physical attractiveness in interpersonal relationships.

Hendrick, C. (Ed.). (1989). *Close relationships.* Newbury Park, CA: Sage.

    Several experts contributed chapters dealing with close friendships, romantic relationships, and marriage.

Hojat, M., & Crandall, R. (1989). *Loneliness: Theory, research, and applications.* Newbury Park, CA: Sage.

    A review and summary of what is known about loneliness and ways to relieve it.

Schwartz, R., & Schwartz, L. J. (1986). *Becoming a couple.* Lanham, Md.: University Press of America.

    The authors offer enlightening information about ways to improve communication between two partners. Relationships strengthen as couples openly discuss issues important to them.

Sternberg, R., & Barnes, M. L. (Eds.). (1988). *The psychology of love.* New Haven, CT: Yale University Press.

    Recent theories and research on love and relationships are discussed by a variety of investigators.

CHAPTER ELEVEN

TECHNIQUES
OF SEXUAL AROUSAL

In the past, masturbation was often viewed as a sinful act stemming from impure thoughts or as a threat to one's health and sanity. We now know that self-stimulation is practiced by most males and females; masturbation is not only harmless, but it constitutes a safe, uncomplicated way to learn about one's sexuality and to experience sexual pleasure. As a young married woman describes in the following account, relatively recent inventions such as vibrators may enhance arousal and provide intense, reliable orgasms.

This whole topic still makes me blush, but I guess it's safe enough to tell my story if no one knows who I am. Tom and I had been married for almost ten years and never once had I experienced a real orgasm with him. We had intercourse many, many times, and everything he did felt nice. From his reactions, though, I knew that his orgasms were something extra special—something that just wasn't part of my own sex life. I read novels that described women whose climaxes were soul-shattering events, but that sure wasn't what happened to me. Tom and I never talked about it, and I learned to moan and sigh at the right time.

Most often, our lovemaking just starts with him touching me and me touching him briefly, followed by intercourse with him on top. When he finishes, I pretend to, and that's the end of it. When we try oral sex, it's just a quick preliminary to intercourse. Let me say again that sex was always a positive thing. I just never reached a climax. When I thought about it, our sex life impressed me as being a little strange, but still it didn't seem to be much of a problem.

Everything changed last year when some of my friends from college decided to have a "women only" reunion just before Christmas. Each person bought one present to put under the tree, and we each picked out one of the gifts at random. Most gifts were jokes of some kind, and I ended up with one that got a big laugh. It was in a box labeled "A GIRL'S BEST FRIEND." Inside was an electric vibrator. I must have looked startled when I unwrapped it, and this set them off—saying things like "now you can give Tom a rest," "that will hit the spot," and so on.

I didn't know what to say but tried to be a good sport. I took the gift home, didn't say anything about it to Tom, and put it away in a dresser drawer. Then, one afternoon, a couple of months later, I spent the day in bed because I had a cold. For some reason, I was feeling kind of sexy, and I thought about the vibrator. I took it out, plugged it into the wall socket by the bed and began rubbing it around my legs and abdomen. When I finally touched myself between my legs, it was like nothing I ever felt before. It sent shivers all through my body and pushed me to my first real orgasm in about a minute. All at once I realized why other people thought that sex was so great. That afternoon, I did it over and over and must have had a dozen climaxes. I only stopped when I was too tired to do it again.

One of these days I'm going to share my secret with Tom—if I can figure out how to bring up the subject without upsetting him. In the meantime, I just look forward to having opportunities to play with my new toy.

Elaine, age 29

There are many ways to create sexual arousal—methods vary, different parts of the body can be the focus, and people differ in what they enjoy as well as in what they accept as appropriate. As Elaine discovered, some forms of stimulation are more effective than others. Despite the variations, the end result should be excitement, pleasure, and orgasm. If you are curious about the kinds of sexual activities most preferred by males and females, Table 11-1 presents the results of one survey (Gerber, 1982).

Among the most personal, private, and often embarrassing aspects of sexuality is *masturbation*. In this chapter, we discuss how males and females practice this very common sexual act alone, as partners engaged in petting, and with the help of such devices as vibrators. We present some of the details of *intercourse* as well as oral and anal sexual practices. The very important role of *sexual fantasy* in eliciting arousal is emphasized. Special sections concentrate on *sexual signals,* the *meaning of touch,* and techniques of *oral-genital stimulation* that can increase the enjoyment of both partners.

Masturbation and Petting

Masturbation is the stimulation of a person's own genitals, most often using the hand but sometimes with various objects. Such stimulation initiates the various stages of the sexual response cycle from arousal to orgasm. Sometimes the term *solo masturbation* is used to distinguish this activity from interpersonal masturbation in which at least two individuals are masturbating simultaneously and mutual masturbation (really petting) in which partners caress each other's genitals.

TABLE 11-1 **These Are a Few of My Favorite Things**

A survey of heterosexual subjects yielded the ten sexual activities most preferred by women and those most preferred by men. Despite some sex differences, males and females generally agree that oral sex and intercourse in a variety of positions are enjoyable. These acts are discussed in some detail in the remainder of this chapter. Note that the data deal with preferences, not necessarily with descriptions of what the respondents regularly do. For example, both males and females give high ratings to sexual interactions with two members of the opposite sex, but very few people have had such an experience even once in their lives (Hunt, 1974); therefore it seems likely that the subjects are indicating a fantasy theme about group sex rather than reflecting their actual experiences with group sex.

SEXUAL ACTIVITIES MOST PREFERRED BY HETEROSEXUAL WOMEN	*SEXUAL ACTIVITIES MOST PREFERRED BY HETEROSEXUAL MEN*
1. Gentle cunnilingus by a male partner, concentrating on the clitoris	**1.** Fellatio to orgasm
2. Gentle stimulation of the clitoris by the male's finger	**2.** Sexual intercourse in a variety of changing positions
3. Sexual intercourse on top of a man	**3.** Engaging in a variety of sexual activities with two women
4. Sexual intercourse in a variety of changing positions	**4.** Petting a woman's breast
5. Engaging in mutual oral-genital sex with a male partner (69)	**5.** Anal intercourse with a woman
6. Massaging a man all over	**6.** Engaging in mutual oral-genital sex with a female partner (69)
7. Masturbating a man	**7.** Performing mild sadomasochistic acts on a woman
8. Being petted, kissed, and stimulated manually and orally by two men, followed by intercourse with one man while being caressed by the other	**8.** Being masturbated by a woman
9. Masturbating	**9.** Performing cunnilingus
10. Performing fellatio	**10.** Masturbating

Source: Gerber, 1982.

■ **Female Masturbation**

Although masturbation is an extremely common activity for females, it occurs less generally and less frequently than among males, and it also is less likely to result in orgasm than is true for males. A major reason for these sex differences rests on cultural beliefs and attitudes about male versus female sexuality. Anatomical differences also may make it more likely for males than for females spontaneously to discover the pleasures of self-stimulation.

Attitudes about Masturbation.   Chapters 7 and 8 discuss the importance of attitudes about masturbation and how they develop as a function of childhood and adolescent experiences. For women, positive attitudes about masturbation are associated with regularly reaching orgasm when they masturbate (Bentler and Peeler, 1979). For both men and women, negative expectations, guilt, and belief in various myths about the practice can prevent the full enjoyment of the sexual excitement and pleasure associated with genital self-stimulation. For example, in Egypt, masturbation is known as "39" because it is believed to be 39 times more exhausting than any other sexual activity (Kalem, 1975).

Female Methods of Masturbation.   The most common technique is to stimulate the genitals manually, concentrating on the clitoral area. Almost half (48 percent) of the subjects studied by Masters et al. (1985) used this technique. Other techniques were practiced by only a small minority (10 percent or less) of the subjects—stimulation by the stream of water in a pulsating shower, alternately tensing and relaxing the thigh muscles to put pressure on the clitoris, and the insertion of blunt objects such as a dildo into the vagina.

Among 100 female undergraduates, masturbation was reported to occur most often in the position shown in Figure 11-1, with orgasm usually resulting. Orgasm was most likely to occur when the woman lay flat on her back, used her fingers to stroke around and on the clitoris, and tensed her body's muscles as excitement rose (Clifford, 1978). The side of the clitoris, its hood, or the clitoris itself is lightly rubbed. Pressure on the mons and gentle tugs on the labia also deliver pleasurable sensations to the clitoris. Females having the most consistent pattern of orgasms reported involuntary hip motion, producing pelvic rocking.

Most females (81 percent) who experience orgasm during masturbation engage in self-stimulation on a regular basis; among women who do not reach orgasm, only half masturbate regularly (Myers et al., 1983). In other words, orgasm is most likely to occur when it is consistently reinforced.

FIGURE 11-1 *FEMALE MASTURBATION* As reported by a group of 100 undergraduates (Clifford, 1978), females reach orgasm most often by masturbating while lying down.

FIGURE 11-2 *MALE MASTURBATION* Male masturbation (whether lying down, sitting, or standing) most often consists of using the hand to stroke up and down the penile shaft until orgasm occurs.

■ Male Masturbation

Most males (82 percent) use one primary method of masturbation, manual stimulation of the penis (Hite, 1981). Another 15 percent rub against the bed while lying on their stomachs. Others use miscellaneous methods such as thigh pressure, pulsating water, and (for those sufficiently limber) oral stimulation of their own penises. Figure 11-2 depicts the most common male masturbatory technique.

Males usually begin masturbating with slow strokes up and down the shaft. Some males initiate the act by pulling their penises away from their bodies to produce an erection. Many find that the use of a lubricant (petroleum jelly, baby oil, and the like) smooths masturbatory friction and enhances sexual pleasure (Zilbergeld, 1978). For some men, using the other hand for anal stimulation adds to the excitement.

Once the penis is fully erect, the strokes usually increase in speed and concentrate more on the glans. Sometimes the glans itself is too sensitive for such stimulation, so the male concentrates on the ridge just below it. Stimulation usually speeds up as orgasm is approached. During ejaculation, some either slow their strokes or stop it altogether; others firmly hold the penis at this point. After orgasm, stimulation usually ceases because it then becomes uncomfortable. There are obviously no rules about how a male

should masturbate. Some prefer light, slow strokes while others enjoy fast, vigorous ones; still others use different styles on different occasions (Barbach, 1978).

■ Petting: Stimulating a Partner

When sexual behavior involves a partner, interpersonal considerations are added to the relatively uncomplicated situation involving sexual desire, self-stimulation, and orgasm. In such an interaction, two individuals have to communicate in some way to indicate that they are mutually interested in sex. The special section, ***Highlighting Research,*** on pages 286 to 287, describes the process of sexual signaling.

Petting: Light and Heavy. Once an interaction is initiated by one partner and accepted by the other, the two individuals are likely to touch one another— holding hands, dancing, placing an arm around the shoulder, gentle patting, and so on. When such contact is designed to stimulate the other person sexually, it is called **petting**. Above the waist, this stimulation has been labeled *necking.* "Light" petting is aimed simply at arousal; "heavy" petting has the goal of inducing orgasm.

A bodily area that, when stroked or kissed, elicits feelings of sexual excitement is called an **eroge-**

Highlighting Research

SEXUAL SIGNALING

How do people initiate a relationship that can potentially develop into a romantic and perhaps sexual interaction? Among the most obvious are direct methods such as asking someone for a date or placing an advertisement in a magazine or newspaper (Lynn and Bolig, 1985). Usually, men initiate contact, though they are pleased when women play the initiator role (Kelley et al., 1981).

Besides these direct, overt actions, both sexes use **sexual signals** to communicate interest in each other. These signals, in-volving behavior and appearance, inform the other person of sexual attraction and interest. For example, smiling, eye contact, and interpersonal touch can serve this function. Males and females differ, however, in how they respond to given behaviors in the opposite sex. In a study of video dating, males were found to dislike expressive, extraverted females, whereas females responded positively to these characteristics in males (Riggio and Woll, 1984). Between married partners, complaints are least when clear signals are sent by each individual and accurately interpreted by the other (Sabatelli et al., 1986).

People who wear revealing clothing may be sending sexual signals—sometimes intentionally, sometimes not. Males, especially, interpret what a female is wearing in this way (Goodchilds and Zellman, 1984). For example, men may assume that a low-cut blouse means that the woman is seeking sexual activity.

What people talk about or where they go can also signal a sexual goal. For example, taking a date to a secluded, private

---

TABLE 11-2 **How Females Signal Sexual Interest in a Male**

Females use a variety of proceptive strategies as sexual signals, indicating their sexual interest in a specific male. Some of the strategies are subtle and some are quite direct.

PROCEPTIVE STRATEGIES USED BY FEMALES

1. VERBAL Talking about sexual or romantic feelings, except love. Examples: Sexy talk, conversation about nonsexual topics, compliments, laughing, or overtly suggesting a sexual interaction.
Percentage of Subjects Using This 57.3

2. ENVIRONMENTAL OR SITUATIONAL Selecting an appropriate social setting or other physical cues. Examples: Invitation to visit one's apartment, wearing sexy clothing, drinking alcohol, playing music, dancing.
Percentage of Subjects Using This 37.6

3. NONVERBAL Acting in ways not involving words. Examples: Making eye contact, kissing.
Percentage of Subjects Using This 13.7 to 21.4

4. CONTINGENCY Signaling interest and indicating the expected response. Examples: Snuggling next to male who is then supposed to put his arm around her, encouraging a shy male to react to her hints, telling the male she likes him.
Percentage of Subjects Using This 6.0 to 41.9

5. NO ASSERTION Spontaneously occurring sexual activity. Example: Influencing the male without using sexual signals.
Percentage of Subjects Using This 29.1

6. SEXUAL LIMITATION Permitting interactions not including intercourse. Example: Engaging only in kissing or petting.
Percentage of Subjects Using This 25.6

7. PREVIOUS EXPERIENCE Telling the male about her other sexual experiences. Examples: Describing how she has seduced other males, saying she has never done this before.
Percentage of Subjects Using This 24.0

8. MASCULINE SEXUAL INITIATIVE Giving the male the responsibility for initiating sexual activity. Example: Male progresses toward increasingly intimate contact, and she does not raise objections.
Percentage of Subjects Using This 14.5

Source: Based on data from Perper and Weis, 1987.

place may be perceived as an invitation to sex; agreeing to go there may be perceived as accepting the sexual invitation. Someone who talks about sex (for example, revealing a considerable amount of past sexual experience) can appear to be coming on to his or her date (Tavris and Wade, 1984).

One difficulty with indirect signals is that our society has no agreed-upon set of rules that everyone follows. A smile, eye contact, a touch on the arm, a low-cut blouse, an invitation to coffee in your apartment, self-disclosure about one's sexual past, or whatever may *not* represent an invitation to intimacy. When there is miscommunication between males and females, problems—such as date rape—may result. It would help, of course, if we could learn to say clearly what we mean rather than using unreliable and easily misunderstood signs and signals.

Sexual signals are employed not only to encourage contact with another person but also to discourage the other person (Graverholz and Serpe, 1985). Perper and Weis (1987) have investigated the **proceptive** (encouraging) and **rejective** (discouraging) **strategies** used by female undergraduates. Subjects wrote essays describing how they would seduce a male and also how they would communicate rejection. Sexual interest was conveyed in eight major ways, using proceptive strategies. Table 11-2 describes these strategies.

Only two major themes were reflected in rejective strategies. When a male is perceived as totally unattractive, complete rejection is communicated by avoiding or ignoring him. Such a rejection is usually not communicated honestly. Instead, the female makes up reasons for not going out with the male, using excuses such as having to study, being previously committed to other plans, or even inventing a nonexistent relationship with another male (Folkes, 1982). The response to some males, in contrast, is incomplete rejection—the female attempts to continue the relationship as a nonsexual one. She may say that she is not ready for an intimate involvement with him or that she likes him as a friend, though she does not love him.

Being rejected by a member of the opposite sex is a common experience. Among undergraduates, 72 percent of the males and 45 percent of the females report having been rejected by someone of the opposite sex (Folkes, 1982). Because males most often take the initiative in such interactions, they experience more rejection than females.

nous zone. Any portion of your body can be an erogenous zone if you interpret it as sexual. Besides the obvious responsiveness of the genitals, nipples, and lips, commonly identified erogenous zones are the face, neck, thighs, hands, feet, arms, and legs. Slow, gentle stroking, kissing, or licking are most likely to be used as sexual stimulation, though a firm touch can be more arousing to some people (Jeffress, 1982). Such contact usually creates positive feelings between consenting partners. Touch indicates caring and affection (Kourany, 1983). One familiar response to this stimulation is "goose flesh" or "goose bumps," caused by the contraction of tiny muscles that cause body hairs to straighten—the same response can be brought about by strong emotions such as fear or elation and also by cold temperature.

Whether or not petting progresses to genital manipulation and orgasm, the pleasure of touching and being touched contributes to feelings of sexual satisfaction (Procci, 1981).

Foreplay: When Petting Is a Prelude to Intercourse. Because society places a great deal of emphasis on intercourse and orgasm, the term **foreplay** is used to refer to petting that is primarily a prelude to more intimate sexual interaction.

Though the importance of foreplay may be overlooked, especially by males, it should be considered as an integral part of sexual behavior (Witkin, 1983). For example, some women stimulate their breasts when they masturbate and enjoy having a partner do the same during intercourse. When manipulation of the breast or nipple is too rough, women may find it painful and react negatively. Breast sensitivity increases as ovulation or menstruation approaches because of increased water retention during these phases of the menstrual cycle.

The breasts and nipples of males also are erotically sensitive, though some men reject being caressed there because they mistakenly interpret such behavior as reflecting negatively on their masculinity.

Sometimes, sexual partners bite one another's necks or bodies, leaving bruise marks known as hickeys. Others scratch or pinch. One purpose of these behaviors is to create signs of "ownership" on the partner's body. For some, minor injuries heighten sexual arousal (Jeffress, 1981b). Less erotic is the fact that broken skin can become the site of an infection (Ericsson, 1983).

Men are sometimes puzzled as to how best to stimulate the clitoris. Many women prefer indirect clitoral stimulation—making contact with the surrounding area—rather than direct, vigorous, and sometimes painful manipulation of the clitoris itself (Perlmutter, 1981). For many women, gentle stimulation of the labia or mons is exciting. Also, the clitoral shaft can be stroked gently, with one finger on each side. Another possibility is to insert one or two fingers (with smoothly trimmed fingernails) gently into the outer third of the vagina (James, 1982d). For maximum pleasure, the woman should tell her partner her preferences as to location, speed, and the amount of pressure applied. She may, for example, prefer to delay vaginal stimulation until later, when sufficient lubrication and muscle relaxation make it more pleasurable.

To stimulate a male manually, his partner can use the same techniques that he himself uses for masturbation. Without feedback, the other person can easily cause pain with a rough approach to the penis and scrotum or, in the opposite extreme, stimulate him too timidly and lightly in an effort to avoid causing discomfort. Both partners need to communicate clearly their sexual likes and dislikes in order to enhance their mutual pleasure.

The longer a couple spends engaged in foreplay, the more likely it is that the woman will experience an orgasm (Gebhard, 1966). Among married couples, after twenty-one minutes of foreplay, only 8 percent of wives failed to have an orgasm during the subsequent sexual interaction. With ten minutes of foreplay, 60 percent did not have an orgasm (Brewer, 1981; Kroop, 1983).

More about the meaning of touch and about sex differences in responding to it is provided in the special section, ***Taking Responsibility and Protecting Yourself,*** on pages 288 to 289.

Taking Responsibility and Protecting Yourself

THE MEANING OF TOUCH

Research indicates that touch plays an important role in communication. For example, touch can signal intimacy, dominance, and playfulness (Thayer, 1986).

Many studies of nonverbal communication are conducted in nonsexual contexts, and the findings are somewhat surprising. For example, when a waitress touches a customer in a restaurant, tipping increases (Crusco and Wetzel, 1984). When a stranger conducting an experiment touches a subject, he or she is more likely

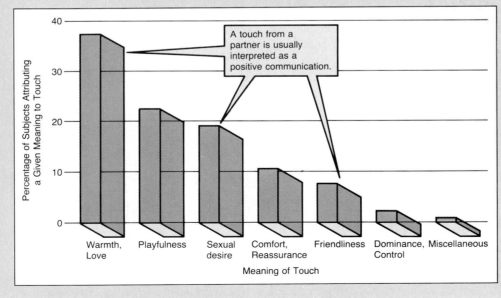

FIGURE 11-3 *REACH OUT AND TOUCH SOMEONE* Touching one's partner can convey any of several meanings. A group of 187 female and 50 male undergraduates described how they typically interpreted thirty-one different kinds of touch (such as stroking the partner's knee) by an opposite-sex partner. Similar meanings were reported by both sexes, and the meanings were not affected by which partner did the touching.
Source: Based on data in Pisano, Wall, and Foster, 1986.

to provide help to the experimenter when asked (Patterson et al., 1986). When a librarian touches a student checking out books, the student evaluates the library more positively (Fisher et al., 1976). It seems clear than a friendly touch from a stranger has positive interpersonal effects. From the time we are born, we need to be touched, hugged, and patted—such interpersonal contact remains physically and psychologically important throughout our lives (Goleman, 1988; Rubenstein, 1990).

Men and women differ in the use of touch and in their response to it. Women are found to touch both sexes more often than men do (Stier and Hall, 1984). Males especially avoid touching other males, presumably to avoid any sign of intimacy with their own gender (Patterson et al., 1981). Same-sex touching is perceived to be more acceptable to both men and women who express feminine rather than masculine attitudes and who think in relatively tolerant, nonauthoritarian ways (Larsen and LeRoux, 1984).

Touch between long-term partners frequently takes on special meaning. Married couples are more positive about touching one another than are single individuals about touching their dates or fiancés (Nguyen et al., 1976). Loving, sexual, pleasant, and friendly feelings are conveyed by touch more often between spouses than between single individuals in a relationship.

In romantic relationships among college students, touch is perceived as a message of warmth and love to a much greater extent than as a message of dominance or control (Pisano et al., 1986). Figure 11-3 illustrates some meanings given to touch between male–female partners. Even the kind of touch that would seem to express dominance (such as gently punching a partner's arm or lightly slapping his or her bottom) is usually interpreted as playfulness. Intimate friends seem to believe that a friendly, pleasurable touch is a positive sign.

■ Sexual Technology: Vibrators and Other Erotic Toys

One characteristic of human beings is to attempt to maximize sexual pleasure by incorporating a wide array of devices into their sexual activities. In recent years, one of the most popular inventions has been the vibrator—used either alone or with a partner.

Positive and Negative Effects of Vibrators. Vibrators come in various shapes and sizes; some are battery operated while others have electric cords and plug into wall sockets. See Figure 11-4 for examples of different models. All vibrate relatively rapidly, and some models permit variations in speed.

Among females who masturbate regularly, approximately one out of four uses an electric vibrator

FIGURE 11-4 *VIBRATOR SEX* Vibrators used for masturbation produce intense stimulation and are the most reliable source of orgasm for women.

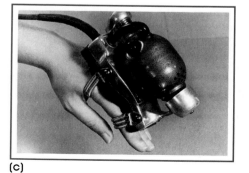

(a)

(b)

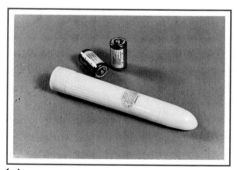

(c)

(d)

at least part of the time. Males, in contrast, usually report that the sensation is too intense, and they are less likely to use these devices.

Most women report that their sexual arousal and sexual pleasure in response to a vibrator is more intense than in response to any other kind of sexual stimulation (Masters and Johnson, 1970). The second most intense response among women is caused by manual stimulation of the genitals, followed by cunnilingus. Vaginal intercourse is the least satisfactory means of stimulation. As the cartoon in Figure 11-5 suggests, women frequently perceive their experiences with a vibrator as more exciting than intercourse with a male.

Masters and Johnson (1970) found that male arousal levels were unaffected by the kind of stimula-

FIGURE 11-5 *INTERCOURSE VERSUS VIBRATORS AS A SOURCE OF PLEASURE* *Women rank intercourse in fourth place behind vibrator masturbation, manual masturbation, and cunnilingus as a source of excitement, pleasure, and satisfaction (Masters & Johnson, 1970). As this cartoon suggests, males may be surprised and threatened when they learn about female preferences.*
Reproduced by Special Permission of Playboy Magazine:
Copyright © 1989 by Playboy.

"It's a beautiful honeymoon, dear, but I still miss my vibrator."

tion. That is, for men, intercourse, masturbation, and fellatio were equally positive sources of excitement and pleasure. Men's ability to have pleasure in a variety of ways coupled with the common belief that women like nothing better than having a penis inserted in their vaginas indicate why women's relatively low evaluation of intercourse is a surprise to men. For this reason, it may be helpful for males to understand why their partners rank intercourse in last place as a source of sexual pleasure and arousal.

As the next section indicates, clitoral stimulation produced by penile thrusting during intercourse usually is insufficient to produce orgasm. A woman can experience more pleasure during intercourse if foreplay is prolonged, manual stimulation of the clitoris (by either partner) is incorporated into the sexual act, or if the clitoris is stimulated by a vibrator. Each of these activities increases the woman's pleasure and the likelihood of her having an orgasm during intercourse.

Two possible negative side effects of using a vibrator should be noted. First, though the uterine contractions caused by the vibrator's intense stimulation are highly pleasurable to many women, it creates painful spasms in others. Second, once a woman becomes accustomed to the intensity of a vibrator, she may become less responsive to and less excited by the slower, gentler stimulation of a hand, penis, or mouth. Her threshold for stimulation changes, so that orgasms occur primarily (or perhaps exclusively) in response to a vibrator. If this preference is perceived as a problem by either the woman or her partner, a solution is to wean herself from the electrical device or to combine it with interpersonal stimulation, thus reversing or reducing the earlier negative effect of the vibrator on her responsivity.

Other Erotic Toys and Variations.   A familiar theme of jokes and literature is the negative effect of marriage on a couple's sexual interaction. Some data do in fact support this stereotype. For example, Ann Landers (1989) asked her readers if their sex life had deteriorated after marriage. Of the more than 140,000 men and women who responded to that question, 82 percent reported that sex after marriage was less exciting than sex before marriage. The most frequently used terms in describing marital sex were *boring, dull, monotonous,* and *routine.*

One possible solution to this problem is to add variety to the sexual interaction. Couples frequently experiment with **sexual aids** such as those shown in Figure 11-6. Such toys by themselves will not improve a dysfunctional or unsatisfying relationship, but they can add to or "spice up" a relatively satisfying sex life. For this reason, there are firms specializing in the distribution of feathers, crotchless underwear, dildos, flavored lubricants, special pillows to affect pelvic positions during intercourse, and countless additional items.

Some erotic devices have negative physical effects. For example, "Ben-wa balls" are made of metal or plastic and are inserted in the vagina to stimulate the woman as she goes about her daily activities. If these balls remain in place for more than a brief time, the result may be a high and sometimes harmful level of blood congestion within the pelvis. Even more dangerous is the "cock ring" placed around the penis. This device is designed to prevent blood from draining out of the penis, thereby prolonging erection. It can, however, cause a type of congestion known as priapism (discussed in more detail in Chapter 16).

Variety in sexual activity also can be provided in ways that do not involve objects or products. Even a minor change in the routine pattern of sexual interaction can help alleviate boredom. Couples may try different settings, such as having sex in the warm water of a shower or a hot tub (Weinberg, 1984), or leaving the lights on (for those who usually engage in sex in the dark) or turning them off (for those who usually have sex in a brightly lighted room) (Coley, 1980).

Additionally, partners can vary the sounds they make during sex. A partner's moans, groans, and cries of pleasure (peaking at orgasm) can be stimulating to both men and women (Ruefli, 1981). These sounds encourage the other partner and let him or her know that pleasure is being experienced. Humans are not alone in accompanying sex with vocalizations. For example, dominant male baboons and gibbons shriek, growl, and smack their lips during intercourse; less powerful males have intercourse quietly (Hamilton and Arrowood, 1978). Some men and women find it sexually exciting to "talk dirty" or even shout obscenities as they interact sexually (Roth, 1981). For variety, noisy partners might try a quieter style, and silent partners might experiment with an

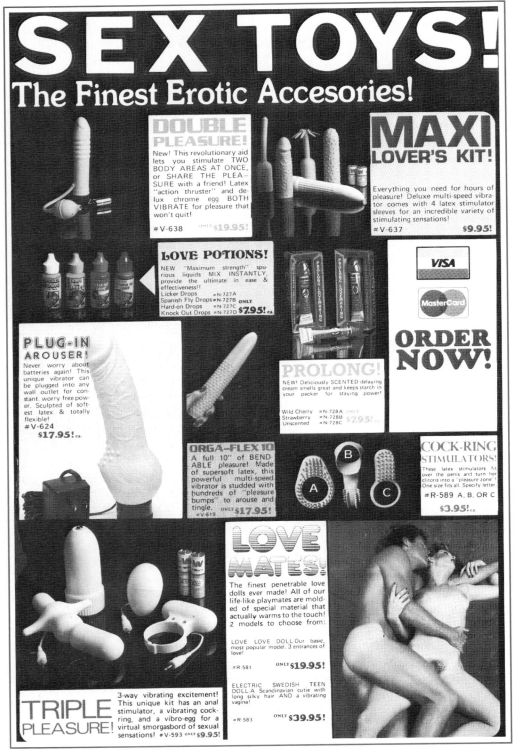

FIGURE 11-6 *SEX—WITH A LITTLE HELP FROM TECHNOLOGY* Couples sometimes enhance their sexual experiences with one or more devices and products including erotic clothing, condoms that provide extra stimulation for the female, vibrators, cock rings, and life-size erotic dolls.

occasional groan. The underlying message is to avoid routine interactions in which sex becomes monotonous and predictable.

Intercourse and Beyond

In ongoing sexual relationships, the most common forms of sexual interaction are genital-genital intercourse and oral-genital stimulation.

■ Vaginal Intercourse

Sexual intercourse is ordinarily defined as the penetration of a vagina by a penis. Because sexual intercourse also can occur with other types of penetration of a body opening by a penis, the specific act is sometimes labeled as **vaginal intercourse. Anal intercourse** refers to the penis penetrating the anus, and **oral-genital intercourse** indicates that the penis penetrates the mouth.

The penis also can be placed within and between other portions of a partner's body, permitting **foration. Interfemoral foration** refers to the friction created when the penis thrusts between the female's inner thighs without penetration of the vagina or anus. **Intermammary foration** occurs when the penis is placed in the cleavage between the partner's breasts. **Interaxial foration** consists of sliding the penis in and out of the partner's armpit, between the arm and the side of the body.

Duration of Intercourse.   A frequent question raised by sexual partners involves intercourse duration. How long does it usually last, and how long *should* it last in order to give both partners the best chance for sexual satisfaction?

In interviews conducted by the Kinsey investigators between 1938 and 1963, males reported that intercourse lasted 5.5 to 7 minutes, whereas females reported it as lasting a full minute less (Levitt, 1980). Pre-intercourse petting is reported to last another 10 to 11 minutes (Huey et al., 1981), so the entire interaction seems to have a duration of about 14.5 to 18 minutes.

Because few people carry stopwatches to bed, it can be assumed that these times are simply subjective estimates. On the basis of other research, we know that people are not very accurate in estimating the passage of time involving sexual interactions. For example, when medical students were shown explicit sexual films and afterward asked how long petting and intercourse lasted, the females in the study perceived longer durations than did the males, and neither were precisely correct (Levitt, 1983).

As Figure 11-7 shows, in a sample of happily married couples, female orgasm tends not to occur when intercourse lasts less than one minute. Beyond the one-minute point, however, these wives said that orgasm occurred during almost every act of intercourse. Women reported the highest frequency of orgasm when intercourse lasted more than eleven minutes (LoPiccolo and LoPiccolo, 1978).

Except for vaginal intercourse lasting less than sixty seconds, clitoral stimulation is more critical than intercourse duration in determining the probability of female orgasm. The location and size of the clitoris, the position of the shaft, and the prominence of the woman's mons pubis all affect whether clitoral stimulation is provided by penile thrusting. Some intercourse positions permit the male's pubic area to press the clitoris, either constantly or intermittently, but other positions do not (Hite, 1976). Lesbian couples understand this, as indicated by the practice of **tribadism,** in which one female lies on top of the other, face-to-face, thrusting and grinding her pelvis against her partner's, providing clitoral stimulation for both. For heterosexual couples, the penis is, of course, stimulated by contact with the vagina, but the clitoris may be left out of the process. One or both partners can nevertheless provide the necessary stimulation as discussed earlier (Kroop, 1982).

■ Positions of Intercourse: Basic Patterns and Cross-Cultural Variations

The Indian sex manual, the *Kaama Suutra,* describes 529 positions for the sexual union of a male and female. Before you try to imagine what they are, note that most of them consist of minor variations in the location and angle of limbs, heads, and bodies. For most people in the Western, industrialized na-

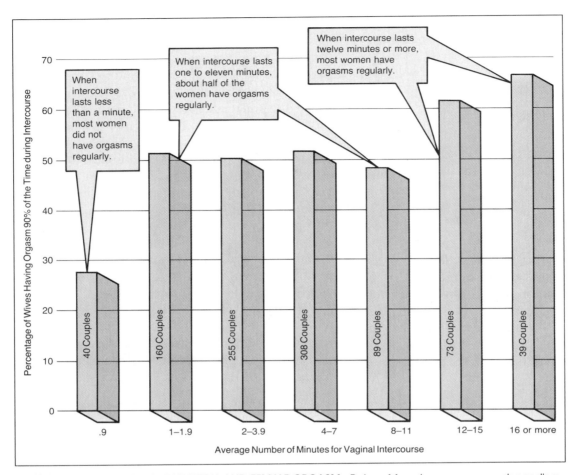

FIGURE 11-7 *INTERCOURSE DURATION AND FEMALE ORGASM*   Rates of female orgasm vary, depending on the duration of vaginal intercourse. Most couples report that intercourse lasts from 2 to 3.9 minutes (26 percent of the subjects) or 4 to 7 minutes (31 percent of the subjects).
Source: Based on data from LoPiccolo and LoPiccolo, 1978.

tions, it is probably more realistic to consider five basic positions (with a few variations for each).

Male-Superior Positions. The word *superior* here simply means "above"; in a similar way, Lake Superior is so named because it is located *above* the other four Great Lakes. The woman lies on her back and spreads her legs apart while the man lies on top of her. This position illustrated in Figure 11-8, is the most popular in the United States. Preference for it has persisted at least since the 1940s when Kinsey et al. (1948) documented American sexual practices. Then, one in ten couples reported using *only* this position for intercourse. By the time of Hunt's (1974) survey, married couples varied their intercourse posi-

tions much more than was true for previous generations, but the male-superior position remained the most popular.

A major advantage of this position is that the partners face one another during intercourse, permitting eye contact and kissing. Also, the male has control over his pelvic movements and can provide extra stimulation to the clitoris by moving his penis back and forth or in a circular fashion within the vagina (Coleman, 1979). This position also increases the chance of conception, because semen is deposited near the cervix. For many, it also is regarded as the most "acceptable" way to have intercourse (Allgeier and Fogel, 1978). Presumably, a major reason for its

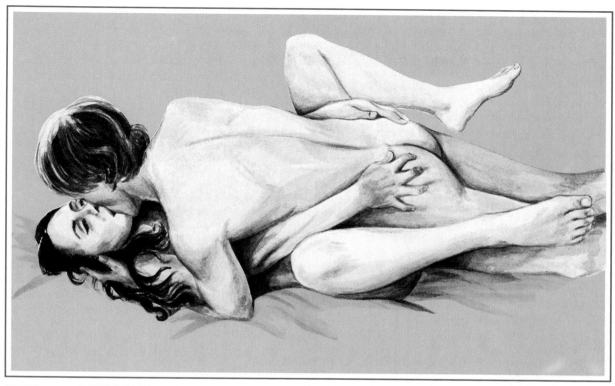

FIGURE 11-8 *MALE-SUPERIOR POSITION: NUMBER ONE IN OUR CULTURE* The male-superior position for vaginal intercourse allows for face-to-face contact between partners. Couples in the United States typically perceive this as the most acceptable position for sexual interaction.

acceptability is the fact that the male is positioned to dominate the interaction, a role considered "natural and proper" by many.

Several disadvantages are associated with the male-superior position. When it—or any other position—is used exclusively, repetition can result in a decrease in excitement and satisfaction. Also, because the male must support his weight on his arms and shoulders, the energy required for this can make it more difficult for him to control the timing of his ejaculation (Tordjman, 1978). For this reason, sex therapists frequently recommend other intercourse positions. A third problem arises if the male does not support himself but rests his entire weight on his partner; the resultant pain and discomfort for the female interferes with her enjoyment, especially if the man is much heavier than his partner. As discussed in Chapter 4, this position is not recommended after the first trimester of pregnancy. When the man lies above the woman, it interferes with her ability to control her pelvic movements. She finds it difficult to change the location or intensity of stimulation to her vagina or clitoris. Finally, manual stimulation of the clitoris is difficult for either partner in this position.

Note that some variety is possible even for couples who restrict themselves to this one position. When the woman's legs are placed between the man's, his penis is held snugly, and is stimulated by her thighs even when partially withdrawn from the vagina between thrusts. Another variation is for the woman to flex her legs toward her chest, causing the penis to penetrate her vagina more deeply. If she raises her legs over her partner's shoulders, penetration becomes even deeper. This may be a positive factor if the male's penis is short relative to the length of the vagina; otherwise, deep penetration may be painful to some women. The pain can be relieved by placing a pillow under her hips; the extra elevation also makes conception slightly less likely (Sloan, 1983). Though most women do not like the feelings caused by the penis stretching the ligaments holding the uterus, some find the movement of their abdominal organs pleasurable (Kroop, 1981b).

Female-Superior Positions. The reverse of the previous position is illustrated in Figure 11-9. The female is above the male, or "superior," and she can lie against him or sit upright. Three fourths of U.S. couples use this intercourse position part of the time. Younger couples are more likely to use it than older ones, presumably because negative reactions to the implication of female dominance are decreasing. One variation involves the female facing the opposite direction, with her back toward the male's head.

One advantage of having the female "on top" is that she can gauge whether her lubrication and relaxation have progressed far enough for penetration to be pleasurable. This position also allows her to con-trol her own pelvic rocking, including its tempo, and the man can participate in the thrusting as well. The woman can raise her torso to a sitting position and use her legs to move herself up and down on the shaft of the penis. By controlling intercourse, she is able to confine penetration and friction to the outer third of her vagina where there is maximum sensitivity.

If she lies down on her partner, the woman may flex her legs toward her chest for a looser grip on the penis or straighten them, especially if placed between the man's legs, to provide tighter pressure on his sexual organ. This tighter grip is generally perceived as positive, especially when the erect penis seems a little small for the expanded vagina (Croft, 1978).

A negative feature is that the woman has to support her own weight with her arms, unless she is light enough simply to rest on her partner (Croft, 1978). Some men (and some women, too) react negatively to

FIGURE 11-9 *FEMALE-SUPERIOR POSITION: PUTTING THE WOMAN IN THE DRIVER'S SEAT* The female-superior intercourse position allows her to control the pelvic movements.

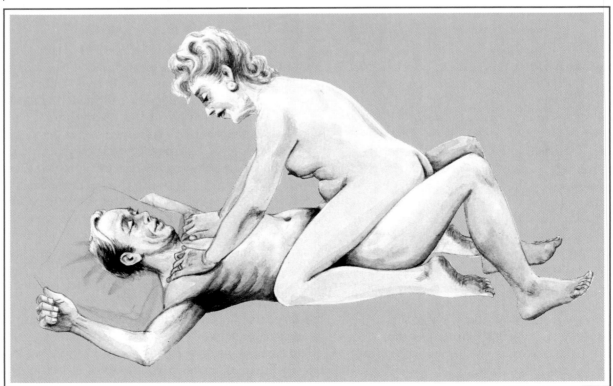

FIGURE 11-10   *LATERAL COITAL POSITION: SEX ON THE SIDE*   In the side-by-side, or lateral, position for vaginal intercourse, each partner can support his or her own weight and freely control pelvic movements.

the woman being above them—the partner is perceived as dominant and threatening. Other couples find this position exciting *because* of the woman's dominant, controlling position.

Side Positions.   In this position, the partners lie on their sides, facing each other. Part of the female's body is placed on top of the male's body, and one of her legs is positioned between his legs, as Figure 11-10 shows. Masters and Johnson (1970) labeled this the **lateral coital position**. This is the third most popular intercourse position in the United States, with half of the couples using it at least occasionally.

Because neither partner has to support much weight, this position is restful and relaxed, permitting both partners freely to control their pelvic movements. Problems may arise however, if the man's penis is relatively short because insertion into the vagina can be difficult. A solution is to begin penetration in a different position and then shift to the lateral coital one. Some couples reject this position because it allows less vigorous thrusting of the pelvis than when either the man or the woman lies above the partner.

Rear-entry Positions.   About four in ten couples sometimes have intercourse in the rear-entry position, primarily for the sake of variety. The man faces the woman's back, and his penis enters her vagina from behind. Thrusting in this position has the advantage of stimulating the woman's perineum between her vagina and anus (Clifford, 1978). Figure 11-11 depicts the most common variation of this position, sometimes known as "doggie style." Other societies apply the names of other animal species—cow, sheep, and so on (Gregersen, 1983).

Variations in rear-entry intercourse include having the man lie on top of the woman, both lying on their sides "like spoons" with the man's front against the woman's back, or the woman bending over from a standing position. When the woman bends over, she is usually more comfortable if the top half of her body can rest on a bed or the back of a chair.

Some object to this position because to them it resembles animal sex or seems too similar to anal intercourse. Others point out that there is no face-to-face contact and that the clitoris is not directly stimulated (Neubardt, 1981). Nevertheless, rear-entry with the couple lying on their sides is the safest and most comfortable way to have intercourse during the last two trimesters of pregnancy. The man can receive increased penile stimulation if the woman draws her legs together. The man's pleasure is also enhanced by thrusting against his partner's naturally padded buttocks.

Sitting Positions.   In the sitting position (Figure 11-12), the partners face one another, and the woman lowers herself onto the penis of her seated partner. One variation is for the woman to face away from the man. In the United States, intercourse in a sitting position is used from time to time by one fourth of the couples for variety and when a bed is unavailable—as in an automobile, for example.

When partners face each other, the woman's clitoris indirectly receives stimulation from the penile thrusting. Manual stimulation of the clitoris is obviously important when the female faces away from the male. Some couples vary the sitting position by rising from it so that, during intercourse, they are standing upright.

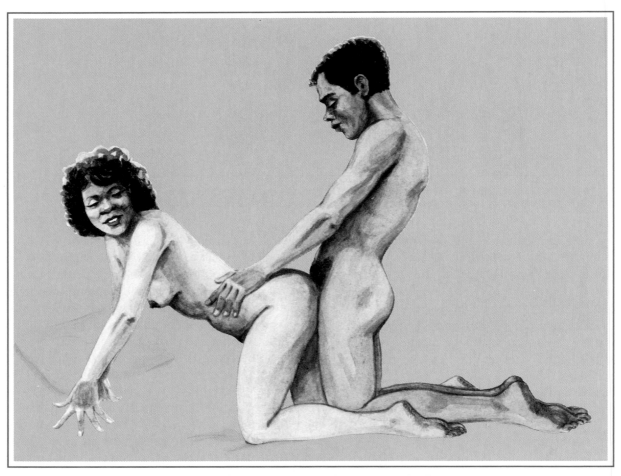

FIGURE 11-11 *REAR-ENTRY VAGINAL INTERCOURSE: DOING AS THE ANIMALS DO*   When the man enters the woman from the rear, many cultures describe the position in terms of a specific animal species. In much of Western society, the term used is *doggie style.*

Cross-cultural Differences in Positions of Intercourse.   Though many assume that everyone does as we do (or that they *should* do so), anthropologists have shown that sexuality is commonly expressed in many different ways (see Chapter 1). It appears that human beings have discovered just about every possibility for obtaining sexual pleasure and reaching orgasm. Whenever a creative individual develops a sexual technique that seems to be truly novel, the odds are that others have engaged in precisely that same behavior, somewhere in the world, for at least several centuries (Davenport, 1977). Six primary positions of heterosexual intercourse occur worldwide.

(1) The most common position is the male-superior or "missionary position." This label origi-nated when Christian missionaries visited other societies and discovered that other positions were used for intercourse. To save souls, they worked hard to persuade their flock to have sex in the "normal" way—as it was practiced in Europe and North America. The ministers defended their beliefs by pointing out that St. Paul proclaimed that a wife should subordinate herself to her husband in every way. With respect to sex, this meant that he should adopt the dominant position over her prone body (Ford and Beach, 1951).

(2) Societies in the Southern Hemisphere more commonly use the side-by-side position for intercourse. In the South Pacific, the Marquesans call it the "gecko-lizard pattern." Gregersen (1983) suggests

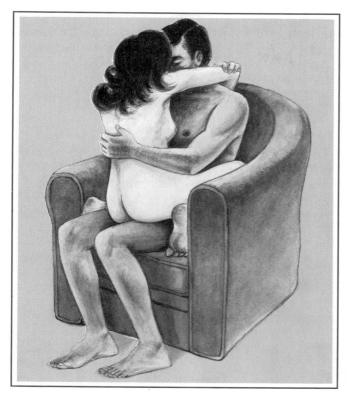

FIGURE 11-12 *SITTING POSITION: CHAIR, COUCH, OR CAR SEAT*
For variety or in situations in which a bed is not readily available, the
sitting position can be used.

FIGURE 11-13 *IN THE SOUTH PACIFIC AND
ELSEWHERE: THE OCEANIC POSITION* The
Oceanic position for intercourse is depicted
here. For women, one advantage of this position—according to the West African Tal-
lensi—is that it enables her to push the male
away by kicking him. The anthropologist
Branislaw Malinowski (1929) described this
style of intercourse among the Trobriand Is-
landers in *The Sexual Life of Savages*. He reportedly entertained his fellow anthropologists at parties by demonstrating how it was
done (Gregersen, 1983).

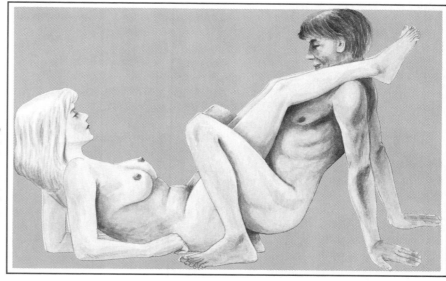

the Vietnamese prefer it to the male-dominant position because kneeling on the bamboo slats of their
beds results in painful scrapes on the male's knees.

(3) Rear-entry intercourse is less common than
the others, perhaps because of its association with animal sexuality.

(4) In the *Oceanic position* illustrated in Figure
11-13, the man squats or kneels between the woman's legs as she lies on her back. He draws her to him
so that her legs straddle his thighs. This position is
used primarily by those living on the islands of the
Pacific.

(5) The position in which the male sits and the female squats facing him is often pictured in Oriental erotic art. This variation of the woman-superior position was recommended in the Chinese Daoist religion; it allows the man to relax and delay his ejaculation while the female plays the active role.

(6) The least common intercourse position involves several variations in which the partners stand and face one another.

In addition to these six positions, anthropologists have been given descriptions of a number of others, but some seem to be attempts by native informants to make jokes at the expense of the inquisitive outsiders. For example, there is a probably fictional account in Fiji of the "flying fox" position in which the man and woman hang by their arms from a beam and copulate by swinging back and forth (Gregersen, 1983).

■ Oral-Genital Stimulation

The specific term applied to oral-genital stimulation (see Figure 11-14) depends on which sex is receiving it. **Fellatio** is the oral stimulation of the man's genitals by his partner. The term derives from the Latin word *felare,* meaning "to suck." **Cunnilingus** is the oral stimulation a female's genitals by her partner. The word *cunnilingus* derives from two Latin words:

FIGURE 11-14 *ORAL SEX: CUNNILINGUS AND FELLATIO*   Cunnilingus is the term for oral stimulation of the female's genitals; fellatio refers to oral stimulation of the male's genitals.

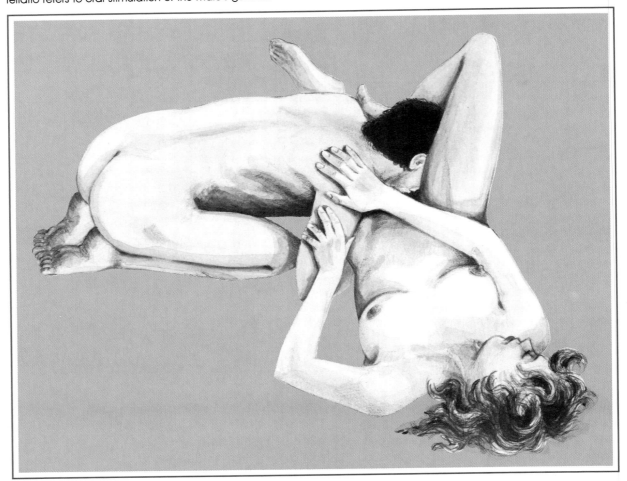

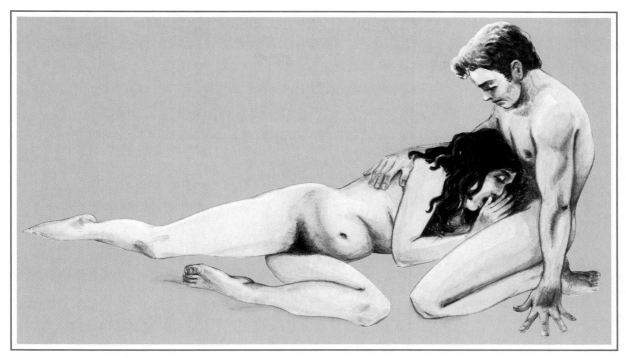

FIGURE 11-14   CONTINUED

cunnus meaning "vulva" and *lingere* meaning "to lick." As the special insert, ***Increasing Enjoyment***, on page 302 indicates, licking and sucking are common elements in both fellatio and cunnilingus.

Further Variations.   Many people enjoy the experience of simultaneous fellatio and cunnilingus; the shape of the two interacting bodies roughly resembles the number 69 (in French, **soixante neuf**). The two partners can engage in such mutual stimulation—either lying side-by-side or one partner lying on his or her back with the other person above.

Although oral sex can be used as foreplay prior to intercourse, couples frequently employ it as an alternative to intercourse and thus continue until orgasm is reached. For many men, the willingness of a partner to let him ejaculate in his or her mouth and then to swallow it is an indication of love. Some partners, however, find the feel and taste of semen objectionable. The important question is whether one likes or dislikes the experience. It is primarily a matter of personal preference; some swallow the ejaculate, while others spit it out and rinse with mouthwash.

Does ingesting semen present any health risks? The answer is that oral-genital sex, including swallowing semen, presents risks similar to kissing on the mouth. If an individual is infected with AIDS, the male's semen or the female's vaginal secretions contain the deadly virus, though this virus probably does not survive in the digestive tract. Like vaginal and anal intercourse, however, AIDS *can* be transmitted by oral sex (Halpern, 1989). For example, infected semen or vaginal secretions can enter the bloodstream through tiny cracks in the lining of the mouth.

Other people express concern about whether semen is fattening: An average ejaculate contains fewer than 100 calories.

An alternative to ejaculation in the partner's mouth is for the man to withdraw his penis prior to orgasm, ejaculating on himself or on some portion of the partner's body (such as the face, breasts, or pubic area). Again, the major concern is how each of the two individuals feels about any of these options, and honest communication between partners can clarify their preferences.

Increasing Enjoyment

METHODS OF ORAL-GENITAL STIMULATION

In 1960, Albert Ellis' book, *The Art and Science of Love,* contained 400 pages dealing with sexual techniques, but only two of these pages discussed oral-genital acts. Even though his coverage was brief, Ellis' treatment of oral sex represented a remarkable change from the pioneering days of Theodore Van de Velde, whose 1926 sex manual, *Ideal Marriage: Its Physiology and Technique,* urged the husband to ignore the sights and smells of the vulva while carefully performing the genital kiss on his young bride. Only after the early stages of marriage was the sexually awakened wife expected to attempt to give her partner a genital kiss. Earlier in the relationship, she might be frightened away from sexual interaction entirely should she prematurely approach ". . . that treacherous frontier between supreme beauty and base ugliness" (p. 171). Only the most experienced partners could possibly gain pleasure from the genital kiss, in Van de Velde's view. Much earlier, in the first century, the Roman poet Martial wrote about the pleasures of being fellated, but felt that a reciprocal act of cunnilingus would be practiced only by the lowest degenerates (Knox, 1988).

Today, oral sex is widely accepted, and such stimulation of a partner's genitals can take several forms. For example, when a partner stimulates a man and his or her mouth is a passive, unmoving receptacle for a thrusting penis, the act is referred to as **irrumation**. The term *fellatio* is used when the mouth actively stimulates the male genitals. Though this act is often called a "blow job," blowing is not what usually occurs. During fellatio, the penis is licked or sucked, and saliva naturally lubricates the skin to produce a smooth contact between lips and penis. The penis or a portion of it may be taken into the mouth, or the stimulation can come primarily from the lips and tongue moving about the shaft. One technique is to begin licking and kissing the underside of the penis at its base and to move slowly up the shaft to the glans; this process is repeated until the man reaches orgasm.

When the partner's mouth engulfs the man's penis, breathing continues through the nose. The gag reflex is likely to occur if the man's erect organ touches the back of the fellator's throat. Linda Lovelace, formerly an actress in erotic films, wrote in her 1980 autobiography, *Ordeal,* that she was forced to learn the "deep throat" technique by her partner. She (as well as others) learned to relax her neck muscles, thus avoiding the tendency to gag and allowing the penis to penetrate more deeply. During fellation, the partner also needs to avoid biting or otherwise injuring the penis with his or her teeth. It is possible to keep the moistened lips over the teeth as a safety measure (Carson, 1982b). The part-

ner's hand also can be placed on the penile shaft and moved up and down in rhythm with the mouth movements, thereby increasing the male's positive sensations.

In cunnilingus, the woman's genitals are orally stimulated. The partner can slowly lick her inner thighs, perineum, and vaginal lips, eventually moving to the clitoris. The term *butterfly tongue* refers to a gentle, fluttering stimulation of the clitoris (Gilmore, 1968). When the clitoris is sucked in a pulsating fashion, the act mimics the timing of orgasmic contractions. Many women find cunnilingus highly arousing.

Oral sex, like intercourse, can be performed in a variety of positions. The recipient can lie on his or her back while the orally active partner approaches the genitals from a variety of directions—kneeling or lying between the legs, lying alongside facing either toward the recipient's head or feet, and so on. The recipient can also be standing, sitting, or kneeling over the face of his or her partner. In the latter instance, the person receiving fellatio or cunnilingus can face toward or away from the partner's head. Besides the pleasure experienced by the recipient of oral sex, his or her partner also can be aroused by the stimulation of the nerve endings in the lips, mouth, and tongue. For many, an excited partner's taste and smell also add to the excitement.

Increased Acceptance of Oral Sex. With the shift toward more liberal sexual attitudes since the 1950s, views about oral-genital sex have become generally quite positive. Those with reservations about fellatio and cunnilingus often perceive them as homosexual acts, even when performed by a heterosexual couple. The enjoyment of oral-genital contact does not, however, have any relationship to the sexual orientation of those who perform it.

College students who have had heterosexual intercourse or who have engaged in oral-genital sex express more positive attitudes about oral sex than students who have done neither (Young, 1980). Oral sex occurs more frequently now than at the time of the Kinsey surveys (1948, 1953), and cunnilingus is slightly more common among adolescents than fellatio (Newcomer and Udry, 1985b). Among high school males (average age of sixteen), 50 percent reported having performed cunnilingus while 44 percent had been fellated. Similarly, high school females who reported having cunnilingus outnumbered those who had fellated males by 41 to 32 percent. Young women, then, appear to be more reluctant to stimulate their partners orally than is true for young men.

For both sexes, feelings of sexual guilt inhibit oral sexuality (Mosher and Cross, 1971). As sexual experience increases, women become more willing to engage in fellatio (Herold and Way, 1983). Fellatio also becomes more acceptable for women once the relationship involves mutual commitment.

■ Anal Sex

The anus can be pleasurably stimulated by the hands, mouth, or penis. Anal intercourse involves the insertion of the penis into the rectum through the anus. Negative attitudes toward anal sex are common, and many consider it disgusting or perverted. Because anal sex was popular among upper-class individuals in ancient Greece, anal penetration by a penis is sometimes referred to as an interest in "Greek culture." There is, by the way, greater historical accuracy connecting anal sex with Greece than in using the terms "French culture" for oral sex and "English culture" for sadomasochistic acts.

Among women in one sample of gynecological patients, 25 percent had experienced anal intercourse at least once, and 15 percent engaged in this form of sex regularly (Bolling, 1978a,b). Half of the regular participants indicated that the practice was initiated by their male partners while half said it was a mutual decision. The women in this sample showed no increase in the incidence of anal diseases or injuries.

Stimulation of the nerve endings around the anus and within the rectum can be pleasurable, but the woman whose anus is penetrated usually does not experience orgasm (Masters and Johnson, 1979). Anal contractions *do* occur during orgasm resulting from other kinds of stimulation.

Chapter 16 discusses the medical hazards associated with anal sex. These include the possibility of sexually transmissible disease, such as syphilis and gonorrhea; even more serious, anal sex is one of the major ways in which AIDS is transmitted. Another

potential problem with anal sex is injury to the tissues (Agnew, 1986). Artificial lubrication is necessary to avoid damaging the lining of the rectum, and the use of condoms is strongly recommended to reduce the chances of infection. The penis should be inserted into the anus and rectum slowly and gently, even when a lubricant is used, to reduce the chances of injury. When heterosexual couples engage in anal intercourse followed by vaginal intercourse, vaginal infections are very likely to occur unless the penis is thoroughly cleaned prior to entering the vagina.

There is another variation of anal sex which doesn't involve pain, but *does* include health risks. When one partner orally stimulates the anus of the other individual, this is known as **analingus.** The term *rimming* is sometimes used to describe a circular movement of the tongue around the rim of the partner's anus. In addition to the general problems of disease transmission described for anal intercourse, analingus presents the additional possibility of bacteria being transferred from the rectal area to the mouth. Extreme care with respect to cleanliness is obviously essential.

■ More about Orgasm

Because orgasm is perceived as the goal of sexual activity by most individuals, it is worth considering this goal more closely. In the 1950s, it was commonly proclaimed that the **simultaneous orgasm** of two partners was the ultimate achievement in sexual interactions. For example, they were supposed to strive to bring about one another's orgasm at the same time (Fracher, 1981). Because orgasmic simultaneity is neither a necessary or even a realistic goal, most individuals today realize that **sequential orgasm** is equally acceptable. Thus, one partner can reach orgasm first, while the other reaches it later in their sexual interaction (Maddock, 1982).

One consequence of assuming that the two orgasms must occur together is the tendency of the partner "in second place" to feel that he or she must fake the response. In Hite's (1976) study of female sexuality, half of her subjects said that they had pretended to have orgasm at least once. Similarly, men whose orgasm is either very rapid or delayed also say that they fake the response in order make the partner believe that it coincides with her climax (Friedman, 1978).

Presumably, sexual activity that is regularly accompanied by orgasms is associated with greater general happiness than is sex without orgasms (Lief, 1980a). Are orgasms the primary indication of sexual enjoyment? In this context, it is interesting to note that an individual's sexual pleasure does *not* depend on whether his or her partner experiences orgasm (Waterman and Chiauzzi, 1982). Couples reported that intercourse and cunnilingus are highly pleasurable with or without orgasm, as Figure 11-15 shows. These and other data have led many sex therapists to conclude that we are overinclined to set unnecessary standards for sexual performance. When it is felt that

one *must* have an orgasm, sexual responding becomes a demanding task rather than a source of enjoyment.

When women were asked to describe the techniques that were most effective in ensuring their orgasms, the following were most frequently mentioned (Kroop, 1979):

1. rubbing the mons pubis using a circular motion
2. pulling down both sides of the inner lips or labia minora
3. having their partner alternate thrusts with circular pelvic movements during intercourse
4. tapping with the flat of the hand against the clitoris and introitus
5. having the partner's penis thrust slowly between the legs

FIGURE 11-15   *IS THE "BIG O" A CRUCIAL PART OF SEX?*   Contrary to general expectations about the essential nature of orgasm as part of a sexual interaction, men and women report that sex is pleasurable without it.
Source: Based on data in Waterman and Chiauzzi, 1982.

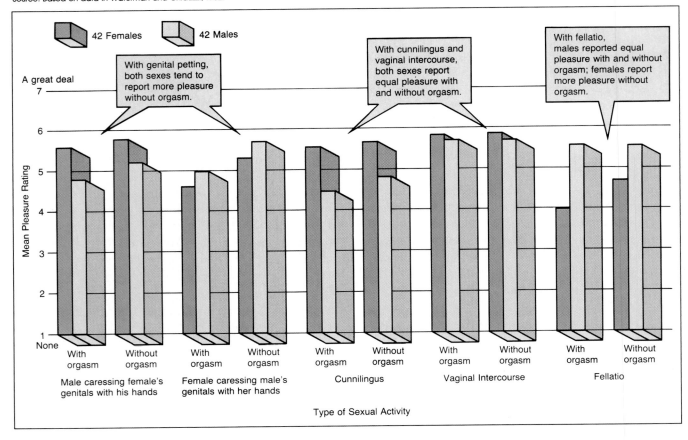

6. experiencing digital stimulation of the anus at the same time as her partner thrusts with his penis
7. gentle pinching of the clitoral foreskin
8. stroking the right side of the clitoral shaft.

The last item raises the question of why the *right* side? The answer may involve the connection between the dominant side of one's brain (for most people, the left side) and its control of responses on the opposite side of the body. If this hypothesis is correct, we should expect left-handed women to prefer stimulation of the left side of the clitoris.

■ Afterplay

What do partners do at the end of a sexual interaction? If they fall asleep almost immediately, as a large percentage of individuals report doing, they risk displeasing their partners no matter how positive the sexual experience might have been (Sherman and Halpern, 1981). A different kind of turn-off was reported by one female undergraduate. While she wanted to continue hugging and kissing, her boyfriend was usually more interested in eating a pizza. Most of the subjects in one investigation indicated that they preferred the partner to remain physically close, talking about intimate topics. Both males and females expressed the desire for **afterplay** such as the following:

1. "I like to be held and cuddled."
2. "I would like touching and caressing."
3. "I like it . . . to be a time to talk about the things I or my partner think about but don't normally convey to other people—one's life, goals, problems, desires."

The worst kind of follow-up to sex is for one or both individuals to provide negative feedback about what just occurred. Neither men nor women like to be criticized about their lovemaking skills. Other topics to be avoided include everyday matters such as money problems or what to feed the cat. Each partner may have sexual dissatisfactions or feel pressure to discuss nonsexual matters—nevertheless, it is a mistake to dwell on these topics during the afterplay period (Laury, 1983). The positive mood and the warm glow of sexual satisfaction can be wiped out when orgasm is followed by receiving a negative "sexual report card" or by hearing your partner express intense concern about who is going to take the dog to the vet tomorrow.

Afterplay generally lasts for a shorter time period than foreplay. In one sample of college students, 40 percent estimated spending five to fifteen minutes in foreplay, while 44 percent estimated sixteen to thirty minutes. In contrast, only 29 percent thought that afterplay lasted more than about fifteen minutes; the majority believed less time was spent. Although males and females gave similar time estimates, the two sexes reported differences in how much they enjoyed foreplay, intercourse, and afterplay. Figure 11-16 indicates that women rated foreplay as the most enjoyable, while men most enjoyed intercourse. Women also said that they wanted to spend more time in foreplay and afterplay than their partners. For

FIGURE 11-16 *BEFORE, DURING, AND AFTER INTERCOURSE* The importance of foreplay to females was indicated in a survey of college students. Males, in contrast, said that they enjoyed intercourse more than either foreplay or afterplay.
Source: Based on data from Denney et al., 1984.

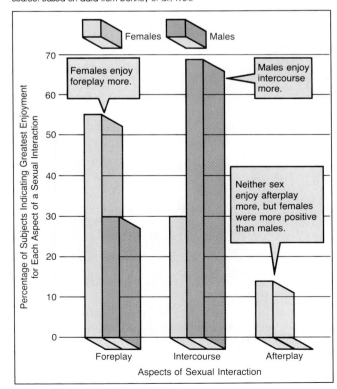

women, then, sexual satisfaction depends as much on what is done before and after intercourse and on how much time is spent in foreplay and afterplay as it does on simply engaging in intercourse and reaching orgasm.

■ Laws Regulating Sexual Techniques

Social beliefs about sexual practices are conveyed in part through laws (see Figure 11-17). When some behaviors are declared illegal while others are not, the limits of acceptable behavior are made clear. For example, sexual acts with children—either in private or as part of pornography—are defined as sexual abuse and a violation of the law in all fifty states of the United States. In contrast, consenting sexual acts within marriage are not normally a part of law enforcement, even when the acts are illegal for others—young people and homosexuals, for example.

Most legislation restricting sexual activity be-

FIGURE 11-17 *LEGAL RESTRICTIONS ON INTIMATE BEHAVIOR* Laws regulating sex-related behaviors define what is acceptable in each society. This cartoon satirizes the restrictiveness of such legislation.
Reprinted by Special Permission of Playboy Magazine. Copyright © 1988 by Playboy.

"I now pronounce you man and wife. Before you kiss the bride, Donald, I think I should remind you that the laws of this state specifically forbid the use of the tongue."

tween consenting adults is aimed at same-sex couples. Oral-genital sex and anal sex are illegal in one third of the states, but the primary targets are gays. The **sodomy laws** that describe these acts use wording that indicates the underlying negative attitudes of those who drafted the legislation:

Crime against nature (Alabama, Louisiana, North Carolina, and Tennessee)

Infamous crime against nature (Arizona, Nevada, and New Jersey—but not for married couples)

Abominable and detestable crime against nature (Massachusetts and Oklahoma)

Deviant sexual intercourse punishable unless the perpetrators are married (Connecticut)

Every person convicted of taking into his or her mouth or anus the sexual organ of any other person or animal (Washington, D.C.)

The penalties for such violations range from monetary fines to twenty years of imprisonment for those convicted.

Legal reformers frequently urge that such laws be updated and liberalized to reflect the current attitudes and behaviors of the majority (Helmer, 1980). In 1986, however, the U.S. Supreme Court affirmed (by a five to four vote) that states have the legal right to regulate and restrict consensual sexual activity between persons of the same sex. This ruling upheld a Georgia law in which a male couple was arrested and convicted for engaging in oral sex in a private bedroom. The police officer was seeking one of these men for not having paid his fine in an unrelated case (public drunkenness), and the officer was given permission to look for him by the person who answered the door. When the officer discovered the couple in the act of fellatio, an arrest was made. In the gay community, and elsewhere as well, the court's decision was perceived as a major setback for civil rights.

Sexual Fantasy

With increasing sexual experience in an ongoing relationship, couples learn the kinds of stimulation and the positions that are most likely to trigger orgasms for each other. Some, for example, focus on the sensations and positive feelings aroused by sexual stimu-

lation, and many use fantasy as a way to facilitate this process (Sholty et al., 1984).

In the preceding sections, this chapter concentrated on the physical activities used to create sexual excitement. At times, such details may be overemphasized, suggesting that each individual should be concentrating on what to touch, where each arm and leg should go, and precisely which movements to make. This *Popular Mechanics* approach to sex leaves out one of the most important aspects of human sexuality. In recent years, research has clearly documented that **sexual fantasy** is a vital component of human sexual responsiveness (Chick and Gold, 1987–88). We will describe some of the research on the role of fantasy, indicate the most common content of these fantasies, and describe how people use erotic images in their sexual lives.

■ Fantasies and Sexual Responding

During sexual interactions, feelings of **involvement** are activated. According to Mosher (1980), involvement consists of the combined processes that promote pleasure in sexual activity. Feelings of involvement are hypothesized to facilitate enjoyment and excitement for all kinds of sexual behavior—masturbation, intercourse, oral sex, or whatever. Involvement is described as having four major components (Mosher, 1981): feelings, thoughts, sexual acts, and interactions with a sexual partner. It is the thought component that includes sexual fantasy, plus memories of past experiences and plans for future interactions.

Those who find it easy to form vivid images of either sexual or nonsexual scenes are more readily aroused by erotic fantasies than those who are less fantasy-prone (Lynn and Rhue, 1986; Smith and Over, 1987). Some people are better able to create exciting fantasies than others (Lynn and Rhue, 1986), but fantasy training can be helpful. Men who do not engage in sexual fantasizing and who have difficulty in maintaining erections can be taught to produce sexual imagery. This increases both their subjective feelings of arousal and their physiological responsiveness (Smith and Over, 1990).

Fantasies often include involvement with a sexual partner. Even during solitary sexual activity, thoughts about a loved one tend to play a dominant role. In Hunt's (1974) large-scale survey of men and women, subjects were asked to describe their thoughts during masturbation. Table 11-3 presents the most common topics reported. Thoughts of intercourse with a loved partner were reported by 75 percent of the men and 80 percent of the women. No other topic even approached this theme in popularity.

Unlike self-created fantasies, external fantasies—presented in erotic films, for example—with themes of casual and uncommitted sex, are more exciting than scenes of sex within a loving relationship. In one experiment, college students were shown an explicit erotic film. Before viewing it, some subjects were told that the couple depicted in it were married, while other subjects were told that the couple were casual acquaintances. Even though all subjects saw the same film, both men and women who thought they were viewing casual sex found the scene more arousing than those who thought they were viewing committed sex (Fisher and Byrne, 1978).

In summary, our spontaneous fantasies seem to focus on a loving partner, but fantasies of uncommitted sex are also enjoyed (Kelley, 1980). A close relationship seems most important in thinking about our own sexuality, but impersonal interactions are exciting when others are involved.

■ Frequency and Content of Sexual Fantasies

You may have noticed in Table 11-3 that men and women differ to some extent in their masturbation fantasies. Thus, although sexual acts with a loved person predominated for both sexes, men fantasized about performing sexual acts with strangers, engaging in group sex, and initiating in coercive sex more frequently than women did. Women, however, were more likely than men to fantasize about doing sexual things they would not want to do in reality, being forced to have sex, and engaging in homosexual acts.

Being excited by a given fantasy does not necessarily indicate the desire to engage in the behavior or the intent to do so. For example, women do *not* want to be raped, but rape fantasies are often enjoyable and arousing. Being a victim of a rapist is neither enjoyable nor arousing. An analogy might help clarify the distinction. Many people enjoy murder mysteries and horror movies, but this does not indicate that they wish to murder anyone, be murdered, or interact with flesh-eating creatures from outer space.

Sexual fantasy is also likely to accompany intercourse, and Table 11-4 provides examples of the themes reported by college students. Women and men fantasized equally often about ten of the thirteen

TABLE 11-3. **Fantasies during Masturbation: Male–Female Comparisons**

Comparisons between males and females indicate that some masturbation fantasies are common to both sexes while others occur more frequently in one sex than the other.

CONTENT OF MASTURBATION FANTASIES	PERCENTAGE REPORTING	
	Females	Males
Both sexes		
Intercourse with a loved person	80	75
Males more frequently than females		
Intercourse with strangers	21	47
Group sexual activity, with more than one		
opposite-sex partner	18	33
Forcing someone to have sex	3	13
Females more frequently than males		
Doing sexual things you would never do		
in reality	28	19
Being forced to have sex	19	10
Interacting with a same-sex partner	11	7

Source: Based on data in Hunt, 1974.

TABLE 11-4 **An Active Fantasy Life during Intercourse**

Sexual fantasies that occur during heterosexual intercourse involve a wide range of themes, as reported in a survey of 116 female and 114 male undergraduates.

SEXUAL FANTASIES DURING INTERCOURSE

The most common fantasies (40 to 60 percent of undergraduates)
  Oral-genital sex
  Others find you sexually irresistible
  Thoughts of a former lover
Moderately common fantasies (20 to 39 percent of undergraduates)
  Thoughts of an imaginary lover
  Being forced to have sex, being overpowered
  Others giving in to you after initial resistance
  Forcing others to have sex
Relatively uncommon fantasies (10 to 19 percent of undergraduates)
  Observing others engage in sex
  Others observing you engage in sex
  Group sex
  Being rejected or sexually abused
Rare fantasies (less than 10 percent of undergraduates)
  Sexual activity with a member of the same sex
  Sexual activity with animals

Source: Based on data from Sue, 1979.

topics (Sue, 1979). Women again differed from men in fantasizing slightly more often about being forced to engage in sexual acts and in having a sexual interaction with someone of the same sex. Men were more likely than women to focus on imaginary lovers. Nevertheless, the sexes were more similar than different in the content of their sexual fantasies.

Sex differences *were* found in the use of fantasies to enhance intercourse. Men more often than women begin utilizing fantasies during their initial experiences with intercourse. Women, in contrast, are more likely to report engaging in intercourse for several months before having any accompanying fantasies. Two years after their first intercourse experience, 21 percent of the women and only 6 percent of the men still did not fantasize during sex (Sue, 1979). Presumably, men receive more permissive fantasy training than women; in effect, males have learned that it is acceptable to think about sex and that such thoughts add to sexual excitement and pleasure.

Evolutionary factors are proposed by Ellis and Symons (1990) to explain sex differences in fantasy content. Their research with over 300 undergraduates found that male fantasies focus on lust while female fantasies emphasize love. Men also report more impersonal fantasies emphasizing the partner's physical attributes while women say that their fantasies are personal with context and emotions as integral elements. Men stress visual cues, and women stress tactile stimulation—being touched by a loving male. Men also imagine a variety of partners, preferably ones who are responsive and lusty; women like to think of themselves as the targets of male excitement and solicitude. These differences are interpreted as reflecting sex differences in the reproductive strategies of our ancient ancestors.

The following two fantasies were written by undergraduates who took part in the research. Can you guess the sex of each person on the basis of the fantasy?

1. My partner and I are lying in bed, fully clothed. Slowly, we begin to caress each other, and to undress each other. We begin to kiss deeply, and to touch each other in sensitive places. Then we fully undress, and manually manipulate each other's genitals. We engage in intercourse. The whole scene is in soft colors and candlelight, scented with our favorite perfume. It is all done gently and lovingly.

2. I have fantasies about engaging in sex underwater. The water is very warm, tropical, salt water, with brightly colored fish around us. My fantasies have never really included a method of breathing underwater, since there is no scuba gear or anything. During intercourse with my partner we have the sensation of floating in a warm liquid, suspended by nothing else than the water.

These two examples involve themes that are very common in sexual fantasies—interaction with a loved partner in the first one and sex *al fresco* (outdoors) in the second. Sex in water (ocean, lake, waterfall, tub, and so forth) is also frequently found in erotic fantasies. Students reported having such fantasies in the classroom, when they came in contact with an attractive member of the opposite sex, and during masturbation, intercourse, or oral sex. The partners consisted of current, former, or imagined lovers. Such thoughts about sexual behavior, sex partners, and the location of these activities play a key role in the sexuality of a great many people (Byrne, 1977). You may be surprised to learn that a young man wrote the first fantasy, and a young woman the second. Contrary to what you might have expected, romance occupied his attention, whereas she focused on sexuality in an exotic setting.

As you might guess, individuals whose sexual interests differ from those of the majority also report fantasies that reflect these differences. Gosselin (1981) examined the fantasies of four groups of men: (1) transvestites (who wear female clothing to increase their sexual pleasure), (2) rubber fetishists (who wear rubber clothing for excitement), (3) leather fetishists (who wear leather garments), and (4) sadomasochists (whose excitement is enhanced by giving or receiving pain). A control group consisted of males who did not express these sexual interests. The four special-interest groups reported fantasies that differed from those of the control group, and Table 11-5 lists the differing themes.

■ Personal Uses of Erotic Imaginings

Not only do sexual fantasies occur during our waking hours but also when we sleep, and such dreams often result in sexual arousal. As described earlier, both men and women can experience orgasm during sleep. In Europe during the Dark Ages, the explanation of these mysterious and powerful events rested on the belief in possession by demons (Money, 1985). An individual who had sexually exciting dreams was assumed to be interacting with supernatural beings.

In the 1700s, this type of **demon theory** was replaced by **degeneracy theory**. A Swiss physician, Simon Andre Tissot, proposed that lustful thoughts during one's waking hours caused sexual dreams and

---

TABLE 11-5 **Different Fantasy Strokes for Different Folks**

Over 500 males with unusual sexual preferences were found to have relatively unusual fantasies reflecting their sexual interests.

SEXUAL FANTASIES REPORTED MORE FREQUENTLY BY MALE TRANSVESTITES, FETISHISTS, AND SADOMASOCHISTS THAN BY MALES IN A CONTROL GROUP

Forcing someone to engage in a sex-related act
Using objects for stimulation
Tying someone up
Being whipped or spanked
Wearing clothing of the opposite sex
Being forced to engage in a sex-related act
Being tied up
Being hurt by a partner
Being excited by a specific kind of material or clothing
Whipping or spanking someone

Source: Based on data from Gosselin, 1981.

hence the harmful loss of body fluids. The evil nature of sexual fantasies (whether they occurred during sleep or while awake) was responsible, he concluded, for the degeneration, or wasting away, of the person's organs.

This curious formulation did contain a germ of truth: The more an individual thinks about sex, the more likely he or she is to have sexual dreams. And, erotic fantasies that occur when we are awake or asleep are likely to cause physical excitement. You might think of such fantasies as the least expensive, most effective, and safest type of aphrodisiac available (Kelley and Byrne, 1978). Among the many research examples supporting this assertion, married couples in one study were asked simply to think about various erotic themes; they reported becoming much more aroused than other couples who were shown sexual photographs or who read sexual stories about those same themes (Byrne and Lamberth, 1971).

The striking power of erotic thoughts leads to the possibility that individual differences in **sex drive** may depend not on some biological factor such as

hormones but rather on the extent to which the person regularly thinks about sex in waking fantasies, dreams, and/or in response to exposure to the erotic fantasies of others in the form of stories, films, and so forth.

Many individuals have learned to utilize erotic fantasies to control or "fine tune" their excitement and to delay or hasten orgasm (Davidson and Hoffman, 1986). Sue (1979) asked college students to describe their use of fantasies during heterosexual intercourse. Figure 11-18 indicates what these subjects reported. Fantasies not only affected level of arousal, Sue found, but also tended to make a sexual partner seem more attractive—he or she acquired some of the perfection typical of fantasy sex.

Fantasies have additional functions. For example, a person may think about and be excited about activities that he or she could or would not actually do for a variety of reasons. If a long-term sexual relationship begins to seem boring, fantasy can solve the problem by providing novelty in images of different partners, activities, settings, and so forth. In each of

FIGURE 11-18 *USING SEXUAL FANTASIES TO INCREASE SEXUAL PLEASURE* According to college undergraduates, sexual fantasies serve many positive functions, thus enhancing pleasure during intercourse. Source: Based on data from Sue, 1979.

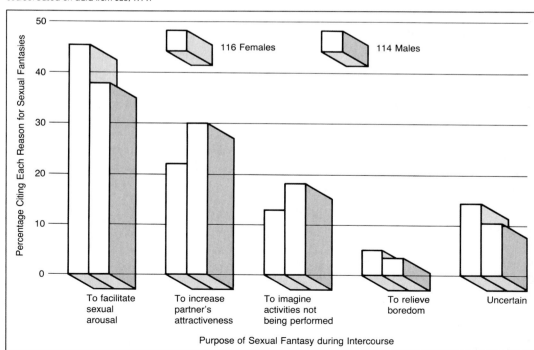

these ways, self-created fantasies serve to make ongoing sexual acts more pleasurable than they might otherwise be. Like batteries, sexual fantasies are ever-ready—available for use. An individual's favorite fantasy can reliably help create sexual arousal; Masters and Johnson (1979) label them "old friends."

When people discuss "sexual aids," or ways to enhance excitement, they usually think of mechanical devices such as vibrators, the consumption of a special substance that is supposed to bring about excitement, or wearing erotic clothing. As we have suggested, our own fantasies may be more effective than any physical creation. Further, many couples have discovered that the fantasies of others can be an exciting prelude to sexual interaction. The availability of explicit videotapes that can be purchased or rented has made it possible for couples to view erotic films as an addition to foreplay. Like self-created fantasies,

erotic scenes can be exciting and add variety to sexual interactions. In addition, erotica provides arousing fantasy material for those who have difficulty forming such images for themselves (Smith and Over, 1987).

This discussion may suggest that fantasies are always a source of pleasure. In fact, individuals with negative sexual attitudes are likely to have negatively toned fantasies that are less enjoyable than the positive fantasies of those with positive sexual attitudes (Kelley, 1985a). More generally, thoughts about any form of sex that the person finds unappealing can evoke negative fantasies (Chick and Gold, 1987; Follingstad and Kimbrell, 1986). To an even greater degree, external fantasies such as those provided by films do not increase sexual pleasure if the response of one or both partners is primarily that of anxiety, disgust, or other negative emotions.

Summarizing the Information about Techniques of Sexual Arousal . . .

Stimulation of a partner's genitals can occur as part of **petting** to orgasm or of **foreplay**. Solitary **masturbation** is frequently used to obtain sexual gratification. There are a numerous ways in which men and women can stimulate themselves to orgasm, and people differ in their preferences for specific techniques. **Erogenous zones** refer to specific portions of the body that elicit sexual arousal in response to caressing or kissing. When foreplay lasts for an extended period, females are subsequently more likely to reach orgasm during intercourse. Also, sexual aids such as vibrators provide stimulation sufficiently strong to produce orgasm, though such stimulation is perceived as enjoyable by women more than men.

Sexual intercourse involves the penetration of the vagina by the penis. Other alternatives provide stimulation primarily to the male; these include **interfemoral** and **intermammary foration**. When vaginal intercourse lasts less than one minute, a woman is not as likely to reach orgasm as when she receives more prolonged stimulation. In the United States, the five main positions for intercourse are male-superior, female-superior, side, rear-entry, and sitting. These

positions differ in the amount of physical strain for one or the other partner, the relative control of pelvic movements, and the degree of stimulation provided to the clitoris.

Oral-genital stimulation has become increasingly common since the 1950s, and **cunnilingus** occurs earlier for most young couples than does **fellatio**. **Anal intercourse** also occurs more frequently today among heterosexuals than in the past, but several health risks are associated with it. The timing and occurrence of orgasm during sexual activity once were regarded as crucial to sexual satisfaction. Now, however, it is believed that the quality of stimulation and the degree of closeness experienced by the two individuals are more important determinants of their enjoyment. An extended period of **afterplay** can enhance the sexual experience considerably. Laws regulating acceptable sexual practices slowly change as societal attitudes and practices change.

Sexual fantasy has been described historically in negative terms, as exemplified by the **demon** and **degeneracy theories**. Today, such fantasies (whether we have them while asleep or awake) are viewed not only as normal human functioning but also as valuable in creating excitement, guiding arousal level during a sexual interaction, relieving boredom, and generally improving sexual experiences. Similarly, external fantasies were (and often still are) condemned and made illegal, but they can serve as a valuable part of foreplay.

To Find Out More about Techniques of Sexual Arousal . . .

Friday, N. (1980). *Men in love: Men's sexual fantasies*. New York: Delacourte.

The erotic fantasies of 3,000 men are described and analyzed. This material is interpreted within a theoretical framework developed by the author of two other books that dealt with the sexual fantasies of women.

Gale, J. (1984). *A young man's guide to sex*. New York: Holt, Rinehart & Winston.

Written as a sourcebook for young adult men, this book provides an understanding of the positive and negative aspects of sexuality.

Kitzinger, S. (1983). *Women's experience of sex*. New York: Putnam.

Using many sensitive illustrations, the author discusses female sexuality.

Peters, B. (1988). *Terrific sex in fearful times*. New York: St. Martin's Press.

A guide to imaginative, but safe, sex. For example, an entire chapter is devoted to methods of masturbating your partner to orgasm.

CHAPTER TWELVE

HOMOSEXUAL AND BISEXUAL BEHAVIOR

For many heterosexuals, the idea of homosexuality can be mysterious and sometimes frightening. Today, an increasing number of the men and women in this sexual minority are willing to acknowledge their sexual orientation openly and to share their experiences, as Jerry does in the following account. One result should be the growing realization that differences in sexual preference are not indicative of other aspects of personality or behavior.

When I was in high school and college, I dated mainly because it was what everyone did. Despite what my friends claimed about their early sexual exploits, my first intimate experience with a female was with my fiance, and it happened during our senior year at the University.

Sex was always intensely important to me. It's hard to know what kind of fantasies other people have, but what turned me on most was a group scene with a lot of men and women interacting. Looking back, I realize now that images of male bodies, erections, and ejaculation were the crucial elements in making a fantasy exciting for me.

On dates, kissing and necking were enjoyable enough, but those things never seemed as good as they were "supposed" to be. Even worse was when Beth and I started having intercourse. There was no problem in functioning sexually, and an orgasm is an orgasm, but I kept asking myself, "Is that all there is?" As graduation and the date of our wedding drew closer, my doubts about the whole situation began to grow. I kept wondering what I was getting myself into.

One day, Beth and I went swimming, and something happened that changed my life. There was a young guy there wearing a brief bikini swimsuit. He was unusually handsome, his body was perfect, and when he came out of the water you could see the outline of his penis through his wet trunks. I stared at this guy so much that Beth said—as a joke—"You're paying more attention to that hunk than to me. You're not gay, are you?"

I laughed, but later, the scene at the pool kept replaying in my head—his body, my excitement in thinking about him, and Beth's question. All of a sudden, it all came together. It seemed so obvious. I'm gay. I've always been gay but never even realized it.

The worst period in my life came next—explaining the situation to Beth, trying to deal with my parents, having some of my "friends" treat me as a kind of freak. There was a lot of other stuff, but you get the idea.

All that has settled down now, and I'm living happily with Paul, someone I met at a Gay and Lesbian Alliance rally during that hectic month after I came out of the closet. We are much more compatible than Beth and I would ever have been.

Jerry, age 23

About one person out of ten defines his or her sexual interest in the way that Jerry does—attraction to same-sex partners. Such a sexual preference often causes concern, and even fear among heterosexuals. We will now examine these and other issues involving sexual orientation.

People differ in defining their sexual preferences, but as yet no one knows with certainty the possible *bases of each person's sexual orientation.* Conflicting explanations tend to focus on biological determinants versus early childhood experiences (Woodman, 1990). Though it is not yet possible to state why a given individual prefers same-sex or opposite-sex partners, studies of the patterns of *homosexual and bisexual relationships* are of interest, and we explore such topics as "coming out," religious and legal restrictions on homosexual activity, and the lifestyles of non-heterosexuals, including parenthood. We also describe the sexual and personality characteristics of *homosexual individuals.* Special sections examine *homophobia and bias against homosexuals* and *male–female differences among homosexuals.*

The Ongoing Search for the Bases of Sexual Orientation

Kinsey, in his 1948 and 1953 books, reported that 37 percent of white males and 19 percent of white females had at least one sexual contact with a same-sex partner during adolescence or adulthood. In the 1970s, Hunt (1974) found that 18 percent of men, 9 percent of married women, and 15 percent of single women had at least one homosexual experience; among students at the University of South Carolina, approximately 15 percent of the men and 8 percent of the women said they had taken part in one or more homosexual interactions (Haynes and Oziel, 1976). More recently, in a survey of over 2,000 college students, about one in twelve reported having engaged in homosexual acts (Segal, 1984), with more men than women having such experiences. A still more recent survey of over 400 students indicated homosexual experiences for about 30 percent of the men and 10 percent of the women (Ellis et al., 1987). These wide variations in percentages are probably based on differences in sampling procedures and in how the question is asked.

Kinsey and his colleagues described sexual behavior as falling along a seven-point scale ranging from exclusively heterosexual (0 on the scale) to exclusively homosexual (6 on the scale), as Figure 12-1 shows. The gradations between 0 and 6 indicate degrees of combined heterosexual and homosexual attraction and overt behavior. A 3 on the scale indicates an equal amount of the two types of experience. Also shown in the figure are the percentages of individuals falling in the three major categories: exclusively heterosexual, exclusively homosexual, and **bisexual**.

These figures have been criticized as being overestimations of the homosexual population in that Kinsey's interviewers contacted subjects in gay bars and other unrepresentative settings. It seems likely that the best estimate of percentages is lower than reported by Kinsey.

Those who engage in a limited number of homosexual acts do not necessarily adopt a homosexual sexual preference, so it is important to differentiate **homosexual behavior** from **sexual orientation**.

■ Sexual Orientation

The term **gay** refers to either a male or female homosexual though it is most often applied to males, while the term **lesbian** specifically indicates a female homosexual. "Gay" originally meant simply merry or carefree. The meaning expanded in the early 1800s to refer to female prostitutes (Sagarin, 1978). From gay women engaged in commercial sex to gay males who engaged in forbidden sexuality, the word gradually acquired its present meaning of a male homosexual. For female homosexuals, *lesbian* refers to residents of the Greek island of Lesbos, the home of the female poet Sappho who lived and wrote around 600 B.C. Gays and lesbians tend to prefer these labels to that of *homosexual,* which describes a person solely on the basis of sexual behavior and is considered derogatory.

What exactly is meant by sexual orientation? In Segal's (1984) survey, college students who reported homosexual experiences did not necessarily view themselves as homosexual. Many clearly maintained strong images of themselves as heterosexual while acknowledging past homosexual acts. We have known since Kinsey's research that most people who have had homosexual experience also have had heterosexual experience. It is now clear that it is more common for an individual to have a bisexual history than an exclusively homosexual one, and we will return to this topic later in the chapter.

The way people describe their own past sexual behavior provides clues to their sexual orientation. Three major components are involved in this description (DeCecco, 1981). The first is physical sexual activity—intimate bodily contact that usually includes sexual excitement and orgasm. The second component is interpersonal affection—the degree of attraction and love directed toward a partner. The third

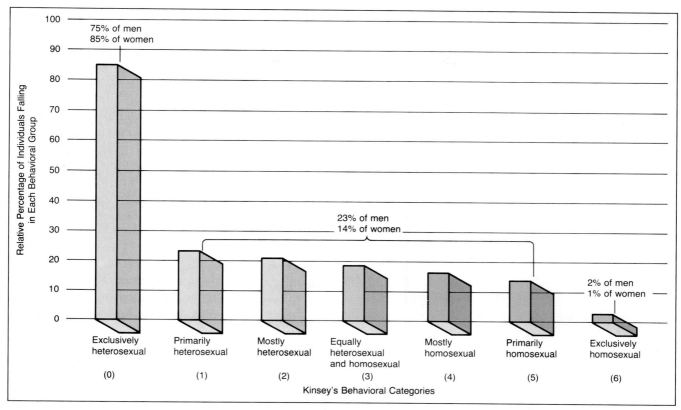

FIGURE 12-1 *SEVEN PATTERNS OF HOMOSEXUAL-HETEROSEXUAL EXPERIENCE* The continuum is based on Kinsey's representation of seven levels of homosexual, bisexual, and heterosexual experiences. The figures above the continuum indicate the probable percentages of the population having had each of the three kinds of sexual interaction. To adjust for sampling errors, these figures are midway between those presented by Kinsey and his colleagues in 1948 and 1953 and those reported by Hunt in 1974.

component is the creation of erotic fantasies involving sex and romance in real or imagined relationships. A person's sexual orientation is defined by the extent to which each of these three components is focused on members of the same or of the opposite sex, as Figure 12-2 suggests.

For some individuals, their sexual activities, feelings of attraction, and fantasies all converge on members of one sex. Often, however, there is a discrepancy between a person's overt sexual acts and his or her private romantic feelings or sexual fantasies. Thus, an individual, like Jerry whose story opened this chapter, may engage in sexual acts with someone of the opposite sex but feel attracted to members of the same sex (Harry, 1984). If the three components do not match in sexual orientation, the discrepancy can create conflicts and anxiety for the individual concerning his or her sexuality. Figure 12-3 illustrates how often behaviors and feelings were reported

FIGURE 12-2 *DEFINING SEXUAL ORIENTATION* The three components of sexual orientation include physical acts, interpersonal affection, and erotic fantasies (DeCecco, 1981). Each component may concentrate on members of the same or of the opposite sex. A person may not be consistent across the three components, and thus his or her sexual preference becomes a matter of definition. A clear homosexual orientation, however, is defined by engaging in physical sexual acts with one or more members of one's own sex, feeling attraction toward and affection for same-sex partners, and having erotic fantasies with homosexual content.

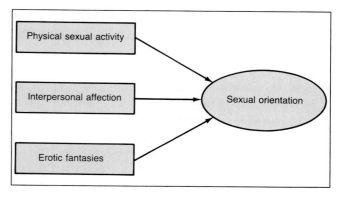

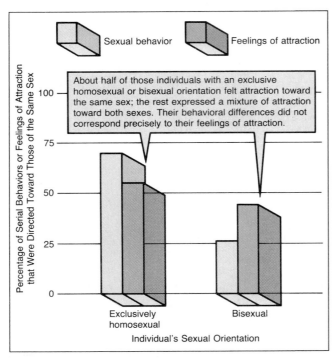

Sexual behavior   Feelings of attraction

About half of those individuals with an exclusive homosexual or bisexual orientation felt attraction toward the same sex; the rest expressed a mixture of attraction toward both sexes. Their behavioral differences did not correspond precisely to their feelings of attraction.

Percentage of Serial Behaviors or Feelings of Attraction that Were Directed Toward Those of the Same Sex

Exclusively homosexual   Bisexual

Individual's Sexual Orientation

FIGURE 12-3 *SEXUAL ORIENTATION: FEELINGS DON'T ALWAYS MATCH BEHAVIOR* In a sample of over 900 persons reporting homosexual or bisexual patterns of behavior, even exclusive homosexuality was not always associated with exclusively homosexual attraction, because many were attracted to members of both sexes. Subjects who engaged in bisexual activity were similarly attracted to both sexes. Approximately one third of this sample indicated a discrepancy between their overt sexual behavior and their interpersonal feelings.
Source: Adapted from Bell & Weinberg, 1978.

to differ from each other as indicated in a survey of bisexuals and exclusive homosexuals.

■ Biological Determinism: Genes and Hormones

Perhaps the most controversial issue about homosexuality concerns its origins. How can we explain why one person develops a heterosexual orientation while another is oriented toward homosexual or bisexual interests? Biological, social, and psychoanalytic theories, as well as combined formulations, have been offered as answers to that question, and none is totally satisfactory (Konner, 1989).

A familiar, and perhaps the simplest, explanation for homosexual behavior is that it is biologically determined.

Gay Genes? Citing evidence that other species—

such as monkeys—engage in homosexual acts in laboratories and zoos (Akers and Conaway, 1979; Chevalier-Skolnikoff, 1976), some scientists have suggested that some portion of our population is innately programmed for same-sex intimacy. In studies of humans, Kallmann (1952) reported that pairs of identical twins tend to be consistently homosexual or heterosexual. More recently, findings by Zuger (1976) failed to replicate those results. Pillard et al. (1982) reported that about 25 percent of the nontwin brothers of homosexual males were also homosexual, but this finding is based on somewhat questionable data (Pillard et al., 1981). If such research produced more reliable results, it would raise the possibility that homosexual behavior is determined by the presence of a gene that somehow affects sexual preference. No specific gene for sexual orientation has been identified to date; if it were, such a gene presumably would be passed on to successive generations by bisexuals who produced children. Current data are not, however, consistent with a genetic explanation of sexual orientation (Zuger, 1989).

Hormonal Determinants of Homosexual Behavior. Experimental studies using mice and rats exposed to different specific hormones before or after birth may not be directly applicable to human behavior, although some of these studies show that levels of prenatal sex hormones can affect the animal's sexual behavior (Birke, 1982). Naturally existing hormone levels do not seem to influence the frequency of sexual behavior among gays of either sex. Conflicting evidence, however, makes it impossible to rule out such factors as possible contributors to sexuality (Dorner, 1988; Meyer-Bahlburg, 1977). For example, in the 1930s and 1940s, androgen was used in an attempt to alter sexual orientation. This approach did not succeed, but it did increase the homoerotic interest of the gays receiving the treatment (Money and Erhardt, 1972). There is also evidence that severe maternal stress during pregnancy increases the chances of a later homosexual orientation in the offspring, presumably because stress affects the prenatal environment of the developing fetus (Ellis et al., 1988).

Evidence has been reported indicating that the sexual orientation of some lesbians may depend partly on exposure to certain sex hormones before birth (Meyer-Bahlburg, 1979). A hormone that has masculinizing effects on female animals (diethylstibestrol or DES) increases masculine sexual patterns in female rats and monkeys. When pregnant rats are given this hormone, they produce female offspring who mount other rats instead of bending over to be mounted by males.

Parallel human data were obtained accidentally. A few decades ago, some pregnant women were given DES during problem pregnancies as a way to prevent spontaneous abortions. (DES was later shown to be ineffective in this respect.) There was evidence, however, that this hormone affected the behavior of the female offspring of these women. Compared to women not exposed to DES while in the womb (including their own sisters), those whose mothers received DES reported more bisexual and homosexual behaviors (Ehrhardt et al., 1985), as Figure 12-4

FIGURE 12-4 *HORMONES AND FEMALE HOMOSEXUALITY* Women aged 17 to 30 whose mothers had been exposed to DES (a masculinizing hormone) during pregnancy reported having more homosexual or bisexual relationships plus more same-sex attraction and fantasies than women whose mothers had not been exposed to the substance. Hormonal variations appear to be one of several quite different factors that may contribute to homosexual behavior.
Source: Based on data from Ehrhardt et al., 1985.

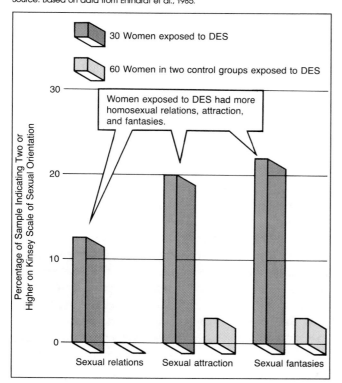

shows. Though the differences between subjects and controls were small, the data indicate that for some women prenatal exposure to this masculinizing hormone increased the likelihood of a later homosexual orientation. It is worth noting, nevertheless, that, "The large majority of homosexuals do not have an abnormal prenatal history" (Gooren et al., 1990, p. 191).

In summary, no purely biological explanations of homosexuality are fully supported by clear-cut evidence (Ruse, 1981). As an example of how biological data dealing with sexual orientation can be reinterpreted, consider a study by Perkins (1981). Lesbians were found to have more muscle tissue, less body fat, and greater arm length and leg circumference than heterosexual women. This could indicate an inborn biological difference associated with sexual orientation. It is equally plausible that homosexual females developed these physical differences because they exercised more and engaged in active sports more often as part of their masculine interests. If so, the physical differences could have been the *result* of behavioral differences rather than the *cause*.

■ Childhood Experiences: Is Sexual Orientation Learned?

At present, an explanation of sexual orientation based entirely on experience seems no more convincing than a biological one (Bell et al., 1981; Suppe, 1982), but let's examine what is known about homosexuality as a learned behavior.

Sexual Experience in Childhood. Most children, given the opportunity, engage in sexual behavior in one form or another. Whether they masturbate or explore sexual possibilities with their peers, their early sexual experiences appear to help shape later sexual attitudes and behavior, as Chapter 7 discusses. It is, therefore, a logical hypothesis that early same-sex sexual experiences may form the basis for later homosexual interests (Freund et al., 1975). A basic question is whether a child's initial sexual contacts with a same-sex peer (or adult) lead to a homosexual orientation in adulthood.

Most of the research on the relationship between childhood sexual experiences and adult preferences has concentrated on males (Jones, 1982). A general finding is that men who report extensive homosexual experiences before puberty are likely to continue it after puberty. Most childhood sex play is limited to mutual genital touching and observation. For some, early childhood also may include oral-genital contact or anal intercourse. These experiences usually are sexually arousing and may even lead to orgasm. The more such experience a young male has, the more likely he is to have a homosexual orientation in adulthood, as Figure 12-5 shows.

It is tempting to accept such findings as strong evidence that sexual orientation is based on an individual's early sexual experiences. Yet, the same sort of doubts that clouded the biological explanations also apply to learning explanations. In a **retrospective** study such as the one just described, the homosexual adults could simply have recalled—or even invented—stories of childhood homosexual experiences that were consistent with their present adult behavior (Schmidt, 1978). Why? Because, we all like to stress the consistency of our behavior, and the homosexual

men in such a study may have been motivated to remember homosexual behavior as a common, stable thread running through their lives. An alternative explanation is that homosexual acts in childhood may in fact be common, but only homosexual men feel comfortable in remembering and reporting them (Ross, 1980).

To rule out such possibilities, **prospective** data are needed in which information about childhood sexual behavior is obtained while subjects are very young; years later, independent information would be gathered concerning adult sexual behavior (Jones, 1982). Actually, even if we had many studies indicating that childhood sexual orientation was strongly related to adult sexual orientation, biological factors could be the key determinants of *both* childhood and adult behavior. Only unethical experimental interventions in which some children were randomly assigned to a group exposed to heterosexual experiences while others were exposed to homosexual experiences could definitively determine whether early learning or biological factors were responsible for adult sexual orientation.

Any explanation of sexual preferences based on early experience is difficult to reconcile with cross-cultural data such as those provided by Baldwin and Baldwin (1989). Among the Sambia in New Guinea, all young males are nourished on mother's milk as infants and on the semen of unmarried adolescent males after age 9. Following 10 years of homosexual interactions (as fellators when they are prepubescent and as fellatees after puberty), they marry young women. Thus, Sambia provide exclusively homosexual experiences for their young males followed by exclusively heterosexual experiences.

Early Maturation as a Determinant of Childhood Sexual Experience. Homosexual orientation could originate from the early development of sexual interests in childhood. How might this take place? Storms (1980, 1981) proposed that sexual images and self-created sexual fantasies are a product of our interpersonal surroundings and constitute an integral part of our sexual development. These images and fantasies in turn help shape our sexual orientation. The content of these fantasies also probably depend in part on the young person's age when the fantasies begin to occur. For example, the prepubertal boy who has sex-

FIGURE 12-5 *HOMOSEXUAL EXPERIENCE BEFORE AND AFTER PUBERTY* In a survey of almost 3,000 male students attending various universities in West Germany, the amount of reported extensive homosexual experience as college students was positively related to the amount of reported homosexual experience prior to puberty.
Source: Based on data from Schmidt, 1978.

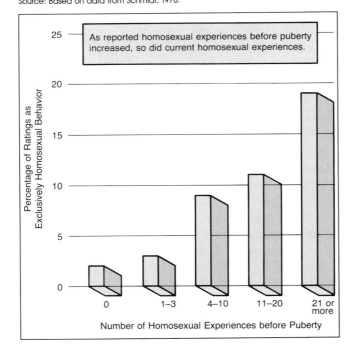

As reported homosexual experiences before puberty increased, so did current homosexual experiences.

Percentage of Ratings as Exclusively Homosexual Behavior

Number of Homosexual Experiences before Puberty

0   1–3   4–10   11–20   21 or more

ual fantasies earlier than his peers very likely has had experience with other males in sex play and in seeing nude male bodies; female partners would ordinarily have been unavailable. Such a boy's thoughts about sex and sexual interactions consequently are likely to involve other boys rather than girls, thus preparing him for later erotic interest in the same sex. In contrast, a boy whose sexual interests developed at a later age probably would have had experiences with both females and males. This difference explains why early maturing boys are likely to have more homosexual masturbatory fantasies in childhood than late maturing boys and, hence, become more likely to have a homosexual orientation in adolescence (Van Wyk and Geist, 1984).

This proposition sounds reasonable, but other research indicates only a few months' difference in the onset of puberty for gays and male heterosexuals (Bell et al., 1981a, b). An additional problem in relating early maturation to homosexuality is that such a formulation is not consistent with what is known about female sexual orientation. For example, girls who develop breasts earlier than their female peers are attractive to older males rather than to other females. Altogether, the early maturation theory is not totally convincing. How else could learning be involved in developing differential sexual interests?

Sissies and Tomboys: Play Behavior.   Do relatively feminine, "sissy" boys and relatively masculine, "tomboy" girls tend to become adult homosexuals? Again, most of the relevant research is based on retrospective data, asking adults to remember their childhood experiences. As a result, we cannot conclude on the basis of such findings that childhood behavior predicts adult behavior.

Nevertheless, there *are* studies indicating a link between feminine play among young boys and later homosexuality, including a prospective investigation of extremely feminine boys and their later sexual development (Green, 1987). Gay males recall playing with girls more often when they were children (Bieber et al., 1962) and playing baseball less (Evans, 1969) than adult heterosexual males. Gay adults generally report fewer masculine behaviors and traits in their childhood than is true for heterosexual men (Hockenberry and Billingham, 1987). A similar association was found for lesbians—they recall being

tomboys (Saghir and Robins, 1973) and playing with guns more than with dolls when they were young (Kaye et al., 1967). Table 12-1 lists some of the play activities recalled by adult homosexual versus heterosexual males and females.

These findings about the relationship between childhood play and adult sexual orientation should be interpreted cautiously. As noted, they too rest on retrospective data and thus may be biased. Also, homosexual males and heterosexual females report that their parents encouraged them to be feminine, so play activity may result from such encouragement. So, even if we tentatively accept the finding that childhood play differs for heterosexuals and homosexuals, it is going too far to conclude that play activities are responsible for later sexual orientation.

The Family Constellation—From Freud to the Homoseductive Mother.   Besides sexual and nonsexual childhood experiences, family relationships—especially interactions between parent and child—have received attention as possible determinants of adult sexual orientation. Freud wrote relatively little about homosexuality, and he never clearly stated his views on its origin. He believed that all people are innately bisexual, though they usually repress these desires. Further, he felt that homosexuals were often extremely creative, that their behavior was biologically determined, and that they were sufficiently well-adjusted to become psychoanalysts (Lewes, 1988). Later psychoanalysts believed that under certain conditions—for example, continued castration anxiety among males—latent homosexual tendencies would appear in overt adult behavior. Freud's beliefs have been largely ignored as analysts describe homosexuality negatively in terms of a neurotic adjustment (Tripp, 1975).

In examinations of family influences, the mother is usually viewed as critical, because she is more likely than the father to be involved in a child's daily activities. Psychoanalyst Irving Bieber (1962) has proposed that interactions between boys and an extremely dominant maternal figure—along with the presence of a relatively nondominant father figure—account for the prevalence of male homosexual orientation compared to the frequency of female homosexual orientation (Lynn, 1969). This type of family was described as creating a fear of heterosexual interac-

TABLE 12-1 **Childhood and Adolescent Interests and Adult Sexual Orientation**

When 396 homosexual and 396 heterosexual adults described their childhood and adolescent activities, some differences were found. For example, among males, homosexuals more often than heterosexuals indicated that they had cooked while more heterosexuals said that they were active in sports. Homosexual males also described their parents as encouraging their feminine play behaviors, while heterosexual males reported the opposite. In an analogous way, lesbian adults described more early masculine activities than did heterosexual women. The fact that these findings are based on retrospective reports raises a caution in that a person's adult sexual orientation may affect what he or she remembers or emphasizes about past events. We are not able to conclude on the basis of such data that particular types of childhood play on adolescent interests *determined* adult sexual orientation.

MALE HOMOSEXUAL ADULTS, AS CHILDREN	*MALE HETEROSEXUAL ADULTS, AS CHILDREN*
Cooked	Played many sports
Listened to records	Made model planes and cars
Played hopscotch and school	Worked on motors and clocks
Play-acted	Played marbles

However, these two groups did not differ in how often they:

Hunted	Went to parties and picnics	Climbed trees
Played cowboys	Built forts	Dated girls

FEMALE HOMOSEXUAL ADULTS, AS CHILDREN	*FEMALE HETEROSEXUAL ADULTS, AS CHILDREN*
Played football	Played school
Built forts	Played with dolls
Played cowboys	Played jacks
Climbed trees	Played hopscotch

However, these two groups did not differ in how often they:

Ran races	Went to movies	Read books
Dated boys	Roller-skated	Played with boys

Source: Adapted from Grellert et al., 1982.

tion, resulting in adult homosexuality. The boy in this situation presumably learns to value femininity rather than masculinity as the appropriate role, but research does not provide consistent support for those propositions (Skeen and Robinson, 1985).

Initial studies of this hypothesis provided support for the importance of the mother's role, but the data were based on homosexual males in therapy for psychological problems (Evans, 1969). In other studies that supported this formulation, subjects were customers at gay bars (Koenig, 1979). The participants in the research, therefore, were not representative of the total homosexual population (Ross and Arrindell, 1988). Some research using less biased samples of gay and straight men has found that ho-

mosexual men rate their mothers *and* fathers as more rejecting and their fathers as less loving (Milic and Crowne, 1986). Also, among college students, gays report more physical abuse by their parents during adolescence than do heterosexual men (Harry, 1989). Consider the possibility that parental rejection and abuse may represent a response to their son's homosexuality rather than a cause of it.

When the family backgrounds of males in four countries—Brazil, Guatemala, the Philippines, and the United States—were examined, only American and Filipino gays described their mothers as stronger and more dominant than their fathers (Whitam and Zent, 1984). Because this relationship did not hold among Guatemalan or Brazilian men, the importance of family background seems to depend on specific cultural factors.

Besides maternal dominance, sexual teasing of a son by his mother (the **homoseductive mother**) has been proposed as a cause of homosexual orientation. However, in the same four-country study, no evidence indicated that mothers of boys who later became homosexual had behaved seductively toward them as children.

Still other studies fail to show any consistent association between women's sexual orientation and their childhood relationships with their parents (Siegelman, 1981b). Some findings suggest that rejection by the mother and/or the father is a critical factor for later development of lesbianism. Possibly an unhappy home situation makes it more difficult for girls to adopt the standard sexual orientation, as one study of lesbians in Hong Kong indicated (Lieh-Mak et al., 1983). An unhappy childhood is not especially unusual, regardless of the person's eventual sexual orientation. A more convincing explanation of female homosexuality based on learning would be one that showed an unhappy childhood combined with pleasurable sexual experiences with another female, but supporting evidence for this is lacking.

After decades of research, we still must say that no definite conclusions about the origins of sexual preference have been reached. One remaining possibility is that some adults are influenced by one set of determinants while others are influenced by totally different factors. It even may be that some individuals are responding to a combination of biological and social factors. For example, Money's (1987) theory of the development of sexual orientation specifies that genetic factors produce prenatal hormonal effects on mammalian brains which become masculinized, feminized, or neither. Subsequent socialization experiences operated to strengthen the existing neurohormonal structure, culminating in a homosexual or heterosexual orientation.

A slightly more complex formulation by Ellis and Ames (1987) suggests that the sexual orientation of all mammals is determined by one or more of five different influences: genetic-hormonal, drugs, maternal stress, individual differences in the offspring's immune system, and socialization.

Keep in mind that the same questions can be asked about either homosexual or heterosexual orientation—how do they develop and why? We know as little about the development of heterosexuality as of homosexuality.

Homosexual and Bisexual Relationships

We know much more about homosexual and bisexual relationships than about the origins of these orientations. In this section, we will explore the individual's awareness of his or her sexual orientation and the process of "coming out," societal attempts to control homosexual behavior, and some of the reasons underlying the negative response to homosexual behavior by formal religions and the legal system. We also will outline how gay and lesbian relationships begin, progress, and are perceived by the participants.

■ Awareness of Sexual Orientation and "Coming Out"

Most people define themselves as heterosexual as a matter of course, and their interactions with the opposite sex conform to what society expects. Those whose sexual orientation does not fit these norms must (1) decide that they differ from the majority and (2) deal with the problem of hiding or publicly revealing this difference.

Self-discovery of Sexual Orientation.   When someone feels that his or her sexual orientation differs from the traditional one, there is often confusion, anxiety, and self-doubt. The decision that one's orientation is homosexual is considered the first step in the process of **coming out**—the recognition, self-acceptance, and communication of a homosexual identity that is integrated into the person's life (Herek, 1985). The initial discovery of homosexual attraction usually occurs during adolescence.

Once the person is clearly aware of his or her homoerotic feelings, the next step is to test this identity and explore sexual interactions with same-sex partners (Coleman, 1982). Gays and lesbians differ in the coming out process (de Monteflores and Schultz, 1978). In a study of several hundred West German homosexuals, males typically experienced their initial awareness of attraction to other men and then interacted sexually with a same-sex partner at age eighteen or nineteen (Schafer, 1977). Among lesbians, these first steps toward coming out were most likely to occur at ages fifteen to seventeen.

Despite the earlier age of homosexual interest among lesbians, male certainty about having a gay orientation is likely to occur at age nineteen, a year and a half earlier than for lesbians. Gay men tend to assume they are homosexual if they experience one sexual act with another male, and one in six decide they are gay without any sexual contact with males (McDonald, 1982). Lesbians are more likely to experience multiple same-sex interactions before identifying their orientation as homosexual. Thus, males define themselves sexually in terms of physical acts (de Monteflores and Schultz, 1978). For females, feelings and the development of attachments to a loved partner are more important than specific sexual behaviors.

Self-acceptance. The homophobic attitudes of others create difficulties for the person who decides that he or she is a member of a disliked minority group (Sophie, 1985/86). The heterosexual peer group is likely to reject the adolescent who is moving toward homosexuality. For this reason, the support of homosexual organizations or partners is emotionally helpful and serves to strengthen the new identity.

Communicating a New Identity. A homosexual orientation usually is disclosed first to sexual partners and fellow homosexuals. The lower the individual's socioeconomic class the more openly sexual orientation is discussed; middle- and upper-class individuals try to hide their homosexuality (Bell and Weinberg, 1978).

Integration of the homosexual identity begins with a separation of the world into gay and straight, "us and them." Gradually, the identity becomes more stable. In a survey of fifty-one gay males, those who felt comfortable about their orientation and who told heterosexuals about it had more positive self-concepts and experienced less depression than those who were uncomfortable and secretive (Schmitt and Kurdek, 1987). The successful resolution of the coming out process is a difficult challenge. At the opposite extreme from maintaining secrecy is the desire to announce one's gay or lesbian orientation by means of lapel pins, buttons, stickers, and flags. Information

"*Really, Mom, there's no need to worry because the dorm's gone coed.*"

FIGURE 12-6 *HOMOSEXUALITY: ANXIETY-AROUSING AND A SOURCE OF HUMOR* At present, homosexual behavior is accepted by many heterosexuals, but there is still a large amount of anxiety and fear about this topic. This cartoon suggests that parental worries about their offspring's heterosexual behavior would be insignificant compared to their reactions to an offspring's homosexual orientation.
Reprinted by Special Permission of Playboy Magazine. Copyright © 1973 by Playboy.

about these items is available from such organizations as Lambda Rising, 1625 Connecticut Ave., N.W., Washington DC 20009.

In a human sexuality course, a lesbian college student and her mother visited the class to discuss the daughter's homosexuality. The student's mother said that she had accepted her daughter's orientation. In response to a question from one of the students about her views, she responded, "My daughter chose a hard way to be a part of society."

The problem of informing parents about being gay or lesbian is a special one, as Figure 12-6 suggests. Gays and lesbians are advised by physicians and others to build up to disclosure slowly, to provide information in the form of books and other reading material or to have a friend discuss the topic with their parents (Deisher, 1982). It is suggested that every attempt be made to maintain the relationship with parents and to recognize that they may accept but not approve of their son or daughter being homosexual. Parents need time to adjust to such information: Their anger or guilt may interfere with acceptance (Myers, 1981), and the problems are especially acute for homophobic parents (Holtzen and Agresti, 1990). Some helpful literature is available from the Federation of Parents and Friends of Lesbians and Gays,

P. O. Box 20308, Denver, Colorado 80220; enclose a long, self-addressed, stamped envelope.

■ **Attempts to Control Homosexual Behavior: Religious and Legal Restrictions**

An astonishing amount of time and energy has been invested over the centuries in attempts to control sexual acts between same-sex partners. Despite these unending efforts, historical accounts indicate that the frequency of homosexual activity has remained unaffected: Between 5 and 15 percent of the population consistently identify themselves as homosexual (Bullough, 1976). The response of Western society to homosexual behavior has varied over time. (Greenberg, 1989), as Table 12-2 outlines.

Religion and Homosexuality. Western religions most often endorse antihomosexual policies because of their generally negative attitudes about sexuality, specifically their negative response to anal sexual acts (Gilbert, 1981). In contrast to Christianity and Judaism, non-Western religions such as Hinduism and Buddhism have been more accepting of homosexual behavior. In this brief space, we will be able to provide only a few examples of the effects of religious thought on homosexuality.

TABLE 12-2   **Responding to Homosexuals: Acceptance or Intolerance?**

Society's response to homosexual behavior and to the rights of homosexuals has a long history of alternations between tolerance and persecution, as this brief historical sample indicates.

EVENTS	PLACE AND TIME
Homosexual relations were allowed for the warrior class among pederasts, or older men with a younger male partner.	Greece, fifth to fourth centuries B.C.
Some social tolerance existed until end of twelfth century A.D., followed by great intolerance and hostility toward homosexuality.	Western Europe, Christian era through thirteenth century
Legal executions of female and male homosexuals occurred.	Europe and America, fourteenth through eighteenth centuries
Laws made conviction for engaging in homosexual acts very difficult.	Massachusetts, 1700s
Male homosexual prostitution was seen as creating the need to make all male homosexual acts illegal.	England, 1800s through early 1900s
Male homosexuals were made to wear a pink triangle on their clothing as special markings; many were executed in Nazi concentration camps.	Germany, 1940s
Gay liberation movement flourished.	United States, 1950 onward
Negative response to gays based on the threat of AIDS.	United States and Western Europe, 1983 onward

Sources: listed chronologically by era in question—Dover, 1978; Boswell, 1979; Crompton, 1981; Oaks, 1981; Weeks, 1977; Lautmann, 1981; Licata, 1981; Landers, 1986.

Ancient Judaism prescribed the death penalty for gays (Crompton, 1981). Christian hostility to homosexuality can be traced to the writings of St. Augustine and St. Thomas Acquinas. Earlier, the Church in Europe was relatively tolerant of homosexuality (Boswell, 1980).

In the Middle Ages, the admission of homosexual acts between males (and often between females) was extracted under torture by the agents of the Inquisition. The punishment was genital mutilation. Religious intolerance and hostility toward homosexuality were common from the Middle Ages through the twentieth century. A different source of negative attitudes was provided by medicine in the eighteenth and nineteenth centuries, viewing homosexuality as an illness rather than a sin (Bullough, 1978). A homosexual was believed to be born with this "defect" that was linked to genetic flaws and neurological weakness (Krafft-Ebing, 1886).

Today, the position of the Roman Catholic Church is that homosexuality is a sin that is condemned on moral grounds (Suro, 1986). Homosexual Catholics are encouraged to recognize the sinfulness of homosexual acts and to remain celibate, but they may practice the sacraments of the church.

Secular Law and Homosexual Behavior. Any perversion of what was assumed to be natural sex (heterosexual intercourse with the aim of reproduction)—such as oral sex and especially anal sex—was labeled as **sodomy**. Literally, *sodomy* means committing whatever acts were committed in Sodom, which, according to Genesis, Chapters 18 and 19, was destroyed along with Gomorrah because of the wicked acts that occurred in both places. Only many centuries later was it concluded that the wickedness consisted of oral and anal sexual acts, and perhaps sex with animals as well. Religious writers frequently have associated the anus with devil and bestiality (Gilbert, 1981). Sodomy laws in the United States vary from state to state, with consensual homosexual acts illegal in half of them. Incidentally, homosexuality was outlawed in the 13 original colonies and in all

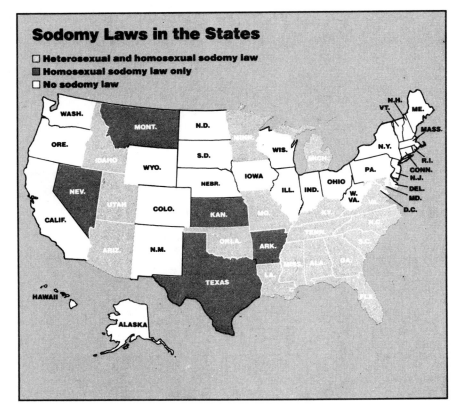

Sodomy Laws in the States

☐ **Heterosexual and homosexual sodomy law**
■ **Homosexual sodomy law only**
☐ **No sodomy law**

FIGURE 12-7 *SODOMY AS A CRIME: IT DE-PENDS ON YOUR LOCATION* In the U.S., sodomy was illegal in 25 states as of 1989. No anti-sodomy laws were on the books in the remaining 25 states or in the District of Columbia.

50 states until 1961 (The rights of . . . , 1986). In China today, homosexuality is prohibited (Ruan and Tsai, 1988). Figure 12-7 identifies those states currently having sodomy laws and whether they apply to everyone or solely to homosexuals. Sodomy is sometimes identified specifically as oral or anal sex acts, and sometimes as any sexual acts involving two males (MacNamara, 1982c). One example is provided by the legal code of Virginia, section 18.1 to 21.2:

> If any person shall carnally know . . . any brute animal . . . any male or female by the anus or with the mouth . . . he or she shall be guilty of a feloney . . .

Three hundred years ago the British legal system introduced the term **buggery** to cover bestiality (sexual contact with animals), child molestation by homosexuals, and homosexual acts (Burg, 1981). Those convicted of buggery could be executed for the crime, although this did not happen often. Many homosexuals, nevertheless, *have* been put to death because of their sexual orientation, including the estimated 100,000 to 400,000 murdered by the Nazi regime in Germany during the 1930s and 1940s (Crompton, 1978). In the United States, persecution was more difficult. The late director of the Federal Bureau of Investigation, J. Edgar Hoover, wanted to prevent or punish such behavior but complained "that we of the FBI are powerless to act in cases of oral-genital intimacy, unless it has in some way obstructed interstate commerce" (Unger and Churcher, 1980, p. 14).

The special section, *Taking Responsibility and Protecting Yourself*, on pages 327 to 328, describes how negative attitudes about homosexuals underlie some of the past and present responses to them.

Taking Responsibility and Protecting Yourself

HOMOPHOBIA AND BIAS AGAINST HOMOSEXUALS

A letter printed in an Ann Landers (1980) column suggested, "Let us, once and for all, get rid of the word 'gay' as a euphemism for homosexual. . . . The homos I have seen are a depressing eyesore on the landscape of humanity."

The person who wrote that letter was undoubtedly expressing more than an interest in terminology. The letter appears to reflect **homophobia**—an irrational fear or intolerance of homosexuals (Morin and Garfinkle, 1978). A homophobic person, as measured by various scales (e.g., Dunbar et al., 1973), tends to agree with such statements as:

Homosexuality is a rotten perversion and ought to be suppressed.

Homosexuals are no better than criminals.

These and similar sentiments are associated with the desire to avoid coming in contact with anyone or anything (a person, artistic depictions, thoughts, or feelings) associated with homosexuality. Those individuals who hold the most traditional beliefs about male-female sex roles are the most negative in evaluating gays and lesbians (Newman, 1989, Whitley, 1987).

The discomfort experienced by those who are homophobic appears to include both anger and guilt (Ernulf and Innala, 1987). The anger leads to derogation, rejection, discrimination, and even physical attacks. The feelings of guilt are less obvious, but they seem to be based on the knowledge that one's prejudice and bigotry are wrong.

A somewhat less intense negative reaction is described as a **homosexual bias**, involving conservative objections to homosexuality on religious and moral grounds (Fyfe, 1983; Herek, 1987). Homosexual bias is frequently based at least partially on myths about homosexuals, such as the belief that child molesters are usually gay, even though this has been shown repeatedly to be untrue (McCaghy, 1971; also, see Chapter 13). An experimental investigation, using a penile plethysmograph, indicated that gays are no more aroused by photographs of immature boys than heterosexual men are by photographs of immature girls (Freund et al., 1989). Homosexual bias leads to the conclusion that homosexual behavior is clearly *deviant,* whatever that term means to the person using it (see Chapter 13). The basic assumption leading to homosexual bias is that homosexuality does not meet the standards for appropriate behavior as defined by the dominant groups in a society.

Like prejudice toward members of a given race or a specific religion, homophobia and homosexual bias grow out of negative emotions and thoughts about the target group. With prejudice based on race or religion, there is no disagreement about the origins of the target group; we know that race is determined genetically and that religious beliefs are learned. Because people differ in their assumptions about the origins of a same-sex orientation, these beliefs must be taken into account along with positive–negative attitudes. Thus, homosexuals are disliked most by people who feel negatively about their sexual behavior *and* who believe that homosexuality is based on learning (Aguero et al., 1984). For these homophobes, the behavior is not only unpleasant but also something that *anyone* could learn. This "fear of contamination" by homosexuals is contrasted with simple social avoidance of homosexuals which is characteristic of those with a negative emotional reaction to homosexuality coupled with the belief that sexual orientation is based on physical determinants.

Other areas of discrimination include employment: twenty-nine percent of gays indicate that their sexual orientation has a negative impact on their careers, and 17 percent report having lost or failed to obtain a job for this reason (Levine, 1980). Perhaps these figures would be even higher if 70 to 75 percent of gays did not hide their sexual orientation from their employer (Bell and Weinberg, 1978; Weinberg and Williams, 1974). On one college campus, derogatory remarks and hostile treatment by other students and university employees were reported by half of the gays and lesbians who responded to a survey. Homosexual bias is also evident in college textbooks, including introductory psychology (McDonald, 1981) and social science (Morin, 1977). Research on this topic is more likely to fo-

cus on male than on female homosexuality, presumably because it is viewed as a more serious "problem". Homophobia is also reflected in housing discrimination, limitations set by the military and by some religious ministries, and by jokes about "queers." Possibly in response to the threat of AIDS, public opinion is shifting toward more negative views. In Great Britain, for example, in the early 1980s, 27 percent of the population felt that private sexual acts between gays should be illegal; by the end of the 1980s, 43 percent endorsed this view (Koenig, 1988).

It may seem surprising, but lesbians in the United States Marine Corps have been discharged on the basis of their sexual activity at a rate of 10 times greater than is true for gay men (Lewin, 1988). Though these figures may represent the presence of more lesbians than gays in the Marines, it is possible that this is an exception to the general rule of greater tolerance for female than for male homosexuality.

Homosexual bias has many interpersonal implications. When a stranger is identified as a homosexual, heterosexuals then view him or her as unlikable (Gross et al., 1980). If, however, the stranger is bisexual with primarily heterosexual interests, he or she *is* deemed likable and even attractive as a sexual partner (Istvan, 1983). Whenever the other person's sexual experience is more than 50 percent homosexual, however, the response is a negative one.

Attitudes about lesbians are much less negative than attitudes about gays (Kelley, 1985a). One possible reason is that our society accepts close friendships between females and behavior such as embracing and kissing more easily than it does be-

tween males; men with very close male friends or those who make physical contact with other men are likely to be labeled as homosexual (Rose, 1985). *Some* negative reactions to lesbians do occur. Homosexual women are believed to be physically unattractive (Dew, 1985), and there is confusion about how they fit female roles (Storms et al., 1981). Generally, heterosexual males are more negative about homosexuality than are heterosexual females, especially with respect to gays (Herek, 1988; Kurdek, 1988).

In the 1980s and 1990s, a new wave of homophobia has been observed, including anti-gay violence (Gutis, 1989). The impetus seems to be an increase in conservatism and the AIDS epidemic that occurs at a higher rate in the gay community.

Strongly held attitudes such as those about homosexuality are resistant to change. Yet, some educational techniques have proven effective in reducing the negative responses. In one study, student nurses participated in a two-hour seminar that dealt with many of the issues discussed in this chapter (Anderson, 1981). Some viewed a film that depicted the sexual interaction of two gays. The nurses were then told of ways to interact positively with gay and lesbian patients. The outcome of this learning experience was positive—homosexual bias was reduced, and this effect persisted for at least the next four months. Decreased bias resulted whether or not the seminar leaders were identified as being homosexual themselves. A similar increased tolerance has been found among students who take a college sexuality course (Larsen et al., 1983; Stevenson, 1988).

■ Couples and Other Relationships

The stereotype of gays and lesbians as sexually hyperactive, desperately seeking anonymous partners for short-term interactions is mostly inaccurate. Heterosexuals find it hard to believe that homosexual

couples can possibly feel as much love or be as satisfied with their relationships as heterosexual couples (Testa et al., 1987). A large-scale study (Bell and Weinberg, 1978) of nearly 1,000 homosexuals living in San Francisco dispelled such myths. Table 12-3 presents the types of relationships reported by these

TABLE 12-3 **Sexual Styles among Gays and Lesbians**

Interviews with almost 1,000 gays and lesbians revealed that most could be classified as fitting one of these five sexual styles.

TYPE OF RELATIONSHIP	BEHAVIOR	PERCENTAGE OF	
		Males	*Females*
Close-coupled	Strong emotional commitment; sexual fidelity	10	28
Open-coupled	Some emotional commitment; partners lived together and also had other sexual partners	18	17
Functional	High level of sexual activity; little or no commitment to a single individual; younger than other subgroups	15	10
Dysfunctional	High level of sexual activity; reported more sexual problems and regrets about homosexual behavior	12	5
Asexual	Little or no interest in sexual activity	16	11

Source: Based on data from Bell and Weinberg, 1978.

individuals. Two of the five subgroups consisted of couples in relationships like heterosexuals—**close-coupled** and **open-coupled**. The close-coupled pairs have a strong emotional commitment to each other and practice sexual monogamy (Warczok, 1988). Open-coupled pairs have some emotional commitment and live together, but they also seek out other sexual partners. Though 28 percent of gays were involved as couples, it is also true that the number of past sexual partners was quite high. Half of these males reported having had at least 500 different sexual partners.

The other sexual styles were **functional** (sexually active and uncommitted to a specific partner), *dysfunctional* (sexually active with sexual problems and regrets), and *asexual* (low interest in sexual activity).

Forming Couples. Legal recognition of gay couples has become increasingly common. In Denmark, for example, gay couples can establish legal partnerships entitling them to most of the advantages and disadvantages of a heterosexual marriage (Rule, 1989).

They become responsible for each other's financial support, including alimony if the partnership is dissolved. If one of the partners should die, the survivor is entitled to receive an inheritance. In New York City, a gay partner of a deceased leaseholder retains the apartment (Gutis, 1989); before 1989, this right applied only to married couples. In that same year, San Francisco granted legal recognition to domestic partners, including homosexuals (Bishop, 1989). Some universities (such as Stanford) now provide the same benefits to gay and lesbian couples as to married or cohabiting heterosexuals—for example, housing and medical care (Johnston, 1990).

Long-term homosexual relationships are less stable than comparable heterosexual ones, perhaps because legal marriage is usually not an option; they have few role models, and do not benefit from societal acceptance and encouragement (Coleman, 1982a). Probably because of the fear of AIDS, close-coupled relationships have increased in frequency among male homosexuals (Martin, 1987).

One characteristic of the behavior of homosexual couples might surprise you. While forced sex is

Highlighting Research

MALE–FEMALE DIFFERENCES AMONG HOMOSEXUALS

Gay men experiment with many more sexual partners than is true for lesbians, and their relationships are often substantially different, paralleling many of the gender differences in attitudes and motives found among heterosexuals (Leigh, 1989). What are some of the other sex differences?

White (1980) found that "cruising" (seeking repeated impersonal contacts in one night) was practiced regularly by 60 percent of homosexual males, while another 25 percent cruised about once a month. Lesbians, in contrast, do not cruise as often as gay men. One possible reason for this sex difference is that women in general place a higher value on fidelity in relationships than men do. Homosexual organizations in large cities provide a private alternative to cruising in public settings such as gay bars.

Another male–female difference is the way they advertise their interests in seeking a same-sex partner. A typical male ad in *Village Voice* reads:

> *Man seeks witty, tall, and lovely man for good times. Ask for Paul, the Adonis of Gleason Street.*

A typical female ad reads:

> *Warm, humorous woman with interest in foreign films and gardening seeks compatible female for roommate.*

As Table 12-4 indicates, the ads of homosexuals and heterosexuals reflect similar sex differences. Sexual orientation, nevertheless, affects the ad content to some extent (Deaux and Hanna, 1984). For example, men seeking a male partner are more likely to emphasize their own attractiveness and general appearance than men seeking a female partner. In contrast, lesbians seeking a female partner stress hob-

---

TABLE 12-4   **Advertising for a Partner: Heterosexuals, Gays, and Lesbians**

The sex and sexual orientation of 800 people who placed personal ads in four publications such as the *Village Voice* were associated with what the advertiser sought and what he or she offered. Compared to lesbians, heterosexual women were more likely to offer physical attractiveness and to seek financial security. Both gays and heterosexual men sought physical attractiveness in a partner, but gays were more likely than heterosexuals to stress their own physical appearance and attractiveness.

GAYS MOST OFTEN SOUGHT:	GAYS MOST OFTEN OFFERED:
Personality traits, 45.5% (e.g., sense of humor)	Certain physical characteristics, 74%
Certain physical characteristics, 38% (e.g., height)	Physical atttractiveness, 53.5%
Physical attractiveness, 29%	Personality traits, 46.5%
Sexual traits, 29% (e.g., lustfulness)	

HETEROSEXUAL MEN MOST OFTEN SOUGHT:	HETEROSEXUAL MEN MOST OFTEN OFFERED:
Personality traits, 62.5%	Certain physical characteristics, 71.5%
Physical attractiveness, 48%	Personality traits, 62.5%
Certain physical characteristics, 33.5%	Hobbies or interests, 43.5% (e.g., cooking)

LESBIANS MOST OFTEN SOUGHT:	LESBIANS MOST OFTEN OFFERED:
Personality traits, 72%	Personality traits, 81%
Physical attractiveness, 18%	Hobbies or interests, 56.5%
Sincerity, 17%	

HETEROSEXUAL WOMEN MOST OFTEN SOUGHT:	HETEROSEXUAL WOMEN MOST OFTEN OFFERED:
Personality traits, 82%	Personality traits, 77%
Financial security, 32%	Physical attractiveness, 69.5%
Sincerity, 32%	Certain physical characteristics, 64%
Similar hobbies or interests, 23.5%	

Source: Based on data from Deaux and Hanna, 1984.

bies and personality traits; heterosexual females stress them, too, but they also express an interest in financial security. Both sex and sexual orientation affect what we expect and seek in a partner.

Sex differences in language also found among gays and lesbians. For example, lesbians are more likely to use words such as clitoris, making love, and suck, while gays are more inclined to say pussy, fuck, and blow job (Wells, 1989). Similar male-female differences are found among heterosexuals.

Once they enter a fairly committed relationship, male and female homosexuals show certain differences. Lesbian partners tend to be relatively similar in income and social status while gay partners are often quite discrepant (Cotton, 1975; Kurdek and Schmitt, 1987). Gays are more likely than lesbians to exclude their partners from their nonsexual activities, presumably because of socioeconomic dissimilarity.

common among heterosexual couples (date rape, marital rape, and so on), it is sometimes assumed that coercion does not occur among gays and lesbians. In fact, recent research indicates that 12 percent of gays and 31 percent of lesbians report being the victims of forced sex by their partners (Waterman et al., 1989). Thus, sexual violence is not limited to heterosexual males and females.

Some of the differences between gays and lesbians are considered in the special section, **Highlighting Research**, on pages 330 to 331.

■ Men: Gay Lifestyles

It seems easier for heterosexuals to picture promiscuous gays cruising for random partners than to imagine gay couples in a committed, loving relationship. What are such couples like?

Gay Couples. Men who *do* form close, intimate gay relationships resemble heterosexual males in the way they develop a caring friendship. Both value such traits in a long-term partner as honesty and affection (Laner, 1978). Like heterosexual couples, most male–male partners are close in age—within five or six years (Harry, 1982). You may have heard that many young gays seek an older man as a father figure, perhaps imitating the ancient Greeks who accepted such man–boy coupling, but this pattern is not common. Just as heterosexuals seek partners who are similar to them in attitudes and personality traits (see Chapter 10), gays also desire a partner similar to themselves (Boyden et al., 1984).

When gays are strongly attached to their partners, feelings of closeness increase, and sexual experimentation with alternative partners decreases. Peplau and Cochran (1981) define attachment by the impor-

tance placed on the following aspects of a relationship:

Sexual fidelity in the relationship
Living together
Spending as much time together as possible
Sharing as many activities with my partner as possible
Knowing that the relationship will endure for a long time
Knowing that my partner depends on me

When close-coupled were compared with open-coupled pairs, the former were more likely to report high attachment, strong feelings of love, and the expectancy of a long-lasting relationship. Attachment also was associated with a high frequency of sexual interactions with the partner and less frequent sexual activity with others. Among the least-attached gays, 80 percent engaged in sex with someone other than the partner during the previous two months; for those whose attachment was high, only 30 percent had an outside sexual interaction.

The most usual patterns among gays are either to begin the relationship with sexual exclusivity or to progress from multiple partners to an exclusive one (Blasband and Peplau, 1985). Few (20 percent) start with an exclusive relationship and then progress to openness. Even when homosexual marriage is not a legal possibility, many have quasi-marriages, relationships that strongly resemble those of heterosexual couples. One pair of men, an artist and a literary critic, were lovers for twenty years; then, one died. During their relationship, they wrote over 3,000 letters to each other in the following vein:

. . . our two lives and personalities have blended into a harmony of understanding affection which brings us closer to the other than we have ever been to anyone else. I did not know that life contained anything so rich and deep . . . . It is a marriage that demands nothing and gives everything [Hyde, 1978, pp. 11, 28].

No relationship runs smoothly all the time, of course, and homosexual partners have disagreements and arguments just as heterosexual couples do. The emphasis on competition that characterizes men in our culture can interfere with a mutually satisfying, supportive gay relationship (Reece and Segrist, 1981). Among sixty gay couples, partners who had recently separated were found to have been less cooperative and helpful toward each other than couples who stayed together. The most successful long-term relationships were characterized by cooperation and close feelings of attachment.

Stages of a Gay Relationship. The development of a close intimate relationship between two males involves positive emotions, financial cooperation, and occasional conflicts.

McWhirter and Mattison (1984) interviewed and observed 156 male couples who had lived together an average of 8.9 years. These investigators described six stages that characterized the relationships over time. First, *blending* occurs in the first year—frequent sexual interactions, strong feelings of love, and the beginning of a working relationship. Second, *nesting* occupies the next two years—sexual activity declines somewhat, financial provisions are made, and areas of compatibility replace the glow of love. Third, the fourth and fifth years are devoted to *maintaining*—conflict resolution is worked out, traditions such as birthday celebrations are established, and there is an independent identity for each partner. Fourth, *building* takes place in the sixth through tenth years as the partners set joint goals, such as a business. Fifth, *releasing* occurs in the second decade of the relationship with increased trust, taking the partner for granted, and a further decline in the frequency of sexual interactions. Sixth, *renewing* takes place in the years beyond the twentieth anniversary—the couple remembers the good and bad times and feel a renewed sense of partnership based on a firm foundation. This description of the six stages seems equally applicable to heterosexual marriages.

Bars and Bathhouses. Participation in a loving relationship with a partner is not the only possible sexual pattern for gays. A large subgroup of homosexual males patronize homosexual bars or bathhouses where a highly impersonal form of sexual interaction occurs, and such activity is most likely in big cities (Harry, 1974). A distinct set of rules and behavioral expectations applies. The bars are a setting for seeking new partners, after careful inspection of the possibilities—much like singles bars for heterosexuals. Part of the ritual for gays is an exaggeration of masculine or feminine behavior (Read, 1980). Gays may make a display of flexing their muscles to emphasize masculinity or of preening in front of a mirror to emphasize femininity, for example. Except for the choice of partners, gay bars and singles bars have a lot in common.

A different homosexual setting, the bathhouse, is more or less analogous to brothels for heterosexual males. In the bathhouse, occupants of a steam room or of small cubicles wait to be selected by a paying customer as a partner in a sexual act (Weiss, 1985). Repeated sexual acts often occur with the same or different partners, all within hearing and frequently in sight of other couples—all strangers to one another. For many gays, these interactions arouse fears of rejection because each person is free to refuse the offer of a sexual encounter. This freedom of choice is one way a bathhouse differs from a brothel; another is in the method of payment. Instead of paying for a prostitute's services, each gay customer simply pays an admission fee plus a charge for the rental of towels and space.

A third pattern of impersonal gay sex has no heterosexual analogy. Public restrooms are used: A "glory hole" is cut in the partition between stalls so that an erect penis can be inserted and fellated by a stranger in the adjoining stall.

These varieties of gay behavior—bars, bathhouses, and restrooms—have become less popular since the mid-1980s because of the fear of AIDS, except among younger, less-educated, and lower-income gay males (Richwald et al., 1988). All are quite different from private homosexual acts between partners involved in an established relationship because they tend not to include concern, affection, and love (Hedblom and Hartman, 1980).

Females: Lesbian Lifestyle

Three elements that help to maintain or dissolve any relationship are the degree of similarity between partners, the degree of their involvement with each other, and the balance of power between them. Such variables are as important for female–female pairs as for heterosexual couples (Peplau et al., 1982). Differences in power suggest a stereotyped **butch-femme** relationship, in which one woman typically behaves in masculine ways while her partner behaves in more obviously feminine ways. Most lesbian couples, in fact, divide such activities as home repair and cooking about equally, and they do not conform to a stereotyped masculine–feminine split (Caldwell and Peplau, 1984).

For female couples, satisfying, loving relationships often grow out of simple friendships (Vetere, 1982). The typical sequence for most lesbians (78 percent) is friendship followed by romantic and sexual involvement. Friendship is perceived as enhancing their mutual romantic feelings, and long-term lesbian relationships are more satisfying to the participants than comparable gay relationships (Kurdek, 1989). Two women expressed their thoughts about friendship and love in this way:

> *When you come down to it, the friendship is a real sizable chunk of the relationship.*

> *I've never had a lover [before] who was my best friend. It adds a whole dimension to the relationship [Vetere, 1982, p. 60].*

Besides relating as couples, lesbians also seek out other social contacts. In a sample of almost 400 lesbians surveyed over a ten-year period in three regions of the United States, most (83 percent) reported going to bars catering primarily to homosexual women (Hedblom and Hartman, 1980). About one in six visited lesbian bars weekly or more often. The respondents indicated that the bars were not used to seek impersonal sexual encounters. Rather, this setting provided a way to meet new friends and talk to other women with common interests—whether or not they currently were involved with a partner.

Gallup (1986) proposed that lesbians experience unsatisfactory sex with men and, as a result, turn to women as an alternative means to achieve gratification. There is some support for this hypothesis in that most lesbians (71 percent) indicate that they have had sexual interactions with a male, usually sexual intercourse, often without great satisfaction (Hedblom and Hartman, 1980). Lesbians, like homosexual males, seem to be more precocious sexually than their heterosexual counterparts. That is, lesbians report having had more male partners and starting sexual activity at an earlier age (sixteen versus seventeen) than heterosexual women (Goode and Haber, 1977), as Figure 12-8 shows. Most lesbians say that they do not enjoy fellating a man—sexually experienced heterosexual women report that both fellatio and intercourse are pleasurable to them. The typical developmental pattern for lesbians is to experiment with heterosexual activity earlier than other women, to discover that intercourse and fellatio are unsatisfactory, and then to seek a female friend as a sexual partner. Some hold the stereotype that lesbian sex is unsatisfactory, but homosexual women report that sexual interactions with another woman is highly pleasurable. Lesbians also report masturbating more frequently and enjoyably than do heterosexual females.

Bisexual Patterns

Our discussion so far has focused on sexual orientation as primarily heterosexual or homosexual, as has much of the research on this topic. Most "homosexuals" are in fact bisexual, and some "heterosexuals" are also bisexual (MacDonald, 1981). The terms *AC/DC* (for alternating current/direct current) or "switch hitter" are sometimes applied to bisexuals. A sizable percentage of the homosexuals in the Bell and Weinberg (1978) study said that they had a bisexual orientation, as Figure 12-9 shows. Sex researchers are increasingly aware of the importance of bisexual behavior, and more information is now available on the topic than previously. The incidence of male bisexuality has decreased in recent years because of the fear of AIDS.

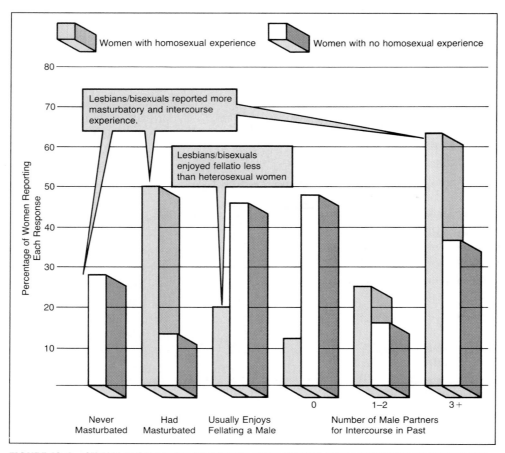

FIGURE 12-8   *SEXUAL EXPERIENCE OF LESBIAN AND BISEXUAL WOMEN VERSUS HETEROSEXUAL WOMEN*   Compared to exclusively heterosexual female students, lesbian or bisexual female students reported masturbating more frequently, engaging in sex with more male partners, and enjoying fellatio less. Their behavior suggests greater interest in sexual stimulation and less gratification in their heterosexual relationships than is true for heterosexual women.
Source: Based on data from Goode & Haber, 1977.

The search for consistency in the backgrounds of bisexuals has been unsuccessful (Blumstein and Schwartz, 1977). For example, only a minority of them report homosexual contacts prior to adulthood, and few of the males had dominant mothers. Most bisexuals had no early, traumatic sexual experiences such as childhood molestation. Instead of a common pattern, there are simply unique, individual paths to bisexual behavior. Whether bisexuality originates accidentally or through deliberate choice, most individuals whose sexual experience includes both men and women nevertheless report a preference for a partner of one sex. Patterns of relationships vary: Sometimes a long-term homosexual relationship occurs before a heterosexual one, sometimes the re-

verse, and sometimes the two types occur during the same time period.

As an example of one specific person's experience, a bisexual woman reported initiating sexual contacts with other girls at pajama parties when she was about seven or eight and being punished for it. In adolescence, she was brutally gang-raped. As a young adult, she defined herself as a lesbian behaviorally and emotionally, but a year later fell in love with a man and planned marriage.

Marriage and Bisexuality.   It is not unusual for bisexuals to marry, sometimes because of social pressures to have a spouse and sometimes simply to experiment with a heterosexual lifestyle (Paluszny,

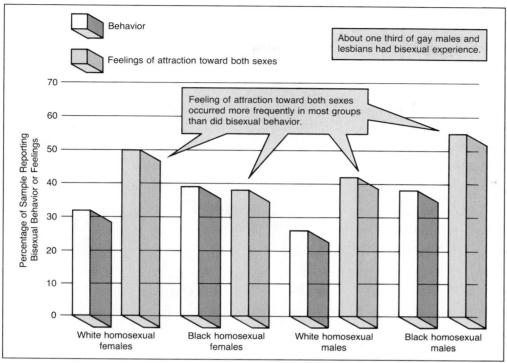

FIGURE 12-9 *HOMOSEXUAL OR BISEXUAL* Bisexual behavior and feelings are commonly reported by gays and lesbians (Bell & Weinberg, 1978). Among "homosexuals"—male and female, black and white—26 to 39 percent had engaged in sexual behavior with both sexes, and 38 to 55 percent reported sexual attraction to both sexes. It appears that a great many individuals who should be classified as bisexual are labeled as homosexual.
Source: Based on data from Bell & Weinberg, 1978.

1982). In Bell and Weinberg's (1978) sample of bisexuals, 30 percent of the women and 20 percent of the men said they married to avoid openly acknowledging a homosexual orientation. When a wife learns of her husband's bisexuality after they are married, her reaction usually is strongly negative (Gochros, 1985). These women feel isolated, confused, and neglected, and the marriage often dissolves (Wolf, 1985).

When a bisexual man is involved in a long-term heterosexual marriage, does his sexual orientation become heterosexual? Apparently, this is not the case. Bisexual males married an average of 7.75 years were found to respond to pictures of nude men with more sexual excitement than to pictures of nude women (McConaghy, 1978). Though a woman may be strongly motivated to change the sexual preferences of her bisexual lover or spouse, she is not likely to succeed.

Compared to heterosexual males, bisexual men express less satisfaction with their marriages even though they had more sexual activity and more orgasms with their wives than did the heterosexual males (D. Dixon, 1985). This finding is complicated by the fact that the heterosexuals in Dixon's study engaged in "swinging" (exchanging partners with other couples; see Chapter 9). Both partners of swinging couples typically interacted with other couples, whereas the bisexual men did not bring their wives along when they had homosexual encounters.

Compared to married bisexual men, bisexual women are usually less aware of their homosexual inclinations and less likely to have had such encounters prior to marriage. Almost all bisexual men report same-sex interactions before they married while only half of the bisexual women do (Coleman, 1985). Bisexual wives are also less likely to disclose to their husbands any attraction toward other women and more likely to have sexual difficulties with their husbands. When bisexual women do reveal their homosexual interests to their husbands, the marriages end more quickly than when bisexual men make similar disclosures to their wives. One caution—these studies are based on clients in psychotherapy. Other evidence suggests that bisexual women not in therapy are able to enjoy sex with their husbands *and* with other women; bisexuality even seems to have a positive effect on the marriage and on feelings of sexual satisfaction (J. K. Dixon, 1985). Perhaps the most general conclusion is that some bisexual women experience significant marital problems and enter therapy, while others report the beneficial effect of bisexuality. As yet, there is no way to predict which outcome to expect.

■ Parenthood

About 20 to 30 percent of bisexuals marry, and some become parents though the exact percentage is unknown (Geist, 1980).

Bisexuals as Parents. Do you think that a person's bisexual orientation has any effect on how children would be raised? Many similarities are reported between heterosexual and bisexual parents. Mothers are likely to hold the same ideals for their children as for themselves, regardless of their sexual orientation. For example, mothers who exemplify traditional, feminine sex roles (see Chapter 6) want their daughters to become as feminine as themselves (Kweskin and Cook, 1982).

Parents differ in how they respond to offspring—some pay more attention to the child than others, some are most concerned with controlling his or her behavior, and so forth. When two children fight, an adult needs to intervene. A comparison of bisexual and heterosexual mothers in this situation indicates no response differences based on sexual orientation (Miller et al., 1981), as Figure 12-10 shows. Both groups of mothers said they would intervene in the fight, and both groups were equally concerned with the welfare of their children.

When a bisexual's marriage ends in divorce, his or her sexual history may interfere with gaining custody of any offspring or even visitation rights (Maddox, 1982). Child custody is ordinarily awarded

FIGURE 12-10 *IS A MOTHER'S BEHAVIOR AFFECTED BY HER SEXUAL ORIENTATION? NO* The maternal behavior of bisexual women is generally similar to that of heterosexual women.

to the mother, but not if she is bisexual. Even if a bisexual mother does gain custody, the court often attempts to control her social and private life (Rand et al., 1982). If these mothers become involved with or live with another woman, affiliate with a lesbian community, or inform their children of their sexual orientation, they risk losing custody. Information that may be helpful to bisexual parents is available from the Lesbian Rights Project in San Francisco and the Gay Fathers Coalition in Washington, D.C.

Parenthood among Gays and Lesbians. Both gays and lesbians sometimes become parents through adoption, and thousands of lesbians have been inseminated artificially so that they could bear their own children (Kolata, 1989).

The fitness of homosexual parents has been challenged in U.S. courts, usually on the basis of general assumptions rather than in response to any direct evidence that a child is harmed by being raised by a homosexual parent. In some states, sexual orientation is no longer automatic grounds for rejecting child custody (Gutis, 1987). When studies compare the intelligence, social behavior, and sexual identity of children brought up by homosexual versus heterosexual parents, more similarities than differences are found (Green et al., 1986; Harris and Turner, 1985/86; Scallen, 1982).

Homosexual Individuals

In our human sexuality classes, it is not unusual for students to ask some version of the question, "What exactly do homosexuals *do* sexually?" Curiosity is understandable, but the facts are not especially mysterious, as will be discussed in the following section.

■ Sexual Interactions

Questions about homosexual acts reflect not only curiosity but also the assumption that penile penetration of a vagina is the most usual and most satisfying form of sexual activity. In 1979, Masters and Johnson exposed the fallacy of this assumption when they investigated the sexual interactions of large numbers of homosexual and heterosexual couples. There were many quite striking differences between the two groups. For example, male and female homosexuals spent more time in close bodily contact and engaged in a slower, less demanding approach to sex. They also communicated more, both verbally and nonverbally. In contrast, heterosexuals spent less time in close body contact and moved more quickly to breast and genital stimulation. Heterosexuals seemed to focus on performance and achieving orgasm with a minimum of communication.

Differences also were found in specific sexual activities, such as breast and nipple stimulation as

TABLE 12-5 Effects of Sex and Sexual Orientation on Giving and Receiving Breast Stimulation

Heterosexual and homosexual couples engaged in sexual interactions while being observed. Clear differences involving breast and nipple stimulation were found. Lesbians showed the most positive response to giving and receiving such stimulation. Heterosexual males were less skillful in stimulating their partners than female–female partners and less likely to want such stimulation than male–male partners.

	LESBIANS	GAYS	HETEROSEXUAL WOMEN	HETEROSEXUAL MEN
Giving breast and nipple stimulation	Generally occurred, both manually and orally, spending equal time on each breast; stimulators excited by doing this, and asked partner for reactions	Less attention to this than by lesbians, but performed it more often than heterosexuals; one fourth of stimulators had erection during it	Three percent did it, very briefly	Paid less attention to it than homosexuals; did not ask partner for her reaction but had erection themselves
Receiving breast and nipple stimulation	Always enjoyed or requested partner to change stimulation	Always enjoyed and had erection	Had less enjoyment and communication than lesbians; one third described their breasts as not being an erogenous zone; considered their partner's pleasure in giving stimulation as more important than their own lack of enjoyment	Usually no erection; did not consider their nipple area sensual

Source: Based on data from Masters and Johnson, 1979.

shown in Table 12-5. This information is potentially helpful to all of us with respect to our own behaviors and to understand the needs and desires of a partner. The general idea is that partners of the same sex probably have greater insight into how best to stimulate one another. Presumably, these insights could be beneficial to the majority of the population whose partners are of the opposite sex.

Manual stimulation of a partner's genitals is a universal practice, but gays and lesbians report more enjoyment from such stimulation. Heterosexual women, for example, report being less sexually excited by manual stimulation than lesbians—primarily because male partners commonly penetrate the vagina with their fingers. This produces less pleasure than stimulation of the clitoris and labia, but heterosexual women usually don't communicate about their preferences because they feel the man likes doing it his way. Similarly, both homosexual and heterosexual men enjoy having their penises stimulated manually, but heterosexuals complain that women often grasp them too loosely or too roughly for maximal enjoyment. They also hesitate to inform their partners about their likes and dislikes.

Another common sexual behavior for both gays and straights is oral-genital stimulation, and here too the two groups differ considerably, as outlined in Table 12-6. According to the findings of Masters and Johnson, in giving oral stimulation, the least involved and least skilled are heterosexual males performing cunnilingus. Analogously, heterosexual women with a male partner are the least satisfied recipients of oral sex.

With respect to the use of sexually explicit images, homosexuals, heterosexuals, and bisexuals sometimes heighten their arousal by reading or viewing erotica. Understandably, gays and lesbians are most excited by pictures and stories involving homo-

TABLE 12-6 **Fellatio and Cunnilingus: Giving and Receiving Oral Sex**

Observation of sexual interactions revealed that sex and sexual orientation affected oral-genital sexual acts. Lesbian couples showed the most positive response to giving and receiving cunnilingus; similarly, gays enjoyed giving and receiving fellatio. Heterosexual males were as positive about being fellated as were gays, but they were relatively less enthusiastic and skillful in performing cunnilingus than lesbians were.

	LESBIANS	GAYS	HETEROSEXUAL WOMEN	HETEROSEXUAL MEN
Giving oral-genital stimulation	High involvement in this technique; slow, nondemanding, empathetic approach; caresses of labia before reaching clitoris; experienced great sexual arousal themselves	Slow, teasing approach; experienced great sexual arousal themselves	Slow, teasing approach (same as homosexual men); regarded this technique as a "challenge to becoming sexually effective woman" but not as a way to lead up to intercourse; experienced some sexual arousal themselves	Lack of involvement in technique; focused almost exclusively and forcefully on clitoris; regarded this technique as a means of leading up to intercourse; experienced some sexual arousal themselves
Receiving oral-genital stimulation	Extreme involvement in high levels of sexual arousal	Extreme involvement in high levels of sexual arousal	Less involvement than lesbians; complained about male's forcefulness but did not communicate this to partner	Extreme involvement in high levels of sexual arousal

Source: Based on data from Masters and Johnson, 1979.

sexual themes, and they are relatively unaroused by themes of heterosexuals engaged in sexual acts (Wincze and Qualls, 1984).

Though self-created internal fantasies play much the same role as external stimuli in creating sexual excitement, there is a lot of overlapping content in the fantasies of homosexuals and heterosexuals. About 30 percent of both sexes say that they occasionally have fantasies about sexual interactions with someone of their own sex (Ellis et al., 1987). When a heterosexual has fantasies about homosexual interactions or being a member of the opposite sex, this is not necessarily a "sign" indicating the person's true sexual orientation; similarly, a homosexual can have heterosexual fantasies without being a closet straight. We described earlier how fantasy, attraction, and behavior are components of sexual orientation. There is obviously a great difference between having fantasies about a given sexual behavior and actually engaging in it, and both homosexual and heterosexual persons report erotic fantasies about both sexes (Masters and Johnson, 1979). As you might guess, the most arousing fantasies tend to be those that are consistent with the person's sexual orientation (Keating and Over, 1990).

■ Stereotypes of Homosexual Behavior

We now will look briefly at the stereotypes about homosexuals that are common in our society. *Masculinity and Femininity.* Lesbians often are believed to be masculine ("bull dikes") while gays are assumed to be feminine ("limp-wristed pansies"). A dictionary definition of *effeminacy* is the "quality or state of being effeminate: a woman-like delicacy, weakness, or softness in a man." Many derogatory terms suggest that male homosexuals are effeminate; these include "swishy," "fags," and "flaming queens."

Early studies found that males who had significant amounts of homosexual experience behaved in more effeminate ways than those without such experience. In laboratory settings they were observed to speak, gesture, and walk in feminine ways (Schatzberg et al., 1975). Further, homosexual men who took the active role of inserter in anal intercourse liked being the dominant, masterful partner in every-day interactions compared to those who took the passive role of being penetrated (Haist and Hewitt, 1974). Seventy-five percent of the passive gays wanted their partner to make the plans for dates and to tell them what to do. Whatever the reasons, these behavior patterns are no longer accurate descriptions of gay behavior.

In the United States today, most gays and lesbians do *not* conform to stereotypes of feminine gays or masculine lesbians. For example, no more than 15 percent of gays act effeminately (Voeller, 1980). Homosexual and heterosexual men are similar in the proportion of individuals with masculine and feminine personality characteristics, and the same is true of women. Rigid masculine–feminine stereotypes occur most often in societies that have even more strongly antihomosexual attitudes than ours (Ross, 1983). The more rigid a society is about differentiating male and female roles, the more homosexuals in that society tend to develop stereotypic opposite-sex roles.

Gays often are described as gravitating toward relatively feminine occupations, but there is inconsistent evidence supporting a link between sexual orientation and vocational choice (Whitam, 1983). In interviews with large numbers of gays in San Francisco, their occupations were not concentrated in such fields as hairdressing, interior decorating, or other so-called "unmasculine" lines of work (Bell and Weinberg, 1978; Bell et al., 1981). It may seem surprising, but many gays are athletes. In a survey at three U.S. universities, 14 to 36 percent of the male athletes had recently engaged in sexual interactions with other men. Nonathletes were not sampled in that investigation, however, so we have no direct comparison of the frequency of homosexual interactions for athletes versus nonathletes.

Is Sexual Orientation a Mental Health Problem? Interest in the mental health of gays and lesbians has a long history in psychology and psychiatry. Until recently, homosexuality was believed to be a sign of emotional disturbance or, at best, a cause of such disturbance. The 1980 revision of the American Psychiatric Association's *Diagnostic and Statistical Manual of Mental Disorders* was the first "official" document to drop homosexuality from the list of psychopathological disorders. Only gays and lesbians who express distress about their sexual orientation are still included among the diagnostic categories: "gender identity disorder." Nevertheless, controversy still continues among some professionals about whether and how to deal with homosexuality in therapy.

Until the late 1970s, therapy designed to change an individual's homosexual orientation to a heterosexual one was an accepted practice. If one assumes that homosexuality is an indication of mental illness, it follows that therapists should attempt to alter that orientation (Socarides, 1978). Psychoanalysis and behavior therapy were equally ineffective in bringing about drastic changes in sexual orientation (Acosta, 1975). There were some reported behavior changes in response to aversion therapy in which arousal to a homosexual stimulus was followed by negative consequences such as electric shock, but the effects were temporary. Other professionals criticized this approach with homosexual clients, emphasizing instead the importance of learning heterosexual skills in interacting with the opposite sex (Phillips et al., 1976).

Most therapists now consider all such therapeutic interventions as misguided (Davison, 1978). Only when a person is dissatisfied with his or her homosexual orientation and expresses the desire to change is therapy appropriate (Sturgis and Adams, 1978). Even here, some argue that the first step is to focus on the difficulties the person is encountering rather than on his or her sexual orientation. As a result, the therapist may find it beneficial to deal with a client's guilt feelings, sexual dysfunction, or attitudes about members of the same or the opposite sex. Such problems can be targeted for treatment without deciding that sexual orientation must be the overriding problem (Everaerd et al., 1982; Russell and Winkler, 1977).

A critical factor affecting treatment is the attitude of the therapist toward homosexuality. For example, male therapists are more likely to view gays and lesbians as psychologically unhealthy than are their female colleagues (Garfinkle and Morin, 1978). More generally, homophobic biases influence judgments about such matters. For example, in an experiment, college students were asked to read a case study about a man who was described as depressed, alcoholic, and having extramarital affairs (Davison and Friedman, 1981). Some were informed that the affairs were with women, some that they were with men. Those who read about homosexual affairs were more curious about the sexual aspects of the case, and they identified the man's homosexual orientation as the cause of his other problems. Eliminating such biases among those in the helping professions is of considerable importance (Gonsiorek, 1982).

Are there any major differences in psychological functioning associated with sexual orientation? The answer is a straightforward *no,* based on studies of men and women in the United States and in Great Britain (Siegelman, 1978, 1979). To consider just one example, sexual orientation is only minimally related to depression (Nurius, 1983). Among all of the factors that cause depression, having a homosexual or bisexual lifestyle accounts for about 2 percent. Even this small effect is probably the result of the negative reaction of others rather than a function of sexual orientation itself (Ross, 1985).

Despite the stigma attached to nonheterosexual behavior, even middle-aged and elderly gays and lesbians do not conform to the stereotype of "lonely, depressed, sexually frustrated" individuals (Kimmel, 1978, p. 113). A general conclusion is that there is no reason to believe that a homosexual orientation is caused by or leads to maladaptive psychological functioning.

Summarizing the Information about Homosexual and Bisexual Behavior . . .

Sexual orientation includes three major components: physical sexual activity, interpersonal affection or attraction, and erotic fantasies that emphasize members of the same or the opposite sex. A small subgroup of individuals interacts sexually only with members of their own sex, but a much larger group reports **bisexual** experience. The determinants of a homosexual orientation are unclear. Some genetic contribution may play a role in male homosexuality, and a slight hormonal influence has been identified for some lesbians. For gay males, there is evidence that early sexual experience can be a contributing factor. Information about play behavior in childhood is consistent with the stereotypes of masculine interests for **lesbians** and feminine interests for **gays**, but the **retrospective** nature of this research casts doubts on whether a cause-effect relationship has actually been identified. The experience of a troubled or otherwise atypical family background is unrelated to sexual orientation.

Antihomosexual religious beliefs and restrictive laws regulating and punishing homosexual behavior have characterized society's response throughout history. Homosexual couples vary in the type of relationship they form (**open-coupled**, **close-coupled**, and **functional**) and in the level of emotional commitment and sexual fidelity. Lesbians tend to establish relationships involving closer, more committed couples and to engage in less sexual activity with strangers than gays do. Other differences between homosexual men and women include a greater male emphasis on appearance in attracting new partners; females emphasize hobbies and personality traits. Lesbians also are likely to go through the **coming out** process at an earlier age than gays. The bisexual lifestyle has been relatively neglected in research and theory until recently.

Among the psychological aspects of homosexual and bisexual orientations is the degree of masculinity and femininity expressed by these individuals. Though heterosexuals who hold attitudes involving **homophobia** or a **homosexual bias** believe that such a lifestyle is overwhelmingly maladaptive, research does not support that assumption. These negative attitudes have contributed to the false belief that homosexuality represents or causes emotional disturbance that should receive psychotherapeutic treatment.

To Find Out More about Homosexual and Bisexual Behavior . . .

Diamant, L. (1987). *Male and female homosexuality.* New York: Hemisphere.

Topics included in this book are: the psychoanalytic, biological, and behavioristic theories of the origins of homosexuality; psychological problems and therapy; and ethical issues.

Duberman, M. B., Vicinus, M., and Chauncey, G. Jr. (Eds.). (1989). *Hidden from history: Reclaiming the gay and lesbian past.* New York: New American Library.

This is a collection of 29 recent historical essays that cover homosexuality across cultures and races in ancient times, medieval Europe, early modern Japan, among Native Americans, in the Third World, and in Europe and North America today.

Fuss, D. (Ed.) (1991). *Inside/out: Lesbian theories, gay theories.* New York: Routledge.

Essays by lesbian and gay intellectuals explore the way sex and sexual differences have been presented in literature, films, music, and photography.

Greenberg, D. (1988). *The construction of homosexuality.* Chicago: University of Chicago Press.

This volume examines societal attitudes, beliefs, and practices about homosexuality and their changes over time.

Money, J. (1988). *Gay, straight, and in-between.* New York: Oxford University Press.

A distinguished behavioral scientist describes his work on the clinical aspects of sexual orientation and its development.

Paul, W., & Weinrich, J. D. (1982). *Homosexuality: Social, psychological, and biological issues.* Beverly Hills, Calif.: Sage.

This book examines homosexuality and mental health issues as well as biological contributions to sexual orientation. Two sections focus on the relationships among gays and lesbians and on societal reactions to people whose sexual orientation is homosexual.

CHAPTER THIRTEEN

IMPERSONAL SEX:
Prostitution, Paraphilias, and Sexual Imagery

A middle-aged male attorney talks about his initial introduction to sex in the following account. As is often the case with a person's first experience with intercourse, this man's memory of his adolescent adventure of visiting a house of prostitution with his friends seems as vivid to him today as when it took place over three decades earlier. While sex with a prostitute was once a common experience for young males, it is now a relatively rare occurrence.

I was in high school when I first had intercourse. A group of us were out drinking beer one night, and somebody said we should go to a "whorehouse." Keep in mind that this was many years ago. I had heard lots of wild stories about a little town on the coast. We started joking about who was still a virgin, and how nobody was a "real man" until he'd had the clap. As you can tell, this was back before there was such a thing as AIDS, or the sexual revolution.

We piled into two cars and headed over the mountains. It turned out to be harder to find prostitutes than we had thought. Ken, who always led the way in whatever we did, went into about a dozen all-night stores, and even to the bus station, to get directions. He finally found out what he wanted to know, and we followed his car to a three-story house out past the city limits.

Ken knocked on the door while the rest of us hung back. I was beginning to feel nervous and wondered how I had gotten myself into this. After a couple of minutes, a small panel in the door opened, and a lady asked what we wanted. Ken told her that we were looking for love. He made up a story about how we were about to join the Air Force. She seemed to be counting heads and must have decided that the money was more important than the risk of letting minors into her establishment.

Once we were inside, she collected $20 from each of us, and the ladies lined up in a kind of waiting room so we could each pick a partner. I remember thinking it was like a junior high dance except these women were older and wore tight shorts with blouses you could see through. My "date" (she said her name was Sherry) took me by the hand to her room. She washed my genitals with some kind of antiseptic soap in a small pan filled with warm water. The medicinal odor and her no-nonsense style were more like an efficient nurse than someone about to make love.

She asked whether I wanted it straight, half and half, or around-the-world. I didn't want to sound naive, so I picked the middle one, and Sherry said that would cost an extra $10.

She went down on me for a few minutes and then lay on her back and told me to get on top. I figured out then what half and half meant—half fellatio and half intercourse. The whole thing was over in a few minutes, and she washed me again and squirted some kind of medicine right into the tip of my penis. I was dressed, back in the waiting room with the other guys, and out the door very quickly. On the way home, we exchanged stories about what we did, making up a few details so we sounded like world-class lovers.

So that was it. I was glad to find out at last what the act of sex was like. It certainly wasn't totally satisfying and I've had better sex since. My partner had a job to do, and she did it. I wanted sex, and I got it. I'm sure Sherry didn't lose any sleep thinking about me.

Warren, age 52

Some aspects of Warren's story have elements in common with the first sexual experience of other adolescents in Western societies—the anxious anticipation, the jokes among young males, and the subsequent feeling of relief about passing a milestone. Such reactions are by no means limited to visiting a prostitute—a kind of sexual initiation that faded into history by the beginning of the 1960s. The fact that Warren's partner used medicinal soap to clean his genitals and some kind of bacterial agent after intercourse are, of course, as meaningful today as they were then, considering the problem of sexually transmissible disease. Also note that his story ended on a slightly sad note. He realized that having a personal involvement with a sexual partner would have been preferable. The difference between impersonal sex with a paid partner and sex with someone you love is analogous to the difference between a meal in a fast-food outlet and a meal in a first-class restaurant. Both may satisfy your basic hunger, but they are quite different experiences otherwise. The remainder of this chapter focuses on impersonal sexual activities.

Impersonal sex refers to sexual acts in which the identity and distinctive personality of the sex object is irrelevant. Perhaps the most ancient and widespread form of impersonal sex is *prostitution,* and we describe this institution from the perspective of the prostitutes and of their customers. We also review attempts to control and restrict this form of commercial sex. *Paraphilias* consist of the compulsive performance of sexual acts with people, animals, or inanimate objects that serve as necessary components of sexual arousal for some individuals. The production of *sexual imagery* is an impersonal sexual business, and we discuss recent controversies as well as research identifying its effects on emotions, attitudes, and behavior. Special sections focus on the *treatment of paraphilic behavior* and the crucial differences in the effects of *violent versus sexual content in depictions of rape.*

Prostitution

Prostitution is the performance of sexual acts in exchange for money or tangible goods. Though some dating and even marital relationships may seem similar, prostitution differs from them in that prostitutes are promiscuous and show little or no discrimination in their choice of sexual partners.

Those Who Sell Sex

When sex is considered as simply a commodity to be sold on the open market, it can be a profitable business for the entrepreneurs—mostly men—and a much less profitable and more dangerous job for those—mostly women—whose bodies are for sale.

Often called the world's oldest profession, prostitution is found in most societies that have been studied by anthropologists. For example, a fourth-century brothel was recently unearthed in Israel, and it contained an ancient hot tub, heart-shaped pillars, and oil lamps decorated with erotic scenes (Richissin, 1987). During the same period in which houses of prostitution proliferated in Western societies, prostitutes were licensed and their incomes taxed in China (Gronewald, 1982). Prostitution varies somewhat across societies (Kalm, 1985), and specific customs differ. For example, in Colombia **pimps** do not play a major role (de Gallo and Alzate, 1976). In Peruvian brothels, economics determine how a customer is treated; wealthy clients drink and dine in groups, while poor clients simply unzip their pants for a hurried encounter (Primov and Kieffer, 1977). Even within the United States, prostitution takes many quite different forms.

Differences among Prostitutes. Prostitutes ("hookers" or "whores") vary in social and financial status and lifestyle. At the upper end is the **call girl**, who dresses expensively, lives in relatively plush surroundings, charges a minimum of $100 an hour, and ordinarily accepts appointments only with recommended clients (usually middle-aged executives or other professionals). You may have read the book *Mayflower Madame*, or watched the TV movie, the true story of a call girl enterprise (see Figure 13-1). Among the items taken on "dates" by these young women was a portable credit card machine for the convenience of the customers (Barrows and Novak, 1986). Call girls have many expenses such as nice clothing, makeup, appropriate furnishings for an apartment, and medical care for sexually transmitted diseases. Such costs come out of the call girl's average annual earnings of about $50,000—though free drinks and meals plus the avoidance of income taxes help to balance the costs.

FIGURE 13-1 *CALL GIRLS: EXPENSIVE SEX* Call girls represent the highest status and most expensive type of prostitute. The *Mayflower Madame* was the true story of one such enterprise.

Often, a call girl is hired to provide a "bonus" for a successful employee or to insure the good will of a company's valued customer. Women who become call girls most often come from a middle-class background and frequently have a college education. Though some operate independently, many work for escort services that are thinly veiled fronts for commercial sex. Some of these businesses stay within the law, charging a customer for the introduction to a date, and then leaving any payment for sexual acts to be negotiated directly between the call girl and the customer.

At a lower status rung are prostitutes who work in **brothels**, a simple version of which was described by Warren at the beginning of this chapter. A more luxurious variety of such "whorehouses" once was very common in the United States—from the 1890s through World War II. The most impressive were located in mansions, featured entertainment, and served customers alcohol and gourmet food. A client (called a "john," "score," or "trick") selected his partner for the evening in the downstairs parlor, and then they retired to an upstairs bedroom to engage in one of several possible sexual activities (Bess and Janus, 1976).

Still lower in status are the women working in a **massage parlor**, a version of prostitution that became popular during the 1960s and 1970s. Although it is legal and respectable to give or to receive a genuine massage, customers visiting massage parlors expect to receive sexual services rather than a rubdown. Many localities have legal restrictions forbidding the use of beds in such establishments, so the man generally lies on a thin massage platform. Intercourse is difficult under these conditions, so fellatio and masturbation are the most common acts performed. Women who work as **hand whores** in these parlors specialize in giving a masturbatory "local," and often do not think of themselves as prostitutes but as masseuses who provide extra services (Bryant and Palmer, 1975). Instead of leisurely sexual interludes, the emphasis in such establishments is on rapid turnover of the paying customers. As one masseuse described it, the guiding philosophy is, "get 'em in, get 'em up, get 'em off, and get 'em out" (Byrne and Byrne, 1977, p. 409).

Women working in a massage parlor are instructed not to offer or even suggest any sexual interaction; the customer has to ask for masturbation or fellatio specifically. Even if the client being massaged breathes heavily, has an erection, and behaves suggestively toward the masseuse, she cannot proposition him. If she does, and the male is an undercover (so to speak) police officer, she would be arrested for **solicitation.** If the officer makes the sexual proposition, he cannot arrest her because that would be defined as **entrapment.** Most clients (61 percent) do request sex, usually masturbation (Armstrong, 1978).

The lowest status, poorest, and most vulnerable prostitutes are the **streetwalkers**—by far the largest group. They may charge as little as $10 for a quickie or slightly more for other acts. Streetwalkers roam the sidewalks of most cities. Their services are performed in automobiles, darkened doorways and alleys, and run-down hotels that rent rooms by the hour. These prostitutes are often young, unhappy runaways (Satterfield, 1981); many are unattractive and from economically depressed backgrounds. They are arrested more frequently and injured by violent clients more often than are higher status prostitutes. **Prostitutes who hang around bars soliciting clients are called bar girls**. When they age, bar girls are called *flea bags,* and their clients are primarily derelicts and skid-row alcoholics.

Many prostitutes have "business managers," or pimps, who function in various ways. A pimp may be in charge of prostitution in a specific area of the city, providing his "stable" of girls with protection against theft and other crimes as well as bail money when required. The pimp also may function as a companion with whom his girls can discuss their work and their problems (Winick, 1980). Figure 13-2 shows one such pair. The sexual interactions between pimp and prostitute are usually of minor importance in their re-

FIGURE 13-2   *THE PIMP'S ROLE IN PROSTITUTION*   For prostitutes such as streetwalkers, a pimp may be the only source of companionship in a life otherwise characterized by impersonal sex with strangers.

lationship. Many pimps appropriate most of the prostitutes' earnings for themselves, and some physically abuse the women for infractions of the rules or for not meeting the evening's financial quota (Milner and Milner, 1972). A pimp usually provides food, clothing, shelter, and drugs such as cocaine for his stable. A *panderer* helps a prostitute find johns, and some pimps also serve this function.

Sexual Orientation of Prostitutes. Most female prostitutes are heterosexual. Interviews with 600 prostitutes indicated that only 3 percent were lesbians while 12 percent were bisexual (James, 1982c). The lesbian subgroup often explain their interest in other women as an outgrowth of negative experiences with customers, pimps, or other men.

Most male prostitutes are either homosexual or bisexual, often beginning their careers at ages ten to thirteen (Allen, 1980). They are called "hustlers," and hustling is defined as either a male or female soliciting a customer for sex. Interviews with ninety-eight male prostitutes revealed that almost one fourth were streetwalkers or **bar boys,** did not use pimps, and were willing to serve customers of either sex. About half as many worked as **call boys** or as **kept boys;** they were maintained for the exclusive pleasure of a homosexual employer. About half of the total group worked as part-time prostitutes to earn extra money by servicing selected customers, usually men. A much smaller group of male hustlers engage in prostitution that includes violence. They coerce others to engage in homosexual acts and then threaten, assault, or blackmail the victims to obtain money or valuable posessions. *Gigolos* prostitute themselves to women, mostly those who are wealthy and older than themselves.

Becoming a Prostitute: Youthful Stress and Continuing Problems. In comparison with other women, female prostitutes frequently have a troubled history. They have experienced more distant relationships with their parents and report more school-related problems, even when compared with women imprisoned for other crimes (Gray, 1973). Adolescent female prostitutes have higher rates of emotional disturbance than their peers, including nonprostitute delinquents (Gibson-Ainyette et al., 1988). Surpris-

ingly, prostitutes are likely to be the firstborn child in their families and to have a strong motivation to complete school (Potterat et al., 1985). When circumstances prevent their progressing toward higher education and successful careers, such women view prostitution as a way to achieve their financial goals.

Personal histories of prostitutes reveal an unusually high incidence of incest and rape, compared to nonprostitutes of similar social and economic backgrounds (Boyer and James, 1981; Janus, 1977). Prostitutes also engage in their first intercourse at earlier ages and are victims of early rape more frequently than nonprostitutes (James and Meyerding, 1977). One survey found that 65 percent had been raped at least once before they became prostitutes (Satterfield, (1981).

The background of young male prostitutes also involves a troubled history—broken and alcoholic homes. Earls and David (1989) surveyed fifty male prostitutes and fifty male controls living in Montreal, Canada, matched for socioeconomic status. The prostitutes were more likely than the controls to live outside their parents' home or to be adopted. They also became sexually active an average of three years earlier than the controls, most often with a male partner. These young men emphasized the financial rewards of prostitution as the primary advantage. They described the disadvantages as dealing with dangerous, violent clients along with the risk of being arrested.

Despite a considerable amount of sexual experience, young prostitutes remain surprisingly unaware of how their own bodies or those of their **johns** function sexually. This lack of knowledge is not a function of low intelligence but is based on a generally immature, dependent approach to life.

The Sexual Activity of Prostitutes. Female prostitutes usually have orgasms only when interacting with their pimps or boyfriends. With clients, they routinely fake excitement and orgasm. Those who ordinarily reach orgasm with their lovers, however, are more likely than nonorgasmic women to enjoy sex with clients and to experience orgasms with them (Savitz and Rosen, 1988).

In a study of almost 500 prostitutes, one third said that they had orgasm during intercourse with a client only occasionally, and the same was true for one fifth during cunnilingus (Diana, 1980). Generally, orgasm with a client is perceived as embarrassing because the prostitute wants to avoid genuine intimacy. For the same reason, kissing, caressing, fondling, and other signs of emotional closeness are also bad business practices because they add to the amount of time required to **turn a trick,** and "time is money" (Auerback, 1979; Pomeroy, 1980).

In an interesting study of the lives of prostitutes, Freund et al. (1989) interviewed twenty streetwalkers in Camden, New Jersey, five or more times daily on at least five different days. The subjects were paid $3 for each five-minute interview. These women averaged four clients a day and worked a four- or five-day week. Half of their clients were repeaters, engaging the woman's services about once a week; vaginal intercourse was more likely with them than with others. Some long-term sexual relationships developed, and they spent several hours together when they interacted—at a motel or in the customer's home. Despite the increased risk of AIDS transmission, condoms were routinely used for intercourse by only six of these women.

A call girl behaves more affectionately toward her clients than other prostitutes because she tends to get to know them, have sex in a date-like atmosphere with only one customer per night, and to expect repeat business (Exner, 1978).

Male prostitutes engaging in homosexual acts report not having orgasms when a client penetrates them anally. Orgasm usually occurs and is expected, however, when a client performs fellatio on them (Auerback and Haeberle, 1981).

■ Customers

One of the more famous historical customers was the French artist Toulouse-Lautrec (1864–1901), who spent much of his adult life among prostitutes. He was less than five feet tall with extremely short

FIGURE 13-3 *BROTHEL LIFE IN PARIS: IMMORTALIZED BY TOULOUSE-LAUTREC* Prostitutes in Paris brothels were featured in a great many of Toulouse-Lautrec's paintings. Because of his physical appearance, the artist's major contact with females was in this setting.

legs, stunted by an accident during early adolescence. His physical appearance repelled most women, so he turned to prostitutes for sex and companionship, also using them as models for many of his paintings, as Figure 13-3 shows. He especially favored lesbian prostitutes as subjects for his art. One of his models also was the likely source of the syphilis that caused his death (Bullough and Servedio, 1983).

As recently as half a century ago, many fathers provided "sex education" for their sons by taking them to visit a local brothel. In the first Kinsey et al. (1948) investigation of male sexual behavior, 69 percent of adult, white males in the United States reported at least one contact with a prostitute. By 1974, Hunt found that only 19 percent of adult males under age thirty-five with some college education had engaged in intercourse with a prostitute. The most obvious reason for the change over time is the increase in sexual permissiveness among American women as premarital sex became the norm. Prostitution is no longer the major sexual outlet for unmarried males.

The typical current customer is a married, white male in his mid-thirties, holding a lower- or middle-class job and attending church on Sunday (Simpson and Schill, 1977). A survey of massage-parlor clients indicated that men say they visit a prostitute out of curiosity and because they lack a sexual partner (45 percent). Customers also report that they want to engage in such acts as fellatio and cunnilingus that are not acceptable to their wives or to engage in sex more frequently than their wives permit.

■ Social Control of Prostitution: Social Embarrassment and Legal Sanctions

Women express more negative and restrictive attitudes toward prostitution than men do, as summarized in Figure 13-4. Male college students say they would be more willing to take or offer money in return for sexual acts than would female students. Women believe that prostitution degrades and exploits their gender. Men support legalizing prostitution more strongly than women do. Neither sex,

FIGURE 13-4 *SEX DIFFERENCES IN EVALUATING PROSTITUTION* Attitudes toward prostitution are more negative among female than among male college students. Compared to women, men express more interest in engaging in sex for money, are less likely to believe that prostitution degrades females, and are more in favor of legalization.
Source: Based on data in Basow and Campanile, 1986.

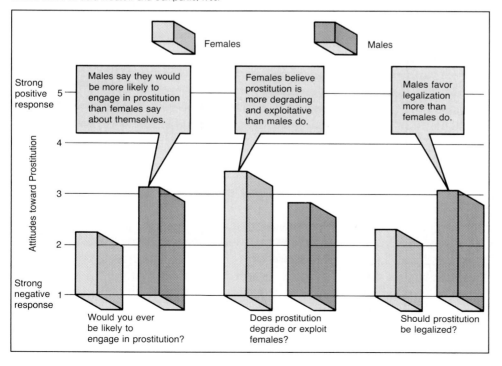

however, feels that greater enforcement of antiprostitution laws would result in its decline (Basow and Campanile, 1986).

Regardless of gender, individuals differ in how negatively they evaluate prostitution. The more negative the attitudes, the harsher the punishment deemed appropriate for violating antiprostitution laws. A study of fifty-one college students with either very positive or very negative attitudes about prostitution asked them to suggest the appropriate bail a prostitute should pay to gain release from jail before going to trial (Rosenblatt et al., 1989). Those with negative attitudes recommended a much higher figure ($414) than those with positive attitudes ($146).

In many societies, negative reactions to prostitution are sufficiently strong that drastic measures are used to discourage its practice. In Iran, prostitutes are executed. In the United States, most states prohibit financial profit from sexual activity. An exception is Nevada, where several counties have legalized prostitution, though the most famous of these brothels, the Mustang Ranch, recently went bankrupt and was forced to close (Lights out . . . , 1990). The FBI's *Uniform Crime Report* describes sex offenses that are criminal in nature; included are prostitution, operating a prostitution-related business, and using or arranging to use women for immoral purposes.

Some countries direct control measures at the prostitutes' customers. An extreme example is provided by Pakistan—where Islamic law is followed—men caught visiting prostitutes receive a public flogging (Twenty-seven Pakistani Johns, 1979). Social embarrassment has been used at various times in the United States. For example, radio stations in some cities set aside a specific time each day to broadcast the names of men who were convicted of having sex with prostitutes (Fallon, 1979; Purnick, 1979). Similarly, some newspapers have published customers' names. Because many of the men so named wield economic or political power, these practices often are quietly and quickly abandoned. In the relatively few instances when a customer is arrested and convicted, the penalty is usually a small fine in contrast to a ten- to thirty-day jail sentence given to convicted prostitutes. It seems that society places much more blame on the women who provide sexual services than on the men who demand and pay for them.

It is common for communities to treat prostitutes as criminals, with periodic roundups of streetwalkers and raids on brothels and massage parlors. Unless prostitutes are operating in residential neighborhoods, however, laws against prostitution are not regularly enforced (Basler, 1981). Enforcement tends, in fact, to occur when there is some external pressure such as an upcoming election or a series of newspaper stories on the issue. Even after arrest, prostitutes typically are bailed out within twenty-four hours unless they are charged with committing some other crime such as robbery or blackmail (MacNamara, 1981).

Prostitution is the only sexual offense for which more women than men are prosecuted, and more than half of them are black. Longstanding debates raise such issues as whether morality should or should not be part of the criminal code, whether prostitution is a victimless crime, and whether it makes any sense to prosecute women—especially black women—for engaging in activities desired and paid for by men. Generally, better arguments can be made against prostitution on the basis of public health issues than on moral grounds.

Among the suggested changes to improve the judicial situation are (1) to *legalize* prostitution, as is common in Europe, so that the government can regulate, license, and tax those that sell sex and (2) to *decriminalize* prostitution. In the latter instance, commercial sex would no longer be against the law and subject to punishment, thus permitting women to decide how they wish to use their own bodies (Miller, 1986).

Paraphilias: Deviant Sex

In discussing **sexual deviance**, it is important to remember that deviance may lie in the eye of the beholder: What is deviant in one culture or at one time may be regarded as perfectly natural in another culture or at some other time in the same culture. Just what is meant by sexually deviant behavior?

Defining Sexual Deviance

What is meant by such terms as *deviant, abnormal, maladjusted,* or *psychopathological?* During the Middle Ages, many behaviors were explained by reference to the supernatural. For example, a person who behaved in unusual and unacceptable ways— sexually or otherwise—was believed to be possessed by the devil or cast under a spell by witchcraft. Sexual dreams and nocturnal orgasms, for example, were attributed to nightly visits by agents of the devil, as Figure 13-5 illustrates. By the nineteenth century, the medical model of deviance generally replaced the supernatural model. Certain kinds of inappropriate and disruptive behavior were viewed as symptoms of an underlying malfunction for which a medical cure was sought. Some believed that heredity was the basic cause; sterilization offered the only solution. In the twentieth century, the psychological model was developed, and many now accept the idea that deviant behavior is learned in the same way that other behavior is learned. In other words, under specific conditions any of us could learn to be paranoid, to hallucinate, or to be sexually aroused only by the smell of dirty sweat socks.

Whatever the best explanation of deviancy, the problem of identifying it remains (Wilson, 1987). What kinds of behavior do we decide are caused by the devil, disease, bad genes, or unfortunate childhood learning experiences? Research suggests that if adults are asked to list the people they regard as deviant, almost everybody would be so labeled by some (Simmons and Chambers, 1965). All too often, there is a tendency to identify normality using ourselves as the yardstick. Many experts believe that we need a standard more defensible than "What I do is normal, and those who behave differently are deviant."

One possible solution is to define deviant behavior as acting in ways that are *inappropriate.* It is not difficult to agree about what this means if the behavior is rare or infrequent, and therefore deviant according to a *statistical definition of deviance.* Thus, you would be deviant if you attended your college class in the nude or became sexually involved with a Great

FIGURE 13-5 *THE DEVIL MADE THEM DO IT* In the Middle Ages, when deviant behavior was believed to have supernatural causes, sexual deviancy was assumed to be the work of the devil. For example, sexual dreams and nocturnal orgasms were caused by demons. A female demon (succubus) was thought to have intercourse with sleeping males and a male demon (incubus) with sleeping females.

Dane. These and a number of other behaviors can easily be identified as unusual and unacceptable in our society. Yet, a case could be made that some common behaviors are inappropriate. An example is engaging in premarital intercourse without contraceptive protection, thereby risking an unwanted pregnancy. You can see that, in defining deviancy, we need first to agree about what is inappropriate even if it is not unusual.

Perhaps we might base a definition of deviancy on what a given society defines as acceptable, known as the *sociological approach to deviance*. A psychiatric category, **dyssocial reaction**, refers to individuals who disregard the usual social codes and often are in conflict with them. That category can easily be applied to the classroom nudist and the person who has intercourse with a dog. One problem with this definition is that it rests on the status quo and rejects the possibility that some people may have different attitudes, beliefs, and values. In addition, deviants who at one time reject what most of society accepts may later be in the majority—people who protested the war in Vietnam in the 1970s and even the Founding Fathers of the United States are examples. With respect to sex, such acts as masturbation, fellatio, and cunnilingus have been defined in the not-too-distant past as deviant and depraved practices that were condemned almost universally. Today, they are accepted as expected aspects of sexuality. Clearly, then, definitions of deviancy shift; current acceptability is therefore questionable as the basis of a definition.

One solution to the problem is to define deviance as **objectionable behavior** that causes unwanted psychological distress or physical pain for the individual engaging in the behavior and/or for an unwilling or unwitting participant. According to this *psychological definition of deviance,* guilt-free masturbation, sexually pleasing acts between consenting unmarried partners, voluntary celibacy, and consensual homosexual acts between adults would be unobjectionable and thus not deviant. You may not want to do any of these things, judge them to be morally offensive, or might even want to persuade others to avoid them. You have every right to react either positively or negatively, but not the right to define these acts as deviant or to interfere with the behavior of those who do not share your views.

This definition clearly fits such acts as rape, exposing one's genitals to disapproving strangers, and engaging in sexual harassment. Note that unwilling participants can be coerced by means other than force or threats of violence—it is equally objectionable to take advantage of another's dependency, poverty, or ignorance. Any acts with a person who is mentally or physically unable to give informed consent are objectionable because such participants are unwitting; for example, children, anyone who is retarded or emotionally disturbed, people who are unconscious, and animals. By this definition, it is also objectionable for a person to engage in sexual acts while deliberately ignoring the possibility of unwanted conception, or to engage in them when carrying a transmittable disease, or to be secretly unfaithful to one's presumably exclusive partner.

The goal of this approach is to base the conception of deviancy on rational grounds that do not depend on a specific culture at a specific time or on wanting everyone to believe the same thing or behave in the same way. All that you have to do is to think before you act and then to act wisely out of concern for the welfare of yourself and of any others who may be involved. Our human capacity for planful foresight permits us to behave in very reasonable ways if only we work at it.

■ Identifying Paraphilias

Rather than affection and mutual desire between two sexual partners, a **paraphilia** consists of sexual attraction toward atypical people, objects, rituals, or situations that are used to satisfy sexual desire. The three major categories of such attraction are (1) a nonhuman object, (2) real or pretended suffering or humiliation experienced by the individual or by a partner, and (3) partners unwilling or unable to give their consent. Because the third category is discussed in Chapter 14, we will cover only the first two here. As with other sexual behavior, fantasies accompany the paraphilia, and they are sufficiently persistent and repetitious that a paraphilic person develops a driving need, or *compulsion,* to engage in the deviant behavior. Because paraphilic men far outnumber paraphilic women, the following discussion will refer almost exclusively to men.

Most sexually active people have preferences about the setting or the activities that they find most sexually arousing. For example, although the typical person engages in sexual intercourse in bed, some find sex more exciting in the shower or outdoors. Similarly, a nonparaphilic man may be especially aroused when a partner wears garter belts, high-heeled shoes, or whatever. As Figure 13-6 suggests, paraphilic desires vary in compulsivity. Individual preferences are common, but when sexual functioning does not occur without the presence of a specific object or act, the term *paraphilia* is applied. Most paraphilias clearly fit the statistical and sociological definitions of deviance; as we describe the major categories, you might want to decide when and under what circumstances the psychological definition should be applied.

We may easily differentiate the man who has a mild preference for redheads from the paraphilic who is driven to steal women's underwear in order to become aroused and masturbate. Between such extremes, however, the dividing line may be arbitrary, depending essentially on the perceptions of others. We can say generally that if sexual functioning is difficult or impossible in the absence of the desired object, a paraphilia is involved. An example would be a man unable to have an erection and engage in sex unless his wife wears black shoes. The problem is more severe if the man substitutes the black shoes for

FIGURE 13-6   *PARAPHILIA: HOW STRONG IS THE NEED?* This continuum indicates variations in the strength of a deviant sexual interest in objects or activities, differentiating preferences from paraphilias. When the object or act is necessary for sexual functioning or serves as a substitute for human contact, the behavior is defined as paraphilia.

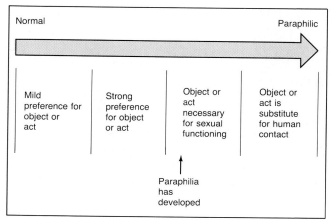

normal human contact—for example, when ejaculation in a shoe replaces sexual interaction with his wife. If, however, the man himself is not disturbed by his behavior and if what he does is acceptable to his wife, the paraphilia does not constitute objectionable behavior by our definition. In contrast, when either the man or his wife *is* unhappy about the behavior or when the paraphilia breaks societal rules—for example, stealing objects or invading the privacy of others—treatment for the deviancy is advisable.

We will now explore some of the major varieties of paraphilias, their possible causes, and how they are treated.

■ Types of Paraphilias

Several categories of paraphilia are based on the nature of the object that sexually arouses the paraphilic.

Fetishism.   When nonliving objects or specific parts of the body are the preferred source of sexual excitement, the paraphilia is labeled **fetishism.**

One of the two major forms of fetishes is **partialism**—desire centers exclusively on a certain part of the body such as the foot or breast. Mild partialism affects many of us; thus, one person may focus on legs, another on buttocks, and another on hairy chests as sexual turn-ons. Beyond these relative preferences, partialism involves concentrating exclusively on these bodily parts and having little interest in the person to whom they are attached. For example, one partialist frequented shopping malls to inspect the feet of women as they walked by. An even stronger partialism is represented by the case of a man whose only sexual interest was in collecting specific mannequin parts (Char and McDermott, 1982).

The second major type of fetish focuses on an inanimate object, and this can be either a **media fetish** or a **form fetish.** A media fetish centers on the hardness or softness of the object. A person with a **hard media fetish** usually is aroused by smooth or slick objects such as plastic, leather, or rubber. These substances are often associated with sadomasochistic paraphilia, and the preferred colors for whips and clothing are black and red. Gags or bonds of this material in these colors can be tightened around the person's body, used to gag the mouth or to bind limbs, or they can be applied to the genitals. In contrast, someone with a **soft media fetish** is not generally aroused by sadomasochistic acts, preferring to use soft, loose things such as hair, fur, or lingerie in pastel colors to elicit arousal. Soft media fetishists often steal clothes or place ads in sexual publications offering to buy used panties or other garments.

Those with a form fetish are aroused by an object's shape, as illustrated in Figure 13-7. In Western, industrialized societies, the shoe has become the most common form fetish, but in the nineteenth century, gloves were the most favored object, with corsets also popular.

The origin of these fetishes is uncertain, but clearly certain objects attract fetishists. Most fetish objects are associated with the body and can be used to provide tactile stimulation (Epstein, 1975). The fetishist seldom shows interest in things that are simply tasted, heard, or smelled. Case histories often re-veal an association between the object and someone who took care of the fetishist in childhood. Sexual fantasies about this adult become transferred to the object, presumably by accident. For example, a boy's mother may have worn black high-heeled shoes when she dressed up, and his unacceptable sexual fantasies about her transferred to less threatening fantasies about her shoes (Stoller, 1977). In part, simple conditioning may be involved; according to learning theory, a fetish can result from simply associating an object with sexual excitement. In any event, the fetish itself usually develops shortly after puberty or during adolescence.

Neither bras nor hats nor doorknobs have ever been reported as common fetish objects. Some objects may lend themselves more readily than others to this role and are said to be more **conditionable**. No one has yet been able to predict exactly which objects will be conditionable.

FIGURE 13-7 *TURNING ON TO SHOES, BOOTS, AND CORSETS* These objects (shoes, boots, and corset) have been popular among form fetishists at various times. The corset was popular in the nineteenth century but not today. Black high-heeled shoes and boots have retained their appeal as fetishes over a much longer period of time.

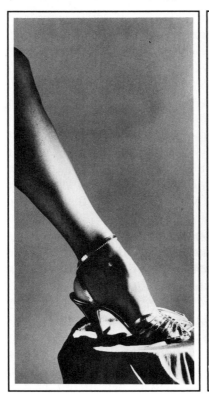  

Transvestism.   Wearing clothing considered appropriate for the opposite sex also qualifies as a fetish, but this behavior is generally classified as a separate paraphilia, **transvestism**. Changing into women's clothes, called cross-dressing, is sexually arousing to the transvestite (Blanchard and Clemmensen, 1988); even tape recordings that describe cross-dressing are arousing to these men (Blanchard et al., 1986). It is common for cross-dressing to be accompanied by sexual fantasies involving scenes of being bound while dressed as a woman (Buhrich and Beaumont, 1981).

Transvestism seems to originate in any of several possible experiences during an individual's youth. Parents and others can feminize a boy by cross-dressing him as a form of punishment for misbehavior, for example (Krueger, 1982). In doing so, they may be acting out their own wishes to have a girl rather than a boy. Cases have also been reported of transvestite fathers encouraging their sons to imitate them (Krueger, 1984). There is no evidence of a physical basis for such clothing preferences; for example, hormone levels of transvestite males do not differentiate them from other males (Buhrich et al., 1979).

Most transvestites are heterosexual men who marry and father children (Krueger, 1982), and they are roughly estimated to comprise about 1 to 3 percent of the U.S. population. Almost all of their cross-dressing occurs in private and results in sexual stimulation. This kind of behavior usually begins in childhood or early adolescence and progresses to a more and more elaborate wardrobe by adulthood. Erections and ejaculation are enhanced by cross-dressing—sometimes occurring only under those conditions—whether by masturbation or intercourse with a partner. Wives of transvestites usually are displeased by this behavior, but some accept and adapt to it by helping the husband apply makeup and select his costumes (Brown and Collier, 1989). Among a group of seventy wives of transvestite husbands, a substantial number (34 percent) reported being upset by their husband's sexual interest in cross-dressing. Others, higher in level of self-esteem, actually were aroused by their husbands' transvestism (Weinberg and Bullough, 1988). Some men prefer to cross-dress

in the company of prostitutes instead of with their wives (Wise, 1982). In large cities, transvestites may join social groups or clubs to be with others with similar sexual interests.

Male transvestites are distinguished from those cross-dressers who are homosexual men in "drag." These gays generally dress as females to ridicule cultural stereotypes. Still another group of cross-dressers consists of heterosexual males who perform as female impersonators, dressing as women as part of their act. Transsexualism, the desire to be a member of the opposite sex, also is characterized by cross-dressing (Buhrich and McConaghy, 1985; McCauley and Ehrhardt, 1980), as Chapter 6 points out. Of these four groups, only transvestites are sexually aroused by cross-dressing.

It is difficult to conceptualize female transvestism, because females in our culture have a much wider latitude in their choice of clothing—from skirts to pants. A woman dressed in a masculine shirt and jeans is commonplace. A man wearing a dress as shown in Figure 13-8, however, would raise eyebrows almost anywhere except in New Orleans during Mardi Gras. Nevertheless, a female transvestite is occasionally identified, such as one woman who reported, "Simply putting on my suit can provoke an orgasm" (Stoller, 1982, p. 101).

Laws against transvestism were first instituted in the early 1800s to punish farmers who disguised themselves as Indians and attacked local officials sent to enforce rent laws. These restrictions dealt with painting one's face and dressing so as to hide one's identity, but they were later applied to transvestites. Several cities now have ordinances that forbid cross-dressing in public places. The transvestite can obtain formal permission to cross-dress in public in some cities, however. Medical pressure has resulted in creating an identification card issued by the health department that permits transvestites and transsexuals to wear women's clothing (Slovenko, 1982c). The card is issued in response to a letter from the health department that explains the individual's condition.

A variation of transvestism is **cisvestism** in which the person wears the clothing of an inappropriate age group or an alternative social role. For example, some cisvestites dress in diapers, or they may

FIGURE 13-8 *PRETENDING TO BE BIKERS* Motorcycle jackets and other garb are exciting for some paraphiles even though they may not own or know how to ride a motorcycle. Sexual interest in inappropriate clothing is known as civestism (Gregersen, 1983).

dress as bikers even though they may never have been around motorcycles. Motorcyclist fashions, as shown in Figure 13-8, were popularized by films such as *The Wild Ones,* starring Marlon Brando (Gregersen, 1983). In homosexual sadomasochistic bars, the exaggerated masculinity of leather plus the Hell's Angels image of toughness have become commonplace not only in the United States but also in Great Britain and Germany.

Sadism and Masochism. **Sadism** is a paraphilia in which sexual gratification is obtained through inflicting mental suffering or physical pain. The term is based on the name of the French author, the Marquis de Sade (1774–1814), who practiced and wrote about such behavior. **Masochism** is defined as a paraphilia in which sexual arousal depends on experiencing mental suffering or physical pain. This term is based on the name of an Austrian novelist, Von Sacher-Masoch (1836–1905), who described in detail the effect of pain on pleasure.

Masochists outnumber sadists, and most are male, despite the stereotype of female masochism.

Each sex plays the dominant or the submissive role equally often (Breslow et al., 1985). Sexual arousal is elicited in both the masochist—who anticipates the effect of the pain—and the sadist—who experiences the power of delivering pain and witnessing its effect. For some sadomasochists, orgasm is possible only during these interactions or in response to fantasies about this kind of scene. Hunt's (1974) survey of U.S. adults found that 10 percent of men and 8 percent of women under age thirty-five reported pleasurably engaging in occasional sadistic or masochistic acts with a partner. In addition, having fantasies about sadomasochism is more common than carrying out such acts.

Sadomasochism as a sexual practice is found only in complex, highly developed societies. The closest analogy in preliterate societies is biting and scratching during foreplay and intercourse (Gebhard, 1969b). Sadomasochism is found in societies that provide time for leisurely pursuits, encourage imaginative creativity, and are characterized by the unequal distribution of power with dominant and submissive social relationships (Weinberg, 1987). Theorists propose that the temporary control of sexual acts through sadomasochistic playacting is an outlet for the participants' frustration at having their impulses socially controlled. Men and women express the need for such an outlet differently, as shown in an analysis of 225 letters to sex-oriented magazines (Baumeister, 1988). Letters from men sought humiliation through pain, loss of status, forced oral sex, and the participation of a third party in their sexual interactions. Women expressed the need for pain as punishment for their misbehavior in a relationship, humiliation through exhibitionism, and the presence of nonparticipating spectators to their sexual activities. Masochists of both sexes say they expect these sexual scenes to provide a short-term release from their cultural roles.

One familiar pattern is for masochistic men to seek sexual partners who will treat them as victims in a carefully scripted scene of sadomasochism. Some masochists will drive hundreds of miles and pay a considerable amount of money to a prostitute willing to enact a sadistic role in their sex games (Gebhard, 1969a). Apparently, many masochists feel intense guilt about their own sexuality, and only the experience of pain to punish their sins seems to justify their engaging in sex (Denko, 1980). A familiar variation of the sadomasochistic interaction involves "petticoat punishment" in which the sadist plays the role of a parent disciplining the "bad child." In such miniplays, the masochist is really the power figure serviced by the sadist who carefully orchestrates the relatively mild pain. Even the number of lashes from a whip is scripted (see Figure 13-9).

In addition to the alleviation of sexual guilt, some aged men may employ sadomasochistic scenes to stimulate their sexual responsiveness weakened by declining physical powers.

In **bondage**, the masochist is physically restrained. The discomfort and total helplessness produced by being bound heightens the effect of the pain psychologically. **Bondage and discipline**, or **B & D**, refers to the combined effects of physical restraint and the administration of emotional or physical pain.

FIGURE 13-9 *SADOMASOCHISTS AT PLAY*   A sadomasochistic interaction enhances the sexual pleasure of some individuals, relieving any guilt associated with sexuality. The sadist's role is to administer discipline, pain, and verbal abuse of the masochist.

The equipment used for these interactions includes whips, chains, handcuffs, ropes, and hooks or bedposts to which the partner can be tied.

About 40 percent of those practicing sadism and masochism locate one another through ads in publications that cater to them, such as *Sugar and Spikes* (Breslow et al., 1985). One fourth report seducing a partner into participating in sadomasochistic acts, while another 10 percent find partners in specialized bars and clubs. The remainder use miscellaneous methods to locate partners, or they simply masturbate while fantasizing or viewing sadomasochistic erotica. Some popular films and novels may give the impression that most sadomasochists are homosexual, but in fact most are heterosexual or bisexual in orientation (Breslow et al., 1985; Spangler, 1977).

A survey of 178 men who engage in sadomasochism revealed most of them to be college graduates, with above average income. They report alternating between playing dominant and submissive roles, and they also engage in other, nonsado-

masochistic sexual activities (Moser and Levitt, 1987). Only a few (6 percent) expressed being unhappy about sadomasochistic interests, and 16 percent had sought counseling. Most of them had practiced and enjoyed spanking and being spanked, bondage, humiliation, and acting out master–slave scenarios. A few had tried the use of a gag, eating or playing with urine or feces, inflicting or receiving burns or branding—such variations were found to be either unexciting or unpleasant.

Exhibitionism. In **exhibitionism** (or "flashing") a person derives sexual pleasure from exposing his genitals to an unwilling viewer, as Figure 13-10 depicts. In contrast, those who wear revealing clothing, let a sexual partner or a physician see their nude bodies, or who work as male or female strippers are *not* exhibitionists. The person who engages in exhibitionistic behavior is sexually gratified by embarrassing or shocking his victims, and the urge to expose himself is compulsive. Some exhibitionists also have the naïve expectation that a female viewing the erection will be-

"I'm sorry. Did I hit a nerve?"

FIGURE 13-10 *EXHIBITIONISM: SURPRISING A STRANGER BY EXPOSING THE GENITALS* Exhibitionists expose their genitals to unwilling strangers and hope to elicit a reaction of shock, fear, or sexual excitement.

come sexually excited. A victim who shows no reaction or who responds with ridicule provides no rewards for the exhibitionist.

Although most exhibitionists pose no physical danger to others, a few are aggressive and dangerous, use verbal abuse, make threatening gestures, or have physical contact with a victim. Some exhibitionists fantasize about raping their victims, although most do not (Gebhard et al., 1965). Exposure can be especially terrifying under certain circumstances—as when the victim is a child or when the setting is an isolated one (such as an elevator) with only the victim and the exhibitionist present (Hackett, 1983).

Many exhibitionists have adequate sex lives with a wife or girlfriend and almost all are heterosexual. The most common age group for exhibitionism is the mid-twenties, with the frequency declining markedly after age forty. One third of a group of almost 300 college women reported having been victimized by a male exhibitionist—by their brother or father before age seventeen and by a stranger at later ages. As many as 20 percent of the men arrested and convicted for exhibitionism subsequently repeat the offense and are rearrested. This rate of **recidivism** is greater than for all other sex offenders. It is suggested that this strongly compulsive act is repeated because there is little additional risk to a man's reputation once he has gone through the public disgrace. Unlike most men, including other types of sex offenders, exhibitionists are sexually aroused by scenes of fully clothed women engaged in nonerotic activity (Fedora et al., 1986).

Exhibitionists typically have had a fairly stable, happy childhood and adolescence; as adults, they are usually timid, shy, and sexually inhibited. Altogether, it is difficult to explain why they engage in this deviant act (Myers and Berah, 1983). It is possible that the risk of being caught is sexually exciting. In experiments comparing exhibitionists and controls, those who expose themselves are found to become more aroused when viewing films that depict a woman exposing and pointing to her genitals (Kolarsky and Madlafousek, 1983). As Figure 13-11 shows, nonexhibitionistic men find such exposure exciting primarily if it is preceded in the movie by other sexual interactions. Learning theory provides one possible explanation, suggesting that exhibitionists have somehow learned an atypical pattern of behavior in which

there is no relationship with the sex object and no foreplay—simply a genital display. In this context, it is interesting to observe that nonhuman primates ordinarily initiate sexual interactions in this way, by showing their genitals to a member of the opposite sex.

Women who expose their breasts or genitals to strangers may have exhibitionistic motives similar to those of male offenders (Procci, 1982). They don't expect to frighten the male viewer; rather, they hope to excite and then frustrate him. Women engaging in this behavior tend to select a protected environment. For example, a woman driving a car may display herself to a male truck driver while stopped at a red light, or a woman at home may deliberately undress in front of a lighted window (Russell, 1982). In such instances, the "victim" seldom files a complaint, and laws against exhibitionism are much less likely to be enforced against a woman than against a man. Analogous male behaviors that tend not to arouse much public concern include streaking (running nude in public) and mooning (exposing one's buttocks as a prank).

Voyeurism. **Voyeurism** (the behavior of a **Peeping Tom**) refers to the compulsive desire to become sexually aroused by viewing other people (usually strangers) engaged in sexual acts or simply undressed without their knowledge or permission. Men are much more likely than women to become voyeurs, as shown in the cartoon in Figure 13-12. Similar voyeuristic motives can be gratified by engaging in group sex or by looking at sexually explicit pictures, without covertly spying on unwilling targets and thus behaving in an unacceptable way.

The true voyeur gets sexual pleasure from watching others but not necessarily from engaging in sexual behavior himself. In fact, he may be unable to function sexually with a partner; thus, many voyeurs restrict their sexual behavior to masturbating while secretly observing others. The typical voyeur is a young male from a low socioeconomic background who possesses poor social skills (Simmons and Moore, 1982; Smith, 1976). Sometimes the voyeur commits other crimes such as theft as part of his activity. There are times when voyeurism escalates into a major criminal act such as rape (Tuteur, 1984) or

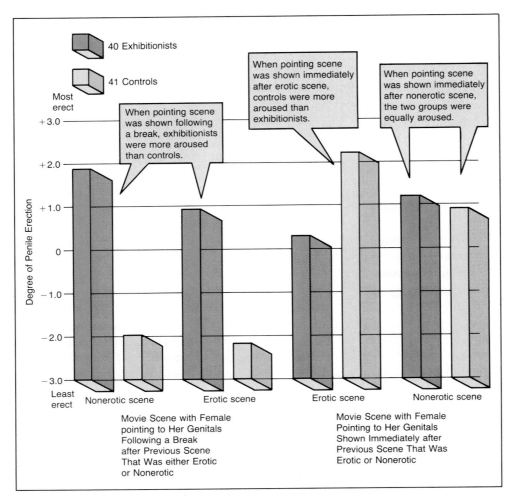

FIGURE 13-11 *EXHIBITIONISTS RESPONDING TO THE DISPLAY OF GENITALS* In an experiment, exhibitionists became more sexually aroused than control-group men when shown a movie scene in which a woman pointed to her genitals. When this scene was immediately preceded by one showing the female behaving sexily, the controls became more excited than the exhibitionists. When the genital-pointing scene was immediately preceded by a scene showing the woman clipping her toenails, the exhibitionists and the controls did not differ in arousal. Such findings suggest that exhibitionists have developed an unusual and immature pattern of sexual responsiveness.
Source: Based on data in Kolarsky and Madlafousek, 1983.

other antisocial acts (Simmons and Moore, 1982), but the exact percentage of voyeurs who commit these crimes is unknown.

For some, voyeuristic behavior lasts for only a short period of time; then, as the novelty wears off, he begins engaging in sex with a partner rather than simply watching others (Groth, 1982). This temporary voyeurism can be relatively harmless unless those being secretly observed discover what is going on.

Telephone Scatalogia. Obscene telephone callers are annoying and sometimes frightening because they repeatedly harass their victims. Such paraphilics arouse anxiety because they know the victim's name and phone number. Most often, such people—usually men—pose no serious threat. When, however, the caller makes additional contact (by mail or by showing up on the doorstep, for example), the danger is greater. As with exhibitionism, the major reward provided by **telephone scatalogia** lies in the

FIGURE 13-12 *NOT THE USUAL RESPONSE TO A VOYEUR*
Voyeurs seek sexual excitement by secretly viewing the nudity or sexual activity of unsuspecting strangers. The reaction of the couple in this cartoon is obviously not the typical response to such an invasion of privacy.

victim's shock or anger. The caller may masturbate during the conversation, and he feels safe from discovery or punishment. The telephone company advises the recipients of such calls to hang up without *any* response. If the annoying caller persists, the police suggest that you click the receiver and say, "Operator, this is the call I want traced" before hanging up. If the calls still continue, they can in fact be traced, but this is a lengthy and bothersome process. Once the caller is caught, his phone can be disconnected, and he can be legally prosecuted (Putrosky, 1981).

A technological innovation, Caller ID, displays the telephone number of the caller on a screen for the person receiving the call. With this device, the number of a telephone scatalogist is identified automatically. The person receiving a call has three options: Call Trace allows the authorities to track the caller, Call Return enables the victim to return the harasser's call immediately, and Call Block makes it possible to block all future calls from that number. Despite its advantage in discouraging obscene phone calls or apprehending the callers, there is pressure to make Caller ID illegal because it "invades the privacy" of the caller.

Zoophilia. When the object of sexual arousal and gratification is an animal, the paraphilia is called **zoophilia** (or **bestiality**). Most often, a man trains the animal to lick his genitals and to participate in anal or vaginal intercourse. In the Kinsey surveys, 8 percent of the men and 4 percent of the women had engaged in bestiality. The typical targets are household pets or farm animals such as cows or sheep. Adolescent boys growing up in rural areas are more likely to engage in bestiality than their counterparts who live in towns or cities, and the behavior tends to last for only a brief period of the person's life. Kinsey et al. (1948) found that about half of the incidents of zoophilia occur among adolescent males and that almost one out of five males in farm settings experience orgasm with an animal. Among women, bestiality usually involves domestic pets; the animal licks their genitals or they masturbate the animal (a male dog, for example). When zoophilia persists over time and in preference to an available human partner, it becomes increasingly difficult to alter. Among the suggested causes of long-lasting bestiality are sadism (when the animal is harmed) and rebellion against societal standards.

In addition to the several paraphilias just described, there are several relatively rare variations that Table 13-1 lists and describes.

■ **Development of Paraphilic Tendencies**

Paraphilias are of concern primarily because of their effect on innocent victims. The frequency of victimization among females is higher than you may expect. In a large random sample of women in their twenties, 59.6 percent reported that they had experienced sexually stressful incidents. These included ha-

rassment (21 percent), attempted rape (14 percent), and rape (10 percent), as will be discussed in Chapter 14. With respect to paraphilias, 31 percent had been confronted by exhibitionists, 12 percent had been touched by frotteurs, 8 percent had been called by telephone scatologists, and 4 percent were aware of being observed by voyeurs. One out of four of the incidents occurred before the female reached age thirteen (DiVasto et al., 1984). Most of the incidents involved strangers, and all of the victims described the experience as anxiety arousing.

Though it has been common medical practice to describe the different categories of paraphilia as though such sexual behavior fits neatly into a series of labels, a paraphilic often commits more than one

TABLE 13-1 **Some Very Different Strokes for Some Very Different Folks**
Among the less common paraphilias are these seven practices.

PARAPHILIA	AROUSED BY	DESCRIPTION
Coprophilia	Feces	Collects own feces and that of others to rub on his face and body
Urophilia	Urine	Urinates ("Golden Showers") on partner or vice versa
Klismaphilia	Enemas	Gives, receives, and observes enemas
Mysophilia	Filth	Attraction to dirt, for example, enjoying mud wrestling as a participant or an observer
Frotteurism	Rubbing	Sexual excitement based on rubbing the genitals against a clothed stranger in a crowded bus, subway, or elevator
Apotemnophilia	Self-mutilation or attraction to someone who is physically damaged, such as an amputee	After mutilating own limbs or genitals, the individual is aroused by the mutilated area; piercing the nipples, scrotum, perineum, or penis represents a slightly less severe version of this paraphilia as does sexual interest in the injuries of others
Necrophilia	Corpse	Those who are excited by seeing or engaging in sexual acts with dead bodies; these paraphilics are usually psychotic

Source: Buhrich, 1983; Greenberg-Englander and Levine, 1981; Hingsburger, 1989; Money et al., 1977; Schaffer, 1984.

kind of deviant act. Exhibitionists, for example, often are also voyeurs, make obscene telephone calls, and engage in frotteurism (Freund et al., 1983). Even paraphilics who deny having ever committed additional deviant acts become aroused in response to descriptions of other deviations. Thus, deviant sexuality may be a single encompassing category, with paraphilic tendencies generalizing from one specific act to others. There are two major theoretical explanations for the origin of paraphilic behavior.

Psychoanalytic Explanation of Paraphilia. According to classical psychoanalytic theory, paraphilia is a defense against castration anxiety, stemming from Oedipal problems. Like all males, the deviant individual during childhood was sexually attracted to his mother but fearful of retaliation by his father who might castrate him.

One way to escape such a fate is to avoid ordinary sexual interactions and to substitute a safer sexual activity. The paraphilic also wants to assure himself that castration has not occurred and will not occur. An exhibitionist, for example, is rewarded by the victim's reaction because it demonstrates that his penis is still in place as an important part of his anatomy. A transvestite cross-dresses to show that women retain penises and are not really castrated males (Nathan, 1982). As with many psychoanalytic proposals, these ideas are interesting but difficult either to confirm or disconfirm.

Social Learning Explanation of Paraphilia. Money (1986) provides evidence that paraphilias begin in childhood as the result of excessive restriction of typical infantile and childhood sex play. He points out that all young mammals, including humans, interact sexually as a way to learn about this bodily function and to rehearse adult sexual activity. Parents are quite content for their children to rehearse adult behavior when they pretend to be teachers, firefighters, police officers, or even robbers. When they rehearse sexual acts, however, the reaction often is quite negative. According to Money, when such behavior is prevented and especially when it is severely punished, the stage is set for paraphilia. In effect, ordinary sexual development is blocked, and alternative sexual outlets are learned.

Learning theorists stress the fact that paraphilias represent learned behaviors. Males are more likely than females to develop these practices because a penis is more likely to be touched and stimulated accidentally than is a clitoris, thus leading to a higher incidence of self-stimulation. During masturbation, erections become associated by chance with specific stimulus events through the process of **classical conditioning.** As a result, the person develops a paraphilia, associating excitement and orgasm with any stimuli present at the same time—his mother's panties or the secret observation of parental lovemaking or his dog. Figure 13-13 illustrates such conditioning. When these events are accompanied by anxiety about sexuality, there is further reason to engage in "safe" paraphilic sex rather than in frightening attempts to attract and interact with an actual partner (McSweeney and Bierley, 1984).

One first-hand description of this kind of learning history was provided by sexologist Havelock Ellis (1859–1939). He revealed that he was a urophile—someone who is excited by contact with urine. He traced this sexual interest to the arousal he felt as a child when his mother urinated in the grass or woods when they were taking a walk (Grosskurth, 1980).

Fetishes can even be produced by classical conditioning in a laboratory experiment. Rachman (1966) created a form fetish in men by repeatedly

FIGURE 13-13 *ACQUIRING A PARAPHILIA THROUGH CONDITIONING* Learning theorists explain paraphilias on the basis of classical conditioning. Through simple association, a previously nonsexual stimulus (e.g., picture depicting a lashing) is present at the same time as a sexual stimulus (masturbation), and it then becomes a stimulus for sexual arousal.

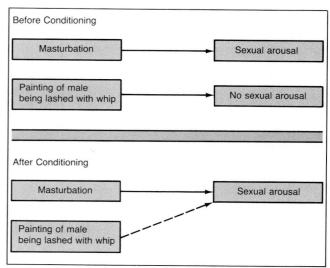

pairing their sexual arousal in response to erotic slides with pictures of black, knee-length women's boots. After a series of conditioning trials, the boot pictures by themselves caused the subjects to become aroused. When the experiment ended, the temporary fetish was extinguished by a series of presentations of the pictures of boots *not* accompanied by erotic slides (Rachman and Hodgson, 1968).

One hypothesis is that paraphilia is more likely to develop when the person has difficulty in attracting and interacting with appropriate sexual partners, and experimental data are consistent with this prediction. In one investigation, when men received two re-

jections from women they wished to date, they were more negative in judging pictures of females than men who had been accepted for dates (LaTorre, 1980). The rejected males did respond positively, however, to pictures of women's legs and panties. In real-life settings, a negative response from females may well lead to a sexual response to a less-threatening substitute object, providing an impetus for a fetish (Freund et al., 1984). In effect, many paraphilias represent confusion and misunderstanding about how to engage in a sexual interaction—designated a *courtship disorder* (Freund and Watson, 1990). Also, sex offenders have a history of frustration that results in in-

Highlighting Research

UNLEARNING PARAPHILIC BEHAVIOR

Behavioral treatments of paraphilias are found to be more successful than psychoanalytic therapy (Smith, 1976). Behavioral therapy generally is designed to associate (1) the unwanted acts with a noxious event so that the paraphilic is motivated to avoid them and (2) the appropriate acts with a rewarding outcome so that the paraphilic is motivated to engage in them.

In *aversion therapy* an unpleasant or painful stimulus is paired with the inappropriate behavior. For example, a transvestite may be instructed to engage in fantasies that include waves of nausea and vomiting as part of a sexual scene in which he is dressed as a woman. Or, a shoe fetishist can learn to think of shoes as evil smelling, covered with fungus, and coated with feces rather than as a source of sexual excitement.

In **shock aversion therapy**, electrodes are attached to a sensitive part of the paraphilic's body, such as the inner thigh. Then, the inappropriate sexual stimulus (fetish object, favorite dress, or whatever) is presented. Whenever the individual responds with an erection, a painful shock is delivered (Kilmann et al., 1982). The procedure is designed to teach the paraphilic

to associate the unacceptable stimulus with pain rather than with sexual pleasure.

Orgasmic reconditioning is designed to associate an acceptable sexual stimulus (such as an adult of the opposite sex) with sexual excitement and pleasure. The person masturbates while fantasizing about the unsuitable target, and then switches to an appropriate fantasy shortly before orgasm occurs. Often, aversion therapy is combined with orgasmic reconditioning so that the paraphilic learns to avoid the unwanted behavior and to substitute more acceptable behavior in its place. In *desensitization*, the person is taught to feel less anxious about nonparaphilic sexual interactions by associating them with pleasant thoughts and muscle relaxation.

Another aspect of behavior therapy is to provide a way for the paraphilic individual to develop effective social skills. Many sexually deviant people need to be taught how to interact with members of the opposite sex in a comfortable and pleasant way, and *social skills training* can help accomplish this goal.

These various techniques, used singly or in combination, can reduce or eliminate paraphilic behavior, at least temporarily.

Among the difficulties for any therapeutic approach to paraphilia, however, is the fact that success is usually judged by what the client reports about his subsequent activity. He is of course motivated to say that the paraphilic acts have not recurred, regardless of the truth. Unless he engages in the behavior and is arrested, there is no way to be certain about the effects of the treatment.

Some paraphilics seek therapy because their behavior is upsetting to themselves or to their family. Therapy is most often provided, however, for those who are caught, convicted, and under a court order to undergo treatment. Offenders who are more adept at avoiding arrest or who are able to afford expensive attorneys are unlikely ever to see a therapist (Croughan et al., 1981).

A final problem gets us back to the definition of deviant behavior and the ethical issue of who should receive therapy. If a person engages in paraphilic behavior in complete privacy (cross-dressing, for example) and feels no guilt or anxiety about what he does, is society justified in forcing him to change? That is not an easy question to answer.

creased arousal and compulsive acts (Konopacki and Oei, 1988).

The special insert, *Highlighting Research,* on page 364, describes the procedures used in guiding paraphilics to learn appropriate sexual responses.

Sexual Imagery: Arousing Words and Pictures

Human sexual behavior is influenced much more by what we have learned, what we think and believe, and how we react emotionally than by physiological variations in hormone levels or a vaguely defined "sex drive" (Kelley, 1986). Words that describe sexual activity and pictures that illustrate this behavior have a powerful impact on our desires, feelings, intentions, preferences, and on what we actually do. As a result, some people spend both time and money in seeking out such imagery as an integral part of their sexual lives while others greatly fear its effects and strive to eliminate it from society. In China, the government has decided that pornography is a Western plot to overthrow the Communist Party; as a result, the death penalty now applies to those who produce or distribute "lewd materials" (Kristof, 1990). What are the facts about this phenomenon?

■ Sexual Imagery as a Legal Issue: From Nudity to Pornography

Legal restrictions on sexual material have taken many forms—what words can be printed, what behaviors can be depicted, what song lyrics are permitted. We will focus attention on just what is meant by terms such as *pornography.*

What is Pornography? Sexual images can take many forms, but our laws and the general public frequently conceptualize all sexually explicit material as falling into a single category: **pornography.** It is as if the painting of a nude were no different from a photograph of a couple engaging in anal intercourse and a sexually explicit film about a brutal rape no different from a sexually explicit film about a loving couple on their honeymoon.

Though the word *pornography* originally referred to material written by or about prostitutes, it has evolved over the centuries into a pejorative term that is applied to any objectionable sexual material. Difficulties arise, of course, because people differ in their definitions of objectionable. Thus, some apply the term *pornography* to the painting "September Morn" depicting a nude female (Eliasberg and Stuart, 1961); others use it in referring to such popular television programs as *Saturday Night Live, Cheers, The Golden Girls,* and the *Oprah Winfrey Show.* Still others confine it to specific erotic content such as domination and violence (Steinem, 1980, 1983).

Pornography and the Law.   Legal attempts to define what is and is not objectionable have reflected changes in public opinion over time. In the United States in the last century, antipornography efforts were spearheaded by Anthony Comstock, who was the self-appointed censor for the New York Society for the Suppression of Vice. His work culminated in the Comstock Act of 1873 that made it a felony to send materials of "indecent character"—including birth control information—through the mail. In the decades that followed, legal sanctions prohibited printing, selling, or importing books containing material that incited lust. One of the first steps in reversing this trend came in 1933 when Judge Woolsey lifted the ban on *Ulysses* by James Joyce, despite its sexual passages. He found the novel acceptable because its primary goal was not to create sexual excitement; rather than representing obscenity, the work had serious artistic and literary value.

In the following decades, the legal system continued to struggle with the question of what precisely constituted acceptable versus unacceptable sexual material. Supreme Court Justice William Brennan "threw his judicial hands up in despair" after he and his fellow justices attempted to develop a working definition (Green, 1985, p. 13). His colleague Potter Stewart added to the judicial confusion about hardcore pornography when he said, "I can't define it, but I know it when I see it." Between 1957 and 1973, the Court arrived at three tests for defining obscenity: The material offends community standards; it has no redeeming social value; and it appeals to a prurient interest in sex.

The Supreme Court now relies primarily on "community standards" to define pornography, but that presents us with three problems. First, how do you define a community—the block you live on, the city, the county, the state, the entire nation, or a group of people who share common political, religious, and cultural beliefs? If someone produces a sexual film that is acceptable in the community where it is made, is it reasonable to arrest that individual in some other community because most people there find it unacceptable? Second, how do you determine what the standards are at a given time in a given place—door-to-door interviews, telephone surveys, questionnaires by mail? Also, what happens if these different methodologies yield different definitions of community standards; how do you then decide what material violates those standards? Third, what do we do when standards change over time? Whenever the standards defining pornography become more permissive, convicted pornographers suddenly would be innocent. Whenever standards become more restrictive, people previously innocent suddenly could be arrested.

Attempting to Develop an Objective Definition.   As difficult as it may be, perhaps it would be helpful to approach the definitional problem in objective rather than subjective terms. The U.S. Attorney General's Commission on Pornography (U.S. Department of Justice, 1986) adopted a system that classified explicit sexual materials into four categories: nonviolent, nonviolent but depicting such themes as degradation and sadomasochism, sexually violent, and sexual depictions of children. This system moves us closer to a definition with clear-cut, identifiable categories.

We believe that this approach has merit, and in Figure 13-14 we present our conceptualization of the varieties of **sexual imagery**—any written or pictorial material with sexual content that has the potential to elicit sexual thoughts, feelings, or physical excitement. Two major subcategories are based on the amount of anatomical or behavioral detail involved: **non-explicit sexual imagery (soft-core)** and **explicit sexual imagery (hard-core)**. Each of these subcategories, in turn, consists of three specific content areas: nudity, sexual activity, and the material we define as pornography—coercion, domination, or any sexual depiction involving children.

Our definition of pornography (like all others) is necessarily based on certain values; for example, we find rape, sexual assault, and the sexual abuse of children unacceptable. Any explicit depiction that causes that kind of behavior to be perceived as less offensive, and hence, more likely to occur is, therefore unacceptable.

Keep in mind others may find simple nudity unacceptable, and some may be offended by any depiction of masturbation, intercourse, oral sex, or homosexual interactions. Considerable debate has been generated among feminists about the negative message communicated by *all* explicit depictions (Green, 1985). Some suggest that the basic point of all such imagery is the use of women as sex objects for male pleasure. One feminist faction approves of sadomasochistic material involving two females because this represents a healthy liberation of female sexuality. Others see such material as further evidence of the oppression of females. Given these and other divergent views about sexual depictions, we don't expect everyone to accept the same definition of pornography in the foreseeable future.

Though some may believe that sexual depictions were invented during the 1960s, the following description of explicit sexual material indicates more accurately its role throughout human history. Figure 13-15 suggests that some of the issues raised in this chapter could have been of equal concern in past centuries.

■ A Capsule History of Sexual Imagery

As soon as human beings discovered how to draw images on the walls of caves, they began to depict nudity and sexual acts. Etruscan art in 600 B.C. included bestiality, oral sex, and intercourse in multiple positions. Much later, artists such as Rembrandt in the seventeenth century created sexually explicit paintings along with their more socially acceptable work. The sexual art was usually purchased by private collectors and ignored by public museums. Sexually explicit images were produced throughout the world. Examples include Japan's "pillow art," designed to provide sex education to newlyweds, and the sacred erotic carvings that decorated India's Hindu temples.

With the introduction of the camera in the nineteenth century, explicit sexual scenes soon were pho-

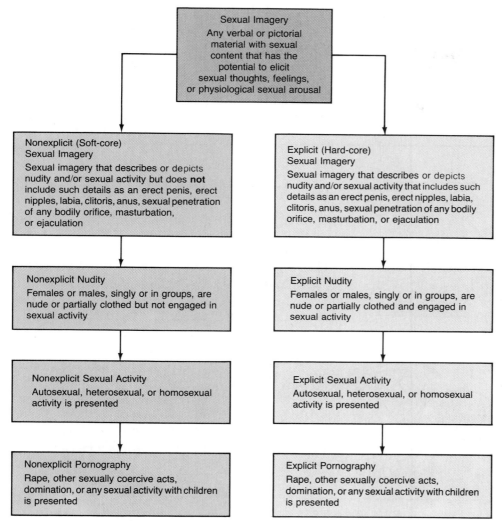

Sexual Imagery
Any verbal or pictorial material with sexual content that has the potential to elicit sexual thoughts, feelings, or physiological sexual arousal

Nonexplicit (Soft-core) Sexual Imagery
Sexual imagery that describes or depicts nudity and/or sexual activity but does **not** include such details as an erect penis, erect nipples, labia, clitoris, anus, sexual penetration of any bodily orifice, masturbation, or ejaculation

Explicit (Hard-core) Sexual Imagery
Sexual imagery that describes or depicts nudity and/or sexual activity that includes such details as an erect penis, erect nipples, labia, clitoris, anus, sexual penetration of any bodily orifice, masturbation, or ejaculation

Nonexplicit Nudity
Females or males, singly or in groups, are nude or partially clothed but not engaged in sexual activity

Explicit Nudity
Females or males, singly or in groups, are nude or partially clothed and engaged in sexual activity

Nonexplicit Sexual Activity
Autosexual, heterosexual, or homosexual activity is presented

Explicit Sexual Activity
Autosexual, heterosexual, or homosexual activity is presented

Nonexplicit Pornography
Rape, other sexually coercive acts, domination, or any sexual activity with children is presented

Explicit Pornography
Rape, other sexually coercive acts, domination, or any sexual activity with children is presented

FIGURE 13-14 *VARIETIES OF SEXUAL IMAGERY* Defining categories of sexual imagery: verbal or pictorial material is divided into two major types (explicit and nonexplicit), each of which consists of three content categories: nudity, sexual activity, and pornography.

tographed. Unlike earlier depictions, photographs made it possible for the viewer to observe real people actually engaged in intercourse, oral sex, and all other forms of human sexuality. A police raid in 1874 in the London suburb of Pimlico resulted in the confiscation of 130,248 photographs that were judged to be obscene. Consistent with the styles and customs of the time, both the male and female performers wore socks (to hide dirty feet and to safeguard their "acting" fees from dishonest photographers) and hats. Throughout the twentieth century,

filmed sex has retained its popularity, and only the clothing and hairstyles have varied over the years.

In the 1950s, *Playboy* magazine first appeared, featuring nonexplicit nudity and sexual activity. An analysis of *Playboy* cartoons and pictures over the past thirty years revealed that violence is rarely shown and that the amount of it has in fact decreased in recent years (Scott and Cuvelier, 1987). Many similar publications, such as *Penthouse,* soon followed. *Screw* anchored the hard-core end of the spectrum, with stories, drawings, and photos depicting vaginal and

FIGURE 13-15 *DEPICTIONS OF SEX AND VIOLENCE: NOT A NEW ISSUE* Though some people seem to believe that sexual imagery is a modern invention and concern, sex and violence have been described and depicted throughout human history. As suggested in this cartoon, such material has frequently led people to question its possible effects on readers or viewers.

anal intercourse, bestiality, and sadomasochism. Occupying the middle of this array were magazines such as *Hustler* that featured, among other things, gynecological close-ups of female genitalia.

The invention of movies quickly led to sexually explicit films. From 1915 until the late 1960s, they were illegal, underground products shown primarily to all-male groups as "stag" films. The shift to semi-respectability began when producer Russ Meyer brought the first of his soft-core sexual movies to the big screen—*Vixen*. Others soon followed, and they captured the imagination of middle-class America. Meyer's films, featuring well-endowed, bare-breasted women and simulated sexual acts, introduced many dating couples to socially acceptable erotica. The first hard-core film to have a similar commercial success was 1973's *Deep Throat,* featuring fellatio, cunnilingus, intercourse, and on-screen ejaculation. With this movie, the flood gates of explicit sexual films had opened, and a wide range of professional, full-length, hard-core movies were soon being shown throughout the United States.

At about the same time, explicit 8 mm loops (lasting about ten to twelve minutes) and later videotapes of varying lengths became available for home viewing. Some channels on cable TV also began to show explicit sexual movies. As a result, many couples could incorporate sexual films as part of their foreplay. Individuals without sex partners also found that such movies added to the pleasure of masturbation. Some adult bookstores provided viewing stalls in which male customers masturbated as they watched (Weatherford, 1985). It is estimated that about 40 million Americans spend about $8 billion each year on explicit sexual materials.

Like earlier forms of sexual imagery, explicit movies primarily show the heterosexual interactions of couples and groups. The next largest content category consists of male homosexual films showing males masturbating or engaging in fellatio and anal intercourse—as couples or in groups. Because we generally prefer viewing other people doing what we do, heterosexuals are the customers for heterosexual material, and gays for gay material. An exception is the popularity among many heterosexuals (though not among lesbians) of films showing female–female sexual interactions.

A very small segment of the market depicts other themes, designed to fit any sexual interest. Thus, some 8 mm loops or videotapes depict sadomasochistic acts, bestiality, and urophilia as well as dwarfs, pregnant women, amputees, obese individuals, and—illegally—children engaged in sexual acts with adults or with other children.

Most of the participants in sex films are white; very few U.S. or European productions show black couples and even fewer feature Oriental couples. Interracial sex is more common, however, and the most popular pairs consist of a white woman with a black man or a white man with an Oriental or black woman.

■ The Effects of Sexual Imagery

It is well established that pictures and verbal material containing explicit sex scenes cause those who view them to become sexually excited, both subjectively and physically (Kelley and Byrne, 1983). As a result, blood congests in the genital region, males have erections, and women experience vaginal lubrication—in the same way that sexual arousal occurs when people interact with sexual partners.

Why Do Sexual Images Cause Arousal?   External images of sexual interactions are apparently translated into internal images in which the viewer imagines himself or herself participating in the scene. Thus, the external fantasy becomes an internal fantasy, and we respond as we do to products of our imagination. In the same way that novels, films, or television programs can make you feel frightened, sad, or angry—also eliciting the appropriate physical reactions to match those emotions—they can cause you to become sexually aroused.

If you cannot process the material cognitively, however, sexual images do not elicit sexual arousal. This was first shown by Geer and Fuhr (1976) who had male subjects listen to a sexually explicit story on tape while they performed nonsexual cognitive tasks that interfered with their fantasy activity. In a **dichotic listening task**, the erotic story was presented through one earphone and a numerical task through the other. The more complex the task to be performed with the numbers, the less sexual arousal these subjects experienced. They heard the sexual stories and knew the content, but they were too busy to process the material and turn it into personal fantasies. In later research, female subjects also responded in the same way (Przybyla and Byrne, 1984). With visual—as opposed to auditory—imagery, however, males and females responded differently. Females were less aroused as cognitive interference increased, but males were unaffected. One possible explanation for this finding is that men may respond more readily than women to visual stimulation (Money, 1985).

Cognitive factors also influence arousal in another way. Both men and women become more aroused in response to sexual images if they are told that others like themselves find the material very arousing (Norris, 1989).

The Effect of Sexual Imagery on Attitudes.   Exposure to sexual images can have effects beyond simply sexual excitement. For one thing, attitudes can be shaped and changed. This is important because an attitudinal change may occur as a preliminary step to a behavioral change. For example, exposure to many scenes of rape could desensitize the viewer to this crime, leading to a less negative attitude about it and about the rapist. Over time, sexual aggression could become more likely because of the attitude shift. Because it is much easier as well as more ethical to study the effects of sexual material on attitudes than to determine its effects on sexually coercive behavior, current research often focuses on these attitudinal effects (Kelley, 1985e).

When male and female subjects view a brief sexually explicit film each day for four days, the result is boredom and a negative emotional response (Kelley and Musialowski, 1986). Following exposure to massive amounts of such films for several weeks, college students express less punitive attitudes about rapists, more negative attitudes about women's liberation, and the perception that unusual sexual practices are common; in addition, the male subjects indicated a more calloused attitude toward women (Zillmann and Bryant, 1984). Table 13-2 summarizes these findings, which suggest that regular viewing of hard-core material could lead to changes in attitude about various sex-related practices.

In addition to general effects, specific attitudes and beliefs often are presented in sexually explicit material. For example, such films—and many nonsexual films as well—glorify male dominance rather than equality between the sexes. In the average

X-rated (or NC–17) movie, concepts such as love, marriage, and family are absent, and the normative behavior is casual sex between strangers. The nonexplicit mass media often portray sexual interactions in a similar fashion (Abramson and Mechanic, 1983).

Bryant (1985) found that explicit films affect moral judgments. College students in the experimental group watched nonviolent, explicit sex films three hours a day for five successive days, while the controls watched nonsexual situation comedies (*Benson, Different Strokes,* and others). Three days after these film sessions ended, both groups were shown brief segments from TV shows depicting questionable behavior. For example, in one scene, a wife slipped into a hotel bed to surprise her husband, whereupon he and his gay lover enter the room after showering together. Subjects who had watched the sex films thought that the man's behavior was less morally wrong than did the subjects in the control group. Similar differences were found in responding to a scene showing a husband having an extramarital affair and to one in which an adult male had sex with a twelve-year-old girl.

Such findings are of considerable interest, but we should be cautious in concluding that explicit sexual depictions have negative effects. The changes in moral judgments may not occur simply because the subjects viewed sex films but rather because certain

TABLE 13-2 The Effects of Massive Exposure to Explicit Sexual Imagery

Exposure to numerous sexually explicit films over a series of days significantly affected the beliefs and attitudes of male and female undergraduates. These effects of sexual imagery may be more important to society in the long run than any dramatic effects on overt sexual behavior.

BELIEFS AND ATTITUDES	EFFECTS OF MASSIVE EXPOSURE TO SEXUAL IMAGERY
Estimates of percentage of adults who engage in oral sex, anal intercourse, group sex, sadomasochism, and bestiality	The greater the exposure, the higher the estimated percentages for each behavior.
Judgments about a film depicting explicit sexual activity	The greater the exposure, the less it was rated as offensive or pornographic and the less objection there was to showing it to minors or broadcasting it on TV.
Recommendations about prison sentence for a convicted rapist	The greater the exposure, the shorter the sentence recommended by both males and females.
Support for women's liberation	The greater the exposure, the less the support for women's liberation by both males and females.
Males' feelings of sexual callousness toward females	The greater the exposure, the more callousness expressed by males.

Source: Based on data in Zillmann and Bryant, 1984.

moral values were expressed in them. For example, on daytime soap operas sexual relationships are commonly depicted, and 94 percent of them involve couples who are not married, at least not to one another (More sex..., 1988). In addition, the themes of non-sexual presentations may be of equal or greater importance in guiding ethical development. Note that the average American child has watched 5,000 hours of television by the time he or she enters school and 19,000 hours by high school graduation (Zoglin, 1990). Even cartoons in magazines such as *Playboy* tend to convey various messages to readers—women are shown as physically attractive victims of sexual coercion as well as being sexually naive and childlike (Matacin and Burger, 1987).

■ Negative Behavioral Effects of Exposure to Sexual Imagery

Of greater general concern than the effect of sexual depictions on arousal or even on attitudes and values is the possibility that they might cause antisocial or even criminal behavior. When campaigns are waged against pornography, the underlying assumption is that explicit sexual content elicits undesirable behavior (Wills, 1977).

Despite centuries of censorship in various parts of the world, there had been almost no research determining the effects of sexual stimuli on behavior until President Johnson appointed the first U.S. Commission on Obscenity and Pornography in 1968. That commission provided encouragement and financial support for a wide range of empirical research. Among the major findings of these correlational and experimental studies was that explicit imagery had only minor, temporary effects on behavior. Partly as a result of the publication of the Commission's technical reports in 1971, sex research became more acceptable, and many investigators began working in this field. In the subsequent research that was carried out in the 1970s and 1980s, some of the data suggested the possibility that at least some kinds of sex-related materials do have negative behavioral effects.

In 1985, U.S. Attorney General Meese appointed a new Commission on Pornography to study the new findings and to recommend legislative action to Congress. Though there was a dissenting minority on the Commission, the majority report was strongly negative about most types of sexual presentations and made a number of suggestions about legal procedures to fight them.

The Meese Report, released in 1986, created considerable controversy. Two leading investigators of the effects of pornography, psychologists Edward Donnerstein and Neil Malamuth, objected to the way research was interpreted in the report. They concluded, for example, that aggressive content was the major cause of the antisocial effects of violent pornography rather than the sexual content. In addition, the report incorrectly portrayed violent pornography as much more common and popular than is actually the case (Linz et al., 1987). Additional criticisms of this commission included the revelation that the majority of the panel members had been selected for their record of bias against sexually explicit material (American Civil Liberties Union, 1986), that the conclusions drawn from the research were simplistic, and that pornography is not contagious (that is, the massive exposure of this material to commission members did not turn them into violent paraphilics).

Surgeon General Koop (1987) convened a Workshop on Pornography and Public Health in 1986. The seventeen behavioral scientists who participated discussed in depth the recent work on the negative effects of hard-core material on behavior; they concluded that the undesirable consequences were attributable primarily to violent erotic material and/or explicit depictions that exploited children.

The use of children in sexually explicit photographs and films clearly has negative consequences on them, but laws already exist to prosecute this activity. While this issue causes no disagreement, the depiction of violence and the degradation of women is more controversial. Even without explicit sexuality, publications such as detective magazines have the theme of women being dominated (76 percent) or in bondage (38 percent) on their covers (Dietz et al., 1986; Linz et al., 1986). Further, pictures of women expressing distress are more sexually arousing to college males than pictures of women expressing positive emotions (Heilbrun and Seif, 1988). Consider also the fact that after viewing violent "slasher" films, males show less sympathy for a rape victim and are less upset by her story than males who had viewed hard- or soft-core sexual films (Linz et al., 1988). Leaving sex aside, the depiction of violence toward women contributes to negative attitudes about women.

Fisher and Barak (1989) suggest that education about the effects of violent sexual imagery can counteract its negative influence. For example, when 105 college men were shown films that emphasized either concern for a sexual partner or the suffering of rape victims, they were empathetic to victims, less favorable toward films depicting violence against women, and more likely to find an accused rapist guilty. Such effects may be temporary, but they point out the value of immunizing people against the familiar negative messages about how women should be treated.

As a result of two decades of research, plus the findings of the two commissions and the workshop, we now know sexual imagery has some effect on interpersonal behavior and on sexual activity, as will be discussed in the following sections.

Effects on Interpersonal Behavior. Sexual excitement alters evaluations of the opposite sex in various ways. For example, after exposure to sexual stimuli, aroused men consider women more physically attractive and sexually responsive than they do without such exposure (Stephan et al., 1971). They also express more love for their female partners under these conditions (Dermer and Pyszcznski, 1978). For both males and females, arousal in response to sexual images leads to more positive evaluations of a physically attractive stranger of the opposite sex and more negative evaluations of an unattractive stranger (Istvan, Griffitt, and Weidner, 1983). Some investigators, however, found a contrast effect; exposure to very attractive females on television or in male sex magazines leads to less positive judgments about average females (Kenrick, Gutierres, and Goldberg, 1989; Kenrick and Gutierres, 1980).

Arousal also affects overt interpersonal behavior. People with negative attitudes about their own arousal avoid looking at or sitting near a stranger of the opposite sex; in contrast, those who respond positively to being aroused are more likely to look at and sit near such a stranger (Griffitt et al., 1974).

Effects on Sexual Activity. Much research indicates an increased likelihood of engaging in sexual acts as a function of being aroused by erotic images. A correlational study found that women who read soft-core sexual romances have sexual intercourse twice as often as those who do not (Coles and Shamp, 1984). In an experiment, unmarried students exposed to explicit images were more likely to masturbate afterward (Amoroso et al., 1971). Similarly, women shown a film depicting female masturbation subsequently masturbated more than controls who did not see the film (Heiby and Becker, 1980). Married couples are more likely to engage in intercourse after viewing a sex film than after viewing a nonsexual film (Cattell et al., 1972).

These and other studies strongly suggest a general motivating effect of sexual stimuli in that viewers become more likely to engage in the kind of sexual activity they ordinarily engage in. Unless one believes that masturbation is bad or that partners should refrain from intercourse, such investigations provide no reason for anyone to become concerned about behavioral effects.

In addition to motivating a person to engage in familiar sexual practices, erotic images can also be used as models to guide future activity (Byrne and Schulte, 1990). In one experiment, for example, sexually inexperienced female undergraduates were shown explicit sexual films. Afterward, they reported a startling increase in their intentions to perform the acts they had viewed, including intercourse. In fact, these subjects said that they expected to engage in eleven out of twelve sexual acts listed by the experimenter (Wishnoff, 1978). Without exception, they expected to engage in their first act of intercourse very soon, while only 15 percent who were shown nonsexual films had such plans. Though explicit sexual productions are not a major source of sex education for most people, males are more likely than females to say that information about some topics was provided by "pornography"—masturbation, arousal, orgasm, oral sex, and anal intercourse (Tjaden, 1988).

The first contact that young people have with sexual films and magazines is of special interest. After their initial exposure, males were more likely than females to believe that the depicted sexual acts were appealing (Bryant, 1985). About half of the females also responded positively, but disgust and revulsion were much more common for them than for males. As Figure 13-16 indicates, males expressed a greater desire than females to imitate the activity. The younger the subjects, the greater the desire to imitate and the more likely they were to engage in the depicted behaviors. Altogether, two thirds of the males and almost half of the females wanted to copy what they had seen, while one fourth of the males and fifteen percent of the females actually did so.

When a depicted sexual act requires a partner, typically the male asks the female to imitate the erotic scene. In a sample of adult females aged eighteen to sixty, 10 to 15 percent said that they were upset when a husband or boyfriend made such a request (Russell and Trocki, 1985).

FIGURE 13-16 *MODELING EFFECTS OF SEXUAL IMAGERY* A young person's first exposure to sexual imagery results in the desire to imitate the activity and the tendency actually to carry out the activity more commonly among boys than girls. More youngsters desire to engage in sexual acts than actually do because of the unavailability of a willing partner and feelings of anxiety and guilt about sex.
Source: Based on data in Bryant, 1989.

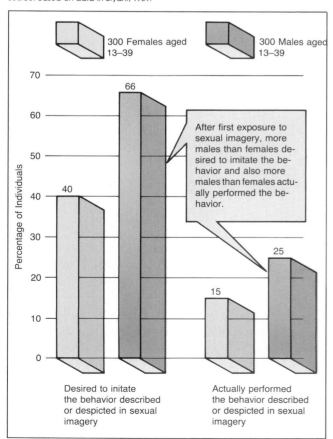

To summarize the findings of these modeling studies, exposure to explicit scenes of sexual activity seems to raise the viewers' desire to imitate the behavior, strengthen their intention to engage in the behavior, and increase the probability of actually doing so. As a result of this line of research, we must consider another element—what behavior is being shown and imitated? This brings us back to our earlier discussion: Values play a major role in how anyone evaluates behavioral effects. Whether you are upset, indifferent, or pleased by the idea of viewers imitating scenes of masturbation, premarital intercourse, or oral sex depends on your attitudes and beliefs about those acts. For example, under pressure from United States Senator Jesse Helms, the National Endowment for the Arts requires grant recipients to guarantee not to produce work involving sadomasochism, the sexual exploitation of children, or homosexual themes (Leavitt, 1990). Do you agree that homoeroticism is as unacceptable as sadism or the use of children as sexual objects? People disagree strongly about such matters, and behavioral science cannot resolve the disagreements. Empirical research can only determine *what* happens, not whether it *should* happen.

One behavioral effect causes concern to almost everyone, however. Sexual images of aggressive acts such as rape are unacceptable if they influence viewers to engage in that kind of antisocial behavior. The special section ***Taking Responsibility and Protecting Yourself,*** on page 374, describes recent research on the effects of sexually violent images.

Sexual Imagery and Sex Crimes: Is There a Link? Almost all sex crimes are committed by men against women. It is obviously of critical importance to know whether sexual materials contribute in any way to such behavior. While it is easy to proclaim either that (1) no one was ever corrupted by a book or movie, or conversely that (2) the rising crime rate clearly reflects the moral breakdown caused by pornography, how can we determine what is actually true? One obviously cannot conduct an experiment in which subjects are exposed to violent pornography to determine how many will commit sex crimes afterward.

One approach is to study convicted sex criminals to find out how much experience they have had with sexual materials. Most such offenders report that they have had less contact with explicit sexual books,

Taking Responsibility and Protecting Yourself

VIOLENT CONTENT VERSUS SEXUAL CONTENT IN RAPE DEPICTIONS

Think about a situation in which someone your age, or younger, views a film that shows the rape of a woman by one or more men. What might that person think and feel while watching such material? More importantly, what lasting effects might result from viewing nonconsensual sex? A number of experimental investigations have explored just such questions. In one study, female undergraduates listened to audiotaped stories in which a woman is overpowered by a rapist; in the struggle, she becomes sexually aroused and enjoys being assaulted (Stock, 1985). This is a common theme in fictional depictions of rape, and it produces higher levels of sexual arousal in those who hear it than in listening to an audiotape of a rape in which the victim expresses only fear, pain, and negative emotions. The myths that suggest that rape is pleasurable to women ("Women don't admit it, but they really want to be raped," "If you're about to be raped, just relax and enjoy it") are already accepted by many people in our society. Depictions of rape as a source of pleasure only strengthen these false beliefs.

A study of sexually explicit videocassettes revealed that over half of the scenes involved domination and exploitation of women by men, sometimes including violence (Cowen et al., 1988).

Some of the negative effects of sexual violence in films and other media can be counteracted through education of the viewers about the falsehood of rape myths depicted in fictional material (Malamuth and Check, 1984). In a postexperimental debriefing, the experimenter explained the goals of the experiment and provided additional information to the subjects. Other research indicates that providing information to differentiate sexuality and violence prior to seeing a violent rape film ("briefing") is equally helpful (Intons-Peterson et al., 1989). In everyday life, of course, viewers exposed to mythical depictions of rape—whether in hard-core pornography or in the soft-core erotica of televised soap operas—there is no briefing or debriefing.

Most people are more aroused by sexual imagery in which one partner is dominated sexually by the other than by imagery showing equality of the partners (Garcia et al., 1984; Kelley et al., 1983). Male college students, for example, are more aroused by a bound woman who experiences distress than by a woman in bondage expressing positive affect (Heilbrun and Seif, 1988). Perhaps this explains why the violent content of rape depictions, not their sexual component, has the most striking effects on behavior and

feelings (Kelley et al., 1989; Malamuth and Donnerstein, 1984). Exposure to violent pornography also produces more negative, stereotypic attitudes about both sexes among its viewers (Kelley, 1985f). Males with a history of exposure to violent sexual stimuli hold pro-rape beliefs that include blaming the victim—whether her appearance or her behavior—for causing the rape (Garcia, 1986).

Depictions of rape and violence also have different effects on different viewers. For example, males who are sexually aggressive are most aroused by fantasies of violence and rape whether these are present externally in a film (Malamuth, 1986) or internally in their own imaginations (Greendlinger and Byrne, 1987). Convicted rapists, for example, are more aroused by rape depictions than by stories of consenting sex, and they are also aroused by nonsexual material in which a female is the victim of violence (Quinsey and Chaplin, 1984). Males who do not have a history of sexual aggression do not respond in this way.

While censorship of violent sexual images may be a mistake, individual citizens can avoid exposing either themselves or their children to such material.

pictures, and films than nonoffenders (Goldstein et al., 1974). Offenders generally describe their childhood experiences and their parents as sexually repressive and restrictive. Other data suggest the possibility that the timing of such exposure may be critical. Between the ages of six and ten, over a third of those who later became rapists had been exposed to explicit materials while only 2 percent of nonoffenders reported that type of early experience.

There is also some indication that potential sex offenders may be especially vulnerable to the effects of sexual presentations, even without early exposure to them (Marshall and Barbaree, 1983). As one step in preparing for committing a criminal offense, 53 percent of child molesters and 33 percent of rapists say they look at sexual pictures. If those findings could be firmly established, perhaps you would conclude that such material must be banned. There is another consideration, however. Given the ability of humans to create their own sexual fantasies, we encounter a seemingly impossible task: How do you ban imagination? For example, rapists and child molesters create more rape fantasies for themselves than male nonoffenders matched for age, intelligence, and socioeconomic background. Even when offenders look at nonviolent scenes of love or the sexual interactions of mutually consenting partners, they translate the material in their own fantasies to stories of rape and domination (Marshall, 1985).

Besides studying sex criminals, another way to investigate the possible link between sexual materials and crime is to find out if a relationship exists between the availability of sexual imagery and the crime rate. Baron (1985) examined the circulation of eight sexual magazines like *Playboy, Penthouse,* and *Hustler* in the United States. Considered on a per capita basis, the circulation rate of these magazines in each state is positively related to the incidence of rape. The incidence of rape also is correlated with the number of adult theaters and bookstores located in a community (Green, 1985).

Before you decide that the evidence is straightforward and clear, consider some additional findings. The incidence of rape is also associated with the circulation of aggressively masculine publications such as *Guns and Ammo* and *Field and Stream* (Scott, 1985) and with a number of factors related to the acceptance of aggression in a given society including the number of hunting licenses sold, an emphasis on football in the schools, enlistments in the National Guard, and the legality of corporal punishment in the schools. Thus, an emphasis on traditional masculine interests (including sex and aggression) in a particular area of the country may have more to do with rape than the specific availability of sexual material. Rape incidence is also associated with community factors such as the degree of urbanization, poverty, and the number of divorced men living there (Baron and Straus, 1984).

What Happens When Pornography Is Legalized? If explicit words and pictures are a cause of criminal behavior, sex crimes should increase when such material is legalized and made widely available. Instead, the experience in Denmark indicated the opposite (Kutchinsky, 1985). When the sale of sexual materials to anyone over age sixteen was made legal in 1969, the sexual abuse of children and homosexual offenses dropped markedly for the next several years. The incidence of rape did not decline, but it also did not increase (Green, 1985). Similarly, West Germany found that the legalization of pornography in 1973 had no effect on rape incidence, but there was an 11 percent drop in the number of other sex offenses over the next seven years (Green, 1985).

Is there any other evidence that the availability of pornography does or does not lead to rape? In Japan, most pornography involves the theme of rape, but the incidence of actual rapes in that country is only one sixteenth of that in the United States on a per capita basis (Abramson and Hayashi, 1984).

Despite all that is now known about the effects of sexual material as determined in laboratory experiments, the study of sex criminals, and the social correlates of sexual offenses, behavioral scientists have been unable to reach agreement about this issue. There is contradictory evidence and considerable uncertainty about basing any crucial legislative actions on any simplistic conclusions (Byrne and Kelley, 1989). Though you may find this answer unsatisfactory, the fact is that no one knows with any degree of certainty the effect of sexual imagery on criminal behavior.

Summarizing the Information about Impersonal Sex . . .

Prostitution has existed throughout the world for thousands of years. Among prostitutes in the United States, **call girls, hand whores, streetwalkers,** and **bar girls** have distinctly different clients and methods of conducting business. Males also become prostitutes, as **call boys, kept boys,** or part-time amateurs, servicing primarily male clients. The background of prostitutes very often reveals a troubled home life and having been sexually exploited. Prostitutes report experiencing little pleasure in their sexual interactions with clients, but they may have a close sexual relationship with a lover, a husband, or a **pimp.** Young males visit prostitutes less frequently now than in the past, because premarital sex is now generally accepted for both sexes. Women have more negative attitudes about prostitution than men. Attempts to limit or ban prostitution involve legal measures and attempts to embarrass clients, but their effectiveness is limited.

Paraphilias consist of a compulsive sexual interest in various stimulus objects or activities that are a necessary accompaniment or substitute for traditional interpersonal sex. **Festishism** is directed at specific forms such as shoes or at hard or soft objects. **Transvestism** is practiced primarily by heterosexual men who find it sexually exciting to dress as a female. Partners who engage in *sadomasochism* enact roles of dominance and submission. One version of this kind of interaction is **bondage and discipline. Exhibitionism** refers to the practice of exposing the genitals to an unwilling stranger, and one of its goals is to shock or frighten that person. This type of paraphilia is more likely than any other to be continued despite arrests, convictions, and public disgrace. **Voyeurism** refers to Peeping Tom behavior, **telephone scatalogia** usually is an attempt to evoke a reaction of disgust or fright from the victim, and **zoophilia** (sex with animals) is usually a passing phase in young males with access to appropriate pets or farm ani-

mals. Psychoanalytic theory has explained paraphilias as originating in childhood castration fears. In contrast, social learning approaches emphasize the failure to acquire appropriate interpersonal skills plus rewards associated with the paraphilic activity. The most successful treatment is behavior therapy in which sexual responses to the paraphilic stimulus are punished while responses to appropriate sexual stimuli are rewarded.

Sexual imagery includes **explicit** and **nonexplicit** verbal and pictorial material that can be categorized as nudity, sexual activity, and **pornography.** The latter category consists of images of rape, other sexually coercive acts, domination, or any kind of sex with children. Public sexual imagery is as old as human history. People respond to such images with sexual arousal; they translate the scene into imaginative fantasies in which they participate. The effects of exposure to sexual images have been systematically investigated only in recent years. Violent content has more negative effects than sexual content, and exposure to either sexual or aggressive imagery can affect attitudes, intentions, and behavior. The evidence about imagery as a cause of sex crimes is unclear.

To Find Out More about Impersonal Sex . . .

Goldman, M. S. (1981). *Gold diggers and silver miners: Prostitution and social life on the Comstock Lode.* Ann Arbor: University of Michigan Press.
    This is an interesting historical account of prostitution in a Western mining town.
Langevin, R. (Ed.). (1984). *Erotic preference, gender identify, and aggression in men.* Hillsdale, N.J.: Lawrence Erlbaum.
    This book, containing chapters by various authors, explores the typical behaviors of those exhibiting paraphilias and the possible causes of such behavior.
Malamuth, N. M., & Donnerstein, E. (Eds.). (1984). *Pornography and sexual aggression.* New York: Academic Press.

    The relationship between pornography and sexual aggression is examined by active investigators in this field of research.
Zillmann, D., & Bryant, J. (Eds.). (1989). *Pornography: Research advances and policy considerations.* Hillsdale, N.J.: Lawrence Erlbaum.
    This book deals with research, theory, and policy involving pornography. The presentations grew out of the Surgeon General's Workshop on this topic. Current controversies and divergent conclusions are well represented.

CHAPTER FOURTEEN

COERCIVE
SEXUAL BEHAVIOR

For most of us, rape is something that we read about, see depicted in fiction, or imagine as part of a sexual fantasy. For the victim, rape is not an abstract, entertaining, or arousing act—it is a brutal, frightening, painful, and degrading physical assault. The following account by one young woman provides a first-hand view of the unpleasant reality of a sexual assault.

It happened when I was fifteen, and now even after ten years have gone by, I still think about it. If my husband gets the least bit aggressive or rough when we're making love, I freeze up. Sometimes I think all men are alike, and they can all go to hell.

The two guys who assaulted me lived in our neighborhood. I had seen them around school, but they weren't friends of mine. I was on my way to the store after dinner when they blocked my way on the sidewalk. We were kidding around at first, but their remarks got more and more crude. I tried to go past them, but they each grabbed one of my arms and pushed me over to a pick-up that was parked by the curb. They opened the door, shoved me in, and crowded in on either side of me.

The one who wasn't driving stuck something in my ribs and said that if I made a sound or caused any kind of trouble, he would blow a hole right through me. Afterward, I decided he didn't have a gun, but I was too scared at the time to know he was talking bull. We drove out of town and into the foothills.

The next four hours were worse than I had ever imagined such an experience could be. They both had intercourse with me on the ground beside the truck. They just kept doing different things, making me change positions while they poked into me. One never had a climax the whole time, and the other only came at the very end when he masturbated all over my breasts.

The worst part, though, was that they made me say things to them like begging for more sex and telling them how great their love making was. I had to ask permission to kiss each one's penis and things like that. The humiliation was awful, more disgusting than having to do the sexual things. They treated me like dirt, and I was forced to say I liked it and wanted more.

Just thinking about all this upsets me even now. My hand is trembling, and I feel like I'm about to scream. Back then, I thought about killing myself, and I thought about killing them. When I went to the police, those two scum were picked up and eventually put on trial. That experience is another miserable story. All they got from the judge was a suspended sentence, and that still makes me angry.

Angela, age 25

Angela's traumatic experience shares a number of characteristics reported by other rape victims—her surprise, fear, humiliation, and the overwhelming feeling of helplessness. Also common are the aftereffects of depression, mistrust of men, and the final insult when she discovers how rapists are treated in the courts. Some may read her story and be annoyed by her passive response to their demands. Why didn't she run away, scream, fight back, or do *something* to resist? In fact, most victims of crime (whether it is a mugging, highjacking, or rape) do not take such actions, regardless of whether they are male or female, young or old. The victim of rape is frequently blamed for what happened, and, even worse, may feel self-blame as well. In evaluating Angela's response, consider that, without warning, she was faced with strong physical force, the threat of a weapon, and what seemed to be the very real possibility of being killed. Would you, or would most people, really be able to respond in some effective and superheroic way? The answer, of course, is no.

Of the many ways people express their sexual needs, the most unacceptable are acts involving an unwilling victim. Through the use of force, power, or persuasion, one person coerces another to engage in a sexual interaction. The most upsetting instances of coercion involve children as victims, and we discuss *incest and the sexual abuse of children*. Though the practice is at least as old as the Industrial Revolution, the concept of *sexual harassment* as an unacceptable and unlawful act of coercion is of relatively recent origin, and we describe such behavior and the steps that can be taken by its victims. When a person is unable or unwilling to consent to engage in sex but nevertheless does so as the result of coercive verbal or physical manipulations, the act is *rape*. This term applies to acts as seemingly different as consensual sex with a minor, date rape, and a violent assault by a stranger. Our discussion also covers rape fantasies, the characteristics of rapists, and the lasting effects of rape on a victim. Special sections explore *rape myths* and possible ways to *prevent rape*.

By the time Americans reach age 18 to 22, seven percent have experienced at least one incident of nonvoluntary sexual intercourse (Moore et al., 1989). Most of the victims are women, and approximately half of the episodes occur before the age of 14. What do we know about who commits these coercive acts and why?

Incest and the Sexual Abuse of Children: The Most Vulnerable Victims

The sex crime that arouses the deepest feelings of disgust and the strongest desire for vengeance is the sexual abuse of children by an adult. In a dramatic incident in 1983 in Buffalo, New York, a ten-year-old girl was taken from her bed and carried out of her apartment by a stranger. When she returned some hours later with only a pillowcase around her hips, she described the man who had abducted her and twice forced her to perform fellatio. Her father and several neighbors thought they recognized the attacker from the girl's description, so they rushed out to find him. A television crew was on hand to cover the story of the missing girl, and they made a vivid photographic record of the alleged child molester being beaten and stabbed, as Figure 14-1 shows.

Though such an attack by a stranger represents a dramatic and fearful incident, another kind of child molestation actually occurs much more frequently. A child is most likely to be sexually coerced by a family member.

▮ Incest: The Secret Crime

Incest refers to sexual interactions between close relatives, and it was once thought to be a rare occurrence (Lester, 1972). When numerous adult patients described such childhood experiences to Freud, he eventually concluded that they were simply expressing fantasies rather than memories of actual events. Even today, a major obstacle to protecting a child who is the victim of incest is the tendency of physicians and others to suspect him or her of lying (Kempe, 1978). Research findings suggest, however, that one child in ten has a sexual interaction with an older relative (Phillips, 1981).

Patterns of Incest.   Incest between brothers and sisters and between first cousins are the most common types (Stark, 1984). Sibling incest usually remains a secret. When the siblings are close in age, adult sexual functioning and satisfaction are not affected by these childhood sexual experiences (Greenwald and Leitenberg, 1989).

Among a sample of 800 undergraduates on six campuses, 15 percent of the females and 10 percent of the males reported having had a sexual experience with a sibling (Finkelhor, 1980). Most (75 percent) of these interactions were by mutual consent, but the remaining 25 percent involved either force or an age difference greater than four years. After such experiences, females more often than males feel exploited

FIGURE 14-1 *REVENGE AGAINST A SUSPECTED CHILD MOLESTER* The most common reaction to sexual attacks on children is outrage. In Buffalo, a television camera was on hand when the father and several neighbors of a ten-year-old victim apprehended the man accused of assaulting her sexually. A family friend is shown attacking the suspect.

and express a negative reaction to this kind of interaction. Long-range effects depended on the circumstances. Only when the experience was unpleasant and when it occurred before age nine did the victims express low sexual self-esteem.

As Figure 14-2 shows, the historical exceptions to prohibitions against incest involved brother–sister marriages among the royal families of ancient Egypt, Peru, and Hawaii, but these marriages were extremely rare (Bixler, 1982).

Mother–son incest is reported very rarely (Loss and Glancy, 1982), and coercion is not likely to be involved. In a study of 128 cases of incest, no instances of mother–daughter sexual interaction were reported (Nelson, 1986). Sex between father and daughter (or stepfather and stepdaughter) occurs less often than sibling incest, but this is the type of incest most likely to be reported to the authorities. This tends not to be an isolated event, but a recurring pattern of interaction typically beginning when the child is eight to twelve years of age and continuing through adolescence, although it can begin as early as infancy.

Most often, the child quietly acquiesces either because she is too young to know that such behavior is unusual or because she is fearful of the consequences of telling anyone about it. One young girl revealed to her counselor, "My dad said this is how kids show their love for them. I figured all my friends were doing it, too, but we just didn't talk about it" (Phillips, 1981, p. E-1).

Usually, the oldest daughter is the target, but sometimes more than one child is abused simultaneously or in sequence as they grow older. Finkelhor (1984b) identified eight facts that increase the probability of young girl being sexually victimized: having a family income under $10,000, a father who doesn't express physical affection, a mother who is not close, a stepfather, living separately from her mother, having a sexually punitive mother, a mother who didn't complete high school, and having two or fewer childhood friends.

Effects of Incest. When adults express their incestuous desires in overt behavior, the negative emotional consequences are borne primarily by the child. According to Kee MacFarlane, director of the sex abuse section of the National Center on Child Abuse and Neglect, the child may respond positively to sexual advances. She craves affection and receives it by engaging in sexual acts. Often, the child's mother is aware of what is going on and either ignores or passively accepts it. The child is trapped between the father's exploitation and the mother's indifference (Gil, 1985; Scott and Flowers, 1988). The mother may fail to take legal action because she fears that her husband will be imprisoned or because the incestuous behavior relieves her from having to engage in sex.

When the child acquiesces to sex repeatedly and feels some pleasure in the activity, she often grows up

FIGURE 14-2 *RARE EXCEPTIONS TO THE INCEST TABOO* Though there are a few historical instances in which royal marriages between brother and sister were acceptable, as in ancient Egypt, such unions were rare, and almost all societies forbid sexual contact between immediate family members.

to feel guilty—she perceives the interaction as her fault and assumes she is as much to blame as her father, perhaps even more so. Many investigations indicate that the incest experience has negative effects on the victim's adult life (La Barbera, 1984). There tend to be adjustment problems, especially sexual adjustment (Meiselman, 1978, 1980). Among a sample of female convicts, it was found that incest victims constituted 52 percent of prostitutes, 36 percent of felons, and 25 percent of those who had been convicted of molesting children (Hinds, 1981).

The man who commits incest often engages in self-deception about his own behavior. One father said, "I kept telling myself that I was doing her a favor. I even told her that I was giving her a head start in life, that it was the best kind of sex education. But I was only fooling myself" (Phillips, 1981, p. E-7). The offender is seldom punished. He usually avoids jail by agreeing to undergo therapy, though there is little evidence that treatment is effective.

■ Incest Taboos

Why are there strong sanctions against incest, and why does it occur anyway?

Evolutionary Advantages of Incest Taboos. Prohibitions against incest in religious doctrine and in legal statutes are almost universal (Murdock, 1949). For that reason, it has been suggested that taboos against it are biologically based. These taboos presumably are of genetic advantage to our species. That is, if closely related individuals mate, any shared maladaptive recessive genetic characteristics are more likely to appear in their offspring. It is found, for example, that the offspring of genetically similar parents have an increased incidence of mental retardation, and their life span is reduced (Adams and Neel, 1967; Morton, 1961; Roberts, 1967; Schull and Neel, 1965). Hall (1979) estimates that 30 to 40 percent of the children of incestuous relationships have genetic defects, and there are apparently *no* reported instances in which inbreeding has resulted in some advantageous physical or behavioral characteristic (Lindzey, 1967), though of course the majority of such children will be normal (Bixler, 1982).

In general, therefore, it is of survival value to the species when individuals refrain from sexual contacts with close relatives. This does not mean that our pre-historic ancestors had to develop genetic theories. It simply means that, over thousands of years, those who did have intercourse with family members produced offspring relatively less equipped to survive and to pass their genes to the next generation; those who found such sexual interactions unattractive produced offspring more likely to survive and pass along their genes.

Studies of various species seem to support the existence of an inborn taboo. Among long-lived, slow-maturing, intelligent animals such as primates or elephants, mating among relatives is rare (Aberle et al., 1963). The same is true for species that form lifelong mating relationships, such as the Canada goose. Among many species—quail (Bateson, 1978), mice (Hill, 1974), rats (Segner, 1968), prairie dogs (Hoogland, 1982), baboons (Packer, 1979), chimpanzees (Pusey, 1980), and human beings (Shepher, 1971)—close association within families decreases sexual attraction. In all of these species, outsiders are preferred as sex partners.

Factors Encouraging Human Incest. The genetic evidence is fairly convincing, but the strength of the incest taboo among humans seems questionable. It is difficult to ignore the high rate of incest discussed earlier. Also, you may recall from Chapter 10 that variables such as propinquity increase attraction. Repeated exposure leads to positive feelings, and such exposure occurs most often within families. Consider also how often family members see one another nude or partially nude, come in close affectionate contact when they hug and kiss, and appear in one another's erotic fantasies and dreams. Playful teasing, kissing, tickling, and wrestling can blend into erotic contact. These factors would seem to increase the potential for sexual attraction.

There is yet another reason that males would focus attention on youthful female relatives. Sociobiological theorists (Cunningham, 1981; Sternglanz et al., 1972) point out that males are most often attracted to young women. This, too, has an evolutionary basis because males remain fertile throughout their lives while females do not. As a result, the chances of producing an offspring are greatest when males of any age have intercourse with young rather than old females. As we discussed in Chapter 10, one type of physically attractive female has features resembling those of infants, as Figure 14-3 suggests. Thus, male's biologically based attraction to youth could enhance incestuous motivation.

If these ideas seem farfetched, note how often

FIGURE 14-3 *MALE ATTRACTION TO YOUNG FEMALES: A BIOLOGICAL IMPERATIVE?* Some sociobiologists suggest that males are genetically programmed to be sexually attracted to young females. Thus, the younger and more childlike the female (large eyes, small nose and chin, large head, smooth skin, and so forth), the higher the probability that she willl attract a mate and be able to bear children, thereby passing on her genes and those of the male attracted to her. Older females are less likely to be fertile, so males attracted to them would be less likely to reproduce. Male attraction to young females is obviously beneficial to survival of the species. A side effect, however, is that some men may be sexually attracted to children.

advertisers attempt to emphasize and exploit the sexuality of young females in selling jeans, cosmetics, and other products as well. Similarly, film presentations of young women, such as *Pretty Baby* and *Baby Doll,* emphasize youthful sexuality. Author Vladimir Nabokov wrote the novel *Lolita* about a twelve-year-old girl who engaged in intercourse and oral sex with a worldly middle-aged man. Clearly, these common themes and images may encourage males to desire young females (Klemesrud, 1981). For similar reasons, some heterosexual males are attracted to prepubescent boys because they have soft bodies, smooth skin, and no body hair (Groth, 1979).

Conflict between Incest Taboos and Incestuous Desires. Whatever the primary reason, it seems that the typical family can easily experience a degree of sexual attraction among its members. There are also powerful constraints on this attraction, including possible genetic inhibitions and religious, legal, and logical prohibitions. Figure 14-4 summarizes these conflicting influences. Most people resolve the conflicts and express them only in myths, dreams, and dramatic fictional accounts such as the ancient Greek

plays, *Oedipus* and *Electra,* as well as in modern literature (Lindzey, 1967). For some, the rejection of incestuous impulses may be sufficiently strong that the overt expression of parental affection is inhibited.

For others, the conflict is resolved by engaging in the forbidden act, often using alcohol or other drugs to reduce the anxiety and guilt (Ellis and Brancale, 1956; Gebhard et al., 1965). Incestuous fathers are dependent, fearful of castration (Martin, 1960), ineffectual, nonaggressive, unsuccessful at earning a living (Gebhard et al., 1965), sexually and emotionally immature (Ellis and Brancale, 1956), and they feel inadequate in personal relationships (Loss and Glancy, 1982). Sexual child abuse is made more likely if the man has developed a paraphilia (see Chapter 13), is rejected sexually and otherwise by a hostile spouse, or is alcoholic (Rosenberg, 1988). Such characteristics suggest a pervasive weakness, and incest is simply one of several maladaptive behaviors typical of these men.

Reporting and Preventing Incest. State laws require that cases of suspected incest be reported by medical personnel, school counselors, or others in contact

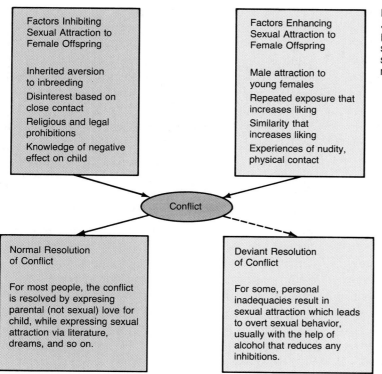

FIGURE 14-4 *THE INCEST CONFLICT: ATTRACTION VERSUS AVERSION* Evidence suggests that human beings (especially males) may experience a conflict between sexual attraction toward an offspring and the rejection of such desires. For those men who are ineffectual and immature, incestuous desires are expressed overtly.

with children. A child is considered unable to give meaningful consent to an adult's sexual advances, so the victim's acquiescence to sex is irrelevant. As awareness of incest frequency has increased since the 1960s, an increasing number of incidents has been reported each decade (Brody, 1987; Derrick, 1979). Note that sexual child abuse refers not only to intercourse but also to oral sex, fondling, and genital exposure.

Preventing incest is obviously very difficult. Perhaps the best that can be done is to provide as much information as possible to potential victims. Children should be taught what is acceptable and unacceptable intimacy on the part of relatives or anyone else. They need to learn to say "no" to adults who want them to do something they dislike. They need to be specifically informed that any genital contact with adults is forbidden. Books, videotapes, and educational posters have been developed to inform children about sexual abuse (Epstein, 1985).

Children should know that there are outside agencies willing to listen to their stories and to provide help. Relatives who know and like the offender are not a good source, because they may doubt the child's story. In contrast, school counselors are much more likely to listen, but children must muster the courage to reveal what is going on. Anyone who suspects such a situation should report it so that an investigation can be made. For example, the New York State Child Abuse and Maltreatment Register has a toll-free number: 800-342-3720. Knowing what behavior to avoid and knowing what to do if it occurs may save a child from years of abuse and exploitation and from a lifetime of unwarranted guilt and self-blame.

■ **Sexual Abuse of Children beyond the Family**

When adults interact sexually with children to whom they are not related, the situation can be similar to that of incest—as when a neighbor or family friend takes advantage of a child. Even more frightening are instances of sexual abuse that refer to a single, traumatic attack on a child. Such attacks usually include aggressive elements as well as sexual ones.

Characteristics of Abusers. **Pedophiles** are adults who are sexually attracted to children and who desire to interact sexually with them. These potential child molesters are almost always married heterosexual men, and three fourths of their victims are girls between eight and eleven years of age (Groth and Birnbaum, 1978). One in five pedophiles who molests a child is a complete stranger to the victim. As is true of men who commit incest, pedophiles are often found to have marital or sexual difficulties and to be alcoholic.

Pederasts, men who are sexually attracted to young boys, are also primarily heterosexual. These men are attracted to partners with feminine characteristics, and, for some, that means attraction to both prepubescent males and females (Groth and Birnbaum, 1978). A specialized subsection of commercially produced sexual imagery (child pornography) portrays relationships between adult males and young boys (Rossman, 1973).

Pedophiles give a variety of explanations to excuse their behavior. For example, some say that the only problem is a repressed society that prevents children from being free to express themselves sexually. Others say they are "addicts," so the behavior is beyond their control. Whatever these individuals say, an attorney familiar with such defendants noted, " . . . the only pedophiles I have ever heard express remorse for their acts are those facing a sentencing court or a parole board." One explanation often proposed is that sexually abused children become sexual abusers as adults. Research with pedophiles confirms this general trend, but the effect is a small one (Freund et al., 1990).

For the worst offenders, *aggressive pedophiles,* the sexual attraction to youngsters includes the desire to torture and, quite often, to murder the victims. The "candy man" in Houston, Texas, was one highly publicized case. He promised children candy, took them to his home, and then subjected them to torture, sexual abuse, and murder. Another notorious series of crimes that occurred in Des Plaines, Illinois, were committed by John Gary. He is shown dressed as a clown performing for kids in Figure 14-5. Gary had been married twice, fathered two children, and was active in the community. Outside this overtly conventional life, he engaged in quite different behavior. After his arrest, he confessed the sexual attacks and murder of thirty-two young males.

FIGURE 14-5 *A SEXUAL CRIMINAL: POGO THE CLOWN* The man shown here is dressed up as Pogo the Clown, a character he created and used to entertain hospitalized children. He married twice and fathered two children. He secretly led a quite different life and eventually confessed to a history of aggressive pedophilia in which he sexually abused young males, murdering thirty-two of them.

Such crimes occur worldwide; the Moors murders in Great Britain provide one example. Another case was reported in the People's Republic of China. A man in his late twenties was charged with molesting children for several years. He finally was arrested after luring a second-grader away from his companions, stripping him, and piercing his eardrums and veins with needles until the boy died (Peking posters accuse aide's son, 1980).

In a study of males convicted of assaulting children, Groth and Birnbaum (1978) differentiated **fixated pedophiles** from **regressed pedophiles**. The sexual interest of the former was fixated exclusively

on children; they could be in charge of the interaction with children but had inadequate social skills to deal with adults. The second category had regressed from normal adult relationships to child partners. Such pedophiles experience sexual failures with adult partners and deal with the resulting stress badly. Despite their different histories, the two groups were found to be quite similar in other respects, as Table 14-1 summarizes. In this study as well as many others, it was found that most molesters of children were under thirty-five years of age (Hicks, 1981).

Summarizing the findings about pedophiles, Finkelhor and Araji (1986) proposed a model with four factors:

1. Molesters attempt to fulfill an emotional need—based on their insecurities and low self-esteem—through emotional identification with children.

2. Sexual arousal is associated with children through conditioning; pedophiles are then excited by children and this learning is rehearsed and strengthened with each incidence of child abuse.

3. Pedophiles have inadequate relationships with adults because they lack social skills and experience social anxiety.

4. Simultaneously, pedophiles lack social inhibitions, and many of them engage in substance abuse. Also common are psychological maladjustments such as sociopathy, involving poor control of impulses and the absence of both guilt and empathy.

Effects of Sexual Child Abuse. When a crime is sex-related, the problem is to obtain accurate information from a young victim about what happened and with whom. Like incest victims, many children who have been sexually abused are unable to talk about it because of fear and guilt (DeVine, 1980). There is also considerable disagreement about the accuracy of children as witnesses, because they often incorporate "facts" suggested by adult questioners (Goleman, 1990). Parents may, however, notice a sudden behavior change in their child—bed-wetting, fear of the dark and of being alone, stomach pains, depression, and an increased interest in sexual topics and in masturbation—which signals the possibility of such abuse (Fontana, 1985). Older children and adolescents may also find it difficult to talk about this

TABLE 14-1 **Child Molesters**

Men who were convicted of sexually molesting children tended to be young heterosexual adults who abused prepubertal victims. Slightly more than half of the 175 offenders were single. The victims were somewhat more likely to be strangers or acquaintances than to be friends or relatives, and most of the attacks used threats or seduction.

	FEMALE VICTIM%	*MALE VICTIM%*	*VICTIMS OF BOTH SEXES%*	*TOTAL%*
Total group	53	29	18	100
Offender single	21.7	22.3	10.9	54.9
Offender married	31.4	6.3	7.4	45.1
Relationship of offender and victim:				
Stranger or acquaintance	27	24	13	64
Friend or relative	27	4	5	36
Method of attack:				
Seduction	15.6	9.2	5.8	30.6
Threat	27.2	11.6	10.4	49.2
Force	9.8	8.1	2.3	20.2
Average age of offender	31.5	29.7	30.1	30.7
Average age of victim	9.4	11	9.4	9.9

Source: Based on data in Groth and Birnbaum, 1978.

kind of experience; instead, they sometimes respond by running away, becoming promiscuous, or even attempting suicide.

Like many other crime victims, children who have been molested may be blamed almost as much as the offender. College students, for example, felt that the young victim "should have resisted" the advances of the adult (Waterman and Foss-Goodman, 1984). Besides being abused and then blamed for letting it happen, the young victims find the courtroom frightening. It can be traumatizing for the child to have to confront the accused attacker while describing the crime (Berliner and Barbieri, 1984). One way to protect a child from this confrontation is to videotape the child's testimony rather than to force him or her to appear in court.

Some pedophiles belong to a network of like-minded individuals, a "sex ring," that locates and recruits young people to be used as sexual partners. Special newsletters contain descriptions of victims or their photographs in which they are nude or engaged in sexual acts (Burgess et al., 1984). Some of these groups, called *solo sex rings,* are organized on the basis of the child's age, including toddlers (aged two to

five), prepubescent children (aged six to twelve), and adolescents (aged thirteen to seventeen) (Lanning and Burgess, 1989). Some of these rings have operated in school and day-care settings.

Among a large group of children and adolescents who had been sexually exploited, three fourths were found to experience negative aftereffects (anxiety, guilt, antisocial behavior) once the ring was exposed. More than 50 percent had spent over a year in the sex ring, and these youngsters had great difficulty in either talking about the experience or in blaming the adults who victimized them. The effects on the victim are usually long lasting. In one investigation, fifty adult women (aged nineteen to fifty-three) who had been molested as children were assessed (Tsai and Wagner, 1978). In another study, 200 streetwalkers (aged ten to forty-six) were interviewed, and 61 percent had been sexually abused during childhood (Silbert, 1989). As Table 14-2 shows, the negative emotional responses and attitudes of these women persisted over many years.

Those who have been abused respond well to group therapy in which victims can share their reactions to their experiences (Tsai and Wagner, 1978).

TABLE 14-2 **Lasting Effects of Child Abuse on the Victims**

The long-lasting effects of abuse on those sexually molested as children were revealed in investigations of fifty women aged nineteen to fifty-three and 200 streetwalkers. The most common reactions to the experience were the seven shown here.

REACTION OF VICTIM	EXAMPLE
Guilt	I felt guilty since I didn't fight as hard, sometimes because it felt good to me.
Low self-esteem	I really feel inferior to other people . . . it's hard to feel good about yourself when you're constantly carrying something with you that can't be talked about.
Mistrust of men	When loving you has been used against you when you're small, you make the association that people who love you mistreat you and you set up barriers.
Inadequate social skills	Socially and sexually I still feel like a little girl.
Seeking inadequate mates	I have a pattern of getting attracted to assholes—my current lover is a Xerox copy of my stepfather.
Sexual dysfunctions	I can't stand for men to touch me or even come near me; I get numb and nauseated.
Psychological paralysis	A severe reaction to stress, characterized by immobility, acceptance of being a victim, rejection of opportunities to change, and feeling trapped and helpless.

Source: Based on data in Silbert, 1989; Tsai and Wagner, 1978.

For those who have been victimized, it is important to be able to identify with others who have undergone similar abuse. In the warm, supportive environment of the group, an emotional closeness develops among those with similar experiences. After six months of such therapy, clients report less guilt, better relationships with their current partners, and better feelings about themselves.

Preventing Child Abuse. Obviously, we want to know how to prevent the sexual abuse of children, and several educational efforts have been designed with this goal (Finkelhor, 1984a). Parents are informed about the potential dangers for their children and about the behavioral signs of victimization.

Children are also taught to be cautious, to recognize "good touch" (like shaking hands) versus "bad touch" (such as genital fondling), and to refuse to cooperate with an adult who behaves in unacceptable ways. Children are given examples of what to do when such situations arise—saying "Don't touch me" or reporting the incident to a parent or another adult. The Clearinghouse of the National Center on Child Abuse and Neglect in Washington, D.C., provides a brochure on this subject entitled, *Child Sexual Abuse*

Prevention: Tips to Parents. Additional information on child sexual abuse is available from the Children's Safety Project, Dept. P, P. O. Box 30201, New York, New York 10011.

Sexual Harassment: Using Power to Elicit Acquiescence

Though it is easy to reach agreement about child abuse or forcible rape as criminal acts, less obvious forms of **sexual aggression** are often misperceived as being acceptable. Most females in our society have been the unwilling targets of male sexual advances. Examples range from the whistles and leering remarks directed at a woman walking along a sidewalk by a group of men to sex-related threats and promises from men in positions of power. Such sexual aggression is an ever-present annoyance and a source of danger to women as they interact with strangers, dates, instructors, bosses, and others. Analogous sexual aggression toward males from females in positions of power can occur, but the vast majority of instances involve female victims and male aggressors. We will examine two major settings in which **sexual harass-**

ment occurs: the work place and academia. Female workers and female students have long been viewed as potential sex objects by men holding positions of authority. Only in recent years, however, has such male behavior been recognized as a criminal act and efforts made to protect the victims and to punish the offenders.

■ The Office as a Male Hunting Ground

Though the problem of sexual harassment by supervisors was recognized from the beginning of the

FIGURE 14-6   *NINE TO FIVE: INCREASING AWARENESS OF SEXUAL HARASSMENT*   The sexual harassment of women has been a common feature of the work place since the Industrial Revolution. Not until the 1970s, however, was the term coined and laws enacted to prohibit it. Today, there is a general awareness of the phenomenon and its implications. The movie *Nine to Five* was a humorous depiction of such sexual aggression against female secretaries and the retaliation of the harassed women.

Industrial Revolution (Bularzik, 1978), the term was first used in the 1970s when such behavior became a social issue (Brewer and Berk, 1982). Among the reasons for the new awareness were the women's movement, the enactment of protective laws, increasing research on the topic by behavioral scientists, and popular films such as *Nine to Five* that dealt with harassment on the job (see Figure 14-6).

Identifying Harassment.   The legal definition of *harassment,* as formulated by the Equal Employment Opportunity Commission in 1980, specifies "unwelcome sexual advances, requests for sexual favors, and other verbal or physical conduct of a sexual nature." Such behavior constitutes unlawful sex discrimination when the employee's job, salary, or promotion is based on acceptance or rejection of a supervisor's advances or when sex-related conduct interferes with job performance or creates an unacceptable working environment (Diamond et al., 1981). Harassment does not refer to harmless flirting or to instances of mutual attraction. A federal study defined three categories of unacceptable sexual intimidation, as Table 14-3 indicates.

Though the definitions and laws apply to either sex, research has indicated significant sex differences in who harasses and is harassed. In one study of employees, 42 percent of the women and only 15 percent of the men reported being sexually harassed at work during the previous two years (Tangri et al., 1982). In other research, over two thirds of the women reported unwanted sexual approaches on the job during a one-year period, and the vast majority disliked the experience (Schneider, 1982).

Being the target of harassment cuts across marital status and type of occupation, but the most likely victims are young women whose status in the organization is low. A survey of almost 500 nurses revealed that 76 percent had been sexually harassed on the job by patients, doctors, coworkers, and supervisors (Grieco, 1987). There is a clear link between the economic vulnerability of women and their sexual vulnerability (MacKinnon, 1979). Those who harass women are most often men (95 percent) who are married (67 percent). Thus, about a third of the harassers are single men, and 5 percent of the instances involve a woman harassing either a male or a female subordinate.

TABLE 14-3   **Sexual Harassment: Coercion on the Job**

The Merit System Protection Board defines three categories of sexual harassment in federal employment. In each instance, the target employee (most often, a woman) is the unwilling recipient of the sexual advances (most often, from a man).

LEVELS OF HARASSMENT		
Less Severe	*Severe*	*Criminal*
Sexual teasing and jokes	Pressure for dates	Rape
Sexual remarks and questions	Touching, leaning over, cornering, pinching	Attempted rape
Suggestive looks and gestures	Pressure for sexual favors	Sexual assault
	Letters, phone calls	
	Showing sexual pictures, stories, or objects	

Source: Based on information in Diamond et al., 1981.

Sex Differences in Perceptions of Harassment. Males and females differ in assessing blame for these incidents. As you may guess, men are more likely to blame the victim, citing her provocative behavior or clothing style that "invited" a sexual approach. Women, in contrast, tend to blame the aggressor (Jensen and Gutek, 1982). Like many other victims of sexual abuse, many who are harassed blame themselves, especially women holding traditional sex-role beliefs.

Men and women also disagree as to what constitutes harassment (Gutek et al., 1980). Everyone agrees about blatant harassing behavior ("You get the job if you go to bed with me"), but less obvious forms (pressure for a date, touching on the arm, staring) elicit different assessments from males and females. Most men (66 percent) believe that the amount of harassment in the work place is greatly exaggerated, but most women (68 percent) do not think it is (Collins and Blodgett, 1981).

One example of how some males respond was provided by former Secretary General of the United Nations, Kurt Waldheim. A committee of women dressed in black called on him to present a report indicating that 25 percent of the women employed at the UN had been approached sexually with the promise of a promotion or other job benefits. Mr. Waldheim listened sympathetically, promised that things would be better in the future, and said that he would prefer to see them dressed in pink or another bright color (Nossiter, 1981).

Harassment as an Economic Burden to Employers. However they might feel ethically about this behavior, both private and governmental organizations have begun to recognize the financial costs of harassment.

One study estimated a two-year expenditure for the federal government of $189 million as the result of sexual aggression against its employees. The expenses include replacing victims who leave because of unpleasant working conditions, paying medical claims for those who suffered emotional reactions in response to the unwanted advances, paying sick leave for employees who miss work to avoid harassers, and loss of productivity (United States Merit Systems Protection Board, 1981).

■   Academia: Students as Sexual Targets

In the academic setting as well as at work, power is misused to obtain sex coercively. Faculty members, for example, control grades, letters of recommendation, and opportunities for research (Reilly et al., 1982). A national survey indicates that sexual harassment of students is increasingly common (National Survey Finds, 1980). Understandably, student targets are frequently upset by the experience and feel less self-confidence and lower self-esteem afterward (Benson and Thomson, 1982). Female students react in various ways to advances by professors (Munich, 1978). Some are very disturbed, seek counseling, or take legal action, while others describe it as a positive experience. One student at Radcliffe indicated that she interpreted intercourse with a faculty member as a "reward" for doing superior work.

Among college undergraduates, 17 percent of the women and only 2 percent of the men reported being sexually harassed by their instructors. In other research, 17 percent of female clinical psychologists revealed that they had sexual relationships with their professors while in graduate school; almost all of these women agreed that the interactions were unethical (Glaser and Thorpe, 1986).

Women who are the victims of academic sexual harassment view such an experience as being almost as stressful as attempted rape (DiVasto et al., 1984). For whatever reasons, moderate verbal and physical harassment from lower status men is viewed as even more unpleasant for victims than the same behavior from those with higher status (Littler-Bishop et al., 1982). When college students read accounts of these incidents, however, harassment is perceived as being only moderately stressful for the victim. College professors are more likely to be labeled as harassers than fellow students when they engage in repeated instances of inappropriate behavior (Pryor, 1985). A consistent finding is that victims view this form of sexual aggression quite differently than do uninvolved observers (Cohen and Gutek, 1985).

■ Fighting Back: How Can Harassment Be Stopped?

Despite the legal protection and the emotional distress of those who are harassed, the victims of unwanted sexual advances usually either put up with the situation or leave it. In a survey of 1,000 working women, half of whom had experienced such advances, 90 percent said that they laughed it off or ignored it. Only 7 percent made a complaint, and 3 percent resigned (Battelle, 1980). The reasons for not fighting back include feelings of guilt and fear of retaliation—losing a job or receiving a low course grade.

The rising awareness of women's rights is, however, resulting in more and more victims willing to take an assertive stand. Male fears of the changing rules of the game were expressed by one vice president of personnel—"A man would be afraid to speak to a woman in the office without first speaking to a lawyer" (Dullea, 1980, p. A-20). Such fears are also expressed in male jokes about harassment:

> *In a fit of anger, the boss snapped at his secretary, "Just because I've slept with you once or twice, who said you could goof off and come in late." "My attorney," she replied (Jeffress, 1980, p. 49).*

Harassment isn't a joke, of course, and numerous positive actions are being taken by employers, special organizations, and the victims themselves (Stessin, 1979). An employer has the legal responsibility to protect all employees by sensitizing both men and women to the meaning of harassment and its consequences, training supervisors and executives to recognize and to avoid such behavior, establishing a grievance mechanism, investigating any charges that are made, and punishing the guilty party when the complaints are verified (Diamond et al., 1981). University administrations are taking increasingly strong stands against intimacy between faculty and students.

For the person who is the target of sexual harassment, whether at work or at school, six recommendations have been made, outlined in Table 14-4.

Rape: Forcing an Unwilling Victim to Engage in Sexual Acts

The word **rape** may suggest a violent sexual assault on a random victim by a vicious male criminal who lurks in dark alleys waiting for a woman, but it refers to any act of nonconsensual sexual interaction. In fact, the rapist is often an acquaintance, a date, a friend, or even a spouse—in addition to the rapists who attack strangers. Sexual coercion may indeed involve threats and physical force, but it also can consist of verbal and emotional manipulations of the victim. We will discuss the different kinds of rape, those who commit this crime, and the effects of rape on the victims.

■ Sexual Pressure on Dates

One type of sexual aggression is perceived by many individuals, males and females alike, as a normal, ethical, expected aspect of dating relationships

TABLE 14-4 **Fighting Back against Sexual Harassment**

The target of sexual harassment, whether at work or school, need not be a passive victim. A series of steps can be taken to stop the coercive behavior and to punish the offender should the behavior continue.

STEPS TO TAKE WHEN YOU ARE THE TARGET OF SEXUAL HARASSMENT

1. A woman must make it clear that she takes her role seriously, whether as an employee or a student.

2. A sexual approach should be met with a firm "no" and not with a feeble excuse that can be misinterpreted.

3. The victim should discuss the problem with fellow employees or fellow students to reduce feelings of isolation and uniqueness. If other victims of the harasser are identified, they can jointly discuss steps to take in dealing with the situation.

4. If the problem continues, the harassed individual should keep a detailed record—a diary with names, possible witnesses, dates, locations, and precisely what was said or done. There should be a careful recording of any negative aftereffects—emotional, economic, or academic.

5. If the harassment continues and the grievances are not acted upon, the woman can contact the state civil rights commission and file a formal grievance with the U.S. Equal Employment Opportunity Commission or the National Advisory Council on Women's Educational Programs. Both are located in Washington, D.C.

6. Several private organizations can provide help, including The Alliance Against Sexual Coercion, Cambridge, Massachusetts; the Working Women's Institute in New York, New York; and the Center Against Sexual Harassment, Women's Legal Clinic, in Los Angeles, California.

Source: Based on suggestions in Diamond et al., 1981; Gillis, 1980; Scott, 1980.

and as much less serious than being raped by a stranger (L'Armand and Pepitone, 1982). **Sexual pressure** refers to aggressive efforts by a male to kiss, to fondle a woman's breasts and genitals, to engage in cunnilingus, to be fellated, and/or to have intercourse with a female companion who does not wish to take part in a sexual interaction.

Dates as Fair Game.   In a dating situation, many males believe that they are supposed to go as far as possible sexually and that it is the woman's responsibility to stop them. If the female does not firmly halt what is going on, it is assumed to mean that she "really" wants him to continue. Further, if she lets him go too far before stopping him, he will be "too excited" to control himself. In effect, anything that happens sexually can be blamed on the female.

As an example of how college students react to accounts of date rape and sexual propositions, the female victim is perceived to be more responsible when such behavior occurs on a date than when the man is a stranger (Bridges and McGrail, 1989). Students believe that the victim should control the situation with her date, regardless of the tactics he uses.

This seemingly naïve perception of male–female interactions may sound like something out of the distant past—perhaps the way one's parents or grand-

parents might have thought. It is true that such behaviors and beliefs *were* first verified in research conducted in the 1950s (Kanin, 1957; Kirkpatrick and Kanin, 1957); however, they do not appear to have undergone any change over the past several decades or to have been affected in any way by variations in sexual attitudes and behaviors over the years (Byrne, 1991, Greendlinger, 1985: Kanin and Purcell, 1977; Murnen et al., 1989).

How Common Is Date Rape?   Over a four-week period, 47 percent of 121 college students of both sexes reported disagreeing with a date about sex; in each instance the man wanted to engage in a given act and the woman did not (Byers and Lewis, 1988). Such disagreements occurred on almost one date out of ten during the month that was studied. The outcome was compliance by the man (61 percent), continued pressure (28 percent), or engaging in the unwanted act (11 percent). In research on sexual pressure among college students, several hundred females on one college campus were asked to describe their experiences anonymously. Over half of this group reported being the target of male sexual pressure during the previous academic year.

Date rape is not limited to college students. Most high school women (63.5 percent) have experienced unwanted sexual pressure, and even more adult women (83 percent) report being the target of unwanted sexual demands at some point in their lives.

Thus, the "normal" expectation of females in our culture is to undergo sexual pressure during their dating years, and **date rape** is a common occurrence. Date rape is a widespread problem on college campuses, and some institutions have undertaken steps to discourage this male behavior and to encourage women to report the incidents when they occur (Parrot, 1989). Nevertheless, among sixteen colleges studied in New York State, for example, most have no such programs (55 percent), nor even any specific policy about date rape (73 percent). Colleges almost always provide individual counseling for the victims, but seldom do they institute disciplinary or legal action against the offender.

This variety of sexual coercion is most likely to occur in a casual dating relationship rather than between emotionally involved individuals. Figure 14-7 identifies the kinds of activity most frequently involved. Being the target of male aggressiveness does not depend on the woman's age, social class, educational level, or past sexual experience.

Recent research investigating both heterosexual and homosexual intercourse reports that a surprising number of college men also engage in sexual acts on dates when they do not want to. Among almost 1,000 students surveyed, more men (63 percent) than women (46 percent) said they had engaged in unwanted intercourse (Muehlenhard and Cook, 1988). The reasons for such unwanted sex differ, however, for men and women. Women report that they were physically coerced, felt they should satisfy their partner's needs, feared the relationship would end, were verbally coerced, or the partner threatened to harm himself. Men report engaging in unwanted sex because the partner was enticing (touched him or removed some of her clothing), they felt it was important to have the experience (to tell others or build self-confidence), they experience peer pressure (friends talked him into it or others were having sex), they believed such behavior would enhance popularity, and they had sex-role concerns (didn't want to appear gay, shy, or inexperienced).

Struckman-Johnson (1988) found that 22 percent of the college women surveyed and 16 percent of the college men had been forced to engage in sexual intercourse at least once. Figure 14-8 indicates the frequencies of various coercion tactics used by dates to obtain sexual intimacy. Again, "force" meant something different to each sex. Women tended to say they were physically forced to have sex while men were responding to psychological pressures. These sex differences are also reflected in the short-term and

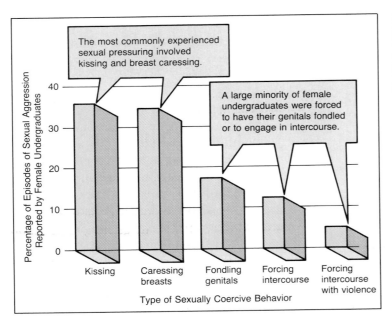

FIGURE 14-7 *UNWANTED SEXUAL PRESSURE ON DATES* On a Midwestern university campus, most of the 282 female undergraduates who were asked about their experiences on dates reported being the targets of male sexual pressure. During the preceding academic year, unwanted acts ranged from kissing to forcible intercourse. Source: Based on data in Kanin and Purcell, 1977.

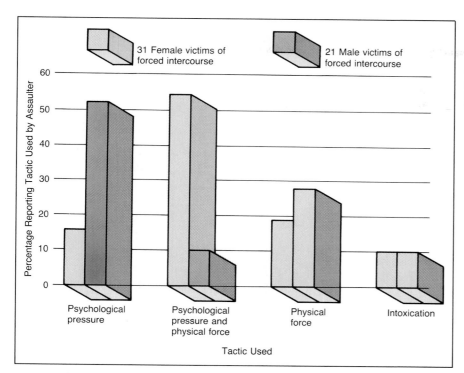

FIGURE 14-8 *TACTICS USED TO FORCE SEXUAL INTERCOURSE* An investigation of both men and women who were the unwilling participants in forced sexual intercourse, the assaulters used psychological pressure, physical restraint or force, a combination of the two, or alcohol.
Source: Based on data from Struckman-Johnson, 1988.

long-term effects of the experience. Most female victims (88 percent) were very upset emotionally after the incident, but most males reported feeling neutral (46 percent) or good (27 percent). Similarly, most women (78 percent) felt that the date rape had a long-term impact on them, but most men (69 percent) denied such effects.

Responding to Sexual Pressure.   According to one survey of college women, in the most serious instances of a date's attempts to force them to engage in sexual activity, 68 percent were successful in resisting the attack (Amick and Calhoun, 1987). Resistance was more likely to be successful if the sexual episode took place in a nonisolated setting, if the man was an acquaintance rather than a steady dating partner, if there was no petting below the waist prior to the attempt to go further, and if the woman made it very clear that she did not want sex. Also, those most successful in resisting sexual pressure scored high on measures of initiative, persistence, leadership, poise, and social skills.

The booklet, "Friends Raping Friends" provides helpful advice about avoiding date rape, how to re-

spond to a pressuring male, and what to do if a date rape actually occurs. This publication is available for $2 from the Project on the Status and Education of Women, Association of American Colleges, 1818 R. St., N.W., Washington, D.C. 20009. This material encourages women to assert clearly their willingness or unwillingness to engage in sex, to be prepared to cover their own expenses on a date, and to stay away from a date who has been drinking too much.

Date Rapists: Macho Male Beliefs.   When male undergraduates are asked about their own sexual behavior on dates, they confirm what females report about sexual pressure. Various studies indicate that from 25 percent to over 50 percent of male undergraduates admit that they have engaged in acts of sexual aggression and used a variety of other tactics in attempting to exploit their dates sexually (Kanin, 1969; Koss and Oros, 1982; Mosher, 1971). In general, men report much more sexually aggressive attitudes and behavior than is true for women (Billingham et al., 1989).

Underlying this male tendency are beliefs about sex and about the sexes that were first identified by Mosher (1971) when he developed the Sex Callousness Scale. In the sample items below, the percentages indicate how many males in one college sample agreed with each statement:

Some girls will screw anything in pants. (84%)

Most women like to be dominated and sometimes humiliated. (58%)

Pickups should expect to put out. (53%)

Prick teasers should be raped. (51%)

A women doesn't mean "no" unless she slaps you. (39%)

You don't *ask* girls to screw, you *tell* them to screw. (25%)

Most women are whores at heart. (23%)

Women are out for all they can get from a man, so a man should get all that he can from a woman. (22%)

Besides asking men about their beliefs and their sexually aggressive behavior on dates, the investigator also asked them to describe the techniques they use to induce a date to have intercourse. Figure 14-9 presents their replies. The higher a man's score on the Sex Callousness Scale, the more likely he was to engage in aggressive and exploitive behavior with females. As the figure indicates, these techniques are often "successful" in achieving the goal of intercourse, so the sexually calloused man receives periodic reinforcement for his beliefs, attitudes, and behavioral tactics.

For some, an exaggerated and stereotyped masculine view of the world assumes that a male is really a man only if he is able to dominate females and to achieve his sexual goals by any means possible (Kanin, 1985). Sexual aggressors on dates expect to be praised for their actions. Forcing sex on a woman picked up in a bar or on any woman perceived as a "prick teaser" enhances the aggressor's reputation with his male friends (Kanin, 1985). Though most behavioral scientists evaluate these macho attitudes and behaviors negatively, no one has yet suggested an effective way to modify them.

The concept of sex callousness was later refined as **hypermasculinity,** or the "macho personality" (Mosher and Sirkin, 1984; Mosher and Tomkins, 1988). The hypermasculine man expresses calloused sexual attitudes toward women, believes that violence is manly, and feels that danger is exciting. As pre-

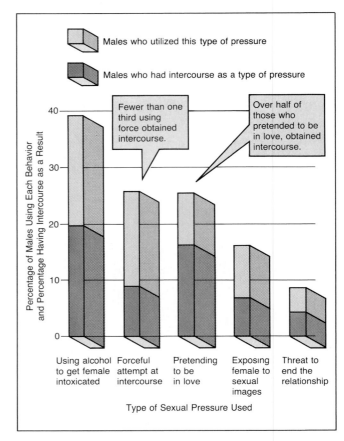

FIGURE 14-9 *MALE SEXUAL PRESSURE ON DATES AND ITS EFFECTS* When college men were asked about their sexually aggressive and exploitive behavior toward dates, the majority (58.2 percent) reported engaging in acts ranging from attempts to get a date drunk to threatening an end to the relationship. Each behavior was associated with some degree of success in obtaining intercourse. False professions of love were the most successful, and the overt use of force was the least successful. Men who used such techniques score high on a measure of sexual callousness toward women.
Source: Based on data in Mosher, 1971.

dicted, such men report engaging in sexually coercive behavior (Mosher and Anderson, 1986) and indicate their willingness to commit rape if they were assured of not getting caught (Smeaton and Byrne, 1987).

Hyperfeminine Females. More recently, a female equivalent of hypermasculinity has been identified as **hyperfemininity** (Murnen and Byrne, 1991). The basic elements of this disposition are the beliefs that relationships with men are of primary importance, attractiveness and sex should be "used" to get a man and keep him, and hypermasculine men are preferable to other men. For example, hyperfeminine women tend to endorse such test items as "I would agree to have sex with a man if I thought I could get him to do what I want" and "It's okay for a man to be a little forceful to get sex."

Research has shown that women high in hyperfemininity are relatively accepting of sexually aggressive behavior and relatively negative about women's liberation. They also are more likely to date hypermasculine men (Smith, 1989) and become the targets of sexual coercion than are women low in hyperfemininity (Murnen et al., 1989).

The beliefs and attitudes that lead to sexual pressure on dates can be carried a step further to the kinds of beliefs and attitudes associated with criminal rape. Recent investigations on this topic are discussed in the special insert, **Highlighting Research,** on pages 395 to 396.

■ Rape: Sex, Violence, or Both?

The proposition that rape is not a sexual act but, rather, a crime of violence that incidentally involves sex (Brownmiller, 1975) originated in part as a reaction to earlier naïve assumptions about male sexual-

Highlighting Research

RAPE MYTHS AND OTHER BELIEFS THAT PERPETUATE SEXUAL VIOLENCE

Before reading this section, turn to Table 14-5 and respond to the test items shown there.

Many acts of sexual aggression are "justified" by the aggressors on the basis of certain beliefs and expectancies, and quite possibly the aggression is guided by them. In discussing sexual pressure on dates, we pointed out that men holding sexually calloused attitudes and those scoring high on the measure of hypermasculinity were most likely to be sexually aggressive and exploitive. In related work, Burt and others (Burt, 1980; Burt and Albin, 1981) have identified a number of **rape myths** that are held by many males (and some females) in our society. The test you just took consisted of part of the scale that measures acceptance of these myths.

Two other sets of beliefs are related to rape myth acceptance. One is the degree to which men and women are viewed as adversaries in a continual struggle. A measure of these adversarial beliefs contains such items as "A man's got to show the woman who's boss right from the start or he'll end up henpecked" and "A lot of men talk big, but when it comes down to it, they can't perform well sexually." The other set involves acceptance of interpersonal violence as measured by such items as "Being roughed up is sexually stimulat-

ing to many women" and "Sometimes the only way a man can get a cold woman turned on is to use force."

In research with several hundred adults, these three belief systems were found to be positively related to one another and negatively related to the amount of education a person had. That is, the more years of schooling, the less the acceptance of rape myths, adversarial beliefs, and interpersonal violence (Burt and Albin, 1981).

When subjects were given brief descriptions of situations in which a man forced a woman to have sex, those high in rape myth acceptance defined fewer situations as "rape" than those low on this dimension. Also, the higher the acceptance of interpersonal violence, the less willing the individual to convict the rapist.

Other research indicates that this cluster of beliefs is associated with the belief that men and women should conform to traditional sex roles (Costin, 1985). These **sex role stereotypes** (Burt, 1980) involve beliefs of the following sort: "A woman should be a virgin when she marries" and "A wife should never contradict her husband in public." Those who are most traditional, especially men, interpret various dating situations as indicating that the woman is leading the man on—thereby

providing the "reason" for his engaging in date rape (Muehlenhard, 1988). Specifically, the most traditional men thought that the woman was indicating willingness to have sex when she initiated the date, accepted an invitation to the man's apartment, or let the man pay the dating expenses.

These belief systems also are associated with overt sexual aggression. For example, a study of almost 2,000 college males found that 40 percent had behaved in sexually aggressive ways toward their dates and female friends. These sexually coercive men expressed attitudes that were more approving of rape and hostility toward women than the remaining 60 percent of male students who had not been sexually coercive (Koss et al., 1985). Men with positive attitudes about sexual aggression also like media presentations of forced sex, feel hostility toward women, and need to be dominant in a relationship (Malamuth, 1989).

These and other investigations (Field, 1978) consistently indicate that people differ greatly in their attitudes and beliefs about male and female behavior, and these differences are related to how rape is defined and rapists and victims are perceived.

TABLE 14-5 **Rape Myth Acceptance Scale**

This scale deals with attitudes and beliefs about rape and women who are rape victims. To obtain your own score, add your responses to each of the ten items. The higher your total score (the closer to 70), the greater is your acceptance of current *rape myths* in our society.

FOR EACH OF THE FOLLOWING STATEMENTS, INDICATE YOUR OPINION ON A SCALE OF 1 TO 7, WITH 7 INDICATING "STRONGLY AGREE" AND 1 INDICATING "STRONGLY DISAGREE."

_____ **1.** A woman who goes to the home or apartment of a man on their first date implies that she is willing to have sex.

_____ **2.** One reason that women falsely report a rape is that they frequently have a need to call attention to themselves.

_____ **3.** Any healthy woman can successfully resist a rapist if she really wants to.

_____ **4.** When women go around braless or wearing short skirts and tight tops, they are just asking for trouble.

_____ **5.** In the majority of rapes, the victim is promiscuous or has a bad reputation.

_____ **6.** If a girl engages in necking or petting and she lets things get out of hand, it is her own fault if her partner forces sex on her.

_____ **7.** Women who get raped while hitchhiking get what they deserve.

_____ **8.** A woman who is stuck-up and thinks she is too good to talk to guys on the street deserves to be taught a lesson.

_____ **9.** Many women have an unconscious wish to be raped, and may then consciously set up a situation in which they are likely to be attacked.

_____ **10.** If a woman gets drunk at a party and has intercourse with a man she's just met there, she should be considered "fair game" to other males at the party who want to have sex with her too, whether she wants it or not.

Source: Burt, 1980, p. 223.

ity. For example, it was once commonly believed that a sexually frustrated man could be overpowered by his physiological needs and driven to have intercourse, even if his partner was unwilling. Much more sophisticated arguments are made by Palmer (1988) that support the proposition that rape is at least partially motivated by sexual needs.

To us, rape does not appear to be simply an act of violence, an uncontrollable expression of masculine sexuality, or a natural product of evolution. Because none of these characterizations of rape is totally accurate, we prefer a definition that describes rape as a violent sexual crime in which threat, force, and intimidation are used to coerce an unwilling victim to engage in sex-related acts to satisfy various needs of the aggressor.

How common are such crimes? In the United States, a Department of Justice survey indicates that 178,000 forcible rapes are reported annually (Anderson, 1983). By way of comparison, one rape occurs every four minutes in this country, while nine nonsexual assaults occur each minute (Crime, 1986). The actual incidence of rape is estimated to be higher than these numbers indicate. Victims often fail to report being raped because (1) they incorrectly believe that no crime was involved (as in date rape), (2) they fear that the offender will retaliate, (3) they expect mistreatment or indifference from police or the courts, or (4) they react with shame or guilt, believing that they are responsible for the attack. Among the victims who fail to report this crime are prostitutes and drug addicts, who feel that they will be treated unfairly by the police and in the courtroom (Gross, 1990).

■ Rape Fantasies versus the Realities of Actual Assaults

Both sexes commonly report having daydreams or masturbatory fantasies that consist of sexual interactions that they label as "rape." Typically, this involves a physically attractive member of the opposite sex who is sexually dominating or who is dominated. The victim is reluctant to have sex, shows resistance, but is finally forced to surrender. The subsequent sexual act is extremely pleasurable, and both partners have orgasms.

Studies of actual instances of rape indicate that real life is quite different from the fantasies. There are also at least three kinds of rape and of rapist (Groth, 1979), and none resemble the images that people create to excite themselves. As Table 14-6 shows, an **anger rape** is likely to be spontaneous and brief. An example is the man who rapes his wife, a former girlfriend, or even a complete stranger as an act of revenge or an expression of hatred toward women. The anger rapist commonly obtains no sexual satisfaction from the assault, often failing either to have an erection or to ejaculate. Quite different is the **power rape,** usually a long-lasting scene in which the rapist is free to act out an elaborate sexual fantasy. Most brutal of all is the **sadistic rape** that involves the infliction of pain and, sometimes, mutilation and murder—the victim's fear and suffering are the rapist's reward. Approximately 5 to 10 percent of rapes are sadistic, and the remainder are about evenly divided between anger and power. Recent studies of incarcerated rapists confirm the fact that men who commit rape fall into different subcategories of the type Groth observed (Kalichman, 1990).

Though the second two categories of rape involve an extended time period, Holmstrom and Burgess (1980) point out that most people imagine an assault to be a brief event involving either forced vaginal intercourse or forced oral sex. In the words of one male undergraduate, "It's not right for anyone to rape a girl, but a twenty-minute screw isn't the end of the world either." He clearly has no conception of the power rape that includes many kinds of traumatic sexual and sex-related humiliations. In fact, all rapes degrade and damage the victims, and it usually takes a long time to recover physically, psychologically, and socially.

Some rapes are committed by two or more men, and these multiple rapists usually do much more to the victim beyond forced intercourse and fellatio. Table 14-7 lists some of the sexual acts forced on rape victims.

An example of multiple rape illustrates the degree to which power is a central part of the crime:

The two assailants, Clyde and Marv, took Molly and David, her date, to an apartment in or near a housing project. A third assailant joined them there. Various

---

TABLE 14-6 **Rape: Anger, Power, or Sadism**

Rapes are categorized into three types on the basis of the rapist's behavior and emotional state. Groth (1979) describes the different patterns of rape as summarized here.

ANGER RAPE

Impulsive and brief assault by an angry and depressed man who feels he is getting even for wrongs done to him by a woman or women. The victim is often cursed and insulted in addition to being raped, and she may also be beaten.

POWER RAPE

A premeditated and extended scene in which an erotic fantasy is acted out by an anxious and insecure man. The rapist gives orders and wants reassurance from the victim that he is sexually skilled and that she is aroused by him. The victim often is terrified and feels humiliated but is not purposely harmed physically.

SADISTIC RAPE

A planned, long-lasting abduction in which the rapist is excited by violence, anger, and the use of force. The victim is degraded and made to undergo bondage, torture, and various bizarre sexual and nonsexual assaults. The victim usually is physically harmed and often mutilated and murdered.

TABLE 14-7 **The Humiliating Scenarios of Rapists**

When either an individual man or two or more men commit rape, the victim is often forced to engage in a variety of sexual and sex-related acts. She is made to submit to sadistic and humiliating demands.

MOST COMMON SEXUAL ACTS FORCED ON VICTIM	PERCENTAGE
Vaginal intercourse	96%
Fellatio	22
Touching victim's genitals	5
Cunnilingus	5
Anal intercourse	5
Kissing	4
Victim touching rapist's penis	3

OTHER SEXUAL ACTS FORCED ON VICTIM	
Rapist masturbating	2%
Licking rapists's body and anus	1
Inserting finger in rapist's anus	1
Victim required to have an orgasm	1

SADISTIC AND HUMILIATING ACTS FORCED ON VICTIM	
Breasts pulled, bitten, touched, or burned	12%
Urinating on victim or on her panties	4
Semen ejaculated on victim's body	2
Victim required to dance in the nude	1
Object inserted in victim's vagina	1
Victim required to perform sexual acts with another female as rapist watches	1

Source: Based on data in Holmstrom and Burgess, 1980.

sex acts were forced on her. Then Clyde came back in and forced Molly to "eat him." Then he made Molly have sex with him by sitting on him. They made her date come in to watch. They turned off all the lights and took a flashlight and played it on Molly when she was having sex—like when she was sitting on one of the men—and then they played it on her date. There was a series of situations—the light would be on her and then would go on David's face (Holmstrom and Burgess, 1980, p. 433).

An even worse example of what the victim must go through is described in a case study of a sadistic rape. A twenty-seven-year-old male abducted a young female at gunpoint and drove her to an isolated spot:

He took her from the car, bound her hands behind her with a rope, disrobed her, attempted to rape her and performed cunnilingus on her. He beat her on the head, rolled her onto her stomach and attempted to assault her from behind. . . . The girl's physical examination revealed bite marks on both her shoulders and privates (Berest, 1970, p. 211).

In the overwhelming majority of instances, rape is committed by males, and the victims are females. It should be noted, however, that males can also be the victims of male rapists. A male victim may be forced to fellate his assailant or to be the recipient of anal intercourse, common events among prison inmates (Nacci and Kane, 1984; Scruton, 1989). Also, in the multiple power rape described previously, the boyfriend was victimized by being forced to watch his girl being raped.

The least frequent, but no less traumatic, type of sexual aggression involves the rape of a male by one or more females (Goyer and Eddleman, 1984). The experience is made worse by the reactions of others to such events because the concept of a female rapist and a male victim seems to strike most people as either impossible or amusing. To others the male victim of heterosexual assault is perceived as initiating or encouraging the act, enjoying it, and suffering no aftereffects (Smith et al., 1988). Because males are raped much less frequently than females, a man who is raped usually feels embarrassed and is very reluctant to report the incident. Nevertheless, men do suffer emotional trauma from being victimized, and sexual dysfunction is common (Myers, 1989).

In reality, the rape of a male by one or more females is quite possible and not at all amusing (Sarrel and Masters, 1982). The following example supports this observation:

> *A 27-year-old divorced truck driver picked up a woman in a bar, took her to a motel, and fell asleep. He awoke to find himself naked, tied hand and foot to the bedstead, gagged, and blindfolded. During the next 24 hours, he was repeatedly forced to have intercourse with four women, threatened with castration by a knife held to his scrotum whenever his performance flagged, and humiliated with derogatory comments* [Timnick, 1983, p. 74].

■ The Rapist

You may think of rapists as violent, abnormal sex maniacs who stalk the city streets each night, but Brownmiller (1975) proposed that *all* males are potential rapists. Studies of male undergraduates suggests that she is at least partially correct.

A substantial minority of male college students report themselves willing to commit a sexual assault. When asked to indicate on a five-point scale (from "very likely" to "not at all likely") whether they would rape a woman if they could be safe from getting caught, over a third report some likelihood of doing so (Malamuth, 1984).

This widespread male willingness to use force to obtain sex is unrelated to sexual frustration or to sexual maladjustment (Briere and Malamuth, 1983). Instead, these men simply accept the belief that violence against women is appropriate (see Figure 14-10). They find it sexually arousing to fantasize about harming women sexually and respond positively to sexually coercive acts such as rape and bondage (Malamuth, 1989). These men also like fantasies of bondage, dominance, and rape (Clegg and Gold, 1988; Greendlinger, 1985; Greendlinger and Byrne, 1987).

FIGURE 14-10 *PROTEST AGAINST RAPE* There is increased anger among women about the prevalence of rape in our society and of widespread beliefs that condone or excuse rape. Protest marches and rallies represent attempts to change attitudes about this crime.

Male undergraduates who have committed sexually aggressive acts, including rape and attempted rape, are found to be angrier toward women, less inhibited about using alcohol, and more likely to disregard societal rules than college men who do not commit sexual aggression (Lisak and Roth, 1988). They also feel inadequate and less powerful than women.

Other studies have investigated the characteristics of convicted rapists, usually some years after the crime was committed. Rapists who are reported, arrested, and convicted tend to be less intelligent and less wealthy than those who avoid legal punishment. As a result, these men probably do not represent *all* rapists. They do, however, have at least two common characteristics.

First, though rapists tend to have more sexual experience at earlier ages than other males (Langevin et al., 1985; Malamuth, 1986), they are unable to recognize interpersonal cues accurately. In an experiment, convicted rapists, other violent criminals, and nonviolent criminals were shown videotaped interactions of a male and a female (Lipton et al., 1987). When the scene was that of a first date, the rapists had the most trouble in identifying any negative reactions expressed by the female. This deficit in social skills quite possibly contributes to a misinterpretation of how females may be responding to their overtures. In other words, when a woman is indicating lack of interest or totally rejecting him, such a man misses the point and doesn't realize what she is communicating.

Second, rapists have difficulty in controlling hostility and violence when aroused. If aggressive men drink significant amounts of alcohol, a relatively minor provocation leads them to acts of aggression toward women (Braucht, 1982). In fact, alcohol use is involved in 40 to 50 percent of reported sexual assaults (Abel et al., 1984; Clark and Lewis, 1977). In a laboratory experiment, some male subjects were given alcohol while others had nonalcoholic drinks. The alcohol group had difficulty in differentiating films of rape and films of mutually consenting sex (Barbaree et al., 1983). Compared to nondrinkers, young male problem drinkers tend to behave more aggressively in sexual situations, like that depicted in Figure 14-11. The use of drugs other than alcohol (for example, marijuana, barbiturates) tends *not* to be associated with rape (Groth, 1979; Rada, 1978a).

FIGURE 14-11 *RAPE: WHEN THE PARTY'S OVER* The use of alcohol in a potentially sexual situation can help set the stage for rape. Lowered inhibitions against aggressive and sexual impulses contribute to the incidence of coercive behavior. This effect is suggested by the brief poem, "Candy is dandy, but liquor is quicker," but the consequences are likely to be criminal rather than amusing.

■ Punishment and Treatment of Rapists

Most rapists are not arrested and brought to trial, but a large number of such men are nevertheless processed by the criminal justice system.

Rape Laws: The Issue of Consent. When the rape victim is over the age of eighteen, it may be difficult for her to convince a judge or jury that she resisted. If she did not resist, it is assumed that she consented to the act and was not the victim of a crime. In most instances, only the rapist and the victim witnessed the interaction, so judicial decision must be based on which individual's testimony is believed. When the victim is injured physically, it becomes much easier to prove that rape occurred.

Consent takes on a different meaning when a male has sex with a female below a certain age. She can be assumed to be too young to give her informed consent, and he can be charged with **statutory rape**, even if she was a willing participant. There are, however, considerable variations in defining what that age might be. In preliterate societies, a female who is able to reproduce is assumed to be old enough to consent. In the United States and other developed societies, legislatures define the appropriate age for making informed, responsible decisions about sexual behavior. In most states of the United States, the age of consent is either sixteen or eighteen, but it ranges from fourteen to twenty-one (McCaghy, 1983).

When the underage partner is very young, the penalties tend to be greater. If the victim lives in Ohio, for example, and is twelve years of age or younger, the offender may be sentenced to a prison term of four to twenty-five years; if she is thirteen to fifteen years of age, the possible penalty is reduced to one to ten years in prison. In some states, the law takes into account the age difference of the participants. In New Jersey, sex with a female below the age of consent (sixteen) is not a crime if the male is less than four years older than she is. When the older person is a female and the younger person a male, their sexual activity is unlikely to be considered a criminal offense.

Rapists and the Criminal Justice System. Rape is most common in societies that promote violence, male dominance, and separation of the sexes (Sanday, 1981). Not surprisingly, the legal establishment in such societies often does little to punish rapists. In the United States, for example, there were no laws defining forcible sex with a spouse as rape until quite recently (Cann et al., 1981).

Examples of legal inadequacies are common throughout the world. Consider a case in India: A sixteen-year-old female was raped by two policemen in a police station in New Delhi (Kaufman, 1980). They were convicted of the crime, but a judge reversed that decision. In making this ruling, he reasoned that the victim did not resist, she had had previous sexual experience, and it is important to maintain police authority. In Japan, police were accused of sexually abusing a female suspect by making her remove her clothes, examining her genitals, and forcing her to urinate as the officers watched (Deardorff, 1989).

In the United States, the laws have gradually changed so that such blatant unfairness to the victim is now unlikely (Loh, 1981). The victim's previous sexual experience is no longer admissible as evidence, for example, unless it bears directly on the case at hand. Resistance is still considered relevant in determining the seriousness of the offense, however. If the victim resists enough to receive a physical injury, it becomes easier to classify the assault as a crime. Try to imagine the analogous argument that a man's failure to fight a burglar indicated a less serious crime or perhaps the man's secret desire to be robbed.

Even in laboratory research, descriptions of a rape in which the victim fights back cause men to assign harsher penalties for the rapist than for a rape in which there is no physical resistance (Scroggs, 1976). Women, however, recommend shorter sentences in such instances, possibly assuming that the passive victim was too frightened and defenseless to fight back. Such findings suggest that a jury would be most fair to the victim and to the defendant if it were composed of equal numbers of men and women.

Women generally evaluate the criminal justice system as highly ineffective in dealing with rape compared to other crimes such a physical assault and murder (Ashworth and Feldman-Summers, 1978), as shown in Figure 14-12. The police, the judicial system, and the prison system were rated as less responsive to the crime of rape than to any other crime. With the passage of time, the rape victim actually be-

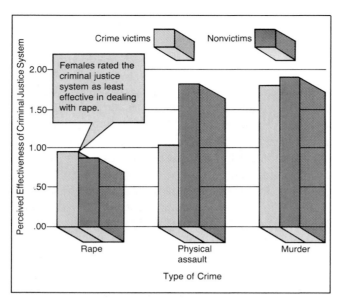

FIGURE 14-12 *WOMEN'S NEGATIVE APPRAISAL OF THE CRIMI-NAL JUSTICE SYSTEM* Whether or not they have been victims of crime, women evaluate the criminal justice system as more inef-fective in dealing with rape than in dealing with other crimes such as physical assault and murder.
Source: Based on data in Ashworth and Feldman-Summers, 1978.

comes increasingly negative about the judicial system in part because the rapist often is not apprehended, not found guilty, nor given a severe penalty. As you might expect, the greater the physical injury to the victim, the more negative the response to the rapist. In a case in North Carolina, the victim committed suicide as the result of her experience, but left a tape recording accusing her attacker. The tape was played during the trial, and the rapist was convicted and sentenced to a life term plus twenty years (Rapist gets life, 1979, p. A-10).

Jurors in rape cases admit that they are influenced by the victim's characteristics. When the victim had had extramarital affairs, was acquainted with the defendant, drank alcohol, or used drugs, members of the jury were less likely to find the accused rapist guilty (LaFree, Reskin, and Visher, 1985).

Because trials can now be televised in the United States, questions have been raised about using this procedure in cases of rape. Public opinion surveys in Minneapolis–St. Paul indicated that most people (60 percent) disapproved of televising any trials, and even more (85 percent) objected to television when the crime was rape (Swim and Borgida, 1987). The major reason given was the belief that such coverage would add to the victim's trauma and invade

her privacy. Most women (63 percent) said they would be less likely to report being raped if they knew they had to face a televised trial.

Treating the Rapist. When a sexual offender is convicted, what is an appropriate punishment? A prison sentence may seem just, but rapists and child molesters have relatively high **recidivism rates** following release. About 35 percent of rapists and 15 to 25 percent of child molesters repeat their criminal behavior and are back in prison within five years (Abel, 1983). When imprisonment emphasizes punishment rather than rehabilitation, recidivism is even higher.

Some argue that the emphasis should be on rehabilitation (Gordon and Verdun-Jones, 1983) such as group therapy, behavioral therapy, or self-help strategies. After evaluation by psychiatrists, psychologists, and/or the judge, the convicted rapist may not be sent to prison but to a therapeutic program as a **nonincarcerated rapist** (Abel et al., 1984; Oliver, 1983).

Studies of those who receive therapy indicate that the average rapist admits to having committed 7.5 assaults. With group therapy, rapists meet with a therapist to explore their past criminal history and to learn how to avoid situations and fantasies that facilitate rape. Though these groups increase the self-esteem of the participants, they do not lead to a reduction in the occurrence of future sexual offenses (Sadoff, 1981). No professionals are able to predict who will or will not rape future victims (Howard et al., 1986). Self-help therapy places the offender in the role of therapist and patient simultaneously in a group setting, but no scientific evidence exists as the effectiveness of this approach (Abel, 1983). Altogether, there is considerable skepticism as to the effectiveness of these approaches. Rapists say that they feel compelled to assault women sexually, and group therapies do not appear to lead to changes in motivation or behavior.

In behavioral therapy, the convicted rapist learns sexual behaviors that are appropriate substitutes for sexual aggression. Through the use of aversive conditioning and reconditioning, sexual excitement in response to inappropriate targets or inappropriate acts results in punishment; excitement in response to appropriate targets and acts is rewarded (Quinsey, 1983). Though the rapist learns to respond sexually to different cues, it is not clear that this means a thorough change of his sexual interests or a change in his future behavior (Lucas et al., 1983; Rosen and Beck, 1986).

There are other, less common treatments such as drugs, psychosurgery, and surgical castration. The offender may volunteer for these procedures as a way to avoid imprisonment, but their effectiveness is not well established. In drug therapy, a synthetic form of progesterone, Depo Provera, is injected in large, long-lasting doses, reducing the level of circulating testosterone and presumably of violent behavior. The same goal is sought by surgical castration in which the testes are removed or badly damaged in order to reduce testosterone levels. Either way, as we discussed in Chapter 3, this hormone does not reliably affect aggressive behavior in humans, so this method cannot be justified scientifically (Heim and Hursch, 1979).

In rare instances, psychosurgery is used, and a portion of the rapist's brain is destroyed or removed. Some surgeons target the hypothalamus because animal research indicates that its removal reduces sexual activity. Others remove portions of the amygdala to produce a decrease in emotional arousal (Schwartz, 1978). No reliable data exist to indicate the effectiveness of either procedure (Schmidt and Schorsch, 1981), and many find these operations highly questionable.

Except for experimental evidence supporting at least short-term effects for behavioral therapy, then, rehabilitation of violent sex offenders has generally failed. Consequently, more attention is now focused on teaching potential victims how to prevent rape—as discussed in the special section. ***Taking Responsibility and Protecting Yourself,*** on pages 403 to 404.

Taking Responsibility and Protecting Yourself

PREVENTING RAPE

No one is safe from rape. When we consider potential victims, young females are the most vulnerable and defenseless (Pepitone-Rockwell, 1980). Rapists are most likely to attack women aged fifteen to forty-four (Hogan, 1980), but rapists also attack those who are younger and those who are older—as well as other men.

Though physically attractive women would seem to be the most likely targets (Seligman et al., 1977), rapists do not limit their targets on the basis of appearance. Some rapists select attractive victims, some select plain ones, and some seek out those who appear the least sexy. For the rapist seeking sex as an expression of violence and domination, the victim's physical attributes and distinctiveness as an individual are irrelevant. Because anyone can be a victim and because the attacker can be a stranger, acquaintance, date, or intimate friend, everyone needs to be prepared to decrease the risk and to respond effectively to attempts at sexual assault.

Despite the unfairness of placing the burden on the innocent, one approach is to make yourself as safe as possible from attack. Outdoors, it helps to stay in well-lighted areas where other people are present. Installing dead-bolt locks on doors and avoiding hitchhiking are among many safety tips offered in a booklet, "How to Protect Yourself against Sexual Assault." This publication is available from the Office of Justice Assistance, Research, and Statistics of the U.S. Department of Justice, Washington, D.C 20537.

If a rapist attacks, what should the victim do? Current advice based on research is to try to resist or escape (Nelson, 1983) unless threatened with a gun or some other form of physical violence (Burnett et al., 1985). Submission to a violent rapist is not the same as consent (Rada, 1978b), and criminal law recognizes this fact.

You may have read of verbal ploys by the victim such as pretending to be pregnant or having a disease, but these tactics often anger the rapist further (Pepitone-Rockwell, 1979). Some rape experts advise the victim to urinate or defecate to repulse the rapist (MacNamara, 1982b), although no one has tested the effectiveness of this type of defensive tactic.

When women who had been raped are compared with women who managed to avoid rape, the factors differentiating the two groups are complex (Bart, 1981; Bart and O'Brien, 1985). Rape is most likely to occur if the attacker is *not* a stranger, if the attempt takes place in the woman's home, and if the victim talks to or pleads with the attacker rather than resisting physically and screaming. Obviously women have control over only the third of these factors, but awareness of the other two can alert them to potential dangers.

Because most rapes occur outdoors or in the victim's home, it is sometimes possible to enlist the aid of others. If it is possible to attract the attention of a passerby or a close neighbor, that person may be able to help by contacting the police. Studies in two major U.S. cities indicate that police respond within three minutes to a crime in progress.

What should the victim shout in order

to get others to help? In an old Smothers Brothers song, "I yelled fire when I fell into the chocolate," Tommy explains that no one would provide help if he yelled, "Chocolate!" The general idea seems reasonable; accuracy is not as important as getting others to respond, but Tommy may be wrong.

In a experimental test of how potential rescuers react to a rape in progress, an attack in an office building was simulated on audiotape (Shotland & Stebbins, 1980). Male students passing by heard an apparent interaction between a man and a woman. She pleaded with the man not to hurt her, and then did one of four things: screamed "Help, rape, call the police"; shouted "Fire!"; blew a whistle; or made

no attempt to summon help. All of those passing by heard the victim pleading with the man who threatened to hurt her; half of them also saw a male actor shove the female actress into a closet. As Figure 14-13 shows, when the males passing by could see what appeared to be a rapist and a victim, it didn't matter what the woman did; most reacted by providing help. When they only heard the interaction, however, they reacted differently; the greatest amount of intervention occurred when they heard the female say "Help, rape, call the police."

In this study, help generally took the form of summoning another person to join in the attempt to save the victim. Very few young men simply rushed in to subdue

the rapist personally, and those who did so tended to have had special training in self-defense. When the actors could not be seen, yelling "Fire" or blowing a whistle only added confusion. Passersby said afterward that a woman wouldn't yell "Fire" when she was being attacked, and they thought the whistle meant someone else was on the way to help.

Most women have been cautioned about the dangers of rape from adolescence onward (Burt and Estep, 1981). It is clearly important to know as much as possible about protecting oneself from attack and about how best to respond should an attack occur.

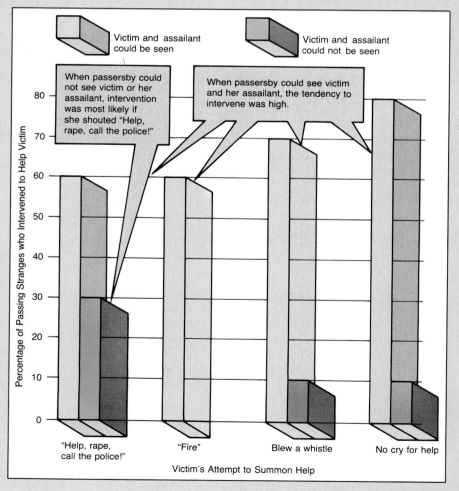

FIGURE 14-13 *WHEN A RAPE VICTIM CALLS FOR HELP* In an experiment, an apparent rape victim who cried for help was more successful when males passing by had seen her and the assailant. When they only heard her cries for help, the passersby were more likely to respond when she shouted, "Help, rape, call the police!" than when she said nothing, shouted, "Fire!" or blew a whistle.
Source: Based on data in Shotland and Stebbins, 1980.

■ The Rape Victim: Aftereffects

What are the short-term and long-term effects of being a rape victim?

Physical Effects. Because rape frequently involves physical injury, the victim must seek treatment for bleeding and torn vaginal tissue (Beazlie, 1981). When a rape crisis center is contacted, a counselor meets the victim at the emergency room of the local hospital to offer emotional support, help her express her feelings, and explore whether she is willing to report what happened to police, friends, or family (Harvey, 1985).

A medical examination not only can determine the extent of the injury but also can provide objective verification that she was attacked. Rape victims should avoid washing or changing clothes or showering before the examination so that no evidence is destroyed (Sproles, 1985). Sperm are present in only about half of all rape victims because the woman successfully resisted her attacker, the rapist was unable to obtain an erection, or he did not ejaculate (Laws, 1982). For this reason, it is important to be able to obtain medical evidence—such as samples of the rapist's blood or skin, one of his pubic hairs, soil from the rape scene—from beneath the victim's fingernails or from her clothing. This physical evidence, the victim's description of what happened and of the rapist, and a photograph of her after the attack are critical data for the police investigation. The cost of the various hospital services and tests are usually paid by city or state agencies.

The risk of pregnancy after one instance of unprotected sexual intercourse in midcycle is 2 to 4 percent (Millen, 1984). If the rape occurs within five days of ovulation, contraceptive pills are administered. Female victims should have their urine tested for pregnancy a few weeks after the attack; the pregnancy can be terminated if they make this decision. Though the danger of contracting AIDS is relatively small, tests for both the victim and the rapist are recommended.

Psychological and Interpersonal Effects. Though physical injuries caused by a rapist heal relatively quickly, other effects linger, sometimes for years (Ellis et al., 1981). Victims often feel depressed about the experience (Atkeson et al., 1982), feel less close to friends and family (Resick et al., 1981), and are less satisfied with subsequent heterosexual activity (Feldman-Summers et al., 1979). With more severe assaults that produce extensive injuries, the emotional reactions afterward are even worse, with frequent crying and mood changes (Norris and Feldman-Summers, 1981). The victim may become reclusive and afraid to be alone, to go out, or to interact with strangers. Anxiety makes the victim unhappy and unable to engage in independent behavior (Myers et al., 1984). Also, the more self-blame the individual experiences, the worse her adjustment is likely to be (Meyer and Taylor, 1986).

The term **rape trauma syndrome** (Burgess and Holmstrom, 1985, 1988) refers to the victim's reactions after an actual or attempted rape. Among the immediate reactions are disorganization, physical symptoms (headaches, nightmares or insomnia), and psychological difficulties, including fear and self-blame (Ellis, 1983).

In the *acute phase* of the syndrome, beginning immediately after the rape and lasting as long as several weeks, the victim typically behaves in either an overcontrolled, subdued manner or with overt expressions of feeling such as crying and emotional turmoil—and sometimes the controlled reaction is followed by the expressive one.

Next, the *long-term phase of reorganization* takes place, and this may last weeks or months. The victim fears that the rapist may return and retaliate. She may move frequently and fear any kind of sexual relationship. Rape victims indicate less sexual satisfaction after the assault (Feldman-Summers et al., 1979). A study (Becker et al., 1986) of women who had recently been attacked found that most (59 percent) reported sexual dysfunctions and fear of sex (54 percent). They also said they felt less sexual desire, found it difficult to become aroused, and experienced pain during intercourse.

Those who have been assaulted report that they have rape flashbacks, dislike being touched, and worry about their partner's reaction. Within a few months after the rape, one third of the victims say that their sexual functioning has returned to normal, another third indicate that such a recovery took years, and the remaining third had not recovered six years later (Burgess and Holmstrom, 1979).

In a survey of over 3,000 women readers of *Ms.* magazine, 328 reported being raped, and another 534 were the victims of attempted rape (Warshaw, 1988). These women also reported over 2,000 additional instances of unwanted sexual contact. Of those who had been raped, about one third sought psychotherapy, 20 percent took self-defense courses, and most (80 percent) said that the rape had changed them by lowering their feelings of self-worth and making them fearful and anxious about the present and the future.

All of these changes in behavior and emotions suggest the terrible price paid by victims. It may be helpful to make sure that judges and jurors are informed about the serious consequences of this crime when they consider how best to deal with a rapist (Frazier and Borgida, 1985).

Beginning in the 1970s, many groups were organized in the United States to protect the welfare of rape victims and to provide information about the high incidence of rape (Harvey, 1985). Such groups provide counseling for victims and educational services to the community dealing with sexual assault laws, the effects of rape, and techniques of prevention. An example of the helpful information generated by such organizations is the pamphlet, "Recovering from Rape: Healing Your Sexuality." It is available from the Seattle Institute for Sex Therapy, Education and Research, 100 N. E. 56th, Seattle, Washington 98105.

Summarizing the Information about Coercive Sexual Behavior . . .

Coercive sexuality includes incest and the sexual abuse of children, harassment, sexual pressuring, and rape. **Incest** often involves a recurring pattern of sexual activity between a father (or stepfather) and his daughter (or stepdaughter). The victim may experience lifelong effects of guilt and self-blame. Explanations for incest range from pathological sexual attraction to sociobiological speculation about males being genetically programmed to seek young, fertile females. **Pedophiles**, adults who are sexually attracted to children, may be either fixated or regressed, and most often are heterosexual men.

Sexual aggression is any sexual act performed without the consent of the victim. **Sexual harassment**—unwelcome sexual advances—has been identified recently as a form of sex discrimination in instances where it affects decisions about an employee or student (who is usually female).

Sexual pressure occurs among acquaintances or close friends, primarily on dates. About half of all female college students report being the target of this form of sexual aggression, called **date rape.** Sexual pressuring is used frequently by males who believe that women really want and need this kind of domination by a "manly" guy in order to express their sexuality. Rape falls into one of three patterns: **anger rape, power rape,** or **sadistic rape.** Rapists lack self-control, believe in the use of violence in personal relationships, and feel callous toward women. Convicted rapists most often are not punished, and our justice system is perceived—especially by rape victims—as ineffective in dealing with rapists. Psychotherapy and physical treatments are employed in programs designed to rehabilitate rapists, but only behavioral therapy has been shown to be even temporarily effective. To prevent rape, potential victims should take various safety precautions. If attacked, resistance is advised unless it appears dangerous to do so, and efforts should be made to attract the attention of others who may provide or summon help. The rape victim faces behavioral, physical, and psychological difficulties—aftereffects termed the **rape trauma syndrome.** These negative effects of rape are often long lasting, underscoring the seriousness of this crime.

To Find Out More about Coercive Sexual Behavior. . .

Abramson, P. H. (1984). *Sarah: A sexual biography*. Albany, N. Y.: SUNY Press.

This is the true story of a college student who was regularly abused in childhood by her stepfather and stepmother. Partly as a result of these experiences, she spent much of her adolescence engaged in promiscuous sexual activity, drug taking, and prostitution. The psychologist who presents her story stresses the way she eventually was able to work out a healthy adjustment.

Diamond, R., Feller, L., & Russo, N. F. (1981). *Sexual harassment action kit*. Washington, D.C.: Federation of Organizations for Professional Women.

This helpful booklet provides information to working women, covering a description of sexual harassment, ways to prevent it, and legal steps to take should it continue. Copies can be obtained for $2.50 from FOPW, 2000 P Street, N.S., No. 403, Washington, D.C. 20036.

Finkelhor, D. (1984). *Child sexual abuse: Theory and research*. New York: Free Press.

A description of research involving the childhood experiences of hundreds of male and female college students. The author discusses incest and child abuse by nonrelatives as well as the effects on the victims.

Mastrosimone, W. (1978). *Extremities*. Garden City, N.Y.: Nelson Doubleday.

The script of a powerful play that involves a brutal attempted rape and the victim's resulting hatred of her assailant. Of special interest is the portrayal for the would-be rapist's attempt to justify his actions, the victim's desire for revenge, and her friends' doubts about what really happened.

Russell, D. E. H. (1984). *Sexual exploitation: Rape, child sexual abuse, and workplace harassment*. Beverly Hills, Calif.: Sage.

Sexually aggressive behavior is the subject of this book, which explores the incidence, causes and effects, as well as the control of child sexual abuse, sexual pressuring, and rape.

Warshaw, R. (1988). *I never called it rape*. New York: Harper & Row.

Acquaintance rape is described, and the discussion includes date rapists and their victims, aftereffects, prevention, and the role society plays.

Wyatt, G.E., & Powell, G.J. (Eds.). *Lasting effects of child sexual abuse*. Newbury Park, CA: Sage.

This book focuses on the consequences of childhood abuse on the victim. Included are chapters on the history of such abuse, theoretical explanations, research findings, treatment, and social policy issues.

CHAPTER FIFTEEN

INFECTIOUS DISEASES ASSOCIATED WITH SEXUALITY

When the danger of AIDS first became widely known in the early 1980s, the homosexual community was especially alarmed. Though no one is immune to this fatal infection, practices such as anal intercourse and promiscuous sex made many gays a prime target. As the number of diagnosed cases and the number of deaths have risen steeply over the years, the fears and the feelings of depression have increased accordingly (Kyle, 1989). The following description provides the first-hand reactions of one individual.

About ten years ago, I went to college in San Francisco and stayed in the city after graduating. I'm gay and proud of it, and the Bay Area in those days was like a sexual Disneyland for us. There was good music and an endless supply of young studs who gathered in the bars and bath houses for uncomplicated, uncommitted pleasure. I worked at a bank during the day and played half the night and all weekend.

One year I kept a sort of diary, and it turned out that I made it with just over 250 different guys, and some of them were more than one-night stands. I once suggested that the K-Y Jelly people should send us some token of appreciation for boosting their profits. It was also a happy time because police harassment had come to an end, and gays were suddenly important to politicians seeking votes.

I first heard about AIDS one evening when a group of us were sitting at an outdoor table in Ghirardelli Square, having a few beers after work. The big news was that a small number of gays in New York had been diagnosed as having this strange new disease that came from Haiti or Africa. It sounded like the plot for a cheap horror movie—one of the first signs was large purple blemishes on your legs and feet. From there, the person just got sicker and weaker because the body couldn't fight off any infections. The worst part of the story was that there was no cure and no way to immunize against it. If you became infected, the only question was how long you might hold on before dying.

In the next several months, we began to hear about people we knew developing the first symptoms. Everyone was terrified. Then the bath houses were closed down. There was still a lot of sex, but most of us began to avoid strangers. Despite the "safe sex" campaigns, it has been difficult to get into using condoms.

Gradually, AIDS has become all too familiar. More and more of my friends have made the same journey: repeated trips to the hospital as they waste away. Those of us who are lucky enough to be alive find ourselves at more and more funerals. The obituaries of famous entertainers and other well-known celebrities frequently give the cause of death as "AIDS-related complications." I'm so scared and depressed that I haven't had sex with anyone for about a year.

One of the worst parts—as if incurable illness isn't bad enough—is the way straight people now feel justified in fearing and hating gays. I can imagine the time when we are forced to wear special arm bands in public or hang bells around our necks. You even read letters in the paper about how God is finally punishing the "queers" for their sins and how the world will soon be cleansed of the sodomites.

Where is it all going to end? I don't know, but the happiest years of my life turned into the most miserable. Unless somebody comes up with a cure, and soon, I'm not at all sure that I want to go on living.

Vincent, age 32

As Vincent indicates, AIDS is the most serious and most life-threatening of the illnesses associated with sexual activity. It is, of course, only one of the many infections that once were known as *venereal diseases* and are now termed **sexually transmissible diseases**, or **STDs**. Obviously, neither AIDS nor the other STDs are limited to homosexuals or to any other group.

Though your first associations to the word *sex* may center on pleasure or reproduction, sexual interactions also involve the possibility of transmitting disease. In this chapter, we describe the many varieties of *infections* that are sexually transmissible and sex-related, including their symptoms and medical treatment. Over the past decade, *AIDS* has provided the world with a frightening spector of an incurable and fatal disease that is transmitted sexually, and we discuss what is known about this viral disease and its effects. Special sections deal with the *effects of sexual attitudes and knowledge on health-care behavior,* the *health concerns of homosexuals and bisexuals,* and a summary of *safer sexual practices.*

Infections: Sexually Transmissible and Sex-Related

It may sound unnecessarily alarming, but STDs are currently infecting record numbers of people. No one can say just how many are infected at any one time, because physicians in the United States, for example, routinely report only cases of syphilis and gonorrhea to health departments (Quinn, 1981). The U.S. Center for Disease Control estimates that one fourth of Americans age fifteen to fifty-five will have a disease transmitted by sexual contact at some point in their lives (White and Felts, 1989).

■ The STD Epidemic

Studies of such STDs as genital herpes indicate that more people are infected each year than the year before.

One indication of the prevalence of these diseases is provided by a study of over 23,000 patients treated at a Denver health clinic over a one-year period (Judson, 1982). As Figure 15-1 shows, sizable numbers of both men and women were found to have several of the infectious diseases that we will discuss in this chapter. AIDS was not yet a factor at the time of that investigation.

As recently as twenty years ago, STDs were concentrated in three groups—the poor, prostitutes, and promiscuous men. When prostitutes are arrested, for example, almost a third typically have at least one

FIGURE 15-1 *STD FREQUENCIES: A GROWING SEXUAL THREAT* This figure shows the frequency with which several sexually transmissable diseases were diagnosed at a Denver health clinic over a one-year period. The data indicate that chlamydia and gonorrhea were the most common STDs. They almost have become the norm among sexually active individuals not involved in a monogamous, sexually exclusive relationship. Note that these data were collected prior to the widespread outbreak of AIDS.
Source: Based on data in Judson, 1982.

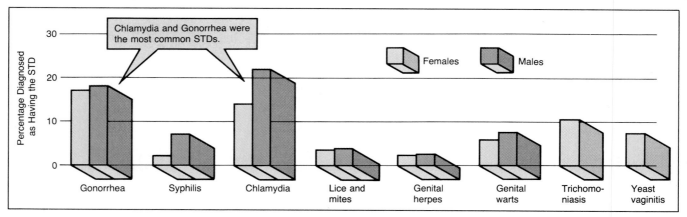

STD (Rothenberg, 1982). These infections, however, no longer discriminate on the basis of social class, occupation, or sexual orientation, as Figure 15-2 suggests.

Among those STDs which are curable, there is still the possibility of recurrence. At present, no immunity or vaccination for STDs exists (James and Brooks, 1981). Also, a person can have more than one such disease at the same time. In the Denver study, over 4 percent of the patients had more than one STD, and some had as many as three or four (Judson, 1982). The most sensible response to this epidemic for a couple contemplating a sexual relationship is to seek a thorough medical inspection beforehand—however unromantic and unexciting that might sound.

We will describe the causes, effects, frequency, and treatment of such infections as well as other sex-related infections.

Many STDs are caused by bacteria and can be cured with antibiotics. When anti-bacterial drugs are taken too frequently, however, antibiotic-resistant strains of the disease can develop and spread worldwide. The old drugs are no longer effective, and stronger drugs are required (Culliton, 1976). STDs have been known throughout much of human history, but some specific varieties are relatively unfamiliar to most people until they discover that they are infected.

The special section, ***Highlighting Research,*** on pages 412 to 414, describes how sexual attitudes and feelings can interfere with sexual health care.

■ Gonorrhea

Incidence and Transmission of Gonorrhea. One bacterium, *Neisseria gonorrhea,* produces the infection **gonorrhea**, sometimes known as "the clap." In the Denver study this was identified as the most common STD among females and the second most common

"*Our group had 20% fewer venereal diseases.*"

© George Dole

FIGURE 15-2 *STDs: AS COMMON AS CAVITIES* STDs show no favoritism as to who is attacked. The term *venereal disease,* used by the young woman in the cartoon, originated from the Latin word for the godess of love, Venus. Currently, and more accurately, it refers to sexually transmissable disease.

Highlighting Research

EFFECTS OF SEXUAL ATTITUDES AND KNOWLEDGE ON HEALTH-CARE BEHAVIOR

One of the strongest barriers to effective prevention of sexually transmissible diseases is an individual's reluctance to acknowlege that he or she has such a disease. Having an STD evokes guilt (Fisher, 1990). Similar in many ways to the steps described in Chapter 5 for effective contraceptive behavior, effective STD behavior also involves five steps, and negative sexual attitudes and feelings can interfere with each step:

1. The individual must know about the various sexually transmissible diseases, including their specific symptoms.

2. It is necessary to examine one's genitals to detect a discharge, rash, growth, and so forth.

3. Medical help must be sought, and this obviously involves communicating in-

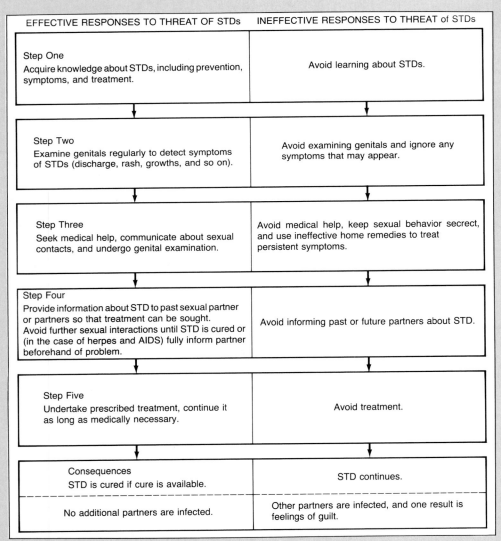

EFFECTIVE RESPONSES TO THREAT OF STDs	INEFFECTIVE RESPONSES TO THREAT of STDs
Step One Acquire knowledge about STDs, including prevention, symptoms, and treatment.	Avoid learning about STDs.
Step Two Examine genitals regularly to detect symptoms of STDs (discharge, rash, growths, and so on).	Avoid examining genitals and ignore any symptoms that may appear.
Step Three Seek medical help, communicate about sexual contacts, and undergo genital examination.	Avoid medical help, keep sexual behavior secrect, and use ineffective home remedies to treat persistent symptoms.
Step Four Provide information about STD to past sexual partner or partners so that treatment can be sought. Avoid further sexual interactions until STD is cured or (in the case of herpes and AIDS) fully inform partner beforehand of problem.	Avoid informing past or future partners about STD.
Step Five Undertake prescribed treatment, continue it as long as medically necessary.	Avoid treatment.
Consequences STD is cured if cure is available.	STD continues.
No additional partners are infected.	Other partners are infected, and one result is feelings of guilt.

FIGURE 15-3 *EFFECTIVE AND INEFFECTIVE RESPONSES TO STD SYMPTOMS* When a person develops symptoms of an STD, he or she can take one of several alternative courses of action. If the symptoms are ignored or treated with ineffective remedies, the disease continues to develop, partners are likely to be infected, and the person then must cope with guilt as well as the disease itself. If, however, the symptoms are treated effectively, the person generally is able to control or cure the disease, any partner is unlikely to become infected, and there is no long-term disease or guilt.

formation about one's sexual behavior as well as undergoing a genital examination.

4. Information about the STD must be provided to any sexual partner or partners to control the disease.

5. Appropriate treatment must be undertaken—in the form of pills, shots, lotions, or whatever—and must be continued as long as medically necessary.

Figure 15-3 contrasts effective versus ineffective responses to the threat of STDs.

Parents of college students sometimes express the belief that schools have the responsibility for educating them about disease prevention, but the responsibility for this education also belongs to the parents and their college-age offspring (Daher et al., 1987). Research has shown the importance of accurate information in avoiding and also in responding appropriately to STDs. For example, college students who received STD instruction in junior high school contracted fewer STDs than those not receiving such instruction (Yarber, 1980). Knowledge about STDs makes it more likely that the individual will seek treatment and avoid infecting others (Arafat and Allen, 1977).

Some studies have focused on specific knowledge about a specific STD. For example, knowledge about herpes is measured with a test consisting of items such as "Anxiety can trigger a herpes recurrence" and "A woman who had genital herpes must have a Cesarean section if she has a baby" (Bruce and McLaughlin, 1986, pp. 78–79). College students who knew the most about herpes tended to express more confidence that they could cope with the disease than those with less knowledge. Studies have also shown that information about STDs and safer sex is learned more effectively if it is combined with fear-producing facts that warn of the dangers of not complying (Baldwin and Baldwin, 1988).

Anyone who contracts STDs experiences quite negative reactions, as would be expected. If a person's general reaction to sexual matters consists of high levels of guilt and erotophobia (see Chapter 8), such reactions would be intensified.

One research finding that may seem surprising at first is that women who contract an STD express less guilt about masturbation than women who do not have a sexually transmissible disease (Houck and Abramson, 1986), as Figure 15-4 shows. Why should this be? Because high sex guilt is associated with avoiding sexual activity, women who are most guilty about masturbation would be less likely to engage in intercourse and thus less likely to contract an STD. If those high in guilt *do* engage in intercourse and become infected, however, they respond to this kind of disease more stressfully than low guilt women.

Lack of accurate information about STDs and negative emotions can raise unnecessary concerns. One example is the turmoil caused by the presence of youngsters with HIV infection in public schools. Most often, they have contracted the infection from a blood transfusion. When fellow students and their parents hold inac-

FIGURE 15-4 *STDs, MASTURBATION GUILT, AND STRESS*
An investigation of sixty women found that those who were diagnosed as having STDs expressed less guilt about masturbation than women without STDs. Among STD patients, masturbation guilt was associated with greater stress about having such a disease.
Source: Houck and Abramson, 1986.

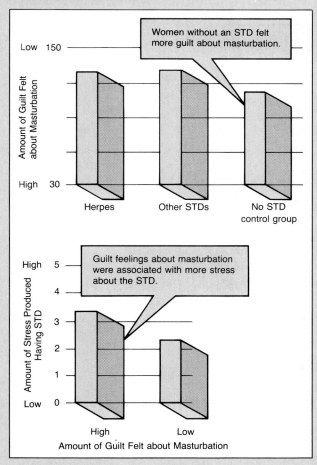

curate beliefs about the risk of contracting the disease from them through casual contact, there is often pressure to remove the infected child from the school, and, if he or she remains in class, to engage in social isolaton (AIDS Fact Book, 1985). Children are in fact more likely to be injured in a school bus accident than to be exposed to HIV from an infected classmate (Murnen, 1985). In fact, the child with the HIV infection runs a greater risk of being infected by his or her classmates than the reverse because of his or her malfunctioning immune system.

To the extent that guilt and embarrassment can be reduced, the likelihood of seeking appropriate information about all aspects of sexuality increases; in addition, people become more likely to take appropriate steps to prevent and treat STDs.

among males. Approximately 1.8 million new cases of gonorrhea occur in the United States every year (Leary, 1988).

Gonorrhea is transmitted quite easily. For example, a man who has intercourse just once with an infected woman has a one in five chance of becoming infected himself. If the woman is menstruating, the odds of infection increase to 50 percent because the bacteria survive easily in menstrual blood (Felman, 1982a). The risks are even higher for women catching it from an infected man (50 to 70 percent) after one act of intercourse, because the gonococcus is deposited directly into the vagina. Gonorrhea is typically transmitted through vaginal or anal intercourse, fellatio, and less commonly, through kissing or cunnilingus. The bacterium that produces gonorrhea can also be transmitted on toilet seats, toilet paper, or wet handtowels, although sexual contact is the most common route.

Symptoms of Gonorrhea. Most men (80 to 90 percent) who contract this disease begin to have symptoms within three to five days after becoming infected (Fleming, 1981)—urination causes pain, and there is a puslike discharge from the urethra. Among infected males, 10 to 20 percent have no symptoms.

About half of the women with gonorrhea have no obvious symptoms because it is concentrated in the cervix. There may be a small discharge through the vagina, but often it is unnoticed or is considered normal. Other mild symptoms of gonorrhea in women include painful urination, increased discharge from the vagina that irritates the labia and causes burning and itching, and changes in menstrual flow. The infection may be present not only in the cervix but also in the rectum, urethra, and/or throat (Di Caprio, 1979). Women can develop *pelvic inflammatory disease* (PID) through infection of the cervix spreading to the uterus, oviducts, and ovaries. Symptoms of PID include fever, pain in the lower abdomen and during intercourse, and nausea or vomiting. PID can cause infertility through scarring of the oviducts. PID is second only to AIDS in importance among STDs affecting women (Hilts, 1990).

Left untreated, gonorrhea can cause infertility, arthritis, and even heart infection (John, 1978). Other parts of the body can be infected if the bacteria are transmitted through the bloodstream, including the joints and the covering of the brain. The presence of gonorrhea in the cervix during delivery can produce an eye infection in newborns, sometimes causing blindness. Fortunately the application of drops such as silver nitrate to the newborn's eyes can prevent infection.

Diagnosis and Treatment of Gonorrhea. Diagnosis is made through tests of a sample of the discharge or of the patient's urine. The man's urethral discharge is expelled for testing by gently but firmly pressing on the glans. The discharge is inspected under a microscope for evidence of N. gonorrhea, and some of it is also transferred to a culture plate to grow for several days to provide a clear identification. Among gays practicing fellatio or anal intercourse, patients should also have a throat culture or a rectal culture because the bacteria may be harbored there. Women are diagnosed by culturing samples from the cervical area, throat, and rectum. A vaginal discharge may infect the rectum even though the woman has not had anal intercourse.

Penicillin is the prescribed treatment. The bacterium that causes gonorrhea has mutated several times, making some strains resistant to penicillin; in such cases other antibiotics are used. The patient may receive an injection of procaine penicillin G with probenecid, and may need to take the antibiotic tetracycline if he or she has chlamydia (also discussed in this chapter) simultaneously with gonorrhea. People with an allergy to penicillin simply take tetracycline as a substitute.

■ Syphilis

Incidence and Transmission of Syphilis. Because **syphilis** seems not to have occurred in Europe until after Columbus returned from the New World, he and his men have been blamed for transmitting it from Native Americans to Europeans (Lobdell and Owsley, 1974). Studies of European skeletal remains show no evidence of syphilis before 1492 (Baker and Armelagos, 1988). There is even evidence that the disease was present in a prehistoric bear living in what is now Indiana about 11,000 years ago (Syphilis in the . . . , 1987). Within Europe, outbreaks were also commonly blamed on various nationalities other than one's own as when the English labeled it the French or Spanish disease, the French called it the Italian or Naples disease, and so forth.

Syphilis occurs less frequently than gonorrhea, but its effects are potentially more serious because in its final stages the disease can be fatal. In the United States, 85,000 people become infected with syphilis every year (Leary, 1988). Syphilis usually is transmitted through sexual contact and less commonly through blood transfusion.

Symptoms of Syphilis. Syphilis is caused by the bacterium, *Treponema pallidum.* Its symptoms usually appear about three weeks after infection occurs, although they can appear anytime from ten days to three months after transmission—also, the early stages of the disease are sometimes entirely free of symptoms (Jacobs, 1981). Following this incubation period, the first sign is usually a lesion (once commonly called a pox) at the point where the bacteria entered the body, most often the genital area. The lesion which can be up to one inch (2.5 cm) in diameter, usually is not painful (Chapel, 1979). This initial stage of the disease is illustrated in Figure 15-5.

The lesion that appears during the *first stage of syphilis* is the **Hunterian chancre,** named for the physician who first described it during the 1800s. Dr. Hunter inoculated himself with the discharge from a patient to test its effects; both died of syphilis

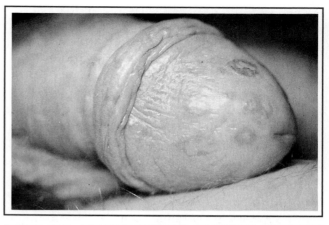

FIGURE 15-5 *THE FIRST SYMPTOM OF SYPHILIS: THE HUNTER-IAN CHANCRE* This Hunterian chancre is the major symptom of the primary stage of syphilis. This usually painless skin lesion has a craterlike appearance and a soft center.

(Kirsner, 1981). Today, syphilis is treated effectively with antibiotics. After several decades of a declining incidence, syphilis has recently rebounded to reach new highs (Altman, 1990b).

The chancre will heal, even without treatment. If antibiotics are not administered, the *secondary stage of syphilis* begins between two weeks and six months after the chancre has healed. A rash that neither itches nor hurts appears on the patient's body, and flu-like symptoms develop. In a few weeks, these signs of the secondary stage subside. Because neither the chancre, the rash, nor the flu appear particularly serious to the victim, only 50 to 60 percent of those who are infected seek medical treatment during the primary or secondary stages of syphilis (Chapel, 1982a). During both of these stages (as well as the tertiary stage), syphilis can be passed on to a sexual partner.

During the *latent stage of syphilis,* the bacteria become dormant, and there are no symptoms (Quinn, 1982a). During this stage the invading organisms live in the infected person's brain, spinal cord, bones, and blood vessels. This stage can last for years, and after the first year of the latent stage the disease is not passed on to sexual partners. A pregnant woman with syphilis may transmit the infection, called *congenital syphilis,* to her fetus during pregnancy, however. Even if the fetus survives the disease, the neonate can be harmed by various defects and deformities of the bones, teeth, and kidneys. Treatment of the pregnant woman before the fifth month of pregnancy can protect the newborn from infection. When a pregnancy test is performed, the woman receives a blood test to determine whether she has syphilis.

Half of those infected with syphilis do not progress past the latent stage, but in the other half, the disease progresses into a more dangerous stage. In the final, or *tertiary stage of syphilis,* the bacteria invade bodily tissues, producing soft, large sores called **gummas.** A gumma forms on internal organs, the skin, and elsewhere, causing extensive damage. If the central nervous system is attacked, the result is *neurosyphilis,* characterized by insanity and paralysis. The tertiary stage is often fatal, and it can appear three to forty years after the initial infection (Greenwood, 1980).

Treating Syphilis. A blood test can detect the presence of the spiral-shaped, syphilitic bacteria, and a physical examination for the presence of chancres is also performed. During the primary or secondary stages, one injection of penicillin cures the disease. In the tertiary stage, syphilis usually can be cured with large doses of the antibiotic over a period of several months, although some irreversible damage to the body or neural system may remain.

Chlamydia

Incidence of Chlamydia. A third form of bacterial STD is **chlamydia,** caused by *chlamydia trachomatis.* In the Denver study, chlamydia was found to be the most common STD among males and the second most common among females. Three to 4 million people are infected with chlamydia every year in the United States, making it America's most common STD (White and Felts, 1989).

Symptoms of Chlamydia. Chlamydia can infect the urinary tract, rectum, or vagina, and it produces a mucus discharge from the penis or vagina. Sometimes, urination is accompanied by a burning sensation. In males, this discharge and pain are labeled *nongonococcal urethritis,* or NGU (Wong and Handsfield, 1983).

Infected pregnant women can transmit chlamydia to their newborns during delivery, producing an eye infection, *conjunctivitis,* or less commonly a lung infection called *chlamydial pneumonia.* Both can be treated with antibiotics.

Diagnosis and Treatment of Chlamydia. Chlamydia can be cured with the broad-spectrum antibiotic, tetracycline, or with erythromycin in cases of tetracycline allergy. But reinfection from a sexual partner can occur even after treatment. Because of this *ping-pong effect,* both sexual partners must be treated to achieve a lasting cure (Jones, 1984). Left untreated, chlamydia can spread throughout the sexual organs and eventually cause PID and infertility (Edwards, 1981).

One type of chlamydia infecting 1,000 people yearly in the United States is called **lymphogranuloma venereum,** transmitted to a sexual partner or to a fetus (Leary, 1988). A small, painless blister appears at the genital or rectal site of entry about two weeks after infection. This is followed by a general illness with fever, and painful lymph nodes in the groin. A very serious disease, called *Reiter's syndrome,* may result. Tetracycline is an effective cure, and its use prevents the development of arthritis or heart disease (Gump, 1985).

Prostatitis

Bacterial infections can reach the male prostate gland and produce **prostatitis.** This is an infection of the prostate involving urinary tract swelling and pain. Urination is frequent and painful, and even sitting down can be uncomfortable. Chronic prostatitis may be free of symptoms, or it can produce pain in the lower back or perineum. This disease is often caused by *E. coli,* which normally exists in the body without causing infection, or less frequently by other organisms that result in genital infections such as chlamydia, mycoplasma (discussed in Chapter 4), trichomoniasis, or gonorrhea. Therefore, before and during treatment, men with prostatitis should avoid intercourse or use a condom to prevent the partner's infection and their own reinfection.

This disease can also interfere with erection and make ejaculation painful (Small, 1984a). Prostatitis may cause infertility by reducing semen production (Shrom, 1982).

Urinary Cystitis

Urinary cystitis is an infection of the urinary tract that can result from sexual activity. It was once called "honeymooner's disease" because frequent sexual interaction sometimes introduces bacteria into the woman's urethra. The specific bacterium causing the infection (often *E. coli*) is quite often present in the genital areas, but the rubbing involved in intercourse or masturbation may force it into the urethra (Melman, 1984). Reduced resistance to disease can also promote urinary cystitis.

The symptoms of cystitis include painful and frequent urination—intercourse also becomes uncomfortable. Males develop cystitis less frequently than females because the greater length of the male urethra helps protect the urinary bladder from bacterial growth. Twenty to 30 percent of women have this infection at some point in their lives (Buckley, 1983).

Eighty-three percent of women have their first case of cystitis soon after they become sexually active. Clearly, prevention is important. Women who urinate only a few times each day are more likely to have the disease, so it is helpful to drink large amounts of water and other fluids each day. Cranberry juice is often recommended to help prevent it because the juice makes the woman's urine acidic. Both sex partners should wash their hands and genitals and use intercourse positions that rub the urethral opening less vigorously; if the woman urinates just before intercourse and within ten minutes afterward she helps reduce the risk. Urination is a preventive measure because the flow of urine removes bacteria from the area. Another such measure for women is to wipe themselves from front to back after either defecating or urinating, rather than the reverse, thereby avoiding the transmission of bacteria from the anal area to the urethra.

Although antibiotics can clear up this disease, recurrence is common unless preventive measures are followed.

Toxic Shock Syndrome

Any sudden illness may be difficult to diagnose, and **toxic shock syndrome**, or **TSS**, conforms to this general rule. Early symptoms resemble those of the flu and include vomiting, diarrhea, and high fever.

This disease is found almost exclusively in women, although occasionally it strikes men and children. The major contributing factor is the use of tampons during menstruation. TSS occurs rarely today, after a sharp rise in 1980 that coincided with the marketing of extra-thick tampons. When thick tampons are used (Cohen and Falkow, 1981), the bacterium *staphylococcus aureus* may multiply and cause TSS. The rapid multiplication of bacteria also occurs when a tampon is left in the vagina for more than six hours. A booklet entitled, "Toxic Shock Syndrome and Tampons," is available from the U.S. Government's Food and Drug Administration, Consumer Information Center, Pueblo, Colorado, 81001. An additional source of infection is a contraceptive diaphragm or sponge left in the vagina for twenty-four hours or longer (Levin, 1984).

A man could theoretically develop toxic shock syndrome after having intercourse with an infected partner, but no such cases have been documented. One unusual instance of male infection has been reported, however. After a maintenance worker injured his knee while fixing a toilet clogged with tampons, bacteria entered the wound, and he developed TSS (Tack, 1985). The same antibiotics used for treating women with TSS were effective in curing his infection. Untreated, the outcome can be serious physical damage to the body and even death.

Genital Ulcers: Granuloma Inguinale and Chancroid

Granuloma inguinale infects about 100 people yearly in the United States, causing small bumps to appear on the genitals or thighs—or in the rectum—after sexual or nonsexual contact with an infected person. The bumps ulcerate and produce a sour odor that infects healthy skin nearby. This infection damages the tissue; treatment with antibiotics such as tetracycline or erythromycin will stop the infection from spreading but will not correct permanent damage such as scarring.

More common are two other bacterial infections of the genitals that result from the presence of hemophilus organisms. *Hemophilus ducreyi* causes **chancroid,** which is transmitted by sexual contact and infects 10,000 people yearly in the United States (Leary, 1988). Three to fourteen days after sexual contact with an infected person, one or more soft, small sores appear in the genital, anal, or perineal area, called **papules.** The papule is painful and resembles a smaller, harder version of the painless Hunterian chancre resulting from syphilis. Papules rupture in a few days and become ulcers with a smelly discharge; lymph nodes in the groin enlarge and also cause pain. Either sexual or nonsexual physical contact can transmit chancroid. Antibiotics such as erythromycin or sulfa are used to cure chancroid.

A related bacterium is *hemophilus vaginalis.* These bacteria do not cause a sore. Instead there is an infection in the vagina which can be transmitted to a male partner. Females can contract this through sexual contact with an infected male or in nonsexual ways. It produces a smelly vaginal discharge and can be cured with antibiotics (Fleury, 1978).

■ Genital Herpes: A Viral Epidemic

In contrast to infections resulting from bacteria, those STDs caused by viruses do not have specific cures. As with the common cold, the illness simply runs its course. Of the three viral STDs we will describe, only genital warts can be cured. To date, genital herpes and AIDS cannot.

Incidence and Transmission of Herpes.   About one out of every six Americans is estimated to have antibodies to **genital herpes** in their bloodstream, and half a million new cases develop each year (Leary, 1988). Because this disease is incurable, the presence of antibodies means that the person will remain infected. Considering that the total number of people infected in 1966 was only 30,000 (Centers for Disease Control, 1982), it is clear that this infection is spreading at epidemic rates.

The type 2 herpes virus survives best in warm, moist environments, so it is most likely to be transmitted through personal contact. This virus survives only about ten to twenty minutes in other locations (such as a toilet seat), making transmission there unlikely, though not impossible.

Usually it is transmitted through intercourse or by oral-genital sex. During a single act of heterosexual intercourse with an infected partner, a woman will get herpes 80 to 90 percent of the time, and a man will contract it 50 percent of the time from an infected woman.

Symptoms of Herpes.   Many people are familiar with *herpes simplex virus type 1,* which usually infects areas above the waist in the form of cold sores or fever blisters; kissing can transmit this disease to others. About 10 to 30 percent of the cases of genital herpes are caused by this virus, presumably through oral-genital contact (Kohl, 1982).

The remaining 70 to 90 percent of the cases are caused by the *herpes simplex virus type 2.* Neither type is curable at present, but prescription drugs are available that reduce the pain and swelling of this infection. After exposure to a herpes virus, symptoms appear within two to twelve days (Vontver, 1979). *Prodromal symptoms* warn of the coming outbreak of herpes, with the infected sites beginning to itch, burn, or tingle in about three-fourths of herpes sufferers. The herpes blisters, called **vesicles,** cluster in a half-inch area on or near the genitalia, as shown in Figure 15-6. These vesicles are painful, especially for women because their genitals are more moist than those of men.

After a few days, the vesicles dry and form crusts, and then disappear from the skin within one to three weeks. The herpes virus found in these vesicles is easily transmitted during close physical contact until healing occurs. During the first year of primary infection, the disease breaks out repeatedly with the vesicles recurring along with fatigue—about once every two to eight weeks. After three years, most sufferers have only about two recurrences each year, and they become less painful over time.

During the dormant stages of the disease (between outbreaks), the virus lives in cells near the base of the spinal cord and produces a mild infection. Stress, illness, and sunburn are among the factors that can activate the virus; it travels to the skin through nerve pathways, producing the next attack of vesicles.

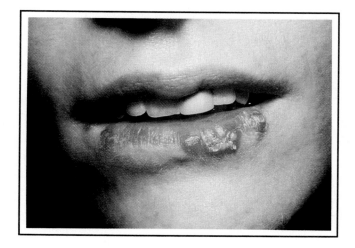

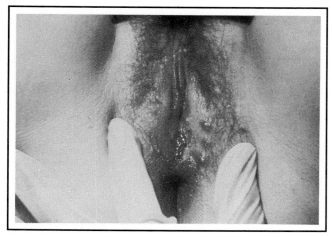

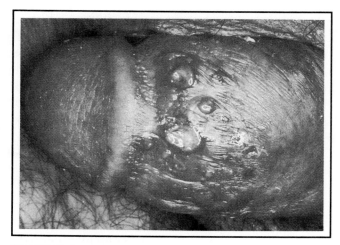

FIGURE 15-6 *HERPES: PAINFUL VESICLES* Herpes vesicles typically appear on the lips or the genitals. Each outbreak lasts about five days, during which the disease is highly contagious.

In a study of fifty-nine women and men with genital herpes, outbreaks occurred in the previous year most frequently among those with the highest number of stressful events in that time period (VanderPlate et al., 1988). After four years, stress-related outbreaks of herpes decrease.

Genital herpes is most contagious when vesicles are present, but 5 percent of the victims can pass on the virus even when they have no symptoms (Chang, 1981). Women may develop vesicles internally (on the cervix) where they remain undetected but are, nevertheless, a source of infection to sexual partners. When a woman with herpes experiences pain during penile thrusting against the cervix, it may indicate an outbreak of internal herpes.

Prevention of Herpes. The herpes virus does not pass through condoms so their use is advisable during the active stage of the disease. When both partners have herpes and want to engage in intercourse, condoms are still recommended if vesicles have erupted. This virus (and others, too) can survive for over four hours on benches and towels around hot tubs, steam rooms, and warm swimming pools; thus, the disease can be contracted even without any sexual contact (Brody, 1987). There are several strains of herpes, and partners may have different varieties of the disease (Felman, 1984). Discussing herpes with a potential sexual partner may be awkward, but essential, as Figure 15-7 suggests. In New York State, a herpes sufferer can be sued by a sexual partner who contracts it and who was not informed of the danger before engaging in sex; other states have not yet established the legal liability for failure to inform a sexual partner.

Some relief from the pain of herpes vesicles can be gained from the prescription drug acyclovir, aspirin, or non-aspirin acetaminophen. Keeping vesicles clean and dry also lessens discomfort and promotes healing.

Two additional health problems can develop if a woman has genital herpes. First, an infected woman has an increased risk of developing cervical cancer. The change to cancerous tissue usually takes several months to develop, so cells from the cervix should be tested by a physician at least once a year. Second,

"But enough about me, let's talk about you. Do you have herpes?"

FIGURE 15-7 *GENITAL HERPES: INFORMING A NEW SEXUAL PARTNER* The issue of who has herpes and who doesn't is not a romantic topic, but truthful disclosures potentially prevent the transmission of an unpleasant and incurable disease. Several legal cases have arisen in which herpes victims have sued former sexual partners for transmitting the disease to them (Brand, 1987). Reproduced by special permission of PLAYBOY Magazine: Copyright © 1983 by PLAYBOY.

herpes can be transmitted to a newborn infant during delivery if vesicles are present in the birth canal or have been there during the previous two weeks (Growdon, 1985). Such exposure leads to herpes in 25 to 40 percent of the infants, and can cause blindness and hearing problems; 60 percent of those infected die (Oriel, 1982). To protect the baby, a Caesarean section may be preferable to a vaginal delivery.

■ Viral Hepatitis

Viral hepatitis in one of its three forms, A, B, and non-A/non-B, usually causes gastrointestinal and other symptoms that can be mild or acute. These symptoms can include mild upset with indigestion and diarrhea, or cause severe illness such as vomiting, abdominal pain, fever, and yellowed skin (called jaundice) resulting from the liver's secretion of excess bile. Hepatitis A is transmitted through fecal-oral contact and incubates two to six weeks. Food contaminated with the virus can be one source, including raw or partially cooked shellfish from contaminated water. Oral-anal contact also spreads hepatitis A, and this is one explanation for the higher percentage of infection among homosexual males than among heterosexuals.

Hepatitis B can be spread in contaminated blood and through the saliva, semen, vaginal secretions, and other bodily fluids of infected persons. Approximately 200,000 cases of hepatitis occur annually in the United States, many of them through sexual transmission. Either anal intercourse, or manual stimulation of the rectum followed by manual contact with the mouth or eyes of a noninfected person, can spread this infection. Having numerous sexual partners increases the risk that this virus will be present in at least one of them, either in an active infection or as one of the half-million or so asymptomatic carriers of hepatitis B. The virus can cause short-term inflammation of the liver and more serious, chronic diseases such as liver disease called cirrhosis and liver cancer. Blood transfusions typically cause non-A/non-B hepatitis.

Following blood tests that distinguish among the three types, treatment of hepatitis is aimed at the symptoms. Partial immunity to hepatitis A is available through a shot of gamma globulin, although persons in intimate contact with an infected person already have been exposed for some time. Safe, effective vaccines for hepatitis B are also available (Kuvin, 1989).

■ Genital Warts

Condyloma acuinatum, also called human papilloma virus, produces **genital warts**, like those shown in Figure 15-8. They appear alone or in groups on the genitals or within the rectum of both sexes and resemble small cauliflowers. Their color is usually red or pink, but they turn hard and yellow on dry skin. In the United States, there are between one half million and one million new cases each year (Boffey, 1987).

FIGURE 15-8 *GENITAL WARTS: A VIRAL STD* Genital warts are caused by a virus. Contrary to myth, frogs and toads are not responsible for the development of warts in humans.

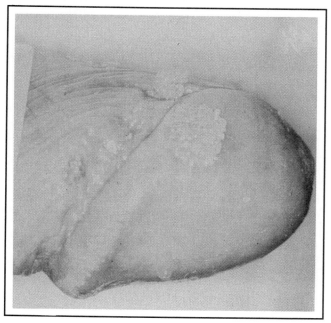

Warts have a long incubation period, and they may not appear until three months to two years after anal, vaginal, or oral-anal contact with an infected partner (Lupulescu, 1979). One or more *cofactors* promote the disease's development once the virus is present. These cofactors include smoking, using birth control pills, and contracting herpes or other STDs. They also can be transmitted through nonsexual contact with other parts of the body. Warts can be removed, using a carbon dioxide laser. An ointment containing podophyllin was used in the past, but it is less effective than removal.

The virus producing warts is genetically similar to the virus responsible for cervical cancer. Women who are infected with genital warts have twice the risk of developing cancer of the cervix than women who have not been infected (Reid et al., 1982). Genital warts sometimes infect the urethra, causing bleeding and obstruction.

■ A Potpourri of Potential Pelvic Invaders: Fungi, Protozoa, Arachnids, and Insects

Besides the bacterial and viral infections, additional organisms thrive in and around human genitals. They, too, can be passed from an individual to his or her sexual partner.

Fungus: Yeast Infection. Many women are familiar with the unpleasantness of a vaginal **yeast infection**, also called *candidiasis* or *moniliasis*. *Candida albicansis* is a fungus that occurs naturally in small amounts in the mouth, digestive tract, and vagina. If this fungus is overly successful and begins to spread, it can infect both sexes whether they are sexually active or not.

This fungus thrives on sugar, and diabetics are prone to yeast infections. The stimulus for its growth is often some change in the person's physical condition that is beneficial to the fungus. For example, women taking oral contraceptives or antibiotics such as tetracyclines may develop a yeast infection (Noble, 1984). Yeast infections also are common during pregnancy because of the hormonal changes; fortunately, the pregnant woman can be treated in order to avoid transmitting *thrush,* or oral yeast infection, to the baby during delivery.

Among the symptoms of vaginal yeast infection are a thick, white or yellow discharge that has a strong odor and resembles cottage cheese. If the discharge is sufficiently heavy, it can coat the introitus and vulva. This causes intense itching in the genitals and sometimes pain during vaginal intercourse until the woman is treated with the prescription drug mico- (or buto-) conazole nitrate; she uses an applicator to place the cream in her vagina for five to ten days. An oral form is available when the mouth and digestive tract are infected. It is important to finish all medication because symptoms may disappear before the drug is finished, making reinfection likely. Men with sexually transmitted yeast infection typically have no symptoms.

If a man has intercourse with an infected partner, he can contract the infection and become a carrier of the fungus. He can then transmit the fungus to other sexual partners (Krantz, 1982). The chances of developing monilia can be reduced by controlling the amount of sugar in the diet, particularly dairy products and sweets. Monilia grows best in warm, damp areas such as the one provided by the moist air between a woman's genitals and her nylon pantyhose, suggesting the value of other styles of hosiery.

Protozoa: Trichomoniasis. **Protozoa** are one-celled organisms, and a specific protozoan that can be transmitted during genital contact is called *Trichomonas vaginalis.* It causes a troublesome infection, **trichomoniasis,** or "the trick" (see Figure 15-9).

Symptoms are an itching, odorous discharge that appears within four weeks after infection. Because this protozoan can survive for thirty to forty-five minutes in a drop of urine at room temperature (Chapel, 1982b), toilet seats are a possible source of trichomoniasis.

This disease can affect the entire range of reproduction, including fertility, recovery from childbirth, and the newborn's health (Hume, 1979). It also increases susceptibility to cervical cancer. Metronidazole is a cure for this infection, but it is important that both sexual partners be treated simultaneously to avoid reinfection. Pregnant women should not use this drug because it adds to the risk of birth defects, particularly during the first trimester. Among the side effects of this drug are a temporary metallic taste in the mouth along with an upset stomach and intestinal difficulties.

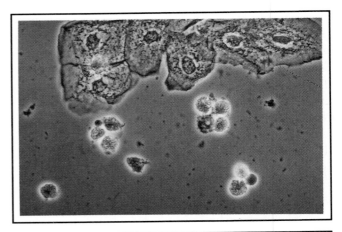

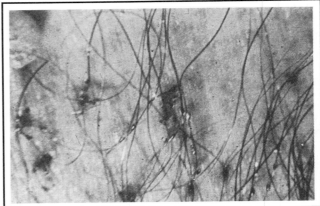

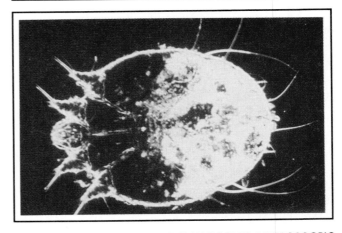

FIGURE 15-9 *WHEN HUMANS PLAY HOST TO MICROSCOPIC PARASITES* Trichomonad protozoa (1), scabies (2), and lice (3) are transmitted primarily through sexual contact with an infected person. The protozoan which causes trichomoniasis has small whips extending from its one cell that propel it through liquid and mucus. The itch mite is an arachnid (related to spiders and ticks) that causes scabies; the parasite burrows into the skin and lays its eggs. Lice are small insects that attach themselves to hair, and live by sucking blood from their hosts.

Scabies: Arachnids under the Skin. The itch mite (also shown in Figure 15-9) causes **scabies**. This tiny arachnid (the class of arthropods consisting of spiders, scorpions, mites, and ticks) is a parasite that travels from one person to another during sexual or nonsexual physical contact. Female scabies burrow under the skin where they lay eggs. An itchy rash develops on the body but not on the face. The link between this mite and the symptoms it causes was discovered in 1654, making it the first human disease with a known cause (Altman, 1990a).

Scabies is highly contagious, but Kwell lotion containing the chemical Lindane effectively eliminates mites.

Lice: Tiny Bloodsucking Insects. Parasitic **lice** (also shown in Figure 15-9) attach themselves to pubic or other hair using their claws. Periodically, they insert their mouthpieces into the person's skin to suck blood for growth and production of eggs and new lice. The major symptom is intense itching (Orkin, 1984). Lice are transmitted through contact with an infected person as well as with his or her clothing or such articles as sheets.

These small wingless insects, popularly known as crabs, are treated with an over-the-counter drug, such as RID, which combines pyrethrins and piperonyl butoxide. The infected person's clothes, sheets, and towels all must be washed after treatment, which is repeated in seven days to kill newly hatched eggs. A less effective, but more humorous, cure has been suggested in folklore. The prescription is to cover the patient's pubic hair with alcohol and sand; the supposed result is that the lice get drunk on the alcohol and kill one another when they start throwing the rocks.

AIDS: HIV Infection

■ Incidence and Transmission of AIDS

Acquired immune deficiency syndrome (AIDS) first appeared in the United States during 1981, in New York City (Bazell, 1983). Similar cases appeared there as early as 1978, although they were not identified as a syndrome at that time. By January 1983, physicians were reporting twenty-four new cases each week (Centers for Disease Control, 1983). So far, half of the victims have died, with death usually occurring within two years of diagnosis. By 1984, awareness of AIDS was sufficiently great that the rate of infections began to drop. Nevertheless, because of the long incubation period, the number of hospital patients with AIDS is expected to rise again and then peak between 1992 and 1995 (Hilts, 1989). As of February 28, 1989, almost 90,000 AIDS cases and over 50,000 deaths had been reported to the U.S. Center for Disease Control. By 1990, more young men had died as the result of AIDS than were killed in the entire Vietnam War (Sullivan, 1990). The prospects are even more grim elsewhere (Carballo et al., 1989; Shannon and Pyle, 1989; Tierney, 1990). In 1990, the World Health Organization projected that because of increases in heterosexual transmission of the disease, 20 million people will have been infected by the year 2000, and Chin (1990) estimates that at least three million women and children will die of this disease during the present decade.

One especially frightening characteristic of AIDS is that as many as eight years may pass between infection by HIV and the appearance of symptoms in the infected person. A study of 288 HIV-infected gays in San Francisco found that half developed AIDS within 9.8 years of the original infection (Moss and Bacchett, 1989). The body's initial response to HIV is to produce antibodies to destroy it. A blood test to detect these antibodies can indicate who has been infected and therefore is at risk for developing the disease (Dodd, 1985).

About one out of every 200 persons in the United States is estimated to have antibodies to the virus causing AIDS (Raeburn, 1989). Without widespread testing, however, no estimate can be considered firm or exact. Among college students, about one per 500 is infected (Leary, 1989). The rate is much higher for specific segments of the population. The highest risk group for developing AIDS consists of men engaging in homosexual or bisexual activity, accounting for 61 to 73 percent of reported U.S. cases. There is also evidence that AIDS risk is greatest among uncircumcised men because the virus may be harbored under the foreskin (Altman, 1988). Seventeen to 20 percent of those infected are intravenous (IV) drug users who share needles. IV drug use, among other factors, explains the high rate of AIDS (62 percent) among homeless men (AIDS facts, 1989). At least half of the 200,000 intravenous drug users in Manhattan are believed to be HIV-infected (Des Jarlais et al., 1989). Heterosexuals with high-risk partners can contract the disease (McCurdy, 1984), most often women who have a high-risk male partner. In addition, men with AIDS transmit the disease more readily during sexual contact than infected women do (Belec et al., 1989). For this reason, AIDS is now the leading cause of death for women aged twenty-five to thirty-four in New York City (AIDS facts, 1989). The AIDS rate is quite high among heterosexual and homosexual prostitutes (Berk, 1990; Pleak and Meyer-Bahlburg, 1990). Research indicates that the risk of catching the AIDS virus from a single act of heterosexual intercourse with a low-risk partner (using a condom) is one in five billion; with an infected partner and no condom, the risk increases to one in five hundred (Boffey, 1988).

The disease is usually transmitted by blood or semen contaminated with the human immunodeficiency virus (HIV, also called the *HTLV-III* or *human T-cell lymphoma virus—Type III*). Less commonly, HIV is also found in tears, saliva, menstrual flow, and vaginal secretions from infected persons, but close, nonsexual contact, which typically does not involve contact with another person's blood or semen, has not led to the transmission of the disease. Anal intercourse is more likely to cause tissue damage than vaginal intercourse, allowing infected semen to mingle with the blood of the person being penetrated. A shared needle is a risk because it can carry the virus from the blood vessels of an infected person to the next one who uses it. Kissing does not appear to transmit HIV because it does not survive in saliva or other digestive fluids (Ho et al., 1985). Very minimal evidence exists that fellatio transmits HIV (Schechter and Saadoun, 1984). Despite understandable fears, nonsexual contacts with an HIV infected patient, even in close family settings, does not seem to result in its transmission.

One to 2 percent of those with HIV infections are hemophiliacs who contracted it when receiving a transfusion of contaminated blood. Before the dangers of HIV infection were widely known, blood transfusions were an obvious danger, but stringent screening procedures are now undertaken to protect against this means of transmission. Nevertheless, because of earlier, nonscreened transfusions, more than half (65 percent) of hemophiliacs have been infected already (AIDS facts, 1989). Transfusions are not totally safe because screening tests are not 100 percent accurate in detecting HIV antibodies. The chances of getting an HIV infection from a blood transfusion today are estimated to be one in 28,000 (Cumming et al., 1989). Those donating blood cannot be infected, however, because their only contact is with a sterile needle.

Many professionals who come in close bodily contact with strangers, including dentists, surgeons, and anyone who performs emergency procedures such as mouth-to-mouth resuscitation, express the fear that they could contract HIV infection. Their fears are justified: As of 1989, twenty-six health-care workers in the United States who were not at risk because of other factors like IV drug use, have HIV infection resulting from their job activity. Seventeen were infected through needle punctures (Navarro, 1989). Many health care professionals rely on "rubber" gloves to protect them during examinations and treatment, but this virus frequently can penetrate such gloves (Klein et al., 1990).

Among the other possible victims of HIV infection are babies born to mothers with the disease. Twenty to 50 percent of babies born to women with HIV infection also will be infected. One-third of the babies born with this infection develop a serious illness or die before they are one year of age (Blanche et al., 1989). Therefore, these women should avoid pregnancy or should consider abortion if pregnancy does occur.

The special section, ***Taking Responsibility and Protecting Yourself,*** on pages 425 to 426, discusses the special health concerns of those who interact sexually with others of their own sex, especially men.

■ Detecting Antibodies to HIV Virus

Two tests detect HIV antibodies; neither directly indicates the presence of HIV in infected persons or asymptomatic carriers. They are the Enzyme-Linked Immunosorbant Assay, or ELISA, and the Western Blot Electrophoretic test. These tests were developed for blood samples as screening devices to lower the risk of transfusing HIV infected blood, but they cannot reveal the status of HIV infection in the individual providing the blood sample. A positive result of either test can show only that a person has been exposed to the virus and has developed antibodies to it. A positive result from ELISA is usually followed by the Western Blot test to confirm it. Among the problems with diagnostic testing has been the long wait between drawing a blood sample and getting the results back from a laboratory. This procedure has also posed a potential threat to the patient's anonymity because of the number of professionals and technicians involved. At the beginning of the 1990s, a simple new test became available that can be carried out in the doctor's office and takes only ten minutes (New AIDS test . . . , 1989). With the single use diagnostic system (SUDS), a small blood sample is drawn from a finger prick, two drops of blood serum are placed on a plastic disk, and a color reactant provides the diagnosis. If a white dot on the disk does not change color, no HIV antibodies are present. If the dot turns blue, the patient has been exposed to the HIV.

Because antibodies are not produced instantaneously following infection, a blood test may be negative if it is given after HIV has invaded the body and before the antibodies are present. Several weeks to several months may elapse before antibodies are produced in a newly infected person. A test is also meaningless if the person afterward engages in high-risk

Taking Responsibility and Protecting Yourself

HEALTH CONCERNS OF HOMOSEXUALS AND BISEXUALS

Men who engage in sexual acts with those of their own sex have special needs for health care. Their sexual lifestyles can make them vulnerable to certain STDs. The outbreak of HIV infection is a dramatic example, because anal intercourse is a common practice among gays and a major means of transmission of the deadly virus. Because the rectum does not expand and lubricate like the vagina, it is more likely to be torn by penile thrusting and thus open to infection. The practice of **handballing,** in which a fist and a portion of the forearm are inserted in the rectum, obviously can have the same effect. The use of lubricants can help prevent tears and abrasions to some extent, but these still can occur. Information about AIDS has resulted in a decrease in high risk sexual behavior (Siegel and Glassman, 1989), though not among gays who are relatively young, less well-educated, and in lower income groups (Richwald et al., 1988).

Though condom use in anal intercourse is safer than not using a condom, these protective devices are far from perfectly effective. The failure rate is sufficiently high that the United States Public Health Service has issued a warning that this form of sex should be avoided entirely (Parachini, 1989).

In addition to HIV infection, other diseases are spread by anal sex. Hepatitis and parasitic diseases, for example, can be transmitted in this way (Felman, 1981; Marr, 1982; Noble, 1982). Women engaging in anal intercourse are also at risk. During anal intercourse men are advised to wear a condom and use a commercially available lubricant. Because physicians do not routinely conduct rectal examinations, men and women who engage in anal intercourse should request it.

One especially high risk group for HIV infection is the male prison population. In New York State prisons, for example,

about 14 percent of the inmates have tested positive. In a nationwide sample of prison and jail inmates, the rate was lower (4.25 percent), while in New York City, the rate is 17.4 percent (Raeburn, 1989). Almost all of the infected individuals (95 percent) are intravenous drug users. Regardless of the precise percentage in a given prison, the rate is much higher than in the general population. This—plus the high frequency of both consensual and coercive homosexual activity in prisons—means that the problem can only get worse. One solution, of course, is to distribute condoms (Prison condom policy, 1989). Most prison officials are reluctant to take this step, however, because it is against the rules for prisoners to engage in fellatio or anal intercourse, and homosexual rape is obviously not condoned. The dilemma for the prison system is to choose betwen admitting that sexual activity between prisoners is rampant so that safer sex practices can be encouraged or forbidding all homosexual acts and thus indirectly giving a death sentence to an unknown number of inmates.

Homosexual females also can contract certain STDs. Trichomoniasis, yeast vaginitis, and hemophilus infections are pelvic diseases that sometimes develop in lesbians. For this reason, good gynecological care is no less important for them than for heterosexual females. It is found that lesbians have Pap smears performed less frequently than heterosexual females, thus exposing themselves to a greater risk of developing undetected cervical cancer (Millen, 1983). If a lesbian is reluctant to be examined by a male physician, she should search for an appropriate female M.D.

activities. For these reasons, it is as important to know about the behavior of a potential sexual partner as to know that he or she tested negative for HIV antibodies. One consequence of fears about this disease has been a decrease in the number of sexual partners among heterosexuals and, especially, among homosexual males, as Figure 15-10 shows. Because an infected individual may be unaware of the fact and because people may lie about their sexual histories, many sexually active individuals are increasingly wary about engaging in sex with anyone unless they know a great deal about their past interactions. Cochran and Mays (1990) reported that 40 to 50 percent of both men and women admit they would lie to a new partner about the number of past partners and about past sexual acts.

Blood tests to detect HIV antibodies are also the center of controversy when they are used to make decisions about employment, marriage, acceptance in the armed services, and the issuance of insurance policies. Should people with HIV antibodies be excluded from various activities and services? It has been argued that this kind of screening represents a massive invasion of privacy and denial of rights (Melton and Gray, 1988). Conversely, it has been argued that unless there is such screening, employers and insurance companies would lose vast amounts of money, marriage partners would be unprotected, and transfusions on the battlefield could cost a life rather than save it. There are no simple, clear-cut answers to these issues.

■ Symptoms and Effects of HIV Infection

One complicating factor is that some—perhaps most—of those with HIV antibodies will develop not AIDS (the life-threatening disease) but, rather, **symptomatic HIV infection** previously known as **AIDS-related complex,** or **ARC.** The patient experiences loss of appetite, diarrhea, weight loss, night sweats, swollen lymph glands, and a variety of infections such as pneumonia more easily and more frequently than usual. Among those so afflicted, an unknown percentage develop a full-blown HIV infection (Murray et al., 1985). In these cases, the antibodies produced by the immune system fail to control the virus, and the victim succumbs to cancer or any of several possible *opportunistic infections* which take advantage of the suppressed immunity, as Table 15-1 shows. This disease is incurable at present, and no vaccine is currently available. An informative booklet, "AIDS: 100 Questions and Answers," is available from the New York State Department of Health in Albany, New York.

FIGURE 15-10 *FEAR OF AIDS LEADS TO FEWER SEXUAL PARTNERS* Patients at a sexual disease clinic in Denver reported having fewer sexual partners per month after learning about HIV infection. Gay men reported the greatest decline in the number of partners, although heterosexual men and women also had fewer partners after they were aware of the dangers of this incurable, fatal disease.
Source: Adapted from McQuay, 1985.

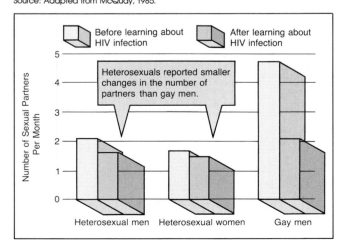

TABLE 15-1 **The Bleak Consequences of AIDS**

Many infections and diseases take advantage of the reduced immunity caused by HIV infection. As such diseases increase in severity and complications mount, death is the eventual result.

DISEASES THAT ATTACK AFTER AIDS WEAKENS IMMUNE SYSTEM	BRIEF DESCRIPTION OF DISEASE
Kaposi's sarcoma	A form of cancer occurring in 30 to 40 percent of AIDS patients, often beginning with a purple lesion on the skin
Pneumocystis pneumonia	An extremely painful, recurrent form of pneumonia with a 50 percent death rate
Recurrent yeast infections	Growth of yeast fungus within the body, including the mouth
Toxoplasmosis	A parasitic disease that attacks the central nervous system, including the brain
Leukemia	Cancer of the blood, characterized by the excessive production of white blood cells
Degeneration of central nervous system	HIV infects the brain and spinal cord, causing paralysis and psychosis

Source: Adapted from Ho et al., 1985; Ognibene, 1984; Resnick et al., 1985.

HIV attacks a certain type of white blood cell, called a T-helper cell, that signals the immune system to produce antibodies against infection (Bridge et al., 1988). HIV attaches to T-helper cells, enters them, and reproduces itself before being released to restart the process in other T-cells and in other cells of the immune system and brain. Patients who test positive for HIV antibodies also receive a blood test to obtain the count of T-helper cells in a milliliter of their blood. Among healthy individuals, the average count is 1000 such cells per milliliter. When the T-helper count ranges between 200 and 500 per milliliter, the patient is diagnosed as having symptomatic HIV infection and should begin drug treatment to delay the onset of a full HIV infection. If the T-helper count falls below 200, the patient is assumed to have an HIV infection.

Cofactors that promote HIV infection include diseases that cause genital ulcers, including herpes, syphilis, chancroid, and granuloma inguinale. These infections have two effects as cofactors—they provide a route of entry for the HIV virus, and they also suppress the immune system's ability to fight it.

One consequence of HIV infection that affects everyone is the cost of detection and treatment (Hilts, 1989). As the 1990s begin, 1 to 1.5 million individuals in the United States have been infected. Over half a million of them have some symptoms and could benefit from treatment. At present the cost of blood tests, physical examinations, counseling, drug treatments, blood monitoring, and so forth, exceeds $10,000 per patient. If only one out of four HIV infected persons were tested and treated, the annual cost in the United States alone would be at least $2.5 billion. If all victims were detected and treated, the cost would be over $10 billion each year. Our present health-care system is unprepared for expenses of such magnitude, and it is difficult to generate public enthusiasm for increased taxes needed to pay the medical expenses of HIV infected patients (Sachs, 1989). The alternative is to decide that only wealthy patients can be treated while all others simply are left to die. These are bleak choices.

The drug azidothymidine (AZT), as of 1990 the only drug approved in the United States for treating HIV infection, is used to delay or lessen its symptoms; it can prolong the life of patients, especially when taken during the early stages of the infection (Volberding et al., 1990). In 1990 the federal government halved the dosage recommended for effectiveness, lowering the cost of treatment with AZT to about $3,000 yearly and reducing the incidence of serious side effects such as severe anemia (Kolata, 1990). Another drug, fluconazole, will soon be available in the United States, having been used in England for years to treat or prevent fungal yeast infections that plague HIV infected persons. Pentamidine is used to fend off pneumocystis pneumonia which is associated with the disease. Despite complaints about the amount of research being devoted to finding a cure for AIDS, the United States Public Health Service is spending more on investigation of this disease than on cancer and heart disease (Wilkenwerder et al., 1989).

HIV infection has been reported in most countries around the world, with the same deadly effects (Ebbesen et al., 1984). Its origin is unknown, and it is possible that, though undiagnosed, it afflicted small numbers of people for decades before the present epidemic occurred. Some have proposed that it originated in the green monkey that lives in central Africa (Benn et al., 1985). This species of monkey transmits several rare diseases to humans, so they are a good suspect (Kanki et al., 1985). More ominous, but undocumented, speculation attributes the disease to germ warfare experiments—by one or more governments—that got out of control (Null, 1989). Whatever the ultimate explanation, HIV probably will remain with us as a threat for the foreseeable future.

In the special insert, *Increasing Enjoyment,* on pages 428 to 429, we outline some of the ways to engage in sexual practices that are safer than others which commonly occurred in the past.

Increasing Enjoyment

SAFER SEXUAL PRACTICES

Given today's reality of rampant STDs, including incurable and fatal varieties, what forms of sexual activity represent safer alternatives? Except for total abstinence or masturbation, there are no alternatives that are risk-free with respect to contracting some of the infections described in this chapter. For most people, interpersonal sex seems to be worth the danger; for example, a survey of almost 2,500 students (mostly college juniors) revealed that only 17 percent of the men and 22 percent of the women were abstaining from intercourse (Segal, 1984). Further, only a minority of sexually active college students use condoms for vaginal or anal intercourse (MacDonald et al., 1990).

Any type of sexual contact can spread STDs. Even moist, passionate kisses transmit disease to a greater degree than dry, chaste ones (Deetz, 1980; Fiumara, 1981). Fingers are not safe, either; if the skin is even slightly broken, bacteria and viruses can enter the bloodstream. In addition, the fingers of an infected individual can transmit disease to a partner's genitals.

Table 15-2 presents some guidelines for sexual practices. This information is least relevant for a person who is confident that he or she has been in an exclusively monogamous relationship since 1978. It is difficult, of course, to be totally certain about the sexual practices and history of one's partner.

Other personal habits should be modified to prevent HIV transmission. For example, no objects should be shared which could be contaminated with blood, including razor blades and toothbrushes. The use of illegal drugs should be avoided, but if drugs are used needles or syringes should not be shared.

Penile-vaginal intercourse can be made safer by using a diaphragm with spermicide applied inside the vagina, in combination with a condom (Felman, 1982b). These protective measures should be taken before and during any penetration. Studies of gonorrhea infection indicate that a spermicide alone has no protective effect. A woman who uses a spermicide containing nonoxynol-9 plus either a diaphragm or a partner's condom is 55 to 59 percent less likely to contract gonorrhea (Austin et al., 1984). Spermicide containing nonoxynol-9 kills HIV in the laboratory (Hicks et al., 1985). It should be noted that oral contraceptives change the chemical balance inside the vagina, increasing the female's susceptibility to STDs. In Chapter 5, variations in the effectiveness of condoms as a birth control device were discussed. Latex condoms offer more protection against pregnancy and STDs than condoms made from skins, for example. However, condoms are not a foolproof protection against HIV transmission; they may break or slip off, whether they are used for contraception or disease prevention or both.

Older generations were advised to wash, urinate, and take antibiotics to avoid STDs. Research has shown that each of these methods is faulty. Washing genitals before intercourse can be a sensual form of foreplay and cleanliness may appeal to both partners, but the organisms that cause disease remain inside the body and in its fluids (Fiumara, 1980). Urinating before and after intercourse may flush away a few organisms and reduce the risk of urinary infections, but it does little to protect the individual from an infected partner (Hooper, 1978; Riggs, 1979).

As suggested earlier in this chapter, the routine use of antibiotics has serious drawbacks. During World War II, many U.S servicemen took antibiotics regularly or after any sexual contact with a stranger. Because drug-resistant STDs developed, the constant use of antibiotics destroyed vari-

TABLE 15-2 **Words to the Wise About Sexual Interactions**

These guidelines for safer sexual practices were developed because of the need to avoid HIV infection and other, less serious STDs. Sexual activity with a partner involves risks and responsibilities.

UNSAFE SEXUAL BEHAVIORS	SAFER SEXUAL PRACTICES
Ejaculation in the mouth	Use of condom or ejaculation outside of mouth
Ejaculation into vagina without a condom	Use of condom and spermicide* during every act of vaginal intercourse
Ejaculation into rectum without a condom	Use of condom, lubrication, and spermicide* during every act of anal intercourse
	Wash and thoroughly dry devices such as a vibrator between uses and do not share "sex toys" with others
	Obtain testing of partners for HIV antibodies if pregnancy is desired
	Kissing
	Massage
	Masturbation, alone or mutual
	Oral-genital contact

	Selectivity in choosing sexual partners, favoring those who:
	  do not inject drugs
	  do not visit prostitutes
	  do not have other partners

*The recommended spermicide is nonoxynol-9.
Source: Nichols, 1986.

ous beneficial bacteria and encouraged superinfections, and also because some individuals became allergic to the drugs over time, this practice was eventually stopped (Chapel, 1981). In general, drug therapy has been abandoned as a **prophylactic**, or preventive, technique.

A useful practice is to inspect your own genitals and those of your partner. If any signs of STDs, such as a discharge or sores, are present, politely retreat and consider nonsexual interactions plus medical treatment. If you (or your partner) have

other sexual relationships, a medical examination for STDs several times a year is recommended (Yarber, 1978). A condom plus spermicide is a wise precaution if your partner is a relative stranger or has been sexually active with others. Any partner unwilling to take precautions or who belittles your concern is best avoided.

In a New York City bathhouse, a poster provided by the Gay Men's Crisis organization reads, "GREAT SEX, Don't Let AIDS stop it" (Weiss, 1985). This same slogan could be adapted to anyone who is sexu-

ally active: "GREAT SEX, Act responsibly."

Those in the United States who need information about STDs quickly and without visiting a physician or clinic can call the following numbers:

STD National Hotline—
800-227-8922.

National AIDS Hotline—
800-342-AIDS.

Herpes Resource Center Hotline—
415-328-7710.

Summarizing the Information about Infectious Disease . . .

Sexually transmissible diseases (STDs) are caused by many different organisms. Bacterial STDs, including **gonorrhea**, **syphilis**, and **chlamydia**, are curable with antibiotics. Other bacterial infections

(**prostatitis**, **urinary cystitis**, and **toxic shock syndrome**) usually originate in ways other than sexual contact, but affect the pelvic area and the sexual organs. Viral STDs have no cure at present, but their symptoms can be partially relieved—**genital herpes**, **genital warts**, and **acquired immune deficiency syndrome (AIDS)**, due to HIV infection. So far, AIDS is an incurable, fatal disease, and the number of infected individuals continues to rise throughout the world. An additional series of STDs are curable, including **yeast infection**, **trichomoniasis**, **scabies**, and **lice**.

The high incidence of STDs and their rapid transmission to others mean that we should all be aware of the meaning of safer sexual activity. This is especially true with respect to the incurable and fatal disease, HIV infection, and the role of anal intercourse and other sexual acts in transmitting it. Effective STD behavior requires accurate information and the willingness to take the necessary steps for prevention and treatment. Sexual guilt and anxiety interfere with each step of the process.

To Find Out More About Infectious Disease . . .

Bridge, T.P., Mirsky, A.F., & Goodwin, F.K. (Eds.). (1988). *Psychological, neuropsychiatric, and substance abuse aspects of AIDS*. New York: Raven Press.

Experts provide information about multiple aspects of AIDS, including its physiological causes and effects, the psychological consequences, risk behaviors, legal issues, and many other topics.

Mandel, B., & Mandel, B. (1985). *Play safe: How to avoid getting sexually transmitted diseases*. Foster City, Calif.: Center for Health Information.

This book has a number of practical suggestions about preventing STDs and avoiding their transmission to others.

Ostrow, D. G., Sandholzer, T. A., & Felman, Y. M. (1983). *Sexually transmitted diseases in homosexual men: Diagnosis, treatment, and research*. New York: Plenum.

Experts on the topic of STDs in sexually active gays present useful research findings. They also discuss treatments of the many medical problems associated with AIDS.

CHAPTER SIXTEEN

DRUGS, DISABILITY, AND DISEASE:
Effects on Sexual Functioning

Most of us are aware of how badly we function when something is wrong with our bodies. For example, a bad headache can interfere with the ability to concentrate. A severe cold can make it almost impossible to do well on an examination. Too much alcohol can turn a good driver into a dangerous one. When similar factors disrupt sexual functioning, however, many people are confused and embarrassed about the effects. The following account by a young woman of her spoiled wedding night is an example of how a common physiological response to alcohol can easily be misinterpreted.

The worst experience I ever had with sex was on the night that was supposed to be the most special. Doug and I had a very nice, informal wedding with our families and a few close friends. We were married by our pastor in the chapel behind the regular church, and then the whole group went out to a lakeside restaurant for the reception.

That was where the trouble started. Doug is not that much of a drinker, but he was hitting the champagne pretty steadily. People kept coming up to congratulate us, raising their glasses for a toast, and Doug drank a little with every one of them. I don't usually drink at all, so I barely sipped mine.

By the time we sat down to eat, my new husband was feeling no pain, and the food didn't slow him down a bit. We tried to dance a couple of times, but he wasn't too steady on his feet. I was getting embarrassed, and my mother was giving him some hard looks.

We finally were ready to leave, and Doug's brother rushed us out the back door to his car so he could drive us to the Marriott. We were gone before anyone had time to make jokes or mess up the car. While Hal drove, the two of us were in the back seat, and Doug was kissing me and trying to touch me under my clothes. I whispered to him to wait and not make a fool of himself.

When we were in our room, Doug had only one thing on his mind, and our clothes were off in the first three minutes. The hotel supplied a bottle of champagne (just what we didn't need), two glasses, and some fruit, so we had one more drink before getting into bed.

This wasn't our first time together, you know, but it was the first time as husband and wife. I felt excited and happy at the same time. After a few minutes, though, I realized that Doug wasn't getting hard. He got on top of me and tried to get started, but there wasn't much he could do. We tried a lot of different things, but nothing worked.

As high as he was, he still was upset and ashamed about his problem. In a few minutes, though, he rolled over and was dead to the world. I lay there crying and wondering if getting married had made him lose interest in me. I felt like going back home to my parents.

Everything was fine the next morning, and now I know that the only problem with Doug was all that champagne. He learned his lesson. I wish we could go back and live our wedding night all over again. Then, we'd do it right.

Laurel, age 23

As Doug and Laurel—and many others—have discovered, alcohol can dramatically affect sexual responding. It is important to learn as much as possible about such influences in order to be able to prevent the kind of incident Laurel described and to know how to interpret such experiences correctly when they do occur.

Sexual functioning can be adversely affected by many of the substances—both legal and illegal—people use and by mental, physical, and emotional disabilities. Though the immediate or short-term effects of alcohol and various psychoactive drugs may facilitate sexual arousal, the eventual effects most often interfere with or prevent sexual activity altogether. We describe *how drugs affect sexual functioning*. The sexual needs of those who are handicapped often are overlooked, but we discuss the importance of recognizing and understanding the relationship between *disability and sexuality*. In addition, many medical conditions ranging from cancer to cardiovascular disease may disrupt the patient's sexual life, and we explore the *effect of illnesses on sexual behavior*. Sexual problems frequently arise as the result of either physical or psychological factors, and a special section describes procedures designed to *distinguish organic and psychogenic causes of sexual difficulties*. We also provide information about ways to *promote sexual health*.

How Drugs Affect Sexual Functioning

Whatever your own attitudes about legal and illegal drugs, sex and drugs are closely associated in American society—as is reflected in movies, songs, television, and advertising. Couples drink alcohol or smoke pot as a sexual preliminary, smoke cigarettes during the resolution phase following orgasm, and use many substances that promise to enhance sexual pleasure. What is known about the relationship between drug use and sexuality?

■ Alcohol Use and Abuse

The most widely used drug is ethanol (alcohol). It has both immediate and long-term effects on sexual functioning.

Immediate, Short-term Effects of Alcohol. When a person drinks, the first effect of alcohol on sexual responses is enhancing. It reduces inhibitions about sexuality—and other behavior as well. This relaxing, anxiety-reducing aspect of alcohol accounts for its popularity in social situations. As more alcohol is consumed, however, its second effect is to reduce sexual responsiveness.

The point at which such interference occurs depends on several factors, including the person's past drinking experience, his or her body weight, and the amount of alcohol consumed. When inhibitions are lowered *and* physiological responses are impaired, it is literally an instance in which the spirit is willing while the flesh is weak.

Because they tend to weigh less than men, women ordinarily require less alcohol to become intoxicated. In both sexes, this drug reduces sexual excitement. Usually, after more than two mixed drinks or glasses of wine, both sexes experience reduced sensitivity, which decreases the pleasure of stimulation and lowers the intensity of arousal and orgasm. With additional drinks, a man may not be able to achieve a full erection or to ejaculate; a woman may not lubricate sufficiently or reach orgasm.

In laboratory experiments, college students were given varying amounts of alcohol and then were asked to masturbate to orgasm (Malatesta et al., 1979, 1982). Figure 16-1 summarizes the findings. Without drinks, both men and women reached orgasm after about six minutes of self-stimulation. After three to five mixed drinks or glasses of wine, stimulation had to continue twice as long in order for the subjects to reach orgasm.

You might be thinking that this experiment indicates that people who are drunk can enjoy sexual stimulation for a longer period than those who are sober. For both men and women, in fact, the stimulation is less pleasurable when they are intoxicated, and it becomes increasingly difficult to remain excited (Hammond, 1984; Wilson and Lawson, 1976). Is it possible that some additional source of stimulation—such as sexual movies—might remedy the problem? The answer is "no." Even in the presence of erotic

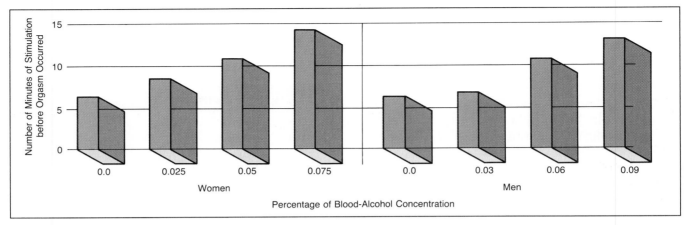

FIGURE 16-1 *THE MORE ALCOHOL CONSUMED, THE MORE DELAYED THE ORGASM* In a laboratory investigation, twenty-four male and eighteen female undergraduates were given controlled amounts of alcohol and then instructed to masturbate to orgasm. As alcohol injection increased, so did the time required to reach orgasm.
Source: Data from Malatesta et al., 1979, 1982.

stimuli, alcohol depresses the physical response to foreplay (Fisher et al., 1986).

Delayed, Long-term Effects of Alcohol. The long-term abuse of alcohol can negatively influence personal relationships. For example, the drinker's attention is directed toward the drug rather than toward the loved one and his or her happiness (Coleman, 1982). Because alcohol reduces inhibitions to aggression as well as to sex, the problem drinker becomes increasingly hostile toward others, sometimes verbally and sometimes physically.

Over time, an alcoholic is likely to experience a deterioration in his or her sex life. Both male and female problem drinkers become less interested in sex and less able to function sexually (Hammond, 1981; Van Thiel, 1980). Half of the alcoholics of both sexes have difficulty in becoming aroused, and one in six experiences problems in reaching orgasm.

Infertility also can occur, and women who drink while pregnant often produce unusually short offspring with mental retardation and abnormal genitals as a result of the **fetal alcohol syndrome** (FAS). Men may develop **alcoholic feminization** because of liver disease and its interference with the body's normal production and use of estrogen and testosterone. They may, as a result, develop large breasts, lose facial hair, and have shrunken testicles (Drucker, 1982).

Psychological and interpersonal problems also impair sexual functioning in that overdrinking leads to depression, low self-esteem, and marital instability. Because the alcoholic is physically and psychologically dependent on this drug, attempts to stop drinking can be painful and beyond his or her ability to accomplish without professional help.

■ Illegal Substances: Psychoactive Drugs

Psychoactive drugs are those that alter mood and thought patterns, remaining in the body for an extended time period. Though alcohol is usually excreted within twenty-four hours, psychoactive drugs require days or even months to be eliminated from the system entirely. We will discuss how marijuana, cocaine, opiates, and other psychoactive drugs affect sexual functioning.

Marijuana: Getting High on Pot. About half of all adolescents and young adults in the United States have used marijuana (also known as "grass," "pot," or "Mary Jane"). Of those who have tried it, approximately 20 percent are frequent users—that is, they smoke it at least once a week. Marijuana's active ingredient, THC, has been investigated extensively in recent years to determine its behavioral effects, including sexual effects (Peterson, 1981). Users report that it enhances their awareness of whatever they are attending to (Fabian and Fishkin, 1981). Research shows that long-term, heavy users do not suffer a loss of mental capacity or the ability to perform psychological tasks (Schaeffer et al., 1981). For some, however, pot produces extreme anxiety, so they tend to discontinue its use (DuPont, 1982).

Like other psychoactive drugs, marijuana's effect on sexuality depends in part on its physical effects and in part on the emotional reactions of the user. Marijuana, like alcohol, is a depressant, but it produces the feeling of euphoria by acting on the pleasure center of the brain—the medial forebrain bund. Because this same area is activated during sexual excitement, marijuana has a direct influence on sexual experience (Nahas, 1981). Marijuana users of both sexes report that the drug heightens sexual desire for their partners, makes sexual acts more pleasurable and satisfying, and enhances the sensations of taste and touch (Weller and Halikas, 1984).

Despite these positive self-reports, marijuana also has some negative sexual effects. Men who regularly smoke more than four marijuana cigarettes (joints) per week have lower levels of testosterone and sperm production, as a result of its negative effect on the hypothalamus (Kolodny et al., 1974). Women who are consistent users may develop irregular menstrual cycles, problems with ovulation, and vaginal dryness because of lowered estrogen production (Nahas, 1981). In short, the pleasures and sexual enhancement described by marijuana users eventually may be followed by physiological problems.

Cocaine: Highs and Lows.   Within fifteen to thirty minutes of sniffing cocaine ("coke"), there is a peak effect, disinhibition, and a euphoric feeling. Such effects quickly dissipate, and the user "crashes," becoming depressed and tired (Mirin, 1982). Crack is a very potent and addictive form of purified cocaine, which can be smoked ("free-basing"), with a general effect similar to that of the powdered form (Morley, 1989). It also enhances sexual functioning in the early stages of its use, but those who continue smoking crack find that sexual desire and arousal sharply decline, and orgasms occur much less frequently.

Cocaine has the reputation of stimulating sexual desire and arousal. An invitation to sniff cocaine usually implies a sexual offer, as well, in that the sexual interest of each user is expected to increase. Although the first stage may have the expected enhancing effect, crashing interferes with sexual performance, including interest, excitement, vaginal lubrication, erection, and orgasm (Cocores and Gold, 1989).

Some men attempt to prolong sexual interactions by rubbing cocaine on the penis, but it has a numbing, anesthetic effect. Sex is less pleasurable, and, when the crashing stage occurs, there is loss of erection (McDonald, 1983).

Another negative effect of continued cocaine sniffing is the decline in sexual attractiveness when the user's nasal septum is destroyed, causing a persistant drip from the nose (Benedek, 1980). Lung disease also may develop. Robin Williams suggests in one of his comedy routines that cocaine is a tremendous drug for a guy who wants to spend a great deal of money to become impotent, develop paranoia, and lose part of his nose.

"Crack babies," those born to mothers who used the drug during pregnancy, tend to have numerous problems including low birth weight, a dysfunctioning immune system, and skeletal deformity (Quindlen, 1990).

Heroin and Other Opiates.   Opiate drugs (such as heroin) lead directly to sexual dysfunction by depressing the central nervous system and the sex centers of the brain. The addicted person eventually loses interest in everything—including sex—except the drug. As with many other psychoactive drugs, 50 to 60 percent of heroin users lose sexual desire, find it difficult to become excited, and cannot reach orgasm.

New male addicts sometimes develop **priapism**—a prolonged, painful erection without ejaculation. Although Priapus was the Greek god of male procreative power, priapism has a negative rather than a positive effect on fertility. Opiates eventually block even this abnormal erectile response (Greenberg, 1984). Though large amounts of heroin interfere with ovulation and conception, pregnancies sometimes occur among addicts, and their newborns experience withdrawal symptoms.

One legal alternative to heroin is the medical use of methodone as a substitute, but this substance has the same negative effects on sexual functioning and fertility as the drug it replaces (Mirin, 1981; Weiss, 1982).

Among the unusual symptoms of heroin withdrawal is the occurrence of **spontaneous orgasm.** The individual has sudden, unintended orgasms, including ejaculation in males. This response occurs without sexual stimulation and is a surprise to the person undergoing withdrawal. Spontaneous orgasm is a positive physical sign that the body is breaking free of opiate addiction.

Other Street Drugs. *Nitrites* ("poppers") are used to heighten and prolong orgasm. In fact, the drug distorts time perception and probably has no effect on the actual duration of orgasm. In order to experience the nitrite effect, the user must have the container in his or her hand as the sexual act occurs in order to be able to release the drug at the moment orgasm begins. The drug dilates the arteries in the abdomen and creates a sensation of warmth.

Amyl nitrate has required a prescription since 1969, so users now rely on a nonprescription form, *isobutyl nitrite*. This substance is sold under various names, including Locker Room, Bullet, and Rush. This drug poses several potential dangers, including a sudden drop in blood pressure (Hollister, 1978).

Barbiturates ("downers") are prescribed for various physical and mental disorders. They can enhance sexual pleasure by reducing inhibitions, much as alcohol does.

For centuries, an amazing array of products has been taken to induce sexual excitement in oneself or in a potential partner. For the most part, money simply has been wasted on these supposed **aphrodisiacs.** Some of these substances, such as oysters and turtle eggs, are harmless and sexually irrelevant. Others are harmful. An example is "Spanish fly" (cantharides), which is extracted from a beetle found in southern Europe. The pulverized bodies of these insects are made into a powder, which can cause diabetes, ulcers, and even death. The false belief in Spanish fly as an aphrodisiac arose because it irritates the urinary bladder and urethra, and the resulting burning sensation can be misperceived as sexual excitement (Cohen, 1982). Because it causes the blood vessels of the penis to widen, one result is priapism. Over time, the bodily irritation negatively affects the genitals and interferes with erection.

Also note that many legal drugs prescribed by physicians to treat specific medical conditions can have side effects that interfere with sexual responding. For example, some of the beta blockers used to lower high blood pressure may impair male sexual functioning. Such problems often can be solved simply by switching to a different drug.

Disability and Sexuality

Though most people do not like to admit it, there is a widespread prejudice against people with mental or physical disabilities. One underlying reason is that the disabled are *different* from others in their appearance or behavior. For example, they are missing a limb, are unable to control their bodily movements, find it difficult to learn or comprehend, or must use a device such as a wheelchair, be guided by a seeing eye dog, or wear a hearing aid.

Negative responses are also based on the presumed *threat* posed by the disabled—"If it could happen to them, it could happen to me!" For this reason, a handicapped person who is most similar to oneself and most likable is especially threatening (Byrne and Lamberth, 1974; Novak and Lerner, 1968). In experiments, it is a common finding that people receive more help when their behavior is pleasant rather than unpleasant. In contrast, Katz et al. (1978) found that a person in a wheelchair actually receives more help after behaving unpleasantly than pleasantly (see Figure 16-2). Apparently, unpleasant disabled persons are perceived as unhappy and deserving of aid, while nice disabled persons pose a threat because they are too much like ourselves.

Although the response to someone who is disabled is seldom overtly negative, it is very common to avoid or ignore such a person—to look the other way. Much of society responds to the sexual interests and rights of the disabled in this same way. People prefer to avoid thinking about such topics and do not even consider sexuality in this context. Institutions, too, seem to assume that anyone who is disabled does not (or should not) be interested in sex. Legal progress has been made in this respect, but there is still less than total sexual freedom for the disabled in institutional settings.

■ Mental Disability

Historically, persons with mental retardation have been discriminated against in being able to express their sexuality. In 1927, the U.S. Supreme Court ruled that the mentally handicapped legally could be required to undergo sterilization. This ruling held for many years, even though heredity plays a

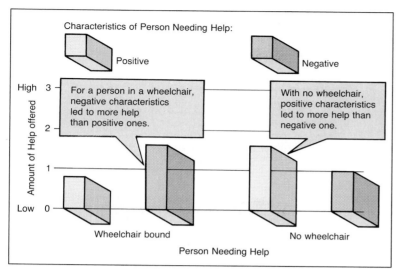

FIGURE 16-2 *HELPING THE HANDICAPPED: ONLY IF THEY ARE UNLIKE ME* A nondisabled person who behaves pleasantly is helped more than one who behaves unpleasantly. When the same person is seated in a wheelchair, unpleasant behavior elicits more help than pleasant behavior. This experiment is one of many that indicate a sometimes subtle reaction to the threat posed by the disabled. The more pleasant a disabled individual is and the more he or she is similar to ourselves, the greater the threat because it raises the possibility that a disability can happen to someone "like us."
Source: Based on data in Katz et al., 1978.

role in only some forms of mental deficiency (Hepner, 1979). Individuals who have mental retardation often have been regarded as either asexual and uninterested in sex or as sexually impulsive and uncontrolled, but neither stereotype is accurate.

Though sterilization is no longer legally mandated, several states prohibit sexual intercourse with a woman having mental retardation (Frankel, 1978). These women are assumed to be incapable of giving informed consent to participate in sex, regardless of their specific intellectual skills. Interestingly, female adolescents with mental retardation do not differ from their intellectually normal peers in the frequency of unwanted pregnancies (Coppolillo, 1984).

Even though many mentally disabled individuals now live and work in semi-independent environments, prejudices about their sexual needs remain widespread. Hall et al. (1973) found that parents of retarded teenagers are fairly accurate in estimating what their offspring know about sex, but are much less accurate in perceiving their children's liberal attitudes about sex.

Those with mental retardation need sex education even more than others in our society, because they usually do not have comparable opportunities to learn about sex from friends or from books. Some individuals with retardation live in institutions; the best of these meet many of their needs, providing work and leisure-time activities. Sexual behavior, however, is most often forbidden. Adolescents who live outside

of institutions know more about sex than institutionalized adolescents matched for IQ, probably because of contact with others (Hall and Morris, 1976).

Abramson et al. (1988) argued that those with retardation should be guaranteed sex education to help them attain sexual expression in socially acceptable ways. They need to be taught, for example, that sexual intercourse causes pregnancy. Those with mild retardation—with an IQ between 51 and 70—function intellectually like a seven- to twelve-year-old, and they can be taught appropriate ways to act responsibly in expressing sexual needs. With moderate retardation, individuals have IQs between 26 and 50, and function like three- to seven-year-olds. They create a greater educational challenge but can be taught to avoid sexual abuse and public exposure. With an IQ below 26, severe retardation leads to intellectual functioning like two-year-olds, and sexual education generally is not possible.

■ Physical Handicaps

Even to the casual observer, physical disabilities are usually immediately apparent, and people respond in much the same way they do to those with mental retardation. Sex is thus seen as somehow inappropriate for them. People who respond in that fashion do not even attempt to justify their reactions. The authors observed one instance in which acquaintances expressed surprise and disapproval when a woman became pregnant while recovering from a broken leg.

Blindness and Deafness. To some degree, sexuality is affected by physical limitations because a person's physical condition may interfere with learning and practicing the necessary interpersonal skills. Blindness, for example, obviously has no effect on physical development or on the timing of puberty and sexual maturation. It does, however, prevent the person from seeing either themself or others in the nude, and sex differences in anatomy may be somewhat mysterious. Blind men are found to have less knowledge than sighted men about sexual anatomy, sexual behavior, and related topics (Welbourne-Moglia, 1984). Deafness can interfere with learning abstract concepts such as femininity, and sex education at home is even more difficult than usual because parents typically do not know sign language.

Blindness and deafness also affect the age at which sexual interactions first begin, in part because parents tend to be overprotective of their blind or deaf children. Another reason for late sexual development is that peers often exclude the blind and the deaf from social activities, presumably because of general prejudices about the handicapped. Parents and peers are even more restrictive in treating disabled girls than boys, assuming that females are more vulnerable than males (Blank, 1982). Given these various impediments to knowledge and the opportunity to learn and practice social skills, it can become difficult for the blind and the deaf to form close relationships.

Spinal-Cord Injury. One kind of physical disability can have a direct effect on sexual functioning in addition to the effects of prejudiced attitudes and beliefs. Spinal-cord injuries (SCIs) are most often caused by automobile and recreational accidents. When there are breaks in the spine, disruption of sexual functioning is one of the possible physical consequences. The specific location and the extent of the break determine whether a paralyzed person can respond to sexual stimulation because all sensation is absent below the level of the break. *Paraplegia* means that the legs are paralyzed; *quadriplegia* indicates that all four limbs are paralyzed.

Men with SCI may have erections but be unable to ejaculate. An erection can occur as a simple reflexive response to physical stimulation (such as rubbing the genitals) but not in response to erotic fantasies or dreams. The man with SCI cannot feel that his penis is erect and is aware of it only if he sees it. Of the male SCI patients whose injury is high enough on the spinal cord, 90 percent have reflex erections; with an injury lower on the cord, only about half experience them. About 5 percent of SCI men are able to ejaculate, but retrograde ejaculation of semen into the bladder is common.

When the injury to the spinal cord is incomplete, four out of five men are able to have intercourse. If erections are a problem, vaginal intercourse can be facilitated with a technique called *stuffing.* The partner places the soft penis in her vagina and thrusts her hips, being careful to avoid letting the penis slip out.

Some SCI patients have a strong sensation of orgasm, even though there is no erection (males) or vaginal lubrication (females). These nongenital climaxes, known as **paraorgasms,** or **phantom orgasms,** are produced by the intact portions of their nervous systems (Webster, 1983). Sometimes, these and other sexual responses return several months or even years following the injury, so counseling about sexual functioning is strongly recommended.

SCI women are commonly misperceived as being less sexually handicapped than SCI men. Some women with such an injury *can* respond physically to sexual stimulation. If, however, the cord is completely severed, she will have little vaginal lubrication or expansion and will not feel the genital sensations associated with orgasm. Like men, women may respond with paraorgasms. Those who have not experienced orgasm prior to the injury tend not to recognize or enjoy this experience (Leyson and Powell, 1979).

In one investigation of SCI women, fifteen out of twenty-four reported that their sexual activity was very enjoyable despite their physical condition. One said, "I feel like a very effective human being and injury has little to do with it except, perhaps, it made me mature faster and gave me an outlook which doesn't get hung up on little things" (Fitting et al., 1978, p. 153).

When the SCI person returns to an active sexual

life, his or her self-concept is likely to receive a boost. Sexual accomplishments following the accident help the individual feel attractive and effective. A sharing, intimate relationship with a partner is extremely beneficial. Many learn to enjoy sexual acts other than intercourse, such as oral-genital and vibrator sex, reporting increased sensitivity in the breasts, face, and so on.

Women with such injuries continue to menstruate and ovulate. Conception and birth are not affected, except that the inability to feel uterine contractions makes it difficult to know when labor has begun (Bleyberg, 1982). As a result, it is advisable for such women to enter the hospital before the due date so they can be monitored and observed. Vaginal delivery is usually possible.

■ Psychological Conditions

As we have described in several contexts, attitudes, beliefs, and emotions can influence sexual behavior. It is not surprising, then, that severe psychological disturbances can have major effects on sexuality. Two examples follow.

Depression. Severe depression often disrupts sexual behavior. The depressed individual usually has less sexual desire, is less able to become sexually excited, and may find it difficult to reach orgasm (Kroop, 1980b). It is estimated that one in five people becomes seriously depressed at some point, and at least half experience a reduced desire for sex until the depression is relieved. Depression interferes with social functioning, including the formation and maintenance of close relationships (Gotlib and Lee, 1989).

The depression-induced changes in sexuality can cause couples to break up. Also, a breakup that occurs for other reasons can cause depression and consequent sexual problems. In either instance, the person can benefit from professional help with both depression and sexual malfunctioning (Garvey, 1985).

Schizophrenia. Schizophrenia is a severe psychotic condition characterized by difficulties in reality-testing and withdrawal into an inner world of fantasy. The term *schizophrenia* (meaning "split personality") is commonly, and inaccurately, applied to those with multiple personalities, but the two conditions are totally unrelated.

Schizophrenics frequently have hallucinations in which fantasy is confused with reality. The person usually develops delusions and functions on the basis of his or her unrealistic beliefs. When the hallucinations and delusions are intense, the person's response to external events may be quite inappropriate from the viewpoint of others.

Given the severity of this emotional disturbance, it is not surprising that schizophrenics have sexual difficulties. The problems partly stem from the condition itself, because it interferes with the ability to enjoy most aspects of everyday life. In addition, schizophrenics tend to withdraw from others, and this isolation makes it hard for them to develop any relationships, including sexual ones (Raboch, 1984).

Schizophrenics who *do* have intimate partners are likely to have unsuccessful sexual interactions. One investigation of schizophrenic women (see Fig-

FIGURE 16-3 *EFFECTS OF SCHIZOPHRENIA ON SEXUAL FUNCTIONING* Schizophrenia is often accompanied by sexual malfunctioning; twenty women with this disorder had greater difficulty in reaching orgasm and felt more turned off about sex than fifteen normal women. The schizophrenic patients did not attribute the problem to an inadequate amount of foreplay; in fact, a much higher percentage of normal women expressed dissatisfaction with the amount of foreplay.
Source: Data from Friedman and Harrison, 1984.

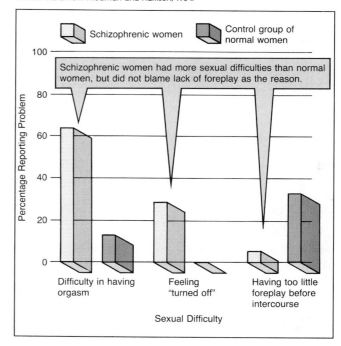

ure 16-3) found that less than half of them experienced orgasm (Friedman and Harrison, 1984).

Even when the psychosis is under control as a function of drug therapy, problems with sexual responding tend to occur as a side effect. These drugs often disrupt sexual functioning because they act to impair vasocongestion (Nestoros, 1981).

Of historical interest is the role played by schizophrenia in reinforcing negative attitudes and beliefs about masturbation. When mental hospitals first were established, staff members observed that schizophrenics frequently masturbated in public despite the inappropriateness of this behavior. The patient engages in such acts, of course, because he or she is absorbed in a world of fantasy as opposed to the reality of the surroundings. Medical observers of that era, however, interpreted such behavior quite differently. They assumed that masturbation was the basic problem that *caused* the psychosis. On the basis of this misconception, the medical profession was in-

strumental in convincing many parents to prevent their offspring from masturbating at all costs in order to avoid insanity.

Illnesses That Affect Sexuality

Besides drugs and disabilities, several illnesses have an impact on sexual functioning. For example, cancer may require surgery to remove malignancies in the genital organs or breasts. In addition to surgical interventions, conditions such as diabetes, neurological disorders, and cardiovascular disease also can influence sexual behavior.

Before describing the specifics of these illnesses, however, we will consider a more general issue that applies to most of the sexual malfunctioning described in this chapter. To what degree is sexual functioning disturbed by the physical effects of a given drug, disability, or illness and to what degree is it

Highlighting Research

DISTINGUISHING BETWEEN ORGANIC AND PSYCHOGENIC CAUSES OF SEXUAL DIFFICULTIES

If a man drinks alcohol, has an injured spinal cord, or develops a severe depression, he may experience interference with having erections. Once he becomes aware of erectile problems, his interpretation of the situation and his worries about it can then make the problem worse. At this point, both physical and psychological factors can act to impair sexual performance, and it becomes important to distinguish between them in order to know how best to deal with the problem (Ford and Levine, 1982).

Organic causes of sexual dysfunction stem from physical factors, while **psychogenic causes of sexual dysfunction** are based on the person's attitudes, beliefs, emotions, and expectancies. Once we know that the person's sexual responses are not typical, how can we determine the cause?

Because personality tests and other common measures cannot provide a reliable answer (Jefferson et al., 1989), the primary way is to assess whether sexual excitement occurs during deep sleep. Penile erection and vaginal vasocongestion usually take place during rapid eye movement (REM) sleep. If there is a physical problem, such responses cannot occur. If the problem is psychological, these sexual reactions usually *do* occur.

For males with erectile difficulties, **nocturnal penile tumescence (NPT)** is measured for three consecutive nights. The more frequently the man has nocturnal erections, the lower the probability that his sexual problems are organic (Marshall et al., 1981; Procci et al., 1983; Procci and Martin, 1984). Often, NPT observations are performed in a sleep laboratory, where the man is attached to a strain

gauge that detects and records the occurrence of any erections. NPT kits also have been developed for home use.

In one investigation, nocturnal erections were observed in three groups—diabetic men who had erectile problems, nondiabetic men with the same dysfunction, and a control group without sexual dysfunction (Zuckerman et al., 1985). Figure 16-4 shows the NPT results. Nocturnal erections were least among the diabetics, and 58 percent were diagnosed as having an organic sexual dysfunction. In contrast, only 23 percent of the nondiabetics with erectile problems were found to have an organic cause, and no one in the control group was so diagnosed. NPT can be a useful technique for distinguishing the causes of sexual dysfunction, although additional tests of the man's responsiveness to sexually explicit films can provide

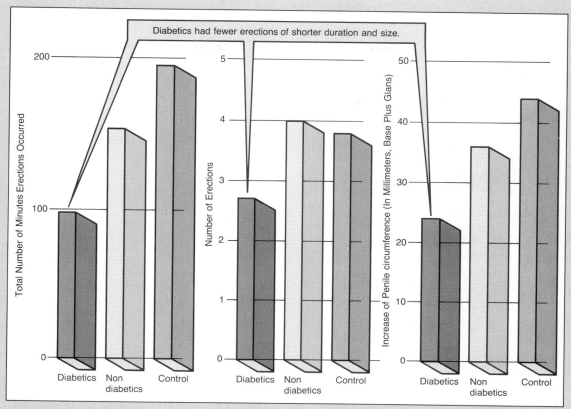

FIGURE 16-4 *NOCTURNAL PENILE TUMESCENCE: ESTABLISHING THE CAUSE OF ERECTILE DYSFUNCTION* Men with erectile problems (a sample of forty-seven diabetics and thirty-one nondiabetics) were compared with twenty-two functional male controls with respect to nocturnal erections. In a sleep laboratory, erections were monitored. The organic basis of such dysfunctions among diabetic patients was confirmed, in that diabetic males had the fewest, briefest, and smallest nocturnal erections of the three groups.
Source: Based on data in Zuckerman et al., 1985.

a more reliable basis for making a correct diagnosis (Wincze et al., 1988).

When women undergo pelvic surgery (to remove the uterus, for example), sexual dysfunction is a common aftereffect (Levine and Yost, 1976). The surgery may or may not be the causal factor because the psychological effects of losing a reproductive organ can have a negative effect on sexuality. Vaginal vasocongestion is mea-sured during sleep to determine whether periods of sexual excitement occur (Rogers et al., 1985). As with men, sexual responding during sleep indicates a psychogenic rather than an organic dysfunction.

Controversies have been generated about the relative roles of psychogenic and organic factors in causing sexual problems. Until recently, most sexual dysfunctions were believed to be psychological in origin (Masters and Johnson, 1970). Most professionals now agree that both physical and psychological elements cause malfunctioning (Martin et al., 1983). For men, sexual problems seem to be based about equally on the two types of causes. For women, sexual problems most often are based on either psychogenic causes or the inadequate sexual techniques of their partners.

caused by the person's reaction to or interpretation of the situation? In the special section *Highlighting Research*, on pages 440 to 441, we discuss how organic and psychogenic causes of sexual problems can be distinguished.

■ Cancer

A major illness such as cancer disrupts many aspects of everyday life. Any illness may affect sexuality by causing weakness, pain, or fatigue, or as the result of the emotional strains of being sick. Sometimes those who are ill believe incorrectly that they cannot engage in sex or enjoy it. In addition, the treatment of illness can affect sexual functioning—for example, the side effects of medications or physical changes produced by surgery. Among cancer patients, most report having less sexual desire than before they became ill (Leiber, 1978).

Uterine and Cervical Cancer. The uterus and cervix are the most common locations for cancer of the reproductive organs among women, followed by cancer of the ovaries and of the vulva (Batts, 1982). About half of the women who develop cancer in one of these organs stop having intercourse, primarily because they no longer desire it (Harris et al., 1982). Figure 16-5 summarizes some of the changes in sexuality among female cancer patients.

Among the factors predisposing women to cervical cancer are smoking (Trevathan, 1984) and contracting STDs repeatedly (Krantz et al., 1984). Sexual practices also can increase the probability of developing cervical cancer; a woman who has multiple partners before the age of eighteen doubles her risk for this disease (Sebastian, 1980).

Breast Cancer.   Cancer of the breast can occur in either sex, as noted in Chapter 15, but women develop it much more frequently than men.

One in ten American women develops breast cancer, which is the second leading cause of cancer deaths among American women (National Cancer Institute, 1989). Of all cancers among women, lung cancer is responsible for the highest number of deaths. Each year, about 142,000 American women are diagnosed as having breast cancer. The disease also affects men; in the United States 900 men are found to have breast cancer annually.

The abnormal growth of cells spreads beyond the breasts to lymph nodes and other areas of the body in half the cases, so this form of cancer is clearly dangerous. Early diagnosis, before the malignancy spreads, can mean the difference between life and death.

As described in the last section of this chapter, female breast cancer can be detected by manual examination of the breasts and by the use of mammograms. For men, there is also a warning sign—

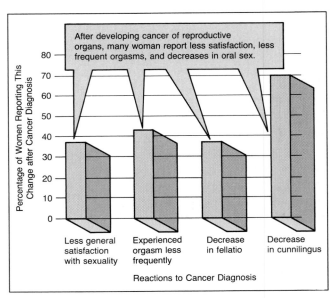

FIGURE 16-5   *THE NEGATIVE EFFECTS OF CANCER ON SEXUAL FUNCTIONING*   In a study of ninety-six women who had cancer of the reproductive organs, they indicated impaired sexual satisfaction, including a decrease in the frequency of orgasms, fellatio, and cunnilingus.
Source: Data from Harris et al., 1982.

nipple discharge, though only 10 percent of women with breast cancer have this symptom (Kinne, 1984).

Among the factors that contribute to the development of breast cancer are fatty diets, some hormonal therapies (Shafie, 1980), facial X-rays (Simon, 1978), and heredity (Kiang et al., 1982).

Cancer of the Prostate.   Despite misplaced fears that cancer can be sexually transmitted, cancers of the penis, testes, or prostate gland are *not* caused by sexual contact (Linton, 1983).

Men over age sixty-five have a 4 percent chance of developing prostate cancer. Treatment consists of surgery (prostatectomy), radiation therapy, and chemotherapy using prescription drugs. The operation and hormone treatments can cause erectile dysfunction and retrograde ejaculation, depending on the extensiveness of the surgery.

Testicular Cancer.   Cancer of a testis occurs infrequently, consisting of approximately 6,000 new cases in the United States each year. The cancerous testis is removed surgically without impairing either sexual functioning or fertility, because the healthy testis continues to function.

■ Surgical Interventions

Any operation that involves the removal of some portion of one's body can affect the self-concept negatively. Some kinds of surgery are more likely than others to have a detrimental effect on sexuality.

Breast Removal. To halt breast cancer, **mastectomy** (surgical removal of the affected breast) may be necessary, though there is medical controversy about precisely how much of the breast should be removed. Radical mastectomy is the most disfiguring, because the muscles underlying the breast are also removed. An alternative surgical procedure, the partial (modified radical) mastectomy, involves removing less muscle tissue, but it may be less effective in eliminating the cancer. Partial mastectomy provides a cure if the cancer has not spread very far, and the woman's sexual adjustment is better than if she undergoes radical mastectomy. A third possibility is lumpectomy, in which only the cancerous tissue is removed. Following this type of surgery, X-ray therapy is administered.

Given our society's emphasis on breasts as a major defining feature of female attractiveness and sex appeal, it is not surprising that many women feel devastated following a mastectomy (Kriss and Kraemer, 1986). Among those who have a breast removed, about 25 percent consider suicide (Pasnau, 1978). Counseling in group sessions with others who have undergone mastectomies can help reduce the feelings of depression.

Some women feel better if they wear an artificial breast under their clothing. A few (about one percent) elect the option of breast reconstruction performed by a plastic surgeon. A silicone implant is placed under the skin, and the new breast is made to resemble the old one in size and shape. A false nipple is constructed from a skin graft. The reconstructed breast is erotically sensitive to touch, though less so than a natural one (Levin, 1981). The woman and her partner are found to adjust better to breast removal with reconstructive surgery than without it (Falik, 1984).

Removal of the Uterus. **Hysterectomy** is the surgical removal of the uterus. This procedure is undertaken when the patient has either cervical or uterine cancer or *fibroid tumors*—large, noncancerous growths within the uterus. This operation once was performed to treat small fibroid tumors within the uterus, but today these growths are removed without hysterectomy, leaving the uterus intact. This surgery, called **myomectomy**, is more difficult to perform than hysterectomy, but is obviously preferable from the point of view of the patient.

Other noncancerous conditions may require hysterectomy if they become severe. These include endometriosis and displaced (prolapsed) uterus.

The precancerous condition *carcinoma in situ* involves the presence of abnormal cells in the surface of the cervix, and it can be treated with surgery or radiation therapy. Once cancerous cells invade the cervix, the disease develops into cervical cancer, called *invasive cancer of the cervix. Endometrial cancer* attacks the lining of the uterus and typically appears after age forty. The symptoms of endometrial cancer include vaginal bleeding following intercourse, cramping or other abdominal pains, and pelvic lumps. Diagnosis of uterine cancer is based on tests of uterine tissue obtained through dilation and curettage (D & C). Four out of five women with endometrial cancer that is confined to the uterus will be cured; that is, the cancer does not recur during the five years following treatment that may include both hysterectomy and radiation therapy.

After a hysterectomy, intercourse can be resumed, and lubrication and vaginal expansion are unaffected. The ovaries still function during the monthly cycle. Because, however, the uterus is gone and the vagina is sealed off at the back, the woman cannot menstruate nor is conception possible. The hysterectomy patient will experience menopause when her ovaries cease to function sometime in her late forties.

Among the aftereffects of this operation are psychological reactions, such as the perceived loss of femininity. Although some members of the medical profession assert that *all* the negative sexual effects of hysterectomy are psychogenic, organic effects may occur as well (Keye, 1984). For example, the vagina may be shortened during surgery or scar tissue may develop after surgery; as a result, the penis cannot penetrate as deeply as before without causing the woman pain. Because uterine contractions no longer occur during orgasm, the woman may experience less satisfaction.

What percentage of hysterectomies are performed unnecessarily is a controversial issue. In 1983, for example, 13,000 of the 670,000 such operations in the United States were carried out to treat premenstrual syndrome (Hufnagel, 1988), even though this condition is ordinarily treated nonsurgically with exercise, diet, and medication. Women (and men) always should be told about alternative treatments for their medical problems, and they should be fully informed about the side effects of each treatment on sexual and nonsexual functioning. The patient, as an informed consumer, needs to be assertive in requesting this information from a physician or obtaining it elsewhere.

Removal of One or Both Ovaries.   **Oophorectomy** is the removal of one or both ovaries. When both are removed, the level of estrogen drops rapidly to about one third of its normal amount. Menopausal symptoms develop almost immediately, with hot flashes, mood changes, and lack of vaginal lubrication. This can be prevented by administering estrogen, but only if the uterus also has been removed; otherwise, estrogen therapy can cause uterine cancer (Martin, 1980).

When only one ovary is removed, the remaining ovary compensates with excess hormonal secretion, thereby preventing menopausal effects.

The ovaries secrete testosterone in addition to estrogen. Estrogen production is halted at menopause, when the woman frequently develops a deeper voice along with unwanted body and facial hair. Thus, for women who are past menopause, ovary removal can have a mildly positive effect. In the absence of ovaries, postmenopausal women have a more feminine appearance and a more feminine voice.

Surgery of the Penis, Prostate, and Testes.   When the penis can no longer become erect because of illness or injury, a permanent surgical solution is possible. Men with spinal-cord injury or penile cancer, for example, are candidates for penile prostheses of the kind shown in Figure 16-6.

A prosthesis is inserted inside the penis, and it can be inflated when an erection is desired and deflated afterward. When a pump placed within the scrotum is pressed, the man is able to control the size of the penile cylinders. Some men who use this kind

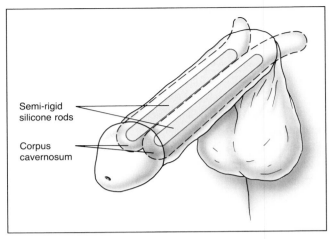

Semi-rigid
silicone rods

Corpus
cavernosum

FIGURE 16-6   *PENILE PROSTHESIS: ONE SOLUTION TO ERECTILE PROBLEMS*   A penile prosthesis makes erection possible for men who have erectile difficulties because of illness or injury. These silicone rods are inserted in each corpus cavernosum in order to produce a permanent, partial erection. Other types of prosthesis are inflatable, allowing the individual to produce an erection and to deflate it.

of implant to have sexual interactions are able to ejaculate, but others are not; the difference seems to depend on the person's medical history (Bullard, 1979). In a survey of fifty-two recipients of penile prostheses, 90 percent said that they would choose to have this surgery again under similar circumstances even though reduced penile sensitivity and size caused sexual satisfaction to be less than before (Steege et al., 1986). Some women complain about the artificial erections, saying that they prefer to be the cause of a partner's excitement rather than a pump inflating a cylinder. In evaluating the necessity of an implant, Shaw (1989) recommends that patients and physicians be made aware of the potential risks and of alternative options.

An alternative to penile prosthesis is the injection of a drug (phenoxybenzanine or papaverine) directly into the penis whenever an erection is needed. The drug causes an erectile response that lasts for ten to fifteen minutes (Szasz et al., 1987). This procedure is effective when the problem is nerve damage, but it cannot be used when circulatory problems prevent erection.

When a cancerous prostate gland must be removed, the surgery (known as **prostatectomy**) can damage the sphincter controlling the passage of urine out of the bladder. As a result, the man experiences retrograde ejaculation of semen into the bladder, and orgasms are not accompanied by an observable ejaculation. Less extensive surgery on the prostate performed to remove noncancerous growths does not necessarily interfere with ejaculation (Gross, 1984). Though such surgery can lead to erectile dysfunction because of damage to pelvic nerves, modern prostatic surgery ordinarily avoids such effects.

Testicular cancer can be treated with surgery, drugs, or radiation. When it is medically necessary to remove both testicles (castration), a reduction in the level of sexual activity often follows, presumably because testosterone drops to prepubertal levels. This sexual problem can be alleviated by administering appropriate hormones (Davidson et al., 1983). For some men, the interference with sexual functioning is based on the belief that their masculinity has been destroyed, and hormonal treatments obviously do not help this emotional response. If a man is concerned about the appearance of his genitals after such surgery, a prosthetic substitute for the testes can be implanted in the scrotum (Small, 1984b).

Despite the seeming importance of testosterone, many castrated men experience *no* change in their sexual activity, and the older a man is when the operation occurs, the less it affects his sexuality. When both testicles are removed—an operation technically known as bilateral orchiectomy—before puberty, such masculine characteristics as facial hair and a deeper voice do not develop.

■ Diabetes

With diabetes, the pancreas is unable to produce a normal amount of insulin. Problems with sexual functioning are more common among diabetic men than diabetic women (see Figure 16-7). The parasympathetic nerves in the diabetic male's pelvis do not control vasocongestion properly, and circulatory difficulties also impair erectile responses (Ellenberg, 1982). The result is erectile difficulty among 50 percent of the men who have diabetes. Once an erection occurs, however, these men are able to ejaculate (Jefferson et al., 1989).

The sexual response cycle of diabetic women is less affected compared to men, but as yet there is no satisfactory explanation for this sex difference. One in

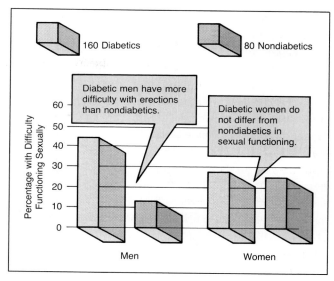

FIGURE 16-7 *SEX DIFFERENCES IN THE EFFECT OF DIABETES ON SEXUALITY* Diabetic men have significantly more difficulty in their sexual functioning than nondiabetic men. Among female patients, diabetics and nondiabetics do not differ in sexual interest, excitement, or the ability to reach orgasm.
Source: Data from Jenson, 1981.

five diabetic women reports reduced sexual desire, and one in seven has orgasmic dysfunction (Jensen, 1986). As with men, the sexual problems are based on malfunctioning of the parasympathetic nerves and the circulatory system.

■ Neurological Disease

Whether sexual behavior is affected by a disease in the central nervous system depends on the specifics of the illness. Even with such serious problems as a stroke, most patients do not lose their sexual desire, and many continue to function sexually (Madorsky, 1983).

Those with the Tourette syndrome, a neurological disorder, progress from blinking excessively to involuntary movements of various parts of the body (tics). One third of the victims of this condition engage in coprolalia—uttering obscene language uncontrollably. The patient may try very hard to stop this behavior, but tension builds and the embarrassing words and phrases are expressed involuntarily. Others engage in copropraxia, making obscene gestures or touching their own or another person's genitals (Shapiro, 1984). These unusual symptoms of the

Tourette syndrome most often occur when the person is frustrated or angry (Shapiro, 1983).

With some neurological disorders, such as epilepsy, there is no predictable effect on sexuality. Sexual interest and activity increases for some, decreases for others, and shows no change in still others (Ehni and Kline, 1981, 1982).

Multiple sclerosis (MS) usually strikes young adults, damaging the tissue that covers nerve cells; approximately 250,000 people in the United States have this disease. About 60 percent of MS patients also experience a decline in one or more of the stages of sexual functioning—desire, arousal, and/or orgasm (Valleroy and Kraft, 1984). A major reason for such effects is that sensory loss reduces the effect of genital stimulation.

■ Cardiovascular Disease

Cardiovascular disease is a major health problem and affects a large proportion of the population. A great many people, consequently, raise questions about the possible effects of high blood pressure (hypertension), clogging and hardening of the arteries, and various heart malfunctions on sexuality.

One of the most dramatic fears among males is the possibility of sudden death occurring during intercourse—*la mort d'amour*. Engaging in sexual activity to orgasm normally raises the heart rate as much as does light to moderate exercise, such as climbing two flights of stairs. These data are based on a laboratory study of men whose heart functions were monitored while they masturbated or engaged in either male-superior or female-superior intercourse (Bohlen et al., 1984).

A study of Seattle residents indicated that only 3.3 percent of sudden deaths among adults occurred during a sexual act. This is possibly an underestimate, however, because the victim's family may be embarrassed to reveal the true circumstances (Cantwell, 1981). A study in Japan showed that men who died during intercourse were found to be interacting with women other than their spouses in most instances (Cantwell, 1981). Besides effects of sexual stimulation, orgasm, or the excitement of a new partner, the physical stress of sexual interaction is increased by such factors as heavy drinking and a big meal. With-

out such complications, however, sex is not risky for most victims of heart disease.

The frequency of developing heart disease also is increasing for women, and they too express concern about the dangers of engaging in sexual activity. One study indicated that in a group of women who had experienced heart attacks, over 60 percent engaged in sexual intercourse less frequently afterward than before (Kolodny, 1981a). The most likely female candidates for cardiovascular disease are career women past the age of menopause when protective estrogen levels have decreased.

Among heart patients, the strain of sexual activity can be reduced by participation in exercise programs. Information is also of value. Sexual activity is most feared by the spouses of heart patients who know very little about the illness and its effect (Weinstein and Como, 1980). Women who lack the appropriate knowledge tend to avoid sex with their husbands in order to protect their spouses from a heart attack. When information is given to patients after a heart attack—for example, when it is safe to resume sexual activity—such fears are greatly reduced (Dhabuwala et al., 1986).

Promoting Sexual Health

It is obvious that knowledge is essential in order to avoid illness if at all possible, to recognize the symptoms of disease when they occur, and to seek prompt, effective treatment. In this section, we will discuss good sexual health habits and describe the details of sex-related medical examinations.

■ Good Health Habits: What We Can Do for Ourselves

As soon as menstrual cycles begin, young girls should be taught how to perform breast self-examinations (BSE). The procedure takes only a few minutes each month and may result in early detection of possibly cancerous growths. Figure 16-8 illustrates how this procedure is performed. The best time for self-examination is a few days after menstruation stops, because the breasts are least likely to be swollen and tender. Most breast lumps (80 to 90 percent) are *not*

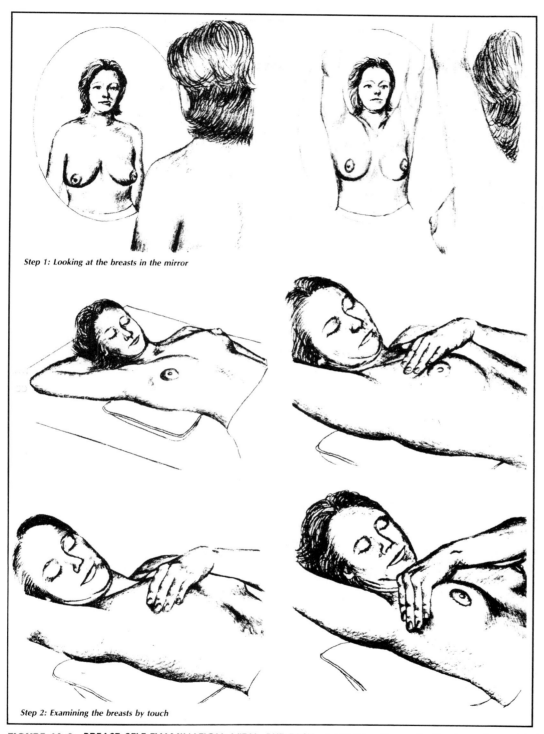

Step 1: Looking at the breasts in the mirror

Step 2: Examining the breasts by touch

FIGURE 16-8 *BREAST SELF-EXAMINATION: VITAL, BUT EASY* A breast self-examination is performed in two steps. The woman observes her breasts in front of a mirror using several positions. Then she feels her breasts to inspect for changes, while lying down with a small pillow or folded towel under the side being examined. Using a circular motion of two flattened fingers, she examines the entire breast area, the area between breast and armpit, and the armpit itself for lumps.

malignant, but the probability of breast cancer increases with age (National Cancer Institute, 1982).

In order to benefit from BSE, the person must perform it regularly and correctly. A survey of 203 female undergraduates found that women who engaged in BSE had more knowledge about the procedure, a stronger belief in its potential payoff for health, and more positive attitudes about it than nonusers (Ronis and Kaiser, 1989). In this instance, knowledge and a positive outlook clearly improves one's chances for good health.

Although we typically think of breast cancer as a female concern, men also should examine their breasts regularly to feel for lumps, changes, or discharge. Breast cancer in males is too often ignored as a potential problem. Also men frequently ignore the possiblity of cancer of the testicles and the importance of testicular self-examination each month. This cancer occurs most frequently among men aged twenty to thirty-four. After a warm bath or shower when the scrotum is loose and relaxed, the man should feel each side for differences in size and for any evidence of lumps. The pair of testicles are normally firm, smooth, and of about the same size. A relatively small number of males develop this type of cancer each year, and it can be cured with early detection and treatment.

As the discussion of STDs in Chapter 15 suggested, it is important to learn to watch for the early signs of the various disorders caused by bacteria, viruses, fungi, and parasites. Any unusual discharge, unexpected pain, persistent itching, or growths are all reasons to visit a physician for a checkup and any necessary treatment. Another sign of a possible disorder is pain during intercourse, especially for women (Huffman, 1982).

It is also essential to keep the genitals clean. Gentle, daily washing between skin folds and under the foreskin of uncircumcised males is required to prevent the collection of smegma caused by the secretion of oil and perspiration (LaFerla, 1982). For the reasons described in Chapter 5, **douching** is not recommended for women. Rinsing and flushing the vagina actually may force disease-causing organisms upward, resulting in a pelvic infection (Neumann, 1979). Attempting to feel and smell "clean" by douching with wine, pepper, or crushed flowers is also unwise (Connell, 1982).

A useful procedure for women is the "dry vulva" regimen to reduce moisture and itching in the genitals (Ingram, 1983). Women using this technique do not wear panties or other underclothing beneath their skirts or nightgowns and should avoid using powders or sprays for "hygiene." They may prefer to wear cotton under-clothing for modesty; synthetic materials reduce ventilation. When not in public, the woman can keep her legs slightly apart in order to maintain dryness. It is unnecessary to go beyond this by using a hair dryer or a fan.

■ The Role of Medical Examinations

Pediatricians usually check their young patients' genitals to look for signs of normal versus abnormal development. By the time a person is eighteen, or earlier if he or she has become sexually active, genital and breast examinations are essential. These procedures may be embarrassing or anxiety evoking initially, but an informative, reassuring physician can be helpful (Brennock, 1981). Unfortunately, many physicians are also embarrassed and anxious about sexual matters, but you can find other doctors who are comfortable in dealing with the subject of sex and the sexual parts of the body.

Gynecologic Exams. Women are more likely to have regular examinations of their genitals and breasts than men because many have learned the importance of a yearly gynecologic exam. During a typical exam, the woman is asked to remove her clothing and is then covered by a sheet. She lies on a flat examining table with stirrups, usually made of metal, to rest her feet. The physician (or nurse practitioner) feels the patient's lower abdomen and inserts two lubricated, gloved fingers to inspect the vagina and cervix. Some doctors also perform a bimanual exam, by pressing one hand on parts of the abdomen from the outside, while probing the vagina or rectum gently with the other hand. The purpose of these procedures is to detect any evidence of disease or swelling.

Because of such genital manipulation, the patient sometimes feels sexual excitement; this need not cause any embarrassment. One physician reported that three out of ten college-age women became sexually aroused during gynecological examinations as shown by vaginal tenting and lubrication (Freeman,

1983). Regardless of the sex of the physician, either lesbian or heterosexual women may experience this effect simply because of the physical manipulation.

Pap Smears. During a **Pap smear**, cells from the external cervical os are scraped painlessly and placed on a glass slide for microscopic examination to detect the presence of abnormalities. It can detect cervical but not uterine or ovarian cancer. This procedure was named for the physician, Papanicolaou, who developed it in 1942. During a Pap smear, a speculum is inserted into the vagina to immobilize the exposed cervix, so that a cotton swab or small spatula can be inserted into the vagina to get a sample of cervical mucus.

Test results are labeled in terms of five classes ranging from Class I, which shows completely normal cells, to Class V, which indicates a high probability of cancer. Class II results usually indicate the presence of infection in the reproductive tract. Class III results suggest that further testing is needed, and Classes IV and V are usually followed by biopsy, surgical removal of a small piece of the cervix to test it microscopically for malignancy.

The test should be performed at least every one to three years (Marx, 1980). Women who have a higher risk of cervical cancer ordinarily are advised to have a Pap smear at least once or twice yearly. For example, any woman with genital herpes or who engages in intercourse with multiple partners should have Pap smears frequently (Gusberg, 1982). Because the risk of cervical cancer decreases beyond age 65, regular tests should be performed at least until that age. Pap smears also can identify problems other than cervical cancer such as infection (Soriero, 1982).

Mammograms. About age thirty-five or forty, a woman needs to have a *baseline mammogram* which produces a picture of her breasts in a normal state. A mammogram consists of X-rays; a procedure known as a *thermogram* gives an indication of heat distribution by means of thermography. Breast tumors are warmer than surrounding tissue, and thermography can detect this difference. A sonogram, also discussed in Chapter 4, can detect the shape of abnormal growths in the breast through their pattern of sound reflection. The results of a mammogram, and perhaps thermogram or sonogram, become an important part of a woman's medical record, because the results can be compared to later tests and reveal any changes that have occurred. Especially for a woman who has a family history of breast cancer on her mother's side, these tests can literally be life-saving.

The amount of radiation from a mammogram has been reduced in the last ten years, and this procedure exposes women to less radiation than a full chest X-ray. Between ages forty and fifty, the mammogram should be repeated every two years and yearly over age 50.

Examining Males. Men over age fifty should have a rectal examination of the prostate each year, and younger men should be examined as part of any routine physical. The physician can detect abnormal growth of the prostate, indicating the possibility of cancer. Cancer of the prostate kills 20,000 men yearly in the United States (Leiter, 1982). Men over fifty also may be given a PAP test that detects high levels of a substance (prostate-specific acid phosphatase) that can indicate prostate cancer (Finck, 1982). With an infected prostate, physicians at one time pressed the organ internally to "milk" it of mucus. This painful procedure is no longer necessary; instead, antibiotics are prescribed (Fordney-Settlage, 1979).

As with women during a pelvic examination, males may find themselves responding sexually to the manipulations of penis, testicles, anus, prostate, breasts, and so forth. Many men feel embarrassed if they have an erection in the presence of either a male or female physician. This is one reason that men often avoid these examinations, no matter how essential they may be (Feigen, 1981).

Summarizing the Information about Drugs, Disability, and Disease . . .

The effects of drugs on sexual functioning depend on the specific drug and the amount used. Alcohol makes the person feel less anxious and inhibited, but it interferes with excitement and orgasm. Illegal **psy-**

choactive drugs such as marijuana, cocaine, and other stimulants initially tend to produce feelings of euphoria and an enhanced response to sexual stimulation. The opiates, such as heroin, tend to eliminate sexual desire and sexual activity. There is no effective substance that acts as an **aphrodisiac,** and substances such as Spanish fly can be physically damaging.

For many disabled individuals, the primary barrier to sexual expression is the prejudice held by the nondisabled. For example, retardation, blindness, and deafness often result in exclusion from participation in a full sexual life. The effects of spinal-cord injuries can interfere directly with sexual functioning, especially in males, but these difficulties can be overcome in a variety of ways. Psychological disorders such as severe depression and schizophrenia tend to reduce sexual interest.

To distinguish between **psychogenic** and **organic causes of sexual dysfunction,** a major criterion is the occurrence of sexual arousal during sleep. The dysfunctional individual who shows **nocturnal penile tumescence** or vaginal vasocongestion while asleep is assumed to be dysfunctional on the basis of psychological rather than physical causes.

A number of physical disorders, such as cancer, decreases the patient's interest in sex. Surgical interventions (for example, **mastectomy** and **hysterectomy**) can interfere with sexuality, but the cause is often the patient's lowered self-esteem and the reactions of the person's sexual partner. The inability to have an erection can be corrected by the insertion of a prosthetic device. The removal of the prostate gland results in **retrograde ejaculation** in which the individual ejaculates semen internally, into his bladder. The removal of both testes—castration—decreases the man's testosterone level, but this does not necessarily affect sexual activity. Diabetes has a greater effect on male sexual functioning (erectile difficulties) than on that of women. Some neurological disorders can affect sexual behavior, as when victims of the Tourette syndrome involuntarily engage in obscene verbalizations or gestures. Cardiovascular disease often evokes the fear that sexual interactions will cause a heart attack, but these fears are greatly exaggerated.

Anyone can (and should) learn and practice good sexual health habits, including self-examination of breasts and genitals. These procedures, performed regularly, make possible the early detection of potentially serious problems. People also should have regular medical examinations, with **Pap smears** for women and prostate examinations for men over fifty.

To Find Out More About Drugs, Disability, and Disease . . .

Cornelius, D. A., Chipouras, S., Makas, E., & Daniels, S. M. (1982). *Who cares? A handbook on sex education and counseling services for disabled people.* Baltimore, Md.: University Park Press.

The sexual rights of the disabled are covered along with their sexual problems and ways to solve them.

Seventeen women doctors. (1980). *Every woman's health, the complete guide to body and mind.* New York: Doubleday.

A wide range of health-care concerns are included in this collection of material authored by a group of female physicians. This book makes helpful suggestions about how to negotiate the health-care system, whether you are male or female.

Taberner, P. V. (1985). *Aphrodisiacs: The science and the myth.* Philadelphia: University of Pennsylvania Press.

The author covers the history and effects of magic charms, potions, and herbs that have been used in the attempt to increase sexual desire and performance. Both quackery and modern drugs are discussed in detail.

CHAPTER SEVENTEEN

SEXUAL DYSFUNCTION AND THERAPY

A male graduate student described the following incident that had taken place some months earlier when he and his girlfriend made love. His account is a good example of the way that a minor sexual dysfunction can be interpreted and perceived in a nonthreatening way. You might consider what would have happened had he or his partner assumed that something was physically wrong with him or that he was seriously dysfunctional.

It's lucky that human beings have a sense of humor and the ability to see that some experiences are funny instead of tragic and shameful. I had been going out with Tracy for a couple of months, and we were beginning to get pretty serious. Heavy petting was as far as we went, though. Both of us had been involved in sexual relationships in the past, but times have changed, and you no longer just hop into bed with someone because he or she is desirable. At least, you don't if you are brighter than an armadillo.

When it became obvious that Tracy and I were moving closer and closer to the main event, we started talking in some detail about our past partners and the fact that neither of us had ever used intravenous drugs. We even went together to a clinic to have blood tests. That may sound strange, but not as strange as catching or passing on an incurable disease. We also talked about birth control, and she told me that she had a diaphragm.

By the time we received a clean bill of health, we were more than ready. I had been thinking about making love to this beautiful woman for many weeks, and now the big day was here. We went out, had a nice dinner, and then went to her apartment. We put on music, dimmed the lights, and stood beside her queen-size bed.

We slowly undressed, kissing and caressing the whole time, and then we were in bed together at last. To my surprise, that was when the unthinkable happened. The moment I entered her, I came. One stroke, and that was it.

We looked at each other for a few seconds, and then we both began laughing. We were almost hysterical. When we quieted down, I told her how much I had fantasized about her and must have been close to the point of ejaculation for days. It wasn't the end of the world, and she soon found that I like cunnilingus as much as she did. At least an hour passed as we lay there talking and kissing. I tried again, and everything was fine. We haven't had that kind of problem since.

To this day she teases me by saying that my name should be Quick Draw McGraw.

Lew, age 26

The fact that both Lew and Tracy reacted to his premature ejaculation with understanding and humor rather than with humiliation and anger suggests that they are mature and knowledgeable enough to be comfortable about their sexuality. These same characteristics also were indicated by their responses to the dangers of STDs and the possibility of unwanted conception.

Lew's experience is not unusual. At any given time, and for a variety of reasons, a man may begin intercourse and then ejaculate too quickly to satisfy his partner. Alternatively, he may have difficulty in becoming fully erect, maintaining an erection, or ejaculating. Similarly, a sexually active woman's vaginal lubrication may be insufficient to permit pleasurable intercourse, the muscles around her vagina may clamp down and prevent penetration by her partner, or she may not reach orgasm. Even when masturbating alone, a person may find that sexual excitement develops too slowly or too quickly, and orgasm may be unsatisfactory.

Sexual dysfunctions refer to difficulties people experience in responding to sexual stimulation and experiencing orgasm. Some types of dysfunction are very common; according to sex therapists Masters and Johnson (1970), half of the married couples in the United States have experienced one or more such incidents in their interactions. This kind of problem can cause acute emotional distress for the dysfunctional individual and negatively affect a couple's relationship. We discuss the major categories of *dysfunctions* involving problems with desire, excitement, and/or orgasm. Many forms of *sex therapy* have been developed over the past few decades to help overcome sexual dysfunctions, some concentrating on *individuals* and some on *couples*. We describe the details of such treatment procedures from the preliminary examination to guided sexual exercises. We also discuss the somewhat controversial topic of the *effects of sex therapy*. Special sections explore *sexual dysfunctions and relationships,* the effects of *emotions on sexual arousal,* and the background and behavior of *sex therapists.*

As we will show, there are many causes of such problems, and many ways to overcome them. To deal with dysfunctions, you need to know as much as possible about sexual functioning, to realize that there *is* an explanation and a solution. Then, it is much easier to respond in an unembarrassed way, as Tracy and Lew did. Sexual activity can't be perfect every time, and we shouldn't be any more surprised or upset about that than we are about our lack of perfection when we play tennis or drive a car.

Dysfunctions

As we discussed in Chapter 16, sexual dysfunctions sometimes have an organic cause. In contrast, **psychosexual dysfunctions** have psychogenic causes;

that is, the basis is primarily psychological (Geer and Messe, 1982). This chapter will focus on such dysfunctions.

■ Sexual Dissatisfaction and the Nature of Dysfunctional Sex

Why do couples seek therapy for sexual problems? A study of middle-aged married couples indicates that husbands and wives differ in their perceptions about what is wrong (Snyder and Berg, 1983). Husbands are most likely to say that their wives are unresponsive to their sexual requests and are nonorgasmic, they do not feel affectionate toward their wives, intercourse occurs too infrequently (or too frequently), and they have difficulty in maintaining an erection. Wives are most likely to express concern about the infrequency of intercourse, their spouse's lack of response, their own lack of response, their lack of affection for their husbands, and pain during intercourse.

Most dysfunctions affect the first three phases of the sexual response cycle (desire, excitement, and orgasm) rather than the last phase (resolution), and we will describe how dysfunctions affect each of those three phases.

There are two other elements that apply to all psychosexual dysfunctions. First, either a dysfunction can characterize the person's lifelong behavior, or it can develop following a period of satisfactory functioning. When the problem has always been present in the person's sexual behavior, it is termed a **primary dysfunction**. In contrast, a **secondary dysfunction** develops later in the person's sexual history. For example, if a woman had never experienced orgasm, she would have a primary dysfunction. If she regularly had orgasms, and then became nonorgasmic, she would have a secondary dysfunction. Most sexual dysfunctions are secondary, among both homosexual and heterosexual couples (Masters and

Highlighting Research

SEXUAL DYSFUNCTIONS AND RELATIONSHIPS: MUTUAL BENEFIT OR RECIPROCAL HARM?

Happily married couples commonly report sexual dysfunctions (Frank et al., 1978). As indicated in Figure 17-1, women complain more often than men about sexual dysfunctions in their marital relationships. For example, women report that sometimes they experience difficulty in becoming sexually excited, in maintaining excitement, or in reaching orgasm. They also are more likely than men to indicate that their sexual interactions are affected by various factors that are either in-

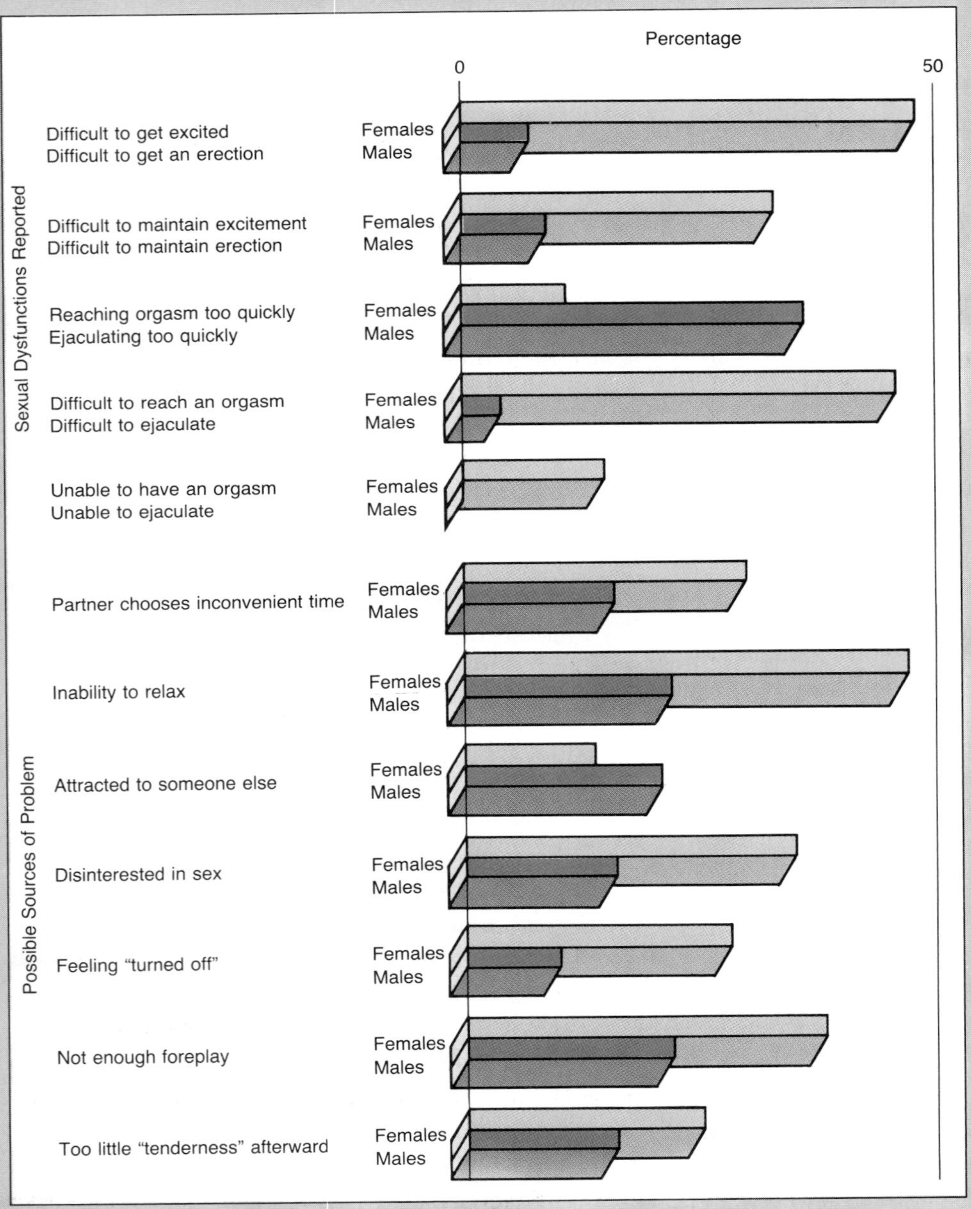

FIGURE 17-1 *SEXUAL DYSFUNCTIONS AMONG MARRIED COUPLES* In a study of 100 happily married couples, spouses reported that dysfunctions occurred frequently in their sexual interactions. Men and women reported different problems and offered different explanations for them.
Source: Based on data from Frank et al., 1978.

Percentage

Sexual Dysfunctions Reported

Difficult to get excited
Difficult to get an erection   Females / Males

Difficult to maintain excitement
Difficult to maintain erection   Females / Males

Reaching orgasm too quickly
Ejaculating too quickly   Females / Males

Difficult to reach an orgasm
Difficult to ejaculate   Females / Males

Unable to have an orgasm
Unable to ejaculate   Females / Males

Possible Sources of Problem

Partner chooses inconvenient time   Females / Males

Inability to relax   Females / Males

Attracted to someone else   Females / Males

Disinterested in sex   Females / Males

Feeling "turned off"   Females / Males

Not enough foreplay   Females / Males

Too little "tenderness" afterward   Females / Males

ternal (the inability to relax, disinterest) or external (inconvenience, inadequate foreplay by spouse). Men complain most about ejaculating too quickly and are more likely than women to identify attraction to another partner as a cause of sexual problems in their marriage.

Obviously sexual difficulties can detract from the quality of a relationship, but is the reverse even more likely? In other words, does an unsatisfactory relationship more often cause sexual malfunctioning than vice versa?

Among 100 couples seeking sex therapy, about one in five of the sexual problems appeared to originate in more general marital conflicts and dissatisfactions, such as disagreement about finances (Lief, 1980b). In a different study, among couples seeking therapy for marital problems, 70 percent were found to have a sexual dysfunction (see Figure 17-2).

The contrast between these groups is clear. A couple seeking help for marital dissatisfaction also is likely to experience sexual dysfunction. A couple seeking help for a sexual dysfunction is not likely to report general dissatisfaction with the marriage. Thus, ". . . it appears that competence in couple-functioning may be preserved in the presence of an unsatisfactory (sexual) relationship" (Hartman, 1980, p. 576). At least for couples seeking

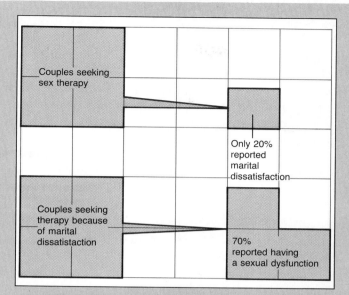

FIGURE 17-2 *MARITAL DISSATISFACTION RESULTS IN SEXUAL DYSFUNCTION, BUT NOT VICE VERSA* Several correlational studies have established the association between relationship problems and sexual problems. A higher percentage of couples seeking marital therapy also report a sexual dysfunction than the reverse; that is, a smaller percentage of couples seeking sex therapy for a dysfunction also report marital dissatisfaction. Based on the reports of 120 couples who sought help for either sexual dysfunctions or marital dissatisfaction, an unhappy marriage seems more likely to lead to a sexual dysfunction than a dysfunction is to bring about an unhappy marriage.
Source: Based on data in Hartman (1980) and Lief (1980).

marital or sex therapy, we can conclude that unhappy marriages lead to sexual dysfunctions more commonly than sexual functions

dysfunctions lead to unhappy marriages (Stuart et al., 1987).

Johnson, 1970, 1979). With a few exceptions, research and theory on dysfunction concentrate on heterosexual couples and individuals (Wilensky and Myers, 1987).

Second, dysfunctions also are classified as either **generalized** or **situational.** If the problem occurs in every sexual situation, it is generalized. For example, a woman who does not reach orgasm in response to masturbation, cunnilingus, or intercourse has a generalized dysfunction. If she is orgasmic when masturbating or engaging in cunnilingus but not during intercourse, she has a situational dysfunction.

Before describing what is known about specific dysfunctions, it may be useful to discuss the interdependence of a person's dysfunction and the quality of

his or her relationship with a partner in the special section *Highlighting Research*, on pages 454 to 455.

■ Low Sexual Desire

Though deciding whether sexual desire is "low" is clearly subjective, most observers would agree that in some instances the term is an accurate one.

Identifying Low Sexual Desire. Adults who have little or no desire for sexual activity and no interest in pursuing it exhibit **inhibited sexual desire,** or **ISD.** Such individuals also tend not to fantasize about sex, avoiding the topic whenever possible.

People may be classified as having ISD if they meet three criteria. First, they must feel that it is inappropriate for them to express sexual interest. If a person's religious beliefs prohibit sexual interactions prior to marriage, his or her avoidance of sexuality while single is understandable and probably is not attributable to a lack of sexual desire. If, in contrast, a young married person lost interest in intercourse, it is reasonable to attribute the reaction to sexual apathy (Booth, 1982). Among couples who stop having intercourse, only 12 percent say that they actually are disinterested in sex. Most such couples say that they avoid sex because of marital discord, anger, and a variety of negative feelings about one another (Martin, 1981).

Second, people with ISD show less interest in sexual activity than others of their age, sex, and occupation. Based on knowledge about normative sexual behavior, for example, we could say that a blue-collar male nearing retirement age would probably engage in sexual acts less often than a young male college graduate (LaFerla, 1984). If a man fitting the latter description desired sex only twice a month, ISD might be indicated. If a man fitting the former description had the same sexual interests, he would probably not be described as having ISD.

Third, ISD is indicated if a person's sexual disinterest is of concern either to self or to a partner. If, for example, a man's sexual apathy distresses him, or his wife, then the term *ISD* could be appropriate. Sometimes, the problem may lie in people's specific beliefs and expectations about their sexual behavior. For example, an elderly Polynesian male complained that something terrible must be wrong with him because he could make love only once a day rather than three times, as he did when he was young. In this instance, sex therapy wasn't the answer; rather, the man benefitted from receiving accurate information about sexuality.

Causes of Sexual Disinterest. Problems within a relationship may cause ISD, as can negative emotions such as anxiety. For example, people who are worried about finances, health, or job-related difficulties may begin to experience ISD. The negative emotions that decrease desire also can be sex-related—fear of pregnancy, previous dysfunctions, or the risk of discovery (Henker, 1984). Additionally, sex therapists have identified boredom and negative attitudes about sexu-

ality as common causes of ISD (Epstein, 1981b; Kaplan, 1979b). Some people severely limit the situations they define as sexual; author Edgar Allen Poe fit this pattern of diminished desire. Throughout his brief life, he was reluctant to engage in sexual acts with women he loved—because he idealized them, Poe experienced difficulty in accepting the possibility that love and sexuality could coexist in a relationship (Bullough, 1983).

Inhibited desire is also known as diminished **libido**, a term first employed by Freud. Libido is distinguished from **potency**, which is the physical ability to become excited enough to engage in the desired sexual act (Jorgensen, 1981). For example, libido may be low in response to a specific partner, but the ability to engage in sex with another partner indicates that potency is unaffected. Such differences in libido in respsonse to different partners indicate a situational form of ISD. An example of situational differences in desire is provided by men in their early forties, who account for 20 percent of ISD cases. Their lack of desire is in response only to their wives, however (Henker, 1981); when they engage in extramarital sex, their libidinal problems disappear (Henker, 1983). This does not, of course, imply that such affairs solve marital problems; in fact, they usually make them worse.

Sexual aversion is a phobia—the fear of sexual activity or the thought of sexual activity (Stout, 1982). Men and women with this aversion are likely to fear dating, touching, undressing, or any other act that could possibly lead to a sexual encounter. When such cues are avoided, the fear is controlled. When sexual cues are encountered, the physical response can be strong—nausea, diarrhea, sweating, or a rapid heart rate. Because these symptoms are extremely unpleasant, a self-perpetuating cycle keeps them away from sex and any experience that might reduce the phobia.

Sexual aversion seems to be caused by negative sexual experiences, often beginning in childhood (Golden, 1988). Examples are a child raised by parents with punitive and restrictive sexual views or one who is the victim of a trauma such as rape or incest. In adulthood, aversion can be created by a partner in a long-term relationship who creates negative feelings about sex through belittling the person's ability or forcing the person to participate in unwanted sexual acts.

At the Opposite Extreme: Excessive Sexual Desire. It is even more difficult to identify what is meant by excessive desire than by inhibited desire. The term is generally applied to people with more sexual experience with more partners than most people, but whose gratification is only short-lived. The term *hypersexuality* (or *sexual addiction*) refers to a pattern of impersonal sex that lacks emotional intimacy and lasting satisfaction, especially when such behavior interferes with other aspects of the person's life (Carnes, 1985, 1988). Terms such as *excessive, addicted,* and *oversexed* may easily be misused. A person is not automatically oversexed because he or she enjoys sex a great deal. Eli Coleman, a sexual educator, considers this type of sexual behavior compulsive rather than addictive (Whitaker, 1991).

Only when someone goes from partner to partner seeking satisfaction is the behavior likely to become a source of concern. The terms **Don Juanism** and **satyriasis** apply to men who seek the sexual conquest of a series of women solely for pleasure. A similar pattern of behavior among women is called **nymphomania.** Sexual partners "exist only as things to be used" (American Psychiatric Association, 1980, pp. 282–283). Although this may sound like an exciting and glamorous way to live, the behavior is dysfunctional because it tends to cause distress both for the individual and for his or her many partners (Hedaya, 1985). Therapists usually focus on the reason underlying the person's compulsion to seek new partners and why each sexual interaction fails to satisfy his or her needs (Denber, 1978; Gerner, 1981; Jeffress, 1984; Liss, 1981; Rosenthal, 1981). Abuse or neglect during childhood may lie at the root of the problem, for example. Note that some insecure men inaccurately label women as nymphomaniacs simply because the women have strong sexual needs and enjoy satisfying them.

With Don Juanism and nymphomania, the needs of the partner do not matter. Sexual adventurers are **hedonists** who strive only to satisfy their own needs (Rand, 1982). Hedonists do not care about the partner's feelings or reactions and are indifferent to the possibilities of conception or disease. In contrast, **healthy adult pleasure-seeking** involves sexual interactions that combine pleasure, acceptance of responsibility, and consideration of the partner.

Parents often fear that that their offspring (especially females) may engage in **promiscuity.** Though this term refers specifically to excessive, impersonal sexual activity, for many people it can take on additional meanings. For example, we knew a mother who believed that her daughter should avoid all premarital sex because once a girl engaged in intercourse, she would become promiscuous because of her inability to refuse the sexual requests of any boy she dated. Undoubtedly, this woman would be shocked to learn that most adolescents now have at least one premarital sexual partner (Walsh, 1980), though few would be labeled promiscuous.

■ Problems Involving Sexual Excitement

Some psychosexual dysfunctions affect a person's ability to become physically aroused. For many years, the terms *impotence* and *frigidity* were applied to such problems. The negative connotations of these terms suggested a powerless male who has lost his manhood and a cold, unresponsive female. Such concepts suggest hostility toward and rejection of those experiencing difficulties in becoming excited, as Figure 17-3 illustrates.

Inhibited Sexual Excitement. To avoid the negative stereotypes, today the term **inhibited sexual excitement** is used to describe various types of excitement disorders. Men with inhibited sexual excitement usually cannot attain or maintain an erection, while women have problems with vaginal lubrication and vasocongestion. These dysfunctions can be total or partial; that is, sexual stimulation may elicit no excitement or only a low level of excitement.

Inhibited sexual excitement is seldom primary; it usually develops after a period during which the person has experienced an adequate level of excitement, and so is labeled secondary. Because it is common to have occasional problems with excitement, Masters and Johnson (1970) suggest that the condition constitutes a dysfunction only if the person is unable to become excited at least one fourth of the time when sexually stimulated.

"*Yes, I screamed for help. Would you like to come in and help him?*"

MARRIAGE
COUNSELOR

"*I'll tell you how frigid she is—when she opens her legs, a little light comes on.*"

FIGURE 17-3 *NEGATIVE STEREOTYPES EVOKED BY DYSFUNCTIONS*   A person's sexual dysfunction is frequently perceived by the partner as a threat, and the result is hostility toward him or her. As these cartoons suggest, a man's erectile failure can provoke scorn and disgust—his partner needs a real man to "help" satisfy her needs. Similarly, the man ridicules his wife's orgasmic dysfunction by comparing her to a refrigerator. (Figure 17-3a Reproduced by Special Permission of PLAYBOY Magazine: Copyright 1981 by PLAYBOY.)

Reduced Excitement in Women. When a woman notices that she is not becoming aroused by her partner's stimulation, a common response is **sexual anxiety.** She feels tense and experiences negative feelings about interacting with her partner (Chambless and Lifshitz, 1981). When women pay close attention to the physical changes caused by stimulation, sex is maximally arousing and satisfying (Hoon and Hoon, 1978). For example, women are pleasantly aware that their nipples are becoming erect, that their genitals are increasingly warm, and that vaginal lubrication is occurring. Women who feel little or no excitement fail to notice these signs of arousal; when they finally notice, their physical responses displease them. Some

are embarrassed or feel that such reactions indicate they are "cheap."

For some women, sexual anxieties center on concerns about how their partner is evaluating them. Such a woman may worry about her bodily (especially vaginal) odors, unattractiveness, the size of her vagina, expelling urine or other fluids, letting air or gas escape from the vagina or rectum, or whether she will appear foolish if she responds freely to excitement and orgasm (Devanesan, 1978). Some of these fears can be reduced if the person realizes that none of these things will lead to terrible consequences, and she need not agonize about any of them.

Sometimes the problem lies in the inadequate

stimulation the woman's partner is providing—too rough, too brief, or in the wrong places. The partner can learn better techniques and even lengthen foreplay to the point that the woman reaches orgasm prior to penetration (Bartusis, 1981).

One especially uncomfortable response to inhibited excitement is **functional dyspareunia** in which the woman experiences pain in her vagina, pelvis, or clitoris during intercourse. The cause may be organic, resulting from disease or scar tissue caused by an infection or surgery. A common cause is lack of lubrication, which may be organic (for example, based on hormonal deficiencies), psychogenic (for example, when excitement is blocked by guilt or anxiety), or the result of inadequate stimulation by the partner (Semmens and Semmens, 1983). Additionally, prolonged vaginal intercourse may reduce lubrication if the clitoris is not stimulated.

Another response to reduced excitement is **functional vaginismus**; the muscles surrounding the outer third of the vagina contract involuntarily, either preventing intercourse or making it extremely painful (Lamont, 1978). A twenty-nine-year-old woman developed a secondary case of functional vaginismus as the aftermath of a pelvic disease. She described her feelings as follows:

> I think about sex every minute my husband is home— I'm afraid he's going to want intercourse. I feel guilty for not wanting to have it very often, but the pain is so bad, I have to force myself to make love [Crenshaw & Kessler, 1985, p. 21]

Vaginismus often develops after a period of dyspareunia. If pain regularly accompanies intercourse over a period of time, the body may respond with vaginismus as a message to avoid intercourse. This dysfunction is relatively uncommon; only 7 percent of the women in the Masters and Johnson (1970) study of dysfunctions were so diagnosed. Vaginismus can affect women of any age, and it may be mild to be quite severe.

A rare excitement disorder, **sexual anesthesia**, is characterized by the absence of erotic sensations during excitement or orgasm. There is controversy about whether the cause is an organic disease (Marmar, 1981) or sexual guilt (Auerback and Auerback, 1984).

Arousal Problems in Men. When a man's erection is insufficient to permit him to perform a sexual act, he is experiencing an **erectile dysfunction**. This disorder is reported worldwide but is especially common in sexually restrictive societies (Welch and Kartub, 1978). Masters and Johnson (1970) reported that 13 percent of their patients with erectile dysfunction were classified as primary; these men had never had an erection that was sufficient to permit intercourse. Cases of secondary erectile dysfunction outnumber the primary type by about seven to one. A secondary dysfunction is defined as the failure to obtain and sustain an erection for successful intercourse at least one fourth of the time.

Besides the organic causes discussed in Chapter 16, psychogenic factors also can cause erectile dysfunction (Burat et al., 1990). Some men with this dysfunction express more guilt about sex, criticize themselves more, and are more sensitive to rejection than functional men (Rosenheim and Neumann, 1981), as depicted in Figure 17-4.

FIGURE 17-4 *THE NEGATIVE FEELINGS OF MALES WITH AN ERECTILE DYSFUNCTION* Males with erectile dysfunction express more guilt, self-criticism, and sensitivity to rejection than do functional males. Whether these characteristics lead to dysfunction or the existence of a dysfunction leads to these characteristics remains unclear.
Source: Based on data from Rosenheim and Naumann, 1981.

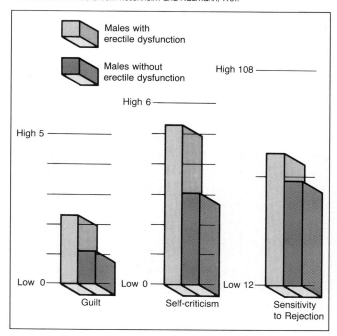

It is also true that guilt, self-criticism, and sensitivity to rejection can sometimes be the result—and not the cause—of the sexual problem. Each of these factors can contribute to an increase in nonsexual responses such as anxiety. In one experiment, men without erectile problems viewed sexually explicit films. Some of the subjects were injected with the drug epinephrine (which produced the symptoms of anxiety) while others were injected with a placebo. As Figure 17-5 shows, those watching the film while experiencing drug-induced anxiety were less physically excited (as indicated by penile circumference) than the men who had been given the placebo injection (Lange et al., 1981). Such findings indicate that nonsexual anxiety can cause erectile dysfunction.

Other kinds of evidence also support this conclusion. Men without erectile dysfunction have increased activity in the nondominant hemisphere of the brain during sexual arousal, but those with erectile dysfunction do not (Cohen et al., 1985). A possible reason is that dysfunctional men engage in self-critical thoughts during sexual interactions while functional men concentrate on the pleasure and the physical sensations of the experience (Coyne and Cross, 1988).

The special section *Increasing Enjoyment*, on pages 461 to 463, explores recent findings showing how specific kinds of distraction may interfere with sexual arousal in men.

The Partner's Role in Male Dysfunction.   A man's partner can contribute to the problem. A woman may misinterpret her partner's erectile difficulties and assume that the absence of an erection indicates his sexual disinterest (Derogatis and Kourlesis, 1981). Even male-female differences in the refractory period can cause misunderstanding between partners. Because women can, after reaching orgasm, respond to continued stimulation and have additional orgasms, they may assume that a man is able to do the same. If he does not, either he isn't a "real man," or she isn't exciting enough to arouse him.

Wives of men with arousal problems are found to express more hostility than other wives (Rosenheim and Neumann, 1981). These women seldom tell their partners that a given sexual experience is enjoyable (Auerback and Auerback, 1982). Some of these women add to the problem by ridiculing their husband's efforts; these men then feel hurt and "castrated" (Deckert, 1981). In one extreme example, a man whose partner made fun of his erectile failure responded by decapitating her (Taylor, 1985). Obviously, most women are not that insensitive, and most men are not that violent.

■   **Difficulties with Orgasm**

Ideally, orgasm is a natural, pleasurable response to sexual stimulation. Yet, human beings frequently make this reflexive response a source of complications and concern.

Among Women, the Absence of Orgasms.   **Orgasmic dysfunction**, called *anorgasmia* among women, is the most common female psychosexual dysfunction. Orgasm does not occur even though the stimulation is sufficient in intensity, duration, and location (Huey et al., 1981).

For many women this dysfunction is identified as situational in that intercourse is the problem; clitoral stimulation *does* lead to orgasm through mastur-

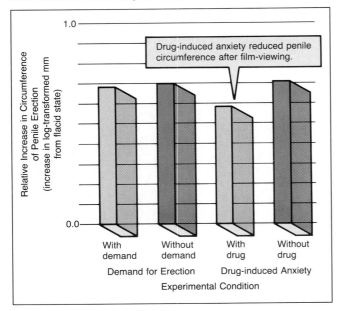

FIGURE 17-5 *ANXIETY AND ERECTILE DYSFUNCTION* Men who did not have an erectile dysfunction experienced reduced erections when they were injected with an anxiety-inducing drug. In contrast, simply receiving instructions designed to arouse performance anxiety did not have this effect. For functional males, anxiety (not performance pressure) interferes with sexual arousal. Source: Based on data from Lange et al., 1981.

bation, cunnilingus, vibrators, and so forth. Although many sex therapists disagree (Wakefield, 1988), situational anorgasmia was labeled "pathological inhibition" by the American Psychiatric Association (1980) on the grounds that manual stimulation of the clitoris "should not be necessary" to reach orgasm. In contrast, Morokoff (1989) suggests that a woman who does not feel aroused in response to vaginal intercourse should be classified as having inhibited arousal rather than an orgasmic disorder.

If orgasm has never occurred, despite adequate clitoral stimulation, the dysfunction is known as *primary anorgasmia;* Masters and Johnson (1970) found that more than 50 percent of anorgasmic women are in this category. If a woman has previously experienced orgasms, but no longer does so, the condition is called *secondary anorgasmia.*

In a large sample of college students, 95 percent of the men and only 50 percent of the women reported that they consistently had orgasms during sexual activity. Among sexually active women, about one in ten have never had an orgasm, and another 10 to 20 percent report having an orgasm less than half the time during intercourse (Kilmann et al., 1984).

Women who consistently have orgasm when they are sexually aroused are more sexually responsive and want to experience more orgasms than dysfunctional women (Loos et al., 1987). Sexual pleasure can be a fulfilling and important part of a person's life. Anorgasmia, whether primary, secondary, or situational, is upsetting to the woman who experiences it. She may become afraid of sexual arousal, thus decreasing her sexual interest and responsiveness. Depression and loss of self-esteem often result. Women

Increasing Enjoyment

DO EMOTIONS INTERFERE WITH OR ENHANCE SEXUAL AROUSAL?

Although anger seems not to affect sexual arousal (Kelley et al., 1983), other emotions such as fear seem to exert an influence. Does fear cause increased or decreased responsiveness to sexual stimulation? Both possibilities have been proposed. For example, sex therapists suggest that general anxieties about sexuality and specific fears about performance interfere with sexual functioning (Hartman, 1985; Norton and Jehu, 1984). In contrast, other evidence suggests that an element of danger enhances sexual excitement (Chambless and Lifshitz, 1984; Roviaro and Holmes, 1980).

In laboratory experiments, fear generally is found to increase sexual arousal in response to sexually explicit films. In two related studies, men and women were shown a film depicting a bloody automobile accident, arousing fear; other subjects were shown a nonarousing, neutral film. Immediately afterward, both groups viewed a sexual film. After seeing the fearinducing movie, both sexes reported

more sexual arousal than after seeing the nonarousing film (Hoon et al., 1977; Wolchik et al., 1980).

These findings could simply indicate the subjects felt relieved when the frightening movie ended. Barlow et al. (1983) designed an experiment to test the hypothesis that sexual arousal is enhanced by the positive feelings of relief rather than by the negative feelings of fear. In this experiment, fear was induced in male subjects by telling them that when a light came on as they watched a sexual film, it indicated they would receive an electric shock soon afterward. The subjects responded to fear with an increase in sexual arousal. Relief was not a factor, because the shock supposedy was soon going to be administered. This research should not be interpreted as encouragement to use fear to enhance sexual arousal. Rather, such experiments help us understand how negative emotions can be involved in dysfunctions.

If fear of traffic accidents or of electric

shock does not inhibit sexual arousal, perhaps a very specific fear—**performance anxiety**—has such an effect. Performance anxiety refers to an individual's tendency to focus on the adequacy of his or her sexual response rather than on the pleasure being experienced. Masters and Johnson (1970) used the term **spectatoring** to describe the distracting effects that occur when people focus on the quality of their sexual arousal and their performance. Spectatoring was hypothesized to increase performance fears, disconnecting the person's sexual feelings from the ongoing sexual activity. Instead of simply enjoying a sensual caress ("That feels good!"), a spectator observes and judges the experience ("Am I aroused yet?" "Is something wrong with me?"). An important goal of sex therapy is to increase the attention people give to feeling pleasure, while decreasing how much they monitor and evaluate performance (Morton and Hartman, 1985).

Abrahamson et al. (1985, 1989) created performance anxiety in a laboratory

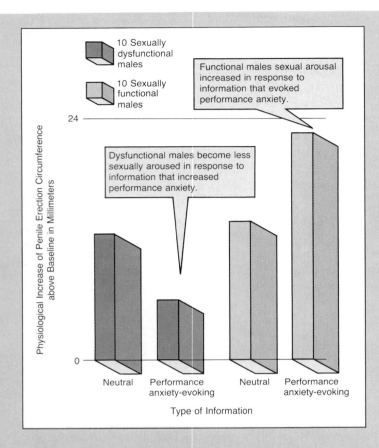

FIGURE 17-6 *PERFORMANCE ANXIETY: NEGATIVE EFFECTS FOR DYSFUNCTIONALS, POSITIVE EFFECTS FOR FUNCTIONALS* Performance anxiety can inhibit or enhance sexual arousal. In an experiment, functional and dysfunctional males were shown a sexual film. Compared to a control condition in which they were given neutral feedback, when subjects received feedback about their erections (as a way to increase performance anxiety), dysfunctional males became less aroused, but functional males actually became *more* aroused.
Source: Based on data from Abrahamson, Barlow, and Abrahamson, 1990.

FIGURE 17-7 *A THEORY OF SEXUAL DYSFUNCTION* A theoretical model outlines the way performance anxiety creates negative feelings and thoughts that interfere with the sexual responses. Because demands for sexual performance are common, the difference between functionals and dysfunctionals is in their emotional and attentional responses to them.
Source: Based on suggestions by Barlow, 1986.

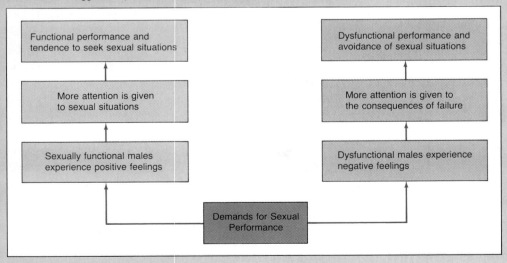

experiment to determine whether sexual arousal would decline as a result. Sexually functional and dysfunctional men viewed either an erotic or a neutral film while receiving visual feedback on a TV monitor showing their degree of physical arousal. The control condition was a neutral task in which the subjects made judgments about the length of lines. Figure 17-6 presents the results. In response to the potentially threatening feedback about performance, the functional males became more aroused, whereas dysfunctionals became less aroused. This finding suggests that most functioning males are not very susceptible to conditions that encourage spectatoring and performance anxiety, while those with erectile dysfunction are highly susceptible.

You might wonder why fear or induced anxiety about performance actually increases arousal in men without sexual problems. Zillmann's (1984) theory of **excitation transfer** provides a convincing explanation. If functional men do not worry about their sexual performance, the experimental manipulation simply raises anxiety level. This anxiety is transferred to sexual arousal, thus increasing its level.

Demands for sexual performance obviously affect sexually functional and dysfunctional men differently, as proposed in Barlow's (1986) theory outlined in Figure 17-7. A major difference between functional and dysfunctional men concerns the focus of their attention during coitus. In sex therapy, dysfunctional men learn not to focus on their performance, but on their sensations and arousal. Without this change of focus, dysfunctionals continue to have negative feelings about sex, expecting to perform inadequately. Without therapy, then, they become even more concerned about the consequences of failure than about pleasure. Eventually, they may find it preferable to avoid sexual interactions altogether. In contrast, functional men respond to the pleasure of sex, without constantly monitoring and evaluating their responses.

Both men and women who repeatedly experience failure respond by continuing to punish themselves (Ferrari, 1990), but less is known about the effects of sexual anxiety on women. In an experiment, sexual anxiety was aroused by providing stories in which sex had to be hurried or there was insufficient privacy. Such anxiety increased the genital vasocongestion of functional women but less so than sexually pleasurable images (Beggs et al., 1987). The latter were created by stories in which sexual interactions were slow and the woman enjoyed orgasm.

frequently blame themselves for not being able to have an orgasm. Such self-blame can only make the problem worse.

The Man's Contribution to a Woman's Dysfunction. By definition, vaginal intercourse consists of penile, but not necessarily, clitoral stimulation. This anatomical difference between the sexes is part of the problem. Factors such as intercourse position, depth of penetration, and the type of movements made by either partner can either result in adequate or inadequate stimulation of the clitoris. Without sufficient stimulation and the accompanying pleasurable sensations, a woman is less likely to reach orgasm.

A knowledgeable and concerned man considers the adequacy of his partner's stimulation an integral aspect of intercourse. Nevertheless, many men believe that penile thrusting alone is enough to evoke pleasure in their partners. These men, as a result, may resent and resist any suggestion by the woman that she needs additional stimulation or a change of position.

Both sexes drive pleasure from their partner's sexual enjoyment. When one partner does not have an orgasm, the other often perceives this as an insult to his or her lovemaking skills. When a woman is unable to reach orgasm, her feelings of "failure" are heightened by these negative reactions from her partner (Nowinski, 1982). To avoid these interpersonal conflicts, some women simply pretend that they experience orgasm. The ability to fool a man by "faking" a climax does not, of course, solve the basic problem.

The Timing of Orgasms as a Special Problem for Men. For men, orgasmic dysfunction usually revolves around the timing of their ejaculation–orgasm. According to Masters and Johnson in 1970, the second most commonly reported male sexual problem (after erectile dysfunction) was **premature ejaculation** (41 percent of the cases). In the 1980s, however, they found that millions of men ejaculate prematurely, making this the most common male sexual dysfunction in the United States.

The precise definition of premature ejaculation can be fuzzy. Both subjective and objective criteria have been used in attempts to define what exactly is meant by an ejaculation being "premature." For example, Meyer (1977) suggests that ejaculation is premature if it occurs before penetration or within the first fifteen thrusts. For Kinsey (1948), the criterion was ejaculation within one minute after insertion. For

Masters and Johnson (1970) the criterion is a pattern (occurring more than half the time) of ejaculating before the partner reaches orgasm.

Because each of these definitions is imperfect, many therapists prefer Kaplan's (1979a) emphasis on whether the man has control over his orgasmic response as the determining factor. Normally, men learn to be aware of the sensations that precede the point of no return—when ejaculation is imminent (Kappelman, 1981). Thus, a man can control the timing of his orgasm by slowing down, speeding up, engaging or not engaging in a particularly exciting fantasy, and so forth. Such control ordinarily increases with sexual experience, enhancing the pleasure of the two partners (Hancock, 1982).

If a man lacks sufficient control of his ejaculation and responds too quickly to please him and/or his partner, his response is dysfunctional. For women, a rapid orgasm creates no problems because there is no refractory period to bring the sexual interaction to a halt. A woman who reaches orgasm quickly is, in fact, praised for her sexual responsiveness, even if her climax occurs during foreplay, prior to penetration.

How upsetting is it for men who ejaculate prematurely? Some question their manliness, while others are not bothered at all. In part, these different reactions are influenced by their partners. Some women express sympathy and understanding, and others respond with anger and rejection.

Why is premature ejaculation a matter of concern? Some speculate that society's increasing awareness of women's rights and needs helped focus attention on this aspect of male sexual responding. Actually, premature ejaculation has been considered a problem since antiquity: In Greek mythology, Hephaestus experienced it with Athena (Ehrentheil, 1974). Biologically, the prematurity of the male orgasm has no meaning; ejaculation into the vagina can result in conception whether the male thrusts for thirty seconds or thirty minutes. In fact, from a sociobiological perspective, rapid ejaculation was originally beneficial. A man who responded quickly during intercourse had a better chance to pass on his genes to the next generation than a man who engaged in leisurely sex, risking attack by other men and wild animals (Bixler, 1986). Today, an emphasis on mutual pleasure and a slower sexual pace have replaced any possible biological advantages for ejaculatory speed (Hong, 1984).

The Origin of Premature Ejaculation. Most cases of premature ejaculation are psychogenic (Derogatis, 1980; Pirke et al., 1979). Many premature ejaculators apparently have learned the wrong cues about their sexual sensation. For example, some young men learn to increase the speed of ejaculation in order to avoid discovery by others (Cooper, 1981). Also, young males who participate in group masturbation often compete to "win" by being the first to ejaculate. On the basis of such experiences, an individual is learning precisely the wrong cues and the wrong responses for pleasurable, mutually satisfying intercourse.

For the inexperienced male, the situational difference between solitary masturbation and sexual interaction with a partner can increase the likelihood of premature ejaculation. Monitoring your sexual sensations is relatively easy when masturbating alone, but the presence of a partner can interfere with the process either by making you anxious or by raising your level of excitement. In either instance, there is less control of ejaculation (Strassberg et al., 1987). If the woman's lubrication decreases (for whatever reason), this can increase penile friction during intercourse, hastening the man's orgasm (Steege, 1981).

When Ejaculation Is Delayed or Absent. A quite different male sexual dysfunction is the delay or complete absence of orgasm, called **inhibited male orgasm,** or *ejaculatory incompetence.* If the problem is temporary and based on drug use, illness, or fatigue, it usually solves itself in time. A typical response by men experiencing this problem is to pretend to climax so that their partner will not react negatively.

One type of inhibited male orgasm is **retarded ejaculation,** or a delay of ejaculation, in which prolonged stimulation is required for orgasm to occur. This condition is rare; according to Masters and Johnson (1970), only 3 percent of their dysfunctional male patients had this problem. Some evidence suggests that retarded ejaculation indicates conflicted feelings about women (Munjack and Kanno, 1979).

The assumption is that the male withholds ejaculation as an act of hostility toward his partner.

Some women respond to retarded ejaculation by assuming that a partner does not find her attractive or enjoy having intercourse with her, or that he is interacting sexually with someone else. These responses add to the man's problem; he needs understanding, sensitivity, and the absence of blame.

Sex Therapy for Individuals

Sexual dysfunctions can be treated individually or with the participation of the two involved partners. Some therapists, such as Masters and Johnson, strongly prefer working with couples. Others feel that it is helpful to work directly with the dysfunctional individual. We will describe both types of sex therapy.

■ Preliminary Examinations: Medical and Sexual

In **sex therapy** for either individuals or couples, participants first are asked to supply the intimate details of their sexual behavior to a therapist. The topics covered in the **sexual history** taken by the therapist range from sex education and childhood sex play to current sexual experiences (Pomeroy et al., 1981). Clinicians have developed questionnaires to record such information (for example, Conte, 1983; McCoy and D'Agostino, 1977). Often, the therapist asks the client to respond to a series of statements by agreeing or disagreeing:

> *I enjoy the sex techniques that my partner likes or uses.*
> *I feel that I should have sex more often.*
> *When we have sex it is too rushed and hurriedly completed [Hudson et al., 1981].*

The person with a sexual dysfunction is likely to disagree with the first statement and agree with the other two.

An example of this kind of measure is the Sexual Experience Scale (Derogatis and Melisaratos, 1979), which asks for frequency estimates with re-

spect to intercourse, kissing, and orgasm over the previous month plus a global rating of satisfaction. The consistency and accuracy of these estimates vary over time and among different individuals (Andersen and Broffitt, 1988). Other scales ask for more detailed reports of the number of minutes and of the outcome of each sexual act occurring over several months (Marks et al., 1988).

Those with sexual dysfunctions also are expected to have a complete medical examination in order to rule out possible organic causes (Weisberg, 1981). The patient with a sexual dysfunction usually brings the problem initially to his or her regular physician, only to find that there is no physical basis for the malfunctioning. At this point, the patient is usually referred to a sex therapist.

The concept of a psychosexual dysfunction seems to be somewhat threatening to men. Combining the various types of dysfunction, only one in five males who are referred actually makes an appointment with a sex therapist. Only one in ten completes such therapy (Segraves et al., 1982).

The next step is a **sexological examination** of the pelvic area to determine its physical condition and responsiveness (Hartman and Fithian, 1973). Some sex therapists instruct each client to touch various parts of his or her own body in private and to describe their feelings afterward. Other therapists direct their clients to stand naked in front of a mirror while touching their bodies and to communicate with the therapist directly. A third variation is for the therapist to touch the client's genitals to determine sexual responsiveness (Hartman and Fithian, 1982).

Considering the intimate nature of the questions in the sexual history questionnaire and the intrusive aspects of the sexological examination, it is not surprising that clients are often initially suspicious of the motives of sex therapists. They may wonder whether the therapist plans to treat the sexual problem or to seduce the client. When a sex therapist gave a guest lecture in one of our college courses, this was one of the questions raised by students. Any sexual approach to a client by a therapist is considered unethical, of course. The special section *Taking Responsibility and Protecting Yourself*, on page 466, discusses this and other issues relevant to sex therapists.

■ Preparing for Sexual Exercises

After the therapist has taken the client's sexual history, the findings are discussed, including the specifics of the dysfunction causing distress. Next, the client is prepared to engage in specific exercises as part of therapy. If the partner is clearly part of the client's problem, he or she is invited to help in resolving it.

Sex education is a critical part of the therapeutic process. The client's knowledge about sexual anatomy, functioning, and techniques—including the material covered in this text—is often faulty. Lack of correct information plus the acceptance of various sexual myths can contribute directly to a dysfunction. For example, some clients believe the following: high levels of sexual arousal are dangerous to one's health; only gays respond sexually to caresses of their nip-

---

Taking Responsibility and Protecting Yourself

THE BACKGROUND AND BEHAVIOR OF SEX THERAPISTS

Although people often turn to a physician when they have sexual problems, the medical training of most doctors includes very little about sexual functioning or dysfunctions (Labby, 1983). Medical schools today often have brief courses on human sexuality, but the content is too limited to prepare physicians to respond to the complex requirements of a patient with sexual problems (Birk, 1981; Mathis, 1981). Because of the need for professional help in this area, an increasing number of sex therapists are being trained to deal with sexual dysfunctions (Babineau and Schwartz, 1977). People of all ages can develop sexual dysfunctions, and increasingly they turn to professional therapists for help.

In evaluating the qualifications of a professional sex therapist, a prospective client should find out whether that person has (1) a valid graduate (postbaccalaureate) degree from a university, (2) clinical training in sex therapy supervised by a trained professional, and (3) the willingness to discuss and verify his or her professional background, training, methods of therapy, and fees. The American Association of Sex Educators, Counselors, and Therapists in Washington, D.C., certifies sex therapists and publishes a national directory listing their names. The Society for the Scientific Study of Sex in Mount Ver-

non, Iowa, provides information on the accreditation of human sexuality programs. Many universities and medical schools are affiliated with sex therapy clinics. In summary, anyone seeking a sex therapist should obtain more information than is available in the Yellow Pages of the telephone book. Some clients express concerns about whether to select a male or female therapist, but no consistent, reliable differences are found in treatment effectiveness based on the gender of the sex therapist (Barak and Fisher, 1989).

Given the highly personal and potentially threatening aspects of sex therapy (Winstead et al., 1988), any indiscretion on the part of a therapist—expecially if sex is involved—is intolerable. Among the early warning signs of potential sexual involvement are self-disclosures by the therapist concerning his or her own personal problems and an excessive amount of physical contact with the client (Goleman, 1990). A pamphlet published by the American Psychological Association, *If Sex Enters into the Psychotherapy Relationship,* defines what is meant by sexual contact, outlines the problems created by sexual contacts between therapists and clients, and lists the options open to the client if such a situation arises, including the notification of state licensing boards and the major national organizations. Copies of

this publication are available from APA, P.O. Box 2710, Hyattsville, MD 20784.

No specific studies of sexual misbehavior by sex therapists have been reported. Nevertheless, investigations of clinical psychologists and physicians suggest that about 9 percent of male professionals and 2 percent of female professionals *do* interact sexually with those they are treating, although the percentage of therapists admitting such contact has dropped in recent years. (Kardener et al., 1973; Pope et al., 1986). Though the percentages seem small, the unethical practitioners tend to repeat the behavior over time and thus victimize a great many clients unless they are stopped.

Among the new responsibilities for those dealing with the sexual problems of clients is responding to the information that the individual tests positive for HIV virus. If so, it is necessary to inform that person's sexual partner(s) of their possible exposure to AIDS (Girardi et al., 1988).

Experts generally agree that all healthcare professionals need better training to prepare them for dealing with sexual problems. Roberts (1981), for example, recommends that future therapists closely examine their own sexual attitudes and values to ensure that their behavior will not harm vulnerable clients.

ples; males have a lifetime quota of ejaculations so they must be rationed "to save for the future"; oral sex is a perversion; or masturbation is a sign of immaturity. Depending on the pervasiveness of such misinformation, the educational aspect of sex therapy may be limited or quite extensive.

The client's current sexual activities are also a matter of concern. Until there is some progress in dealing with the dysfunction, the therapist usually instructs the person to avoid intercourse. This advice may seem strange, but the rationale is that unreasonably early attempts to engage in sexual activity may create problems and undermine what has been accomplished. For example, if a man has a problem with premature ejaculation and is beginning to learn sensual relaxation, he may decide that he is ready for intercourse. If the result is—once again—premature ejaculation, his failure could convince him that he is incurable, thus delaying or preventing further progress (Hartman and Fithian, 1973; Kaplan, 1974; Lobitz and LoPiccolo, 1972; Masters and Johnson, 1970).

Sexual Exercises: Women

The exercises prescribed by the therapist depend on the specific dysfunction. The client performs them privately, as therapeutic "homework."

Masturbation Training. Masturbation is an important step in treating sexual dysfunctions. A woman who is dysfunctional needs to learn how to obtain maximal sexual pleasure during self-stimulation. In **masturbation training,** the therapist first instructs a female patient to masturbate manually. If this does not lead to orgasm, the therapist suggests using a vibrator. Learning to enjoy masturbation does not mean that this act becomes a substitute for intercourse; rather, it makes intercourse more enjoyable (Leff and Israel, 1983).

The thoughts that accompany masturbation are all-important determinants of whether the experience is pleasurable. **Orgasmic reconditioning** consists of guiding the client toward exciting and enjoyable thoughts and away from those involving anxiety, guilt, or boredom. During sexual stimulation, a nonorgasmic woman may focus, for example, on worries about her attractiveness or whether she will be

able to reach orgasm. With reconditioning, she learns to avoid those unpleasant thoughts and to substitute fantasies about pleasurable sexual interactions. Simply learning to have and to enjoy guilt-free fantasies while masturbating to orgasm is a crucial step in overcoming many dysfunctions. A common procedure is for the woman to begin masturbating alone and later to include her partner. Women who devote a lot of time to such masturbation exercises receive the greatest benefit (Van Wyk, 1982).

Part of masturbation training may include film viewing. Appropriate movies provide information and have positive effects on sexual thoughts, emotions, and behavior. One such film, *The Sexually Mature Adult,* describes the sensual pleasure that accompanies clitoral stimulation. When married women viewed this film and heard a lecture on methods of clitoral stimulation, they were more knowledgeable afterward about reasons for female orgasmic difficulties during intercourse than women in a control group (Wilcox and Hager, 1980). As Figure 17-8 shows, exposure to the film and lecture led to greater agreement that the absence of an orgasm was caused by insufficient clitoral stimulation rather than the woman's failure to feel free and relaxed.

Increased Muscle Control. The PC (pubococcygeal) muscle surrounds the introitus, as described in Chapter 2. A device inserted into the vagina can measure the strength of the muscle (Logan, 1975). Women with sexual dysfunction can perform **Kegel exercises** to strengthen the muscle by repeatedly contracting and relaxing it, monitoring their progress with the measuring instrument.

Even among women without sexual dysfunctions, those engaging in Kegel exercises begin to respond to erotic fantasies with increased sexual excitement (Messe and Geer, 1985). Despite their usefulness, these exercises do not increase orgasm frequency, and orgasms can occur in the absence of strong PC muscles (Chambless et al., 1982, 1984).

Treating Vaginismus. In treating vaginismus, the first step is to deal with the physical problem and then to provide sex therapy. The therapist may use vaginal dilators, illustrated in Figure 17-9. First, the smallest are briefly inserted, then gradually replaced by larger dilators for longer time periods.

A related technique is the insertion of a finger—initially, that of the therapist, eventually the client's, and later her partner's—into the vagina as she alternately relaxes and contracts her vaginal muscles (Kaufman, 1982). The goal of each technque is for the woman to learn that penetration can be painless and that she can control her muscle contractions.

■ Sexual Exercises: Men

Historically, sexually dysfunctional men were punished rather than treated. In the twelfth century A.D., for example, a woman could annul her marriage if her husband was unable to impregnate her because he had an erectile dysfunction. In sixteenth- and seventeenth-century France, a man accused of this "weakness" could defend himself of the charge of impotence only by performing sexually with his spouse in front of a medical tribunal (Darmon, 1986). The level of performance anxiety under such circumstances was no doubt unusually high, and today's sex therapy appears to be a preferable approach.

Therapy for Erectile Dysfunction. Most men (51 percent) with erectile dysfunction do not enter sex therapy or seek other types of treatment for their problem. When sex therapy is recommended to them, only about 35 percent comply; when a penile prosthesis is recommended, less than 30 percent obtain one (Tiefer and Melman, 1987).

Sex therapists use two major techniques to treat erectile dysfunction (Kilmann and Auerbach, 1979). One of these guides men through an extensive re-learning process. They are taught to masturbate without feeling anxious and to talk honestly with their partner about sexual problems (Lobitz and Baker, 1979). They also learn how to have more enjoyable sexual fantasies and to detect their physical sensations during lovemaking (Price et al., 1981).

The second technique, used by behavior therapists, is **systematic desensitization.** The man is instructed to practice deep relaxation while creating erotic fantasies that become increasingly more exciting as he masturbates. Sometimes he is shown explicit sexual films to augment his own fantasies and to reduce anxiety. The goal is to teach him to fantasize and to enjoy stimulation in a nonthreatening, guilt-free atmosphere.

Learning to Control the Ejaculatory Response. Therapy for premature ejaculation focuses on the behavior and sensations that accompany the high levels of excitement preceding orgasm. In 1956 a urologic physician, James Semans, developed a procedure, called the **stop** (or **pause**) **method,** to prolong sexual arousal and delay ejaculation. Semans instructed his patients to masturbate to a full erection and then stop for several seconds until they were able to experience further stimulation without ejaculating. Such pauses were repeated, each time reaching higher levels of arousal. After practicing this procedure, patients were able to remain excited for an extended period of time

FIGURE 17-8 *LEARNING WHY ORGASMS DO NOT OCCUR* Married women were shown an educational film on sexuality, heard a talk about techniques of clitoral stimulation, and received information supplementing the lecture. The additional information discussed the research in detail and pointed out the importance of clitoral stimulation for a woman's orgasmic response. The control group simply viewed the film and heard the lecture—without further explanation. Compared to a control group, the women receiving the supplementary information correctly identified the cause of a female's lack of orgasm during intercourse as insufficient clitoral stimulation. Women in the experimental group also placed less blame on their own tense feelings as the reason for not having an orgasm. Such educational information can help correct misconceptions about the causes of sexual problems.
Source: Based on data from Wilcox and Hager, 1980.

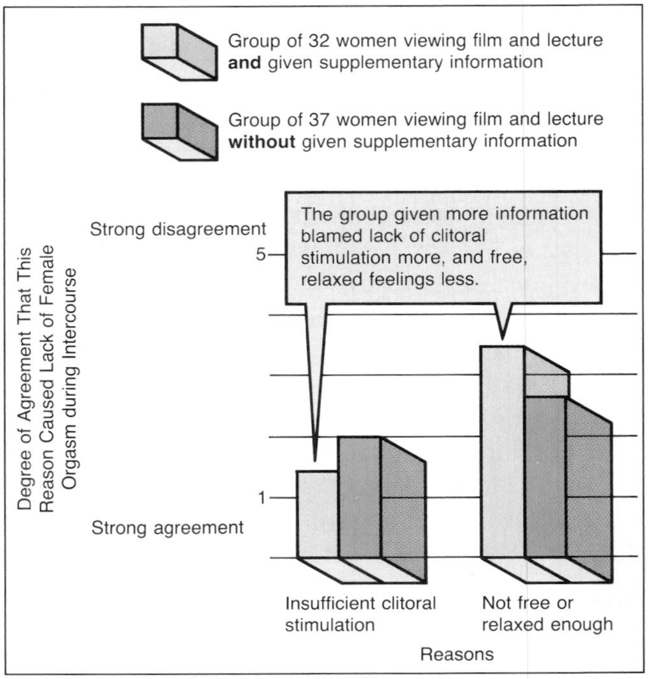

Group of 32 women viewing film and lecture **and** given supplementary information

Group of 37 women viewing film and lecture **without** given supplementary information

The group given more information blamed lack of clitoral stimulation more, and free, relaxed feelings less.

Degree of Agreement That This Reason Caused Lack of Female Orgasm during Intercourse

Strong disagreement — 5

Strong agreement — 1

Insufficient clitoral stimulation

Not free or relaxed enough

Reasons

FIGURE 17-9 *VAGINAL DILATION FOR VAGINISMUS* As part of the treatment for vaginismus, the therapist uses vaginal dilators to help the woman learn to control and relax the muscles surrounding the outer third of her vagina.

prior to orgasm. Then, they were told to attempt intercourse, pausing if necessary to delay ejaculation (Kaplan et al., 1974).

Adapting Semans' basic idea, Masters and Johnson (1970) developed the **squeeze method** as a substitute for the pause. When the man feels on the brink of ejaculating, either he or his partner presses the penis under the coronal ridge, just beneath the rim, as Figure 17-10 illustrates. The man lies on his back in order to reduce myotonia and thus have better control over his arousal level. When interacting with a partner, he is encouraged to communicate about his arousal. The squeeze is firm, but not hard enough to cause pain. This is an easy procedure to learn, even from written instructions (Zeiss, 1978),

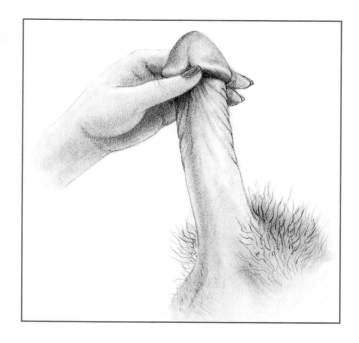

FIGURE 17-10 *THE SQUEEZE TECHNIQUE: LEARNING TO CONTROL EJACULATION* The squeeze technique for treating premature ejaculation was developed by Masters and Johnson (1970), who adapted it from Semans' (1956) pause (stop) method. Just as the male feels he is about to ejaculate, he or his partner firmly squeezes the penis for three to four seconds to prevent orgasm. After fifteen to thirty seconds, stimulation is resumed.

and any couple can use it as long as is necessary until ejaculatory control is achieved.

For generalized retarded ejaculation, therapy involves practice in stimulating the penis manually to orgasm until it occurs reliably. Then, intercourse is substituted for masturbation. If the patient has had no difficulty with masturbation, only with intercourse, the therapist suggests an alternative procedure. The client's female partner participates in his therapy by learning to masturbate the man until just before he ejaculates, then she quickly inserts the penis in her vagina so that he ejaculates inside her. The couple repeats this process over time until penetration and thrusting gradually replace the lengthy period of masturbation (O'Connor and Flax, 1981; Oziel, 1978).

Sex Therapy with Couples

Couples often participate jointly in sex therapy. In some of the exercises just described, the partner's co-operation is necessary. Whenever the partner is contributing to the dysfunction (with criticism or ridicule, for example), his or her participation is even more important so that the therapist can attempt to alter the maladaptive behavior.

As in treating individuals, therapists generally employ four steps with couples: sexological examination, sex education, sexual exercises, and the application of the new knowledge and skills to intercourse. Table 17-1 summarizes these steps. Each of the different models of sex therapy shares this same general structure, while incorporating specific variations.

■ The PLISSIT Model

Psychologist Jack Annon (1974, 1975) developed the **PLISSIT** model of sex therapy, organized into educational, practical, and therapeutic aspects. The letters stand for individual portions of the procedure. *P* refers to *permission*. The therapist instructs each client to examine his or her own thoughts, fantasies, and feelings that contribute to sexuality; the goal is to realize that the person is permitted to have a highly arousing sex life. Many people hold irrational beliefs or unrealistic expectations that interfere with sexual behavior, and they need to learn how to control and change these cognitions (Epstein, 1981b). The treatment at this state constitutes **rational-emotive therapy**, designed to substitute rational cognitions for irrational ones (Ellis and Harper, 1975).

Next, each client receives *LI,* or *limited information,* about sexuality. This includes educational mate-

---

TABLE 17-1   **The Steps Involved in Sex Therapy**

Most forms of sex therapy are built around these four basic steps.

I. SEXUAL HISTORY: THE COLLECTION OF INFORMATION

Following a medical examination, the therapist obtains a sexual history from the client, performs a sexological examination, and identifies the sexual dysfunction.

II. PREPARATION FOR SEXUAL EXERCISES: SEX EDUCATION

Discussions clear up misinformation and provide basic knowledge about anatomy and functioning prior to sexual exercises.

III. SEXUAL EXERCISES: BEHAVIOR THERAPY FOR THE DYSFUNCTION

The therapist prescribes exercises specific to each type of dysfunction, and the client practices them.

IV. INTERCOURSE: APPLICATION OF WHAT HAS BEEN LEARNED

If the the treatment is successful, successful and satisfying vaginal intercourse takes place in this last stage of therapy.

rial dealing with sexual anatomy, masturbation, and other basic factual content. Then, at the *SS (specific suggestions)* level, the therapist talks to the couple about their sexual concerns and tells them how to correct the dysfunction. The procedure is designed to improve communication, increase sexual arousal, and reduce anxiety. If the result is successful functioning, therapy is discontinued. If not, a final step is necessary—*IT, or intensive therapy.* Most clients do not require IT with the focus on masturbation training and orgasmic reconditioning.

■ Kaplan: Therapy for Sexual Apathy

Psychiatrist Helen Kaplan (1974, 1979a) regards psychological therapy as critical to stimulate sexual desire. According to Kaplan (as discussed in Chapter 3), human sexual response involves three phases consisting of desire, arousal, and orgasm. *Sexual apathy,* or lack of desire, is hypothesized to stem from deep conflicts about sexuality developed in childhood—as a result, this is the most difficult dysfunction to treat. Sexual apathy is unaffected by the partner's pleading for or demanding a sexual response, or by wearing sexy underclothing and providing candlelight. Instead, intensive psychotherapy is required (Lehman, 1986).

Kaplan's theory and therapy combine psychoanalytic principles and the techniques of behavior therapy. Other therapists place less emphasis on long-term, intensive therapy in treating desire disorders, favoring short-term treatment focusing on the thoughts, feelings, and behaviors that interfere with sexuality (Leiblum and Rosen, 1988; LoPiccolo and Friedman, 1988). While Kaplan agrees that some causes of sexual dysfunction may be relatively obvious and accessible, others—such as unconscious guilt and anxiety—lie deeply hidden and require prolonged psychoanalysis. One way to reach them is to combine hypnosis with more traditional forms of sex therapy. While hypnotized, the client can set aside self-criticism and allow pleasurable erotic feelings to surface (Araoz, 1982).

When the effects of combined hypnosis–sex therapy were compared with sex therapy alone in treating women with primary anorgasmia, the combined procedure was found to be more effective

(Obler, 1982). A follow-up study indicated that those receiving hypnotic sex therapy still showed improvement four years later.

You may be interested to learn that Dr. Kaplan is married to the owner of Toys 'R Us, should the question arise while playing a trivia game.

■ Body-work Sex Therapy: Paraprofessionals and Surrogates

Sex therapist Bernard Apfelbaum (1977; 1984) describes **individual body-work sex therapy** in which paraprofessionals interact with each dysfunctional client in sexual exercises. These assistants receive short-term training in body work to enable them to engage in a "standard sexual encounter" with a client. The paraprofessional is trained to proceed slowly enough to make it possible to recognize any anxieties that may arise during the encounter and to calm them. The assistant, as part of the sexological examination, stimulates the partner sexually and masturbates to orgasm while being observed by the client.

An individual who enters sex therapy but does not have a partner also may be provided with a **surrogate partner** for the various exercises, including intercourse. Most often, the surrogate is a woman, but some male surrogates are used. Most surrogates receive about $50 to $60 for a two-hour session. Dauw (1988) describes the successful use of surrogates in therapy with male clients having erectile and orgasmic dysfunctions, premature ejaculation, and inhibited sexual desire; 84 to 98 percent had positive results.

Many who learn about the use of paraprofessionals and surrogates perceive the practice as being closer to prostitution than to therapy. Because of the nature and the goals of their work, surrogates are not prosecuted for prostitution in most states. The International Professional Surrogates Association maintains that, as members of a therapy team, surrogates must closely follow the therapist's instructions and regularly report as to progess and problems.

Other legal and ethical objects are also raised. What if a personal relationship develops between client and surrogate? What if pregnancy results? What if either partner transmits a disease to the other? These and other concerns have persuaded many sex therapists to avoid the use of surrogates altogether.

Behavior Therapy

For decades psychologists have applied learning theory to alter behavior problems with the techniques of *behavior therapy* (once called behavior modification). At the most basic level, desirable acts are reinforced; as a result, they occur more frequently. As introduced by Wolpe in the 1950s, the therapist also treats unwanted fears and anxieties through desensitization procedures, first extinguishing them and then substituting positive responses. This approach is commonly used in sex therapy (Heiman et al., 1976; Leiblum and Pervin, 1980).

How, specifically, is behavior therapy used to treat sexual problems? For example, in treating an anorgasmic woman, the therapist leads her toward orgasmic intercourse through a series of steps (LoPiccolo and Lobitz, 1972). Table 17-2 summarizes these procedures. Therapy begins at step 1 with the client engaging in nonthreatening fantasies while she masturbates manually. Once she has become thoroughly comfortable with this step, her partner joins her in step 2 to observe as she fantasizes and masturbates,

but he does not participate (Zeiss et al., 1977). The purpose of his presence is to help her learn to feel comfortable about being aroused and having an orgasm in his presence; also, he is able to learn exactly how she caresses herself to produce the greatest pleasure. Various intermediate steps, known as **bridge maneuver**, include manual masturbation by the client and engaging in pelvic rocking as a way of reaching orgasm (Kaplan, 1974).

In step 3, the patient is again alone, but this time she uses a dildo to masturbate and to penetrate her vagina. The phallic object is used so that she can become familiar and comfortable with the sensations that accompany vaginal stimulation. In step 4 she engages in intercourse fantasies while gently thrusting with the dildo (see Figure 17-11).

In step 5 the male partner returns, and he again simply observes how she stimulates herself. She learns to relax with him present; it is important that she controls all aspects of the penetration and thrusting until reaching orgasm, coaching him about what feels best to her. Finally, in step 6 the couple engages in foreplay and intercourse as the woman fantasizes and focuses on the sensations elicited by the penis in her vagina. Orgasm may or may not occur in the early sessions of this step; of greater importance is for the couple to become lovingly involved with each other's pleasure.

TABLE 17-2   **Learning to Associate Sexual Pleasure, Fantasies, and Vaginal Penetration**

Female orgasmic dysfunction can be treated by a six-step course of behavior therapy such as the one presented here. The goal is to teach the woman to associate masturbatory orgasms with intercourse fantasies and the sensations of vaginal penetration. Afterward, she and her partner apply these lessons to intercourse itself. These steps take place over a series of sessions lasting several weeks, interspersed with consultations with the therapist.

A BEHAVIOR THERAPY PLAN FOR FEMALE ORGASMIC DYSFUNCTION

Step 1. The woman fantasizes about intercourse while masturbating to orgasm.
Step 2. The male partner observes her self-stimulation to learn what pleases her most.
Step 3. She uses a dildo to masturbate.
Step 4. She fantasizes about intercourse with her partner while masturbating with a dildo.
Step 5. The male partner returns to observe and learn as she masturbates to orgasm.
Step 6. The couple has intercourse, and penile penetration occurs while the woman engages in pleasurable fantasies.

Source: Based on Zeiss et al., 1977.

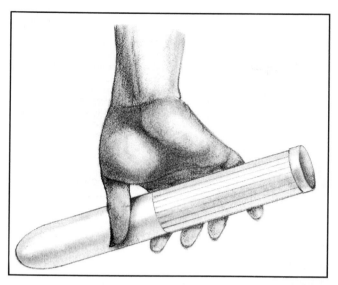

FIGURE 17-11 *DILDO: ONE OF THE TOOLS USED IN SEX THER-APY* During behavior therapy for orgasmic dysfunction, the woman uses a dildo as a penis substitute.

Women who participate in this type of therapy typically experience an increase in intercourse-induced orgasms. A manual provided by the therapist provides information about each of the therapeutic steps (Dodge et al., 1982).

■ **The Techniques of Masters and Johnson**

Undoubtedly the best known therapy used to treat sexual dysfunctions is that developed by the husband–wife team of physician William Masters and psychologist Virginia Johnson. Their procedures have evolved since their work began in 1959, combining many of the elements already discussed in this chapter with innovations of their own.

Instead of long-term therapy, Masters and Johnson prefer a relatively rapid approach involving a two-week treatment program in which couples participate in daily sessions. This format is designed to reduce anxiety and to correct any mistakes that clients may be making. A primary aim is to eliminate concerns about sexual performance. The message is that sexual acts are done for pleasure rather than to achieve a goal involving certain standards and the possibility of failure.

Perhaps the most notable feature of the Masters and Johnson program is **sensate focus**, in which ". . . subjective appreciation of sexual responsivity derives return from positive pleasure in sensory experiences that, in turn, derive their individual meaning and value from the patient's psychosocial sexual background" (Masters and Johnson, 1970, p. 65). Put in less formidable terms, the couple take turns giving and receiving pleasure from touching different parts of each other's bodies (avoiding genitals and breasts) without pressure to respond in any specified way, as Figure 17-12 illustrates.

Couples engaging in sensate focus use moisturizing lotions on their bodies to increase the enjoyable sensations. Until the co-therapists (a male and a female) decide that the time is appropriate, sexual intercourse and other sexual acts are ruled out. The reasoning underlying such rules is that the couple needs to learn about the sensual pleasures of mutual caresses without the threat of having to perform sexually.

This therapy is performed at the Masters and Johnson Institute in St. Louis, Missouri. From a large pool of applicants, couples are selected for the treatment, which costs several thousand dollars. At one time, surrogates were available for single clients or those with nonparticipating spouses, but this aspect of treatment has been abandoned.

Table 17-3 outlines the course of therapy. As in other therapies, the clients provide sexual histories and undergo a medical examination. The probable cause of the dysfunction is discussed, and homework assignments are given. The latter sessions alternate with sex education and discussions that focus on the couple's reaction to the experience. The therapists ordinarily prescribe some combination of Kegel exercises, the squeeze technique, masturbation, the use of a vibrator, and mutual exploration of genitals before vaginal intercourse is resumed.

Evaluating the Effectiveness of Sex Therapy

As with any treatment procedure, it is essential to ask, "Does it work?" or "How effective is it?" As you may expect, there is some disagreement about the value of sex therapy.

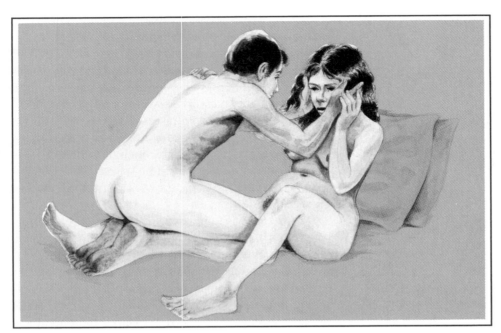

FIGURE 17-12 *SENSATE FOCUS: NONDEMAND PLEASURING* In sensate focus, sexual partners take turns giving and receiving sensual pleasure, avoiding genitals and breasts. This couple is also using the "hand-riding" technique in which one of them places a hand over the other's hand to provide nonverbal feedback about what provides the greatest pleasure.

TABLE 17-3   **The Two-week Sex Therapy of Masters and Johnson**

The outline for the Masters and Johnson program for sex therapy consists of the components outlined here. A male–female co-therapist team conducts the program.

Day 1	The initial interview is conducted by a therapist of the same sex as the client, gathering a sexual and a life history.
Day 2	A second interview is conducted by a therapist of the opposite sex to assess the client's motivation for sex therapy. Both partners are interviewed.
Day 3	A medical examination is completed. The therapists and the clients discuss the probable cause of the sexual dysfunction. Sensate focus is assigned for homework.
Day 4	There is a discussion of reactions to sensate focus, and information about sexual anatomy is provided. Sensate focus that includes breast and genital stimulation is assigned.
Days 5 to 14	The therapists direct the couple to perform specific sexual exercises for the particular dysfunction in private.

Source: Masters and Johnson, 1970.

■   **Factors That Affect Success**

Definitions of "success" vary from study to study, but generally an outcome is considered successful if there is improvement in the sexual dysfunction, lasting for an extended period of time after therapy ends, usually several months or years. To what extent is success affected by the person seeking therapy and to what extent by the therapy itself?

Characteristics of the Clients.   Some dysfunctional clients are more likely to benefit from therapy than others. For example, couples with a marginally functioning marriage respond less well than happily married couples (Abramowitz and Sewell, 1980). Because sex therapy deals only with the couple's sexual interaction, marital therapy may be necessary as a separate procedure.

Even within a smoothly functioning marriage, a person who is flexible and open to change is best able to benefit from sex therapy. Such people find it easier to change, and they are more likely to persist in therapy than those who are rigid (Sewell and Abramowitz, 1979). Those clients who do persist in pursuing sex therapy experience some beneficial side effects. In a study of a large group of couples in which either the man or the woman was dysfunctional, both the clients and their partners were less depressed and socially inhibited after therapy than before (Clement and Pfafflin, 1980).

Such results occur because people feel better about themselves and their marriage when a dysfunction improves. In discussing intimate matters with a therapist, clients learn how to express their feelings more openly to their partners and to be more assertive in making their needs known (Tullman et al., 1981). Thus, sex therapy not only enhances sexual enjoyment but also leads to improved social skills.

The Therapy Itself. Studies of other kinds of therapy sometimes find that the crucial element is not the treatment itself but the process of acknowledging that a problem exists and seeking help for it. Even with physical illness, this effect is often observed. You may have had the experience of feeling terrible, visiting a physician, being told that your problem is a sinus infection or whatever, receiving a prescription, and discovering on the way to the pharmacist that you feel 100 percent better even before taking the first dose of medication. Sexual dysfunctions can be affected in a similar way by entering sex therapy, but the gains sometimes disappear a few months after therapy ends (Kilmann et al., 1986).

In each variety of sex therapy, many different specific procedures are combined, so there is no way to know which are essential and which are irrelevant. For example, is it really important for the therapist to prohibit intercourse during the early stages of therapy? In an experiment designed to answer this question, males with secondary erectile dysfunction and their spouses were treated in one of two different procedures (Takefman and Brender, 1984). All couples were trained to communicate their sexual preferences, but half were instructed not to have intercourse while the other half were told that it was permitted. Contrary to expectations, sexual functioning improved to

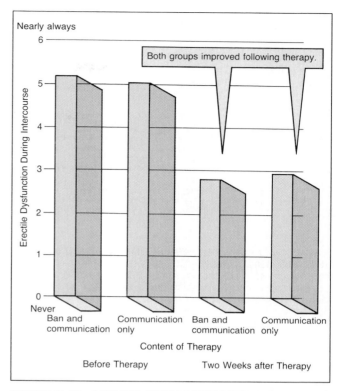

FIGURE 17-13 *BANNING INTERCOURSE DURING SEX THERAPY: AN IRRELEVANT PROCEDURE?* In this study of sex therapy, intercourse was either banned or not banned during sex therapy for secondary erectile dysfunction, and all 116 couples were instructed to communicate their sexual preferences. Regardless of the intercourse ban, dysfunctional men improved. It appears that the common practice of instructing couples to refrain from intercourse during the early stages of sex therapy is unnecessary.
Source: Based on data from Takefman and Brender, 1984.

an equal extent in both groups, as Figure 17-13 indicates.

Prohibiting intercourse, thus, had no effect. Further analysis indicates, however, that some of the dysfunctional males in both groups improved and some did not. The differentiating factor, as Figure 17-14 shows, was the degree of sexual satisfaction expressed by the couple prior to therapy. Erectile dysfunction was much more likely to improve if the couple was satisfied rather than dissatisfied.

This experiment indicates that communication training with sexually satisfied couples was helpful in treating erectile problems primarily in sexually satisfied couples and that a ban on intercourse neither enhanced nor interfered with the treatment. More research of this type is needed to identify precisely

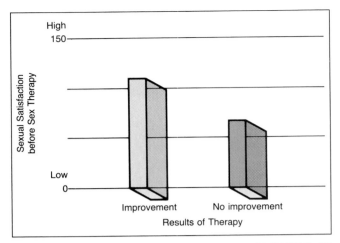

FIGURE 17-14 *MARITAL SATISFACTION AS A PREDICTOR OF WHO WILL BENEFIT FROM SEX THERAPY* In a study of sex therapy for erectile dysfunction, some of the 116 male clients improved and some did not. Following therapy, those men who benefited from the treatment had erections during 94 percent of their sexual interactions; those who did not improve had erections only 25 percent of the time. Men in the improved group reported greater sexual satisfaction in their marriage before therapy began than did those who failed to improve.
Source: Based on data from Takefman and Brender, 1984.

which therapeutic techniques are effective and which clients are most able to benefit from them.

■ Outcomes and Criticisms of Sex Therapy

Research designed to evaluate therapy outcome is difficult because the meaning of success is not always clear. If we set aside that problem and assume that success means improved sexual functioning as judged by the therapist or reported by the client, we can summarize the relative success of sex therapy with different dysfunctions.

A comparison of success rates for specific dysfunctions is presented in Table 17-4. Of the male dysfunctions, premature ejaculation responds most readily to treatment. For women, vaginismus and primary orgasmic dysfunction have better outcome prospects than secondary orgasmic dysfunction. Though detailed figures are not available, inhibited sexual desire in either men or women is consistently reported to be extremely resistant to improvement (De Amicis et al., 1985). Even when the client shows positive gains immediately after therapy, the dysfunction returns (Schover and LoPiccolo, 1982).

Strong criticism of sex therapy and its effectiveness raises questions about the data just presented. Zilbergeld and Evans (1980) charged that Masters and Johnson bias their outcome data in two significant ways. First, they select only those therapy clients most likely to benefit from it, thereby inflating their success rates. Second, the criteria for "success" is perceived as far too lenient. Responding to these arguments, Masters and Johnson argue that only 2 percent of the applicants to the St. Louis clinic are rejected for treatment and that their measures of long-term success are quite strict (Kolodny, 1981b).

Psychiatrist Thomas Szasz (1980) criticizes sex therapy in more general terms. The moral values of the clients are ignored, he asserts, and impersonal standards are applied in judging whether a person's sexual responses are dysfunctional. From his perspective, masturbation guilt or sexual repression are personal matters, not the concern of sex therapists. According to Szasz, a male who ejaculates prematurely simply has a different sexual style, not necessarily a dysfunction. By analogy, some people eat their meals quickly while others linger over each dish, but we don't label either group as dysfunctional and prescribe therapy for them.

The counterargument is that sex therapy is not forced on anyone. People who are unhappy about their sexual functioning seek it out. Sex therapy is popular because many people feel that it has helped their sexual functioning. Also note that the kind of behavioral sex therapy described in this chapter is much more effective in dealing with sexual problems than is traditional psychotherapy (Howard et al., 1986).

■ What the Individual Can Do to Prevent Sexual Dysfunctions

People who have been exposed to very restrictive, negative information about sex in childhood are more likely to have sexual dysfunctions than others. Anyone with this kind of background who wishes to change his or her beliefs or emotional responses can take steps to do so—learning more about sex by taking courses and reading books, for example. If a dysfunction does develop, some of the information

TABLE 17-4   **How Successful Is Sex Therapy?**

The percentage of clients for whom sex therapy was a success, as reported by various therapists, varies as a function of the specific dysfunction for each sex. The first column is based on data from almost 3,000 clients, two to five years after being treated in the Masters and Johnson Institute. The second column is based on reports of other therapists and consists of varying lengths of time following therapy.

TYPE OF DYSFUNCTION	PERCENTAGE OF CLIENTS FOR WHOM THERAPY WAS SUCCESSFUL	
	Masters and Johnson	Other Investigators
Males		
Primary erectile dysfunction	67%	77%
Secondary erectile dysfunction	78	43–66
Premature ejaculation	96	100
Retarded ejaculation	76	50
Females		
Primary orgasmic dysfunction	79%	100%
Secondary orgasmic dysfunction	71	33–37
Vaginismus	99	66

Source: Based on data from Cooper, 1971; Kolodny, Masters, and Johnson, 1979; Lobitz and LoPiccolo, 1972; Masters and Johnson, 1970; Milan, Kilmann, and Boland, 1988; O'Connor and Stern, 1972; Ovesay, cf. Kaplan, 1974; Semans, 1956.

presented in this chapter may help. If self-help procedures are ineffective, the person may decide to seek the aid of a qualified sex therapist.

On another note, it is wise to be skeptical about the claims of self-appointed experts as to how you can improve your sex life. A great deal of money is made in selling books and articles telling you what to do and how to do it, but little or no scientific effort is made to determine whether this advice is useful, useless, or harmful.

Instead, some general recommendations seem to be of greater value: Learn as much as possible about sexuality, discover how to communicate with a partner, learn to recognize and express your genuine feelings, and strive to provide yourself and your partner as much enjoyment as possible.

Summarizing the Information about Sexual Dysfunction and Therapy . . .

Sexual dysfunctions often are associated with general marital dissatisfactions, but not as the basic cause. A **psychosexual dysfunction** can be **primary** (a lifelong problem) or **secondary** (developing after a period of normal functioning). The dysfunction can be a **generalized** one affecting all sexual expression or a **situational** one affecting only specific interactions. **Inhibited sexual desire** is a lack of interest in sex; at the opposite extreme is a compulsive interest in interacting sexually with as many partners as possible, known as **Don Juanism** in men and **nymphoma-** nia in women. **Inhibited sexual excitement**, when not based on organic factors, is associated with **sexual anxiety**. The pain of **functional dyspareunia** can result in **functional vaginismus**, the clamping of vaginal muscles that prevents penetration. **Erectile dysfunction** can be caused by anxiety and made worse by the negative reactions of a partner. For women, **orgasmic dysfunction** is the most common sexual problem, and it is often based on negative personal feelings about sexuality. Among men, **premature ejaculation** develops in response to performance pressures and inattention to the internal sensations of excitement and impending orgasm. **Retarded ejaculation** is less common and can be caused by fatigue, drugs, or nonsexual worries.

Sex therapy begins with a **sexual history** and an educational program relevant to the client's dysfunction. Among the common exercises prescribed are **masturbation training** and **orgasmic reconditioning**, with the goal of using fantasies and improving sexual responsiveness. Some therapists recommend **Kegel exercises** for women. Anxieties and fears can be treated with **systematic desensitization** to replace negative emotional responses with positive ones. For premature ejaculation, the **squeeze method** is very effective.

Couples often participate in sex therapy even though only one individual is dysfunctional. Most sex therapies have a common structure, but specific variations include the **PLISSIT** model, Kaplan's emphasis on sexual desire, **individual body-work sex therapy** with a trained paraprofessional or surrogate, behavior therapy, and the procedures of Masters and Johnson, including **sensate focus**.

The success of sex therapy depends on the characteristics of the client, the specific dysfunction, the therapy itself, and whether the client is involved in a successful sexual relationship. Critics of sex therapy attack the procedures, the outcome data, and the values communicated to the clients. People can take steps to avoid developing dysfunctions by becoming knowledgeable about sex, learning to communicate, recognizing and expressing feelings, and attempting to give and receive as much enjoyment as possible.

To Find Out More about Sexual Dysfunction and Therapy . . .

Cameron-Bandler, L. (1985). *Solutions: Practical and effective antidotes for sexual and relationship problems*. San Rafael, Calif.: Future Press.

Written by a therapist, this book examines a method of self-help for relationship and sexual problems. The author emphasizes the cognitive aspects of these difficulties.

Cranston-Cuebas, M.A., & Barlow, D.H. (1990). Contributions to sexual functioning. In J. Bancroft, C.M. Davis, & D. Weinstein (Eds.), *Annual review of sex research*, Vol. I, (pp. 114-161). Mt. Vernon, IA: Foundation for the Scientific Study of Sexuality.

This is an up-to-date review of theory and research dealing with the way thought processes and emotions affect human sexual responsiveness.

Grosskopf, D. (1983). *Sex and the married woman*. New York: Simon & Schuster.

This book paints a lively picture of the lives of over 1,200 adult women who were surveyed about their fantasies, preferences, and practices. These women also describe what affects sexual desire and enjoyment at different stages of the life cycle.

Kaplan, H. S. (1989). *How to overcome premature ejaculation*. New York: Brunner/Mazel.

A leading sex therapist provides detailed instructions that enable a man to control his ejaculatory response.

Killmann, P. R., & Mills, K. H. (1983). *All about sex therapy*. New York: Plenum.

This manual should be useful to anyone who is contemplating sex therapy. The authors examine the possibilities, as well as the limits, of these therapeutic procedures.

APPENDIX A

These Drugs May Reduce the Effectiveness of Oral Contraceptives:

ampicillin
analgesics
anti-migraine
   preparations
barbiturates
chloramphenicol
griseofulvin
isoniazid
neomycin
nitrofurantoin

penicillin V
phenylbutazone
phenytoin
primidone
rifampin
sulfonamides
tetracycline
tranquilizers, such as
    diazepam

Oral Contraceptives May Alter the Effectiveness of These Drugs:

acetaminophen
anti-convulsants
anti-hypertensive
   agents, such as
   guanethidine
clofibrate
glucocorticoids

hypoglycemic agents
oral anticoagulants
theophylline
tricyclic
   anti-depressants
vitamins

GLOSSARY

abortion   The termination of a pregnancy.

Acquired Immune Deficiency Syndrome (AIDS)   A viral STD which is sexually transmissible. To date, there is no cure, and the disease is fatal.

adolescence   The period of human development following childhood, characterized by rapid social, physical, and emotional changes.

affective state   Emotions, feelings, or mood.

afterplay   The physical and verbal interactions between two individuals following orgasm.

agape (ah gáh pay)   Expressing charity and concern toward others.

AIDS-related complex (ARC)   An illness which may precede AIDS in which the body has difficulty in fighting infections. It is now called *symptomatic HIV infection*.

alcoholic feminization   The tendency of alcoholic males to develop some of the physical characteristics of women.

alimony   Support payments made to a former spouse following divorce.

amniocentesis (am nee oh sen tee´sis)   A procedure in which a sample of amniotic fluid is drawn in order to test for genetic problems in the fetus.

amniotic fluid (am knee oht´ ic)   The fluid that surrounds the developing embryo (and later, fetus).

analingus   Oral stimulation of the partner's anus.

anal intercourse   Penile penetration of the male or female partner's anus.

anal stage   The developmental stage proposed in psychoanalytic theory that involves interest in anal functioning, including toilet training.

androgen (an´ droh jen)   A group of hormones that are secreted by the testes, ovaries, and adrenal glands. They stimulate the growth of male sex structures.

androgenital syndrome (an droh jen´ ih tul)   Female pseudo-hermaphroditism that is caused by excessive androgen.

androgyny   The gender role in which both masculine and feminine traits are present.

andrologist (an droll´ oh jist)   A physician specializing in urology and the male reproductive system.

anger rape   Rape performed as an act of revenge or expression of hate, usually an interaction of relatively short duration.

anorexia   An eating disorder in which weight loss is carried to life-threatening extremes.

antecedent-consequent relationship   When changes in one variable are regularly followed by changes in a second variable, they are said to have an antecedent-consequent (or "cause and effect") relationship.

aphrodisiac (af row dee´ zee ak)   A substance assumed to enhance sexual desire or sexual enjoyment.

apotemnophilia   A paraphilia in which there is self-inflicted mutilation of one's body.

areola (ah ree´ oh lah)   The pigmented area surrounding the nipple.

attitude similarity   The extent to which two people agree about a series of topics.

autocratic tactics   An influence tactic characterized by insisting, asserting authority, or claiming greater knowledge than the other person.

bar boys   Male prostitutes who contact customers in bars; they ordinarily are willing to provide sexual services to either men or women.

bargaining   An influence tactic using reasoning and compromise.

bar girls   Prostitutes of relatively low status who contact prospective partners in bars.

Barr bodies (sex chromatin)   Inactive X-chromosome material, found in all normal females.

Bartholin's glands (Barth´ oh lins)   The two glands on either side of the vaginal introitus, which secrete a small amount of mucus.

bilateral orchiectomy (or kee ek´ toe mee)   The surgical removal of both testicles, also known as castration.

bisexual   Referring to a sexual orientation in which sexual behavior, affection, and fantasies are directed toward members of both sexes.

B-love (being-love)   Maslow's theoretical concept that focuses on the needs of the loved person.

bondage   A sadomasochistic activity involving physical restraint.

bondage and discipline (B & D)   Sadomasochistic activities involving physical restraint, domination, and humiliation.

breech position   When the fetus' feet or buttocks move through the birth canal before the head does.

bridge maneuver   A technique in sex therapy in which the client masturbates manually, followed by pelvic rocking to produce orgasm.

brothel   A house of prostitution in which clients purchase sexual favors and, in some instances, also are served drinks, food, and music.

buggery   The legal term in Great Britain for bestiality, homosexual child molestation, and homosexual acts.

bulbocavernosus muscle (bulb oh cav ur noh´ sus)   The muscle at the base of the penis that stimulates penile contractions in the expulsion stage.

bulbourethral (Cowper's) glands (bulb oh you ree´ thrul) A pair of glands near the entrance to the male urethra that secrete a mucus that lubricates the urethra and neutralizes its acidity.

bullying An influence tactic involving threatening, insulting, becoming violent, or ridiculing.

butch-femme A stereotype of a lesbian relationship in which one of the individuals is relatively more powerful and dominant than the other.

calendar method of family planning A birth control method of scheduling intercourse in which fertile days are identified by charting the menstrual cycle.

call boys Young male prostitutes who have some selectivity about their sexual dates.

call girl The highest status prostitute who dates and engages in sex with selected clients.

capacitation (cuh pass ih tay´ shun) The final stages of sperm maturation in which they become able to fertilize an ovum.

castration anxiety The term from psychoanalytic theory that refers to a boy's fears concerning the loss of his genitals.

celibate marriage A marriage in which the couple avoids all sexual interaction.

cervical cap A smaller and more effective version of the diaphragm.

cervical os (sir´ vick uhl oss) The cervical openings—the internal os leads to the uterus, and the external os to the vagina.

cervix (sir´ vicks) The lower part of the uterus that connects it to the vagina.

chancroid (shang´ kroid) A bacterial STD that causes a painful skin lesion.

chlamydia (kluh mid´ ee uh) A very common bacterial STD that can be treated with antibiotics.

chorionic villus biopsy (core ee ohn´ ik vil´ us by´ op see) A procedure in which a sample of the tissue surrounding the eight-to ten-week-old embryo is obtained to test for genetic problems.

chromosomes (chroh´ moh soams) The thin, stringlike structures on which the genes are located in each body cell.

circumcision Removal of the foreskin from the penis for medical or (more often) cultural reasons.

cisvestism A paraphilia in which the individual wears clothing inappropriate for his age or social role.

classical conditioning A type of learning in which a neutral stimulus is repeatedly paired with one that elicits a specific response. As a consequence, the neutral stimulus acquires the ability to elicit that response.

clitoral hood (klit´ ohr uhl) The fold of skin covering the clitoris.

clitoris (klit´ ohr iss) In females, the erotically sensitive external tissue at the top juncture of the labia majora.

clonic (kloh´ nick) The characteristic of repeated contractions during orgasm which continue until vasocongestion is sufficiently reduced.

close-coupled A couple characterized by a strong emotional commitment and by sexual fidelity.

cognitive therapy A type of psychotherapy that attempts to restructure the client's thought processes into a more positive and realistic form.

cohabitation The arrangement in which an unmarried couple lives together in a sexual relationship.

coitus interruptus An ineffective method of birth control in which the penis is withdrawn from the vagina before ejaculation.

colostrum (koh law´ strum) The nutritionally rich milk secreted by the mother following delivery.

comarital sexual behavior (swinging) The practice in which a married couple jointly engage in recreational sexual activity with at least one other person.

coming out The process in which a homosexual recognizes his or her sexual orientation and communicates this knowledge to those involved in the other personal and social aspects of life.

companionate love The type of love characterized by caring, emotional closeness, and friendship.

conditionable The property of objects that indicates their suitability as neutral stimuli in classical conditioning.

control group In research, the group of subjects similar in every way to the experimental group except for the absence of exposure to the experimental manipulation of the independent variable.

conventional level of moral reasoning Moral reasoning characterized by conformity with the existing norms of behavior.

coprolalia (coh proh layl´ ya) The involuntary use of obscene language.

coprophilia A paraphilia in which the sexual object is feces.

copropraxia (coh proh prax´ ya) The involuntary expression of obscene gestures or movements.

corona (core oh´ nuh) The area where the glans penis attaches to the shaft.

corpora cavernosa (core´ pore uh cav ur noh´ suh) A pair of spongy bodies running along the side of the clitoral and penile shafts.

corpus luteum (core´ puss loo´tee uhm) A gland, yellow in color, which develops out of the wall of a follicle.

corpus spongiosum (core´pus sponge i oh´ sum) The spongy tissue containing the urethra, found inside the penile shaft.

correlation The extent to which two or more events vary in a similar fashion. Two variables may increase together and decrease together (positive correlation) or one may increase when the other decreases and vice versa (negative correlation).

correlational research Research which assesses variables and determines relationships between and among them rather than manipulating them in any way.

couvade (koo vahd´) The experience by a male of some symptoms like those of pregnancy and perhaps childbirth.

crowning The appearance of a portion of the fetus' head at the cervix during labor.

cryptorchidism (kryp tor´ chih dizm) Undescended testes.

cultural scenarios In script theory, societal information about how we should behave sexually.

cunnilingus Oral stimulation of the female's genitals.

data The information obtained in empirical research.

date rape Coerced sexual activity that occurs in the context of a date.

degeneracy theory The eighteenth-century belief that the occurrence of sexual fantasies and sexual dreams resulted in the wasting away (or degeneration) of bodily organs.

demographic variables Variables characteristic of large groups of people such as those belonging to different social classes or different races.

demon theory The belief that persisted from the Middle Ages through the Inquisition that sexual dreams were the result of witchcraft and possession by demons.

dependent variable A variable under investigation that is assessed to determine how it is affected by changes in the independent variable.

dichotic listening task An experimental procedure in which a subject receives two different auditory messages (one in each ear) through earphones.

dilation (die lay´shun) Widening of the cervical opening.

dilation and curettage (dilatation and curettage) Widening of the cervical opening in order to scrape out the contents of the uterus with a curette. This is used as a form of induced abortion as well as a standard gynecological procedure.

distributive justice A style of moral decision making based on intention to do no harm.

D-love (deficiency-love) Maslow's theoretical concept that focuses on the satisfaction of one's own needs.

Don Juanism The behavior pattern in which a man interacts sexually with a series of partners, seeking only his own sexual pleasure.

douching (do´shing) Rinsing and flushing the vagina with a liquid preparation.

dysmenorrhea (dis´men oh ree´ah) Painful menstruation caused by uterine contractions.

dyssocial reaction A psychiatric category describing individuals who disregard and frequently clash with accepted social codes.

eclampsia (e klamp´see uh) A serious disease of pregnancy, involving high maternal blood pressure.

ectopic pregnancy (eck tóp ick) The development of a fertilized ovum within the abdomen but outside of the uterus.

effacement (eh face´ment) Thinning of the cervix.

effleurage (ef´luh ahj) Massaging of the abdomen during childbirth, one portion of the Lamaze method.

egocentrism Viewing the world from one's own perspective to the exclusion of that of others.

ego-defensive bias The tendency to respond in such a way as to defend oneself against anxiety.

ejaculatory inevitability (ee jack´you luh tore ee) The feeling that ejaculation is unavoidable, occurring just before ejaculation.

empirical Investigations that involve observable phenomena.

endometrium (en doh mee´tree um) The lining of the uterus.

entrapment A punishable offense in which a law enforcement officer encourages or entices an individual to break the law.

epididymis (epp ih did´ee muss) The area at the back of each testicle that briefly stores the newly produced sperm cells.

episiotomy (eh pee zee ot´oh mee) An incision made in the perineum during childbirth to enlarge the opening through which the neonate emerges and thus to reduce tearing of the tissues.

erectile dysfunction The sexual dysfunction in which a man is unable to achieve or maintain an erection that is sufficient for completing a sexual act.

erogenous zones Areas of the body whose stimulation produces sexual arousal.

eros Romantic, passionate love.

erotophilic Having primarily positive, approving attitudes toward a variety of sexual topics and a tendency to approach sexual cues.

erotophobic Having primarily negative, disapproving attitudes toward a variety of sexual topics and a tendency to avoid sexual cues.

ethnocentric bias The culturally centered orientation which assumes that one's own culture is the normal, natural one by which other cultures should be evaluated.

excitation transfer Zillmann's theory that one form of emotional arousal can transfer to another, thus increasing its strength.

exhibitionism A paraphilia in which the individual exposes his genitals to unwilling viewers.

experimental Refers to research procedures and methodology in which an independent variable is manipulated in order to determine its effect on a dependent variable.

experimental group In research, the group of subjects exposed to the experimental manipulation of the independent variable.

explicit (hard-core) sexual imagery Verbal or pictorial material that includes such details as an erect penis, erect nipples, labia, clitoris, anus, sexual penetration of any bodily orifice, masturbation, or ejaculation.

fellatio Oral stimulation of the male's genitals in which the partner's mouth is active while the penis remains relatively passive.

fetal alcohol syndrome Fetal and infant abnormalities produced by chronic alcohol use during pregnancy, including small body size and mental retardation.

fetal monitoring Testing the vital signs (for example, heart rate) of the fetus during labor.

fetishism The use of inanimate objects as the preferred source of sexual excitement.

fetus (fee´tus) The designation for the child during the prenatal stage of development from the ninth week after conception until delivery.

fixated pedophile A pedophile whose sexual interest has always focused exclusively on children.

follicles (fahl´i kals) The sacs in each ovary containing immature or maturing ova.

follicle stimulating hormone (FSH) The hormone secreted by the pituitary that affects the functioning of the ovaries and testes.

follicular phase (fahl lik´you lur) The middle phase of the menstrual cycle during which ovulation occurs.

foration Rubbing the penis against various parts of the partner's body.

foreplay The physical and verbal interactions between two individuals prior to engaging in a primary sexual act such as intercourse, fellatio, cunnilingus, etc.

foreskin The loose layer of skin which encircles the glans penis; the foreskin is often removed by circumcision for religious, medical, or aesthetic reasons.

form fetish   A fetish in which the shape of the sexual object is the basis for its appeal.

frenulum (fren´ you lum)   A small triangle of skin which connects with the foreskin on the underside of the penis.

frotteurism   A paraphilia in which a clothed male rubs his body and genital area against the body of a female in a public place such as a crowded bus or elevator.

functional   A person with a high level of sexual activity who has little or no commitment to any specific partner.

functional dyspareunia   A sexual dysfunction in which intercourse causes pain for the woman.

functional vaginismus   A sexual dysfunction in which the vaginal muscles contract involuntarily and either prevent intercourse or make it painful.

gay   A man with a homosexual orientation.

gender   The personal characteristics assumed to correspond to one's sex.

gender identity   Labeling of oneself as male or female.

gender role   The pattern of traits associated with masculinity or with femininity.

generalized dysfunction   A dysfunction that occurs across situations, regardless of the sexual acts being attempted.

genital herpes (gen´ ih tul   her pees)   A viral STD caused by herpes simplex type 2. To date, no cure has been found, but the symptoms that accompany its repeated outbreaks can be alleviated.

genital stage   The developmental stage proposed in psychoanalytic theory that involves the search for a mature sexual partner.

genital tubercle (jen´ ih tul too´ bur kull)   The embryo's genitalia which develop into either the penis or clitoris.

genital warts   A viral STD that induces growths on the genitals.

glans clitoris   The outer tip of the clitoris.

glans penis   The enlarged, outer section of the penis.

gonadotropins (go nad oh troh´ pins)   Pituitary hormones including FSH and LH.

gonorrhea (gahn or ee´ uh)   A bacterial STD characterized by a mucus discharge and painful urination. The symptoms are more noticeable in males than in females.

Grafenberg spot (or **G spot**) (graff´ in burg)   An erotically sensitive area in the anterior wall of the vagina.

gumma (guhm´ muh)   A soft, large sore that appears during the tertiary stage of syphilis.

gynecomastia (gie neh koh mass´ tee uh)   Enlarged breasts in the male.

handballing   The practice of inserting a fist and a portion of the forearm into a partner's rectum.

hand whores   Prostitutes in massage parlors who masturbate their male clients.

hard media fetish   A fetish for smooth or slick objects.

healthy adult pleasure-seeking   Behavior combining sexual pleasure, acceptance of responsibility, and consideration of the partner's needs in deciding whether to engage in sexual activity.

hedonist   A person whose primary motivation is the maximal satisfaction of his or her own needs.

hermaphroditism (intersexuality) (her maf´ roh die tism)   The condition in which a person has ambiguous genitals.

homophobia   The irrational fear or intolerance of those who engage in homosexual acts.

homoseductive mother   An hypothesized, but probably incorrect, causative factor in male homosexuality—a mother who behaves seductively toward her son.

homosexual behavior   Sexual interaction between members of the same sex.

homosexual bias   Religious and moral objections to homosexuality, the belief that such behavior is deviant, and the acceptance of various myths about homosexuals.

Hunterian chancre (hunt ehr´ee un shang´kre)   The skin lesion that appears during the primary stage of syphilis.

hymen (high´ men)   The tissue that partially covers the vaginal introitus in young females.

hyperfemininity   A dispositional cluster of female attitudes and beliefs involving an emphasis on the importance of relationships with males, the tendency to use attractiveness and sex to get and keep a man, and a preference for hypermasculine males.

hypermasculinity   A dispositional cluster of male attitudes and beliefs involving sexual callousness toward women, acceptance of violence as manly, and the belief that danger is exciting.

hypothalamus (high poe thal´ uh muss)   A part of the brain that controls functions such as hunger, thirst, and the neuroendocrine system.

hysterectomy (hiss tur ek´ tuh mee)   The surgical removal of the uterus.

hysterosalpingogram (hiss tur oh sal pin´ joh gram)   An X-ray of the oviducts and uterus.

incest   Sexual interaction between individuals who are closely related genetically.

independent variable   A variable that is deliberately manipulated by an experimenter in order to determine its effect on a dependent variable.

individual body-work sex therapy   Sex therapy in which the client interacts sexually with a trained paraprofessional.

induced abortion   The deliberate termination of pregnancy by medical or surgical means.

infertility   Failure to conceive after one year of regular intercourse without using contraceptives.

inhibited male orgasm   A sexual dysfunction in which orgasm and ejaculation are delayed or absent, despite an adequate period of stimulation and excitement.

inhibited sexual desire (ISD)   A sexual dysfunction in which the person has little or no desire for sexual activity.

inhibited sexual excitement   A sexual dysfunction in which there is difficulty in attaining or maintaining an erection (men) or in responding with vaginal lubrication and vasocongestion (women).

interaxial foration   Rubbing the penis in the partner's armpit.

interfemoral foration (in tur fem´ or uhl four ay´ shun)   The sexual act in which the penis is rubbed between a partner's thighs.

intermammary foration   Rubbing the penis between the partner's breasts.

interpersonal attraction   The degree to which another person is liked or disliked.

interpersonal scripts   In script theory, the adaptation of cultural norms about sexual behavior to the situations we encounter.

intrapsychic scripting In script theory, our internal fantasies, thoughts, and feelings about sexual behavior.

intrauterine device (IUD) A contraceptive method in which a copper- or hormone-bearing device is inserted into the uterus as a long-term way to prevent pregnancy.

in vitro fertilization (in vee´troe) A procedure in which a mature egg is removed from the ovary surgically, fertilized in the laboratory, and then placed in the uterus to develop.

involvement The processes that facilitate sexual enjoyment and excitement: feelings, thoughts, sexual acts, and interactions with partner.

irrumation Oral stimulation of the male's genitals, in which the penis actively thrusts in and out of the partner's mouth.

jealousy The negative thoughts, feelings, and actions aroused by a real or imagined rival for a love object.

john Prostitutes' term for a male customer.

Kegel exercises A therapeutic exercise in which women's PC (pubococcygeal) muscles are strengthened by practicing contraction and relaxation of them.

kept boy A young male prostitute who engages in sexual acts with a sponsor who provides him with a place to live, college tuition, or other tangible rewards.

Klinefelter's syndrome (Kline´ fell turz) Males with an extra X chromosome, associated with undeveloped genitalia.

klismaphilia A paraphilia in which enemas are used as a source of sexual pleasure.

kolpograph (coal´ poe graf) In an early attempt to measure female arousal directly, this balloon-like device was inserted in the vagina to detect muscle contractions.

labia majora (lay´ bee uh ma johr´uh) The large, outer lips surrounding the inner lips or labia minora.

labia minora lay´ bee uh mi nohr´ uh) The small, inner lips surrounding the female's vestibule.

labor The process through which a fetus leaves the uterus to emerge from the vagina as a newborn child.

laparoscopic sterilization A method of female sterilization in which a lighted instrument is inserted into the abdomen in the process of cutting and tying the oviducts.

laparoscopy (lap uh ross´cup ee) A telescopic, surgical examination of the female reproductive tract.

laparotomy A method of female sterilization in which the oviducts are cut and the ends tied through an abdominal incision.

latency period The developmental period proposed in psychoanalytic theory that involves repression and lack of interest in sexual needs.

lateral coital position Intercourse in which the two partners lie on their sides.

lesbian A woman who has a homosexual orientation.

Leydig cells (lay´ dig) Cells in the interstitial spaces within the testes that secrete androgen.

libido The innate drive for sexual gratification, as proposed by Freud.

lice Parasitic insects that infest the body, most often among pubic hairs.

loneliness A negative emotional experience that occurs when existing social relationships fail to meet one's expectations.

love Liking, sexual attraction, and strong emotional responses shared by two individuals.

luteal phase (loo´tee uhl) Phase of the menstrual cycle between ovulation and menstruation.

luteinizing hormone (LH) (loo´ tin eye zing) Hormone secreted by the pituitary gland that affects the functioning of the ovaries and testes.

luteinizing hormone-releasing hormone (LHRH) Hormone secreted by the hypothalamus that causes the release of LH and FSH.

lymphogranuloma venereum (lim´ foe gran yu loh muh veh neer´ ee um) A bacterial STD which is a type of chlamydia.

madonna-whore syndrome A set of attitudes toward women as being either chaste or excessively sexual.

male climacteric The period of life when physical and hormonal decline affects male sexual behavior.

manipulation An influence tactic characterized by hinting, flattering, behaving seductively, or reminding the other person of past favors.

marital dissatisfaction Negative feelings concerning the thoughts, feelings, or behaviors involved in the marital relationship.

marital satisfaction Positive feelings concerning the thoughts, feelings, or behaviors involved in the marriage.

marital therapy The helping process which has the goal of improving interactions within a marriage.

masochism A paraphilia in which sexual arousal depends on experiencing mental or physical pain or humiliation.

massage parlor An establishment that provides massages and, in recent years, sexual services such as masturbation, fellatio, and sometimes intercourse.

mastectomy (mass tek´ toh mee) The surgical removal of a breast.

masturbation Manual stimulation of the genitals.

masturbation training Therapy designed to teach the individual to obtain pleasure through masturbating to orgasm.

mate-swapping A form of comarital sexual behavior in which married couples exchange partners in order to engage in sexual interactions.

meatus (mee a´tus) The urethral and seminal opening at the tip of the glans penis.

media fetish A fetish in which the substance of a sexual object is the basis of its appeal.

menarche (men nar´ kee) First menstruation.

menopause The point in the reproductive life cycle in which a woman's fertility ends as the ovaries cease to produce eggs, hormonal activity changes, and menstruation ceases.

menstrual phase The phase of the menstrual cycle during which menstruation occurs.

menstruation (men stray´ shun) The discharge of blood and cells from the endometrium of the uterus through the vagina, usually at monthly intervals whenever fertilization has not taken place.

microphallus (my kroh fahl´ us) (micropenis) An abnormally small penis.

monogamy Marriage between one woman and one man.

mons pubis (veneris) (mons pyu´bis or ven uhr is) The tissue and fat covered by pubic hair and lying just over the female pubic bone.

Müllerian ducts (myu lehr´ee un dukts) Embryonic ducts that form a portion of the female's sexual organs.

multiple orgasms Repeated orgasms that occur, most often in women, without a pause in stimulation and without loss of excitement.

myomectomy The surgical removal of growths from the uterus.

myotonia (my´oh tone ee uh) Increased muscle tension.

mysophilia A paraphilia in which filth is the sexual object.

natural (Billings) method of family planning A birth control method of scheduling intercourse developed by the Drs. Billings, in which fertile days are identified by the appearance and consistency of cervical mucus.

necrophilia A paraphilia in which the individual interacts sexually with a corpse.

need for affiliation The motive to seek friendships and other interpersonal relationships.

negative affect Emotional responses characterized by discomfort and displeasure.

negative feedback loop The decrease in hormone production that results from a rise in hormone level—a thermostat-like process that maintains hormones at a relatively constant level.

nipple The part of the breast containing the opening of the mammary ducts through which milk is excreted.

nocturnal emission An orgasm ("wet dream") that occurs during sleep among males. Females also experience such nocturnal orgasms.

noctural penile tumescence (NPT) The occurrence of penile erections during deep sleep.

no-fault divorce laws Laws which permit divorce without focusing the blame on either partner.

nonexplicit (soft-core) sexual imagery Verbal or pictorial material that describes or depicts nudity or sexual activity but does *not* include such details as an erect penis, erect nipples, labia, clitoris, anus, sexual penetration of any bodily orifice, masturbation, or ejaculation.

nonincarcerated rapist A convicted rapist who participates in a treatment program, avoiding imprisonment.

nymphomania The pattern of behavior in which a woman engages in sexual interactions with a series of partners, seeking only her own sexual pleasure.

objectionable behavior A definition of deviance that is based on its causing unwanted psychological distress or physical pain for the individual and/or for an unwilling or unwitting partner.

oogenesis The production of a mature egg.

oophorectomy (oh oh four ek´ toe mee) The surgical removal of an ovary or ovaries.

open-coupled A couple charactized by some emotional commitment, living together but without sexual fidelity.

open marriage Marriage in which partners agree that each is free to establish sexually and emotionally intimate relationships with other individuals.

oral-genital intercourse Sexual interaction in which the penis penetrates the partner's mouth.

oral stage The developmental stage proposed in psychoanalytic theory that involves interest in oral stimulation.

organic causes of sexual dysfunction Physical bases for an individual's inability to function sexually.

orgasm The pleasurable and rapid loss of vasocongestion and the related muscle contractions that are produced by sexual stimulation.

orgasmic dysfunction A sexual dysfunction in which orgasm does not occur (usually among women) or is mistimed (usually among men).

orgasmic platform Swelling of the labia minora and the outer third of the vagina just before orgasm.

orgasmic reconditioning Therapy in which positive sexual responses and sexual fantasies are substituted for negative ones.

ova (oh´ vuh) Eggs, produced by the female, which contain half of the genetic material necessary for conception.

ovaries (oh´ vuh rees) The two organs which produce ova and secrete female sex hormones.

oviducts (oh´ vih dukts) The two tubes that extend from the uterus to the vicinity of each ovary.

ovulation (avh you lay´ shun) The process in which a mature follicle expels an egg.

oxytocin (ox ee toe´ sin) A hormone secreted by the pituitary gland that causes contractions of smooth muscles in the female's reproductive organs.

Pap smear A medical diagnostic test in which a sample of cells is taken from the cervix for examination.

papule (pap´ yule) A sore produced by the STD chancroid.

paraorgasm A strong sensation of orgasm experienced by some people with spinal-cord injuries, despite the inability to ejaculate (in males) and the lack of vaginal lubrication (in females).

paraphilia Behavior involving atypical sexual objects or behavior that are substituted for human affection.

partialism A fetish in which a specific part of the human body is the primary source of sexual excitement.

passionate love The type of love involving intense emotional responses and preoccupation with the loved person.

pederast A man who is sexually attracted to young boys.

pedophile An individual who is sexually attracted to children.

penile plethysmograph (pee´nyle plu thiz´ moe graf) A device that measures changes in the volume or circumference of the penis, thus assessing sexual arousal.

penile shaft (pee´ nyle) The cylindrical part of the penis which becomes erect during sexual arousal.

penis (pee´ niss) The male genital organ serving a sexual and urinary function.

penis envy The concept in psychoanalytic theory that girls feel inferior to boys anatomically, being envious of the male's genitals.

performance anxiety The negative feelings and expectancies that are based on the fear of failing to meet certain standards of sexual performance.

perineal sponge (pehr ih nee´ ul) An area of spongy tissue between the vagina and the perineum.

perineum (pehr ih nee´ uhm)   The area between the vaginal introitus and the anus in females. In males, it is the area between the scrotum and the anus.

petting   Sexual stimulation by a partner up to, but not including, intercourse.

Peyronie's disease (Pey roh´ neez)   Curvature of the penis resulting from the growth of foreign tissue inside the penis.

phallic stage   The developmental stage proposed in psychoanalytic theory that involves interest in the clitoris or penis plus sexual interest in the opposite-sex parent.

phantom orgasm   Another term for paraorgasm.

philia (fill´ yah)   Interpersonal attraction.

physical attractiveness   The combination of facial features, body shape, and general appearance defined as pleasing by a given culture at a given time.

pimp   An individual who serves as the business manager for one or more prostitutes.

pituitary gland (pit oo´ it air ee)   The gland lying at the base of the hypothalamus in the brain.

placenta (pluh sen´ tuh)   The organ which forms during pregnancy to help nourish the fetus.

plateau phase (plah toe´ faze)   The portion of the Masters and Johnson model of the sexual response cycle. It follows excitement and precedes orgasm.

PLISSIT   A model of sex therapy involving permission to engage in enjoyable sex, limited information, specific suggestions, and (if necessary) intensive therapy.

polyandry   Marriage of one woman to more than one man.

polygamy   Marriage between a person of one sex and more than one person of the opposite sex.

polygynandry   Marriage between multiple men and multiple women simultaneously.

polygyny   Marriage between one man and more than one woman.

polythelia (pahl ee theel´ ee uh)   A condition in which a person has extra breasts or nipples.

pornography   Sexual imagery in which rape, other sexually coercive acts, domination, or any sexual activity with children are described or depicted.

positive affect   Emotional responses characterized by comfort and pleasure.

positive feedback loop   The increase in hormone production that results from a drop in hormone level—a thermostat-like process that maintains hormones at a relatively constant level.

postconventional level of moral reasoning   Moral reasoning characterized by a search for justice apart from rigid rules.

postpartum depression   Depression experienced by a mother soon after childbirth.

potency   The physical ability to become sufficiently excited to engage in a sexual act.

power rape   The enactment of an elaborate sexual fantasy of domination and humiliation with an unwilling victim, usually taking place over a relatively long period of time.

precocious puberty   The condition in which reproductive capability occurs before age nine in females or age ten in males.

preconventional level of moral reasoning   Moral reasoning characterized by egocentric thoughts.

premature ejaculation   A sexual dysfunction in which men reach orgasm too quickly because of an inability to recognize and control the sensations occuring just prior to ejaculation.

premenstrual syndrome   A pattern of symptoms reported to be associated with the menstrual cycle; they decrease significantly during the week following menstruation.

priapism (pry´ uh pizm)   A prolonged, painful, and nonorgasmic erection.

primal scene   When a child perceives his or her parents engaging in sexual intercourse or other sexual acts.

primary dysfunction   A dysfunction that the individual has experienced throughout his or her sexual life.

primary sexual characteristics   Genital organs and internal sexual anatomy.

proceptive (proh cep´ tiv)   Anything that makes conception more likely to occur.

proceptive strategies   Behaviors that encourage sexual interaction.

procreational orientation   The attitude toward sexuality that considers reproduction within marriage as the only justification for sexual interaction.

promiscuity   Sexual activity judged to be excessive, impersonal, and immoral.

prophylactic (proh fil lak´ tik)   A preventive measure or device.

propinquity   Proximity or nearness.

prospective   A scientific study in which the investigator observes the behavior of subjects at one point in time and later observes the same subjects at a second point in time.

prostate gland (pros´ tait)   A gland at the base of the male urinary bladder that secretes part of the seminal fluid.

prostatitis (pros tuh tie´ tiss)   Infection of the male's prostate gland.

prostatectomy (pross tek´ tuh mee)   The surgical removal of the prostate gland.

prostitution   The performance of sexual acts in exchange for money or tangible goods.

protozoa (proh toe zoe´ uh)   One-celled organisms.

pseudohermaphrodite (soo´ doh her maf roh dite)   A type of hermaphroditism in which the person's internal sex organs are of one sex while the genitalia are of the opposite sex.

psychoactive drugs   Drugs that alter mood and thought patterns.

psychoanalysis   The procedures and theoretical framework of the psychotherapeutic technique developed by Freud.

psychoanalytic theory   Freud's personality theory, including his description of sexual development.

psychogenic causes of sexual dysfunction   Psychological bases for an individual's inability to function sexually.

psychosexual dysfunction   A dysfunction based primarily on psychological factors.

pubococcygeus muscle (pyu boh kok see´ gee us)   The layer of muscle encircling the vaginal introitus in females and encircling the base of the penis in males.

puberty (pew' bur tee)   The physical maturation of reproductive capability.

purdah (pur' dah)   The social customs practiced by many Moslems which dictate the separation of the sexes and the seclusion or hiding of women from the sight of males not members of their families.

random assignment   The procedure of assigning subjects randomly to experimental and control groups in order to insure that the subjects in each group do not differ in any systematic way.

rape   A violent crime in which a nonconsenting victim is forced to engage in unwanted sexual activity.

rape myths   A series of beliefs that identify rape and other forms of sexual aggression as appropriate ways for males and females to interact.

rape trauma syndrome   The consequences suffered by a rape victim, including behavioral, physical, and psychological problems.

raphe (ray' fee)   The seam running down the middle of the scrotum, separating its two halves.

rational-emotive therapy   A form of therapy which attempts to substitute rational thoughts for the irrational and unrealistic ones that contribute to sexual and other problems.

recidivism   Committing a criminal act for which the individual was previously arrested, convicted, and punished.

recidivism rate   The rate of return to prison for repeating a criminal act for which the individual had previously been convicted and punished.

reciprocity   A fair exchange in interpersonal behavior.

recreational orientation   The attitude that physical pleasure is the primary justification for sexual interaction.

refractory period   The period of time during which the male is physically unresponsive to sexual stimulation following orgasm.

regressed pedophile   A pedophile whose sexual interest is focused on children but who previously was sexually attracted to adults.

reinforcement-affect model of interpersonal attraction   The theory that identifies positive and negative emotions as the basis for interpersonal evaluations such as attraction.

rejective strategies   Behaviors that discourage sexual interaction.

relational orientation   The belief that sexual interaction is justified by the quality of a relationship.

reliability   The consistency of a measuring device. A reliable measure is internally consistent, consistent over time, and any two or more investigators obtain consistent results when using it.

repeated exposure   The phenomenon whereby evaluations of a person or object become increasingly positive as a function of a series of repeated contacts.

replevin   A judicial process seeking the return of a partner's property following separation or divorce.

replicate   When the exact procedures of previous empirical research are repeated in order to determine whether precisely the same results can be obtained in a second sample.

representative sample   A sample of the total population being investigated that accurately reflects the composition of that population.

research   Procedures involved in seeking knowledge and information. Research can be differentiated into *library research* in which one seeks to discover and organize what others have written, and *empirical research,* in which new observations are made. When scientists speak of research, they most often mean empirical research.

resolution phase   The portion of the sexual response cycle during which sexual excitement gradually dissipates over a one- to two-hour period.

retarded ejaculation   A male sexual dysfunction in which orgasm and ejaculation are delayed despite an adequate period of stimulation and excitement.

retributive justice   A type of moral decision making in which the positive versus negative outcome determines whether an action is taken.

retrograde ejaculation   Internal ejaculation into the urinary bladder.

retrospective   A scientific study in which subjects at one point in time report what they remember about behavior and events at an earlier point in time.

rhythm method   The general term for scheduling intercourse at "safe" times when a mature egg is not present to be fertilized.

Romeo and Juliet effect   Increased feelings of passionate love resulting from anger about parental interference with the love affair.

sadism   A paraphilia in which sexual arousal depends on causing mental or physical pain or humiliation.

sadistic rape   The most brutal form of rape, in which the victim is physically harmed, and sometimes mutilated and murdered.

sampling   Selecting a specific portion of the total population who will serve as research subjects.

satyriasis   The pattern of behavior in which a male engages in sexual interactions with a series of partners, seeking only his own sexual pleasure.

scabies (scay' bees)   A parasitic itch mite that infests the skin, most often among pubic hairs.

scrotum (scroh' tum)   A pouch consisting of skin and muscle that contains the testes in two separate compartments.

secondary dysfunction   A sexual dysfunction that develops following a period of normal functioning.

secondary sexual characteristics   Physical aspects of sexual development other than the primary sexual characteristics—for example, a female's breasts and a male's deep voice.

semen (seminal fluid) (see' min, sehm' in ul)   The substance that is ejaculated from the penis—a mixture of sperm and the secretions of various organs.

seminal vesicles (sehm' in ul ves' ih culs)   A pair of glands that contribute fructose to the ejaculate.

seminiferous tubules (sehm ih nih' fur us tuh' byuls)   Structures in the testes where sperm are produced.

sensate focus   A sex therapy technique developed by Masters and Johnson in which partners caress one another to provide pleasure without engaging in a sexual act or reaching orgasm.

sequential orgasm   When the orgasms of two interacting partners occur separately in time, one preceding the other.

serial monogamy Having more than one spouse over time through repeated marriages and divorces.

sex The biological fact of being either male or female.

sex chromosomes (kroh´ moh soamz) Genetic material that determines an individual's sex and sex-linked characteristics.

sex drive The motivation to engage in sexual activity. The strength of this drive is probably a combination of biological and learned factors.

sex flush Reddening of the skin (especially on the face, back, and chest) during sexual excitement as a result of vasocongestion.

Sex Guilt Scale Test that measures sex guilt—the response evoked by the violation of one's sexual standards or the thought of violating these standards.

sexism A prejudiced attitude associated with the derogation of others on the basis of their sex.

sexological examination An examination of the condition of a client's genitals and his or her responsiveness to sexual stimulation.

sex-role stereotype Strong belief that males and females are supposed to behave according to their respective, traditional roles.

sex therapy Treatment procedures designed to change sexual attitudes and behavior.

sex-typing Defining the categories of maleness and femaleness and learning to value the culturally approved qualities considered appropriate for one's sex.

sexual aggression Any sexual behavior performed without the consent of a victim.

sexual aids Products which are used to produce or enhance sexual excitement.

sexual anesthesia A rare sexual dysfunction in which the individual feels no erotic sensations.

sexual anxiety A negative emotional response occurring during sexual acts.

sexual asphyxia (as fix´ ee uh) Sexual excitement and orgasm produced by depriving the brain of an adequate amount of oxygen through such means as suffocation or electrocution.

sexual attraction The erotic response to a person who is perceived as exciting.

sexual aversion A strong fear of situations or thoughts involving sex.

sexual compatibility Similarity between partners in sexual attitudes and preferences.

sexual deviance Activity which is performed with a nonconsenting or unwitting partner or which causes unwanted pain or distress to a sexual partner.

sexual dysfunction Any problem a person has in engaging in normal sexual activity.

sexual fantasy Imagining erotic activity in one's daydreams.

sexual harassment Unwelcome sexual advances or requests for sexual acts, and other unwanted verbal or physical contact of a sexual nature.

sexual history The information obtained by a sex therapist about a client's past sexual experiences.

sexual imagery Any verbal or pictorial material with sexual content that has the potential to elicit sexual thoughts, feelings, or physiological sexual arousal.

sexually transmissible disease (STD) An infection which can be transmitted through sexual contact.

Sexual Opinion Survey Test that measures positive (erotophila) versus negative (erotophobia) feelings and attitudes about a variety of sexual topics.

sexual orientation The combination of physical sexual activity, interpersonal affection, and erotic fantasies that are directed either at the members of the opposite sex, the same sex, or both.

sexual pheromones Chemical sexual attractants that are common to many species.

sexual pressure Unwelcome efforts by one person (usually a man) to kiss, fondle, and/or engage in some kind of sexual activity with another person (usually a woman).

sexual revolution Changes during the twentieth century in the direction of greater sexual permissiveness and tolerance along with more frequent and varied sexual activities.

sexual scripts In script theory, roles which guide our sexual behavior.

sexual signals Cues that communicate one person's sexual interest or disinterest with respect to another individual.

shock aversion therapy A treatment in which painful electric shock is associated with an undesirable behavior; the goal is to reduce or eliminate that behavior.

significant A statistical term indicating that a given finding is probably replicable rather than simply a matter of chance.

simultaneous orgasms When the orgasms of two interacting partners occur at the same time.

situational dysfunction A sexual dysfunction that occurs during some types of sexual activity but not others.

situation ethics A moral philosophy that emphasizes love and concern as the basis for rational decision making.

social categorization A prejudiced way of thinking which results in perceiving individuals as members of categories with certain stereotypic attributes.

social comparison The process of evaluating ourselves by comparing various physical and behavioral characteristics with those of others.

social skills training Psychotherapy in which the client is instructed in ways to alter maladaptive social behavior.

sociobiological perspective on sexual attraction The theory that human sexual attraction is based on inherited tendencies that evolved because they represented the best reproductive strategies.

sociobiology The field based on the theory emphasizing the contribution of inherited factors to complex social behavior.

sodomy A criminal act defined differently by the laws of different nations and of various states in the United States. Such laws generally refer to either homosexual or heterosexual anal intercourse, homosexual or heterosexual oral sex, and/or sexual relations between males. Historically, it refers to the unspecified wicked acts of the residents of Sodom.

sodomy laws Laws that restrict various types of consensual sexual activity, usually aimed at oral and/or anal sexual acts. Statutes differ from state to state in the United States as to the specific acts and the sex and marital status of the partners which constitute illegality.

soft media fetish A media fetish for soft, smooth objects.

soixante neuf (swa´ sahnt nufe) The French term for "69"—when both partners engage in oral-genital stimulation at the same time.

solicitation A punishable offense in which a prostitute asks a potential client if sexual services are desired.

spectatoring Monitoring and evaluating one's own sexual performance.

sperm The small tadpole-like cells that contain half of the genetic material necessary for conception.

spermatids (spur´muh tids) The male germ cells after undergoing spermatogenesis in the seminiferous tubules.

spermatogenesis (spur matt oh jen´eh sis) The period of sperm formation in which the developing germ cells become spermatids.

spermiogenesis (spur mee oh jen´eh sis) The maturation of a spermatid into a sperm.

spontaneous abortion Termination of pregnancy through natural causes.

spontaneous orgasm An unexpected orgasm occurring without direct stimulation—one of the symptoms of withdrawal from heroin.

squeeze method A technique for treating premature ejaculation in which the male or his partner presses the penis just below the glans when he senses the approach of ejaculatory inevitability.

status orgasmus Continuation of orgasmic contractions in the female for a longer period than usual, up to one minute.

statutory rape Sexual interaction with a person below the legal age of consent, usually sixteen or eighteen years of age.

sterilization The cessation of fertility, usually through irreversible surgical procedures.

stop (pause) method A technique for treating premature ejaculation in which the male temporarily stops all penile stimulation when he senses the approach of ejaculatory inevitability.

storge (store´gay) An affectionate form of love.

streetwalker A low-status prostitute who contacts prospective clients in public places.

subincision A cultural rite performed at puberty in which the penis is slit lengthwise along the urethral canal.

supernumerary breast (sue pur nuh´ mur ar ee) An extra breast in addition to the usual pair.

supplication An influence tactic involving pleading, crying, or acting ill and helpless.

surrogate partner A professional sexual partner who substitutes for an actual partner during sex therapy.

survey A series of specific research questions to which subjects respond orally or in writing.

symptomatic HIV infection The early symptoms of an HIV infection (formerly known as ARC) that can develop into AIDS.

syphilis (si´ fil iss) A bacterial STD that, left untreated, progresses through three increasingly serious stages.

systematic desensitization The extinction process in which there is a gradual reduction in negative responses to specific cues, and their replacement by positive responses.

telephone scatologia A paraphilia in which the individual makes obscene telephone calls to unwilling recipients.

temperature method of family planning A birth control method of scheduling intercourse in which fertile days are identified by recording the fall and rise of body temperature expected at the time of ovulation.

teratogen (ter´ at oh jin) A toxic substance that damages fetal growth or development.

testes (tes´ tees) The testicles, the two glands of the male genitalia that produce sperm.

testosterone (tess toss´tur own) The major hormone of the androgen group.

thermography (thur mog´ruh fee) The procedure using a heat-sensitive device to assess changes in skin temperature that are associated with vasocongestion and sexual excitement.

thorarche (thor are´kuh) First ejaculation of semen.

three-factor theory of passionate love The theory that passionate love occurs when an individual has been exposed to the necessary cultural expectations, is in the presence of an appropriate love object, and is experiencing emotional arousal that can be labeled as love.

toxemia (tox ee´ mee uh) A life-threatening complication of pregnancy involving elevated blood pressure, water retention and severe swelling, rapid weight gain, and premature delivery. Because eclampsia sometimes results, toxemia is also termed pre-eclampsia.

toxic shock syndrome (TSS) A disease caused by bacteria that can multiply in certain tampons and also in contraceptives such as the diaphragm and sponge if they are left in the vagina for a long period of time.

transsexual An individual whose gender identity does not match his or her sex.

transvestism A paraphilia in which the clothing of the opposite sex is worn to stimulate sexual excitement.

tribadism The act in which a woman rubs her genitals against the genitals of another woman.

trichomoniasis (trick oh moh neye´ us siss) A protozoan infection that affects both sexes, but in women the symptoms include an itchy, odorous discharge.

trimester (try´mess tur) One of the three 3–month segments of pregnancy.

true hermaphrodite (her maf´ roh dite) A type of hermaphroditism in which both an ovary and a testis develop in the abdomen.

tubal ligation Surgical sterilization involving severing the female's oviducts.

turn a trick Prostitutes' term for a sexual and financial interaction with a customer.

Turner's syndrome Females with this syndrome lack one sex chromosome, and they tend to be very short and infertile.

UCLA Loneliness Scale A scale developed at the University of California at Los Angeles to assess feelings of loneliness.

umbilical cord (um bil´ ee kuhl) The tube connecting the fetus to the placenta.

urethra (you ree´thruh) A tube through which urine is expelled by both sexes and through which males ejaculate semen.

urinary cystitis (you´ih nair ee sis tie´tiss) An infection of the urinary tract.

urophilia   A paraphilia involving urine as the source of sexual excitement.

uterus (you´ tur us)   The pear-shaped internal sexual organ which contains the developing fetus during pregnancy.

vacuum aspiration   A method of induced abortion in which the uterine contents are sucked out by means of a vacuum device.

vagina (vuh jih´ nuh)   An internal sexual organ in females consisting of a long tube located between the urinary bladder and the rectum.

vaginal intercourse   Sexual interaction in which the man's penis penetrates his partner's vagina.

vaginal introitus (vah jih´ nuhl in troy´ tuss)   The vaginal opening.

vaginal photoplethysmograph (vu´h jih nuhl foe tow plu thiz´ moe graf)   A device which measures the degree of sexual excitement and orgasm in women, using a light source and light sensor to assess vasocongestion.

validity   The accuracy of a measuring device. A valid measure is one that actually assesses what it purports to measure.

vas deferens (vaz def´ uh rens)   A tube that transports sperm from the testes to the urethral area.

vasectomy   Surgical sterilization involving severing and tying the male's vas deferens.

vasocongestion   Engorgement of tissues with blood.

vesicles (vess´ih cals)   Clusters of herpes blisters.

voyeurism (Peeping Tomism)   A paraphilia in which the individual secretly observes a stranger's nudity or sexual interactions.

vulva (vul´ vah)   The external female genitalia: the mons, the labia, the clitoris, and the vaginal opening.

Wolffian ducts (Wool´ fee un)   Ducts found in the embryo which form a portion of male's sexual organs.

yeast infection   A vaginal infection produced by a fungus.

zona pellucida (zoe´ nuh pell loo´ sih duh)   A layer covering the ovum through which a sperm penetrates.

zoophilia (bestiality)   A paraphilia in which the sexual object is an animal.

zygote (zeye´ goat)   An egg after it is fertilized by a sperm.

REFERENCES

Abbey, A. (1982). Sex differences in attributions for friendly behavior: Do males misperceive females' friendliness? *Journal of Personality and Social Psychology, 42,* 830–838.

Abbey, A., Cozzarelli, C., McLaughlin, K., & Harnish, R.J. (1987). The effects of clothing and dyad sex composition on perceptions of sexual intent: Do women and men evaluate these cues differently? *Journal of Applied Social Psychology, 17,* 108–126.

Abbott, A.R., & Sebastian, R.J. (1981). Physical attractiveness and expectations of success. *Personality and Social Psychology Bulletin, 7,* 481–486.

Abel, G.G. (1983). The relationship between treatment for sex offenders and the court. In S.N. Verdun-Jones and A.A. Keltner (Eds.), *Sexual aggression and the law* (pp. 15–26). Vancouver, B.C.: Criminology Research Centre, Simon Fraser University.

Abel, G.G., Mittleman, M.S., & Becker, J. V. (1984). *Sexual offenders: Results of assessment and recommendations for treatment.* Unpublished manuscript, New York State Psychiatric Institute and College of Physicians and Surgeons, Columbia University, New York.

Abelson, P.H. (1985). Use of research on pheromones. *Science, 229,* 1343.

Aberle, D., Bronfenbrenner, U., Hess, E., Miller, D., Schneider, D., & Spuhler, J. (1963). The incest taboo and the mating patterns of animals. *American Anthropologist, 65,* 253–265.

Abortion, intimidation and death. (1988, October 28). *New York Times,* A 34.

Abraham, G.E. (1983). Nutritional factors in the etiology of the pre-menstrual tension syndromes. *Journal of Reproductive Medicine, 28,* 446–464.

Abrahamson, D.J. (1985). *The effects of two types of distracting tasks on sexual arousal in sexually functional and dysfunctional males.* Unpublished doctoral dissertation, University at Albany, State University of New York.

Abrahamson, D.J., Barlow, D.H., & Abrahamson, L.S. (1989). Differential effects of performance demand and distraction on sexually functional and dysfunctional males. *Journal of Abnormal Psychology, 98,* 241–247

Abrahamson, D.J., Barlow, D.H., Beck, J.G., & Sakheim, D.K. (1985). The effects of attentional focus and partner responsiveness on sexual responding: Replication and extension. *Archives of Sexual Behavior, 14,* 361–371.

Abramowitz, S.I., & Sewell, H.H. (1980). Marital adjustment and sex therapy outcome. *Journal of Sex Research, 16,* 325–337.

Abramson, P.R. (1982). *The sexual system: A theory of human sexual behavior.* San Francisco: Academic Press.

Abramson, P.R. (1984). *Sarah: A sexual biography.* Albany, N.Y.: State University of New York Press.

Abramson, P.R., and Hayashi, H. (1984). Pornography in Japan: Cross-cultural and theoretical considerations. In N.M. Malamuth and E. Donnerstein (Eds.), *Pornography and sexual aggression* (pp. 173–183). New York: Academic Press.

Abramson, P.R., & Imai-Marquez, J. (1982). The Japanese-American: A cross-cultural, cross sectional study of sex guilt. *Journal of Research in Personality, 16,* 227–237.

Abramson, P.R., & Mechanic, M.G. (1983). Sex and the media: Three decades of best-selling books and major motion pictures. *Archives of Sexual Behavior, 12,* 185–206.

Abramson, P.R., Moriuchi, K.D., Waite, M.S., & Perry, L.B. (1983). Parental attitudes about sexual education: Cross-cultural differences and covariate controls. *Archives of Sexual Behavior, 12,* 381–397.

Abramson, P.R., & Mosher, D.L. (1975). Development of a measure of negative attitudes toward masturbation. *Journal of Consulting and Clinical Psychology, 43,* 485–490.

Abramson, P.R., Parker, T., & Weisberg, S.R. (1988). Sexual expression of mentally retarded people: Educational and legal implications. *American Journal of Mental Retardation, 93,* 328–334.

Abramson, P.R., Perry, L.B., Seeley, T.T., Seeley, D.M., & Rothblatt, A. (1981a). Thermographic measurement of sexual arousal: A discriminant validity analysis. *Archives of Sexual Behavior, 10,* 171–176.

Abramson, P.R., Perry, L.B., Rothblatt, A., Seeley, T.T., & Seeley, D.M. (1981b). Negative attitudes toward masturbation and pelvic vasocongestion: A thermographic analysis. *Journal of Research in Personality, 15,* 497–509.

Abstemious Dani. (1976). *Time, 108*(5), 58.

Acosta, F.X. (1975). Etiology and treatment of homosexuality: A review. *Archives of Sexual Behavior, 4,* 9–29.

Adams, C.G., & Turner, B.F. (1985). Reported change in sexuality from young adulthood to old age. *Journal of Sex Research, 21,* 126–141.

Adams, M.S., & Neel, J.V. (1967). Children of incest. *Pediatrics, 40,* 55–62.

Adelmann, P.K., Antonucci, T.C., Crohan, S.E., & Coleman, L.M. (1989). Empty nest, cohort, and employment in the well-being of midlife women. *Sex Roles, 20,* 173-189.

Adler, J.D., & Boxley, R.L. (1985). The psychological reactions to infertility: Sex roles and coping styles. *Sex Roles, 12,* 271–279.

Adler, N.E. (1976). Sample attrition in studies of psychosocial sequelae to abortion: How great a problem? *Journal of Applied Social Psychology, 6,* 240–259.

Agnew, J. (1986). Hazards associated with anal erotic activity. *Archives of Sexual Behavior, 15*, 307–314.

Aguero, J.E., Block, L., & Byrne, D. (1984). The relationships among sexual beliefs, attitudes, experience, and homophobia. *Journal of Homosexuality, 10*, 95–107.

AIDS Fact Book. (1985). New York: GCR Publishing Company.

AIDS facts. (1989, October). *Playboy,* 45.

Aiman, J., & Boyar, R.M. (1982). Testicular function in transsexual men. *Archives of Sexual Behavior, 11*, 171–179.

Akers, J.S., & Conaway, C.H. (1979). Female homosexual behavior in macaca mulatta. *Archives of Sexual Behavior, 8*, 63–80.

Albright, L., Kenny, D.A., & Malloy, T.E. (1988). Consensus in personality judgments at zero acquaintance. *Journal of Personality and Social Psychology, 55*, 387–395.

Aldrich, N.W., Jr. (1988), *Bloom town. 21* (23), 40–46.

Alexander, N.J., & Clarkson, T.B. (1978). Vasectomy increases the severity of diet-induced atherosclerosis in macaca fascicularis. *Science, 201*, 538–541.

Allee, W.C. (1938). *The social life of animals.* New York: W.W. Norton.

Allen, D.M. (1980. Young male prostitutes: A psychosocial study. *Archives of Sexual Behavior, 9*, 399–426.

Allen, J.B., Kenrick, D.T., Linder, D.E., & McCall, M.A. (1989). Arousal and attraction: A response-facilitation alternative to misattribution and negative-reinforcement models. *Journal of Personality and Social Psychology, 57*, 261–270.

Allen, T.D. (1979). Penis size in infancy vs. adulthood. *Medical Aspects of Human Sexuality, 13* (6), 74, 79.

Allgeier, A.R. (1978, May). *Attitudinal and behaviorial correlates of sexual knowledge.* Paper presented at the convention of the Midwestern Psychological Association in Chicago.

Allgeier, A.R., & Byrne, D. (1973). Attraction toward the opposite sex as a determinant of physical proximity. *Journal of Social Psychology, 90*, 213–219.

Allgeier, E.R. (1982). Correlates of sex education: Promiscuity and pregnancy or contraceptive use? *SIECUS Report, 11* (2), 7.

Allgeier, E.R., & Fogel, A.F. (1978). Coital positions and sex roles: Responses to cross-sex behavior in bed. *Journal of Consulting and Clinical Psychology, 46*, 588–589.

Allgeier, E.R., & Murnen, S.K. (1985). Perceptions of parents as sexual beings: Pocs & Godow revisited. *Siecus Reports, 13*, 11–12.

Altman, L.K. (1988a, July 5). Pregnant women and hepatitis B: New policy reflects fears. *New York Times,* C 3.

Altman, L.K. (1988b, August 4). African study finds AIDS risk to be higher in uncircumcised men. *New York Times,* B 7.

Altman, L.K. (1990a, October 23). Tiny mite causes overwhelming itch: Elusive scabies. *New York Times,* C 3.

Altman, L.K. (1990b, November 13). Syphilis fools a new generation. *New York Times,* C 3.

Alzate, H. (1982). Effect of formal sex education on the sexual knowledge and attitudes of Colombian medical students. *Archives of Sexual Behavior, 11*, 201–214.

Alzate, H. (1984). Sexual behavior of unmarried Colombian University students: A five-year follow-up. *Archives of Sexual Behavior, 13*, 121–132.

Alzate, H. (1985). Vaginal eroticism: A replication study. *Archives of Sexual Behavior, 14*, 529–537.

Alzate, H. (1989). Sexual behavior of unmarried Columbian university students: A follow-up. *Archives of Sexual Behavior, 18*, 239–250.

Alzate, H., & Londono, L. (1987). Subjects' reactions to a sexual experimental situation. *Journal of Sex Research, 23*, 362–400.

Amabile, T.M. (1983). Brilliant but cruel: Perceptions of negative evaluators. *Journal of Experimental Social Psychology, 19*, 146–156.

Ambert, A.-M. (1988). Relationship between ex-spouses: Individual and dyadic perspectives. *Journal of Social and Personal Relationships, 5*, 327–346.

Amberson, J.I., & Hoon, P.W. (1985). Hemodynamics of sequential orgasm. *Archives of Sexual Behavior, 14*, 351–360.

American adults' approval of legal abortion has remained virtually unchanged since 1972. (1985). *Family Planning Perspectives, 17*, 181.

American Civil Liberties Union. (1986). *Polluting the censorship debate.* Washington, DC: American Civil Liberties Union.

American Psychiatric Association. (1987). *Diagnostic and statistical manual of mental disorders—III–Revised.* New York: American Psychiatric Association.

Ames, B.N. (1983). Dietary carcinogens and anticarcinogens. *Science, 221*, 1256–1264.

Amoroso, D.M., Brown, M., Pruesse, M., Ware, E.E., & Pilkey, D.W. (1971). An investigation of behavioral, psychological, and physiological reactions to pornographic stimuli. In *Technical report of the Commission on Obscenity and Pornography,* Vol. 8. Washington, DC: U.S. Government Printing Office.

Andersen, B.L., & Broffitt, B. (1988). Is there a reliable and valid self-report measure of sexual behavior? *Archives of Sexual Behavior, 17*, 509–525.

Anderson, C.L. (1981). The effect of a workshop on attitudes of female nursing students toward male sexuality. *Journal of Homosexuality, 7*, 57–69.

Anderson, K. (1983). Private violence. *Time, 122* (10), 18–19.

Anderson, S.A. (1985). Parental and marital role stress during the school entry transition. *Journal of Social and Personal Relationships, 2*, 59–80.

Anderson, S.M. & Bem, S.L. (1981). Sex typing and androgyny in dyadic interaction: Individual differences in responsiveness to physical attractiveness. *Journal of Personality and Social Psychology, 41*, 74–86.

Andres, D., Gold, D., Berger, C., Kinch, R., & Gillett, P. (1983). Selected psychosocial characteristics of males: Their relationship to contraceptive use and abortion. *Personality and Social Psychology Bulletin, 9*, 387–396.

Andrews, L.B. (1980). Inside the genius farm. *Parents, 55* (10), 81–84, 148.

Andrews, L.B. (1981). Embryo technology. *Parents, 56* (5), 63–70.

Angier, N. (1990, October 2). Seasons sway human birth rates. *New York Times,* C 6.

Angier, N. (1991, January 22). A potent peptide prompts an urge to cuddle. *New York Times*, C 1, C 10.

Annon, J.S. (1974). *The behavioral treatment of sexual problems: Volume 1 brief therapy*. Honolulu, Hawaii: Enabling Systems.

Annon, J.S. (1975). *The behavioral treatment of sexual problems: Volume 2 intensive therapy*. Honolulu, Hawaii: Enabling Systems.

Ansbacher, R. (1982). Coitus during menses. *Medical Aspects of Human Sexuality*, 16(12) 17–18.

Ansbacher, R. (1983). Median age for menopause. *Medical Aspects of Human Sexuality*, 17(8), 143.

Ansbacher, R. (1984). No effect of adoption on fertility. *Medical Aspects of Human Sexuality*, 18(6), 260.

Ansong, K., & Smith, A.D. (1982). Fate of sperm in vasectomized men. *Medical Aspects of Human Sexuality*, 16(12), 17.

Antonovsky, H.F. (1982). Adolescent sexuality: A study of attitudes and behavior. *Contemporary Psychology*, 27, 375–376.

Antonovsky, H.F., Shoham, I., Kavenocki, S., Modan, B., & Lancet, M. (1978). Sexual attitude-behavior discrepancy among Israeli adolescent girls. *Journal of Sex Research*, 14, 260–272.

Apfelbaum, B. (1977). The myth of the surrogate. *Journal of Sex Research*, 13, 238–249.

Apfelbaum, B. (1978). Prostitutes no "cure" for impotence. *Medical Aspects of Human Sexuality*, 12(4), 7, 11.

Apfelbaum, B. (1983). *Expanding the boundaries of sex therapy* (2nd ed.). Berkeley, Calif.: Berkeley Sex Therapy Group.

Apfelbaum, B. (1984). The ego-analytic approach to individual body-work sex therapy: Five case examples. *Journal of Sex Research*, 20, 44–70.

Appleton, W.S. (1983). Women at middle age: Effects on marital relationships. *Medical Aspects of Human Sexuality*, 17(10), 188–190, 192–194.

Apuzzio, J. (1980). Clitoral response to tight jeans. *Medical Aspects of Human Sexuality*, 14(12), 16.

Arafat, I., & Allen, D.E. (1977). Venereal disease: College students' knowledge and attitudes. *Journal of Sex Research*, 13, 223–230.

Araoz, D.L. (1982). Hypnosis and sex therapy. *Erotic uses of hypnosis*. New York: Brunner/Mazel.

Arendell, T. (1986). *Mothers and divorce*. Berkeley, Calif.: University of California.

Arentewicz, G., & Schmidt, G. (1983). *The treatment of sexual disorders*. New York: Basic Books.

Argyle, M., & Henderson, M. (1985). The rules of friendship. *Journal of Social and Personal Relationships*, 1, 211–238.

Arias, I., & Beach, S.R.H. (1986, April). *The role of social desirability in reports of marital violence*. Paper presented at the meeting of the Eastern Psychological Association, New York City.

Armstrong, E.G. (1978). Massage parlors and their customers. *Archives of Sexual Behavior*, 7, 117–125.

Aron, A., Dutton, D.G., Aron, E.N., & Iverson, A. (1989). Experiences of falling in love. *Journal of Social and Personal Relationships*, 6, 243–257.

Aronson, M.E., & Nelson, P.K. (1967). Fatal air embolism in pregnancy resulting from an unusual sexual act. *Obstetrics and Gynecology*, 30, 127–130.

Artson, B.S. (1988). Judaism and homosexuality. *Tikkun*, 3(2), 52–54, 92–93.

Asayama, S. (1976). Sexual behavior in Japanese students: Comparisons for 1974, 1960, and 1952. *Archives of Sexual Behavior*, 5, 371–390.

Asendorpf, J.B. (1989). Shyness as a final common pathway for two different kinds of inhibition. *Journal of Personality and Social Psychology*, 57, 481–492.

Ashworth, C.D., & Feldman-Summers, S. (1978). Social and legal issues. *Criminal Justice and Behavior*, 5(3), 227–240.

Assaad, M.B. (1980). Female circumcision in Egypt: Social implications, current research, and prospects for change. *Studies in Family Planning*, 11(1), 3–16.

Asso, D. (1983). *The real menstrual cycle*. Chichester, Pa.: John Wiley.

Athanasiou, R., & Sarkin, R. (1974). Premarital sexual behavior and postmarital adjustment. *Archives of Sexual Behavior*, 3, 207–225.

Athanasiou, R., Shaver, P., & Tavris, C. (1970). Sex. *Psychology Today*. 4(7), 39–52.

Atkeson, B.M., Calhoun, K.S., Resick, P.A., & Ellis, E.M. (1982). Victims of rape: Repeated assessment of depressive symptoms. *Journal of Consulting and Clinical Psychology*, 50, 96–102.

Atkinson, L., Schearer, S.B., Harkavy, O., & Lincoln, R. (1980). Prospects for improved contraception. *Family Planning Perspectives*, 12, 173–175, 178–192.

Atkinson, L.E., Lincoln, R., & Forrest, J.D. (1985). Worldwide trends in funding for contraceptive research and evaluation. *Family Planning Perspectives*, 17, 196–199, 202–207.

Auerback, A. (1979). Why prostitutes don't kiss. *Medical Aspects of Human Sexuality*, 13(2), 35.

Auerback, A., & Auerback, M.L. (1982). How should a woman react to a man's occasional episode of impotence? *Medical Aspects of Human Sexuality*, 16(8), 97–100.

Auerback, A., & Auerback, M.L. (1984). Pleasureless ejaculation. *Medical Aspects of Human Sexuality*, 18(4), 228–231.

Auerback, A., & Haeberle, E.J. (1981). Orgasmic prostitutes. *Medical Aspects of Human Sexuality*, 15(3), 29.

Austin, H., Louv, W.C., & Alexander, W.J. (1984). A case-control study of spermicides and gonorrhea. *Journal of the American Medical Association*, 251, 2822.

Austrom, D., & Hanel, K. (1985). Psychological issues of simple life in Canada: An exploratory study. *International Journal of Women's Studies*, 8, 12–23.

Averill, J.R., & Boothroyd, P. (1977). On falling in love in conformance with the romantic ideal. *Motivation and Emotion*, 1, 235–247.

Babineau, R., & Schwartz, A.J. (1977). The treatment of sexual dysfunction in a university health service setting. *Journal of the American College Health Association*, 25, 176.

Bachmann, G.A. (1983). How sexual arousal varies during the menstrual cycle. *Medical Aspects of Human Sexuality*, 17(6), 186, 188, 191, 192, 194, 195.

Bachrach, C.A. (1984). Contraceptive practice among American women. *Family Planning Perspectives, 16*(6), 253–259.

Baie, J. (1988). *APA Monitor, 19*(1), 32.

Bak. J.S., & Greene, R.L. (1980). Changes in neuropsychological functioning in an aging population. *Journal of Consulting and Clinical Psychology, 48,* 395–399.

Bakaitis, R.F., & Abramson, P.R. (1986). *Cognitive control processes, sex guilt, and memory for erotic prose.* Unpublished manuscript, Loyola Marymount University, Los Angeles.

Baker, B.J., & Armelagos, G.J. (1988). The origin and antiquity of syphilis: Paleopathological diagnosis and interpretation. *Current Anthropology, 29*(5), 703–737.

Baker, S., Thalberg, S., & Morrison, D. (1988). Parents' behavioral norms as predictors of adolescent sexual activity and contraceptive use. *Adolescence, 23,* 278–281.

Baldwin, J.D., & Baldwin, J.I. (1988). AIDS information and sexual behavior on a university campus. *Journal of Sex Education and Therapy, 14,* 24–28.

Baldwin, J.D., & Baldwin, J.I. (1989). The socialization of homosexuality and heterosexuality in a non-Western society. *Archives of Sexual Behavior, 18, 13–29.*

Bales, J. (1984). Parents' divorce has major impact on college students. *APA Monitor, 15*(8), 13.

Balswick, J. (1978). Comparative earnings of Greek Cypriot women and men. *Sex Roles, 4,* 877–885.

Barak, A., & Fisher, W.A. (1989). Counselor and therapist gender bias? More questions than answers. *Professional Psychology: Research and Practice, 20,* 001–007.

Barbach, L. (1982). The nipple during female orgasm. *Medical Aspects of Human Sexuality, 16*(9), 21.

Barbach, L.G. (1978). Preferred type of clitoral stimulation. *Medical Aspects of Human Sexuality, 12*(5), 27.

Barbaree, H.E., Marshall, W.L., Lightfoot, L.O., & Yates, E. (1983). Alcohol intoxication and deviant sexual arousal in male social drinkers. *Behaviour Research and Therapy, 21,* 365–373.

Barfield, R., Wilson, C., & McDonald, P. (1975). Sexual behavior: Extreme reduction of postejaculatory refractory period by midbrain lesions in male rats. *Science, 189,* 147–149.

Barlow, D.H. (1986). The causes of sexual dysfunction: The role of anxiety and cognitive interference. *Journal of Consulting and Clinical Psychology, 54,* 140–148.

Barlow, D.H., Becker, R., Leitenberg, H., & Agras, W.S. (1970). A mechanical strain gauge for recording penile circumference change. *Journal of Applied Behavior Analysis, 3,* 73–76.

Barlow, D.H., Hayes, S.C., Nelson, R.O., Steele, D.L., Meeler, M.E., & Mills, J.R. (1979). Sex role motor behavior: A behavioral checklist. *Behavioral Assessment, 1,* 119–138.

Barlow, D.H., Sakheim, D.K., & Beck, J.G. (1983). Anxiety increases sexual arousal. *Journal of Abnormal Psychology, 92,* 49–54.

Baron, L. (1985, September). *Toward an integated theory of rape.* Paper presented at the U.S. Justice Department Hearings, Houston.

Baron, L., & Straus, M.A. (1984). Sexual stratification, pornography, and rape in the United States. In N.M. Malamuth and E. Donnerstein (Eds.), *Pornography and sexual aggression* (pp. 186–209). New York: Academic Press.

Baron, R.A., & Byrne, D. (1987). *Social psychology: Understanding human interaction* (5th ed.). Boston: Allyn and Bacon.

Barr, S.J. (1979, November 4). Doctors did it. *Parade,* p. 27.

Barrett, F.M. (1980). Sexual experience, birth control usage, and sex education of unmarried Canadian University students: Changes between 1968 and 1978. *Archives of Sexual Behavior, 9,* 367–390.

Barringer, F. (1990, November 10). More girls are sexually active, study finds. *New York Times,* 11.

Barrows, S., & Novak, W. (1986). *Mayflower madam: The secret life of Sydney Biddle Barrows.* New York: Arbor House.

Bart, P.B., (1981). A study of women who both were raped and avoided rape. *Journal of Social Issues, 37*(4), 123–137.

Bart, P.B., & O'Brien, P.H. (1985). *Stopping rape: Successful survival strategies.* Elmsford, N.Y.: Pergamon Press.

Bartell, G.D. (1970). Group sex among mid-Americans. *Journal of Sex Research, 6,* 113–130.

Bartusis, M.A. (1981). Need for extended foreplay. *Medical Aspects of Human Sexuality, 15*(6), 91.

Basler, B. (1981, August 15). City's prostitutes moving into residential sections. *New York Times,* 1, 13.

Basow, S.A., & Campanile, F. (1986, April). *Attitudes toward prostitution as related to attitudes toward feminism.* Paper presented at the meeting of the Eastern Psychological Association, New York City.

Bateson, P. (1978). Sexual imprinting and optimal outbreeding. *Nature, 273,* 659–660.

Batra, S.K., & Lue, T.F. (1990). Physiology and pathology of penile erection. In J. Bancroft, C.M. Davis, & D. Weinstein (Eds.), *Annual review of sex research* (Vol. 1) (pp. 251–263). Mount Vernon, IA: Foundation for the Scientific Study of Sexuality.

Battelle, P. (1979, November 12). Living together: Is economics the heart of it? *Albany Knickerbocker News,* 1–C.

Battelle, P. (1980, July 31). The "office pass" enters a new age. *Albany Knickerbocker News,* B–1.

Batts, J.A. (1982). Vulvar tumors: Impact on sexual function. *Medical Aspects of Human Sexuality, 16*(2), 34a–34b.

Baucom, D.H., Sayers, S.L., & Duhe, A. (1989). Attributional style and attributional patterns among married couples. *Journal of Personality and Social Psychology, 56,* 596–607.

Baum, S.K. (1983). Older women feel lonelier than older men. *Medical Aspects of Human Sexuality, 17*(1), 170–171.

Bauman, K.E., & Wilson, R.R. (1974). Sexual behavior of unmarried university students in 1968 and 1972. *Journal of Sex Research, 10,* 327–333.

Bauman, K.E., & Wilson, R.R. (1976). Premarital sexual attitudes of unmarried university students: 1968 vs. 1972. *Archives of Sexual Behavior, 5,* 29–37.

Baumeister, R.F. (1988). Gender differences in masochistic scripts. *Journal of Sex Research, 25,* 478–499.

Baxter, L.A. (1984). Trajectories of relationship disengagement. *Journal of Social and Personal Relationships, 1,* 29–48.

Baxter, L.A. (1990). Dialectical contradictions in relationship development. *Jounal of Social and Personal Relationships, 7,* 69–88.

Baxter, L.A., & Wilmot, W.W. (1985). Taboo topics in close relationships. *Journal of Social and Personal Relationships, 2,* 253–270.

Bazell, R. (1983). The history of an epidemic. *New Republic, 189*(5), 14–15, 17–18.

Bazell, R. (1988, February 15). In vitro veritas. *New Republic,* 11–13.

Beach, F.A. (1976). *Human sexuality in four perspectives.* Baltimore, Md.: Johns Hopkins University Press.

Beach, L.R., Hope, A., Townes, B.D., & Campbell, F.L. (1982). The expectation-threshold model of reproductive decision making. *Population and Environment, 5,* 95–108.

Beazlie, F.S., (1981). Coital injuries of genitalia. *Medical Aspects of Human Sexuality, 15,* 112, 116–117, 120–121.

Beck, J.G., & Barlow, D.H. (1983). Unraveling the nature of sex roles: A behavioral approach. In E. Blechman (Ed.), *Behavioral modification with women* (pp. 34–59). New York: Guilford Press.

Beck, J.G., Barlow, D.H., & Sakheim, D.K. (1983). The effects of attentional focus and partner arousal on sexual responding in functional and dysfunctional men. *Behaviour Research and Therapy, 21,* 1–8.

Beck, J.G., & Davies, D.K. (1987). Teen contraception: A review of perspectives on compliance. *Archives of Sexual Behavior, 16,* 337–368.

Beck. J.G., Sakheim, D.K., & Barlow, D.H. (1983). Operating characteristics of the vaginal photoplethysmograph: Some implications for its use. *Archives of Sexual Behavior, 12,* 43–58.

Beck, S.B., Ward-Hall, C.I., & McLear, P.M. (1976). Variables related to women's somantic preferences of the male and female body. *Journal of Personality and Social Psychology, 34,* 1200–1210.

Becker, M.A., & Byrne, D. (1984). Type A behavior and daily activities of young married couples. *Journal of Applied Social Psychology, 14,* 82–88.

Becker, M.A., & Byrne, D. (1985). Self-regulated exposure to erotica, recall errors, and subjective reactions as a function of erotophobia and Type A coronary–prone behavior. *Journal of Personality, 48,* 228–235.

Becker, J.V., Skinner, L.J., Abel, G.G., & Cichon, J. (1986). Level of postassault sexual functioning in rape and incest victims. *Archives of Sexual Behavior, 15,* 37–49.

Beckman, L.J. (1987). Changes in motivation for parenthood among young married couples. *Population and Environment, 9,* 96–110.

Beckwith, D. (1985). Solo Americans. *Time, 126*(22), 41.

Beggs, V.E., Calhoun, K.S., & Wolchik, S.A. (1987). Sexual anxiety and female sexual arousal: A comparison of arousal during sexual anxiety stimuli and sexual pleasure stimuli. *Archives of Sexual Behavior, 16,* 311–319.

Belcastro, P.A. (1985). Sexual behavior differences between black and white students. *Journal of Sex Research, 21,* 56–67.

Belec, L., Georges, A., Steenman, G., & Martin, P. (1989). Anti-bodies to human immunodeficiency virus in the semen of heterosexual men. *Journal of Infectious Diseases, 159,* 324–327.

Bell, A.P., & Weinberg, M.S. (1978). *Homosexualities: A study of diversity among men and women.* New York: Simon & Schuster.

Bell, A.P., Weinberg, M., & Hammersmith, S. (1981a). *Sexual preference: Statistical appendix.* Bloomington, Ind.: Indiana University Press.

Bell, A.P., Weinberg, M.S., & Hammersmith, S.K. (1981b). *Sexual preference: Its development in men and women.* Bloomington, Ind.: Indiana University Press.

Belsky, J., & Rovine, M. (in press). Patterns of marital change across the transition to parenthood: Pregnancy to three years postpartum. *Journal of Marriage and the Family.*

Belsky, J., Rovine, M., & Fish, M. (1990, in press). The developing family system. In M. Gunnar (Ed.), *Systems and development, Minnesota Symposium on Child Psychology* (Vol. 22). Hillsdale, N.J.: Lawrence Erlbaum.

Belzer, E.G., Jr., Whipple, B., & Moger, W. (1984). On female ejaculation. *Journal of Sex Research, 20,* 403–406.

Bem, S.L. (1975). Sex role adaptability: One consequence of psychological androgyny. *Journal of Personality and Social Psychology, 31,* 634–643.

Benassi, M.A. (1982). Effects of order of presentation, primacy, and physical attractiveness on attributions of ability. *Journal of Personality and Social Psychology, 43,* 48–58.

Benderly, B.L. (1988, October). For cancer, try marriage. *Psychology Today,* 14.

Benditt, J. (1979). Second-trimester abortion in the United States. *Family Planning Perspectives, 11,* 358–361.

Benditt, J.M. (1980). Current contraceptive research. *Family Planning Perspectives, 12,* 149–152, 154–155.

Benedek, E.P. (1983). Breast development in adolescent females. *Medical Aspects of Human Sexuality, 17*(1), 16U, 16V, 16X, 16CC, 16FF, 16KK, 16NN, 16PP.

Benedek, T. (1980). Cocaine damage to nasal mucosa. *Medical Aspects of Human Sexuality, 14*(12), 6.

Ben Franklin's advice to a young man. (1983). *Medical Aspects of Human Sexuality, 17*(3), 161–162.

Benn, S., Rutledge, R., & Folks, T. (1985). Genomic heterogeneity of AIDS retroviral isolates from North America and Zaire. *Medical Aspects of Human Sexuality, 230,* 949–951.

Bennett, N.G. (1990, May 27). How to calculate the U.S. divorce rate, correctly. *New York Times,* 12 E.

Bennett, P., & Mannis, T. (1986, March). A few words about breasts. *Playboy,* 20.

Bensimon, H. (1981). Infertility caused by frequent ejaculation. *Medical Aspects of Human Sexuality, 15*(12), 81.

Bensimon, H. (1984). Orgasm vs. ejaculation. *Medical Aspects of Human Sexuality, 18*(3), 252.

Benson, D.J., & Thomson, G.E. (1982). Sexual harassment on a university campus: The influence of authority relations, sexual interest, and gender stratification. *Social Problems, 29,* 236–251.

Bentler, P.M., & Newcomb, M.D. (1978). Longitudinal study of marital success and failure. *Journal of Consulting and Clinical Psychology, 46,* 1053–1070.

Bentler, P.M., & Peeler, W.H. (1979). Models of female orgasm. *Archives of Sexual Behavior, 8,* 405–423.

Berardo, F.M., Vera, H., & Berardo, D.H. (1983). Age-discrepant marriages. *Medical Aspects of Human Sexuality, 17*(1), 57–58, 63, 64, 72, 73, 76.

Berenstain, S., & Berenstain, J. (1974). *He bear, she bear.* New York: Random House.

Berest, J.J. (1970). Report on a case of sadism. *Journal of Sex Research, 6,* 210–219.

Berg, J.H., & McQuinn, R.D. (1989). Loneliness and aspects of social support setworks. *Journal of Social and Personal Relationships, 6,* 359–372.

Berg, J.H., & Peplau, L.A. (1982). Loneliness: The relationship of self-disclosure and androgyny. *Personality and Social Psychology Bulletin, 8,* 624–630.

Berger, M.M. (1978). Fathers' discomfort at daughters' sexual maturation. *Medical Aspects of Human Sexuality, 12*(9), 141.

Bergquist, C., Nillius, S.J., & Wide, L. (1982). Long-term intranasal luteinizing hormone-releasing hormone (LHRH) agonist treatment for contraception in women. *Fertility and Sterility, 38,* 190.

Berk, R.A. (1990). Drug use, prostitution and the prevalence of AIDS: An analysis using census tracts. *Journal of Sex Research, 27,* 607–621.

Berliner, L., & Barbieri, M.K. (1984). The testimony of the child victim of sexual assault. *Journal of Social Issues, 40,* 125–137.

Berman, P.W., O'Nan, B.A., & Floyd, W. (1981). The double standard of aging and the social situation: Judgments of attractiveness of the middle-aged woman. *Sex Roles, 7,* 87–96.

Bernhard, L. (1986). Methodology issues in studies of sexuality and hysterectomy. *Journal of Sex Research, 22,* 108–128.

Bernstein, A.C., & Cowan, P.A. (1975). Children's concepts of how people get babies. *Child Development, 46,* 77–92.

Bernstein, B.E. (1977). Effect of menstruation on academic performance among college women. *Archives of Sexual Behavior, 6,* 289–296.

Bernstein, I.C. (1983). Terminating contraception when menopause nears: A psychiatric review. *Medical Aspects of Human Sexuality, 17*(2), 32A, 32D, 32F.

Bernstein, I.L. (1984). Hypersensitivity reactions to semen. *Medical Aspects of Human Sexuality, 18*(10), 16, 95.

Bernstein, W.M., Stephenson, B.O., Snyder, M.L., & Wickland, R.A. (1983). Causal ambiguity and heterosexual affiliation. *Journal of Experimental Social Psychology, 19,* 78–92.

Berscheid, E., Dion, K., Walster, E., & Walster, G.W. (1971). Physical attractiveness and dating choice: A test of the matching hypothesis. *Journal of Experimental Social Psychology, 7,* 173–189.

Bess, B.E., & Janus, S.S. (1976). Prostitution. In B.J. Sadock, H.I. Kaplan, & A.M. Freedman (Eds.), *The sexual experience* (pp. 564–610). Baltimore, Md.: Williams and Wilkens.

Betts, K. (1984). The Billings method of family planning: An assessment. *Studies in Family Planning, 15*(6), 253–266.

Bieber, I., Dain, H.J., Dince, P.R., Drellich, M.G., Grand, H.G., Gundlach, R.H., Kremer, M.W., Rifkin, A.H., Wilbur, C.B., &

Bieber, T.B. (1962). *Homosexuality: A psychoanalytic study.* New York: Basic Books.

Billingham, R.E., Smith, K.A., & Keller, J. (1989). The effect of chronological and theoretical birth order on sexual attitudes and behaviors. *Archives of Sexual Behavior, 18,* 109–116.

Birk, L. (1981). What a physician can learn from a sex therapist. *Medical Aspects of Human Sexuality, 15*(8), 105, 109.

Birke, L.I.A. (1982). Is homosexuality hormonally determined? *Journal of Homosexuality, 6*(4), 35–49.

Bishop, K. (1987, November 1). Getting permission to have an abortion. *New York Times,* E 7.

Bishop, K. (1989, May 31). San Francisco grants recognition to partnerships of single people. *New York Times,* A 17.

Bixler, R.H. (1982). Sibling incest in the royal families of Egypt, Peru, and Hawaii. *Journal of Sex Research, 18,* 264–281.

Bixler, R.H. (1986). Of apes and men (including females). *Journal of Sex Research, 22,* 255–267.

Blaivas, J.G. (1981). Test for sterility after vasectomy. *Medical Aspects of Human Sexuality, 15*(11), 23.

Blaivas, J.G. (1982). Ejaculatory impotence with erection. *Medical Aspects of Human Sexuality, 16*(4), 16–17.

Blakeslee, S. (1989, July 25). Data suggest that implants may pose risk of later harm. *New York Times,* C 1, C 8.

Blakeslee, S. (1991, January). Research on birth defects turns to flaws in sperm. *New York Times Medical Science, 1,* 36.

Blanchard, R. (1985). Typology of male-to-female transsexualism. *Archives of Sexual Behavior,* pp. 247–261.

Blanchard, R. (1989). The classification and labeling of nonhomosexual gender dysphorias. *Archives of Sexual Behavior, 18,* 315–334.

Blanchard, R., & Clemmensen, L.H. (1988). A test of the DSM-III-R's implicit assumption that fetishistic arousal and gender dysphoria are mutually exclusive. *Journal of Sex Research, 25,* 426–432.

Blanchard, R., Clemmensen, L.H., & Steiner, B.W. (1983). Gender reorientation and psychosocial adjustment in male-to-female transsexuals. *Archives of Sexual Behavior, 12,* 503–509.

Blanchard, R., Clemmenson, L.H., & Steiner, B.W. (1987). Heterosexual and homosexual gender dysphoria. *Archives of Sexual Behavior, 16,* 139–152.

Blanchard, R., McConkey, J.G., Roper, V., & Steiner, B.W. (1983). Measuring physical aggressiveness in heterosexual, homosexual, and transsexual males. *Archives of Sexual Behavior, 12,* 511–524.

Blanchard, R., Racansky, I.G., & Steinder, B.W. (1986). Phallometric detection of fetishistic arousal in heterosexual male cross-dressers. *Journal of Sex Research, 22,* 452–462.

Blanche, S., et al. (1989). A prospective study of infants born to women seropositive for human immunodeficiency virus type I. *New England Journal of Medicine, 320,* 1643.

Blank, H.R. (1982). Sexuality in the blind. *Medical Aspects of Human Sexuality, 16*(6), 137–140.

Blankenship, V., Hnat, S.M., Hess, T.G., & Brown, D.R. (1984). Reciprocal interaction and similarity of personality attributes. *Journal of Social and Personal Relationships, 1,* 415–432.

Blasband, D., & Peplau, L.A. (1985). Sexual exclusivity versus openness in gay male couples. *Archives of Sexual Behavior, 14,* 395–412.

Bleier, R. (1984). *Science and gender: A critique of biology and its theories on women.* New York: Pergamon Press.

Bleyberg, L.S. (1982). Sexuality and the rehabilitation process. *Medical Aspects of Human Sexuality, 16*(3), 34L, 34N–34P, 34T, 34U.

Bloch, D. (1979). Sex education practices of mothers. *Journal of Sex Education and Therapy, 4*(1), 7–12.

Block, J.H. (1973). Concepts of sex roles: Some cross-cultural and longitudinal perspectives. *American Psychologist, 28,* 512–526.

Blood, R.O. (1982). Marriages of older men to younger women. *Medical Aspects of Human Sexuality, 16*(7), 9.

Bloom, D.E. (1981, March), *What's happening to the age at first birth in the United States? A study of recent white and nonwhite cohorts.* Paper presented at the meeting of the Population Association of America in Washington, D.C.

Blue for boys. . . (1989, August 13). *Albany Times Union,* F–7.

Blumberg, N.L. (1980). Effects of neonatal risk, maternal attitude, and cognitive style on early postpartum adjustment. *Journal of Abnormal Psychology, 89,* 139–150.

Blumstein, P.W., & Schwartz, P. (1976). Bisexuality in women. *Archives of Sexual Behavior, 5,* 171–181.

Blumstein, P.W., & Schwartz, P. (1977). Bisexuality: Some social psychological issues. *Journal of Social Issues, 33*(2), 30–46.

Blumstein, P.W., & Schwartz, P. (1983). *American couples: Money, work, sex.* New York: William Morrow.

Body fat and infertility. (1980, January). *Harvard Medical School Health Letter, 5*(3), 5.

Boffey, P.M. (1987, November 17). The latest concern about sex: The perils of the papilloma virus. *New York Times,* C 3.

Boffey, P.M. (1988, April 22). Researchers list odds of getting AIDS in heterosexual intercourse. *New York Times,* A 1, A 18.

Bogue, R., & Sigelman, D.W. (1979, July 17). *Sterilization report number 3: Continuing violations of federal sterilization guidelines by teaching hospitals in 1979.* Washington, D.C.: Public Citizen Health Research Group.

Bohlen, J.E. (1982). "Female ejaculation" and urinary stress incontinence. *Journal of Sex Research, 18,* 360–363.

Bohlen, J.G., Held, J.P., Sanderson, M.O., & Ahlgren, A. (1982). The female orgasm: Pelvic contractions. *Archives of Sexual Behavior, 11,* 367–387.

Bohlen, J., Held, J., Sanderson, M., & Patterson, R. (1984). Heart rate, rate-pressure product, and oxygen uptake during four sexual activities. *Archives of Internal Medicine, 144,* 1745–1748.

Bolling, D. (1978). Pain and trauma of anal coitus. *Medical Aspects of Human Sexuality, 12*(6), 41. (a)

Bolling, D.R. (1978). Women's interest in anal coitus. *Medical Aspects of Human Sexuality, 12*(8), 80, 116.(b)

Bongaarts, J. (1984). Building a family: Unplanned events. *Studies in Family Planning, 15*(1), 14–19.

Boone, M.S., Farley, J.U., & Samuel, S.J. (1985). A cross-country study of commercial contraceptive sales programs: Factors that lead to success. *Studies in Family Planning, 16,* 30–39.

Booth, A. (1982). When intercourse ceases in young couples. *Medical Aspects of Human Sexuality, 16*(2), 70AA, 70EE.

Booth, A., & Duvall, D. (1981). Sex roles and the link between fertility and employment. *Sex Roles, 7,* 847–856.

Bornstein, R. F., Leone, D. R., & Galley, D. J. (1987). The generalizability of subliminal mere exposure effects: Influence of stimuli perceived without awareness on social behavior. *Journal of Personality and Social Psychology, 53,* 1020–1079.

Boswell, J. (1979). *Christianity, social tolerance, and homosexuality: Gay people in western Europe from the beginning of the Christian era to the fourteenth century.* Chicago: University of Chicago Press.

Boswell, J. (1980). *Christianity, social tolerance, and homosexuality.* Chicago: University of Chicago Press.

Bouton, K. (1982, June 13). Fighting male infertility. *New York Times Magazine,* pp. 86–91, 100.

Boyar, R.M., & Aimen, J. (1982). The 24-hour secretory pattern of LH and the response to LHRH in transsexual men. *Archives of Sexual Behavior, 11,* 157–169.

Boyden, T., Carroll, J.S., & Maier, R.A. (1984). Similarity and attraction in homosexual males: The effects of age and masculinity–feminity. *Sex Roles, 10,* 939–948.

Boyer, D., & James, J. (1981). Prostitutes' incest experience. *Medical Aspects of Human Sexuality, 15*(8), 96.

Brabant, S. (1976). Sex role stereotyping in the Sunday comics. *Sex Roles, 2,* 331–337.

Bradbard, M.R., & Endsley, R.C. (1983). The effects of sex typed labeling on preschool children's information-seeking and retention. *Sex Roles, 9,* 247–261.

Bradley, R.A. (1981). *Husband-coached childbirth* (3rd ed.). New York: Harper & Row.

Bradsher, K. (1990, January 17). For every five young women, six young men. *New York Times,* pp. C-1, C-10.

Brand, D. (1987). The cost of kissing and not telling. *Time, 129*(24), 78.

Brandt, J.L. (1892). *Marriage and the home.* Chicago: Laird and Lee.

Braucht, G.N. (1982). Problem drinking among adolescents: A review and analysis of psychological research. In *Alcohol and Health Monograph No. 4: Special Populations.* U.S. Department of Health and Human Services.

Breast-feeding linked to straighter teeth. (1987, June 2). *New York Times,* C 5.

Brecher, E.M. (1969). *The sex researchers.* Boston: Little, Brown.

Brender, W., Libman, E., Burstein, R., & Takefman, J. (1983). Behavioral sex therapy: A preliminary study of its effectiveness in a clinical setting. *Journal of Sex Research, 19,* 351–365.

Brennan, T. (1982). Loneliness at adolescence. In L.A. Peplau and D. Perlman (Eds.), *Loneliness: A sourcebook of current theory, research, and therapy* (pp. 269–290). New York: John Wiley.

Brennan, T., & Auslander, N. (1979). *Adolescent loneliness: An exploratory study of social and psychological pre-dispositions and theory* (Vol. 1). Prepared for the National Institute of Mental Health, Juvenile Problems Division, Grant No. R01—MH 289 12–01, Behavioral Research Institute, 1979.

Brennock, W.E. (1981). Initial gynecologic examination. *Medical Aspects of Human Sexuality, 15*(11), 21.

Brennock, W.E. (1982). Fertility at menarche. *Medical Aspects of Human Sexuality, 16*(12), 21, 24.

Breslow, N., Evans, L., & Langley, J. (1985). On the prevalence and roles of females in the sadomasochistic subculture: Report of an empirical study. *Archives of Sexual Behavior, 14*, 303–317.

Bretschneider, J.G., & McCoy, N.L. (1988). Sexual interest and behavior in healthy 80- to 102-year olds. *Archives of Sexual Behavior, 17*, 109–129.

Brewer, J.S. (1981). Duration of foreplay and female orgasm rates. *Medical Aspects of Human Sexuality, 15*(4), 70.

Brewer, M.B., & Berk, R.A. (1982). Beyond Nine to Five: An introduction. *Journal of Social Issues, 38*(4), 1–4.

Brick, P. (1985). Sexuality education in the elementary school. *SIECUS Report, 13*(3), 1–4.

Bridge, T.P., Mirsky, A.F., & Goodwin, F.K. (Eds.). (1988). *Psychological neuropsychiatric, and substance abuse aspects of AIDS.* New York: Raven Press.

Bridges, C.F., Critelli, J.W., & Loos, V.E. (1985). Hypnotic susceptibility, inhibitory control, and orgasmic consistency. *Archives of Sexual Behavior, 14*, 373–376.

Bridges, J.S., & McGrail, C.A. (1989). Attributions of responsibility for date and stranger rape. *Sex Roles, 21*, 273–286.

Briere, J., & Malamuth, N.M. (1983). Self-reported likelihood of sexually aggressive behavior: Attitudinal versus sexual explanations. *Journal of Research in Personality, 17*, 315–323.

Brigham, J.C. (1980). Limiting conditions of the "physical attractiveness stereotype": Attributions about divorce. *Journal of Research in Personality, 14*, 365–375.

Bringle, R.G., & Williams, L.J. (1979). Parental offspring similarity on jealousy and related personality dimensions. *Motivation and Emotion, 3*, 265–286.

Brinn, J., Kraemer, K., Warm, J.S., & Paludi, M.A. (1984). Sex-role preferences in four age levels. *Sex Roles, 11*, 901–910.

Broderick, C.B. (1966). Sexual behavior among preadolescents. *Journal of Social Issues, 22*(1), 6–21.

Brodsky, C.M. (1976). *The harassed worker.* Lexington, Mass.: D.C. Heath.

Brody, J.E. (1983, October 4). Relations: Americans on conservative side. *Albany Times-Union,* A–1, A–8.

Brody, J.E. (1987a, January 13). Therapists seek causes of child molesting. *New York Times,* C 1, C 12.

Brody, J.E. (1987b, January 28). As saunas, hot tubs, and steam rooms multiply, so do disease-causing organisms. *New York Times,* C 10.

Brody, J.E. (1987c, March 4). Few sexually active people are properly informed about the correct use of condoms. *New York Times,* C 8.

Brody, J.E. (1987d, November 4). Personal health: Today more people than in the 1940s say they approve of masturbation or practice it. *New York Times,* C 8.

Brody, J.E. (1989, January 5). How women can begin to cope with premenstrual syndrome, a biological mystery. *New York Times,* B 12.

Brody, J.E. (1990, November 8). Taking the mystery out of child-

birth: Prenatal diagnoses for sex selection. *New York Times,* B 25.

Brody, L.R. (1985). Gender differences in emotional development. A review of theories and research. *Journal of Personality, 53*, 102–149.

Brooks, J.B. (1984). When children witness parental coitus. *Medical Aspects of Human Sexuality, 18*(8), 16, 77.

Brooks–Gunn, J., & Ruble, D.N. (1982). Development processes in the experience of menarche. In A. Baum & J.E. Singer (Eds.), *Handbook of psychology and health* (Vol. 2, pp. 117–147). Hillsdale, N.J.: Lawrence Erlbaum.

Brooks–Gunn, J.B. (1986). The relationship of maternal beliefs about sex typing to maternal and young children's behavior. *Sex Roles, 14*(1/2), 21–35.

Brosman, S.A. (1982). Current thinking on vasectomy. *Medical Aspects of Human Sexuality, 16*(9), 16A, 16D, 16H, 16J.

Brown, D.G. (1956a). Masculinity-feminity development in children. *American Psychologist, 11*, 415.

Brown, D.G. (1956b). Sex-role preference in young children. *Psychological Monographs, 70*, 1–19.

Brown, G. (1980). *Why more men and women are abstaining from sex—and enjoying it.* New York: McGraw-Hill.

Brown, G.R., & Collier, L. (1989). Transvestites' women revisited: a nonpatient sample. *Archives of Sexual Behavior, 18*, 73–83.

Brown, I.S. (1984). Development of a scale to measure attitude toward the condom as a method of birth control. *Journal of Sex Research, 20*, 255–263.

Brown, J.L. (1989a). When do boys become fertile? *Child, 4*(4), 32.

Brown, J.L. (1989b). Prenatal tests. *Child, 4*(6), 42, 44, 46.

Brown, S. (1985). Which birth style is best for you? *Parents, 60*(8), 53–56.

Brown, W. (1987). Hormones and sexual aggression in the male: Commentary. *Integrative Psychiatry, 5*, 91–93.

Brown, W.A. (1982). Males nursing infants. *Medical Aspects of Human Sexuality, 16*(10), 43, 47.

Brownmiller, S. (1975). *Against our will: Men, women, and rape.* New York: Simon & Schuster.

Bruce, J. (1981). Women-oriented health care: New Hampshire Feminist Health Center. *Studies in Family Planning, 12*, 353–363.

Bruce, K.E.M., & McLaughlin, J. (1986). The development of scales to assess knowledge and attitudes about genital herpes. *Journal of Sex Research, 22*, 73–84.

Bruch, M.A., Gorsky, J.M., Collins, T.M., & Berger, P.A. (1989). Shyness and sociability reexamined: A multicomponent analysis. *Journal of Personality and Social Psychology, 57*, 904–915.

Bryant, C.D., & Palmer, C.E. (1975). Massage parlors and "hand whores": Some sociological observations. *Journal of Sex Research, 11*, 227–241.

Bryant, J. (1985, September). *Testimony on the effects of pornography: Research findings.* Paper presented at the U.S. Justice Department Hearings, Houston, Texas.

Bryant, J., & Brown, D. (1989). Uses of pornography. In D. Zillmann & J. Bryant (Eds.), *Pornography: Research advances and policy considerations* (pp. 25–55). Hillsdale, N.J.: Lawrence Erlbaum.

Buckley, R.M. (1983). Sexual intercourse and subsequent urinary tract infections in women. *Medical Aspects of Human Sexuality, 17*(8), 249, 253, 256, 257.

Budell, J.W. (1981). Congenital syphilis. *Medical Aspects of Human Sexuality, 15*(10), 72G, 72K.

Buhrich, N. (1983). The association of erotic piercing with homosexuality, sadomasochism, bondage, fetishism, and tatoos. *Archives of Sexual Behavior, 12*, 167–171.

Buhrich, N., & Beaumont, T. (1981). Comparison of transvestism in Australia and America. *Archives of Sexual Behavior, 10*, 269–279.

Buhrich, N., & McConaghy, N. (1985). Preadult feminine behaviors of male transvestites. *Archives of Sexual Behavior, 14*, 413–419.

Buhrich, N., Theile, H., & Crawford, A. (1979). Plasma testosterone, serum FSH, and serum LH levels in transvestism. *Archives of Sexual Behavior, 8*, 49–53.

Buie, J. (1988). *APA Monitor, 19*(1), 32.

Bularzik, M. (1978). Sexual harassment at the workplace. Historical notes. *Radical America, 12*(4), 25–43.

Bullard, D. (1979). Male sexual experience with penile prosthesis. *Medical Aspects of Human Sexuality, 13*(5), 85–86.

Bullough, V.L. (1975). Transsexualism in history. *Archives of Sexual Behavior, 4*, 561–571.

Bullough, V.L. (1976). *Sexual variance in society and history.* New York: John Wiley.

Bullough, V.L. (1977). Sex education in Medieval Christianity. *Journal of Sex Research, 13*, 185–196.

Bullough, V.L. (1978). Variant life styles: Homosexuality. In B.I. Marstein (Ed.), *Exploring Intimate Life Styles* (pp. 245–257). New York: Springer.

Bullough, V.L. (1983). Edgar Allan Poe. *Medical Aspects of Human Sexuality, 17*(3), 231–232.

Bullough, V.L. (1989). *The Society for the Scientific Study of Sex: A brief history.* Mt. Vernon, IA: Foundation for the Scientific Study of Sexuality.

Bullough, V.L., Bullough, B., & Smith, R. (1983). A comparative study of male transvestites, male to female transsexuals, and male homosexuals. *Journal of Sex Research, 19*, 238–257.

Bullough, V.L., & Servedio, L. (1983). Toulouse–Lautrec. *Medical Aspects of Human Sexuality, 17*(1), 143, 146.

Bulut, A. (1984). Acceptance of effective contraceptive methods after induced abortion. *Studies in Family Planning, 15*, 281–284.

Bunge, W.R. (1984). Athletic support's protection and comfort. *Medical Aspects of Human Sexuality, 18*(6), 247, 250.

Burden, D. (1989). First year of marriage: Down to real. *Psychology Today, 23*(5), 13.

Burg, B.R. (1981). Hohum, another work of the devil: Buggery and sodomy in early Stuart England. *Journal of Homosexuality, 6*(1/2), 69–78.

Burg, B.R. (1988). Nocturnal emission and masturbatory frequency relationships: A 19th-century account. *Journal of Sex Research, 24*, 216–220.

Burger, J.M., & Burns, L. (1988). The illusion of unique invulnerability and the use of effective contraception. *Personality and Social Psychology Bulletin, 14*, 264–270.

Burger, J.M., & Inderbitzen, H.M. (1985). Predicting contraceptive behavior among college students: The role of communication, knowledge, sexual anxiety, and self-esteem. *Archives of Sexual Behavior, 14*, 343–350.

Burgess, A., & Holmstrom, L. (1974). Rape trauma syndrome. *American Journal of Psychiatry, 131*, 980–986.

Burgess, A., & Holmstrom, L.L. (1979). Adaptive strategies and recovery from rape. *American Journal of Psychiatry, 136*, 1278–1282.

Burgess, A., & Holmstrom, L. (1985). Rape trauma syndrome and post traumatic stress response. In A.W. Burgess (Ed.), *Rape and sexual assault: A research handbook* (pp. 46–60). New York: Garland.

Burgess, A., & Holmstrom, L. (1988). Treating the adult rape victim. *Medical Aspects of Human Sexuality, 22*(1), 36–43.

Burgess, A.W., Hartmann, C.R., McCausland, M.P., & Powers, P. (1984). Response patterns in children exploited through sex rings and pornography. *American Journal of Psychiatry, 141*, 656.

Burgess, J.K. (1983). The widower. *Medical Aspects of Human Sexuality. 17*(6), 158, 160, 162, 163, 166, 167.

Burgoyne, D. (1982). Sexual attitudes of lower socioeconomic men. *Medical Aspects of Human Sexuality, 16*(12), 30.

Burnett, R.C., Templer, D.I., & Barker, P.C. (1985). Personality variables and circumstances of sexual assault predictive of a woman's resistance. *Archives of Sexual Behavior, 14*, 183–188.

Burns, G.L., & Farina, A. (1984). Social competence and adjustment. *Journal of Social and Personal Relationships, 1*, 99–114.

Burns, K.A., Deddish, R.B., Burns, W.J., & Hatcher, R.P. (1983). Use of oscillating waterbeds and rhythmic sounds for premature infant stimulation. *Developmental Psychology, 19*, 746–751.

Burros, M. (1990, October 10). Eating well. *New York Times,* C 3.

Burt, M.R. (1980). Cultural myths and supports for rape. *Journal of Personality and Social Psychology, 38*, 217–230.

Burt, M.R., & Albin, R.S. (1981). Rape myths, rape definitions, and probability of conviction. *Journal of Applied Social Psychology, 11*, 212–230.

Burt, M.R., & Estep, R.E. (1981). Apprehension and fear: Learning a sense of sexual vulnerability. *Sex Roles, 7*, 511–522.

Burton, S. (1988). The sexual revolution hits China. *Time, 132*(11), 65.

Burton, S. (1990a). Straight talk on sex in China. *Time, 135*(20), 82.

Burton, S. (1990b). Condolences, it's a girl. *Time, 136*(19), 36.

Buss, D.M. (1984). Toward a psychology of person-environment (PE) correlation: The role of spouse selection. *Journal of Personality and Social Psychology, 47*, 361–377.

Buss, D.M. (1988). Love acts. The evolutionary biology of love. In R.J. Sternberg & M.L. Barnes (Eds.), *The psychology of love* (pp. 100–118). New Haven, CT: Yale University Press.

Buss, D.M. (1989a). Conflict between the sexes: Strategic interference and the evocation of anger and upset. *Journal of Personality and Social Psychology, 56*, 735–747.

Buss, D.M. (1989b). Sex differences in human mate preferences: Evolutionary hypotheses tested in 37 cultures. *Behavioral and Brain Sciences, 12,* 1–49.

Buss, D.M., & Barnes, M. (1986). Preferences in human mate selection. *Journal of Personality and Social Psychology, 50,* 559–570.

Butler, R.N., & Lewis, M. (1983). Sexual frustration of older women. *Medical Aspects of Human Sexuality, 17*(4), 65, 69, 71.

Butterfield, F. (1980, January 13). Love and sex in China. *New York Times Magazine,* 15–17, 43–44., 46–49.

Buunk, B. (1982). Anticipated sexual jealousy: Its relationship to selfesteem, dependency, and reciprocity. *Personality and Social Psychology Bulletin, 8,* 310–316.

Buunk, B., & Bringle, R.G. (1987). Jealousy in love relationships. In D. Perlman & S. Duck (Eds.), *Intimate relationships. Development, dynamics, and deterioration* (pp. 123–147). Newbury Park, CA: Sage.

Buvat, J., Buvat-Herbaut, M., Lemaire, A., Marcolin, G., & Quitterlier, E. (1990). Recent developments in the clinical assessment and diagnosis of erectile dysfunction. In J. Bancroft, C.M. Davis, & D. Weinstein (Eds.), *Annual review of sex research,* Vol. 1, (pp. 265–308). Mt Vernon, IA: Foundation for the Scientific Study of Sexuality.

Buys, C.J., Word, E.D., Jank, D.R., Ligon, R.W., Mauritz, M.N., Pena, R.H., & Vogt, M.B. (1977). Ministers' attitude toward overpopulation. *Personality and Social Psychology Bulletin, 3,* 567–570.

Byard, R.W., & Bramwell, N.H. (1988). Autoerotic death in females: An underdiagnosed syndrome? *American Journal of Forensic Medical Pathology, 9,* 252–254.

Byers, E.S., & Heinlein, L. (1989). Predicting initiations and refusals of sexual activities in married and cohabiting heterosexual couples. *Journal of Sex Research, 26,* 210–231.

Byers, E.S., & Lewis, K. (1988). Dating couples' disagreements over the desired level of sexual intimacy. *Journal of Sex Research, 24,* 15–29.

Byrne, D. (1961). The influence of propinquity and opportunities for interaction on classroom relationships. *Human Relations, 14,* 63–69.

Byrne, D. (1971). *The attraction paradigm.* New York: Academic Press.

Byrne, D. (1977). The imagery of sex. In J. Money and H. Musaph (Eds.), *Handbook of sexology* (pp. 327–350). Amsterdam: North-Holland.

Byrne, D. (1979). The people glut: Societal problems and the sexual behavior of individuals. *Journal of Sex Research, 15,* 1–5.

Byrne, D. (1983). Sex without contraception. In D. Byrne and W.A. Fisher (Eds.), *Adolescents, sex, and contraception* (pp. 3–31). Hillsdale, N.J.: Lawrence Erlbaum.

Byrne, D. (1991). Double standard or *macho* myopia? *Playboy, 38*(2), 42.

Byrne, D., & Buehler, J.A. (1955). A note on the influence of propinquity upon acquaintanceships. *Journal of Abnormal and Social Psychology, 51,* 147–148.

Byrne, D., & Byrne, L.A. (Eds.). (1977). *Exploring human sexuality.* New York: Harper and Row.

Byrne, D., Cherry, F., Laniberth, J., & Mitchell, H.E. (1973). Husband–wife similarity in response to erotic stimuli. *Journal of Personality, 41,* 385–394.

Byrne, D., Clore, G.L., & Smeaton, G. (1986). The attraction hypothesis: Do similar attitudes affect anything? *Journal of Personality and Social Psychology, 51,* 1167–1170.

Byrne, D., Ervin, C.R., & Lamberth, J. (1970). Continuity between the experimental study of attraction and real-life computer dating. *Journal of Personality and Social Psychology, 16,* 157–165.

Byrne, D., & Fisher, W.A. (Eds.). (1983). *Adolescents, sex, and contraception.* Hillsdale, N.J.: Lawrence Erlbaum.

Byrne, D., & Kelley, K. (1984a). The role of case histories in psychosexology. In P.R. Abramson, *Sarah: A sexual biography* (pp. 1–12). Albany, N.Y.: State University of New York Press.

Byrne, D., & Kelley, K. (1984b). Pornography and sex research. In N.M. Malamuth and E. Donnerstein (Eds.), *Pornography and sexual aggression* (pp. 1–15). New York: Academic Press.

Byrne, D., & Kelley, K. (Eds.). (1986). *Alternative approaches to the study of sexual behavior.* Hillsdale, N.J.: Lawrence Erlbaum.

Byrne, D., & Kelley, K. (1989). Basing legislative action on research data: Prejudice, prudence, and empirical limitations. In D. Zillmann & J. Bryant (Eds.), *Pornography: Research advances and policy considerations* (pp. 363–385). Hillsdale, NJ: Lawrence Erlbaum Associates.

Byrne, D., & Lamberth, J. (1971a). Cognitive and reinforcement theories as complementary approaches to the study of attraction. In B.I. Murstein (Ed.), *Theories of attraction and love* (pp. 59–84). New York: Springer.

Byrne, D., & Lamberth, J. (1971b). The effect of erotic stimuli on sex arousal, evaluative responses, and subsequent behavior. In *Technical Report of the Commission on Obscenity and Pornography* (Vol. 8). Washington, D.C.: U.S. Government Printing Office.

Byrne, D., & Murnen, S. (1988). Maintaining loving relationships. In R.J. Sternberg and M.L. Barnes (Eds.), *The psychology of love* (pp. 293–310). New Haven, Conn.: Yale University Press.

Byrne, D., Murnen, S., Greendlinger, V., & Kelley, K. (1990, in press). Content, sex of viewer, and dispositional variables as predictors of affective and evaluative responses to erotic films. *Journal of Applied Social Psychology.*

Byrne, D., & Schulte, L. (1990). Personality dispositions as mediators of sexual responses. In J. Bancroft, C.M. Davis, & D. Weinstein (Eds.), *Annual review of sex research,* Vol. 1 (pp. 93–117). Mt. Vernon, IA: Foundation for the Scientific Study of Sexuality.

Cahill, S.E. (1983). Reexamining the acquisition of sex roles: A social interactionist approach. *Sex Roles, 9,* 1–15.

Caldwell, B.M. (1964). The effects of infant care. *Review of Child Development Research, 1,* 9–88.

Caldwell, M.A., & Peplau, L.A. (1984). The balance of power in lesbian relationships. *Sex Roles, 10,* 587–599.

Calhoun, L.G., Selby, J.W., & King, H.E. (1981). The influence of pregnancy on sexuality: A review of current evidence. *Journal of Sex Research, 17,* 139–151.

Callan, V.J., & Kee, P. (1981). Sons or daughters? Cross-cultural comparisons of the sex preferences of Australian, Greek, Italian, Malay, Chinese and Indian parents in Australia and Malaysia. *Population and Environment, 4,* 97–108.

Calvert, J.D. (1988). Physical attractiveness: A review and reevaluation of its role in social skills research. *Behavioral Assessment, 10,* 29–42.

Campden–Main, B.C., & Sara, M.L. (1983). Sex in the later years. *Medical Aspects of Human Sexuality, 17*(3), 81, 84, 86, 91.

Campion, N.R. (1989, March 26). Half a century of sex education. *New York Times Magazine, 22,* 24.

Cann, A., Calhoun, L.G., Selby, J.W., & King, H.E. (1981). Rape: A contemporary overview and analysis. *Journal of Social Issues, 37,* 1–4.

Cantrell, W.A. (1979). Height and penis size. *Medical Aspects of Human Sexuality, 13*(5), 76.

Cantrell, W.A. (1982). Privacy of the parents' bedroom. *Medical Aspects of Human Sexuality, 16*(8), 17.

Cantwell, J.D. (1981). Sex and the heart. *Medical Aspects of Human Sexuality, 15*(9), 14, 19, 23, 29.

Can you rely on condoms? (1989, March). *Consumer Reports,* pp. 135–141.

Carballo, M., Cleland, J., Carael, M., & Albrecht, G. (1989). A cross national study of patterns of sexual behavior. *Journal of Sex Research, 26,* 287–299.

Carns, D.E. (1973). Talking about sex: Notes on first coitus and the double sexual standard. *Journal of Marriage and the Family, 35,* 677–688.

Carnes, P. (1985). *Out of the shadows: Understanding sexual addiction.* Minneapolis, MN: CompCare.

Carnes, P. (1988). *Contrary to love: Helping the sexual addict.* Minneapolis, MN: Compcare.

Carson, K.F. (1981). How to know if a female reaches orgasm. *Medical Aspects of Human Sexuality, 15*(6), 92. (a)

Carson, K.F. (1981). Women's failure to lubricate. *Medical Aspects of Human Sexuality, 15*(12), 60A, 60E. (b)

Carson, K.F. (1982). Female premature ejaculation. *Medical Aspects of Human Sexuality, 16*(6), 165. (a)

Carson, K.F. (1982). Fellatio. *Medical Aspects of Human Sexuality, 16*(1), 68. (b)

Carter, D.B. (1986). AIDS and the sex therapist: "Just the facts please ma'am." *Journal of Sex Research 22,* 403–408.

Cash, T.F., & Derlega, V.J. (1978). The matching hypothesis: Physical attractiveness among same-sexed friends. *Personality and Social Psychology Bulletin, 4,* 240–243.

Castelnuevo-Tedesco, P. (1979). Sexual self-image and signs of aging. *Medical Aspects of Human Sexuality, 13*(6), 40–41.

Catania, J.A., & White, C.B. (1982). Sexuality in an aged sample: Cognitive determinants of masturbation. *Archives of Sexual Behavior, 11,* 237–245.

Cattell, R.B., Kawash, G.F., & De Young, G.E. (1972). Validation of objective measures of ergic tension: Response of the sex erg to visual stimulation. *Journal of Experimental Research in Personality, 1,* 103–114.

Centers for Disease Control. (1982, March 26). *Morbidity and mortality weekly report.* U.S. Department of Health and Human Services, Public Health Service. Washington D.C.: U.S. Government Printing Office.

Centers for Disease Control. (1983, August 5). *Morbidity and mortality weekly report.* U.S. Department of Health and Human Services. Washington, D.C.: U.S. Government Printing Office.

Cesarean Birth Task Force. (1981). National Institute of Health consensus development statement on Cesarean childbirth. *Obstetrics and Gynecology, 57,* 537.

Chambers, K.C., & Phoenix, C.H. (1982). Sexual behavior in old male rhesus monkeys: Influence of familiarity and age of female partners. *Archives of Sexual Behavior, 11,* 299–308.

Chambless, D.L., & Lifshitz, J.L. (1981, April). *The expanded sexual arousability inventory: Validation of a scale measuring sexual anxiety.* Paper presented at the meeting of the Eastern Psychological Association, New York.

Chambless, D.L., & Lifschitz, J.L. (1984). Self-reported sexual anxiety and arousal: The Expanded Sexual Arousability Inventory. *Journal of Sex Research, 20,* 241–254.

Chambless, D.L., Stern, T., Sultan, F.E., Williams, A.J., Goldstein, A.J., Lineberger, M.H., Lifshitz, J.L., and Kelly, L. (1982). The pubococcygeus and female orgasm: A correlational study with normal subjects. *Archives of Sexual Behavior, 11,* 479–490.

Chambless, D.L., Sultan, F.E., Stern, T., O'Neill, C., Garrison, S., & Jackson, A. (1984). Effect of pubocorrygeal exercise on coital orgasm in women. *Journal of Consulting and Clinical Psychology, 52,* 114–118.

Chang, T. (1981). When herpes genitalis is most contagious. *Medical Aspects of Human Sexuality, 15*(6), 91–92.

Chapel, T.A. (1979). Presenting signs and symptoms of primary syphilis. *Medical Aspects of Human Sexuality, 13*(6), 99–100.

Chapel, T.A. (1981). Antibiotic prophylaxis after exposure to venereal disease. *Medical Aspects of Human Sexuality, 15*(11), 16.

Chapel, T.A. (1982). Secondary syphilis: A disease that is difficult to diagnose. *Medical Aspects of Human Sexuality, 16*(4), 60E, 60F. (a)

Chapel, T.A. (1982). Dissemination of trichomoniasis. *Medical Aspects of Human Sexuality, 16*(8), 145, 149. (b)

Char, W.F., & McDermott, J.F. (1982). Fetishism. *Medical Aspects of Human Sexuality, 16*(6), 169.

Chartrand, S. (1989, April 11). Experts assess a decade of in vitro fertilization. *New York Times,* C 5.

Check, J.V.P., Perlman, D., & Malamuth, N.M. (1985). Loneliness and aggressive behavior. *Journal of Social and Personal Relationships, 2,* 243–252.

Cherlin, R.S. (1984). Male hypogonadism. *Medical Aspects of Human Sexuality, 18*(3), 195–198, 199.

Chevalier–Skolnikoff, S. (1976). Homosexual behavior in a laboratory group of stumptail monkeys (macaca arctoides): Forms, contexts, and possible social functions. *Archives of Sexual Behavior, 5,* 511–527.

Chick, D., & Gold, S.R. (1987–88). A review of influences on sexual fantasy: Attitudes, experience, guilt, and gender. *Imagination, Cognition and Personality, 7,* 61–76.

Chin, J. (1990). Current and future dimensions of the HIV/AIDS pandemic in women and children. *Lancet, 336,* 221.

Chisholm, D.D. (1981). Total sexual ignorance. *Medical Aspects of Human Sexuality, 15*(4), 52I.

Chlamydial, mycoplasmal infections may cause some complications of pregnancy and childbirth. (1984). *Family Planning Perspectives, 16,* 94–95.

Christakos, A.C. (1983). Vaginals permicidal agents. *Medical Aspects of Human Sexuality, 17*(3), 129, 132.

Christensen, H.T. (1969). Normative theory derived from cross-cultural family research. *Journal of Marriage and the Family, 31,* 209–222.

Christopher, F.S., & Cate, R.M. (1984). Factors involved in premarital sexual decision-making. *Journal of Sex Research, 20,* 363–376.

Christopher, F.S., & Cate, R.M. (1985). Premarital sexual pathways and relationship development. *Journal of Social and Personal Relationships, 2,* 271–288.

Cibley, L.J. (1980). Trichomonas vaginalis vaginitis. *Medical Aspects of Human Sexuality, 14*(3), 53–54.

Clark, L., Bean, A., Swicegood, G., & Ansbacher, H. (1979). The decision for male versus female sterilization. *The Family Coordinator, 18,* 250–254.

Clark, L., & Lewis, D. (1977). *Rape: The price of coercive sexuality.* Toronto: The Women's Press.

Clark, L.A., & Watson, D. (1988). Mood and the mundane: Relations between daily life events and self-reported mood. *Journal of Personality and Social Psychology, 54,* 296–308.

Clark, M.S., & Waddell, B. (1985). Perceptions of exploitation in communal and exchange relationships. *Journal of Social and Personal Relationships, 2,* 403–418.

Clay, D.C., & Zuiches, J.J. (1980). Reference groups and family size norms. *Population and Environment, 3,* 262–278.

Cleek, M., & Pearson, T. (1985). Perceived causes of divorce: An analysis of interrelationships. *Journal of Marriage and the Family, 47,* 179–183.

Clegg, C.L., & Gold, S.R. (1988, March). *Sexual fantasies of students with coercive experiences and attitudes.* Paper presented at the meeting of the Southeastern Psychological Association, New Orleans.

Clement, U. (1989). Profile analysis as a method of comparing intergenerational differences in sexual behavior. *Archives of Sexual Behavior, 18,* 229–237.

Clement, U. (1990). Surveys of heterosexual behavior. In J. Bancroft, C.M. Davis, & D. Weinstein (Eds.), *Annual review of sex research,* Vol. 1 (pp. 45–74). Mt. Vernon, IA: Foundation for the Scientific Study of Sexuality.

Clement, U., Pfafflin, F. (1980). Changes in personality scores among couples subsequent to sex therapy. *Archives of Sexual Behavior, 9,* 235–244.

Clement, U., Schmidt, G., & Kruse, M. (1984). Changes in sex differences in sexual behavior: A replication of a study on West German students (1966–81). *Archives of Sexual Behavior, 13,* 99–120.

Clifford, R. (1978). Development of masturbation in college women. *Archives of Sexual Behavior, 7,* 559–573.

Clifford, R. (1979). Timing of orgasm. *Medical Aspects of Human Sexuality, 13*(4), 33.

Clifford, R.E. (1978). Favored coital positions. *Medical Aspects of Human Sexuality, 12*(11), 52–55.

Clore, G.L., & Byrne, D. (1974). A reinforcement-affect model of attraction. In T.L. Huston (Ed.), *Foundations of interpersonal attraction* (pp. 143–170). New York: Academic Press.

Coale, A.J. (1983). Recent trends in fertility in less developed countries. *Science, 221,* 828–832.

Cochran, S.D., & Mays, V.M. (1990). Sex, lies, and HIV. *New England Journal of Medicine, 322,* 774.

Cocores, J., & Gold, M. (1989). Substance abuse and sexual dysfunction. *Medical Aspects of Human Sexuality, 23*(2), 22–31.

Cohen, A., Rosen, R., & Goldstein, L. (1985). EEG hemispheric asymmetry during sexual arousal: Psychophysiological patterns in responsive, unresponsive, and dysfunctional men. *Journal of Abnormal Psychology, 94*(4), 580–590.

Cohen, A.G., & Gutek, B.A. (1985). Dimensions of perceptions of social-sexual behavior in a work setting. *Sex Roles, 13,* 317–327.

Cohen, D. (1979). *J.B. Watson: The founder of behaviorism.* London: Routledge & Kegan Paul.

Cohen, H.D., & Shapiro, A. (1970). A method of measuring sexual arousal in the female. *Psychophysiology, 8,* 251.

Cohen, J.B., Severy, L.J., & Ahtola, O.T. (1978). An extended expectancy-value approach to contraceptive alternatives. *Journal of Population, 1,* 22–41.

Cohen, M.L., & Falkow, S. (1981). Protein antigens from Staphylococcus aereus strains associated with toxic-shock syndrome. *Science, 211,* 842–844.

Cohen, M.M. (1987). Long-term risk of hysterectomy after tubal sterilization. *American Journal of Epidemiology, 125,* 410.

Cohen, S. (1982). Patterns of lethal drug abuse and sexuality. *Medical Aspects of Human Sexuality, 16*(2), 132, 133, 136, 137.

Cohn, D.L. (1983). Genital mycoplasmas. *Medical Aspects of Human Sexuality, 17*(12), 196, 198, 203, 204.

Colangelo, N., Rosenthal, D.M., & Dettmann, N. (1984). Maternal employment and job satisfaction and their relationship to children's perceptions and behaviors. *Sex Roles, 10,* 693–702.

Cole, D. (1987, August 9). The cost of entering the baby chase. *New York Times,* 9 F.

Cole, L.P., Fortney, J.A., Kennedy, K.I. (1984). Menstrual patterns after female sterilization: Variables predicting change. *Studies in Family Planning, 15,* 242–250.

Coleman, E. (1982a). Developmental stages of the coming-out process. In W. Paul, J.D. Weinrich, J.C. Gonsiorek, & M.E. Hotvedt (Eds.), *Homosexuality* (pp. 149–158). Beverly Hills: Sage.

Coleman, E. (1982b). How chemical dependency harms marital and sexual relationships. *Medical Aspects of Human Sexuality, 16*(10), 42N, 42P, 42U, 42X, 42Z, 42EF.

Coleman, E. (1985). Bisexual women in marriages. *Journal of Homosexuality, 11*(1/2), 87–99.

Coleman, L.M., Jussim, L., & Abraham, J. (1987). Students reactions to teachers' evaluations: The unique impact of negative feedback. *Journal of Applied Social Psychology, 17,* 1051–1070.

Coleman, M., & Ganong, L.H. (1985). Love and sex role stereotypes: Do macho men and feminine women make better lovers? *Journal of Personality and Social Psychology, 49,* 170–176.

Coleman, M.J. (1979). Coital motions preferred by women. *Medical Aspects of Human Sexuality, 13*(2), 30.

Coleman, R.O. (1983). Acoustic correlates of speaker sex identification: Implications for the transsexual voice. *Journal of Sex Research, 19,* 293–295.

Coles, C.D., & Shamp, M.J. (1984). Some sexual, personality, and demographic characteristics of women readers of erotic romances. *Archives of Sexual Behavior, 13,* 187–209.

Coley, S.B. (1980). Sexual relations with lights on. *Medical Aspects of Human Sexuality, 12*(9), 7.

Collins, E.G.C., & Blodgett, T.B. (1981). Sexual harassment: Some see it—some won't. *Harvard Business Review, 59,* 77–95.

Colt, E. (1981). Sex and athletics. *Medical Aspects of Human Sexuality, 15*(2), 25.

Comarr, A.E. (1982). Sexual function in paraplegics. *Medical Aspects of Human Sexuality, 16*(3), 19.

Comfort, A. (1973). Sexuality in a zero growth society. *Current, 148,* 29–34.

Condoms. (1979, October). *Consumer Reports,* pp. 583–589.

Condon, J.W., & Crano, W.D. (1988). Inferred evaluation and the relation between attitude similarity and interpersonal attraction. *Journal of Personality and Social Psychology, 54,* 789–797.

Conn, J. M. (1947). Children's awareness of the origins of babies. *Journal of Child Psychology, 1,* 140–176.

Connell, E.B. (1982). Vaginal douching. *Medical Aspects of Human Sexuality, 16*(3) 34I, 34J.

Connell, E.B. (1983). What practical advice can physicians give patients on avoiding genital herpes? *Medical Aspects of Human Sexuality, 17*(8), 157–158, 160, 163–164, 169, 173, 176–177.

Conte, H.R. (1983). Development and use of self-report techniques for assessing sexual functioning: A review and critique. *Archives of Sexual Behavior, 12,* 555–576.

Cook, E.P. (1985). *Psychological androgyny.* New York: Pergamon Press.

Cook, L.C. (1989). Girls: Just say "not now". *Psychology Today, 23*(2), 59.

Cooper, A.J. (1971). Treatments of male potency disorders: The present status. *Psychosomatics, 12,* 235–244.

Cooper, A.J. (1981). Causes of premature ejaculation. *Medical Aspects of Human Sexuality, 15*(3), 76A, 76C, 76H, 76I, 76L, 76M.

Cooper, K., Chassin, L., & Zeiss, A. (1985). The relation of sex-role self-concept and sex-role attitudes to the marital satisfaction and personal adjustment of dual-worker couples with preschool children. *Sex Roles, 12,* 227–241.

Coppolillo, H.P. (1984). Sexuality of the retarded. *Medical Aspects of Human Sexuality, 18*(9), 199–200.

Cordero, J.F., & Layde, P.M. (1983). Vaginal spermicides, chromosomal abnormalities and limb reduction defects. *Medical Aspects of Human Sexuality, 15*(1), 16–18

Cornog, M. (1981, November). *Genital pet names.* Paper presented at the meeting of the Society for the Scientific Study of Sex, New York City.

Cory, C.T. (1980, November). The withdrawal method advances among teenagers. *Psychology Today, 14*(6), 100–101.

Coryllos, E. (1980). Counseling parents about girls' participation in sports. *Medical Aspects of Human Society, 14*(11), 19–20.

Costa, F., Jessor, R., & Donovan, J.E. (1987). Psychosocial correlates and antecedents of abortion: An exploratory study. *Population and Environment, 9,* 3–23.

Costin, F. (1985). Beliefs about rape and women's social roles. *Archives of Sexual Behavior, 14,* 319–325.

Costos, D. (1986). Sex role identity in young adults: Its parental antecedants and relation to ego development. *Journal of Personality and Social Psychology, 50,* 602–611.

Cotton, W.L. (1975). Social and sexual relationships of lesbians. *Journal of Sex Research, 11,* 139–148.

Courter, G. (1982). Rebirth of the American midwife. *Parents, 57*(2), 59–63.

Covey, H. (1989). Perceptions and attitudes toward sexuality of the elderly during the Middle Ages. *Gerontologist, 29,* 93–100.

Cowan, A.L. (1990, November 17). A case for no new tummies: The tax on cosmetic surgery. *New York Times,* 29.

Cowan, G. (1984). The double standard in age-discrepant relationships. *Sex Roles, 11,* 17–23.

Cowan, G., Lee, C., Levy, D., & Snyder, D. (1988). Dominance and inequality in X-rated videocassettes. *Psychology of Women Quarterly, 12,* 299–311.

Cox, C.L., & Glick, W.H. (1986). Resume evaluations and cosmetics use: When more is not better. *Sex Roles, 14*(1/2), 51–58.

Cox, D.J. (1988). Incidence and nature of male genital exposure behavior as reported by college women. *Journal of Sex Research, 24,* 227–234.

Coyne, B.J., & Cross, H.J. (1988). Effects of social pressure on erections and evaluations of erotica. *Journal of Sex Research, 25,* 397–411.

Crabbe, P., Disczfalusy, E., & Djerassi, C. (1980). Injectable contraceptive synthesis: An example of international cooperation. *Science, 209,* 992–994.

Cramer, R.E. (1985). Attraction in context: Acquisition and blocking of person-directed action. *Journal of Personality and Social Psychology, 49,* 1221–1230.

Cranston-Cuebas, M.A., & Barlow, D.H. (1990). Cognitive and affective contributions to sexual functioning. In J. Bancroft, C.M. Davis, & D. Weinstein (Eds.), *Annual review of sex research,* Vol. 1, (pp. 119–161). Mt. Vernon, IA: Foundation for the Scientific Study of Sexuality.

Crenshaw, T.L., & Kessler, J. (1985). Vaginismus. *Medical Aspects of Human Sexuality, 19*(1), 21, 22, 27, 32.

Crime by the minute in U.S. (1986, December 2). *Albany Times-Union,* C-1.

Crist, T. (1984). Coitus without penetration. *Medical Aspects of Human Sexuality, 18*(8), 139.

Croft, H.A. (1978). Most popular coital positions. *Medical Aspects of Human Sexuality, 12*(5), 26, 27.

Crompton, L. (1978). Gay genocide: From Leviticus to Hitler. In L. Crew (Ed.), *The Gay Academic* (pp. 67–91). Palm Springs, Calif.: Etc. Publications.

Crompton, L. (1981). The myth of lesbian impunity capital laws from 1270 to 1791. *Journal of Homosexuality, 6*(1/2), 11–25.

Cross, R.J. (1983). Sex education in medical schools. *Medical Aspects of Human Sexuality, 17*(12), 92.

Croughan, J.L., Saghir, M., Cohen, R., & Robins, E. (1981). A comparison of treated and untreated male cross-dressers. *Archives of Sexual Behavior, 10,* 515–528.

Crusco, A.H., & Wetzel, C.G. (1984). The Midas touch: The effects of interpersonal touch on restaurant tipping. *Personality and Social Psychology Bulletin, 10,* 512–517.

Culliton, B.J. (1976). Penicillin-resistant gonorrhea: New strain spreading worldwide. *Science, 194,* 1395–1397.

Cumming, P.D., Wallace, E.L., Schorr, J.B., & Dodd, R.Y. (1989). Exposure of patients to human immunodeficiency virus through the transfusion of blood components that test antibody-negative. *New England Journal of Medicine, 321,* 941.

Cunningham, M.R. (1981). Sociobiology as a supplementary paradigm for social psychological research. In L. Wheeler (Ed.), *Review of personality and social psychology* (Vol. 2, pp. 69–106). Beverly Hills, Calif.: Sage.

Cunningham, M.R. (1986). Measuring the physical in physical attractiveness: Quasi-experiments on the sociobiology of female facial beauty. *Journal of Personality and Social Psychology, 50,* 925–935.

Cunningham, M.R. (1988). Does happiness mean friendliness? Induced mood and heterosexual self-disclosure. *Personality and Social Psychology Bulletin, 14,* 283–297.

Curran, J.W. (1980). VD and fertility. *Medical Aspects of Human Sexuality, 14,* 118.

Cutler, W.B., Garcia, C.R., & McCoy, N. (1987). Perimenopausal sexuality. *Archives of Sexual Behavior, 16,* 225–234.

Cvetkovich, G., & Grote, B. (1983). Adolescent development and teenage fertility. In D. Byrne & W.A. Fisher (Eds.), *Adolescents, sex, and contraception* (pp. 109–123). Hillsdale, N.J.: Lawrence Erlbaum.

Daher, D., Greaves, C., Supton, A. (1987). Sexuality in the college years. Special Issue: Parental concerns in college student mental health. *Journal of College Student Psychotherapy, 2,* 115–126.

Dalton, J.E. (1983). Sex differences in communication skills as measured by a modified relationship inventory. *Sex Roles, 9,* 195–204.

Dalton, K. (1982). Premenstrual tension: An overview. In R.C. Friedman (Ed.), *Behavior and the menstrual cycle* (pp. 217–242). New York: Dekker.

Darmon, P. (1986). *Damning the innocent: A history of the persecution of the impotent in pre-Revolutionary France.* New York: Viking.

D'Augelli, J.F., & Cross, H.J. (1975). Relationship of sex guilt and moral reasoning to premarital sex in college women and in couples. *Journal of Consulting and Clinical Psychology, 43,* 40–47.

Daugherty, L.R., & Burger, J.M. (1984). The influence of parents, church, and peers on the sexual attitudes and behaviors of college students. *Archives of Sexual Behavior, 13,* 351–359.

Dauw, D.C. (1988). Evaluating the effectiveness of the SECS' surrogate assisted sex therapy model. *Journal of Sex Research, 24,* 269–275.

Davenport, W.H. (1965). Sexual patterns and their regulation in a society of the Southwest Pacific. In F. Beach (Ed.), *Sex and behavior.* New York: John Wiley.

Davenport, W.H. (1977). Sex in cross-cultural perspective. In F.A. Beach (Ed.), *Human sexuality in four perspectives* (pp. 115–163). Baltimore, MD.: Johns Hopkins University Press.

David, H.P., Rasmussen, N.K., & Hoist, E. (1981). Postpartum and postabortion psychotic reactions. *Family Planning Perspectives, 13,* 88–92.

Davidson, J.K., Sr. (1983). Age of one's second wife. *Medical Aspects of Human Sexuality, 17*(6), 22–23.

Davidson, J.K., Sr., & Darling, C.A. (1988). The sexually experienced woman: Multiple sex partners and sexual satisfaction. *Journal of Sex Research, 24,* 141–154.

Davidson, J.K., Sr. & Hoffman, L.E. (1986). Sexual fantasies and sexual satisfaction: An empirical analysis of erotic thought. *Journal of Sex Research, 22,* 184–205.

Davidson, J.M., Camargo, C., Smith, E.R., & Kwan, M. (1983). Maintenance of sexual function in a castrated man treated with ovarian steroids. *Archives of Sexual Behavior, 12,* 263–276.

Davidson, J.M., Kwan, M., & Greenleaf, W.J. (1982). Hormonal replacement and sexuality in men. In J. Bancroft (Ed.), *Clinics in endocrinology and metabolism, diseases of sex and sexuality* (pp. 599–624). Philadelphia: Saunders.

Davis, C.M., Yarber, W.L., & Davis, S.L. (Eds.). (1988). *Sexuality related measures.* Mt Vernon, IA: Foundation for the Scientific Study of Sexuality.

Davis, D. (1981). Implications for interaction versus effectance as mediators of the similarity-attraction relationship. *Journal of Experimental Social Psychology, 17,* 96–116.

Davis, K.B. (1929). *Factors in the sex life of 2,200 women.* New York: Harper & Row.

Davis, M.H., & Franzoi, S.L. (1986). Adolescent loneliness, self-disclosure, and private self-consciousness: A longitudinal investigation. *Journal of Personality and Social Psychology, 51,* 595–608.

Davis, M.H., & Kraus, L.A. (1989). Social contact, loneliness, and mass media use: A test of two hypotheses. *Journal of Applied Social Psychology, 19,* 1100–1124.

Davison, G.C. (1978). Not can but ought: The treatment of homosexuality. *Journal of Consulting and Clinical Psychology, 46,* 170–172.

Davison, G.C., & Friedman, S. (1981). Sexual orientation stereotypy in the distortion of clinical judgment. *Journal of Homosexuality, 6*(3), 37–44.

Dawes, R.M. (1989). Statistical criteria for establishing a truly false consensus effect. *Journal of Experimental Social Psychology, 25,* 1–17.

Dawson, D.A. (1980). Early contraceptive methods. *Medical Aspects of Human Sexuality, 14*(5), 139.

Dawson, D.A., Meny, D.J., Ridley, J.C. (1980). Fertility control in the United States before the contraceptive revolution. *Family Planning Perspectives, 12,* 76–78, 80–86.

De Amicis, L.A., Goldberg, D.C., LoPiccolo, J., Friedman, J., & Davies, L. (1985). Clinical follow-up of couples treated for sexual dysfunction. *Archives of Sexual Behavior, 14,* 467–489.

Dean, S.R. (1980). Nonmarital sex in retirement areas. *Medical Aspects of Human Sexuality, 14*(5), 107.

Deardorff, T. (1989, November). Japan's finest. *Penthouse,* 143.

Deaux, K. (1984). From individual differences to social categories. *American Psychologist, 39,* 105–116.

Deaux, K., & Hanna, R. (1984). Courtship in the personals column: The influence of gender and sexual orientation. *Sex Roles, 11,* 363–375.

Debrovner, C.H. (1983). When a woman patient regrets sterilization. *Medical Aspects of Human Sexuality, 17*(3), 196, 201.

DeCecco, J.P. (1981). Definition and meaning of sexual orientation. *Journal of Homosexuality, 6*(4), 51–67.

DeCecco, J.P., & Ricketts, W. (1982). Physical changing of gender. *Medical Aspects of Human Sexuality, 16,* 97.

Deckert, G.H. (1981). "Castrating" women. *Medical Aspects of Human Sexuality, 15*(6), 91.

Deetz, T.R. (1980). Contracting VD via mouth-to-mouth resuscitation. *Medical Aspects of Human Sexuality, 14*(3), 4, 6.

deGallo, M.T., & Alzate, H. (1976). Brothel prostitution in Colombia. *Archives of Sexual Behavior, 5,* 1–7.

Deisher, R.W. (1982). When parents learn their child is homosexual. *Medical Aspects of Human Sexuality, 16*(6), 16U–16V.

DeLamater, J. (1981). The social control of sexuality. *Annual Review of Sociology, 7,* 263–290.

DeLamater, J. (1987). Gender differences in sexual scenarios. In K. Kelley (Ed.), *Females, males, and sexuality* (pp. 127–140). Albany, N.Y.: State University of New York Press.

DeLamater, J., & MacCorquodale, P. (1978). Premarital contraceptive use: A test of two models. *Journal of Marriage and the Family, 40,* 235–247.

DeLamater, J., & MacCorquodale, P. (1979). *Premarital sexuality: Attitudes, relationships, behavior.* Madison, Wis.: University of Wisconsin Press.

Delumeau, J. (1990). *Sin and fear: The emergence of a Western guilt culture.* New York: St. Martin's Press.

DeMare, C. (1982, July 14). Woman testifies to sitter's abuse of child. *Albany Times-Union,* 4.

DeMartino, M. (1974). *Sex and the intelligent woman.* New York: Springer.

de Monteflores, C., & Schultz, S.J. (1978). Coming out: Similarities and differences for lesbians and gay men. *Journal of Social Issues, 34*(3), 59–72.

de Moya, A. (1984). Lack of response to breast stimulation. *Medical Aspects of Human Sexuality, 18*(4), 218.

de Moya, A., & de Moya, D. (1981). Variability of nipple response during stimulation. *Medical Aspects of Human Sexuality, 15*(9), 119.

Denber, H.C.B. (1978). Treatment of excessive sexual desire. *Medical Aspects of Human Sexuality, 12*(5), 131–132.

D'Encarnacao, P., & D'Encarnacao, P. (1979). Pleasurable areas of female genitalia. *Medical Aspects of Human Sexuality, 13*(5), 7, 76.

Denko, J.D. (1980). Genesis of masochism. *Medical Aspects of Human Sexuality, 14*(8), 15.

Denmark, F.L., Shaw, J.S., & Ciali, S.D. (1985). The relationship among sex roles, living arrangements, and the division of household responsibilities. *Sex Roles, 12,* 617–625.

Denney, N.W., Field, J.K., & Quadagno, D. (1984). Sex differences in sexual needs and desires. *Archives of Sexual Behavior, 13,* 233–245.

Derlega, V.J., Durham, B., Gockel, B., & Sholis, D. (1981). Sex differences in self-disclosure: Effects of topic content, friendship, and partner's sex. *Sex Roles, 7,* 443–447.

Derlega, V.J., Winstead, B.A., Wong, P.T.P., & Hunter, S. (1985). Gender effects in an initial encounter: A case where men exceed women in disclosure. *Journal of Social and Personal Relationships, 2*(1), 25–44.

Dermer, M., & Pyszczynski, T.A. (1978). Effects of erotica upon men's loving and liking responses for women they love. *Journal of Personality and Social Psychology, 36,* 1302–1309.

Derogatis, L.R. (1975). *Derogatis Sexual Functioning Inventory.* Baltimore, Md.: Clinical Psychometric Research.

Derogatis, L.R. (1980). Etiologic factors in premature ejaculation. *Medical Aspects of Human Sexuality, 14*(6), 32, 35, 39, 43, 47.

Derogatis, L.R., & Kourlesis, S.M. (1981). Women's contributions to men's sexual dysfunction. *Medical Aspects of Human Sexuality, 15*(6), 76, 80, 81, 82, 84, 86, 87.

Derogatis, L.R., & Melisaratos, N. (1979). The DSFI: A multidimensional measure of sexual functioning. *Journal of Sexual and Marital Therapy, 5,* 244–281.

Derrick, F.C., Jr. (1979). Incidence of childhood molestation. *Medical Aspects of Human Sexuality, 13*(10), 135.

Des Jarlais, J.C., et al. (1989). HIV-1 infection among intravenous drug users in Manhattan, New York City, from 1977–1987. *Journal of the American Medical Association, 261,* 1008.

Detjen, J. (1990, November 5). Female condoms undergo final testing stages. *Albany Times Union,* B-16.

Deutsch, C. (1981). Dating after divorce. *Parents, 56*(2), 26, 28.

Devanesan, M. (1978). Countering anxiety which inhibits women's sexual responses. *Medical Aspects of Human Sexuality, 12*(7), 131–132.

DeVine, R. (1980). Discovering and treating sexual abuse of children. *Medical Aspects of Human Sexuality, 14*(10), 25–26.

Dew, M.A. (1985). The effect of attitudes on inferences of homosexuality and perceived physical attractiveness in women. *Sex Roles, 12,* 143–155.

Dhabuwala, C.B., Kumar, A. & Pierce, J.M. (1986). Myocardial infarction and its influence on male sexual function. *Archives of Sexual Behavior, 15,* 499–504.

Diamant, L. (Ed.). (1987). *Male and female homosexuality*. New York: Hemisphere Publishing.

Diamond, M. (1979). Sexual continence and nocturnal emissions. *Medical Aspects of Human Sexuality, 13*(3), 147, 151.

Diamond, M. (1982). Sexual identity, monozygotic twins reared in discordant sex roles and a BBC follow-up. *Archives of Sexual Behavior, 11*, 181–186.

Diamond, R., Feller, L., & Russo, N.F. (1981). *Sexual harassment action kit*. Washington, D.C.: Federation of Organizations for Professional Women.

Diamond, S., & Maliszewski, M. (1985). Headache, sexual functioning, and marital status. *Medical Aspects of Human Sexuality, 19*(1), 77, 81, 89, 92.

Diamond, S.A. (1985). *Helping children of divorce: A handbook for parents and teachers*. New York: Schocken Books.

Diana, L. (1980). Prostitutes and orgasm. *Medical Aspects of Human Sexuality, 14*(11), 5–6.

DiCaprio, J.M. (1979). Pharyngeal infections from cunnilingus. *Medical Aspects of Human Sexuality, 13*(3), 151.

Dickman, I. (1982). *Winning the battle for sex education*. New York: Sex Information and Education Council of the United States.

Dietz, P.E., Harry, B., & Hazelwood, R.R. (1986). Detective magazines: Pornography for the sexual sadist? *Journal of Forensic Sciences, 31*, 197–211.

Dingfelder, J.R. (1979). Coitus and spontaneous abortion. *Medical Aspects of Human Sexuality, 13*(11), 115.

Dion, K.K. & Dion, K.L. (1975). Self-esteem and romantic love. *Journal of Personality, 43*, 39–57.

Dion, K.L., & Dion, K.K. (1987). Belief in a just world and physical attractiveness stereotyping. *Journal of Personality and Social Psychology, 52*, 775–780.

Dion, K.L., & Dion, K.K. (1988). Romantic love: Individual and cultural perspectives. In R.J. Sterberg & M.L. Barnes (Eds), *The psychology of love* (pp. 264–289). New Haven, CT: Yale University Press.

DiVasto, P.V., Pathak, D., & Fishburn, W.R. (1981). The interrelationship of sex guilt, sex behavior, and age in an adult sample. *Archives of Sexual Behavior, 10*, 119–122.

DiVasto, P.V., Kaufman, A., Rosner, L., Jackson, R., Christy, J., Pearson, S., & Burgett, T. (1984). The prevalence of sexually stressful events among females in the general population. *Archives of Sexual Behavior, 13*, 59–67.

Dixit, N. (1985). *The effect of verbal contact and spatial positioning on job satisfaction, job performance, and interpersonal attraction: An experimental investigation*. Unpublished doctoral dissertation, University at Albany, SUNY.

Dixon, A.F. (1990). Neuroendocrine regulation of sexual behavior in female primates. In J. Bancroft, C.M. Davis, & D. Weinstein (Eds.), *Annual review of sex research*, Vol. 1 (pp. 197–226). Mt Vernon, IA: Foundation for the Scientific Study of Sexuality.

Dixon, D. (1985). Perceived sexual satisfaction and marital happiness of bisexual and heterosexual swinging husbands. *Journal of Homosexuality, 11*(1/2), 209–222.

Dixon, J.K. (1984). The commencement of bisexual activity in swinging married women over age thirty. *Journal of Sex Research, 20*, 71–90.

Dixon, J.K. (1985). Sexuality and relationship changes in married females following the commencement of bisexual activity. *Journal of Homosexuality, 11*(1/2), 115–133.

Dodd, R.Y. (1985). Detection of AIDS in donor blood. *Medical Aspects of Human Sexuality, , 19*(1), 202–203.

Dodge, L.J.T., Glasgow, R.E., & O'Neill, H.K. (1982). Bibliotherapy in the treatment of female orgasmic dysfunction. *Journal of Consulting and Clinical Psychology, 20*, 442–443.

Doniger, W. (1990, September 23). Why the body is disgusting. *New York Times Book Review*, 27–28.

Donovan, P. (1982). Airing contraceptive commercials. *Family Planning Perspectives, 14*, 321–324.

Donovan, P. (1983). When does personhood begin? *Family Planning Perspectives, 15*, 40–44.

Donovan, P. (1984). Wrongful birth and wrongful conception: The legal and moral issues. *Family Planning Perspectives, 16*, 64–69.

Dorman, R.L., & Olds, D.L. (1983). *Antepartum worries as predictors of maternal caregiving and perceptions of infant temperament during the first year of life*. Paper presented at the meeting of the American Psychological Association, Anaheim, California.

Dorner, G. (1988). Neuroendocrine response to estrogen and brain differentiation in heterosexuals, homosexuals, and transsexuals. *Archives of Sexual Behavior, 17*, 57–75.

Dover, K.J. (1978). *Greek homosexuality*. Cambridge, Mass.: Harvard University Press.

Downey, L. (1980). Intergenerational change in sex behavior: A belated look at Kinsey's studies. *Archives of Sexual Behavior, 9*, 267–317.

Downs, A.C., & Harrison, S.K. (1985). Embarrassing age spots or just plain ugly? Physical attractiveness stereotyping as an instrument of sexism on American television commercials. *Sex Roles, 13*, 9–20.

Drachman, D., de Carufel, A., & Insko, C.A. (1978). The extra credit effect in interpersonal attraction. *Journal of Experimental Social Psychology, 14*, 458–465.

Dranov, P. (1980, September). The "artificial" baby game. *Cosmopolitan, 282*, 311–314.

Driscoll, R., Davis, K.E., & Lipetz, M.E. (1972) Parental interference and romantic love: The Romeo and Juliet effect. *Journal of Personality and Social Psychology, 24*, 1–10.

Drucker, W.D. (1982). Endocrine abnormalities caused by alcoholism. *Medical Aspects of Human Sexuality, 16*(12), 34E, 34K, 34N.

Dryfoos, J. (1985). School-based health clinics: A new approach to preventing adolescent pregnancy? *Family Planning Perspectives, 17*, 70–75.

Duberman, M.B., Vicinus, M., & Chauncey, G., Jr. (Eds.). (1989). *Hidden from history: Reclaiming the gay and lesbian past*. New York: New American Library.

Duchin, S., Ledger, W., Schulze, R., & Speroff, L. (1989, March 30). OCs: Risks, benefits, guidelines. *Patient Care*, 89–111.

Duck, S., Lock, A. McCall, G., Fitzpatrick, M.A., & Coyne, J.C. (1984). Social and personal relationships: A joint editorial. *Journal of Social and Personal Relationships, 1,* 1–10.

Duenhoelter, J.H. (1978). Sex and pregnancy. *Medical Aspects of Human Sexuality, 12* (5), 45–50.

Duffy, M. (1990). I'm working late tonight, dear. *Time, 136* (22), 99.

Dullea, G. (1980, October 24). Sexual harassment at work: A sensitive and confusing issue. *New York Times,* A 20.

Dunbar, J., Brown, M., & Amoroso, D.M. (1973). Some correlates of attitudes toward homosexuality. *Journal of Social Psychology, 89,* 271–279.

Dunn, M.E., & Trost, J.E. (1989). Male multiple orgasms: A descriptive study. *Archives of Sexual Behavior, 18,* 377–387.

DuPont, R.L. (1982). Adverse reactions to marijuana. *Medical Aspects of Human Sexuality, 16* (9), 21.

Durova, N. (1988). *The memoirs of a woman soldier of 1812.* Ann Arbor, Mich.: Ardis.

Dutton, D.G., & Aron, A.P. (1974). Some evidence for heightened sexual attraction under conditions of high anxiety. *Journal of Personality and Social Psychology, 30,* 510–517.

Earls, C.M., & David, H. (1989). A psychosocial study of male prostitution. *Archives of Sexual Behavior, 18,* 401–419.

Earls, C.M., Quinsey, V.L., & Castonguay, L.G. (1987). A comparison of three methods of scoring penile circumference changes. *Archives of Sexual Behavior, 16,* 493–500.

Ebbesen, E.B., Kjos, G.L., & Konecni, V.J. (1976). Spatial ecology: Its effects on the choice of friends and enemies. *Journal of Experimental Social Psychology, 39,* 460–470.

Ebbesen, P., Melbye, M., & Biggar, R.J. (1984). Sex habits, recent disease, and drug use in two groups of Danish male homosexuals. *Archives of Sexual Behavior, 13,* 291–300.

Edelman, D.A., North, B.B., & Bernstein, G.S. (1985). Parity, pregnancy, and the sponge. *Family Planning Perspectives, 17,* 284.

Edmonds, E.M., & Cahoon, D.D. (1984). Female clothes preference related to male sexual interest. *Bulletin of the Psychonomic Society, 22,* 171–173.

Edmondson, D. (1984). "Carrying high" and other myths of sex prediction. *Parents, 9,* 53.

Edwards, L.D. (1981). Nongonococcal urethritis and related syndromes. *Medical Aspects of Human Sexuality, 15* (9), 137–138.

Eheart, B.K. & Martel, S.K. (1983). *The fourth trimester: On becoming a mother.* New York: Appleton-Century-Crofts.

Ehni, B.L., & Kline, D.G. (1981). Hypersexuality caused by neurologic dysfunction. *Medical Aspects of Human Sexuality, 15* (6), 95–96.

Ehni, B.L., & Kline, D.G. (1982). Hyposexuality caused by neurologic dysfunction. *Medical Aspects of Human Sexuality, 16* (7), 101–102.

Ehrentheil, O.F. (1974). A case of premature ejaculation in Greek mythology. *Journal of Sex Research, 10,* 128–131.

Ehrhardt, A.A., Grisanti, G., & McCauley, E.A. (1979). Female-to-male transsexuals compared to lesbians: Behavioral patterns of childhood and adolescent development. *Archives of Sexual Behavior, 8,* 481–490.

Ehrhardt, A.A., Ince, S.E., & Meyer-Bahlburg, H.F.L. (1981). Career aspiration and gender role development in young girls. *Archives of Sexual Behavior, 10,* 281–299.

Ehrhardt, A.A., Meyer-Bahlburg, H.F.L., Feldman, J.F., & Ince, S.E. (1984). Sex-dimorphic behavior in childhood subsequent to prenatal exposure to exogenous progestogens and estrogens. *Archives of Sexual Behavior, 13,* 457–477.

Ehrhardt, A.A., Meyer-Bahlburg, H.F.L., Rosen, L.R., Feldman, J.F., Veridiano, N.P., Zimmerman, I., & McEwen, B.S. (1985). Sexual orientation after prenatal exposure to exogenous estrogen. *Archives of Sexual Behavior, 14,* 57–77.

Eidelson, R.J. (1980). Interpersonal satisfaction and level of involvement: A curvilinear relationship. *Journal of Personality and Social Psychology, 39,* 460–470.

Eiger, M.S. (1987). *The complete book of breastfeeding.* New York: Bantam.

Einigenberg, E.M. (1968). "How new is the new morality?" In H. Cox (Ed.), *The situation ethics debate.* Philadelphia: Westminister Press.

Eisen, M., & Zellman, G.L. (1987). Changes in incidence of sexual intercourse of unmarried teenagers following a community-based sex education program. *Journal of Sex Research, 23,* 527–533.

Eisen, M., Zellman, G.L., & McAlister, A.L. (1990). Evaluating the impact of a theory-based sexuality and contraceptive education program. *Family Planning Perspectives, 22,* 261–271.

Eisenman, R. (1982). Sexual behavior as related to sex fantasies and experimental manipulation of authoritarianism and creativity. *Journal of Personality and Social Psychology, 43,* 853–860.

Elias, S. (1980). Advising patients about genetic amniocentesis. *Medical Aspects of Human Sexuality, 14* (8), 51–52.

Eliasberg, W.G., & Stuart, I.R. (1961). Authoritarian personality and the obscenity threshold. *Journal of Social Psychology, 55,* 143–151.

Ellenberg, M. (1982). Different sexual effects of diabetes. *Medical Aspects of Human Sexuality, 16* (4), 75.

Ellenbogen, R. (1979). Selection of bras. *Medical Aspects of Human Sexuality, , 13* (9), 159.

Ellenbogen, R. (1982). Asymmetric breasts. *Medical Aspects of Human Sexuality, 16* (8), 32A, 32G.

Ellis, A. (1960). *The art and science of love.* New York: Lyle Stuart.

Ellis, A., & Brancale, R. (1956). *The psychology of sex offenders.* Springfield, Ill.: Charles C. Thomas.

Ellis, A., & Harper, R.A. (1975). *A new guide to rational living.* Englewood Cliffs, N.J.: Prentice Hall.

Ellis, B.J., & Symons, D. (1990). Sex differences in sexual fantasy: An evolutionary psychological approach. *Journal of Sex Research, 27,* 527–555.

Ellis, E. (1983). A review of empirical rape research: Victim reactions and response to treatment. *Clinical Psychology Review, 3,* 473–490.

Ellis, E.M., Atkeson, B.M., & Calhoun, K.S. (1981). An assessment of long-term reaction to rape. *Journal of Abnormal Psychology, 90,* 263–266.

Ellis, H. (1899). *Studies in the psychology of sex.* New York: Random House.

Ellis, H. (1936). *Studies in the psychology of sex.* New York: Random House. (Original work published 1899).

Ellis, H. (1942). *Studies in the psychology of sex* (Vols. 1 & 2). New York: Random House. (Original work published in seven volumes, 1896–1928).

Ellis, L., & Ames, M.A. (1987). Neuro-hormonal functioning and sexual orientation: A theory of homosexuality–heterosexuality. *Psychological Bulletin, 101,* 233–258.

Ellis, L., Ames, M.A., Peckham, W., & Burke, D. (1988). Sexual orientation of human offspring may be altered by severe maternal stress during pregnancy. *Journal of Sex Research, 25,* 152–157.

Ellis, L., & Beattie, C. (1983). The feminist explanation for rape. *Journal of Sex Research, 19,* 74–93.

Ellis, L., Burke, D., & Ames, M.A. (1987). Sexual orientation as a continuous variable: A comparison between the sexes. *Archives of Sexual Behavior, 16,* 523–529.

Ellwood, D.T., & Bane, M.J. (1985). The impact of AFDC on family structure and living arrangements. *Research in Labor Economics, 7,* 137.

Elwin, V. (1968). *The kingdom of the young.* London: Oxford University Press.

Elmer-Dewitt, P. (1990). A revolution in making babies. *Time, 136*(20), 76–77.

Emery, R.D., & Wyer, M.M. (1987). Divorce mediation. *American Psychologist, 42,* 472–480.

Emlen, S.T., & Oring, L.W. (1977). Ecology, sexual selection, and the evolution of mating systems. *Science, 197,* 215–223.

Epstein, A.W. (1975). The fetish object: Phylogenetic considerations. *Archives of Sexual Behavior, 4,* 303–308.

Epstein, C.C. (1985). Teaching kids to be safe. *Parents, 60*(9), 180, 182, 184, 186.

Epstein, N. (1981a). How partners "collaborate" to avoid sex. *Medical Aspects of Human Sexuality, 15*(7), 68I, 68M.

Epstein, N. (1981b, November). *Cognitive-behavioral therapy in the treatment of sexual disorders.* Paper presented at the meeting of the Society for the Scientific Study of Sex, New York.

Epstein, N. (1982). Sexual problems as symptoms of marital or family dysfunction. *Medical Aspects of Human Sexuality, 16*(9), 24E, 24H, 24I.

Ericsson, C.D. (1983). Consequences of bites. *Medical Aspects of Human Sexuality, 17*(3), 15–16.

Ernulf, K.E., & Innala, S.M. (1987). The relationship between affective and cognitive components of homophobic reaction. *Archives of Sexual Behavior, 16,* 501–509.

Erwin, J., & Maple, T. (1976). Arobisexual behavior with male--male anal penetration on male rhesus monkeys. *Archives of Sexual Behavior, 5,* 9–14.

Evans, R.B. (1969). Childhood parental relationships of homosexual men. *Journal of Consulting and Clinical Psychology, 33,* 129–135.

Evans, R.G. (1984). Hostility and sex guilt: Perceptions of self and others as a function of gender and sex-role orientation. *Sex Roles, 10,* 207–215.

Everaerd, W., Dekker, J., Dronkers, J., Van der Rhee, K., Staffeleu, J., & Wiselius, G. (1982). Treatment of homosexual and heterosexual sexual dysfunction in male-only groups of mixed sexual orientation. *Archives of Sexual Behavior, 11,* 1–10.

Exner, J.E. (1978). Prostitutes' enjoyment of sex acts. *Medical Aspects of Human Sexuality, 12*(12), 105.

Ex-unwed couples found more likely to divorce. (1987, December 7). *New York Times,* A 25.

Faber, M.M. & Rosenblum, S.E. (1978). Sexual asphyxia. *Medical Aspects of Human Sexuality, 12*(4), 146–147.

Fabian, W.D., Jr., & Fishkin, S.M. (1981). A replicated study of self-reported changes in psychological absorption with marijuana intoxication. *Journal of Abnormal Psychology, 90,* 546–553.

Failure rate for sponge higher than for diaphragm; parous sponge users are most likely to conceive. (1985). *Family Planning Perspectives, 17,* 80–81.

Falbo, T., & Shepperd, J.A. (1986). Self-righteousness: Cognitive, power, and religious characteristics. *Journal of Research in Personality, 20,* 145–157.

Falik, L.A. (1984). Sexual crisis after mastectomy. *Medical Aspects of Human Sexuality, 18*(6), 97, 101.

Fallon, B. (1979). The mind boggles over john hour "hysterics." *Daily News,* 12c.

Farber, B. (1964). *Family: Organization and interaction.* San Francisco: Chandler.

Farrell, W. (1986). *Why men are the way they are: The male–female dynamic.* New York: McGraw-Hill.

Fausto-Sterling, A. (1985). *Myths of gender.* New York: Basic Books.

Fedders, C. (1987). *Shattered dreams.* New York: Harper & Row.

Feder, H.H. (1984). Hormones and sexual behavior. *Annual Review of Psychology, 35,* 165–200.

Fedora, O., Reddon, J.R., & Yeudall, L.T. (1986). Stimuli eliciting sexual arousal in genital exhibitionists: A possible clinical application. *Archives of Sexual Behavior, 15,* 417–427.

Feigen, G. (1981). Resistance to rectal examination. *Medical Aspects of Human Sexuality, 15*(6), 93.

Feild, H.S. (1978). Attitudes toward rape: A comparative analysis of police, rapists, crisis counselors, and citizens. *Journal of Personality and Social Psychology, 36,* 156–179.

Feinberg, R.A., Miller, F.G., & Ross, G.A. (1981). Perceived and actual locus of control similarity among friends. *Personality and Social Psychology Bulletin, 7,* 85–89.

Feinman, S. (1981). Why is cross-sex-role behavior more approved for girls than for boys? A status characteristic approach. *Sex Roles, 7,* 289–300.

Feinsilber, M., & Mead, W.B. (1980). *American averages: Amazing facts of everyday life.* New York: Doubleday.

Feldman, S.S., & Nash, S.C. (1984). The transition from expectancy to parenthood: Impact of the firstborn child on men and women. *Sex Roles, 11,* 61–78.

Feldman-Summers, S. (1985). Sexual behavior following divorce. *Medical Aspects of Human Sexuality, 19*(1), 216.

Feldman-Summers, S., Gordon, D., & Meagher, D. (1979). The impact of rape on sexual satisfaction. *Journal of Abnormal Psychology, 88*, 101–105.

Feldstein, M. (1983). *Inflation, tax rules, and capital formation.* Chicago: University of Chicago Press.

Feingold, A. (1988). Matching for attractiveness in romantic partners and same-sex friends: A meta-atalysis and theoretical critique. *Psychological Bulletin, 104*, 226–235.

Feingold, A. (1989). *Gender differences in effects of attractiveness and similarity on opposite-sex attraction: Integration of self-report and experimental findings.* Unpublished manuscript, Yale University, New Haven, CT.

Felman, Y. (1981). Hepatitis from oral-anal sex. *Medical Aspects of Human Sexuality, 15*(1), 30.

Felman, Y. (1984). When both partners have herpes. *Medical Aspects of Human Sexuality, 18*(3), 86.

Felman, Y.M. (1982a). Risk of acquiring gonorrhea in single coital contact. *Medical Aspects of Human Sexuality. 16*(11), 34.

Felman, Y.M. (1982b). Effects of contraceptives in reducing the risk of STD. *Medical Aspects of Human Sexuality, 16*(5), 102, 103.

Felman, Y.M., & William, D.C. (1979). Homosexuals' preference for term "gay." *Medical Aspects of Human Sexuality, 13*(8), 100.

Fennema, E. (1980). Sex-related differences in mathematics achievement: Where and why. In L.H. Fox, L. Brady, & D. Tobin (Eds.), *Women and the mathematical mystique.* Baltimore, Md.: Johns Hopkins University Press.

Ferrari, J.R. (1990). Choosing to suffer after failure: Effects of frequent failure on self-administered shock. *Journal of Social Behavior and Personality, 5*, 163–174.

Fertel, N.S. (1983a). Coital positions during pregnancy. *Medical Aspects of Human Sexuality, 17*(2), 170.

Fertel, N.S. (1983b). Detection of diaphragm during coitus. *Medical Aspects of Human Sexuality, 17*(4), 276.

Festinger, L., Schachter, S., & Back, K. (1950). *Social pressures in informal groups: A study of a housing community.* New York: Harper.

Fichten, C.S. (1984). See it from my point of view: Videotape and attributions in happy and distressed couples. *Journal of Social and Clinical Psychology, 2*, 125–142.

Fiedler, D.E. (1978). Menarche and the onset of sexual activity. *Medical Aspects of Human Sexuality, 12*(5), 149.

Field, H.S. (1978). Attitudes toward rape: A comparative analysis of police, rapists, crisis counselors, and citizens. *Journal of Personality and Social Psychology, 36*, 156–179.

Fincham, F.D., Beach, S.R., & Baucom, D.H. (1987). Attribution processes in distressed and nondistressed couples: 4. Self-partner attribution differences. *Journal of Personality and Social Psychology, 52*, 739–748.

Fincham, F.D., & Bradbury, T.N. (1989). The impact of attributions in marriage: An individual difference analysis. *Journal of Social and Personal Relationships, 6*, 69–85.

Finck, F.M. (1982). Male PAP test. *Medical Aspects of Human Sexuality, 16*(3), 105.

Finkelhor, D. (1979). *Sexually victimized children.* New York: Free Press.

Finkelhor, D. (1980). Sex among siblings: A survey on prevalence, variety, and effects. *Archives of Sexual Behavior, 9*, 171–197.

Finkelhor, D. (1984a). The prevention of child sexual abuse: An overview of needs and problems. *SIECUS Report, 13*(1), 1–5.

Finkelhor, D. (1984b). *Child sexual abuse: Theory and research.* New York: Free Press.

Finkelhor, D., & Araji, S. (1986). Explanations of pedophilia: A four-factor model. *Journal of Sex Research, 22*, 145–161.

Finn, J. (1986). The relationship between sex role attitudes and attitudes supporting marital violence. *Sex Roles, 14*, 235–244.

Finney, J.C. (1983). Definition of premature ejaculation. *Medical Aspects of Human Sexuality, 17*(1), 175.

Firth, M. (1982). Sex discrimination in job opportunities for women. *Sex Roles, 8*, 891–901.

Fischer, E.H. (1979). Student nurses view an abortion client: Attitude and context effects. *Journal of Population, 2*, 33–46.

Fischman, J. (1986). Women and divorce: Ten years after. *Psychology Today, 18*(1), 15.

Fisher, A. (1984). Allergic reactions to condom. *Medical Aspects of Human Sexuality, 18*(9), 200.

Fisher, C., Cohen, H.D., Schiavi, R.C., Davis, D., Furman, B., Ward, K., Edwards, A., & Cunningham, J. (1983). Patterns of female sexual arousal during sleep and waking: Vaginal thermo-conductance studies. *Archives of Sexual Behavior, 12*, 97–122.

Fisher, C., Gross, J., & Zuch, J. (1965). Cycle of penile erection synchronous with dreaming (REM) sleep. *Archives of General Psychiatry, 12*, 27–45.

Fisher, J.D., Rytting, M., & Heslin, R. (1976). Hands touching hands: Affective and evaluative aspects of an interpersonal touch. *Sociometry, 39*, 416–421.

Fisher, T. (1986). Parent-child communication about sex and young adolescents' sexual knowledge and attitudes. *Adolescence, 21*, 517–527.

Fisher, T. (1987). Family communication and the sexual behavior and attitudes of college students. *Journal of Youth and Adolescence, 16*, 481–495.

Fisher, T. (1988). The relationship between parent-child communication about sexuality and college students' sexual behavior and attitudes as a function of parental proximity. *Journal of Sex Research, 25*, 305–311.

Fisher, T., Pollack, R.H., & Malatesta, V.J. (1986). Orgasmic latency and subjective ratings of erotic stimuli in male and female subjects. *Journal of Sex Research, 22*, 85–93.

Fisher, W.A. (1984). Predicting contraceptive behavior among university men: The roles of emotions and behavioral intentions. *Journal of Applied Social Psychology, 14*, 104–123.

Fisher, W.A. (1990). Understanding and preventing adolescent pregnancy and sexually transmissible disease. In J. Edwards et al. (Eds.), *Social influence processes and prevention* (pp. 71–101). New York: Plenum.

Fisher, W.A., & Barak, A. (1989). Sex education as a corrective: Immunizing against possible effects of pornography. In D. Zillmann & J. Bryant (Eds.), *Pornography: Research advances and policy considerations* (pp. 298–320). Hillsdale, N.J.: Lawrence Erlbaum.

Fisher, W.A., & Byrne, D. (1978). Sex differences in response to erotica: Love versus lust. *Journal of Personality and Social Psychology, 36,* 117–125.

Fisher, W.A., Byrne, D., Edmunds, M., Miller, C.T., Kelley, K., & White, L.A. (1979). Psychological and situation-specific correlates of contraceptive behavior among university women. *Journal of Sex Research, 15,* 38–55.

Fisher, W.A., Byrne, D., & White, L.A. (1983). Emotional barriers to contraception. In D. Byrne & W.A. Fisher (Eds.), *Adolescents, sex, and contraception* (pp. 207–239). Hillsdale, N.J.: Lawrence Erlbaum.

Fisher, W.A., Byrne, D., White, L.A., & Kelley, K. (1988). Erotophobia-erotophilia as a dimension of personality. *Journal of Sex Research, 25,* 123–151.

Fisher, W.A., Fisher, J.D., & Byrne, D. (1977). Consumer reactions to contraceptive purchasing. *Personality and Social Psychology Bulletin, 3,* 293–296.

Fisher, W.A., & Gray, J. (1988). Erotophobia-erotophilia and sexual behavior during pregnancy and postpartum. *Journal of Sex Research, 25,* 379–396.

Fisher, W.A., Grenier, G., Watters, W.W., Lamont, J., Cohen, M., & Askwith, J. (1988). Students' sexual knowledge, attitudes toward sex, and willingness to treat sexual concerns. *Journal of Medical Education, 63,* 379–385.

Fisher, W.A., Miller, C.T., Byrne D., & White, L.A. (1980). Talking dirty: Responses to communicating a sexual message as a function of situational and personality factors. *Basic and Applied Social Psychology, 1,* 115–126.

Fitting, M.D., Salisbury, S., Davies, N.H., & Mayclin, D.K. (1978). Self-concept and sexuality of spinal cord injured women. *Archives of Sexual Behavior, 7,* 143–156.

Fiumara, N.J. (1980). Postcoital washing and urination for VD prophylaxis. *Medical Aspects of Human Sexuality, 14*(5), 109.

Fiumara, N.J. (1981). Infectivity of "moist" vs. "dry" kiss. *Medical Aspects of Human Sexuality, 15*(9), 47.

Fleming, A.T. (1989, March 15). When a loving nest remains empty. *New York Times,* C 8.

Fleming, M., Macgowan, B., & Costos, D. (1985). The dyadic adjustment of female-to-male transsexuals. *Archives of Sexual Behavior, 14,* 47–55.

Fleming, W.L. (1981). Onset of manifestations of gonorrhea vs. syphilis. *Medical Aspects of Human Sexuality, 15*(8), 92.

Fletcher, G.J.O., Fitness, J., & Blampied, N.M. (1990). The link between attributions and happiness in close relationships: The roles of depression and explanatory style. *Journal of Social and Clinical Psychology, 9,* 243–255.

Fletcher, J. (1966). *Situation ethics: The new morality.* Philadelphia: Westminster Press.

Fleury, F.J. (1978). Characteristic vaginal odor. *Medical Aspects of Human Sexuality, 12*(5), 31, 75.

Flowers, J.S., & Flowers, C.E. (1978). Anorgasmia after childbirth. *Medical Aspects of Human Sexuality, 12*(4), 154.

Floyd, F.J., & Markman, H.J. (1984). An economical observational measure of couples' communication skill. *Journal of Consulting and Clinical Psychology, 52,* 97–103.

Folkes, V.S. (1982). Forming relationships and the matching hypothesis. *Personality and Social Psychology Bulletin, 8,* 631–636.

Follingstad, D.R., & Kimbrell, C.D. (1986). Sex fantasies revisited: An expansion and further classification of variables affecting sex fantasy production. *Archives of Sexual Behavior, 15,* 475–486.

Fontana, V.J. (1985). Finding the hidden signs of child sexual abuse. *Medical Aspects of Human Sexuality, 19*(1), 156–158.

Ford, A.B., & Levine, S.B. (1982). Sexual behavior of chronically ill patients. *Medical Aspects of Human Sexuality, 16*(2), 138, 142, 143, 148–150.

Ford, C., & Beach, F. (1951). *Patterns of sexual behavior.* New York: Harper & Row.

Fordney-Settlage, D.S. (1979). Pelvic examination of women: Genitorectal examination of men. In R. Green (Ed.), *Human sexuality: A health practitioner's text* (2nd ed.) (pp. 33–45). Baltimore, Md.: Williams & Wilkins.

Foreit, K.G., & Foreit, J.R. (1978). Correlates of contraceptive behavior among unmarried U.S. college students. *Studies in Family Planning, 9,* 169–174.

Forrest, J.D. (1987). Unintended pregnancy among American women. *Family Planning Perspectives, 19,* 76.

Forsyth, D., & Clark, R.D. (1975). The effects of frustration and social desirability on heterosexual attraction. *Representative Research in Social Psychology, 6,* 114–118.

Forsyth, D.R., & Nye, J.L. (1990). Personal moral philosophies and moral choice. *Journal of Research in Personality, 24,* 398–414.

Foss-Goodman, D. (1984). *Summary of Masters and Johnson's relevant findings and predictions for the sexual interaction inventory.* Unpublished manuscript, University at Albany, State University of New York.

Foster, D., Klinger-Vartabedian, L., & Wispe, L. (1984). Male longevity and age differences between spouses. *Journal of Gerontology, 39*(1), 117–120.

Fox, C.A., & Knaggs, G.S. (1969). Milk ejection activity (oxytocin) in peripheral venous blood in man during lactation and in association with coitus. *Journal of Endocrinology and Metabolism, 45,* 145–146.

Fox, G.L., & Inazu, J. (1980). Mother–daughter communication about sex. In E. Roberts (Ed.), *Family life and sexual learning* (p. 347). Cambridge, Mass.: Population Education.

Fox, J.L. (1983). In vitro fertilization goes commercial. *Science, 221,* 1160–1162.

Fracher, J.C. (1981). Simultaneous vs. sequential orgasms. *Medical Aspects of Human Sexuality, 15*(11), 113.

Frank, E., Anderson, C., & Rubinstein, D. (1978). Frequency of sexual dysfunction in "normal" couples. *New England Journal of Medicine, 299,* 111.

Frank, E., Anderson, C., & Rubinstein, D. (1979). Marital role strain and sexual satisfaction. *Journal of Consulting and Clinical Psychology, 47,* 1096–1103.

Frank, S. (1983, October 16). "We" conquering "me" era, as sexual revolution fades. *Albany Times Union,* C-1, C-3.

Frankel, C.J. (1978). Legality of coitus with mentally retarded. *Medical Aspects of Human Sexuality, 12*(5), 139.

Franzoi, S.L., & Herzog, M.E. (1987). Judging physical attractiveness: What body aspects do we use? *Personality and Social Psychology Bulletin, 13,* 19–33.

Frauman, D.C. (1982). The relationship between physical exercise, sexual activity, and desire for sexual activity. *Journal of Sex Research, 18,* 41–46.

Frazier, P., & Borgida, E. (1985). Rape trauma syndrome evidence in court. *American Psychologist, 40,* 984–993.

Freed, R.S., & Freed, S.A. (1989). Beliefs and practices resulting in female deaths and fewer females than males in India. *Population and Environment, 10,* 144–161.

Freedman, J. (1978). *Happy people.* New York: Harcourt Brace Jovanovich.

Freeman, M. (1983). Stimulating effect of pelvic examination. *Medical Aspects of Human Sexuality, 17*(12), 13.

Freese, M.P., & Levitt, E.E. (1984). Relationships among intravaginal pressure, orgasmic function, parity factors, and urinary leakage. *Archives of Sexual Behavior, 13,* 261–268.

Freud, S. (1949). *An outline of psychoanalysis.* New York: W.W. Norton.

Freud, S. (1955). From the history of an infantile neurosis. In *Standard edition of the complete psychological works of Sigmund Freud* (Vol. 17). London: Hogarth Press. (Originally published in 1918).

Freud, S. (1962). *Three contributions to the theory of sex.* New York: Dutton. (Original work published in 1905).

Freund, K., Langevin, R., Wescom, T., & Zajac, Y. (1975). Heterosexual interest in homosexual males. *Archives of Sexual Behavior, 4,* 509–518.

Freund, K., Scher, H., & Hucker, S. (1983). The courtship disorders. *Archives of Sexual Behavior, 12,* 369–379.

Freund, K., Scher, H., & Hucker, S. (1984). The courtship disorders: A further investigation. *Archives of Sexual Behavior, 13,* 133–139.

Freund, K., & Watson, R. (1990). Mapping the boundaries of courtship disorder. *Journal of Sex Research, 27,* 589–606.

Freund, K., Watson, R., & Dickey, R. (1990). Does sexual abuse in childhood cause pedophilia: An exploratory study. *Archives of Sexual Behavior, 19,* 557–568.

Freund, K., Watson, R., & Rienzo, D. (1989). Heterosexuality, homosexuality, and erotic age preference. *Journal of Sex Research, 26,* 107–117.

Freund, K.A. (1963). A laboratory method diagnosing predominance of homo- or hetero-erotic interest in the male. *Behavior Research and Therapy, 1,* 85–93.

Freund, K.A., Sedlacek, F., & Knob, K. (1965). A simple transducer for mechanical plethysmography of the male genital. *Journal of the Experimental Analysis of Behavior, 8,* 169–170.

Freund, M., Leonard, T.L., & Lee, N. (1989). Sexual behavior of resident street prostitutes with their clients in Camden, New Jersey. *Journal of Sex Research, 26,* 460–478.

Fried, P. (1982). Effect on neonate of mother's use of marijuana. *Medical Aspects of Human Sexuality, 16*(1), 13, 17.

Friedman, M. (1978). Men who fake orgasms. *Medical Aspects of Human Sexuality, 12*(6), 33.

Friedman, N. (1983, April). Condoms: They're new and improved. *Playgirl, 11*(11), 9.

Friedman, S., & Harrison, G. (1984). Sexual histories, attitudes, and behavior of schizophrenic and "normal" women. *Archives of Sexual Behavior, 13,* 555–567.

Fuchs, A., Fuchs, F., Husslein, P., Soloff, M.S., & Fernstrom, M.J. (1982). Oxytocin receptors and human parturition: A dual role for oxytocin in the initiation of labor. *Science, 215,* 1396–1398.

Furstenberg, F.F., Jr. (1976). Premarital pregnancy and marital instability. *Journal of Social Issues, 32*(1), 67–86.

Furstenberg, F.F., Jr., Herceg-Baron, R., Shea, J., & Webb, D. (1984). Family communication and teenagers' contraceptive use. *Family Planning Perspectives, 16,* 163–170.

Furstenberg, F.F., Jr., & Spanier, G.B. (1984). *Recycling the family: Remarriage after divorce.* Beverly Hills, CA: Sage.

Fuss, D. (Ed.). (1991). *Inside/out: Lesbian theories, gay theories.* New York: Routledge.

Futterweit, W. (1984). Is there a male climacteric? *Medical Aspects of Human Sexuality, 18*(4), 147, 148, 153, 157, 160.

Fyfe, B. (1983). "Homophobia" or homosexual bias reconsidered. *Archives of Sexual Behavior, 12,* 549–554.

Gagnon, J.H. (1975). Sex research and social change. *Archives of Sexual Behavior, 4,* 111–141.

Gagnon, J.H. (1985). Attitudes and responses of parents to preadolescent masturbation. *Archives of Sexual Behavior, 14,* 451–466.

Gagnon, J.H. (1990). The explicit and implicit use of the scripting perspective in sex research. In J. Bancroft, C. M. Davis, & D. Weinstein (Eds.), *Annual review of sex research,* Vol. 1 (pp. 1–43). Mt. Vernon, IA: Foundation for the Scientific Study of Sexuality.

Gagnon, J., & Simon, W. (1987). The sexual scripting of oral genital contacts. *Archives of Sexual Behavior, 16,* 1–25.

Gall, S.A. (1983). Effect of breast-feeding on breasts. *Medical Aspects of Human Sexuality, 17*(1), 173–174.

Galle, P.S., Freeman, M.G., Mitchell, D.E., & Reindollar, R.H. (1984). Endocrinologic aspects of female sexuality: Hirsuitism androgen excess. *Medical Aspects of Human Sexuality, 18*(3), 60, 62–65.

Gallup, A. (1984). The Gallup poll of teachers' attitudes toward the public schools—I. *Phi Delta Kappan, 66,* 97.

Gallup, A. (1985a). The 17th annual Gallup poll of the public's attitudes toward the public schools. *Phi Delta Kappan, 67,* 35.

Gallup, A. (1985b). The Gallup poll of teachers' attitudes toward the public schools—II. *Phi Delta Kappan, 67,* 323.

Gallup, A. (1985c). Premarital sex. *The Gallup Report*, No. 237, 28.

Gallup, G.G., Jr. (1982). Permanent breast enlargement in human females: A sociobiological analysis. *Journal of Human Evolution*, 11, 597–601.

Gallup, G.G., Jr. (1986). Unique features of human sexuality in the context of evolution. In D. Byrne & K. Kelley (Eds.), *Alternative approaches to the study of sexual behavior* (pp. 13–42). Hillsdale, N.J.: Lawrence Erlbaum.

Gallup, G.G., Jr. & Suarez, S.D. (1983). Unpublished survey. University at Albany, State University of New York.

Galton, L. (1972). VD: Out of control? *Sexual Behavior*, 2(1), 17–24.

Gamson, J. (1990). Rubber wars: Struggles over the condom in the United States. *Journal of the History of Sexuality*, 1, 262–282.

Gangestad, S., & Snyder, M. (1985). On the nature of self-monitoring: An examination of latent causal structure. In P. Shaver (Ed.), *Review of personality and social psychology* (Vol. 6, pp. 65–85). Beverly Hills: Sage.

Ganong, L., Coleman, M., & Kennedy, G. (1990). The effects of using alternate labels in denoting stepparent or stepfamily status. *Journal of Social Behavior and Personality*, 5, 453–463.

Garcia, L.T. (1982). Sex role orientation and stereotypes about male–female sexuality. *Sex Roles*, 8, 863–876.

Garcia, L.T. (1983). Sexual stereotypes and attributions about sexual arousal. *Journal of Sex Research*, 19, 366–375.

Garcia, L.T. (1984). Sexual evaluation of women with feminist attitudes. *Journal of Sex Research*, 20, 91–96.

Garcia, L.T. (1986). *Exposure to pornography and attitudes about women and rape: A correlational study*. Manuscript submitted for publication, Rutgers University.

Garcia, L.T., Brennan, K., DeCarlo, M., McGlennon, R., & Tait, S. (1984). Sex differences in sexual arousal to different erotic stories. *Journal of Sex Research*, 20, 391–402.

Garcia, L.T., & Derfel, B. (1983). Perception of sexual experience: The impact of nonverbal behavior. *Sex Roles*, 9, 871–878.

Garcia, L.T., Kowal, E., DeCosmo, K., & Bacha, A. (1983). *Informational requests for male and female targets: The importance of sexual information*. Manuscript submitted for publication, Rutgers University.

Garfinkle, E.M. & Morin, S.F. (1978). Psychologists' attitudes toward homosexual psychotherapy clients. *Journal of Social Issues*, 34(3), 101–112.

Garn, S.M. (1981). Smoking for two. *Parents*, 56(10), 8.

Garner, B., & Smith, R.W. (1977). Are there really any gay male athletes? An empirical survey. *Journal of Sex Research*, 13, 22–34.

Gartrell, N., & Mosbacher, D. (1984). Sex differences in the naming of children's genitalia. *Sex Roles*, 10, 869–876.

Garvey, M.J. (1985). Decreased libido in depression. *Medical Aspects of Human Sexuality*, 19(12), 30–32, 34.

Gay, P. (Ed.). (1989). *The Freud reader*. New York: W.W. Norton.

Gaylin, J. (1977). Choosing a life without children. *Psychology Today*, 11(6), 97.

Gaylin, J. (1985). Childbirth news. *New York*, 18(2), 62, 64, 65.

Gebhard, P.H. (1966). Factors in marital orgasm. *Journal of Social Issues*, 27, 88–95.

Gebhard, P.H. (1969). Fetishism and sadomasochism. *Science and Psychoanalysis*, 15, 71–80. (a)

Gebhard, P.H. (1969). Fetishism and sadomasochism. In J.H. Masserman (Ed.), *Dynamics of deviant sexuality* (pp. 71–80). New York: Grune & Stratton. (b)

Gebhard, P.H. (1971). Human sexual behaviors: A summary statement. In D.S. Marshall & R.C. Suggs (Eds.), *Human sexual behavior: Variations in the ethnographic spectrum* (pp. 206–217). New York: Basic Books.

Gebhard, P.H. (1976). The institute. In M.S. Weinberg (Ed.), *Sex research: Studies from the Kinsey Institute*. New York: Oxford Press.

Gebhard, P.H. (1977). The acquisition of basic sex information. *Journal of Sex Research*, 13, 148–169.

Gebhard, P.H. (1985). Sexuality in cross-cultural perspective. In W.H. Masters, V.E. Johnson, & R.C. Kolodny, *Human Sexuality* (pp. 620–637). Boston: Little, Brown.

Gebhard, P.H., Gagnon, J.H., Pomeroy, W.B., & Christenson, C.V. (1965). *Sex offenders*. New York: Harper & Row.

Gebhard, P.H., & Johnson, A.B. (1979). *The Kinsey data*. Philadelphia: Saunders.

Geer, J.H. (1975). Direct measurement of genital responding. *American Psychologist*, 30, 415–418.

Geer, J.H., & Fuhr, R. (1976). Cognitive factors in sexual arousal: The role of distraction. *Journal of Consulting and Clinical Psychology*, 44, 238–243.

Geer, J., Heiman, J., & Leitenberg, H. (1984). *Human sexuality*. Englewood Cliffs, N.J.: Prentice-Hall.

Geer, J.H., & Messe, M. (1982). Sexual dysfunctions. In R.J. Gatchel, A. Baum, & J.E. Singer (Eds.), *Handbook of psychology and health* (Vol. 1, pp. 329–370). Hillsdale, N.J.: Lawrence Erlbaum.

Geer, J.H., & O'Donohue, W. (Eds.). (1987) *Theories of human sexuality*. New York: Plenum.

Geist, C.S. (1980). Lesbians' desire for motherhood. *Medical Aspects of Human Sexuality*, 14(8), 107.

Gelman, R., & McGinley, H. (1978). Interpersonal liking and self-disclosure. *Journal of Consulting and Clinical Psychology*, 46, 1549–1551.

George, L.K. & Weiler, S.J. (1981). Sexuality in middle and late life. *Archives of General Psychiatry*, 38, 919–923.

Gerber, A.B. (1982, February). *The book of sex lists*. Quoted in *Playboy*, 47.

Gerdes, E.P., & Garber, D.M. (1983). Sex bias in hiring: Effects of job demands and applicant competence. *Sex Roles*, 9, 301–319.

Gerner, R.H. (1981). Hypersexuality of manics. *Medical Aspects of Human Sexuality*, 15(3), 99.

Gerrard, M. (1980). Sex guilt and attitudes toward sex in sexually active and inactive female college students. *Journal of Personality Assessment*, 44, 258–261.

Gerrard, M. (1982). Sex, sex guilt, and contraceptive use. *Journal of Personality and Social Psychology*, 42, 153–158.

Gerrard, M. (1987). Are men and women really different? Sex differences in emotional and cognitive factors associated with contraceptive behavior. In K. Kelley (Ed.), *Females, males, and sexuality: Theories and research* (pp. 213–242). Albany, N.Y.: State University of New York Press.

Gerrard, M., & Gibbons, F.X. (1982). Sexual experience, sex guilt, and sexual moral reasoning. *Journal of Personality, 50,* 345–359.

Gerson, M. (1984). Feminism and the wish for a child. *Sex Roles, 11,* 389–399.

Gibbons, F.X, & Wright, R.A. (1981). Motivational biases in causal attributions of arousal. *Journal of Personality and Social Psychology, 40,* 588–600.

Gibson-Ainyette, I., Templer, D.I., Brown, R., Veaco, L. (1988). Adolescent female prostitutes. *Archives of Sexual Behavior, 17,* 431–438.

Gil, V.E. (1985, September). *In thy father's house: Incest in conservative Christian homes.* Paper presented at the meeting of the Society for the Scientific Study of Sex, San Diego.

Gil, V.E. (1990). Sexual fantasy experiences and guilt among conservative Christians: An exploratory study. *Journal of Sex Research, 27,* 629–638.

Gilbert, A.N. (1981). Conceptions of homosexuality and sodomy in Western history. *Journal of Homosexuality, 6*(1/2), 57–68.

Gilliam, A., & Seltzer, R. (1989). The efficacy of educational movies on AIDS knowledge and attitudes among college students. *Journal of American College Health, 37,* 261–265.

Gilligan, C. (1982). *In a different voice.* Cambridge, Mass.: Harvard University Press.

Gilligan, C., Kohlberg, L., Lerner, J., & Belenky, M. (1970). Moral reasoning about sexual dilemmas. In *Technical report of the Commission on Obscenity and Pornography* (Vol. 1, pp. 141–174). Washington, D.C.: U.S. Government Printing Office.

Gillin, F.D., Reiner, D.S., & Wang, C. (1983). Human milk kills parasitic intestinal protozoa. *Science, 221,* 1290–1292.

Gillis, J.S., & Avis, W.E. (1980). The male-taller norm in mate selection. *Personality and Social Psychology Bulletin, 6,* 396–401.

Gillis, P. (1980, August). Sexual harassment—no longer a dirty joke. *Parents,* 24.

Gilmartin, G.B. (1977). Swinging: Who gets involved and how? In W. Libby & R.N. Whitehurst (Eds.), *Marriage and alternatives* (pp. 80–111). Glenview, Ill.: Scott, Foresman.

Gilmore, D.H. (1968). *Soixante neuf 69: A study of an old yet hushed-up sex practive.* Torrance, Calif.: Monogram.

Gintzler, A.R. (1980). Endorphin-mediated increases in pain threshold during pregnancy. *Science, 210,* 193–195.

Girardi, J.A., Keese, R.M., Traver, L.B., & Cooksey, D.R. (1988). Psychotherapist responsibility in notifying individuals at risk for exposure to HIV. *Journal of Sex Research, 25,* 1–27.

Glaser, R.D., & Thorpe, J.S. (1986). Unethical intimacy: A survey of sexual contact and advances between psychology educators and female graduate students. *American Psychologist, 41,* 43–51.

Glasner, S. (1961). Judaism and sex. In A. Ellis & A. Abarbanel (Eds.), *The encyclopedia of sexual behavior* (Vol. 2). New York: Hawthorn Books.

Glass, S.P., & Wright, T.L. (1985). Sex differences in type of extramarital involvement and marital dissatisfaction. *Sex Roles, 12,* 1101–1120.

Glenn, J.F. (1980). Libido after vasectomy. *Medical Aspects of Human Sexuality, 14*(10), 67, 70.

Glenn, N. (1979). Most people condemn extramarital sex. *Medical Aspects of Human Sexuality, 13*(7), 93.

Glenn, N.D., & Weaver, C.N. (1979). Attitudes toward premarital, extramarital, and homosexual relations in the United States in the 1970s. *Journal of Sex Research, 15,* 108–118.

Glick, P.C. (1980). Years of marriage most prone to divorce. *Medical Aspects of Human Sexuality, 14*(7), 11.

Glick, P.C. (1983). Seventh-year itch. *Medical Aspects of Human Sexuality, 17*(5), 103.

Goben, R. (1990). Hope for fertility problems. *Stanford Observer, 25*(1), 17.

Gochros, J.S. (1985). Wives' reactions to learning that their husbands are bisexual. *Journal of Homosexuality, 11*(1/2), 101–113.

Goethals, G.R. (1986). Social comparison theory: Psychology from the lost and found. *Personality and Social Psychology Bulletin, 12,* 261–278.

Goh, H.H., & Ratnam, S.S. (1990). Effect of estrogens on prolactin secretion in transsexual subjects. *Archives of Sexual Behavior, 19,* 507–516.

Gold, J.A., Ryckman, R.M., & Mosley, N.R. (1984). Romantic mood induction and attraction to a dissimilar other: Is love blind? *Personality and Social Psychology Bulletin, 10,* 358–368.

Goldberg, A.S., & Shiflett, S. (1981). Goals of male and female college students: Do traditional sex differences still exist? *Sex Roles, 7,* 1213–1222.

Goldberg, D.C., Whipple, B., Fishkin, R.E., Waxman, H., Fink, P., & Weisberg, M. (1983). The Grafenberg spot and female ejaculation: A review of initial hypotheses. *Journal of Sex and Marital Therapy, 9,* 27–37.

Goldberg, M. (1981). Effects of children on marital satisfaction. *Medical Aspects of Human Sexuality, 15*(1), 50–51, 57, 58, 63, 64, 66, 71.

Golden, J. (1988). A second look at a case of inhibited sexual desire. *Journal of Sex Research, 25,* 304–306.

Goldfarb, L., Gerrard, M., Gibbons, F.X., & Plante, T. (1988). Attitudes toward sex, arousal, and the retention of contraceptive information. *Journal of Personality and Social Psychology, 55,* 634–641.

Goldman, R., & Goldman, J. (1982). *Children's sexual thinking: A comparative study of children aged 5 to 15 years in Australia, North America, Britain, and Sweden.* London: Routledge & Kegan Paul.

Goldman, R., & Goldman, J. (1983). Children's perceptions of sex differences in babies and adolescents: A cross-national study. *Archives of Sexual Behavior, 12,* 277–294.

Goldsmith, J. (1981). Sadistic partners. *Medical Aspects of Human Sexuality, 15*(3), 93–94.

Goldsmith, J. (1982). When functional young couples choose abstinence. *Medical Aspects of Human Sexuality, 16*(4), 45.

Goldstein, B. (1976). *Human sexuality*. New York: McGraw-Hill.

Goldstein, M.J., Kant, H.S., & Hartman, J.J. (1974). *Pornography and sexual deviance*. Berkeley, Calif.: University of Chicago.

Goleman, D. (1988, February 2). The experience of touch: Research points to a critical role. *New York Times*, C 1, C 4.

Goleman, D. (1990a, November 6). Doubts rise on children as witnesses. *New York Times*, C 1, C 6.

Goleman, D. (1990b, December 20). New guidelines issued on patient-therapist sex. *New York Times*, B 21.

Golub, S., & Harrington, D.M. (1981). Premenstrual and menstrual mood changes in adolescent women. *Journal of Personality and Social Psychology*, *41*, 961–965.

Gonsiorek, J.C. (Ed.). (1982). Homosexuality and psychotherapy. *Journal of Homosexuality*, 7(2/3), 1–21.

Goodall, J. (1971). *In the shadow of man*. New York: Dell.

Goodchilds, J.D., & Zellman, G.L. (1984). Sexual signaling and sexual aggression in adolescent relationships. In N.M. Malamuth & E. Donnerstein (Eds.), *Pornography and sexual aggression* (pp. 233–243). New York: Academic Press.

Goode, E. (1981). Remarriage rates. *Medical Aspects of Human Sexuality*, 15(12), 81, 84.

Goode, E., & Haber, L. (1977). Sexual correlates of homosexual experience: An exploratory study of college women. *Journal of Sex Research*, *13*, 12–21.

Gooren, L., Fliers, E., & Courtney, K. (1990). Biological determinants of sexual orientation. In J. Bancroft, C.M. Davis, & D. Weinstein (Eds.), *Annual review of sex research* (pp. 175–196). Mt Vernon, IA: Foundation for the Scientific Study of Sexuality.

Gordon, H.L. (1981). Problems with "withdrawal" technique. *Medical Aspects of Human Sexuality*, 15(9), 47.

Gordon, M. (1988). College coaches' attitudes toward pregame sex. *Journal of Sex Research*, *24*, 256–262.

Gordon, M., & Bernstein, M.C. (1970). Mate choice and domestic life in the nineteenth-century marriage manual. *Journal of Marriage and the Family*, 32(11), 665–674.

Gordon, R., & Verdun-Jones, S.N. (1983). Ethics and ethical dilemmas in the treatment of sexual offenders. In S.N. Verdun-Jones & A.A. Keltner (Eds.), *Sexual aggression and the law* (pp. 73–96). Vancouver, B.C.: Criminology Research Centre, Simon Fraser University.

Gordon, S. (1986, October). What kids need to know. *Psychology Today*, 22–26.

Gosselin, C. (1981). The influence of special sexual desires. In M. Cook (Ed.), *The bases of human sexual attraction* (pp. 65–92). London: Academic Press.

Gotlib, I.H., & Lee, C.M. (1989). The social functioning of depressed patients: A longitudinal assessment. *Journal of Social and Clinical Psychology*, *8*, 223–236.

Gottman, J., Notarius, C., Gonso, J., & Markman, H. (1976). *A couple's guide to communication*. Champaign, Ill.: Research Press.

Gottman, J.M. (1980). Consistency of nonverbal affect and affect reciprocity in marital interaction. *Journal of Consulting and Clinical Psychology*, *48*, 711–717.

Gouaux, C. (1971). Induced affective states and interpersonal attraction. *Journal of Personality and Social Psychology*, *20*, 37–43.

Gough, H.G. (1975). An attitude profile for studies of population psychology. *Journal of Research in Personality*, *9*, 122–135.

Gould, S.J. (1981). *The mismeasure of man*. New York: W.W. Norton.

Gould, S.J. (1991, March). The Great Seal principle. *Natural History*, 4, 6, 8–12.

Goyer, P.F., & Eddleman, H.C. (1984). Same-sex rape of nonincarcerated men. *American Journal of Psychiatry*, *141*, 576–579.

Graber, B. (Ed.). (1982). *The circum-vaginal musculature and sexual function*. New York: Karger.

Graber, B., & Kline-Graber, G. (1979). Clitoral foreskin adhesions and female sexual function. *Journal of Sex Research*, *15*, 205–212.

Grace, E. (1981). Areas of sexual misunderstanding among adolescents. *Medical Aspects of Human Sexuality*, 15(1), 81–82.

Grady, D. (1988). Another sexual blight to fight. *Time*, *131* (14), 69.

Grafenberg, E. (1950). The role of urethra in female orgasm. *International Journal of Sexology*, *3*, 145–148.

Grauer, H. (1978). Deviant sexual behavior associated with senility. *Medical Aspects of Human Sexuality*, 12(4), 127–128.

Graverholz, E., & Serpe, R.T. (1985). Initiation and response: The dynamics of sexual interaction. *Sex Roles*, *12*, 1041–1059.

Gray, D. (1973). Turning out: A study of teenage prostitution. *Urban Life and Culture*, *1*, 401–425.

Graziano, W., Brothen, T., & Berscheid, E. (1978) Height and attraction: Do men and women see eye-to-eye? *Journal of Personality*, *46*, 128–145.

Green, F.C. (1978). Incidence of child molesters. *Medical Aspects of Human Sexuality*, 12(6), 111.

Green, R. (1985, September). *Exposure to explicit sexual materials and sexual assault: A review of behavioral and social science research*. Paper presented at the U.S. Justice Department Hearings, Houston.

Green, R. (1987). *The "sissy boy syndrome" and the development of homosexuality*. New Haven, CT: Yale University Press.

Green, R., & Fleming, D.T. (1990). Transsexual surgery follow-up: Status in the 1990s. In J. Bancroft, C.M. Davis, & D. Weinstein (Eds.), *Annual review of sex research*, Vol. 1 (pp. 163–174). Mt. Vernon, IA: Foundation for the Scientific Study of Sexuality.

Green, R., Mandel, J.B., Hotvedt, M.E., Gray, J., & Smith, L. (1986). Lesbian mothers and their children: A comparison with solo parent heterosexual mothers and their children. *Archives of Sexual Behavior*, *15*, 167–184.

Green, R., & Stoller, R.J. (1971). Two monozygotic (identical) twin pairs discordant for gender identity. *Archives of Sexual Behavior*, *1*, 321–327.

Green, R., Williams, K., & Goodman, M. (1982). Ninety-nine "tomboys" and "non-tomboys": Behavioral contrasts and demographic similarities. *Archives of Sexual Behavior*, *11*, 247–266.

Green, S.E., & Mosher, D.L. (1985). A causal model of sexual arousal to erotic fantasies. *Journal of Sex Research*, *21*, 1–23.

Green, S.K., Buchanan, D.R., & Heuer, S.K. (1984). Winners, losers, and choosers: A field investigation of dating initiation. *Personality and Social Psychology Bulletin*, *10*, 502–511.

Green, V. (1985). Experiential factors in childhood and adolescent sexual behavior: Family interaction and previous sexual experiences. *Journal of Sex Research, 21*, 157–182.

Greenberg, A. (1984). Effects of opiates on male orgasm. *Medical Aspects of Human Sexuality, 18*(5), 207, 211.

Greenberg, D.F. (1989). *The construction of homosexuality.* Chicago: University of Chicago Press.

Greenberg, J. (1981, July 31). Study finds widowers die more quickly than widows. *New York Times,* A 1, A 10.

Greenberg-Englander, S., & Levine, S.B. (1981). Significance of enemas. *Medical Aspects of Human Sexuality, 15*(11), 116.

Greenblatt, R.B. (1980). Casanova. *Medical Aspects of Human Sexuality, 14*(7), 91.

Greendlinger, V. (1985). *Dispositional and situational variables as predictors of rape proclivity in college men.* Unpublished doctoral dissertation, University at Albany, State University of New York.

Greendlinger, V., & Byrne, D. (1985). *Propinquity and affiliative needs as joint determinants of classroom friendships.* Unpublished manuscript, University at Albany, State University of New York

Greendlinger, V., & Byrne, D. (1987). Coercive sexual fantasies of college men as predictors of self-reported likelihood to rape and overt sexual aggression. *Journal of Sex Research, 23*, 1–11.

Greene, B.L., & Grossman, M.G. (1979). Divorce attributable to sex problems. *Medical Aspects of Human Sexuality, 13*(7), 11.

Greenhouse, L. (1988, January 21). New poll finds wide support for abortion rights. *New York Times,* A 18.

Greenwald, E., & Leitenberg, H. (1989). Long-term effects of sexual experiences with siblings and nonsiblings during childhood. *Archives of Sexual Behavior, 18*, 389–399.

Greenwood, R.J. (1980). Diverse presenting symptoms of neurosyphilis. *Medical Aspects of Human Sexuality, 14*(4), 31–32.

Gregersen, E. (1982). *Sexual practices: The story of human sexuality.* London: Mitchell Beazley.

Gregersen, E. (1983). *Sexual practices: The story of human sexuality.* New York: Franklin Watts.

Gregersen, E. (1986). Human sexuality in cross-cultural perspective. In D. Byrne & K. Kelley (Eds.), *Alternative approaches to the study of sexual behavior* (pp. 87–102). Hillsdale, N.J.: Lawrence Erlbaum.

Grellert, E.A., Newcomb, M.D., & Bentler, P.M. (1982). Childhood play activities of male and female homosexuals and heterosexuals. *Archives of Sexual Behavior, 11*, 451–478.

Grieco, A. (1987). Scope and nature of sexual harassment in nursing. *Journal of Sex Research, 23*, 261–265.

Griffin, E., & Sparks, G.G. (1990). Friends forever: A longitudinal exploration of intimacy in same-sex friends and platonic pairs. *Journal of Social and Personal Relationships, 7*, 29–46.

Griffen, J. (1977). A cross-cultural investigation of behavioral changes at menopause. *The Social Science Journal, 14*(2), 49–55.

Griffitt, W. (1970). Environmental effects on interpersonal affective behavior: Ambient effective temperature and attraction. *Journal of Personality and Social Psychology, 15*, 240–244.

Griffitt, W. (1973). Response to erotica and the projection of response to erotica in the opposite sex. *Journal of Experimental Research in Personality, 6*, 330–338.

Griffitt, W. (1981). Sexual intimacy in aging marital partners. In J. Marsch & S. Kiesler (Eds.), *Aging: Stability and change in the family* (pp. 301–315). New York: Academic Press.

Griffitt, W. (1986). Females, males, and sexual responses. In K. Kelley (Ed.), *Females, males, and sexuality: Theories and research* (pp. 141–174). Albany, N.Y.: State University of New York Press.

Griffitt, W., & Kaiser, D.L. (1978). Affect, sex guilt, gender, and the rewarding-punishing effects of erotic stimuli. *Journal of Personality and Social Psychology, 36*, 850–858.

Griffitt, W., May, J., & Veitch, R. (1974). Sexual stimulation and interpersonal behavior: Heterosexual evaluative responses, visual behavior, and physical proximity. *Journal of Personality and Social Psychology, 30*, 367–377.

Grimes, D.A. (1980). Amount of blood shed in menses. *Medical Aspects of Human Sexuality, 14*(3), 143.

Grimes, D.A. (1984). Second-trimester abortions in the United States. *Family Planning Perspectives, 16*, 260–266.

Grisanti, M.L. (1989). The Cesarian epidemic. *New York, 22*(8), 56–61.

Grobstein, C., Flower, M., & Mendeloff, J. (1983). External human fertilization: An evaluation of policy. *Science, 222*, 127–133.

Gronewald, S. (1982). *Beautiful merchandise: Prostitution in China, 1860–1936.* New York: Hayworth Press.

Gross, A.E., Green, S.K., Storck, J.T., & Vanyur, J.M. (1980). Disclosure of sexual orientation and impressions of male and female homosexuals. *Personality and Social Psychology Bulletin, 6*, 307–314.

Gross, J. (1990, October 12). Prostitutes and addicts: Special victims of rape. *New York Times,* A 14.

Gross, P.L. (1984). Sexual effects of radical vs. simple prostatectomy. *Medical Aspects of Human Sexuality, 18*(8), 134.

Grosskopf, D. (1983). *Sex and the married woman.* New York: Simon & Schuster.

Grosskurth, P. (1980). *Havelock Ellis: A biography.* New York: Alfred A. Knopf.

Grossman, J.H., III. (1985). Incidence of genital herpes. *Medical Aspects of Human Sexuality, 19*(2), 9.

Grossman, K., Thane, K., & Grossman, K.E. (1981). Maternal tactual contact of the newborn after various postpartum conditions of mother–infant contact. *Developmental Psychology, 17*, 158–169.

Groth, A.N. (1979). *Men who rape: The psychology of the offender.* New York: Plenum.

Groth, A.N. (1982). Voyeurism. *Medical Aspects of Human Sexuality, 16*(1), 65.

Groth, A.N., & Birnbaum, H.J. (1978). Adult sexual orientation and attraction to underage persons. *Archives of Sexual Behavior, 7*, 175–181.

Groth, A.N., & Hobson, W.F. (1982). Male rape. *Medical Aspects of Human Sexuality, 16*(6), 163–164.

Growdon, W.A. (1985). Herpes in third trimester. *Medical Aspects of Human Sexuality, 19*(1), 215–216.

Grudzinskas, J.G., & Atkinson, L. (1984). Sexual function during the puerperium. *Archives of Sexual Behavior, 13*, 85–91.

Grush, J.E., & Yehl, J.G. (1979). Marital roles, sex differences, and interpersonal attraction. *Journal of Personality and Social Psychology, 37*, 116–123.

Guidubaldi, J., Perry, J.D., & Nastasi, B.K. (1987). Growing up in a divorced family: Initial and long-term perspectives on children's adjustment. In S. Oskamp (Ed.), *Family processes and problems: Social psychological aspects* (pp. 202–237). Beverly Hills, Calif.: Sage.

Gump, D.W. (1985). Lymphogranuloma venereum. *Medical Aspects of Human Sexuality, 19*(6), 90, 92, 94.

Gunderson, B.H., Melas, P.S., & Skar, J.E. (1981). Sexual behavior of preschool children: Teachers' observations. In L.L. Constantine & F.L. Martinson (Eds.), *Children and sex: New findings, new perspectives* (pp. 45–62). Boston: Little, Brown.

Gunning, J.E. (1981). Common errors in use of the diaphragm. *Medical Aspects of Human Sexuality, 15*(9), 43.

Gusberg, S.B. (1982). Promiscuity and the frequency of Pap smears. *Medical Aspects of Human Sexuality, 16*(4), 25.

Gutek, B.A., Nakanura, C.Y., Gahart, M. Handschumacher, I., & Russell, D. (1980). Sexuality and the workplace. *Basic and Applied Social Psychology, 1*, 255–265.

Gutis, P.S. (1987, January 21). Homosexual parents winning some custody cases. *New York Times,* C 1, C 16.

Gutis, P.S. (1989a, April 27). How to define family: Court hears case of a gay tenant. *New York Times,* B 1, B 2.

Gutis, P.S. (1989b, June 8). Attacks on U.S. homosexuals held alarmingly widespread. *New York Times,* A 24.

Hacker, A. (1980, February 10). The technocrat in the bedroom. *New York Times Book Review,* 7, 24, 26.

Hackett, T. (1983). Dangerousness of exhibitionists. *Medical Aspects of Human Sexuality, 17*(5), 86.

Haddad, K. (1986, December 17). TV blamed for pregnancies. *Albany Times Union,* B-8.

Hahlweg, K., & Markman, H.J. (1988). Effectiveness of behavioral marital therapy: Empirical status of behavioral techniques in preventing and alleveating marital distress. *Journal of Consulting and Clinical Psychology, 56*, 440–447.

Haist, M., & Hewitt, J. (1974). The butch-fem dichotomy in male homosexual behavior. *Journal of Sex Research,* 10, 68–75.

Hall, J.A., & Braunwald, K.G. (1981). Gender cues in conversations. *Journal of Personality and Social Psychology,* 40, 99–110.

Hall, J.E., & Morris, H.L. (1976). Sexual knowledge and attitudes of institutionalized and noninstitutionalized retarded adolescents. *American Journal of Mental Deficiency, 80*, 382–387.

Hall, J.E., Morris, H.L., & Barker, H.R. (1973). Sexual knowledge and attitudes of mentally retarded adolescents. *American Journal of Mental Deficiency, 77*, 706–709.

Hall, J.G. (1979). Offspring of incest. *Medical Aspects of Human Sexuality, 13*(11), 121.

Halpern, S. (1989, May). AIDS: Rethinking the risk. *Ms.,* 80–87.

Halverson, H. (1940). Genital and sphincter behavior of the male infant. *Journal of Genetic Psychology, 56*, 95–136.

Hamilton, G.V. (1929). *A study in marriage.* New York: Boni.

Hamilton, W.J., & Arrowood, P.C. (1978). Copulatory vocalizations of chocma baboons (Papio ursinus), gibbons (Hylebates hoolock), and humans. *Science, 200*, 1405.

Hammond, C.B. (1981).. Hormonal treatment of loss of libido. *Medical Aspects of Human Sexuality, 15*(6), 90–91.

Hammond, D.C. (1981). Sexual dysfunction in women alcoholics. *Medical Aspects of Human Sexuality, 15*(11), 32A, 32E.

Hammond, D.C. (1984). Alcohol: An impediment to erection and orgasm. *Medical Aspects of Human Sexuality, 18*(6), 191, 195.

Hanauer, G. (1985). Celibacy chic. *Penthouse, 17*(4), 80–82, 186–187, 190, 192.

Hancock, J.C. (1982). Defining premature ejaculation. *Medical Aspects of Human Sexuality, 16*(3), 105.

Hands, J., Herbert, V., & Tennent, G. (1974). Menstruation and behavior in a special hospital. *Medicine, Science, and the Law, 14*, 32–35.

Hansen, C.H., & Hansen, R.D. (1988). How rock music videos can change what is seen when boy meets girl: Priming stereotypic appraisal of social interactions. *Sex Roles, 19*, 287–316.

Hansen, G.L. (1985). Dating jealousy among college students. *Sex Roles, 12*, 713–721.

Hansson, R.O., Jones, W.H., & Carpenter, B.N. (1984). Relational competence and social support. In P. Shaver (Ed.), *Review of personality and social psychology 5: Emotions, relationships, and health* (pp. 265–284). Beverly Hills, Calif.: Sage.

Hansson, R.O., Jones, W.H., & Chernovetz, M.E. (1979). Contraceptive knowledge: Antecedents and implications. *Family Coordinator, 28*, 29–39.

Harbison, J.J.M., Graham, P.J., Quinn, J.T., McAllister, H., & Woodward, R. (1974). A questionnaire measure of sexual interest. *Archives of Sexual Behavior, 3*, 357–366.

Harlan, W.R. (1980). Age of male puberty. *Medical Aspects of Human Sexuality, 14*(8), 103, 107.

Harlap, S. (1979). Gender of infants conceived on different days of the menstrual cycle. *New England Journal of Medicine, 300*, 1445–1448.

Harlow, H.F. (1975). Lust, latency, and love: Simian secrets of successful sex. *Journal of Sex Research, 11*, 79–90.

Harlow, H.F., & Rosenblum, L.A. (1971). Maturational variables influencing sexual posturing in infant monkeys. *Archives of Sexual Behavior, 1*, 175–180.

Harman, S.M. (1981). Testosterone replacement therapy. *Medical Aspects of Human Sexuality, 15*(9), 111–112.

Harrell, T.H., & Stolp, R.D. (1985). Effects of erotic guided imagery on female sexual arousal and emotional response. *Journal of Sex Research, 21*, 292–304.

Harris, C.S. (1983). The case of the vanishing twin. *Science 83, 4*(2), 84.

Harris, M.B., Harris, R.J., & Bochner, S. (1982). Fat, four-eyed, and female: Stereotypes of obesity, glasses, and gender. *Journal of Applied Social Psychology, 12*, 503–516.

Harris, M.B., & Turner, P.H. (1985/86). Gay and lesbian parents. *Journal of Homosexuality, 12,* 101–113.

Harris, P.R., & Wilshire, P. (1988). Estimating the prevalence of shyness in a "global village": Pluralistic ignorance or false consensus? *Journal of Personality, 56,* 405–415.

Harris, R., Good, R.S., & Pollack, L. (1982). Sexual behavior of gynecologic cancer patients. *Archives of Sexual Behavior, 11,* 503–510.

Harry, J. (1974). Urbanization and the gay life. *Journal of Sex Research, 10,* 238–247.

Harry, J. (1982). Decision making and age differences among gay male couples. *Journal of Homosexuality, 8*(2), 9–21.

Harry, J. (1984). Sexual orientation as destiny. *Journal of Homosexuality, 10*(3/4), 111–124.

Harry, J. (1989). Parental physical abuse and sexual orientation in males. *Archives of Sexual Behavior, 18,* 251–261.

Hartman, L.M. (1980). The interface between sexual dysfunction and marital conflict. *American Journal of Psychiatry, 137,* 576–579.

Hartman, L.M. (1985). Attentional focus, sexual responding, and metacognitions. *Journal of Sex Research, 21,* 211–217.

Hartman, M.S. (1976). *Victorian murderesses.* New York: Schocken.

Hartman, W.E., & Fithian, M.A. (1973). *Treatment of sexual dysfunction.* New York: Jason Aronson.

Hartman, W.E., & Fithian, M.A. (1974). *Treatment of sexual dysfunction* (2nd ed.). New York: Jason Aronson.

Hartman, W.E., & Fithian, M.A. (1982). Additional comment on the sexological examination: A reply to Hoch. *Journal of Sex Research, 18,* 64–71.

Hartman, W., & Fithian, M. (1984). *Any man can: The multiple orgasmic technique for every loving man.* New York: St. Martin's Press.

Harvey, M.R. (1985). *Exemplary rape crisis programs: A cross-site analysis and case studies.* Rockville, Md.: National Institute of Mental Health.

Harvey, P.H., & May, R.M. (1989). Out for the sperm count. *Nature, 337,* 508–509.

Harvey, S.M., & Scrimshaw, S.C.M. (1988). Coitus-dependent contraceptives: Factors associated with effective use. *Journal of Sex Research, 25,* 364–378.

Hass, A. (1979). *Teenage sexuality: A survey of teenage sexual behavior.* New York: Macmillan.

Hatcher, R.A., Stewart, F., Trussell, J., Kowal, D., Guest, F., Stewart, G.K., & Cates, W. (1990). *Contraceptive technology, 1990–1992, with special section on AIDS and condoms* (15th rev. ed.). New York: Irvington.

Hatfield, E. (1983). What do women and men want from love and sex? In E.R. Allgeier & N.B. McCormick (Eds.), *Changing boundaries: Gender roles and sexual behavior.* Palo Alto, Calif.: Mayfield.

Hatfield, E. (1988). Passionate and companionate love. In R.J. Sternberg & M.L. Barnes (Eds.), *The psychology of love* (pp. 191–217). New Haven, CT: Yale University Press.

Hatfield, E., Greenberger, D., Traupmann, J., & Lambert, P. (1982). Equity and sexual satisfaction in recently married couples. *Journal of Sex Research, 18,* 18–32.

Hatfield, E., & Rapson, R.L. (1987). Passionate love/sexual desire: Can the same paradigm explain both? *Archives of Sexual Behavior, 16,* 259–278.

Hatfield, E., & Sprecher, S. (1986a). Measuring passionate love in intimate relations. *Journal of Adolescence, 9,* 383–410.

Hatfield, E., & Sprecher, S. (1986b). *Mirror, mirror . . . The importance of looks in everyday life.* Albany, N.Y.: State University of New York Press.

Hatfield, E., Sprecher, S., Pillemer, J.T., Greenberger, D., & Wexler, P. (1988). Gender differences in what is desired in the sexual relationship. *Journal of Psychology and Human Sexuality, 1,* 39–52.

Hatfield, E., Traupmann, J., & Sprecher, S. (1984). Older women's perceptions of their intimate relationships. *Journal of Social and Clinical Psychology, 2,* 108–124.

Hatfield, E., & Walster, G.W. (1981). *A new look at love.* Reading, Mass.: Addison-Wesley.

Hawkins, J.L. (1982). Continued sex relations after divorce. *Medical Aspects of Human Sexuality, 16*(4), 25.

Hay, W.M., Barlow, D.H., & Hay, L.R. (1981). Treatment of stereotypic cross-gender motor behavior using covert modeling in a boy with gender identity confusion. *Journal of Consulting and Clinical Psychology, 49,* 388–394.

Hayes, S.C., & Leonard, S.R. (1983). Sex-related motor behavior: Effects on social impressions and social cooperation. *Archives of Sexual Behavior, 12,* 415–426.

Hayes S.C., Nelson, R.O., Steele, D.L., Meeler, M.E., & Barlow, D.H. (1984). Instructional control of sex-related motor behavior in extremely masculine or feminine adults. *Sex Roles, 11,* 315–331.

Haynes, S.N., Jensen, B.J., Wise, E., & Sherman, D. (1981). The marital intake interview: A multimethod criterion validity assessment. *Journal of Consulting and Clinical Psychology, 49,* 379–387.

Haynes, S.N., & Oziel, L.J. (1976). Homosexuality: Behaviors and attitudes. *Archives of Sexual Behavior, 5,* 283–289.

Hays, R.B. (1984). The development and maintenance of friendship. *Journal of Social and Personal Relationships, 1,* 75–98.

Hazelwood, R.R., & Burgess, A.W. (1984). Autoerotic fatalities. *Medical Aspects of Human Sexuality, 18*(8), 9.

Heath, D.H. (1978). Marital sexual enjoyment and frustration of professional men. *Archives of Sexual Behavior, 7,* 463–476.

Hedaya, R. (1985). The womanizer. *Medical Aspects of Human Sexuality, 19*(1), 113–114.

Hedblom, J.H., & Hartman, J.J. (1980). Research in lesbianism: Selected effects of time, geographic location, and data collection technique. *Archives of Sexual Behavior, 9,* 217–234.

Heiby, E., & Becker, J.D. (1980). Effect of filmed modeling on the selfreported frequency of masturbation. *Archives of Sexual Behavior, 9,* 115–121.

Heider, K.G. (1976). Dani sexuality: A low energy system. *Man, 11,* 188–201.

Heilbrun, A.B., Jr., & Seif, D.T. (1988). Erotic value of female distress in sexually explicit photographs. *Journal of Sex Research, 24,* 47–57.

Heim, N., & Hursch, C.J. (1979). Castration for sex offenders: Treatment or punishment? A review and critique of recent European literature. *Archives of Sexual Behavior, 8,* 281–304.

Heiman, J., LoPiccolo, L., & LoPiccolo, J. (1976). *Becoming orgasmic: A sexual growth program for women.* Englewood Cliffs, N.J.: Prentice Hall.

Heiman, J.R., & Hatch, J.P. (1980). Affective and physiological dimensions of male sexual response to erotica and fantasy. *Basic and Applied Social Psychology, 1,* 315–327.

Heimberg, R.G., & Hope, D.A. (1989). Dating anxiety. In H. Leitenberg, (Ed.), *Handbook of social anxiety.* New York: Plenum.

Heinicke, C.M. (1984). Impact of prebirth parent personality and marital functioning on family development: A framework and suggestions for further study. *Developmental Psychology, 20,* 1044–1053.

Helmer, W.J. (1980). The laws against love. *Playboy, 27*(10), 56.

Helmreich, R.L., Spence, J.T., & Wilhelm, J.A. (1981). A psychometric analysis of the personal attributes questionnaire. *Sex Roles, 7,* 1097–1108.

Helsing, K.J., Szklo, M., & Comstock, G.W. (1981). Factors associated with mortality after widowhood. *American Journal of Public Health, 71,* 802.

Hembree, W.C. (1980). Marijuana and male fertility. *Medical Aspects of Human Sexuality, 14*(1), 11, 121.

Hendershot, G.E., Mosher, W.D., & Pratt, W.F. (1982). Infertility and age: An unresolved issue. *Family Planning Perspectives, 14,* 287–288.

Henderson, D.K. (1984). Transmission of AIDS to health care workers. *Medical Aspects of Human Sexuality, 18*(8), 9, 13.

Hendrick, C. (Ed.) (1989). *Close relationships.* Newbury Park, CA: Sage.

Hendrick, C., & Hendrick, S. (1986). A theory and method of love. *Journal of Personality and Social Psychology, 50,* 392–402.

Hendrick, C., Hendrick, S., Foote, F.H., & Slapion–Foote, M.J. (1984). Do men and women love differently? *Journal of Social and Personal Relationships, 1,* 177–195.

Hendrick, S. (1981). Self-disclosure and marital satisfaction. *Journal of Personality and Social Psychology, 40,* 1150–1159.

Hendrick, S., & Hendrick, C. (1987). Multidimensionality of sexual attitudes. *Journal of Sex Research, 23,* 502–526.

Hendrick, S., Hendrick, C., & Adler, N.L. (1988). Romantic relationships: Love, satisfaction, and staying together. *Journal of Personality and Social Psychology, 54,* 980–988.

Henker, F.O. (1981). Diminished libido. *Medical Aspects of Human Sexuality, 15*(2), 25.

Henker, F.O., III. (1982). Men's concern about penis size. *Medical Aspects of Human Sexuality, 16*(8), 149.

Henker, F.O. (1983). Diminished libido in middle-aged women. *Medical Aspects of Human Sexuality, 17*(6), 247, 250, 251, 254.

Henker, F.O. (1984). Sudden disappearance of libido. *Medical Aspects of Human Sexuality, 18*(1), 167, 171, 172.

Henshaw, S.K., Binkin, N.J., Blaine, E., & Smith, J.C. (1985). A portrait of American women who obtain abortions. *Family Planning Perspectives, 17,* 90–96.

Hensley, W.E., & Spencer, B.A. (1985). The effect of first names on perceptions of female attractiveness. *Sex Roles, 12,* 723–729.

Hepner, P.J. (1979). Sexual expression and the mentally retarded: The lawyer's role. *Sexuality and Disability, 2*(1), 38–45.

Herek, G.M. (1985). On doing, being, and not being: Prejudice and the social construction of sexuality. *Journal of Homosexuality, 12*(1), 135–151.

Herek, G.M. (1987). Religious orientation and prejudice: A comparison of racial and sexual attitudes. *Personality and Social Psychology Bulletin, 13,* 34–44.

Herek, G.M. (1988). Heterosexuals' attitudes toward lesbians and gay men: Correlates and gender differences. *Journal of Sex Research, 25,* 451–477.

Herjanic, B. (1984). How adolescents can deal with pressures to engage in sex. *Medical Aspects of Human Sexuality, 18*(6), 204, 209–211, 214, 217–218.

Hernandez. D.J. (1985). Fertility reduction policies and poverty in Third World countries: Ethical issues. *Studies in Family Planning, 16,* 76–87.

Herold, E.S., & Way, L. (1983). Oral-genital sexual behavior in a sample of university females. *Journal of Sex Research, 19,* 327–338.

Hicks, D. (1981). Age of child molesters. *Medical Aspects of Human Sexuality, 15*(9), 47, 111.

Hicks, D., Martin, L., Getchell, J., Heath, J., Francis, D., McDougal, J., Curran, J., Voeller, B. (1985). Inactivation of HTLV-III/LAV infected cultures of normal human lymphocytes by nonoxynol-9 in vitro. *Lancet, I-8469-70,* 1422–1423.

Hill, C.A. (1987). Affiliation motivation: People who need people but in different ways. *Journal of Personality and Social Psychology, 52,* 1008–1018.

Hill, C.T., Rubin, Z., & Peplau, L.A. (1976). Breakups before marriage: The end of 103 affairs. *Journal of Social Issues, 32,* 147–168.

Hill, C.T., & Stull, D.E. (1981). Sex differences in effects of social and value similarity in same-sex friendship. *Journal of Personality and Social Psychology, 41,* 488–502.

Hill, G.J. (1989). An unwillingness to act: Behavioral appropriateness, situational constraint, and self-efficacy in shyness. *Journal of Personality, 57,* 871–890.

Hill, J.L. (1974). Peromyscus: Effect of early pairing on reproduction. *Science, 186,* 1042–1044.

Hill, W.C. (1985). Indications for performance of breast stimulation stress test. *Medical Aspects of Human Sexuality, 19*(1), 115, 118.

Hillard, P.A. (1982). Iron-deficiency anemia in pregnancy. *Parents, 57*(10), 96, 98.

Hillard, P.A. (1983). Preeclampsia. *Parents, 58*(2), 82, 85.

Hillard, P.A. (1984). Forceps delivery. *Parents, 5*(7), 94, 96.

Hillard, P.A. (1985). Coping with the pain of labor. *Parents, 60*(1), 102. (a)

Hillard, P.A. (1985). Breech presentation. *Parents, 60*(10), 154–156. (b)

Hillard, P.A., & Hillard, J.R. (1983). The expectant father. *Parents, 58*(4), 80, 82.

Hiller, D.V. (1984). Power dependence and division of family work. *Sex Roles, 10,* 1003–1019.

Hilts, P.J. (1989, September 15). Early treatment of AIDS seen as costing billions. *New York Times,* D-17.

Hilts, P.J. (1990a, October 11). Growing concern over pelvic infection in women. *New York Times,* B 12.

Hilts, P.J. (1990b, December 11). U.S. approves 5-year implants to curb fertility. *New York Times,* A 1, B 10.

Hinds, M. deC. (1981, June 15). The child victim of incest. *The New York Times,* B-9.

Hingsburger, D. (1989). Motives for coprophilia: Working with individuals who had been institutionalized with developmental handicaps. *Journal of Sex Research, 26,* 139–140.

Hite, S. (1976). *The Hite report.* New York: Dell.

Hite, S. (1981). *The Hite report on male sexuality.* New York: Alfred A. Knopf.

Hite, S. (1987). *Women and love: A cultural revolution in progress.* New York: Alfred A. Knopf.

Ho, D., Byington, R., Schooley, R., Flynn, T., Rota, T., & Hirsch, M. (1985). Infrequency of isolation of HTLV-III virus from saliva in AIDS. *New England Journal of Medicine, 313,* 1606.

Ho, D.D., Rota, T.R., Schooley, R.T., et al. (1985). Isolation of HTLV-III from cerebrospinal fluid and neural tissues of patients with neurologic syndromes related to the acquired immunodeficiency syndrome. *New England Journal of Medicine, 313,* 1493–1497.

Hoch, Z. (1980). The sensory arm of the female orgasmic reflex. *Journal of Sex Education and Therapy, 6,* 4–7.

Hochschild, A.R. (1987, November 15). Why can't a man be more like a woman? *New York Times Book Review,* 3, 34.

Hock, E., Christman, K., & Hock, M. (1980). Factors associated with decisions about return to work in mothers of infants. *Developmental Psychology, 16,* 535–536.

Hockenberry, S.L., & Billingham, R.E. (1987). Sexual orientation and boyhood gender conformity: Development of the Boyhood Gender Conformity Scale (BGCS). *Archives of Sexual Behavior, 16,* 475–492.

Hodges, W.F. (1986). *Interventions for children of divorce.* New York: John Wiley.

Hoebel, E.A. (1960). *The Cheyennes: Indians of the Great Plains.* New York: Holt, Rinehart & Winston..

Hoenig, J., & Kenna, J.C. (1974). The nonsociological position of transsexualism. *Archives of Sexual Behavior, 3,* 273–287.

Hofmann, A.D. (1982, March). *Biological and psychological correlates of contraception in adolescence: A review.* Paper presented to the Maternal and Child Health Division of the World Health Organization, Geneva.

Hogan, W.L. (1980). Types of women most likely to be raped. *Medical Aspects of Human Sexuality, 14*(10), 63, 66.

Hogue, C.J.R., Cates, W., Jr., & Tietze, C. (1983). Impact of vac-uum aspiration abortion on future childbearing: A review. *Family Planning Perspectives, 15,* 119–126.

Hojat, M., & Crandall, R. (Eds.). (1987). *Loneliness: Theory, research, and applications.* Newbury Park, CA: Sage.

Holden, C. (1979). Sex change operations of dubious value. *Science, 205,* 1235.

Hollander, J.B. (1984). Wife's dissatisfaction with penile prosthesis. *Medical Aspects of Human Sexuality, 18*(10), 16, 103.

Hollerbach, P.E. (1980). Power in families, communication, and fertility decision-making. *Population and Environment, 3,* 146–173.

Hollister, L., (1978). Amyl nitrite to enhance sexual experiences. *Medical Aspects of Human Sexuality, 12*(3), 14.

Holmstrom, L.L., & Burgess, A.W. (1980). Sexual behavior of assailants during reported rapes. *Archives of Sexual Behavior, 9,* 427–439.

Holtzen, D.W., & Agresti, A.A. (1990). Parental responses to gay and lesbian children: Differences in homophobia, self-esteem, and sex-role stereotyping. *Journal of Social and Clinical Psychology, 9,* 390–399.

Holub, D.A. (1982). Untoward effects of androgens used by athletes. *Medical Aspects of Human Sexuality, 16*(10), 47, 48.

Hong, L.K. (1984). Survival of the fastest: On the origin of premature ejaculation. *Journal of Sex Research, 20,* 109–122.

Hoogland, J.L. (1982). Prairie dogs avoid extreme inbreeding. *Science, 215,* 1639–1641.

Hoon, E.F., & Hoon, P.W. (1978). Styles of sexual expression in women: Clinical implications of multivariate analyses. *Archives of Sexual Behavior, 7,* 105–116.

Hoon, P., Wincze, J., & Hoon, E. (1977). A test of reciprocal inhibition: Are anxiety and arousal in women mutually inhibitory? *Journal of Abnormal Psychology, 86,* 65–74.

Hooper, R.R. (1978). Postcoital urination and VD prevention. *Medical Aspects of Human Sexuality, 12*(6), 41–82.

Hoose, P. (1990, September 19). Vasectomy vets. *New York Times Magazine,* 28, 30.

Horgan, D. (1983). The pregnant woman's place and where to find it. *Sex Roles, 9,* 333–339.

Horn, J.C. (1979). For men, splitting is easier. *Psychology Today, 13*(2), 97–98.

Hornick, J.P. (1978). Premarital sexual attitudes and behavior. *Sociological Quarterly, 19,* 535–544.

Horton, C.E., & Devine, C.J. (1981). Hypospadias. *Medical Aspects of Human Sexuality, 15*(9), 89, 93.

Horvath, T. (1979). Correlates of physical beauty in men and women. *Social Behavior and Personality, 7,* 145–151.

Houck, E.L., & Abramson, P.R. (1986). Masturbatory guilt and the psychological consequences of sexually transmitted diseases among women. *Journal of Research in Personality, 20,* 267–275.

House, E.A. (1986). Sex role orientation and marital satisfaction in dual- and one-provider couples. *Sex Roles, 14,* 245–259.

Howard, J.A., Blumstein, P., & Schwartz, P. (1986). Sex, power, and influence tactics in intimate relationships. *Journal of Personality and Social Psychology, 51,* 102–109.

Howard, K.I., Kopta, S.M., Krause, M.S., & Orlinsky, D.E. (1986). The dose-effect relationship in psychotherapy. *American Psychologist, 41,* 159–164.

Howe, M. (1980, December 21). Couple's suicide over "bride price" shocks Turks. *New York Times,* 24.

Howe, M. (1989, June 19). Experts call for rehabilitation and tough penalties for rapists. *New York Times,* B 2.

Hoyt, M.F. (1978). Children's exposure to parental coitus. *Medical Aspects of Human Sexuality, 12,* 82–83.

Hoyt, M.F. (1979a). Primal-scene experiences: Quantitative assessment of an interview study. *Archives of Sexual Behavior, 8,* 225–245.

Hoyt, M.F. (1979b). An experimental study of the thematic structure of primal-scene imagery. *Journal of Abnormal Psychology, 88,* 96–100.

Hudson, J.W. (1980). College men's attitudes regarding female chastity. *Medical Aspects of Human Sexuality 14*(1), 137.

Hudson, W., Crosscup, P., & Harrison, D. (1990). *Sexual discord in dyadic relationships.* Unpublished manuscript, University of Hawaii.

Hudson, W.W., Harrison, D.F., & Crosscup, P.C. (1981). A short-form scale to measure sexual discord in dyadic relationships. *Journal of Sex Research, 17,* 157–174.

Hudson, W.W., Murphy, G.J., & Nurius, P.S. (1983). A short-form scale to measure liberal vs. conservative orientations toward human sexual expression. *Journal of Sex Research, 19,* 258–272.

Huey, C.J., Kline-Graber, G., & Graber, B. (1981). Time factors and orgasmic response. *Archives of Sexual Behavior, 10,* 111–118.

Huff, B.B. (1982). *Physicians' desk reference.* Oradell, N.J.: Medical Economics Co.

Huffman, J.W. (1982). Coitus during vaginal infection. *Medical Aspects of Human Sexuality 16*(7), 145, 148, 152.

Huffman, S.L. (1984). Determinants of breastfeeding in developing countries: Overview and policy implications. *Studies in Family Planning, 15,* 170–183.

Hufnagel, V. (1988, October 4). Women need to know risks of hysterectomy. *New York Times,* A 30.

Hughes, R. (1984, February 27). Beyond the skin's frontier. *Time,* 92.

Hume, J.C. (1979). Sequelae of trichomoniasis. *Medical Aspects of Human Sexuality, 13*(2), 47.

Hunt, M. (1974). *Sexual behavior in the 1970s.* Chicago: Playboy Press.

Hunt, M. (1986, March 2). Teaming up against AIDS. *New York Times Magazine,* 42–44, 46, 51, 78–83.

Hutchings, J.E., Benson, P.J., Perkin, G.W., & Soderstrom, R.M. (1985). The IUD after 20 years: A review. *Family Planning Perspectives, 17*(6), 244–255.

Hutz, C.S. (1990, October 10). Personal communication.

Hyde, L. (Ed.) (1978). *Rat & the devil: Journal letters of F.O. Matthiessen and Russell Cheney.* Hamden, Conn.: Archon Books.

Imber, G. (1980). Advising patients about the advisability and procedures involved in breast augmentation. *Medical Aspects of Human Sexuality 14*(3), 25–26.

Imperato-McGinley, J., Guerrero, L., Gautier,, T., & Peterson, R.E. (1974). Steroid 5-a-reductase deficiency is man: An inherited form of male pseudohermaphroditism. *Science, 186,* 1213–1215.

Imperato-McGinley, J., Peterson, R.S., & Gautier T. (1976). Gender identity and hermaphroditism. *Science, 191,* 872.

Improved copper IUD receives FDA approval for four years of use. (1985). *Family Planning Perspectives, 17,* 81.

Inazu, J., & Fox, G.L. (1980). Maternal influences on the sexual behavior of teenage daughters. *Journal of Family Issues, 1,* 81.

Ingram, J.M. (1983). "Dry vulva" regimen. *Medical Aspects of Human Sexuality, 17*(3), 178.

Innala, S.M., & Ernulf, K.E. (1989). Asphyxiophilia in Sweden. *Archives of Sexual Behavior, 18,* 181–189.

Intons-Peterson, M.J., & Crawford, J. (1985). The meanings of marital surnames. *Sex Roles, 12,* 1163–1171.

Intons-Peterson, M.J., Roskos-Ewoldsen, B., Thomas, L., Shirley, M., & Blut, D. (1989). Will educational materials reduce negative effects of exposure to sexual violence? *Journal of Clinical and Social Psychology, 8,* 256–275.

Istvan, J. (1983). Effects of sexual orientation on interpersonal judgment. *Journal of Sex Research, 19,* 173–191.

Istvan, J., & Griffitt, W. (1980). Effects of sexual experience on dating desirability and marriage desirability. *Journal of Marriage and the Family, 42,* 377–385.

Istvan, J., Griffitt, W., & Weidner, G. (1983). Sexual arousal and the polarization of perceived sexual attractiveness. *Basic and Applied Social Psychology, 4,* 307–318.

Jaccard, J. (1981). Attitudes and behavior: Implications of attitudes toward behavioral alternatives. *Journal of Experimental Social Psychology, 17,* 286–307.

Jaccard, J., Hand, D., Ku, L., Richardson, K., & Abella, R. (1981). Attitudes toward male oral contraceptives: Implications for models of the relationship between beliefs and attitudes. *Journal of Applied Social Psychology, 11,* 181–196.

Jacklin, C.N., Dipietro, J.A., & Maccoby, E.E. (1984). Sex-typing behavior and sex-typing pressure in child/parent interaction. *Archives of Sexual Behavior, 13,* 413–425.

Jacob, K.A. (1979). Clelia Duel Mosher. *Johns Hopkins Magazine,* 8–16.

Jacobs, L.I. (1980). Variations in penile tumescence during sex activity. *Medical Aspects of Human Sexuality, 14*(2), 11.

Jacobs, N.F., Jr. (1981). VD incubation time. *Medical Aspects of Human Sexuality, 15*(7), 16.

Jacobson, J.L., Jacobson, S.W., Fein, G.G., Schwartz, P.M., & Dowler, J.K. (1984). Prenatal exposure to an environmental toxin: A test of the multiple effects model. *Development Psychology, 20,* 523–532.

Jacobson, M.J. (1981). Effects of victim's and defendant's physical attractiveness on subject's judgments in a rape case. *Sex Roles, 7,* 247–255.

Jacobson, N.S., Follette, W.C., & McDonald, D.W. (1982). Reactivity to positive and negative behavior in distressed and nondistressed married couples. *Journal of Consulting and Clinical Psychology, 50,* 706–714.

Jahoda, G. (1979). A cross-cultural perspective on experimental social psychology. *Personality and Social Psychology Bulletin, 5,* 142–148.

Jain, A.K., & Bongaarts, J. (1981). Breastfeeding: Patterns, correlates, and fertility effects. *Studies in Family Planning, 12,* 79–99.

James, B.E. (1982a). Women's readiness for penile entry. *Medical Aspects of Human Sexuality, 16* (10), 49, 75.

James, B.E. (1982b). Retention of maiden name after marriage. *Medical Aspects of Human Sexuality, 16* (9), 17.

James, B.E. (1982c). Lesbian prostitutes. *Medical Aspects of Human Sexuality, 16* (8), 149.

James, B.E. (1982d). Digital stimulation of vagina. *Medical Aspects of Human Sexuality, 16* (5), 98.

James, J., & Meyerding, J. (1977). Early sexual experience as a factor in prostitution. *Archives of Sexual Behavior, 7,* 31–42.

James, J.F., & Brooks, G.F. (1981). Patients subject to recurrent sexually transmitted infections. *Medical Aspects of Human Sexuality, 15* (12), 97, 103.

James, W.H. (1981). The honeymoon effect on marital coitus. *Journal of Sex Research, 17,* 114–123.

Jamieson, D.W., Lyndon, J.E., & Zanna, M.P. (1987). Attitude and activity preference similarity: Differential bases of interpersonal attraction for low and high self-monitors. *Journal of Personality and Social Psychlogy, 53,* 1052–1060.

Jamison, P.L., & Gebhard, P.H. (1988). Penis size increase between flaccid and erect states: An analysis of the Kinsey data. *Journal of Sex Research, 24,* 177–183.

Janda, L. (1982). How college males evaluate coeds. *Medical Aspects of Human Sexuality, 16* (11), 34–35.

Janman, K. (1989). One step behind: Current stereotypes of women, achievement, and work. *Sex Roles, 21,* 209–230.

Janowsky, D.S., Berens, S.C., & Davis, J.M. (1973). Correlations between mood, weight, and electrolytes during the menstrual cycle: A renin-angiotensin-aldosterone hypothesis of premenstrual tension. *Psychosomatic Medicine, 35,* 143–154.

Janus, S. (1977). Prostitutes' emotional needs. *Medical Aspects of Human Sexuality, 11* (11), 102.

Janus, S.S., & Bess, B.E. (1981). Latency: Fact or fiction? In L.L. Constantine & F.L. Martinson (Eds.), *Children and sex: New findings, new perspectives* (pp. 75–82). Boston: Little, Brown.

Jayne, C. (1981, November). *Freud, Grafenberg, and the neglected vagina: An examination of an historical omission in sexology.* Paper presented at the meeting of the Society for the Scientific Study of Sex, New York City.

Jayne, C. (1983). Sexual withholding in marriage. *Medical Aspects of Human Sexuality, 17* (6), 81, 85–86.

Jazwinski, C., & Byrne, D. (1978). The effect of a contraceptive theme on response to erotica. *Motivation and Emotion, 2,* 287–297.

Jefferson, T.W., Glaros, A., Spevak, M., Boaz, T.L., & Murray, F.T. (1989). An evaluation of the Minnesota Multiphasic Personality Inventory as a discriminator of primary organic and primary psychogenic impotence in diabetic males. *Archives of Sexual Behavior, 18,* 117–126.

Jeffress, J.E. (1980). Psychodynamics of sexual humor: Sex at the office. *Medical Aspects of Human Sexuality, 14* (7), 49–50, 52.

Jeffress, J.E. (1981a). Vaginal lubrication during sleep. *Medical Aspects of Human Sexuality, 15* (11), 24.

Jeffress, J.E. (1981b). Backscratching during intercourse. *Medical Aspects of Human Sexuality, 15* (4), 28.

Jeffress, J.E. (1982). Sensitivity to touching. *Medical Aspects of Human Sexuality, 16* (6), 170–171.

Jeffress, J.E. (1984). Satyriasis. *Medical Aspects of Human Sexuality, 18* (10), 13.

Jenks, R.J. (1985a). Swinging: A replication and test of a theory. *Journal of Sex Research, 21,* 199–210.

Jenks, R.J. (1985b). Swinging: A test of two theories and a proposed new mode. *Archives of Sexual Behavior, 14,* 517–527.

Jennings, J.W., Geis, F.L., & Brown, V. (1980). Influence of television commercials on women's self-confidence and independent judgment. *Journal of Personality and Social Psychology, 38,* 203–210.

Jensen, G. (1981). Helplessness during period of ejaculatory inevitability. *Medical Aspects of Human Sexuality, 15* (1), 21.

Jensen, G.D. (1978). Masturbation by married men. *Archives of Sexual Behavior, 12,* 37.

Jensen, I.W., & Gutek, B.A. (1982). Attributions and assignment of responsibility in sexual harassment. *Journal of Social Issues, 38* (4), 121–136.

Jensen L.C., Christensen, R., & Wilson, D.J. (1985). Predicting young women's role preference for parenting and work. *Sex Roles, 13,* 507–514.

Jensen, N.F. (1978). Limits to growth in world food production. *Science, 201,* 317–324.

Jensen, S. (1986). Sexual dysfunction in insulin-treated diabetics. *Archives of Sexual Behavior, 15,* 271–283.

Jensen, S.B. (1981). Diabetic sexual dysfunction: A comparative study of 160 insulin treated diabetic men and women and an age-matched control group. *Archives of Sexual Behavior, 10,* 493–504.

Jessor, R., Costa, F., Jessor, L., & Donovan, J.E. (1983). Time of first intercourse: A prospective study. *Journal of Personality and Social Psychology, 44,* 608–626.

John, J.F., Jr. (1978). Gonococcal endocarditis. *Medical Aspects of Human Sexuality, 12* (5), 32

Johnson, C.B., Stockdale, M.S., & Saal, F.E. (1987, August). *Men perceive more sexuality—except when it's really there?* Paper presented at the meeting of the American Psychological Association, New York.

Johnson, D.J., & Rusbult, C.E. (1989). Resisting temptation: Devaluation of alternative partners as a means of maintaining commitment in close relationships. *Journal of Personality and Social Psychology, 57,* 967–980.

Johnson, J.H. (1982). Tubal sterilization and hysterectomy. *Family Planning Perspectives, 14,* 28–30.

Johnson, J.H. (1983). Vasectomy—An international appraisal. *Family Planning Perspectives, 15,* 45–48.

Johnson, J.H. (1984). Contraception—The morning after. *Family Planning Perspectives, 16,* 226–270.

Johnston, J.A., Roberts, D.B., & Spencer, R.B. (1980). A survey evaluation of the efficacy and efficiency of natural family planning services and methods in Australia. *Family Planning Perspectives, 12,* 214–215.

Johnston, T. (1990). Domestic partners. *Stanford Observer, 25* (1), 3.

Jones, E.F., Forrest, J.D., Goldmen, N., Henshaw, S.K., Lincoln, R., Rosoff, J.I., Westoff, C.F., & Wulf, D. (1985). Teenage pregnancy in developed countries: Determinants and policy implications. *Family Planning Perspectives, 17,* 53–62.

Jones, G.P. (1982). The social study of pederasty: In search of a literature base. *Journal of Homosexuality, 8,* 61–95.

Jones, J.C., & Barlow, D.H. (1987, November). *Self-reported frequency of sexual urges, fantasies, and masturbatory fantasies in heterosexual males and females.* Paper presented at the meeting of the Association for the Advancement of Behavior Therapy, Boston.

Jones, M.E., & Stanton, A.L. (1988). Dysfunctional beliefs, belief similarity, and marital distress: A comparison of models. *Journal of Social and Clinical Psychology, 7,* 1–14.

Jones, R.B. (1984). Chlamydia: The most common sexually transmitted pathogen. *Medical Aspects of Human Sexuality, 18*(2), 238, 243, 247, 250, 252, 257, 261.

Jones, W.H., Freeman, J.A., & Goswick, R.A. (1981). The persistence of loneliness: Self and other determinants. *Journal of Personality, 49,* 27–48.

Jones, W.H., Hannson, R.C., & Philips, A.L. (1978). Physical attractiveness and judgments of psychotherapy. *Journal of Social Psychology, 105,* 79–84.

Jorgensen, V. (1981). A womans' view of men's sexual problems. *Medical Aspects of Human Sexuality, 15*(9), 32M, 32N.

Jovanovic, V.J. (1971). The recording of physiological evidence of genital arousal in human males and females. *Archives of Sexual Behavior, 1,* 309–320.

Judson, F.N. (1980). Coexisting sexually-transmitted diseases. *Medical Aspects of Human Sexuality, 14*(6), 138.

Judson, F.N. (1982). Concurrent sexually transmitted diseases. *Medical Aspects of Human Sexuality, 16*(2), 77–79, 86.

Juni, S., & Cohen, P. (1985). Partial impulse erogeneity as a function of fixation and object relations. *Journal of Sex Research, 21,* 275–291.

Kafka, D., & Gold, R.B. (1983). Food and drug administration approves vaginal sponge. *Family Planning Perspectives, 15,* 146–148.

Kagel, S.A., & Schilling, K.M. (1985). Sexual identification and gender identity among father-absent males. *Sex Roles, 13,* 357–370.

Kalem, T.E. (1975, August 25). Bard from Bysantium. *Time,* 63–64.

Kalichman, S.C. (1990). Affective and personality characteristics of MMPI profile subgroups of incarcerated rapists. *Archives of Sexual Behavior, 19,* 443–459.

Kalick, S.M., & Hamilton, T.E. (1986). The matching hypothesis reexamined. *Journal of Personality and Social Psychology, 51,* 673–682.

Kallen, D.J., Stephenson, J.J. & Doughty, A. (1983). The need to know: Recalled adolescent sources of sexual and contraceptive information and sexual behavior. *Journal of Sex Research, 19,* 137–159.

Kallmann, F.J. (1952). Comparative twin study on the genetic aspects of male homosexuality. *Journal of Nervous and Mental Diseases, 115,* 283–293.

Kalm, F. (1985). The two "faces" of Antillean prostitution. *Archives of Sexual Behavior, 14,* 203–217.

Kalmuss, D., Lawton, A.I., & Namerow, P.B. (1987). Advantages and disadvantages of pregnancy and contraception: Teenagers' perceptions. *Population and Environment, 9,* 23–40.

Kandel, D.B., Single, E., & Kessler, R.C. (1976). The epidemiology of drug use among New York State high school students: Distribution, trends, and change in rates of use. *American Journal of Public Health, 66,* 43–53.

Kanin, E.J. (1957). Male aggression in dating–courtship relations. *American Journal of Sociology, 63,* 197–204.

Kanin, E.J. (1985). Date rapists: Differential sexual socialization and relative deprivation. *Archives of Sexual Behavior, 14,* 219–231.

Kanin, E.J., & Purcell, S.R. (1977). Sexual aggression: A second look at the offended female. *Archives of Sexual Behavior, 6,* 67–76.

Kanki, P.J., Alroy, J., & Essex, M. (1985). Isolation of T-lymphotropic retrovirus related to HTLV-III/LAV from wild-caught African green monkeys. *Science, 230,* 951–954.

Kaplan, H.S. (1974). *The new sex therapy.* New York: Brunner/Mazel.

Kaplan, H.S. (1979a). *The new sex therapy, Volume II.* New York: Brunner/Mazel.

Kaplan, H.S. (1979b). *Disorders of sexual desire.* New York: Brunner/Mazel.

Kaplan, H.S. (1989). *How to overcome premature ejaculation.* New York: Brunner/Mazel.

Kaplan, H.S., Kohl, R.N., Pomeroy, W.B., Offit, A.K., & Hogan, B. (1974). Group treatment of premature ejaculation. *Archives of Sexual Behavior, 3,* 443–452.

Kappelman, M. (1978). Father taking adolescent son to prostitute. *Medical Aspects of Human Sexuality, 12*(7), 125.

Kappelman, M. (1981). Premature ejaculation among young men. *Medical Aspects of Human Sexuality, 15*(8), 91.

Kardener, S., Fuller, M., & Mensh, I. (1973). A survey of physician's attitudes and practices regarding erotic and non-erotic contact with patients. *American Journal of Psychiatry, 130,* 1077.

Karpas, A.E. (1981a). Hypogonadism in males. *Medical Aspects of Human Sexuality, 15*(9), 32A, 32E.

Karpas, A.E. (1981b). Use and abuse of anabolic steroids by athletes. *Medical Aspects of Human Sexuality, 15*(5), 29–30.

Karpas, A.E. (1982). Gynecomastia in adolescent boys. *Medical Aspects of Human Sexuality, 16*(8), 101, 104, 105.

Katz, I., Farber, J., Glass, D.C., Lucido, D., & Emswiller, T. (1978). When courtesy offends: Effects of positive and negative behavior by the physically disabled on altruism and anger in normals. *Journal of Personality, 46,* 506–518.

Katzman, E.M., Mulholland, M., & Sutherland, E.M. (1988). College students and AIDS: A preliminary survey of knowledge, attitudes, and behavior. *Journal of American College Health, 37,* 127–130.

Kaufman, J.E. (1981). What do most men and woman like their partners to do immediately after intercourse? *Medical Aspects of Human Sexuality, 15*(1), 158, 163, 167, 170.

Kaufman, M.T. (1980a, April 20). Rape case reversal infuriates Indian women's groups. *New York Times,* p. 3.

Kaufman, M.T. (1980b, November 16). Love upsetting Bombay's view of path to altar. *New York Times,* p. 12.

Kaufman, S.A. (1982). Physical clues to sexual maladjustment in women. *Medical Aspects of Human Sexuality, 16*(3), 70B, 70F, 70G, 70I, 70N, 70P, 70U.

Kavich-Sharon, R. (1984). The mixed sexual dysfunction syndrome: A team approach to total sexual health care. *Journal of Sex Research, 20,* 407–414.

Kaye, C.I. (1981). Genetic counseling. *Medical Aspects of Human Sexuality, 15*(3), 164, 169, 172, 177, 178, 180.

Kaye, C.I. (1983). Genetic problems in marriages between relatives. *Medical Aspects of Human Sexuality, 17*(1), 117, 118, 120.

Kaye, H.E., Berl, S., Clare, J., Eleston, M.R., Gershwin, B.S., Gershwin, P., Kogan, L.S., Torda, C., & Wilbur, C.B. (1967). Homosexuality in women. *Archives of Sexual Behavior, 17,* 626–634.

Keating, J., & Over, R. (1990). Sexual fantasies of heterosexual and homosexual men. *Archives of Sexual Behavior, 19,* 461–475.

Keeney, I.G. (1986, February 21). If you're considering divorce, think before you leave home. *Albany Times Union,* B-6.

Keeney, I.G. (1990, December 6). Living together. *Albany Times Union,* C-1, C-20.

Keith, L. (1979). Diaphragm to retain menses. *Medical Aspects of Human Sexuality, 13*(9), 153.

Keller, D.E. (1985). Ability to discern orgasm in partner. *Medical Aspects of Human Sexuality, 19*(2), 161–164.

Kellerman, J., Lewis, J., & Laird, J.D. (1989). Looking and loving: The effects of mutual gaze on feelings of romantic love. *Journal of Research in Personality, 23,* 145–161.

Kelley, K. (1979). Socialization factors in contraceptive attitudes: Roles of affective responses, parental attitudes, and sexual experience. *Journal of Sex Research, 15,* 6–20.

Kelley, K. (1980). Sexual fantasies of multiple partners. *Medical Aspects of Human Sexuality, 14,* 109.

Kelley, K. (1982a). Predicting attraction to the novel stimulus person: Affect and concern. *Journal of Research in Personality, 16,* 32–40.

Kelley, K. (1982b). Playing roulette with pregnancy. In L.H. Gross (Ed.), *The parents' guide to teenagers* (pp. 309–310). New York: McGraw-Hill.

Kelley, K. (1983). Adolescent sexuality: The first lessons. In D. Byrne & W.A. Fisher (Eds.), *Adolescents, sex, and contraception* (pp. 125–142). Hillsdale, N.J.: Lawrence Erlbaum.

Kelley, K. (1985a). Sexual fantasy and attitudes as functions of sex of subject and content of erotica. *Imagination, Cognition, and Personality, 4,* 339–347.

Kelley, K. (1985b). Sexual attitudes as determinants of the motivational properties of exposure to erotica. *Personality and Individual Differences, 6,* 391–393.

Kelley, K. (1985c). Sex, sex guilt, and authoritarianism: Differences in responses to explicit heterosexual and masturbatory slides. *Journal of Sex Research, 21,* 68–85.

Kelley, K. (1985d). Nine social indices as functions of population size or density. *Bulletin of the Psychonomic Society, 23,* 124–126.

Kelley, K. (1985e, September). *Testimony presented to the U.S. Attorney General's Commission on Pornography.* Paper presented at the hearings of the U.S. Attorney General's Commission on Pornography in Houston.

Kelley, K. (1985f). The effects of sexual and/or aggressive film exposure on helping, hostility, and attitudes toward women and men. *Journal of Research in Personality, 19,* 472–482.

Kelley, K. (1985g). Sexuality and hostility of authoritarians. *The High School Journal, 68,* 173–176.

Kelley, K. (1986). Integrating sex research. In D. Byrne & K. Kelley (Eds.), *Alternative approaches to the study of sexual behavior* (pp. 201–207). Hillsdale, N.J.: Lawrence Erlbaum.

Kelley, K. (1987a). Perspectives on females, males, and sexuality. In K. Kelley (Ed.), *Females, males, and sexuality* (pp. 1–12). Albany, N.Y.: State University of New York Press.

Kelley, K. (Ed.). (1987b). *Females, males, and sexuality.* Albany, N.Y.: State University of New York Press.

Kelley, K. (1987c). Applying social psychology. In R.A. Baron & D. Byrne, *Social psychology: Understanding human interaction* (5th ed.). Boston: Allyn & Bacon.

Kelley, K. (1987d). *Health correlates of sexual attitudes.* Manuscript submitted for publication, University at Albany, State University of New York.

Kelley, K., & Byrne, D. (1977). Strength of instigation as a determinant of the aggression-attraction relationship. *Motivation and Emotion, 1,* 29–38.

Kelley, K., & Byrne, D. (1978). The function of imaginative fantasy in sexual behavior. *Journal of Mental Imagery, 2,* 139–146.

Kelley, K., & Byrne, D. (1983). Assessment of sexual responding: Arousal, affect, and behavior. In J. Cacioppo & R. Petty (Eds.), *Social psychophysiology* (pp. 467–490). New York: Guilford Press.

Kelley, K., Dawson, L., & Musialowksi, D.M. (1989). Three faces of sexual explicitness: The good, the bad, and the useful. In D. Zillmann & J. Bryant (Eds.) *Pornography: Recent research, interpretations, and policy considerations.* Hillsdale, N.J.: Lawrence Erlbaum.

Kelley, K., Miller, C.T., Byrne, D., & Bell, P.A. (1983). Facilitating sexual arousal via anger, aggression, or dominance. *Motivation and Emotion, 7,* 191–202.

Kelley, K., & Musialowski, D. (1986). Repeated exposure to sexually explicit stimuli: Novelty, sex, and sexual attitudes. *Archives of Sexual Behavior, 15,* 487–498.

Kelley, K., Pilchowicz, E., & Byrne, D. (1981). Response of males to female initiated dates. *Bulletin of the Psychonomic Society, 17,* 195–196.

Kelley, K., & Rolker-Dolinsky, B. (1986). The psychosexology of female initiation and dominance. In S. Duck & D. Perlman (Eds.), *Intimate relationships 6: Heterosexual relationships, marriage, and divorce* (Vol. 6, pp. 63–88). London: Sage Publications.

Kelley, K., Smeaton, G., Byrne, D., Przybyla, D.P.J., & Fisher, W.A. (1987). Sexual attitudes and contraception among females across five college samples. *Human Relations, 40,* 237–254.

Kelley, K., & Streeter, D. (1990, June). *Chronic self-destructiveness, sexual attitudes, and the risk of HIV infection.* Paper presented at the meeting of the American Psychological Society, Dallas.

Kelly, C., Huston, T.L., & Cate, R.M. (1985). Premarital relationships correlates of the erosion of satisfaction in marriage. *Journal of Social and Personal Relationships, 2,* 167–178.

Kempe, C.H. (1978). Sexual abuse by child's father. *Medical Aspects of Human Sexuality, 12*(5), 135.

Kennel, J. (1981). Childbirth made easier. *Parents, 56*(1), 7.

Kenny, J.A. (1973). Sexuality of pregnant and breastfeeding women. *Archives of Sexual Behavior, 2,* 215–229.

Kenrick, D.T., & Gutierres, S.E. (1980). Contrast effects and judgments of physical attractiveness: When beauty becomes a social problem. *Journal of Personality and Social Psychology, 38,* 131–140.

Kenrick, D.T., Gutierres, S.E., & Goldberg, L.L. (1989). Influence of popular erotica on judgments of strangers and mates. *Journal of Experimental Social Psychology, 25,* 159–167.

Kenrick, D.T., & Keefe, R.C. (in press). Age preferences in mates reflect sex differences in reproductive strategies. *Behavioral and Brain Sciences.*

Kenrick, D.T., & Trost, M.R. (1986). A biosocial model of heterosexual relationships. In K. Kelley (Ed.), *Females, males, and sexuality: Theories and research.* Albany, N.Y.: State University of New York Press.

Kerrison, R. (1988, November 28). Sex-ed class is way off course. *New York Post,* 2.

Kestenberg, J. (1979). Orgasm in prepubertal children. *Medical Aspects of Human Sexuality, 13*(7), 92–93.

Keye, W.R. (1983). Vaginal dryness during coitus. *Medical Aspects of Human Sexuality, 17*(11), 38.

Keye, W.R., Jr., (1984). Posthysterectomy sexual changes. *Medical Aspects of Human Sexuality, 18*(5), 86.

Khaw, K.-T, & Peart, W.S. (1982). Blood pressure and contraceptive use. *British Medical Journal, 285,* 403.

Kiang, D.T., King, M., Zhang, H., Kennedy, B.J., & Wang, N. (1982). Cyclic biological expression in mouse mammary tumors. *Science, 216,* 68–70.

Kilmann, P.R., & Auerbach, R. (1979). Treatments of premature ejaculation and psychogenic impotence: A critical review of the literature. *Archives of Sexual Behavior, 8,* 81–99.

Kilmann, P.R., Mills, K.H., Caid, C., Bella, B., Davidson, E., & Wanlass, R. (1984). The sexual interaction of women with secondary orgasmic dysfunction and their partners. *Archives of Sexual Behavior, 13,* 41–49.

Kilmann, P.R., Mills, K.H., Caid, C., Davidson, E., Bella, B., Milan, R., Drose, G., Boland, J., Follingstad, D., Montgomery, B., & Wanlass, R. (1986). Treatment of secondary orgasmic dysfunction: An outcome study. *Archives of Sexual Behavior, 15,* 211–229.

Kilmann, P.R., Sabalis, R.F., Gearing, M.L., II, Bukstel, L.H., & Sovern, A.W. (1982). The treatment of sexual paraphilias: A review of the outcome research. *Journal of Sex Research, 18,* 193–252.

Kilmann, P.R., Wanlass, R.L., Sabalis, R.F., & Sullivan, B. (1981). Sex education: A review of its effects. *Archives of Sexual Behavior, 10,* 177–205.

Kilpatrick, A.C. (1987). Childhood sexual experiences: Problems and issues in studying long-range effects. *Journal of Sex Research, 23,* 173–196.

Kimmel, D.C. (1978). Adult development and aging: A gay perspective. *Journal of Social Issues, 34*(3), 113–130.

King, K., Balswick, J.O., & Robinson, I.E. (1977). The continuing premarital sexual revolution among college females. *Journal of Marriage and the Family, 39,* 455–459.

King, P. (1989, March). Living together: Bad for the kids. *Psychology Today,* 77.

Kinne, D.W. (1984). Nipple discharge in men. *Medical Aspects of Human Sexuality, 18*(6), 259.

Kinsey, A.C., Pomeroy, W.B., & Martin, C.E. (1948). *Sexual behavior in the human male.* Philadelphia: W.B. Saunders.

Kinsey, A.C., Pomeroy, W.B., Martin, C.E., & Gebhard, P.H. (1953). *Sexual behavior in the human female.* Philadelphia: W.B. Saunders.

Kirchler, E. (1988). Marital happiness and interaction in everyday surroundings: A time-sample diary approach for couples. *Journal of Social and Personal Relationships, 5* 375–382.

Kirkpatrick, C., & Kanin, K. (1957). Male sex aggression on a university campus. *American Sociological Review, 22,* 52–58.

Kirsner, A.B. (1981). John Hunter and the "Hunterian chancre." *Medical Aspects of Human Sexuality, 15*(7), 11.

Kisker, E.E. (1985). Teenagers talk about sex, pregnancy, and contraception. *Family Planning Perspectives, 17,* 83–90.

Klaus, H. (1984). Natural family planning. *Medical Aspects of Human Sexuality, 18*(6), 59, 63, 67, 70.

Kleck, R.E., & Strenta, A. (1980). Perceptions of the impact of negatively valued physical characteristics on social interaction. *Journal of Personality and Social Psychology, 39,* 861–873.

Klein, R.C., Party, E., & Gershey, E.L. (1990). Virus penetration of examination gloves. *BioTechniques, 9,* 196–199.

Kleinke, C.L., & Kahn, M.L. (1980). Perceptions of self-disclosers: Effects of sex and physical attractiveness. *Journal of Personality, 48,* 190–205.

Kleinke, C.L., & Staneski, R.A. (1980). First impressions of female bust size. *Journal of Social Psychology, 110,* 123–134.

Klemesrud, J. (1981, March 3). "Lolita syndrome" is denounced. *New York Times*, B 14.

Klerman, L.V., & Jekel, J.F. (1978). Teenage pregnancies. *Science, 199*, 1390.

Kligman, A. (1977). Androgens and acne vulgaris. *Medical Aspects of Human Sexuality, 11*(11), 102.

Klitsch, M. (1982). Sterilization without surgery. *Family Planning Perspectives, 14*, 324–327.

Knapp, J.J. (1976). An exploratory study of seventeen sexually open marriages. *Journal of Sex Research, 12*, 206–219.

Knaub, P.K., Eversoll, D.B., & Voss, J.H. (1983). Is parenthood a desirable adult role? An assessment of attitudes held by contemporary women. *Sex Roles, 9*, 355–362.

Knodel, J. (1977). Breast-feeding and population growth. *Science, 198*, 1111–1115.

Knox, B. (1988, February). The scorpion's sting. *New Republic*, 38–40.

Koch, J.P. (1982). The Prentif contraceptive cervical cap: A contemporary study of its clinical effectiveness. *Contraception, 25*, 135.

Kockott, G., & Fahrner, E.-M. (1988). Male-to-female and female-to-male transsexuals: A comparison. *Archives of Sexual Behavior, 17*, 539–548.

Kockott, G., Feil, W., Revenstorf, D., Aldenhoff, J., & Besinger, U. (1980). Symptomatology and psychological aspects of male sexual inadequacy: Results of an experimental study. *Archives of Sexual Behavior, 9*, 457–475.

Koenig, F. (1979). Dominant parent as projected by homosexual and heterosexual males. *Journal of Sex Research, 15*, 316–320.

Koenig, R. (1988). Lords of discipline. *New York, 21*(7), 26.

Kohl, S. (1982). Transferring oral herpes. *Medical Aspects of Human Sexuality, 16*(8), 50.

Kohlberg, L. (1966). A cognitive-developmental analysis of children's sex-role concepts and attitudes. In E.E. Maccoby (Ed.), *The development of sex differences* (pp. 53–85). Stanford, Calif.: Stanford University Press.

Kohlberg, L. (1981). *The philosophy of moral development*. San Francisco: Harper & Row.

Kohlberg, L. (1984). *The psychology of moral development*. San Francisco: Harper & Row.

Kohut, H. (1977). *The restoration of the self*. New York: International University Press.

Kolarsky, A., & Madlafousek, J. (1983). The inverse role of preparatory erotic stimulation in exhibitionists: Phallometric studies. *Archives of Sexual Behavior, 12*, 123–148.

Kolata, G. (1980a). How safe is Bendectin? *Science, 210*, 518–519.

Kolata, G. (1980b). NIH panel urges fewer Cesarean births. *Science, 210*, 176–177.

Kolata, G. (1983a). In vitro fertilization goes commercial. *Science, 221*, 1160–1161.

Kolata, G. (1983b). First trimester prenatal diagnosis. *Science, 221*, 1031–1032.

Kolata, G. (1988a, July 27). Study finds 31% rate of miscarriage. *New York Times*, A 14.

Kolata, G. (1988b, December 25). Fetal sex test used as step to abortion. *New York Times*, 1, 38.

Kolata, G. (1989, January 30). Lesbian partners find the means to be parents. *New York Times*, A 13.

Kolata, G. (1990a, January 17). U.S. halves dosage for AIDS drug. *New York Times*, B-6.

Kolata, G. (1990b, November 28). Study links estrogen to cancer, but risk is slight. *New York Times*, A 18.

Kolbert, E. (1987, February 15). Baby M adds urgency to search for equitable laws. *New York Times*, 22 E.

Kolodny, R.C. (1981a). Female sexuality after myocardial infarction. *Medical Aspects of Human Sexuality, 15*(1), 156.

Kolodny, R.C. (1981b). Evaluating sex therapy: Process and outcome at the Masters & Johnson Institute. *Journal of Sex Research, 17*, 301–318.

Kolodny, R.C. (1981c, February). *Effects of marijuana on sexual behavior and function*. Paper presented at the Midwestern Conference on Drug Use, St. Louis.

Kolodny, R.C., Masters, W.H., Kolodny, R.M., & Toro, G. (1974). Depression of plasma testosterone levels after chronic intensive marijuana use. *New England Journal of Medicine, 290*, 873.

Kolodny, R.C., Masters, W.H., & Johnson, V.E. (1979). *Textbook of sexual medicine*. Boston: Little, Brown.

Konner, M. (1987, December 27). Childbearing and age. *New York Times Magazine*, 22–23.

Konner, M. (1989, April 2). Homosexuality: Who and why? *New York Times Magazine*, 60–61.

Konopucki, W.P., & Oei, T.P.S. (1988). Interruption in the maintenance of compulsive sexual disorder: Two case studies. *Archives of Sexual Behavior, 17*, 411–419.

Koop, C.E. (1987). Report of the Surgeon General's workshop on pornography and public health. *American Psychologist, 42*, 944–945.

Koss, M.P., & Leonard, K.E. (1984). Sexually aggressive men: Empirical findings and theoretical implications. In N.M. Malamuth & E. Donnerstein (Eds.), *Pornography and sexual aggression*. New York: Academic Press.

Koss, M.P., Leonard, K.E., Beezley, D.A. & Oros, C.J. (1985). Nonstranger sexual aggression: A discriminant analysis of the psychological characteristics of undetected offenders. *Sex Roles, 12*, 981–992.

Koss, M.P., & Oros, C.J. (1982). Sexual experiences survey: A research instrument investigating sexual aggression and victimization. *Journal of Counseling and Clinical Psychology, 50*, 455–457.

Kothari, P. (1989). *Orgasm—New dimensions*. Bombay: VRP.

Kourany, R.F.C. (1983). The need for body contact. *Medical Aspects of Human Sexuality, 17*(10), 204, 209, 212, 214.

Krafft-Ebing, R. von (1886). *Psychopathia sexualis*. Philadelphia: F.A. Davis. (Reprinted in 1978).

Krantz, K.E. (1982). Consequences to the male of contracting moniliasis. *Medical Aspects of Human Sexuality, 16*(1), 17.

Krantz, K.E., Magrina, J.F., & Capen, C.V. (1984). Sexual risk factors for developing cervical cancer. *Medical Aspects of Human Sexuality, 18*(11), 144, 148, 150, 153, 154.

Krassner, P. (December, 1987). How times change. *Playboy*, p. 46.

Krause, C.A. (1978). Generational contrasts in sex attitudes. *Medical Aspects of Human Sexuality, 12*(12), 108.

Kressel, K. (1985). *The process of divorce.* New York: Basic Books.

Kretchmer, A. (1986). Can sex survive AIDS? *Playboy, 33*(2), 48–49.

Kriss, R.T., & Kraemer, H.C. (1986). Efficacy of group therapy for problems with postmastectomy self-perception, body image, and sexuality. *Journal of Sex Research, 22,* 438–451.

Kristof, N.D. (1987, April 29). In China, beauty is a big Western nose. *New York Times,* C 4.

Kronsberg, S., Schmaling, K., & Fagot, B.I. (1985). Risk in a parent's eyes: Effects of gender and parenting experience. *Sex Roles, 13,* 329–341.

Kroop, M. (1979). Female "trigger spots" for orgasm. *Medical Aspects of Human Sexuality, 13*(6), 39.

Kroop, M. (1983). Importance of foreplay. *Medical Aspects of Human Sexuality, 17*(1), 17, 21.

Kroop, M.S. (1980a). Pleasureless orgasm. *Medical Aspects of Human Sexuality, 14*(9), 15.

Kroop, M.S. (1980b). Depression manifested by sexual symptoms. *Medical Aspects of Human Sexuality, 14*(12), 87.

Kristof, N.D. (1990, October 28). Beijing condemns pornography as subversive. *New York Times,* International Section, 6.

Kroop, M.S. (1981a). Introital vs. vaginal sensitivity. *Medical Aspects of Human Sexuality, 15*(6), 29.

Kroop, M.S. (1981b). Shallow vs. deep penetration. *Medical Aspects of Human Sexuality, 15*(2), 20.

Kroop, M.S. (1982). Coital positions. *Medical Aspects of Human Sexuality, 16*(3), 99.

Krueger, D.W. (1982). Transvestites. *Medical Aspects of Human Sexuality, 16*(6), 17, 20.

Krueger, D.W. (1984). Transvestites. *Medical Aspects of Human Sexuality, 18*(8), 142, 144.

Knudsin, R.V., Driscoll, S.G., & Pelletier, P.A. (1981). Ureaplasma urealyticum incriminated in perinatal morbidity and mortality. *Science, 213,* 474–476.

Kulik, J.A., & Mahler, H.I.M. (1989). Stress and affiliation in a hospital setting: Preoperative roommate preferences. *Personality and Social Psychology Bulletin, 15,* 183–193.

Kupfer, D.J., Rosenbaum, J.F., & Detre, T.P. (1977). Personality style and sexual functioning among psychiatric outpatients. *Journal of Sex Research, 13,* 257–266.

Kupperman, H. (1983). Hormones to augment penile dimensions. *Medical Aspects of Human Sexuality, 17*(4), 247, 250.

Kupperman, H. (1981). When patients forget to take birth control pills. *Medical Aspects of Human Sexuality, 15*(8), 91–92.

Kurdek, L.A. (1988). Correlates of negative attitudes toward homosexuals in heterosexual college students. *Sex Roles, 18,* 727–738.

Kurdek, L.A. (1989). Relationship quality in gay and lesbian cohabiting couples: A 1-year follow-up study. *Journal of Social and Personal Relationships, 6,* 39–59.

Kurdek, L.A., Blisk, D., & Siesky, A.E., Jr. (1981). Correlates of children's long-term adjustment to their parents' divorce. *Developmental Psychology, 17,* 565–579.

Kurdek, L.A., & Schmitt, J.P. (1987). Partner homogamy in married, heterosexual cohabiting, gay, and lesbian couples. *Journal of Sex Research, 23,* 212–232.

Kuriansky, J.B. (1977). Delaying female climax. *Medical Aspects of Human Sexuality, 11*(11), 37, 93.

Kutchinsky, B. (1985). Pornography and its effects in Denmark and the United States. *Comparative Social Research, 8.*

Kutner, L. (1989a, May 11). The myths of puberty are much exaggerated. *New York Times,* C 8.

Kutner, L. (1989b, October 12). What to expect when a teen-ager starts to date. *New York Times.*

Kuvin, S.F. (1989, April 9). Vaccination can halt epidemic of hepatitis B, a cousin of AIDS. *New York Times,* 24 E.

Kwan, M., VanMaasdam, J., & Davidson, J.M. (1985). Effects of estrogen treatment on sexual behavior in male-to-female transsexuals: Experimental and clinical observations. *Archives of Sexual Behavior, 14,* 29–40.

Kweskin, S.L., & Cook, A.S. (1982). Heterosexual and homosexual mothers' self-described sex-role behavior and ideal sex-role behavior in children. *Sex Roles, 8,* 967–975.

Kyle, G.R. (1989). AIDS and the new sexual order. *Journal of Sex Research, 26,* 276–278.

LaBarbera, J.D. (1984). Seductive father–daughter relationships and sex-roles in women. *Sex Roles, 11,* 941–951.

Labby, D.H. (1983). Iatrogenic effects on sexual function. *Medical Aspects of Human Sexuality, 17*(6), 170–173, 176–178.

LaFerla, J. (1982). Severe genital hygiene problem. *Medical Aspects of Human Sexuality, 16*(11), 188.

LaFerla, J. (1984). When couples stop having intercourse. *Medical Aspects of Human Sexuality, 18*(5), 203.

LaFree, G., Reskin, B., & Visher, C. (1985). Jurors' responses to victims' behavior and legal issues in sexual assault trials. *Social Problems, 32*(4), 389–407.

Lamont, J.A. (1978). Vaginismus. *American Journal of Obstetrics and Gynecology, 131,* 632.

Landers, A. (1980, July 15). Let them call themselves "gay." *Albany Knickerbocker News,* 2-B.

Landers, S. (1986, December). Violence in the wake of AIDS. *APA Monitor.*

Lane, M.E. (1980). Care and inspection of diaphragms. *Medical Aspects of Human Sexuality, 14*(8), 107, 110.

Laner, M.R. (1978). Qualities homosexuals seek in partners. *Medical Aspects of Human Sexuality, 12*(10), 85, 86.

Lange, J.D., Wincze, J.P., Zwick, W., Feldman, S., & Hughes, K. (1981). Effects of demand for performance, self-monitoring of arousal, and increased sympathetic nervous system activity on male erectile response. *Archives of Sexual Behavior, 10,* 443–464.

Langevin, R., Paitich, D., & Russom, A.E. (1985). Are rapists sexually anomalous, aggressive, or both? In R. Langevin (Ed.), *Erotic preference, gender identity, and aggression in men: New research studies* (pp. 17–38). Hillsdale, N.J.: Lawrence Erlbaum.

Langmyhr, G.J. (1981). Quiz: Coital patterns and fertility. *Medical Aspects of Human Sexuality, 15*(1), 12, 14, 19.

Lanning, K.W., & Burgess, A.W. (1989). Child pornography and sex rings. In D. Zillmann & J. Bryant (Eds.), *Pornography: Research advances and policy considerations* (pp. 235–255). Hillsdale, N.J.: Lawrence Erlbaum.

Lantz, H.R., Schultz, M., & O'Hara, M. (1977). The changing American family from the preindustrial to the industrial period: A final report. *American Sociological Review, 42,* 406–421.

L'Armand, K., & Pepitone, A. (1982). Judgments of rape: A study of victim–rapist relationship and victim sexual history. *Personality and Social Psychology Bulletin, 8,* 134–139.

Larrick, R.P., Morgan, J.N., & Nisbett, R.E. (1990). Teaching the use of cost-benefit reasoning in everyday life. *Psychological Science, 1,* 362–370.

Larsen, K.S., Cate, R., & Reed, M. (1983). Anti-black attitudes, religious orthodoxy, permissiveness, and sexual information: A study of the attitudes of heterosexuals toward homosexuality. *Journal of Sex Research, 19,* 105–118.

Larsen, K.S., & LeRoux, J. (1984). A study of same sex touching attitudes: Scale development and personality predictors. *Journal of Sex Research, 20,* 264–278.

Larsen, V.L. (1965). College students and menstrual facts. *Journal of American Medical Woman's Association, 20.*

Lasswell, M. (1983). Marrying too early. *Medical Aspects of Human Sexuality, 17*(7), 20, 22, 24, 25, 29, 32, 41.

Lasswell, M. (1985). Illusions regarding marital happiness. *Medical Aspects of Human Sexuality, 19*(2), 144, 151, 154, 158.

LaTorre, R.A. (1980). Devaluation of the human love object: Heterosexual rejection as a possible antecedent to fetishism. *Journal of Abnormal Psychology, 89,* 295–298.

Lau, S. (1989). Sex role orientation and domains of self esteem. *Sex Roles, 21,* 415–422.

Laudenslager, M.L., & Reite, M.L. (1984). Losses and separations: Immunological consequences and health implications. In P. Shaver (Ed.), *Review of personality and social psychology 5: Emotions, relationships, and health* (pp. 285–312). Beverly Hills, Calif.: Sage.

Lauer, J., & Lauer, R. (1985, June). Marriages made to last. *Psychology Today,* 22–26.

Laukaran, V.H., & Winikoff, B. (1985). Contraceptive use, amenorrhea, and breastfeeding in postpartum women. *Studies in Family Planning, 16,* 293–302.

Laury, G.V. (1978). Influences on childhood sexuality. *Medical Aspects of Human Sexuality, 12*(11), 97–102.

Laury, G.V. (1981). Difficulty in reaching orgasm by aging men. *Medical Aspects of Human Sexuality, 15*(3), 29, 32.

Laury, G.V. (1982). Ejaculatory changes in aging men. *Medical Aspects of Human Sexuality, 16*(8), 136, 145.

Laury, G.V. (1983). Women's negative feelings after intercourse. *Medical Aspects of Human Sexuality, 17*(3), 191, 195.

Lautmann, R. (1981). The pink triangle: The persecution of homosexual males in concentration camps in Nazi Germany. *Journal of Homosexuality, 6*(1/2), 141–160.

Lavrakas, P.J. (1975). Female preferences for male physiques. *Journal of Research in Personality, 9,* 324–334.

Laws, D.R. (1982). Sexual dysfunctions of rapists. *Medical Aspects of Human Sexuality, 16*(6), 171, 175.

Laws, S. (1983). The sexual politics of premenstrual tension. *Women's Studies International Forum, 6,* 19–31.

Lawson, C. (1989, June 15). Toys: Girls still apply make-up, boys fight wars. *New York Times,* C 1, C 10.

Lawson, C. (1990, August 12). Couples' own embryos used in birth surrogacy. *New York Times,* 1, 24.

Leary, W.E. (1988, July 14). Sharp rise in sex-related diseases. *New York Times,* B 6.

Leary, W.E. (1989a, March 10). In vitro fertilization clinics vary widely in success rates. *New York Times,* A 16.

Leary, W.E. (1989b, May 23). Campus AIDS survey finds threat is real but not yet rampant. *New York Times,* C 12.

Leavitt, D. (1990, August 19). Fears that haunt a scrubbed America. *New York Times,* Section 2, 1, 27.

Leavitt, F., & Berger, J.C. (1990). Clinical patterns among male transsexual candidates with erotic interest in males. *Archives of Sexual Behavior, 19,* 491–505.

Leavitt, J.W. (1987). *Brought to bed: Childbearing in America, 1750–1950.* Oxford University Press.

Leboyer, F. (1975). *Birth without violence.* New York: Knopf.

Lee, L. (1984). Sequences in separation: A framework for investigating endings of the personal (romantic) relationships. *Journal of Social and Personal Relationships, 1,* 49–73.

Lee, P.A. (1985). Cryptorchidism. *Medical Aspects of Human Sexuality, 19*(2), 48, 50–52, 56, 59, 62.

Lee, R.B. (1974). Male–female residence arrangements and political power in human hunter-gatherers. *Archives of Sexual Behavior, 3,* 167–173.

Lee, R.V. (1980). The case for chastity. *Medical Aspects of Human Sexuality, 14*(12), 57–58.

Leff, J.J., & Israel, M. (1983). The relationship between mode of female masturbation and achievement of orgasm in coitus. *Archives of Sexual Behavior, 12,* 227–236.

Lehfeldt, H. (1982). Dyspareunia caused by episiotomy. *Medical Aspects of Human Sexuality, 16*(11), 42A, 42F.

Lehman, B.A. (1986, March 20). When sexual desire is gone: Therapy helps. *Albany Times Union,* C-1, C-8.

Lehman, B.A. (1989, March 7). New test for birth defects offers advantages and possible risks. *Albany Times Union,* C-1, C-2.

Lehne, G.K. (1978). Gay male fantasies and realities. *Journal of Social Issues, 34*(3), 28–37.

Leiber, L. (1978). Sexual relationships of cancer patients. *Medical Aspects of Human Sexuality, 12*(5), 139, 144.

Leiblum, R.C., & Rosen, R.C. (Eds.). (1988). *Sexual desire disorders.* New York: Guilford Press.

Leiblum, S.R., & Pervin, L.A. (Eds.) (1980). *Principles and practices of sex therapy.* New York: Guilford Press.

Leigh, B.C. (1989). Reasons for having and avoiding sex: Gender, sexual orientation, and relationship to sexual behavior. *Journal of Sex Research, 26,* 199–209.

Leitenberg, H., Greenwald, E., & Tarran, M.J. (1989). The relation between sexual activity among children during preadolescence and/or early adolescence and sexual behavior and sexual adjustment in young adulthood. *Archives of Sexual Behavior, 18,* 299–313.

Leitenberg, H., & Slavin, L. (1983). Comparison of attitudes toward transsexuality and homosexuality. *Archives of Sexual Behavior, 12,* 337–346.

Leiter, E. (1982). Detecting prostate cancer: Importance of the rectal examination. *Medical Aspects of Human Sexuality, 16*(6), 181–182.

Lemery, C.R. (1983). *Children's sexual knowledge of parent's affective orientation to sexuality and parent–child communication about sex: A causal analysis.* Unpublished master's thesis, University of Western Ontario.

Lemkau, J.P. (1988). Emotional sequelae of abortion. *Psychology of Women Quarterly, 12,* 461–472.

Lennon, M.C. (1987). Is menopause depressing? An investigation of three perspectives. *Sex Roles, 17,* 1–16.

Lentz, S.L., & Zeiss, A.M. (1984). Fantasy and sexual arousal in college women: An empirical investigation. *Imagination, Cognition, and Personality, 3,* 185–202.

Leo, J. (1980). Cacophony in Copenhagen. *Time, 125*(29), 52.

Leo, J. (1983). Waterbeds and willow worlds. *Time, 122*(5), 71.

Leo, J. (1985). Getting a headlock on wedlock. *Time, 126*(19), 96.

Lesbian hails legal ruling restoring daughters. (1981, January 30). *Albany Times Union,* 14.

Leslie, G.R. (1978). Sexual behavior of college men: Today vs. 30 years ago. *Medical Aspects of Human Sexuality, 12*(7), 102, 107, 111, 115.

Lester, D. (1972). Incest. *Journal of Sex Research, 8,* 268–285.

Levenson, R.W., & Gottman, J.M. (1983). Marital interaction: Physiological linkage and affective exchange. *Journal of Personality and Social Psychology, 45,* 587–597.

Levin, A.A., Schoenbaum, S.C., Monson, R.R., & Ryan, K.J. (1980). Association of induced abortion with subsequent pregnancy loss. *Journal of the American Medical Association, 243,* 2495.

Levin, J., & Arluke, A. (1985). An exploratory analysis of sex differences in gossip. *Sex Roles, 12,* 281–286.

Levin, N. (1981). Erogenicity of reconstructed breast. *Medical Aspects of Human Sexuality, 15*(6), 29.

Levin, N. (1984). Toxic shock. *Medical Aspects of Human Sexuality, 18*(9), 200.

Levin, R.J. (1976). Thorarche—a seasonal influence but no secular trend. *Journal of Sex Research, 12,* 173–179.

Levin, R.J., & Wagner, G. (1985). Orgasm in women in the laboratory—Quantitative studies on duration, intensity, latency, and vaginal blood flow. *Archives of Sexual Behavior, 14,* 439–449.

Levine, B. (1990, September 30). The new battle of the sexes. *Albany Times Union,* 3.

Levine, E.M., Gruenewald, D., & Shaiova, C.H. (1976). Behav-ioral differences and emotional conflict among male-to-female transsexuals. *Archives of Sexual Behavior, 5,* 81–86.

Levine, M.P. (1980). Employment discrimination of homosexuals. *Medical Aspects of Human Sexuality, 14*(11), 123–124.

Levine, R. (1959). Gusii sex offenses: A study in social control. *American Anthropologist, 61,* 965–990.

Levine, S. (1987). More on the nature of sexual desire. *Journal of Sex and Marital Therapy, 13,* 35–44.

Levine, S.B., & Shumaker, R.E. (1983). Increasingly Ruth: Toward understanding sex reassignment. *Archives of Sexual Behavior, 12,* 247–261.

Levine, S.B., & Yost, M.A., Jr. (1976). Frequency of sexual dysfunction in a general gynecological clinic: An epidemiological approach. *Archives of Sexual Behavior, 5,* 229–238.

Levinger, G. (1970). Husbands' and wives' estimates of coital frequency. *Medical Aspects of Human Sexuality, 4*(9), 42.

Levinger, G. (1980). Toward the analysis of close relationships. *Journal of Experimental Social Psychology, 16,* 510–544.

Levinger, G. (1988). Can we picture "love"? In R.J. Sternberg & M.L Barnes (Eds.), *The psychology of love* (pp. 139–158). New Haven, CT: Yale University Press.

Levitan, S.A., & Belous, R.S. (1981). Divorce rate appears to be stabilizing. *Medical Aspects of Human Sexuality, 20*(2), 198.

Levitt, E.E. (1980). Duration of intercourse. *Medical Aspects of Human Sexuality, 14*(10), 7.

Levitt, E.E. (1983). Estimating the duration of sexual behavior: A laboratory analog study. *Archives of Sexual Behavior, 12,* 329–335.

Levitt, E.E., Konovsky, M., Freese, M.P. & Thompson, J.F. (1979). Intravaginal pressure assessed by the Kegel perineometer. *Archives of Sexual Behavior, 8,* 425–430.

Levy, G.D. (1989). Developmental and individual differences in preschoolers' recognition memories. The influences of gender schematization and verbal labeling of information. *Sex Roles, 21,* 305–324.

Lewes, K. (1988). *The psychoanalytic theory of male homosexuality.* New York: Simon & Schuster.

Lewin, R. (1981a). Genetic link with human behavior causes stir. *Science, 211,* 373.

Lewin, R. (1981b). Cultural diversity tied to genetic differences. *Science, 212,* 908–910.

Lewin, T. (1988, December 4). Gay groups suggests Marines selectively prosecute women. *New York Times,* 34.

Lewis, C.S. (1960). *The four loves.* New York: Harcourt Brace Jovanovich.

Lewis, J.S. (1986, March 23). Genetic counselors multiply. *New York Times,* Section 12, 22–23.

Lewis, J.W. (1990). Premenstrual syndrome as a criminal defense. *Archives of Sexual Behavior, 19,* 425–441.

Lewis, R.J., & Janda, L.H. (1988). The relationship between adult sexual adjustment and childhood experiences regarding exposure to nudity, sleeping in the parental bed, and parental attitudes toward sexuality. *Archives of Sexual Behavior, 17,* 349–363.

Leyson, J.F.J., & Powell, R.B. (1979). Counseling the female spinal cord–injured patient. *Medical Aspects of Human Sexuality, 13*(7), 59–60.

Licata, S.J. (1981). The homosexual rights movement in the United States: A traditionally overlooked area of American history. *Journal of Homosexuality, 6*(1/2), 161–189.

Lief, H.I. (1979). Status of sex education in medical schools. *Medical Aspects of Human Sexuality, 13*(2), 44.

Lief, H.I. (1980a). Comments on current thinking on the orgasm experience. *Medical Aspects of Human Sexuality, 14*(7), 55, 59, 62.

Lief, H.I. (1980b). Marital disharmony and sexual dysfunction. *Medical Aspects of Human Sexuality, 14*(12), 6.

Lieh-Mak, F., O'Hoy, K.M., & Luk, S.L. (1983). Lesbianism in the Chinese of Hong Kong. *Archives of Sexual Behavior, 12,* 21–30.

Lifton, P.D. (1985). Individual differences in moral development: The relation of sex, gender, and personality to morality. *Journal of Personality, 53,* 306–334.

Lights out. Bankruptcy filing puts Nevada brothel to bed for good. (1990, September 20). *Albany Times Union,* A-4.

Lii, S., & Wong, S. (1982). A cross-cultural study on sex-role stereotypes and social desirability. *Sex Roles, 8,* 481–491.

Lincoln, R. (1984). The pill, breast, and cervical cancer, and the role of progestogens in arterial disease. *Family Planning Perspectives, 16,* 55–63.

Lindzey, G. (1967). Some remarks concerning incest, the incest taboo, and psychoanalytic theory. *American Psychologist, 22,* 1051–1059.

Linker, D.G. (1981). Sources of seminal fluid. *Medical Aspects of Human Sexuality, 15*(11), 40.

Linnet, L., Moller, N.P.H., Bernth-Peterson, N., Ehlers, I., Brandslund, I., & Svehag, S.E. (1982). No increase in arteriolosclerotic retinopathy or activity tests for circulating immune complexes 5 years after vasectomy. *Fertility and Sterility, 37,* 798.

Linton, E. (1982). Vaginal exercises. *Medical Aspects of Human Sexuality, 16*(4), 103.

Linton, E. (1983). Transmission of genital cancer. *Medical Aspects of Human Sexuality, 17*(4), 103.

Linton, E. (1984). First gynecologic examination. *Medical Aspects of Human Sexuality, 18*(2), 280.

Linton, E.B. (1981). Vaginal depth. *Medical Aspects of Human Sexuality, 15*(5), 101.

Linz, D.G., Donnerstein, E., Bross, M., & Chapin, M. (1986). Mitigating the influence of violence on television and sexual violence in the media. In R. Blanchard (Ed.), *Advances in the study of aggression* (Vol. 2, pp. 165–194). New York: Academic Press.

Linz, D.G., Donnerstein, E., & Penrod, S. (1987). The findings and recommendations of the Attorney General's Commission on Pornography. Do the psychological "facts" fit the political fury? *American Psychologist, 42,* 946–953.

Linz, D.G., Donnerstein, E., & Penrod, S. (1988). Effects of long-term exposure to violent and sexually degrading depictions of women. *Journal of Personality and Social Psychology, 55,* 758–768.

Lipnick, R.J., et al. (1986). Oral contraceptives and breast cancer. *Journal of the American Medical Association, 255,* 58–61.

Lipton, D.N., McDonel, E.C., & McFall, R.M. (1987). Heterosexual perception in rapists. *Journal of Consulting and Clinical Psychology, 55,* 17–21.

Lisak, D., & Roth, S. (1988). Motivational factors in nonincarcerated sexually aggressive men. *Journal of Personality and Social Psychology, 55,* 795–802.

Liss, J.L. (1981). Compulsive sex. *Medical Aspects of Human Sexuality, 15*(11), 40–41.

Littlel, L. (1981, August 17). Sad country tunes may turn your brown eyes red. *Albany Times Union,* 1.

Littler-Bishop, S., Seidler-Feller, D., & Opaluch, R.E. (1982). Sexual harassment in the workplace as a function of initiator's status: The case of airline personnel. *Journal of Social Issues, 38*(4), 137–148.

Lloyd, S.A., & Cate, R.M. (1985a). The developmental course of conflict in dissolution of premarital relationships. *Journal of Personality and Social Psychology, 2,* 179–194.

Lloyd, S.A., & Cate, R.M. (1985b). Attributions associated with significant turning points in premarital relationship development and dissolution. *Journal of Social and Personal Relationships, 2*(4), 419–436.

Lobdell, J.E. (1975). Considerations on ritual subincision practices. *Journal of Sex Research, 11,* 16–24.

Lobdell, J.E., & Owsley, D. (1974). The origin of syphilis. *Journal of Sex Research, 10,* 76–79.

Lobitz, W.C., & Baker, E.L. (1979). Group treatment of single males with erectile dysfunction. *Archives of Sexual Behavior, 8,* 127–138.

Lobitz, W.C., & LoPiccolo, J. (1972). New methods in the behavioral treatment of sexual dysfunctions. *Journal of Behaviour Therapy and Experimental Psychiatry, 3,* 265–271.

Lochman, J.E., & Allen, G. (1981). Nonverbal communication of couples in conflict. *Journal of Research in Personality, 15,* 253–269.

Loeb, M.B. (1979). Sex in nursing homes. *Medical Aspects of Human Sexuality, 13*(5), 135.

Logan, T.G. (1975). The vaginal clasp: A method of comparing contractions across subjects. *Journal of Sex Research, 11,* 353–358.

Loh, W.D. (1981). What has reform of rape legislation wrought? *Journal of Social Issues, 37,* 28–52.

Lohr, S. (1988, May 30). F.D.A. move aids tiny company. *New York Times,* 33.

Loos, V.E., Bridges, C.F., & Critelli, J.W. (1987). Weiner's attribution theory and female orgasmic consistency. *Journal of Sex Research, 23,* 348–361.

LoPiccolo, J., & Friedman, J.M. (1988). Broad-spectrum treatment of low sexual desire: Integration of cognitive, behavioral, and systemic therapy. In S.R. Leiblum & R.C. Rosen (Eds.), *Sexual desire disorders.* New York: Guilford Press.

LoPiccolo, J., & Lobitz, W.C. (1972). The role of masturbation in the treatment of orgasmic dysfunction. *Archives of Sexual Behavior, 2,* 163–171.

LoPiccolo, J., & LoPiccolo, L. (1978). *Handbook of sex therapy.* New York: Plenum.

LoPresto, C.T., Sherman, M.F., & Sherman, N.C. (1985). The effects of a masturbation seminar on high school males' attitudes, false beliefs, guilt, and behavior. *Journal of Sex Research, 21,* 142–156.

Lorenz, K. (1966). *On aggression.* New York: Harcourt, Brace, & World.

Loss, P., & Glancy, E.M. (1982). Men who sexually abuse their children. *Medical Aspects of Human Sexuality, 16*(10), 35, 38.

Lott, B. (1985). The devaluation of women's competence. *Journal of Social Issues, 41*(4), 43–60.

Lovelace, L., with M. McGrady. (1980). *Ordeal.* Secaucus, N.J.: Citadel Press.

Lovenheim, B. (1987). Brides at last, *New York, 20*(30), 20–28.

Lowe, S.G. (1982). Birthing chairs make labor easier. *Playgirl, 11*(6), 28.

Lucas, L., Abel, G.G., Mittelman, M.S., & Becker, J.V. (1983). *Pupillometry to determine the sexual preferences of paraphiliacs.* Poster presented to the World Congress of Behavior Therapy, Washington, D.C.

Lumsden, C.J., & Wilson, E.O. (1981). *The channeling of social behavior.* Cambridge, Mass.: Harvard University Press.

Lund, M. (1985). The development of investment and commitment scales for predicting continuity of personal relationships. *Journal of Social and Personal Relationships, 2,* 3–24.

Lupulescu, A.P. (1979). Genital warts. *Medical Aspects of Human Sexuality, 13*(5), 159–160.

Lutz, D.J., Roback, H.B., & Hart, M. (1984). Feminine gender identity and psychological adjustment of male transsexuals and male homosexuals. *Journal of Sex Research, 20,* 350–362.

Lynn, D.B. (1969). *Parental and sex-role identification: A theoretical formulation.* Berkeley, Calif.: McCutcheon Publishing.

Lynn, D.B. (1973). The process of learning parental and sex-role identification. In A.M. Juhasz (Ed.), *Sexual development and behavior: Selected readings* (pp. 78–92). Homewood, Ill.: Dorsey.

Lynn, M. (1989a). Race differences in sexual behavior: A critique of Rushton and Bogaert's evolutionary hypothesis. *Journal of Research in Personality, 23,* 1–6.

Lynn, M. (1989b). Criticisms of an evolutionary hypothesis about race differences: A rebuttal to Rushton's reply. *Journal of Research in Personality, 23,* 21–34.

Lynn, M., & Bolig, R. (1985). Personal advertisements: Sources of data about relationships. *Journal of Social and Personal Relationships, 2,* 377–383.

Lynn, M., & Shurgot, B.A. (1984). Responses to lonely hearts advertisements: Effects of reported physical attractiveness, physique, and coloration. *Personality and Social Psychology Bulletin, 10,* 349–357.

Lynn, S.J., & Rhue, J.W. (1986). The fantasy-prone person: Hypnosis, imagination, and creativity. *Journal of Personality and Social Psychology, 51,* 404–408.

Maccoby, E.E., & Jacklin, C.N. (1974). *The psychology of sex differences.* Stanford, Calif.: Stanford University Press.

MacDonald, A.P., Jr. (1981). Bisexuality: Some comments on research and theory. *Journal of Homosexuality, 6*(3), 21–35.

MacDonald, N.E., Wells, G.A., Fisher, W.A., Warren, W.K., King, M.A., Doherty, J.-A.A., & Bowie, W.R. (1990). High-risk STD/HIV behavior among college students. *Journal of the American Medical Association, 283,* 3155–3169.

MacFarlane, D.F. (1984). Transsexual prostitution in New Zealand: Predominance of persons of Maori extraction. *Archives of Sexual Behavior, 13,* 301–309.

MacKie, J. (1979). Unwanted births: 1/6 of recent growth. *ZPG Reporter, 11*(6), 1.

MacKinnon, C.A. (1979). *Sexual harassment of working women: A case of sex discrimination.* New Haven, Conn.: Yale University Press.

Macklin, E. (1978). Review of research on non-marital cohabitation in the United States. In B.I. Murstein (Ed.), *Exploring intimate life styles.* New York: Springer.

Macklin, E.C. (1983). Effect of changing sex roles on the intimate relationships of men and women. *Marriage and Family Review, 6,* 97–113.

MacNamara, D.E.J. (1981). Prostitution and crime. *Medical Aspects of Human Sexuality, 15*(8), 16.

MacNamara, D.E.J. (1982a). Raped while "high." *Medical Aspects of Human Sexuality, 16*(3), 99.

MacNamara, D.E.J. (1982b). Resisting a rapist. *Medical Aspects of Human Sexuality, 16*(6), 47.

MacNamara, D.E.J. (1982c). Meaning of "sodomy." *Medical Aspects of Human Sexuality, 16*(3), 95.

Macovsky, S.J. (1979, May). Coping with cohabitation. *Money,* 66–68, 70, 72.

MacShane, F. (1985). Into eternity: The life of James Jones, American writer. *The New Republic, 193*(49), 31–34.

Maddock, J. (1982). Simultaneous orgasm. *Medical Aspects of Human Sexuality, 16*(9), 91, 93.

Maddox, B. (1982). Homosexual parents. *Psychology Today, 16*(2), 62, 66–69.

Madorsky, J.G.B. (1983). Sexuality of the physically disabled. *Medical Aspects of Human Sexuality, 17*(7), 45, 48, 53.

Magoun, H.W. (1981). John B. Watson and the study of human sexual behavior. *Journal of Sex Research, 17,* 368–378.

Mahoney, E.R. (1979). Sex education in the public schools: A discriminant analysis of characteristics of pro and anti individuals. *Journal of Sex Research, 15,* 264–275.

Mahoney, E.R. (1980). Religiosity and sexual behavior among heterosexual college students. *Journal of Sex Research, 16,* 97–113.

Maier, R.A., & Lavrakas, P.J. (1984). Attitudes toward women, personality rigidity, and idealized physique preferences in males. *Sex Roles, 11,* 425–433.

Major, B., Carnevale, P.J.D., & Deaux, K. (1981). A different perspective on androgyny: Evaluations of masculine and feminine personality characteristics. *Journal of Personality and Social Psychology, 41,* 988–1001.

Majority of Americans oppose overturning Roe v. Wade and banning abortion outright, polls show. (1989). *Family Planning Perspectives, 21*(3), 138–139.

Malamuth, N.M. (1984). Aggression against women: Cultural and individual causes. In N.M. Malamuth & E. Donnerstein (Eds.), *Pornography and sexual aggression* (pp. 19–52). New York: Academic Press.

Malamuth, N.M. (1986). Predictors of naturalistic sexual aggression. *Journal of Personality and Social Psychology, 46.*

Malamuth, N.M. (1989). The attraction to sexual aggression scale: Part one. *Journal of Sex Research, 26,* 26–49.

Malamuth, N.M., & Check, J.V. (1984). Debriefing effectiveness following exposure to pornographic rape depictions. *Journal of Sex Research, 20,* 1–13.

Malamuth, N.M., & Donnerstein, E. (Eds.). (1984). *Pornography and sexual aggression.* New York: Academic Press.

Malatesta, V.J., Pollack, R.H., Crotty, T.D., & Peacock, L.J. (1982). Acute alcohol intoxication and female orgasmic response. *Journal of Sex Research, 18,* 1–17.

Malatesta, V.J., Pollack, R.H., Wilbanks, W.A., & Adams, H.E. (1979). Alcohol effects on the orgasmic-ejaculatory response in human males. *Journal of Sex Research, 15,* 101–107.

Male lovebug. (1984, May 5). Believe it or not! *Albany Times-Union,* p. 5.

Malinowski, B. (1929). *The sexual life of savages of Northwestern Melanesia.* New York: Halcyon House.

Mamay, P.D., & Simpson, R.L. (1981). Three female roles in television commercials. *Sex Roles, 7,* 1223–1232.

Mandell, A., & Mandell, M. (1967). Suicide and the menstrual cycle. *Journal of the American Medical Association, 200,* 792–793.

Mandell, G.L. (1984). Chancroid. *Medical Aspects of Human Sexuality, 18*(12), 25, 28.

Manson, W.C. (1986). Sexual cyclicity and concealed ovulation. *Journal of Human Evolution, 15,* 21–30.

Mangan, J.A., & Walvin, J. (Eds.). (1987). *Manliness and morality: Middle-class masculinity in Britain and America, 1800–1940.* New York: St. Martin's Press.

Marangoni, C., & Ickes, W. (1989). Loneliness: A theoretical review with implications for measurement. *Journal of Social and Personal Relationships, 6,* 93–128.

Marchant, D.J. (1980). Fundamentals of diagnosing breast disease. *Medical Aspects of Human Sexuality, 14*(7), 29–30.

Marchant, D.J. (1983). Breast anomalies. *Medical Aspects of Human Sexuality, 17*(10), 253–255.

Marciano, T.D. (1977). Upper classes more liberated sexually. *Medical Aspects of Human Sexuality, 11*(11), 98.

Marcil-Gratton, N., & Lapierre-Adamcyk, E. (1983). Sterilization in Quebec. *Family Planning Perspectives, 15,* 73–78.

Margolick, D. (1990, September 26). Divorce court quandary: Is fame property? *New York Times,* B 1, B 3.

Margolin, G., John, R.S., & O'Brien, M. (1989). Sequential affective patterns as a function of marital conflict style. *Journal of Social and Clinical Psychology, 8,* 45–61.

Markman, H.J. (1981). Prediction of marital distress: A 5-year followup. *Journal of Consulting and Clinical Psychology, 49,* 760–762.

Markman, H.J., Floyd, F.J., Stanley, S.M., & Storaasli, R.D. (1988). Prevention of marital distress: A longitudinal investigation. *Journal of Consulting and Clinical Psychology, 56,* 210–217.

Marks, I.M., Cordess, C., & Verde, F. (1988). A notation for sexual activity. *Journal of Sex Research, 25,* 555–562.

Marmar, J.L. (1980). Necessity for millions of sperm. *Medical Aspects of Human Sexuality, 14*(4), 52, 105.

Marmar, J.L. (1981). Man's lack of pleasurable sensation during coitus. *Medical Aspects of Human Sexuality, 15*(8), 87, 91.

Marr, J.S. (1982). How hepatitis B is transmitted sexually. *Medical Aspects of Human Sexuality, 16*(7), 171–172.

Marshall, D.S. (1971). Sexual behavior in Mangaia. In D.S. Marshall & R.C. Suggs (Eds.), *Human sexual behavior* (pp. 103–162). Englewood Cliffs, N.J.: Prentice Hall.

Marshall, E. (1981). Ethical risks in biomedicine. *Science, 212,* 307–309.

Marshall, P., Surridge, D., & Delva, N. (1981). The role of nocturnal penile tumescence in differentiating between organic and psychogenic impotence: The first stage of validation. *Archives of Sexual Behavior, 10,* 1–10.

Marshall, W.L. (1985, September). *The use of pornography by sex offenders.* Paper presented at the U.S. Justice Department Hearings, Houston.

Marshall, W.L., & Barbaree, H.E. (1983). A behavioral perspective of rape. *International Journal of Law and Psychiatry, 7,* 51–77.

Marsiglio, W. (1987). Adolescent fathers in the United States: Their initial living arrangements, marital experience, and educational outcomes. *Family Planning Perspectives, 19,* 240–256.

Marsiglio, W., & Menaghan, E.G. (1987). Couples and the male birth control pill: A future alternative in contraceptive selection. *Journal of Sex Research, 23,* 34–49.

Martin, C.E. (1981). Factors affecting sexual functioning in 60–79-year-old married males. *Archives of Sexual Behavior, 10,* 399–420.

Martin, J.L. (1987). The impact of AIDS on gay male sexual behavior patterns in New York City. *American Journal of Public Health, 75,* 493–496.

Martin, J.O. (1960). A psychological investigation of convicted incest offenders by means of projective techniques. *Dissertation Abstracts, 21,* 241.

Martin, L.M. (1981). Effect of conflict on lovemaking. *Medical Aspects of Human Sexuality, 15*(10), 93.

Martin, L.M., Rodgers, D.A., & Montague, D.K. (1983). Psychometric differentiation of biogenic and psychogenic impotence. *Archives of Sexual Behavior, 12,* 475–485.

Martin, M.W. (1985). Satisfaction with intimate exchange: Gender-role differences and the impact of equity, equality, and rewards. *Sex Roles, 13,* 597–605.

Martin, P.A. (1981). Happy sexless marriages. *Medical Aspects of Human Sexuality, 15*(1), 25.

Martin, P.L. (1980). Sexual desire and response after oophorectomy. *Medical Aspects of Human Sexuality, 14*(7), 115–116.

Martini, F. (1989). *Fundamentals of anatomy and physiology.* Englewood Cliffs, N.J.: Prentice Hall.

Marx, J.L. (1979). Hormones and their effects in the aging body. *Science, 206,* 805–806.

Marx, J.L. (1980). Consensus—more or less—on the Pap smear. *Science, 209,* 672.

Maschhoff, T.A., Fanshier, W.E., & Hansen, D.J. (1976). Vasectomy: Its effect upon marital stability. *Journal of Sex Research, 12,* 295–314.

Masheter, C., & Harris, L.M. (1986). From divorce to friendship: A study of dialectic relationship development *Journal of Social and Personal Relationships, 3,* 177–189.

Masters, W.H., & Johnson, V.E. (1966). *Human sexual response.* Boston: Little, Brown.

Masters, W.H., & Johnson, V.E. (1970). *Human sexual inadequacy.* New York: Little, Brown.

Masters, W.H., & Johnson, V.E. (1976). *The pleasure bond.* New York: Bantam.

Masters, W.H., & Johnson, V.E. (1979). *Homosexuality in perspective.* Boston: Little, Brown.

Masters, W.H., Johnson, V.E., & Kolodny, R.C. (1985). *Human sexuality* (2nd ed.). Boston: Little, Brown.

Mastrosimone, W. (1978). *Extremities.* Garden City, N.Y.: Nelson Doubleday.

Matacin, M.L., & Burger, J.M. (1987). A content analysis of sexual themes in *Playboy* cartoons. *Sex Roles, 17,* 179–186.

Mathes, E.W., Adams, H.E., & Davies, R.M. (1985). Jealousy: Loss of relationship rewards, loss of self-esteem, depression, anxiety, and anger. *Journal of Personality and Social Psychology, 48,* 1552–1561.

Mathew, R.J., & Weinman, M.L. (1982). Sexual dysfunctions in depression. *Archives of Sexual Behavior, 11,* 323–328.

Mathis, J.L. (1981). Iatrogenic sexual disturbances. *Medical Aspects of Human Sexuality, 15*(7), 96, 101, 105, 106, 108.

Maugh, T.H., II. (1981a). Alcohol: The ultimate birth control drug. *Science, 214,* 643–644.

Maugh, T.H., II. (1981b). Male "pill" blocks sperm enzyme. *Science, 212,* 314.

Maugh, T.H.II. (1990, February 19). Love, American style. *Albany Times Union,* A-1, A-12.

Mauldin, W.P. (1980). Population trends and prospects. *Science, 209,* 148–159.

Maxwell, G.M. (1985). Behaviour of lovers: Measuring the closeness of relationships. *Journal of Social and Personal Relationships, 2,* 215–238.

May, J.L., & Hamilton, P.A. (1980). Effects of musically evoked affect on women's interpersonal attraction and perceptual judgments of physical attractiveness of men. *Motivation and Emotion, 4,* 217–228.

Mazor, M.D. (1980). Psychosexual problems of the infertile couple. *Medical Aspects of Human Sexuality, 14*(12), 32, 39, 43, 47, 49.

McAdams, D.P. (1982). Experiences of intimacy and power: Relationships between social motives and autobiographical memory. *Journal of Personality and Social Psychology, 42,* 292–302.

McAdams, D.P., & Powers, J. (1981). Themes of intimacy in behavior and thought. *Journal of Personality and Social Psychology, 40,* 573–587.

McCabe, M.P., & Collins, J.K. (1983). The sexual and affectional attitude and experiences of Australian adolescents during dating: The effects of age, church attendance, type of school, and socioeconomic class. *Archives of Sexual Behavior, 12,* 525–539.

McCaghy, C. (1983). Age of consent. *Medical Aspects of Human Sexuality, 17*(6), 275.

McCaghy, C.H. (1971). Child molesting. *Archives of Sexual Behavior, 1,* 16–24.

McCann, M.F., & Cole, L.P. (1980). Laparoscopy and minilaparatomy: Two major advances in female sterilization. *Studies in Family Planning, 11,* 119–127.

McCarley, R. (1978). Cause of sleep erections. *Medical Aspects of Human Sexuality, 12*(5), 135.

McCarthy, J., & Radish, E.S. (1982). Education and childbearing among teenagers. *Family Planning Perspectives, 14,* 154–155.

McCauley, E.A., & Ehrhardt, A.A. (1980). Sexual behavior in female transsexuals and lesbians. *Journal of Sex Research, 16,* 202–211.

McConaghy, N. (1970). Penile response conditioning and its relationships to aversion therapy in homosexuals. *Behavior Therapy, 1,* 213–221.

McConaghy, N. (1978). Heterosexual experience, marital status, and orientation of homosexual males. *Archives of Sexual Behavior, 7,* 575–581.

McConaghy, N. (1989). Validity and ethics of penile circumference measures of sexual arousal: A critical review. *Archives of Sexual Behavior, 18,* 357–369.

McConnell, J.V. (1974). *Understanding human behavior: An introduction to psychology.* New York: Holt, Rinehart and Winston.

McCormack, A. (1985). The sexual harassment of students by teachers: The case of students in science. *Sex Roles, 13,* 21–32.

McCormack, P. (1980, January 4). Sex creates stress on college campuses. *Albany Knickerbocker News,* p. 1-B.

McCormick, N.B., & Gaeddert, W. (1989). Power in college students' contraceptive decisions. *Archives of Sexual Behavior, 18,* 35–48.

McCoy, N., Cutler, W., & Davidson, J.M. (1985). Relationships among sexual behavior, hot flashes, and hormone levels in perimenopausal women. *Archives of Sexual Behavior, 14,* 385–394.

McCoy, N.N., & D'Agostino, P.A. (1977). Factor analysis of the Sexual Interaction Inventory. *Archives of Sexual Behavior, 6,* 25–35.

McCray, G.M. (1981). Flagrant masturbation by children. *Medical Aspects of Human Sexuality, 15*(2), 60S, 60T.

McCully, R.S. (1976). A Jungian commentary on Epstein's case (wet-shoe fetish). *Archives of Sexual Behavior, 5,* 185–188.

McCurdy, P.R. (1984). Blood transfusion and AIDS. *Medical Aspects of Human Sexuality, 18*(11), 10, 12.

McDonald, G. (1981). Misrepresentation, liberalism, and heterosexual bias in introductory psychology textbooks. *Journal of Homosexuality, 6*(3), 45–60.

McDonald, G.J. (1982). Individual differences in the coming out process for gay men: Implications for theoretical models. *Journal of Homosexuality, 8*(1), 47–60.

McDonald, K. (1988). Sex under glass. *Psychology Today, 22*(3), 58–59.

McDonald, R.H. (1983). Medical hazards of cocaine usage. *Medical Aspects of Human Sexuality, 17*(1), 24C, 24I.

McDonald, P., & McDonald, D. (1978). *53 contributing causes of infidelity.* Milwaukee, Wis.: WISN-TV.

McGee, E. (1982). *Too little, too late: Services for teenage parents.* New York: Ford Foundation.

McGinnis, T. (1981). *More than just a friend: The joys and disappointments of extramarital affairs.* Englewood Cliffs, N.J.: Prentice Hall.

McGloshen, T.H., & O'Bryant, S.L. (1988). The psychological well-being of older, recent widows. *Psychology of Women Quarterly, 12,* 99–116.

McGuire, W.J., McGuire, C.V., & Winton, W. (1979). Effects of household sex composition on the salience of one's gender in the spontaneous self-concept. *Journal of Experimental Social Psychology, 15,* 77–90.

McKenry, P.C. (1979). Success of second marriages. *Medical Aspects of Human Sexuality, 13*(9), 150.

McLaughlin, P.C. (1990, November 12). Sis-boom-bah, humbug. *Albany Times Union,* C–1.

McQuay, D. (1985, December 1). It's hard to identify winners of the sexual revolution. *Albany Times Union,* D–1, D–10.

McSweeney, F.K. & Bierley, C. (1984). Recent developments in classical conditioning. *Journal of Consumer Research, 11,* 619–631.

McWalter, K. (1987, December 6). Couch dancing. *New York Times Magazine,* 138.

McWhirter, D.P., & Mattison, A.M. (1984). *The male couple: How relationships develop.* Englewood Cliffs, N.J.: Prentice Hall.

Mead, M. (1928). *Coming of age in Samoa.* New York: William Morrow.

Mead, M. (1935). *Sex and temperament in three primitive societies.* New York: William Morrow.

Mead, M. (1969). *Sex and temperament in three primitive societies.* New York: Dell.

Meeker, B.F. (1983). Equality and differentiation in time spent in paid work in two-income families. *Sex Roles, 9,* 1023–1033.

Mehrabian, A. (1970). The development and validation of measures of affiliative tendency and sensitivity to rejection. *Educational and Psychological Measurement, 30,* 417–428.

Meiselman, K.C. (1978). *Incest: A psychological study of causes and effects with treatment recommendations.* San Francisco: Jossey-Bass.

Meiselman, K.C. (1980). Personality characteristics of incest history among psychotherapy patients: A research note. *Archives of Sexual Behavior, 9,* 195–197.

Melman, A. (1984). Sexual intercourse: A forerunner of female urinary-tract infections. *Medical Aspects of Human Sexuality, 18*(2), 186, 191, 192.

Melton, G.B., & Gray, J.N. (1988). Ethical dilemmas in AIDS research. *American Psychologist, 54,* 60–64.

Mendelsohn, M.J., & Mosher, D.L. (1979). Effects of sex guilt and premarital sexual permissiveness on role-played sex education and moral attitudes. *Journal of Sex Research, 15,* 174–183.

Mendonsa, E.L. (1981). The status of women in Sisala society. *Sex Roles, 7,* 607–625.

Mercer, G.W., & Kohn, P.M. (1979). Gender differences in the integration of conservatism, sex urge, and sexual behaviors among college students. *Journal of Sex Research, 15,* 129–142.

Merriam, S.B., & Hyer, P. (1984). Changing attitudes of women towards family-related tasks in young adulthood. *Sex Roles, 10,* 825–835.

Messe, M.R., & Geer, J.H. (1985). Voluntary vaginal musculature contractions as an enhancer of sexual arousal. *Archives of Sexual Behavior, 14,* 13–28.

Messenger, J.C. (1971). Sex and repression in an Irish folk community. In D.S. Marshall & R.C. Suggs (Eds.), *Human sexual behavior* (pp. 3–37). Englewood Cliffs, N.J.: Prentice Hall.

Meyer, C.B., & Taylor, S.E. (1986). Adjustment to rape. *Journal of Personality and Social Psychology, 50,* 1226–1234.

Meyer, J.K. (1977). The treatment of sexual dysfunction. *Medical Clinics of North America, 61*(4), 811.

Meyer, J.P., & Pepper, S. (1977). Need compatibility and marital adjustment in young married couples. *Journal of Personality and Social Psychology, 35,* 331–342.

Meyer, W.J., Finkelstein, J.W., Stuart, C.A., Webb, A., Smith, E.R., Payer, A.F., & Walker, P.A. (1981). Physical and hormonal evaluation of transsexual patients during hormonal therapy. *Archives of Sexual Behavior, 10,* 347–356.

Meyer, W.J., III, Webb, A., Stuart, C.A., Finkelstein, J.W., Lawrence, B., & Walker, P.A. (1986). Physical and hormonal evaluation of transsexual patients: A longitudinal study. *Archives of Sexual Behavior, 15,* 121–138.

Meyer-Bahlburg, H.F.L. (1977). Sex hormones and male homosexuality in comparative perspective. *Archives of Sexual Behavior, 6,* 297–325.

Meyer-Bahlburg, H.F.L. (1979). Sex hormones and female homosexuality: A critical examination. *Archives of Sexual Behavior, 8,* 101–119.

Meyer-Bahlburg, H.F.L., Feldman, J.F., Ehrhardt, A.A., & Cohen, P. (1984). Effects of prenatal hormone exposure versus pregnancy complications on sex-dimorphic behavior. *Archives of Sexual Behavior, 13,* 479–495.

Milan, R., & Kilmann, P. (1987). Interpersonal factors in premarital conception. *Journal of Sex Research, 23,* 289–321.

Milan, R.J., Jr., Kilmann, P.R., & Boland, J.P. (1988). Treatment outcome of secondary orgasmic dysfunction: A two- to six-year follow-up. *Archives of Sexual Behavior, 17,* 463–480.

Milardo, R.M., Johnson, M.P., & Huston, T.L. (1983). Developing close relationships: Changing patterns of interaction between pair members and social networks. *Journal of Personality and Social Psychology, 44,* 964–976.

Milic, J.H., & Crowne, D.P. (1986). Recalled parent-child relations and need for approval of homosexual and heterosexual men. *Archives of Sexual Behavior, 15,* 239–246.

Millard, C.E. (1980). Adolescent sexual preoccupations. *Medical Aspects of Human Sexuality, 14*(9), 99–102.

Millen, A.K. (1982). Stretch marks postpartum. *Medical Aspects of Human Sexuality, 16*(8), 126–127.

Millen, A.K. (1983). Lesbian patients. *Medical Aspects of Human Sexuality, 17*(5), 194, 217.

Millen, A.K. (1984). Medication for rape victim. *Medical Aspects of Human Sexuality, 18*(8), 138.

Miller, A., & Byrne, D. (1985). Husband and wife arousal in response to erotica and marital adjustment. *KACD Journal, 5,* 4–12.

Miller, B. (1991, January 9). Birthrate dropped at schools with contraception information. *New York Times,* A 20.

Miller, B.C., Higginson, R., McCoy, J.K., & Olson, T.D. (1987). Family configuration and adolescent sexual attitudes and behavior. *Population and Environment, 9,* 111–123.

Miller, B.C., & Olson, T.D. (1988). Sexual attitudes and behavior of high school students in relation to background and contextual factors. *Journal of Sex Research, 24,* 194–200

Miller, C.T., & Byrne, D. (1978, May). *A possible risk in using contraceptives: Observers' perceptions of contraceptives.* Paper presented at the meeting of the Midwestern Psychological Association, Chicago.

Miller, H.C. (1981). Constriction of scrotum. *Medical Aspects of Human Sexuality, 15*(10), 15, 93.

Miller, H.C. (1984). Deviation of penis on erection. *Medical Aspects of Human Sexuality, 18*(10), 98.

Miller, J. (1986, October 2). Prostitutes convene on rights. *New York Times,* A 10.

Miller, J.A., Jacobsen, R.B., & Bigner, J.J. (1981). The child's home environment for lesbian vs. heterosexual mothers: A neglected area of research. *Journal of Homosexuality, 7*(1), 49–56.

Miller, P.C., Lefcourt, H.M., Holmes, J.G., Ware, E.E., & Saleh, W.E. (1986). Marital locus of control and marital problem solving. *Journal of Personality and Social Psychology, 51,* 161–169.

Miller, W.B. (1976). Sexual and contraceptive behavior in young unmarried women. *Primary Care, 3,* 427–453.

Milner, C., & Milner, R. (1972). *Black players: The secret world of black pimps.* Boston: Little, Brown.

Mincer, J. (1988, November 30). Baby baby boom boom: Later pregnancies mean more twins. *New York Times,* C 1, C 16.

Mindick, B., Oskamp, S., & Berger, D.E. (1977). Prediction of success or failure in birth planning: An approach to prevention of individual and family stress. *American Journal of Community Psychology, 5,* 447–459.

Mirin, S.M. (1981). Methadone and sexual performance. *Medical Aspects of Human Sexuality, 15*(3), 99, 103.

Mirin, S.M. (1982). Adverse sexual effects of cocaine. *Medical Aspects of Human Sexuality, 16*(4), 13–14.

Mirkin, G. (1980). Sexual activity before athletic competition. *Medical Aspects of Human Sexuality, 14*(1), 4, 6.

Mischell, D. (1989). Medical progress: Contraception. *New England Journal of Medicine, 320,* 777–787.

Mitchell, D.E. (1982). Delayed menarche. *Medical Aspects of Human Sexuality, 16*(11), 34E, 34I, 34L.

Money, J. (1976). Gender identity and hermaphroditism. *Science, 191,* 872.

Money, J. (1985, September). *Pornography as related to criminal sex offending and the history of medical degeneracy theory.* Paper presented at the U.S. Justice Department Hearings, Houston.

Money, J. (1986). *Lovemaps: Clinical concepts of sexual/erotic health and pathology, paraphilia, and gender transposition in childhood, adolescence, and maturity.* New York: Irvington.

Money, J. (1987). Sin, sickness, or status? Homosexual gender identity and psychoneuroendocrinology. *American Psychologist, 42,* 384–399.

Money, J., Cawte, J.E., Bianchi, G.N., & Nurcombe, B. (1970). Sex training and traditions in Arnhem Land. *British Journal of Medical Psychology, 43,* 383–399.

Money, J., & Ehrhardt, A. (1972). Prenatal hormonal exposure: Possible effects on behavior in man. In R. Michael (Ed.), *Endocrinology and human behavior.* London: Oxford University Press.

Money, J., Jobaris, R., & Furth, G. (1977). Apotemnophilia: Two cases of self-demand amputation as a paraphilia. *Journal of Sex Research, 13,* 115–125.

Money, J., & Mathews, D. (1982). Prenatal exposure to virilizing progestins: An adult follow-up study of twelve women. *Archives of Sexual Behavior, 11,* 73–83.

Moore, C. (1984). Sexual turnoffs and hypoactive sexual desire. *Medical Aspects of Human Sexuality, 18*(9), 149, 150, 152, 154.

Moore, K.A., Nord, C.W., & Peterson, J.L. (1989). Nonvoluntary sexual activity among adolescents. *Family Planning Perspectives, 21,* 110–114.

Moore, K.L. (1977). *The developing human.* Philadelphia: Saunders.

Moos, R.H. (1969). Typology of menstrual symptoms. *American Journal of Obstetrics and Gynecology, 103,* 390–402.

More sex on TV. (1988). *Psychology Today, 22*(10).

More single women found sexually active. (1988, July 28). *Albany Times Union,* A-8.

Moreland, R.L., & Zajonc, R.B. (1979). Exposure effects may not depend on stimulus recognition. *Journal of Personality and Social Psychology, 37,* 1085–1089.

Moreland, R.L., & Zajonc, R.B. (1982). Exposure effects in person perception: Familiarity, similarity, and attraction. *Journal of Experimental Social Psychology, 18,* 395–415.

Morin, S.F. (1977). Heterosexual bias in psychological research on lesbianism and male homosexuality. *American Psychologist, 32,* 629–637.

Morin, S.F., & Garfinkle, E.M. (1978). Male homophobia. *Journal of Social Issues, 34*(1), 29–47.

Morley, J. (1989). What crack is like. *New Republic, 201*(14), 12–13.

Morokoff, P.J. (1989). Sex bias and POD. *American Psychologist, 44,* 73–78.

Morris, W.N., Worchel, S., Bois, J.L., Pearson, J.A., Rountree, C.A., Samaha, G.M., Wachtler, J., & Wright, S.L. (1976). Collective coping with stress: Group reactions to fear, anxiety, and ambiguity. *Journal of Personality and Social Psychology, 33,* 674–679.

Morrison, E.S., Starks, K., Hyndman, C., & Ronzio, N. (1980). *Growing up sexual.* New York: D. Van Nostrand.

Morton, N.E. (1961). Morbidity of children from consanguinous marriages. In A.G. Steinberg (Ed.), *Progress in medical genetics* (Vol. 1, pp. 261–291). New York: Grune and Stratton.

Morton, R.A., & Hartman, L.M. (1985). A taxonomy of subjective meanings in male sexual dysfunction. *Journal of Sex Research, 21,* 305–321.

Moser, C., & Levitt, E.E. (1987). An exploratory-descriptive study of a sadomasochistically oriented sample. *Journal of Sex Research, 23,* 322–337.

Mosher, D.L. (1968). Measurement of guilt in females by self-report inventories. *Journal of Consulting and Clinical Psychology, 32,* 690–695.

Mosher, D.L. (1971). Sex callousness toward women. In *Technical report of the Commission on Obscenity and Pornography* (Vol. 8, pp. 313–325). Washington, D.C.: U.S. Government Printing Office.

Mosher, D.L. (1979). Sex guilt and sex myths in college men and women. *Journal of Sex Research, 15,* 224–234.

Mosher, D.L. (1980). Three dimensions of depth of involvement in human sexual response. *Journal of Sex Research, 16,* 1–42.

Mosher, D.L. (1981). Reply to Money's, Izard's, and Bullough's comments on Mosher's "Three dimensions of depth of involvement in human sexual response." *Journal of Sex Research, 17,* 179–181.

Mosher, D.L. (1988). Balancing the rights of subjects, scientists, and society: 10 principles for human subject committees. *Journal of Sex Research, 24,* 378–385.

Mosher, D.L. (1989). Advancing sexual science: Strategic analysis and planning. *Journal of Sex Research, 26,* 1–14.

Mosher, D.L., & Anderson, R.D. (1986). Macho personality, sexual aggression, and reactions to guided imagery of realistic rape. *Journal of Research in Personality, 20,* 77–94.

Mosher, D.L., & Cross, H.J. (1971). Sex guilt and premarital sexual experiences of college students. *Journal of Consulting and Clinical Psychology, 36,* 27–32.

Mosher, D.L., & O'Grady, K.E. (1979a). Homosexual threat, negative attitudes toward masturbation, sex guilt, and males' sexual and affective reactions to explicit sexual films. *Journal of Consulting and Clinical Psychology, 47,* 860–873.

Mosher, D.L., & O'Grady, K.E. (1979b). Sex guilt, trait anxiety, and females' subjective sexual arousal to erotica. *Motivation and Emotion, 3,* 235–249.

Mosher, D.L., & Sirkin, M. (1984). Measuring a macho personality constellation. *Journal of Research in Personality, 18,* 150–163.

Mosher, D.L., & Tomkins, S.S. (1988). Scripting the macho man: Hypermasculine socialization and enculturation. *Journal of Sex Research, 25,* 60–84.

Mosher, D.L., & Vonderheide, S.G. (1985). Contributions of sex guilt and masturbation guilt to women's contraceptive attitudes and use. *Journal of Sex Research, 21,* 24–39.

Mosher, D.L., & White, B.B. (1980). Effects of committed or casual erotic guided imagery on females' subjective sexual arousal and emotional response. *Journal of Sex Research, 16,* 273–299.

Mosher, W.D. (1982). Infertility trends among U.S. couples: 1965–1976. *Family Planning Perspectives, 14*(1), 22–27.

Mosher, W.D. (1985). Reproductive impairments in the United States, 1965–1982. *Demography, 22,* 415.

Mosley, J.L. (1984). Turner's syndrome and the H-Y antigen: A response to Silvers, Gasser, and Eicher (1982). *Journal of Sex Research, 20,* 97–101.

Moss, A.R., & Barchett, P. (1989). Natural history of HIV infection. *AIDS, 3,* 55.

Mozley, P.D. (1983). Atrophic vaginitis. *Medical Aspects of Human Sexuality, 17*(1), 76D, 76F, 76H, 76K, 76O.

Muehlenhard, C.L. (1988). Misinterpreted dating behaviors and the risk of date rape. *Journal of Social and Clinical Psychology, 6,* 20–37.

Muehlenhard, C.L., & Cook, S.W. (1988). Men's self-reports of unwanted sexual activity. *Journal of Sex Research, 24,* 58–72.

Mulligan, T., & Moss, C.R. (1991). Sexuality and aging in male veterans: A cross-sectional study of interst, ability, and activity. *Archives of Sexual Behavior, 20,* 17–25.

Mumford, S.D. (1983). The vasectomy decision-making process. *Studies in Family Planning, 14,* 83–89.

Mumford, S.D., Bhiwandiwala, P.P., & Chi, I.C. (1980). Laparoscopic and minilaparotomy female sterilization compared in 15,167 cases. *Lancet, II,* 1066.

Munich, A. (1978). Seduction in academe. *Psychology Today, 11,* 82–108.

Munjack, D.J., & Kanno, P.H. (1979). Retarded ejaculation: A review. *Archives of Sexual Behavior, 8,* 139–150.

Munjack, D.J., Oziel, L.J., Kanno, P.H., Whipple, K., & Leonard, M.D. (1981). Psychological characteristics of males with secondary erectile failure. *Archives of Sexual Behavior, 10,* 123–131.

Munro, H.H. (reprinted 1988). The watched pot. In *The complete works of Saki* (pp. 865–944). New York: Dorset.

Murdock, G.P. (1949). *Social structure.* New York: Macmillan.

Murdock, G.P. (1981). *Atlas of world cultures.* Pittsburgh: University of Pittsburgh Press.

Murnen, S.K. (1985). *Homophobia, erotophobia, and processing information about AIDS.* Unpublished manuscript, University at Albany, State University of New York.

Murnen, S.K., & Byrne, D. (1991). Hyperfemininity: Measurement and initial validation of the construct. *Journal of Sex Research.*

Murnen, S.K., Perot, A., & Byrne, D. (1989). Coping with unwanted sexual activity: Normative responses, situational determinants, and individual differences. *Journal of Sex Research, 26,* 85–106.

Murnen, S.K., & Allgeier, E.R. (1986). *Estimations of parental sexual frequency and parent-child communication.* Manuscript submitted for publication, State University of New York at Albany.

Murphy, E.A. (1978). Inherited baldness. *Medical Aspects of Human Sexuality, 12*(6), 131, 136.

Murphy, J. (1986). The month-after pill. *Time, 128*(26), 64.

Murray, H.W., Hillman, J.K., Rubin, B.Y., et al. (1985). Patients at risk for AIDS-related opportunistic infections. *New England Journal of Medicine, 313,* 1504–1510.

Murray, J., Harvey, S.M., & Beckman, L.J. (1989). The importance of contraceptive attributes among college students. *Journal of Applied Social Psychology, 19,* 1327–1350.

Murray, J.L. (1979). "False pregnancy." *Medical Aspects of Human Sexuality, 13*(3), 133–134.

Murstein, B.I. (1972). Physical attractiveness and marital choice. *Journal of Personality and Social Psychology, 22,* 8–12.

Murstein, B.I. (1974). Sex drive, person perception, and marital choice. *Archives of Sexual Behavior, 3,* 331–348.

Musician's death at 74 reveals he was a woman. (1989, February 2). *New York Times,* A 18.

Myers, D., Jr., Kilmann, P.R., Wanlass, R.L., & Stout, A. (1983). Dimensions of female sexuality: A factor analysis. *Archives of Sexual Behavior, 12,* 159–166.

Myers, J.G. (1981, November). *An investigation of the relationship between marital and sexual satisfaction.* Paper presented at the meeting of the Society for the Scientific Study of Sex, New York.

Myers, L. (1981). Sex researchers and sex myths: A challenge to activism. *Journal of Sex Research, 17,* 84–89.

Myers, M.B., Templer, D.I., & Brown, R. (1984). Coping ability of women who become victims of rape. *Journal of Consulting and Clinical Psychology, 52,* 73–78.

Myers, M.F. (1989). Men sexually assaulted as adults and sexually abused as boys. *Archives of Sexual Behavior, 18,* 203–215.

Myers, R.G., & Berah, E.F. (1983). Some features of Australian exhibitionists compared with pedophiles. *Archives of Sexual Behavior, 12,* 541–547.

Myers, W.A. (1981). Advising parents of a teenage homosexual. *Medical Aspects of Human Sexuality, 15*(6), 92.

Nacci, P.L., & Kane, T.R. (1984). Sex and sexual aggression in federal prisons: Inmate involvement and employee impact. *Federal Probation, 48,* 46–53.

Nachtigall, L.E. (1980). Menopause and hysterectomy. *Medical Aspects of Human Sexuality, 14*(7), 93–96.

Nadelson, C. (1978). Relation of vaginal lubrication to sexual desires. *Medical Aspects of Human Sexuality, 12*(9), 98.

Nadelson, C.C. (1978). The emotional impact of abortion. In M.T. Notman & C.C. Nadelson (Eds.), *The woman patient* (Vol. 1, pp. 173–179). New York: Plenum.

Nahas, G.G. (1981). Marijuana and sex. *Medical Aspects of Human Sexuality, 15*(12), 30, 39.

Nakashima, I.I. (1980). Pregnancy risk vs. frequency of coitus. *Medical Aspects of Human Sexuality, 14*(10), 11.

Nathan, S.G. (1982). Sexual paraphilias of males. *Medical Aspects of Human Sexuality, 16*(11), 35.

Nathanson, C.A., & Becker, M.H. (1980). Obstetricians' attitudes and hospital abortion services. *Family Planning Perspectives, 12,* 26–32.

National Cancer Institute. (1982). Breast self-examination. *Medical Aspects of Human Sexuality, 16*(2), 125–126.

National Cancer Institute. (1989, September). *What you need to know about breast cancer.* Bethesda, MD: U.S. Department of Health and Human Services, Public Health Service, National Institutes of Health.

National Center for Health Statistics. (1987a, June 26). Birth in America: A fact sheet. *New York Times,* A 20.

National Center for Health Statistics. (1987b, December 1). Contraceptive choices. *New York Times,* C 3.

National Research Council Committee on Contraceptive Development. (1990, October). Methods of contraception available outside the U.S. *American Health,* 41.

National survey finds the sexual harassing of students is rising. (1980, October 12). *New York Times,* 47.

Navin, H. (1981). Medical and surgical risks in handballing: Implications of an inadequate socialization process. *Journal of Homosexuality, 6*(3), 67–76.

Navarro, M. (1989, December 7). With AIDS, doctor plans for a trial, not a career. *New York Times,* B 1, B 10.

Neff, L. (1985). Test-tube baby: A mother's diary. *Parents, 60*(10), 119, 187–190, 194–195, 197.

Nelson, B. (1983, August 16). Psychologists determine best ways to talk to assailants. *New York Times,* C 1, C 11.

Nelson, J.A. (1986). Incest: Self-report findings from a nonclinical sample. *Journal of Sex Research, 22,* 463–477.

Nelson, J.B. (1978). *Embodiment: An approach to sexuality and Christian theology.* Minneapolis: Augsburg Publishing.

Nelson, J.H. (1982). Post-pill amenorrhea. *Medical Aspects of Human Sexuality, 16,* 99.

Nelson, J.H. (1983). Women's loss of desire after childbirth. *Medical Aspects of Human Sexuality, 17*(7), 172.

Nemec, E.D., Mansfield, L., & Kennedy, J.W. (1976). Heart rate and blood pressure during sexual activity in normals. *American Heart Journal, 92,* 274.

Nestoros, J.N., Lehmann, H.E., & Ban, T.A. (1981). Sexual behavior of the male schizophrenic: The impact of illness and medications. *Archives of Sexual Behavior, 10,* 421–422.

Nettles, E.J., & Loevinger, J. (1983). Sex role expectations and ego level in relation to problem marriages. *Journal of Personality and Social Psychology, 45,* 676–687.

Neubardt, S. (1981). Vaginal coitus via rear entry. *Medical Aspects of Human Sexuality, 15*(5), 25.

Neuliep, J.W. (1987). Gender differences in the perception of sexist and nonsexist humor. *Journal of Social Behavior and Personality, 2,* 345–351.

Neumann, H.H. (1979). Potential hazards of douching. *Medical Aspects of Human Sexuality, 13*(5), 84.

Nevid, J.S. (1984). Sex differences in factors of romantic attraction. *Sex Roles, 11,* 401–411.

New AIDS test quickens diagnosis. (1989, September 16). *Albany Times Union,* A-8.

Newcomb, M.D. (1986). Sexual behavior of cohabitors: A comparison of three independent samples. *Journal of Sex Research, 22,* 492–513.

Newcomb, M.D., Huba, G.J., & Bentler, P.M. (1986). Determinants of sexual and dating behaviors among adolescents. *Journal of Personality and Social Psychology, 50,* 428–438.

Newcomb, P.R. (1979). Cohabitation in America: An assessment of consequences. *Journal of Marriage and the Family, 41,* 597–603.

Newcomb, T.M. (1961). *The acquaintance process.* New York: Holt, Rinehart and Winston.

Newcomer, S.F., & Udry, J.R. (1985). Parent–child communication and adolescent sexual behavior. *Family Planning Perspectives, 17,* 169–174. (a)

Newcomer, S.F., & Udry, J.R. (1985). Oral sex in an adolescent population. *Archives of Sexual Behavior, 14,* 41–46. (b)

Newman, B.S. (1989). The relative importance of gender role attitudes to male and female attitudes toward lesbians. *Sex Roles, 21,* 451–465.

Newman, H.M. & Langer, E.J. (1981). Post-divorce adaptation and the attribution of responsibility. *Sex Roles, 7,* 223–232.

Newman, J. (1990, October). A brief history of contraception. *American Health,* 38.

Newton, D.E. (1982). A note on the treatment of homosexuality in sex education classes in the secondary school. *Journal of Homosexuality, 8,* 97–99.

Newton, N., & Newton, M. (1978). Psychologic aspects of lactation. *New England Journal of Medicine, 297,* 1180.

Nguyen, M.L., Heslin, R., & Nguyen, T.D. (1976). The meaning of touch: Sex and marital status differences. *Representative Research in Social Psychology, 7,* 13–18.

Nichols, E.K. (1986). *Mobilizing against AIDS.* Cambridge, MA: Harvard University Press.

Nickerson, C.A., & McClelland, G.H. (1987). Beliefs and values and the sterilization decision. *Population and Environment, 9,* 74–95.

Nida, S.A., & Koon, J. (1983). They get better looking at closing time around here, too. *Psychological Reports, 52,* 657–658.

Noble, R.C. (1982). Sexually transmitted diseases common in homosexual men. *Medical Aspects of Human Sexuality, 16*(1), 37, 41.

Noble, R.C. (1984). Causes of vaginal infections due to Candida. *Medical Aspects of Human Sexuality, 18* (8), 144.

Nolan, K. (1988). Sorry, Planned Parenthood. *Playboy, 35*(8), 33.

Noller, P. (1980). Misunderstandings in marital communication: A study of couples' nonverbal communication. *Journal of Personality and Social Psychology, 39,* 1135–1148.

Noller, P. (1981). Gender and marital adjustment level differences in decoding messages from spouses and strangers. *Journal of Personality and Social Psychology 41,* 272–278.

Noller, P. (1985). Negative communications in marriage. *Journal of Social and Personal Relationships, 2,* 289–302.

Norris, J. (1989). Normative influence effects on sexual arousal to nonviolent sexually explicit material. *Journal of Applied Social Psychology, 19,* 341–352.

Norris, J., & Feldman-Summers, S. (1981). Factors related to the psychological impacts of rape on the victim. *Journal of Abnormal Psychology, 90,* 562–567.

Norton, G.R., & Jehu, D. (1984). The role of anxiety in sexual dysfunctions: A review. *Archives of Sexual Behavior, 13,* 165–183.

Norwood, C. (1982). Delivering babies the old-fashioned way. *New York, 15*(8), 66–67.

Nossiter, B.D. (1981, March 16). One in 4 women at U.N. reports sexual harassment. *New York Times,* A 4.

Notelovitz, M. (1978). Coitus as prophylaxis for vaginal atrophy. *Medical Aspects of Human Sexuality, 12*(12), 23.

Novak, D.W., & Lerner, M.J. (1968). Rejection as a consequence of perceived similarity. *Journal of Personality and Social Psychology, 9,* 147–152.

Novicki, D.E. (1983). Involuntary urination with sexual activity. *Medical Aspects of Human Sexuality, 17*(2), 105, 109–110.

Nowinski, J. (1982). Men's reaction to women's anorgasmia. *Medical Aspects of Human Sexuality, 16*(2), 16, 19.

Null, G. (1989, January). AIDS: A man-made plague? *Penthouse,* 160–162, 164–165, 200.

Nurius, P.S. (1983). Mental health implications of sexual orientation. *Journal of Sex Research, 19,* 119–136.

Nyquist, L., Slivken, K., Spence, J.T., & Helmreich, R.L. (1985). Household responsibilities in middle-class couples: The contribution of demographic and personality variables. *Sex Roles, 12,* 15–34.

Oakes, J.R. (1980, August 29). China's people problem. *New York Times,* A 19.

Oaks, R.F. (1981). Defining sodomy in seventeenth-century Massachusetts. *Journal of Homosexuality, 6*(1/2), 79–83.

Obler, M. (1982). A comparison of a hypnoanalytic/behavior modification technique and a cotherapist-type treatment with primary orgasmic dysfuntional females: Some preliminary results. *Journal of Sex Research, 18,* 331–345.

O'Connell, M., & Rogers, C.C. (1982). Differential fertility in the United States: 1976–1980. *Family Planning Perspectives, 14,* 281–287.

O'Connell, M., & Rogers, C.C. (1984). Out-of-wedlock births, premarital pregnancies, and their effect on family formation and dissolution. *Family Planning Perspectives, 16,* 157–170.

O'Conner, J.F., & Flax, C.C. (1981). Retarded ejaculation. *Medical Aspects of Human Sexuality, 15*(10), 93.

O'Conner, J.F., & O'Conner, D.O. (1980). Pleasureless orgasms. *Medical Aspects of Human Sexuality, 14*(3), 122–130.

O'Conner, J.F. & Stern, L.O. (1972). Results of treatment in the behavioral treatment of sexual dysfunctions. *Journal of Behaviour Therapy and Experimental Psychiatry, 3,* 265–271.

Ognibene, F.P. (1984). Complications of AIDS. *Medical Aspects of Human Sexuality, 18*(10), 83.

O'Grady, K.E. (1982a). Affect, sex guilt, gender, and the rewarding–punishing effects of erotic stimuli: A reanalysis and reinterpretation. *Journal of Personality and Social Psychology 43,* 1064–1071.

O'Grady, K.E. (1982b). Sex, physical attractiveness, and perceived risk for mental illness. *Journal of Personality and Social Psychology, 43,* 1064–1071.

Ogus, E.D., Greenglass, E.R., & Burke, R.J. (1990). Gender-role differences, work stress and depersonalization. *Journal of Social Behavior and Personality, 5,* 387–398.

Okum, L. (1986). *Woman abuse: Facts and myths.* Albany, N.Y.: State University of New York Press.

O'Leary, K.D., & Smith, D.A. (1991). Marital interactions. In M.R. Rosenzweig & L.W. Porter (Eds.), *Annual review of psychology,* Vol. 42 (pp. 191–212). Palo Alto, CA: Annual Reviews, Inc.

Oliver, H.G. (1983). Sentencing the sexual offender. *Sexual aggression and the law* (pp. 97–112). Vancouver, B.C.: Criminology Research Centre, Simon Fraser University.

Olson, L. (1983). *Costs of children.* Lexington, Mass.: Lexington Books.

O'Neil, J.M., Helms, B.J., Gable, R.K., David, L., & Wrightsman, L.S. (1986). Gender-role conflict scale: College men's fear of feminity. *Sex Roles, 14,* 335–350.

O'Neill, N., & O'Neill, G. (1972). *Open marriage.* New York: Evans.

Oriel, J.D. (1982). Sex and herpes. *Medical Aspects of Human Sexuality, 16*(10), 34C, 34D, 34K, 34L.

Orinova, G. (1981, November). A woman's-eye view of Russia. *Cosmopolitan,* 194, 196.

Orkin, M. (1984). Pediculosis pubis. *Medical Aspects of Human Sexuality, 18*(1), 47, 50–51.

Orr, M.T., & Forrest. J.D. (1985). The availability of reproductive health services from U.S. private physicians. *Family Planning Perspectives, 17,* 63–69.

Orr, M.T., Forrest, J.D., Johnson, J.H., & Tolman, D.L. (1985). The provision of sterilization services by private physicians. *Family Planning Perspectives, 17,* 217–220.

Ortner, S.B., & Whitehead, H. (Eds.). (1981). *Sexual meanings— The cultural construction of gender and sexuality.* New York: Cambridge University Press.

Ory, H.W. (1983). Mortality associated with fertility and fertility control: 1983. *Family Planning Perspectives, 15,* 57–63.

Ory, H.W., Rosenfeld, A., & Landman, L.C. (1980). The pill at 20: An assessment. *Family Planning Perspectives, 12,* 278–283.

O'Shea, M. (1989, May 7). Guide to better fitness. *Parade,* 12.

Ostling, R.N. (1990, December 17). Fury of a feminist scorned. *Time,* 92.

Oswald, P.J., & Cleary, P.J. (1986). Effects of pelvic muscle tension and expectancy on general and specific indicators of sexual arousal. *Archives of Sexual Behavior, 15,* 247–260.

Oziel, L.J. (1978). Treating retarded ejaculation in the male. *Medical Aspects of Human Sexuality, 12*(11), 111–112.

Packer, C. (1979). Inter-troop transfer and inbreeding avoidance in *Papio anubis. Animal Behavior, 27,* 1–36.

Padilla, E.R., & O'Grady, K.E. (1983). *Sexuality among Mexican-Americans: An empirical approach.* Unpublished manuscript, University of New Mexico.

Paitich, D., Langevin, R., Freeman, R., Mann, K., & Handy, L. (1977). The Clarke SHQ: A clinical sex history questionnaire for males. *Archives of Sexual Behavior, 6,* 421–436.

Palmer, C.T. (1988). Twelve reasons why rape is not sexually motivated: A skeptical examination. *Journal of Sex Research, 25,* 512–530.

Paloutzian, R.F., & Ellison, C.W. (1979, May). *Emotional, behavioral, and physical correlates of loneliness.* Paper presented at the UCLA Research Conference on Loneliness, Los Angeles.

Paluszny, M.J. (1982). Fear of homosexuality as a cause of marriage. *Medical Aspects of Human Sexuality, 16*(5), 63, 93.

Panter, G.G. (1980). What starts labor? *Parents, 55*(10), 94, 96.

Panter, G.G. (1981a). Confirming your pregnancy. *Parents, 56*(5), 88, 91.

Panter, G.G. (1981b). Varicose veins and hemorrhoids. *Parents, 56*(11), 120, 122.

Panter, G.G. (1981c). Endometritis—postpartum infection. *Parents, 56*(12), 78, 80.

Panter, G.G. (1981d). Circumcision: Making the choice. *Parents, 7,* 82, 84.

Panter, G.G. (1982). Nausea and vomiting in pregnancy. *Parents, 57*(1), 74, 76.

Parachini, A. (1989, February 18). U.S. warns of condom failure more emphatically than before. *Albany Times Union,* A-6.

Parlee, M.B. (1974). Stereotypic beliefs about menstruation: A methodological note on the Moos menstrual distress questionnaire and some new data. *Psychosomatic Medicine, 36,* 229–240.

Parrot, A. (1989). *A comparison of acquaintance rape patterns and services in rural and urban colleges in New York State.* Paper presented at the meeting of the Society for the Scientific Study of Sex.

Pasnau, R.O. (1978). Psychosexual impact of mastectomy. *Medical Aspects of Human Sexuality, 12*(12), 108–109.

Passmore, J. (1980). Sex education. *New Republic, 183*(14), 27–32.

Patterson, M.L., Jordan, A., Hogan, M.B., & Frerker, D. (1981). Effects of nonverbal intimacy on arousal and behavioral adjustment. *Journal of Nonverbal Behavior, 5,* 184–198.

Patterson, M.L., Powell, J.L., & Lenihan, M.G. (1986). Touch, compliance, and interpersonal affect. *Journal of Nonverbal Behavior, 10,* 41–50.

Paul, R. (1988, April 24). Sex education manual prompts moral outrage. *New York Times,* 39.

Paulsen, C.A. (1981). Male taking the "pill." *Medical Aspects of Human Sexuality, 15,* 14.

Pauly, I.B. (1974). Female transsexualism: Part I. *Archives of Sexual Behavior, 3,* 487–507.

Pauly, I.B. (1974). Transsexualism. In D.R. Laub & P. Gandy (Eds.), *Proceedings of the second interdisciplinary symposium on gender dysphoria syndrome* (pp. 49–55), Stanford, CA.

Paxton, A.L., & Turner, E.J. (1978). Self-actualization and sexual permissiveness, satisfaction, prudishness, and drive among female undergraduates. *Journal of Sex Research, 14,* 65–80.

Peel, J., & Potts, M. (1970). *Textbook of contraceptive practice.* Cambridge, Mass.: Cambridge University Press.

Peking posters accuse aide's son. (1980, January 10). *New York Times,* A 4.

Pelletier, L.A., & Herold, E.S. (1988). The relationship of age, sex guilt, and sexual experience with female sexual fantasies. *Journal of Sex Research, 24,* 250–256.

Pennebaker, J.W., Dyer, M.A., Caulkins, R.S., Litowitz, D.L., Ackerman, P.L., Anderson, D.B., & McGraw, K.M. (1979). Don't the girls get prettier at closing time: A country and western application to psychology. *Personality and Social Psychology Bulletin, 5,* 122–125.

Pepitone-Rockwell, F. (1979). Dissuading a rapist. *Medical Aspects of Human Sexuality, 13*(6), 39–40.

Pepitone-Rockwell, F. (1980). Counseling women to be less vulnerable to rape. *Medical Aspects of Human Sexuality, 14*(1), 145–146.

Peplau, L.A., & Cochran, S.D. (1981). Value orientations in the intimate relationships of gay men. *Journal of Homosexuality, 6*(3), 1–19.

Peplau, L.A., Padesky, C., & Hamilton, M. (1982). Satisfaction in lesbian relationships. *Journal of Homosexuality, 8*(2), 23–35.

Peplau, L.A., Rubin, Z., & Hill, C.T. (1977). Sexual intimacy in dating relationships. *Journal of Social Issues, 33*(2), 86–109.

Perdue, C.W., & Gurtman, M.B. (1990). Evidence for the automaticity of ageism. *Journal of Experimental Social Psychology, 26,* 199–216.

Perkins, M.W. (1981). Female homosexuality and body build. *Archives of Sexual Behavior, 10,* 337–345.

Perlman, D., Josephson, W., Hwang, W.T., Begum, H., & Thomas, T.L. (1978). Cross-cultural analysis of students' sexual standards. *Archives of Sexual Behavior, 7,* 545–558.

Perlman, S.D., & Abramson, P.R. (1981). *Sexual satisfaction in married and cohabiting individuals.* Unpublished manuscript, University of California, Los Angeles.

Perlmutter, J.F. (1981). Foreplay. *Medical Aspects of Human Sexuality, 15*(8), 56E, 56H, 56I, 56M.

Perper, T., & Weis, D.L. (1987). Proceptive and rejective strategies of U.S. and Canadian college women. *Journal of Sex Research, 23,* 455–480.

Perrucci, C.C., Potter, H.R., & Rhoads, D.L. (1978). Determinants of male family-role performance, *Psychology of Women Quarterly, 3,* 53–66.

Perry, J.D., & Whipple, B. (1981). Pelvic muscle strength of female ejaculators: Evidence in support of a new theory of orgasm. *Journal of Sex Research, 17,* 22–39.

Peters, B. (1988). *Terrific sex in fearful times.* New York: St. Martin's Press.

Peterson, J., Kretchmer, A., Nellis, B., Lever, J., & Hertz, R. (1983, March). The *Playboy* readers' sex survey, Part 2. *Playboy,* 90–92, 178–184.

Peterson, R. (1981). Marijuana now more potent. *Medical Aspects of Human Sexuality, 15*(12), 20.

Peterson, R.A. (1983). Attitudes toward the childless spouse. *Sex Roles, 9,* 321–331.

Pettiti, D.B. (1982, November). *Atherosclerotic disease in men 10 or more years after vasectomy.* Paper presented at the meeting of the Associaiton of Planned Parenthood Professionals, Baltimore.

Pfaus, J.G., Myronuk, L.D.S., & Jacobs, W.J. (1986). Soundtrack contents and depicted sexual violence. *Archives of Sexual Behavior, 15,* 231–237.

Pfeffer, W.H. (1980). An approach to the diagnosis and treatment of the infertile female. *Medical Aspects of Human Sexuality, 14*(4), 121–122.

Pfost, K.S., Lum, C.U., & Stevens, M.J. (1989). Feminity and work plans protect women against postpartum dysphoria. *Sex Roles, 21,* 423–431.

Philliber, S.G. (1980). Socialization for childbearing. *Journal of Social Issues, 36*(1), 30–44.

Philliber, S.G., & Philliber, W.W. (1985). Social and psychological perspectives on voluntary sterilization: A review. *Studies in Family Planning, 16*(1), 1–28.

Phillips, D., Fischer, S.C., Groves, G.A.,& Singh, R. (1976). Alternative behavioral approaches to the treatment of homosexuality. *Archives of Sexual Behavior, 5,* 223–228.

Phillips, R. (1981, November 1). Incest. *Albany Times Union,* E-1, E-7.

Phillis, D.E., & Gromko, M.H. (1985). Sex differences in sexual activity: Reality or illusion? *Journal of Sex Research, 21,* 437–448.

Piaget, J. (1951). *Plays, dreams, and imitation in childhood.* New York: W.W. Norton.

Piaget, J. (1965). *The moral judgment of the child.* New York: Free Press.

PID risk increased sharply among IUD users, British cohort, U.S. case-control studies affirm. (1981). *Family Planning Perspectives, 13*(4), 183–184.

Pietropinto, A., & Simenauer, J. (1981). *Husbands and wives.* New York: Berkeley Books.

Pike, G.R., & Sillars, A.L. (1985). Reciprocity of marital communication. *Journal of Social and Personal Relationships, 2,* 303–324.

Pillard, R.C., Poumadere, J., & Carretta, R.A. (1981). Is homosexuality familial? A review, some data, and a suggestion. *Archives of Sexual Behavior, 10,* 465–475.

Pillard, R.C., Poumadere, J., & Carretta, R.A. (1982). A family study of sexual orientation. *Archives of Sexual Behavior, 11,* 511–520.

Pines, A., & Aronson, E. (1983). Antecedents, correlates, and consequences of sexual jealousy. *Journal of Personality, 51,* 108–136.

Pirke, K.M., Kockott, G., Aldenhoff, J., Besinger, U., & Feil, W. (1979). Pituitary gonadal system function in patients with erectile impotence and premature ejaculation. *Archives of Sexual Behavior, 8,* 41–48.

Pisano, M.D., Wall, S.M., & Foster, A. (1986). Perceptions of nonreciprocal touch in romantic relationships. *Journal of Nonverbal Behavior, 10* 29–40.

Pittenger, J.B., Mark, L.S., & Johnson, D.F. (1989). Longitudinal stability of facial attractiveness. *Bulletin of the Psychonomic Society, 27,* 171–174.

Planned Parenthood. (1986). *How to talk with your child about sexuality.* New York: Doubleday.

Playboy interview: Donald Sutherland. (1981, October). *Playboy.*

Pleak, R.R., & Meyer-Bahlburg, H.F.L. (1990). Sexual behavior and AIDS knowledge of young male prostitutes in Manhattan. *Journal of Sex Research, 27,* 557–587.

Plomin, R. (1990). *Nature and nurture: An introduction to human behavior genetics.* Pacific Grove, CA: Brooks/Cole.

Pocs, O., & Godow, A.G. (1977). Can students view parents as sexual beings? *The Family Coordinator, 26,* 31–36.

Polit, D.F., & Kahn, J.R. (1985). Project Redirection: Evaluation of a comprehensive program for disadvantaged teenage mothers. *Family Planning Perspectives, 17,* 150–155.

Pollitt, K. (1990). Georgie Porgie is a bully. *Time, 136*(19), 24.

Pomeroy, W.B. (1966). The Masters-Johnson report and the Kinsey tradition. In R. Brecher & E. Brecher (Eds.), *An analysis of human sexual response.* Boston: Little, Brown.

Pomeroy, W.B. (1972). *Dr. Kinsey and the Institute for Sex Research.* New York: Harper & Row.

Pomeroy, W.B. (1980). Prostitutes' refusal to kiss. *Medical Aspects of Human Sexuality, 14*(9), 14.

Pomeroy, W.B., Flax, C.C., & Wheeler, C.C. (1981). *Taking a sex history: Interviewing and recording.* Riverside, N.J.: Free Press.

Pope, K.S., Keith-Spiegel, P., & Tabachnick, B.B. (1986). Sexual attraction to clients: The human therapist and the (sometimes) inhuman training system. *American Psychologist, 41,* 147–158.

Porterfield, E. (1973). Mixed marriage. *Psychology Today, 7*(1), 71–78.

Potkay, C.E., Potkay, C.R., Boynton, G.J., & Klingbeil, J.A. (1982). Perceptions of male and female comic strip characters using the adjective generation technique (AGT). *Sex Roles, 8,* 185–200.

Potterat, J.J., Phillips, L., Rothenberg, R.B., & Darrow, W.W. (1985). On becoming a prostitute: An exploratory case-comparison study. *Journal of Sex Research, 21* 329–335.

Potts, M., & Wheeler, R. (1981). The quest for a magic bullet. *Family Planning Perspectives, 13,* 269–271.

Power, T.G., & Parke, R.D. (1984). Social network factors and the transition to parenthood. *Sex Roles, 10,* 949–972.

Prager, K.J. (1976). Intimacy status: Its relationship to locus of control, self-disclosure, and anxiety in adults. *Personality and Social Psychology Bulletin, 12,* 91–109.

Prager, K.J., & Bailey, J.M. (1985). Androgyny, ego development, and psychosocial crisis. *Sex Roles, 13,* 525–536.

Pratt, W.F., Mosher, W.D., Bachrach, C.A., & Horn, M.C. (1984). Understanding U.S. fertility: Findings from the National Survey of Family Growth, Cycle III. *Population Bulletin, 39.*

Prendergast, A. (1990, October). Beyond the pill. *American Health,* 37–44.

Price, S.C., Reynolds, B.S., Cohen, B.D., Anderson, A.J., & Schochet, B.V. (1981). Group treatment of erectile dysfunction for men without partners: A controlled evaluation. *Archives of Sexual Behavior, 10,* 253–268.

Primov, G., & Kieffer, C. (1977). The Peruvian brothel as sexual dispensary and social arena. *Archives of Sexual Behavior, 6,* 245–253.

Prior, J.C., Vigna, Y.M., & Watson, D. (1989). Spironolactone with physiological female steroids for presurgical therapy of male-to-female transsexualism. *Archives of Sexual Behavior, 18,* 49–57.

Prison condom policy draws fire. (1989, September 19). *Albany Times Union,* B-3.

Procci, W.R. (1981). Benefits of nonorgasmic sex. *Medical Aspects of Human Sexuality, 15*(4), 90, 95, 99, 103, 107.

Procci, W.R. (1982). Women exhibitionists. *Medical Aspects of Human Sexuality, 16*(8), 17, 23.

Procci, W.R., & Martin, D.J. (1984). Preliminary observations of the utility of portable NPT. *Archives of Sexual Behavior, 13,* 569–580.

Procci, W.R., Moss, H.B., Boyd, J.L., & Baron, D.A. (1983). Consecutive-night reliability of portable nocturnal penile tumescence monitor. *Archives of Sexual Behavior, 12,* 307–316.

Pryor, J.B. (1985). The lay person's understanding of sexual harassment. *Sex Roles, 13,* 273–286.

Przybyla, D.P.J., & Byrne, D. (1981). Sexual relationships. In S. Duck & R. Gilmour (Eds.), *Personal relationships 1: Studying personal relationships* (pp. 109–130). New York: Academic Press.

Przybyla, D.P.J., & Byrne, D. (1984). The mediating role of cognitive processes in self-reported sexual arousal. *Journal of Research in Personality, 18,* 54–63.

Przybyla, D.P.J., & Byrne, D. (1989). *The negative response of college students to geriatric sex.* Unpublished manuscript, University at Albany, State University of New York.

Przybyla, D.P.J., Byrne, D., & Allgeier, E.R. (1988) Sexual attitudes as correlates of sexual details in human figure drawing. *Archives of Sexual Behavior, 17,* 99–105.

Przybyla, D.P.J., Murnen, S.K, & Byrne, D. (1985). *Arousal and attraction: Anxiety reduction, misattribution, or response strength?* Unpublished manuscript, University at Albany, State University of New York.

Purnick, J.H. (1979, November 9). WNYC may discontinue broadcasts of "John Hour." *New York Times,* B 3.

Pursell, S., Banikiotes, P.G., & Sebastian, R.F. (1981). Androgyny and the perception of marital roles. *Sex Roles, 7,* 201–215.

Pusey, A.E. (1980). Inbreeding avoidance in chimpanzees. *Animal Behavior, 28,* 543–552.

Putrosky, S. (1981, June 8). Dial H for help. *New York,* 38–39.

Quindlen, A. (1987, March 4). Life in the 30s. The name is mine: This is why I have never changed it. *New York Times,* C 12.

Quindlen, A. (1990, October 7). Hearing the cries of crack. *New York Times,* E 19.

Quinn, R.W. (1981). Patterns shifting in STDs. *Medical Aspects of Human Sexuality, 15*(12), 20.

Quinn, R.W. (1982a). Dormancy of sexually transmitted diseases. *Medical Aspects of Human Sexuality, 16*(7), 161–162.

Quinn, R.W. (1982b). Latent trichomoniasis. *Medical Aspects of Human Sexuality, 16*(11), 39.

Quinsey, V.L. (1983). Prediction of recidivism and the evaluation of treatment programs for sex offenders. In S.N. Verdun-Jones & A.A. Keltner (Eds.), *Sexual aggression and the law.* Ottawa: Criminology Research Centre.

Quinsey, V.L., & Chaplin, T.C. (1984). Stimulus control of rapists' and non-sex offenders' sexual arousal. *Behavioral Assessment, 6,* 169–176.

Raboch, J. (1984). The sexual development and life of female schizophrenic patients. *Archives of Sexual Behavior, 13,* 341–349.

Raboch, J., & Bartok, V. (1980). Changes in the sexual life of Czechoslovak women born between 1911 and 1958. *Archives of Sexual Behavior, 9,* 495–502.

Raboch, J., Mellan, J., & Starka, L. (1977). Adult cryptorchids: Sexual development and activity. *Archives of Sexual Behavior, 6,* 413–419.

Rachman, S. (1966). Sexual fetishism: An experimental analogue. *Psychological Record, 16,* 293–296.

Rachman, S. & Hodgson, R.J. (1968). Experimentally induced "sexual fetishism": Replication and development. *Psychological Record, 18,* 25–27.

Rachman, S.J. , & Wilson, G.T. (1980). *The effects of psychological therapy* (2nd ed.). New York: Pergamon Press.

Rada, R.T. (1978a). *Clinical aspects of the rapist.* New York: Grune & Stratton.

Rada, R.T. (1978b). Resisting rape attempts. *Medical Aspects of Human Sexuality, 12,* 65.

Rader, G.E., Bekker, L.D., Brown, L., & Richardt, C. (1978). Psychological correlates of unwanted pregnancy. *Journal of Abnormal Psychology, 87,* 373–376.

Radwanska, E. (1980) Regimens to induce ovulation. *Medical Aspects of Human Sexuality, 14*(3), 111.

Raeburn, P. (1988, October 14). Acne drug as harmful to fetus as thalidomide. *Albany Times Union,* B-12.

Raeburn, P. (1989, September 19). One in 24 inmates infected with AIDS. *Albany Times Union,* A-1, A-8.

Rajashekhar, T.P. (1979). Phantom breast in mastectomized women. *Medical Aspects of Human Sexuality, 13*(8), 93.

Ramey, E. (1972, Spring). Men's cycles (they have them too, you know). *Ms. Magazine,* 8–14.

Rand, C., Graham, D.L.R., Rawlings, E.I. (1982). Psychological health and factors the court seeks to control in lesbian mother custody trials. *Journal of Homosexuality, 8*(1), 27–39.

Rand, C.S.W. (1982). Hedonism. *Medical Aspects of Human Sexuality, 16*(11), 125–128.

Randolph, B.J., & Winstead, B. (1988). Sexual decision making and object relations theory. *Archives of Sexual Behavior, 17,* 389–409.

Ranke-Heinemann, U. (1990). *Eunuchs for the Kingdom of Heaven.* New York: Doubleday.

"Rapist gets life as suicide's tape is heard." (1979, October 10). *New York Times,* A-10.

Ravenson, T.A. (1981). Coping with loneliness: The impact of causal attributions. *Personality and Social Psychology Bulletin, 7,* 565–571.

Read, K.E. (1980). Other voices: The style of a male homosexual tavern. Novato, Calif.: Chandler and Sharp.

Reage, P. (1965). *Story of O.* New York: Grove Press.

Reamy, K.J., & White, S.E. (1987). Sexuality in the puerperium: A review. *Archives of Sexual Behavior, 16,* 165–186.

Redondi, P. (1987). *Galileo heretic.* Princeton, N.J.: Princeton University Press.

Reece, R., & Segrist, A.E. (1981). The association of selected "masculine" sex-role variables with length of relationship in gay male couples. *Journal of Homosexuality,* 7(1), 33–47.

Reed, D., & Weinberg, M.S. (1984). Premarital coitus: Developing and establishing sexual scripts. *Social Psychology Quarterly, 47,* 129–138.

Reed, J. (1870). *Man and woman.* Boston: Nichols and Noyes.

Reeder, G.D., & Coovert, M.D. (1986). Revising an impression of morality. *Social Cognition, 4,* 1–17.

Reevy, W.R. (1972). Petting experience and marital success: A review and statement. *Journal of Sex Research, 8,* 48–60.

Reichelt, P.A. (1978). Changes in sexual behavior among unmarried teenage women utilizing oral contraception. *Journal of Population, 1,* 57–68.

Reichelt, P.S. (1986). Public policy and public opinion toward sex education and birth control for teenagers. *Journal of Applied Social Psychology, 16,* 95–106.

Reid, R., Stanhope, C.R., Herschman, B.R. (1982). Genital warts and cervical cancer. *Cancer, 50,* 377.

Reilly, T., Carpenter, S., Dull, V., & Bartlett, K. (1982). The factorial survey: An approach to defining sexual harassment on campus. *Journal of Social Issues, 38*(4), 99–110.

Reindollar, R.H., & McDonough, P.G. (1981). Sexual infantilism in girls. *Medical Aspects of Human Sexuality, 15*(11), 84, 86, 91, 97.

Reinhold, R. (1980, February 23). Virginia hospital's chief traces 50 years of sterilizing the "retarded." *New York Times,* 6.

Reinisch, J. (1984, April 19). "Natural" birth control often fails. *Albany Times Union,* B-7.

Reis, H.T., Nezlek, J., & Wheeler, L. (1980). Physical attractiveness in social interaction: *Journal of Personality and Social Psychology, 38,* 604–617.

Reis, H.T., Wheeler, L., Spiegel, N., Kernis, M.H., Nezlek, J., & Perri, M. (1982). Physical attractiveness in social interaction: II. Why does appearance affect social experience? *Journal of Personality and Social Psychology, 54,* 979–996.

Reis, J., & Herz, E.J. (1989). An examination of young adolescents' knowledge of and attitude toward sexuality according to perceived contraceptive responsibility. *Journal of Applied Social Psychology, 19,* 231–250.

Reiss, I.L. (1960). *Premarital sexual standards in America.* New York: Free Press.

Reiss, I.L. (1967). *The social context of premarital permissiveness.* New York: Holt, Rinehart and Winston.

Reiss, I.L. (1990). *An end to shame: Shaping our next sexual revolution.* Buffalo, N.Y.: Prometheus.

Reiss, I.L., & Miller, B.C. (1979). Heterosexual permissiveness: A theoretical analysis. In W.R. Burr, R. Hill, F.I. Nye, & I.L. Reiss (Eds.), *Contemporary theories about the family: Vol. 1, Research based theories* (pp. 57–100). New York: Free Press.

Reiter, E.O. (1981). Delayed puberty in boys. *Medical Aspects of Human Sexuality, 15*(1), 79–80.

Renshaw, D.C. (1982). Divorce and loneliness. *Medical Aspects of Human Sexuality, 16*(7), 23–25, 29–32.

Renshaw, D.C. (1984). Effects of diabetes on female sexuality. *Medical Aspects of Human Sexuality, 18*(4), 235, 238, 243.

Research and Forecasts, Inc. (1981). *The Connecticut Mutual Life report on American values in the '80s: The impact of belief.* Hartford, Conn: Connecticut Mutual Life Insurance Co.

Researchers confirm induced abortion to be safer for women than childbirth; refute claims of critics. (1982). *Family Planning Perspectives, 14,* 271–272.

Resick, P.A., Calhoun, K.S., Atkeson, B.M., & Ellis, E.M. (1981). Social adjustment in victims of sexual assault. *Journal of Consulting and Clinical Psychology, 49,* 705–712.

Resnick, L., diMarzo-Veronese, F., Schupbach, J., et al. (1985). Intra-blood-brain barrier synthesis of HTLV-III-specific IgG in patients with neurologic symptoms associated with AIDS or AIDS-related complex. *New England Journal of Medicine, 313,* 1498–1504.

Reyniak, J.V. (1983). Third nipple. *Medical Aspects of Human Sexuality, 17*(5), 218.

Reyniak, J.V. (1984). Onset of fertility in girls. *Medical Aspects of Human Sexuality, 18*(2), 278–280.

Rhoden, N.K. (1985). Late abortion and technological advances in fetal viability. *Family Planning Perspectives, 17,* 160–164.

Richards, J.M. (1978). An ecological analysis of the impact of the U.S. Supreme Court's 1973 abortion decision. *Journal of Applied Social Psychology, 8,* 15–28.

Richissin, T. (1987, August 3). Hot-tub history. Ancient brothel found in Israel resort town. *Albany Times Union,* A-12.

Richwald, G.A., Morisky, D.E., Kyle, G.R., Kristal, A.R., Gerber, M.M., & Friedland, J.M. (1988). Sexual activities in bathhouses in Los Angeles County: Implications for AIDS prevention education. *Journal of Sex Research, 25,* 169–180.

Riding, A. (1990, February 28). France is to pay 80 percent of cost of abortion pill. *New York Times,* A 7.

Ridley, C.A., & Nelson, R.R. (1985). The behavioral effects of training premarital couples in mutual problem-solving skills. *Journal of Social and Personal Relationships, 1,* 197–210.

Rierdan, J., & Koff, E. (1984). Age at menarche and cognitive functioning. *Bulletin of the Psychonomic Society, 22,* 174–176.

Riggio, R.E. (1986). Assessment of basic social skills. *Journal of Personality and Social Psychology, 51,* 649–660.

Riggio, R.E., & Friedman, H.S. (1986). Impression formation: The role of expressive behavior. *Journal of Personality and Social Psychology, 50,* 421–427.

Riggio, R.E., & Woll, S.B. (1984). The role of nonverbal cues and physical attractiveness in the selection of dating partners. *Journal of Social and Personal Relationships, 1,* 347–357.

Riggs, W.M. (1979). Postcoital urination and VD prophylaxis. *Medical Aspects of Human Sexuality, 13*(2), 38.

Rindfuss, R.R., Gortmaker, S.L., & Ladinsky, J.L. (1978). Elective induction and stimulation of labor and the health of the infant. *American Journal of Public Health, 68,* 872.

Rindfuss, R.R., Ladinsky, J.L., Coppock, E., Marshall, V.W., & Macpherson, A.S. (1979). Convenience and the occurrence of births: Induction of labor in the United States and Canada. *International Journal of Health Services, 9,* 439.

Rindskopf, S. (1981, November). *Content analysis of sex education primers.* Paper presented at the meeting of the Society for the Scientific Study of Sex, Philadelphia.

Riordan, C.A., Quigley-Fernandez, B., & Tedeschi, J.T. (1982). Some variables affecting changes in interpersonal attraction. *Journal of Experimental Social Psychology, 18,* 358–374.

Riordan, C.A., & Tedeschi, J.T. (1983). Attraction in aversive environments: Some evidence for classical conditioning and negative reinforcement. *Journal of Personality and Social Psychology, 44,* 684–692.

Risk of developing primary infertility is at least twice as high for IUD users as for never-users. (1985). *Family Planning Perspectives, 17*(4), 182.

Roback, H.B., Felleman, E.S., & Abramowitz, S.I. (1984). The mid-life male sex-change applicant: A multiclinic survey. *Archives of Sexual Behavior, 13,* 141–153.

Robbins, M.B., & Jensen, G.D. (1978). Multiple orgasm in males. *Journal of Sex Research, 14,* 21–26.

Robertiello, R.C. (1970). The "clitoral versus vaginal orgasm" controversy and some of its ramifications. *Journal of Sex Research, 6,* 307–311.

Roberto, L.G. (1983). Issues in diagnosis and treatment of transsexualism. *Archives of Sexual Behavior, 12,* 445–473.

Roberts, B.M. (1981, November). *The catch 22 in sex therapy: How unexamined values adversely affect diagnosis, treatment, and the measurement of success.* Paper presented at the meeting of the Society for the Scientific Study of Sex, New York City.

Roberts, D.F. (1967). Incest, inbreeding, and mental abilities. *British Medical Journal, 4,* 336–337.

Robertson, N. (1980, September 21). A primer on sex, circa 1912. *New York Times,* 71.

Robinson, E.A., & Price, M.G. (1980). Pleasurable behavior in marital interaction: An observational study. *Journal of Consulting and Clinical Psychology, 48,* 117–118.

Robinson, I., & Jedlicka, D. (1983). Change in sexual attitudes and behavior of college students from 1965 to 1980: A research note. *Journal of Marriage and the Family, 44,* 237–240.

Robinson, W.L.V., & Calhoun, K.S. (1983). Sexual fantasies, attitudes, and behavior as a function of race, gender, and religiosity. *Imagination, Cognition, and Personality, 2,* 281–290.

Rode, S.S., Chang, P., Fisch, R.O., & Sroufe, L.A. (1981). Attachment patterns of infants separated at birth. *Developmental Psychology, 127,* 188–191.

Rodgers, J.L., Billy, J.O.G., & Udry, J.R. (1984). A model of friendship similarity in mildly deviant behaviors. *Journal of Applied Social Psychology, 14,* 413–425.

Roemer, R. (1985). Legislation on contraception and abortion for adolescents. *Studies in Family Planning, 16,* 241–250.

Roemer, R., & Paxman, J.M. (1985). Sex education laws and policies. *Studies in Family Planning, 16,* 219–230.

Roen, P.R. (1978). Angle of erection at different ages. *Medical Aspects of Human Sexuality, 12*(4), 7.

Roen, P.R. (1981). Effect of condom on sexual sensation. *Medical Aspects of Human Sexuality, 15*(2), 20.

Roen, P.R. (1982). The condom. *Medical Aspects of Human Sexuality, 16*(2), 35–36.

Roen, P.R. (1983). Coitus interruptus. *Medical Aspects of Human Sexuality, 17*(6), 255, 259.

Rogak, L. (1987, January 5). When Mommy moves out: Women who choose to give up custody of their children. *New York,* 36–41.

Rogers, G.S., Van de Castle, R., Evans, W.S., & Critelli, J.E. (1985). Vaginal pulse amplitude response patterns during erotic conditions and sleep. *Archives of Sexual Behavior, 14,* 327–342.

Rogers, L., & Walsh, J. (1982). Shortcomings of the psychomedical research of John Money and co-workers into sex differences in behavior: Social and political implications. *Sex Roles, 8,* 269–281.

Rogers, L.J. (1983). Hormonal theories for sex differences—Politics disguised as science: A reply to DeBold and Luria. *Sex Roles, 9,* 1109–1113.

Roland, M. (1984). Withdrawal as a contraceptive method. *Medical Aspects of Human Sexuality, 18*(4), 215.

Rolker-Dolinsky, B. (1987a). The premenstrual syndrome. In K. Kelley (Ed.), *Females, males, and sexuality.* Albany, N.Y.: State University of New York Press.

Rolker-Dolinsky, B. (1987b). *The influence of stress, neuroticism, and chronic self-destructiveness on premenstrual symptom change.* Unpublished dissertation, University at Albany, State University of New York.

Rollin, S. (1980). Sexual misconceptions of teenage boys. *Medical Aspects of Human Sexuality, 14*(4), 52.

Rollins, J., & White, P.N. (1982). The relationship between mothers' and daughters' sex-role attitudes and self-concepts in three types of family environments. *Sex Roles, 8,* 1141–1155.

Romero, M. (1985). A comparison between strategies used on prisoners of war and battered wives. *Sex Roles, 13,* 537–549.

Ronis, D.L., & Kaiser, M.K. (1989). Correlates of breast self-examination in a sample of college women: Analyses of linear structural relations. *Journal of Applied Social Psychology, 19,* 1068–1084.

Rook, K.S. (1984). Research in social support, loneliness, and social isolation: Toward an integration. In P. Shaver (Ed.), *Review of personality and social psychology 5: Emotions, relationships, and health* (pp. 239–264). Beverly Hills, Calif.: Sage.

Rook, K.S., & Peplau, L.A. (1982). Perspectives on helping the lonely. In L.A. Peplau & D. Perlman (Eds.), *Loneliness: A sourcebook of current theory, research, and therapy* (pp. 351–378). New York: John Wiley.

Rose, S.M. (1985). Same- and cross-sex friendships and the psychology of homosociality. *Sex Roles, 12,* 63–74.

Rosen, A.-S., & von Knorring, K. (1989). Attitudes to abortion methods and participation effects. *Social Behaviour, 4,* 71–82.

Rosen, R.C., & Beck, J.G. (1986). Models and measures of sexual response: Psychophysiological assessment of male and female arousal. In D. Byrne & K. Kelley (Eds.). *Alternative approaches to the study of sexual behavior* (pp. 43–86). Hillsdale, N.J.: Lawrence Erlbaum.

Rosen, R.C., Goldstein, L., Scoles, V., III, & Lazarus, C. (1986). Psychopyhsiologic correlates of nocturnal penile tumescence in normal males. *Psychosomatic Medicine, 48,* 423–429.

Rosen, R.C., & Kopel, S.A. (1977). Penile plethysmography and biofeedback in the treatment of a transvestite–exhibitionist. *Journal of Consulting and Clinical Psychology, 45,* 908–916.

Rosen, R.C., & Kostic, J.B. (1985). Biobehavioral sequellae associated with adrenergic-inhibiting antihypertensive agents: A critical review. *Health Psychology, 4,* 579–604.

Rosen, R.H. (1977, September). *Teenage pregnancy and parental involvement.* Paper presented at the meeting of the Society for the Study of Social Problems, Chicago.

Rosen, R.H., Ager, J.W., & Martindale, L.J. (1979). Contraception, abortion, and self concept. *Journal of Population, 2,* 118–139.

Rosen, R.H., Herskovitz, L., & Stack, J.M. (1982). Timing of the transition to nonvirginity among unmarried adolescent women, *Population Research and Policy Review, 1,* 153–170.

Rosenbaum, K.N. (1982). Ambiguous genitalia in the neonate. *Medical Aspects of Human Sexuality, 16*(1), 36A, 36E.

Rosenbaum, M.E. (1986). The repulsion hypotheses: On the non-development of relationships. *Journal of Personality and Social Psychology, 51,* 1156–1166.

Rosenberg, C.E. (1987). *The care of strangers: The rise of America's hospital system.* New York: Basic Books.

Rosenberg, M. (1988). Adult behaviors that reflect childhood incest. *Medical Aspects of Human Sexuality, 22*(5), 114–124.

Rosenblatt, A., Greenberg, J., Solomon, S., Pyszczynski, T., & Lyon, D. (1989). Evidence for terror management theory: I. The effects of mortality salience on reactions to those who violate or uphold cultural values. *Journal of Personality and Social Psychology 57,* 681–690.

Rosenblum, C. (1979, January). Parenthood by choice. *Human Behavior,* 58–59.

Rosenfeld, A. (1974). If Oedipus' parents had only known. *SR/World, 1*(26), 49, 52.

Rosenfeld, A. (1984). When children witness parental coitus. *Medical Aspects of Human Sexuality, 18*(8), 13, 16.

Rosenfeld, D.L. (1980). Emotional aspects of artificial insemination. *Medical Aspects of Human Sexuality, 14*(7), 111.

Rosenfeld, R.G. (1983). Management of boys with delayed growth and maturation. *Medical Aspects of Human Sexuality, 17*(12), 17, 21, 25.

Rosenheim, E., & Neumann, M. (1981). Personality characteristics of sexually dysfunctional males and their wives. *Journal of Sex Research, 17,* 124–138.

Rosenthal, S. (1984). Premarital prognosis: Factors that make for a good marriage. *Medical Aspects of Human Sexuality, 18*(6), 91–94.

Rosenthal, S.H. (1981). Nymphomania. *Medical Aspects of Human Sexuality, 15*(9), 119.

Rosenwasser, S.M., Wright, L.S., & Barber, R.B. (1987). The rights and responsibilities of men in abortion situations. *Journal of Sex Research, 23,* 97–105.

Rosenzweig, J.M., & Daley, D.M. (1989). Dyadic adjustment/sexual satisfaction in women and men as a function of psychological sex role self-perception. *Journal of Sex and Marital Therapy, 15,* 42–56.

Ross, J., & Kahan, J.P. (1983). Children by choice or by chance: The perceived effects of parity. *Sex Roles, 9,* 69–77.

Ross, L., Anderson, D.R., & Wisocki, P.A. (1982). Television viewing and adult sex-role attitudes. *Sex Roles, 8,* 589–592.

Ross, M.W. (1980). Retrospective distortion in homosexual research. *Archives of Sexual Behavior, 9,* 523–531.

Ross, M.W. (1983). Societal relationships and gender role in homosexuals: A cross-cultural comparison. *Journal of Sex Research, 19,* 273–288.

Ross, M.W. (1985). Actual and anticipated societal reaction to homosexuality and adjustment in two societies. *Journal of Sex Research, 21,* 40–55.

Ross, M.W., & Arrindell, W.A. (1988). Perceived parental rearing patterns of homosexual and heterosexual men. *Journal of Sex Research, 24,* 275–281.

Ross, M.W., & Need, J.A. (1989). Effects of adequacy of gender reassignment surgery on psychological adjustment: A follow-up of fourteen male-to-female patients. *Archives of Sexual Behavior, 18,* 145–153.

Rossi, A., & Rossi, P. (1980). Body time and social time: Mood patterns by menstrual cycle phase and day of week. In J. Parsons (Ed.), *The psychobiology of sex differences and sex roles.* New York: McGraw-Hill.

Rossman, G.P. (1973). Literature on pederasty. *Journal of Sex Research, 9,* 307–312.

Roth, N. (1981). Crude language during coitus. *Medical Aspects of Human Sexuality, 15*(3), 28.

Rothenberg, R. (1982). Role of prostitutes in the dissemination of STDs. *Medical Aspects of Human Sexuality, 16*(3), 94A, 94E.

Rothman, K.J. (1978). Twinning rate after discontinuing oral contraceptives. *Medical Aspects of Human Sexuality, 12*(8), 118.

Roviaro, S.E., & Holmes, D.S. (1980). Arousal transfer: The influence of fear arousal on subsequent sexual arousal for subjects with high and low sex guilt. *Journal of Research in Personality, 14,* 307–320.

Rowan, R.L. (1982). Irrelevance of penis size. *Medical Aspects of Human Sexuality, 16* (7), 153–156.

Ruan, F.-f., & Bullough, V.L. (1988). The first case of transsexual surgery in mainland China. *Journal of Sex Research, 25,* 546–547.

Ruan, F.-f., & Tsai, Y.-m. (1988). Male homosexuality in contemporary mainland China. *Archives of Sexual Behavior, 17,* 189–199.

Rubenstein, C. (1990). The power of touch. *Child, 5*(9), 86–87, 89, 91, 120.

Rubin, Z. (1982). Children without friends. In L.A. Peplau & D. Perlman (Eds.), *Loneliness: A sourcebook of current theory, research, and therapy* (pp. 379–406). New York: John Wiley.

Ruble, D.N. (1977). Premenstrual symptoms: A reinterpretation. *Science, 197,* 291–292.

Ruble, T.L. (1983). Sex stereotypes: Issues of change in the 1970s. *Sex Roles, 9,* 397–402.

Ruefli, T. (1981, November). *Gender differences in sound making during sex.* Paper presented at the meeting of the Society for the Scientific Study of Sex, New York City.

Ruefli, T. (1985). Explorations of the improvisational side of sex: Charting the future of the sociology of sex. *Archives of Sexual Behavior, 14,* 189–199.

Ruff, C.F., Templer, D.I., & Ayers, J.L. (1976). The intelligence of rapists. *Archives of Sexual Behavior, 5,* 327–329.

Rule, S. (1989, October 2). Denmark permits gay "partnerships." *New York Times,* A 8.

Rusbult, C.E. (1983). A longitudinal test of the investment model: The development (and deterioration) of satisfaction and commitment in heterosexual involvements. *Journal of Personality and Social Psychology , 45,* 101–117.

Rusbult, C.E., Johnson, D.J., & Morrow, G.D. (1986). Impact of couple patterns of problem solving on distress and nondistress in dating relationships. *Journal of Personality and Social Psychology, 50,* 774–753.

Rusbult, C.E., Morrow, G.D., & Johnson, D.J. (1990). Self-esteem and problem-solving behavior in close relationships. *British Journal of Social Psychology.*

Rusbult, C.E., & Zembrodt, I.M. (1983). Responses to dissatisfaction in romantic involvements: A multidimensional scaling analysis. *Journal of Experimental Social Psychology, 19,* 274–293.

Ruse, M. (1981). Are there gay genes? Sociobiology and homosexuality. *Journal of Homosexuality, 6*(4), 5–34.

Rushton, J.P. (1988a). Race differences in behaviour: A review and evolutionary analysis. *Personality and Individual Differences, 9,* 1009–1024.

Rushton, J.P. (1988b). The reality of racial differences: A rejoinder with new evidence. *Personality and Individual Differences, 9,* 1035–1040.

Rushton, J.P. (1989a). Race differences in sexuality and their correlates: Another look and physiological models. *Journal of Research in Personality, 23,* 35–54.

Rushton, J.P. (1989b). The evolution of racial differences: A response to M. Lynn. *Journal of Research in Personality, 23,* 7–20.

Rushton, J.P., & Bogaert, A.F. (1987). Race differences in sexual behavior: Testing an evolutionary hypothesis. *Journal of Research in Personality, 21,* 529–551.

Rushton, J.P., & Bogaert, A.F. (1988). Race versus social class differences in sexual behavior: A follow up test of the r/K dimension. *Journal of Research in Personality, 22,* 259–272.

Russell, A., & Winkler, R. (1977). Evaluation of assertive training and homosexual guidance service groups designed to improve homosexual functioning. *Journal of Consulting and Clinical Psychology, 45,* 1–13.

Russell, D.. (1982). The measurement of loneliness. In L.A. Peplau & D. Perlman (Eds.), *Loneliness: A sourcebook of current theory, research, and therapy* (pp. 379–406). New York: John Wiley.

Russell, D., Peplau, L.A., & Cutrona, C.E. (1980). The revised UCLA Loneliness Scale: Concurrent and discriminant validity evidence. *Journal of Personality and Social Psychology, 39*, 472–480.

Russell, D.E.H. (1984). *Sexual exploitation: Rape, child sexual abuse, and workplace harassment.* Beverly Hills, Calif.: Sage.

Russell, D.E.H., & Trocki,. K.F. (1985, September). *The impact of pornography on women.* Paper presented at the U.S. Justice Department Hearings, Houston.

Russell, D.H. (1982). Motives of women exhibitionists. *Medical Aspects of Human Sexuality, 16*(4), 47.

Sabatelli, R.M., Buck, R., & Kenny, D.A. (1986). A social relations analysis of nonverbal communication accuracy in married couples. *Journal of Personality, 54*, 513–527.

Sachs, A. (1988). Swinging —— and ducking —— singles. *Time, 132*(10), 54.

Sachs, A. (1989). Who should foot the AIDS bill? *Time, 134*(16), 88.

Sachs, A. (1990). Handing out scarlet letters. *Time, 136*(14), 98.

Sack, A.R., Billingham, R.E., & Howard, R.D. (1985). Premarital contraceptive use: A discriminant analysis approach. *Archives of Sexual Behavior, 14*, 165–182.

Sadalla, E.K., Kenrick, D.T., & Vershure, B. (1987). Dominance and heterosexual attraction. *Journal of Personality and Social Psychology, 52*, 730–738.

Sadoff, R.L. (1981). Treatment of the sexual offender. *Medical Aspects of Human Sexuality, 14*(10), 72A, 72D, 72F.

Safir, M.P., Peres, Y., Lichtenstein, M., Hoch, Z., & Shepher, J. (1982). Psychological androgyny and sexual adequacy. *Journal of Sex and Marital Therapy, 8*, 228–240.

Sagarin, E. (1978). Origin of the word "gay." *Medical Aspects of Human Sexuality, 12*(8), 79.

Saghir, M.J., & Robins, E. (1973). *Male and female homosexuality: A comprehensive investigation.* Baltimore, Md.: Williams & Wilkins.

Sai, F.T. (1984). The population factor in Africa's development dilemma. *Science, 226*, 801–805.

Sakheim, D.K., Barlow, D.H., Beck, J.G., & Abrahamsom, D.J. (1984). The effect of an increased awareness of erectile cues on sexual arousal. *Behavior Research and Therapy, 22*, 151–158.

Sakheim, D.K., Barlow, D.H., Beck, J.G., & Abrahamson, D.J. (1985). A comparison of male heterosexual and male homosexual patterns of sexual arousal. *Journal of Sex Research, 21*, 183–198.

Saltz, G. (1981). Cervical infection by Chlamydia Trachomatis in female adolescents. *Medical Aspects of Human Sexuality, 15*(8), 127, 128.

Samuels, R.M. (1982). Asexual marriages. *Medical Aspects of Human Sexuality, 16*(2), 87, 91.

Sanday, P.R. (1981). The socio-cultural context of rape: A cross-cultural study. *Journal of Social Issues, 37*, 5–27.

Sanders, G.S. (1982). Social comparison as a basis for evaluating others. *Journal of Research in Personality, 16*, 21–31.

Sanfilippo, J.S. (1984). Precocious puberty. *Medical Aspects of Human Sexuality, 18*(4), 196, 198–201.

Sarason, B.R., Sarason, I.G., Hacker, T.A., & Basham, R.B. (1985). Concomitants of social support: Social skills, physical attractiveness, and gender. *Journal of Personality and Social Psychology, 49*, 469–480.

Sarrel, P.M., & Masters, W.H. (1982). Sexual molestation of men by women. *Archives of Sexual Behavior, 11*, 117–131.

Sattem, L., Savells, J., & Murray, E. (1984). Sex-role stereotypes and commitment of rape. *Sex Roles, 11*, 849–860.

Satterfield, S.B. (1981). Clinical aspects of juvenile prostitution. *Medical Aspects of Human Sexuality, 15*(9), 126, 130, 131, 136.

Saunders, D., Fisher, W., Hewitt, E., & Clayton, J. (1985). A method for empirically assessing volunteer selection effects: Recruitment procedures and responses to erotica. *Journal of Personality and Social Psychology, 49*, 1703–1712.

Savitz, L., & Rosen, L. (1988). The sexuality of prostitutes: Sexual enjoyment reported by "streetwalkers." *Journal of Sex Research, 24*, 200–208.

Scales, P., & Gordon, S. (1979). Preparing today's youth for tomorrow's family. *Impact '79, 1*(2), 3.

Scales, P., & Kirby, D. (1983). Perceived barriers to sex education: A survey of professionals. *Journal of Sex Research, 19*, 309–326.

Scallen, R. (1982). An investigation of paternal attitudes and behavior in homosexual fathers (Doctoral dissertation, California School of Professional Psychology, Los Angeles, 1981). *Dissertation Abstracts International, 42*, 3809B.

Schachter, S. (1959). *The psychology of affiliation.* Stanford, Calif.: Stanford University Press.

Schaeffer, J., Andrysiak, T., & Ungerleider, J.T. (1981). Cognition and long-term use of ganja (cannabis). *Science, 213*, 465–466.

Schafer, S. (1977). Sociosexual behavior in male and female homosexuals: A study in sex differences. *Archives of Sexual Behavior, 6*, 355–364.

Schaffer, C.B. (1984). Self-mutilation. *Medical Aspects of Human Sexuality, 18*(4), 231.

Schatzberg, A.F., Westfall, M.P., Blumetti, A.B., & Birk, C.L. (1975). Effeminacy. I. A quantitative rating scale. *Archives of Sexual Behavior, 4*, 31–41.

Schechter, J.A., & Saadoun, S. (1984). The acquired immune deficiency syndrome: A discussion of etiologic hypotheses. *AIDS Research, 1*, 107–120.

Schenk, J., Pfrang, H., & Rausche, A. (1983). Personality traits versus the quality of the marital relationship as the determinant of marital sexuality. *Archives of Sexual Behavior, 12*, 31–42.

Schiavi, R.C. (1990). Sexuality and aging in men. In J. Bancroft, C.M. Davis, & D. Weinstein (Eds.), *Annual review of sex research*, Vol. 1 (pp. 227–249). Mt. Vernon, IA: Foundation for the Scientific Study of Sexuality.

Schlesselman, J., Stadel, B., Murray, P., & Lai, S. (1988). Breast cancer in relation to early use of oral contraceptives. *Journal of the American Medical Association, 259*, 1828–1833.

Schmeck, H.M., Jr. (1987, December 23). Single gene may determine the sex of a fetus. *New York Times,* 1, B 12.

Schmeck, H.M., Jr. (1989, January 17). Sexual response is studied in rats. *New York Times,* C 6.

Schmid, R.E. (1988, January 21). One-parent homes on rise in U.S. *Albany Times Union,* A-1, A-12.

Schmidt, G. (1978). Letter to the editor. *Archives of Sexual Behavior,* 7, 73–75.

Schmidt, G., & Schorsch, E. (1981). Psychosurgery of sexually deviant patients: Review and analysis of new empirical findings. *Archives of Sexual Behavior,* 10, 301–323.

Schmitt, J.P., & Kurdek, L.A. (1987). Personality correlates of positive identity and relationship involvement in gay men. *Journal of Homosexuality,* 13(4), 101–109.

Schnarch, D.M. (1981). Impact of sex education on medical students' projection of patients' attitudes. *Journal of Sex and Marital Therapy,* 7(2), 141–155.

Schnarch, D.M., & Jones, K. (1981). Efficacy of sex education courses in medical school. *Journal of Sex and Marital Therapy,* 7, 141–155.

Schneider, B. (1978, November 27). Stop-gap measures: *Screw* chronicles the make-do methods which spawned modern-day birth control. *Screw,* 4–7.

Schneider, B.E. (1982). Consciousness about sexual harassment among heterosexual and lesbian women workers. *Journal of Social Issues,* 38(4), 75–98.

Schneidmen, B., & McGuire, L. (1976). Group therapy for nonorgasmic women: Two age levels. *Archives of Sexual Behavior,* 5, 239–247.

Schoof-Tams, K., Schlagel, J., & Walczak, L. (1976). Differentiation of sexual morality between 11 and 16 years. *Archives of Sexual Behavior,* 5, 353–370.

Schover, L.R. (1981). Male and female therapists' responses to male and female client sexual material: An analogue study. *Archives of Sexual Behavior,* 10, 477–492.

Schover, L.R., & LoPiccolo, J. (1982). Treatment effectiveness for dysfunctions of sexual desire. *Journal of Sex and Marital Therapy,* 8, 179–197.

Schreiner-Engle, P., & Schiavi, R. (1986). Lifetime psychopathology in individuals with low sexual desire. *Journal of Nervous and Mental Disease,* 174, 646–651.

Schull, W.J., & Neel, J.V. (1965). *The effects of inbreeding on Japanese children.* New York: Harper & Row.

Schullo, S.A., & Alperson, B.L. (1984). Interpersonal phenomenology as a function of sexual orientation, sex, sentiment, and trait categories in long-term dyadic relationships. *Journal of Personality and Social Psychology,* 47, 983–1002.

Schultz, N.R., & Moore, D. (1986). The loneliness experience of college students: Sex differences. *Personality and Social Psychology Bulletin,* 12, 111–119.

Schultz, W.C.M.W., van de Wiel, H.B.M., Klatter, J.A., Sturm, B.E., & Nauta, J. (1989). Vaginal sensitivity to electric stimuli: Theoretical and practical implications *Archives of Sexual Behavior,* 18, 87–95.

Schwartz, M. (1978). *Physiological psychology* (2nd ed.). Englewood Cliffs, N.J.: Prentice Hall.

Schwartz, S. (1973). Effects of sex guilt and sexual arousal on the retention of birth control information. *Journal of Consulting and Clinical Psychology,* 41, 61–64.

Scott, F.B. (1979). Innervation of penis vs. testes. *Medical Aspects of Human Sexuality,* 13(8), 93.

Scott, F.B. (1981). Nerve endings in glans clitoris vs. glans penis. *Medical Aspects of Human Sexuality,* 15(7), 88.

Scott, J. (1985). *Violence and erotic material: The relationship between adult entertainment and rape.* Paper presented at the meeting of the American Association for the Advancement of Science, Los Angeles.

Scott, J.E., & Cuvelier, S.J. (1987). Violence in Playboy magazine: A longitudinal analysis. *Archives of Sexual Behavior,* 16, 279–288.

Scott, J.P. (1961). Animal sexuality. In A. Ellis & A. Abarbanel (Eds.), *The encyclopedia of sexual behavior* (pp. 132–144). New York: Hawthorn Books.

Scott, N. (1979a, November 9). Pregnancy affects future at work. *Albany Times Union,* 10.

Scott, N. (1979b, December 29). What qualities make a wife ideal? Here's what men say. *Albany Times Union,* 5.

Scott, N. (1980, June 22). Where help is available for harassment victims. *Albany Times Union,* F-4.

Scott, R.L., & Flowers, J.V. (1988). Betrayal by the mother as a factor contributing to psychological disturbance in victims of father-daughter incest: An MMPI analysis. *Journal of Social and Clinical Psychology,* 6, 147–154.

Scott, W.J., & Morgan, C.S. (1983). An analysis of factors affecting traditional family expectations and perceptions of ideal fertility. *Sex Roles,* 9, 901–914.

Scrimshaw, S.C.M. (1981). Women and the pill: From panacea to catalyst. *Family Planning Perspectives,* 13, 254–262.

Scroggs, J.R. (1976). Penalties for rape as a function of victim provocativeness, damage, and resistance. *Journal of Applied Social Psychology,* 6, 360–368.

Scruton, B.A. (1989, September 6). Reported rape of man second in two months. *Albany Times Union,* B-1, B-6.

Scruton, R. (1986). *Sexual desire: A moral philosophy of the erotic.* New York: Free Press.

Seagraves, K. (1989). Extramarital affairs. *Medical Aspects of Human Sexuality,* 23(4), 99–105.

Searle removes 2 IUDs from market. (1986, February 1). *Albany Times Union,* A-4.

Sebastian, J.A. (1980). Cervical cancer: A sexually transmitted disease. *Medical Aspects of Human Sexuality,* 14(10), 75, 124.

Seeley, T.T., Abramson, P.R., Perry, L.B., Rothblatt, A.B., & Seeley, D.M. (1980). Thermographic measurement of sexual arousal: A methodological note. *Archives of Sexual Behavior,* 9, 77–85.

Segal, J. (1984). *The sex lives of college students.* Wayne, Pa.: Miles Standish Press.

Segal, M.W. (1974). Alphabet and attraction: An unobtrusive

measure of the effect of propinquity in a field setting. *Journal of Personality and Social Psychology, 30,* 654–657.

Segner, L.L. (1968). Two studies of the incest taboo. *Dissertation Abstracts, 29B,* 796.

Segraves, R.T. (1985). Questions about orgasm. *Medical Aspects of Human Sexuality, 19*(11), 118, 122.

Segraves, R.T., Schoenberg, H.W., Zarins, C.K., Knopf, J., & Camic, P. (1982). Referral of impotent patients to a sexual dysfunction clinic. *Archives of Sexual Behavior, 11,* 521–528.

Seidler, V.J. (1989). *Rediscovering masculinity: Reason, language, and sexuality.* New York: Routledge, Chapman & Hall.

Seims, S. (1980). Abortion availability in the United States. *Family Planning Perspectives, 12,* 88–101.

Sekaran, U. (1986). Significant differences in quality-of-life factors and their correlates: A function of differences in career orientations or gender? *Sex Roles, 14,* 261–279.

Seligman, C., Brickman, J., & Koulack, D. (1977). Rape and physical attractiveness: Assigning responsibility to victims. *Journal of Personality, 45,* 554–563.

Selnow, G.W. (1985). Sex differences in uses and perceptions of profanity. *Sex Roles, 12,* 303–313.

Selnow, J.H. (1956). Premature ejaculation: A new approach. *Southern Medical Journal, 49,* 353–358.

Semans, J. (1956). Premature ejaculation, a new approach. *Southern Medical Journal, 49,* 353–358.

Semmens, J.P., & Semmens, E.C. (1983). Termination of vaginal lubrication after penile entry. *Medical Aspects of Human Sexuality, 17*(8), 271.

Sevely, J.L., & Bennett, J.S. (1978). Concerning female ejaculation and the female prostate. *Journal of Sex Research, 14,* 1–20.

Sewell, H.H., & Abramowitz, S.I. (1979). Flexibility, persistence, and success in sex therapy. *Archives of Sexual Behavior, 8,* 497–506.

Sexual survey #4: Current thinking on homosexuality. (1977). *Medical Aspects of Human Sexuality, 11*(11), 110–111.

Sexy soaps distorting teens' values, study finds. (1981, August 10). *Albany Times Union,* 16.

Shafie, S.M. (1980). Estrogen and the growth of breast cancer: New evidence suggests indirect action. *Science, 209,* 701–702.

Shakin, M., Shakin, D., & Sternglanz, S.H. (1985). Infant clothing: Sex labeling for strangers. *Sex Roles, 12,* 955–964.

Shannon, G.W., & Pyle, G.F. (1989). The origin and diffusion of AIDS: A view from medical geography. *Annals of the Association of American Geographers, 79,* 1–24.

Shapiro, A. (1983). Obscene language and the Tourette syndrome. *Medical Aspects of Human Sexuality, 17*(6), 271.

Shapiro, A., Cohen, H., Dibianco, P., & Rosen, G. (1968). Vaginal blood flow changes during sleep and sexual arousal. *Psychophysiology, 4,* 394.

Shapiro, E. (1984). Tourette syndrome and female sexual behavior. *Medical Aspects of Human Sexuality, 18*(10), 71–72.

Shapiro, H.I. (1988). *The new birth-control book: A complete guide for women and men.* Englewood Cliffs, N.J.: Prentice Hall.

Shapiro, J.L. (1987, January). The expectant father. *Psychology Today,* 36–39, 42.

Shapiro, J.P. (1988). Relationships between dimensions of depressive experience and evaluative beliefs about people in general. *Personality and Social Psychology Bulletin, 14,* 388–400.

Shapiro, S.S. (1980). Artificial insemination. *Medical Aspects of Human Sexuality, 14*(5), 97–98.

Shaw, J. (1989). The unnecessary penile implant. *Archives of Sexual Behavior, 18,* 455–460.

Shearer, L. (1989, September 24). Sex and teenagers. *Parade,* 12.

Shearn, M.A., & Shearn, L. (1983). Louis XVI. *Medical Aspects of Human Sexuality, 17*(2), 139–140.

Sheehy, G. (1981). *Pathfinders.* New York: William Morrow.

Shephard, M. (1980). Nonsurgical methods of contraception. In R.N. Shain & C.J. Pauerstein (Eds.), *Fertility control: Biologic and behavioral aspects.* New York: Harper & Row.

Shepher, J. (1971). Mate selection among second generation kibbutz adolescents and adults: Incest avoidance and negative imprinting. *Archives of Sexual Behavior, 1,* 293–307.

Sheppard, J.A., & Strathman, A.J. (1989). Attractiveness and height: The role of stature in dating preference, frequency of dating, and perceptions of attractiveness. *Personality and Social Psychology Bulletin, 15,* 617–627.

Sheppard, N. (1980, February 1). Two rulings limit "palimony" rights. *New York Times,* A 14.

Sheppard, N., Jr., (1979, November 11). Private morals of public aides set off debate. *New York Times,* 2.

Sherman, J. (1980). Mathematics, spatial visualization, and related factors: Changes in girls and boys, grades 8–11. *Journal of Educational Psychology, 72,* 476–482.

Sherman, M.A., & Halpern, J. (1981). What do most men and women like their partners to do immediately after intercourse? *Medical Aspects of Human Sexuality, 15*(1), 163, 167.

Sherwin, R., & Corbett, S. (1985). Campus sexual norms and dating relationships: A trend analysis. *Journal of Sex Research, 21,* 258–274.

Shettles, L., & Rorvik, D. (1970). *Your baby's sex: Now you can choose.* New York: Dodd, Mead.

Shinkle, F. (1990, October 23). What's dangerous during pregnancy. *Albany Times Union,* C-1, C-4.

Sholty, M.J., Ephross, P.H., Plauts, S.M., Fischman, S.H., Charnas, J.F., & Cody, C.A. (1984). Female orgasmic experience: A subjective study. *Archives of Sexual Behavior, 13,* 155–164.

Shostak, A., McLouth, G., & Seng, L. (1984). *Men and abortions: Lessons, losses, and love.* New York: Praeger.

Shotland, R.L., & Stebbins, C.A. (1980). Bystander response to rape: Can a victim attract help? *Journal of Applied Social Psychology, 10,* 510–527.

Shrom, S.H. (1982). Prostatitis, prostatosis, and prostatodynia. *Medical Aspects of Human Sexuality, 16*(9), 44E, 44H, 44M.

Sidanius, J., & Crane, M. (1989). Job evaluation and gender: The case of university faculty. *Journal of Applied Social Psychology, 19,* 174–197.

Siegal, D.L. (1990). Women's reproductive changes: A marker, not a turning point. *Generations, 14*(3), 31–32.

Siegel, J.M. (1986). The multidimensional anger inventory. *Journal of Personality and Social Psychology, 51,* 191–200.

Siegel, K., & Glassman, M. (1989). Individual and aggregate level change in sexual behavior among gay men at risk for AIDS. *Archives of Sexual Behavior, 18,* 335–348.

Siegelman, M. (1978). Psychological adjustment of homosexual and heterosexual men: A cross-national replication. *Archives of Sexual Behavior, 7,* 1–11.

Siegelman, M. (1979). Adjustment of homosexual and heterosexual women: A cross-national replication. *Archives of Sexual Behavior, 8,* 121–125.

Siegelman, M. (1981a). Parental backgrounds of homosexual and heterosexual men: A cross-national replication. *Archives of Sexual Behavior, 10,* 505–513.

Siegelman, M. (1981b). Parental backgrounds of homosexual and heterosexual women: A cross-national replication. *Archives of Sexual Behavior, 10,* 371–378.

Siegfried, W.D. (1982). The effects of specifying job requirements and using explicit warnings to decrease sex discrimination in employment interviews. *Sex Roles, 8,* 73–82.

Sigelman, C.K., Sigelman, L., & Goodlette, M. (1984). Sex differences in the moral values of college students and their parents. *Sex Roles, 10,* 877–883.

Signorielli, N..(1989). Television and conceptions about sex roles: Maintaining conventionality and the status quo. *Sex Roles, 21,* 341–360.

Sigusch, V., & Schmidt, G. (1973). Teenage boys and girls in West Germany. *Journal of Sex Research, 9,* 107–123.

Silber, T.J. (1985). Some medical problems common in adolescence. *Medical Aspects of Human Sexuality, 19*(2), 79, 82, 83.

Silbert, M.H. (1989). The effects on juveniles of being used for pornography and prostitution. In D. Zillmann & J. Bryant (Eds.), *Pornography: Research advances and policy considerations* (pp. 215–234). Hillsdale, N.J.: Lawrence Erlbaum.

Silverstein, B., Perdue, L., Peterson, B., & Kelly, E. (1986). The role of the mass media in promoting a thin standard of bodily attractiveness for women. *Sex Roles, 14,* 519–532.

Simmons, J.E., & Moore, G.W. (1982). The teenage exhibitionist and voyeur. *Medical Aspects of Human Sexuality, 16*(1), 145, 149.

Simmons, J.L., & Chambers, H. (1965). Public stereotypes of deviants. *Social Problems, 13,* 223–232.

Simmons, R.G., & Rosenberg, M. (1975). Sex, sex-roles, and self-image. *Journal of Youth and Adolescence, 4,* 229–258.

Simon, J.L. (1980). Resources, population, environment: An oversupply of false bad news. *Science, 208,* 1431–1437.

Simon, N. (1978). Breast cancer after radiaton therapy for acne. *Medical Aspects of Human Sexuality, 12*(10), 88.

Simon, W., & Gagnon, J. (1968). *Youth cultures and aspects of the socialization process: College study marginal book.* Bloomington, Ind.: Institute for Sex Research.

Simon, W., & Gagnon, J.H. (1986). Sexual scripts: Permanence and change. *Archives of Sexual Behavior, 15,* 97–120.

Simpson, M., & Schill, T. (1977). Patrons of massage parlors: Some facts and figures. *Archives of Sexual Behavior, 6,* 521–525.

Singer, B. (1984). Conceptualizing sexual arousal and attraction. *Journal of Sex Research, 20,* 230–240.

Singer, B. (1985). A comparison of evolutionary and environmental theories of erotic response. *Journal of Sex Research, 21,* 229–257.

Singer, D., Avedon, J., Hering, R., McCann, A., & Sacks, C. (1977). Sex differences in the vocabulary of college students. *Journal of Sex Research, 13,* 267–273.

Singh, B., & Forsyth, D.R. (1989). Sexual attitudes and moral values: The importance of idealism and relativism. *Bulletin of the Psychonomic Society, 27,* 160–162.

Sintchak, G., & Geer, J.H. (1975). A vaginal plethysmographic system. *Psychophysiology, 12,* 113–115.

Sivin, I. (1983). IUDs and ectopic pregnancy. *Studies in Family Planning, 14*(2), 57–62.

Sivin, I., Diaz, S., Holma, P., Alvarez-Sanchez, F., & Robertson, D.N. (1983). A four-year clinical study of NORPLANT implants. *Studies in Family Planning, 14,* 185–191.

Skeen, P., & Robinson, B.E. (1985). Gay fathers' and gay nonfathers' relationship with their parents. *Journal of Sex Research, 21,* 86–91.

Skinner, B.F. (1981). Selection by consequences. *Science, 213,* 501–504.

Skinner, B.F. (1986). What is wrong with daily life in the Western world? *American Psychologist, 41,* 568–574.

Sklar, J., & Berkov, B. (1974). Abortion, illegitimacy, and the American birthrate. *Science, 185,* 909–915.

Slater, E.J., & Haber, J.D. (1984). Adolescent adjustment following divorce as a function of familial conflict. *Journal of Consulting and Clinical Psychology, 52,* 920–921.

Sloan, D. (1982a). Pseudocyesis. *Medical Aspects of Human Sexuality, 16*(8), 23, 27.

Sloan, D. (1982b). Conflict over coital frequency. *Medical Aspects of Human Sexuality, 16*(9), 79.

Sloan, D. (1983). Pillow under hips during coitus. *Medical Aspects of Human Sexuality, 17*(1), 49.

Slovenko, R. (1982a). Suits for breach of promise. *Medical Aspects of Human Sexuality, 16*(7), 157.

Slovenko, R. (1982b). Absconding mate. *Medical Aspects of Human Sexuality, 16*(7), 33.

Slovenko, R. (1982c). Cross-dressing. *Medical Aspects of Human Sexuality, 16*(8), 145.

Small, M.P. (1984a). Sexual discomfort in prostatitis. *Medical Aspects of Human Sexuality, 18*(5), 211.

Small, M.P. (1984b). Testicular prosthesis. *Medical Aspects of Human Sexuality, 18*(10), 127, 130, 132.

Smeaton, G., & Byrne, D. (1987). The effects of R-rated violence and erotica, individual differences, and victim characteristics on acquaintance rape proclivity. *Journal of Research in Personality, 21,* 171–184.

Smeaton, G., Byrne, D., & Murnen, S.K. (1989). The revulsion hypothesis revisited: Similarity irrelevance or dissimilarity bias? *Journal of Personality and Social Psychology, 56,* 54–59.

Smith, C.G., Almirez, R.G., & Berenberg, J. (1983). Tolerance develops to the disruptive effects of delta-9-tetrahydrocannabinol on primate menstrual cycle. *Science, 219,* 1453–1455.

Smith, D., & Over, R. (1987). Correlates of fantasy-induced and film-induced male sexual arousal. *Archives of Sexual Behavior, 16,* 395–409.

Smith, D., & Over, R. (1990). Enhancement of fantasy-induced sexual arousal in men through training in sexual imagery. *Archives of Sexual Behavior, 19,* 477–489.

Smith, E.R. (1989). *Interpersonal attraction as a function of similarity and assumed similarity in traditional gender role adherence.* Unpublished doctoral dissertation, University at Albany, State University of New York.

Smith, E.R., Becker, M.A., Byrne, D., & Przybyla, D.P.J. (1990, June). *Sexual attitudes of males and females as predictors of interpersonal attraction and marital compatibility.* Paper presented at the meeting of the American Psychological Society, Dallas.

Smith, E.R., & Byrne, D. (1988, June 11). *Differential perceptions of sexism.* Paper presented at the Society for the Scientific Study of Sex, Midcontinent Region, Chicago.

Smith, G.J. (1985). Facial and full-length ratings of attractiveness related to the social interactions of young children. *Sex Roles, 12,* 287–293.

Smith, H.W. (1976). Status inconsistency effects on sexual liberalness. *Journal of Sex Research, 12,* 321–329.

Smith J., & Russell, G. (1984). Why do males and females differ? Children's beliefs about sex differences. *Sex Roles, 11,* 1111–1120.

Smith, K.D. (1978). Declining sperm counts in recent years. *Medical Aspects of Human Sexuality, 12*(11), 57–63.

Smith, R.E., Pine, C.J., & Hawley, M.E. (1988). Social cognitions about adult male victims of female sexual assault. *Journal of Sex Research, 24,* 101–112.

Smith, R.H., Kim, S.H., & Parrot, W.G. (1988). Envy and jealousy: Semantic problems and experimental distinctions. *Personality and Social Psychology Bulletin, 14,* 401–409.

Smith, R.S. (1976). Voyeurism: A review of the literature. *Archives of Sexual Behavior, 5,* 585–608.

Smith, T.W. (1985). Working wives and women's rights: The connection between the employment status of wives and the feminist attitudes of husbands. *Sex Roles, 12,* 501–508.

Smolowe, J. (1990). What price love? Read carefully. *Time, 136*(16), 94–95.

Snary, J., Son, L., Kuehne, V.S., Hauser, S., & Vaillant, G. (1987). The role of parenting in men's psychosocial development: A longitudinal study of early adulthood infertility and midlife generativity. *Developmental Psychology, 23*(4), 593–603.

Snell, W.E., Jr., & Papini, D.R. (1989). The Sexuality Scale: An instrument to measure sexual-esteem, sexual-depression, and sexual-preoccupation. *Journal of Sex Research, 26,* 256–263.

Snider, A.J. (1973). Mixed marriage. *Psychology Today, 7*(4), 4.

Snow, L.F., & Johnson, S.M. (1978). Menstrual myths. *Medical Aspects of Human Sexuality, 12*(10), 85.

Snyder, D.K., & Berg, P. (1983). Determinants of sexual dissatisfaction in sexually distressed couples. *Archives of Sexual Behavior, 12,* 237–246.

Snyder, D.K., & Regts, J.M. (1982). Factor scales for assessing marital disharmony and disaffection. *Journal of Consulting and Clinical Psychology, 50,* 736–743.

Snyder, D.K., Wills, R.M., & Keiser, T.W. (1981). Empirical validation of the marital satisfaction inventory: An actuarial approach. *Journal of Consulting and Clinical Psychology, 49,* 262–268.

Snyder, M., & Ickes, W. (1985). Personality and social behavior. In G. Lindzey & E. Aronson (Eds.), *The handbook of social psychology,* 3rd ed. (Vol. I, pp. 883–947). New York: Random House.

Snyder, M., & Simpson, J.A. (1984). Self-monitoring and dating relationships. *Journal of Personality and Social Psychology, 47,* 1281–1291.

Socarides, C.W. (1978). *Homosexuality.* New York: Jason Aronson.

Solano, C.H., Batten, P.G., & Parish, E.A. (1982). Loneliness and patterns of self-disclosure. *Journal of Personality and Social Psychology, 43,* 524–531.

Solberg, D.A., Butler, J., & Wagner, N.N. (1973). Sexual behavior in pregnancy. *New England Journal of Medicine, 288,* 1098–1103.

Sollie, D.L., & Fischer, J.L. (1985). Sex-role orientation, intimacy of topic, and target person differences in self-disclosure among women. *Sex Roles, 12,* 917–929.

Solnick, R.L., & Birren, J.E. (1977). Age and male erectile responsiveness. *Archives of Sexual Behavior, 6,* 1–9.

Solomon, R.C. (1981). The love lost in cliches. *Psychology Today, 15*(10), 83–85, 87–88.

Sonenschein, D. (1987). On having one's research seized. *Journal of Sex Research, 23,* 408–414.

Sonenstein, F.L., & Pittman, K.J. (1984). The availability of sex education in large city school districts. *Family Planning Perspectives, 16*(1), 19–23, 25.

Sophie, J. (1985/86). A critical examination of stage theories of lesbian identity development. *Journal of Homosexuality, 12*(2), 39–51.

Sorensen, R.C. (1973). *Adolescent sexuality in comtemporary America.* New York: World.

Sorensen, T., & Hertoft, P. (1982). Male and female transsexualism: The Danish experience with 37 patients. *Archives of Sexual Behavior, 11,* 133–155.

Sorg, D.A. (1982). Stimulation of female mons. *Medical Aspects of Human Sexuality, 16*(11), 125.

Soriero, O.M. (1982). Cytologic screening for cervical cancer. *Medical Aspects of Human Sexuality, 16*(7), 68EE, 68HH.

Spanier, G.B., & Margolis, R.L. (1983). Marital separation and extramarital sexual behavior. *Journal of Sex Research, 19,* 23–48.

Spengler, A. (1977). Manifest sadomasochism of males: Results of an empirical study. *Archives of Sexual Behavior, 6,* 441–456.

Spencer, J. (1987, July 18). Domestic violence peaks in hot weather. *Albany Times Union,* B-4.

Spitz, A.M., Rubin, G.L., McCarthy, B.J., Marks, J., Burton, A.H., & Berrier, E. (1983). The impact of publicly funded perinatal care programs on neonatal outcome, Georgia, 1976–1978. *American Journal of Obstetrics and Gynecology, 147,* 295.

Spitz, C.J., Gold, A.R., & Adams, D.B. (1975). Cognitive and hormonal factors affecting coital frequency. *Archives of Sexual Behavior, 4,* 249–263.

Spitz, I.M., & Bardin, C.W. (1985). Antiprogestins: Prospects for a once-a-month pill. *Family Planning Perspectives, 17,* 260–262.

Spitz, R. (1949). Autoeroticism: Some empirical findings and hypotheses on three of its manifestations in the first year of life. *Psychoanalytic study of the child 3, 4.* New York: International Universities Press.

Spitzberg, B.H., & Canary, D.J. (1985). Loneliness and relationally competent communication. *Journal of Social and Personal Relationships, 2,* 387–402.

Spitze, G., & South, S.J. (1985). Women's employment, time expenditure, and divorce. *Journal of Family Issues, 6*(3), 307–329.

Sprecher, S. (1985). Sex differences in bases of power in dating relationships. *Sex Roles, 12,* 449–462.

Sprecher, S. (1989). Premarital sexual standards for different categories of individuals. *Journal of Sex Research, 26,* 232–248.

Sprecher, S., DeLamater, J., Neuman, N., Neuman, M., Kahn, P., Orbuch, D., & McKinney, K. (1984). Asking questions in bars: The girls (and boys) may not get prettier at closing time and other interesting results. *Personality and Social Psychology Bulletin, 10,* 482–488.

Springer, J.F., & Gable, R.W. (1981). Modernization and sex roles: The status of women in Thai bureaucracy. *Sex Roles, 7,* 723–737.

Sproles, E.T., III. (1985). *The evaluation and management of sexual abuse: A physician's guide.* Rockville, Md.: National Institutes of Mental Health.

Stafford, R., Backman, E., & Dibona, P. (1977). The division of labor among cohabitating and married couples. *Journal of Marriage and the Family, 39,* 43–57.

Stake, J.E., & Noonan, M. (1985). The influence of teacher models on the career confidence and motivation of college students. *Sex Roles, 12,* 1023–1031.

Stark, E. (1984, May). The unspeakable family secret. *Psychology Today,* 42–46.

Stark, E. (1989). Teen sex: Not for love. *Psychology Today, 23*(5), 10, 12.

Stayton, W.R. (1983). Preventing infidelity. *Medical Aspects of Human Sexuality, 17*(5), 36C, 36D.

Stayton, W.R. (1984). Lifestyle spectrum. *SIECUS Report, 12*(3), 1–5.

Steck, L., Levitan, D., McLane, D., & Kelley, H.H. (1982). Care, need, and conceptions of love. *Journal of Personality and Social Psychology, 43,* 481–491.

Stedman's Medical Dictionary (20th ed.). (1961). Baltimore, Md.: Williams & Wilkins.

Steege, J.F. (1981). Female factors which contribute to premature ejaculation. *Medical Aspects of Human Sexuality, 15*(1), 73–74.

Steege, J.F., Stout, A.L., & Carson, C.C. (1986). Patient satisfaction in Scott and Small-Carrion penile implant recipients: A study of 52 patients. *Archives of Sexual Behavior, 15,* 393–399.

Steinberg, L. (1984). *The sexuality of Christ in renaissance art.* New York: Pantheon/October Books.

Steinberger, E. (1981). Quiz: Patients' most common questions about sexual anatomy. *Medical Aspects of Human Sexuality, 15*(8), 110–111.

Steinem, G. (1980). Erotica and pornography. In L. Lederer (Ed.), *Take back the night: Women on pornography.* New York: Morrow.

Steinem, G. (1983). Erotica vs. pornography. In G. Steinem (Ed.), *Outrageous acts and everyday rebellions* (pp. 219–230). New York: Holt, Rinehart & Winston.

Steinfels, P. (1990, November 10). Beliefs. *New York Times,* 11.

Steinhorn, A.I. (1984, January). On lesbian mothers. *SIECUS Report,* pp. 7–8.

Stephan, W., Berscheid, E., & Walster, E. (1971). Sexual arousal and heterosexual perception. *Journal of Personality and Social Psychology, 20,* 93–101.

"Sterilized children." (1980, September 28). *Parade,* 17.

Sterling, T.D., & Kobayashi, D. (1975). A critical review of reports on the effect of smoking on sex and fertility. *Journal of Sex Research, 11,* 201–217.

Stern, P.N. (Ed.). (1989). *Pregnancy and parenting.* New York: Hemisphere.

Sternberg, R.J. (1986). A triangular theory of love. *Psychological Review, 93,* 119–135.

Sternberg, R.J. (1988). Triangulating love. In R.J. Sternberg & M.L. Barnes (Eds.), *The psychology of love* (pp. 119–138). New Haven, CT: Yale University Press.

Sternberg, R.J., & Barnes, M.L. (1988). *The psychology of love.* New Haven, CT: Yale University Press.

Sternglanz, S.H., Graz, J.L., & Murakami, M. (1972). Adult preferences for infantile facial features: An ethological approach. *Animal Behavior, 25,* 108–115.

Stessin, L. (1979, December 23). Two against harassment. *New York Times,* F 7.

Stetson, D.M. (1979). Relation of divorce laws to divorce rate. *Medical Aspects of Human Sexuality, 13*(4), 117, 120.

Stevenson, M.R. (1988). Promoting tolerance for homosexuality: An evaluation of intervention strategies. *Journal of Sex Research, 25,* 500–511.

Stier, D.S., & Hall, J.A. (1984). Gender differences in touch: An empirical and theoretical review. *Journal of Personality and Social Psychology, 47,* 440–459.

Stock, W. (1985, September). *The effect of pornography on women.* Paper presented at the U.S. Justice Department Hearings, Houston.

Stock, W.E., & Geer, J.H. (1982). A study of fantasy-based sexual arousal in women. *Archives of Sexual Behavior, 11,* 33–47.

Stockard, J., & Wood, W. (1984). The myth of female underachievement: A reexamination of sex differences in academic underachievement. *American Educational Research Journal, 21,* 825–838.

Stockton, W. (1989, March 27). Researchers study effects of exercise during pregnancy. *New York Times,* C 11.

Stokes, K., Kilmann, P.R., & Wanlass, R.L. (1983). Sexual orientation and sex role conformity. *Archives of Sexual Behavior, 12,* 427–433.

Stolk, Y., & Brotherton, P. (1981). Attitudes toward single women. *Sex Roles, 7,* 73–78.

Stoller, R.J. (1977). Sexual deviations. In F. Beach (Ed.), *Human sexuality in four perspectives* (pp. 190–214). Baltimore, Md.: Johns Hopkins University Press.

Stoller, R.J. (1979). *Sexual excitement: Dynamics of erotic life.* New York: Pantheon.

Stoller, R.J. (1982). Transvestism in women. *Archives of Sexual Behavior, 11,* 99–115.

Stoller, R.J., & Herdt, G. (1985). Theories of origins of male homosexuality. *Archives of General Psychiatry, 42,* 399–404.

Stone, A. (1982). Breasts. *Playgirl, 10*(3), 90–95, 97, 107.

Stone, L. (1989). Dead end kids. *New Republic, 200*(9), 31–34.

Storms, M.D. (1980). Theories of sexual orientation. *Journal of Personality and Social Psychology, 38,* 783–792.

Storms, M.D. (1981). A theory of erotic orientation development. *Psychological Review, 88,* 340–353.

Storms, M.D., Stivers, M.L., Lambers, S.M., & Hill, C.A. (1981). Sexual scripts for women. *Sex Roles, 7,* 699–707.

Story, M.D. (1979). A longitudinal study of the effects of a university human sexuality course on sexual attitudes. *Journal of Sex Research, 15,* 184–204.

Stout, A.L. (1982). Sexual phobias. *Medical Aspects of Human Sexuality, 16*(10), 88, 90, 91, 93.

Stout, H.R. (1885). *Our family physician.* Peoria, Ill.: Henderson and Smith.

Strassberg, D.L., & Mahoney, J.M. (1988). Correlates of the contraceptive behavior of adolescents/young adults. *Journal of Sex Research, 25,* 531–536.

Strassberg, D.S., Kelly, M.P., Carroll, C., & Kircher, J.C. (1987). The psychophysiological nature of premature ejaculation. *Archives of Sexual Behavior, 16,* 327–336.

Straus, M.A., & Gelles, R.J. (1986). Societal change and change in family violence from 1975 to 1985 as revealed by two national surverys. *Journal of Marriage and the Family, 48,* 465–479.

Strause, M.A., & Gelles, R.J. (1989). *Physical violence in American families: Risk factors and adaptations to violence in 8,145 families.* New Brunswick, NJ: Transaction.

Streissguth, A.P., Martin, D.C., Barr, H.M., Sandman, B.M., Kirchner, G.L., & Darby, B.L. (1984). Intrauterine alcohol and nicotine exposure: Attention and reaction time in 4-year-old children. *Developmental Psychology, 20,* 533–541.

Strickland, B. (1983, August). *Sex differences.* Paper presented at the meeting of the American Psychological Association, Anaheim, California.

Struckman-Johnson, C. (1988). Forced sex on dates: It happens to men, too. *Journal of Sex Research, 24,* 234–241.

Stuart, F.M., Hammond, D.C., & Pett, M.A. (1987). Inhibited sexual desire in women. *Archives of Sexual Behavior, 16,* 91–106.

Sturgis, E.T., & Adams, H.E. (1978). The right to treatment: Issues in the treatment of homosexuality. *Journal of Consulting and Clinical Psychology, 46,* 165–169.

Suarez, J.M., & Weston, N.L. (1978). Postdivorce sexual involvements. *Medical Aspects of Human Sexuality, 12*(8), 85–86.

Sue, D. (1979). Erotic fantasies of college students during coitus. *Journal of Sex Research, 15,* 299–305.

Suedfeld, P. (1982). Aloneness as a healing experience. In L.A. Peplau & D. Perlman (Eds.), *Loneliness: A sourcebook of current theory, research, and therapy* (pp. 54–67). New York: John Wiley.

Sullivan, A. (1990). Gay life, gay death. *New Republic, 203*(25), 19–25.

Sullivan, P. (1984). First coitus. *Medical Aspects of Human Sexuality, 18*(9), 200.

Sullivan, P.R. (1982). Sex perceived as too much work. *Medical Aspects of Human Sexuality, 16*(2), 19.

Sullivan, W. (1987, September 23). New way devised to pick child's sex. *New York Times,* D 30.

Sun, M. (1984). Panel says Depo-Provera not proved safe. *Science, 226,* 950–951.

Suppe, F. (1982). The Bell and Weinberg study: Future priorities for research on homosexuality. *Journal of Homosexuality, 6*(4), 69–97.

Suro, R. (1986, October 29). Vatican guidelines on homosexuals. *New York Times,* A 12.

Survey says men do more housework, but still trail women. (1988, December 1). *Albany Times Union,* C-12.

Svare, B., & Kinsley, C.H. (1987). Hormones and sex-related behavior: A comparative analysis. In K. Kelley (Ed.), *Females, males, and sexuality: Theories and research.* Albany, N.Y.: State University of New York Press.

Swallow, S.R., & Kuiper, N.A. (1987). The effects of depression and cognitive vulnerability to depression on judgments of similarity between self and others. *Motivation and Emotion, 11,* 157–161.

Swap, W.C. (1977). Interpersonal attraction and repeated exposure to rewarders and punishers. *Personality and Social Psychology Bulletin, 3,* 248–251.

Sweet, A.Y. (1988, July 15). Lyme disease hazards during pregnancy. *New York Times,* A 30.

Swim, J., & Borgida, E. (1987). Public opinion on the psychological and legal aspects of television rape trials. *Journal of Applied Social Psychology, 17,* 507–518.

Symons, D. (1979). *The evolution of human sexuality.* New York: Oxford.

Szasz, G., Stevenson, R.W.D., Lee, L., & Sanders, H.D. (1987). Induction of penile erection by intracavernosal injection: A double-blind comparison of phenoxybenzamine versus paverine-phentolamine versus saline. *Archives of Sexual Behavior, 16,* 371–378.

Szasz, T. (1980). *Sex by prescription.* New York: Anchor Press/Doubleday.

Szasz, T. (1981). The case against sex education. *Penthouse, 12*(5), 124–125.

Syphilis in the New World. (1987, September 8). *New York Times,* C 9.

Tack, K.J. (1985). Possible tampon-associated toxic shock syndrome in a man. *Medical Aspects of Human Sexuality, 19*(2), 236.

Takefman, J., & Brender, W. (1984). An analysis of the effectiveness of two components in the treatment of erectile dysfunction. *Archives of Sexual Behavior, 13*, 321–340.

Talking about sex...parent to child. (1989, March). *Psychology Today*, 18.

Tangri, S.S., Burt, M.R., & Johnson, L.B. (1982). Sexual harassment at work: Three explanatory models. *Journal of Social Issues, 38*(4), 33–54.

Tanner, J.M. (1962). *Growth at adolescence*. Oxford: Blackwell Scientific Publications.

Tanner, J.M. (1981). Menarcheal age. *Science, 214*, 604.

Tavris, C., & Wade, C. (1984). *The longest war: Sex differences in perspective* (2nd ed.). San Diego: Harcourt, Brace, Jovanovich.

Taylor, G. (1985, November 22). Retrial OK'd in murder by decapitation. *Albany Times Union*, B-16.

Taylor, S.E. & Langer, E.J. (1977). Pregnancy: A social stigma. *Sex Roles, 3*, 27–35.

Teenage pregnancies out of control. (1979). *Science, 204*, 597.

Teen-age pregnancy and birth rate drop. (1987, October 2). *New York Times*, A 29.

Teen childbearing costs U.S. $16.6 B. (1986, February 19). *Albany Times Union*, A-3.

Tennov, D. (1979). *Love and limerance*. New York: Stein and Day.

Terman, L.M., Buttenwieser, P., Ferguson, L.W., Johnson, W.B., & Wilson, D.P. (1938). *Psychological factors in marital happiness*. New York: McGraw-Hill.

Tesch, S.A. (1984). Sex-role orientation and intimacy status in men and women. *Sex Roles, 11*, 451–465.

Tesch, S.A. (1985). The Psychosocial Intimacy Questionnaire: Validational studies and an investigation of sex roles. *Journal of Social and Personal Relationships, 2*, 471–488.

Tesser, A., & Paulhus, D.L. (1976). Toward a causal model of love. *Journal of Personality and Social Psychology, 34*, 1095–1105.

Testa, R.J., Kinder, B.N., & Ironson, G. (1987). Heterosexual bias in the perception of loving relationships of gay males and lesbians. *Journal of Sex Research, 23*, 163–172.

Thayer, S. (1986). History and strategies of research on social touch. *Journal of Nonverbal Behavior, 10*, 12–28.

The history of abortion in America. (1989). *Playboy, 36*(3), 50.

Thelen, M.H., Fishbein, M.D., & Tatten, H.A. (1985). Interspousal similarity: A new approach to an old question. *Journal of Social and Personal Relationships, 2*, 437–446.

The rights of homosexuals. (1986, July 2). *Albany Times Union*, A-9.

Thoits, P.A. (1984). Coping, social support, and psychological outcomes: The central role of emotion. In P. Shaver (Ed.), *Review of personality and social psychology 5: Emotions, relationships, and health* (pp. 219–238). Beverly Hills, Calif.: Sage.

Thomas, C. (1985). The age of androgyny: The new views of psychotherapists. *Sex Roles, 13*, 381–392.

Thompson, A.P. (1983). Extramarital sex: A review of the research literature. *Journal of Sex Research, 19*, 1–22.

Thompson, D. (1989). A setback for pro-life forces. *Time, 133*(13), 82.

Thornton, A., & Freedman, D. (1982). Changing attitudes toward married and single life. *Family Planning Perspectives, 14*(6), 297–303.

Tice, A.D. (1987). Informed consent: VIII. Biasing of sensitive self-report data by both consent and information. *Journal of Social Behavior and Personality, 2*, 369–373.

"Thou shalt not"—And shall. (1976). *Time, 125*(3), 41.

Tiefer, L., & Melman, A. (1987). Adherence to recommendations and improvement over time in men with erectile dysfunction. *Archives of Sexual Behavior, 16*, 301–309.

Tierney, J. (1990, October 19). AIDS in Africa: Experts study role of promiscuous sex in the epidemic. *New York Times*, A 10.

Tietze, C. (1981). Condom leakage test. *Medical Aspects of Human Sexuality, 15*(2), 47.

Tietze, C. (1984). The public health effects of legal abortion in the United States. *Family Planning Perspectives, 16*, 26–28.

Timnick, L. (1983). When women rape men. *Psychology Today, 17*(9), 74–75.

Tippins, T. (1986). *When you face divorce*. Albany, N.Y.: Timothy M. Tippins.

Tjaden, P.G. (1988). Pornography and sex education. *Journal of Sex Research, 24*, 208–212.

Tolstedt, B.E., & Stokes, J.P. (1984). Self-disclosure, intimacy, and the depenetration process. *Journal of Personality and Social Psychology, 46*, 84–90.

Tomer, S.E. (1989, March 7). Grounding mothers-to-be. *Albany Times Union*, C-1, C-3.

Tordjman, G. (1978). Loss of erection in male-superior position. *Medical Aspects of Human Sexuality, 12*(9), 103.

Torres, A., & Forrest, J.D. (1983). The costs of contraception. *Family Planning Perspectives, 15*, 70–72.

Toufexis, A. (1987a, February 2). Ads that shatter an old taboo. *Time*, 63.

Toufexis, A. (1987b, November 30). Season of autumn-summer love. *Time*, 75.

Toufexis, A. (1988). Comeback of a contraceptive. *Time, 131*(23), 67.

Toufexis, A. (1989a). New perils of the pill? *Time, 133*(3), 73.

Toufexis, A. (1989b). Abortions without doctors. *Time, 134*(9), 66.

Townsend, J.M. (1987). Sex differences in sexuality among medical students: Effects of increasing socioeconomic status. *Archives of Sexual Behavior, 16*, 425–444.

Trainer, J. (1981). Clitoral sensitivity. *Medical Aspects of Human Sexuality, 15*(4), 27.

Trainer, J.B. (1980). Disadvantages of abstinence. *Medical Aspects of Human Sexuality, 14*(1), 11.

Trent, R.B. (1980). Evidence bearing on the construct of "ideal family size." *Population and Environment, 3*, 309–327.

Trevathan, E. (1984). Cigarette-induced diseases. *Medical Aspects of Human Sexuality, 18*(7), 159–160.

Tribe, L.H. (1990). *Abortion: The clash of absolutes*. New York: W.W. Norton.

Tripp, C.A. (1975). *The homosexual matrix*. New York: McGraw-Hill.

Troiden, R.R., & Jendrek, M.P. (1987). Does sexual ideology correlate with level of sexual experience? Assessing the construct validity of the SAS. *Journal of Sex Research, 23,* 255–261.

Trounson, A.O., Leeton, J.F., Wood, C., Webb, J., & Wood, J. (1981). Pregnancies in humans by fertilization in vitro and embryo transfer in the controlled ovulatory cycle. *Science, 212,* 681–682.

Trump, D. (1983). Chest hair in women. *Medical Aspects of Human Sexuality, 17*(4), 273.

Truxal, B. (1983). Nocturnal emissions. *Medical Aspects of Human Sexuality, 17*(7), 128, 132, 133, 136.

Tryon, G.S. (1984). Effects of client and counselor sex on client attendance at counseling. *Sex Roles, 10,* 387–393.

Tsai, M., & Wagner, N.N. (1978). Therapy groups for women sexually molested as children. *Archives of Sexual Behavior, 7,* 417–427.

Tsoi, W.F. (1990). Developmental profile of 200 male and 100 female transsexuals in Singapore. *Archives of Sexual Behavior, 19,* 595–605.

Tucker, L.A. (1983). The structure and dimensional satisfaction of the body cathexis construct of males: A factor analytic investigation. *Journal of Human Movement Studies, 9,* 189–194.

Tucker, L.A. (1985). Dimensionality and factor satisfaction of the body image construct: A gender comparison, *Sex Roles, 12,* 931–937.

Tullman, G.M., Gilner, F.H., Kolodny, R.C., Dornbush, R.L., & Tullman, G.D. (1981). The pre- and post-therapy measurement of communication skills of couples undergoing sex therapy at Masters & Johnson Institue. *Archives of Sexual Behavior, 10,* 95–109.

Turner, B.F., & Adams, C.G. (1988). Reported change in preferred sexual activity over the adult years. *Journal of Sex Research, 25,* 289–303.

Tuteur, W. (1984). Dangerousness of Peeping Toms. *Medical Aspects of Human Sexuality, 18*(10), 97.

Twenty-seven Pakistani "Johns" flogged in public. (1979, October 26). *Albany Times Union,* 16.

Tyre, P. (1989). Holy war. *New York, 22*(17), 48–51.

Tyrer, L.B. (1981). Checking for IUD strings. *Medical Aspects of Human Sexuality, 14*(12), 21, 87.

Tyrer, L.B. (1981). Changes in size of diaphragm needed. *Medical Aspects of Human Sexuality, 15*(10), 99.

Tyrer, L.B. (1982). Effect of petroleum jelly on condoms. *Medical Aspects of Human Sexuality, 16*(3), 105.

Tyrer, L.B. (1984). Contraceptive effectiveness of breastfeeding. *Medical Aspects of Human Sexuality, 18*(2), 9. (a)

Tyrer, L.B. (1984). Precautions in diaphragm use. *Medical Aspects of Human Sexuality, 18*(4), 243, 247. (b)

Uchitelle, L. (1990, November 24). Women's push into work force seems to have reached plateau. *New York Times,* 1, 28.

Udry, J.R. (1980). Changes in the frequency of marital intercourse from panel data. *Archives of Sexual Behavior, 9,* 319–325.

Udry, J.R., & Talbert, L.M. (1988). Sex hormone effects on personality at puberty. *Journal of Personality and Social Psychology, 54,* 291–295.

Umberson, D., & Hughes, M. (1984, August). *The impact of physical attractiveness on achievement and psychological well-being.* Paper presented at the meeting of the American Sociological Association, San Antonio, TX.

Unger, C., & Churcher, S. (1980, October 6). Intimate sex lives' revealed. New York, 14.

Unger, R.K., Hilderbrand, M., & Madar, T. (1982). Physical attractiveness and assumptions about social deviance. *Personality and Social Psychology Bulletin, 8,* 293–301.

United States Merit Systems Protection Board. (1981). *Sexual harassment in the Federal workplace: Is it a problem?* Washington, D.C.: U.S. Government Printing Office.

Urberg, K.A. (1982). The development of the concepts of masculinity and femininity in young children. *Sex Roles, 8,* 659–668.

U.S. Bureau of the Census. (1981a, March). Marital status and living arrangements. *Current population reports,* Series P20, No. 372, Table B.

U.S. Bureau of the Census. (1981b). *Report of the U.S. Bureau of the Census.* Washington, D.C.: U.S. Government Printing Office.

U.S. Bureau of the Census. (1982). *Current population survey data.* Washington, D.C.: U.S. Government Printing Office.

U.S. Bureau of the Census. (1988a). Marital status and living arangements: March 1988. *Current population reports,* Series P-20, No. 433. Washington, D.C.: U.S. Government Printing Office.

U.S. Bureau of the Census. (1988b). *Statistical Abstract of the United States in 1988.* Washington, D.C.: U.S. Government Printing Office.

U.S. Department of Justice. (1986). *Attorney General's Commission on Pornography: Final report.* Washington, DC: U.S. Government Printing Office.

U.S. population is 60 million too high, Dr. Pauling says. (1976, February 7). *Indianapolis Star,* 15.

Utne, M.K., Hatfield, E., Traupmann, J., & Greenberger, D. (1984). Equity, marital satisfaction, and stability. *Journal of Social and Personal Relationships, 1,* 323–332.

Valleroy, M., & Kraft, G. (1984). Sexual dysfunction in multiple sclerosis. *Archives of Physical Medicine and Rehabilitation, 65,* 125–128.

Van Buren, A. (1986, March 28). Man is moving. *Albany Times Union,* B-7.

Vance, E.B., & Wagner, N.N. (1976). Written descriptions of orgasm: A study of sex differences. *Archives of Sexual Behavior, 5,* 87–98.

VanderPlate, C., Aral, S.O., & Magder, L. (1988). The relationship among genital herpes simplex virus, stress, and social support. *Health Psychology, 7*(2), 159–168. 557–559.

Van de Velde, T.H. (1926). *Ideal marriage: Its physiology and technique.* New York: Random House.

Van Thiel, D.H. (1980). Basis for alcoholics' impotence. *Medical Aspects of Human Sexuality, 14*(7), 15, 66.

Van Wyk, P.H. (1982). Relationship of time spent on masturbation assignments with orgasmic outcome in preorgasmic women's groups. *Journal of Sex Research, 18,* 33–40.

Van Wyk, P.H., & Geist, C.S. (1984). Psychosocial development of heterosexual, bisexual, and homosexual behavior. *Archives of Sexual Behavior, 13,* 505–544.

Veitch, R., & Griffitt, W. (1976). Good news, bad news: Affective and interpersonal effects. *Journal of Applied Social Psychology, 6,* 69–75.

Ventura, S.J. (1982). Trends in first births to older mothers, 1970–1979. *Monthly Vital Statistics Report,* National Center for Health Statistics, Department of Health and Human Services, *31*(2).

Vetere, V.A. (1982). The role of friendship in the development and maintenance of lesbian love relationships. *Journal of Homosexuality, 8*(2), 51–65.

Vinick, B.H. (1983). Remarriage by the elderly. *Medical Aspects of Human Sexuality, 17*(10), 111, 115, 116.

Vital statistics of the planet. (1979, December 30). *New York Times, 2.*

Volberding, P.A., et al. (1990). Zidovudine in asymptomatic human immunodeficiency virus infections. *New England Journal of Medicine, 322,* 941.

Vontver, L.A. (1979). Incubation period for herpes. *Medical Aspects of Human Sexuality, 13*(8), 102.

Wagner, G., & Green, R. (1981). *Impotence: Physiological, psychological, and surgical diagnosis and treatment.* New York: Plenum.

Wakefield, J. (1988). Female primary orgasmic dysfunction: Masters and Johnson versus DSM-III-R on diagnosis and incidence. *Journal of Sex Research, 24,* 363–377.

Walfish, S., & Myerson, M. (1980). Sex role identity and attitudes toward sexuality. *Archives of Sexual Behavior, 9,* 199–203.

Walker, J. (1983). *Sexual activities and fantasies of university students as a function of sex role orientation.* Unpublished honors thesis, University of Western Ontario, London, Ontario, Canada.

Walker, R.H. (1982). Accuracy of paternity testing. *Medical Aspects of Human Sexuality, 16*(10), 16, 35.

Wallace, R.B. (1980). Likelihood of menopause when three menstrual periods are missed. *Medical Aspects of Human Sexuality, 14*(7), 67, 102.

Walling, W.H. (1904). *Sexology.* Philadelphia: Puritan.

Walling, W.H. (1912). *Sexology.* Philadelphia: Puritan.

Walsh, R. (1980). Nonvirginity vs. promiscuity. *Medical Aspects of Human Sexuality, 14*(1),11.

Walster, E., Traupmann, J., & Walster, G.W. (1978). Equity and extramarital sexuality. *Archives of Sexual Behavior, 7,* 127–142.

Wanlass, R.L., Kilmann, P.R., Bella, B.S., & Tarnowski, K.J. (1983). Effects of sex education on sexual guilt, anxiety, and attitudes: A comparison of instruction formats. *Archives of Sexual Behavior, 12,* 487–502.

Warczok, R. (1988). Correlates of sexual orientation in the German Democratic Republic. *Archives of Sexual Behavior, 17,* 189–199.

Warshaw, R. (1988). *I never called it rape.* New York: Harper & Row.

Washington, A.E., Gove, S., Schachter, J., & Sweet, R.L. (1985). Oral contraceptives, chlamydia trachomatis infection, and pelvic inflammatory disease: A work of caution about protection. *Journal of the American Medical Association, 253,* 2246–2250.

Waterman, C.K., & Chiauzzi, E.J. (1982). The role of orgasm in male and female sexual enjoyment. *Journal of Sex Research, 18,* 146–159.

Waterman, C.K., Chiauzzi, E., & Gruenbaum, M. (1979). The relationship between enjoyment and actualization of self and sexual partner. *Journal of Sex Research, 15,* 253–263.

Waterman, C.K., Dawson, L.J., & Bologna, M.J. (1989). Sexual coercion in gay male and lesbian relationships: Predictors and implications for support services. *Journal of Sex Research, 26,* 118–124.

Waterman, C.K., & Foss-Goodman, D. (1984). Child molesting: Variables relating to attribution of fault to victims, offenders, and nonparticipating parents. *Journal of Sex Research, 20,* 329–349.

Watson, J.B. (1929). Introduction. In G.V. Hamilton & K. Macgowan, *What is wrong with marriage?* New York: Boni.

Watson, J.B., & Lashley, K.S. (1919). The opinion of doctors regarding venereal disease. *Social Hygiene, 4,* 769–847.

Watson, R.E.L. (1983). Effect of premarital cohabitation. *Medical Aspects of Human Sexuality, 17*(8), 13, 16.

Watts, B.L. (1982). Individual differences in circadian activity rhythms and their effects on roommate relationships. *Journal of Personality, 50,* 374–384.

Weatherford, J. (1985). *Porn row.* New York: Arbor House.

Weathersbee, P., & Lodge, J.R. (1980). Coffee ingestion and infertility. *Medical Aspects of Human Sexuality, 14*(10), 124.

Webster, G.D. (1983). Sexual dysfunction in the paraplegic patient. *Medical Aspects of Human Sexuality, 17*(1). 32M, 32P, 32S, 32T, 32W, 32AA.

Weeks, D.G., Michela, J.L., Peplau, L.A., & Bragg, M.E. (1980). Relation between loneliness and depression: A structural equation analysis. *Journal of Personality and Social Psychology, 39,* 1238–1244.

Weeks, J. (1977). *Coming out: Homosexual politics in Britain from the nineteenth century to the present.* New York: Quartet Books.

Weeks, M.O., & Gage, B.A. (1984). A comparison of the marriage-role expectations of college women enrolled in a functional marriage course. *Sex Roles, 11,* 377–388.

Weinberg, M.S., & Williams, C.J. (1974). *Male homosexuals: Their problems and adaptations.* New York: Oxford University.

Weinberg, M.S., & Williams, C.J. (1988). Black sexuality: A test of two theories. *Journal of Sex Research, 25,* 197–218.

Weinberg, P.C. (1984). Sex in the bath. *Medical Aspects of Human Sexuality, 14*(7), 15.

Weinberg, T.S. (1987). Sadomasochism in the United States: A review of recent sociological literature. *Journal of Sex Research, 23,* 50–69.

Weinberg, T.S., & Bullough, V.L. (1988). Alienation, self-image, and the importance of support groups for the wives of transvestites. *Journal of Sex Research, 24,* 262–268.

Weinstein, S.A., & Como, J. (1980). The relationship between knowledge and anxiety about postcoronary sexual activity among wives of postcoronary males. *Journal of Sex Research, 16,* 316–324.

Weis, D. (1975, December). *Sexual learning in adolescence: Agents of learning and sources of sexual information.* Paper presented at the meeting of the Indiana Home Economics Association, Muncie.

Weis, D.L. (1983a). Affective reactions of women to their initial experience of coitus. *Journal of Sex Research, 19,* 209–237.

Weis, D.L. (1983b). "Open" marriage and multilateral relationships: The emergence of nonexclusive models of the marital relationship. In E.D. Macklin & R.H. Rubin (Eds.), *Contemporary families and alternative lifestyles: Handbook on research and theory* (pp. 194–215). Beverly Hills, Calif.: Sage.

Weis, D.L. (1985). The experience of pain during women's first sexual intercourse: Cultural mythology about female sexual initiation. *Archives of Sexual Behavior, 14,* 421–438.

Weis, D.L., & Slosnerick, M. (1981). Attitudes toward sexual and nonsexual extramarital involvements among a sample of college students. *Journal of Marriage and the Family, 43,* 349–358.

Weisberg, M. (1981). Eliciting sexual data from women patients. *Medical Aspects of Human Sexuality, 15*(1), 124G, 124K.

Weiss, H.W. (1984, January). On gay fathers. *SEICUS Report.* 7–8.

Weiss, L., & Meadow, R. (1979). Women's attitudes toward gynecologic practices. *Obstetrics and Gynecology, 54,* 110.

Weiss, P. (1985). Inside a bathhouse. *New Republic, 193*(48), 12–13.

Weiss, R.D. (1982). Effects of opiates on orgasm. *Medical Aspects of Human Sexuality, 16*(11), 29.

Weitzman, L. (1985). *The divorce revolution.* New York: Free Press.

Welbourne-Moglia, A. (1984). Sexuality of the blind. *Medical Aspects of Human Sexuality, 18*(10), 176.

Welch, M.R., & Kartub, P. (1978). Sociocultural correlates of incidence of impotence: A cross-cultural study. *Journal of Sex Research, 14,* 218–230.

Weldon, V.V. (1980). Topical testosterone. *Medical Aspects of Human Sexuality, 14*(8), 99.

Weller, R.A., & Halikas, J.A. (1984). Marijuana use and sexual behavior. *Journal of Sex Research, 20,* 186–193.

Wells, B.L. (1986). Predictors of female nocturnal orgasms: A multivariate analysis. *Journal of Sex Research, 22,* 421–437.

Wells, J.W. (1989). Sexual language usage in different interpersonal contexts: A comparison of gender and sexual orientation. *Archives of Sexual Behavior, 18,* 127–143.

Wentzel, K.R. (1988). Gender differences in math and English achievement: A longitudinal study. *Sex Roles, 18,* 691–699.

Wertz, R.W., & Wertz, D.C. (1977). *Lying-in: A history of childbirth in America.* New York: Free Press.

Wessel, M.A. (1980). Coping with acne. *Parents, 55*(10), 42.

Westoff, C.F. (1976). The decline of unplanned births in the United States. *Science, 11,* 38–41.

Westoff, C.F. (1980). Women's reactions to pregnancy. *Family Planning Perspectives, 12,* 135-139.

Westoff, C.F., Delung, J.S., Goldman, N., & Forrest, J.D. (1981). Abortion preventable by contraceptive practice. *Family Planning Perspectives, 13,* 218-223.

Westoff, C.F., & Rundfuss, R.R. (1974). Sex preselection in the United States: Some implications. *Science, 184,* 633–636.

Whalen, R.E. (1984). Multiple actions of steroids and their antagonists. *Archives of Sexual Behavior, 13,* 497–502.

Wheeler, J., & Kilmann, P.R. (1983). Comarital sexual behavior: Individual and relationship variables. *Archives of Sexual Behavior, 12,* 295–306.

Whelan, E.M. (1975). Attitudes toward menstruation. *Studies in Family Planning, 6,* 104–108.

Whipple, B., & Komisaruk, B.R. (1988). Analgesia produced in women by genital self-stimulation. *Journal of Sex Research, 24,* 130–140.

Whitaker, R. (1991, February 3). Addicted to love: Self-help groups bring hidden lives to light. *Albany Times Union, 41,* 44.

Whitam, F.L. (1983). Culturally invariable properties of male homosexuality: Tentative conclusions from cross-cultural research. *Archives of Sexual Behavior, 12,* 207–226.

Whitam, F.L. & Zent, M. (1984). A cross-cultural assessment of early cross-gender behavior and familial factors in male homosexuality. *Archives of Sexual Behavior, 13,* 427–439.

Whitbourne, S.K. (1990). Sexuality in the aging male *Generations, 14*(3), 28–30.

White, C.B. (1980). Sex in nursing homes. *Medical Aspects of Human Sexuality, 14*(7), 102.

White, C.B. (1982a). A scale for the assessment of attitudes and knowledge regarding sexuality in the aged. *Archives of Sexual Behavior, 11,* 491–502.

White, C.B. (1982b). Sexual interest, attitudes, knowledge, and sexual history in relation to sexual behavior in the institutionalized aged. *Archives of Sexual Behavior, 11,* 11–21.

White, D.M., & Felts, W.M. (1989, Spring). Chlamydial infection: The quiet epidemic. *Our Sexuality Update, 1,* 4.

White, G. (1981). Jealousy and partner's perceived motives for attraction to a rival. *Social Psychology Quarterly, 44*(1), 24–30.

White, G.L. (1980a). Physical attractiveness and courtship progress. *Journal of Personality and Social Psychology, 39,* 660–668.

White, G.L. (1980b). Inducing jealousy: A power perspective. *Personality and Social Psychology Bulletin, 6,* 222–227.

White, G.L., & Mullen, P.E. (1990). *Jealousy: Theory, research, and clinical strategies.* New York: Guilford.

White, G.L., & Shapiro, D. (1987). Don't I know you? Antecedents and social consequences of perceived familiarity. *Journal of Experimental Social Psychology, 23,* 75–92.

White, J.M. (1985). Perceived similarity and understanding in married couples. *Journal of Social and Personal Relationships, 2,* 45–58.

White, R. (1985). Thoughts on social relationships and language in hominid evolution. *Journal of Social and Personal Relationships, 12,* 95–116.

White, S.E., & Reamy, K. (1982). Sexuality and pregnancy: A review. *Archives of Sexual Behavior, 11,* 429–444.

Whitley, B.E., Jr. (1987). The relationship of sex-role orientation to heterosexuals' attitudes toward homosexuals. *Sex Roles, 17,* 103–113.

Wielandt, H., Boldsen, J., & Jeune, B. (1989). Age of partners at first intercourse among Danish males and females. *Archives of Sexual Behavior, 18,* 449–454.

Wholey, J. (1983). Breast-beating. *New York, 16*(43), 84–86.

Wiest, W.M., & Webster, P.C. (1988). Effects of a contraceptive hormone, danazol, on male sexual functioning. *Journal of Sex Research, 24,* 170–177.

Wiggins, J.S., Wiggins, N., & Conger, J.C. (1968). Correlates of heterosexual somatic preference. *Journal of Personality and Social Psychology, 10,* 82–90.

Wilcox, D., & Hager, R. (1980). Toward realistic expectations for orgasmic response in women. *Journal of Sex Research, 16,* 162–179.

Wilcox, S., & Udry, J.R. (1986). Autism and accuracy in adolescent perceptions of friends' sexual attitudes and behavior. *Journal of Applied Social Psychology, 16,* 361–374.

Wild, R.A. (1981). Exercise-delayed menarche as a contraceptive. *Medical Aspects of Human Sexuality, 15,* 86.

Wild, R.A. (1983). Lack of usefulness of foam after condom breakage. *Medical Aspects of Human Sexuality, 17*(121), 112–113.

Wilensky, M., & Myers, M.F. (1987). Retarded ejaculation in homosexual patients: A report of nine cases. *Journal of Sex Research, 23,* 85–105.

Wilkenwerder, W., Kessler, A.R., & Stolec, R.M. (1989). Federal spending for illness caused by the human immunodeficiency virus. *New England Journal of Medicine, 320,* 1598.

Williams, J.E., & Best, D.L. (1990). *Measuring sex stereotypes: A multination study.* Newbury Park, CA: Sage.

Williams, J.G., & Solano, C.H. (1983). The social reality of feeling lonely: Friendship and reciprocation. *Personality and Social Psychology Bulletin, 9,* 237–242.

Williams, R.M. (1979). The power of fetal politics. *Saturday Review, 6*(12), 12–15.

Wills, G. (1977). Measuring the impact of erotica. *Psychology Today, 11*(3), 30–31, 33–34, 74, 76.

Wills, T.A., Weiss, R.L., & Patterson, G.R. (1974). A behavioral analysis of the determinants of marital satisfaction. *Journal of Consulting and Clinical Psychology, 42,* 802–811.

Willscher, M.K. (1980). Reversing vasectomy. *Medical Aspects of Human Sexuality, 14*(8), 6.

Wilson, G.D. (1987). *Variant sexuality: Research and theory.* Baltimore, Md.: John Hopkins University Press.

Wilson, G.T., & Lawson, D.M. (1976). Effects of alcohol on sexual arousal in women. *Journal of of Abnormal Psychology, 85,* 489–497.

Wincze, J.P., Bansal, S., Malhotra, C., Balko, A., Susset, J.G., & Malamud, M. (1988). A comparison of nocturnal penile tumescence and penile response to erotic stimulation during waking states in comprehensively diagnosed groups of males experiencing erectile difficulties. *Archives of Sexual Behavior, 17,* 333–348.

Wincze, J.P., & Qualls, C.B. (1984). A comparison of structural patterns of sexual arousal in male and female homosexuals. *Archives of Sexual Behavior, 13,* 361–370.

Winer, D.L., Bonner, T.O., Jr., Blaney, P.H., & Murray, E.J. (1981). Depression and social attraction. *Motivation and Emotion, 5,* 153–166.

Winick, C. (1980). Functions of a pimp. *Medical Aspects of Human Sexuality, 14*(5), 138.

Winick, C. (1983). Arousal potential of pubic hair. *Medical Aspects of Human Sexuality, 12*(4), 11, 14.

Winick, C. (1985). A content analysis of sexually explicit magazines sold in an adult bookstore. *Journal of Sex Research, 21*(2), 206–210.

Winn, M. (1981, January 25). What became of childhood innocence? *New York Times Magazine,* 15–17, 44–46, 54–55, 58, 68.

Winn, R.L., & Newton, N. (1982). Sexuality in aging: A study of 106 cultures. *Archives of Sexual Behavior, 11,* 283–298.

Winstead, B.A., Derlega, V.J., & Margulis, S.T. (1988). Understanding the therapeutic relationship as a personal relationship. *Journal of Social and Personal Relationships, 5,* 109–125.

Wise, T.N. (1978). Variations in male orgasm. *Medical Aspects of Human Sexuality, 12*(8), 72.

Wise, T.N. (1979). Sex before sports. *Medical Aspects of Human Sexuality, 13*(11), 7.

Wise, T.N. (1982). Heterosexual men who cross-dress. *Medical Aspects of Human Sexuality, 16*(11), 174, 176, 178, 179, 182.

Wise, T.N., & Mayer, J.K. (1980). Transvestism: Previous findings and new areas for inquiry. *Journal of Sex and Marital Therapy, 6,* 116.

Wishnoff, R. (1978). Modeling effects of explicit and nonexplicit sexual stimuli on the sexual anxiety and behavior of women. *Archives of Sexual Behavior, 7,* 455–461.

Witkin, M.H. (1983). Importance of clitoral stimulation. *Medical Aspects of Human Sexuality, 17*(1), 158, 160, 161, 165, 168.

Wittenberg, M.T., & Reis, H.T. (1986). Loneliness, social skills, and social perception. *Personality and Social Psychology Bulletin, 12,* 121–130.

Witters, W.L., & Jones-Witters, P. (1980). *Human sexuality: A biological perspective.* New York: D. Van Nostrand.

Wolchik, S., Brauer, S., & Jensen, K. (1985). Volunteer bias in erotica research: Effects of intrusiveness of measure of sexual background. *Archives of Sexual Behavior, 14,* 93–107.

Wolchik, S.A., Beggs, V., Wincze, J.A., Sakheim, D.K., Barlow, D.H., & Mavissakalian, M. (1980). The effects of emotional arousal on subsequent sexual arousal in men. *Journal of Abnormal Psychology, 89,* 595–598.

Wolf, T.J. (1985). Marriages of bisexual men. *Journal of Homosexuality, 11*(1/2), 135–148.

Wolfe, L. (1980, September). The sexual profile of that Cosmopolitan girl. *Cosmopolitan,* 247–257, 263–265.

Wolkoff, A.S. (1977). Penile girth and female pleasure. *Medical Aspects of Human Sexuality, 11*(11), 28.

Wolpe, J. (1958). *Psychotherapy by reciprocal inhibition.* Stanford, Calif.: Stanford University Press.

Women began 61.5% of U.S. divorces in '86. (1989, June 8). *Albany Times Union*, A-2.

Wong, E., & Handsfield, H.H. (1983). Nongonococcal urethritis. *Medical Aspects of Human Sexuality, 17*(8), 149–152.

Woo, E. (1981, August 19). Solution to shortage of men: Women wed younger spouse. *Albany Times Union*, 14.

Woodman, S. (1990). Will your child be straight? *Child, 5*(9), 104–105, 112–113.

World Health Organization Special Programme of Research, Development and Research Training in Human Reproduction. (1978). *7th Annual Report*. Geneva: United Nations Publication.

World Health Organization Task Force. (1981a). Women's bleeding patterns: Ability to recall and predict menstrual events. *Studies in Family Planning, 12*(1), 17–27.

World Health Organization Task Force. (1981b). A cross-cultural study of menstruation: Implications for contraceptive development and use. *Studies in Family Planning, 12*(1), 3–16.

World Health Organization Task Force on Psychosocial Research in Family Planning, Special Programme of Research, Development and Research Training in Human Reproduction. (1982). Hormonal contraception for men: Acceptability and effects on sexuality. *Studies in Family Planning, 13*, 328–342.

World's people total 4.7 billion. (1983, September 4). *New York Times*, 9.

Worley, R.J. (1979). Female orgasm and contraception. *Medical Aspects of Human Sexuality, 13*(4), 39, 43.

Worley, R.J. (1980). Significance of 35-day menstrual cycles. *Medical Aspects of Human Sexuality, 14*(8), 11.

Worley, R.J. (1983). Cessation of fertility after menopause. *Medical Aspects of Human Sexuality, 17*(4), 71, 76.

Worthington, E.L., Martin, G.A., Shumate, M., & Carpenter, J. (1983). The effect of brief Lamaze training and social encouragement on pain endurance in a cold pressor tank. *Journal of Applied Social Psychology, 13*, 223–233.

Wright, B.A. (1983). *Physical disability—A psychosocial approach*. New York: Harper & Row.

Wright, P.H. (1984). Self-referent motivation and the intrinsic quality of friendship. *Journal of Social and Personal Relationships, 1*, 115–130.

Wyatt, G.E. (1989). Reexamining factors predicting Afro-American and white American women's age at first coitus. *Archives of Sexual Behavior, 18*, 271–298.

Wyatt, G.E., Peters, S.D., & Guthrie, D. (1988). Kinsey revisited, part II: Comparisons of the sexual socialization and sexual behavior of black women over 33 years. *Archives of Sexual Behavior, 17*, 289–332.

Wyatt, G.E., & Powell, G.J. (Eds.). (1988). *Lasting effects of child sexual abuse*. Newbury Park, CA: Sage.

Wyers, E.J., Adler, H.E., Carpen, K., Chiszar, D., Demarest, J., Flanagan, O.J., Jr., Glasersfeld, E.V., Glickman, S.E., Mason, W.A., Menzel, E.W., & Tobach, E. (1980). The sociobiological challenge to psychology: On the proposal to "cannibalize" comparative psychology. *American Psychologist, 35*, 955.

Wyshak, G., & Frisch, R.E. (1982). Evidence for a secular trend in age of menarche. *New England Journal of Medicine, 306*, 1033.

Xinzhong, Q. (1983). China's population policy: Theory and methods. *Studies in Family Planning, 14*, 295–301.

Yarber, W.L. (1978). Preventing venereal disease infection: Approaches for the sexually active. *Health Values, 2*(2), 61–67.

Yarber, W.L. (1980). Value of VD education. *Medical Aspects of Human Sexuality, 14*(8), 103.

Yarber, W.L., & McCabe, G.P. (1981). Teacher characteristics and the inclusion of sex education topics in grades 6–8 and 9–11. *Health Education, 51*, 288–291.

Yarber, W.L., & McCabe, G.P. (1986). *Importance of sex education topics: Correlates with teacher characteristics and inclusion of topics of instruction*. Unpublished manuscript, Purdue University.

Yarber, W.L., & Whitehill, L.L. (1981). The relationship between parental affective orientation toward sexuality and responses to sex-related situations of preschool-age children. *Journal of Sex Education and Therapy, 82*, 47–57.

Yogev, S. (1982). Happiness in dual-career couples: Changing research, changing values. *Sex Roles, 8*, 593–605.

Yogev, S., & Vierra, A. (1983). The state of motherhood among professional women. *Sex Roles, 9*, 391–396.

Young, B.K. (1983). Sexual changes caused by adrenal virilizing syndromes in women. *Medical Aspects of Human Sexuality, 17*(1), 56R, 56V, 56AA, 56EE.

Young, G.H., & Bramblett, C.A. (1977). Gender and environment as determinants of behavior in infant common baboons (Papio cynocephalus). *Archives of Sexual Behavior, 6*, 365–385.

Young, J.E. (1982). Loneliness, depression, and cognitive therapy: Theory and application. In L.A. Peplau & D. Perlman (Eds.), *Loneliness: A sourcebook of current theory, research, and therapy* (pp. 379–406). New York: John Wiley.

Young, M. (1980). Attitudes and behavior of college students relative to oral-genital sexuality. *Archives of Sexual Behavior, 9*, 61–67.

Youngs, D.D. (1979). Postpartum sexual problems. *Medical Aspects of Human Sexuality, 13*(2), 111–112.

Yulsman, T. (1990, October 7). A little help for creation. *New York Times Magazine*, 22–24, 26–29.

Zabin, L.S., & Clark, S.D., Jr. (1983). Institutional factors affecting teenagers' choice and reasons for delay in a family planning clinic. *Family Planning Perspectives, 15*, 25–29.

Zabin, L.S., Hirsch, M.B., Smith, E.A., & Hardy, J.B. (1984). Adolescent sexual attitudes and behaviors: Are they consistent? *Family Planning Perspectives, 16*, 181–185.

Zajonc, R.B. (1968). Attitudinal effects of mere exposure. *Journal of Personality and Social Psychology Monographs Supplement, 9*, 1–27.

Zajonc, R.B., Adelmann, P.K., Murphy, S.T., & Niedenthal, P.M. (1987). Convergence in the physical appearance of spouses. *Motivation and Emotion, 11*, 335–346.

Zammichieli, M.E., Gilroy, F.D., & Sherman, M.F. (1988). Relation between sex–role orientation and marital satisfaction. *Personality and Social Psychology Bulletin, 14*, 747–754.

Zarem, H.A. (1982). Advising patients who ask about cosmetic surgery. *Medical Aspects of Human Sexuality, 16*(5), 76E, 761, 76J.

Zaviacic, M., Zaviacicova, A., Holoman, I.K., & Molcan, J. (1988). Female urethral expulsions evoked by local digital stimulation of the G-spot: Differences in the response patterns. *Journal of Sex Research, 24,* 311–318.

Zeiss, A.M. (1982). Expectations for the effects of aging on sexuality in parents and average married couples. *Journal of Sex Research, 18,* 47–57.

Zeiss, A.M., Rosen, G.M., & Zeiss, R.A. (1977). *Journal of Consulting and Clinical Psychology, 77,* 891–895.

Zeiss, R.A. (1978). Self-directed treatment for premature ejaculation. *Journal of Consulting and Clinical Psychology, 46,* 1234–1241.

Zelnik, M. (1980). Second pregnancies to premaritally pregnant teenagers, 1976 and 1971. *Family Planning Perspectives, 12,* 69–76.

Zelnik, M., & Kantner, J.F. (1979). Probabilities of intercourse and contraception among U.S. teenage women, 1971–1976. *Family Planning Perspectives, 11,* 177–183.

Zelnik, M., & Kim, Y.J. (1982). Sex education and its association with teenage sexual activity, pregnancy, and contraceptive use. *Family Planning Perspectives, 14* (3), 117–126.

Zelnik, M., & Shah, F.K. (1983). First intercourse among young Americans. *Family Planning Perspectives, 15* (2), 64–70.

Ziff, R.A. (1984). Increasing rates of ectopic pregnancies. *Medical Aspects of Human Sexuality, 18* (12), 14, 16.

Zigler, E., & Child, I.L. (1968). Socialization. In G. Lindsey & E. Aronson (Eds.) *Handbook of social psychology* (Vol. 3, pp. 450–589). London: Addison Wesley.

Zilbergeld, B. (1978). *Male sexuality.* Boston: Little, Brown.

Zilbergeld, B., & Evans, M. (1980). The inadequacy of Masters and Johnson. *Psychology Today, 14* (8), 29, 30, 33–38, 40, 42–43.

Zillmann, D. (1984). *Connections between sex and aggression.* Hillsdale, N.J.: Lawrence Erlbaum.

Zillmann, D., & Bryant, J. (1984). Effects of massive exposure to pornography. In N.M. Malamuth & E. Donnerstein (Eds.), *Pornography and sexual aggression* (pp. 115–138). New York: Academic Press.

Zillmann, D., & Mundorf, N. (1986, April). *Effects of sexual and violent images in rock-music videos on music appreciation.* Paper presented at the meeting of the Broadcast Education Association, Dallas.

Zoglin, R. (1990). Is TV ruining our children? *Time, 136* (16), 75–76.

Zohn, D.A. (1979). Pain caused by large breasts. *Medical Aspects of Human Sexuality, 13* (8), 9.

Zucker, K.J., Doering, R.W., Bradley, S.J., & Finegan, J.K. (1982). Sex-typed play in gender-disturbed children: A comparison to sibling and psychiatric controls. *Archives of Sexual Behavior, 11,* 309–321.

Zucker, K.J., Finegan, J.K., Doering, R.W., & Bradley, S.J. (1984). Two subgroups of gender-problem children. *Archives of Sexual Behavior, 13,* 27–39.

Zuckerman, M., & Brody, N. (1988). Oysters, rabbits and people: A critique of "Race Differences in Behavior" by J.P. Rushton. *Personality and Individual Differences, 9,* 1025–1033.

Zuckerman, M., Neeb, M., Ficher, M., Fishkin, R.E., Goldman, A., Fink, P.J., Cohen, S.N., Jacobs, J.A., & Weisberg, M. (1985). Nocturnal penile tumescence and penile responses in the waking state in diabetic and nondiabetic sexual dysfunctionals. *Archives of Sexual Behavior, 14,* 109–129.

Zuckerman, M., Tushup, R., & Finner, S. (1976). Sexual attitudes and experience: Attitude and personality correlates and changes produced by a course in sexuality. *Journal of Consulting and Clinical Psychology, 44,* 7–19.

Zuger, B. (1989). Homosexuality in families of boys with early effeminate behavior: An epidemiological study. *Archives of Sexual Behavior, 18,* 155–166.

CREDITS

NAME INDEX

SUBJECT INDEX

Some terms in the subject index are italicized; you will find the italicized terms defined in the glossary.

Male sexual anatomy:
Cowper's glands, 41
ejaculation and, 55–57
erection and, 49–51
penis, 36–38
prostate gland, 41
puberty and, 175
raphe, 38
scrotum, 38–39
semen, 37, 49, 55, 56, 57, 72
seminal vesicles, 39, 41
sexual response cycle and, 49–51, 55–59
testicles, 36, 38, 39–41
vas deferens, 41
vocabulary for, 38, 185–86
(see also Sex differences; specific parts)
Male superior position, 294–96
cross-cultural study of, 298
eye contact and, 294–95
Mammary alveoli, 35
Mammary glands, 35–36, 75
(see also Breasts)
Mammography, 442, 449
Mammoplasty, 263
Mangaia society:
homosexual behavior in, 199
sexual behavior in, 45
Manipulation, 234
Manual stimulation, 198–99
Marijuana, 207
pregnancy and, 83
sexual arousal and, 434–35
Marital compatibility, 13, 214
androgyny and, 166–67
Marital dissatisfaction, 231–32, 237
Marital satisfaction, 214, 231–32
bisexual behavior and, 335
communication and, 233–34
conflict and, 272
extramarital sex and, 237
parenthood and, 232
remarriage and, 248–49
Marital therapy, 234
Marquesans, 298–99
Marriage:
abstinence or celibacy in, 231
age at, 225–26
androgyny and, 166–67
bisexual behavior and, 334–36
bride price and, 224
cohabitation and, 223–24
communication in, 232–36
culture and, 228–29
decision to marry, 224–26
divorce and, 239–44
extramarital relationships and, 236–39
group marriage, 229
homosexual behavior and, 329, 331
household duties and, 162–63, 225
legal issues and, 306–7
maintaining, 271–73, 332
open, 237–39
parenting and, 232
preparation for, 79–80
rape and, 235–36, 401
reasons for, 224–26
relationship contract and, 224
religious views of, 202–3
sexual attitudes and, 214
sexuality and, 229–31
swinging and, 237–39, 335
woman's last name and, 227–28
(see also Cohabitation; Divorce; Love; Marital dissatisfaction; Marital satisfaction; Marital therapy; Relationships)
Masculinity:
(see also Androgyny; Gender role; Sex differences)

attractiveness and, 261
culture and, 12, 149–52
homosexual behavior and, 339
measuring, 153
perception of, 165, 322
sexual attitudes and, 211–12
socialization of, 155
Masochism, 356
(see also Sadomasochism)
Massage parlor, 345
Massage, sensate focus and, 473
Mastectomy, 443
Masturbation:
adolescence and, 181
aging and, 250
AIDS and mutual, 428
anal, 285
attitudes toward, 136, 215–18, 284
childhood and, 5, 19, 172–73, 179
clitoris and, 33
contraception and, 136
fantasy, 208
frequency of, 13–14, 181, 207, 210, 216, 217, 230
goals of, 283–84
group, 464
guilt about, 412–13
history, 7, 202
infancy and, 171
insanity and, 440
Jewish religion and, 202
latency period and, 179
marriage and, 230–31
medical field and, 215
mental disability and, 436–37
methods of, 284–85
monkeys and, 9
mutual, 283, 428–29, 473
orgasm and, 284–85
paraphilias and, 363
premature ejaculation and, 464
psychosexual development and, 172–73, 179, 215–18
puberty and, 175, 176
public, 217
safer sexual practices and, 428
semen analysis and, 99
sex differences in, 181
sex education about, 216, 218–19
sex therapy and, 467, 472, 473
sexual adjustment and, 218–19
sexual attitudes and, 210
sexual knowledge and, 188
sexually transmissible diseases and, 412–13
sin and, 215
solo, 283, 429
techniques, 238, 284–85, 290–91
thermography and, 61
vibrator and, 289–91
Victorian England and, 215
Masturbation training, 467
Maternal age, 74, 84
Mate selection, 224–26
Mate-swapping, 237
Mathematical ability, 161
Measurement:
of love, 267, 268
of sexual arousal, 59–61
Meatus, 37, 51
Mechanical strain gauge, 59
Meconium, 85
Media:
love and, 268, 275
violence in, 371–72, 375
Media fetish, 353
Medial forebrain bund, 435
Medical examination:

sex therapy and, 465, 473–74
Medical model of deviance, 351
Medical students, 211, 214
Medication (see Antibiotics; Drugs)
Meese Report, 371
Melanesian society:
homosexual behavior in, 199
Memory:
menstruation and, 70
sexual explicitness and, 212
Menarche, 176–77
Menopause:
amenorrhea, 97, 244–45
heart disease and, 446
hormone therapy and, 245
hysterectomy and, 443
oophorectomy and, 444
physical changes in, 30, 245
sexuality and, 245
sterilization and, 443
vaginal lubrication and, 30, 245
Menstrual cramps, 70
Menstrual cycle:
contraception and, 108–9
difficulties during, 69
hormones and, 35, 67–69
hypothalamus and, 67
luteal phase of, 67–69
marijuana and, 435
menarche, 176
menstrual phase of, 67–69
ovulation and, 67–69
sexual arousal and, 70
(see also Menstrual cycle; Premenstrual syndrome)
Menstrual flow:
AIDS and, 424
blockage of, 32
composition of, 67–68
endometrium and, 33
Menstrual phase, 67–69
Menstruation:
amenorrhea, 75
cross-cultural study of, 70
dysmenorrhea, 70–72
myths and taboos about, 8, 69–70
onset of, 176–77
oral contraception and, 119
physiology of, 67–69
premenstrual syndrome (PMS), 70–72
sex education about, 19, 176
sexual behavior during, 8, 70
toxic shock syndrome (TSS) and, 416
(see also Menstrual cycle; Ovulation; Premenstrual syndrome)
Mental disability, sexuality and, 144, 436–37
(see also Mental retardation)
Mental retardation, 78, 144, 436–37
sexual knowledge and attitudes, 437
Methadone, sexual arousal and, 435
(see also Heroin)
Methods of sexual arousal (see Techniques)
Metronidazole:
birth defects and, 422
trichomoniasis and, 422
Mexico, 247
Mico-conazole nitrate, 422
Micropenis (see Microphallus)
Microphallus, 143
Middle age:
marriage and, 226
sexual behavior and, 164, 249–50, 326
sexual interest and, 45
Middle Ages, 351
Midwifery, 89–90
Mifegyne, 123
Milk, breast:
AIDS and, 35, 94–96